THE OXFORD ENCYCLOPEDIA OF
THE MODERN WORLD

EDITORIAL BOARD

THE OXFORD ENCYCLOPEDIA
OF
THE MODERN WORLD

Peter N. Stearns

Editor in Chief

Volume 3

Earth Day–Heart Disease

OXFORD

UNIVERSITY PRESS

2008

OXFORD
UNIVERSITY PRESS

Oxford University Press, Inc., publishes works that further
Oxford University's objective of excellence
in research, scholarship, and education.

Oxford New York
Auckland   Cape Town   Dar es Salaam   Hong Kong   Karachi
Kuala Lumpur   Madrid   Melbourne   Mexico City   Nairobi
New Delhi   Shanghai   Taipei   Toronto

With offices in
Argentina   Austria   Brazil   Chile   Czech Republic   France   Greece
Guatemala   Hungary   Italy   Japan Poland   Portugal   Singapore
South Korea   Switzerland   Thailand   Turkey   Ukraine   Vietnam

Copyright © 2008 by Oxford University Press

Published by Oxford University Press, Inc.
198 Madison Avenue, New York, NY 10016
www.oup.com

Oxford is a registered trademark of Oxford University Press

The Library of Congress Cataloging-in-Publication Data
The Oxford encyclopedia of the modern world / Peter N. Stearns, editor in chief.

p. cm.
Includes bibliographical references and index.
ISBN 978-0-19-517632-2 (hbk.: alk. paper)
1. History, Modern—Encyclopedias.
2. Civilization, Modern—Encyclopedias.
I. Stearns, Peter N.
D205.O94 2008
909.0803—dc22
2007039891

1 3 5 7 9 8 6 4 2
Printed in the United States of America
on acid-free paper

COMMON ABBREVIATIONS USED IN THIS WORK

b.	born	n.	note
B.C.E.	before the common era (= B.C.)	n.d.	no date
c.	*circa,* about, approximately	no.	number
C.E.	common era (= A.D.)	n.p.	no place
cf.	*confer,* compare	n.s.	new series
d.	died	p.	page (pl., pp.)
diss.	dissertation	pt.	part
ed.	editor (pl., eds), edition	rev.	revised
f.	and following (pl., ff.)	ser.	series
fl.	*floruit,* flourished	supp.	supplement
l.	line (pl., ll.)	vol.	volume (pl., vols.)

THE OXFORD ENCYCLOPEDIA OF
THE MODERN WORLD

E

EARTH DAY. The first Earth Day celebration, widely hailed as a turning point in American environmentalism, was the culmination of years of heightened concern about pollution, pesticides, and additional ecological health threats. Rachel Carson's *Silent Spring* (1962) raised public consciousness with its detailed exposition on the dangers of environmental pollution to human health.

Concern about pollution from factories and power plants, misuse of land and resources, toxic dumps, synthetic substances, air and water quality, and environmental degradation all spurred an avalanche of protests. Activists helped draft federal legislation, including the Wilderness Act (1964); the Air Quality Act (1967); the National Trails System Act (1968); and the Wild and Scenic Rivers Act (1968).

By 1969 public awareness of ecological crises reached a critical threshold. The Santa Barbara oil spill shocked people with images of oil-covered beaches. The People's Park protests at Berkeley further heightened environmental awareness. In June, Cleveland's Cuyahoga River, a waterway inundated with oil and toxic chemicals, burst into flames. The river fire captured national attention and affected popular perceptions of the environment.

Later that year, Gaylord Nelson, a U.S. senator from Wisconsin, proposed a nationwide teach-in and protest to raise awareness of the environmental crisis. He incorporated a nonprofit, nonpartisan organization called Environmental Teach-In. Nelson enlisted Denis Hayes, a graduate student, to spearhead a campaign for raising funds and attracting volunteers. They purchased a full-page advertisement in the *New York Times* in February 1970, announcing plans for the impending demonstrations. Funds for Earth Day came from organized labor groups, such as the United Auto Workers, as well as personal and corporate contributions.

David Brower, an active conservationist who founded Friends of the Earth in 1969, helped compile a book to serve as a source of ideas and tactics for the teach-in. The *Environmental Handbook* went through three printings between January and April 1970, and became a virtual bible for the consciousness-raising activities associated with Earth Day.

National newspapers gave front-page coverage to the roster of scheduled events. Congress recessed that week so that members could return to their constituencies and address Earth Day rallies. Other prominent speakers included Barry Commoner, Paul Ehrlich, Ralph Nader, and Allen Ginsberg.

The first Earth Day, held on 22 April 1970, made "ecology" a household word. A national shift in priorities helped lead to the creation of the U.S. Environmental Protection Agency in 1970. Congress passed a series of environmental laws in the 1970s, including the 1972 Federal Water Pollution Control Act Amendments, the 1973 Endangered Species Act, and the 1974 Safe Drinking Water Act. The Sierra Club, the National Wildlife Federation, the Audubon Society, and other conventional conservation groups played little role in Earth Day, since many feared that it would distort the traditional focus on wilderness protection in favor of urban and social justice issues. In the aftermath of Earth Day, new institutions such as Greenpeace emerged that combined social sensibility with concern for nature. Environmental Action, formed in 1970 to coordinate Earth Day activities, stayed in business as an aggressive lobbying and public information group.

Coverage of environmental issues in the media increased dramatically in the 1970s. A series of toxic chemical episodes brought greater publicity, energy, and momentum to the movement. The first wave of environmental concern began to subside by the mid-1970s. By the 1980s, however, "mainstream environmentalism" had emerged, in which concerns about urban problems like pollution and energy sustainability were more integrated with traditional anxieties about wilderness and wildlife.

Denis Hayes helped organize the 1990 Earth Day celebration, which promoted recycling efforts worldwide and helped pave the way for the 1992 United Nations Earth Summit in Rio de Janeiro. Hayes also served as chairman of the international Earth Day Network, which operates in 160 countries and links more than 4,000 affiliated organizations. Earth Day has evolved into an international holiday, celebrated with performances, exhibits, demonstrations, grassroots activism, and street fairs around the globe. On 22 April 1990, more than 200 million people in over 140 nations observed the twentieth anniversary of Earth Day. By Earth Day 2000, 5,000 environmental groups and 500 million people around the world were on board, participating in over 180 countries.

[*See also* Climate and Climate Change *and* Environment.]

BIBLIOGRAPHY

De Bell, Garrett, ed. *The Environmental Handbook: Prepared for the First National Environmental Teach-In.* New York: Ballantine, 1970.

Hayes, Denis. "Earth Day! A Call To Unite in Defense of Our Planet." *Mother Earth News* (April/May 2005): 25–31.

Matthiessen, Peter, "Rachel Carson." *Time* (29 March 1999): 187–189.

Oelschlaeger, Max, ed. *After Earth Day: Continuing the Conservation Effort.* Denton: University of North Texas Press, 1992.

Shabecoff, Philip. *A Fierce Green Fire: The American Environmental Movement.* New York: Hill and Wang, 1992.

ROBIN O'SULLIVAN

EARTH SUMMITS. Earth summits are exceptional, historical meetings that bring together more than one hundred heads of state in order to discuss the protection of the environment through mutual cooperation, international law, and international development. Although there have been a few such world meetings, only two Earth summits were held as such, in 1992 and 2002.

A Preview of Earth Summits. Before the era of Earth summits, the first-ever world summit to discuss environmental issues was held in Stockholm, Sweden, in June 1972. Even though the meeting focused on environmental risks and topics such as limits to growth, the Stockholm event was not labeled an "Earth summit"; it was known as the United Nations Conference on the Human Environment. The still-active United Nations Environment Programme (UNEP) was created on that occasion; its *Report* set a series of twenty-six founding principles related to "the capacity of the earth to produce vital renewable resources," plus "the sovereign right [of states] to exploit their own resources pursuant to their own environmental policies" (principle 21), calling for a greater awareness of

"the effects of nuclear weapons and all other means of mass destruction" (principle 26). It declared as well that "States shall ensure that international organizations play a coordinated, efficient and dynamic role for the protection and improvement of the environment" (principle 25). Another principle stated that "Education in environmental matters, for the younger generation as well as adults, giving due consideration to the underprivileged, is essential" (principle 19).

The First Earth Summit. The United Nations Conference on Environment and Development (UNCED) organized the 1992 Earth Summit, which was held in Rio de Janeiro, Brazil, from 3 June to 14 June 1992. It was also known as Sommet de la Terre (in French) or Eco 92 (in Portuguese). The conclusions and to do list for the Earth were published in a book, *Agenda 21 Earth Summit* (1992), by the United Nations and translated into many languages, including a short version for children (*Rescue Mission—Planet Earth: A Children's Edition of Agenda 21*). *Agenda 21* was intended as a nonbinding framework for future summits.

The United Nations Framework Convention on Climate Change, which began with preparatory meetings in 1992, became known as the Kyoto Protocol in 1997. The Kyoto Protocol was adopted by 191 countries in December 1997.

The Second Earth Summit. An even bigger event, the second Earth Summit, was in fact labeled the World Summit on Sustainable Development (WSSD). It was held in Johannesburg, South Africa, and lasted from 26 August to 4 September 2002. Among many conclusions of the UN's *Report*, the 2002 World Summit recognized that sustainable development of the globe was critically dependent upon achieving sustainable development in Asia and the Pacific.

The Earth summits confirmed that environmental issues are matters of domestic politics and policies, international development, and good will from all countries. If the June 1972 United Nations Conference on the Human Environment clearly defined the main issues, concepts, and directions, the two Earth summits were places for discussions and negotiations of concrete measures, such as the Kyoto Protocol.

[*See also* Climate and Climate Change; Green Movement; *and* Kyoto Protocol.]

BIBLIOGRAPHY

Agenda 21: Earth Summit—United Nations Programme of Action from Rio. Geneva, Switzerland: United Nations, 1993. Available at http://www.un.org/esa/sustdev/documents/agenda21/index.htm.

Foster, John Bellamy. "The Ecology of Destruction." *Monthly Review* 58, no. 8 (February 2007). Available at http://www.monthlyreview.org/0207jbf.htm.

Hens, Luc, and Bhaskar Nath, eds. *The World Summit on Sustainable Development: The Johannesburg Conference.* Dordrecht, The Netherlands: Springer, 2005.

"The 1972 Conference on the Human Environment in Stockholm." Available at http://www.unep.org/Documents.Multilingual/Default.asp?DocumentID=97.

YVES LABERGE

EASTER RISING. The 1916 Easter Rising in Ireland was an outgrowth of the cultural nationalism of the late nineteenth century, the pressures of World War I, and the machinations of advanced physical-force nationalists. However, Ireland's revolutionary potential in 1916 can be easily overstated. Moderate Irish nationalism seemed on the verge of success, not revolt, in the prewar years. The Irish Parliamentary Party (IPP) enjoyed broad support, and the overtly revolutionary Irish Republican Brotherhood (IRB) was barely emerging from decades of decline. Most rebelliousness in Ireland came from Ulster, where unionists pledged violent resistance to home rule, and from organized labor, which fought Dublin employers in a bitter 1913 lockout.

However, there were storm clouds on the horizon. Home rule's implementation had been suspended in 1914, the Ulster issue had not been resolved, and various conferences had repeatedly failed to reach a solution. The IRB, although numerically insignificant, had infiltrated larger groups such as the Gaelic League and the Irish Volunteers. The IPP's support for the war also sowed the seeds of later discord. Nearly 150,000 Irishmen had volunteered by 1916, but enthusiasm waned as the war dragged on, and eventually there was widespread opposition within Ireland to British threats of conscription.

Most directly, the Easter Rising was engineered by a handful of men on the IRB's Military Council, primarily Tom Clarke (1857–1916) and Sean MacDermott (1883–1916). These men believed in using force to achieve a republic. They also adhered to the old maxim that England's difficulty was Ireland's opportunity, and they saw the war as their chance to strike at England. By January 1916 the council had co-opted the labor leader James Connolly (1868–1916), who pledged the support of his tiny Irish Citizen Army. The details of Connolly's accession are still debated, because his Marxist internationalism did not always harmonize with the views of his co-conspirators.

The goals of the Easter Rising are a matter of controversy among historians. Much emphasis has been placed on the mysticism of Patrick Pearse (1879–1916), a somewhat unorthodox Catholic schoolmaster who was obsessed with the revival of the Irish language, as well as traditional Irish legends. He had little grasp of military matters, but his speeches and writings transmitted the rising's ideology to a broader public. Those historians who emphasize Pearse's role in the rising tend to portray it as a deliberate blood sacrifice, because Pearse rhetorically glorified violence, claiming that Ireland was sinful and in need of redemption. Given the paucity of participants, the static military strategy, and the bloody references in Pearse's canon, the depiction of the rising as a deliberate sacrifice seems tenable.

However, Pearse was not the most important member of the Military Council, and others made more pragmatic military plans, which depended largely on Connolly's erroneous assumption that the arch-capitalist British would not shell Dublin for fear of destroying private property. The rebels also hoped that their heroism would spark a general revolt in the countryside, fueled by the arrival of a cache of German weapons. If all else failed, the rebels wanted to hold out long enough to achieve belligerent status, thereby gaining a seat at the postwar peace conference.

The planning was kept secret from the IRB's Supreme Council, the chief of staff of the Irish Volunteers (Eoin MacNeill, 1867–1945), and the rank and file. All of the careful planning came unraveled in the days before the rising was to begin on Easter Sunday. The German arms did not land, and MacNeill, upon first learning of the plans, wavered in his support. Feeling misled, and fearing that the rising had no chance of success, MacNeill issued a public order canceling all "maneuvers."

The council decided to go on with the rising anyway, postponing it one day, but turnout was low because of the confusion caused by MacNeill's order, and there were no German arms to distribute. Only the tremendous torpor of British intelligence allowed for any element of surprise as 1,300 Volunteers and 200 Citizen Army men and women mustered. They were later joined by units of Cumann na mBan, the women's nationalist organization. The rebels occupied key buildings and waited for the British response. For the most part, Volunteers outside of Dublin were quiet, and the expected countrywide rising never took place.

Symbolically, the greatest success of the Easter Rising—aside from its surprising duration—was the reading of the Proclamation of the Republic on Easter Monday. After the rebels occupied the General Post Office as their headquarters, Pearse emerged and read the proclamation to a few puzzled Dubliners. The proclamation declared an Irish Republic, established vaguely communal economic goals, and called on Irish citizens to pledge their allegiance to the republic. Any hope for military success disappeared rapidly. The British, initially caught off guard, brought in gunboats and artillery to shell rebel positions. By the end of Easter week, central Dublin was burning. On Saturday, 29 April, Pearse formally surrendered. The rebel leaders were distraught at the civilian casualties and looting, and they hoped that surrender could save the lives of their followers. About 450 people, half of them civilians, lost their lives. The British quickly declared martial law and arrested thousands of people, a number far exceeding the number of participants. Military authorities tried a number of key rebels in secret and executed fifteen of them. Another seventy-five death sentences were commuted after the government decided that further executions were unwise. The remaining rebels were hauled off to prison camps.

The effects of the Easter Rising are controversial. Nationalists claimed that although initial public response was hostile, the executions boosted the rebels' cause, eventually leading to the independence movement. The rising also anchored a republic as the goal of many Irish nationalists, and it elevated Pearse, Connolly, and the others into the pantheon of Irish heroes. There is much to commend this conventional view, because the political and military manifestations of Irish nationalism were certainly strengthened by the rising. However, a linear progression from Pearse and Clarke to Michael Collins (1890–1922) and Eamon de Valera (1882–1975) obscures the fact that although the memories of the rising leaders were sanctified, their actions were not emulated. The 1916 rebels largely showed their successors what did not work militarily. Another school of thought questioned whether the rising was necessary at all, noting that Britain had already promised home rule before 1916. This argument hinges on the sincerity of British intentions, as well as on interpretations of the differences between prewar British offers and the eventual treaty of 1921. Regardless of whether the Easter Rising was strictly necessary, it was a significant crack in the British wartime consensus, and its ideologies shaped the direction of Irish nationalism for the rest of the century.

[See also Home Rule; Ireland; Irish Nationalism; Irish Republican Army; Northern Ireland; and Troubles, The.]

BIBLIOGRAPHY

Edwards, Ruth Dudley. *Patrick Pearse: The Triumph of Failure.* London: Victor Gollancz, 1977.

Foster, Roy F. *Modern Ireland, 1600–1972.* London: Penguin, 1998.

Foy, Michael, and Brian Barton. *The Easter Rising.* Thrupp, U.K.: Sutton, 1999.

Ní Dhonnchadha, Máirín, and Theo Dorgan, eds. *Revising the Rising.* Derry, U.K.: Field Day, 1991.

Taillon, Ruth. *When History Was Made: The Women of 1916.* Dublin, Ireland: Beyond the Pale, 1996.

                                        JASON KNIRCK

EAST GERMANY. *See* Germany.

EAST INDIA COMPANY, BRITISH. A global trading power and the early modern world's largest commercial concern, the British East India Company implemented change in bureaucracy, consumerism, culture, learning, and state policies. A benevolent enterprise that had its own navy, army, administration, and social welfare service, the company affected many parts of the world.

The beginnings were rather different. On 31 December 1600, Elizabeth I (r. 1558–1603) granted a charter to "The Company of Merchants of London trading into the East Indies." Synonymy between the company and the government of England or India, absent at this innovative stage, became apparent only later. Rather, reference was made to the East Indies and to London, from where 218 men, mostly merchants and tradesmen, emerged as initial subscribers. Circumstances both at home and overseas were propitious. The Reformation spirit, the Elizabethan Age's creative urge and talent, the idea of a sea-dependent island nation, and the influence at court of Dr. John Dee (1527–1608) formed a heady mixture. By the same token, shipping spices directly from the East, thereby avoiding both Ottoman and Venetian blocs, while also outwitting Portuguese and Dutch rivals, appealed greatly to commercial men. Though the company developed all the necessary operational attributes, the key to its success was strong organizational structure. The court of directors, often called the Little Parliament, presided over the company; answerable to it was a series of specialist committees, each responsible for an area such as correspondence, shipping, or warehouses. Employment opportunities were considerable and included agency work at home and overseas, bureaucratic positions, or positions in the company's military and maritime services.

Company sea captains, recruited widely from the British Isles, commanded hired East Indiamen that were armed and crewed by 65 to 130 hands. Captains were responsible for bringing to England cargoes valued, in the early 1800s, at £10 million per fleet. Regulations, seniority, and other changes reduced the captain's status after 1818. On homeward voyages the company retained native Indian sailors, called lascars, to compensate for crew shortfalls. The religious principles of the lascars were respected, exemplified in the Mohammedan Jubilee of April 1805 in London. The company retained agents in such British ports as Kinsale, Milford Haven, and Portsmouth and overseas in Cairo, Lisbon, Rio de Janeiro, Vienna, and elsewhere. Some captains added to maritime and meteorological knowledge. Captain James Horsburgh (1762–1836), company hydrographer in 1810, corresponded with Matthew Flinders (1774–1814), Sir John Herschel (1792–1871), and Charles Darwin (1809–1882), thereby rendering the company's maritime operations safer.

Many men made their mark through company employment after 1750. Warren Hastings (1732–1818), the enlightened and reformist governor-general of Bengal, underwent a lengthy trial for corruption, and he was acquitted. John Cleland (1709–1789) and Thomas Babington Macaulay (1800–1859) became literary figures. Employed in the company's Bombay legal department, Cleland was notorious for his novel *Memoirs of a Woman of Pleasure* (1748–1749). Macaulay spent five years examining educational and judicial policies in the company's Indian territories; later he became a statesman and a noted essayist and historian. Sir Elijah Impey (1732–1809), educated at Westminster with Warren Hastings and Edward Gibbon (1737–1794), became Bengal's first lord chief justice. He and his wife commissioned paintings of Indian customs and the local flora and fauna. Harford Jones (1764–1847), proficient linguist and Baghdad's company representative in 1800, collected Babylonian antiquities and wrote about Persia. Dr. Patrick Russell (1727–1805), physician and botanist in the Madras Medical Service in the 1780s, published a work on Indian snakes in 1795. James Rennell (1742–1830), surveyor-general of Bengal, became the founding father of Indian geography. Stamford Raffles (1781–1826), lieutenant-governor of Java, subsequently established Singapore.

To defend its growing interests, the company maintained an army, based at Bengal, Bombay, and Madras. The army grew by almost ten-fold between 1760 and 1805 to 154,500 men, making it much larger than either Spain's or Sweden's land forces. Composed of Indian troops, mixed regardless of religion or race, and soldiers recruited from Switzerland and some German states, the army had British commanders and frequently went to war. The Nawab of Arcot had its support in the first Mysore War (1767–1769). Governor-General Hastings used the American struggle of 1775–1783 as an opportunity to exploit company interests further. Similarly, Richard Wellesley, second Earl of Mornington (1760–1842), governor-general from 1798 to 1805, achieved glory defeating Tipu, sultan of Mysore (1799), and the Marathas (1803), but he increased company debts. The military became a juggernaut, waging war against China in 1837, Afghanistan in 1838, and the fearsome Sikhs in the 1840s, and in 1856–1857 it was involved in the Anglo-Persian War to deter Russia from supporting Persian interests. The Anglo-Persian War was the last time that the company's directors declared war on a power.

Such struggles unfolded against a backdrop of changes to the company's framework, legislative basis, and responsibilities, these coinciding with charter renewal. In 1765, the Mogul emperor Shah Alam II (r. 1761–1805) granted the company revenue-collecting powers in Bengal, Bihar, and Orissa, inevitably undermining effective control from London. Company directors, many ignorant of Indian culture and institutions and disliking Hastings's extravagant policies, grew increasingly remote. Westminster politics affected company affairs, and 1763–1784 saw the loss of company control. The Regulating Act of 1773 appointed a governor-general based in Bengal and responsible for the whole of India. A supreme court was created in Bengal, with Crown-appointed judges dispatched from England. William Pitt's India Act of 1784 brought further reforms and improvements. A London-based board of control, under royal direction, approved all company dispatches. A robust governor-general, in the person of General Charles Cornwallis (1738–1805) who had surrendered at Yorktown in 1781, was appointed to India. Lacking political and diplomatic powers, company personnel were now free to concentrate on trade.

Between then and 1813 the company's attitude to India and the East changed, confidence and conquest being replaced by less positive views. The rise in Indian debt from £18 million in 1802 to £32 million by 1809 did not help the company's monopoly cause. Though trade and administration—the latter helped by alumni from Haileybury, a company-founded school—remained the company's preserve, charter renewal in 1813 removed all company monopolies and privileges save for that of the Canton tea trade. The 1833 charter opened Eastern trade and removed all commercial activities from the company; charter renewal in 1853 simply confirmed the status quo. The one remaining significant element, the army, managed to annoy both company leaders and India's vast population. Attempts to control military activity failed, and attitudes hardened, eventually erupting in the revolt of 1857 (also known as the Great Mutiny). Both in England and India, at Velore (1806) and Barrackpore (1824), low-key mutinies had occurred, while Hindu sepoys grew restless from the late 1830s. What was new was the scale and ferocity. In May 1857 the mutiny broke out at Mirath (Meerut), followed by savage massacres at Cawnpore and Lucknow. Though Delhi was sacked extensively, Bombay and Madras presidencies, Sind, and the Punjab went untouched. Particularly notable was the rise of the Rani of Jhansi's force with 14,000 soldiers, some of them women, in her army. The company was shaken to its foundations. Inefficient and devoid of its former considerable powers, it faced overwhelming and intractable problems, including a potentially hostile population of 40 million, while its total responsibilities extended to 250 million people. By the India Act of 1858, full company powers were transferred to the English Crown, and on 1 June 1874 the charter granted in 1854 lapsed. With that the company was dissolved, becoming part of the heritage of many different countries.

[*See also* Colonialism; East India Company, Dutch; Empire and Imperialism; India; Myanmar; *and* Plassey, Battle of.]

BIBLIOGRAPHY

Keay, John. *The Honourable Company: A History of the English East India Company.* London: HarperCollins, 1991. A deep, incisive, and revealing study.

Lawson, Philip. *The East India Company: A History.* London: Longman, 1993. This insightful work offers both breadth and depth.

Marshall, Peter J., ed. *The Oxford History of the British Empire*, Vol. II: *The Eighteenth Century.* Oxford: Oxford University Press, 1998. A thorough, wide-ranging, and impressive work.

Wild, Antony. *The East India Company: Trade and Conquest from 1600.* New London, Conn.: HarperCollins, 1999. A useful and comprehensively illustrated study.

JAMES H. THOMAS

EAST INDIA COMPANY, DUTCH. The Dutch East India Company, or VOC (Vereenigde Oostindische Compagnie), chartered in 1602, stood out as a remarkable contemporary monument of commercial capitalism. In addition to engaging in a large-scale trade between Europe and Asia throughout the seventeenth and the eighteenth centuries, it was also a major participant in maritime trade within the Indian Ocean. At the turn of the eighteenth century the average annual value of the company's exports from Asia to Europe stood at £420,000; the corresponding figure of its principal rival, the English East India Company, was £380,000. The value of the Dutch East India Company's trade within Asia broadly matched that of its Euro-Asian trade. By 1780 or so, however, the overall picture had undergone a massive change. Though the average annual value of the Dutch Euro-Asian trade had gone up only to £580,000, the corresponding English figure had reached a staggering £1.9 million. The closing decades of the eighteenth century were even worse for the Dutch East India Company. The Fourth Anglo-Dutch War (1780–1784) made the position of the company untenable, leading to its eventual liquidation at the end of the century.

It was essentially during the second half of the eighteenth century that the position of the company underwent a great deal of erosion both in Asia as well as at home. In Asia the company had two distinct kinds of presence. In the Indonesian archipelago and Ceylon (now Sri Lanka), the company enjoyed extensive monopsonistic and monopolistic privileges arising essentially out of its territorial authority there. In other regions, however, where an extensive amount of trade was carried on, the company operated simply as an ordinary merchant group. The most important among these regions were the Indian subcontinent, the Persian Gulf, and Japan. The second half of the eighteenth century witnessed major upheavals in the company's position in both these sets of regions.

In the Indonesian archipelago, the power and influence of the company increased during the second half of the eighteenth century. But with a severe reduction in the relative weight of the spice trade, the overall importance of the region in the company's trade was on the decline. Ceylon, the other area where the company had enjoyed territorial and monopoly rights for a long time, also witnessed important changes in the decades after 1750. An attempt to have the amount of land under cinnamon increased—to the detriment of land under other crops—led to widespread unrest that could be contained only after intense military and diplomatic intervention. In the course of the Fourth Anglo-Dutch War, the English managed to take Trincomalee from the Dutch, and in 1796 the entire island passed under English control.

A region such as India where the company had no special privileges—except in Malabar on the southwest coast of India—but operated strictly within a market-determined framework had always been extremely important for the company's trade. An overwhelming proportion of textiles and raw silk, by far the most important of the Asian goods the company traded in the eighteenth century, originated in India. The second half of the eighteenth century, however, was a period of great stress for the company in all parts of the subcontinent, but most of all in Bengal, which was by far the most important source for both textiles and raw silk. The reason for the stress was the political ascendancy of the English East India Company, which enabled it to marginalize its principal rival. The English used their authority to insist that the textile weavers work for no one other than themselves.

The Fourth Anglo-Dutch War had further disastrous consequences for the Dutch East India Company in the subcontinent. Following the outbreak of the war at the end of 1780, all the Dutch establishments in India were annexed by the English and not given back until 1784. On the Coromandel coast, the company's factory at Nagapattinam was never given back, which forced the company to move its Coromandel headquarters back to Pulicat. In Gujarat, the factory at Broach, the only factory the company had other than the chief factory at Surat, was also not returned to the Dutch but was instead handed over to Madhav Rao Scindia. Finally, the Dutch connection with Malabar came to an end in the 1790s.

Things were not going particularly well for the company in Europe, either, during the second half of the eighteenth century. For one thing the control of the government over the company was gradually on the increase. Stadtholder William V took over as chief director in 1766, reflecting growing financial support that the company was obliged to seek from the state. Also, there were serious complaints about increasing corruption among the company's employees in Asia, voiced through various pamphlets published on the issue. The Fourth Anglo-Dutch War in some sense served to act as the final nail in the company's coffin. The company's finances were in a state of near bankruptcy. A so-called Fifth Department was added to the Amsterdam chamber in 1783 with a view to remedy the situation.

But matters did not improve, and in 1790 it was decided to set up a State Committee for the Affairs of the East India Company. The Batavian Revolution of 1795 led to the promulgation on 24 December of the Decree for the Annulment of the Present Management of the VOC. On 1 March 1796 the directors had to make way for a Committee for the East Indies Trade and Possessions. In 1798 it was decided that the Batavian Republic would take over all the assets and liabilities of the company, which was formally wound up on 1 January 1800.

[*See also* Empire and Imperialism, *subentry* The Dutch Colonial Empire; Indonesia; *and* Java War.]

BIBLIOGRAPHY

Gaastra, Femme S. *The Dutch East India Company: Expansion and Decline.* Zutphen, The Netherlands: Walburg Pers, 2003.

Jacobs, Els M. *Merchant in Asia: The Trade of the Dutch East India Company during the Eighteenth Century.* Translated by Paul Hulsman. Leiden, The Netherlands: CNWS Publications, 2006.

Prakash, Om. *The Dutch East India Company and the Economy of Bengal, 1630–1720.* Princeton, N.J.: Princeton University Press, 1985.

Prakash, Om. *European Commercial Enterprise in Pre-colonial India.* Cambridge, U.K., and New York: Cambridge University Press, 1998.

OM PRAKASH

EAST PAKISTAN. *See* Bangladesh; Pakistan.

EAST TIMOR. East Timor has a geographic size that approximates that of Northern Ireland or the U.S. state of Connecticut. In 2005 its population was estimated to be 925,000 people, over 90 percent of whom are Catholic. East Timor, or Timor-Leste as it is officially known, is located at the eastern end of the Indonesian archipelago.

The half-island nation, as a political-geographic entity, is the creation of Portuguese imperialism. The Portuguese appear to have first arrived on the island in 1511. Along with Portuguese traders, the Dutch were occasionally visiting the territory to obtain sandalwood and slaves by the early 1600s. Eventually conflict ensued between the two as both tried to extend their influence on the island and throughout the region. The Netherlands ultimately prevailed, leaving Portugal with the eastern half of the island, in addition to an enclave (called Oecussi) in the western half, which became part of the Dutch East Indies, the colony out of which Indonesia emerged.

"Portuguese Timor" remained firmly within Lisbon's empire until April 1974, when left-leaning military officials overthrew Portugal's fascist government, and immediately announced the decolonization of Lisbon's overseas territories. Prior to that, Jakarta had shown only occasional interest in East Timor, while often publicly stating that Indonesia had no claim to it. By 1974, however, the Indonesian military intelligence service had decided that it could not allow an independent East Timor lest it serve as a base of leftist subversion or as an example for regionally based secessionist movements within Indonesia. Indonesia's military and intelligence apparatus then launched a campaign to subvert the decolonization process, one that culminated in a full-scale invasion on 7 December 1975.

As documented by East Timor's official truth commission, there were at minimum 102,800 East Timorese civilian deaths—mostly from hunger and illness—attributable to Indonesia's actions, which included widespread torture, extrajudicial killings, "disappearances," politically created famine, and indiscriminate bombing. And possibly, according to the commission, there were as many as 201,900 conflict-related civilian fatalities—this in a territory with an estimated population in 1975 of less than 700,000. The commission also estimates that Indonesian forces committed "thousands" of acts of sexual violence against women on a systematic basis.

Western governments provided Indonesia with billions of dollars worth of weapons, military equipment and training, and economic aid, as well as diplomatic cover throughout the period. The West's collective assistance—especially that of the United States—was decisive in allowing Indonesia's 1975 invasion to go forward and its illegal occupation to continue until late 1999. The commission thus recommended that Jakarta's Western backers—in addition to Indonesia—provide reparations to East Timor.

East Timor formally achieved independence on 20 May 2002 after about two-and-one-half years of United Nations transitional government. It is a country "chained by poverty" in the words of a January 2006 United Nations Development Program (UNDP) report and the poorest country in Asia. According to the UNDP, 90 out of 1,000 children die before their first birthday, half the population is illiterate, 64 percent suffer from food insecurity, half lack access to safe drinking water, and 40 percent live below the official poverty line of fifty-five cents a day.

In 2003 East Timor's income from exports was US$7 million, 85 percent of which was generated through the sale of coffee. The country's government hoped that large deposits of oil and natural gas in the Timor Sea would provide the revenues needed to break out of its "underdeveloped" state.

[See also Indonesia.]

BIBLIOGRAPHY

"Chega! Final Report of the Commission for Reception, Truth, and Reconciliation in East Timor (CAVR)." http://etan.org/news/2006/cavr.htm.

Nevins, Joseph. *A Not-So-Distant Horror: Mass Violence in East Timor.* Ithaca, N.Y.: Cornell University Press, 2005.

JOSEPH NEVINS

ECOLOGY. *See* Environment and Pollution.

ECONOMIC AND MILITARY AID IN THE MIDDLE EAST, NORTH AFRICA, AND CENTRAL ASIA.

The Persian and Ottoman empires dominated the Middle East, the Caucasus, Central Asia, and parts of Europe for many centuries. However, the Ottoman Empire's emerging industrial and economic capability could not resist the expanding power of western Europe, and the Ottoman Empire, like all great empires, crumbled. Already competing for more influence, the European powers became increasingly divided until their incompatible imperialistic, territorial, and economic interests collided in World War I. The Great War resulted in the fall of the Ottoman Empire and the advent of a new regional order, dominated by western Europe through colonial rule.

Aid to Turkey. Since then the Republic of Turkey resolutely joined the Western camp, despite the observation by Kemal Atatürk, the founder and first president of the Republic of Turkey: "The West has always been prejudiced against the Turks . . . but we Turks have always consistently moved towards the West. . . . In order to be a civilized nation, there is no alternative." Despite the start of Turkish-American relations in 1927, the United States supported Soviet demands to revise the Montreux Convention (1936) governing the status of the Turkish Straits. The United States changed its policy only after World War II. With the advent of the Cold War, Turkey, a neighbor to the USSR, became an indispensable strategic ally for U.S. interests in seeking to prevent the spread of (or at least "contain") communism. For nearly sixty years, Turkey has received significant economic, military, and diplomatic support from the United States. The British government's postwar inability to continue its military and economic aid to Greece and Turkey incited an anxious President Harry S. Truman to launch an initiative, which came to be known as "the Truman Doctrine," to protect these countries as well as the eastern Mediterranean and the Near East against communist domination. The United States gave Turkey $100 million in military and economic aid—an investment that the recipient rewarded. Turkish troops fought in the Korean War, and in 1952 Turkey became a full member of NATO. In 1955, Turkey signed the Baghdad Pact as part of the American policy to contain the Soviet Union. The pact was transformed into the Central Treaty Organization after the Iraqi departure and the arrival of Iran and Pakistan as new members.

Beginning in the late 1940s, considerable infusions of U.S. aid accelerated industrialization in Turkey and helped the nation's predominantly agricultural economy to diversify in the 1970s and 1980s. By 1971, the United States had given Turkey about $5.7 billion in aid under various programs. The 1980 Defense and Economic Cooperation Agreement between the United States and Turkey allowed the installation of United States military bases in Turkey in exchange for help in modernizing Turkey's military and transfers of U.S. arms. Since 1980 Washington has shipped $9 billion of arms to Turkey and provided $6.5 billion in military aid in the form of grants and loans to purchase U.S. equipment. In 1990, the George H. W. Bush administration stated: "Turkey is a key country for support of U.S. strategic interests in the European, Southwest Asia and Middle East areas." In fiscal year 1989, U.S. aid to Turkey was $563 million ($503 million in military aid and $60 million in economic aid). For fiscal year 1990, the Bush administration requested $553 million in military assistance and $60 million in economic aid.

In the spring of 1994, U.S. President Bill Clinton agreed to assist Turkey in obtaining EXIMBANK and World Bank credit to overcome an economic crisis and to transfer the $1.2 billion Gulf Fund (to which Saudi Arabia, Kuwait, and the United Arab Emirates contributed to finance continuing Turkish production of F-16 airplanes) from the U.S. Treasury to Turkey.

By fiscal year 1999, Congress phased out this type of military aid to Turkey out of recognition that it was able to finance its own arms purchases. Before fiscal year 1999, Turkey had been the third largest recipient of U.S. military aid after Israel and Egypt.

The U.S. Congress used its aid as leverage by linking aid to Turkey to progress toward a settlement with Greece over the contested island of Cyprus. Congress has also established linkage between aid and military sales, human rights, and other concerns.

U.S. military aid and arms sales to Turkey between 1980 and 1999 amounted to $11.5 billion (arms imports), $4.6 billion (grant aid), and $1.9 billion (direct loans) for a total of $18 billion.

To overcome Turkey's reluctance to be involved in the invasion of Iraq in 2003, Washington promised $18 billion in financial aid to Ankara in order to address a portion of Turkish losses in the case of war. Of that amount, $14 billion would consist of low-interest loans to be paid over the long term, and $4 billion would take the form of donations. Washington also hinted at other economic incentives if Turkey would collaborate with the "coalition of the willing."

Aid to Iran. Iran was also the focus of imperial rivalry. Reza Shah Pahlavi (r. 1925–1941), an enlightened nationalist dictator, negotiated the withdrawal of the Soviet and British forces stationed in Iran since World War I. Shunning the United States, Britain, and the Soviet Union, Reza Shah sought out technical assistance from Germany, France, Italy, and other European countries to implement his reforms and modernize Iran. With the start of World War II, Britain pressured Reza Shah to put an end to his cooperation with Germany. His refusal cost him his throne. He died in exile in South Africa. His son and successor, Mohammad Reza Pahlavi, adopted an American model of development and spent billions of dollars in purchasing U.S. arms. From 1950 to 1974 Iran imported 35 percent of the total U.S. arms exported to the Middle East, which made Iran the most powerful military state in the region. In 1979 the Islamic Revolution put an end to the country's monarchy and the American influence in Iran. Instead, Iran made purchases of arms from the Soviet Union, China, and North Korea rather than from the United States.

U.S.-Israeli Relations. U.S. Middle East policy is focused on Israel. Both the White House and the U.S. Congress maintain a close and supportive relationship with Israel through aid. U.S. secretary of state Henry Kissinger reinforced the institutionalization of the U.S. aid to Israel in the mid-1970s by connecting it to peace with Arabs. Each territorial concession by Israel to the Arabs is accompanied by U.S. aid to address Tel Aviv's security needs. Following the Camp David Accord in 1979, the United States granted Israel $3 billion for redeploying its settlers and troops from Sinai. Additionally, during the Wye River Accords in 1998, the U.S. Congress approved $1.2 billion in special aid to help fund Israel's pullout from the West Bank and Gaza Strip, yet an effective withdrawal of the Israel Defense Forces from Palestinian territories did not take place. Between 1949 and 1965, 95 percent of the roughly $65 million in annual U.S. aid to Israel went toward economic assistance and food aid. In recent years leading up to 2005, Israel received approximately $3 billion per year toward economic and military assistance, over 30 percent of the total U.S. foreign aid budget.

Europe was Israel's main arms supplier in the 1950s and 1960s. A modest U.S. military aid program started in 1959. From 1966 through 1970, the United States increased its assistance to approximately $102 million per year, although 47 percent of this amount included military loans. Since 1987 the U.S. Congress has approved foreign aid to Israel totaling an average of $3 billion per year,

75 percent of which was related to military-assistance programs. During the administration of U.S. president Ronald Reagan, the two countries reached a variety of strategic and defense agreements. Israel was granted status as a major non-NATO ally, which granted the country access to major weapon systems and the opportunity to bid on U.S. defense contracts. This alliance also hastened a bilateral free-trade agreement in 1985.

In 1992 Washington approved loan guarantees of $400 million to settle one million Soviet Jewish immigrants expected to arrive in Israel between 1991 and 1995. U.S. housing-loan guarantees between 1972 and 1990 were worth $600 million in total. The U.S.-Israeli relationship has thus evolved away from sympathy for the creation of Israel to the settlement of Jewish refugees.

Following the Persian Gulf War in 1991, the United States gave Israel $2 billion annually in federal loan guarantees, which brought annual U.S. foreign aid to Israel to approximately $5 billion. The Clinton administration granted $300 million in aid to Israel for antiterrorist activities and its antimissile system. In 2003 the administration of U.S. president George W. Bush announced a reduction in loan guarantees to Israel from $3 billion per year to about $300 million as a result of Israeli settlement activity. Under an agreement between the two countries, the U.S. economic assistance program was phased out while its military aid was increased to $2.16 billion for the year 2004. Additionally, the 2003 Congressional Emergency Wartime Supplemental Appropriations Act granted Israel an additional $1 billion in military assistance to help it fight terrorism. Congress also approved more than $8 billion in loan guarantees to help Israel's declining economy, battered by the continuing Palestinian intifada (uprising).

Notwithstanding its significant power in the Middle East, the Israeli military remains dependent on U.S. assistance. Despite their close collaboration, the United States and Israel had significant disagreements over the nature of U.S. military assistance. The Arms Export Control Act states that Washington may stop U.S. military assistance used for purposes other than legitimate self-defense. The administration has indicated to Congress that Israel may have violated provisions of that act four times between 1978 and 1982 and asked for a congressional investigation.

From 1994 to 1998, $29 billion in U.S. loans have been waived for Israel. The Congressional Research Service has put total U.S. loans and grants to Israel from 1949 to 2005 at $189 billion: $157 billion in military aid and $32 billion in economic aid.

U.S.-Egyptian Relations. U.S. assistance to Egypt is directly related to security issues. In the years since Egypt signed a peace agreement with Israel in 1979, the country has received over $45 billion in economic assistance from the U.S. government, in comparison to $4.2 billion over the roughly equal number of years (twenty-six) prior to the peace agreement. Egypt remains the largest recipient of conventional U.S. military and economic aid after Israel. In the 1990s the United States forgave $7.1 billion in past Egyptian military debt since Cairo supported the United States in the Persian Gulf War. In 1999 Egypt received a $3.2 billion grant from the United States to modernize its military. U.S. military assistance accelerated peace efforts between Egypt and Israel.

Since 1992 the United States Agency for International Development has supported Egypt with approximately $1.8 billion per year to liberalize its economy. Egypt also received $1.3 billion in military aid and $615 million for social programs in 2003. In March 2005 a new memorandum of understanding allowed the United States to monitor Egypt's reforms in the financial sector and to release funds only after those reforms are completed. The Egyptian government, however, fears the impact of these reforms on domestic stability.

U.S.-Saudi Relations. The United States and Saudi Arabia have a long-standing economic and defense relationship. As of 2005, Saudi Arabia provides approximately 20 percent of total U.S. crude-oil imports. The United States is Saudi Arabia's largest trading partner, while the Saudi kingdom is the largest U.S.-export market in the Middle East. U.S.-Saudi military cooperation dates back to 1953, with America providing training and support to the Saudi military.

Between World War II and 1975, the United States gave the Saudis a total of $329 million in military and economic assistance. This aid ended in 1979, however, when Saudi oil revenue increased significantly. Thereafter, the United States and Saudi Arabia reached an array of bilateral security agreements, and the United States deployed military forces in the Saudi kingdom. Following several Islamic groups' denunciation of foreign soldiers' presence in Saudi Arabia, the United States withdrew its forces in August 2003 but remains the kingdom's largest arms supplier, with the total value of bilateral arms agreements and transfers amounting to $127 billion between 1950 and 2004. Deeply affected by the events of 11 September 2001, Saudi Arabia has closely collaborated with the United States in the campaign against terrorism.

The United States, Russia, and Caspian Basin. During the Cold War, the slogan of successive American administrations was the development of democratic institutions, the rule of law, and the promotion of liberal economies in Central Asia and the Caucasus. Since the collapse of the Soviet Union in 1991, the United States has actively sought to eliminate weapons of mass destruction and has provided some security assistance to the region for its combat against terrorism, proliferation of weapons of mass destruction, and arms trafficking. In 1994 the Clinton administration created a fund to lend up to $150 million to countries in the region to promote market economies. However, the U.S. assistance was dropped in September 2000 and then increased to about $45.5 million for 2001.

In the aftermath of 9/11 the U.S. State Department increased its security assistance, but the amount decreased in 2003–2004. Security and law-enforcement aid was $187.55 million in 2002, $100.98 million in 2003, and an estimated $68.62 million in 2004. All the states received International Military Education and Training and also Foreign Military Financing and are eligible to receive grants of American Excess Defense Articles. U.S. cumulative foreign assistance to Central Asia was $3.188 billion from 1992 to 2003 ($266 million per year) and $695 million in 2003–2005 ($232 million per year).

Russia feels threatened and does not welcome U.S. interference in its "near abroad." Moscow remains interested in maintaining strategic security and economic ties with Central Asia and discourages regional collaboration with the United States through debt forgiveness, military incentives, and political intimidation. The Russian view of Central Asia favors reintegration of Soviet space and remains imperialistic.

The Soviet Union/Russia and the Middle East. The Middle East was very important for the Soviet Union during the Cold War. Egypt (until 1972), Syria, the People's Republic of South Yemen, Iraq, Algeria, and Libya were tactical allies of the Soviet Union, receiving significant military and economic assistance from Moscow. Soviet military assistance was crucial for Arab states, providing them with some tactical advantage, but not giving them military parity with Israel.

If ideology and political considerations played a major role in Soviet military cooperation with the Arab states, Russia's approach to arms transfers is purely business-oriented. The demise of the Soviet Union put Syria at a serious disadvantage vis-à-vis Israel, which has unlimited access to U.S. arms imports. Syria remains the only Arab client of Russia, which lost influence in the region to the United States and its allies.

[*See also* Arab-Israeli Conflict; Arms, Armaments, and the Armaments Industry, *subentry* The Middle East, North Africa, and Central Asia; Caspian Sea; Development, Industrial, *subentry* The Middle East and North Africa; Iran; Iran-Iraq War; Israel; Middle East; Modernization, *subentry* The Middle East and North Africa; Saudi Arabia; Trade, International, *subentry* The Middle East, North Africa, and Central Asia; Turkey; *and* Westernization, *subentry* The Middle East, North Africa, and Central Asia.]

BIBLIOGRAPHY
Aydin, Mustafa, and Çagri Erhan, eds. *Turkish-American Relations: Past, Present and Future.* New York, Routledge, 2004.
Brands, H. W., ed. *The Use of Force After the Cold War.* College Station: Texas A&M University Press, 2000.
Cohen, Warren I. *America's Failing Empire: U.S. Foreign Relations since the Cold War.* Blackwell, 2005.
The Columbia Gazetteer of the World Online. Saul B. Cohen, ed. New York: Columbia University Press, 2005. http://www.columbiagazetteer.org/
Riemer, Andrea. *A Triangle of Tensions: U.S.-Europe-Turkey.* Peter Lang, 2003.
Satterthwaite, Joseph C. "The Truman Doctrine: Turkey." *Annals of the American Academy of Political and Social Science,* Vol. 401, America and the Middle East (1972): 74–84.

HOUCHANG HASSAN-YARI

ECONOMICS. Adam Smith created the first systematic analysis of the economy, *Inquiry into the Nature and Causes of the Wealth of Nations,* in 1776. From the beginning, economics was international. Arguing that the source of wealth lies in the division of labor and that the extent of the division of labor is limited only by the extent of the market, Smith criticized protectionist policies and colonialism, which brought great riches but even greater costs to metropoles. Across Europe, classical economists influenced reformers in many countries. While Smith had criticized colonialism, later economists—such as John Stuart Mill (1806–1873) and Thomas Robert Malthus (1766–1834)—would work for the British East India Company, interpreting Smith's work to support policies that further reinforced the dominance of the European colonial powers.

Until the late 1800s, these scholars had called their field "political economy," reflecting their interest in the state's role in the economy. In his 1890 *Principles of Economics,* Alfred Marshall replaced the term "political economy" with "economics" to emphasize a turn to microeconomics—the study of markets and households rather than the study of the whole economy—and the use of mathematics. European economists recognized the usefulness of the concept "marginal utility," the satisfaction gained from each additional unit of a commodity. Using calculus, economists could now compare marginal utilities of various goods and find prices that would produce the exact amount of goods that is demanded, achieving general equilibrium. While historians debate whether this was a revolution or merely an innovation that was incorporated into classical economics, general equilibrium analysis provided an important tool for economists.

The Professionalization of Economics. Throughout the nineteenth century, scholars across the disciplines sought new status through scientific methods, professional associations and journals, and standardized training. While Continental European political economists had typically been trained in law, American and British political economy was a branch of moral philosophy, with many scholars and instructors trained for the ministry. Political economists began to distance themselves from theology and advocacy, through the mathematical rigor of general equilibrium analysis and by privileging the expertise of economists working in universities over nonacademic practitioners. In the 1880s and 1890s, new academic economic journals and professional associations abounded, which developed these new scientific methods and a more unified economics community.

In the nineteenth century, economists from Europe and the United States flocked to Germany because it was the only country offering systematic training in political economy. However, German economists rejected the new general equilibrium analysis and mathematics. Instead, German economists formed the "historical school," which conducted empirical research, was suspicious of abstract mathematical models, and focused on the role of the nation-state in encouraging economic growth. American economists combined the historical school with the American tradition of progressive reformism, creating institutionalism. Other economists had less-systematic classical economics training. While American and British universities offered a few political economy courses, they did not establish separate economics departments until the 1890s. Economics departments then sprouted up around the world.

In response to the Great Depression, economists developed tools for governments to direct the economy away from market failures, smooth out business cycles, promote economic growth, and provide full employment.

In his *General Theory of Employment, Interest, and Money* (1935), John Maynard Keynes built a model of the national economy that allowed economists to examine the main elements of the economy—income, interest rates, investment levels, consumption levels, and government expenditures—and how changes in these elements could increase output and provide full employment. Over the next several decades, economists worked out the details of this model, which provided a shared project to unite economists professionally.

The Globalization of American Economics. The center of the economics discipline then shifted from Continental Europe to the United States. As a result of the Great Depression, Stalinist persecution, and Nazi terror, many high-caliber economists left Continental Europe for the United States and England, bringing the traditions of their own economics professions with them and changing the economics disciplines in their new homes. American economics became dominant worldwide because of the large-scale investment in economics and universities by the U.S. government, the expanded opportunities for economists inside and outside the universities, and the concentration of so many great minds in economics.

As E. Roy Weintraub has discussed, economists and mathematicians from central Europe brought highly developed mathematical economics to the United States in the 1930s and 1940s. The new generation of economists began to be trained in high-level mathematics and statistics. Economists brought together the Keynesian model, general equilibrium analysis, and mathematics to create the neoclassical synthesis. Many economists saw the neoclassical synthesis as providing the means to create a better world through planning. In contrast to Soviet planning, which eradicated prices and markets, American economists sought to plan with mainstream economic tools.

The American economics profession found its most supportive environment not in private industry, but in the wartime and postwar state, as Michael Bernstein (2004) has shown. During World War II, economists had discovered that general equilibrium analysis could be applied to governmental and military allocation decisions. Kenneth Arrow and Gerard Debreu proved mathematically that models of competitive economies and models run by planners could provide the same results. Innovations in linear programming, game theory, and other mathematical applications were encouraged by large-scale U.S. government and private foundation funding. The U.S. government also hired economists in large numbers to work in the expanding state bureaucracy.

Mathematical economics, econometrics, and the invention of the computer provided a common language for a global economic discussion and tools to unify the economics profession globally. Scholars have debated whether the diffusion of these methods constitutes the Americanization or the internationalization of economics around the world (Coats). On the one hand, American economics was exported as a way to support the American Cold War effort. The U.S. government and large foundations promoted curriculum reform outside the United States based on American economics training. Economists and graduate students from around the world enrolled in American universities or studied for short periods through academic exchange programs funded by the U.S. government, bringing American economics home when they returned. On the other hand, American economics was already globalized and contained a wide range of tools, including planning. Intergovernmental organizations also encouraged a broader range of economic work through conferences and research projects. The United Nations, for example, supported the world input-output modeling efforts of Wassily Leontief, which he had begun in the Soviet Union.

The United Nations supported the Economic Commission for Latin America in the 1950s, which made Latin America a center for the study of development. The Argentinean economist Raúl Prebisch argued that the world economy made the third world underdeveloped—providing only raw materials and not industrializing—and dependent on developed countries. The Brazilian Celso Furtado and the Chilean Osvaldo Sunkel provided further support for policies to end underdevelopment, including import substitution, arguing against the unrestricted international trade first promoted by Adam Smith. Latin American economics prompted the World Bank to pursue programs of poverty eradication in the 1970s. With decolonization in Africa, a different form of dependency theory found a home within African socialism.

During the 1940s and early 1950s, economists in the Soviet Union and Eastern Europe were forbidden to use mainstream economic tools to analyze the economy; they were required, instead, merely to implement plans or provide ideological support to Communist Party policies. With the death of Joseph Stalin in 1953, Soviet and East European economists rebuilt their professional associations, journals, and international connections. Encouraged by military and planning agencies, as well as by professional interest, Soviet bloc economists developed mathematical economics. Through international conferences, exchanges, and a common mathematical language, leading economists from the United States and the Soviet Union saw themselves working on a common project of creating planning models. Reflecting the parallel paths of Soviet and American economics, Leonid Vitaliyevich Kantorovich of the USSR and Tjalling C. Koopmans of the United States won the Noble Prize in 1975.

In addition to mathematical economics, East European economists in the 1960s developed market socialism, incorporating markets and competitive prices within the socialist planning system. Economists around the world were interested in these reforms because of a widespread belief that capitalism with its large-scale corporations and socialism with these newly introduced incipient markets were converging. East European market socialism seemed to bring together the best parts of capitalism and socialism.

Throughout the twentieth century, economists had questioned the assumptions of the neoclassical synthesis. Economists of the Austrian and Chicago schools questioned the abilities of planners to obtain reliable information about the economy and called instead for the end of state intervention in the economy. Milton Friedman argued that money supply fluctuations had a greater impact on output than the fiscal policies advocated by Keynesians. Robert Lucas further criticized Keynesian policy by arguing that people anticipate changes in fiscal policies and thus make these policies ineffective. These economics schools did not fundamentally alter academic economics, which had long been interested in decisions made under uncertainty and asymmetrical information. The Austrian and Chicago schools did, however, transform economic policy.

Starting in the 1970s in Latin America, elites sought to realize the ideas of the Chicago school by privatizing public companies, deregulating the economy, liberalizing trade, focusing on monetary supply, and decreasing the size of the state. This package of policies came to be known as neoliberalism or the Washington Consensus. The International Monetary Fund (IMF) and World Bank spread neoliberalism worldwide through structural adjustment programs that demanded economic restructuring in exchange for loans. In spite of its antistate rhetoric, neoliberalism required strong, authoritarian states to be implemented.

With the end of socialism in Eastern Europe, the Soviet Union, and Africa, economists faced a new problem: how to create capitalism. Many economists believed capitalism would emerge naturally through neoliberal policies. However, the transitions of the 1990s showed that capitalism did not emerge naturally with the removal of the state, but rather required the creation of institutions, such as the rule of law, clear property rights, and a social safety net. The financial crises from 1994 to 2002 in Mexico, Asia, Russia, Brazil, Turkey, and Argentina brought into further doubt the policy recommendations of the IMF and World Bank, as seen in Joseph E. Stiglitz (2003).

Globalization has continued to change the economics profession worldwide. With such a concentration of world-renowned economists, American universities have been able to attract many economists and graduate students from abroad, thus further globalizing the American economics profession. Transnational connections and collaborations have increased because economists can more easily work across national borders. Economists carry with them the concerns and interests of their own economies, bringing the economics of transition, development, political economy of poverty, and international finance to the center of the field. Leaders in economics such as Amartya Sen, the Indian Nobel laureate, or Mahbub ul Haq, the Pakistani inventor of the United Nations Human Development Index, move easily between elite universities worldwide and expand the fields of interest to economists, further globalizing American economics and exporting this evolving field worldwide.

[*See also* Business; Capitalism; Depressions and Economic Crises; Development, Economic; Industrialization; International Monetary Fund; Keynesianism; Laissez-faire; Market Revolution; Marxism; Mercantilism; Physiocrats; Planning, Economic; *and* World Bank.]

BIBLIOGRAPHY

PRIMARY WORKS

Marshall, Alfred. *Principles of Economics: An Introductory Volume.* Philadelphia: Porcupine Press, 1982. First published in London in 1890. Classic text in the marginalist tradition.

Smith, Adam. *An Inquiry into the Nature and Causes of the Wealth of Nations.* Edited by Edwin Cannan. New York: Modern Library, 1965. First published in London in 1776. The first systematic study of the economy.

SECONDARY WORKS

Bernstein, Michael. *A Perilous Progress: Economics and Public Purpose in Twentieth-Century America.* Princeton, N.J.: Princeton University Press, 2004. The best work in the field. In an enjoyable readable style and based on rigorous archival research, this book explains the development of the American economics profession.

Coats, A. W., ed. *The Post-1945 Internationalization of Economics.* Annual Supplement to History of Political Economy 28. Durham, N.C.: Duke University Press, 1996. Explores economics professions in numerous countries to understand whether they have been Americanized, have been internationalized, or have retained their national character.

"The History of Economic Thought." http://cepa.newschool.edu/het/. An excellent resource that summarizes the major schools of thought and the ideas of major economists worldwide.

Niehans, Jürg. *A History of Economic Theory: Classic Contributions, 1720–1980.* Baltimore: Johns Hopkins University Press, 1990. Detailed analysis of the history of economic thought and methodology, as well as biographical sketches of major economists.

Stiglitz, Joseph E. *Globalization and Its Discontents.* New York: W. W. Norton, 2003. Criticism of World Bank policy by the former chief economist of the World Bank and Nobel laureate.

Weintraub, E. Roy. *General Equilibrium Analysis: Studies in Appraisal.* Cambridge, U.K.: Cambridge University Press, 1985. While the technical explanations require mathematical knowledge, this book provides insight into the history of general equilibrium analysis and its long-term influence on economics.

JOHANNA K. BOCKMAN

ECONOMY [*This entry includes two subentries, on the economy of South Asia and the economy of Southeast Asia.*]

South Asia

One in five people in the early twenty-first century lives in South Asia. The three most populous nations—India, Pakistan, and Bangladesh—have 1.31 billion people. The smaller nations—Nepal, Sri Lanka, Bhutan, and the Maldives—account for 48 million.

Though there are variations in livelihood patterns among these nations, they also share common characteristics. For example, agriculture is still the largest employer, though manufacturing and services have grown faster than agriculture since the early twentieth century. Agricultural conditions vary. Tropical dry climate prevails, summers are hot, and winters are dry, giving rise to desert and semiarid zones in the west and in the southern peninsula. The monsoon winds bring much rain, which, together with the Himalayas, create great river systems in both the east (Ganges) and the west (Indus) and turn eastern and coastal India, Bangladesh, and Sri Lanka wet or humid. Among exceptions to this pattern, Nepal and Bhutan are largely highland, and the Maldives is a group of islands. Livelihoods in the dry zones tend to be precarious and are characterized by low income and high risk of famine. Livelihoods in the wet regions are dominated by settled, high-valued agriculture. In India, Pakistan, and Sri Lanka, highland zones sustain plantations.

The Eighteenth-Century Transition. Historically, the river valleys were seats of powerful empires sustained by land taxes, whereas the arid areas tended to see unstable politics. Somewhat on the margin of these territorial powers, littoral South Asia took part in the maritime trade within Asia. For four centuries after the Portuguese mariner Vasco da Gama discovered the sea route between Europe and India in 1497, European traders took a prominent part in the Indian Ocean trade, increasingly directing Asian trade toward Europe. Cotton textiles from the Gujarat, Bengal, and the Coromandel coast began to define new standards of consumption in the West.

From early in the eighteenth century the Mughal Empire started breaking up into a number of successor states, one of which was Bengal. Bengal was also the major center of operation of the British East India Company. On 23 June 1757 an English force defeated Siraj-ud-Dawlah, the nawab of Bengal, in the battle of Plassey. Eight years later the East India Company became the sovereign ruler of Bengal. A century later, 60 percent of land area in South Asia belonged to British India, now under the rule of the Crown. The remaining states maintained peace with the British and participated in a more or less integrated system of trade. Whereas the decline of the Mughal Empire saw a degree of political chaos in the region, historians now believe that it also created new economic possibilities and consolidated a merchant class in northern India. The successor states were fiscally weak and innovated on finances. The resultant tax farming and market borrowings made the commercial classes powerful enough to meddle in state affairs. Indeed, their collaboration was an element of the British success at Plassey.

A merchant firm thus inherited a state dependent on land taxes. Initially a part of these taxes was used to carry out trade, but soon declining demand for Indian cottons in Europe closed that option, and the regime settled down as a territorial power. From the beginning the taxation system was seen as inefficient. Tax farming, it was felt, needed to make way for a regime wherein proprietors would pay taxes. In the zamindari system introduced in 1793, tax collection became an administrative function of the state, and legislation was introduced to make peasantry's right on the land a clear proprietary title. The irony of this reform was that property rights were granted to the former tax collectors or zamindars, turning the actual peasants into tenants. By 1790 the British in Bengal were not secure enough to imagine a reform without the cooperation of the elite. When territories in southern and western regions fell to British hands in the early nineteenth century, property-right reforms were carried out with greater information and confidence. Therefore it was easier to consider peasant proprietorship in these regions, and the individual peasant or a peasant kinship unit became responsible for taxation and received proprietary rights in exchange.

Nineteenth-Century Integration. As these events took shape the Atlantic economy experienced the Industrial Revolution. By 1820 the export trade in cotton textiles had almost ceased, and South Asia had begun to import cotton cloth from Lancashire. Export of agricultural goods accelerated, beginning with indigo, opium, and cotton and diversifying into wheat and rice later in the century. The peasant, rather than the artisan, forged the new link between South Asia and the world economy. The transition was complete by the last third of the nineteenth century after transportation costs had fallen dramatically because of steamships, railway development, and the Suez Canal (opened in 1869). Grain export more than doubled in volume between 1870 and 1914. There was great regional variation in the extent of agricultural commercialization. By and large the zamindari areas, consisting of the wet agricultural zones such as Bengal, and the dry areas participated little in the export boom. The most successful were a subset of the dry areas that saw extension of state investment in canal irrigation, chiefly Punjab.

The merchant classes adapted well to the globalization of the economy. Opium and cotton trades, inland transportation and the trade of export goods, and a great deal of banking and finance were conducted by local groups. The colonial connection now brought the technology and technical manpower needed to process cotton or jute fibers within easy reach of these classes. The American Civil War (1861–1865) offered huge profit opportunities to cotton merchants of Bombay. After the war ended, a part of these profits found its way to the construction of cotton mills. Employment in factories in South Asia increased from four hundred thousand in 1891 to 1.57 million in 1938. Impressive as this record was, the growth initially was uneven. Industries around Bombay (Mumbai) and Calcutta (Kolkata) accounted for about half of factory employment. Cities that pulled a number of key resources together—ports, resident capitalists, European settlement, railway terminals, water and power, financial and labor markets—saw the beginnings of industrialization. These resources did disperse, if slowly at first.

Dispersal was quickened after World War I, which led to large gains for Indian industries. After the war the government began to look toward local sources and became more open to promoting such sources. The use of protective tariffs for industrial promotion was sanctioned. This measure led to growth in sugar, steel, cement, matches, paper, and woolen textiles. Despite colonialism, foreign capital remained restricted to a few sectors of the economy, of which tea plantations in Bengal, Assam, and Ceylon (Sri Lanka) were important.

The nineteenth-century world economy offered the South Asian artisan many opportunities. Machine-made products offered only a few articles of consumption. The artisan supplied the bulk of consumer goods, as well as major new exports such as semiprocessed leather. Technological advances in Europe cheapened and simplified the use of inputs for traditional industry in the region, a process best illustrated by cotton yarn and dyes. On the consumption side, the Industrial Revolution, by cheapening cotton textiles, stimulated demand for other goods. Some crafts such as carpets and leather found markets abroad. Cheaper transportation made some other goods, such as silks or carpets, more accessible to the urban middle class. These changes served as a foundation for the impressive growth of small-scale industry in the twentieth century.

The combination of industrialization and agricultural change in the fifty years before World War I produced comfortable economic growth rates. Per capita income increased at a rate of between 1 and 2 percent a year. Regional inequality, however, increased. The export boom had not made a significant difference to the dry areas, which were periodically convulsed in violent famines (1876, 1896, and 1898). Further, the agrarian expansion slowed in the interwar period because the two principal ingredients that sustained the boom—arable land expansion through irrigation, and world demand for food and raw materials—slowed after 1920. Population growth, long stable in the region, began to accelerate from this decade. Rural wages and incomes stagnated, and possibly even fell in Bengal. Industrialization was unable to stem a gathering rural crisis. The nationalist movement, founded on an economic critique of colonial rule, gathered strength.

Planning and Industrialization. In 1947, British colonial rule in South Asia ended, and South Asia saw the birth of several independent nations, principally India, Pakistan, and Ceylon (Sri Lanka). The map of the region was redrawn in 1971 with the birth of Bangladesh from Pakistan.

Already before independence a broad political consensus had emerged on the need to restrain trade and build a strong government. It was held that free trade and a non-interventionist state, tenets of classical liberalism to which the colonial government adhered, had impoverished the region and drained local resources. Over the next decade an import-substituting industrialization strategy was designed and was implemented by means of five-year plans. With minor variations, all nations followed the same path. Pakistan and Sri Lanka, the relatively less industrialized nations, shared the same interest in state-directed industrialization and self-reliance as India did.

The policy choice was framed in the Mahalanobis model adopted in India in the 1950s. Emulating Soviet experience, industrial policy placed emphasis on the development of machinery and material production. Since domestic production of capital-intensive goods in a capital-scarce economy could lead to high cost of production, tariffs were steeply raised. Capital needed to be rationed, which was done by means of industrial licensing and nationalization of banking and insurance. In order to direct credit better, interest rates were controlled. The government was the sole channel for the import of essential raw materials and food. To reduce the fiscal burden, exchange rates were fixed and overvalued. Later, government securities that offered tax concessions became another handy way to raise funds. Since the government had privileged access to scarce resources, the public sector established industries or nationalized them. In Sri Lanka the mainstay plantations sector was seminationalized. Encouragement to export was provided by export bonus and entitlement schemes, often at high fiscal costs.

Agriculture fell in priority in this period. The thrust of agricultural policy was institutional reform and irrigation. The zamindari system was abolished in India, land ceilings were introduced, and cooperatives in credit and marketing were encouraged. In Pakistan, irrigation schemes and an increased supply of arable land sustained agricultural growth in the 1960s. But in India, production and yield lagged when a severe crop failure occurred in 1966–1967. Following this episode agricultural technology became a priority and paved the way for the first green revolution based on a combination of new and improved seeds, chemical fertilizers, and water. The package was a remarkable success in Punjab, both in Pakistan and in India. In the 1980s the package succeeded in a few other regions, notably the poorer, rice-growing areas of Bangladesh and West Bengal in India. Although large segments of poor agricultural conditions persisted, especially in the dry zones, by the 1980s the specter of food shortages had more or less disappeared from South Asia. This "revolution," however, was bought at a high fiscal cost. It was enabled everywhere by huge state aid doled out as subsidized water, electricity, fertilizers, credit write-offs, price support, and zero taxes.

Import-substituting industrialization generated quick returns for about a decade and a half, followed by a slowdown. The point of transition came in the early-1970s when prospects of manufacturing growth by selling at the limited home market were exhausted. The high cost and poor quality of goods depressed even domestic demand. The extreme form of import protection practiced in the region, with average tariff rates nearing 100 percent, hurt exports because new technologies were not allowed in. Poor export effort and high budget deficits worsened inflation and the balance of payments. As resources were channeled into capital goods, potentially exportable labor-intensive manufactures such as textiles and clothing were denied capital. The later years of import substitution were thus characterized by low levels of factor productivity and low employment potentials.

Liberalization. Between 1985 and 1995 a package of trade and industrial reforms was introduced in India, Pakistan, and Bangladesh. In Sri Lanka liberalization had begun as early as 1967. Starting with the liberalization of exchange rates and a reduction in tariffs, the reforms extended to industrial and financial deregulation and privatization. The end of the regime saw a dramatic rise in income, employment, and export growth rates. Important examples of export success include textiles and clothing throughout South Asia in the 1990s and information technology and pharmaceuticals in the 2000s in India. In India, export success was a joint outcome of the strengths of the old regime and those of the new. For example, implicit protection in the old regime in the shape of process patents had fostered indigenous research and development in pharmaceuticals. After the reforms this nurturing stood India in good stead as several firms emerged from this experience with superior research capability. The emphasis on higher and technical education as part of the industrialization strategy of the old regime also helped build capability in information technology.

Assessment. Students of economic development often find it hard to explain South Asian economic performance. The tenacious mix of extreme poverty and world-class enterprise makes most abstract models fail fully to explain economic change in South Asia. By and large, manufacturing and services responded efficiently to opportunities offered by globalization of the nineteenth century, protection in the mid-twentieth, and globalization again from the late twentieth century. That said, two long-standing features explain to a large extent the persistence of poverty: high rates of population growth and poor quality of land resources, especially the universal and acute scarcity of water. The struggle to overcome these geographical and social constraints is far from over.

[*See also* Agriculture, *subentry* South Asia; Child Labor, *subentry* South Asia; Environment, *subentry* Environment and Pollution in South Asia; Industrialization, *subentry* South Asia; Labor and the Labor Movement, *subentry* South Asia; Land, *subentry* Land Use and Land Reform in South Asia; Middle Class, *subentry* South Asia; Peasants, *subentry* South Asia; Railroads, *subentry* South Asia; South Asian Association for Regional Cooperation; Tourism, *subentry* South Asia; Trade, International, *subentry* South Asia; Urbanism and Urbanization, *subentry* South Asia; *and entries on countries mentioned in this article.*]

BIBLIOGRAPHY

Athukorala, Prema-chandra, and Sarath Rajapatirana. *Liberalization and Industrial Transformation: Sri Lanka in International Perspective.* New Delhi, India: Oxford University Press, 2000.

Hasan, Parvez. *Pakistan's Economy at the Crossroads: Past Policies and Present Imperatives.* Karachi, Pakistan: Oxford University Press, 1998.

Jahan, Rounaq, ed. *Bangladesh: Promise and Performance.* London: Zed, 2000.

Kumar, Dharma, ed. *The Cambridge Economic History of India.* Vol. 2: *c. 1757–c. 1970.* Cambridge, U.K.: Cambridge University Press, 1983.

Roy, Tirthankar. *The Economic History of India, 1857–1947.* 2d ed. New Delhi, India: Oxford University Press, 2006.

Srinivasan, T. N., and Suresh D. Tendulkar. *Reintegrating India with the World Economy.* Washington, D.C.: Institute for International Economics, 2003.

TIRTHANKAR ROY

Southeast Asia

"Southeast Asia," as a term signifying a distinct and coherent subregion of Asia, alongside (or between) South Asia and East Asia, is relatively recent, dating from World War II. It is now generally identified as coterminous with the Association of Southeast Asian Nations (ASEAN), comprising Indonesia, Malaysia, Singapore, the Philippines, and Thailand (the 1967 founding members), plus Brunei (1984), Vietnam (1995), Cambodia, Laos, and Burma (1997). East Timor and Papua New Guinea are associate members, eventually likely to join.

The history of the political economy of the region and its commercial and industrial development is as complex as its geography. Southeast Asia is the world's most fragmented and exotically diverse region (including the 26,000 islands of Indonesia and the Philippines), encompassing an immense variety of country situations in terms of land areas, population sizes, histories, ethnographies, languages, religions, social arrangements, and cultural practices.

The region's rich and diverse resources have made it a magnet for migrants, traders, and investors, as well as conquerors, evangelists, smugglers, pirates, spies, and most recently (after 2001) Islamic terrorists. This diversity allows for a wide range of perspectives, interpretations, and endlessly fascinating debates. Southeast Asian politicians, commentators, and scholars are thus challenged to frame this formidable range of contrasts within a manageable comparable context.

Indonesia. Indonesia accounts for around 43 percent of Southeast Asia's population and land area, and 32 percent of its combined gross domestic product (see Tables 1 and 2 for these and other selected socioeconomic indicators). It is the prototype "export economy" with a long experience of staple-led growth from spices and indigo, tea, coffee, tobacco, copra, sisal, rubber, tin, palm oil, tropical hardwoods, fish, copper, urea, bauxite, and petroleum, among many other primary exports. The large caches of Chinese coins discovered in many parts of Indonesia indicate that overseas trading goes back to several centuries B.C.E., and suggest that local producers ran trade surpluses and kept the coins to facilitate local and other international transactions (or as security against the contingencies of poor harvests, sickness, or other natural or man-made disasters). As leading international traders, the Chinese thus profited, since they were able to run balance-of-payments deficits by letting their currency circulate overseas, while less developed countries, such as Indonesia, generally ran trade surpluses, with some of the financial surplus being

extracted by powerful interlopers as taxes, tribute, plunder, or "protection payments" against being plundered.

Around the twelfth century, a few Indonesian trade goods had reached Europe via a tortuous land route across India, Arabia, and Italy, with middlemen making monopoly profits (appropriating economic rents) all along the way. When Columbus went astray in the Caribbean in 1492, he was seeking a shortcut to Ambon for the spices, to capture this conduit of profits. In 1448 the Portuguese rounded the Cape of Good Hope but encountered a formidable "Indonesian" navy that outmaneuvered them and, with bronze cannons, outgunned them. They limped home, took another century to improve their technology, returned, and conquered. In 1602 the Dutch, after some rival colonial skirmishes, began their occupation, which lasted 340 years, but Indonesia's fragmentation and intense local identities and revolts meant that they never fully subjugated all regions. The Dutch introduced new export staples, coerced local cultivators, and appropriated the surplus. Decade by decade, export earnings often increased by over 50 percent, but with barely perceptible improvements in local farmers' incomes or the living standards of the indigenous population.

After the Japanese occupation (1942–1945) and a bitter struggle against the Dutch (1945–1948), Indonesia achieved independence. Its trade and development

TABLE 1. *Southeast Asia: area, population, and human development indicators*

COUNTRY	LAND AREA (1,000s OF SQ. KM.) (1)	POPULATION SIZE, 2006 (MILLIONS) (AND % GROWTH RATE, 2006) (2)	LIFE EXPECTANCY AT BIRTH IN 2004 (YEARS) (3)	LITERACY, 2004 (% OF POPULATION OVER AGE 15) (4)	SCHOOL ENROLLMENT IN 2004, PRIMARY, SECONDARY, TERTIARY (% OF AGE COHORTS) (5)	HDI RANK 2004 (AND PER CAPITA GDP PPP RANK, 2005) (6)
Indonesia	1,919.4	234.7 (1.2)	67.2	90.4	94, 57, 16	108 (114)
Malaysia	329.7	24.8 (1.8)	73.4	88.7	93, 76, 26	61 (60)
Philippines	300.0	91.1 (1.8)	70.7	92.6	94, 61, 29	84 (103)
Singapore	0.7	4.6 (1.3)	78.9	92.5	100, 59, 9	25 (17)
Thailand	513.0	65.1 (0.7)	70.3	92.6	85, 77, 41	74 (70)
Vietnam	332.0	85.3 (1.0)	70.8	90.3	93, 65, 10	109 (121)
Brunei	5.7	0.38 (1.8)	76.6	92.7	100, 94, 13	34 (29)
Burma (Myanmar)	677.0	47.4 (0.8)	60.5	89.9	87, 37, n.a.	130 (142)
Cambodia	181.0	14.0 (1.7)	56.5	73.6	98, 26, 3	129 (123)
Laos	236.0	6.5 (2.4)	55.1	68.7	84, 37, 6	133 (137)

NOTES: HDI = Human Development Index. The Human Development Index is based on a calculation involving (a) life expectancy (column 3), (b) literacy (column 4) and net school enrollment rates at the primary, secondary, and tertiary levels (column 5), and (c) gross domestic product per capita adjusted for purchasing power parity (table 2, column 2). GDP = gross domestic product. PPP = purchasing power parity. The HDI ranking in Column 6 is out of 177 countries; the GDP PPP per capita ranking is out of 179 countries.
SOURCES: Column 1, and Columns 3–6: United Nations Development Programme, *Human Development Report, 2007* that includes data on many other economic and social indicators. Source for GDP PPP per capita rankings in column 6: International Monetary Fund, *World Economic Outlook*, April 2007. Estimates for tertiary level enrollment in Column 5: United Nations Development Programme, *Country Fact Sheets*, 1995. SOURCE for Column 2: Central Intelligence Agency, *Factbook* (updated online, 27 July 2007), that provides a constantly updated data source; however, the population size and growth rate data can differ somewhat from United Nations, World Bank, and other estimates, having been adjusted for AIDS mortality rates, often not included in national data for some countries. C.f. also, for selected countries: Economist Intelligence Unit, *Country Fact Sheets* (quarterly).

TABLE 2. *Southeast Asia: selected economic indicators*

COUNTRY	GDP (US$ BILLIONS), 2006, (SAME PER CAPITA)	GDP PPP (US$ BILLIONS), 2006, (SAME PER CAPITA)	REAL GDP GROWTH RATES, 2001–2005, AND 2006 (% PER YEAR)	INFLATION, 2001–2005, AND 2006 (% PER YEAR)	AVERAGE REAL GDP GROWTH RATES, 1970s, 1980s, 1990s (% PER YEAR)	SHARES OF GDP OF AGR., IND., SERV., 2006 (%)	EXPORTS/GDP, IMPORTS/GDP, 2006 (%)
	(1)	(2)	(3)	(4)	(5)	(6)	(7)
Indonesia	264.7 ($1,127)	948.3 ($3,900)	2.6 (5.5)	5.9 (13.2)	8.9, 6.3, 4.4	13, 46, 54	39, 29
Malaysia	132.3 ($5,323)	313.8 ($12,900)	4.9 (5.9)	1.7 (3.8)	9.6, 6.0, 7.3	8, 48, 44	120, 96
Philippines	116.9 ($1,283)	449.8 ($5,000)	4.3 (5.4)	5.4 (6.2)	6.0, 3.0, 3.1	14, 32, 54	40, 44
Singapore	122.1 ($26,543)	141.2 ($31,400)	3.3 (7.9)	0.6 (1.0)	9.1, 7.4, 7.8	0.1, 34, 66	232, 202
Thailand	197.7 ($3,037)	596.5 ($9,200)	5.0 (4.8)	2.2 (5.1)	6.8, 7.9, 4.6	10, 45, 45	62, 60
Vietnam	48.4 ($568)	262.8 ($3,100)	7.5 (8.2)	4.5 (7.5)	−0.4, 5.6, 7.6	20, 42, 38	82, 81
Brunei	9.5 ($25,600)	9.5 ($53,600)	n.a.(0.4)	n.a.(1.1)	8.3, −1.8, 0.9	3, 61, 36	66, 16
Burma (Myanmar)	9.6 ($203)	85.2 ($1,800)	n.a.(3.0)	n.a.(21.4)	4.4, 1.4, 7.1	50, 15, 35	37, 21
Cambodia	6.6 ($471)	37.7 ($2,700)	n.a.(7.2)	n.a.(5.0)	−6.7, 0.5, 3.6	35, 30, 35	51, 67
Laos	2.8 ($427)	13.6 ($2,100)	n.a.(7.4)	n.a.(6.8)	0.0, 5.5, 6.3	43, 31, 26	35, 49

NOTES: GDP = gross domestic product. PPP = purchasing power parity. Column 1: Nominal gross-domestic-product estimates converted to U.S. dollars at prevailing currency exchange rates. Column 2: Gross domestic product adjusted for purchasing power parity, to take into account lower domestic commodity prices vis-à-vis the United States. Column 3: Nominal GDP growth rates have been adjusted to eliminate the influence of yearly commodity price inflation. The result is real GDP growth. Column 4: Inflation (or the GDP deflator applied in column 3). (adding real GDP growth rates and inflation will yield nominal GDP growth rates). Column 5: Average GDP growth rates in constant 1990 prices. Note that some growth rates are negative. Column 6: Value-added shares in the gross domestic product of (a) agriculture (including forestry and fisheries), (b) industry (mining, manufacturing, and construction), and (c) service-sector activities. Column 7: Total values of exports and imports as a percentage of the gross domestic product. High levels of total exports (e.g., for Singapore) can include exports with high import content (as in processing and assembly, wholesale retailing, and simple transshipment).

SOURCES: Data for columns 1–4 and 6–7: Central Intelligence Agency, *Factbook* (online, 27 July 2007; a convenient source that is constantly updated). Somewhat different estimates can be found in the Economist Intelligence Unit, *Country Fact Sheets* (1997), the World Bank, *World Development Indicators* (2007), the Asian Development Bank, *Key Indicators* (2006), and the *ASEAN Statistical Yearbook* (2005).

Data for column 5: United Nations, Department of Economic and Social Affairs, *Statistical Database*, September 2005, and links to national statistical data sources.

strategy under President Sukarno can be broadly characterized as (a) a continuation of primary-export-led growth, but with efforts to diversify the commodity composition and to transfer ownership and control from foreign to indigenous operators (to extract economic rents), and (b) a reaction to foreign trade and investment dependency, with attempts to build up and integrate the indigenous economy and especially to promote industrialization (for value-added productivity). Sukarno's disillusionment with what he saw as continuing neocolonial dominance over Indonesia's terms of trade and access to global finance led him to strive for a more regulated and economically self-reliant approach. This failed, owing in part to international isolation and hostility, but mainly because Sukarno and his advisers lacked a coherent and practical model of alternative development on which to base their strategy, and by 1960 the economy had virtually collapsed.

In 1967 President Suharto's New Order reinstated Indonesia's outward-looking orientation: revitalizing primary-export-led growth, attracting foreign aid and investment, and promoting many large-scale joint-venture projects. Especially after 1973, a bonanza in foreign exchange earnings from oil (courtesy of OPEC, the Organization of the Petroleum Exporting Countries, which engineered a tenfold increase in crude oil prices from 1973 to 1978) and provided a gusher of tax revenues that enabled the government to mortgage this wealth through extensive international borrowing. This enabled it to promote a "green revolution" (transforming Indonesia from the world's largest rice importer to a virtually self-sufficient country by the 1980s); to undertake extensive irrigation, road improvement, electrification, and other infrastructure projects; to subsidize food and petroleum prices and imported fertilizers and chemicals; and to make significant outlays on education, health facilities, and other social investments. However, this development bonanza also encouraged megaproject mania, extravagant urban office, housing, and hotel construction, and other schemes of questionable productivity or social merit. The profit-seeking frenzy created a pervasive culture of cronyism, nepotism, and corruption, of monopoly franchises and preferential credit, with bank lending increasingly politicized and lack of transparency obscuring misappropriation, insolvency, and nonperforming loans.

Oil revenues declined in the 1980s, and chronic deficits were incurred in the financial (or capital) account as debt-service costs escalated, foreign profits were repatriated, and the elite increasingly banked or invested their wealth overseas. Rather than seek appropriate ways to reduce its dependency on foreign exchange, the government took the easy way out: systematically devaluing the rupiah (by 34 percent in 1978, 28 percent in 1983, 31 percent in 1986; and on average by 5 percent per year between 1987 and 1996). The International Monetary Fund routinely endorsed such devaluations as a legitimate response to Indonesia's chronic inflation and balance-of-payments deficits, but it was a short-term palliative, not a root-cause solution. The Fund also promoted economic-reform packages to attract foreign loans and investment, especially in plantations, mining, fisheries, and tourism. The government promoted some import substitution, but mainly pushed non-oil exports by any means possible, often involving cheap resource giveaways with disastrous environmental impacts, especially on forests and around mining sites. Attempts to increase value-added export processing included transforming Indonesia from the world's largest tropical hardwood exporter to its largest plywood exporter (though the trees came down just the same). Export tax-free zones, industrial-park subsidies, and other incentives did succeed in attracting foreign investment into labor-intensive industries such as textiles, footwear, and other manufacturing, and this boosted employment and export earnings, but the repressive labor practices were widely criticized as perpetuating a "cheap-labor mentality," and hence as being "antidevelopmental."

The 1997 Asian Financial Crisis, which originated in Thailand, hit Indonesia especially hard, and its economic recovery was more prolonged than that in other countries. Student-led demonstrations ousted Suharto in 1998; he was followed by a sequence of four presidents in six years, culminating in October 2004 with President Susilo Bambang Yudhoyono, the first to be directly elected. Yudhoyono initiated a new era of political and institutional reform, but economic recovery remained problematic, with efforts to attract foreign investment hampered by judicial and bureaucratic obstacles, endemic corruption, sectarian violence, street crime, recurrent Al-Qaeda–type terrorist bombings, and anti-U.S. (and anti-Western) hostility exacerbated by events in Iraq. Demands for local autonomy have also made securing "Unity in Diversity" (Indonesia's national motto) a formidable challenge. The December 2004 Indian Ocean tsunami, the most disastrous in recorded history, wreaked social and economic havoc in Aceh, but also helped end decades of bloody conflict and fostered a surge in international assistance.

Malaysia. Since at least 1400, the port city of Malacca has played a strategic role in facilitating commerce in the Malacca Straits. It was captured by Portugal in 1511, by

Holland in 1641, and by Britain in 1785, being annexed from 1819 to 1826 with Penang and Singapore as the Straits Settlements. By 1874 Britain controlled most of the Malay sultanates by indirect rule and had superimposed export enclaves, notably tin mines and rubber plantations, alongside the local subsistence economy. This socioeconomic dualism was intensified by the fact that the mines and plantations employed mostly Chinese and Indian migrants, rather than local Malays. Malaya became the world's largest exporter of rubber, tin, palm oil, and later tropical hardwoods and other forest products, to which were added substantial exports of oil and natural gas. Export revenues often grew by 5 percent or more per year, but the income mostly benefited landowners, foreign investors, import-export firms, local sultans, and a rentier elite, as well as manufacturers and consumers in more developed countries. Hence, even in 1965, 49 percent of Malaysia's population was officially recorded as living below the poverty line.

Malaya achieved independence in 1957, becoming Malaysia by adding Sabah and Sarawak in 1963 (along with Singapore, which then separated in 1965). Malays and aboriginal inhabitants composed around 55 percent of the population and were assigned a special status (as *bumiputera,* or "sons of the soil"), while Chinese and Indian citizens comprised around 35 percent and 10 percent respectively. Most Malays were rural subsistence farmers or smallholder rubber producers, while significant numbers of Chinese and Indians pursued urban occupations (with Chinese being dominant in commerce and finance, and Indians in the legal profession and other service sectors, although many earned modest livelihoods). In the 1960s the government sought to boost rural incomes by subsidizing the research and transplanting of high-yielding rubber and rice strains (a green revolution), but the productivity gains mostly reduced prices rather than raising farmers' incomes (especially since similar innovations were being implemented in neighboring countries). In 1965, as Malaya redefined itself as Malaysia, the government shifted its strategy toward promoting industrial development and securing Malay participation. Quotas favoring Malays for university entrance, civil service, and army recruitment were increased, and the New Economic Policy required businesses to give hiring preference to Malays and corporations to assign 30 percent of their stock shares to *bumiputera* institutions for eventual transfer to Malay ownership. Malaysia's still bountiful primary-export revenues were used to subsidize import substitution and other pioneer industries, and through tax relief, industrial-park development and other incentives that induced foreign corporations to locate their processing and export assembly platforms in Malaysia, especially producing electronic equipment, garments, footwear, sports equipment, and cosmetics. Malaysia also invested heavily in Silicon Valley–type development, which fostered indigenous computer-based industries and a highly skilled sector of its labor force, while also promoting a "national-car project" and other components of a modern industrial and service-sector economy. This fostered national pride and significant multiracial harmony, creating a substantial urban middle class, and generating linkage benefits to the rural sector. These admirable achievements remain highly dependent, however, on state patronage and investment subsidies, which also help perpetuate a relatively autocratic political system, an extensive bureaucracy, an economic–rent-seeking quasi-service sector, and a rent-absorbing privileged elite.

Singapore. In sharp contrast to Malaysia, the small island city-state known as Singapore was virtually devoid of natural resources, with only its location conferring a natural comparative advantage, which colonial and Chinese enterprise built into a major import-export entrepôt. Singapore became de facto self-governing in 1959, briefly joined Malaysia in 1963, but separated in 1965, leaving it feeling like a besieged economy threatened by nationalist animosities from Malaysia and Indonesia ("a Chinese island in a hostile Muslim sea," as it was described at the time). The analogy prompted Prime Minister Lee Kuan Yew to look to Israel as a model for strategy, both in acquiring military advice, weapons, and training, and in molding its people into a cohesive, well-educated, highly motivated, and patriotic nation (a strategy that also involved repressing labor unions, left-wing parties, and student protests, all regarded as "subversive"). Yet Singapore also developed its own version of the East Asian model, beginning with import substitution and value-added processing of regional primary imports for re-export. By the mid-1970s Singapore had become the region's most well-equipped, secure and healthy environment, the preferred location for multinational corporate regional headquarters, with a wide range of financial, commercial, and high-tech activities. In 2007 it ranked as one of the world's most globalized economies, with total export earnings (including re-exports) often registering two or three times the total value of gross domestic product, and with a per capita gross domestic product higher than most European nations. This outstanding performance evidently emanated from Singapore's very special circumstances and from its process of social engineering that was not likely to be easily replicated by neighbors, such as Indonesia, with entrenched rural poverty and much larger, diverse, and dispersed populations.

Thailand. Thailand was known as Siam until 1939, when it took its present name. The country, through history and mythology, traces its national identity to the kingdoms of Sukhothai (1238–1438) and Ayutthaya (1351–1767). During the height of its imperial conquest, it controlled most of today's Cambodia and Laos, and parts of Burma and Malaysia. Burmese invasions fostered national unity and consolidated an absolute monarchy (1768–1932), which then created princely trading monopolies and excluded foreigners. Portuguese and Spanish traders were active in Siam since the sixteenth century, and Dutch, British, and French traders since the seventeenth century. By the early nineteenth century, Britain, based in Malaysia and Burma and expanding its regional ambitions, sent missions to Siam in 1821 and 1825 demanding commercial access and extraterritoriality (immunity for its citizens from local laws). It gained partial acquiescence in 1826 and virtual full compliance with the 1855 Bowring Treaty (helped by the intimidating example of the 1840–1842 Opium War through which China had been coerced to open up its markets to foreign traders). Threats from France and the United States soon led to a full opening of the country to foreign commerce. Subsequently, in 1909 Siam's possessions in Malaya were annexed by Britain, while France, having occupied Saigon in 1859 and all of Vietnam by 1867, sent gunboats in 1893 to force Siam to surrender the remainder of Laos, and by 1907 all of Cambodia had been annexed into French Indochina. Thailand was able to avoid colonization—a unique feat among Southeast Asian nations—in part because it formed a convenient buffer zone between the British and French empires.

As Southeast Asia's largest mainland nation, Thailand has a long history of rivalry with Vietnam, and this continues in efforts to lay claim to Cambodian and Laotian resources, and in border disputes over fishing rights, oil exploration, and other strategic interests. This helps explain Thailand's willingness to serve as a major U.S. staging base during the Second Indochina War (also known as the Vietnam War), especially after Thailand was alleged to be the next domino under threat from Communist China's expansionism. Rice production made Thailand one of the region's major rice bowls, but as the green revolution spread across Southeast Asia in the 1960s and 1970s, rice prices plummeted, and this prompted efforts to diversify exports and promote industrialization through subsidized import substitution. Thailand had a relatively well-educated, low-wage, and disciplined workforce, and it set up industrial parks and duty-free export zones that encouraged East Asian firms to outsource their textile, garment, footwear, sports equipment, and other labor-intensive manufacturing. To diversify resources for export, efforts were also made to promote forestry products, shrimp farming, and gemstone production. Catering to U.S. military bases during the Second Indochina War also dramatically expanded Thailand's hospitality and related service sectors, including cultural attractions, elaborate beach resorts, and extensive golf courses, all of which now make Thailand one of Asia's leading tourist destinations.

The military has long played a prominent role in Thailand's political and economic affairs. A 1932 coup established a constitutional monarchy, and there have been seventeen subsequent political coups. High levels of foreign military and economic aid helped boost the military's influence in creating a secure corporate business environment, but such aid also encouraged pervasive corruption and repression of labor unions and social and political activism. Industrial and service-sector development, including large corporate conglomerates and thousands of small enterprises (often dependent on corporate outsourcing), has always been highly concentrated in and around Bangkok. Thailand's rapidly expanding middle class and its well-funded financial sector (including military banks) also stimulated indigenous entrepreneurship and locally financed business initiatives. By the 1980s Bangkok had created a sophisticated capital and financial intermediation sector to rival Singapore and Hong Kong. The substantial urban middle class and wealthy elite enjoyed lifestyles in stark contrast to the bare subsistence and modest living standards in the rest of the country. New industrial sectors had a high import content (including raw materials, equipment, technology, and components for local assembly), while urban consumerism also boosted imports of high-tech and luxury goods. By the 1990s, rising wages and other production costs were also slowing export performance, and this added to a chronic balance-of-payments deficit, which in 1997 triggered capital flight, a currency collapse, and a major financial and economic crisis that precipitated a wider Asian Financial Crisis and fears of a global economic recession. Since then Thailand has steadily recovered, resuming essentially the same economic strategy, but with more accountability, financial safeguards, and a somewhat more democratic political system. Corruption and special-interest manipulation remain endemic, however, and in March 2006 scandals and vote buying again polarized the disaffected rural poor against Bangkok's affluent urban-industrial enclave. In September 2006, while Prime Minister Thaksin Shinawatra was attending the United Nations General Assembly in New York, the military engineered another political coup, citing the need to avoid political turmoil and curb corruption, and promising to restore democracy within twelve months. As of 2007 the government was focusing so much on controlling a brewing conflict in the country's Muslim-majority southern provinces that it tended to neglect the many other pressing socio-economic issues jeopardizing the nation.

Philippines. The Philippine archipelago comprises over 7,000 islands (of which 2,000 are inhabited year-round). Chinese trade with coastal villages dates from the tenth century, and in the fifteenth century Muslim traders brought Islam to Mindanao and Luzon. In 1521 Ferdinand Magellan's "discovery" of the archipelago led to Spanish colonial domination from 1565 to 1898 (when the United States took control following the Spanish-American War). Spain did little to develop the indigenous resource potential of its only Asian colony beyond making huge land grants to Catholic missionaries and to a Spanish and local rentier class. Exclusive state monopolies effectively isolated the Philippines from global trade, while Manila flourished as a transshipment port for galleons plying the China–Mexico–Spain import-export trade. A substantial local Chinese merchant community also prospered in these entrepôt activities and, through mixed marriages, formed part of an emerging Filipino elite and middle class of bankers, landowners, civil servants, and other professionals. The galleon trade came to an end in 1815, and the lifting of foreign trade restrictions in 1834 led to a more systematic development of a primary-export economy, featuring plantation crops such as sugar, tobacco, hemp, and copra, and with sugar refining, rum, and cigars as value-added exports.

After the Spanish-American War, the U.S. occupation met with a tenacious guerrilla insurrection (1899–1913) demanding national independence, after which U.S. control was rationalized as a temporary tutelage until democratic institutions and the rule of law could be established. A parliament was elected in 1907 with broad autonomy over domestic affairs (but subject to the veto power of a U.S. governor general), and in 1935 the Philippines was declared a commonwealth with the promise of full independence by 1945 (when it became a republic). English became the official language, American-style institutions and culture became dominant, and several major U.S. naval and military bases were established. U.S. citizens

were assured equal legal rights with Filipinos, for example in regard to resource ownership, and U.S. firms predominated in financial and many other service sectors. Under preferential free-trade agreements, Philippine primary exports surged, while U.S. manufactured imports outcompeted local producers.

After independence, the Philippines continued to receive special consideration in U.S. economic assistance and in the military buildup during the Korean War and the Second Indochina (or Vietnam) War. By 1965 rapid economic growth was being encouraged by the country's high educational standards, facility with the English language, and familiarity with Western technology, making the Philippines appear as the most likely candidate, after Japan, to become Asia's next NIC (newly industrializing country). High levels of imports also suggested obvious sectors for import substitution, if only foreign investors could be induced to outsource their assembly plants, or if the nation could somehow free itself from neocolonial dependency. While the male-dominated elite continued to control local politics and the national legislature, a series of strong presidents, backed by economic nationalists and popular anticolonial sentiment, succeeded in playing the anticommunist threat to gain leverage with the U.S. government and its corporate establishment to assist to some degree in this industrial transition. President Ferdinand Marcos was most adroit in gaining U.S.-endorsed economic and military support. However, under his autocratic and corrupt regime, the allocation of industrial subsidies, tariffs, quotas, and franchises became increasingly politicized in favor of a crony financial clique. There was a sharp conflict of interest between the aspiring urban industrial elite and the entrenched quasi-feudal landowning class benefiting from primary-export economic rents and their close links with U.S. corporations and import-export firms. Yet here too Marcos found ways to divide and compensate the landowning elite by playing one subgroup against another. Moreover, all elite classes had an interest in perpetuating a cheap-labor advantage, which created a widening polarization of incomes and wealth. In consequence, the Philippines under Marcos became a "beat-NIC" rather than a "miracle economy," and, even after Marcos's ouster in 1986 by a remarkable nonviolent, people-power coup, the persistence of political patronage, corruption, industrial inertia, and bureaucratic inefficiency has saddled the nation with one of the worst levels of persistent poverty in Southeast Asia.

Vietnam. Vietnam's elongated coastline makes it a natural seafaring nation, and its 74 percent mountainous terrain has made its coastal zones and many valleys some of Asia's most densely populated regions. Ethnic Vietnamese (Kinh) account for 85 percent of its 85 million people, the remainder consisting of Chinese (3 percent) and 52 other ethnic minorities. Chinese dynasties ruled northern Vietnam for over a thousand years (111 B.C.E.–938 C.E.), introducing Buddhism and Confucianism, but also a legacy of animosity, suspicion, and periodic conflict (most recently in 1979 during the Sino-Vietnamese War, after Vietnam attacked the Khmer Rouge regime in Cambodia). French colonization began in 1858, was completed in 1885, and ended with the battle of Dien Bien Phu and the 1954 Geneva Convention. Plans for unification failed in 1955 when South Vietnam, with U.S. support, declared itself a republic, and the North, led by Ho Chi Minh and backed by the Soviet Union, established a Communist regime. In the subsequent conflict, the Second Indochina War (known in the United States as the Vietnam War), U.S. military support built up to 534,000 troops, of whom 58,000 were killed, while Vietnamese troop fatalities amounted to over 1 million on each side, plus an estimated 3 million civilians.

Following reunification, Vietnam was effectively isolated from global trade and finance by a U.S.-imposed embargo that included denial of eligibility for World Bank, International Monetary Fund, and most other multilateral and bilateral loans and assistance. It depended heavily on barter trade with the Soviet Union, East Germany, and other Comintern countries, and on credit and technical assistance from these and other Communist countries, notably Cuba. After a decade of sluggish economic performance and resistance to its efforts to impose collectivized farming and state-planning on the previously free-enterprise South, the government in 1986 began a sequence of learning-by-doing economic reconstruction (known as the *doi moi* reforms) that, by stages, transformed Vietnam into a multisector, market-oriented–socialist economy and opened it up to foreign trade and investment. The domestic and international response was dramatic, and from 1990 to 2005 Vietnam's gross domestic product grew at an average of over 8 percent per year. Agriculture production doubled, transforming Vietnam from a country of chronic food shortages to the world's second-largest rice exporter, and exports of coffee, tea, rubber, fish, crude oil, and other minerals rapidly expanded. Foreign investment also dramatically increased exports of such labor-intensive products as textiles, garments, shoes, and handicrafts. The United States lifted its embargo in 1994 and negotiated the U.S.-Vietnam Bilateral Trade Agreement in 2001. Vietnam joined the Association of Southeast Asian Nations in 1995, the forum for Asia-Pacific Economic Cooperation (APEC) in 1999; in 2007 Vietnam achieved full membership in the World Trade

Vietnamese Factory. Workers assemble shoes at a Nike factory on the outskirts of Ho Chi Minh City, Vietnam, October 2000. Photograph by Richard Vogel. AP IMAGES

Organization. Shortly after entry, however, fears of imbalanced growth and exposure to the volatility, intense competition, and unequal terms of trade often operating in world markets raised concern in some official circles over the burdens of membership.

Brunei. Brunei is a small, wealthy oil-producing Islamic Sultanate located on Borneo Island, surrounded by Malaysia. The sultanate, dating from the ninth century, became a British Protectorate in 1888, became self-governing in 1959, and gained full independence in 1984. Brunei is Southeast Asia's third-largest oil producer, and the world's fourth-largest exporter of liquefied natural gas, resources that are estimated to account for 90 percent of export revenues, although national secrecy restricts access to this and other economic data. The government is appointed by the sultan, not elected, but provides free education and medical services, and subsidizes rice and housing. The population comprises 67 percent Malays, 15 percent Chinese, 6 percent aboriginals, and 12 per cent other ethnicities. Underemployment is relatively high and the government is seeking to upgrade skills and diversify its economic sectors, especially in tourism and financial services.

Cambodia. Khmer kingdoms date from the first century C.E., eventually expanding over most of today's Cambodia, Laos, Vietnam, and parts of Thailand, especially during the Angkor Empire, from the ninth century to the fifteenth (reaching its climax in the thirteenth), but finally succumbed to a Siamese invasion in 1431. With Siam and Vietnam vying for its territory, the Khmer civilization and local economy went into decline. In 1863 it became a French protectorate and in 1907 part of French Indochina, until it gained independence in 1953. From the mid-1960s North Vietnamese troops used its border region as a haven and conduit while waging war on South Vietnam, and U.S. bombing raids killed more than a million Cambodians. Subsequent political instability, exacerbated by Vietnamese and U.S. intervention, climaxed in 1975 with a Khmer Rouge military coup. This monstrous regime emptied cities and towns and killed around one-third of Cambodia's 7.3 million people by assassination, starvation, forced labor, or lack of medical attention. In December 1978 Vietnam invaded, driving the Khmer Rouge army out of Phnom Penh and into the northwest region. Civil war continued until a Paris peace conference in 1989–1991, after which U.N. peacekeepers organized elections in 1993 that installed a coalition government which eventually achieved a Khmer Rouge surrender in 1998.

After three decades of war and turmoil, 1999 was the first year of relative normalcy for Cambodia. The economy began to recover, boosted by foreign economic assistance, and preferential quotas for textile exports under the Agreement on Textiles and Clothing, sponsored by the World Trade Organization. (These quotas expired in January 2005, however, and Cambodia must compete with China and other low-cost exporters.) A major restoration of Angkor Wat (1994–2005), funded mostly by Japan, has made Cambodia one of Asia's leading tourist attractions and has become a major source of foreign exchange. However, three-quarters of Cambodians are still engaged in subsistence agriculture, while narcotics, gem smuggling, and money laundering remain pervasive. Future progress will also require reducing institutionalized corruption and improving occupational skills, especially of the 75 percent of its population under age twenty.

Laos. Dating from 1353, the Lan Xang kingdom reached its zenith in the sixteenth century and fell under Siamese control in the eighteenth century. It was absorbed by stages into French Indochina from 1893 to 1904, fell to Japan during World War II (along with most of Southeast Asia), and achieved independence under the 1954 Geneva Convention. A series of unstable coalition governments and army coups in the 1950s led to a second Geneva Convention (1961–1962), which confirmed its independence and political neutrality, but the agreement was subverted by both Vietnam and the United States, which supported proxy parties and militias and dragged Laos into the Second Indochina (or Vietnam) War. From 1965 to 1975 Laos sustained the heaviest bombing in the history of warfare, inflicted by the United States, with casualty estimates ranging from 50,000 to 500,000, and with thousands of unexploded bombs continuing to cripple children and adults.

Laos became a Communist state in 1975 when Pathet Lao rebels forced the king to abdicate. Both politically and economically, it depended heavily on Vietnam until the late 1980s, when Vietnamese troops were withdrawn. Foreign trade, aid, and investment remained minuscule, and the economy stagnated. Drug production and trafficking provide a major source of (unrecorded) income and revenues, perpetuating corruption and criminality. In 1986 the government began to decentralize decision making and encourage private enterprise (following Vietnam's example, but without its dramatic success). Tourism did improve, but is deterred by lack of security from robberies and kidnappings. Over 40 percent of Laotians live below the poverty line, while 80 percent rely on subsistence agriculture.

Burma (Myanmar). Burma was a flourishing Buddhist kingdom from the eleventh to thirteenth centuries. It then fell to Mogul invaders, became a Chinese vassal state, and was colonized by Britain (1824–1886) and later incorporated into its Indian empire. Burma became a self-governing colony in 1937, gained independence in 1948, and declined membership in the British Commonwealth. From 1962 to 1988, General Ne Win imposed his ill-fated Burmese way to socialism, effectively isolating the nation and its economy. Multiparty elections in 1990 gave a landslide majority to the National League for Democracy, headed by Aung San Suu Kyi, but the military junta refused to cede power, put her under house arrest, and imprisoned many of her followers. (They also changed the country's name to Myanmar, but this is not recognized by the United States and several other nations.) Aung San Suu Kyi was awarded the Nobel Peace Prize in 1991, as Burma continues to be widely condemned for human-rights violations, persecution of ethnic minorities (which comprise half the population), endemic corruption, environmental degradation, and narcotics trafficking. Many nations canceled economic aid and imposed economic sanctions on Burma. Thailand has given sanctuary to thousands of Karen and other ethnic-minority refugees, but the code of the Association of Southeast Asian Nations requiring member states not to criticize one another's domestic affairs has, until recently, muted regional condemnation. Eventually in July 2005 a meeting of ASEAN foreign ministers voiced concern over Burma's human-rights record and suggested it forgo its turn as chair of ASEAN in 2006, and in February 2006 a meeting of Southeast parliamentarians urged the association to expel Burma unless democracy is restored and Aung San Suu Kyi and other political prisoners are released. In mid-2007, steps were being taken to establish an ASEAN-wide Human Rights Commission. In September 2007, saffron-robed Buddhist monks led a group of thousands in protests of sharp hikes in gasoline and kerosene prices; these demonstrations escalated to include demands for the release of political prisoners such as Aung San Suu Kyi and a restoration of democratic government. Images of demonstrations from Rangoon, Mandalay, and other urban centers were transmitted globally via e-mail and cell phone cameras, and the military junta's violent response was condemned by the United Nations Security Council and many Asian and Western governments. This led to further tightening of economic sanctions.

Burma's exceptionally rich resource endowments, including forestry products, many types of minerals, precious stones, and hydroelectricity have attracted substantial trade and investment with China and Thailand, but at least 70 percent of the population is engaged in subsistence agriculture. Official export earnings of US$3 billion (mainly from clothing, natural gas, forest products, fish, and rice) are probably exceeded by earnings from smuggling (both informal and officially organized), especially of timber, gems, narcotics, and rice.

Key Issues Facing Southeast Asia. Economically, each nation needs to devise an appropriate commercial and industrial strategy that balances the potential gains from globalization with the need to protect against neocolonial dependency and volatile financial crises, and that identifies and promotes distinctive comparative advantages to secure employment, diversify production, and upgrade skills and technologies. The Association of Southeast Asian Nations has performed a useful role in promoting regional cooperation, resolving border disputes, and harmonizing economic policies, but has been less successful in promoting intra-ASEAN trade and industrial complementarity. China's spectacular industrial and technological development evidently makes it a dominant presence, a major trading partner, and a formidable competitor in virtually every manufacturing sector. Its ravenous need for primary imports raises the specter of its absorbing Southeast Asia into yet another neocolonial Greater East Asia Co-prosperity Sphere. Participation in broader pan-Asian and pan-Pacific organizations that promote common markets and broader economic integration might offset this bilateral dependency, but also requires that countries carefully balance the risks and benefits of such exposure and the loss of national autonomy from the rules and pressures being imposed.

The boost to economic nationalism triggered by the 1997 Asian Financial Crisis has subsequently been tempered in most Southeast Asian nations by the governments' perceived need to attract foreign investment again to reignite export-led growth and create industrial jobs. Fostering this perception is the fact that the bulk of global capital is now being absorbed by China and India, attracted by their low-wage and technologically adept workforces and by generous investment incentive packages. However, the people-power democracy movements that ousted autocratic regimes in several Southeast Asia countries in the aftermath of the Asian Crisis have made it difficult for the new administrations to follow their previous, or China's current, strategies of export-led growth based on cheap labor and cheap resource comparative advantages, particularly when accompanied by government cutbacks in social amenities provided by the public sphere. The informal economy, including smuggling and piracy, as well as extensive individual and small-business operations, has long accounted for the major share of people's livelihoods and income opportunities throughout Southeast Asia, but such activities do not generally form part of governmental priorities or perspectives, and more generally have been discouraged or repressed.

The "new economic imperatives" (or ideologies) of globalization, privatization, and more stringent self-reliance can thus be seen by local citizens as reneging on a social contract, dating from the struggle for independence, under which government promised to sustain local autonomy, secure employment and balanced economic growth, and promote social equity. Evidence of failure to fulfill such state responsibilities is also manifest in the endemic corruption that still permeates the political, administrative, and judicial systems in most Southeast Asian countries, which further stifles "faith in the system," hinders individual enterprise, and kills incentives for foreign and domestic investment. This sense of betrayal especially resonates in Indonesia, where recollections of the Sukarno regime's abuse of power are still vivid, and where Suharto's socialist legacy and ideals still resonate. Since 2001, potential investors and joint-venture partners have also been further discouraged by anti-Western (and especially anti-U.S.) sentiments inflamed by events in Iraq and Afghanistan, and by Al-Qaeda–inspired terrorism and intersectarian violence, that also jeopardize social stability and national integrity. These developments fundamentally undermine respect for the rule of law and for public agencies in general, and create serious impediments to civil society organization, self-help, and communal mutual assistance. Finding the will and viable means to promote political, social, and legal reform, to empower civil society initiatives, to promote tolerance and mutual respect, and to reconcile interreligious and other intersectarian tensions, thus rank among the highest priorities for government, religious, and civil society leaders in Southeast Asia seeking to secure social stability, sustainable development, economic prosperity, and genuine participatory democracy.

[*See also* Agriculture, *subentry* Southeast Asia; Angkor; ASEAN; Child Labor, *subentry* Southeast Asia; Environment, *subentry* Environment and Pollution in Southeast Asia; Labor and the Labor Movement, *subentry* Southeast Asia; Land, *subentry* Land Use and Land Reform in Southeast Asia; Peasants, *subentry* Southeast Asia; Sex Tourism; *and* Tourism, *subentry* Southeast Asia.]

BIBLIOGRAPHY

Anderson, Benedict. *Spectre of Comparisons: Nationalism, Southeast Asia and the World.* London: Verso, 1998.

Chandler, David. *A History of Cambodia.* 4th ed. Boulder, Colo.: Westview Press, 2007.

Crouch, Harold. *Government and Society in Malaysia.* Ithaca, N.Y.: Cornell University Press, 1996.

Dixon, Chris. *South-East Asia in the World Economy.* Cambridge, U.K.: Cambridge University Press, 1991.

Fforde, Adam, and S. de Vylder. *From Plan to Market: The Economic Transition in Vietnam.* Boulder, Colo.: Westview Press, 1996.

Hainsworth, Geoffrey B. "Economic Growth, Basic Needs, and Environment in Indonesia: The Search for Harmonious Development." *Southeast Asian Affairs 1985.* Singapore: Institute of Southeast Asian Studies, 1985.

Hainsworth, Geoffrey B., ed. *Globalization and the Asian Economic Crisis: Indigenous Responses, Coping Strategies, and Governance Reform in Southeast Asia.* Vancouver: Centre for Southeast Asia Research, University of British Columbia, 2000.

Hainsworth, Geoffrey B., ed. *Village-Level Modernization in Southeast Asia: The Politics of Rice and Water.* Vancouver: University of British Columbia Press, 1982.

Hawes, Gary. *The Philippine State and the Marcos Regime: The Politics of Export.* Ithaca, N.Y.: Cornell University Press, 1987.

Hewison, Kevin, Richard Robison, and Garry Rodan, eds. *Southeast Asia in the 1990s: Authoritarianism, Democracy and Capitalism.* Sydney, Australia: Allen and Unwin, 1993.

Hirsch, Philip. *Development Dilemmas in Rural Thailand.* Singapore: Oxford University Press, 1990.

Jamieson, Neil L. *Culture and Development in Vietnam.* Honolulu Hawai'i: East-West Center, 1991.

Jomo, K. S., ed. *Tigers in Trouble: Financial Governance, Liberalisation and Crises in East Asia.* New York: Zed Books, 1998.

Kingsbury, Damien. *Politics of Indonesia.* 3d ed. Singapore: Oxford University Press, 2005.

Keyes, Charles F. *Thailand: Buddhist Kingdom as Modern Nation State.* Boulder, Colo.: Westview Press, 1987.

Kunio, Yoshihara. *The Rise of Ersatz Capitalism in South-East Asia.* Singapore: Oxford University Press, 1988.

Reid, Anthony. *Southeast Asia in the Age of Commerce, 1450–1680.* New Haven, Conn.: Yale University Press, 1988.

Rigg, Jonathan. *Southeast Asia: The Human Landscape of Modernization and Development.* 2d ed. London and New York: Routledge, 2003.

Robison, Richard. *Indonesia: The Rise of Capital.* Canberra, Australia: Asian Studies Association of Australia, 1986. Sixth Impression. Sydney, Australia: Allen and Unwin, 1990.

Rodan, Garry. *The Political Economy of Singapore's Industrialisation: National State and International Capital.* Basingstoke, U.K.: Macmillan, 1989.

Rodan, Garry, Kevin Hewison, and Richard Robison, eds. *The Political Economy of South-East Asia: Markets, Power and Contestation.* Melbourne, Australia: Oxford University Press, 2006.

Southeast Asian Affairs [annual review]. Singapore: Institute of Southeast Asian Studies.

Tarling, Nicholas. *Southeast Asia: A Modern History.* New York: Oxford University Press, 2001.

Tarling, Nicholas, ed. *The Cambridge History of Southeast Asia.* Four volumes. Cambridge, U.K.: Cambridge University Press, 1993.

World Bank. *The East Asian Miracle: Economic Growth and Public Policy.* Oxford: Oxford University Press, 1993.

GEOFFREY B. HAINSWORTH

ECOTOURISM. As a concept ecotourism is often misunderstood as being synonymous with sustainable tourism, or other environmentally friendly tourism initiatives. It is, however, a distinct form of tourism that first evolved in the 1990s and sought to incorporate tourist education and indigenous groups with environmental and cultural conservation concerns as a means to promote sustainable development. While providing enjoyment to the tourists who visit, ecotourism is meant to be a mutually beneficial arrangement where visitors spend tourist dollars to boost local economies. The recipients of such funding in turn are provided with financial incentives to help preserve the local environment. As discussed below, the ecotourism concept has a long pedigree, is a specific aspect of the broader term sustainable development, and faces an uncertain future.

The evolution of ecotourism has to be viewed within the context of the emerging consciousness over the previous fifty years of the impact of tourism on local populations and ecosystems. Tourism has grown from approximately 25 million global visits in 1950 to 740 million in 2004, with projections indicating global growth in tourist visits to hit 1.56 billion in 2020. Meanwhile, since the 1960s, when books such as Rachel Carson's *Silent Spring* (1962) and Barbara Ward and René Dubos's *Only One Earth* (1972) were published, the world has become increasingly aware of the damaging impact of human activities on the human environment. The two developments are related in that tourists can often damage or destroy local ecologies. Furthermore, the danger increases with the number of tourists visiting local areas. Large numbers of tourists visiting sites can place pressures on the local environment that would not otherwise have existed.

For example, the world-famous Ecuadorian Galápagos Islands, whose unique creatures inspired Charles Darwin's theory of evolution, are in peril. The islands are now under threat owing chiefly to the large numbers of visitors to the islands.

The ecotourism concept evolved after the idea of sustainable tourism. The latter is a broad-based concept focusing on tourism as an industry and ensuring that operations do not endanger the future enjoyment of tourist areas. The concept of ecotourism is more restricted. Ecotourism differs from sustainable tourism in its attention to the conservation of both natural and cultural heritages; involvement of local indigenous populations; the maintenance of indigenous interests as a focal point; the obligation to explain the natural and cultural value of an area to all visitors; and, finally, its greater suitability to smaller tourist groups at any given time.

Ecotourism evolved to ensure that the primary beneficiaries of tourist developments are populations and local ecosystems. A major milestone for the ecotourism movement came in 2002 when the United Nations General Assembly declared the International Year of Ecotourism. In preparation, in 1999 the World Tourism Organization and United Nations Environment Programme were instructed by the Commission on Sustainable Development to prepare a series of events around the world to draw attention to ecotourism, including its contribution to sustainable development in lesser-developed nations.

A series of conferences, information campaigns, as well as attempts to convince governments to develop national ecotourism strategies permeated the year's events. A highlight of the year came in May 2002 at the World Ecotourism Summit in Quebec, Canada. Nearly 1,200 participants from 132 countries representing a wide range of interests, including national governments, nongovernmental organizations, development agencies, business organizations, and indigenous groups, met for four days. The end result was the nine-page Quebec Declaration on Ecotourism that was signed by all participants.

The Quebec Declaration defined the term "ecotourism" and made specific recommendations. The declaration was meant for the UN-sponsored World Summit on Sustainable Development (WSSD) to be held in Johannesburg, South Africa, in August and September of that year, 2002. Ecotourism advocates wished to ensure the topic received attention at the WSSD as they believed it provided a means of helping to alleviate poverty in specific areas while contributing to environmental protection of delicate and often endangered ecosystems.

The ecotourism concept held out great promise for developing nations, but its application is much broader. In 1990 The International Ecotourism Society (TIES) was formed to promote ecotourism as a tool for sustainable development and conservation and to help develop common standards and practices for the emerging ecotourism industry. It worked with international experts, domestic governments, indigenous groups, and others to develop a wide range of ecotourism guidelines for those responsible for national parks and protected areas; small tourism businesses; the running of ecolodges; and marine ecotourism areas. In addition, manuals and standards for the development of ecotourism policies, practices, and principles were developed and distributed to public and private sector organizations. However, TIES has not yet been able to fully establish an international accreditation program for the ecotourism industry. Nonetheless, regional organizations, such as the

Ecotourism Association of Australia, the European Network for Sustainable Tourism Development, and the Green Globe Asia Pacific group have successfully developed certification and label programs to inform potential tourists that company operations meet strict ecotourism (or sometimes the broader dictates of sustainable tourism) standards.

The future of ecotourism is likely to become problematic in the context of global effort to fight the growth of greenhouse gas (GHG) emissions. As the world attempts to advance global efforts to reduce GHGs, in the post–Kyoto Protocol era, modes of transportation have come under increasing scrutiny, especially air travel. With ecotourism being predicated upon heightened sensitivity to environmental issues, having minimal negative impacts, and educating visitors on their ecological impact, it may become difficult to promote and justify travel to distant places.

BIBLIOGRAPHY

Dubois, Ghislain, and Jean Paul Ceron. "The Interactions between Climate Change and Tourism." In *Climate Change, the Environment, and Tourism: The Interactions, Final Report*, edited by David Viner, Bas Amelung, Pim Martens, and Maureen Agnew. Norwich, U.K.: eCLAT Climate Research Unit, 2003. http://www.tec-conseil.com/docsPDF/climamil.pdf.

Secretary General of the World Tourism Organization. *Assessment of the Results Achieved in Realizing the Aims and Objectives of the International Year of Ecotourism.* New York: United Nations General Assembly, 2003. http://www.world-tourism.org/sustainable/IYE/IYE-Rep-UN-GA-2003.pdf.

"The International Ecotourism Society." *Global List of University Ecotourism and Sustainable Tourism Programs.* http://www.ecotourism.org/webmodules/webarticlesnet/templates/eco_template_news.aspx?articleid=293&zoneid=18.

Wood, Megan Epler, ed. *Ecotourism Emerging Industry Forum.* Burlington, Vt., 2005. http://www.eplerwood.com/im ages/Emerging-Industry-Full-Report.doc.

World Ecotourism Summit. *The World Ecotourism Summit Final Report.* Madrid: World Tourism Organization and the United Nations Environment Programme, 2002.

JASON L. CHURCHILL

ECUADOR. The intertwined histories of export-driven economics, the search for a viable nation-state, and less-powerful groups' quest for equality have moved Ecuadorian history forward in ways that both parallel and diverge from the histories of other nations in Latin America.

Colonial State. The late eighteenth century in Ecuador—then the Audiencia of Quito—was a period of economic transition and rising strain within the colonial state. The once prosperous textile production of the north-central highlands was in decline because of Bourbon trade policies that allowed the influx of European-manufactured cloth. Along the coast around Guayaquil, however, these same trade policies spurred a boom in cocoa exports. José García de León y Pizarro brought the heavy hand of Bourbon reforms and taxation to the region, multiplying and raising taxes in both the prosperous coast and the declining highlands. Taxes hit indigenous peoples especially hard because their tribute burden doubled, a rise that far exceeded population growth.

Adding to resentment toward the Bourbon state were León y Pizarro's corrupt methods of ruling and the outflow of profits to Spain, which inhibited economic development. By the time of the Napoleonic takeover of Spain, the capital city of Quito was ripe for rebellion. From 1809 to 1810, Creoles in Quito strove for independence; Guayaquil Creoles did the same in 1820. Independence was finally achieved with Antonio José de Sucre's victory in the 1822 battle of Pichincha.

Independence and Nation-building. Ecuador became a sovereign country after a brief period as the southern province of Gran Colombia from 1822 to 1830. The goal of making Ecuador into a true nation-state, however, was far more difficult than achieving independence. Regional divisions and competition, particularly among Quito, Guayaquil, and Cuenca, plagued early-nineteenth-century politics and precluded national integration. At least as disturbing was the maintenance of Indian tribute and slavery in the republican era. Independence and early republican leaders had asserted that they would put an end to colonial exploitation and legally sanctioned racial inequalities, yet in Ecuador—as in Bolivia and Peru—slavery and tribute were not eliminated until the 1850s. Tribute was especially difficult to abolish because it accounted for 15 to 36 percent of government revenue. Once alternate sources of national income were available, making abolition possible, other aspects of nation-building could be addressed.

Gabriel García Moreno (r. 1859–1865, 1869–1875) embarked on Ecuador's first significant nation-making project, using Catholicism both to support his own authoritarianism and to unite Ecuadorians into "a single family"; Catholicism was even a citizenship requirement in the 1869 constitution. Though his emphasis on religion was conservative, many other aspects of Garcianismo were quite modern, such as the many state-financed road and railway construction projects. Infrastructure projects encouraged economic growth, leading coastal and highland landowners to compete for access to indigenous workers.

Though elite men benefited from Garcian rule, the same cannot be said for women or Indians. Women could not vote, and the 1860 civil code gave husbands control of all marital goods and power to represent their wives' civil interests. Indians were even worse off, losing land to large-estate owners and shouldering heavier tax burdens than they had under the tribute system. This situation led to an indigenous rebellion in the central highlands in December 1871, known as the Daquilema uprising after one of its leaders. Manuela León was an important leader in the rebellion and was executed for her role. She was not alone: in Ecuador, as in many other Latin American nations, women regularly participated in, and sometimes led, peasant rebellions. This 1871 uprising was harshly repressed, but nevertheless it reminded ruling elites that they could push Indians only so far.

In 1895 the coastal native Eloy Alfaro led the Liberal Revolution, which marked the beginning of the next era of nation-state formation, from 1895 to 1925. Liberals envisioned a secular nation-state, and many of their laws reduced the church's power in Ecuadorian society: secular public schools were created, civil marriage laws were passed, and a 1908 law put church property in the hands of the state. Liberals also claimed that they would liberate women, passing divorce laws in 1902 and 1910, and a 1911 law gave married women the right to control goods they brought into marriage—but not any wealth accumulated during marriage. Female suffrage was not granted, though lawmakers did debate it.

Reformers were also concerned with Indians, but their actions were delayed and limited: liberals focused on debt peonage as the Indians' main problem, but they did nothing about it until they passed a law in 1918 that made it illegal to imprison estate workers for their debts. Though this law did help indigenous workers, it did not break up the large-estate system, nor did it challenge the landowners' right to exploit indigenous workers.

The Search for Stability. International economics greatly influenced national politics from the 1920s to the 1940s. Liberal rule did not officially end until the 1925 July revolution, when military officers overthrew president Gonzalo Segundo Córdova y Rivera, but it had been in decline since World War I, when the cocoa market collapsed. During the military-backed rule of Isidro Ayora (r. 1926–1931) the government focus was on economic and labor reforms—though the labor reforms failed to reach the majority of poor workers in the countryside. Notably, the 1929 constitution made Ecuadorian women the first in Latin America to gain the right to vote in nationwide elections. This government also fell victim to the global economy when it could not weather the 1929 stock market crash.

There were twenty-one governments between 1931 and 1948, none of them finishing its term. The foundation for sociopolitical unrest was the massive inflation resulting from the depreciation of Ecuadorian currency (the sucre) on the world market; the poor—especially nonwhites—were literally at the risk of starving. Indigenous peoples actively sought to improve their situation in the mid-twentieth century, and women often led the way. Most noteworthy was Dolores Cacuango, wife of an indebted estate worker in Cayambe. Cacuango not only established a bilingual school where indigenous children could learn in their native Quichua as well as in Spanish but also was a founding member of the Federación Ecuatoriana de Indios (Federation of Ecuadorian Indians, FEI), the first national indigenous organization in Ecuador.

Intertwined economic, social, and political crises led to popular uprisings—the Glorious Revolution—in 1944 that brought the former president José María Velasco Ibarra back into power. Ibarra was a populist leader whose authoritarian tendencies were balanced by his charisma and ability to address the socioeconomic grievances of the poor without alienating wealthier classes. This brought Ibarra to the presidency five times in all, and his platform greatly influenced Ecuadorian politics for three decades.

Economy and Society. Other important developments in the middle of the twentieth century focused on the economy and culture, with a strong military influence on events. The banana boom of the 1950s gave rise to a new landed elite along the coast and increased revenue for government programs. Economic growth in the 1960s focused on the Amazon region, where the Texaco and Gulf oil companies discovered rich oil reserves. Ecuador then became an oil-producing nation, joining OPEC in 1967; over the next two decades, oil production and exports expanded to make this small north-Andean nation the fifth-largest oil producer in South America.

Similar growth did not occur, however, in the highlands, and when military officers took over the national government in the 1960s they tried to modernize and strengthen the highland economy through land reform. The 1964 Agrarian Reform and Colonization Law broke up the system of highland large estates, distributing subsistence plots of land to former estate workers. Agrarian reform was gender biased: the government distributed land only to men who were former estate workers, assuming that they were the heads of households. This left many women heads of households struggling to maintain subsistence.

The law did not solve the problem of poverty in the highlands, but it did weaken the landowners' political and economic power and allowed indigenous peoples to become prominent actors in local politics. By the 1970s, Indians—now involved in regional politics—demanded more and better social programs. Thanks to the oil boom, the military leadership was able to oblige with many new services.

Economic Challenges and Indigenous Activism. Since the 1980s, Ecuador has been home to a complicated mix of economic decline, neoliberal policies, and indigenous activism. Falling oil prices and natural disasters in the 1980s led to government cutbacks in social services at precisely the time that the poor sought expanded relief programs. In 1992, Ecuador also pulled out of OPEC, unable to meet the organization's annual membership fee and frustrated by its production quotas.

To consolidate and increase their political power, indigenous activists created an umbrella organization in 1986, naming it the Confederation of Indigenous Nationalities of Ecuador (CONAIE). As government leaders embraced neoliberal open-trade policies and proposed cutbacks on earlier programs, indigenous activists became more adamant in their demands. By the 1990s, Indians began staging roadblocks (*paros*) to protest government policies. One of the most outstanding confrontations occurred in June 1994 when state officials tried to reverse aspects of agrarian reform: indigenous peoples brought interregional transportation to a halt for a month and forced the government to maintain earlier reforms.

Nina Pacari is one of Ecuador's most prominent indigenous activist leaders. The first indigenous lawyer in Ecuador, she has served as legal counsel to CONAIE and has participated in the Ecuadorian national government both as a congressional representative and as a cabinet minister. She has also been a member of the United Nation's Permanent Forum of Indigenous Peoples.

By the late 1990s the political situation was intense: Ecuador had lost oil-producing territory in a 1995 war with Peru, inflation was soaring, and there was a strong divide between conservative neoliberals and indigenous activists over how to address the nation's problems. By late 1999, President Jorge Jamil Mahuad proposed to abandon the sucre and adopt the U.S. dollar as the Ecuadorian national specie. This, among other policies, led a coalition of indigenous and military leaders to overthrow Mahuad in January 2000. However, within days the vice president, Gustavo Noboa Bejarno, took over the presidency and dollarized the Ecuadorian economy.

In short, Ecuador is a land of contrasts. This nation so rich in resources faces huge problems with poverty. Oil remains the country's most valuable export and is a critical source for funding social services. With these concerns in mind, Ecuador rejoined OPEC in February 2007. The country has one of the strongest indigenous activist movements in all of Latin America, and indigenous leaders are prominent players in national politics. Yet Indians remain among the poorest and most deeply exploited of all Ecuadorians. Women have made great strides in politics, achieving high posts in government and within the indigenous movement—yet they also face deeply embedded sexism that limits many of their personal and political goals. Ecuadorian history teaches both the dangers of the modern world economic system for Third World nations and the rising strength and capability of poor men and women to effect political change and challenge elite rule.

[*See also* Andean Pact; Ecuador, Indigenous Uprisings in; *and* Indigenous Movements in Latin America.]

BIBLIOGRAPHY

Clark, A. Kim. *The Redemptive Work: Railway and Nation in Ecuador, 1895–1930.* Wilmington, Del.: SR Books, 1998. This study of the importance of the railroad to the liberal regime offers an excellent discussion of the political and cultural aspects of nation-making in Ecuador.

Pallares, Amalia. *From Peasant Struggles to Indian Resistance: The Ecuadorian Andes in the Late Twentieth Century.* Norman: University of Oklahoma Press, 2002. A first-rate study that follows how and why the Indian movement shifted from class-to ethnic-based politics from about 1960 to 1990.

Rodríguez, Linda Alexander. *The Search for Public Policy: Regional Politics and Government Finances in Ecuador, 1830–1940.* Berkeley: University of California Press, 1985. This path-breaking examination of Ecuadorian fiscal history explores how economics, regionalism, and politics affected each other in the nineteenth and early twentieth centuries.

Spindler, Frank MacDonald. *Nineteenth Century Ecuador: An Historical Introduction.* Fairfax, Va.: George Mason University Press, 1987. This invaluable source is the most comprehensive overview of nineteenth-century Ecuadorian history available in English.

Torre, Carlos de la. *Populist Seduction in Latin America: The Ecuadorian Experience.* Athens, Ohio: Ohio University Press, 2000. An important survey of Ecuadorian populism that places it within a broader Latin American context.

ERIN E. O'CONNOR

ECUADOR, INDIGENOUS UPRISINGS IN. In June 1990, in a powerful *levantamiento*, or uprising, the largest ever in Ecuador's history, indigenous peoples blocked roads with boulders, rocks, and trees that paralyzed the transport system, effectively cutting off the food supply to the cities and shutting down the country for a week. Frustrated by stagnated talks with the government over bilingual education, agrarian reform, and demands to recognize the plurinational nature of Ecuador, the Confederación de Nacionalidades Indígenas del Ecuador (CONAIE, Confederation of Indigenous Nationalities of Ecuador) launched the uprising to force the government to negotiate.

Indigenous militants began to refer to this uprising as a *pachakutik*. In the Kichwa language, *pacha* means "time or land," and *kutik* means "return to," hence the word *pachakutik* implies a return in time or a cultural rebirth. It implies a process of change, rebirth, transformation, or cataclysm intended to rid the world of injustice and restore order. In a nutshell, *pachakutik* was the Kichwa word for the Andean concept of "revolution," and it shook Ecuador's white elite power base.

The 1990 *levantamiento* is commonly seen as representing the emergence of indigenous peoples as new political actors, but it formed part of a political engagement that evolved in a variety of ways throughout the twentieth century. In the 1920s indigenous activists organized peasant syndicates to fight for higher wages and better working conditions on haciendas (landed estates). With leftist support and encouragement, activists founded the Federación Ecuatoriana de Indios (FEI, Ecuadorian Federation of Indians) in 1944. The FEI was the first successful attempt to establish a national organization for and by indigenous peoples. It flourished from the 1940s through the 1960s but began to decline after realizing its main objective of agrarian reform in 1964.

In the 1960s new indigenous organizations surfaced that emphasized ethnic aspects of their struggle, including a defense of culture, religion, medicine, and bilingual education. Rather than being allied with labor unions and the political left, progressive sectors of the Catholic Church under the influence of liberation theology encouraged their development. The first significant ethnic organization was the Shuar Federation that Salesian missionaries helped establish in the early 1960s. After the passage of agrarian reform legislation, progressive priests also helped found the Federación Nacional de Organizaciones Campesinas (FENOC, National Federation of Peasant Organizations) and Ecuarunari (Ecuador Runacunapac Riccharimui, a Kichwa phrase that means to awaken the Ecuadorian Indians). In both cases religious workers sought to create these federations as alternatives to the Communist-dominated FEI. Both organizations soon distanced themselves from their religious base and began to move leftward, increasingly engaging class and economic issues of land reform and better living conditions.

Indigenous Nationalities. In the 1980s indigenous intellectuals, returning to concepts that the Communist International had introduced in the 1920s, organized

Uprising in Ecuador. Demonstrators run from tear gas during a protest against President Jamil Mahuad in Guayaquil, Ecuador, 21 January 2000. AP IMAGES

around the concept of indigenous nationalities. In 1980 the Shuar Federation joined other organizations to form the Confederación de Nacionalidades Indígenas de la Amazonía Ecuatoriana (CONFENIAE, Confederation of Indigenous Nationalities of the Ecuadorian Amazon) to battle for the common interests of the indigenous peoples (Kichwa, Shuar, Achuar, Siona, Secoya, Cofan, and Huaorani) in the Amazon basin. In 1986, CONFENIAE joined Ecuarunari in the highlands to form the Confederación de Nacionalidades Indígenas del Ecuador (CONAIE, Confederation of Indigenous Nationalities of Ecuador) to combine all indigenous peoples into one large national pan-indigenous movement. Whereas leftists and religious workers assisted in the formation of earlier federations, CONAIE increasingly benefited from alliances with nongovernmental organizations (NGOs). CONAIE's central and most controversial demand was to revise the constitution to recognize the plurinational character of Ecuador, a proposal that elites repeatedly rejected as undermining the unity and integrity of the country.

Although CONAIE attempted to position itself at the head of a unified movement, other currents and organizations competed for representation of indigenous concerns. FENOC renamed itself the Federación Nacional de Organizaciones Campesinas Indígenas y Negras (FENOCIN, National Federation of Indigenous, Peasant, and Black Organizations) to reflect its broadened scope of struggling for the rights of peasant, indigenous, and Afro-Ecuadorian communities. The Federación Ecuatoriana de Indígenas Evangélicos (FEINE, Ecuadorian Federation of Evangelical Indians) promoted the holistic development of evangelical indigenous peoples, focusing on both their spiritual and their cultural identity. CONAIE, FENOCIN, FEINE, and occasionally FEI coordinated efforts as they struggled for common goals. Sometimes they competed for the allegiance of the same people. It would be a mistake to conceptualize this as a unified indigenous movement, for in reality Ecuador had numerous indigenous movements representing competing interests, concerns, and cultures.

Scholars commonly paint the history of Ecuador's indigenous movements as moving from a focus on local concerns to regional, national, and finally international issues, and transitioning through constructing indigenous demands in the language of class, then ethnicity, and finally nationality. This is too simplistic an interpretation, for since the 1920s indigenous organizations have often simultaneously engaged local, regional, national, and international issues, and organized on the basis of class, ethnic, and national identities. In the 1920s peasant federations used the language of indigenous nationalities, whereas in the 1990s an authentic and democratic land reform continued to be one of CONAIE's key economic demands. In April 1992, two thousand Kichwa, Shuar, and Achuar peoples began a 240-mile (385-kilometer) *caminata* (march) from the Amazon to the capital city of Quito to demand legalization of land holdings. In June 1994 indigenous organizations again organized a "Mobilization for Life" campaign in protest of neoliberal economic reforms that would take away their land, privatize water resources, and undermine their economic livelihood.

Pachakutik. The formation in 1995 of the Movimiento Unidad Plurinacional Pachakutik–Nuevo País (MUPP-NP, Pachakutik Movement for Plurinational Unity–New Country) to campaign for political office represented a shift in strategies from a focus on civil society to a focus on electoral campaigns. Activists had long debated whether indigenous organizations should put forward their own candidates for political office, or whether they should support existing parties. Pachakutik represented the emergence of a third option in which indigenous peoples and other sectors of Ecuador's popular movements organized together as equals to form a new political movement. It explicitly identified itself as part of a new Latin American left that embraced principles of community, solidarity, unity, tolerance, and respect. Pachakutik opposed the government's neoliberal economic policies and favored a more inclusive and participatory political system. It represented a culmination of CONAIE's drive to insert indigenous peoples directly into debates, giving them a voice and allowing them to speak for themselves.

Pachakutik experienced moderate success on both local and national levels, and achieved significant gains in the 1998 constitutional assembly. Most significantly, in January 2000, indigenous leaders allied with lower ranking military officials in a coup that removed President Jamil Mahuad from power after he had implemented unpopular neoliberal economic policies. In 2002, Pachakutik first allied with coconspirator Colonel Lucio Gutiérrez in a bid for the presidency, but once he was in power Pachakutik broke from his government after he implemented the same neoliberal reforms that hurt poor and indigenous peoples. Indigenous movements had learned how to bring governments down, but it proved more difficult to construct viable and sustainable alternatives.

[*See also* Ecuador *and* Indigenous Movements in Latin America.]

BIBLIOGRAPHY

Pallares, Amalia. *From Peasant Struggles to Indian Resistance: The Ecuadorian Andes in the Late Twentieth Century.* Norman: University of Oklahoma Press, 2002.

Sawyer, Suzana. *Crude Chronicles: Indigenous Politics, Multinational Oil, and Neoliberalism in Ecuador.* Durham N.C.: Duke University Press, 2004.

Selverston-Scher, Melina. *Ethnopolitics in Ecuador: Indigenous Rights and the Strengthening of Democracy.* Boulder, Colo.: Lynne Rienner Publishers, 2001.

Whitten, Norman E., Jr., ed. *Millennial Ecuador: Critical Essays on Cultural Transformations and Social Dynamics.* Iowa City: University of Iowa Press, 2003.

MARC BECKER

ECUMENISM, CHRISTIAN. Ecumenism relies on the impulse to seek unity among Christian churches around the world. The Greek root is *oikoumenē*, "the whole inhabited world." Though many Christians through nineteen centuries have desired such unity, the term ordinarily refers to the modern ecumenical movement. Historians point to an international conference of missionary agencies in Edinburgh, Scotland, in 1910 as a starting point. Many missionaries from Europe and North America were shocked when they saw the competition among their agencies. If the nineteenth century had been called "the great century" for such missions, especially to Asia and Africa, the twentieth was to recognize the ecumenical reality as "the great new fact of our era," to use the language that advocates regularly used.

The Christian churches through the century overcame many obstacles to union and invented an array of forces that demonstrated that the ecumenical movement had organizational and practical consequences. Though in the first half of the century most of the energies resulted from efforts by the European and American Protestant missionaries, there were some indications that Eastern Orthodoxy, divided from Western Christian churches after 1054, would be conciliatory, and some elements in Eastern Orthodoxy became active in ecumenical agencies, notably the World Council of Churches, formed in 1948. Roman Catholicism remained off by itself until Vatican II (1962–1965), after which time it became a major player in ecumenical moves.

The movement derived in part from shock experienced over Christian disunity, yet its leaders were inspired by positive theological motifs. Because the Bible was recognized as a source and norm of teaching and practice by believers everywhere, ecumenical advocates were motivated by a prayer of Jesus as it appeared in the Gospel of John. In it, Jesus was quoted as beseeching his divine Father that "they"—his disciples then but now believers gathered in separate churches—"might all be one" (John 17:11). The leaders also cited the writings of the apostle Paul, who saw the Christian church as "the body of Christ," and as a body it could not be divided.

Some ecumenists dreamed of a day when all the churches would become one. Official Roman Catholic teachers contended that unity would be achieved only among those who acknowledged the authority of and were obedient to the pope at Rome. Such a vision meant a stipulation that the Eastern Orthodox could not accept, congenial though they found much Catholic teaching to be. They would not yield the authority of their patriarchs to the bishop of Rome. If the Orthodox could not unite with Rome, Protestants certainly could not. They were separated from both Orthodoxy and Roman Catholicism since the sixteenth century, and they were not interested in themes such as "the return to Rome."

The Protestant churches, lacking a pope or patriarchs and a theology that supported their governance, were themselves divided from each other. Early in the twenty-first century it was estimated that more than twenty-five thousand church bodies, most of them Protestant, worked their separate ways around the world. Yet most of them were clustered in a smaller number of large families, such as the Anglican—never quite content to be labeled "Protestant"—Lutheran, Baptist, and the like.

Efforts at Merging. All through the century there were efforts, a few of them successful, at merging once separated bodies. These included the United Church of Canada (1925), the Church of South India (1947), and one or two in the United States, such as the United Church of Christ (1957). Such mergers came at the high price of the possible loss of cherished traditions, and frustration over failed efforts to merge was among the bases for the search for models other than full reunion.

Some Christian ecumenism meant tidying up bonds among churches within communions, as in the Lutheran World Federation and similar Reformed and Baptist clusters. These served to reduce competition and to provide a clearer witness to the claimed essential unity of Christians.

More ambitious and often successful were ecumenical efforts that followed "confessional" or "creedal" lines in the formation of federations and councils. In these the participants did not yield their particulars at most points, but they accented and worked with what they could generally support. Scandalized, as many of them said they were, by the fact that they could not share what some called Holy Communion, others the Lord's Supper, and still others the Eucharist, some effected policies in which they shared communion without having settled all issues of doctrine and practice.

As for the federations and councils, often these were geographically fixed, as in the National Council of Churches in the United States of America (1951) and, on a grander scale, the World Council of Churches (1948). No one pretended that these represented satisfying fulfillments of the ecumenical desire and call. Yet they provided several channels for common life. Thus at its formation the council drew on energies of one movement called Life and Work and another called Faith and Order, names that more or less explain themselves. There have also been numberless regional and local councils of churches, many of them designed more for common witness and service than for formal progress in settling theological differences.

Because Roman Catholicism, which includes more than half of the 1.8 billion Christians, is the most geographically extended and the most highly organized on such a scale, its entry onto the ecumenical stage resulted in a shift of expectations and strategies. If some Protestant ecumenical activities had once been, as its critics suggested, aimed at "bigness," to counter Catholic power, now there were amazing strides expressing friendliness across Protestant-Catholic boundaries, and common activities often resulted. The one major impermissible practice was sharing at the sacrament of unity, the Lord's Supper or Mass.

Challenges. Though the Protestant-Orthodox-Catholic discussions deepened, two new challenges arose to jostle the ecumenical forces and agencies among them. One was the startling growth of Pentecostal movements, most of which paid no heed to the ecumenical movement and agencies. A second was the prosperity of Christian churches and agencies that remained distant from and often aggressive against ecumenists. These included churches often called "fundamentalist" or "evangelical." Their leaders regarded ecumenical ententes as shallow or even offensive compromises, which muffled Christian witness. These reactionaries sometimes organized themselves in associations that appeared to be anti-ecumenical, though in some respects, when they cooperated with each other, they were manifesting still another form of the ecumenical spirit.

The third major challenge to often relaxed and indifferent Christians in their separated churches came from what many called "postmodernity." However else one defines such a term, in Christianity it tends to mean eclecticism in religious choices—perhaps favoring individualized "spirituality" over "the organized church," and not showing loyalty to or making use of denominations.

It challenges models in which churches as bodies try to overcome their antagonisms and differences.

After a century, however, any balanced assessment would reveal that the ecumenical movement, no longer a subject of curiosity and enthusiasm as it once was, had succeeded in creating a climate in which mutuality, dialogue, and cooperation exceeded anything realized a century before.

[*See also* Christianity; Interreligious Dialogue; *and* World Council of Churches.]

BIBLIOGRAPHY
An indispensable three-volume work is *A History of the Ecumenical Movement*, published in Geneva, Switzerland, by the World Council of Churches: Vol. 1, *1517–1948*, edited by Ruth Rouse and Stephen C. Neill (1954); Vol. 2, *1948–1968*: *The Ecumenical Advance*, edited by Harold E. Fey (1970); and Vol. 3, *1968–2000*, edited by John Briggs, Mercy Amba Oduyoye, and Georges Tsetsis (2004).
Goosen, Gideon. *Bringing Churches Together: A Popular Introduction to Ecumenism*. Geneva, Switzerland: World Council of Churches, 2001.
Kinnamon, Michael, and Brian E. Cope, eds. *The Ecumenical Movement: An Anthology of Key Texts and Voices*. Geneva, Switzerland: World Council of Churches, 1997.
Wainwright, Geoffrey. *The Ecumenical Movement: Crisis and Opportunity for the Church*. Grand Rapids, Mich.: W. B. Eerdmans, 1983.

MARTIN E. MARTY

EDUCATION [*This entry includes nine subentries, an overview and discussions of education in Africa, East Asia, China, Europe, Japan, Latin America, the Middle East, and the United States. See also* Literacy and Reading; Schools and Schooling; *and* Universities.]

Overview

The modern history of education is a story of how "education" came to mean "schooling," and of how schooling came to be something coordinated by the government for entire populations rather than for a few elites. Education, broadly conceived, has always been practiced. For most of human history it took place primarily within the home: parents communicated to their children the knowledge they needed to live and work in local, mainly agricultural, settings. Parents taught children how to farm, cook, trade, and fight, as well as whatever else they might need to know in order to become productive members of society. Families living in towns often arranged for apprenticeships outside the home, in which children could acquire specialized skills in handicraft production.

Education in Chad. Schoolchildren in their classroom in École Mani, Chad, Feburary 2006. Photograph by Sayyid Azim. AP Images

Formal schooling was available in most premodern societies, but it was restricted to extremely small segments of the population—for the most part, clergy and political elites. In East Asia, schooling was the preserve of elites who spent years mastering classical Confucian texts in order to pass examinations that qualified them for government positions. In Islamic areas of Africa and the Middle East, a small number of elites underwent years of intensive study that revolved around the Qur'an but extended to Arabic language, law, and medicine. In Asia, Buddhist priests devoted themselves to the study of sacred texts and turned monasteries into islands of immense learning surrounded by largely illiterate societies. Sometimes clergy made efforts to provide religious schooling for the local lay population, but these efforts had little overall effect on the gap in formal schooling between elites and ordinary people. Governments perceived little benefit to be gained by providing schooling for ordinary people, and in any case they did not possess the administrative reach necessary to engage in such a far-reaching project.

These circumstances began to change in a few areas of the world during the seventeenth century because of a set of social and economic developments that historians have labeled "early modern." These developments include the growth of large cities, the emergence of an expansive commercial market, and the integration of distant regions through commercial and cultural exchange. Under such conditions, growing numbers of people could benefit from achieving literacy, while the commercial market provided some people with surplus wealth that could be used to pay tuition or hire tutors. Meanwhile, advancements in printing technologies made possible the saturation of society, especially urban society, with the written word. Daily life increasingly involved the production or consumption of written materials, therefore raising the potential costs of illiteracy.

Such conditions could be found in parts of Europe, North America, and East Asia during the seventeenth and eighteenth centuries, prompting a significant expansion in the availability of schooling. In China the number of schools increased rapidly during this period; one scholar estimates that basic literacy rates for men reached 30–40 percent. In Japan some fifty thousand schools for commoners were established beginning in the eighteenth century, with virtually no support from the government. In Europe, religious wars provided additional stimulus for the growth of schooling: the Catholic and Protestant churches opened local schools in an effort to convert the masses to their side or to keep them there. By the late eighteenth century, areas of England, France, Germany, and Italy became highly literate. This also occurred in Scandinavia and the northeastern United States, where local governments had begun to assume an active role in promoting schooling.

This early modern growth of schooling involved a significant departure from earlier educational patterns, but its limitations should be recognized. First, the growth was uneven, even in those areas where early modern changes had made the furthest inroads. By the end of the eighteenth century more than 70 percent of men in northeast France could read; in the southern part of the country, however, only 27 percent could. In the United States, New England possessed the highest literacy rates in the world, but the rates were much lower in the South and were extremely low among the slave population. Everywhere, schooling was much more common in cities than in the countryside, where education still meant the transmission of essential skills from parents to children, conducted within the context of daily life rather than in an institution outside the home.

A significant gender gap in schooling remained, too. Throughout Europe girls were far less likely to attend school than boys were, and those who attended did so for a much shorter period. In China, literacy rates had by the late eighteenth century reached almost 40 percent for men, but they remained as low as 2 percent for women. Governments had begun to invest more money into the schooling of elites, but their involvement in mass schooling was minimal; most schools for ordinary people were run by clergy or local elites. There was, in other words, no such thing as a comprehensive educational system.

Industrialization and the Rise of the Nation-State. Beginning around the mid-eighteenth century two factors set the stage for a fundamental transformation in the practice of schooling. The first was the emergence of industrial capitalism, which appeared first in Britain and soon after in other parts of western Europe. The relations among industrialization, schooling, and literacy is complex, and historians have debated the issue at length—in particular the question of whether industrialization necessarily leads to a growth in schooling and, if so, how. In Europe, however, what is clear is that the demographic shifts and social dislocations associated with industrialization motivated governments to expand schooling opportunities for the general population. The flood of unschooled people into cities to work in factories created a number of unfamiliar social problems that social and political elites believed might be fixed through schooling.

Some reformers, informed by Enlightenment ideas about the capacity of each individual for learning and improvement, felt compassion for the urban poor and hoped to use schools to better their lives. Others worried about social disorder: old fears about the danger of overeducated commoners gave way to the even more threatening specter of unschooled urban masses outside the influence and regulation of social elites. In general, elites realized that schools could be used as a vehicle for teaching the lower classes the values and skills conducive to their new role in an industrializing society.

The second major factor behind the transformation in schooling in the eighteenth and nineteenth centuries was the emergence of the nation-state. The nation-state was different from earlier political formations in that it was premised on the active involvement of the entire population in the life of the nation. Officials came to believe that the strength of a nation was determined by the collective strength of its people. In turn, governments sought to integrate people into the institutions of the state, mobilize them for various kinds of service to the nation, and teach them loyalty to the nation. Governments recognized that schools could serve all of these purposes. In an era of international competition, the fate of the nation depended on such preparation. Schooling therefore became a task too important to be addressed in a hit-or-miss fashion. Nor could the responsibility for schooling continue to be relegated to local elites or the church, who were themselves often rivals of the centralizing state. Thus was conceived an idea that is commonplace in the early twenty-first century but was, in the late eighteenth century, unprecedented and revolutionary: nationwide, government-run, government-funded school systems.

Building such systems was an enormous undertaking. In Europe and North America, which were home to the earliest experiments in publicly funded mass schooling, these systems emerged over a period of many decades. Governments began in the late eighteenth century by issuing laws concerning primary education. These laws were early expressions of governmental intent to intervene in mass schooling—but with the exception of Germany, governments did not back up these laws with substantive efforts to control and fund schools for the general population. For the most part, reforms were still focused on schooling for elites.

In France, for example, Napoleon (r. 1804–1815) devoted much effort to reforming and centralizing secondary education, but he was content for the time being to leave mass schooling in the hands of churches. In the 1830s the French government turned its attention to mass schooling by providing for teacher training and requiring the establishment of a public primary school in every commune. But it was not until the 1880s that a series of laws made schooling free and compulsory. Other countries moved toward compulsory public schooling in a similarly gradual, lurching manner, though their school systems varied in important ways. A particularly strong contrast can be seen in the United States, where early efforts to fund and control mass schooling were initiated mainly by local governments. It was only in the twentieth century that the central government began to intervene in primary schooling, and even then its role remained comparatively limited—a pattern that continues.

Imperialism and the Global Spread of Public Schooling. Despite such variations, the general model of government-funded and government-regulated public schooling had taken root in Europe and North America by the late nineteenth century. The emergence of this model in the West coincided with the rise of Western imperialism. As Western nations used their newfound economic wealth and military might to extend their influence throughout the world, they carried with them this model of schooling. In the process this "local" model became truly global in its influence.

For much of Africa, Western imperialism came in the form of direct colonial control. At first, however, colonial governments in Africa did not take an active role in encouraging or regulating schooling. Private schools were available for the children of white settlers and were not significantly different from those in Europe. Schooling was not available to most African children, but a small minority had access to schools run by European missionaries. The missionary schools provided African children with the tools of literacy in an attempt improve their economic circumstances, convert them to Christianity, and inculcate in them the habits and mores of European society. Until around the mid-nineteenth century they were privately funded and largely free from government supervision.

As occurred within Europe, however, European colonial governments in Africa soon recognized the potential value of schools in serving their political goals and began taking steps to assert control over preexisting schools. This process was gradual, as it had been in Europe, and the nature of government regulation in a given area generally depended on which European nation controlled it. For example, French colonial schools in Africa were closely regulated by the government in Paris and were required to conform closely to schools in France: African children studied French history and geography, sang French songs, and recited French poems. In those areas controlled by Britain, colonial governments adopted a more decentralized model of regulation. British colonial governments in sub-Saharan Africa allowed missionary schools to flourish, supporting them through grants while gradually exercising

more control over them. The legacy of these distinctive colonial patterns continued to influence educational thought and practice even after decolonization. What also persisted was the pattern of inequality: both during and after the period of European colonial rule, the vast majority of African children did not have access to schooling.

Countries that did not experience direct colonial control during this era of imperialism were nonetheless deeply influenced by the model of schooling that had taken shape in Europe and North America. In Japan, as in many countries, the threat of Western imperialism created a powerful impetus for all kinds of reform. Though Western strength presented itself in the form of guns and ships, many Japanese leaders believed that this strength was, more fundamentally, the product of a united, disciplined, mobilized population. Such a population, they argued, could be created only through schooling. The new Meiji government began in the 1870s to devote its attention to the creation of a centralized school system, even at a time when the government was unstable and barely solvent. The government had the benefit of examining the various school systems in the West as relatively finished products, and then it could pick and choose from multiple models. Its first plan for centralized schooling borrowed heavily from the French model, calling for a highly centralized, hierarchical school system directed by a Ministry of Education in Tokyo. Reforms in the late 1870s were informed by the decentralized American system, but in the 1880s the Ministry of Education moved back toward a more centralized model—this time, that of Germany.

At the same time, the Japanese government sought to differentiate its school system from these Western models by infusing it with values that Japan's leaders argued were distinctive to Japan. By the end of the nineteenth century, Japan possessed a fully functioning school system with enrollment rates of more than 90 percent—though as in all countries, the effort to convince rural families that their children should attend regularly, and for the duration recommended by the government, took much longer. This extraordinary burst of effort was motivated by the widespread belief that the key to national independence and strength lay in the nation-state—which, in turn, could be built through mass schooling.

Governments in other nations were similarly convinced of the value of mass schooling and carefully observed the various systems in the West when formulating educational policies for their own countries. China and Russia offer two interesting comparisons. Both countries turned their attention to mass schooling in the late nineteenth century in an effort to strengthen the nation and experienced significant growth in the number of primary schools. However, both the Qing dynastic government and the tsarist government faced financial limitations and, more broadly, obstacles to political centralization. These limited the extent to which new ideas for educational reform could be implemented across the country, particularly in distant and populous rural areas.

In both countries, free, compulsory schooling was achieved only after highly centralized Communist governments, each possessing a much larger administrative apparatus than its predecessor, had come to power in the twentieth century. These governments defined themselves in opposition to the capitalist West, and therefore they sought to deviate from the West's educational model. The content of schooling emphasized socialist values in opposition to those in the West, and in the Soviet Union schooling was integrated with work in a way that was consistent with Marxist ideology. But the structure of the two systems was based on essentially the model that had originally emerged in Western Europe: that of government-regulated and government-funded schooling in the service of the nation-state. Indeed, by placing control over schooling more completely within the hands of the government and tying it more closely to the interests of the state, these countries can be said to have carried the logic of the modern school system to its furthest extent.

The Social Impact of Schooling. Much of the above discussion focuses on the advent of modern school systems from the perspective of those who constructed them. This is an important part of the story of modern education, but the impact of such systems on ordinary people is also part of the story. This impact cannot be overstated. First, mass schooling represented a basic change in how societies raised children. Children now spent a large portion of their time in an institution outside the home, away from their parents and extended family, under the supervision of unfamiliar people. At the age of seven or eight—an age when children would previously have begun participating actively in household work—children now entered institutions that segregated them from the world of work. The primary responsibility of children was now to study, which required very different skills and structured children's days according to very different rhythms.

Schools also segregated children from adults. For the most part, children had once lived in an adult world, spending their time in the company of adults and participating in most of the same activities. Schools had the effect of taking children out of that adult world and placing them into a world of peers. This new children's world was created with the child in mind, constructed around the interests and inclinations of children rather than those of adults. Schools both reflected and contributed to the new notion that children should be sheltered from adult knowledge—that they were unique and vulnerable, and therefore they needed to be treated differently. The changes wrought by schools were not just in the social experience of being children but also in the concept of childhood.

Schools also expanded children's social and intellectual horizons. In most cases, schools pulled children out of the context of family and neighborhood and into a much broader peer group, allowing them to interact with people whom they normally would not have had the opportunity to interact with—children from other villages or, in some cases, other social classes. The knowledge that children were exposed to in the schools also transcended family and work. Even where governments designed primary education to dampen unrealistic life aspirations and keep poor children in agricultural or industrial work, schools inevitably exposed children to information that was not specific to the life and work of their own families and communities—unfamiliar places, different kinds of jobs, new skills. In many cases the schools also taught children a language different from the local dialect spoken at home. It was also at school that children learned about the nation. Schools taught children to identify with the nation and to unite with and sacrifice for people they did not know and would never meet. Schools pulled children out of their local community and taught them to belong to a new, national community.

Families did not always see the benefit of these expanded horizons. Often they perceived them—perhaps correctly—as a threat to the continuity of the household and as a challenge to parental and community authority. On a more concrete level, families often viewed school attendance as an economic loss. Sending children to school was, in part, a decision about the potential benefits of schooling versus the cost of a child's lost labor contributions to the household—after all, children could not farm, weave silk, or babysit younger siblings while in school. Consequently, so long as parents believed that schooling was unlikely to benefit the household, they were reluctant to send their children. Historians of education have shown that even the most powerful governments have had enormous difficulties trying to convince poor, especially rural, families to send their children to school when they did not believe in its benefit to the household.

Enduring Issues in Education. The onset of modern school systems has generated two key political and cultural issues that persist to the present day. The first is inequality. Of course, inequality has always existed. Indeed, the limited access to schools in premodern societies reflected this inequality: in general, elite men went to school, and the rest of society did not. But the creation of free, compulsory, and relatively standardized schooling opened up the possibility for unprecedented upward mobility. It had the potential of eliminating one of the key markers of social distinction that preserved inequality in premodern societies. Elites were aware of this possibility; as a result, even as they opened up schools to the masses, they designed the school systems in such a way that social distinctions could be maintained. For example, many countries made provisions for mass schooling at the primary level while limiting secondary and higher education to those with means. Other countries created separate schooling tracks, designing most elementary schools to provide basic skills and moral instruction for the general population and others as preparatory schools for children who were likely to progress to the higher schools that served as gateways to wealth and power. Even where there were no formal mechanisms for exclusion, the costs of schooling limited its leveling effects. Schooling almost always carried with it additional expenses even if no tuition was charged, not to mention the opportunity cost of labor contributions that children could otherwise make to the household if they did not go to school.

Similar patterns of inequality played out along gender lines. Most families were particularly unwilling to sacrifice the labor contributions of female children to send them to school. In part this was because the household labor of girls was less dispensable, particularly in their roles as caregivers for younger children. It was also more difficult for parents to recognize the benefits of educating girls who, it was assumed, would grow up to perform functions within the household that did not require literacy. As a result, rates of school attendance and retention for girls consistently lagged far behind those for boys—and continue to do so in many parts of the world.

Recognizing that many people felt this way about compulsory schooling for girls—and usually sharing many of those thoughts—governments often designed specific schooling tracks designed to provide girls only with the skills and knowledge they would need to fulfill traditional roles within the household. Even in the United States, which was unusually progressive in providing girls with opportunities for postprimary schooling in the form

of coeducational public high schools, girls were usually expected to learn (among other things) subjects like sewing and cooking. Indeed, in the United States and elsewhere the value of schooling for girls gained widespread recognition only when society began to emphasize the mother's role in the education of children.

In the long run public educational systems have served as a tool of upward mobility—that is, within those societies that have them. On a global scale, however, there is a tremendous gap in access to schooling that reaffirms other forms of inequality. Whereas rates of literacy and school enrollment are well over 90 percent in most industrialized nations, in many poorer nations they remain under 40 percent. Narrowing this gap has proved extremely difficult. Even where there are stable societies with governments willing and able to provide mass schooling, for many families around the world there remains the obstacle presented by the opportunity cost of children's labor contributions to the household—the same obstacle that governments in industrialized countries faced when they first attempted to convince the general population to send their children to school. Where such popular resistance to schooling has been overcome, it has been accomplished not by policy or rhetoric but by basic social and economic changes that transformed the way of life of ordinary people and altered their calculation of schooling's benefits. As a result, efforts to use schooling to address social and economic inequality are hindered by the fact that this inequality often poses an obstacle to widespread access to schooling.

A final issue concerns the content of education. Wherever there is a public educational system, governments must determine what is important for its citizens to know. Before the eighteenth century, the content of schooling was overwhelmingly religious. Since then the advent of state-run school systems has brought with it a gradual shift in emphasis toward secular content, paralleling the shift in control over schooling from the church to the state. This shift was more decisive in some societies than in others—in France, for example, as well as in Communist states such as China and the Soviet Union. By contrast, the content of public education in some Islamic states continues to be dominated by religion. In still others, religion is largely excluded from the public school system but still plays a significant role in education because of its influence in private schools. And regardless of the status of religious education, all school systems are involved in the transmission of some kind of value system. Education is never solely about skills; it usually aims to shape children into good people—the definition of which, of course, differs widely from one society to the next.

The definition of a good person also varies within societies. This has always been the case, but today social groups, usually organized around a common ethnicity or religion, tend to assert their separate identities and political interests more clearly. Defining a good person thus becomes an increasingly difficult matter, resulting in contentious debates about various aspects of educational policy— everything from content and language to dress codes. And when social groups feel that their interests are not reflected in the public education system, they often respond by seceding from that system and choosing some form of private or even home schooling.

This dynamic is the opposite of what was happening two hundred years ago in Europe when governments were first attempting to negotiate (or suppress) competing interests in order to create a unified, public education system. It is also the opposite of what is happening in the twenty-first century in many developing nations, where governments seeking to modernize are pinning their hopes on such public systems. Indeed, the secession from public schooling, though an important development, can be seen as a reminder of how dominant the model of government-run schooling has become, despite its recent historical vintage. Even more dominant is the equation of education with schooling. The last two hundred years have ensured that education will for the foreseeable future continue to be thought of mostly as something that takes place within the walls of the school.

[See also Children and Childhood; Literacy; and Universities.]

BIBLIOGRAPHY
Abdi, Ali A. *Culture, Education, and Development in South Africa: Historical and Contemporary Perspective.* Westport, Conn.: Bergin and Garvey, 2001.

Anderson-Levitt, Kathryn M., ed. *Local Meanings, Global Schooling: Anthropology and World Culture Theory.* London: Palgrave Macmillan, 2003.

Baker, David P., and Gerald K. LeTendre. *National Differences, Global Similarities: World Culture and the Future of Schooling.* Stanford, Calif.: Stanford Social Sciences, 2005.

Chisick, Harvey. *The Limits of Reform in the Enlightenment: Attitudes toward the Education of the Lower Classes in Eighteenth-Century France.* Princeton, N.J.: Princeton University Press, 1981.

Eklof, Ben. *Russian Peasant Schools: Officialdom, Village Culture, and Popular Pedagogy, 1861–1914.* Berkeley and Los Angeles: University of California Press, 1986.

Elman, Benjamin A., and Alexander Woodside. *Education and Society in Late Imperial China, 1600–1900.* Berkeley and Los Angeles: University of California Press, 1994.

Fortna, Benjamin C. *Imperial Classroom: Islam, the State, and Education in the Late Ottoman Empire.* Oxford: Oxford University Press, 2002.

Goodman, Joyce, and Jane Martin, eds. *Gender, Colonialism, and Education: The Politics of Experience.* London: Woburn Press, 2002.

La Vopa, Anthony J. *Grace, Talent, and Merit: Poor Students, Clerical Careers, and Professional Ideology in Eighteenth-Century Germany.* 2d ed. Cambridge, U.K.: Cambridge University Press, 2002.

Marshall, Byron K. *Learning to Be Modern: Japanese Political Discourse on Education.* Boulder, Colo.: Westview Press, 1994.

Maynes, Mary Jo. *Schooling in Western Europe: A Social History.* Albany: State University of New York Press, 1985.

Pepper, Suzanne. *Radicalism and Education Reform in 20th-Century China: The Search for an Ideal Development Model.* Cambridge, U.K.: Cambridge University Press, 1996.

Platt, Brian. *Burning and Building: Schooling and State Formation in Japan, 1750–1890.* Cambridge, Mass.: Harvard University Asia Center, 2004.

Pulliam, John, and James Van Patten. *History of Education in America.* 9th ed. New York: Prentice Hall, 2006.

Rawski, Evelyn Sakakida. *Education and Popular Literacy in Ch'ing China.* Ann Arbor: University of Michigan Press, 1979.

Ridder-Symoens, Hilde de. *A History of the University in Europe.* Cambridge, U.K.: Cambridge University Press, 2003.

Stearns, Peter N. *Schools and Students in Industrial Society: Japan and the West, 1870–1940.* Boston: Bedford Press, 1998.

Stone, Lawrence, ed. *Schooling and Society: Studies in the History of Education.* Baltimore: Johns Hopkins University Press, 1976.

Vaughan, Mary Kay. *Cultural Politics in Revolution: Teachers, Peasants, and Schools in Mexico, 1930–1940.* Tucson: University of Arizona Press, 1997.

BRIAN PLATT

Africa

Since the early nineteenth century, formal classroom-based education in sub-Saharan Africa has changed from a foreign institution, extremely limited in both geographical scope and demographic impact, into a widespread and normative institution that aspires to universality. Though formal education expanded dramatically under the period of colonial occupation as a result of missionary, government, and independent African efforts, it became a much more developed and widespread institution in the period following political independence.

Education in Africa, c. 1800. At the beginning of the modern period, education in Africa took one of three major forms: traditional or oral systems of education, Islamic education, and Western-style education, which was often identified with Christianity. The first of these was the most widespread and diverse in its forms. In addition to the diffuse work of character training and instruction in life skills, performed by a child's relatives or members of the community, oral systems of education had more formal structures and institutions through which individuals were trained for particular professions or were marked as properly prepared adults. Rites of passage into adulthood, whether performed by secret societies such the Poro or Sandé of Sierra Leone, Liberia, and Guinea, or by relatives, contained elements of formal instruction concerning the adult responsibilities of women or men as well as practical skills. Long periods of training through apprenticeship were standard both for crafts such as textile making, metalworking, and ceramics and for professions such as the priesthood, healing, or royal counseling. In some cases these systems of instruction were disrupted or dissolved during the colonial period, but often they continued alongside the new educational systems.

Islamic education included instruction in Islamic texts, literacy in Arabic, and, for those who demonstrated particular aptitude, advanced study through apprenticeship to a particular Islamic scholar or through passage into one of the institutions of higher learning. This advanced study included mathematics and law alongside deeper consideration of religious texts and commentaries, and it connected scholars, particularly through Islamic fraternal organizations, to discussions and debates in the wider Islamic world. Elements of this system had been present in sub-Saharan Africa since the introduction of Islam in the ninth and tenth centuries C.E., but it expanded in both reach and importance during the eighteenth and nineteenth centuries as the result of increased trade and political interaction with groups from the Arabian Peninsula and the wider Indian Ocean world on the one hand and West African jihadist movements of religious reform and political consolidation on the other. Shehu Usman dan Fodio, who in 1804 led the Fulani jihad that established the Sokoto Caliphate in what is now Nigeria, was an established scholar before he became a political and military leader, and his daughter, Nana Asmau, became an advocate for women's education, as well as a scholar and instructor herself. Islamic education continued to hold a special position of authority in the British Protectorate of Northern Nigeria, but generally it existed alongside mission or secular schooling during the colonial period.

Outside Ethiopia, where Christian education had been present since the conversion of the region in the fourth century, efforts at Christian education in Africa were almost entirely associated with the slave trade or limited to areas of European settlement before the revival of missionary efforts in the nineteenth century. Though their initial success was limited, Christian missionary efforts included the construction of schools and allowed at least a few individuals to pursue advanced study in Europe.

Colonial Education. The conquest of African territories and their division among European powers in the 1880s was followed by a longer period of political consolidation that allowed for a further spread and development of educational efforts. Though some colonial powers, such as the Belgian and short-lived German administrations, relied almost entirely on missionary efforts, missionary societies were the predominant force for establishing schools throughout colonial Africa and were only gradually joined by or absorbed into centralized measures for funding and regulating education. Mission schools had to balance their own educational goals against the expectations of the colonial administrations, the support or at least toleration of local African officials, and their ability to convince a sufficient number of students to attend.

Differences in the systems of education in African colonies were determined primarily by two major factors: (1) the existing domestic system of education for each of the colonial powers and the powers' philosophies for education's role in empire and (2) the possible presence of European settlers, who generally experienced a separate system of education. As is the case for colonial rule more generally, historical understandings of the differences in education among the various colonial powers have moved from an emphasis on the differences among their official policies to a consideration of the commonalities that emerged in the face of similar local challenges.

Although all colonial powers regarded education as a part of the civilizing mission, a doctrine of cultural assimilation was more pronounced in the French, Belgian, and Portuguese territories, where education was regarded as a primary route through which colonial knowledge and beliefs could be inculcated. The British, in keeping with their policy of indirect rule, sought to slow the rate of cultural change. In the wake of the Phelps-Stokes Commission's report, British policymakers in the 1920s embraced an approach known as adapted education. Based largely on models drawn from U.S. education of African Americans, adapted education emphasized moving education for Africans away from a European model and toward an emphasis on technical and agricultural education, as well as an attempt to bridge the gap between educated and uneducated Africans by emphasizing a pride in local history and culture alongside knowledge of European institutions. In reality, however, this model was only partially implemented as local administrators made their own decisions regarding curricular changes, as funds for expansion or reform dried up during the Depression of the 1930s, and as an adapted or technical education was rejected by many Africans, for whom such training offered little advantage within the colonial economy.

Similarly, in attempting to provide primary education for the masses, rather than just for the elite who could be granted a form of French citizenship, French administrators embraced a policy of adaptation themselves, just as they did in the political arena. Though the French employed greater centralized control over education and more widespread use of the colonial language as the language of instruction than other colonizers did, the curriculum of rural primary schools deviated significantly from that of metropolitan France and embraced technical and agricultural training and, in some cases, an interest in local culture.

Although education was meant to serve the cultural and political aims of colonial powers, its primary purpose for them was economic, allowing for the training of Africans who could work within the bureaucracy and within the colonial economy. Some educated Africans aspired to rise to positions of authority within the colonial order, but they often found that their possibilities for advancement past a certain point were extremely limited and that, in political conflicts, colonial officials tended to favor uneducated local rulers over their educated challengers. Women's education was much more limited than men's and was motivated primarily by the desire to provide educated wives for literate men. Secondary schooling was much less available than primary schooling was, particularly in the Portuguese and Belgian colonies, and aside from teacher training, postsecondary instruction was almost completely absent, with universities not created until after World War II.

In the postwar period, most colonial powers sought to reform and expand their educational systems. Many Africans, however, found these efforts inadequate and instead embraced political independence as the means for achieving educational reform.

Independence and Postcolonial Education. The rise of a new generation of educated Africans, as well as an expanded number of Africans who had received at least some primary education, was a key factor in the emergence of more activist nationalist movements in the period following World War II. When these movements rose to power, they were committed to the goal of universal education and engaged in vigorous efforts in educational expansion. In many cases this involved the rapid training of teachers, as well as significant government spending. By 1961, Ghana declared universal and fee-free primary education, with Kenya and Nigeria following in the 1970s. By 1980 most African nations had at least one university. However, in the 1980s, economic recession and political turmoil produced severe cutbacks in educational spending. Especially during this period Africa suffered from a brain drain, with many of its most skilled and educated choosing to work and live abroad.

In the twenty-first century African education continues to face many challenges, including poverty, disease, and armed conflicts. Though they have at least partially recovered from the setbacks of the 1980s, many nations remain dependent on international funding and subject to conditions set by lending agencies. Education for African women has improved significantly and has benefited from international support, but it continues to lag behind education for men. The achievements in educational expansion, however, remain considerable.

[*See also* Brain Drain, *subentry* Africa; Civilizing Mission; Colonialism, *subentry* Africa; *and* Missions, Christian, *subentry* Africa.]

BIBLIOGRAPHY

Fafunwa, A. Babs, and J. U. Aisiku, eds. *Education in Africa: A Comparative Study*. London and Boston: Allen & Unwin, 1982. Case studies of ten African nations, covering both colonial and postcolonial history.

Nwauwa, Apollos O. *Imperialism, Academe, and Nationalism: Britain and University Education for Africans, 1860–1960*. London and Portland, Ore.: Frank Cass, 1997. Study of the debates and political conflicts in both Africa and Great Britain surrounding the establishment of universities in Africa.

Summers, Carol. *Colonial Lessons: Africans' Education in Southern Rhodesia, 1918–1940*. Portsmouth, N.H.: Heinemann, 2002. Study of social, cultural, and political conflicts around education in the settler-colony of Southern Rhodesia (Zimbabwe).

UNESCO Regional Office for Education in Africa. *EFA, Paving the Way for Action: Education for All in Africa*. Dakar, Senegal: UNESCO, 2005. Analyzes current conditions and efforts to improve and expand education.

Zachernuk, Philip S. *Colonial Subjects: An African Intelligentsia and Atlantic Ideas*. Charlottesville: University Press of Virginia, 2000. A history of both the development of colonial pedagogy and the emergence of an educated class in British West Africa, with particular attention to Nigeria.

JEREMY POOL

Traditional Education in East Asia

Premodern East Asian societies placed a strong cultural emphasis on education. This emphasis stemmed in part from the Confucian belief that education led to moral self-cultivation, social harmony, and good government. It also stemmed from the adoption in China of an examination system to select government officials. Because any man could sit for the exams and because government positions translated into power and wealth, families saw education as a means of social mobility. Predictably, the content of education revolved around what was covered in the exams: Confucian texts. Study consisted primarily of memorizing those texts.

Candidates prepared for the exams mainly in private academies or under tutors. Success required years of full-time study. As a result, the cost of acquiring the level of education necessary to pass the exams was prohibitive for most, and upward mobility through education remained closed off to most families. This was especially true for women, although aristocratic families usually equipped their daughters with some formal education.

In Japan and Korea, too, education consisted mainly of mastering classical texts in private schools built around the master-pupil relationship. Not all educational sites were Confucian-oriented, however. In all three countries Buddhist temples served as important sites of learning and in some cases provided formal education for the local populace. And there were differences among the three countries. In Japan the Heian-era imperial government (794–1185) adopted a Chinese-style examination system but soon discarded it, mainly because hereditary political elites did not embrace its meritocratic implications. In Korea an examination system remained in place, but only aristocrats could take the exams. As a result, education served to affirm status rather than offer a means of social mobility.

The seventeenth through nineteenth centuries brought a marked expansion of popular education in East Asia. In China the number of schools increased rapidly during this period; one scholar estimates that basic literacy rates reached 30 to 40 percent for men and 2 to 10 percent for women. In Japan some fifty thousand schools for commoners were established during the eighteenth and early nineteenth centuries with virtually no support from the government. Scholars attribute this expansion to the growth of the commercial economy and the diffusion of print-based popular culture, as well as to the public activism of local elites, who hoped to stabilize society by educating the local masses.

In the nineteenth century, Western imperialism brought to East Asia a very different model of schooling. In this model the primary goal of education was not to train elites but to mobilize the general population to participate actively in the life of the nation. This meant government-funded schooling for the entire population. The threat of imperialism led to calls for educational reform, and previous schooling arrangements came under sharp criticism. In Japan, after overthrowing the Tokugawa regime in 1867, the Meiji government established a new education system in 1872 modeled closely on systems in Europe and the United States. In China, political fragmentation prevented the creation of a centralized system, but local initiatives resulted in the creation of thousands of modern elementary schools late in the nineteenth century. In addition, critiques of traditional educational practices led ultimately to the abolition of the examination system in 1905.

[*See also* Universities, *subentry* East Asia.]

BIBLIOGRAPHY

Elman, Benjamin, and Alexander Woodside, eds. *Education and Society in Late Imperial China.* Berkeley: University of California Press, 1994.

Platt, Brian. *Burning and Building: Schooling and State Formation in Japan, 1750–1890.* Cambridge, Mass.: Harvard University Asia Center, 2004.

BRIAN PLATT

China

For some eight hundred years prior to the mid-nineteenth century, formal education in China focused on Confucian learning and was generally available only to males. Most children received their educations from private tutors and later entered private academies to prepare for the state-run Confucian examinations. Because this was expensive, the vast majority of pupils came from well-to-do families. Girls and children from modest backgrounds sometimes achieved basic literacy, but the education system was not designed for them. Within the formal system, a student's goal was to pass the state examinations so as to become eligible to serve within the imperial bureaucracy. To pass the three levels of the Confucian examinations, a man had to be thoroughly familiar with Confucian ethical learning and with the arts of composition, calligraphy, and poetry. This system was fundamentally elitist: access was limited by income, and it assumed that educated men were morally superior to ordinary people and thus were society's rightful leaders. Learning that fell outside the boundaries of the dynasty's mandated curriculum was useless when it came to the Confucian examinations, so there was little incentive for wealthy families to concentrate on anything other than the orthodox curriculum. Educational thought and practice were neither static nor uniform during the late imperial period, but in the main it was organized around this structural reality. By controlling the examinations, the imperial state enforced its own ideological preferences and created a pool of potential officials indoctrinated in a worldview that upheld dynastic interests.

This system was not significantly challenged until Western imperialists defeated the Qing imperial armies in the Opium Wars of the mid-nineteenth century. Reformers shocked by the military power of the imperialists and by the foreigners' success in gaining trading and other privileges in China persuaded the court to found a handful of schools to train Chinese officials in Western languages and military techniques. They hoped these schools would graduate men who could help the Chinese state defend itself against further imperialist advances. Nevertheless, during the late nineteenth century the vast majority of students continued to study the traditional Confucian curriculum. Not until the end of the century, after additional military defeats at the hands of the foreign powers, including a humiliating defeat at the hands of Westernized Japan in 1894–1895, did a new generation of reformers conclude that the Chinese education system needed to be fundamentally revamped.

In the late nineteenth and early twentieth centuries, a number of officials, many influenced by foreign missionaries, opened private academies whose curricula went beyond Western languages and military technology to include study of Western political thought, history, and society. By promoting this type of education, these officials implicitly questioned the relevance of the Confucian system of thought to the internationalized world of their day. At the same time, foreign missionaries began to found schools at all levels to teach Western thought and religion to Chinese students. Eventually, the Qing court too concluded that the traditional education system could no longer meet China's needs. In 1905 it abandoned the Confucian examination system in favor of a nationwide system of schools that taught a mixture of Western and Confucian learning. The government sent thousands of students to Japan, Europe, and the United States for schooling, and many others paid their own ways. Thus by the beginning of the twentieth century Chinese education had entered a period of fundamental transformation.

The pluralization of Chinese education that began in the late Qing period (1644–1911) continued apace until the Communist revolution of 1949. During the Republican era (1911–1949) there was a wide variety of schools, and education for girls and women became more widespread. At every level, primary through college, there were state-run schools and Chinese- and foreign-run private ones. There was also an explosion in the number of specialty schools. This was truer in cities than in rural areas, and schooling continued to be available mainly to those with means, but in general, during the first half of the twentieth century, educational opportunity expanded. During that period, high schools and colleges, many of whose Chinese faculty had received education abroad, graduated a generation of liberal-minded students familiar with Western science and humanistic learning, and they also produced China's first professional lawyers, doctors, engineers, and academic specialists.

The rise of the Nationalist and Communist parties in the 1930s led to an even greater diversity in education. Both revolutionary parties established schools at every level to indoctrinate students in their separate political ideologies. As in the imperial period, education in these schools was centered on the needs of those in, or aspiring to be in, political power. Party schools coexisted with missionary and private Chinese institutions in the 1930s and 1940s, but their appearance foreshadowed the complete governmental takeover of education that came about after the Communist revolution.

When the Communist Party took power in 1949, it ended educational pluralism. Schooling became more widely available than ever before, but it also became narrower in focus. The party abolished all private educational institutions and used schools to propagate its Marxist worldview. Every discipline was affected, especially the humanities and social sciences. The education system continued to be meritocratic, but success for students now depended on political, as much as academic, criteria. During the Cultural Revolution (1966–1976), education was totally disrupted. Schools closed down altogether as students and faculty got caught up in the political campaigns of the period; and when they reopened in the 1970s, they focused more on political indoctrination than on academic training. A generation of people missed out on educations that could provide them with practical knowledge.

After 1978 the Communist Party repudiated the complete politicization of education and rebuilt an academically based school system. The party was now seeking to modernize the country and needed a vast number of well-trained people for that gargantuan task. It invited foreign experts to teach in

China and sent many thousands of students abroad for study, mostly in the natural and applied sciences. Political education continued, but Chinese schools experienced definite liberalization of the curriculum in the 1980s. Since then this process has accelerated rapidly. At the beginning of the twenty-first century in China there are again private schools, and many educational institutions have academic partnerships with foreign high schools and colleges. Although in theory the Chinese government provides universal education, its retreat from socialism has resulted in reduced funding for schools. In many parts of the country, especially in poor rural regions, education is too expensive for ordinary families to afford. Thus schooling has become less accessible as it has become more pluralized and connected to intellectual trends in the outside world. This is a major problem that the Communist Party is seeking to remedy.

[See also Civil Service, subentry East Asia; Confucianism; and Universities, subentry East Asia.]

BIBLIOGRAPHY

Elman, Benjamin A., and Alexander Woodside, eds. *Education and Society in Late Imperial China, 1600–1900.* Berkeley: University of California Press, 1994.

Hayhoe, Ruth. *China's Universities, 1895–1995: A Century of Cultural Conflict.* New York: Garland, 1996.

Peterson, Glen D., and Ruth Hayhoe and Yongling Lu, eds. *Education, Culture, and Identity in Twentieth-Century China.* Ann Arbor: University of Michigan Press, 2001.

Weston, Timothy B. *The Power of Position: Beijing University, Intellectuals, and Chinese Political Culture, 1898–1929.* Berkeley: University of California Press, 2004.

Yeh, Wen-Hsin. *The Alienated Academy: Culture and Politics in Republican China, 1919–1937.* Cambridge, Mass.: Council on East Asian Studies, Harvard University, 1990.

Timothy B. Weston

Europe

Revolutionary ideas about education spread across Europe by the late eighteenth century. These ideas were part of a set of new attitudes toward politics and society conceived within the philosophical movement called the Enlightenment. Implementation was cautious, however. Schooling changed modestly, cumulatively, and primarily where the Enlightenment had a toehold.

Enlightenment philosophers postulated a sensationalist epistemology that envisioned human behavior as malleable and dependent on childhood experiences. Knowledge and reason defined humanity. The French

Jansenist J. B. L. Crevier observed, "In villages where there is no school, human beings appear to differ from animals only in their shape" (Chisick, p. 97). Education became the way to free minds, improve life, produce useful members of society, and inaugurate an era of human progress. Often quoted is the French philosopher Claude-Adrien Helvétius's hyperbolic 1773 claim: "L'éducation peut tout" (Education can do everything).

After the serendipitous publication of Jean-Jacques Rousseau's *Émile* in 1762, the expulsion from France that year of the Jesuits who conducted elite schools in Catholic Europe—and the 1763 publication by Louis-René Careduc de la Chalotais' *Essai d'éducation nationale*, which called for a national system of education and was translated into English—philosophers, notables, and government officials intensified the discussion of schooling. Their proclamation that governments establish public educational systems which would both expand schooling and take it out of the hands of churches and home was revolutionary. In the 1760s such principles disseminated from west to east. By the 1770s so-called enlightened despots, monarchs in central and eastern Europe attuned to Enlightenment concepts and wanting to inculcate common values among their subjects, announced plans for national schooling. French legislation in 1792 proposed state schooling as a means of forming citizens loyal to the Revolution; in 1794 Prussia declared the state "guardians of children."

The assumption of a social chasm that divided "the people" from their social superiors restricted innovation. Schooling should assure that each individual had proper skills but also attitudes appropriate to one's predetermined station in life. Most reformers envisioned mass education as limited to morality and basic literacy. The few who advocated democratic schooling held little sway. Among aristocratic circles in England and Germany, a minority opposed popular schooling for fear that it would make the masses dissatisfied with farm or industrial labor and encourage sedition. Obscurantism delayed the implementation of reform; it could not reverse direction. Charges by some philosophes that the church was obscurantist is belied by the fact that churches were the main suppliers of schooling until the late nineteenth century.

In the second half of the eighteenth century Enlightenment ideals, commercial needs, and state-building produced a wave of educational reform. A huge gap remained between the spread of ideas, efforts to construct programs, and actual outcomes.

Higher Education. Three levels of schools existed in Europe: university, secondary, and elementary, with divisions between the former two and the latter by gender, class, and curriculum. Although the philosophes championed learning, the number of European universities remained constant at 143, most founded centuries earlier. Two-thirds were in Catholic territories, only two in England, none in emerging cities. Upper-class Oxford and Cambridge retained a traditional emphasis on theology; more than half of their graduates entered the clergy. Elsewhere, theology receded, supplemented by law. The suppression of the Jesuits, first in Portugal in 1759 and by Rome in 1774, allowed southern universities to separate from the church and train state administrators. German universities were a conduit for ideas from England and France. French universities declined. There, a parallel system of technical schools developed, including those teaching agriculture and surgery.

Secondary education was largely the preserve of the gentry and the bourgeoisie; nevertheless, as much as one-third of secondary enrollment in England, Prussia, and France consisted of the children of well-to-do tradesmen and farmers. Boarding was the main expense; children of modest means could attend as day students. Grammar schools in England included both a secondary and an elementary division. In the late eighteenth century English grammar schools modified their classical curriculum to suit the practical needs of nonelites. Only in the nine great private schools such as Eton and Westminster did classical education still dominate. Two-thirds of English peers attended one of these elite schools. Only a few aristocratic young women received secondary schooling, either from a tutor or in a convent.

In Prussia, every major town had a secondary school intended to produce civil servants. Languages, history, geography, the natural sciences, and mathematics supplanted Latin and religion as the subjects of study. Curricula reform in 1774 coincided with severe measures that reinforced the aristocratic nature of these schools, separating the gymnasium from elementary schooling. Ordinances in Austria similarly curtailed advancement from elementary to secondary schools, which decreased in number. In Catholic states, the expulsion of the Jesuits disrupted secondary schooling.

The exception was France, which had Europe's widest network of secondary schools and of which a full study was made in the twentieth century (Palmer). On the eve of the Revolution, there were 347 *collèges*, two-thirds of them founded before 1650 and 33 affiliated with universities.

Organization and methods dated from the foundation of the Jesuits during the Catholic Reformation. The vernacular and natural sciences were gradually added to classical studies. About 50,000 students attended—a participation rate of 1 in 50 males not surpassed until the 1860s. The 1762 expulsion of Jesuits from their 105 *collèges* did not lead to closure, for other clergy took their place. After the Revolution, between 1795 and 1802, governments attempted to establish a state system of secondary schools, called central schools. This first attempt to create a nationwide uniform system of secondary education foundered, but it anticipated the centralization of the nineteenth century.

Proposals for Public Schools. Although the idea of the national direction of schooling originated in France, it was in central and eastern Europe, where schooling lagged, that national governments first established schools. Schooling needed a boost. Sound education required direction by the civil power. Frederick the Great of Prussia promulgated the General School Regulation of 1763. The decree was historic in its aim to establish a state-controlled, uniform system of compulsory elementary education for all children aged five to thirteen. Children were to attend six hours a day year-round. Each village had to pay for those too poor to attend school. Elementary attendance increased from 30,000 to 120,000 over 50 years, but local initiatives mattered as much as legislation. Recognizing that expanded schooling required trained teachers, Prussian officials established the first "normal" schools in central Europe, but only 4 percent of teachers had graduated from one in 1800.

The general school ordinance of 6 December 1774 reorganized schooling throughout the Habsburg Monarchy. Its preamble stated that "the education of youth of both sexes is vital to the happiness of the nation." The ordinance's provisions were similar to those existing in Prussia. Upper Austria had 13,000 schools in 1774, 19,300 a decade later. About one-third of school-age children attended schools there, as compared to 5 percent in Gallicia and a lower percentage in other eastern provinces. Lombardy, Piedmont, and Parma (in Italy) passed similar legislation without immediate results.

Following Catherine the Great's guideline of March 1764, the statute of public schools in Russia, dated 5 August 1786, transferred responsibility for schooling from the church and family to the state. Alexander I's decree of January 1802 stipulated as follows: "Public instruction . . . is a special function of the State." Schools were established primarily in towns in an attempt to create a commercial class. The number of schools rose from 8 in 1782 to 316 in 1796, but this was a paltry number given Russia's vastness. Poland established the first supervisory national education board in 1773, but in those provinces partitioned to Prussia from 1793 to 1795, a mere 712 schools served 9,400 communes.

Monarchs were more interested in strengthening the state than in promoting mass learning. In 1779 Frederick the Great worried that if students "learn too much they will run off to the cities to become secretaries or some such thing." Initiatives faltered primarily because of poverty in the countryside, inadequate communication and transportation, lack of public funding, and a shortage of teachers. Absolutist goals and local conditions were apposite.

The French Revolution spawned the most ambitious attempt to introduce a national school system. Marquis de Condorcet's Report on Education to the National Assembly in April 1792 included a philosophy of education and curricula for each grade. It avowed, "Public education is a duty that society owes to all citizens." Napoleon implemented the plan a decade later. The eighteenth century conceived the notion of national schooling. The nineteenth century realized it.

Expansion of Elementary Schooling. Western Europe had established a network of elementary schools independent of the state by the late eighteenth century. Demand preceded compulsion. Evangelization and competition between religions were principal motivations in the initial spread of schooling. Churches conducted most schools. Private school masters often served as assistants to clergymen. A few towns had charitable endowments to support schooling, but ultimately parents or the community were responsible for paying teachers.

The main impediment to enrollment was the absence of a school in small villages. Intensive local studies show that the establishment of schools led immediately to enrollment. A population threshold of 400 to 500 seems to have been crucial in the ability to afford schools. Making schools free helped because about 10 to 20 percent of the population was too poor to afford even nominal tuition. There were also labor costs involved in sending children to school in a familial farm economy. In one case, where a local board awarded grants to the families of poor children to compensate them for their children's labor, attendance doubled. Absences were most common during the harvest and planting seasons. Since the labor of younger children was less important, children often started school at age four or five, attended irregularly for a few years, then returned in their early teens to finish. Learning was one-to-one, so students of different skills could join in the heterogeneous one-room classroom with some ease. Getting to school in the winter off-season could be a challenge, however. The French National Archives contain reports of schoolchildren, like intrepid mountain climbers, tying themselves together in order to walk to school. That so many communes and individuals made sacrifices to establish and attend school argues that school attendance was demand driven and not resisted in the countryside. Inadequate transportation and communication, lack of funds, weak civil power, a paucity of qualified teachers, and different dialects or even languages put practical limits on success.

Charity schools in England aimed to increase piety and industriousness among the poor, but the free aspect of schooling brought in many who otherwise could not have attended. Most schools—about twenty thousand in total—depended on local initiative. About two-thirds of school-age children attended English schools in 1800—representing a modest increase from midcentury—but nearly all attended in Scotland, which operated a church-state partnership. The densely populated northeast achieved universal enrollment when a minority of children in the poorer western and central areas of France attended.

Considerable variations in schooling remained from western to eastern Europe, between towns and isolated rural areas, by class and sex. Eastern and southern Europe lagged behind the west, but there were great internal differences too—between the lowlands and highlands of Scotland, among Italian principalities, between German and non-German areas in the Habsburg Monarchy, and between the northeast and the west of France. The process of educational advance was cumulative, with each generation building on the achievements of another. By the late eighteenth century a majority of school-age children attended school in England, lowland Scotland, northeastern France, the Netherlands, southwestern German states and capital cities—the most advanced areas.

Popular schooling for girls lagged behind that of boys. The late eighteenth century was a period of catch-up for areas that earlier had established schools for boys. Girls' schools tended to follow. They outnumbered boys' schools in rural France in 1789. Teaching orders of nuns that had been established following the Catholic Reformation provided the personnel. Nuns constituted the first cadre of women teachers. They intended to produce good Christian mothers and wives with literacy as a by-product. In the late eighteenth century profane subjects were added to curricula in response to parental demands.

German philosophers posited a polarization in the sexual division of labor and the natures of men and women in the late eighteenth century at the very time girls' schooling, which had been rare, was expanding rapidly in German states. In Catholic Germany, like France, nuns established schools. Pietist groups and philanthropists took the initiative in Protestant areas. Protestants pioneered coeducation, whereas the schooling of boys and girls was separated throughout Catholic Europe. Both systems produced similar literary rates. In western Europe, girls' schooling expanded more than boys' in the late eighteenth century; in eastern and southern Europe, it remained in its infancy.

Content of Schooling. Elementary schooling involved the four R's of reading, religion, writing, and arithmetic—in that order of importance. The method was memorization. The alphabet, block letters, was taught first; then reading of the Bible or catechism. Religion was an integral part of educational purpose, a vehicle to salvation. Not included in the curriculum of early years, writing reached fewer students; thus, some who could not write possessed rudimentary reading skills. For girls, sewing and needlework were taught prior to writing. The final R, arithmetic, was a capstone. Teachers of writing or arithmetic put feathers in their caps to advertise these skills (hence the phrase "another feather in your cap"). Many classrooms remained rooms within a house. Most private teachers lacked training and had outside trades. Improvements in quality were only gradual.

Three revolutionary developments in pedagogy occurred in the later years of the eighteenth century. The schools operated by the Christian Brothers became influential in France, Belgium, and Italy. Supported by endowments, these schools charged no tuition. Their pedagogy, outlined in 1720 by the Christian Brothers founder, Jean-Baptiste de la Salle, in *Conduit des Écoles Chrétiennes* (Direction of Christian Schools), set out a progression to follow from one topic to another and stressed the deportment of students and the conjunctive teaching of reading and writing. This pedagogy permeated French boys' schools throughout the nineteenth century. Around 1798 the Monitorial School movement, led by the educator Joseph Lancaster, began in England. It taught writing to the youngest students and encouraged the use of older students to tutor young ones because teachers were scarce. The ideas of the Swiss educator Johann Heinrich Pestalozzi influenced pedagogy into the twentieth century. Convinced that social ills resulted from poverty and ignorance, he conceived of the human personality as developing in stages that schools could nurture. Prussia and Switzerland were the first to introduce his methods.

Literacy. Literacy became increasingly linked with formal schooling by the late eighteenth century. Even trivial amounts of schooling produced rudimentary skills. Mathematical correlations for both eighteenth- and early-nineteenth-century France show a .9 association between literacy and enrollment in elementary schools. Since literacy was defined as the ability to sign one's name, official literacy rates underestimate those who possessed basic reading skills. Writing and reading differentials might have been 10 percent in the French countryside. In Hungary as late as 1870, 14 percent of women and 7 percent of men could read but not write. Similar differences existed elsewhere.

Sweden was a unique exception to the link between schooling and literacy. Following the Reformation, the Lutheran State Church supervised home and parish schooling that taught reading but not writing so that people could internalize the biblical message. Reading but not writing was universal in Sweden prior to the establishment of public schools in the eighteenth century.

Outside Scandinavia, England had the highest literacy rates in 1750: some 60 percent for males and 40 percent for females. This 3 to 2 ratio was common in the West. English literacy rose little for the remainder of the century, probably because of internal migration to emerging towns, which lacked schools. Male literacy rates in Scotland, which did not industrialize, surpassed England's by the end of the eighteenth century. In 1982 François Furet and Jacques Ozouf conducted the most detailed study of literacy—for France. Literacy rates there stood at 47 percent for men and 27 percent for women in 1786, representing a 10 percent increase for each since midcentury. National averages obscure notable differences among classes, between town and country, and among regions. The clergy, high nobility, and commercial classes were universally literate. Most gentry and artisans could read; agricultural laborers—the bulk of the population—could not. Above the St. Malo–Geneva line across northeastern France, the universal literacy rates for men were above 70 percent and sometimes rose higher than 90 percent, whereas literacy stood at approximately 15 percent for men in Britanny and 5 percent for women in the Massif Central. In England, one parish had 97 percent literacy, the lowest only 17 percent.

Extrapolating from local studies, one determines that literacy rates in Spain, northern Italy, and western German states were similar to those in southern France—a middle tier. Rates for southern Italy, Ireland, and eastern Europe were the lowest. Serfs in eastern Europe remained universally illiterate. In Austria-Hungary, two-thirds of conscripts, three-quarters in the east, were still illiterate in 1867. At the end of the eighteenth century only 7 percent of Russian men and 3 percent of women could read; 15 percent of the nobility remained illiterate. Many of those who achieved literacy did so outside of school because only about 1 percent of the school-age population in Russia, Poland, and the Balkans attended school. Informal means of acquiring literacy persisted in those areas where schools did not exist.

By the beginning of the twentieth century nearly all children in western and central Europe attended school and a majority of youth were literate for the first time. Illiteracy became a social disability. The gap between advanced areas and eastern Europe had widened. The educational system became more class-defined. With compulsion at the elementary level came a rigid divide from higher schooling. Girls' literacy and schooling closely matched those of boys in advanced areas. Gender differences were widest where low participation rates existed. Nuns began the feminization of elementary teaching, universal by the twentieth century. The eighteenth century introduced state supervision, which would become state control of schooling a hundred years later. Schooling had evolved into a social and political issue, the primary means to inculcate knowledge.

Key developments during the twentieth century involved the extension of the school-leaving age (particularly after World War II), building mass secondary education. Most European countries further emphasized testing to screen students into different types of secondary schools and, from them, a minority gained access to universities or colleges. Again after World War II, the percentage of the relevant age group attending a university expanded rapidly, and women's access improved also. The Communist Revolution and takeover in Russia and other parts of Eastern Europe greatly stimulated educational expansion. Although Communist indoctrination was a special feature of the system, broad aspects of the educational experience, and its centrality in children's lives, drew closer to patterns already established in the West.

[See also Universities, subentry Europe.]

BIBLIOGRAPHY

Baker, Donald N., and Patrick J. Harrigan, eds. *The Making of Frenchmen: Current Directions in the History of Education in France, 1679–1979.* Waterloo, Ontario: Historical Reflections Press, 1980. Includes important French scholars' studies of regions and of girls' schooling.

Chisick, Harvey. *The Limits of Reform in the Enlightenment: Attitudes toward the Education of the Lower Classes in Eighteenth Century France.* Princeton, N.J.: Princeton University Press, 1981. Demonstrates class prejudices of the philosophes, arguing that their faith in progress and education was mitigated by disdain for the ignorant masses.

Furet, François, and Jacques Ozouf. *Reading and Writing: Literacy in France from Calvin to Jules Ferry.* Cambridge, U.K.: Cambridge University Press, 1982. The most sophisticated study of literacy and schooling. Quantitative analysis by regions, class, and gender. Contains the most complete information for any country.

Gay, Peter. *The Enlightenment: An Interpretation.* 2 vols. New York: Norton, 1977. The standard for Europe as a whole. Argument that it was the "first modern age" and constituted a sharp break with the past has been nuanced by later scholars.

Graff, Harvey J. *The Legacies of Literacy: Continuities and Contradictions in Western Culture and Society.* Bloomington: Indiana University Press, 1987. Overview from classical times to the present. Chapter 6 presents a clear overview of the eighteenth century, summarizing local and national studies.

Houston, Robert Allan. *Literacy in Early Modern Europe: Culture and Education, 1500–1800.* London: Longman, 1988. Survey of early modern period, integrating secondary literatures for all European states.

Lebrun, Francois, Marc Venard, and Jean Quéniart. "De Gutenberg aux lumières." In *Histoire générale de l'enseignement et de l'éducation en France,* edited by Louis Henri-Parias, chap. 2. Paris: Nouvelle Librarie de France, 1981. Best survey of French scholarship for the period.

Maynes, Mary Jo. *Schooling in Western Europe: A Social History.* Albany: State University of New York Press, 1985. Still the standard text, with a focus on France and Germany. Uniquely considers the social constraints and impact of schooling rather than legislation.

Melton, James Van Horn. *Absolutism and the Eighteenth-Century Origins of Compulsory Schooling in Prussia and Austria.* Cambridge, U.K.: Cambridge University Press, 1988. More concerned with the origins and development of legislation than impact. Best survey of central Europe.

Palmer, Robert Roswell. *The Improvement of Humanity: Education and the French Revolution.* Princeton, N.J.: Princeton University Press, 1985. Examines both theory and practice from the Enlightenment through the Revolution. Considers teachers and officials as well as philosophers. Argues that they believed education was the means to reform society and humanity.

Ridder-Symoens, Hilde de, ed. *A History of the University in Europe.* Vol. 2, *Universities in Early Modern Europe, 1500–1800.* Cambridge, U.K.: Cambridge University Press, 1996. Standard history of universities. Different authors survey various topics and times.

Schleunes, Karl A. *Schooling and Society: The Politics of Education in Prussia and Bavaria, 1750–1900.* Oxford: Berg Publishers, 1989. Covers states in what is now Germany. More concerned with outcomes than Melton.

Tóth, István György. *Literacy and Written Culture in Early Modern Central Europe.* New York: Central European University Press, 2000. Excellent discussion. Unique information based on regional archival research for the practice of literacy and schooling in the eastern provinces of the Habsburg Monarchy.

PATRICK J. HARRIGAN

Japan

For most of Japan's history, education was not tied exclusively to schooling. As in most parts of the world before the eighteenth century, education took place primarily within the home: parents transmitted to their children the knowledge necessary to live and work in local, mainly agricultural, settings. Those living in towns often arranged apprenticeships outside the home, through which children acquired skills in the production of handicrafts. Aristocratic and elite samurai families, who made up the country's political leadership, gave their children a more formal education designed to help them master classical texts and gain proficiency in elite cultural practices.

Political consolidation under the Tokugawa regime (1603–1867) brought many changes to Japanese education. First, the creation of an extensive bureaucracy led to the growth of schools to train government officials. These consisted of private academies and public institutions funded by central and regional governments. These schools were limited almost exclusively to samurai, who in the Tokugawa period functioned as a hereditary ruling caste.

The eighteenth century saw the expansion of schooling to new segments of the Japanese population. The explosive growth of cities fueled this development, contributing to the formation of a commercialized economy and generating an ever-increasing variety of documents: contracts, record books, lawsuit-related materials, and diverse forms of literary entertainment. Well-to-do commoners in both urban and rural settings responded to this new environment by pursuing the kind of private schooling previously limited to elites.

An even greater numerical increase in schooling began in the early nineteenth century and penetrated more deeply into the Japanese population. During the last several decades before the fall of the Tokugawa regime in 1867, some thirty thousand schools were established, with essentially no support from political authorities. Many children who began attending school at this time were from ordinary farm families. This increase in schools was partly because of an acceleration of the developments mentioned above: commercialization and the spread of literate culture, which stimulated a demand for literacy. In addition, the widespread perception of a social crisis in late Tokugawa Japan prompted thousands of community leaders to open schools as a means of stabilizing local society.

A new phase of transformation in Japanese education, brought on by the impact of Western imperialism, began in the mid-nineteenth century. Following Matthew Perry's arrival in Japan in 1853, the threat of colonization destabilized the Tokugawa regime and prompted people to consider radical alternatives to the existing order. During this time Japan was also exposed to a new model of schooling, one tied to the political rationale of the modern nation-state. In this model, the primary goal of schooling is to mobilize the general population to participate actively in the life of the nation. This meant government-led, government-funded schooling for the entire population—an idea as revolutionary in Japan then as it had been in Europe a century earlier.

Soon after overthrowing the Tokugawa regime in 1867, the Meiji government, convinced that centralized schooling was a key to progress and national strength, created a plan for such a system of education, modeled closely on contemporaneous systems in Europe and the United States. It was highly centralized, forming a pyramid of elementary schools, middle schools, and public universities, all headed by the Ministry of Education in Tokyo. Central and local governments established teacher-training schools, which adopted new textbooks and embraced recent pedagogical theories of reformers in Europe and the United States.

These initiatives met with much dissent, both from ordinary people and from local activists and educators. Over the next twenty years the system took shape not by government fiat but though vigorous debate and compromise. By the 1890s the basic concept of a centralized, compulsory school system had taken root in Japanese society. Although poorer children, particularly girls, continued to attend school only sporadically and usually dropped out after a few years, almost all children were enrolled. People had begun to believe that the new schools were the key to social advancement—which was partly true, although only a select few (and only males) could realistically hope to get into the higher schools and universities that served as entryways into the nation's government and business elite.

In addition to training Japanese children to participate in an industrializing economy, the new schools inculcated in them a sense of national identity. The 1890 Imperial Rescript on Education, which became a pledge repeated daily by Japanese children, called upon each child to "Offer yourself courageously to the state, and thus guard and maintain the prosperity of Our Imperial Throne." The schools also played an important role in creating new gender roles by stressing the value of women's contributions to the nation, though confining those contributions to the home. Debates about content, pedagogy, and other education-related issues continued, as did larger debates about politics and society. These were fueled by the emergence in the 1910s and 1920s of mass media and an urban middle class. Especially by the 1930s, schools functioned as a powerful instrument by which the state could mobilize popular support for its goals, which by that time had turned to aggressive imperialism and war.

After Japan's defeat in World War II, the United States occupied the country and seized control over public policy. Occupation authorities believed that the education system had been partly responsible for Japan's wartime behavior. They criticized in particular the nationalistic, overly centralized, and elitist nature of prewar education. Accordingly, the occupation authorities carried out a series of reforms to expunge the schools of all traces of wartime ideology, limit the power of the Ministry of Education and give power to locally elected school boards, and guarantee academic freedom. They also adopted an American-style 6-3-3 structure for elementary, middle, and high school and took various steps to encourage educational equality between men and women. Many of these reforms took root, but others were unsuccessful—most notably, the effort to decentralize the education system. Some defining features of the postwar system, like the high-pressure exams that determine entry into the universities, continued prewar patterns.

[*See also* Textbook Controversy in Japan; *and* Universities, *subentry* East Asia.]

BIBLIOGRAPHY
Amano, Ikuo. *Education and Examination in Modern Japan.* Translated by William K. Cummings and Fumiko Cummings. Tokyo: University of Tokyo Press, 1990.
Beauchamp, Edward, ed. *Windows on Japanese Education.* New York: Greenwood Press, 1991.
Marshall, Byron K. *Learning to Be Modern: Japanese Political Discourse on Education.* Boulder, Colo.: Westview Press, 1995.
Platt, Brian. *Burning and Building: Schooling and State Formation in Japan, 1750–1890.* Cambridge, Mass.: Harvard University Asia Center, 2004.

BRIAN PLATT

Latin America

Though the Catholic Church played a significant role in education during the colonial period, its broad influence waned in the nineteenth and twentieth centuries. The development of formal education in Latin America is closely tied with the development of the state and the region's economic prosperity.

During the colonial period, schooling was offered by private lay teachers and the church. Originally, private tutors exclusively instructed the elites, providing the sole source of lay education. Subsequently, nonreligious individuals started to offer what was called "public education" even though they charged a fee. At this time, public education was the enterprise of an individual working in a room provided by the *Cabildo* or town council; in return, teachers provided free instruction for a certain number of students.

Convents and other orders supplied education. Unlike in Europe, church orders in Spanish America not only maintained their traditional role in secondary and higher education but instructed at the elementary levels as well. Especially prominent were the Jesuits, whose main task was to offer such education. Thus when they were expelled in 1767, many schools closed down, and colonial education suffered considerably.

Upper-class women's formal education was enhanced in the eighteenth century through the influence of the Convents of La Enseñanza founded in Mexico City (1753), Bogotá (1770), and Mendoza (1760). Lay schools, funded by confraternities or laypersons, followed, offering morning or evening classes to poor girls. Finally, the establishment and expansion of municipal schools further advanced women's education. However, it was not until the mid-nineteenth and early twentieth centuries that there was a major effort to school women.

Demand for reading skills increased as printing presses became more commonplace and books more readily available at the end of the eighteenth century, and as education started to become a public concern.

Whereas in the colonial period education served to expand religion and legitimize the existing social structure, the independence movements of the early nineteenth century promoted an egalitarian ethic and independence of thought. Government leaders challenged the dominance of the church in education and asserted that access to education should be universal and a state responsibility.

Thus during the nineteenth century, as new nation-states established themselves and overcame their initial political turmoil, elites perceived education as a way to modernize and civilize the population. Ministries of education were established, and using the European model, the first teacher-training schools were established. Although education expanded, it was not nearly as significant as in, for example, the United States and Canada; the difference was that, unlike the governments of the United

States and Canada, local and state governments took little interest in education. By the late nineteenth century immigration increased literacy. A major limitation for expanding the schools further was a scarcity of teachers.

The twentieth century was the era of education for Latin America, and it produced the national education systems used in the early twenty-first century. Teacher-training schools were developed, there was a significant territorial expansion of public schools to outlying areas, and greater resources were allocated to education.

During the first half of the twentieth century there was a massive state-led expansion of elementary education. As a result, literacy rates increased from an average of 32.8 percent in 1900 to 60.8 percent in 1950, though many regional differences persisted. Secondary education based on the French model and leading exclusively to university was also developed. Increased literacy was key to the diffusion of democracy because throughout the nineteenth and most of the twentieth centuries citizenship was linked to literacy: only those who knew how to read and write could vote.

In the 1940s and 1950s, as Latin America engaged in import-substituting industrialization, public education systems became a major concern for governments as human capital was recognized as a major component of economic growth and development. In the 1960s rates of educational growth soared. Education plans helped coordinate aid to the education sector from agencies such as USAID, the World Bank, and the Inter-American Development Bank, whose main thrust during this period was developing educational infrastructures. In the 1990s education was seen as a strategy to reduce poverty, and multilateral organizations promoted and financed reforms that sought to modernize educational systems: national standardized testing was developed, curricula were revised so as to be more student-centered and focused on learning, new financing mechanisms were promoted, and teacher training was revamped, among other measures.

Education systems in Latin America were very centralized until the 1980s. In response to national efforts to provide subregions with greater autonomy regarding policies and service provision, education was often decentralized. Decentralization increased school autonomy and parental participation as school boards were instituted and strengthened.

Despite the achievements in Latin American education, dissatisfaction with quality and equity remains. Test results show that the cognitive level of students in Latin America lags behind the levels in developed countries, as well as the levels in countries in eastern Europe and Asia that have similar levels of per capita income. Differences in years of schooling between genders have decreased, except for indigenous women. Indigenous people are still less successful in school: they use it less, have higher dropout rates, and have lower test scores. Multicultural and bilingual education at the national level started only in the 1990s. Although in the 1960s the average number of years of schooling in Latin America and Asia was identical, by the end of the century the average in Asian countries exceeded seven years, while in Latin America it hovered below six.

Cuba demonstrates a greater level of educational attainment than the rest of Latin America largely because of its social and political contexts. The nonexistence of child labor, better overall nutrition and school readiness owing to larger preschool enrollment, greater principal autonomy, and the possibility of being able to attract "the best and the brightest" to the teaching profession—because of the higher prestige of teachers and the marginal wage difference between them and other professions—account for the better educational achievement.

At the start of the twenty-first century, gross enrollment is 100 percent in primary schools and around 70 percent in secondary schools. Expansion of secondary enrollment has increased demand for higher education. Preschool has increased over the last years but still reaches only 54 percent of children age four to five. Dropout rates constitute a major factor for explaining failures in primary and secondary schools.

The educational situation of Latin America is diverse. Though for some countries the major challenges are how to expand preschool and primary education, in others it is secondary school enrollment. Quality, greater equity, and pertinence to the job market are still pending issues for all countries.

[*See also* Universities, *subentry* Universities and University Reforms in Latin America.]

BIBLIOGRAPHY

"Inter-American Development Bank." *Expanding Knowledge Capital of Latin America and the Caribbean: An IDB Strategy for Education and Training.* Available at http://www.iadb.org. 22 August 2006.

Newland, Carlos. "Spanish American Elementary Education before Independence: Continuity and Change in a Colonial Environment." *Itinerario* 15 (1991): 79–92.

Torres, Carlos Alberto, and Adrian Puiggrós. "Introduction: The State and Public Education in Latin America." In *Latin American Education: Comparative Perspectives*, edited by Carlos Alberto Torres and Adriana Puiggrós, pp. 1–28. Boulder, Colo.: Westview Press, 1997.

MANUEL E. CONTRERAS

The Middle East, North Africa, and Central Asia

The Middle East, North Africa, and Central Asia, because of their shared Islamic heritage, similar relationship with imperialism, and trajectory of modernization, have undergone comparable—if not identical—paths of educational transformation since the eighteenth century. Educational institutions and social actors therein have been key figures in the perpetuation of tradition and have been harbingers of change and innovation. The pursuit of knowledge (*ilm*) within a context of culturally relevant forms of socialization has been the cornerstone of educational endeavors for the populations of this region. Prior to the modern period, when formal institutionalized schooling became the norm, education, understood as the formal transmission of knowledge and codes of behavior to the young, had diverse manifestations.

Indigenous Education in Muslim Societies. Prior to the mid-twentieth century, the most widespread arrangement for the elementary learning of children was the *maktab* or *kuttab*. The terms, both derived from the Arabic root "k-t-b," which means "to write," are indicative of the high value placed on textual authority and the written word in Muslim cultures. Although often roughly translated as "school," a *maktab* can more accurately be translated as a place for learning religious and cultural literacy. *Maktab*s are associated with Islam, but a Christian variety also existed. Spatially, the *maktab* did not necessarily constitute a separate building but rather constituted a designated space for instruction, whether a section of a mosque, a room in a private home, or an area in a religiously endowed (*waqf*) building such as a public fountain or library. Though boys made up the overwhelming majority of pupils, *maktab*s catering to girls were not uncommon, yet these were more likely to be located in the homes of a female teacher (*shaykha* or *atin*) than in a public building.

The pedagogic techniques of teaching by rote through recitation, repetition, and memorization, reinforced through the rod, attempted to instill deference in the young for their learned elders and discipline and reverence for formal learning. The level of knowledge and skills acquired in the roughly two to three years of instruction varied because *maktab*s operated independently of one another throughout vast geographic territories and did not follow a fixed or unified curriculum. Ideally, a pupil would have committed the entirety of the Qur'an to memory and learned rudimentary writing and mathematic skills. Some *maktab*s such as those in Iran exceeded these norms by proving additional instruction in Persian poetry and calligraphy. In addition to formal knowledge, pupils were also expected to acquire *adab*, codes of ethical conduct and moral dispositions and behavior. Indeed, *adab* was considered inseparable from knowledge (*ilm*), for, as a medieval jurist elucidated, "Knowledge without *adab* is like fire without firewood. *Adab* without knowledge is like a spirit without a body" (cited in Rosenthal, p. 252).

Advanced education by way of apprenticeships was provided by the craft and merchant guilds, government bureaus, hospitals, astrological observatories, and Sufi monasteries. At the stage of puberty a boy would apprentice with a master, *ustaz* (the same term used to denote "professor"), to follow a path of initiation for a particular trade. More than mere vocational training, apprenticeships contained their own sacralized worldviews and often included the study of Islamic law and mysticism. Boys learned their place in professional hierarchies, were socialized into the proper codes of behavior (*adab*), and gradually mastered the skills and sacred knowledge necessary to participate as productive members of a given professional community.

The institution for higher study, the madrassa (*madrasa*), trained the Muslim scholarly class, the ulema (*ulama*), and since its spread in the ninth century served to bind the Muslim community (*umma*) in a unified cultural project. With its approach to knowledge (*ilm*) as intricately connected to action (*amal*), the madrassa prepared its ranks for active roles in social and political life as religious scholars, preachers, teachers, jurists, and political leaders. The madrassa enjoyed protected status as a religious endowment (*waqf*) and consisted of anything from a room in a modest structure to an elaborate mosque university complex with boarding facilities. Celebrated madrassas such as al-Azhar in Cairo (established in 969) and Qarawiyyin in Fez, Morocco (established in 859), which survive in the early twenty-first century, attracted itinerant scholars from throughout the Muslim world and served as vibrant cosmopolitan centers of learning.

A madrassa specialized in one or more of the four schools of Islamic law (Sharia). The course of study therein, although not standardized, was likely to include Arabic, Islamic law (*fiqh*), jurisprudence (*usul al-fiqh*), interpretation (*tafsir*), and possibly philosophy, theology, mathematics, or astronomy. Similar to *maktab* education, the madrassa was characterized by a high degree of institutional informality and centered on the primacy of the relationship between teacher and pupil. Who one studied with was more important than where one studied. A small study circle (*halqa*) in a private home under the leadership of a renowned teacher, an *alim* (plural ʿ*ulama* or ulema), would have been as coveted as a comparable course in a famous madrassa. It was the individual *alim* rather than the institution that conferred on the pupil a diploma or, more precisely, the license to teach (*ijaza*) a subject or particular mastered text. In this way, the ulema determined who could join their ranks and act as legitimate religious authorities and carriers and transmitters of the religious sciences.

Modern Education for Political and Cultural Reform. From the eighteenth century institutions and cultures of learning in the Muslim East reformed in response to broader socioeconomic and political transformations. The rise of European and Russian imperial expansion and military supremacy and the effects of the Industrial Revolution on modes of economic production and exchange impelled political leaders in the region to reform their military, political, economic, and cultural institutions. Models of formal learning from Europe—and in the case of Central Asia, from Russia—were perceived as containing the blueprint for attaining military power, scientific advancement, and economic development in the new world order. The indigenous Islamic educational institutions and their gatekeepers, the ulema, were perceived as ill-suited for the task.

Leaders sought ways to acquire foreign expertise, knowledge, and institutional models, initially for the sake of modernizing their military apparatuses. As early as 1720 an Ottoman delegation sent by Sultan Ahmed III (r. 1703–1730) traveled to Europe on an expedition to study Europe's education systems. Soon thereafter a bureau for the translation of European works of history and philosophy into Turkish and Arabic was established. In Egypt in 1809 the viceroy Muhammad Ali Pasha (r. 1805–1849) dispatched the first of many student missions to Europe. He subsequently established numerous technical schools of veterinary medicine, pharmaceutics, chemistry, agriculture, translation, and midwifery, all of which were related in some way to strengthening the military. In a similar vein, the Tunisian reformer Ahmad Bey (r. 1837–1855) founded the École Polytechnique to train military officers, and in Iran the elite francophone military institution Dar al-Funun was established in 1851 during the reign of the Qajar shah Nasir al-Din (r. 1848–1896) as part of the New Order reforms. These early military institutions had little bearing on the general population but were significant in that they provided a new prototype for schooling and set in motion a process of broader state-led educational change.

Sweeping programs for modernizing reform in the Ottoman Empire, beginning with the *Nizam al-Jadid* (New Order) of Sultan Selim III (r. 1789–1807) and continuing with the more comprehensive and secularizing Tanzimat reforms (1839–1876) under the reigns of Sultan Mahmud II (r. 1808–1839) and Sultan Abdülmecid (or Abdelmejid; r. 1839–1861), propelled more penetrating educational changes. Early legislation from Istanbul in 1824 called for compulsory education for boys, and the Tanzimat Education Regulation of 1869 (Maarif Nizamnamesi) stipulated a plan for a centrally organized network of schools throughout the empire.

In Egypt the first modern education ministry to regulate primary schooling, the Department of Schools (Diwan al-Madaris), was established in 1836. Calls for compulsory schooling were fraught with challenges because of the noncompliance of local populations and because states lacked both the resources for universal schooling and a pool of skilled lay teaching professionals to staff the schools. Yet the administrative and legislative infrastructure for the expansion and management of a new education sector was put firmly in place. In Iran and Morocco, where the ulema held greater political sway, Islamic institutions maintained positions of eminence, and educational reform was resisted because it would entail an erosion of the ulema's power and their loss of control over the production and transmission of knowledge.

Colonialism and Alternative Modernities. Colonial governments and foreign missionaries also played a pivotal role in the spread of new schooling, especially among minority (*millet*) Christian and Jewish communities. Autonomous networks of foreign and sectarian schools, distinct from the incipient modern state schools and the indigenous *maktab*s and madrassas, dotted the educational terrain of North Africa and the Levant. Run by religious missions, foreign governments, and private associations, these largely European and American schools proliferated at a rapid pace throughout the nineteenth century and into the first decades of the twentieth and served tens of thousands of students—including a growing number of Muslims—far surpassing the reach of state schools. Collectively, they left an indelible mark on, among other things, girls' education and higher education. The earliest modern universities rooted in principles of liberal education were the Syrian Protestant College, later named the American University of Beirut, established in 1866; the Université Saint-Joseph, established in Beirut in 1875;

and the American University in Cairo, established in 1919. These were founded by Christian missionaries.

The conditions of colonialism facilitated the spread of these institutions, yet colonial education policies were inconsistent and at times obstructionist regarding the value of schooling for native populations. The British mandate government (1882–1922) in Egypt, for example, wary of the political consequences of an educated public, supported only a minimum level of schooling necessary to train civil servants and curbed press and political freedoms. The French, with their *mission civilatrice*, actively founded schools to facilitate the spread of French language and culture, but the French institutions—whether schools, courts, or hospitals—intersected with a predatory imperialism that spurred growing dissent. Leaders of proto-nationalist and anti-imperial movements took issue with the foreign schools, which they viewed as contributing to sectarianism and Western elitism and as serving imperial interests.

Within a context of imperialism and the wide-ranging sociocultural modernist changes emerged a growing class of native public intellectual reformers. They were instrumental in the local cultural production of newspapers, journals, theater, literary fiction, and new schooling and grappled with forging alternative modernities. These reformers included figures from the three major religious communities, and although they were mostly men, women played prominent roles in the growing women's press and as educators. Out of this movement grew a vocal and active group of what has been called Islamic modernists; the figure of Sayyid Jamal ad-Din al-Afghani (1838–1897), itinerant scholar, Mason, and revolutionary reformer, looms large among them. They preached the compatibility of Islam with modernity—or more specifically the compatibility among Islam, the Enlightenment, and rational sciences. Central to their societal vision was the need for a syncretic schooling that emphasized Arabic and other native languages, regional history, rational sciences, vocational training, religion, and morals.

Indeed, throughout the region and up until the postwar era of national independence, numerous indigenous movements advocated for a modern native education that was distinct from the foreign and government-controlled schools. The schools of Islamic benevolent societies in Greater Syria and Egypt, the Maqasid School of Beirut founded in 1878 by ʿAbd al-Qadir al-Qabbani, the Islamic Benevolent Society School of Alexandria founded in 1879 by Abdallah al-Nadim, and the Maqasid schools of Egypt from 1892 associated with Sheikh Mohammed Abduh

provided early prototypes of Islamic modernist schooling. Later examples of schooling for alternative modernities include the Moroccan Free Schools, which flourished in the 1920s as a substitute to French colonial schools, institutions of the Central Asian Muslim modernists, the Jadids, who operated in a Russian colonial context, and the Muslim Brotherhood schools in Egypt, which proliferated from the group's founding in 1928 until its first banning in 1948.

Educating and Reeducating the Nation. With the lead-up to and eventual end of direct colonial rule, national education systems underwent vigorous expansion and centralization. Education figured prominently in national constitutions, which, with the exception of Saudi Arabia and Bahrain, mandated compulsory primary schooling for boys and girls. Compulsory schooling was supposed to serve as the great social equalizer. On this point, the outcomes have been mixed, especially in poorer autocratic states where—because of a combination of population stress, authoritarian governance, paltry resources, and deteriorating quality—mass education systems are under enormous strain.

At the level of higher education, national universities assumed tremendous symbolic and practical significance. The earliest national university in the region, Cairo University, represented a liberal ideal and the promise of regional power. Initially a private university, the university was nationalized in 1925. It opened branches in Beirut and Khartoum and provided much of the staff for the newly established universities in the Arab states. National universities were subsequently established throughout the region, including in Lebanon (1949), Libya (1954), Jordan (1962), and Saudi Arabia (1962). In Tunisia, Iran, and Turkey, already existing institutions were reorganized and nationalized.

During periods of radical change the education system has been swiftly revised in the service of reeducating the nation. Such was the case in Turkey during the secularization and Turkification that took place under the leadership of Kemal Atatürk (r. 1923–1938) and also in Iran, which underwent a contrary process of state Islamization following the Islamic Revolution of 1979.

Globalization and Fragmented Futures. The efforts to build a cohesive system of national education have been tested in recent decades by globalization, Islamization, and the fragmentation that has come about from free-market reforms. International bilateral and multilateral organizations including the World Bank, the International Monetary Fund, and the United Nations have a great

Elementary Education. Schoolchildren display their answers during a mathematics lesson in Laayoune, Western Sahara, December 1992. Photograph by Terrill Jones. AP IMAGES

degree of influence in setting educational agendas, which are often not in the interests of local communities. In a related vein, free-market economic policies have resulted in the growing privatization of education at all stages.

Higher education, for its part, has vastly expanded and diversified. More than fifty new private universities opened in the region in the 1990s alone. The oil-rich Arab Gulf countries are taking a lead in higher education that is to a greater extent being modeled on the American credit system. The 2,500-acre Education City in Doha, Qatar—which houses branches of several U.S. universities and offers a smorgasbord of educational offerings—is representative of this trend. On the other hand, there has been an unmistakable grassroots Islamization of education, as evidenced in the revitalization of Islamic-oriented secondary Imam Hatip schools in Turkey, the spread of fully accredited Islamic private schools, the revival of *maktabs* for qur'anic study, and the establishment of new Islamic universities in several countries.

The kind of education that has arisen in the region since the early eighteenth century has variously been described as "modern," because subjects and skills deemed necessary to contribute to a changing economy and global social order are taught, and as "Western," because western Europe provided much of the early expertise and institutional

prototype for the new schools. Some have designated the new schooling as "secular" because religion is no longer the organizing principle around which knowledge revolves but rather is a discrete subject in the curriculum; some have designated the schooling as "new method" because learning is structured through pedagogic arrangements that rely less on the individual teacher–pupil relationships than on standardized institutional norms and practices. The matter of what to call the modern kind of education continues to be a subject of debate; what is clear is that contemporary institutionalized schooling, in all its diversity, vigor, and mixed ideological underpinnings, has validated new forms of knowledge, given legitimacy to new figures of authority, and provided opportunities for emerging and continuously changing modes of social mobility, economic activity, and political and cultural engagement in the region and in the world.

[*See also* American University in Cairo; Civilizing Mission; Islamic Revivalism; Madrassa; *and* Missions, Christian, *subentry* Missions and Missionary Schools in the Middle East and North Africa.]

BIBLIOGRAPHY

Berkey, Jonathan. *The Transmission of Knowledge in Medieval Cairo: A Social History of Islamic Education.* Princeton, N.J.: Princeton University Press, 1992.

Chamberlain, Michael. *Knowledge and Social Practice in Medieval Damascus, 1190–1350*. Cambridge, U.K.: Cambridge University Press, 1994.

Fortna, Benjamin C. *Imperial Classroom: Islam, the State, and Education in the Late Ottoman Empire*. Oxford: Oxford University Press, 2002.

Herrera, Linda. "Higher Education in the Arab World." In *International Handbook of Higher Education*, edited by James J. F. Forest and Philip Altbach, pp. 409–421. Dordrecht, The Netherlands: Springer, 2006.

Herrera, Linda, and Carlos Alberto Torres, eds. *Cultures of Arab Schooling: Critical Ethnographies from Egypt*. New York: State University of New York Press, 2006.

Heyworth-Dunne, J. *An Introduction to the History of Education in Modern Egypt*. London: Luzac, 1939.

İhsanoğlu, Ekmeleddin. "Genesis of Learned Societies and Professional Associations in Ottoman Turkey." *Archiuum Ottomanicum* 14 (1995/1996): 160–190.

Khalid, Adeeb. *The Politics of Muslim Cultural Reform: Jadidism in Central Asia*. Berkeley: University of California Press, 1998.

Mottahedeh, Roy. *The Mantle of the Prophet: Religion and Politics in Iran*. New York: Simon and Schuster, 1985.

Reid, Donald Malcolm. *Cairo University and the Making of Modern Egypt*. Cambridge, U.K.: Cambridge University Press, 1990.

Rosenthal, Franz. *Knowledge Triumphant: The Concept of Knowledge in Medieval Islam*. Leiden, The Netherlands: E. J. Brill, 1970.

Tibawi, A. L. *Islamic Education: Its Traditions and Modernization into the Arab National Systems*. London: Luzac, 1972.

UNESCO Regional Bureau for Education in the Arab States. *Higher Education in the Arab Region: 1998–2003*. Paris: UNESCO, 2003. http://unesdoc.unesco.org/images/0013/001303/130341e.pdf.

United Nations Development Programme. *Arab Human Development Report 2003: Building a Knowledge Society*. New York: United Nations Development Programme, Regional Bureau for Arab States, 2003.

Waardenburg, Jean Jacques. *Les universités dans le monde arabe actuel*. Vol. 1. Paris: Mouton, 1966.

LINDA HERRERA

The United States

The history of education in what is today the United States of America reaches back to the early 1600s. In examining its goals, methods, and outcomes, and how social, political, and religious trends have affected it, the following topics will be considered: educational philosophies, the rise of public schooling, religious schools, elite universities, land grant colleges, historically black colleges, and the charter and homeschooling movements. It will be seen that the history of American education, especially its early history, has been shaped by the desire to create good Protestants who come to know their God in an unmediated fashion through the study of the Bible. This history has also been shaped by the desire to create good citizens who need a broad balance of skills and knowledge.

Educational Philosophies. Educational philosophies are especially influenced by social, political, and religious views. The first peoples of the North American continent were organized along tribal lines. They had no schools; instead, boys and girls were educated for their roles in tribal life by role models on a one-to-one basis.

European settlers came to the continent in the 1600s and settled in various parts of what is now the United States. For example, the French settled in Louisiana, the Spanish in the Southwest, and the British in New England. It was the British whose philosophy of education eventually became the dominant one, in the sense that it came to have the greatest impact on how the subsequent structure and methods of education developed.

Perhaps the most notable group of early British settlers was the Puritans. They landed in the early 1600s and settled mainly in Massachusetts and Connecticut. They had been exiled from England for their religious views and went first to France and then to New England in order to practice their religion without persecution. They founded the first public schools in order to teach children reading so that they could read the Bible and learn moral lessons. These schools were public in the sense that the Commonwealth of Massachusetts gave money for the schools, in addition to the tuition that parents and apprentice masters contributed. The goals of these schools were to educate children who could, as the Massachusetts Education Law of 1642 said, read and understand the principles of religion and the capital laws of the country. The Puritans had a great belief in fines and punishments as a cure for wrongdoing and began the tradition of corporal punishment in the schools. They also believed in memorizing verses from the Bible and from *The New England Primer*.

The Puritan idealistic view of education held sway until the late 1700s, after which realism became more dominant. Realism was gradually replaced by the pragmatic views of educators like John Dewey (1859–1952), who promoted the view that the student learns by doing rather than by memorizing.

The Rise of Public Schooling. Education was originally a parental activity. However, as the Massachusetts "Old Deluder Satan" law of 1647 indicated, parents were not doing their duty in this regard, and so there was a need for schools to provide religious and civic education. This law mandated that elementary schoolmasters were to be hired in towns with fifty or more families to teach children to read and write. Grammar schoolmasters were to be hired in towns with one hundred or more families to prepare students to attend Harvard College.

Elementary schoolmasters were not highly qualified. It was thought that a man was able to teach whatever level of school he had completed. Teachers were poorly paid. Sometimes their pay included room and board, with their stay being rotated among the families of their students.

An exception to the new emphasis on schooling was found in the southern colonies. There tutoring was favored in place of schools, largely because of the dispersed nature of the population. Southern planters also considered education to be more of a private matter than a concern of the state. Slaves were present in large numbers in the South, but by law they were forbidden to be educated. Any master who presumed to educate his slaves faced severe penalties.

With the coming of independence for the American colonies, there was a need to enculturate children along more American lines. Noah Webster (1758–1843) authored *A Grammatical Institute of the English Language: Part I* (1783), which was basically a spelling book and later became known as *The American Spelling Book* or, more simply, *Webster's Blue-Backed Speller.* Webster's aim was to foster "literary improvements" and, with the dictionaries he published later, to standardize an American dialect of the English language.

Several Founding Fathers were involved in education. Benjamin Franklin (1706–1790), noted as a statesman, inventor, and publisher, was concerned that education should become more practical in its orientation, that is, be given more useful and commercial goals. To this end he proposed the founding of the Philadelphia Academy, which would be not a grammar school but rather a boarding school where students would learn agriculture and mechanics in addition to such subjects as history and morality.

Thomas Jefferson (1743–1826) was also deeply involved in education. While a member of the Virginia legislature in 1779, he proposed "A Bill for the More General Diffusion of Knowledge," which essentially outlined a plan of public education for Virginia, with three years of tax-paid education to be provided for every child. It also involved a scholarship plan, about which he commented in his *Notes on the State of Virginia* (published in 1787 in the United States): "By this means twenty of the best geniuses will be raked from the rubish annually and be instructed at the public expense so far as the grammar schools go." He was known as the father of the University of Virginia for his work in designing the campus, as well as the curriculum, of that institution.

The one person who by most accounts made the greatest individual contribution to public education in the United States was Horace Mann (1796–1859). He served in the Massachusetts legislature and eventually became president of the Massachusetts Senate. He resigned this position in 1837 to become secretary of the newly created State Board of Education. In that position, which was somewhat comparable to a state superintendent of education, he spent twelve years (1837–1848) devoting himself to the reform of public education with an almost missionary zeal.

Mann feared political, class, and religious discord. He felt that if all children could be educated in a common school, they would learn to be good citizens of the republic and would come to understand their responsibilities toward each other: those of the rich toward the poor and those of the poor toward the rich. The common school would become the "balance wheel of the social machinery" (Horace Mann, *Twelfth Annual Report of the Secretary of the Board of Education of Massachusetts,* 1848).

The curriculum that Mann proposed for the common school consisted of arithmetic, English grammar, geography, reading, writing, spelling, human physiology, and vocal music. He did not believe that any one particular religion should be taught in the common school but believed that a kind of general Protestantism with emphasis on the moral teachings of the Bible and generic Christian prayers was appropriate. He never quite understood why certain religious groups, notably Roman Catholics, had problems with his religious synthesis.

In 1852, four years after Mann left office, Massachusetts became the first state to pass a law compelling children to attend school. It required them to attend school three months a year, but only half of that time had to be continuous. All states had compulsory attendance laws by 1918, the southern states being the last to adopt them. These laws were not effectively enforced until well into the twentieth century because of the lack of truant officers to enforce attendance and the lack of a school census that would indicate how many children should be attending.

The last major accomplishment in the rise of public education was the development of the public high school, which gradually replaced the Latin grammar school and the academy as the dominant form of secondary education. In 1875 the high school was still fairly new, and relatively few people went on from elementary school to attend it. Those who did so were usually the children of rich parents who could afford the tuition. When the town of Kalamazoo, Michigan, suggested supporting its high school with tax funds, many citizens objected on the grounds that a high school was an elite institution that provided a specialized education for which the general public should not be taxed.

American School. Classroom scene, 1945. NATIONAL ARCHIVES, SPECIAL MEDIA DIVISION/U.S. CENSUS BUREAU

The "Kalamazoo case" went to the Michigan Supreme Court, which ruled in 1874 that taxes could be used to support a high school.

Elementary schools began to be called "grade" schools toward the end of the nineteenth century when the original one-room schools were divided into multiple rooms on the basis of students' ages. This division resulted in the need for multiple teachers, the most senior of whom was designated the "principal" teacher. Eventually the noun "teacher" was dropped and the "principal" became concerned primarily with administration.

Religious Schools. Most European nations at the time of the American Revolution had a tradition of religiously sponsored elementary schools, and the United States followed suit for most of the first century of its history. This practice did not become contentious until the mid-nineteenth century. At that time large-scale immigration brought large numbers of Catholics to the United States, first from northern and western Europe and later from southern and eastern Europe. Many of these immigrants were from the lower socioeconomic classes. The established Anglo-Saxon Protestants in the United States feared this influx and saw the immigrants' Catholic

allegiance as a threat to democracy. The political cartoons of Thomas Nast in the second half of the nineteenth century give ample evidence of this attitude.

Other groups, such as the Missouri Synod of the Lutheran Church, established a system of parochial schools in America. The Roman Catholic system has been historically the largest.

Elite Universities. Harvard College was the first college in what is now the United States. It was founded in 1636 as a Puritan seminary so that the Puritans would not have to send their future ministers back to England and have them exposed to what they perceived to be the heretical views that were rampant in Oxford and Cambridge. The original curriculum at Harvard included philosophy, natural science, ancient history, Hebrew, and Greek—the latter two being the languages of the Old and New Testaments of the Bible.

Another early college to be established in what is now the United States was Yale College. It was founded in 1701 in reaction to what some Puritans thought was too much liberalism at Harvard. Colleges throughout the eighteenth and most of the nineteenth centuries were sponsored by religious denominations, had clergymen as their presidents, and required their students to attend daily chapel exercises. The first state-sponsored university was the University of Georgia, chartered in 1785.

In 1815 the New Hampshire legislature attempted to turn Dartmouth College—which had been established in 1769 by a charter from George III of England (r. 1760–1820)—into a state college. The members of the legislature believed that it was proper to do this because even though Dartmouth was a private institution, the legislature had been supporting it with public funds for many years. The case went to the U.S. Supreme Court, which ruled, in *Trustees of Dartmouth College v. Woodward* (1819), that as a private institution, Dartmouth could not be taken over by the state. The Court's reasoning was that what makes a school public or private is not where its funding comes from but rather who has title to it. In other words, a school is public if it is owned by a federal, state, or municipal government, even if it happens to receive most of its funding from a private source. It is private if it is owned by a private entity, even if it happens to receive most of its funding from a public source.

In the late 1820s there was growing concern that the traditional college curriculum, which taught the classics through Latin and Greek and required students to listen to lectures and recite from memory, was not practical enough. In 1828 the faculty of Yale College deliberated this question and issued a report that said that the old ways were still the best ways and that collegiate educational practice should not change. The classical approach, with its aim of forming a "gentleman," was retained. The faculty ruled that "the skills of the counting house should be learned in the counting house." This report effectively deferred vocational education—that is, education that could be applied to a job—for more than half a century. Also deferred was the higher education of women in the United States. It was argued well into the late 1800s that women did not have the physical strength to endure a college education.

Land Grant Colleges. The Morrill Land Grant Act of 1862 gave thirty thousand acres of federally owned land to each state for every member that the state had in Congress. The states used this land to establish colleges whose purpose would be to teach the agricultural and mechanical arts. Hence, these institutions were known as A&M colleges. The land grant college in Illinois originally had the title "Illinois Industrial University" and later became the University of Illinois. The Morrill Act was important for two reasons. First, it shifted the purpose of higher education in the United States from the classical preparation of a gentleman to the more applied, vocationally oriented purpose of preparing the student for the world of work. Second, this was the first time that the federal government gave tangible support to higher education.

Historically Black Colleges. If higher education was slow in coming for women, it was even slower for African Americans. Only one college, Alcorn State University in Mississippi, was created as a land grant college specifically for African Americans. The Second Morrill Act, passed in 1890, opened up greater opportunities for African Americans to attend college by specifying that states using Morrill funds must either be nondiscriminatory in admissions or create land grant colleges specifically for African American students.

A great debate was waged in the African American community after the Civil War regarding what kind of higher education was best for African Americans. On one side, Booker T. Washington (1856–1915), a former slave, advocated a practical curriculum emphasizing agriculture and the mechanical arts. On the other, W. E. B. Du Bois (1868–1963), the first African American to earn a PhD from Harvard, argued that African Americans should receive the same kind of liberal arts education that white Americans received.

The *Plessy v. Ferguson* decision handed down by the U.S. Supreme Court in 1896 said, "The object of the [Fourteenth] amendment was undoubtedly to enforce the absolute equality of the two races before the law, but in the nature of things it could not have been intended to abolish distinctions based upon color, or to enforce social, as distinguished from political, equality, or a commingling of the two races upon terms unsatisfactory to either." This decision gave the legal sanction of the highest court in the land to the theory of separate but equal education for the races. This separation was maintained until 1954 when the *Brown v. Board of Education* case reversed *Plessy*. In *Brown*, the Court said, "We conclude that, in the field of public education, the doctrine of 'separate but equal' has no place. Separate educational facilities are inherently unequal."

Charter Schools. Charter schools have their roots in the educational reform movement of the 1970s. About three thousand of them have appeared since states began passing legislation in the 1990s to allow for their creation.

Charter schools are nonsectarian public schools of choice. That is, they are operated by a sponsor (usually a state or local school board) and are free from many of the rules and regulations that govern regular public schools. These schools are granted charters that usually run from three to five years and that specify the format and structure of the school and how students will be assessed. If the school evidences success during this period, its charter may be renewed. Thus charter schools are granted freedom from myriad regulations in return for the production of educational results, including meeting state and federal standards of achievement.

Homeschooling. A moment's reflection will reveal that the term "homeschooling" is an oxymoron. Yet the fact that most people use it without such reflection is understandable, since education was historically done at home but, for a number of social, political, and religious reasons, was eventually handed over to the school. There were many complaints in the 1970s and 1980s that schools were not doing their jobs. Ivan Illich, in his book *Deschooling Society* (1970), said that schools serve the economic interests of the rich and do more harm than good to the poor. One reaction to these complaints was the charter school movement. Another more radical answer was the homeschooling movement.

It is estimated that in 1981 only 15,000 to 20,000 children were being taught at home. In 2003, the National Center for Educational Statistics (NCES) reported that 1.1 million children were being homeschooled. As to the reasons for homeschooling, the NCES said,

> Thirty-one percent of homeschoolers had parents who said the most important reason for homeschooling was concern about the environment of other schools. Thirty percent said the most important reason was to provide religious or moral instruction. The next reason was given about half as often; 16 percent of homeschooled students had parents who said dissatisfaction with the academic instruction available at other schools was their most important reason for homeschooling.

Education is a state responsibility, and so each state makes its own rules and regulations governing homeschooling with regard to such things as curriculum, amount of required instruction, and qualifications of the parent-teachers. Because of the press of responsibilities for operating regular schools, these regulations concerning homeschooling are sometimes not well policed.

Legacy. Americans have been paradoxical about their relation to education. They have held teachers in high regard, yet they have paid them low wages. They have expected schools to inculcate morality in children, yet they have excluded religious bases of morality from public schools. They have sought to be inclusive, yet they have not always provided equitable treatment with regard to race, gender, religion, ethnic origin, and handicapped status.

Education in the United States is a state responsibility. All states except Hawai'i have passed on much of that responsibility to the local level. Assuming that this status quo continues, it is likely that education in the United States will continue to be a basically democratic activity.

[*See also* Catholicism; Protestantism; Slavery, *subentry* The United States; United States, *subentries* Colonial Settlement, The Early Republic, Nation Building and Westward Expansion, *and* The Regulatory State; *and* Universities.]

BIBLIOGRAPHY

Dewey, John. *Democracy and Education: An Introduction to the Philosophy of Education*. New York: Macmillan, 1916. Arguably, this book was responsible for a change in the purpose and methods of education in the United States.

Illich, Ivan. *Deschooling Society*. New York: Harper and Row, 1970. An influential book in educational reform by a leading social critic.

Mann, Horace. *The Republic and the School: On the Education of Free Men*. Edited by Lawrence A. Cremin. New York: Teachers College, Columbia University, 1957. Contains an excellent introduction to Mann's work, together with selections from his twelve annual reports.

National Center for Educational Statistics. "1.1 Million Homeschooled Students in the United States in 2003." http://nces. ed.gov/nhes/homeschool/. A brief report concerning numbers of students that were homeschooled in 2003 and parents' most important reasons for homeschooling them.

National Commission on Excellence in Education. *A Nation at Risk, the Imperative for Educational Reform: A Report to the Nation and the Secretary of Education, United States Department of Education*. Washington, D.C., 1983. The federal report that spurred a wave of educational reform at the elementary and secondary levels in the last decades of the twentieth century.

The New England Primer. Boston, 1727. The classic first text for children used by the Puritans. It contained a catechism and an introduction to the alphabet employing religious examples. No copies of the editions before 1727 have survived.

Rudolph, Frederick. *The American College and University: A History*. New York: Vintage Books, 1962. A classic history of American higher education.

U.S. Charter Schools. http://www.uscharterschools.org. This site features sections on news, online dialogue, state profiles, federal support, and resources for charter schools.

Webster, Noah. *A Grammatical Institute of the English Language: Part I*. Hartford, Conn., 1783. This book, also known as the *Blue-Backed Speller*, was one of the first textbooks in the newly independent United States.

ROBERT NEWTON BARGER

EGYPT. In the mid-eighteenth century Egypt was still an Ottoman state, as it had been ever since its invasion in 1517 by Sultan Selim I. It was ruled by a wali (pasha), the sultan's deputy from Istanbul, for one year unless extended by a *faraman* (decree). The wali had a military force and was assisted by the Mamluks, who had ruled Egypt with Ottoman permission.

The Emergence of the Mamluks. As the Ottoman state weakened, the power of the Mamluks increased. The most outstanding was ʿAli Bey, who in 1763 became the country's sheikh with the title "al-Kabir" (the Great). His ambition was to become the independent ruler of Egypt, and in 1768 he took the opportunity of war between Russia and the Ottomans to declare Egypt's independence. He deposed the Ottoman wali and refused to pay the *kheraj* (tax). He sent his follower, Muhammad Abu al-Dhahab, to conquer Syria and advance toward Hejaz.

The Ottoman state overthrew ʿAli Bey al-Kabir by turning his deputy, Abu al-Dhahab, against him. After ʿAli Bey was killed in 1773, Abu al-Dhahab became the country's sheikh, and the Ottoman wali returned from Istanbul. Following the death of Abu al-Dhahab in 1775, Ibrahim Bey became the country's sheikh, sharing authority with Murad Bey. Hampering its efforts to regain power over Egypt, the Ottoman state remained preoccupied with war with Russia until the French expedition arrived in Egypt in July 1798, led by Napoleon Bonaparte.

On the eve of the French invasion, Egypt was administratively divided into sixteen *muderiyyas*, called *iqlim* (provinces). Egypt's population was approximately 3 million, with about 300,000 living in Cairo. The basic source of wealth was agricultural, and the land was owned by the state. Peasants were tasked to farm in order to pay taxes, and they benefited from the surplus. Taxes were collected by the *multazim* (tax collector), who competed for the post in a specific region. The state granted the tax collector a piece of land that was around 5 percent of the size of the arable land that he collected taxes from, and peasant serfs farmed it. Industry was manual, undertaken by craftsmen organized in small groups. Trade was conducted across the Red Sea.

Socially, Egyptians were divided into religious sects, with a Muslim majority and a minority of Copts and Jews. The Azhar mosque was a religious establishment that practiced Sharia (Islamic law), specialized in Islamic studies, and produced famous scholars. The Monophysite Orthodox Church represented the predominant sect among Egyptian Copts.

The French Invasion and Experience. On 1 July 1798 the French army led by Napoleon landed in Alexandria. They were resisted by the citizens led by Muhammad Korayim, the governor of the city, whom the French arrested, imprisoned on a warship, and then shot on 6 September 1798. The army advanced toward Cairo, defeating the Mamluk forces. Ibrahim Bey fled to the Sharqiyya region and from there to Acre, while Murad Bey fled to Upper Egypt, where he continued resistance. In October 1798, while battles were fought in Upper Egypt, a revolution broke out in Cairo led by Azhar scholars. The French army rode their horses into the Azhar mosque, enraging the Muslim majority. Around two hundred Frenchmen and two thousand Egyptians died in the battle.

Napoleon secretly departed Egypt on 12 August 1799, leaving in his place Jean-Baptiste Kléber, who was unenthusiastic about staying in Egypt because of the constant resistance and the arrival of an Ottoman expedition to expel the French. He proposed peace with the Ottoman state in return for his safe departure with his soldiers, but the Ottomans did not honor the agreement and requested that the French disarm. When fighting broke out again, the Egyptians took the opportunity, and the second revolution arose in Cairo in March–April 1800; it was quickly curbed. Kléber was assassinated by Sulayman al-Halabi, an Azhar scholar. He was succeeded by Jacques-François de Menou, who sought to stay in Egypt and transform it into a colony. He declared his conversion to Islam and married an Egyptian from Rosetta. In February 1801, Britain sent its fleet, which was joined by the Ottoman army, to Abu Qir near Alexandria, and ultimately the French were unable to resist and departed on 18 December 1801.

In politics and management Napoleon established in each *muderiyya* in Egypt a local council known as the diwan to resolve complaints and keep the peace. A central diwan was established in Cairo, consisting of delegates from the other diwans. After the first revolution of Cairo, Napoleon divided the diwans into two, while General Menou merged them again, adding to the function of each a judiciary role.

Agricultural experiments were made to farm coffee and sugarcane, windmills were built, the Giza *tarsana* (arsenal) was repaired, and Red Sea trading was revived. On the social front, health centers were established. The judiciary system was Egyptianized, and court cases became better organized. Menou added another reform when he established a courthouse for every religious sect.

The French expedition had a noticeable impact through the scholars from all branches of the sciences, arts, and literature who accompanied Napoleon. He also established the Institut d'Égypte, which first met on 23 August 1798 in Cairo and issued two newspapers, *Courier de l'Égypte* and *Le Decade Égyptienne*.

The Selection of Muhammad ʿAli as Wali of Egypt. After the departure of the French, a conflict arose between the Ottoman state and the Mamluks over regaining power in Egypt. Chaos prevailed, and soldiers looted because their salaries could not be paid. Muhammad ʿAli Pasha arrived in Egypt as the leader of a troop of Arnawut (Albanians) as part of the Ottoman forces to expel the French. His neutral attitude toward the conflict attracted the attention of the Egyptian leaders headed by Omar Makram, and on 13 May 1805 they decided to depose the Ottoman wali and replace him with Muhammad ʿAli. The Ottoman sultan at first refused, but he ultimately agreed to their request, and Muhammad ʿAli officially became wali of Egypt.

Challenges facing Muhammad ʿAli included the British expedition to Egypt in March 1807, then the crisis with Omar Makram about tax estimation, which ended in 1809 with his removal as head of the Alids. Next, Muhammad ʿAli got rid of the Mamluks in the citadel massacre of 1 March 1811, before he departed for the Arabian Peninsula to fight the Wahhabis.

Muhammad ʿAli, who ruled until 1848, is described by historians as the founder of modern Egypt. In agriculture he abolished the *multazim* tax system and created a direct relation between his department and peasants. Land was surveyed, and a new system was established for peasants to farm the land in return for tax payment and usufruct. He also improved irrigation methods and introduced new crops. He established military industries directly affiliated with the state, recruited foreign experts to support them, and sent missions abroad for training. He monopolized the marketing of crops and discouraged imports.

Muhammad ʿAli was also concerned with education. From 1813 he nurtured experts in industry and related sciences. He built a systematic military force analogous to the French army, conscripted Egyptians, and built factories (for weapons, ammunition, sails) and fortresses.

As for the political system, Muhammad ʿAli personally took over both the legislative and the executive authorities. He changed the existing administrative divisions whereby each of the sixteen regions was divided into seven *muderiyya*s, further divided into a number of *markaz* (districts), with each of those divided into *nahiya* (canton) and villages. Each village had a *sheikh balad* or mayor.

Because Muhammad ʿAli was a wali of the Ottoman state, he did not have independent relations with foreign powers. Upon the request of the sultan, he fought the Wahhabi sect (1811–1819) in the Arabian Peninsula, expanded his control to Sudan (1820–1822), and sent his army to Greece to assist the sultan during the Greek war of independence (1821–1828). Muhammad ʿAli also aspired to acquire Syria, so his army advanced there in October 1831, entered Anatolia, and threatened the Ottoman sultan.

Developments worked to his disadvantage. In August 1838, Britain signed the Balta Liman agreement with the Ottoman state, allowing British products to enter Ottoman-ruled countries, including Egypt, but Muhammad ʿAli refused to implement the agreement. Simultaneously, his army clashed with the sultan's, and the sultan's forces were defeated at Nezib (or Nizip), north of Aleppo, on 24 June 1839. However, the European nations stood by the sultan to protect the balance of power. The European powers defeated Muhammad ʿAli, forcing him into an unfavorable settlement in London on 15 July 1840 and restraining his ambitions. As a consequence, monopoly was abolished, and Egyptian markets were opened to European products and investments. This led to construction of the railway during the era of Muhammad ʿAli's successor Abbas I (r. 1849–1854) and of the Suez Canal during the era of Saʿid Pasha (r. 1854–1863).

Foreign Interference in Egyptian Affairs. During the reigns of Abbas I and Saʿid, Egypt did not clash with foreign powers. Clashes began during the reign of Ismaʿil Pasha (r. 1863–1879) when his ambitions conflicted with Anglo-French interests. During his era the nation witnessed a cultural renaissance, with the establishment of schools and a new emphasis on the education of girls. The Christian missionary schools increased to seventy and admitted Egyptian children. The same period saw the establishment of various learned societies and institutions.

Ismaʿil expanded his territories to the southeast of Sudan, fought with Ethiopia (1875–1876), and was defeated. With Egypt indebted to various nations, Britain sent a financial mission in December 1875, while a separate mission sent by France examined Egypt's financial situation. Thus began a period of foreign interference in the internal affairs of Egypt. Ismaʿil, who opposed such interference, was deposed in July 1879 and was replaced by his son Tawfiq (r. 1879–1892), who was unable to resist the Anglo-French meddling.

The Urabi Revolution and the British Occupation. A group of nationalists formed a resistance society in Helwan, south Cairo. Its first statement was published on 4 July 1879, and in mid-1881 it demanded a system of national surveillance to replace the foreign control. The Misr al-Fatah (Young Egypt) society, which was formed in Alexandria, demanded liberty, and the unrest spread to the Egyptian army, whose leadership positions were occupied by Turks. Finally, the Egyptian officers, led by Ahmad Urabi (*urabi* [head officer] of the Egyptian army), combined forces with the civil movement and the so-called Urabi Revolt (1881–1882) broke out. The events ended with the British occupation of Egypt on 14 September 1882.

Under the British occupation, a new era began with a British counselor placed in every ministry. After ten years of occupation Tawfig died and was succeeded by his son Abbas II on 8 January 1892. Abbas took measures—including the release of prisoners held since the Urabi Revolt—that brought him closer to the people. At first secretly supported by Abbas, Mustafa Kamil, a law school graduate, led the Egyptians against the British occupation in 1894. France supported him and requested that Britain leave Egypt.

On 13 June 1906, the Dinshaway incident occurred at this small village near the city of Tanta in the Nile Delta. On 13 June 1906 a party of British officers set out for the village to shoot pigeons. As often happened in such cases, the officers trampled the crops underfoot, and the village peasants asked them to leave. In reply the Englishmen opened fire, and the peasants then used their wooden staffs. Because the temperature that day was more than a hundred degrees, one of the British officers died of sunstroke. The peasants were charged with the murder of a British officer and were arrested and tried. Four of them were sentenced to death by hanging and nine to penal servitude, and the others were flogged at the foot of the gallows.

By 1907 there were ten political parties, the most famous, the National Party, founded near the end of 1907 by Mustafa Kamil. Kamil died in February 1908 and was succeeded by Muhammad Farid, who continued to lead the resistance despite his imprisonment. Farid left Egypt in 1912 and continued his activities at international gatherings in Geneva and Berlin.

The nationalist movement increased its demand for establishing a genuine system of political parties. Consequently in July 1913 the British authority formed the Legislative Assembly through free, direct elections. When World War I broke out in August 1914 the Ottoman state allied with Germany against Britain, and soon after Britain established Egypt as a protectorate, deposing Abbas II and appointing Prince Hussein Kamil with the title "sultan." The Legislative Assembly stopped meeting, law school students boycotted classes, and Sultan Hussein's entourage was twice attacked in protest against rule under the protectorate. The British continued to pursue opponents under martial law.

March 1919 Revolution. On 13 November 1918, Saʾd Zaghlul, Abdul Aziz Fahmy, and Aly Shaʿ met with the British commissioner to request permission to attend the peace conference in Paris as a *wafd* (delegation). These delegates hoped to express Egypt's right to self-determination, in keeping with the principles outlined by the American president Woodrow Wilson on 8 January 1918. The British authorities refused to grant permission, and Zaglul became the leader of the new nationalist Wafd Party. On 9 March 1919 revolution broke out when Zaghlul and his companions were arrested and exiled to the island of Malta. After a period of unrest, Britain announced Egypt's independence as a constitutional kingdom on 28 February 1922, with Sultan Ahmed Fuad designated as King Fuad.

Political Life under the Constitution. Elections under the constitution resulted in the formation in January 1924 of a so-called people's government led by Zaghlul. The new government sought to negotiate unresolved issues with the British but failed because Britain insisted that Egypt should remain a military base. Moreover, Zaghlul fought with the king over authority and with British authorities over the assassination on 19 November 1924 of the general marshal of the Egyptian army; days later the British disbanded Zaghlul's government. Elements of a class struggle emerged based on the means of production and wealth, resulting in the establishment of the Bank Misr (1920), the Egyptian Industries Union (1922), the General Egyptian Agricultural Union (1922), and the Chamber of Commerce (1927). The ʿayyan were members of both councils of parliament, were represented in *muderiyya* councils, and formed different cabinets. The government opposed calls for a workers' trade union (the Egyptian Industries Union and the General Egyptian Agricultural Union were for the large landowners and the owners of industrial and commercial projects, not for workers). The Socialist Party, which was formed in 1921, became the Communist Party in 1923. The Muslim Brotherhood was formed in 1928 under the leadership of Hassan al-Banna and sought to have the existing authorities declared as infidels.

In the midst of these transformations, in 1930 the prime minister, Ismaʿil Sedki, abolished the constitution and set about creating another, giving the king absolute authority. The political parties sought to remove him from office and bring back the 1923 constitution; Sedki was forced to resign in 1933. Subsequently, a treaty was signed with Britain on 26 August 1936, and in the following year foreign capitulations were abolished by a treaty signed in Montreux, Switzerland, in May 1937.

The Political Situation until 23 July 1952. After the 1936 treaty was signed, a new phase of Egyptian history began, distinguished by extreme turmoil. The treaty did not achieve any of the national aspirations, and conflict among parties was increasing. Mustafa an-Nahhas, the Wafd Party leader, was asked to form a government by Miles Lampson, the British ambassador, on 4 February 1942. During a sixteen-year period, from 1936 until 23 July 1952, Egypt was ruled by eighteen different governments. There were notable divisions among the major political parties, including among the Communists. Political assassination became the norm.

On 20 December 1945 the Egyptian government of Mahmoud Fahmi an-Nukrashi submitted a memorandum to Britain concerning a renegotiation of the 1936 treaty. Britain's tepid response led to further demonstrations and the demand for Britain's departure. A period of politicalchaos ensued, while negotiations with the British failed with successive governments. The situation was aggravated by the failure of the Arabs to save Palestine from the Zionists in 1948. On 8 October 1951 the prime minister, Mustafa an-Nahhas, declared the abolition of the treaty, which led to clashes with the British forces in the Suez Canal area—clashes that reached their climax on 25 January 1952 when the British besieged the headquarters of the Egyptian police in Ismailiyya. On the next day, fires broke out in Cairo, and the country was exposed to a sharp political crisis until the army, led by Gamal Abdel Nasser, a leader of the Free Officers organization, suddenly seized power on 23 July 1952.

July 1952–September 1970. The existing political parties were abolished in January 1953, and a one-party system was established. The republic was declared on 18 June 1953, and a treaty was signed with Britain that led to eventual British evacuation. In January 1956 the constitution was issued, along with economic decisions affecting the restructuring of Egypt, including agricultural reform and the formation of a public sector. Iron and steel factories, military factories, and the Aswan Dam were built; free education was instituted; and imports were restricted as the state took on the economic and social role in five-year plans starting in 1960. The National Charter was issued

Egyptian Leaders. Some of the Egyptian military leaders who led the coup d'état in 1952. From left to right seated: Lieutenant Colonel Zacharia Mohieddin, Squadron Leader Hassan Ibrahim, Lieutenant Colonel Youssef Saddick, Lieutenant Colonel Anwar el-Sadat, Wing Commander Aly Baghdady, Lieutenant Colonel Gamal Abdel Nasser, General Mohamed Neguib, and Colonel Ahmed Sawki. Left to right standing: Major Kamal El Din Hussein and Major Abdel Hakim Amer. Nasser became president of Egypt in 1956 and president of the United Arab Republic in 1958, a post he held until his death in 1970. Sadat succeeded him as president of Egypt in 1970. AP Photo

in July 1962 as a way to transform Egypt into a socialist society.

In the Arab world Nasser was viewed as leader of freedom, unity, and dignity as he stood by Arab revolutions. He declared a union between Egypt and Syria, establishing the short-lived United Arab Republic in 1961. Until his death on 28 September 1970 he supported adamantly the rights of Palestinians to establish a nation-state on their land, a position that led to armed conflict with Israel, culminating in the 1967 Six-Day War. Nasser is remembered as a leading voice in the nonalignment movement.

September 1970–October 1981. Anwar el-Sadat, one of the Free Officers and a man whom Nasser appointed vice president in 1969, succeeded Nasser upon his death. In October 1970, following a public referendum, Sadat was nominated as president. Sadat fought with members of the supreme executive committee of the Arab Socialist Union, the existing political organization, and on 15 May 1971, Sadat arrested the members of the group and brought them to trial. He released the Muslim Brothers to create a balance with the Nasserites and changed the name of the Nation's Assembly to the People's Assembly; the United Arab Republic became the Arab Republic of Egypt, and a new constitution was issued in July 1971.

One of Sadat's first tasks was to liberate Sinai from Israeli occupation, and in coordination with Syria the attack began on the Israeli forces on the east side of the Suez Canal on 6 October 1973. Subsequent negotiations between Egypt and Israel, under international sponsorship, disengaged the combatants, and the United States sought to settle many of the issues between the two countries while seeking a lasting peace in the Middle East. Sadat traveled to Israel on 19 November 1977 and addressed the Knesset, expressing his desire for peace. In September 1978, Sadat went to Washington, D.C., where discussions led to the Camp David Accords with the Israeli prime minister Menachem Begin. With the assistance of the American president Jimmy Carter, a framework for a treaty was signed on 26 March 1979.

Sadat faced strong opposition both within Egypt and among the larger Arab community. Iraq, Algeria, Libya, Sudan, and Yemen formed a resistance front, and the Arab League was moved from Cairo to Tunisia. The internal opposition came from a wide range of political powers. The political crisis was exacerbated by a socioeconomic crisis when Sadat declared an open-door policy in April 1974 in which the state relinquished its economic and social role, allowing market mechanisms to flourish and abolishing subsidies for basic goods. The political forces increasingly moved against Sadat, using the new, open political environment that had replaced Nasser's one-party system. Political parties emerged on the left, the right, and the center. The Muslim Brothers agitated among students, particularly within the military colleges, and new groups were formed, most notably al-Gihad. In response to increasing opposition, including threats on Sadat's life, he arrested a large number of prominent political figures on 5 September 1981. On 6 October 1981 members of the military shot and killed Sadat, and a state of emergency ensued.

After Sadat. After Sadat's assassination, the speaker of the People's Assembly, Sufi Aboutaleb, became president of the republic in accordance with the constitution. A public referendum resulted in the nomination as president of Hosni Mubarak, who had been appointed vice president in 1975. A new page of modern Egyptian history began, in many ways an extension of the Sadat era. Emphasis was placed on the open-door policy, the state relinquished its former economic and social role, privatization was implemented by selling public sector companies, and there was a commitment to continued peace with Israel. These measures led to much unrest and increased opposition, especially the violent actions of some Muslim groups, and a corresponding increase in security control over political movements.

The opposition forces demanded the change of article 76 of the constitution, which allows the appointment of the vice president as president, arguing instead for a general election for the presidency from among several nominees. On 26 February 2005 this change was instituted, but the change restricted the chances of other nominees, and the elections concluded with Mubarak's victory in the October 2005 elections. The opposition continued to demand the rephrasing of article 76 and the alteration of article 77. (In 1980, Sadat had changed article 77 to increase the number of terms allowed for the presidency from two to "several.") As the pace of opposition increased, with new groups joining—including judges, lawyers, and other civil groups—the president proposed reviewing thirty-four articles of the constitution, but not the contentious article 77.

[See also Alexandria; American University in Cairo; Arab League; Arabs and the Arab World; Cairo; Condominium Agreement; Dinshaway Incident; Institut d'Égypte; Mamluks; Mixed Courts of Egypt; Ottoman Empire; Sudan, Anglo-Egyptian; Suez Canal; Suez Crisis; and United Arab Republic.]

BIBLIOGRAPHY

Baer, Gabriel. *Studies in the Social History of Modern Egypt.* Chicago: University of Chicago Press, 1969.

Burrell, R. Michael, and Abbas R. Kelidar. *Egypt: The Dilemmas of a Nation, 1970–1977.* Washington, D.C.: Georgetown University Press, 1977.

Cooper, Mark. *The Transformation of Egypt.* Baltimore, Md.: Johns Hopkins University Press, 1982.

Gran, Peter. *Islamic Roots of Capitalism 1760–1840.* Modern Middle East Series 4. Austin: University of Texas Press, 1979.

Harris, Christina Phelps. *Nationalism and Revolution in Egypt.* The Hague, The Netherlands: Mouton, 1964.

Holt, P. M., ed. *Political and Social Change in Modern Egypt: Historical Studies from the Ottoman Conquest to the United Arab Republic.* London: Oxford University Press, 1968.

Hussein, Mahmoud. *Class Conflict in Egypt, 1945–1970.* New York: Monthly Review Press, 1973.

Issawi, Charles. *Egypt in Revolution.* London: Oxford University Press, 1963.

Mansfield, Peter. *Nasser's Egypt.* London: Penguin, 1965.

Lacouture, Jean, and Simonne Lacouture. *Egypt in Transition.* London: Methuen, 1958.

Lutfi al-Sayyid-Marsot, Afaf. *Egypt's Liberal Experiment 1922–1936.* Berkeley: University of California Press, 1977.

Safran, Nadav. *Egypt in Search of Political Community, 1804–1952.* Cambridge, Mass.: Harvard University Press, 1961.

Tignor, Robert. *Modernization and British Colonial Rule in Egypt: 1882–1914.* Princeton, N.J.: Princeton University Press, 1966.

Vatikiotis, P. J. *A Modern History of Egypt.* New York: Praeger, 1969.

Zayid, Mahmud. *Egypt's Struggle for Independence.* Beirut, Lebanon: Khayats, 1965.

ASSEM EL-DESSOUKI

1830, REVOLUTIONS OF.

Since the peace treaties of 1814 (Treaty of Ghent) and 1815 (Treaty of Paris), the Metternich or Vienna system had sought to prevent a resurgence of the liberal challenge of the French and European revolutions of the decade after 1789 by maintaining a European balance of power of mainly autocratic regimes. The revolutions of 1830 were a dramatic, widespread—and partly successful—challenge to that system.

Causes. The causes of the revolutions lay above all in middle-class aspirations for political reform and national self-determination, especially among educated young men resentful of the social exclusiveness of post-1815 regimes. Widespread harvest failures across the period 1827–1832 also fueled popular anger, and in some places, protests at food shortages and urban unemployment developed into demands for more radical social and political change.

The impulse for revolution came from France. There the revolution of 1789–1799 had ended absolute monarchy and noble privilege but not noble power. Society and politics continued to be dominated by great landed magnates, whether noble or wealthy bourgeois: the *grands notables*. The vote was limited to the wealthiest 1 percent of males, but even within that narrow elite there was liberal opposition to the autocratic pretensions of Charles X (r. 1824–1830).

Political friction coincided with a protracted economic slump. After a decisive liberal electoral victory in July 1830, Charles introduced severe controls on the press and slashed the size of the electorate. Mass protest culminated on 27 July, when barricades were erected in the streets of Paris; in the ensuing fighting two thousand insurgents and soldiers were killed. The liberal Louis-Philippe d'Orléans (r. 1830–1848) accepted the crown as "king of the French," and Charles was forced to flee the country.

This rapidly became a nationwide revolution, as peasants and artisans welcomed revolution as a chance to express their grievances and uncertainties. Hopes for radical change were soon dashed. The Orléanist regime's new charter offered guarantees only against infringement of civil liberties, restored the tricolor as the national flag, and asserted the primacy of parliament over the king.

News of the July revolution swept the continent and was the pretext for both peaceful and insurrectionary demands for political reform and national self-determination in many areas. In Belgium religious and linguistic differences had fueled demands for independence from the United Netherlands. On 25–26 August workers in Brussels joined a middle-class protest; there and in other towns the authority of the Dutch king William I (r. 1815–1840) collapsed. Tsar Nicholas I (r. 1825–1855) offered to provide a quarter of a million troops to restore Dutch rule, but within months he himself was confronted by a nationalist rising in Poland. Belgian independence was accepted by the Netherlands in December, but ultimately only British and French intervention in August 1831 secured Dutch acceptance of Belgium's new frontiers.

In Switzerland, in some German states—such as Brunswick, Saxony, and Hanover—and in Portugal successful demands were made for more liberal constitutional forms. Upheavals in the Italian and German states were undermined by divisions between liberals and democrats and by an inability of states to cooperate. Mass meetings including artisans and workers demanded a democratic and united Germany, but in the face of this radical challenge, elites preferred liberal reform or no reform at all. In Italy this lack of strategic unity against the Habsburg Monarchy gave the Austrian foreign minister Klemens Wenzel von Metternich the opportunity to reimpose order with the Austrian army.

There was in fact no common set of demands across the continent. At one extreme the 1832 Reform Act in Britain, enfranchising one-fifth of adult men, only narrowly diverted radical demands for universal suffrage fueled by the intransigence of the House of Lords. At the other extreme, in Spain, the constitutional government of Ferdinand VII (r. 1808, 1814–1833) was instead opposed by a militantly royalist and populist Carlist revolt that lasted in the north until 1840.

Such was the geographic extent and popular involvement in revolutionary movements that conservatives feared that demands for constitutional government and national self-determination might spill over into a renewed revolutionary upheaval as in 1789–1795. This was not to be: new regimes were quick both to absorb their predecessors into slightly broader ruling elites and to repress more democratic challenges.

The bloodiest example of repression was in Poland, where limited parliamentary autonomy had provided the shelter for more radical demands for self-government. Tsar Nicholas dispatched an army of a hundred and twenty thousand troops in February 1831, and after spirited military resistance until September, the parliament, the Polish army, and universities were closed, and eighty thousand Poles were imprisoned or exiled to Siberia. The most protracted battle over the outcomes of revolution was in France itself, where the consolidation of the Orléanist or July Monarchy was achieved only after a prolonged, often violent struggle in which large numbers of workers and peasants sought to push the regime in more radical directions before the new elite finally succeeded in driving opposition underground in 1835.

Outcomes. The major outcome of the revolutions of 1830 was the division of Europe between states that had some type of representative, parliamentary regime (Belgium, Britain, France, Portugal, Spain) and those that remained essentially autocratic (most of Germany and the Habsburg Monarchy, Italy, and Russia). Even successful upheavals did not significantly alter the ongoing social and political preeminence of great landed magnates, many of them noble. Large landowners continued to dominate the British Parliament.

In France itself, the revolution had resulted in only a slight widening of the electorate, to about 2 percent of adult men. In local government, however, the vote was extended to about 40 percent of men, and this, together with François Guizot's 1833 education laws, was the basis for a new democratic culture in ensuing decades. Everywhere, the revolutions of 1830 were a powerful precedent, leaving a legacy of memories of popular participation in politics and, in some areas, social radicalism.

[*See also* Belgium; Carlism; Conservatism, *subentry* Europe; 1848, Revolutions of; French Revolution; Liberalism, *subentry* Europe; *and* Nationalism.]

BIBLIOGRAPHY
Broers, Michael. *Europe after Napoleon: Revolution, Reaction, and Romanticism, 1814–1848.* Manchester, U.K.: Manchester University Press, 1996.
Church, Clive H. *Europe in 1830: Revolution and Political Change.* London: G. Allen and Unwin, 1983.
Gildea, Robert. *Barricades and Borders: Europe 1800–1914.* 2d ed. Oxford: Oxford University Press, 1996.
Rapport, Michael. *Nineteenth-Century Europe.* Basingstoke, U.K.: Palgrave Macmillan, 2005.
Sperber, Jonathan. *Revolutionary Europe, 1780–1850.* Harlow, U.K.: Longman, 2000.

PETER MCPHEE

1848, REVOLUTIONS OF. The "revolutions of 1848" is an umbrella term for a protracted political, social, and economic crisis affecting most of Europe in the period from 1846 to 1851. These were the most significant revolutionary upheavals in Europe between the French Revolution and the Eastern European revolutions of 1989 to 1991, but although the revolutions of 1848 were more widespread than either, the results were more modest. The revolutions of 1848 were also marked by greater popular involvement, more radical demands, and sharper class divisions than the revolutions of 1830.

Background. The crisis stemmed in part from severe harvest failure in 1845, of which the Irish famine was the most extreme manifestation. Food shortages and collapse of demand for manufactures caused mass unemployment in rapidly growing cities, in many of which new work practices had transformed the language of the workplace from occupational to class solidarities. Political and social tensions were aggravated throughout the mid-century upheaval by deep-seated economic crisis.

As in 1830, a combination of political opposition, economic crisis, and governmental ineptitude brought down the monarchy in Paris. On 23 February 1848 nervous troops fired shots into crowds of protestors; barricades were erected all over the city, and King Louis-Philippe fled. Crowds invaded the Chamber of Deputies and named a provisional government that proclaimed the Second Republic. Such action was mirrored in popular seizure of power in thousands of towns and villages. The new government guaranteed subsistence to the urban unemployed through "national workshops" opened in Paris, Marseille, and other cities. It also introduced universal manhood suffrage and freedom of the press and association.

Though the initial upheavals had been in Palermo and Switzerland, as in 1830 it was the overthrow of the French monarchy that was the spark for revolts elsewhere. Constitutions were granted in Tuscany, Piedmont, and the Papal States. After violent insurrection in Vienna, the emperor dismissed Klemens Wenzel von Metternich and promised a constitution, sparking similar uprisings in Prague, Venice, Milan, and Budapest. Hungary was guaranteed autonomy, and its parliament began to implement Lajos Kossuth's reform agenda. Constitutions were also promised for German states, and leading liberals organized an all-German assembly that convened in Frankfurt on 31 March.

Not all popular upheavals succeeded: though a constitution was promised in Denmark, in Sweden and Norway demonstrations were repressed, as were disparate movements for reform in Spain, Russia, and Britain, where a massive Chartist demonstration on 10 April was confronted by one hundred thousand "special constables." The February Revolution in Paris also inspired the large-scale but unsuccessful democratic Praieira revolt in Brazil.

The mixture of shock and elation at the rapidity of the collapse of established governments in so many places engendered optimism about a harmonious Europe of democratic, independent states, dubbed "the springtime of the peoples." Across much of the continent there was an unprecedented expression of a new political culture characterized by democratic clubs, workers' associations, a cheap and uncensored press, and, in places, demands for women's rights.

Reaction. Such optimism was not to last, and conflicting visions of the future polarized liberal reformers and social radicals, ultimately impelling new regimes to turn to the armed forces to suppress the democratic challenge. Though 84 percent of adult males voted in France and Europe's first elections by direct, universal manhood suffrage on 23 April, the outcome was a conservative French Assembly dominated by landed proprietors. After this assembly decided on 21 June to close the workshops for the unemployed, an unprecedented civil war tore Paris in two. The government lost eight hundred troops, and perhaps three thousand insurgents were killed. Contemporaries such as Karl Marx and Alexis de Tocqueville were struck by the manifestation of a new type of class conflict.

Similar social demands were articulated by the delegates from workers' associations that convened in Berlin in August. But they and workers in the large cities of Europe

Revolution of 1848 in Paris. "Scène de barricade, Paris, Juin 1848," etching by Adolphe Hervier (1821–1879). PRINTS AND PHOTO-GRAPHS DIVISION, LIBRARY OF CONGRESS

had little success in reaping tangible gains beyond temporary unemployment relief. The most significant gains were won by the peasantry of central and eastern Europe, for across much of Germany and the Habsburg Monarchy peasants were freed from all seigneurial dues and obligations. In the Pyrenees, Alps, and Jura, in contrast, there had been massive invasions of state and private forests in the spring of 1848, but these were ultimately unsuccessful protests.

Violent clashes in Frankfurt between radical democrats and troops called in by a nervous assembly undermined the reform agenda: to many liberals, social order seemed preferable to radical menace. Radicals also bridled at the legislature's preparedness to accept compromise over national boundaries, as in a dispute with Denmark over Schleswig-Holstein. Despite the numerical strength of support on which constitutional regimes in Germany and Austria could count, the parliament was increasingly unable to control resurgent conservatives in Prussia and other strong states.

The outbreak of war between Hungary and the Habsburg Monarchy impelled the imperial regime to confront radicalism simultaneously: the Viennese revolution was destroyed in late October by troops commanded by Josip Jelačić and Alfred Windischgrätz, at a cost of two thousand lives. Increasing conflict in Berlin impelled Frederick William IV to take action to restore social order, and in November, General Wrangel's troops dissolved the Prussian parliament, declared martial law, and closed down newspapers and clubs. This was a decisive moment in the history of the revolutions of 1848. The king spurned "the crown from the gutter" offered to him in by the Frankfurt Assembly in March 1849, and the assembly itself was dissolved ignominiously in May. Karl Marx was one of those deported. After a republic proclaimed in Baden was bloodily crushed in July, some eighty thousand Badenese chose to emigrate to America, abandoning their hopes for change at home.

National Unity. The revolutions in central and southern Europe were undermined not so much by class and ideological division as by "the national question." The collapse of authority in the Habsburg Monarchy in the spring of 1848 had enabled its Italian territories to win political freedom, but appeals for national unity foundered on division over the leadership of Charles Albert of Piedmont, opening the way for Joseph Radetzky's forces to reassert control against revolutionary regimes. In August 1849 the Venetian Republic, under its president Daniele Manin, was the last to fall.

In central and southeastern Europe, hopes for autonomous Czech, Hungarian, Transylvanian, and Croatian constitutional regimes dissipated in antipathy between ethnic minorities; Romanian demands ultimately led to forty thousand deaths. In June 1849, Russian troops invaded Hungary and ruthlessly repressed its new institutions; a renewed rising in Poland was similarly crushed. The reestablishment of Habsburg authority also ended hopes for a united greater Germany. The ethnic divisions that undermined the possibilities of peaceful constitutional reform in central Europe prefigured some of the horrors of the twentieth century.

Reaction in France was less bloody but ultimately as effective. In the presidential elections of 10 December 1848, Louis-Napoleon won a staggering 74 percent. Though popular opinion had often identified him with the promise of radical social change, it soon became apparent that he stood above all for social order. When France again went to the polls in May 1849 the party of order won easily, but the emergence of a strong rural constituency for the Left raised republican hopes for electoral victory in 1852. Louis-Napoleon further alienated the Left by his decision to support militarily the crushing of the short-lived Roman Republic (in which Giuseppe Mazzini and Giuseppe Garibaldi were prominent) in July 1849 and the reinstatement of the pope. Republican hopes were dashed by increasingly repressive restrictions on political freedoms, then by Louis-Napoleon's military coup d'état on 2 December 1851. Most people welcomed the coup as the way to end social and political instability; however, in specific areas of southern and central France up to one hundred thousand peasants and artisans took up arms against it.

Outcome. This resistance was crushed, and a subsequent plebiscite gave massive post facto approval to the coup. Neither it nor earlier reaction elsewhere could reverse some durable changes. In France, the revolutions of 1848 marked the end of royalist regimes, the definitive victory of universal manhood suffrage, and the end of slavery in France's colonies. In Prussia and Piedmont there were new forms of constitutional government. The peasantry in much of Germany and the Habsburg Monarchy had been freed from the vestiges of feudalism, like their French counterparts in the 1789–1793 period. More radical social demands from urban workers and feminists had been crushed or ignored. The revolutions bequeathed a rich legacy of regional political traditions. Just as important, however, elites horrified by the eruption of working-class challenges to the existing social order had begun to learn—like Louis-Napoleon—that universal suffrage could create a mass base for conservative politics.

[See also Conservatism, *subentry* Europe; Constitutionalism; 1830, Revolutions of; Liberalism, *subentry* Europe; *and* Nationalism.]

BIBLIOGRAPHY

Agulhon, Maurice. *The Republican Experiment, 1848–1852.* Translated by Janet Lloyd. Cambridge, U.K., and New York: Cambridge University Press, 1983.

Deák, István. *The Lawful Revolution: Louis Kossuth and the Hungarians 1848–1849.* New York: Columbia University Press, 1979.

Esdaile, Charles J. *Spain in the Liberal Age: From Constitution to Civil War, 1808–1939.* Oxford and Malden, Mass: Blackwell, 2000.

Evans, R. J. W., and Hartmutt Pogge von Strandmann, eds. *The Revolutions in Europe, 1848–1849: From Revolution to Reaction.* Oxford and New York: Oxford University Press, 2000.

Gildea, Robert *Barricades and Borders: Europe 1800–1914.* 2d ed. Oxford and New York: Oxford University Press, 1996.

Ginsborg, Paul. *Daniele Manin and the Venetian Revolution of 1848–49.* Cambridge, U.K., and New York: Cambridge University Press, 1979.

Rath, R. John. *The Viennese Revolution of 1848.* New York: Greenwood Press, 1969.

Saunders, David. *Russia in the Age of Reaction and Reform 1801–1881.* London and New York: Longman, 1992.

Sewell, William H., Jr., *Work and Revolution in France: The Language of Labor from the Old Regime to 1848.* Cambridge, U.K., and New York: Cambridge University Press, 1980.

Sked, Alan. *The Survival of the Habsburg Empire: Radetzky, the Imperial Army, and the Class War, 1848.* London and New York: Longman, 1979.

Sperber, Jonathan. *The European Revolutions, 1848–1851.* Cambridge, U.K., and New York: Cambridge University Press, 1994.

Sperber, Jonathan. *Rhineland Radicals: The Democratic Movement and the Revolution of 1848–1849.* Princeton, N.J.: Princeton University Press, 1991.

Stearns, Peter N. *1848: The Revolutionary Tide in Europe.* New York: Norton, 1974.

PETER MCPHEE

EIRE. *See* Ireland.

ELECTRICITY. In ancient times people recognized that some materials could hold light and a magnetic charge, but it took thousands of years for these phenomena to be explained. In the seventeenth century, Europeans began to experiment with the conduction of electricity. In the nineteenth century, Americans and Europeans began to harness the power of electricity. The control of electricity gave people a readily available and reliable power source as well as the ability to seemingly change night into day. More so than almost any other scientific development, the harnessing of electricity dramatically altered the patterns of daily living around the globe.

Electricity gave birth to a new technological system as networks of interrelated products and devices appeared. In 1882 there was only one electrical-power generating plant in the United States. By 1902 there were 2,250 American plants and two of the nation's largest firms, General Electric and Westinghouse, specialized in the design and manufacture of electrical goods. Electricity made electronic communications such as the telegraph and the telephone possible. By 1920 there were 13 million telephones in the United States, giving geographically separated individuals the ability to hold conversations. The changes proved startling to most people.

Many different inventors contributed to the electrical revolution. Thomas Edison, however, stands at the forefront. Edison, an American, developed the incandescent lightbulb in the 1870s. It consisted of a conducting filament mounted in a glass bulb. Passing electricity through the filament caused it to heat up and radiate light. A vacuum in the tube prevented the filament from burning up. Edison always had an eye on the commercial prospects for his inventions. He realized that he needed to develop not just the bulb but the ability to provide electricity to it. He developed an electrical system that included not only appliances but also power generators, transmission lines, relay stations, and electromagnetic devices such as thermostats.

Public supply of electricity at the end of the nineteenth century generally could be found only in larger towns and cities where either a local entrepreneur or a municipality established relatively small generating stations to supply local lighting loads. Electric street lighting provided much brighter light than gas and kerosene lamps. It had been installed in most American and European cities by the 1890s. Electric light permitted businesses to work longer hours, and entertainments, such as amusement parks, to remain open at night.

The American entrepreneur Samuel Insull developed two technologies that made possible the electrification of entire cities. He converted alternating current (AC) into direct current (DC), which allowed electricity to be conveyed throughout a city at a reasonable cost. He then developed a demand meter that could measure not only a customer's energy consumption but also the timing and size of the customer's peak demand. Insull was thus able to apportion costs equitably while offering lower rates to those who used more kilowatts or who used them at off-peak hours. The result, early in the twentieth century, was the electrification of nearly all American commercial buildings and a growing number of residences.

While the lightbulb is the most important electrical device of the nineteenth century, the vacuum tube is one of the most significant devices of the first half of the twentieth century. The vacuum tube has its roots in Edison's work. When developing his lightbulb, Edison noticed that electric current would flow from the filament to a positively charged metal plate inside the tube. He regarded this effect (known as the Edison effect, or thermionic emission) as interesting but not worth pursuing. In 1897 Joseph John Thomson, an English physics professor, discovered the electron. He immediately realized that the filament flow was a particle stream of electrons. John Ambrose Fleming, an employee of the British Wireless Telegraphy Company, then attached a bulb with two electrodes to a radio receiving system in order to improve the reception of radio signals. He patented the first electronic rectifier, the Fleming valve, or diode, in 1904. The vacuum tubes were indispensable to switch currents and became an integral element in the Italian physicist Guglielmo Marconi's long-distance radio system. However, the Fleming valves consumed large amounts of power and were insensitive to electromagnetic changes. In 1906 the American inventor Lee De Forest added a third electrode, a network of small wires around the cathode, to control the electron stream. This triode made possible the amplification of music and voice, thereby making long-distance calling practical.

Vacuum tubes continued to use large amounts of power. This characteristic created heat that shortened the life of the tubes. By the 1930s devices such as radios and telephones needed receivers that required high power. Early digital computers, such as the U.S. Army's ENIAC in the late 1940s, required about nineteen thousand vacuum tubes, which simply generated too much heat. In 1904, the Indian physicist Jagadis C. Bose patented the first solid-state point-contact detector of electromagnetic waves. Other inventors engaged in efforts to improve detection. The 1947 invention of the transistor by the Americans Walter H. Brattain and John Bardeen of Bell Laboratories meant that smaller, reliable, and less power-hungry devices could be produced. This point-contact transistor, a type of semiconductor, used a small amount of electrical current to control a larger change in voltage. With this development, the semiconductor became the key to further developments in electronics.

The United States became the leader in semiconductor development chiefly through the efforts of Bell Laboratories and Texas Instruments. These two competing firms developed semiconductors from germanium and silicon. However, since silicon could operate at higher temperatures than germanium, it became the favored material. The one-way conductance of semiconductors is the quality that makes them useful, and by the end of the twentieth century they could be found in nearly every electrical device.

The electrical revolution missed large swaths of Latin America, Asia, and especially Africa. At the start of the twenty-first century the glow of electric light on Earth was visible from space. Europe and the United States emitted a bright light. Some areas of the planet, however, stood strikingly dark as an indication of a lack of industrial development.

[*See also* Industrialization, *subentry* Overview; Radio; Science and Technology, *subentry* Overview; Telegraph; Telephone and Cell Phone; *and* Television.]

BIBLIOGRAPHY

Bordeau, Sanford P. *Volts to Hertz—The Rise of Electricity: From the Compass to the Radio through the Works of Sixteen Great Men of Science Whose Names Are Used in Measuring Electricity and Magnetism.* Minneapolis, Minn.: Burgess, 1982.

Meyer, Herbert W. *A History of Electricity and Magnetism.* Cambridge, Mass.: MIT Press, 1972.

Sharlin, Harold I. *The Making of the Electrical Age: From the Telegraph to Automation.* London and New York: Abelard-Schuman, 1964.

Simon, Linda. *Dark Light: Electricity and Anxiety from the Telegraph to the X-Ray.* Orlando, Fla.: Harcourt, 2004.

CARYN E. NEUMANN

ELECTRONICS INDUSTRY. Remarkably broad, the modern electronics industry includes all manufacturers of business, consumer, and heavy machinery based on electronic circuits, as well as producers of individual electronic components like circuit boards, vacuum tubes, and microchips. In 2006, global sales of these various electronics goods totaled nearly 1,150 billion U.S. dollars.

The roots of an independent electronics industry can be traced to the late-nineteenth-century drive to harness and commercialize electrical power. The earliest firms to dominate the generation and supply of electricity, beginning in the 1880s, in turn dominated the introduction of the first mass-produced electronics device, the vacuum-tube radio, which debuted in 1920. Some firms, such as Westinghouse in the United States, nurtured their expertise in radio production through government-sponsored radar and wireless telegraphy research during World War I. All involved built upon a shared baseline of scientific and technical knowledge that spanned from Heinrich Hertz's 1888 demonstration of electromagnetic waves to Lee De Forest's triode vacuum tube for amplifying wireless signals, patented in 1907.

The Radio Industry. Radio's commercial success drove electronics production into a life of its own, separate from the electrical supply industry. By 1925, Britain reported several hundred small-scale radio and components manufacturers, together employing some forty thousand workers, whereas in the United States hundreds more smaller firms competed with the New York–based Radio Corporation of America, formed in 1919, and its main competitors, Zenith (1923) and Galvin (1928; Motorola after 1947). By 1940, however, the industry had streamlined significantly, and only the highest ranks of a narrowing oligarchy could undertake a massive research and development project like the invention of television—headed in the 1930s by EMI, Marconi, RCA, Philco (U.S.), and Telefunken.

Modern Electronics. World War II dismantled Berlin, the onetime "electrical capital of the world," and marked the acme of Britain's role in early electronics innovation. Within the United States, on the other hand, wartime funding for electronics research and production continued to increase in the late 1940s, and it continued to do so throughout most of the Cold War. Few historians question that the 1947 invention of the amplifying transistor at Bell Labs, New Jersey, was the landmark moment in modern electronics. From this point onward, the extravagance of U.S. military and space programs continued to lessen the risk of investing in newer microelectronics breakthroughs such as the silicon transistor (1954), the planar etching process (1959), and the integrated circuit (1959). As late as 1970 when the first computer microprocessor chips (CPUs) were in development, government purchasing continued to represent the largest part of U.S. new electronics component sales.

As the industry miniaturized, transitioning from using wired assemblies of vacuum tubes to printed circuit boards with plug-in semiconductor components, long-standing U.S. industry leaders such as General Electric and Sylvania lost their advantage. Producing semiconductors, essentially a chemical refining process, required machinery and materials well outside the scope of the traditional electrical or radio suppliers. Moreover, small yet durable semiconductor components lent themselves to a much different, increasingly global division of labor. Postwar newcomers to the U.S. electronics industry like Texas Instruments and Fairchild capitalized on this context, as well as on new U.S. tariff structures that minimized duties on overseas electronics assembly, to become pioneers in the use of inexpensive foreign assembly operations.

By the late 1970s most U.S. electronics production, from stereo equipment to military guidance systems, had passed at some point through an offshore assembly site, which at that time were concentrated in Hong Kong, Taiwan, South Korea, and Singapore. Along with this reliance on internationalized production, leading electronics firms of the postwar era differentiated themselves from their vacuum-tube predecessors by frequent offshoots and mergers, a smaller, highly educated domestic workforce, and closer ties to major research institutions. This unique business structure came to be symbolized in the mid-1970s by the booming cluster of computer and microchip companies found in California's Santa Clara "Silicon" Valley.

Global Competition and the Information Revolution. Contrasting with the turbulence of America's postwar electronics industry, older vacuum-tube companies in western Europe and Japan took the lead in adopting U.S. innovations like the transistor. Many also experimented with automating their labor-intensive manufacturing processes before shifting to the widespread use of foreign assembly in the late 1970s. In the burgeoning market for low-cost, semiconductor-based consumer electronics, Japanese manufacturers alone rivaled U.S. companies, offering remarkably inexpensive goods from radios, microwaves, and calculators to individual memory chips. Historians have credited Japan's postwar strength in the widening consumer electronics market to a combination of general and industry-specific national policies, including its native cartelized *keiretsu* business structure, strong financing from its Ministry of International Trade and Industry (MITI), inexpensive labor, and a ban until 1974 on foreign-owned plants. U.S. companies at various times alleged undervalued dumping by Japanese firms, including a successful trade suit over color televisions in the 1970s, but any resulting effort to limit Japanese imports ran up against the growing internationalization of the electronics industry as a whole. By the early 1980s most large Japanese companies—like their foreign counterparts—shipped from numerous overseas plants.

Once established in the 1960s, the offshore assembly model, offering tax incentives, low plant costs, and inexpensive, largely nonunionized labor, continued to shape electronics industry development throughout Southeast Asia, South and Central America, and Mexico. Beginning in the late 1970s some of the earliest hosts to multinational assembly operations attempted, with varying success, to develop more comprehensive electronics industries. Taiwan and South Korea, though not innovators, gradually became significant exporters of their own brands of televisions, videocassette recorders, and computer peripherals. Meanwhile those more developed countries attempting to lure foreign electronics investment, such as India, China, and Brazil, sought to leverage their greater political and economic authority to structure this investment around nationalistic goals, like sophisticated technology transfer. Similarly, the United States and many western European countries adopted their own national electronics development programs in the 1970s and 1980s, particularly in research fields considered strategic, like computers and microchips. For the most part such initiatives failed to counterbalance the momentum toward multinational ownership, investment, and production in the industry, as with world trade in general at the close of the twentieth century.

By the mid-1990s the so-called information revolution—merging data processing and telecommunications—represented a significant part of the largest growth period yet in global electronics sales. In developed nations, electronics manufacturers found an apparently insatiable demand for new media technologies such as cellular phones and Internet-equipped personal computers, each in turn requiring an underlying electronic infrastructure, also powered by advances in microchips. In this climate of "pervasive computing," as the sociologist Manuel Castells characterized the 1990s and early 2000s, the industry in its full breadth—semiconductors, computers, consumer electronics, telecommunications, navigation and industrial equipment—seemed destined to grow only more turbulent, capital intensive, and geographically dispersed. Though the United States, western Europe, and Japan continued to be leaders in new electronics innovation and sales, in 2006 the industry's true weight fell further across Asia and the Pacific—with growing assembly regions in Thailand, Malaysia, the Philippines, and Indonesia—and, increasingly, into Mexico's maquiladora havens for direct foreign investment. Mexico in particular drew a windfall of relocated and new electronics manufacturing facilities following the North American Free Trade Agreement (NAFTA, 1994).

[*See also* Computers; Foreign Investment; Information Technology; Radio; *and* Television.]

BIBLIOGRAPHY

Braun, Ernest, and Stuart Macdonald. *Revolution in Miniature: The History and Impact of Semiconductor Electronics Re-explored and Updated.* Rev. 2d ed. Cambridge, U.K., and New York: Cambridge University Press, 1982.

Castells, Manuel. *The Rise of the Network Society.* 2d ed. Oxford and Malden, Mass.: Blackwell, 2000.

Chandler, Alfred D., Jr. *Inventing the Electronic Century: The Epic Story of the Consumer Electronics and Computer Industries.* New York: Free Press, 2001.

Hall, Peter, and Paschal Preston. *The Carrier Wave: New Information Technology and the Geography of Innovation, 1846–2003.* London and Boston: Unwin Hyman, 1988.

Todd, Daniel. *The World Electronics Industry.* London and New York: Routledge, 1990.

JOSHUA PALMER

ELITES IN THE MIDDLE EAST. The upper classes in the Middle East, called *al-Khassa*—literally "the special" in Arabic—can be divided into roughly three, often overlapping, categories. First, there were elites who rose to prominence because of specific religious connections to the prophet Muhammad, most notably those with a direct, patrilineal blood relationship with the family of the Prophet, the *shurafa*, or sharifs. Also, especially in the early Islamic period, the *ansar*—the "helpers" or first followers of the Prophet—and the *muhajirun*—those Muslims who first fled with Muhammad from Mecca to Madina in 622 C.E.—both had a special status in the Muslim community and were consulted regularly as sources of Hadith, sayings of the Prophet that often held the authority of law.

Descendants of the sharifs continue to hold positions of power and authority in the early twenty-first century, perhaps the most famous examples being the Hashemite dynasty that rules Jordan and the ʿAlawid dynasty that has ruled Morocco since the seventeenth century. Shia Islam also puts primary importance in descent from the Prophet, especially from the offspring of the Prophet's daughter Fatima and his cousin ʿAli, the fourth caliph, or successor to the Prophet. The first eleven recognized male descendents of ʿAli and Fatima are considered by most Shiites to be the true imams, or leaders, of the Islamic community. The twelfth imam, known as the Mahdi, born in 868 C.E. and fearing persecution from the authorities, went into hiding or occultation. Most Shiites believe that the true imam has yet to emerge from occultation.

The second category of upper class in the Middle East included those elites with preexisting, pre-Islamic power who often attempted to use Islam to legitimate their authority. The leaders of the elite Quraysh tribe in Mecca were some of the most vehement opponents of the prophet Muhammad. After the Prophet conquered Mecca under favorable terms that allowed the Quraysh to maintain much of their economic power, the Quraysh and their descendants rapidly adopted Islam and maneuvered into positions of political and religious authority. The Umayyad dynasty, founders of the first great empire of Islam, originated from an elite Qurayshi family. Most elites attempted to convert as rapidly as possible as the new faith of Islam spread to various lands. In addition to its spiritual dimension, Islam promised many economic and political benefits to non-Arab elites who had no connections with the historical blood or life of the Prophet. Some non-Arab elites, such as the Persians, attempted to recast Islam in local, regional terms, claiming to be even better stewards of the religion than were the Arabs to whom Muhammad first preached his message.

Finally, there are those Middle Eastern elites who have risen to power largely out of their own initiative, education, or economic savvy. Although many religious positions could pass down from father to son, great jurists or ulema were judged and respected not merely according to their name or tribe but according to the extent and authority of their writings and the depth of their memorization of the Qur'an, the Hadith, and commentaries on the sources of Islam. Trade, government, modern education, and more recent bursts of economic development have opened new avenues to those not born with tribal connections. Under the Mamluks in Egypt and later under the Ottoman Empire, for example, rulers were chosen specifically outside the existing tribal framework. The Mamluks were originally slaves, captured in various raids outside Egypt and placed in positions of authority. *Askari*s, or military bureaucrats, and ulema, Islamic bureaucrats, ruled the Ottoman Empire like mandarins. Sometimes even Jews and Christians could use their status as middlemen between Muslims to reap vast sums and gain the confidence of kings and sultans as *wazir*s, or ministers.

With their vast deserts, Arabia and the Middle East in general have been infamous as a place of enormous potential risk but also enormous potential reward for the intrepid merchant or raider. Vast fortunes could sometimes befall the poorest of merchants, who would then often seek to construct the legitimacy of a sharifian heritage—even if, in fact, no such elite connection existed. Also, from the earliest periods, true sharifs have been known to fall into desperate poverty. Although seemingly rigidly determined by tradition, tribe, and faith, the elite categories of the Middle East are, in fact, remarkably fluid. Moreover, Islam mandates the fundamental equality of all believers before God. During the pilgrimage to Mecca a billionaire prince and a poor shoemaker will wear the same humble, white cloak and perform the same ceremonies. It is this belief in the fundamental equality of all believers that has made power, wealth, and status both a blessing for this world and a potential curse in the eyes of God. Many Muslim elites choose to hide their wealth within the confines of their home and tribe.

During the colonial period elites across the three different classes, as well as across borders, had to make the difficult choice of whether to collaborate with or resist European rule. Under the intellectual guidance of Pan-Arabists and Pan-Islamic writers, Arabs, often educated in the West, were able to construct the basis for effective anticolonial resistance. The dream of Pan-Arabism and Pan-Islamism still lives, if weakened by the death of the icon of Pan-Arabism, Gamal Abdel Nasser (1918–1970), president of Egypt, and the defeat of the Arabs by Israel in the 1967 war. More recently, leaders of terrorist organizations such as Al-Qaeda, including Osama bin Laden and Ayman al-Zawahiri, have been drawn from the wealthy and educated elite of Middle Eastern society, even as they send their less fortunate cousins to die as suicide bombers. This Al-Qaeda elite is connected across borders by globalization. There is a much larger group of Middle Eastern elites, however, an elite represented by the moderate to reformist governments under the king of Morocco, the emirs of Qatar and the United Arab Emirates, the sultan of Oman, and the king of Jordan, who are engaged in the much more productive, much less self-defeating, task of creating Middle Eastern forms of modernity that do not fundamentally threaten the distinctive, Islamic character of the region.

[*See also* Arabs and the Arab World *and* Islam.]

BIBLIOGRAPHY
Baraka, Magda. *The Egyptian Upper Class between Revolutions, 1919–1952*. Reading, U.K.: Ithaca Press, 1998.
Findley, Carter Vaughn. *Ottoman Civil Officialdom: A Social History*. Princeton, N.J.: Princeton University Press, 1989.
Petry, Carl F. *The Civilian Elite of Cairo in the Later Middle Ages*. Princeton, N.J.: Princeton University Press, 1981.
Zartman, I. William. *Political Elites in Arab North Africa*. New York: Longman, 1982.

ALLEN FROMHERZ

EL SALVADOR. El Salvador is the smallest Central American state in area but historically one of the region's most densely populated and productive. Conquered by Pedro de Alvarado, a lieutenant of Hernán Cortés, in 1524, it remained a marginal territory of the Kingdom of Guatemala (part of New Spain) until the eighteenth century, when Bourbon economic reforms led to a sustained boom in the production of indigo. Salvadoran growers turned to Guatemalan traders to finance and distribute their crops, and resulting disputes over the merchants' lending policies laid the foundation for a longstanding antagonistic relationship between the two regions. Economic decline and ideological clashes between Salvadoran Liberals and Guatemalan Conservatives only exacerbated these problems, which continued to plague the Kingdom of Guatemala even after it had declared independence from Spain (1821) and Mexico (1823) and had adopted a new name: the United Provinces of Central America. A weak endeavor from the outset, the coalition of former Spanish territories lasted only three short decades before succumbing to intraterritorial tensions and the powerful Conservative Guatemalan caudillo Rafael Carrera. El Salvador declared itself an independent republic in 1856, the last of the Central American states to do so.

The Rise of Coffee. By the time the Liberals regained power in the 1860s under General Gerardo Barrios

Espinoza, coffee had begun to challenge indigo as El Salvador's primary cash crop. Liberal reformers threw the weight of the state behind the coffee revolution, abolishing municipal and indigenous communal landholdings previously used to plant subsistence crops in an attempt to create a nation of independent coffee producers. A class of entrepreneurial smallholding peasants did manage to survive well into the early twentieth century, but most lost their lands soon after as a result of population pressures and a more forceful project of agrarian expropriation carried out by an increasingly powerful landed elite tied to the Meléndez-Quiñónez dynasty that ruled El Salvador from 1912 until 1927. These disenfranchised peasants swelled the numbers of a fledgling rural proletariat, providing fertile ground for the Salvadoran Communist Party that, led by the firebrand Agustín Farabundo Martí, proceeded to build a strong following among the primarily indigenous laborers on the coffee plantations, or *fincas.*

President Pío Romero Bosque (1928–1931) broke with the ruling Liberal oligarchy in relaxing restrictions on political opposition and implementing gradual electoral reforms. But the social and economic instability that plagued the tenure of his democratically elected successor, the populist Arturo Araujo, led a nervous military to stage a coup d'état, bringing El Salvador's brief experiment in democracy to an abrupt end with the appointment of Araujo's vice-president, General Maximiliano Hernández Martínez, to the presidency in December of 1931. One month later, thousands of indigenous subsistence farmers and coffee-pickers rose up in an ill-planned rebellion following blatant electoral fraud perpetrated by Hernández Martínez during recent elections. While the rebels killed no more than one hundred persons (civilian and military), the Hernández Martínez regime responded by slaughtering between ten thousand and thirty thousand indigenous Salvadorans. This massacre, known as the *matanza* (slaughter), marked the end of outwardly recognizable indigenous identity in most of the country. Its effectiveness in quieting the countryside became a rationale for wealthy Salvadoran landowners to employ mass murder as a political tool in the years to come.

Dictatorship, Development, and Revolution. The Hernández Martínez dictatorship ushered in a half-century of military rule during which the Salvadoran armed forces guaranteed their upper-class benefactors protection from similar civilian uprisings in return for the right to govern the country. Mixing reform with heavy-handed repression, Hernández Martínez successfully co-opted the urban working classes and cultivated

El Salvador. Street vendors sell grinding stones at a street market in San Salvador, mid-twentieth century. PRINTS AND PHOTOGRAPHS DIVISION, LIBRARY OF CONGRESS

the support of wealthy landowners and industrialists while brutally suppressing the rural proletariat. His successors followed similar strategies, ensuring that political opposition would never challenge elite hegemony over the state apparatus. Following World War II, El Salvador attempted to reduce its dependence on coffee by diversifying its agricultural sector. By the late 1950s, state capital investment and profits from coffee exports had given rise to a modern, mechanized system of cotton production, followed by booms in the sugar and cattle industries in the 1960s and 1970s. Such promising economic advances, however, were offset by negative social trends: the rapidly expanding cotton and sugar plantations and cattle ranches forced thousands of peasants off their lands, leading to a crisis of subsistence in which an overpopulated and underemployed agrarian sector could not produce enough basic foodstuffs to sustain itself.

The Salvadoran military regime attempted to assuage an increasingly restless population by promoting gradual electoral reforms during the 1960s. This opened up space for opposition groups such as the fledgling Christian Democratic Party (PDC), which gained a strong foothold among the urban middle classes with its platform of progressive reforms based on Catholic social teachings. The regime also sought to create jobs by increasing manufacturing sector outputs. The creation of the Central

American Common Market in 1961 and the succeeding aid provided by the U.S.-sponsored Alliance for Progress considerably boosted Salvadoran industrial output. These manufactured goods flooded the markets of less industrialized nations like Honduras and Nicaragua, stifling their attempts at domestic modernization. The unwelcome influx of goods, combined with a history of border disputes and the destabilizing presence of 300,000 Salvadorans in Honduras (mainly economic refugees displaced by the expanding agro-export sector and population pressures) led to the 100-hour Soccer War between El Salvador and its northern neighbor in July of 1969. For a brief moment, disparate political groups and social classes united in patriotic fervor against the Hondurans, providing the military government a respite from dealing with the crisis of subsistence. Yet as thousands of refugees poured back across the borders into El Salvador in the months following the war, social reformers renewed their calls for land redistribution, social equality, and a more transparent and democratic political process.

Successive fraudulent presidential elections in 1972 and 1977 proved the government's rhetoric of democratic reform to be hollow, leading to increasingly militant actions by peasant unions, urban workers, and students. These groups attempted to persuade Salvadoran state officials to carry out meaningful structural reforms that would close the gap between the few wealthy and the hundreds of thousands of poor. Powerful landowners responded by organizing paramilitary death squads to silence them, and by the late 1970s the countryside was awash in the blood of peasant activists. In 1979, a reformist group of junior military officers staged a successful coup d'état and promised to address popular grievances, but they were quickly shunted aside by members of the army's old guard, who were determined to block any reforms. By 1980, a full-fledged revolution was under way in El Salvador. Led by the Farabundo Martí National Liberation Front (FMLN), a coalition of leftist guerrilla groups that culled the majority of its support from the rural poor, the revolutionary forces fought the military to a draw over the course of the next decade. The United States, fearful of the political repercussions of another Marxist victory in Central America following the 1979 Sandinista triumph over the U.S.-sponsored Somoza dictatorship in Nicaragua, poured an estimated $1.5 million per day into economic and military aid to the Salvadoran government from 1980 to 1992. The United States also heavily subsidized the 1984 election campaign of the Christian Democrat José Napoleón Duarte in his successful bid to become the first civilian president in over half a century. Yet for all intents and purposes, the armed forces still ruled the country. By the late 1980s, accusations of widespread corruption had combined with Duarte's failure to make good on his promises of peace and economic prosperity to bring about the downfall of the Christian Democrats.

Democratization and the Peace Process. The victory of the conservative National Republican Alliance (ARENA) over the moribund PDC in the presidential elections of 1989 brought to power a party founded by the reactionary Major Roberto D'Aubuisson, a former death squad leader and the man who had ordered the assassination of Catholic Archbishop Oscar Romero in 1980. Conceived of as a means to combat the perceived threat of Communism through the electoral processes, ARENA had during the course of the war shifted from the control of wealthy coffee growers to a more moderate group of industrialists and coffee-processing elites, who promoted Alfredo Cristiani to the party's leadership position. Tapping into fears of the extreme Left and the sheer exhaustion resulting from a decade of war, Cristiani handily defeated his PDC opponent and set about negotiating a peaceful end to the conflict with the FMLN, which had also undergone internal changes that made it more likely to negotiate with the government. Despite the high-profile executions of six Jesuit priests at the Central American University in San Salvador in 1989 by the Salvadoran military, the two sides came together and signed the Peace Accords at Chapultepec in 1992.

The signing of the peace accords did not, however, bring about an end to violence in El Salvador. During the 1970s and 1980s, hundreds of thousands of Salvadorans had fled to the United States in search of temporary asylum from political persecution. Many found legitimate employment and eventually obtained residency, but others—lacking money, family, and stable employment—joined gangs in cities like Los Angeles and Washington, D.C., and were deported back to El Salvador after the end of the war. There, in a region plagued by high unemployment, ravaged by a decade of civil war, and bristling with arms left over from the conflict, these gangs reconstituted themselves on the streets of the capital, making San Salvador one of the most violent cities in the Western Hemisphere in the twenty-first century. Those Salvadorans who remain in the United States (approximately 2.5 million, over one-third of El Salvador's total population) send back approximately $2.8 billion yearly in monetary gifts to family members or friends in El Salvador, keeping the country's economy afloat. Yet El Salvador still suffers from a polarized political climate, joblessness, and violent crime, leading thousands to make the perilous journey north each year, seeking better lives in the meat processing plants, on the construction sites, and in the homes of families across the United States.

[*See also* Caribbean, *subentry* United States Relations with Caribbean Nations.]

BIBLIOGRAPHY

Anderson, Thomas P. *Matanza: El Salvador's Communist Revolt of 1932*. Lincoln: University of Nebraska Press, 1971.

Browning, David. *El Salvador: Landscape and Society*. Oxford: Clarendon Press, 1971.

Durham, William H. *Scarcity and Survival in Central America: Ecological Origins of the Soccer War*. Stanford: Stanford University Press, 1979.

Lauria-Santiago, Aldo. *An Agrarian Republic: Commercial Agriculture and the Politics of Peasant Communities in El Salvador*. Pittsburgh: University of Pittsburgh Press, 1999.

Lindo-Fuentes, Héctor. *Weak Foundations: The Economy of El Salvador in the Nineteenth Century*. Berkeley: University of California Press, 1990.

Montgomery, Tommie Sue. *Revolution in El Salvador: From Civil Strife to Civil Peace*. 2d ed. Boulder, Colo.: Westview Press, 1995.

Stanley, William. *The Protection Racket State: Elite Politics, Military Extortion, and Civil War in El Salvador*. Philadelphia: Temple University Press, 1996.

Webre, Stephen A. *José Napoleón Duarte and the Christian Democratic Party in Salvadoran Politics, 1960–1972*. Baton Rouge: Louisiana State University Press, 1979.

PATRICK D. SCALLEN

EMANCIPATION OF SERFS IN RUSSIA. The Russian serf emancipation law has been called the greatest legislative act in history. The law of 19 February 1861 freed more than 50 million peasants—nearly half of the Russian Empire's population—from the bonds of serfdom. The Thirteenth Amendment in the United States, in contrast, liberated around 4 million slaves.

Up to the middle of the nineteenth century, Russian social life and economy were based on the institution of serfdom. Serfs worked the land, thereby producing a surplus that allowed Russian landowners to serve the Russian state as officers and administrators. Serfs also made up the bulk of the Russian army. While voices of moral outrage such as Alexander Radishchev's in *Journey from St. Petersburg to Moscow* (1790) denounced the institution, and even the conservative tsar Nicholas I (r. 1825–1855) expressed moral misgivings, serfdom was so central to the Russian economy and social order that Nicholas did not dare touch it.

The Russian defeat in the Crimean War (1854–1856) shocked the new tsar, Alexander II (1818–1881; r. 1855–1881), into action. Upon ascending the throne, Alexander declared that it would be better to abolish serfdom from above than to have it destroyed from below by social revolution. The primary motivation behind the serf emancipation—and the so-called Great Reforms of the 1860s and 1870s in Russia—was that Russia needed a freer economic and social order to compete with European powers. By emancipating the serfs the Russian government hoped to increase agricultural efficiency, free up labor to work in industry, and increase prosperity—and thereby its tax base. Connected with the emancipation was also a thoroughgoing military reform that called on all male Russians—in theory, at least—to serve in the armed forces. Such a reform would have been impossible before the legal bonds of serfdom had been severed.

And yet the realities of serf emancipation were far from ideal. Though emancipated serfs did receive allotments of land, the former serfs received only a part of the land that they had tilled, and they were obliged to pay for it over forty-nine years. Peasants could not freely move to the city or to another province. No longer under the landlord's supervision, post-emancipation peasants remained dependent upon the good will of the leadership of the peasant community (*mir*).

Landowners were also dissatisfied with the emancipation. Though they received payment for their land, this came in the form of government bonds that would reach maturity (the face value) after more than a decade. In any case, half of the "redemption payments" immediately went to paying debts. The hoped-for revitalization of Russian agriculture did not occur; the use of technology and the agricultural yield remained very low into the twentieth century.

Nonetheless, the scope and ambition of the emancipation must be recognized. In the United States some four million slaves were freed in 1865, in Brazil perhaps seven hundred thousand in 1888—numbers far lower than in Russia. For all its weaknesses, the serf emancipation did narrow legal disabilities on serfs and paved the way for industrialization in Russia in the late nineteenth century.

[*See also* Land, *subentry* Land Reform, An Overview; Peasants, *subentry* Europe; Russia, the Russian Empire, and the Soviet Union; *and* Serfdom.]

BIBLIOGRAPHY

Eklof, Ben, John Bushnell, and Larissa Zakharova, eds. *Russia's Great Reforms, 1855–1881*. Bloomington, Ind.: Indiana University Press, 1994. Collection of articles on the Great Reforms, including serf emancipation.

Emmons, Terence. *The Russian Landed Gentry and the Peasant Emancipation of 1861*. London: Cambridge University Press, 1967. A thorough and detailed study on landowners' reactions to emancipation.

Field, Daniel. *The End of Serfdom: Nobility and Bureaucracy in Russia, 1855–1861*. Cambridge, Mass.: Harvard University Press, 1976. The classic work on serf emancipation.

Lincoln, W. Bruce. *The Great Reforms: Autocracy, Bureaucracy, and the Politics of Change in Imperial Russia*. DeKalb: Northern Illinois University Press, 1990. Discusses emancipation in the broader context of reforming Russia.

THEODORE R. WEEKS

EMOTIONS. Although emotions are to some degree hardwired into the human constitution, they are also deeply affected by cultural systems, which may reflect additional factors deriving from politics or business or family life. As such, emotions also have a history, in that cultural signals can and do change.

To date, historical work has focused particularly on western Europe and the United States. A major theory about a "civilizing process" at work in Europe during the seventeenth and eighteenth centuries, authored initially by Norbert Elias, has led to significant findings about new constraints on expressions of anger, particularly within the family. During the eighteenth century also, romantic love began to gain a more positive evaluation, with parents paying increasing attention to their children's emotional reactions to potential spouses and with courts of law sometimes releasing young people from an engagement if they claimed to be unable to love their proposed mate.

Grief also won new attention, at least by the nineteenth century, with elaborate mourning etiquette and vivid expressions of sorrow at the deaths of children. By the 1870s in the United States, girls could buy mourning kits for their dolls, complete with black clothing and caskets, to help train them in this emotion. The nineteenth century also saw unusual emphasis on the gendered basis for emotion. Women were urged to refrain from anger, on grounds that it was unladylike, whereas boys and men were supposed to retain anger as a motivation but curb its expression with the family. Words like "sissy" began to describe boys who were incapable of appropriate anger or who were too fearful.

Twentieth Century. Changes in emotional rules continued in the twentieth century. In the United States, excessive grief began to be seen as a liability, possibly requiring psychiatric therapy; this change went along with the decline in the death rate and a new emphasis on fighting death medically, rather than emphasizing

consolation. Experts also began to attack anger at work; foremen were trained to prompt workers to repeat a grievance several times, so that they would become embarrassed about the anger involved and possibly retreat entirely. American politicians learned that open expressions of anger (save, perhaps, against a foreign enemy) were taken as signs of weakness. At the same time, experts also cautioned against too much reliance on courage in dealing with fear. Children were now seen as extremely fearful, and parents were advised to try to prevent fear-inducing situations and to console rather than to urge children to handle this emotional burden on their own.

Guilt was also regarded as harmful; many parents tried to avoid inflicting this emotion, and by the 1960s, school programs, bent on bolstering self-esteem rather than using guilt or shame as motivations, moved in the same direction. Jealousy also came in for new comment in Western societies where men and women now mingled more freely. American parents were urged to prevent jealousy in children, lest the emotion fester and disfigure adulthood, and comparative studies suggested that Americans became particularly eager to conceal this emotion.

All in all, as manners became more relaxed in the twentieth century, Americans and West Europeans nevertheless had to learn some complicated rules about what kinds of emotions could be appropriately expressed and in what contexts. Many people relied increasingly on witnessing vivid emotions in movies or sporting events as an alternative to admitting these emotions into their own daily lives.

Comparative Analysis. The most obvious way to approach emotions from a world historical perspective involves comparison. Different societies view particular emotions in highly varied fashion, often reflecting cultural orientations developed before the modern period. Honor-based societies, such as those around the Mediterranean, express particular interest in emotions surrounding respect; they also see positive value in emotions like anger and jealousy. Within western Europe and North America, a recent study shows pronounced differences in contemporary reactions to jealousy: when jealous, Dutch people become sad, Frenchmen become angry, but Americans, reflecting the new attitudes toward this emotion that had formed earlier in the twentieth century, are inclined to check with friends and acquaintances to see if they seemed too revealing.

Other comparisons are significant in world historical turns. According to one study, Chinese see more value in what Americans regard as negative emotions, such as fear, than do people in several other societies; Chinese were much less likely, however, in the 1970s, to claim to experience love. It is not far-fetched to see in this balance strong traces of a Confucian value system, including ideas about family. In another instance, even as Japan moved strongly to new educational commitments for children, it maintained a distinctive emphasis on shame. Children who faltered in mathematics, for example, were identified before their classmates. American schools, in contrast, had moved away from shame, even outlawing the public posting of grades. In this instance, an intriguing emotional divergence had measurable consequences: the Japanese approach, however emotionally stressful, worked better in terms of mathematics achievement. Several societies systematically discouraged anger. Tahitians were seen by eighteenth-century travelers as "slow to anger and easily appeased," and contemporary anthropological studies confirm this finding.

Emotional comparisons of this sort call upon serious efforts at historical explanation, even when their origins predate modern times. Their consequences also invite assessment. Differences in law may follow from variations in emotional culture. The contemporary American concept of a no-fault divorce, which gained ground from the 1970s onward, followed from the idea of minimizing emotional distress, but it also encouraged a higher divorce rate than that found in societies like Japan's that were less eager to avoid guilt or shame. An American eagerness for friendliness and cheerfulness, which can be traced back to emotional changes in the eighteenth century, could even have diplomatic implications. Faced with a consistently sullen demeanor from the Soviet Union's Joseph Stalin at the Yalta conference late in World War II, Franklin Roosevelt of the United States expended considerable energy in abortive efforts to make his counterpart smile. On yet another front, in the wake of the terrorist attack on the United States in 2001, and the ensuing American response, several authorities speculated that American culture might be more vulnerable to fear than was true in societies more accustomed to threat and uncertainty, with policy consequences that included unusually elaborate fortifications and warning systems.

Comparative analysis is not, however, the only approach in dealing with the modern history of emotions from a world historical perspective. Several larger developments involved changes in emotional standards that could cut across diverse cultures. It is premature to claim a fully systematic set of findings, but several trajectories have been established.

Contact among different societies can yield changes in emotional experience. In the late eighteenth century, visitors reported dramatic rituals concerning grief in Tahiti. Women often cut themselves to express their deep feelings, but though the cuts led to quite a bit of bloodshed, they were carefully controlled. After the work of Christian missionaries in the nineteenth century, however, these expressions of grief disappeared.

Effects of Consumerism and Demographics. Commercial contacts could also lead to emotional change. When the McDonald's fast-food chain set up operations in Russia in the 1980s, managers carefully trained their new service employees to maintain a cheerful, friendly demeanor. This emotional style was not customary in Soviet commerce, where ambivalence about consumerism and pro-labor policies had often led to surly, unresponsive sales personnel in restaurants and department stores, so the transformation was quite real.

As protest movements spread among different groups in various parts of the world, leaders often exhorted their constituencies to cast off emotional deference in favor of anger and emotional assertiveness. This was an explicit message of Mao Zedong to Chinese peasants, as against more traditional Confucian emotional values. African American parents in the 1970s were advised to train their children in assertiveness, and feminist leaders spread the same message.

Demographic changes could have emotional consequences. Reductions in birthrates often led to great emotional attachment between parents and individual children; this is particularly true when infant death rates fall as well, making emotional investments less risky. These developments were noted in western Europe and the United States in the later eighteenth century, and again in China at the end of the twentieth century.

Finally, the spread of consumerism often had emotional implications. In the United States, early in the twentieth century, consumerism was tied to a reevaluation of envy; the emotion was now seen as a desirable consumer motivator, rather than, in more traditional Christian terms, a sign of bad character. Consumerism also tended to discredit emotions associated with sadness or displeasure, like grief, in favor of at least superficial cheerfulness that could accompany efforts at acquiring more material goods. Consumerism was also often associated with romantic love and love for children, both because these emotions could motivate the purchases of gifts and of attractive clothing and because both love and consumerism expressed a sense of pleasure-seeking. This linkage was evident even in the early stages of modern consumerism in western Europe, in the eighteenth century. It also was evident as urban China moved toward a more consumerist society after 1978.

Emotions in modern world history follow no tidy formulas. There are always variations, and some of them—like the unusual American commitment to self-esteem in children—were recent products, creating new differentiations along with more traditional ones. There were nevertheless some intriguing crosscutting tendencies, developing from the late eighteenth century onward. Contacts, the apparent demands of modern commerce and consumerism, new family forms, and in some instances protest currents all could generate reconsideration of emotional values across cultural lines.

[*See also* Children and Childhood; Consumption and Consumerism; Etiquette and Manners; *and* Psychology.]

BIBLIOGRAPHY

Matt, Susan J. *Keeping Up with the Joneses: Envy in American Consumer Society, 1890–1930.* Philadelphia: University of Pennsylvania Press, 2002.

Reddy, William M. *The Navigation of Feeling: A Framework for the History of Emotions.* Cambridge, U.K., and New York: Cambridge University Press, 2001.

Sommers, Shula. "Understanding Emotions: Some Interdisciplinary Considerations." In *Emotion and Social Change: Toward a New Psychohistory*, edited by Carol Z. Stearns and Peter N. Stearns. New York: Holmes & Meier, 1988.

Stearns, Peter N. *American Cool: Constructing a Twentieth-Century Emotional Style.* New York: New York University Press, 1994.

PETER N. STEARNS

EMPERORS IN EAST ASIA. In the nineteenth century, European empires frequently invoked the notion of "oriental despotism" to characterize the political structures of the non-West. Applied most liberally to the Chinese and Ottoman empires, the mistaken assumption of governments in the thrall of an unenlightened, omnipotent ruler came to characterize kingdoms throughout the Pacific, and provided justification for the often aggressive means with which Western actions were carried out under the pretext of imparting civilization. Yet such fanciful stereotyping obfuscates the complexities of the monarchical institutions in China and Japan, each of which faced challenges of rulership and historical conditions particular to its national context. The impact of European imperialism varied widely as well, hastening the decline of dynastic rule in China, but mobilizing modern nationalism in Japan in ways that revitalized the institution.

There were, to be sure, commonalities that connected the kingdoms throughout northeast and southeast Asia. China, Japan, Korea, and Vietnam adopted as their state ideology Confucianism, a political, social, and moral framework that prized filial piety, loyalty, and hierarchical order. Within the Pacific world, Chinese hegemony was acknowledged through a tributary system that paid homage to the "son of heaven." Neither attribute persevered in the twentieth century.

China. The last emperors of China who formed the Qing dynasty (1644–1911) were in fact Manchu, a northeast Asian people with a history, language, and cultural practices distinct from the Han Chinese majority. Whereas earlier historiography describes a government that replicated the administrative and social institutions of the Chinese dynasties, recent scholarship has undermined the theory of "sinicization" to emphasize the self-conscious ways in which the ruling elite maintained their ethnic identity. Thus, even as they continued the system of bureaucratic recruitment through the civil service examination, patronized Chinese art and literature, issued Confucian decrees, and promoted filiality as a principal criterion of rulership, the Manchu elite also perpetuated their martial heritage by institutionalizing archery, horsemanship, and imperial hunts in the daily life at court. With territorial boundaries extending beyond China proper to encompass present-day Manchuria, Mongolia, Eastern Turkestan (Xinjiang Uyghur), and Tibet, the Qing rulers acknowledged the disparate ethnic groups under their control by establishing a rotating system of capitals and imperial villas that required them to spend significant time away from the Forbidden City in Beijing. Manchu rulers learned the languages (Chinese, Mongolian, Tibetan, and Uyghur) and cultural practices (shamanism, Buddhism, even Islam) of the conquered peoples. Although the court's closest advisory roles were assigned to imperial kinsmen, an innovative system allowed members of the conquered elite loyal to the throne to be awarded important administrative, military, and diplomatic positions.

Through political consolidation, economic prosperity, and charismatic leadership, the Qing dynasty attained its peak over the course of a "long eighteenth century." Yet the underlying structure that privileged Manchu over the empire's other ethnic populations ultimately proved to be unsustainable in the face of social, military, and foreign pressures. In the nineteenth century rapid population growth and a series of widespread rebellions placed strains on government revenues, while the growing Western presence—in the forms of opium, wars, treaty ports, and indemnity payments—compounded fiscal woes and social turmoil. In an effort to regain popular confidence by tapping into the zeitgeist of modernization, the Qing court suggested the possibility of transitioning to a constitutional monarchy. The government itself reneged on its offer, but reformers and revolutionaries seized on the opportunity to oust the Manchu ruling house in 1911. The subsequent establishment of a presidency and republic put an end to two thousand years of monarchical government.

Japan. By contrast, the fortunes of the Japanese imperial house improved greatly in the modern era, owing as much to its dynastic legitimacy as adaptability. Despite having an "unbroken line" of succession that can be traced back to the fifth century C.E., from the ninth century onward the Chinese-style imperial office had atrophied, and the monarchy's primary function was largely ceremonial. When political fragmentation finally came to an end in 1600, it was a succession of generals and their descendants who ruled as military governors (shogun) from Tokyo, while the emperor resided in isolation in the Kyoto Palace, deprived even of the privilege to ennoble the ranks of aristocracy that formed his extensive court. In 1853 the arrival of American ships demanding a commercial treaty sparked a national crisis over imminent foreign encroachment; a political revolution ensued, whereby the leaders toppled the discredited Tokugawa shogunate in 1868 and returned Japan nominally to direct imperial rule.

The Meiji Restoration jump-started the island kingdom's transformation into a modern state and colonial empire. Advisors to the court implemented a wildly successful program of social and economic change that touched all aspects of society through education, conscription, and taxation. Despite the promulgation of a modern constitution that invested in him supreme authority, the emperor's role in formulating policy remained peripheral, yet he conferred legitimacy and official sanction to the new projects and actively popularized them. Although late-nineteenth-century Japan embraced all things Western and modern, paradoxically the emperor's mystique rested in large part on his ability to evoke a timeless Japanese spirit. By the early twentieth century, both Shintoism and the broader emperor cult had achieved a level of orthodoxy, supported in no small part by successive military victories against China (1894–1895) and Russia (1904–1905).

The extent of the emperor's authority and policy engagement throughout Japan's imperial expansion and the Pacific War remains ambiguous to this day, in part because of the inaccessibility of archival records. At the conclusion of World War II, Japanese policy makers insisted on the preservation of the imperial office as a condition of the country's surrender, and Cold War exigencies led their American counterpart to retain the wartime emperor Hirohito (1901–1989; r. 1926–1989). The seven-year military occupation that followed framed a number of institutions that aided Japan's transition to a democratic society, chief among them a new constitution that stipulated popular—not imperial—sovereignty. By the early 2000s, the monarchy had returned to fulfilling a largely symbolic role, irrelevant to, and only marginally revered by, mainstream Japanese society.

[*See also* Confucianism; Conservatism; *and* Monarchy.]

BIBLIOGRAPHY

Crossley, Pamela Kyle. *A Translucent Mirror: History and Identity in Qing Imperial Ideology.* Berkeley: University of California Press, 1999. With its focus on the Qianlong emperor (r. 1735–1796) and Inner Asian aspects of the Qing empire, this work highlights the formation of ethnic and national identities and provides a compelling refutation of the Chinese assimilation paradigm.

Fujitani, Takashi. *Splendid Monarchy: Politics and Pageantry in Modern Japan.* Berkeley: University of California Press, 1996. An historical ethnography of the imperial institution in the late nineteenth and early twentieth centuries that makes inventive use of visual and archival sources.

Gluck, Carol. *Japan's Modern Myths: Ideology in the Late Meiji Period.* Princeton, N.J.: Princeton University Press, 1985. A classic study on the evolution of the emperor ideology in the late nineteenth century.

Rawski, Evelyn S. *The Last Emperors: A Social History of Qing Imperial Institutions.* Berkeley: University of California Press, 1998. Examines the material culture, social organization, and court rituals of the Manchu rulers.

CHRISTINE KIM

EMPIRE AND IMPERIALISM [*This entry includes ten subentries, an overview and discussions of the Spanish, Portuguese, Dutch, British, French, Belgian, and German colonial empires; imperialism in East Asia; and imperialism and the environment. See also Colonialism; Decolonization; Gender and Empire; Informal Empire; Missionary Movements; Missions, Christian; Popular Imperialism, British; Postcolonialism; and Racism.*]

Overview

Empires were not new to the modern world. Indeed, they featured regularly in the history of the ancient, medieval, and early modern worlds. Yet even though modern empires shared continuities with these older empires, modern empires have been distinguished by their unprecedented size, the percentage of the world's landmasses they have included, the number of states involved in empire-building, and their reliance on modern technologies such as steam and mass production. Moreover, modern empires have fundamentally shaped the contemporary world by contributing to the global economic and political dominance of particular states, by transforming social relationships in far-distant parts of the globe, and by the legacies of exploitation against subject populations as well as the natural environment.

Definitions. Even though empires have existed for millennia, the term "empire" itself is often ambiguously defined or confused with related terms such as "imperialism" or "colonialism." Moreover, discussions of modern empires often refer to a host of secondary terms—including "informal imperialism," "cultural imperialism," and "indirect empire"—without clearly defining their relationship to one another. Here, "empire" is a structural term that refers to the extension of control from a dominant polity to a subordinate polity (or polities). The control exerted by the dominant power is frequently political in nature—often expressed by the claim of sole sovereignty over subordinate areas—but generally also includes significant economic as well as social control. Although obviously related to "empire," "imperialism" refers to the ideologies held within the dominant polity that support and encourage the creation of empires. It is, in other words, the force behind empire that translates expansionist sentiment into action. "Imperialism" is frequently confounded with "colonialism," but in fact the two terms are not synonymous. Rather, "colonialism" refers not to the driving ideology behind empire, but to the policies and practices set in motion within imperial territories in order to maintain order and to realize economic and social objectives.

Until the mid-twentieth century, most historical works about empire focused solely on relationships in which the dominant state claimed political sovereignty over its subordinates. Since then, however, a variety of historians have come to see this type of "formal empire" as only one expression of imperial relationships. These historians claim that a state of empire can be said to exist when a dominant polity exerts decisive economic, political, and social power over subordinate polities even when it does *not* claim sovereignty. This relationship, now commonly known as "informal empire," does not require the formal structures of colonial governments, but instead functions through the threat of military action or economic sanctions if the demands of the dominant polity are not met. Thus historians claim that the treatment of nineteenth-century China by the European powers constituted an imperial relationship because the level of control exerted by the latter was extensive even though China never formally lost its sovereignty.

Just as there were differences between "imperialism" and "colonialism" and "formal" and "informal" empire, there were also qualitative differences in styles of "formal" imperial rule. "Direct" imperial rule refers to a structure in which the dominant polity substitutes the subordinate polity's government, army, and systems of law, taxes, and education with its own. British rule over large parts of India was a prime example of this style, which was cost intensive both in terms of financial and human resources. Much less expensive was the style of formal empire known as "indirect rule" (sometimes known as "empire on the cheap"), in which the dominant polity left the governmental, economic, and social structure of the subordinate polity largely intact and instead simply placed a small group of officials at its head to ensure compliance with imperial wishes. Colonial Nigeria was an excellent example of this style of imperial rule: indeed, much of sub-Saharan Africa was ruled in this way in the nineteenth and twentieth centuries.

Styles of colonial rule also differed significantly between settler and nonsettler colonies. In settler colonies, such as Australia, New Zealand, Canada, Algeria, Kenya, and South Africa, tensions between newcomers from the dominant polities and the original inhabitants of the colony frequently exploded into violent clashes over land and rights. Laws controlling the movement, education, occupation, and political participation of indigenous groups also tended to be particularly restrictive in such colonies. In nonsettler colonies like Ghana and India, by contrast, indigenous populations outside of urban areas frequently had far more limited day-to-day contact with colonizers.

In addition to the terms above, media and scholarly commentators since the mid-twentieth century have increasingly popularized the notion of "cultural imperialism." This term, which does not imply political control, refers to a process by which the cultural forms of dominant states—in this case primarily the United States—come to permeate the cultures of other areas to the point where indigenous cultural expressions are lost. According to this idea, the extension of institutions like McDonald's, Starbucks, and Kentucky Fried Chicken, as well as the global reach of pop music, American television, and Hollywood, constitute a form of economic and social control in itself. Although this term remains controversial among historians, it is nevertheless useful to keep in mind that relationships of empire frequently included expressions of cultural power in addition to political, economic, and social power.

Major Epochs in the Modern History of Empire. Since 1750, the structure, players, justifications, and fortunes of modern empires have shifted dramatically. In the mid-eighteenth century, European powers focused their imperial ambitions on the Americas, hoping to fuel state coffers through plantation agriculture, slavery, and resource extraction. By the late nineteenth century, powerful states had turned their attention to larger and larger swathes of Asia, and had begun to divide Africa between themselves. At the turn of the twentieth century, a whole host of European powers as well as the United States, Japan, and Russia had divided most of the world among them. Yet by the mid-twentieth century, nearly all of these empires were crumbling, and most completely disappeared by 1970. In the post–World War II Cold War era, however, a new form of expansion developed as the Soviet Union extended its frontiers and added satellite states, while the United States used pressure, covert operations, and monetary influence to build anticommunist alliances. Finally, after the dissolution of the Soviet Union beginning in 1989, the United States came under increased criticism for its heavy-handed tactics in strategic areas of the world, especially the Middle East. At the beginning of the twenty-first century, some scholars as well as media pundits have branded the United States as a neo-imperial power, bent on global economic, political, and cultural domination. While such claims are controversial, they nevertheless have brought renewed vigor to discussions of empire and imperialism around the world. At the same time, such discussions highlight important discontinuities and changes in the history of modern empires.

1750–1815. In 1750 the dominant empires of the early modern era—particularly the Spanish, Portuguese, and Ottoman empires—were in decline. During the seventeenth century the British, French, and the Dutch states wrested territory and imperial influence away from both the Spanish and the Portuguese, although by the mid-eighteenth century only the French and the British were serious contenders for imperial dominance. Much imperial expansion in this period focused on the Americas, where the Atlantic slave trade provided labor for highly lucrative plantation agriculture in commodities such as sugar, tobacco, and cotton.

Imperial competition between the French and the British led to a series of wars fought on several continents in this period. The French defeat in the Seven Years' War (1756–1763) resulted in the loss of huge territories in the Americas, including all of Canada. By the end of the French Revolutionary and Napoleonic Wars in 1815—particularly after Napoleon sold the Louisiana Territory to the United States in 1803 and the French island of Saint-Domingue gained its independence in 1804—French colonial territories in the Americas were minuscule. As a result, Britain became the dominant imperial power in North America and the Caribbean, even after the loss of its thirteen American colonies in the American Revolution (1776–1783). In particular, the slave-sugar economy of the Caribbean was highly lucrative for British plantation owners, many of whom became enormously rich.

In most of the rest of the world, Europeans were not strong enough to stake out large territorial empires in the face of existing states. Exceptions included the Dutch East India Company, which had ousted the Portuguese in the spice islands of modern Indonesia in the seventeenth century, and was in the midst of building an empire centered on the island of Java. In India too, the British East India Company made the transition from a trading company to a territorial power in 1757, when it wrested control over Bengal from the Mughal Empire. Elsewhere in Asia as well as in Africa, European merchants and businessmen set up trading posts in coastal areas, while missionaries sought to spread Christianity in a variety of locations. For the most part, however, the goal of territorial expansion was secondary to the goal of making a profit.

1815–1880. Historians conventionally refer to the years between 1815 and 1880 as a period of "absent-minded imperialism," when the desire for territorial expansion was limited among those states that already held colonies. In Europe, much of the continent was enveloped in nationalist struggles or nation-building programs, which left little money or energy for imperial expansion. In eastern Europe and north Africa, the Ottoman Empire was steadily losing territory. In China, the once-powerful Qing Empire battled internal rebellions as well as encroachments by European and American powers. Given this global situation, Britain was able to capitalize on the resources and profits it had made in the Americas, its newly industrialized machine power, and its strong navy to pursue trading interests all over the world without fear of serious competition from other powers. Thus, official policy did not tend toward imperialist sentiment in this period because it did not need to: British interests could efficiently pursue the goals of trade and profit-making without resorting to formal expansion. In many cases, whether in China or Latin America, the mere threat of British military might—especially when coupled with the use of economic incentives—was enough to secure access to trade and resources. For this reason, historians often dub this period as the high point of "informal imperialism."

It is important to note, however, that despite the absence of strong imperialist sentiments in most states strong enough to expand, this period did in fact witness persistent formal expansion. For example, even though British policy favored informal influence, the East India Company continued to acquire huge territories in India. In fact, by 1857—when the Indian Army rebelled and the British government assumed direct control over India—the East India Company had assumed control over nearly the entire subcontinent. British expansion in South Africa also occurred in this period, as it did in Australia and New Zealand. The French, too, were expanding formally in Algeria beginning in the 1830s, and in Indochina by the middle of the century. The Dutch continued to consolidate their formal control over the Indonesian islands, while the Russian government sponsored aggressive moves to acquire territory in central Asia.

1875–1914. By the end of the nineteenth century, the easy dominance of the British was shattered by the increasing power—and appetite for territories—of France and Russia as well as new competitors like Germany, Japan, and the United States. With British imperial success as their model, newly industrialized states sought to squeeze their own fortunes from resource-rich areas of the world through access to foreign markets and trading concessions. Even small states such as Italy, Belgium, and Portugal sought to profit from foreign resources through territorial expansion. Additionally, in contrast to the mid-nineteenth century, this period was marked by increasing popular interest in imperial conquest. In many states civilian interest groups formed to lobby for imperial expansion, while newspapers, books, and theaters were replete with stories of imperial conquest. Indeed, this period became marked by a distinct ideology of "imperialism" in metropolitan centers, which in turn fueled further imperial expansion. Because of this combination of imperialist ethos and the rapid imperial expansion that subsequently occurred, it has become known as the era of "High Imperialism."

Increased competition among the world powers also dramatically increased the political tensions between them. Now, it seemed that global resources were finite and needed to be hoarded by those powerful enough to acquire them. Moreover, it seemed clear that the only way to ensure access to resources was to claim sovereignty over territory; informal pressure would no longer suffice. Thus, when the British government seized control over Egypt in 1882 in order to protect the Suez Canal, this action triggered a process of land grabbing among the other states aspiring to imperial power that quickly resulted in the colonial division of most of the world, adding 11 million square miles (28.5 million square kilometers) to European possessions alone.

So high were the political tensions after the British occupation of Egypt that a general European war seemed likely. To avoid this, fourteen European states and the United States came together at a conference in Berlin (1884–1885) in order to plan the orderly division of global territory. Thereafter, they set about claiming and conquering territories in Asia, the Pacific, and especially in Africa. Indeed, in the short span between 1885 and 1914 known as the "Scramble for Africa," the African continent was nearly completely colonized by foreign powers. Conquest was greatly aided by the technologies made possible by the Industrial Revolution: steamboats, railroads, accurate weapons, and telegraphs all allowed small numbers of colonizers regularly to defeat large, indigenous armies. In fact, technological innovation was so important in the division of the world between the expanding powers in this period that it is sometimes referred to as the era of "industrial imperialism." Especially when compared to the era of "informal imperialism," this period was marked by rapid, extensive, and popular formal expansion at an unprecedented level.

1914–1945. The period from 1914 to 1945 was bookended by two of the most destructive wars in the history of humanity, both of which were partly caused by imperial ambitions, and both of which had tremendous consequences for modern empires. In 1914 the tensions between the aspiring global powers—for years expressed in colonial expansion—exploded in warfare on the European continent. As both sides settled into trench warfare on the western front, millions of colonial subjects were called on to give their labor, their service, and their lives to the war effort. Many of these soldiers and workers, along with their fellow colonial subjects, expected that their service would be rewarded with increased participation in colonial governments. When the colonial powers by and large did not fulfill these expectations, discontent with imperial rule soared. In India, for example, at the start of the war nationalist leaders like Mohandas K. Gandhi urged soldiers to enlist in the army, whereas by the war's end he was advocating Indian independence. Colonial subjects belonging to every empire took note: the imperial powers had shown the world their weaknesses and had demonstrated their poor faith in the people they ruled. In response, resistance movements grew into increasingly well-organized and stronger nationalist organizations.

While nationalism became a feature of the interwar years in all of the empires, World War I did not bring about the end of the formal empires. Instead, the imperial powers functioned as if they would rule indefinitely, and fought nationalist movements all over the world—in the Dutch East Indies (Indonesia), Algeria, Indochina, India, among others—by imprisoning their leaders, censoring the media, and using force against demonstrators. Yet World War II, itself caused by imperial expansion in both Europe and Asia, changed imperial relationships irrevocably. For one thing, the successful Japanese assault against nearly every Asian colonial territory shattered European and American confidence, especially when some colonial subjects welcomed the Japanese invaders. Additionally, some nationalist groups used their bargaining power to leverage their desire for independence, insisting that their support during the war must translate into progress toward decolonization. Finally, the financial and human cost of the war was so great that even the victorious powers could scarcely afford to expend the resources to fight organized nationalist movements once it was over. In 1946 the United States withdrew from the Philippines, which became the first former colony to achieve its independence in the twentieth century. Even more significantly, the British withdrew from India in 1947 and began making plans for decolonizing its other colonial territories. Colonial nationalists all over the world took this as inspiration for their own causes, and prepared to fight even harder for self-determination.

1945–1989. Ironically, the period between 1945 and 1989 witnessed the dissolution of nearly all of the formal empires of the modern world even while the struggles of the Cold War built a new empire in Eastern Europe and resulted in massive interference in the affairs of newly independent nations by both the Soviet Union and the United States. Between 1946 and 1980, more than ninety nations gained independence from the imperial powers, in most cases bringing to fruition years of resistance and organization against imperial domination. In some cases, the transition from colony to independent nation was relatively smooth, as in French West Africa and British sub-Saharan Africa. In other cases, as in India and Pakistan, independence unleashed civil strife that resulted in mass violence after the imperial powers departed. In still

other cases where the imperial powers were loath to relinquish control over their colonies, the fight for independence was long and bloody, as it was in Indonesia, Vietnam, Angola, and Algeria. Yet by the 1960s it was clear that the empires consolidated in the period of high imperialism were vanishing.

Even as world maps became dotted with tens of newly independent nations in this period, the Cold War struggle between the USSR and the United States led to formal territorial expansion in Eastern Europe as well as both blatant and informal intervention in much of the rest of the world. Seeking to protect itself from hostile forces in Europe, the Soviet Union sought to annex or control all the states on its borders. Elsewhere, desperate to win the ideological battle between Communism and capitalism, the Soviet Union and the United States sought to win influence among veteran as well as newly independent nations. When it seemed that weaker nations might support the other side, both powers used covert operations, economic incentives, and force to ensure the victory of their own ideology. As a result, some new nations like Vietnam won their independence only to find themselves in the midst of a power struggle between the United States and the Communist powers. While Cold War interference cannot be conflated with the formal expansion of High Imperialism, it is nevertheless clear that these powerful polities controlled subordinate polities in significant and enduring ways for their own interests.

Since 1989. The dissolution of the Soviet Union beginning in 1989 led to the end of the Cold War and left only one dominant world power: the United States. Since then, criticisms that the United States was attempting to consolidate its control over the rest of the world economically, culturally, and politically became increasingly sharp. U.S. intervention in Iraq during the Persian Gulf War (1990–1991) was decried in many circles as an unabashed attempt to control crucial oil reserves in the Middle East. Following the invasion of Iraq in 2003, many voices both inside and outside the United States saw the war as an even more flagrant example of the United States flexing its muscles to protect its own interests.

In addition to apprehensions of U.S. imperialism in the Middle East, private, internationally owned corporations as well as a variety of entertainment industries have attracted attention from different quarters as exhibiting imperialist tendencies. While the precise meaning of this type of imperialism is frequently ill defined, such claims seem to imply that corporate intervention in national sovereignty constitutes expansionism, and that the spread of cultural forms—like pop music—represents attempts to change societies at a fundamental level. Whether these post–Cold War apprehensions about a "new imperialism" led by the United States and capitalist ventures represent viable continuities with the imperial past is still hotly debated: what remains clear is that many of the world's populations seem to believe such continuities exist.

Continuities across Empires and Epochs. Although the structure and composition of modern empires have changed significantly over the last 250 years, there are nevertheless unifying factors shared by nearly all of them over time and across space. Indeed, taken together modern empires share far more similarities than they do differences, especially in terms of methods, motivations, and justifications.

Violence and resistance. One of the most basic continuities in modern as well as ancient empires is that imperial conquest is rarely achieved without the use—or at least the threat—of violence. Unless a colonial territory is uninhabited, claims to rule must be made in the presence of existing populations. And whether in New Zealand, Ghana, Indochina, or Indonesia, colonial occupation invariably elicits resistance from such populations. For this reason, imperial powers backed up their claims to sovereignty with military force, and then were obliged to continue to bolster their rule through the use of police forces and military units to protect against the ever-present threat of rebellion. While the daily use of violence varied over time and from colony to colony (with the Belgian Congo as an extreme example of sustained colonial violence), every imperial power regularly used violence as a way to counter resistance and maintain control. In addition, initial resistance to colonial rule continued to develop over time, so that nearly every colony experienced the growth of organized resistance movements.

Collaboration. While resistance to colonial rule was ubiquitous across time and space, power could not have been maintained without some level of collaboration from colonial populations. Every colonial power attempted to entice particular indigenous groups to support its rule by allowing them access to wealth, power, prestige, or all three. In the Dutch East Indies, for example, Dutch colonizers gave a small class of Javanese elites the power to collect taxes, which in turn afforded these elites tremendous power and wealth at the expense of Javanese farmers and laborers. In India, the British set up institutions for European-style education, and then used the recipients of such education to staff the lower-level bureaucratic positions necessary for running the territory. Indeed,

without collaboration it would have been impossible for any colony to survive resistance and rebellion for long.

Profit and exploitation. For the most part, the primary raison d'être for modern colonial expansion was profit—either in the form of resource extraction, taxation, or agriculture. Exceptions to this generality tended to occur in the period of high imperialism, when colonial territory was feverishly claimed and occupied just to keep it out of the hands of competitors. Even in those cases, however, most imperial powers at least tried to create profit from their newfound territories, introducing cash-crop agriculture whose commodities could be sold at controlled prices, or utilizing indigenous labor for colonial projects. This profit mentality led to countless instances of environmental destruction and human exploitation, whether from voracious big-game hunting, the harvesting of wood or metals, or the use of human labor on farms, on colonial projects, in homes, or in mines. Both human and environmental exploitation were greatly accelerated through the use of industrial-era technologies, modern transport and communications, and global trade networks.

Othering. Whether in eighteenth-century slave economies in North America or in twentieth-century Ghana, all of the modern imperial powers justified their colonial acquisitions by distinguishing themselves from their colonial subjects. In the eighteenth century, colonial rulers frequently depicted themselves as superior in terms of civilizational standards, arguing that their own forms of political, religious, social, and economic organization were more advanced than those of conquered territories. By the mid-nineteenth century, colonial rulers increasingly described their superiority in terms of inherent racial superiority. By this logic, colonial subjects could not hope to rise to the level of their colonial rulers because their inferiority was inborn and unchangeable. Indeed, by the late nineteenth century a variety of "sciences" had arisen in the colonial metropolitan centers that sought to describe, classify, and rank the various "races" of the world. In addition to civilizational and racial superiority, colonizers also tended to believe that their own religions and gender ideals were more advanced than those of the people they colonized, and they used these differences to justify colonial domination.

Civilizing mission. Modern colonial rulers in nearly every era and place also sought to justify their rule by arguing that it was good for their subjects. Known broadly as the "civilizing mission," colonial rulers tended to believe that their cultural, political, social, and (eventually) racial superiority gave them a special obligation to help societies all over the world achieve similar standards. Even if equality was not generally considered a real possibility, the influence of superior societies alone was considered an improvement over preexisting conditions. As a result, most modern imperial powers sought to establish religious missions and schools that would educate colonial subjects in the customs, mores, and values of the ruling society.

Conclusion. The desire for territorial expansion has been a regular feature of human communities since ancient times, as has the building of empires. In the modern period, empire building has been especially intense, and modern empires have played a critical role in the history of nearly the entire world. Indeed, modern empires fundamentally transformed economic relationships, political relationships, and cultural relationships on every continent; they were responsible for massive migrations of people to distant parts of the earth; they set in motion major inequalities between dominant and subordinate polities whose effects are still being felt today; and they made possible large-scale operations of labor and environmental exploitation. And even though imperial relationships altered significantly between the mid-eighteenth and twenty-first centuries, enough commonalities exist over time and across space for contemporary commentators to see historical continuities as well as historical change.

[*See also* Civilizing Mission; Collaboration; Colonialism; Decolonization; Gender and Empire; Informal Empire; Missionary Movements; Missions, Christian; Popular Imperialism, British; Postcolonialism; Racism; *and* Resistance Movements.]

BIBLIOGRAPHY

Adas, Michael. *Machines as the Measure of Men: Science, Technology, and Ideologies of Western Dominance.* Ithaca, N.Y.: Cornell University Press, 1989.

Bayly, C. A. *The Birth of the Modern World, 1780–1914: Global Connections and Comparisons.* Malden, Mass.: Blackwell, 2003.

Bayly, C. A. *Imperial Meridian: The British Empire and the World, 1780–1830.* London and New York: Longman, 2004.

Blue, Gregory, Martin Bunton, and Ralph Crozier, eds. *Colonialism and the Modern World: Selected Studies.* Armonk, N.Y.: M. E. Sharpe, 2002.

Chamberlain, M. E. *Decolonization: The Fall of the European Empires.* Oxford and Malden, Mass.: Blackwell, 1999.

Cook, Scott B. *Colonial Encounters in the Age of High Imperialism.* New York: Talman, 1996.

Curtin, Philip D. *The World and the West: The European Challenge and the Overseas Response in the Age of Empire.* Cambridge, U.K., and New York: Cambridge University Press, 2000.

Hamm, Bernd, and Russel Smandych, eds. *Cultural Imperialism: Essays on the Political Economy of Cultural Domination.* Peterborough, Ont.: Broadview, 2005.

Harvey, David. *The New Imperialism.* Oxford and New York: Oxford University Press, 2003.

Osterhammel, Jürgen. *Colonialism: A Theoretical Overview.* 2d ed. Translated by Shelley L. Frisch. Princeton, N.J.: Markus Weiner, 2005.

Rajan, Balachandra, and Elizabeth Sauer. *Imperialisms: Historical and Literary Investigations, 1500–1900.* New York: Palgrave Macmillan, 2004.

Samson, Jane. *Race and Empire.* Harlow, U.K., and New York: Pearson Longman, 2005.

Semmel, Bernard. *The Rise of Free Trade Imperialism: Classical Political Economy, the Empire of Free Trade, and Imperialism.* Cambridge, U.K.: Cambridge University Press, 2004.

Smith, Bonnie G. *Imperialism: A History in Documents.* New York: Oxford University Press, 2000.

Smith, Woodruff D. *European Imperialism in the Nineteenth and Twentieth Centuries.* Chicago: Nelson-Hall, 1982.

HEATHER STREETS

The Spanish Colonial Empire

Spain was commercially active in the Mediterranean Sea and down the Atlantic coast of Africa for many decades before 1492. Most notably, it had begun its takeover of the Canary Islands nearly a century before Columbus's voyage. The only valuable resource on the Canaries was orchilla, a dyestuff, but the Spanish established sugar plantations, complete with black slaves imported from Africa, producing for the European market soon after taking over.

Like the Portuguese Atlantic islands, the Canary Islands under Spain were primarily military ventures and trading centers where a small number of proprietors profited from the efforts of sharecroppers and paid laborers. The Spanish introduced livestock and Mediterranean plants to the Canaries, which in turn provided sugar and fish.

It was during the reign of Isabella I of Castile and Ferdinand V of Aragon, whose marriage in 1469 had united their separate kingdoms into one, that the pace of expansion quickened. Isabella and Ferdinand supported exploration of distant parts in order to spread Christianity and increase Spain's trading possibilities with the Far East.

Initial Discoveries in the Americas. In the Americas, Spain first colonized the major islands of the Caribbean, but by 1550, after turning out only modest amounts of gold, these islands had become an economic backwater in the still-expanding empire. In 1494, with the Treaty of Tordesillas, Portugal and Spain ended their emerging rivalry over the South Atlantic. Portugal protected its exclusive sea route to India, and Spain assured its dominance in the Americas. Spanish expeditions conquered Mexico in 1521 and Peru in 1532. These lands, rich with silver and large Native populations, would be Spain's primary centers of trade until the 1700s, when the emergence of other Spanish American colonial economies, including Cuba, Venezuela, and Buenos Aires, required a shift in Spain's trading patterns. By the 1570s the colonies of Central America, Colombia, Paraguay, and Chile had been established, but their primary products, including indigo, yerba maté (a kind of tea), and wheat, were marketed primarily to other American colonies rather than overseas, which limited their growth and prosperity.

Regulation of Trade. Spain soon established a monopoly over trade with its American colonies. In 1503 the Casa de la Contratación (House of Trade) was established in Seville to govern commercial relations with the colonies. In 1543 the crown legally incorporated the powerful merchant houses of Seville into a merchants guild (*consulado*) in which a monopoly over trade was formally invested. It was also granted juridical authority covering civil disputes over trade, a tremendous legal advantage.

In the 1560s, to protect its trade with its colonies against marauding ships from other European powers, Spain established the fleet system, wherein two substantial fleets escorted by warships departed Spain each year, one bound to Mexico's primary port of Veracruz and the other to the Isthmus of Panama, where its goods were offloaded to be shipped down the Pacific coast to Peru. The two fleets remained at their American ports until loaded with silver from Mexico and Peru, whereupon they departed for Spain. Although very expensive and limiting in the amount of merchandise that the colonies could legally receive, the fleet system worked quite well for Spain's purposes. European rivals seized the fleets only twice, in 1628 and 1656.

The Manila galleon. In 1561 an expedition organized in Mexico sailed across the Pacific Ocean and occupied the Philippines. This gave Mexico access to prized Chinese goods, which had been shipped to Manila for centuries by Chinese merchant houses, and spices from the Indonesian archipelago. Each year the major Mexican trading houses that dominated the trade dispatched from Acapulco one galleon loaded with silver to Manila, where the contents were exchanged for Chinese fineries for the shipment back. Each voyage lasted six to nine months, so long that disease often ran rampant among the crew and passengers, with the total number of fatalities commonly exceeding one hundred persons.

By at least the eighteenth century, merchandise arriving in Mexico from Spain typically found no consumers if a galleon had recently arrived from Manila. Also by that time, the Mexico City trading houses that dominated the trade were not content just to finance the galleons; they also stationed commercial agents, often close relatives, in Manila itself. The Manila galleon trade endured until 1815. This trade route was so lucrative that often more than a third of Mexico's annual silver production was routed to Manila rather than to Spain.

The emerging problem of contraband. Contraband trade sprung up in Spanish America against the crown's restrictive trading system and spread rapidly. Spain could control neither the vast American coastline nor its profit-seeking colonial officials. Contraband clearly worsened in the second half of the seventeenth century and throughout the eighteenth. By the early seventeenth century, Spain's economy had declined compared to those of the Netherlands, England, and France, and after midcentury these latter countries seized lightly occupied Spanish Caribbean islands to establish their own complexes of sugar plantations.

The first notable loss was England's seizure of Belize in 1638. In 1655 Spain was forced to yield Jamaica, by then a center of piracy and illicit trade, to England, which already had effective control over the island. Around the same time, France occupied the western third of the island of Santo Domingo, which was renamed Haiti. Also in the seventeenth century, the English, Dutch, and French occupied the Guianas, England seized Barbados, and France captured Martinique and Guadeloupe.

The slave trade. Around 3 million African slaves were imported into Spanish America over the course of the colonial period, largely to work on plantations. But Spain itself shipped very few slaves from the African mainland. Instead it entered into agreements (*asientos*) with other European nations whose traders were more firmly based in Africa. Portugal was the first country to gain such an *asiento.* That Spain and Portugal were ruled by the same monarch between 1580 and 1640 facilitated that agreement. After Portugal successfully rebelled against Spain to gain a Portugal-based ruling family, Spain turned eventually to France and then England as replacement suppliers.

Slaves labored on plantations and other types of agricultural estates, in cities as artisans, transporters, and household servants, and in both gold and silver mining. Although Spanish America retained a great number of slaves, many earned their freedom. Free blacks actually outnumbered slaves at some point in the eighteenth century.

Spanish Colonial Society. The nearly all-embracing social concept in the Spanish colonies was that of a hierarchy in which the three major ethnic components—European, African, and Native American—each held a fixed position. This is, of course, a Spanish perspective, and the more an ethnic group resembled the Spanish in any fashion, the higher it ranked. These three major groupings were commonly described in ethnic terms: Spaniard, Black, and Indian. The dominant descriptors embraced both culture and racial phenotype. The Native peoples were notably reluctant to accept "Indian" as a descriptor. They insisted on being called by their individual ethnic terms.

A critical component of this Spanish American ethnic scheme was that it recognized mixture. The most important intermediate categories were mestizo, recognizing a mixture of Spanish and Indian, and mulatto, a mixture of Spanish and black. Overall, these intermediate categories were placed between the parent ethnicities.

Perhaps the way in which the major ethnic groups most approximated group realities was in constituting marriage pools. Other things being equal, most members of the distinct ethnic groups chose marriage partners from within the same group. However, when an adequate mate was not available within the group, as dictated by wealth and rank, people married from within neighboring groupings, either higher or lower. Studies have shown that in the mid-to-late colonial period, a third to half of the marriages might occur outside the ethnic category.

Another social group, small in numbers but quite influential, made their presence felt in the late colonial era. Immigrant Spaniards, termed *peninsulares*, numbered only some tens of thousands in any individual colony. But many of them came in groups of poor, young men, invited by their related *peninsulares* of an earlier generation who had prospered in commerce or mining. These newcomers were dispersed throughout the main and provincial cities to work long hours and long years as agents for their older relatives.

Some of them eventually prospered and married, typically a Creole cousin some years younger than they, and were designated to succeed to the directorships of their family's commercial houses. Yet others became prosperous, but at a lower level, controlling commerce in a provincial city or some specialized aspect of trade. A substantial number of these immigrant Spaniards never succeeded, and lived out their lives directing a provincial store or as peddlers.

The increased number of *peninsular* bureaucrats who came to the colonies in the eighteenth century engendered resentment among local Creole families. For at least a century previously, the crown had treated the issue of patronage in the colonies with considerable disregard. The upshot was that local Creoles were appointed to many positions in the colonial government, up to posts as judges in the colonial appeals courts. In the early eighteenth century, the royal government began an initiative to fill most colonial governmental positions with *peninsulares* to tighten control over colonial administration. The local colonial elites took umbrage with this new government policy, and were able to limit its effectiveness. They did this by their control over investment funds and emerging business opportunities, assets the *peninsular* officials prized. Officials frequently came to understandings with the local elite families, including through intermarriage, to use their positions for the benefit of both parties.

Bourbon Reforms. The gold and, predominantly, silver that was extracted from numerous Spanish American mines transformed the European economy: banking expanded, commerce increased, and prices became inflated. However, little of Spain's colonial wealth benefited its own economy; rather, its riches were squandered in other countries to pay for such imperial ventures as extended wars, campaigns against heresy, luxury goods for the nobility, and the administration of Spain's global empire.

By the early eighteenth century Spain's economy had continued to decline, because it did not participate in the incipient Industrial Revolution and suffered from a weak governmental financial system and a flagging navy. Spain had been unable to prevent a rapid expansion of contraband trade with its colonies. The fleet system was badly outdated and was gradually abandoned until its final dissolution in the 1760s.

By the mid-eighteenth century, Spain realized that its military and economic weakness relative to its European rivals derived in part from the little revenue that it earned from its colonies. During the Seven Years' War, the English easily seized the port of Havana in 1762, held it for a year, and greatly enhanced its foreign commerce during this time. This embarrassed the Spanish government and galvanized it to commence a program of reform.

Commonly known as the Bourbon Reforms, these shifts in colonial regulation are most closely identified with King Charles III (1716–1788; r. 1759–1788). Their goals were to strengthen the Spanish economy and military through deriving substantially more revenue from the colonies. This in turn would be accomplished by stimulating sectors of the colonial economies and by establishing royal monopolies over especially profitable colonial industries, such as tobacco, explosives, alcohol, and playing cards. These monopolies, unpopular in the cities, incited numerous urban uprisings that sometimes combined elements of the elite and commoners made up of different ethnicities. Although some of these revolts enjoyed limited success, most were repressed through the use of an unprecedented level of violence by military units.

The intendancy reform. Spain greatly increased the size of its administration in the colonies, particularly in outlying regions, bringing them firmly under governmental control for the first time. Cuba became a captaincy general in 1764. Formerly substantially ignored by Spain, in 1776 the Viceroyalty of La Plata was created, with its capital in Buenos Aires. But the Bourbons' most dramatic change in the administration system was the introduction of intendants, provincial administrators with substantial staffs and more authority than any of their predecessors. Intendants inherited the crucial task of administering Indian districts. They also extended royal rule to outlying provinces that had never been effectively placed under the central government. Most intendants were *peninsulares* appointed directly from Spain.

Seeking to limit the authority of the Catholic Church in the colonies, Charles III ordered the expulsion of the Jesuits from all Spanish territories in 1767, and mandated that the control of rural parishes be turned over from the powerful orders of priests to the less independent secular branch of the church.

The crown also established the first substantial military presence in Spanish America after the stunning British seizure of Havana. Spain could not afford to sustain massive numbers of Spanish troops in the Americas, though some few thousands did come. It relied instead on a colonial militia.

Reformist administrators. The colonial administrators most associated with instituting the Bourbon Reforms are José de Gálvez, and Juan Vicente Güemes-Pacheco de Padilla y Horcasitas, the Conde de Revillagigedo. Gálvez made use of a quality education and court patronage to rise rapidly in the Spanish colonial administration. In 1765 he was appointed *visitador* (royal inspector general) of New Spain. His primary charge was to maximize tax remittances to Spain and to use funds generated in New Spain to subsidize Spain's Caribbean colonies. Gálvez immediately came into conflict with the viceroy of New Spain, Joaquín de Montserrat, the Marquis of Cruillas, who would lose much of his power during Gálvez's inspectorship, which lasted until 1771.

Gálvez achieved some major reforms during his tenure, including establishment of a new sales tax code that increased royal tax revenues by 9 percent. He strengthened the mining sector by establishing the Royal Mining Tribunal. Perhaps his most notorious reform was the creation of a royal tobacco monopoly. He created a similar monopoly on the production and sale of playing cards.

When the crown ordered the expulsion of the Jesuits from New Spain, Gálvez took the lead in enforcing the decree. He used his military forces to put down local uprisings and ordered the execution or imprisonment of rebel leaders. Gálvez followed the French model of government administration by dividing New Spain into eleven provinces, or intendancies. After completing his inspectorship, Gálvez returned to Spain and a guaranteed appointment to the Council of the Indies, the governing body of Spain's American colonies.

Güemes-Pacheco de Padilla was one of the few non-*peninsular* viceroys, having been born in Cuba in 1740. His father was a lifelong colonial administrator, serving as viceroy of New Spain between 1746 and 1755. Güemes-Pacheco de Padilla in turn was appointed viceroy of New Spain in 1789.

Considered one of the most effective viceroys of the Bourbon era, Güemes-Pacheco de Padilla combated administrative corruption by reforming public administration. He initiated a campaign of public works to improve sanitation in Mexico City, while providing jobs for the commoners. He cleared the main square and set up more orderly public markets. Güemes-Pacheco de Padilla angered the Catholic Church by forbidding burials inside churches and encouraging cemetery construction instead. He sought to repair the decrepit road system that interlaced New Spain. He also created the National Archives and founded the Royal Mining College. His tenure as viceroy ended in 1794.

Free trade. Finally, after repeatedly losing both military conflicts and trading concessions to its more innovative and productive rivals, Spain undertook various trading reforms with its colonies. Far and away the most important was permitting free trade within the empire. In 1778 all colonies except for Mexico and Venezuela were allowed to trade with each other, plus any port in Spain could now send any number of ships at any time of the year to any colonial ports. The free trade system was finally extended to Mexico and Venezuela as well in 1789. Nonetheless, because of Spain's enduring industrial weakness, the amount of foreign-made goods shipped to the Americas continued to increase. Moreover, Spain never entertained allowing its colonies to trade legally outside of the empire.

In the eighteenth century, colonies that had been of peripheral economic importance to Spain over the previous two centuries saw their economies expand quite rapidly because of western Europe's commercial revolution and heightened demand for primary products, including sugar from Cuba, cacao from Venezuela and Ecuador, and cattle hides from the Buenos Aires region.

Fall of the Spanish Empire in America. Economic and political forces largely drove the Spanish American independence movements. The colonial elites, leaders of most of the revolts, sought free trade with all countries and political autonomy under the Spanish monarchy. Spain's maritime and military weakness was increasingly visible. As early as 1796, England blockaded trade between Spain and its colonies. The nearly continuous series of wars after 1790 created an almost insurmountable obstacle to Spanish efforts at imperial reform. Crises in many colonial economies required the expenditure of more tax revenue locally and minimized the funds being shipped back to Spain.

The crown's intervention in colonial affairs was increasingly perceived as arbitrary. For the Spanish Americans, the prime function of their ruler was to maintain legal equity. Few in Spanish America thought that the crown was fulfilling this function in the final decades before independence. The Creoles' loyalty to the crown was based on the subjects' right to review new laws and to dismiss those that they found harmful to their region. Indian visions of an alternative to colonial society were almost entirely self-generated and parochial and often harked back to their glorified memories of a pre-Hispanic past.

Following the Napoleonic invasion of Spain in 1808, most of the American colonies moved quickly to independence, Mexico and Venezuela gaining their freedom in 1821, Ecuador in 1822, Peru in 1824, and Bolivia in 1825. Cuba, Puerto Rico, and the Philippines remained as colonies until 1898. As Spain lost its political control over its former colonies, it also lost most of its trade with them to its major commercial rivals, England, France, and the United States.

Colonial political structures collapsed during the independence struggles. The militarization of society also brought about political dislocations. The removal of the monarch left only the weakest forms of nationalism in its place. The primary loyalty became that to the separate regional societies. The breakdown of internal markets, the lack of overseas markets, and the shortage of investment capital doomed most of the new Latin American countries to poverty.

A comparison of Spain's balance of trade in 1792 and 1827 reveals that Spain's total foreign trade fell by nearly three-quarters. Comparisons with its former colonies reveal even worse drop-offs. Exports to the Americas had fallen to nearly negligible proportions.

Impact of Colonial Independence on Spain. Many Creoles had conceived of the empire as a single family under a father king. This personalized concept of a political relationship became especially strong after the defeat of Napoleon, during the reign of Ferdinand VII (1784–1833; 1814–1833). The revenue-enhancing aspects of the Bourbon Reforms were so successful that every viceroyalty in the Americas produced a profit. But Spain itself, unable to revitalize its economy, remained an undeveloped metropolis.

Even when Spain was ruled by a liberal government in the early 1810s, it showed that its fundamental attitude toward the American colonies was the same as that under the royalists: it refused free trade with any countries outside of Spain and its territories; and it refused to consider political autonomy for the colonies under the ultimate authority of Spain. Once the continental American colonies achieved their independence, Spain adamantly refused to recognize the fact until 1833. The country resolutely and impractically drew up plans of reconquest until then. Spanish citizens, whether liberal or conservative, comforted themselves with the belief that no country had ever treated their colonists in a more magnanimous fashion, and that Spain had never attempted to inhibit its American colonies in any field of activity.

Philippine independence. Spain had extended its control over the Philippines by playing local groups against one another and encouraging feuds. Manila remained a crucial port for the Spanish Empire, where Spanish silver from the American colonies was turned over to Asian traders for Chinese ceramics, silk, tea, gold, and spices. Spanish control over trade in the Philippines declined in the nineteenth century, leaving space for the Filipinos to cultivate export crops, such as indigo, sugar, and hemp, which were marketed through English and American merchants.

Filipinos began to demand social, political, and religious reforms from the Spanish government, but Spain's response ranged from conciliation to repression. By the early 1890s, Filipinos were organizing secret societies to take action against Spanish officials. The most notable of these societies was the Philippine League, which was organized by the famed novelist José Rizal in 1891. Rizal militated more for equality for the Filipinos than he did independence for the islands. But in 1896, the Spanish charged him with inciting rebellion and executed him. The Spanish-American War erupted in 1898 before the Filipinos could achieve their own victory, and following the American victory, Spain ceded the Philippines to the United States.

Cuba's independence struggle. Cuba did not mount much of an independence struggle in the early part of the nineteenth century, when the colonies of continental Spanish America successfully gained their independence from Spain. As an island separated from the mainland, Cuba did not participate in the developments witnessed there. It also labored under the presence of large units of the Spanish military and, dominated by slave-labor–based sugar plantations, its master class feared an uprising of the slaves if action was taken against Spain. Further, alone among the Spanish American colonies, Cuba had to deal with the substantial possibility during the first two-thirds of the century that the United States would seek to annex it from Spain. American efforts only ended with the Civil War and the abolition of slavery.

In 1868 the *Grito de Yara* (the formal declaration of independence by Cuban patriots) announced a rebellion in support of independence, but it was largely contained in the eastern end of the island, away from the big, slave-populated sugar plantations. The rebel leadership, largely landowners, refused to attack slavery in order to keep the support of the sugar plantation owners. The war continued on an off-and-on basis for ten years, with the rebel leadership fearful of recruiting slaves to its cause. Negotiations ensued between the two sides in 1878 and concluded that same year with the Pact of Zanjón. In it, Spain promised a range of political reforms and promised a general amnesty to all insurgents.

Independence movements remained quiescent until the late 1880s, when José Martí y Pérez, a noted Cuban writer, poet, and patriot, rose to leadership of the cause and subordinated all other issues to that of independence. In early 1895 an insurrection broke out once again, but again it enjoyed little success. In the fall of that year, however, insurgent armies erupted out of the eastern mountains and marched into the western valleys. Martí was killed in combat in 1895.

Spain responded by increasing its troops and consigning insurgents to concentration camps. Nonetheless, a rebel victory appeared inevitable by late 1897. The outbreak of the Spanish-American War in 1898 determined that the Spanish would be expelled, however, and the Cubans were subsequently denied full independence by the Americans.

Gibraltar. In 1713 Spain ceded this rocky promontory on its south coast to England in the Treaty of Utrecht, which ended the War of the Spanish Succession. Since the 1980s, Spain has made fervent demands that Gibraltar be returned to it, but despite all of its protests and legal actions, in 2007 the promontory remained in English hands.

Spanish Africa. Spain established a number of small enclaves along the North African coast in the fifteenth and early sixteenth centuries. They ran from Tripoli in the east to Ifni in the west. Spain added more coastal areas in the nineteenth century, most notably the Spanish Sahara (Western Sahara) in 1884. In 1921, a leader of the tribesmen of the Rif led an uprising against a Spanish military base and massacred some sixteen thousand soldiers after capturing it.

After French Morocco gained its independence in 1956, Spain realized that it would have a difficult time holding onto Spanish Morocco. Spain withdrew from the territory between 1956 and 1958 and moved out of the Western Sahara in 1975.

Comparisons with British North America. The revolution that impelled the thirteen colonies of North America to break with the British Crown in 1776 reflected disappointed expectations. After the Seven Years' War, the British simply did not behave toward the colonists as the latter had come to expect in the years before the war. Likewise, the Creoles of Spanish America felt a sense of profound disappointment at the policies of the king's ministers. Eventually, this distrust of policies in the two sets of colonies transformed itself into a distrust of their respective monarchs, who came to be seen as despotic and illegitimate themselves.

When such disillusionment circulated among the British colonists, they were fortified by a gamut of political and intellectual treatises that spoke to the issues. But little scope for public debate existed in the more controlled atmosphere of the Spanish American world. The Spanish American Enlightenment lagged seriously behind its British American counterpart, and its impact would only be widely felt during the last two decades of the eighteenth century. The problems involved in mobilizing and coordinating resistance over the vast American areas occupied by Spain were of an order that British North America never had to deal with.

The thirteen British colonies, though quite diverse in character, joined together in a common act of defiance against the British Crown. The Spanish American colonies gained their independence without a similar experience of close and enduring collaboration. Independence came to them in different times and in different ways.

[*See also* Bourbon Reforms; Buenos Aires; Colombia; Cuba; Ecuador; Gibraltar; Latin American Wars of Independence; Mexico; Panama; Peru; Philippines; Spanish-American War; Túpac Amaru Rebellion; Venezuela; *and* Western Sahara.]

BIBLIOGRAPHY
Anna, Timothy A. "Spain and the Breakdown of the Imperial Ethos: The Problem of Equality." *Hispanic American Historical Review* 62, no. 2 (May 1982): 254–272.

Anna, Timothy A. *Spain and the Loss of America.* Lincoln: University of Nebraska Press, 1983.

Bailyn, Bernard. *Atlantic History: Concept and Contours.* Cambridge, Mass.: Harvard University Press, 2005.

Brading, D. A. *The First America: The Spanish Monarchy, Creole Patriots, and the Liberal State, 1492–1867.* Cambridge, U.K., and New York: Cambridge University Press, 1991.

Burkholder, Mark A., and Lyman L. Johnson. *Colonial Latin America.* 4th ed. New York: Oxford University Press, 2001.

Costeloe, Michael P. *Response to Revolution: Imperial Spain and the Spanish American Revolutions, 1810–1840.* Cambridge, U.K., and New York: Cambridge University Press, 1986.

Elliott, J. H. *Empires of the Atlantic World: Britain and Spain in America, 1492–1830.* New Haven, Conn.: Yale University Press, 2006.

Kamen, Henry. *Empire: How Spain Became a World Power, 1492–1763.* New York: HarperCollins, 2003.

Lockhart, James, and Stuart B. Schwartz. *Early Latin America: A History of Colonial Spanish America and Brazil.* Cambridge, U.K., and New York: Cambridge University Press, 1983.

Pagden, Anthony. *European Encounters with the New World: From Renaissance to Romanticism.* New Haven, Conn.: Yale University Press, 1993.

Pagden, Anthony. *Lords of All the World: Ideologies of Empire in Spain, Britain, and France, c. 1500–c. 1800.* New Haven, Conn.: Yale University Press, 1995.

Parry, J. H. *The Spanish Seaborne Empire.* New York: Alfred A. Knopf, 1966.

Pérez, Louis A., Jr. *Cuba: Between Reform and Revolution.* 2d ed. New York: Oxford University Press, 1995.

Seed, Patricia. *Ceremonies of Possession in Europe's Conquest of the New World, 1492–1640.* Cambridge, U.K., and New York: Cambridge University Press, 1995.

Stein, Stanley J., and Barbara H. Stein. *Apogee of Empire: Spain and New Spain in the Age of Charles III, 1759–1789.* Baltimore: Johns Hopkins University Press, 2003.

Van Young, Eric. *The Other Rebellion: Popular Violence, Ideology, and the Mexican Struggle for Independence, 1810–1821.* Stanford, Calif.: Stanford University Press, 2001.

Voss, Stuart F. *Latin America in the Middle Period, 1750–1929.* Wilmington, Del.: Scholarly Resources, 2002.

JOHN E. KICZA

The Portuguese Colonial Empire

On 21 August 1415, the burning African sun caught the quick, the dying, and the dead, Muslim and Christian alike, in a furious day of conflict that contested the future of the ancient North African trade center of Ceuta. The Portuguese army of John I (r. 1385–1433) prevailed, and his force of Christians proceeded to sack the city. Here they found extensive treasures of gold, silver, and jewelry, as well as merchandise from across the world. Six hundred pillars of alabaster and marble were seized by the king's third son, Peter, were shipped to Portugal, were spiritually cleansed and blessed, and were incorporated into Christian churches and palaces. Four days after the battle

the sons of the king, Duarte, Peter, and Henry, knelt in the now purified and Christianized mosque to be knighted by their father. A week later, on 2 September, the Portuguese fleet sailed home and left behind a governor and a garrison of twenty-seven hundred men to hold this tiny beachhead on the rim of the Muslim world. It was this rude act that announced the beginning of the Portuguese empire.

The First Empire. Portuguese interest in these treasures had begun long before with a commercial fascination over the golden thread that linked the Iberian Peninsula through the western Maghreb with the sub-Saharan regions of Africa. Gold and slaves had provided the main elements of the northbound trade from the Sudan and the Gulf of Guinea. During the fourteenth century, Europeans had begun to understand the sources of this wealth, and this understanding led the Portuguese push into African affairs.

There had developed a powerful and independent class of merchants who put great trust in the new Avis dynasty, and John I could ill afford to neglect their welfare. The crown also had to find a solution to the monetary ills of the nation, and entry into Africa provided the hope of securing a reliable solution to bullion shortages. The successful operation against Ceuta had been aimed at gaining a share of the fabled Saharan gold trade. Unfortunately, this seizure caused the Muslim merchants to shun Ceuta, and it was not until Tangier and the other ports of the western Maghreb were secured that Portugal could dominate the local trade. It was, however, the source of this wealth that fascinated the merchants and government of Portugal, and it was one of the royal brothers at Ceuta, Henry, who would solve the riddle and help realize the dreams of his countrymen. He became famous as Henry the Navigator: his vision led to the new discoveries, and his science happily married the mathematical learning and practical seamanship that made such accomplishments possible.

Following the fall of Ceuta, Portugal became engaged in three enterprises in Africa: the conquest of the coastal reaches of the western Maghreb, the settlement of the Atlantic islands, and the tentative exploration south along the West African coast. These latter two initiatives led to the mastery of the African and Atlantic trade routes and the beginning of Portugal's African and Brazilian holdings. This earlier era of prosperous exploration that led to the Gulf of Guinea was advanced in 1497 when Vasco da Gama rounded the Cape of Good Hope, discovered Mozambique, and established trading contacts in India. Portugal proceeded to develop this new route unchallenged in the short term. Great wealth had awaited the European nation that could directly tap the source of Eastern goods and eliminate the middlemen along the fabled Silk Route, and Portugal succeeded in this challenge.

The trade was immensely profitable, and wealth poured into Portugal on an unprecedented scale. The Portuguese defeated challenges from both the Europeans and the Muslims to their new monopoly and proceeded to establish a systematic arc of enclaves strategically ringing the Indian Ocean. These bases commanded both the sources of trade and the sea routes themselves. As the Portuguese secured their dominance in this area, profits from their localized trade, as well as from the Cape route, increased accordingly.

Portugal reached its height of power and influence during the first half of the sixteenth century. Its decline can be marked from June 1578, the month of the disastrous North African campaign in which King Sebastian (r. 1557–1578) and his army were destroyed in four hours by Moroccan forces at Alcázarquivir (El-Ksar el-Kebir). The Portuguese army totaled some fifteen thousand foot soldiers and fifteen hundred cavalry, along with nine thousand camp followers. Five hundred vessels were required to transport the army. Eight thousand were killed, fifteen thousand were taken prisoner and sold into slavery, and perhaps only one hundred eventually reached the safety of Portugal. The might of Portugal was wasted with this disaster, and the next year Portugal's great epic poet and inspirer of nationalistic sentiment, Luis de Camões (c. 1524–1580), wrote to a friend from his deathbed in Lisbon that not only was he dying but his country was dying with him.

Though leaving an indelible imprint on the European perspective of the world, the Portuguese had exhausted themselves in the process. They were never able to regain their sixteenth-century stature, and from that time until 1974 and the final, complete, and irremediable loss of its empire, Portugal experienced an irregular path of decline with episodes of partial recovery. As a nation, the Portuguese historically have looked back on this time, which they call *O Século Maravilhoso* (The Marvelous Century), and have longed to regain their former height of glory and greatness. Although this first empire was short-lived, it created a permanent nostalgia that gave Portuguese leaders a vibrant chord of imperial grandeur around which to rally colonial support. Conversely, though politicians and colonial ideologues were able to play strongly on this period of grandeur, the Portuguese citizens themselves were never unanimous in their attitudes toward Portuguese Asia, and many saw it as a hollow triumph that drained Portugal of resources and left it impotent in its defense against Spain.

The Second Empire. In the period between 1497 and 1578 the Portuguese had established a new concept of empire based on a mastery of the ocean routes. Trade, not territory, was the prime objective. Portugal was unable to sustain such a grand enterprise with its very limited resources, particularly in manpower, and when Spain annexed it in its depleted state between 1580 and 1640, this trade dominance was effectively lost. When Portugal recovered its independence in 1640, it was a wonder that it retrieved so much of its overseas holdings as well, particularly Brazil.

Whereas spices were the single most lucrative commodity of the sixteenth century, Brazilian sugar was the single most lucrative commodity in the seventeenth century. Just when West Indian sugar production threatened to supplant that of Brazil, gold was discovered there in 1694. In 1728 diamonds were also discovered. The revenue from this colonial wealth maintained the continuity of Portuguese prosperity until Brazil declared its independence in 1822. It was the memory of Brazil and the wealth that it had provided that generated a twentieth-century hope for a similar prosperity from the African colonies. Brazil was a far different enterprise than the earlier Asian experience in that it had provided raw materials, and in turn Portugal had supplied manufactures. It also had been a colony of settlement rather than one where immigrants died of tropical diseases and melted into the local population. This Brazilian model, where Portuguese language and culture were firmly entrenched, became a far more influential guide for the development of Angola and Mozambique than *O Século Maravilhoso*. These two colonies were seen potentially as modern-day Brazils and the prized keys to renewed prosperity and greatness.

Elusive domestic prosperity also reinforced the commitment to the African colonies and their economic promise. Metropolitan Portugal from the earliest times remained economically underdeveloped and was dependent on overseas commerce and colonial wealth to maintain more than a subsistence standard of living. Lisbon in the first half of the sixteenth century was a spectacularly opulent city, yet Portugal as a whole did not produce enough goods to feed and clothe its population, and staples had to be purchased abroad. Slaves were imported from the Guinean coast to supply labor, and rural Portuguese immigrated to western Spain in search of employment. The wealth of Lisbon seemed useless to the population at large. Because

Portugal had never developed a domestic economy of any consequence during the years of plenty, there was no alternative to the stagnation at home when the wealth from abroad evaporated. Portugal's economy persisted at subsistence levels, and because it was so weak, it failed to participate significantly in the Industrial Revolution of the nineteenth century. This signal failure made the promise of Africa increasingly important.

Portugal began the nineteenth century with such an anemic domestic economy that it could not convert the raw materials of its colonies into manufactured goods to the same degree that its European trading partners could. With the loss of Brazil and the loss of access to its readily salable commodities, Portugal was left to survive on its weak economic capability. Portugal's trade patterns during this period give insight into its problem. Portugal's share of trade with its main European partners was a mere 1.2 percent in 1820 and experienced steady erosion through the century to 0.78 percent in 1899. Portugal's relatively small share of world trade declined from 0.88 percent in 1820 to 0.53 percent in 1899. Though world trade was expanding tenfold during this span, Portugal's share expanded only sixfold from a very small base. It is instructive to note that the greatest increase in worldwide trade during the nineteenth century was the 80 percent increase in the 1850s. Portugal lagged the average with a 60 percent performance, while its European trading partners were beating the average with a 100 percent increase during the decade. Because Portugal was not developing its economic engine, it was unable to employ the resources of its colonies on any appreciable scale or to exploit any relative trading advantage in international commerce.

The Third Empire. In the last two decades of the nineteenth century at the height of the Industrial Revolution, there occurred a spontaneous Scramble for Africa, a frantic, largely irrational rush among the European powers to establish colonial claims. This scramble was prompted by an increasing awareness in Europe about Africa, coupled with a speculative search for new opportunities by Europe's more prosperous powers. Approximately 80 percent of the territorial acquisitions in Africa during this time were made by the three most industrialized nations of Europe: Britain, France, and Germany. Portugal, although having been established in Africa since the fifteenth century, was not an economic or military powerhouse and was thus vulnerable to challenge. Portugal's confrontation with Britain over its coast-to-coast colonial ambitions became an unfortunate face-off.

Portugal intended to join Angola and Mozambique through austral Africa potentially to form a second Brazil. After Brazilian independence in 1822, the development of the vast colonies of Angola and Mozambique remained the last hope for any substantial renewal of prosperity. If one considers the territory that was lost to Britain and its imperial developer Cecil Rhodes from a twenty-first-century perspective, it is easy to see that the hinterland wealth of the Rhodesias and portions of the Belgian Congo, when connected to the Atlantic and Indian ocean outlets of Angola and Mozambique, would have indeed given Portugal a second Brazil. The magnitude of this loss became a Portuguese preoccupation thereafter and steeled its national attitude in the absolute sacredness of its remaining territories abroad.

Portugal had launched expeditions by Alexandre Serpa Pinto, Hermenegildo Brito Capelo, Roberto Ivens, and Henrique de Carvalho between 1877 and 1885 to explore its claimed territory in Central Africa, and thus it viewed itself as already in possession of this land. Consequently, following the 1885 treaties with Germany and France resulting from the Berlin West Africa Conference on the ownership of Africa, Portugal published the "Rose-Colored Map," which showed Angola and Mozambique united in a coast-to-coast colony. Britain became alarmed both at the vigor and direction of Portuguese colonial policy, which seemed so unprecedented, and also at the unusual success of Portugal's military operations. At the insistence of the opportunist Rhodes, Britain took strong exception to Portuguese claims, and in June 1887, Lord Salisbury, the prime minister, stated that the British would "not recognize Portuguese sovereignty in territories not occupied with sufficient forces to maintain order." To Salisbury's government it did not matter how many ruined forts, churches, and other relics the Portuguese could show. It mattered only whether the Portuguese could keep law and order in the areas.

Portugal nevertheless proceeded with its colonial expansion plans, and the ardent imperialist Serpa Pinto boldly advanced into a British preserve near Lake Nyasa in what is now southern Malawi. As a consequence, on 11 January 1890, Salisbury demanded Portugal's immediate withdrawal from the area in question and backed the demand with a threat of force in mobilizing the British fleet. Portugal withdrew accordingly in great humiliation. This action became known as the "ultimatum," and its consequences were to make Mozambique a coastal colony with no hinterland and to make British territory landlocked with no outlet to the sea. Mozambique remained separated from Angola by between 300 and

430 miles (500 and 700 kilometers), and Portugal's ambition for a grand coast-to-coast colony remained unrealized. Portugal's claims were far superior to those of Britain. When Portugal established what was clearly effective occupation, Salisbury switched tack and condemned the occupation of areas claimed by Britain even when unsupported by any presence.

British colonial ambitions in the area were a reflection of those of Rhodes, an inveterate territorial privateer. The ultimatum had struck at the roots of the Portuguese monarchy, whose popular support rested in part on the assumption that the Portuguese crown was a magic link to British protective power, a link that dated from the initial Anglo-Portuguese alliance of 13 June 1373. The ultimatum undermined this concept, contributed to the downfall of the monarchy in 1910, and brought into relief one British view of imperialism: if Portugal was unable to fulfill its colonizing mission, then the "white man's burden" should pass to those more capable.

It was often assumed that the disintegration of Portuguese Africa was simply a matter of time and that the British would be its heirs. Such attitudes and assumptions spawned a number of secret agreements, the key one being between Britain and Germany to divide Portuguese possessions should its empire crumble. Germany, a relatively late arrival in Africa, had at the time a number of widely separated territories. It sought to link them through further acquisitions and thus ensure what it viewed as its rightful place in the modern colonial expansion. This linking was to occur in great part through the liquidation of the Portuguese possessions; specifically, Britain and Germany would divide them so that Germany would receive southern and northern Angola, and Britain its center. Northern Mozambique and Timor would also go to Germany, while southern Mozambique would go to Britain.

The German government then initiated a policy of *pénétration pacifique*, in which it began a diplomatic and financial offensive to weaken Portugal's hand in Africa. Portuguese leadership was aware of this scheming and remained determined, as a national policy, to stay in Africa. Portugal thus began to take the concept of effective occupation seriously as part of its national strategy, particularly in light of the lesson of the ultimatum—that the rules applied to the Great Powers would be different from those applied to Portugal.

World War I. The Portuguese entry into the European theater of World War I was seen by its government first as a shortcut to popular acceptance by its European neighbors and second as a means to secure its colonial interests.

As it evolved, this national strategy was ill-considered, was poorly executed, and—not surprisingly—achieved none of its goals.

Portugal remained an unsettled and impoverished nation. By the early twentieth century and World War I, Portugal still could neither feed nor clothe its population and depended on imports and credit from its European neighbors, particularly Great Britain, to function as a country. From the outside it was viewed as unable to govern itself in a civilized way, considering its coups, assassinations, and political imprisonments that resulted in some thirty changes in government during the republican era between 1910 and 1926. This was the period from the overthrow of the constitutional monarchy to the entry of Dr. Antonio de Oliveira Salazar, an economics professor from Coimbra University, and his Estado Novo (New State) to solve the fiscal problems of the government.

The misplaced notion of becoming a belligerent alongside the Allies was born in September 1914 when the French requested that Portugal supply a number of French-manufactured 75mm field guns for the Flanders front. The Portuguese position was that if the Allies wanted the guns, then they must accept Portugal as a cobelligerent and accept the presence of a Portuguese division on the western front. Ultimately the guns proved not to be useful: they were not compatible with similar weapons in the French inventory, and they got to France too late. Nevertheless, Portugal insisted on sending a reinforced division that Portugal could not afford, that could be destroyed in a single day of fighting, that would have no significant impact on the outcome of the war, and that would pose a burden on the Allies because of its low state of readiness. After a long and sad drama, all of these weaknesses proved true, and despite the individual bravery of the troops involved, Portugal had not improved its political position in the least. It had failed in Europe and on the two fronts in Africa and as a result held an empty hand at the Versailles peace negotiations.

In Africa, Portugal had confronted Germany in both Angola and Mozambique. Germany had always coveted the southern portion of Angola and the northern portion of Mozambique. World War I provided the long-sought opportunity for it to take what it wished. The key German aim in Africa at this time had centered on the concept of a German Central Africa in which a zone of economic opportunity would be acquired principally from the French, Belgian, and Portuguese possessions—carved from the French West Coast, the Congo Free State, Angola, and Mozambique. The reason for demanding Angola was to connect the mining area of Katanga to the west coast ports of Moçâmedes (Namibe), Benguela, and Luanda. British colonies were avoided in this plan because Germany did not believe that Britain could be defeated as could France and Belgium. The German strategy with Portugal, a neutral, was to compel it to abandon its position of neutrality through a contrived border dispute and associated incident in southern Angola. This action would serve as a pretext to provoke a break with Portugal, so that it could be among the defeated German adversaries and be forced to part with its colonies when a victorious Germany dictated the peace terms.

German designs under its *pénétration pacifique* became less subtle in November 1913 with an agreement to open Angolan ports to its commerce and establish a consul general in Luanda. Though these moves might seem innocuous, the Portuguese government was intimidated by Germany and agreed further to the establishment of a joint German-Portuguese mission for scientific studies in the south of Angola. When the mission arrived in Luanda, Governor-General Luís Norton de Matos was taken by surprise, not having been consulted or informed by Lisbon. The vastness of Angola, the long uncontrolled southern border, and the relatively primitive communications made it particularly vulnerable to any German offensive. Norton de Matos had few troops with which to police the frontier, much less to defend the colony. With the German mission traveling through the area gathering intelligence on every aspect of the colonial defenses and able to engage in other activities, and the consul general vigorously pursuing German interests, it was not difficult to foresee trouble.

As the implementation of German war aims in Africa became more obvious, anxiety grew in Lisbon and Luanda. Even though the borders between Angola and German Southwest Africa had been fixed by a treaty dated 30 December 1886, the Germans sought certain convenient interpretations. For instance, in the treaty a portion of the southern border ran from the Ruacaná Cataract on the Cunené River along the east-west parallel until it intersected with the Cubango River. The Germans insisted that the border originated at the Nanguari Rapids farther upriver. This claim had the effect of moving a 275-mile (445-kilometer) border about 6.8 miles (11 kilometers) north and giving Germany about 3,100 square miles (5,000 square kilometers) of additional territory for which no battle had to be fought. Although this zone was disputed by Portugal, German intimidation moved the de facto border.

From 1900, German patrols had penetrated the southern areas of Angola on reconnaissance missions and stirred trouble with the local population. This irregular activity increased with the advent of war, and finally on 19 October 1914 there was a shooting incident in which three Germans were killed at the Portuguese border post of Naulila. This was the incident that Germany sought. Retribution was swift, and on 31 October a German patrol seized and massacred the occupants of the Portuguese border post of Cuangar. The German rampage continued, and Portugal was forced to abandon four additional posts in the area. A final German strike was organized against Naulila on 18 December, and in this engagement the Portuguese were forced to retreat. The Germans immediately withdrew to defend Southwest Africa from the assaults of General Louis Botha and the Union of South Africa, but the tenuous Portuguese hold over the south of Angola had been disrupted and required almost a year to reassert. The German activity achieved little other than humiliating the Portuguese.

The World War I German offensive into northern Mozambique had its roots in two dynamics: the German colonial ambitions of 1914 and the fighting withdrawal and survival of the German colonial force under Lieutenant Colonel Paul Emil von Lettow-Vorbeck. The Portuguese strategic situation in Mozambique in August 1914 was driven by three factors: the progress in gaining control over the colony and its indigenous people, the means available for its defense, and the nature of the potential external threat. By 1914, Portugal effectively controlled all of Mozambique with the exception of the Maconde people in the north. This region was also where the fewest Europeans lived, where the Portuguese military had the least presence, where government administrative posts were few and scattered, and where the frontier with German East Africa was largely uncontrolled. Great portions of Mozambique were at the time managed under various agreements by several large charter companies funded by foreign capital. Of these, the Niassa Company controlled the northern portion of the colony that abutted German territory. Because the commercial interests of the charter companies did not necessarily coincide with the interests of the Portuguese government, the areas under contract were invariably underdeveloped, underexplored, and underpoliced. Indeed, it is said that with the arrival of the 1914 military expedition in the Niassa Company area the European population increased tenfold. Government control of northern Mozambique was thus tenuous at best, and it was vulnerable to both outside mischief and local resistance to pacification.

As in the south of Angola, Portugal had yielded border concessions to the Germans and allowed the enclave of Quionga to be established at the mouth of the Rovuma River in Mozambique. As the war unfolded, German colonial aims in East Africa shifted to defense and to becoming a distraction for Allied resources in an attempt to provide relief to the European front. In this forgotten theater Portuguese and British forces expended enormous resources for limited gains in chasing down the elusive foe of von Lettow-Vorbeck and his relatively small Schutztruppe of native soldiers.

Portugal consequently fought the Germans in Angola and Mozambique with the same disappointing results as in Europe. Had Portugal not participated on the Flanders front and used all of its resources in Africa to gain victories over the Germans and particularly over von Lettow-Vorbeck in East Africa, the British would have been most grateful at a time when a victory on any front would have been welcomed.

New Colonial Vision. During and following World War I the colonies may have had potential, but Portugal was unable to capitalize significantly on their promise in the traditional mercantilist sense to the betterment of its overall economy. Through inadequate colonial policies the colonies became less important to the metropolis in economic terms between 1910 and 1926. This colonial decline contributed to the downfall of the republican regime in 1926 and the subsequent emergence of Salazar, who introduced both fiscal and political discipline.

In Portuguese eyes the colonies nevertheless continued to hold the ultimate potential for prosperity in their underdeveloped state. On coming to power, Salazar moved decisively to reinforce economic links between the colonies and the metropolis, and by the eve of the last colonial war in 1961 the African colonies appeared finally to be realizing their true promise. It was at this point that Portugal deeply believed in its African colonial potential. Salazar saw the colonies as an important part of Portugal's ability to emerge from the fiscal chaos of the previous republican government. If Portugal was to rediscover itself, then it would have to reestablish its identity. Salazar thus sought to promote a new imperial consciousness that came to be known as Lusotropicalism. It could not be born in an atmosphere of ignorance and lack of interest. Consequently, it was based on the Portuguese ideology of imperial greatness with which everyone was familiar. Lusotropicalism was defined in terms of three elements: geography, heroism, and trade. The first element was supported by the notion that the Portuguese flag flew over vast territories spreading over three continents and making a small European state the third largest colonial power, the second lay in the discoveries by Portugal's epic sailors and warriors during *O Século Maravilhoso*, and the third focused on the hardships that the Portuguese people had endured in carving the hidden riches from remote lands and establishing centers of production and profit there.

Salazar viewed the colonies as a vehicle to give Portugal stature in a world where the preceding republican government had removed all such standing with the number and volatility of its administrations. In Lusotropicalism he attempted to create a colonial mentality within the Portuguese people by drawing on the sense of achievement in *O Século Maravilhoso* and relating it to the present colonial ownership. Salazar's Lusotropical vision embodied a sense of unity between the colonies and the metropolis that had genuine foundations in national heritage and psychology and in past colonial policy.

On assuming full and complete power in 1933, Salazar initially put the colonies on hold until he could get control of the national budget and navigate the country through the Depression. By 1937 he had established the colonial development fund, which would be financed primarily through colonial budget surpluses and other colonial monopoly profits. These measures enabled Portugal and its colonies to participate in the economic emergence from the Depression of the 1930s and the expansion associated with World War II.

Salazar's programs were designed largely to improve colonial infrastructure and were in step with Salazar's neo-mercantilist view of the empire. His theoretical aim was to construct a form of autarky that allowed Portugal to develop its economy without the use of foreign investment, thus reducing the potential for any foreign obligation or intrusion. Salazar was provincial in character and temperament despite his sophisticated education. In fact, he was so suspicious of foreigners and resistant to change that at first he refused U.S. aid under the Marshall Plan following World War II. The error in judgment was so apparent that he reversed himself. He held the view that foreign sources of funding could dwarf Portugal's investment at home and in its colonies and that any such change, even for the sake of progress, would threaten both the economic and political status quo. This isolationist doctrine of self-reliance was unrealistic in a postwar system of increasing interdependence among nations; however, Salazar saw any change as a potential threat to the forces that kept him in power. With economic freedom would come the desire for political freedom.

The initial rigidity of Salazar's position softened as he gained an understanding of the impact that foreign capital could make on Portugal's domestic and overseas economies. This softening allowed a significant but belated development of colonial industries. Expertise and supporting funds came from established firms for any significant or complicated undertaking, particularly mining. Belgian (diamond mining), British (railroads), and U.S. (oil exploration) investments dominated and were largely exempt from exchange controls. They strengthened and stabilized the colonial economies in the years between 1945 and 1961, deepening Portugal's economic reliance on the colonies and its commitment to defend them. In 1961 private foreign investment accounted for about 15 percent of gross fixed capital formation in the colonies and had grown to almost 25 percent in 1966. By 1961 the colonies had finally become an economically worthy possession.

Also by 1961, Portugal's economy had shifted from a partial autarky under orthodox economic practices to a fledgling but rapidly growing industrialized one. The shift away from an agriculturally based economy in the metropolis and the colonies meant that there was a decreasing dependence on peasant labor and its attendant policies. As the metropolis developed in this direction, so the first moves were made to foster complementary development in the colonies. Mining, oil exploration and refining, textiles, and cashew processing were in place by 1961, and other basic industries were in the planning stages. These activities reflected a break with the past and a new Salazar policy fueled by colonial promise. Education received renewed and expanded attention as literate workers with skills were in increasing demand. The paranoia in regard to foreign investment had evaporated, and French, German, U.S., and South African participation in the economy was welcomed.

The gathering momentum of the colonial economies continued to accelerate well past 1961 and became a welcome support for the political element in fighting its colonial wars of the period from 1961 to 1974. The colonies were thus developing into substantial economic engines in their own right, and not only were their citizens beginning to benefit individually but Portugal itself was also reaping substantial rewards from this growing prosperity. The colonies' historic potential was being realized, a fact that reinforced their longtime importance to Portugal and Salazar's commitment of the nation to their defense.

The year 1961 was a difficult one for Portugal because in March there was an enormous invasion and uprising in the north of Angola by one of several nationalist movements based in the former Belgian Congo, which had received its independence the preceding year. The Portuguese were caught off guard, and it took the better part of six months to restore order. This event highlighted the Portuguese position of continuing as a colonial power while Britain and France were dissolving their empires.

Consequent and unwanted attention at the United Nations in December resulted in a resolution condemning Portuguese African policy. Portugal became a semi-pariah state, politically isolated with its colonial neighbors of South Africa and Rhodesia. That same month India, sensing a diplomatically isolated and vulnerable Portugal, invaded and seized the colony of Goa. Portugal next faced an open armed assault on its African colonies of Angola, Guinea, and Mozambique launched from the newly independent neighboring states that now surrounded its territories. Though Salazar suffered a stroke in 1968, his successor Marcel Caetano continued Salazar's policies unchanged. The war to preserve ownership proved long and debilitating for Portugal, and it reached its culmination in 1974 when disaffected elements of Portugal's military overthrew the government in a coup and liberated the colonies.

In the final analysis, though Portugal fought an imaginative campaign between 1961 and 1974 to retain its colonies in an anticolonial era, no amount of military verve could overcome the twentieth-century political problem of Portugal's legitimacy in Africa. Portugal's political leadership during this time, however, had remained shortsighted and removed from reality. The true hope for the regeneration of Portugal lay in releasing its colonies to resolve both the domestic and international dissent stemming from the thirteen-year conflict and to embrace the European prosperity then under way. When the politicians failed to provide the necessary complementary support, it was the military that intervened on 25 April 1974 and provided the political solution of ending the Portuguese empire—a solution that not only freed the colonies but also ultimately liberated Portugal and made possible its transition to a democracy.

[See also Angola; Brazil; Colonialism; Decolonization, subentry Africa; Latin American Wars of Independence; Macau; Mozambique; Portugal; and World War I, subentry Africa.]

BIBLIOGRAPHY
Atkinson, William C. "Introduction" to *The Lusiads*, by Luis Vaz de Camões. Translated by William C. Atkinson. Harmondsworth, U.K., and New York: Penguin Books, 1952. Atkinson's introduction gives a sound and interesting overview of the early Portuguese empire.

Birmingham, David. *A Concise History of Portugal.* Cambridge, U.K., and New York: Cambridge University Press, 1993. A well-written, concise history of the Portuguese empire by a noted scholar.

Boorstin, Daniel J. *The Discoverers.* New York: Random House, 1983. This extensive volume covers the early explorations. Chapters 21, 22, and 23 put the Portuguese in proper context and are particularly relevant.

Bruce, Neil. *Portugal: The Last Empire.* London: David and Charles, 1975. This highly readable volume gives a sound contemporary picture of the final days of the Portuguese empire and how Portugal came to be in such straits in Africa.

Cann, John P. *Counterinsurgency in Africa: The Portuguese Way of War, 1961–1974.* Westport, Conn.: Greenwood Press, 1997. A comprehensive account of the Portuguese African campaigns of 1961–1974 that examines this complex subject as part of a coherent whole.

Clarence-Smith, W. Gervase. *The Third Portuguese Empire, 1875–1975: A Study in Economic Imperialism.* Manchester, U.K.: Manchester University Press, 1985. The best book of its kind on the economic development of overseas Portugal from the Scramble for Africa to the final days of empire.

Farwell, Byron. *The Great War in Africa, 1914–1918.* London: W. W. Norton and Company, 1986. This lively and dependable account of the African front in World War I is an impressive blend of action and analysis.

Newitt, Malyn. *A History of Mozambique.* London: C. Hurst & Co.; Bloomington: Indiana University Press, 1995. This highly readable book from a preeminent scholar gives an interesting and balanced account of the Portuguese settlement and fight for control of Mozambique until the final days of empire.

Newitt, Malyn. *Portugal in Africa, the Last Hundred Years.* London: Longman, 1981. Gives a balanced account of the Portuguese empire in Africa up to its final colonial war.

Pélissier, René. *La colonie du Minotaure: Nationalismes et révoltes en Angola, 1926–1961.* Orgeval, France: Pélissier, 1978. Describes the development of nationalism in Angola; the most complete account available in any language.

Pélissier, René. *Les guerres grises: Résistance et révoltes en Angola, 1885–1941.* Orgeval, France: Pélissier, 1977. This six-hundred-page volume is the most complete account of the Portuguese pacification of Angola in any language.

Pélissier, René. *Naissance de la Guiné: Portuguais et Africains en Sénégambie, 1841–1936.* Preface by Léopold Sédar Senghor. Orgeval, France: Pélissier, 1989. This French-language work is the most detailed of any on the Portuguese pacification of its tiny colony of Guinea.

Pélissier, René. *Naissance du Mozambique: Résistance et révoltes anticoloniales (1854–1918).* 2 vols. Orgeval, France: Pélissier, 1984. Addresses the pacification of Mozambique in a two-volume work that is the most complete in any language.

Pélissier, René. *Le naufrage des caravelles: Études sur la fin de l'empire Portugais (1961–1975).* Orgeval, France: Pélissier, 1979. Conclusion of Pélissier's trilogy on Portuguese pacification of Angola and the demise of the Portuguese empire.

Ribeiro de Meneses, Filipe. *Portugal 1914–1926: From the First World War to Military Dictatorship.* Bristol, U.K.: Hispanic, Portuguese, and Latin American Monographs, University of Bristol, 2004. The author takes an original look in a highly readable account at why Portugal engaged in World War I and relates how the war was perceived and waged by the Portuguese government.

Russell-Wood, A. J. R. *The Portuguese Empire, 1415–1808: A World on the Move.* Baltimore: Johns Hopkins University Press, 1998. This well-written and insightful volume provides the background to Portugal's continued search for modern prosperity.

Strachan, Hew. *The First World War in Africa.* Oxford and New York: Oxford University Press, 2004. Addresses the war from the perspectives of all the nations who fought in Africa during World War I.

Wheeler, Douglas L., and René Pélissier. *Angola.* London: Pall Mall Press, 1971. This highly readable book from two preeminent scholars gives a balanced account of the Portuguese empire in Africa up to the mid-1960s, with a prognosis for the future.

JOHN P. CANN

The Dutch Colonial Empire

The Dutch Empire of the nineteenth and twentieth centuries was constructed on the remnants of the possessions acquired by the Dutch East India Company and the Dutch West India Company in Asia and around the Atlantic during early modern times. The Dutch East India Company had been founded in 1602 and had become a sovereign statelike organization in Asia, with strongholds and territorial possessions from the Cape of Good Hope in the west to the little island of Dejima in Japan in the east. The center of the company's empire was the city of Batavia on Java. While extending its influence in Southeast Asia, the company experienced a deteriorating commercial position at the end of the eighteenth century. The British East India Company in particular was much more successful in the trade of tea and textiles than the Dutch East India Company. In 1799 the Dutch Batavian Republic took over the possessions of the company. The Dutch government, in 1791, had already bought the stocks of the Dutch West India Company, which had taken part in the African slave trade and at one time governed New Netherland (New York, New Jersey, and Connecticut), several Caribbean islands, Suriname, Guyana, and Brazil and had trading posts on the Gold Coast (now Ghana) and in Angola. During the Napoleonic Wars (1803–1815), the Dutch colonies around the world were occupied by the United Kingdom, with the exception of Dejima in Nagasaki Bay.

After the Napoleonic Wars, the major powers of Europe envisioned a strong Netherlands at the northern border of France. To create such a strong Dutch state, some colonies were returned to the Netherlands, most notably the Indonesian archipelago. Parts of the Atlantic empire were also returned, but the six little islands in the Caribbean, the colony of Suriname, and the posts on Africa's Gold Coast never rose to any importance for the Netherlands, especially after the Dutch finally abolished slavery in 1863. In 1871 the Netherlands even sold its possession on the Gold Coast to the United Kingdom, giving up any ambition to create a colonial empire on the African continent. The Netherlands was a small power in Europe, and subsequent Dutch governments realized that they could have only limited colonial ambitions in the world. Hence, in the nineteenth and twentieth centuries the Netherlands concentrated its energies on a potentially rich part of the world: the Indonesian archipelago.

War and Exploitation. In the East Indies the Dutch took over power from the British on 19 August 1816. Java had been ruled since 1811 by a young and ambitious English lieutenant-governor, Thomas Stamford Raffles. He had modernized the colonial state by abolishing the Dutch East India Company's system of forced deliveries of coffee and introducing freedom of trade and a new system of taxation, the land rent, which was premised upon the rights of the sovereign to ownership of all the land. The land was rented to village chiefs on Java, who in turn were responsible for collecting taxes on it. In 1816 the Dutch authorities retained the land-rent system, hoping the Javanese would start to produce cash crops for exports. However, this economic policy failed. Prices for coffee and sugar on the world market dropped, and this drop diminished both the income of Javanese farmers and the land-rent revenue of the colonial government. The Dutch East Indies became a financial burden for the Netherlands.

The Dutch position on Java further deteriorated in 1825. On central Java, a prominent prince in the court of Yogyakarta, Dipanagara, started an uprising against the Dutch presence that evolved into a full-scale war, the Java War (1825–1830). Dipanagara tried to defend the traditional position of the Javanese aristocracy and also believed that he had been chosen by divine powers to fight the Dutch by starting a holy war against them. He was widely believed to be Ratu Adil, the mythical Just King of old Javanese stories. It took the Dutch five years to defeat the guerrilla forces of Dipanagara, but finally their authority on Java was undisputed. During the war, an estimated 200,000 Javanese soldiers and 15,000 Dutch soldiers lost their lives.

Both the difficult financial position of the Dutch East Indies and the Java War led to a fundamental change in colonial policy. An influential Dutch military officer, Johannes van den Bosch, had already argued for a return to the old policies of the Dutch East India Company, claiming that these policies were much more suitable for an oriental society than the more liberal policies of the English lieutenant-governor Raffles and his immediate Dutch successors. In 1830 King William I appointed van den Bosch governor-general. Five years later he returned to the Netherlands to become minister of the colonies. Van den Bosch introduced the Cultivation System to Java. Rural villages were forced to allocate a maximum of one-fifth of their land to export crops like coffee, sugar, indigo, and tea,

The Dutch East India Company. The Dutch East India Company's ships docked in the harbor of Jepara, Java. *Recueil des voyages qui ont servi à l'établissement et aux progrez de la Compagnie des Indes Orientales*, by Constantin de Renneville, Rouen, 1725. COURTESY OF THE NEW YORK PUBLIC LIBRARY, ASTOR, LENOX, AND TILDEN FOUNDATIONS

and villagers had to supply labor for a maximum of one-fifth of the year. After 1836 villagers received full payment for their produce, with which they could pay their taxes, and eventually they were exempted from the land rent.

In practice, the Cultivation System was not a system at all. There occurred wide local and regional variations in applying the regulations, partly owing to differences in producing the different crops. The implementation of the Cultivation System was carried out by Dutch civil servants and local rulers, the so-called regents and their subordinate officials. Both colonial and Javanese officials received a percentage of the revenues, to stimulate them to make the system work.

For the Dutch and their Javanese collaborators, the Cultivation System became a huge success. Profits from the system amounted to between 19 and 31 percent of Dutch state revenues between 1834 and 1877. These profits erased the colonial government's deficits, financed the building of the Dutch railroad system, and funded the compensation of slaveholders after the abolition of slavery in the colony of Suriname. At a time when colonialism was rather unpopular in Europe, the Netherlands ran a very profitable colonial enterprise. After the British experienced a bloody revolt in India, a Calcutta-based British lawyer, J. W. B. Money, published a book titled *Java, or How to Manage a Colony* (1861).

Despite the success, critics of the Cultivation System argued for reform. Some of them pointed at the negative consequences for the Javanese population, but more important, the monopoly of the Dutch state in the trade of export crops was resented by an increasingly important liberal political party in the Netherlands. (Formal parties did not exist; there are political groupings within the parliament.) In 1870 the Dutch parliament passed two important laws, the Sugar Act and the Agrarian Act, mandating gradually abolishing the Cultivation System and opening the Dutch East Indies to private enterprise.

Dutch Imperialism in the Indonesian Archipelago. The opening of the Dutch East Indies to private enterprise coincided with the opening of the Suez Canal and the growth of colonial ambitions of other European powers. These three developments made the Dutch government discontinue its policy of concentrating on Java while leaving most other parts of the Indonesian archipelago more or less to themselves. Sumatra especially became of great importance in the latter part of the nineteenth century. Extensive rubber and tobacco plantations were established on Sumatra's East Coast, petroleum was found, and the main shipping route between Europe and East Asia went through the Strait of Malacca. In North Sumatra the independent sultanate of Aceh controlled a large portion of the pepper trade and challenged the Dutch by actively seeking relations with other Western countries.

In 1871 the Netherlands and the United Kingdom signed a treaty that gave the Dutch a free hand in Sumatra concerning Aceh. Two years later the Netherlands decided to incorporate Aceh into the Dutch East Indies. The capital was attacked, but the Acehnese continued to resist the Dutch by waging guerrilla warfare, which would last until 1903. The Aceh War was the longest and bloodiest in the history of the Dutch East Indies.

Many Acehnese saw their struggle against the Dutch as a holy war of Islam against a Christian power. The colonial authorities were very aware that they ruled a predominantly Islamic population. Hence, the promotion of Christianity was restricted to those parts of the archipelago with non-Muslim populations. The principal architect of colonial Islamic policy became Christiaan Snouck Hurgronje, a Leiden-trained scholar of Arabic who had gone to Mecca to study Indonesian pilgrims and served as adviser to the Netherlands Indies government from 1891 to 1904. With regard to the war in Aceh, he advocated persecuting extremist Muslim teachers and strengthening the position of local chiefs. Together with the new antiguerrilla tactics of the Dutch colonial army, Snouck Hurgronje's policy succeeded in defeating the Acehnese.

After successfully ending the Aceh War, the Dutch colonial government, under Governor-General J. B. van Heutsz, established its full authority on all the islands of the Indonesian archipelago. Sometimes this expansion of Dutch authority met with fierce resistance. On Bali, several military expeditions were necessary to suppress the opposition of local Hindu kings. Some of the kings and their families, including women and children, realizing that their ancient world was crumbling, committed suicide on a massive scale. In the end, van Heutsz created a powerful and centralized colonial state, with an extensive colonial civil service that in many parts of the archipelago used local elites to rule. One can argue that modern-day Indonesia in large part was created by the Dutch at the beginning of the twentieth century.

In the meantime, other European powers established vast new empires in Africa and greatly extended their power in Asia. The Netherlands was a minor player in this game. Being a small power in Europe, it deliberately did not take part in the Scramble for Africa, but rather concentrated its energy on the Indonesian archipelago, building up a strong colonial state and making sure that other powers did not conquer parts of it.

Toward a Modern Colonial State. The first part of the twentieth century saw an expansion of the Dutch presence in Southeast Asia. The colonial state intervened more and more in the indigenous society, Western companies became more active in the region, and the number of Europeans in the colony rose dramatically. In 1880 fewer than 60,000 Europeans lived in the Dutch East Indies, a number that would rise to more than 240,000 by 1930. The number of European women rose even more dramatically. In 1880 only 481 European women for every 1,000 European men lived in the Dutch East Indies, a ratio that would increase to 884:1,000 by 1930. A significant consequence of this development was the increasingly segregated nature of European colonial society. In the nineteenth century, many European men had relations with indigenous women, making them familiar with the nature of the local society. In the twentieth century most Europeans lived in segregated neighborhoods in the cities.

Many Europeans worked for large companies producing raw materials for the world economy. Rubber plantations were established on a large scale in the early twentieth century, particularly on Sumatra's East Coast, with American and other foreign investment playing a major role. Besides rubber, petroleum became the most important export product. In 1890 the Royal Dutch Petroleum Company (Koninklijke Nederlandse Petroleum Maatschappij) was established, and in 1907 it merged with Shell Transport and Trading Company, a British company, to become Royal Dutch Shell, which controlled around 85 percent of oil production in the Indonesian archipelago before World War II.

One Dutch group did maintain close relations with the indigenous society: the colonial civil servants. Many of them were inspired by the famous novel *Max Havelaar* (1860), by Multatuli, the pen name of a colonial civil servant, Eduard Douwes Dekker. In the novel, the protagonist, Max Havelaar, tries to battle against a corrupt government system in Java that allowed the local aristocratic elite to suppress the population in exchange for cooperation with the colonial state. The solution advocated by Multatuli was a more direct and just rule by unselfish colonial civil servants like himself. At the end of the nineteenth century, more and more inspired young Dutchmen went to Southeast Asia to develop and "civilize" the indigenous population.

This attitude even became official government policy in 1901, when the so-called ethical policy was inaugurated.

Christian parties in the Netherlands had already called for a more just colonial policy, and liberal politicians had argued for returning the profits of the Cultivation System to the colony. The latter spoke of a "debt of honor." The growing poverty among the Javanese at the end of the nineteenth century finally made the Dutch government change its policy. The ethical policy had two main objectives. First, it tried to develop Indonesian society by promoting irrigation, better agricultural techniques, and education. Second, it sought to develop the colonial state in the direction of self-government. The first, more technical part of the ethical policy would be a partial success. The densely populated island of Java would again become an exporter of rice, many Indonesians would receive an elementary education for the first time, a system of microcredit would empower small indigenous farmers and businessmen, and the public-health situation would improve.

Many realized that education was the key to developing Indonesian society. Some, such as Snouck Hurgronje, advocated an "association policy," which meant educating only the indigenous elite, but the colonial government under van Heutsz choose a much more basic education for the masses. Only a small group of Indonesians could enter schools of higher education. Some of them went to the Netherlands, but many of them were trained at institutions like the Bandung Institute of Technology (Technische Hogeschool Bandung, founded in 1920), the Law School at Batavia (founded in 1924), the Medical School (1927), or the School for Arts and Humanities (1940).

However limited, a small modern Indonesian elite emerged in the first decades of the twentieth century. It did not take long for members of this elite to realize that they were still considered second-class citizens, despite their education. They were not accepted in European social circles and the highest positions in the colonial civil service remained reserved for the Dutch. Despite the partial success of the ethical policy, the Dutch failed to convince the emerging modern Indonesian elite of their good intentions.

The Rise of a Nationalist Movement. Slowly an Indonesian national identity emerged among the modern elite, although its members originated in different parts of the archipelago and had different ethnic and religious backgrounds. As a group, they were treated by the Dutch as inlanders or natives. Treated as a group, they reacted as a group, and developed a common Indonesian identity.

On 20 May 1908 a group of Javanese medical students founded the Budi Utomo Society, which advocated modernizing Javanese culture and providing greater educational opportunities for the elite. Although Budi Utomo never became a mass movement, it is considered to be a forerunner of later, more explicitly nationalist political organizations, such as Sarekat Islam, which was founded in 1911. The founding of the latter society was a response to the economically more successful Chinese, who challenged the position of the indigenous Javanese in the marketplace. This society quickly developed into a political organization that strove democratic reform of the colonial state.

At first colonial administrators and politicians welcomed the emergence of the nationalist movement. They saw it as a success of their ethical policy. In response, the liberal minister of the colonies Thomas B. Pleijte, together with Governor-General Johan Paul graaf van Limburg Stirum (count of Limburg Stirum), developed plans for a more democratic colonial state, with autonomous districts, and for more democratic municipalities, with elected councils. In 1916 a semiparliament was created. Called the Volksraad, or People's Council, it had a chairman, nineteen appointed members, and nineteen elected members; fifteen of them representing the indigenous population. The Volksraad first convened in 1918.

In the meantime, the nationalist movement, of which Sarekat Islam was the most important party, quickly radicalized. Riots between Chinese and Javanese in the town of Kudus, rumors about the activities of a secretive revolutionary Section B of Sarekat Islam, and pressure from conservative Dutch citizens living in Indonesia made the Dutch government and the colonial authorities in Indonesia rethink their policies. After 1919 a much more conservative policy was implemented, and this policy eventually turned the Dutch East Indies into a police state.

In December 1925 radical nationalists led by the leadership of the small Communist Party of Indonesia (Partai Komunis Indonesia) planned a general strike, to be followed by an uprising against the Dutch. This revolt was started on 12–13 November 1926, but was quickly suppressed by the colonial authorities, who arrested some 13,000 persons, of whom some 4,500 eventually received jail sentences. Some 800 nationalists were exiled for an indefinite period to a remote camp on New Guinea: Boven-Digoel.

All the measures taken by the colonial authorities could not defeat the nationalist movement. Even though the colonial state took all kinds of repressive actions, it still had to act within the legal limits of the colonial constitution, which was based on European democratic and liberal models. Careful nationalists still had room to maneuver, for instance in the Volksraad. After the failed Communist revolution, a new generation of nationalist leaders came to the forefront. One of them was Sukarno, or Soekarno (1901–1970), in 1921 one of the first six indigenous students of the Bandung Institute of Technology. While at this institute, he became convinced that the nationalist movement should pursue a policy of noncooperation and should base its ideology on a mixture of nationalism, Islam, and Marxism. On 4 July 1927, U.S. Independence Day, Sukarno founded the Union of Indonesian Nationalists (Perserikatan Nasional Indonesia), which openly strove for Indonesian independence. The leaders of the party, including Sukarno, were arrested in 1929. They were sentenced to relatively short jail terms, but in 1933 the colonial authorities decided to arrest them once again and exile them to various remote places in the archipelago.

The deeper reasons for the change in Dutch colonial policies were complex. One reason was that after 1900 most Dutch in Indonesia lost touch with the indigenous society because the sharp rise in the number of European women resulted in Europeans being segregated in certain sections of the cities. Many Dutch did not notice important changes in Indonesian society and started to consider nationalists as peripheral and hence negligible. Another reason was the desire of many colonial administrators to control the development of the indigenous society on a more or less permanent basis. Nationalists, whose ambition was to become independent, also from the well-meaning colonial administrators, were considered dangerous for the future of the country. Finally, Dutch cognoscenti of colonial affairs increasingly stressed the "oriental" character of Indonesian society, which Western-educated nationalists would never be able to lead. They considered the traditional elites to be the true leaders of Indonesia.

War, Revolution, and Decolonization. World War II struck a mortal blow to the Dutch empire. In Europe the Netherlands was occupied by Germany; in Southeast Asia, Japan defeated the Dutch in a short period of time. The Dutch surrendered in Indonesia on 8 March 1942. The Japanese occupation of Indonesia had many important consequences. Europeans were imprisoned in special camps and lost their prewar prestige. To mobilize the Javanese for the Japanese war effort, nationalist leaders such as Sukarno were set free and could address the Javanese population over the radio. Javanese youths were trained in a semimilitary fashion. But the Japanese occupation also meant hardship for the Indonesian population. Many Indonesians were sent as laborers to other parts of Southeast Asia to work under very difficult circumstances. During the last year of the war, the Indonesian economy collapsed, bringing hunger and devastation, especially to the urban areas of Java. An estimated number of 4 million Indonesians died as a consequence of Japanese occupation.

In September 1944, Japanese Prime Minister Koiso Kuniaki promised the occupied countries of Asia a form of independence. However, the preparations for the independence of Indonesia were only shortly under way when Japan surrendered on 15 August 1945. As a consequence, Sukarno did not know how to proceed on to road to independence. In the end, radical youths persuaded him and his fellow nationalist Mohammad Hatta to proclaim Indonesia's independence unilaterally on 17 August.

The Netherlands did not recognize this declaration of independence. For many Dutch, Sukarno came close to being a war criminal for his collaboration with the Japanese during the war. Under the leadership of Lieutenant-Governor-General H. J. van Mook, the Dutch tried to regain their position in Southeast Asia. They quickly realized that the Republic of Indonesia was paramount on the islands of Java and Sumatra. Van Mook eventually followed the same course as the French in Indochina, proposing the establishment of a "United States of Indonesia," which would become part of the "Netherlands-Indonesian Union." The Indonesian Republic would be only one state of these proposed United States. In November 1946, in the mountain village of Linggadjati, a commission-general representing the Dutch government agreed with the government of the Republic of Indonesia on forming a *sovereign* United States of Indonesia. However, the Dutch parliament changed this agreement and asked the Dutch government to work for the establishment of a sovereign Netherlands-Indonesian Union with a *subordinate* United States of Indonesia. Clearly, this was not acceptable to the government of Indonesia. Efforts to reach a compromise failed, and in July 1947 a war broke out between the Netherlands and Indonesia and lasted well into 1949. It was not a continuous war: the United Nations stopped the first Dutch assault on the Republic of Indonesia already in August 1947. The second all-out attack of the Dutch army took place in December 1948 and sought to destroy the Republic of Indonesia completely. The Dutch failed, for several reasons. First, even those members of the Indonesian elite who were willing to cooperate with the Dutch in the end sided with Sukarno. Second, the Dutch army failed to defeat the Indonesian army. And third, the United States of America forced the Dutch to accept Indonesian independence, since it was confident that Sukarno could be a reliable anti-Communist Third World leader. Sovereignty over the archipelago was finally handed over on 27 December 1949.

Postcolonial Netherlands. It was difficult for the Netherlands to leave its colonial past behind. In 1949 it held onto the western part of New Guinea. There the Dutch government started a massive development project to prepare the territory for full independence, separate from Indonesia. After Indonesia threatened with an invasion and the United States applied strong pressure, the Dutch handed over the territory to a temporary UN administration in 1962.

In the meantime, relations between the Netherlands and its colonies in the Caribbean were transformed. In 1954 both the Netherlands Antilles and Suriname became self-governing, with the Netherlands retaining control of defense and foreign affairs. In the 1970s a progressive Dutch government wanted to free itself from its colonial legacy. It found an ally with the Creole Party in Suriname, which dominated the local government. Negotiations resulted in independence for Suriname in 1975. However, roughly half the population, fearing that the new country would see violent ethnic conflict, immigrated to the Netherlands. The Netherlands Antilles resisted Dutch attempts to make them independent. The people of these islands remained Dutch citizens, a status that gave them the right to settle in the Netherlands, which many of them eventually did.

Ironically, at the end of the twentieth century the Netherlands had more problems in coming to terms with its colonial activities in the Atlantic than in its colonial past in Southeast Asia, although the latter had been much more important. Hundreds of thousands of immigrants from Suriname and the Netherlands Antilles reminded the Dutch of a long-forgotten past in which the Netherlands had been actively engaged in the Atlantic slave trade. At a time when Indonesia became, for most Dutch, nothing more than a popular vacation destination, their history with regard to slavery started to haunt them. An attempt to put this past to rest was made on 1 July 2002, when a National Monument Commemorating Slavery was dedicated in Amsterdam. Nevertheless, the impact of Dutch imperialism remains visible, not only in the Netherlands, but also on the Netherlands Antilles, in Suriname, and in Indonesia.

[*See also* Caribbean, *subentry* The Dutch Caribbean; Decolonization, *subentry* Belize; East India Company, British; East India Company, Dutch; *and* Java War.]

BIBLIOGRAPHY
Anderson, Benedict. *Java in a Time of Revolution: Occupation and Resistance, 1944–1946.* Ithaca, N.Y.: Cornell University Press, 1972.

Carey, Peter. "Waiting for the 'Just King': The Agrarian World of South-Central Java from Giyanti (1755) to the Java War (1825–30)." *Modern Asian Studies* 20 (1986): 59–137.

Cheong, Yong Mun. *H. J. van Mook and Indonesian Independence: A Study of His Role in Dutch-Indonesian Relations, 1945–48.* The Hague, The Netherlands: Martinus Nijhoff, 1982.

De Jong, Louis. *The Collapse of a Colonial Society: The Dutch in Indonesia during the Second World War.* Leiden, The Netherlands: KITLV Press, 2002.

Elson, Robert E. *Village Java under the Cultivation System, 1830–1870.* Sydney, Australia: Allen and Unwin, 1994.

Fasseur, C. *The Politics of Colonial Exploitation: Java, the Dutch, and the Cultivation System.* Ithaca, N.Y.: Southeast Asia Program, Cornell University, 1992.

Kahin, George McTurnan. *Nationalism and Revolution in Indonesia.* Ithaca, N.Y.: Cornell University Press, 2003.

Kartodirdjo, Sartono. *Modern Indonesia, Tradition and Transformation: A Socio-historical Perspective.* 2d ed. Yogyakarta, Indonesia: Gadjah Mada University Press, 1988.

Kuitenbrouwer, Maarten. *The Netherlands and the Rise of Modern Imperialism: Colonies and Foreign Policy, 1870–1902.* Translated by Hugh Beyer. New York: Berg, 1991.

Legge, John D. *Sukarno: A Political Biography.* 3d ed. Singapore: Archipelago Press, 2003.

Locher-Scholten, Elisabeth. *Women and the Colonial State: Essays on Gender and Modernity in the Netherlands Indies, 1900–1942.* Amsterdam: Amsterdam University Press, 2000.

Oostindie, Gert, and Inge Klinkers. *Decolonising the Caribbean: Dutch Policies in a Comparative Perspective.* Amsterdam: Amsterdam University Press, 2003.

Ricklefs, Merle C. *A History of Modern Indonesia since c. 1200.* 3d ed. Basingstoke, U.K.: Palgrave, 2001.

Shiraishi, Takashi. *An Age in Motion: Popular Radicalism in Java, 1912–1926.* Ithaca, N.Y.: Cornell University Press, 1990.

Van den Doel, H. W. *Afscheid van Indië: De val van het Nederlandse imperium in Azië.* 3d ed. Amsterdam: Prometheus, 2001.

Van Niel, Robert. *The Emergence of the Modern Indonesian Elite.* The Hague, The Netherlands: W. van Hoeve, 1960.

Van Niel, Robert. *Java under the Cultivation System: Collected Writings.* Leiden, The Netherlands: KITLV Press, 1992.

WIM VAN DEN DOEL

The British Colonial Empire

The British Empire began in the late sixteenth century and ended in the mid- to late twentieth century. At its height, it ruled over 450 million people, covering over 14 million square miles (22.5 million square kilometers). The "first" British Empire began in the late sixteenth century and was comprised of Ireland, the West Indian colonies, and British North America. It lasted until the American Revolutionary War ended in 1783. The "second" British Empire began at this date, passing through several phases. In the first phase, Britain focused on expansion in South and Southeast Asia, extending its hegemony over the Indian subcontinent and capturing several Asian territories. The British also acquired territory in the Pacific, particularly Australia and New Zealand. This phase ended in the 1880s, when a period of "new imperialism" emerged that saw Britain expand its empire dramatically in Africa and the Middle East. The British Empire had several important effects on world history, heavily influencing political, social, and economic relationships around the globe. It continues to explain and provide context to many issues facing the postcolonial world, including economic development in nonindustrialized states, ethnic or religious rivalries in India, the Middle East, and Malaysia, and social problems relating to gender and racial equity and the development of civil society.

The Emergence of the Second Empire. The mid-eighteenth century represents a watershed in British imperial history. The first empire, beyond its American and Irish possessions, consisted of numerous coastal trading stations, the most important of which were those along the West African coast used as collection and exchange points for slaves destined for plantations in the New World. Also important were those in the littoral areas of India, owned by the British East India Company (EIC) and intended to channel some of the lucrative South Asian trade in spices, minerals, and textiles to Britain and away from European rivals.

The Seven Years' War resulted in a dramatic expansion of British imperial territory. This conflict pitted the colonial states of France and Spain against Britain and thus the war became a global affair. When Britain emerged as the victor in 1763, the French gave up any claims on North America east of the Mississippi River, recognized the new reality of British supremacy in the West Indies, and gave up its West African colony of Senegal, a crucial departure point for slaves. The Spanish ceded Florida to the British in return for the restoration of their colonies in the Philippines and Cuba. Thus in the course of a few years, the British had almost doubled the territory of its empire.

Meanwhile, in India, the British East India Company changed its role on the subcontinent from a trading company to a territorial power after the Battle of Plassey in 1757, which resulted in the company's acquisition of Bengal. By 1765 the EIC had obtained the sole right to collect taxes, and in the next few decades it introduced new taxation schemes that enriched collectors, undermined the ability of farmers to maintain small holdings, and virtually eliminated communal forms of land ownership. In 1773, economic and political difficulties stemming from the rapid extension of power caused the British government to pass the Regulating Act, which increased its direct role in India by approving company directors and appointing a governor responsible for overseeing what had grown to the three presidencies of Bengal, Bombay, and Madras.

Slavery and Abolition. The institution of slavery was critical for the first British Empire. By the eighteenth century, British sugar colonies in the West Indies produced nearly 50 percent of all the sugar consumed in the world. Until the 1820s, sugar was Britain's largest import. The intensive labor required for sugar production stimulated the African slave trade to the New World. Britain was the most active slave-trading state by the late eighteenth century, but at the same time organizations developed in Britain itself opposed to slavery and calling for abolition. As early as the 1770s, Quakers instituted a boycott of businesses involved with the trade and in 1787 the Society for the Abolition of the Slave Trade was formed. However, West Indian planters had considerable political power, and it was not until much later that abolition was seriously considered by Parliament. The West Indies gradually started to diminish in economic importance, a process accelerated by the loss of the American colonies and industrialization in Britain. This fact, combined with the emerging doctrine of free trade that criticized forced labor and the overwhelming evidence of the brutalities of the slave system, led to the abolition of the slave trade in 1807. Still, slavery continued to exist in the British Americas until 1834 and when it was finally abolished, slave owners were compensated with millions of pounds and were guaranteed labor through the "apprenticeship" program that forced slaves to stay with their masters for at least seven years.

The Napoleonic Wars. The chaotic conditions in Europe caused by the French Revolution and the Napoleonic period led to new challenges and opportunities for British imperialism. In Ireland, uprisings by Catholics against the ruling class of Protestant Anglicans resulted in the formal annexation of Ireland by Britain. The British desire to protect its commerce and its territories in India during the wars also led the government to sanction the capture of remaining French and Dutch possessions in the West Indies, as well as Dutch colonies in Southeast Asia and southern Africa. At the Congress of Vienna, several of these colonies were returned, but those considered crucial to the protection of India and British trade, including Cape Colony in South Africa and parts of the Malaysian peninsula, were retained. In South Africa, the formalization of Cape Colony as British territory created the context for future confrontations between Britons, Dutch Afrikaners who had settled there in the seventeenth century, and indigenous Africans. In the Malayan peninsula, the British

split the area into several administrative regions, some of which—like the Straits Settlements—were controlled directly by the British Crown, and others that were allied to Britain under indigenous leaders.

The direct control of the Straits Settlements under the Crown represented an important shift in British imperial policy. Previously, the British had taken two approaches to political administration in their colonies. Either settlers were allowed to form institutions of limited self-rule, as was the case in the Americas, or territory was administered by a proxy, such as by the EIC in India. This period saw the emergence of the "Crown Colony," areas directly controlled by the metropolitan government with an administration not answerable to any peoples (indigenous or otherwise) living therein. Crown colonies would become a common way to organize new territorial acquisitions, especially in places with large indigenous populations considered "unfit" to control their own affairs.

India Under the EIC. India increasingly came under the authority of the EIC between the late eighteenth century and 1857. After the loss of the American colonies, the importance of India to the empire increased dramatically. In 1784, the India Act enlarged government oversight of the EIC and established a Board of Control charged with overseeing the activities of the company. Its character shifted from a mere trading company to a full-blown government as more and more territory came under its direct rule, including the Carnatic in 1801, Sind in 1843, and Oudh in 1856. By the 1850s, the British had established direct rule even in central India, in Saugor and Narbada. Those territories not directly controlled still found themselves under British influence through treaties that severely limited the ability of local rulers to exert much control outside of religious or cultural issues. Some growth occurred outside of India proper, such as in parts of Burma in the 1820s, Ceylon in 1815, and Mauritius in 1810. Eventually, these territories were reorganized as separate political entities, but for several decades they were administered as part of EIC India rather than Crown colonies or protectorates. These expansions were supported by the growth of the EIC armed forces that, by the middle of the nineteenth century, boasted almost 250,000 troops. The army was comprised primarily of Indian soldiers, known as sepoys, who were commanded by a small cadre of British officers.

While approaches to local religious, cultural, and political structures in India were as diverse as those structures themselves, it is possible to identify two major strands of imperial thought. Paternalism stressed maintaining local structures as much as possible under the belief that significant social reform would not only be expensive, but ultimately unsuccessful due to the inability of "backward" indigenous people to comprehend enlightened Western society. This view typically predominated in newly established colonies where serious attempts at reform could only be of a limited nature and thus was the preferred approach of the EIC before the 1820s. However, by 1813 when the EIC charter renewal allowed missionaries into India, a shift toward more direct interference developed. New EIC administrators, trained at institutions emerging in Britain designed specifically to produce colonial elites, saw little value in maintaining local political and social structures and instead sought to Westernize India. Thomas Macaulay, a member of the Bengali government, published a statement against traditional forms of Indian education in 1835 that proposed the substitution of a Western curriculum in order to create an indigenous administrative class. Women were often the target of reforms. Blind to their own patriarchal culture, the British increasingly tried to "protect" Indian women from their "oppressive" society by passing laws against the relatively rare and high-caste practice of sati (widow burning) and restructuring the ability of women to remarry. A fundamental problem with these reforms is that they tended to be based on practices of the highest castes (being the most familiar to administrators) and had the effect of reifying social institutions that had been more diverse and flexible.

China and Informal Empire. By the early nineteenth century, mercantilist economic policies were beginning to fall out of favor. Britain, now the clear leader among European colonial powers, no longer benefited from strict controls on most goods. Industrialization created an environment where Britain was the main supplier of manufactured goods and the primary importer of raw materials, a situation that made it the main beneficiary of free exchange. Over the course of the nineteenth century, Britain began to loosen its grip on economic exchanges and demanded that other nations follow suit. This new economic policy precipitated a subtle change in British imperial policy. It was no longer necessary to politically control sources of raw materials if local leaders agreed to the principles of free-trade. This marked the beginning "informal empire." The dominance of British economic power was visible in many parts of the world, such as in Argentina and Brazil, the Persian Gulf state of Bahrain, and the Kingdom of Siam (Thailand) that signed a free-trade treaty with Britain in 1855, but perhaps there is no greater example of "informal empire" than China.

Direct access to Chinese markets had long been the ultimate goal of European merchants. However, Europe produced few products that interested China, and using cash was prohibitively expensive. The answer was found in opium, an addictive product that, after a time, created its own self-sustaining market. This was a key reason why India was so important to the British Empire. Poppies could be grown there, and indeed as soon as Bengal was captured, opium production began in earnest. By the 1820s, India shipped over nine hundred tons of opium to China annually, even though its importation was illegal. The Chinese Qing government objected to this and in 1839 confiscated an entire year's worth of Indian opium. This sparked the first of two Opium Wars. The EIC army, supported by the Royal Navy, quickly defeated Chinese forces around Canton and coerced the Chinese into signing the Treaty of Nanjing in 1842. This granted the British access to several ports with low tariffs as well as the island of Hong Kong. However, importation of opium remained illegal until the Second Opium War of 1856–1860, in which a combined force of British, French, and American troops forced China to open up even more treaty ports, allow foreign missionaries, and legalize opium importation. China did not become a formal British colony at the conclusion of the Opium Wars, but its sovereignty with respect to trade was seriously compromised.

The Consolidation of Empire. Despite the shift toward Asian expansion and non-settler colonies, Britain still maintained several settler colonies in various parts of the world. By the middle of the nineteenth century, these colonies had significantly increased in population and began to exhibit an equalized distribution of men and women. Over time, calls for greater self-government were being heard. The British were ambivalent toward this movement. On one hand, self-government took much of the administrative and economic burden away from Britain. However, it could also open the door to independence and increase the chance of political and social instability.

British North America was the first territory to experiment with self-government. Two rebellions broke out in 1837, both concerned to some degree with the lack of political freedom. The solution was found in an 1839 report by Lord Durham, the new Governor General of Canada, which recommended "responsible government." Responsible government was political reorganization that established local lawmaking bodies responsible to the electorate rather than to metropolitan Britain or colonial officials. As these legislatures only had authority over internal affairs, foreign policy and trade continued to be controlled centrally. In 1840, the United Province of Canada was formed, uniting Lower and Upper Canada in a bid to weaken the power of French Catholics. This action was unpopular among Canadians and was repealed in 1867, when the British North America Act joined Upper and Lower Canada, New Brunswick, and Nova Scotia into the federal Dominion of Canada. In the next decade, the Dominion was augmented by British Columbia and Manitoba.

Australia grew rapidly as well in this period. Despite the struggles of the first convict colonies, settler populations increased. This encouraged the growth of new colonies outside of New South Wales, such as Van Diemen's Land (Tasmania) in 1825 and South Australia in 1836. Initially, colonists were greeted with generous grants of land to encourage settlement and agricultural production. Even convicts could obtain land after their sentences were completed. In the 1830s, the British government provided more fiscal incentives to bolster colonization and these were successful in encouraging viable families to settle there. However, this growth had a catastrophic impact on indigenous Australians, also called Aborigines, who numbered about 350,000 in the late eighteenth century. As more land was appropriated for settled agriculture and more colonists moved toward the interior, Aborigine numbers drastically declined from disease and malnutrition. The antagonism of the settlers exacerbated this decline; Aborigines were considered by many to be subhuman and were expelled from productive land with virtually no concern about their well-being or survival. By the 1850s, settler colonies had grown sufficiently to warrant self-rule. Responsible government spread rapidly with New South Wales, Victoria, Tasmania, and South Australia gaining parliaments in 1855, followed by Queensland and the Northern Territory at the end of the decade. Beginning in the 1790s, New Zealand was visited by various European ships engaged in whaling or sealing. For the next several decades, Europeans interacted with the indigenous Maori sporadically and without any government oversight. Some bought land from the Maori but different conceptions of land ownership caused conflict. Importation of European firearms led to a series of Musket Wars between various Maori groups in the 1830s until the technology spread to most indigenous communities. Missionaries became increasingly concerned about the lawless nature of European and Maori interaction, and encouraged the British, who had a technical claim on the islands since 1788, to intervene. In 1840, the Treaty of Waitangi was signed between the Maori and the British government, recognizing British sovereignty over New Zealand but also, unusually, recognizing Maori ownership of land. British settlement activities increased rapidly in the post-treaty period and by the 1850s most of the individual colonies were granted self-rule, culminating in the New Zealand Constitution Act of 1852 that united the island under responsible government. Demands for the Maori to sell more land increased, leading to many communities being completely dispossessed. Maori anger resulted in the New Zealand Land Wars of the 1860s and the 1870s that saw the defeat of organized Maori military resistance but established a small number of Maori seats in the New Zealand parliament. New Zealand's economy grew rapidly, shifting from wool to meat production in the late nineteenth century with the advent of refrigerated ships. It was granted dominion status in 1907.

Imperial Motivations. The British had no single motivation driving the expansion of their empire. The reasons for growth were as diverse as the territories governed. However, there are several general categories of motivation that can be identified. A central concern for Britain was finding new opportunities to encourage economic growth. Britain had a limited set of products it could produce, either for domestic or foreign consumption. Conquering other regions with different climates, geology, and biospheres allowed Britain access to a much wider variety of goods.

Direct political control is not necessary to obtain foreign goods, but Britain often chose this path in order to maximize profitability and minimize interference from local governments. Exchanges of goods depended upon stability and expansion of British territory was tied to concerns about weak local governments and the aggressive postures of neighboring states. How the empire benefited Britain economically is debated among historians. Indeed, some scholars argue that imperialism only benefited a small cadre of wealthy capitalists and was largely detrimental to the general populace of Britain.

Strategic concerns regarding intra-European rivalries also played a role. By the nineteenth century, for example, Britain and Russia vied for control over central Asia in what became known as the "Great Game," where the British government in India funneled financial and military resources into India's northwest frontier and Afghanistan to protect British India from Russian incursions. Yet while economic and strategic concerns represented pragmatic motivations for empire, they did little to dissipate moral qualms regarding the subjugation of vast numbers of the global population. Throughout the nineteenth century, but particularly toward its close, the idea of the civilizing mission emerged as a powerful moral justification for empire. Britons were convinced of the superiority of their culture and race, and sought to expand the benefits of their enlightened society to the rest of the world. Throughout the empire, doctors, feminists, missionaries, and engineers worked to reform what they saw as backward, barbaric societies.

Concerns about the plight of indigenous women often played a major role in the civilizing mission. From the British perspective, most colonial women were oppressed by patriarchal societies that condoned such practices as child marriage, polygamy, and limitations on remarriage. Without understanding either the cultural reasons why such institutions existed or their own poor track record with women's rights, the British attacked indigenous conceptions of gender in multiple ways, through legislation or educational institutions developed for girls to be trained in how to be "proper" women.

Often the vanguard of colonial reformist movements was the spread of missionaries. By the end of the nineteenth century over ten thousand missions had been established in various parts of the empire. However, missionaries frequently faced lukewarm receptions from colonial administrators as their presence was seen to undermine social stability and conflicted with the policy of paternalism. Indeed, missionaries were often quite critical of colonial policies they saw as exploitative, including unfair economic processes, the sexual exploitation of women by indigenous or colonial men, and lack of access to educational or medical services. They even meddled with the society of the colonial administrative class, undermining the masculine culture of drinking and womanizing that typified colonies where British women were few. While the missionaries believed themselves to have the best interests of colonial subjects in mind, they were nonetheless constrained by their own worldview and rarely gave support to existing social or cultural structures.

The Scramble for Africa. All of these motivations and justifications appeared in the most rapid era of expansion of the British Empire, the Scramble for Africa. Before the late nineteenth century, British influence in Africa rarely extended much beyond a collection of coastal trading forts. There were some exceptions: Sierra Leone, established as a colony for freed slaves in 1787, the southern African territories such as the Cape Colony, and the Gambia River estuary, which had been under British control since 1783 and was incorporated as a Crown Colony in 1843. In the mid-nineteenth century, Africa represented

one of the last unexplored regions of the world. Mungo Park explored the watershed of the Niger River in 1795, but more famous expeditions such as David Livingstone's travels across Africa to trace the Zambezi River and find the source of the Nile, Richard Burton's discovery of the African Great Lakes, and John Speke's discovery of Lake Victoria all occurred in the late 1840s to early 1860s. However, concerted attempts to gain new territory did not develop until the 1880s. As was often the case, the first steps of British expansion were reactionary.

For several decades Europeans had enjoyed unequal trading treaties and immunity from local laws in Ottoman Egypt. In 1855 the Suez Canal was constructed and in 1875 Britain purchased a 44 percent share of the company that controlled it. However, the Ottoman Empire was weakening and the situation in Egypt became chaotic. Fearful that British interests would no longer be respected and that investments would be lost, the British directly intervened in Egyptian affairs in 1882. Limited military action only worsened the situation, so Britain occupied Egypt, although it remained formally under Ottoman control.

This began a process of land-grabbing on the African continent unparalleled in history. There were two primary reasons for this. First was the growing balance of trade deficit that most European countries, especially Britain, were facing. To some, Africa seemed to represent a huge marketplace that could solve the problem of overproduction of manufactured goods. More importantly, new imperial powers were beginning to make their mark, particularly Belgium and a newly unified Germany. Africa was the preferred location for these new imperial powers to expand, as it was one of the few regions remaining that was not already divided into formal empires or spheres of influence. In 1882, Belgium under King Leopold II entered into treaties with various Congolese communities that laid the groundwork for the establishment of the Congo Free State. Amid European concerns that such land-grabbing might provoke war between European powers, in 1884 the Berlin Conference determined how to divide Africa among the various European claimants. Britain was hesitant about this process, believing that the costs of large-scale territorial acquisitions would outweigh any benefits. Nonetheless, the British did establish a number of companies operating under charters, such as the Royal Niger Company and the Imperial British East African Company, both established in 1886, and the British South Africa Company in 1889 to administer the future Rhodesia under the leadership of Cecil Rhodes. This was necessary because the Berlin Conference required "effective occupation" and for half a decade British intervention in its new territories was slight. However, by the mid-1890s the British were flexing their muscle, establishing new forms of agricultural production, sending white settlers to Rhodesia and British East Africa (Kenya) and building railroads and telegraph networks to link their vast African holdings.

British expansion in Africa led to a conflict with serious ramifications for the public perception of empire. This conflict was not between indigenous Africans and European imperialists, but between two different waves of European settlers. The Afrikaners, who had established several independent states north of British South Africa and were allowed to remain outside the sphere of British political control, faced increased tensions with Britain owing to the discovery of gold in Transvaal and the entrance of British settlers into the Afrikaner republic.

War between the Afrikaner states and Britain broke out in 1899 (the Second Boer War) after it was clear that neither side would back down over demands relating to sovereignty and the place of British immigrants in Afrikaner territory. The war initially went poorly for the British, but when reinforcements arrived, the British captured the capital cities of the republics. However, the Afrikaners launched a campaign of guerrilla warfare that lasted for two years. The British response was brutal. They pursued a scorched earth policy and established concentration camps where thousands of Afrikaners and indigenous Africans were interred under terrible conditions. Slowly, the British extended their control over the hinterlands and sapped Afrikaner resolve. The war ended in 1902, but the large number of British deaths (about seven thousand due to conflict and fourteen thousand due to disease) and the brutality of the British campaign made the war quite unpopular back home. It was at this point that serious questions about the desirability and morality of empire began to be raised in earnest in Britain.

India under the Raj. Developments in India continued to be crucial to the British Empire. In 1857 the Indian Rebellion broke out in several parts of the colony. The putative cause was both Hindu and Muslim objections to the use of pork and beef grease on the cartridges given to the Indian Army, but deeper causes included racism, anger over the considerable tax burden imposed by the EIC, reforms aimed at the army, and further territorial encroachments. It took the British over a year to suppress the revolt and it made clear how ineffectual company governance was. In 1858 the East India Company was dissolved and replaced with direct British rule, inaugurating the British Raj, which controlled India until independence.

Fear of further revolts of indigenous armies led to a substantial increase in British-born troops until independence, numbering at least sixty thousand. Administrative changes were introduced as well, although largely a process of codifying laws, clarifying legal gray areas, and amassing considerable data concerning population, revenues, land ownership and tenure, and agricultural production.

More intensive rule meant more British administrators, thus increasing the British population in India. Although never a significant portion of the overall population, this led to the emergence of an elite class of Britons who grew xenophobic toward their colonial charges. The tension caused by the growing white population manifested itself in the debate on the Ilbert Bill in 1883. The bill proposed allowing Britons to be tried by juries of indigenous Indians in an attempt to ameliorate institutionalized racism. The outcry by British settlers against the bill was severe, and the final version of the bill was significantly watered down in reaction to British protests.

This move angered the growing Indian middle class that had developed out of the growth of the Indian Civil Service (ICS), an administrative institution headed by whites but managed by Western educated Indians. Increased Western education for Indians meant introduction to important Enlightenment ideals such as individual freedom, self-determination, and legitimate rule. These elites spread beyond the ICS and took up jobs as lawyers, journalists, and teachers. Thus, having been promised that Indians would be granted equal rights as soon as they were sufficiently "civilized," the defeat of the Ilbert Bill in its original form was perceived as a significant step backward. In response, educated Indians created the Indian National Congress (INC) in 1885, which was designed to advocate for stronger Indian participation in British government. By 1905, the INC was making more radical demands against British rule, and was forming into an important nationalist organization.

What is more, the INC was not the only emerging nationalist group. It failed to attract large numbers of Muslims who instead formed the All India Muslim League in 1906. Many Indians joined nationalist groups that emphasized religion or indigenous cultural forms and rejected Westernization. Indian nationalist groups continued to grow into the early twentieth century, and the British were forced to grant limited self-representation in the colonial administration. The Government of India Act of 1909 established seats in various legislatures for indigenous Indians and contested through elections, including a certain number of seats reserved for Muslims.

While necessary in order to avoid permanent Hindu control of legislatures, the act also had the effect of increasing sectarian divisions in India.

Imperialism in the Metropole. The impact of the British Empire was not limited to colonized territories. The experience of conquering and ruling diverse regions of the world affected the metropole as well. British life was materially impacted in several ways. A number of products produced in overseas possessions became important to the British populace. Sugar and tea emerged as crucial dietary supplements, and many historians argue that these goods were indispensable for industrialization and urbanization. The cheap energy they provided kept workers going even if the rest of their diet was inadequate. Although governments rarely rose or fell on imperial topics, the Liberals, Conservatives, and later Labour, remained aware of developments in the empire and all three parties generally supported Britain's role in maintaining it. Financially, the empire generated wealth for a small group of capitalists, in part serving as the foundation for industrialization.

Empire impacted the social sphere as well, particularly toward the end of the nineteenth century. An example of this impact was the colonial exhibition. By the late nineteenth century, exhibitions specifically concerned with colonies appeared. Generally, each possession had its own display, explaining the products that the colony produced, a triumphalist version of the colony's history, and information on the indigenous peoples of the colony. These latter displays were occasionally augmented by "human zoos" of indigenous people living in "authentic" and "traditional" villages. These zoos were constructed based on a faulty, Eurocentric worldview that denied the ability of any non-European society to change over time. They stressed notions of scientific racism emerging out of misinterpretations of Charles Darwin's work on natural selection and celebrated the British role in bringing enlightenment and Christianity to barbarian heathens.

The Twilight of Empire. World War I had numerous effects on the British Empire. In Africa, British colonial soldiers played the primary role in capturing German colonies like Cameroon and German East Africa (Burundi, Rwanda, and Tanganyika), although they suffered thousands of deaths. In the Middle East, Indian soldiers were responsible for British gains in Palestine and Mesopotamia (Iraq) at the expense of the crumbling Ottoman Empire. The Dominions were also crucial to the British war effort. Canada suffered fifty-seven thousand deaths in the war, while Australia and New Zealand combined lost seventy-seven thousand men. On the western

front, Dominion soldiers augmented British troops, but in the struggle against the Ottomans, they comprised the majority of British forces. Beyond merely providing men, the colonies also exported a myriad of goods to support Britain, perhaps most importantly vast quantities of food. Toward the end of the war, Germany was starving, but Britain survived in part due to imported food.

The Growth of Nationalism. The war had ramifications for Dominion unity. Nationalism existed in the Dominions before the war, but the shared experience of the front and colony-wide remembrances of the war dead contributed greatly to a feeling of national unity that was increasingly divergent from and more important than affinities with the imperial center. Australia and New Zealand were deeply affected by the Battle of Gallipoli, a disaster that resulted in many deaths and encouraged a sense of national loss. The failure of Britain to support these troops in their most desperate hour also contributed to the weakening of affinities to the imperial core.

Non-Dominion troops participating on the European front were exposed to Europeans not conditioned to operate in the imperial sphere. The carefully cultivated "white myth" of European superiority and aloofness found in the colonies was not as rigid in Europe itself and colonial troops found themselves interacting with lower-class Britons who were less likely to dismiss non-Europeans on account of race. What is more, they were tended to by female nurses and some even had relationships with British women. Finally, the carnage of the front convinced many that European superiority was obviously a myth, as the viciousness of the war undermined the ideal of the civilized West.

These changing global perceptions, combined with other developments, increased non-European nationalism in the early twentieth century. Many Indian nationalists were appalled that they had been forced into the war without consultation. The war represented real costs to India, not only in terms of soldiers sent overseas, but also financially, as taxes were increased to bolster the war effort. By 1917, the satyagraha (soul-force) movement, founded by the lawyer and nationalist Mohandas Gandhi, was rapidly growing. Satyagraha stressed nonviolent resistance to British rule in the hopes that their own brutality would become apparent. The British were alarmed by the growth of Indian nationalism and during the war promised to move toward self-government. However, after the war the restrictive Rowlatt Acts kept emergency measures, like internment without trial, alive. This, combined with the lack of movement toward self-rule, inspired several large-scale demonstrations against Britain. In 1919, a large crowd in Amritsar was dispersed by a British army that indiscriminately opened fire, killing at least 380 Indians. Indians reacted by stepping up their agitation and civil disobedience. By the mid-1920s resistance had grown to an unprecedented extent. The British tried to meet some nationalist demands in the Government of India Act of 1935, but elections for new legislative councils produced a huge Congress Party victory that increasingly called for independence. When India was once again forced into a world war against its will in 1939, nationalist leaders inaugurated the Quit India campaign that, while ruthlessly suppressed by the British, made it clear that continued British rule was an impossibility. After World War II, decolonization of India would proceed at a rapid pace.

As in India, nationalist agitation elsewhere was inspired by World War I. In the Home Rule Act of 1914, the British agreed to partition Ireland into two self-governing regions. Owing to the war this was delayed, and radical nationalists decided to take advantage of the British military's overcommitment, launching the Easter Rising of April 1916. The rebellion was unsuccessful, crushed in a matter of days, and the British began a campaign of terror against nationalists, first by executing the ringleaders of the Rising and then by arresting large numbers of nationalists with no regard to legal niceties. These actions radicalized many Catholic nationalists who did not initially support the rebellion, and they became further alarmed by the attempts of the British to initiate conscription in Ireland in 1918. That same year, elections in Ireland for the British Parliament resulted in a watershed victory for Sinn Fein, a republican group blamed by the British for the Rising. Sinn Fein declared an Irish Republic free from British control, inaugurating the Anglo-Irish War of 1919–1921 that resulted in partition and the creation of the Irish Free State as a Dominion colony.

The Last Expansion. Despite increased nationalist agitation in some colonies, the postwar years saw the last great expansion of the British Empire. The defeat of the Ottomans and the Germans meant that their former territories needed political oversight. The solution was the League of Nations' 1919 mandate system. A mandate was not technically part of any formal empire, but was paternalistically administered by European authorities with the eventual goal of achieving independence. The British were granted mandates for several regions.

During the war, the British encouraged Arab groups to rise up against the Ottomans, promising, in the correspondence between Sharif Hussein of Mecca and the British High Commissioner in Egypt, Henry McMahon, self-determination after the war. Conflicting agreements were made with other parties, however. The 1916 Sykes-Picot Agreement divided the Middle East among France, Russia, and Great Britain, and the 1917 Balfour Declaration promised a "national home" for the Zionist cause. After the war, in Iraq the British faced anticolonial sentiment and it was not until the 1921 establishment of the Hashemite kingdom that violence died down. Britain tried to limit its entanglement with Iraq, and through a series of agreements that protected British oil and military interests the country gained some modicum of self-rule by 1932. In 1921, the Transjordan came to be governed separately from the Palestine Mandate, and achieved a degree of self-rule, gaining full independence in 1946. In Palestine, however, the British had to contend with growing Jewish immigration and unrest among local Arabs. The British tried to limit Jewish immigration with little success. Conflict between Arabs and Jews grew and several terrorist organizations formed on both sides. In 1936, the British faced a surge of Arab nationalism that resulted in three years of intermittent fighting. During World War II the British increased their efforts to limit Jewish immigration in the hopes of gaining the loyalty of the Arabs, but again this was ineffectual. By the end of World War II growing sectarian violence and the results of the Holocaust convinced the British that it was time to evacuate Palestine, which they did in 1948.

World War II and Dissent. Between the wars, Britain faced growing nationalism in almost every part of its empire. Previously, nationalism in its most developed form had been limited due to weak connections between small groups of urban elites and the masses. However, the situation changed as colonials became more aware of economic inequalities and the Great Depression placed greater pressure on existing forms of economic production and taxation systems. Many workers were, in turn, driven to urban centers where they were exposed to nationalist ideology. The growth of trade unions, sometimes accompanied by Marxist ideology, strengthened calls for improved conditions in mines and plantations and intensified labor unrest. In 1912, the African National Congress was formed in South Africa, based on the INC model. In the next two decades it organized several labor strikes that paralyzed the country. In Kenya and Rhodesia, two white settler African colonies, the economic disparity between white and black was obvious and inspired calls for more protection of African land rights. Eventually, under the leadership of Africans like Jomo Kenyatta, disparate labor strikes and riots coalesced into nationalist movements demanding not just the gradual reformation of British administrative policies but outright independence. In Kenya, this culminated in the Mau Mau Uprising of 1952. In Burma and Malaya as well, nationalist movements formed. Various nationalist groups in Burma had different agendas, but they were all in agreement in demanding political separation from India and the establishment of home rule. In Malaya, ethnic divisions in the region made the situation more complex. Large numbers of Chinese immigrants to Malaya during the imperial period had now come into conflict with ethnic Malayans amid the fight for self-determination. British tenacity in the face of resistance tended to support the view that Britain had no intention of letting their empire merely fade away.

It took the catastrophe of World War II and the political and economic realities that followed to fatally undermine the empire. Once again, colonies played their role in the war, sending troops and supplies to the metropole. However, many "colonies," particularly the Dominions, now had the ability to set terms more to their liking in exchange for their support. Australia, New Zealand, South Africa, and Canada all entered the war on their own accord and did so as united allied nations rather than as imperial colonies. Conversely, colonies like India continued to have no say. After the war, these colonies agitated further for more say in their own affairs, a perceived just reward for being entangled in another European conflict. Britain tried to save the empire after the war, investing heavily in economic development schemes that largely failed thanks to anger over the increased interference in local economies that they necessarily entailed. Beyond internal problems, outside forces were at work to ensure the empire's demise. The United Nations was intrinsically opposed to imperialism, and both the United States and the Soviet Union opposed it, at least on paper. The United States was suspicious of protectionist imperial trade patterns and believed that courting moderate nationalists was preferable to colonies forcefully separating themselves under Communist leadership. Moreover, European integration was moving rapidly forward, and it soon became clear that closer ties with Europe would be more economically beneficial than the increasingly unprofitable relationships with colonies. The stage for decolonization was now set.

[*See also* British Raj; Caribbean, *subentry* The British Caribbean; Decolonization, *subentry* The British Empire; East India Company, British; Great Game; *and* Popular Imperialism, British.]

BIBLIOGRAPHY

Cain, P. J., and A. G. Hopkins. *British Imperialism: 1688–2000.* Harlow, U.K., and New York: Longman, 2001. This text introduced the idea of "gentlemanly capitalism" and stressed the importance of the growth of financial institutions to the expansion of empire.

Curtin, Philip D. *The World and the West: The European Challenge and the Overseas Response in the Age of Empire.* Cambridge, U.K., and New York: Cambridge University Press, 2000. While not exclusively focused on the British Empire, this text has enlightening sections on gender, technology, and resistance to imperialism.

Devine, T. M. *Scotland's Empire, 1600–1815.* London and New York: Allen Lane, 2003. Discusses the impact of Scottish Union, the commercial nature of Scotland, and the role of the Scottish Enlightenment.

Galbraith, J. S. "The 'Turbulent Frontier' as a Factor in British Expansion." *Comparative Studies in Society and History* 2 (1960): 150–168. The article that first introduced the concept of the "man on the spot" as an important motor behind imperial expansion.

Gallagher, John, and Ronald Robinson. "The Imperialism of Free Trade." *The Economic History Review* 6 (1953): 1–15. Introduced to a wide audience the idea of "informal empire" as well as describing how free trade could be just as much a tool of empire as mercantilist policies.

Hobson, J. A. *Imperialism: A Study.* London: J. Nisbet, 1902. An early work produced shortly after the Second Boer War arguing that imperialism benefited a small group of capitalists to the detriment of British society in general.

Jeffery, Keith, ed. *"An Irish Empire"? Aspects of Ireland and the British Empire.* Manchester, U.K.: Manchester University Press; New York: St. Martin's Press, 1996. A collection of essays discussing the role of Ireland in the British Empire.

Judd, Denis. *The Lion and the Tiger: The Rise and Fall of the British Raj, 1600–1947.* Oxford and New York: Oxford University Press, 2004. A concise and accessible text that, despite its title, discusses British involvement in India from the late sixteenth century to 1947.

Levine, Phillipa. *The British Empire: Sunrise to Sunset.* Harlow, U.K., and New York: Pearson Longman, 2007. An excellent survey of the British Empire that synthesizes a significant amount of research into a single volume. Organized thematically, it includes a detailed timeline in the appendix useful for new scholars as well as imperial specialists.

Lloyd, T. O. *The British Empire: 1558–1995.* 2d ed. Oxford and New York: Oxford University Press, 1996. A general survey of British imperialism that has strong sections on Dominion colonies and the metropolitan political decision-making process as it pertained to the empire.

Lloyd, T. O. *Empire: The History of the British Empire.* London and New York: Hambledon and London, 2001. An accessible general survey of the empire.

Louis, William Roger, ed. *The Oxford History of the British Empire.* 5 vols. Oxford and New York: Oxford University Press, 1998–1999. Covers most aspects of the British Empire in detail but is somewhat constrained by a conservative approach that neglects less dominant narratives of British imperial history.

Mackenzie, John M., ed. *Imperialism and Popular Culture.* Manchester, U.K., and Dover, N.H.: Manchester University Press, 1986. A fascinating text that focuses on the portrayal of empire in the popular culture of metropolitan Britain.

Mangan, J. A., ed. *Benefits Bestowed? Education and British Imperialism*. Manchester, U.K., Manchester University Press; New York: St. Martin's Press, 1988. A collection with strong essays on Irish education (by John Coolahan) and African schools (by Clive Whitehead).

Marshall, P. J., ed. *The Cambridge Illustrated History of the British Empire*. Cambridge, U.K., and New York: Cambridge University Press, 2001. A textbook that begins with a chronological explanation of the empire and continues with thematic chapters. Includes illustrations and maps.

Mintz, Sidney W. *Sweetness and Power: The Place of Sugar in Modern History*. New York: Viking, 1985. An early example of "commodity studies," this book traces the importance of sugar from a global perspective. Sections on slavery and European dietary changes are particularly related to British imperialism.

Porter, Bernard. *The Lion's Share: A Short History of British Imperialism 1850–2004*. 4th ed. Harlow, U.K., and New York: Pearson Longman, 2004. In this Anglo-centric work, Porter sees the expansion of British formal imperialism as a sign of British economic weakness rather than strength.

Sinha, Mrinalini. *Colonial Masculinity: The "Manly Englishman" and the "Effeminate Bengali" in the Late Nineteenth Century*. Manchester, U.K.: Manchester University Press; New York: St. Martin's Press, 1995. An academic work that examines gender construction in British India.

White, Nicholas. *Decolonisation: The British Experience since 1945*. New York: Longman, 1999. A short text that describes internal metropolitan changes and external international pressures.

Williams, Eric. *Capitalism and Slavery*. Chapel Hill: University of North Carolina Press, 1944. Williams argues that slavery ended because it no longer meshed with industrialization and current economic theories. It represents a seminal work in the field of slavery studies.

AARON D. WHELCHEL

The French Colonial Empire

The period from the outbreak of the Revolution in 1789 to the collapse of the Napoleonic regime in 1815 was a watershed in French imperialism. France lost most of its first overseas empire, situated mainly in North America and the Caribbean, and set in motion the processes that would lead to its territorial expansion into Africa and Asia and the establishment of its second colonial empire. It was not just a shift in geographical emphasis, however. The events and rhetoric of the Revolutionary era altered the concepts on which its new imperialism would be founded.

On the eve of the Revolution, France possessed territories in the Caribbean, North America, the Indian Ocean, and West Africa, producing coffee, indigo, and sugar. The most important economically was Saint-Domingue (now known as Haiti), where African slaves worked large sugar plantations. Slaves in French territories were regulated by the Code Noir (the Black Code), which was established by edict under Louis XIV in 1685. Although the code required slave owners to care for sick and aged slaves, it laid down strict rules for their policing and control. The harsh conditions to which slaves were subjected caused concern among the more liberal-minded members of colonial society, who saw them as an impediment to productivity. As a result, a series of decrees were promulgated under Louis XV introducing limited ameliorations. In the metropole the emphasis was toward abolition rather than amelioration, with Abbé Raynal (Guillaume-Thomas-François de Raynal) and like-minded philosophes questioning the morality of enslaving men, whatever their race. In 1788 they founded the Société des Amis des Noirs, whose purported aim was to abolish slavery while maintaining the colonies. The events of 1789–1799 would lead to an altogether different outcome.

Although at the outset of the Revolution the slaves' situation was little improved, the move toward radical change had been set in motion. On 4 August 1789 the newly founded National Constituent Assembly swept away the rights and privileges that had buttressed the absolutist state and between 20 and 26 August adopted the Declaration of the Rights of Man, which stated that "all men were born and remain free and equal in rights." It thus triggered the events that would culminate in the demise of France's first overseas empire. In the same month there was a slave rebellion in Martinique; a year later there was another in Saint-Domingue; and in 1791 disturbances started in Guadeloupe. Only Saint-Domingue achieved independence (1804), but the revolts prompted the French revolutionaries to take steps to alleviate the troubling situation. Between May 1791 and April 1792 a series of decrees granted political rights to *gens de couleur* (people of color). When this did not stem the uprisings, the First Republic (September 1792–October 1795) abolished slavery: first in Saint-Domingue on 29 August 1793 and then in the whole of the French Empire on 4 February 1794. With the advent of the Directory (1795–1799) and the creation of a new constitution, the colonies were transformed into French departments, a measure that was ratified by the 1798 law on the colonies. By the end of the Revolution, therefore, the foundations of the slave economy in the Caribbean had been shattered.

If these events had a direct impact on the way France's second overseas empire took shape, the expansionary and anticlerical movements that developed during the Revolution influenced the way in which imperialism was conceived. The Revolutionary Wars started defensively but culminated in an expansionary movement to spread revolutionary ideas across Europe. As such, they prefigured the discourse of the *mission civilisatrice* (civilizing mission), in which the vaunted progressive nature of France's civilization became a justification for domination and the spread of French ideas. The anticlericalism of the Revolution set in motion a century-long struggle to separate church from state, which was reflected in the colonies by privileging the juridical colonial state over local religious codes. Additionally, as the struggle between church and state waxed and waned in France, the church sought to spread its influence beyond the metropole, greatly increasing missionary activity.

French Imperialism under Napoleon Bonaparte. The Napoleonic period (1799–1815) was prefaced by an overseas venture that set the tone for much of France's nineteenth-century imperialism. The expedition to Egypt (1798–1800) ended in military failure and yet it had a significant ideological impact. Napoleon considered Egypt to be the strategic foothold in the eastern Mediterranean that would provide France with a base from which to survey more closely and, if necessary, disrupt British activities in the Ottoman Empire and in India. Members of the Directory who had become alarmed by Napoleon's meteoric rise encouraged his designs, and in 1798 he set sail for Egypt. The expedition included professors and students from the École Polytechnique, whose mission was to explore and examine every aspect of Egypt, from its society to its topography. The result was the establishment of the Institut d'Égypte and the multivolume *Déscription de l'Égypte*. This scholarly activity paved the way for the development of Egyptology and nineteenth-century Orientalism, but, more importantly, scholarly activity also became attached to military conquest. Soldier-scholars in Algeria and other parts of the empire would become involved in similar activities. The ideological importance of the period to future imperial activity was also related to the development of Saint-Simonianism, a doctrine that stressed the superiority of European civilization and envisaged a hierarchical society, where an educated elite (industrialists, scientists, and technocrats) would guide the less fortunate through the creation of a progressive society.

The Convention had founded the École Centrale des Travaux Publics in 1794 and a year later changed its name to the École Polytechnique, with the motto *Pour la patrie, les sciences et la gloire* (For the homeland, sciences, and glory). Thus, the First Republic emphasized the importance of scientific education, which was seen to be emblematic of a progressive state. In 1804 a Napoleonic decree militarized the school, thus directly establishing the link between science and the military. In 1812 this trend was reinforced when the best graduates in mathematics were recruited by the Ministry of War. During the Napoleonic period the school became closely connected to the Utopian philosophy of Claude-Henri de Rouvroy, comte de Saint-Simon. Until the last quarter of the nineteenth century it remained France's premier *grande école*.

Napoleon's sense of personal and national grandeur left little room for revolutionary concepts of equality, and in 1802 he reinstated the institution of slavery and sent troops to Saint-Domingue in an attempt to regain French control over the entire island of Hispaniola. Decimated by disease, his troops were defeated, and France withdrew from Hispaniola, where the independent republic of Haiti was formed in 1804. The previous year, fearful of American involvement in Saint-Domingue and in need of revenue to finance his expansionary projects in Europe, Napoleon had sold France's Louisiana territories to the United States. The combination of these two events effectively put an end to the importance of its first overseas empire. At the Congress of Vienna, France was deprived of more of its overseas possessions, although it retained Martinique and Guadeloupe in the Caribbean, French Guiana, Réunion, and its *comptoirs* (trading or commercial outposts) in India and Senegal.

The events of the Revolutionary and Napoleonic periods radically reshaped France's imperial paradigm. Although slavery was not definitively abolished until 1848, a slave-based economy would no longer be the mainstay of French colonial possessions. Furthermore, the different regimes of the 1789–1815 period gave rise to contradictory principles that would contribute to the paradoxical nature of nineteenth-century French imperial ideology and practice. In the first place, the Declaration of the Rights of Man, which posited freedom and equality for all men, was counteracted by the authoritarian and centralizing discourses of the First Republic and Napoleon I. Secondly, the assimilatory logic behind the transformation of overseas territories into French departments was belied by the reinstatement of slavery. Although as an institution its importance diminished after the loss of Saint-Domingue, the revival of the colonial master–slave hierarchy between 1802 and 1804 created a precedent that would be reenacted in various forms throughout France's empire. Finally, the loss of national and military prestige that followed Napoleon's final defeat in 1815 would fuel France's quest to regain influence and honor through military conquest overseas.

Expansion under the July Monarchy (1830–1848). In 1830 France embarked on a punitive expedition to

Algiers. The rationale for the invasion was retaliation for a slight to its consul, whom the dey of Algiers had swatted with a fly whisk three years earlier. The probable causes, however, were unresolved economic tensions created over grain payments during the Napoleonic period and a desire to divert attention from the political problems besetting Charles X's regime. What started as a brief disciplinary action ended in 132 years of colonial rule. The conquest of Algeria lasted twenty-seven years. The French encountered fierce resistance, first from the Arabs, under the leadership of Abdelkader, and then from the Kabyles, Berbers from Kabylia. In the first decade the military made slow headway, and it was only the appointment in 1840 of Thomas-Robert Bugeaud de la Piconnerie as governor-general and commander of the military that enabled the French to prevail. Bugeaud (later marshal of France) took up his post in 1841 and immediately undertook the pacification of the Arabs by means of a brutal scorched earth policy, which led to the surrender of Abdelkader in 1847 and opened the way to the conquest of Kabylia. Algeria was finally deemed "pacified" in 1857. Military administration persisted until 1870.

In the early years, when colonial policy was one of limited occupation (*occupation restrainte*), the military discouraged civilian colonization, which they saw as too exploitative and detrimental to the maintenance of security. After 1848, when Algeria was converted into three French departments, colonization proceeded, albeit at a fairly slow pace. Migrants from France and the northern shores of the Mediterranean started to settle in the "pacified" areas. Bugeaud, who believed in military colonization, had advocated colonization "by the sword and the plow." Although some military officers of the Arab Bureaux, the administrative units established to control the pacified areas, had followed this dictum by trying to sedentarize nomadic tribes and introduce agricultural innovations, the sword was used more often than the plow.

If Algeria was the most noteworthy site of French expansion, it was not the only one. In the first fifteen years of Louis-Philippe's reign, France acquired a number of outposts (*points d'appui*) along the West African coast (Grand Bassam and Assinie in the Ivory Coast and port access in Gabon) and took over a number of small islands in the Indian Ocean. In an 1842 speech to the National Assembly, François Guizot, Louis-Philippe's chief minister at the time, declared that France needed such colonial sites in order to be both strategically and commercially competitive at the international level. By the time the July Monarchy fell, France had a network of bases in Asia, Africa, and the Mediterranean.

Imperialism under Napoleon III (1852–1870). When Louis-Napoleon transformed the Second Republic (1848–1852) into the Second Empire (1852–1870), making himself emperor, imperialism as a nineteenth-century concept came into being. Napoleon III surrounded himself with a number of prominent Saint-Simonians, one of whom was Ismail Urbain, a convert to Islam. Urbain, who had been to Egypt and had worked in Algeria as an interpreter and adviser on "native" affairs, had come to the conclusion that educating Muslims would make them amenable to French rule. His influence prompted Napoleon III to write two open letters to the Algerians, in 1863 addressed to Maréchal Pélisser and 1865 addressed to Maréchal de Mac-Mahon, in which he set out his aims for the territory. Rather than a colony, he declared, Algeria should be an Arab kingdom (*royaume arabe*), in which the French would live side by side with the local population, whose practices and religion they were to respect. The French were to administrate rather than exploit, in order to reconcile the local population to the settlers, who would serve as guides, and initiate the former to French law, morality, and justice.

The settler population was small, comprising a motley collection of individuals who had emigrated from France and countries along the northern shores of the Mediterranean for economic or political reasons. Algeria was also conveniently close as a site of exile for undesirables and had been used as such from the earliest days of conquest, first for military and then for political firebrands. After the closing in June 1848 of the National Workshops, established five months earlier to combat unemployment, and the upheavals of the 1848 revolution in France (and later following the annexation of Alsace-Lorraine in 1870) political refugees added to the European population. Mortality was high, however, and it was only in the last quarter of the nineteenth century, with the introduction of prophylactics, improved hygiene, and the clearing of the mosquito-infested swamplands, that it stabilized. The last decade of military rule was a period of rising tension, with the growing civilian population reacting negatively to what it saw as the pro-Arab policies of Napoleon III's regime. The Civil War (1861–1865) in the United States encouraged settlers to plant cotton, and the decade of the 1860s was the period when cotton production peaked. The period was also one of increased land sequestration, although its high point would only be attained after the civilian administration was established in 1871.

Napoleon III's interest in overseas ventures did not stop at Algeria. It was during his reign that the real push into Africa and Southeast Asia began. Because of the importance of slaves to its first overseas empire, France had established trading posts in Senegal to handle the business of the slave trade. When the slave trade was abolished in 1807, the French and African merchants and middlemen involved in the trade were obliged to find new sources of income. They focused on two products that soon developed in importance: groundnuts and palm oil. Following on the treaties drawn up with chiefs from the neighboring Ivory Coast (1842–1843) to allow them access to the area, in 1849 the French negotiated protectorate status for Guinea, and in 1857 they founded Dakar, now the capital of Senegal. In 1854, General Louis Faidherbe was appointed governor of Senegal, at the request of the merchants of Bordeaux, the commercial center for trade with Africa. Faidherbe expanded inland, attacking the Tukulor chiefs and conquering their kingdoms. Faidherbe's thrust into the hinterland of West Africa set in motion the expansion that would culminate, in the 1880s, in the acquisition of the vast territory of French West Africa (Afrique Occidentale Française).

French involvement in what was to become Indochina started when France intervened ostensibly to protect Catholic missionaries who were seen to be under threat. In fact the move had more to do with rivalry with the British and French economic interests than with religious concerns. British power in India was consolidated when the British Crown took over the government of India in 1858, following the revolt of 1857 (also known as the Great Mutiny). Britain had also gained Hong Kong and secured the opening of a number of ports in China following the First Opium War (1839–1842), thus increasing its influence in the area. French participation in the Second Opium War (1856–1860) established France's military presence in the region and encouraged its economic presence when the Treaty of Tianjin (1858) provided for the opening of a further eleven Chinese ports to foreign trade. A year later, in 1859, the French navy occupied Saigon and, from there, moved into Cochin China, thus establishing control over southern Vietnam. Admiral Louis-Adolphe Bonard, who was appointed governor of Cochin China, expressed French determination to maintain its presence in the area and prevent potential interference from neighboring countries. Negotiations with neighboring Cambodia led to the establishment of a French protectorate in 1863. The French, who were tantalized by the possibilities of trade with China, believed that controlling the Mekong River would establish a gateway to Yunnan. In 1866, Lieutenant Ernest-Marc-Louis de Gonzague Doudart de Lagrée was designated to lead an expedition up the Mekong. Although the expedition did not achieve its original aim as the river was not navigable after Laos, the "discovery" of the Khmer temples in Siem Reap and the publicity surrounding the beauties of Angkor Wat raised French public awareness of and official interest in the area.

Napoleon III's ventures in the Levant (1860–1861) and Mexico (1861–1867) were less successful. As in Southeast Asia, French activities in the Levant were ostensibly to protect the Maronite Christians who were involved in a sectarian war with the Druze, but domestic political and economic interests also underlay the move. Politically it was an attempt to mollify Catholic constituents disturbed by the Druze massacres of Christians, and to maintain the Catholic vote in the south of France, where trade between Catholic and Levantine merchants was important. Economically it was a response to the silk workers of Lyon, who did not want the supply of raw silk interrupted by disturbances in the Levant. French influence would persist in the area, culminating in the interwar years in protectorate status for Syria and Lebanon.

Economic interests were also at stake in Napoleon III's Mexican "adventure." Civil war in Mexico (War of Reform, 1858–1861) led to the suspension of the payment of international debt. Although France, Britain, and Spain decided to intervene militarily in order to protect their interests, Spain and Britain soon realized that France had expansionary intentions and withdrew their support. Napoleon III envisioned creating a Catholic empire in Mexico under French hegemony. He believed it would provide markets and raw materials and enable the promotion of *latinité*, a concept whose aim was to bind areas whose culture was connected to the Romance languages. He also envisaged building a canal linking the Pacific and the Atlantic, a project designed by the Saint-Simonians. French troops marched on Mexico City, occupying it in June 1863. Napoleon then appointed Archduke Maximilian of Austria emperor of Mexico. For the next four years French support kept Maximilian on the throne, but in 1866–1867, under pressure from the United States, the French withdrew, leaving the hapless Maximilian to his fate. He was executed shortly afterward, thus ending France's Mexican episode.

Even though the Panama Canal did not materialize during Napoleon III's reign, the Suez Canal did. The French had withdrawn from Egypt in 1801, but French cultural and economic influence continued and it was this that led to

French involvement in a number of public works projects, including the building of the canal. Also a scheme of the Saint-Simonians, it was originally drawn up by Henri Fournel but was abandoned, only to be reassigned to Ferdinand de Lesseps, who completed the project in 1869.

By the time the Second Empire collapsed in 1870, France had acquired the aura and influence of an imperial power. Napoleon III may have lost an empire at home but he had laid the foundation of an overseas empire that would, at its apogee, be matched only by that of the British. The Third Republic (1870–1940) would consolidate and enlarge on the overseas gains made by Napoleon III.

The French Empire under the Third Republic (1870–1940). The switch from a military to a civilian regime in Algeria (1870–1871) was accompanied by a major rebellion in Kabylia that nearly succeeded in overthrowing French rule. The repression was brutal, and Kabylia, which had been protected by the military from excessive land expropriation, was now subjected to extensive sequestration. It signaled the implementation of an exploitative and often punitive relationship that would only end with decolonization. Although the high mortality rates that characterized the early years of French occupation diminished, the European population remained low. The Kabyle rebellion of 1870 increased fears engendered by the demographic disparity between the Muslims and Europeans, most of whom were of Italian, Spanish, or Maltese origin. The Crémieux Decree of 1870 had granted citizenship to the Jews. In 1889 a further law granted citizenship to children born in Algeria of non-French settlers.

The land expropriations that so benefited the Europeans pauperized the Arabs and Berbers, who migrated, first to the urban centers and then to France, in search of the means with which to support their families. The settlers used the expropriated land to cultivate citrus, wheat, and vines. The phylloxera epidemic, which ruined the wine industry in France, proved a boon for the settlers, who planted resistant cuttings that flourished, thus establishing wine as one of the colony's leading industries. By driving the local population off its land, the settlers were assured of cheap labor, but there was always the fear of discontents rebelling. As a means of control the settlers relied on the *code de l'indigénat* ("native" code). First introduced in Algeria in 1834 as a temporary measure, it was regularly renewed and during the civilian regime acquired an increased number of punishable offenses.

During the last quarter of the nineteenth century French expansion was stepped up, thanks in large part to the statesman and exponent of imperialism Jules Ferry (1832–1893). Ferry rose to prominence as minister of education but it was during his two premierships (1880–1881; 1883–1885) that he became a strong advocate of colonial expansion and this in the face of popular disinterest and political opposition. Backed by a small coterie of like-minded imperialists, he formulated an expansionary policy justified by economic, political, and cultural necessities. In a speech to the National Assembly he drew attention to German and U.S. protectionist policies, the threat of British naval power, and the "duty" of the "superior" races to civilize "inferior" races, declaring that to maintain its position as a leading power France had to respond to these challenges by expanding its territorial acquisitions. He pointed to the potential of South America as a huge market for North American goods and stated that colonies would allow France to compete economically in a world of expanding markets where free trade and the laws of supply and demand prevailed. During his premierships France extended its empire in North Africa, Southeast Asia, and Africa.

In the 1881 Treaty of Bardo, France gained protectorate status over Tunisia, and in 1883 the French forces moved northward in Vietnam, finally acquiring Annam and Tonkin, which they had unsuccessfully tried to capture a decade earlier. In 1883 France started its incursion into Madagascar, securing the island as a protectorate in 1885 in an agreement with the British, who retained Zanzibar and the Mauritius. But Madagascar did not accept French suzerainty and it was only in 1898, two years after the National Assembly voted to send troops under the command of Governor-General Joseph-Simon Gallieni, that the island was finally "pacified."

France's territorial acquisitions during the Scramble for Africa were vast. The process was set in motion during 1884–1885, when France acquired part of the Congo, and by the time war was declared in 1914 France had acquired the bulk of its colonies in Equatorial Africa (Gabon, French Congo, Oubangui-Chari [now Central African Republic], and Chad) and in West Africa (French Guinea, Senegal, Ivory Coast, Dahomey [now Benin], French Sudan [now Mali], Upper Volta [now Burkina Faso], Niger, and Mauritania).

Sub-Saharan Africa was not the only focus of French expansion in Africa. France's final prize was the acquisition of protectorate status over Morocco in 1912. Nineteenth-century imperial rivalry among the great powers, for which the Berlin Conference (1884–1885) was but a palliative measure, was also evident in the Mediterranean, where

France and Britain had competed for influence since Napoleon Bonaparte's unsuccessful bid to occupy Egypt. Although French influence remained strong, it was the British who occupied Egypt in 1882. French acquiescence to this move was motivated by a desire to secure Tunisia and eventually Morocco without British interference. But Britain was not the only rival to French influence. Since unification, Germany's interest in overseas colonies had sharpened and with it a desire to curb further French expansion. The tension came to a head in Morocco, where the French financial and military presence had grown considerably at the century's end. The military sorties from Algeria that characterized the initial French incursion into the area culminated in 1903, when Louis-Hubert-Gonzalve Lyautey, who had served with Gallieni in Indochina and Madagascar, marched westward, taking territory along the coast. The move violated boundary treaties established between the French and Moroccans and alarmed the international powers. In 1905 and again in 1911 Germany intervened to try and stop French encroachment. In both instances France gained ground, and in 1912 Morocco became a French protectorate.

The Moroccan crises of 1905 and 1911 were significant internationally as they brought the European powers to the brink of war. In 1905 the German kaiser, or emperor, William II visited Morocco. The sultan, seriously in debt to France, found in the kaiser an ally against the French. The brinksmanship that followed was resolved at the Algeciras Conference in 1906, when France recognized Moroccan sovereignty but won advantageous rights over Moroccan ports. In July 1911 the Germans used gunboat diplomacy to try, once again, to check French influence. War was averted when France agreed to cede some of its territory in the Congo to Germany in exchange for a free rein in Morocco.

The thirty-five years preceding World War I had seen France extend its power across the globe in an empire that surpassed that of the British in size, if not in might. Unlike the British Empire, where the flag followed trade, the French Empire had as much to do with national prestige and military bravura as it did with trade. Military officers, far from the metropole and out of reach of communication, took many of the initiatives that led to increased territorial acquisition.

While France was gaining control over an extraordinary range of "subject" peoples, ideas about human races had coalesced into an ideology of white superiority and domination. In the place of assimilation, French colonial policy shifted to one of association, whereby the culture and practices of its "subject" peoples would be respected and allowed to develop at their own rhythm. In 1910 Jules Harmand, a naval doctor and diplomat, published *Domination et colonisation*, in which he argued that assimilation was a profound error. France's right of domination was determined by its superior morality and civilization and inspired by its need for enrichment. Colonies should not be seen as an extension of the metropole but as semi-autonomous entities to be governed in response to local circumstance. Harmand's work was a reflection of current ideas rather than a blueprint of association. French colonial policy had always been haphazard, and association did not develop into a blanket policy any more than assimilation had. There was a small percentage of assimilated individuals, the *évolués*, but even among this group many did not have French nationality. The vast majority of its colonized peoples were subjects, not citizens.

World War I and the Interwar Years. On the surface the 1914–1918 war did not change much in the colonies. France's colonial subjects were called on to fight alongside its citizens. Large numbers of colonial troops were conscripted to this end with the help of local dignitaries, who informed them that military service would lead to increased rights and even equality. The colonial troops fought and died with the French and after the war medals and pensions were proffered instead of rights. The leveling impact of the trenches and the horrors of the war made many realize that France's much-vaunted moral and cultural superiority was a myth.

The interwar years are generally considered to be the colonial apogee, and yet the seeds of imperial decline had already been sown. The devastation of the war brought France to its knees, and it turned to its colonies for help in fulfilling its labor needs and in the hope of reaping economic benefits. In 1923 Albert Sarraut published *La mise en valeur des colonies françaises*, in which he encouraged the economic exploitation of France's colonies. Although only Algeria had a fully developed settler society, small settler populations grew up in Tunisia, Morocco, Indochina, the islands of Madagascar and Réunion, and some of the territories in the Indian Ocean and the Pacific. Whereas the settler population in Algeria was large, multiethnic, and socially diverse, with multigenerational roots in the land, the number of settlers in other colonies was much smaller. (The French settler population of Algeria was over a million; in Indochina it was no more than twenty thousand; in French Equatorial Africa only two thousand.) Furthermore, with the exception of the French who owned and ran the plantations and estates, the connections to the colonies of most of the French were transitory. They were administrators, civil servants, or fortune seekers, who came to the colonies for limited periods of time.

For all the apparent confidence of the French people in their colonial empire, the interwar years were not tranquil. The colonized peoples, many of whom had been exposed to socialist ideas during the war and had come into contact with trade unions for the first time, were further inspired by the Russian Revolution. In 1919 there was a workers' strike at Thiès, an important depot for groundnuts in Senegal. It was the first in a series of strikes and disturbances that heralded the beginning of sustained nationalist activity both in France and in the colonies during the interwar period. In France the North African workers joined the Étoile Nord-Africaine (ENA), headed by the charismatic Algerian Ahmed Messali Hadj. The ENA reformed in Algeria as the Parti du Peuple Algérien (PPA). The PPA would eventually be taken over by the Front de Libération Nationale (FLN), which led the country to independence. In Tunisia, the Tunisian youth movement came together with other groups to form the Destour, which in the 1930s was transformed into the Neo-Destour Party by Habib Bourguiba, who became the first president of independent Tunisia. In Morocco, religious and intellectual leaders formed the Istiqlal, the party that would be instrumental in gaining Morocco its independence. In Indochina, Ho Chi Minh, inspired by the French Communist Party, formed the Revolutionary Youth League of Vietnam. Two years later, in 1927, the first organized nationalist movement, Viet Nam Quoc Dan Dang (VNQDD), was founded, with the express aim of getting rid of the French. In 1930 Vietnamese soldiers turned on their French officers, killing them and starting the Yen Bay uprising. Although the revolt was short-lived, the repression virtually destroyed the VNQDD and left a lasting impression on the Vietnamese. The events and aftermath of Yen Bay prompted Ho Chi Minh to create the Vietnamese Communist Party, whose resistance to the French would eventually be successful. In North Africa the Rif War (War of Melilla, 1919–1926) was a further reminder that many parts of the empire were not secure.

With few exceptions the French, in both the metropole and the colonies, appeared oblivious to the potential gravity of nationalist developments. The colonies were glorified (and promoted) in a series of colonial exhibitions in Paris, the most flamboyant of which was held in 1931. At the same time, colonial Algeria celebrated the 1930 centenary of French presence with more pomp than tact. Maurice Violette, one of the few colonial governors to realize that reform was essential if France was to keep its empire, proposed a bill to enlarge the franchise for a limited number of Algerians, only to have it rejected by the settler lobby. Throughout the empire évolué demands for greater suffrage or improved rights were ignored or denied by powerful colonial lobbies. The Popular Front (1936–1938) brought with it renewed hope for reform. The Blum-Violette Bill was reintroduced to the National Assembly, only to be blocked once more. By 1939 there were a mere twenty thousand naturalized citizens in the whole of the empire, all proposals for improved enfranchisement or naturalization having been blocked. Whereas the 1920s had seen something of an economic boom in the colonies, the 1930s were years of depression and want throughout the empire. The colonized peoples were the hardest hit, and many more migrated to urban centers or to France, where they often gravitated toward nationalist movements.

World War II and Its Aftermath. If World War I created the first fissures in the imperial edifice, World War II was the decisive blow that would bring it down. The rapid collapse of France and its occupation by Germany was crippling to France's image of superiority and signaled the metropole's weakness, while the overrunning of much of Southeast Asia, including Indochina, by the Japanese was an indication of France's inadequacies in its colonies. The divided loyalties in the metropole between General Charles de Gaulle's Free French and Marshal Philippe Pétain's Vichy government were mirrored in the colonies as some rallied to the former and some to the latter. Eric Jennings has demonstrated the way in which three colonies, Indochina, Madagascar, and Guadeloupe, used Vichy's National Revolution to their own ends, but North Africa and French West Africa also rallied to the Vichy government. As early as October 1940, Algeria repealed the Crémieux Decree, which had granted Jews French citizenship and soon afterward barred Jews from a number of professions. Anti-Semitic laws were similarly passed in other colonies. The pro-Vichy administrations in the colonies followed a logic of their own, but discrimination did increase. Those who suffered most were the évolués, who began to realize that their struggles had been and would be fruitless. Resistance in the colonies at this time was complex. Both the Free French and the colonized peoples opposed the regimes, but within these two groups there were numerous factions ranging from radical revolutionaries to independence-minded moderates. By the war's end, therefore, the resistance movements in the colonies had been greatly strengthened.

The "wind of change" that swept the French empire after World War II started well before the British prime minister, Harold Macmillan, made his now-famous speech in the parliament of South Africa in 1960. In 1945, Ho Chi Minh declared Vietnamese independence, setting in motion a series of wars that were fought first by the French, as they tried to regain control of their Southeast Asian territories, and then by the Americans, as they tried to "contain" the spread of Communism. The same year in Algeria, demonstrations by Algerians in Sétif and Guelma degenerated as demonstrators were fired on. The ensuing massacre of just over one hundred settlers by the Algerians was followed by a brutal repression, out of all proportion to the initial events. Similar events occurred in Madagascar in 1948. The early 1950s saw pro-independence manifestations in nearly all French colonies, although none provoked a response of the magnitude of those in Algeria and Madagascar. The Algerian War of Independence (1954–1962) was one of the most brutal and bitter of the European wars of decolonization. It pitted not only the Algerians against the French, but also Algerian against Algerian and French against French. As a result of the war two new regimes came into being, the French Fifth Republic and the People's Democratic Republic of Algeria. The war's political, cultural, and social legacy is still being played out in both countries. During the period in which the war was being fought, most of France's overseas territories were granted independence. Those that opted to maintain strong ties to France now form the French overseas departments and territories, better known as the DOM-TOM (Départements d'Outre-mer–Territoires d'Outre-mer).

[*See also* Africa; Brazzaville Conference; Cambodia; Caribbean, *subentry* The French Caribbean; Civilizing Mission, *subentry* French Empire; Cochin China; Decolonization, *subentry* The French Empire; French Union; Indochina War, First; Laos; *Loi Cadre; and* Vietnam.]

BIBLIOGRAPHY

Ageron, Charles-Robert. *Les algériens musulmans et la France: 1871–1919.* Paris: Presses Universitaires de France, 1968.

Aldrich, Robert. *The French Presence in the South Pacific, 1842–1940.* London: Macmillan, 1990.

Aldrich, Robert. *Greater France: A History of French Overseas Expansion.* Basingstoke, U.K.: Macmillan, 1996.

Betts, Raymond F. *Assimilation and Association in French Colonial Theory, 1890–1914.* 2d ed. Lincoln: Nebraska University Press, 2005.

Cantier, Jacques, and Eric Jennings, eds. *L'empire colonial sous Vichy.* Paris: Odile Jacob, 2004.

Conklin, Alice L. *A Mission to Civilize: The Republican Idea of Empire in France and West Africa, 1895–1930.* Stanford, Calif.: Stanford University Press, 1997.

Connelly, Matthew. *A Diplomatic Revolution: Algeria's Fight for Independence and the Origins of the Post–Cold War Era.* New York: Oxford University Press, 2003.

Dubois, Laurent. *A Colony of Citizens: Revolution and Slave Emancipation in the French Caribbean, 1787–1804.* Chapel Hill: University of North Carolina Press, 2004.

Hoisington, William A. *Lyautey and the French Conquest of Morocco.* New York: St. Martin's, 1995.

James, C. L. R. *The Black Jacobins: Toussaint L'Ouverture and the San Domingo Revolution.* 2d rev. ed. New York: Vintage, 1989. First published 1938.

Jennings, Eric. *Vichy in the Tropics: Petain's National Revolution in Madagascar, Guadeloupe, and Indochina, 1940–1944.* Stanford, Calif.: Stanford University Press, 2001.

Julien, Charles-André. *La conquête et les débuts de la colonisation (1827–1871).* Vol. 1 of *L'histoire de l'Algérie contemporaine.* Paris: Presses Universitaires de France, 1968.

Kanya-Forstner, A. S. *The Conquest of the Western Sudan: A Study in French Military Imperialism.* Cambridge, U.K.: Cambridge University Press, 1969.

Le Sueur, James D. *Uncivil War: Intellectuals and Identity Politics during the Decolonization of Algeria.* 2d ed. Lincoln: University of Nebraska Press, 2006.

Lorcin, Patricia M. E. *Imperial Identities: Stereotyping, Prejudice, and Race in Colonial Algeria.* London: I. B. Tauris, 1999.

Martin, Jean. *Maghreb, Indochine, Madagascar, iles et comptoirs.* Vol. 2 of *L'empire triomphante, 1871–1936.* Paris: Denoël, 1990.

Meyer, Jean, Jean Tarrade, Annie Rey-Goldzeiguer, et al. *Histoire de la France Coloniale.* 2 vols. Paris: Armand Colin, 1991.

Osborne, Milton E. *The French Presence in Cochinchina and Cambodia: Rule and Response (1859–1905).* Bangkok: White Lotus Press, 1997.

Pennell, C. R. *Morocco since 1830: A History.* New York: New York University Press, 2000.

Porch, Douglas. *The Conquest of the Sahara.* New York: Knopf, 1984.

Ruedy, John. *Modern Algeria: The Origins and Development of a Nation.* 2d ed. Bloomington: Indiana University Press, 2005.

Thomas, Martin. *The French Empire between the Wars: Imperialism, Politics, and Society.* Manchester, U.K.: Manchester University Press, 2005.

Thompson, Elizabeth Helen. *Colonial Citizens: Republican Rights, Paternal Privilege, and Gender in French Syria and Lebanon.* New York: Columbia University Press, 2000.

PATRICIA M. E. LORCIN

The Belgian Colonial Empire

Belgium became an independent state in 1830, having successfully freed itself from periods of successive colonial rule by Spain, Austria, France, and Holland. In an age in European history when monarchical rule was the popular institution of governance, the new state selected a German prince related to Britain's Queen Victoria as its first king. He took the title of Leopold I, king of the Belgians (1790–1865; r. 1831–1865). The new kingdom, ridiculed by the future Leopold II (1835–1909; r. 1865–1909) as "Petit pays, petits gens" (small country, small people), was less than half the size of America's West Virginia. Sandwiched between France and Germany, the new kingdom's first priority was military and economic survival. The founding of a colonial empire was not Leopold I's concern.

And yet, by 1885, Leopold II, who ascended the Belgian throne in 1865, was to play a major role in the scramble for, and the partition of, Africa. Even before he became king, he had become convinced that his insignificant country needed colonies if it hoped to succeed economically. Moreover, successful colonial enterprises might make Belgium "one of the richest countries in the world" (cited in Hochschild, p. 36), thus raising its diplomatic profile. From 1853, when he was only eighteen years old, founding a Belgian colonial empire became an obsession with him. After he came to power, he embarked on several unsuccessful and, sometimes, bizarre colonial ventures. His opportunity came when the European interests in the geographical exploration of Africa, the planting of Christianity there, and the suppression of both the Atlantic and the Indian Ocean slave trade fostered the colonizing of the continent. Determined to help himself to "a slice of this magnificent African cake," Leopold convened in 1876 the Brussels Geographical Conference on African exploration. The result of the conference was the founding of the International African Association (IAA) for the lofty philanthropic mission of exploring the African interior and bringing the benefits of Christianity and Western civilization to the people. He carefully masked his colonial ambition from which he hoped to reap economic benefits and achieve power and recognition both at home and abroad. He was aware that if he made his intentions known at this early stage the major European powers would have stopped him emphatically.

The king benefited from his association with Henry Morton Stanley, the celebrated explorer; General Henry Shelton Sanford, a member of a wealthy American family, who had served as President Abraham Lincoln's envoy to Belgium; and members of a rather shadowy body that was called the Committee For Upper Congo Studies, which consisted of British and Dutch businessmen who served as the king's proxies. In 1879 Stanley finally agreed to serve as Leopold's agent in the Congo for five years. His mission ostensibly was to explore, on behalf of the IAA, the Congo River. Leopold and Stanley cleverly shielded their political ambition thoroughly from the public; inquisitive journalists and individuals were told that they were simply concerned with "scientific explorations." Leopold's aim was to ease the anxieties of critics in Belgium who felt that for their small country to get involved in the

acquisition and administration of a colonial empire would be financially ruinous. Shortly afterwards, he formed another so-called philanthropic organization called the International Association of the Congo (IAC), making it clear that the new association was quite distinct from the IAA, although the IAC was allowed to use the flag of the IAA. By this time also, the Committee for Upper Congo Studies had become moribund. Leopold's imperial enterprise was a tangled web of deceptions, outright lies, and disgraceful duplicity. As soon as Leopold's true intentions were discovered, his ambition in Africa fueled French and Portuguese interest in colonizing Africa.

Between 1876 and 1883, indeed, France, Portugal and Leopold had committed themselves to founding colonies in Central Africa. Consequently, Britain and Germany abandoned their ideal of informal control and influence in Africa. When this happened, the Scramble for Africa turned into a dangerous steeplechase. Afraid that it was only a matter of time before the leading European powers pushed it out of Africa totally, Portugal proposed the summoning of an international conference to settle European territorial disputes in Central Africa. Otto von Bismarck, the German chancellor, having sounded the opinion of the powers, was encouraged to invite them to Berlin to discuss these issues as well as the slave trade and the other elements of humanitarian idealism that it was claimed inspired the conference. The news that the conference was to be held between 15 November 1884 and 23 February 1885 quickened the pace of the Scramble. Far from seriously discussing the slave trade and humanitarian issues, the Berlin West Africa Conference, as it was officially called, laid down "the rules to be observed in future with regard to the occupation of territory on the coasts of Africa" (cited in Uzoigwe, p. 29). Although technically the Berlin conference did not partition Africa, for all practical purposes, appropriation of African territory did not only take place but also regulations for future territorial acquisitions were clearly spelled out.

A major result of the Berlin West Africa Conference was the recognition of the Congo Free State created by Leopold, thanks to the persuasive ability of Stanley, the diplomatic dexterity of Leopold, and the not insignificant support of Bismarck. "The new Congo state," Bismarck gloated, "is destined to be one of the most important executors of the work we intend to do, and I express my best wishes for its speedy development, and for the realization of the noble aspirations of its illustrious creator" (cited in Hochschild, p. 86). For Leopold the Berlin conference was a great personal triumph. With determination, lies, hard work, skillful diplomacy, and monetary expenditure, he was able to obtain a territory eighty times the size of Belgium with 1.3 million square miles of river basin (an area larger than the Indian subcontinent or about the size of Europe itself).

The Strange History of the Congo Free State. The short history of the Congo Free State (CFS) was as strange as it was tumultuous. Founded in 1885 and recognized by both European powers and the United States as a civilizing agent in Central Africa, the Belgian government refused to claim it as their country's colony. In April 1885, the Belgian parliament therefore authorized "His Majesty Leopold II, King of the Belgians . . . to be chief of the State founded in Africa by the International Association of the Congo. The Union between Belgium and the new State of the Congo shall be exclusively personal" (cited in Legum, p. 26), implying that the CFS was Leopold's personal possession. On 29 May, Leopold officially became king-sovereign of the CFS as well as simultaneously retaining his position as king of the Belgians. This strange arrangement came to an ignominious end in 1908 when the Belgian parliament was forced by internal opposition and extraordinary foreign pressure to terminate the CFS's sorry and shameful existence.

What went wrong? First, Leopold was above all a businessman. The profit motive was his god. If he were not a king, he would have performed splendidly as a ruthless chief executive of a major business conglomerate. Second, the "civilizing mission" he claimed that inspired his proceedings in the Congo turned out to be, unbeknownst to contemporaries who applauded his remarkable philanthropy, a grand mask for largely mundane purposes. He knew, or should have known, that philanthropy and successful business do not mix. In fairness to him, having invested himself a considerable personal fortune in the Congo enterprise, he was entitled to make some profit. But had he made his intentions clear from the beginning, he would not have received much support from home or abroad; and the CFS would not have received the diplomatic recognition given to it at the Berlin conference.

When the international community finally saw through Leopold's smoke screen, and the CFS had been turned into the equivalent of an enormous slave plantation, its opposition to the regime became relentless and implacable. From the beginning Leopold also realized that establishing and administering his vast colonial estate was a formidable task; more important, it required much more money that he could mobilize from his considerable personal wealth.

In the Congo, his estate property of unoccupied land, estimated to be the size of Poland, was undeveloped. Therefore, he allotted huge chunks of these lands to private concessionaire companies, offering them monopoly rights to exploit their natural resources, notably rubber, ivory, and palm oil. At the same time, he decreed secretly that the resources of these vacant lands belonged to him, thus forcing the companies to pay for both receiving the concessions and for exploiting their products. He further forbade the Congolese to enter his possessions and thus restricted them to the lands allocated to them. Those who disobeyed these orders were suppressed by force.

The autocratic rule he could not exercise in Belgium, he exercised without restraint in the CFS where he ruled by decree. He ignored the Free Trade provisions of the Berlin Act, forced the Congolese to sell their products only to his agents, and imposed a suffocating monopoly over the state's economy. He was even accused of "directly encouraging slave raids" and at the same time funding anti-slavery conferences in Europe (Nzongola-Ntalaja, pp. 20–21). In addition, the CFS and the concessionaires were excused of severe human rights violations against the Congolese. These allegations caused an international scandal and led to the founding of the Congo Reform Association (CRA) headed by the British human rights activist Edmund Dene Morel, author of *Red Rubber* and *King Leopold's Rule in Africa* in which these atrocities were detailed. The CRA grew to become a global association. Its most prominent members and supporters included Mark Twain, who satirized what was going in his classic *King Leopold's Soliloquy*; Joseph Conrad, who depicted these crimes in his classic novel *Heart of Darkness*; Roger Casement, British diplomat and Irish nationalist whose dispatches outraged the British government; George Washington Williams, African American journalist-historian; and Hezekiah Andrew Shanu, a Nigerian who worked for the CFS, then turned against it when he could no longer stand the atrocities. Although Leopold denied all these allegations, available evidence suggests strongly that he knew most of what was going on and did, in fact, authorize some of it.

Finally, led by Britain, the international community, taking note of criticism within Belgium as well as that of the CRA and Congolese revolts, pressured Belgium to take over the administration of the Congo Free State from Leopold. This was done on 28 August 1908. The role of the Belgian government throughout the life of the CFS left a lot to be desired. It derived enormous advantages from the exploitation of the Congolese while refusing to shoulder imperial responsibilities. "Leopold," one author wrote,

> displayed exceptional generosity in the disbursement of the newfound wealth. The Congo profits were used to fund a grandiose policy of public works and urban improvement—in Belgium. The magnificent Arcade du Cinquantenaire in Brussels, the famous Tervuren Museum, extensions to the Royal Palace, public works at Ostend, various urban building schemes—all were funded by the Congo Free State
> (cited in Nzongola-Ntalaja, p. 23).

Belgian Colonial Rule. Most scholars agree that the new managers of the Congo Free State, now called Belgian Congo, having no previous experience of colonial governance, followed closely the system put in place under Leopold's rule; the major difference was that they refined it for the purpose of winning Belgian and international support. It was not until 1913 that the CRA, satisfied that a tolerable set of civilized laws had been enacted in the colony, ceased to exist. These laws included the *charte coloniale*, a sort of constitution that was to be a guide for colonial administration. Since among those who drafted the constitution were major shareholders in the great concessionaire companies, however, departure from past practices was more apparent than real.

The Belgian government did set out to develop a professional, high quality colonial service. The goal was to be state paternalism: in other words, the civilized, highly trained and benevolent Belgian elite was to govern the supposedly uncivilized Congolese for their own good. The church was actively involved in promoting Belgian's paternalism. Its missionaries worked hand in hand with the state and business to transform the Congolese and yet keep them in their subservient place. The energetic evangelization of the people yielded fantastic results. By 1954 Congolese Christians were estimated to number 3.5 million; by 1959 there were six hundred Congolese Catholic priests; Congolese Protestant clergy were almost as many. In line with Belgian colonial policy, they were all accorded subordinate statuses in the priestly hierarchy. The congregations were separated by color. The church, granted virtual monopoly over education, carried religious indoctrination to the classroom. The pupils were taught that their cultures and values were barbarous and must be eradicated; and that because the Congolese were inferior to the Europeans, they were obligated to be subservient tothem. Instruction was in the vernacular languages; technical and agricultural training were emphasized; secondary school education was discouraged until the 1950s;

and discouraged also was the opportunity to study in Belgium. Indeed, on the eve of independence in 1960 the entire colony had less than twenty Congolese college graduates.

The economic system was based on the concept of state capitalism, that is, the state was a shareholder in, and was represented on the board of directors of, the concessionaires who had been granted monopolies to exploit the colony's resources. The economic policy, like those of other Europeans, was to ensure that the colony paid its way and yielded a profit for the state and for the companies. To make this possible, Congolese land continued to be appropriated without regard for land tenure systems. A head tax introduced in 1914 to be paid in cash led to periodic rural-urban migration in search of paid employment in order to pay the tax, or to flight to neighboring states to escape taxation. The state also continued to pursue vigorously a labor policy based on forced labor, compulsory cultivation of economic crops, plantation agriculture, and mineral resources utilization. This policy produced the desired results: the rise of infrastructure in some areas; the rise of urban centers; the emergence of a class of controlled peasant producers and factory proletariat; and a rise in the standard of living. On the other hand, the abuses the policy generated, the sufferings endured by the Congolese, and the dislocation that resulted negated most of whatever benefits the policy brought. In the final analysis, state capitalism produced no Congolese commercial or middle class; it merely created a dissatisfied "working class in the making" and an artisan class that had no hope of rising to the top.

Nationalism and Independence. Throughout the colonial period, the Congo was passed off by the Belgian authorities as a "blue chip" colony in which all Belgians should take national pride; that economically and socially the civilizing mission had worked splendidly; and that the Congolese honored the Belgians and were eternally grateful to them for benevolently guiding them into civilization. The average Belgian, hardly imperialistically minded, was satisfied with allowing the small circle of colonial administrators to continue their good and commendable work. The Congolese, of course, who wore the colonial shoe, knew where it pinched. However, until the 1950s, all that the few Congolese *evolues* wanted was colonial amelioration and not independence. Sheltered from democratic influences, denied freedom of association, given no opportunity to gain parliamentary experience by serving in a legislative assembly, and not allowed to gain administrative experience in the senior ranks of the civil service, it is no surprise that their aspirations were so limited. The Belgian government was not unaware of the wind of political change blowing all over Africa after World War II.

Thus, the formation of the Alliance des Bakongo (ABAKO) in 1957, a cultural organization dedicated to the preservation of ancient Congolese traditions, which denounced those who preached moderation and demanded immediate independence, came as a great surprise to the government. As a response urban communes in the three biggest cities of Leopoldville, Elizabethville, and Jadotville, each headed by a burgomaster and run by an elected council, were immediately created. The ABAKO, then led by Joseph Kasavubu, transformed itself into an ethnic political party and won the election to the Leopoldville commune. It demanded a federal constitution for the Congo. The Elizabethville (Katanga) communal election was won by Baluba (Kasai) elements who were immigrants in Katanga. The surprise victory caused the so-called "authentic Katangans" (Balunda, Yeke, and northern Baluba) to form their own political party, the Confederation des associations Tribales du Katanga (CONAKAT). Led by Moise Tshombe, a businessman who claimed descent from the old royal family of the Mwata Yamvo, CONAKAT stood for a federal constitution. Opposed to these two parties was the Mouvement National Congolais (MNC) led by Patrice Lumumba. The party was formed in 1958 in response to General Charles de Gaulle's dramatic offer of immediate independence to France's Congo-Brazzaville colony in the same year. It demanded immediate independence for Belgian Congo and stood for a unitary constitution. Lumumba, a former postal clerk who had served a year's sentence for embezzlement, turned out to be a charismatic leader, a skillful politician, and a spellbinding orator. His party was the only Congolese pan-national movement.

Apparently confused by what was taking place, Belgium abandoned its gradualist policy and agreed to grant independence to the colony without delay. At once, various Congolese ethnic groups rushed to form their own political parties in order to protect the interests of their respective peoples. The most important of the parties was Albert Kalonji's faction of the MNC. Kalonji, a Muluba, had broken away with his Baluba supporters to form the MNC-Kalonji. These parties fought furious battles among themselves and practically brought the machinery of the colonial government to a halt. A helpless Belgium government called a Round Table Conference in Brussels for January 1960 to work out the machinery for independence.

At the conference, with the sniff of freedom in the air, the warring parties miraculously patched up their differences, and threw the Belgium negotiators who had anticipated a deadlock into total confusion. A dizzy Belgium government, outflanked and outmaneuvered by the "African barbarians" who were now riding the political horses in the colony, dramatically set 30 June 1960 as the independence date for Belgian Congo. Lumumba's MNC won the independence election. His party's slogans—"Independence means total equality between blacks and whites" and "If you must travel by foot to go somewhere and happen to meet a European who drives a car, he must stop and pick you up if you think there is room for you"—struck a very receptive chord with a people who had been subjected to apartheid-like segregation throughout their lives. Within a week Lumumba surprised observers by forming a broad-based coalition government.

King Baudouin of the Belgians attended the ceremonies. Unfortunately, his paternalistic and eulogistic speech recounting tremendous Belgian achievements in the former colony demonstrated that the leaders of Belgium still knew little about the Congo and, worse still, learned nothing from the Congolese. Lumumba, regarding the king's speech as a great insult to the Congolese people, threw all diplomatic niceties to the wind, and bitterly responded: "We are no longer your monkeys." The die was cast. The new Congo-Belgium relationship had started on the wrong foot. The consequences were to be dire.

[*See also* Belgian Congo *and* Berlin West African Conference.]

BIBLIOGRAPHY

Conrad, Joseph. *Heart of Darkness.* Edited by Robert Kimbrough. New York: W.W. Norton and Co., 1988.

Cookey, S. J. S. *Britain and the Congo Question: 1885–1913.* London: Longmans, 1968.

Emerson, Barbara. *Leopold II of the Belgians: King of Colonialism.* New York and London: St. Martin's, 1979.

Hochschild, Adam. *King Leopold's Ghost: A Story of Greed, Terror, and Heroism in Colonial Africa.* Boston: Houghton Mifflin, 1998.

Legum, Colin. *Congo Disaster.* Baltimore: Penguin Books, 1961.

Lemarchand, René. *Political Awakening in the Belgian Congo.* Berkeley: University of California Press, 1964. Reprint. Westport, Conn.: Greenwood, 1982.

Morel, Edmund D. *King Leopold's Rule in Africa.* London: Heinemann, 1904.

Nzongola-Ntalaja, Georges. *The Congo: From Leopold To Kabila: A People's History.* London and New York: Zed Books, 2002.

Slade, Ruth. *The Belgian Congo: Some Recent Changes.* London and New York: Oxford University Press, 1960.

Twain, Mark. *King Leopold's Soliloquy.* Boston: P. R. Warren, 1905.

Uzoigwe, G. N. *Britain and the Conquest of Africa: The Age of Salisbury.* Ann Arbor: University of Michigan Press, 1974.

G. N. Uzoigwe

The German Colonial Empire

Germany was a relative latecomer to overseas empire and administered some of its colonies quite harshly. Its colonial empire was seized after the loss in World War I. Unlike other European states, Germany played no direct role in the expansion of European influence abroad beginning in the early sixteenth century. Fragmented by dynastic and confessional divisions into the feudal petty states of the Holy Roman Empire, suffering relative economic decline since the fall of Constantinople and the rise of Atlantic trade routes, and then ravaged by the Thirty Years' War (1618–1648), Germany did not emerge as a modern unified state until 1871. By that time the lion's share of colonial territory in the Americas, Africa, Asia, and Australasia had been divided among the English, Dutch, French, Portuguese, and Spanish. Minor exceptions to this narrative were a number of short-lived mercantilist initiatives by German princes, of which only the exploits of Frederick William, Elector of Brandenburg (called the Great Elector; 1620–1688), in securing the trading post Gross-Friedrichsburg on the coast of present-day Ghana and outposts on St. Thomas in the Antilles for triangular trade, are worth mentioning. Even these minor possessions were sold to the Dutch in 1717. That is not to say that individuals from various German states did not contribute to European imperialism; quite the contrary. German sailors, cartographers, naturalists, missionaries, physicians, merchants, bankers, and mercenaries took an active part in various imperial enterprises. Likewise German farmers and craftspeople were a significant profile in a number of colonial populations, notably in British North America (for example, the Pennsylvania "Dutch"). Indeed, by the nineteenth century the flow of German immigrant settlers to the Americas in particular would assume massive dimensions and spark efforts within German aristocratic and bourgeois circles to create autonomous German settler colonies in the United States (Texas) and Brazil in order to secure this population for Germany. Such proposals were explored in some detail by the liberal 1848 revolutionaries under Heinrich von Gagern (1799–1880) as part of plans for a unified German state. In the absence of a navy, however, these plans remained speculative at best, and the subsequent collapse of the Frankfurt National Assembly in May of 1849 put a definitive end not only to the dream of a German colonial presence but to a liberal-democratic German state. The failure of the 1848 revolution and continued strong population growth would in turn accelerate this German emigration, which led to no fewer than 6 million settling in the United States before 1914.

The Origins of German Colonial Expansion.

Following the wars of German unification of 1864, 1866, and 1870–1871, Chancellor Otto von Bismarck was very sensitive to the fact that the new German Empire had disrupted the traditional European balance of power and that maintaining this unstable status quo required careful diplomacy to prevent a hostile bloc of states from forming against the Reich. Of those European states, France was least likely to be accommodated given its loss in the Franco-Prussian War of 1870–1871, which resulted in a high punitive indemnity and the loss of Alsace-Lorraine. The isolation of France and the maintenance of an alliance with Russia became cornerstones of German foreign policy under Bismarck to which all other ambitions were subordinated. To this end Bismarck took pains to emphasize that Germany was territorially satiated and devoted to stability in central Europe. The precarious fiscal structure of the imperial government—the Reich could not levy direct taxes—also put strict bounds on German foreign policy.

Despite this unpromising start, the late 1870s and early 1880s witnessed the effervescence of German procolonial interests and organizations. These began to articulate a complex of ambitions that reflected a peculiar set of anxieties about Germany at a time of economic change and societal flux. Among the most prominent and influential publicists and organizers of this movement were Friedrich Fabri (1824–1891), a Lutheran pastor and missionary, Wilhelm Hübbe-Schleiden (1846–1916), a Hamburg lawyer and former diplomat, the theoretician Ernst von Weber (1830–1902), the journalist Hugo Zöller (1852–1933), and the explorer, writer, and radical nationalist Carl Peters (1856–1918). These men shared an acute awareness of Germany as a belated nation-state and of the danger of missing what few opportunities remained to establish a presence overseas. Explicit or implicit in this was the ambition of establishing a colonial empire that could rival Great Britain's. Colonial ambitions were thus perceived as a "school of the nation" that would help fulfill a great national destiny and bring Germans the prestige and status of their British cousins. Like their predecessors during the 1848 revolution, they were also concerned about the social implications of rapid population growth and the need to capture the vast stream of emigrants heading to the Americas in German settler colonies. Indeed, colonial expansion was perceived as a way of defusing domestic German political tensions stoked by the rise of a large industrial working class and revolutionary Social

So kolonisiert der Deutsche,

So kolonisiert der Engländer,

"Colonial Powers." Drawing by Thomas Theodor Heine from the German satirical magazine *Simplicissimus*, 3 May 1904: "Here's how the German colonizes / Here's how the Englishman colonizes / and so the Frenchman / and so the Belgian."

Democratic Party. Another theme uniting some of these colonial advocates was the perceived need to secure colonies as sources of tropical products, raw materials and, especially, as a sales market for German industry, which at the time was suffering from heightened competition, overcapacity, and falling prices. That is, emphasis was placed on creating trading colonies, but this did not preclude a settler presence per se.

Over the course of the 1870s colonial ambitions shifted from more traditional sites of German colonial aspiration in the Americas, Asia, and the Near East to the African continent. Increasingly expansive and utopian dreams were projected upon West Africa by men like Hübbe-Schleiden and others who imagined creating a "German India." Colonial associations were also founded to promote these aims. Friedrich Fabri, Wilhelm Hübbe-Scheeiden, and Hugo Zöller were active in the West German Association for Colonization and Export (co-founded by Fabri in 1879). Prominent members of Germany's business establishment, including industrialists, bankers, shipping magnates, and trading company owners founded the German Colonial Association in 1882, while Carl Peters created the Society for German Colonization in 1884. The latter two organizations were amalgamated into the German Colonial Society in 1887, which became the most important of the German procolonial organizations. Even so, the colonial cause was never the exclusive purview of these and other colonial societies. An extraordinary variety of nationalist organizations were created over the course of the 1880s and 1890s that made German colonies a cause of their own and distanced themselves from the established colonial bodies by their even more strident expansionist aims, shrill language, and broader middle class base. One of the most prominent of these was the Pan-German League founded in 1894. These groups and others expressed grave concerns about rapid German industrialization and urbanization and the threats they posed to rural life and thus also to German identity and political culture. Settler colonies came to figure centrally as a panacea to these and other ills of modern life, and as importantly, as a means to spread German influence to all corners of the earth.

Given what is known about Bismarck's consistent rejection of colonial ambitions, his entry on the colonial stage in the spring of 1884 has presented something of a puzzle that historians have been trying to piece together for more than a century. Most agree that a German colonial gambit was enabled by the very favorable foreign circumstances in 1884, notably the existing tensions between Russia and Britain over Afghanistan as well as French and British disputes over Egypt. German involvement in Africa thus worked to further distract the European Great Powers, particularly France, from central Europe. Some have suggested that Bismarck's strategy was calculated to lead to some kind of accommodation or even alliance with France. Evidence also points to the fact that Bismarck was increasingly concerned about securing German export markets and commercial interests in the periphery in a climate of economic depression, increasing protectionism and possible exclusion from colonial markets. The Anglo-French Sierra Leone Agreement of 1882, which granted French and English traders reciprocal rights within their respective colonial spheres, as well as the expansion of French and Belgian interests along the Congo River, made such fears credible. There was particular concern about access to West Africa, and to a lesser extent Southwest Africa, New Guinea, and Samoa, where North German merchants and traders were active. Even so, Bismarck's initial ambitions were modest: at most he envisioned self-financed and self-administered trading colonies in various overseas outposts turned into Reich protectorates along a laissez-faire model of the flag following trade. No grand colonial strategy informed Bismarck's perspective—least of all did he envision settler colonies—and only the most minimal financial commitments were envisioned.

Domestic political calculations also seem to have played a significant role in Bismarck's decision. While he was no doubt responsive to the rise of procolonial sentiments in Germany, he saw a chance to exploit these for his own purposes in the 1884 autumn Reichstag elections, which afforded the opportunity to isolate the Progressive Liberals and Social Democrats by appealing to middle and lower middle class sentiments supportive of colonies, something both parties opposed on principle. At the same time he sought the cooperation of the National Liberals, many of whom were colonial supporters. Whether this is evidence of "social imperialism"—colonial empire as a deliberate ploy to diffuse domestic tensions and shore up middle class support for conservative policies serving the Junker elite—is a matter of dispute. Bismarck's own conflicting statements about what ends the colonies served add little clarity to this issue. Like much else Bismarckian, the colonies presented a political opportunity to address several problems simultaneously, ones not necessarily related. The picture presented by the "social imperialism" thesis, while suggestive, is too monolithic a picture that does not adequately account for multiplicity of forces and interests in evidence in the creation of the colonies.

German Southwest Africa. German Southwest Africa, declared a German protectorate in April 1884, would turn out to be Germany's most important colony in terms of economic value, as a destination for settlers and because of its boarder impact on German society. This was in what today constitutes the territory of Namibia, one of the driest countries of sub-Saharan Africa and one that had attracted little interest from the European powers before 1875. A German missionary presence had been active along Angra Pequena (Lüderitz Bay) and Walvis Bay on the coast and in Windhoek in the interior for some decades, but it was not until the ventures of Adolf Lüderitz (1834–1886) that this region gained official attention. A Bremen tobacco merchant and gun trader who managed to amass vast territory in the region through self-financed expeditions and questionable treaties, Lüderitz was after gold and diamonds but strained his personal resources and successfully lobbied for Reich protection over these lands in 1884. A year later he sold the territories to the newly founded Deutsche Kolonialgesellschaft für Südwest-Afrika (German Colonial Society for Southwest Africa, DKGSWA), As a concession company, it was entrusted with administering the colony, raising investment capital and, it was hoped, making profits, while the Reich provided a commissioner, a few civil administrators, and, despite initial reluctance, a small defensive force (Schutztruppe). The initial hopes for Southwest Africa were, however, quickly dashed by the realties of this sprawling, arid territory, of which only about 1 percent was suitable for arable farming and that required heavy port and railway investments before any of its anticipated mineral bounty could be exploited. The DKGSWA quickly revealed that it was incapable of shouldering these costs alone and the Reich was forced to fill the financial breach.

While sparsely populated, the native people of Southwest Africa numbered about 200,000 in 1884 and included the Owambo, Herero, Nama and Orlam (Hottentots), and San (Bushmen), of which the pastoralist Herero and Nama in the central and southern part of the country, respectively, were the largest groups. In classic imperial fashion tensions between the Herero and Nama were exploited in consolidating rule, with the Germans playing the Herero off against the Nama yet aiming to preserve tribal self-governance. This was greatly complicated by the migration of German settlers to the colony in the 1890s, something neither planned when the protectorate was created nor encouraged by the Colonial Section of the Foreign Office. This highlights both the unpredictable dynamic of colonies and the relative autonomy of the colonial movement within Germany, which found increasing support from radical nationalist and conservative circles in 1890s. Between 1891 and 1904, for example, the white population of Southwest Africa grew from 539 to 4,500. This influx of settlers produced many tensions with natives over cattle and grazing and undermined the administration's aim of preserving tribal integrity and self-governance. Railway investments added to these tensions by accelerating the dispossession of land while undermining the traditional structures of Herero and Nama society through the use of native labor. A catastrophic rinderpest epidemic in 1897 then destroyed about half of all native cattle and forced many more Herero to work for wages or depend on credit extended by German settlers. This in turn led to yet more losses of land and the creation of reservations. Legal insecurity and abusive colonial justice added much to these woes.

The tensions with the German population over land and the resulting loss of autonomy led to an organized uprising by the chief of the Herero, Samuel Maherero (1854–1923), and the slaughter of some 123 white farmers in January 1904. The rebellion caught the colonial administration flat-footed and precipitated the replacement of Governor Theodor Leutwein (1849–1921) by the uncompromising Friedrich von Lindequist (1862–1945) and the mustering of military reinforcements from Germany. The commander of the reinforced Schutztruppe, General Lothar von Trotha (1848–1920), a veteran of other colonial wars, conducted the campaign against the Herero people with a notorious ruthlessness, defeating the main Herero force at Waterberg in August 1904 and driving the survivors into the arid Omaheke steppe where most died of exposure. The war waged against the Herero people culminated in von Trotha's infamous "Extermination Decree" of October 1904, which put a cash prize on Maherero's head, refused peace negotiations, and declared that every Herero man, woman, and child was to be driven into exile or shot on sight. Around this time the Nama under Hendrik Witbooi (c. 1830–1905) also went to war against the Germans. Better armed and trained than the Herero, they managed to continue their struggle until March 1907.

The consequences of this war of extermination were catastrophic for both peoples. Those Herero who managed to survive landed in a system of camps and forced labor whose conditions killed nearly half of the remaining population. By 1911 they had been reduced by 75–80 percent of their prewar numbers, while the Nama suffered losses of nearly 60 percent. Tribal structures were dissolved, lands confiscated, and native populations were now subject to draconian legal restrictions and penal transportation. On the German side, the war cost some 1,500 men and 585 million marks. It also exacted a toll on Germany's self-image as a humane, civilized and orderly colonial power. Indeed the brutality of von Trotha's campaign and the long duration and high costs of the war produced fierce criticism from the Social Democrats, Catholic Center, and left liberal parties in the Reichstag. This precipitated a crisis of confidence in the entire colonial endeavor in 1906 and new elections early in 1907.

An illustration entitled *"Kolonialmächte"* (Colonial powers) by Thomas Theodor Heine offers an admittedly satirical but nonetheless revealing image of German self-perceptions of its style of colonial rule at this time. In the top image, entitled "This is how the German colonizes," the giraffes are numbered consecutively and march in lock-step before a colonial official. A palm to the right bears a sign that reads, "Dumping rubbish and snow here is prohibited." The crocodile in the foreground wears a tax collar and is being fitted with a muzzle by a colonial soldier. Like all stereotypes, there is a grain of truth here about German colonial rule, yet the colonial experience in German Southwest Africa and elsewhere also showed how the German taste for law and order was repeatedly warped to serve the aim of dominating native populations by local interventions into the rule of law. Examples of this included the extraordinary escalation in the use of corporal punishment as well as arbitrary restrictions on intermarriage, movement, the disposal of property, and not least, the suspension of the rules of war in dealing with native uprisings. It is very ironic, although not any less true, that despite the coercion of the colonial regime—indeed, perhaps because of the regime's uncompromising subordination of the natives—many German settlers, including many women, came to view Southwest Africa as a place of freedom, opportunity, social mobility, and emancipation. But this was hardly the first or last time in African history that the freedom of a white minority was secured at the expense of the native population.

For obvious reasons, it has been tempting to see in the genocidal war waged against the Herero and Nama and the system of camps developed to control and exploit their remnant populations an important precedent for the murderous policies of the Nazi regime less than forty years later. As suggestive are the continuities in German military thinking that enabled this first of three "wars without mercy" in the twentieth century. At the same time, comparative studies reveal an unsettling pattern of "frontier genocide"

with much in common between the Herero experience and, for example, the destruction of the Tasmanians in Australia and the Yuki Indians of California. With this in mind, it may be most accurate to interpret the Herero and Nama war as both fitting prior historical patterns and, through its scale and brutality, setting a disturbing precedent for twentieth-century genocide.

Following the 1907 Reichstag elections, a reform course was begun by the director of the newly created Colonial Office, Bernhard Dernburg (1865–1937), which aimed at better treatment of native populations, fostering indigenous farming and a more scientific and economically rational approach to developing the colonies. The expansion of railways figured centrally in this new thinking. Numerous railway lines were completed in Southwest Africa in 1907–1909 and enabled much expanded copper and diamond mining. By 1913 these two commodities alone comprised well over 90 percent of the value of Southwest Africa's exports, and the colony's economy accounted for no less than 65 to 75 percent of all colonial trade with Germany. But measured against the enormous administrative and military outlays and heavy state investments in railways, the colony remained a net liability for the Reich until its loss in World War I. Thereafter it was administered by South Africa as a League of Nations mandate.

German East Africa. Next in importance as a German colony was East Africa, which comprised the present-day territories of Tanzania, Rwanda, and Burundi. German Hanseatic traders had been active in Zanzibar and its adjacent African coast for some time, but Reich protection over what came to be German East Africa was not extended until the independent exploits of the adventurer Carl Peters. A man of pathological ambition animated by the reports of the explorer David Livingstone (1813–1873), Peters managed to acquire a vast coastal hinterland through dubious treaties in February of 1885. These were then offered Reich protection with some reluctance by Bismarck. Later that month, Peters founded the Deutsch-Ostafrikanische Gesellschaft (German East Africa Company, DOAG), which subsequently gained sovereign rights to operate and administer the territory. In years following Peters continued his exploits to expand the territory under delusions of creating a "German India" that would extend from Somaliland to Mozambique, much to the chagrin of Bismarck, who saw German relations with Britain threatened by such reckless moves and rescinded Peters' letter of safe conduct. As it turned out, Peters' DOAG conducted it affairs quite heavy-handedly and generated frictions with

Arab coastal traders, which led to a major uprising in 1888–1889 that the DOAG was in no position to suppress. Troops had to be dispatched from Germany, and by 1891 the territory came under direct control of its first German colonial governor, Julius von Soden (1846–1921).

German East Africa had a complex ethnic composition that included Arab and Indian traders, Swahili, and a variety of Bantu and Tutsi peoples that made imperial submission, much less effective economic exploitation, a challenging endeavor. Indeed, extensive military campaigns had to be waged between 1891 and 1897 just to pacify the territory, with much of the eastern parts of the country remaining under indirect rule or ungoverned. The region around Mount Kilimanjaro was particularly troublesome in this respect because of the influx of white settlers into this area in the 1890s. The DOAG and the colonial government had sought to develop large-scale plantation cash-crop production and to systematically exploit the human and natural resources of the colony to this end. Village cotton production was made compulsory by the administration and traditional hunting was prohibited or restricted. Lands were expropriated and native labor was recruited, often forcibly, to work the plantations. Crushing hut and head taxes were imposed and collected with great brutality by the Askari mercenary forces employed by the Germans. More often than not, these taxes were paid in the form of extensive labor services sold to plantation owners. Large railway projects connecting the coast to the Kilimanjaro region and the banks of Lake Tanganyika were also undertaken. Native social structure changed dramatically as a consequence of the labor recruitment policies that were part of the plantation economy and railway construction, a process that eventually undermined peasant agriculture and led to the abandonment of many villages. At the same time the activities of missionaries threatened traditional customs and sources of authority.

Under these circumstances, it was not altogether surprising that German East Africa witnessed a major native revolt in 1905. The Maji Maji uprising spearheaded by the Ngoni, Pangwa, and other Bantu peoples of the south and articulated through the idiom of traditional religious cults sought to restore the older order being destroyed by the colonial presence. The uprising was met with a harsh response that cost the lives of some 75,000 and nearly annihilated the Pangwa. Punitive measures after the war killed many more. But the uprising, coinciding as it did with the Herero and Nama wars, shook the colonial administration to its core and reverberated all

the way back to Berlin. Under Bernhard Dernburg in the Imperial Colonial Office and the new governor of East Africa, Albrecht von Rechenberg (1861–1935), a dramatic change in policy was ushered in which aimed at restricting settler and plantation activities in the interest of fostering native peasant agriculture. To this end Rechenberg prohibited whites from purchasing native lands, reformed taxes, ended compulsory village cultivation of cotton, restricted corporal punishment, and reformed local government to include native interests. These progressive reforms did defuse tensions and resulted in considerable increases in native cash crop production, especially of copra, coffee, and rubber. In reality, however, there were limits to how much could be done to restore native agriculture given the wrenching changes witnessed in the colony as well as deep white settler hostility to Rechenberg's policies. Despite the inroads made by planters and cash crops in the colony, it is worth mentioning that before World War I German East Africa ran consistent trade deficits with Germany and, like nearly all of the Reich's other colonies save Togo, could not pay its own keep. Following the war, German East Africa was divided between Britain, Belgium, and Portugal.

Togo and Cameroon. Both Togo and Cameroon were seized for Germany in an extraordinary bit of gunboat diplomacy in July of 1884. Bremen and Hamburg merchants and traders and German missionaries had established a presence in both West African territories, but given the pace of Belgian, British, and French annexations along the Congo, Niger, and Volta rivers, concern grew about eventual German exclusion. Togo was brought under Reich protection by treaties of 4–6 July 1884 to secure the interests of the pious Bremen merchant family Vietor, involved in the lucrative palm product trade, as well as to protect the North German Mission. Togo's coastal Ewe people had been in touch with European missionaries and traders for generations and did not violently oppose the German presence. Bringing the northern peoples— the Dagomba, Kabre, Konkomba, and Tykossi, among others—under German administration proved more difficult and led to an indirect form of rule.

In marked contrast to the other African colonies, Togo's colonial history was not punctuated by major uprisings or marked by severe mistreatment of its native populations, although the Togolese, like other people under German colonial rule, were subject to rigid colonial justice that made much use of corporeal punishment. Vietor and the missionaries opposed the alcohol and gun trade on principle (albeit unsuccessfully), and along with Governor Julius von Zech (1868–1914), successfully resisted the encroachment of large-scale plantations by land reforms that secured native title, intent as they were to protect and foster traditional indigenous farming. Togo also had a very high concentration of mission schools and the highest rate of school attendance and literacy in West Africa. Nevertheless, its economy was dominated by exports of palm nuts and oil (76 percent of exports in 1911), which only accounted for less than 8 percent of German colonial trade before World War I. Quite remarkably, Togo was the only German colony that was able to bear its own administrative costs. Following World War I, Togo was divided between France and Britain.

Cameroon became a Reich protectorate through a treaty with the Duala people on 14 July 1884 just days before it was to be annexed by the British. This move was made in order to secure the interests of the C. Woermann Company, a major alcoholic spirits exporter to West Africa. German colonial activities were confined largely to the coastal region with some forays made into the immediate southern hinterland resulting in fighting with the Bakoko, Bane, and other peoples, who took years to subdue. Indeed, fighting and uprisings of various kinds were a running theme in Cameroon's colonial history, and eastern Cameroon was only indirectly ruled by the Germans. In fact, many of the colony's export products such as rubber and ivory were collected by native peoples in the ungoverned hinterland and carried to the coast. In some contrast to Togo, however, large plantations came to figure importantly in Cameroon's economy with many of the same abuses already enumerated in the discussion of German East Africa. Worth mentioning here is the West African Plantation Company Victoria, the single most important planter company operating in Cameroon and a favorite of the colonial governor Jesko von Puttkamer (1855–1917), who was a shareholder. With the connivance of the colonial government, the company systematically expropriated native lands in the Cameroon highlands, destroying village life and removing the natives to reservations or turning them into plantation laborers subject to much coercion and cruelty. Complaints about Puttkamer's abusive and corrupt regime reached a chorus during the series of colonial crises that wracked Germany in 1905–1906, and in 1907 he was replaced by Theodor Seitz (1863–1949). Like his counterpart von Rechenberg in East Africa, Seitz tried to accommodate the native population by reforming the administration and improving the working conditions of plantation laborers, albeit with only rather modest success. The primary exports of Cameroon were rubber, cacao, palm oil, and ivory, in that order of significance, but it ran continued trade deficits with Germany and relied heavily on Reich subsidies to finance its administration. Cameroon's territory was divided between the French and British following World War I.

The Pacific Colonies and Kiaochow. Since the 1860s German Hanseatic traders and merchants had gained a prominent position in the South Pacific. But with British expansion into Fiji in 1874, American dominance of Hawaii beginning in 1875, and Australian influence spreading to New Guinea, concerns were raised about possible German exclusion from this trade, which centered on copra, coconut oil, cotton, tortoise shell, and mother of pearl. Most prominent in this trade was the Hamburg firm Johann Cesar Godeffroy & Son (later Deutsche Handels und Plantagen Gesellschaft [German Trade and Plantation Company, DHPG]), with a sprawling network of coconut and cotton plantations dotted over many islands in the South Pacific and headquartered in Apia, Samoa, where the German navy also had a base. As a result of these interests and the threats posed to them by the warring factions of Samoa, the DHPG, supported by the German consulate, overthrew the Samoan government in 1887, and following a series of negotiations and conferences with the British and Americans, jointly governed the islands until 1900. In that year Samoa was divided between the Americans and Germans, with Western Samoa becoming a German colony. By all accounts the first German governor, Wilhelm Solf (1862–1936), was an outstanding administrator who rarely resorted to violence and did much to bring about reconciliation between Samoa's opposing factions. Solf worked to foster indigenous cash crop production by encouraging coconut cultivation, restricted the sale of land to white planters, and prohibited forced labor on existing plantations. He also sought to protect Samoan cultural integrity by restricting permanent immigration of foreign laborers to Samoa. Samoa's main export to Germany was copra, but the Pacific colonies, including Samoa, only accounted for less than 8.5 percent of Germany's copra imports and as little as 0.15 percent of Germany's overall trade in 1909. After World War I, New Zealand administered German Samoa as a League of Nations mandate.

Around the same time that German influence was growing in Samoa, the New Guinea Consortium (later renamed the New Guinea Company) was formed by the prominent German bankers Adolf von Hansemann (1826–1903) and Gerson von Bleichröder (1822–1893)—the latter Bismarck's private banker—with the aim of developing

TABLE 1. *Colonial territories and their German populations, 1910*

	LAND AREA (THOUSAND KM$[^2]$)	GERMAN INHABITANTS
Southwest Africa	835.1	9,283
East Africa	995	2,384
Cameroon	495.6	986
Togo	87.2	300
New Guinea	240	549
Caroline, Palau, Mariana and Marshall Islands	2.47	236
Samoa	2.57	270
Kiaochow	0.5	1,412
Total	2,658.44	15,420

SOURCE: Kaiserliches Statistisches Amt, ed., *Statistisches Jahrbuch für das Deutsche Reich*, 1910 (Berlin: Puttkammer & Mühlbrecht, 1911), p. 396

plantations on the northeastern part of the island of New Guinea. In 1883 this territory was claimed and in the autumn of 1884 it gained Reich protection. The company was given a concession to administer New Guinea and the New Britain Archipelago. To this was then added a series of islands in Micronesia including the Marshall Islands, which were administered by the Jaluit Company. Negotiations with the British in 1885 affirmed Germany's claim over northeastern New Guinea (renamed Kaiser Wilhelmsland), the New Britain Archipelago (renamed the Bismarck Archipelago), and the Marshall Islands. In 1899 the Caroline, Mariana, and Palau islands were purchased from Spain and added to this sprawling oceanic empire. However, by then the New Guinea Company had failed to develop viable plantations in New Guinea producing only tensions with the indigenous population over land and the treatment of plantation workers. Thus the Reich was forced to administer these territories as a colony starting in 1899. The first governor, Albert Hahl (1868–1945), addressed these problems by protecting existing native land claims, regulating plantation work, encouraging native cash crop production and improving medical care and schooling. Before 1914 New Guinea showed remarkable increases in exports of copra, rubber, guttapercha, and phosphates, but the colony was only ever a tiny component of German overall trade. New Guinea was seized by Australia during World War I and was administered as a League of Nations mandate thereafter.

The final part of the German colonial empire was the Chinese treaty port of Kiaochow on the Shantung peninsula. German merchants, traders, and manufacturers had been much lured by the promise of the China market since its opening in the 1840s. By the 1890s German trade with China exceeded trade with its own colonial possessions and it began to greatly overshadow the relatively disappointing African colonies. In 1897 the killing of German

missionaries was used as a pretext for seizing a base of operation in the Bay of Kiaochow centered on the small port city of Tsing-tao on the Shantung peninsula. Through negotiation with the Chinese, this territory was then leased to Germany for ninety-nine years. Kiaochow, unlike the other colonies, was administered by the Imperial Navy, and the Naval Secretary Admiral Alfred von Tirpitz (1849–1930) took a special interest in it not only as a naval base but also as a spearhead from which Germany could begin to economically penetrate China. It was also to serve as a model treaty port demonstrating Germany's superiority over Britain and the other imperial powers. To that end enormous sums of money were invested into Kiaochow for such things as modern sewage and water works, port facilities, telegraphs, and roads. The German Shantung Mining Company and the Railway Company were created and granted monopoly concessions to develop railway lines into the interior and open up modern coal mines to supply Kiaochow and export markets in East Asia. By 1913 Kiaochow had received some 200 million marks in investments and subsidies from the Reich making it by far the most expensive single colonial project. However, Shantung Mining remained a loss-making enterprise and the hoped for economic penetration of China by Germany did not materialize. What is more, Germany trailed the Japanese, British, and Americans in terms of their share of exports to the port of Tsing-tao. Shortly after the outbreak of World War I, Japan occupied Kiaochow. It reverted to Chinese rule in 1922.

[*See also* Cameroon; Herero Revolt; Maji Maji Rebellion; Papua New Guinea; Southwest Africa; *and* Tanzania.]

BIBLIOGRAPHY

Arendt, Hannah *The Origins of Totalitarianism.* 2d enl. ed. New York: Meridian, 1958. The first work to draw parallels between colonial violence and the rise of National Socialism. While some of its claims are problematic, it is still a very stimulating book.

Bernhardi, Friedrich von. *Germany and the Next War*. Translated by Alan H. Powles. New York: Longmans, Green, and Co., 1914. English translation of *Deutschland und der Nächste Krieg*, first published in 1912. Influential statement of the aims of German "world policy" shortly before World War I.

Bley, Helmut. *South-West Africa under German Rule, 1894–1914*. Translated by Hugh Ridley. Evanston, Ill.: Northwestern University Press, 1971. English translation of *Kolonialherrschaft und Sozialstruktur in Deutsch-Südwestafrika*, first published in 1968. An important study of the most significant German settler colony including analysis of the causes and consequences of the Herero and Nama wars.

Bridgman, Jon M. *The Revolt of the Hereros*. Berkeley, Los Angeles, and London: University of California Press, 1981. A very useful history of the Herero revolt and its consequences.

Eley, Geoff. *Reshaping the German Right: Radical Nationalism and Political Change After Bismarck*. New Haven, Conn.: Yale University Press, 1980. The definitive study of the noisy politics of Germany's radical nationalists, their impact on Germany's political culture and influence on policy-making after 1890.

Eley, Geoff, and James Retallack, eds. *Wilhelminism and Its Legacies: German Modernities, Imperialism, and the Meanings of Reform, 1890–1930: Essays for Hartmut Pogge von Strandmann*. New York and Oxford: Berghahn Books, 2003. Contains a number of important contributions on German imperialism and Wilhelmine politics and culture.

Fabri, Friedrich. *Bedarf Deutschland der Colonien/Does Germany Need Colonies?* Translated, edited, and introduced by E. C. M. Breuning and M. E. Chamberlain. 3d ed. Lewiston, N.Y.: Edwin Mellen, 1998. English translation of *Bedarf Deutschland der Colonien*, first published in 1879. One of the most influential tracts written advocating German colonial expansion abroad.

Friedrichsmeyer, Sara, Sara Lennox, and Susanne Zantop, eds. *The Imperialist Imagination: German Colonialism and Its Legacy*. Ann Arbor: University of Michigan Press, 1998. Contains many stimulating chapters on the impact of the colonial experience on German literature, culture, and politics.

Gall, Lothar. *Bismarck, the White Revolutionary*. 2 vols. Translated by J. A. Underwood. London and Boston: Allen & Unwin, 1986. English translation of *Bismarck: Der weisse Revolutionär*, first published in 1980. A brilliant study of Bismarck's style of politics and the complex of motives driving his bid for colonies.

Grimmer-Solem, Erik. "The Professors' Africa: Economists, the Elections of 1907, and the Legitimation of German Imperialism." *German History* 25, no. 3 (2007): 313–347. Analyzes the transformation of German imperialist ideology following the colonial crisis of 1906–1907.

Iliffe, John. *Tanganyika under German Rule, 1905–1912*. London: Cambridge University Press, 1969. An important study of the colonial administration of German East Africa shortly before World War I.

Kennedy, Paul M. *The Rise of Anglo-German Antagonism, 1860–1914*. Boston and London: Allen & Unwin, 1980. A thorough analysis of the sources of friction, colonial and other, between Germany and Britain that led to World War I.

Madley, Benjamin. "Patterns of Frontier Genocide 1803–1910: The Aboriginal Tasmanians, the Yuki of California, and the Herero of Namibia." *Journal of Genocide Research* 6, no. 2 (June 2004): 167–192. Reveals the common processes at work in the genocidal confrontation between native peoples and settlers over resources.

Moses, John A., and Paul M. Kennedy, eds. *Germany in the Pacific and Far East, 1870–1914*. St. Lucia, Australia: University of Queensland Press, 1977. Contains many valuable chapters on German imperialism in China, New Guinea, and the Pacific.

Perras, Arne. *Carl Peters and German Imperialism, 1856–1918: A Political Biography*. New York: Oxford University Press; Oxford: Clarendon Press, 2003. A valuable recent biography of the adventurer and Pan-German nationalist who founded German East Africa.

Smith, Woodruff D. *The German Colonial Empire*. Chapel Hill: University of North Carolina Press, 1978. A very useful and reliable survey of German colonial history.

Taylor, A. J. P. *Germany's First Bid for Colonies 1884–1885: A Move in Bismarck's European Policy*. New York: W.W. Norton, 1970. A provocative book that argues for the central role of Bismarck's European diplomacy in German colonial expansion.

Townsend, Mary Evelyn. *The Rise and Fall of Germany's Colonial Empire, 1884–1918*. New York: Howard Fertig, 1966. A thorough history of Germany's colonial empire.

Wildenthal, Lora. *German Women for Empire, 1884–1945*. Durham, N.C., and London: Duke University Press, 2001. Reveals the extent to which German women became materially, politically and intellectually invested in the German colonial empire.

Erik Grimmer-Solem

East Asia

Before the nineteenth century, East Asia was dominated by the last of a series of powerful land empires centered on the Chinese mainland. The Manchu rulers of the Qing Empire (1644–1912) not only conquered the territory controlled earlier by the Chinese Ming dynasty (1368–1644) but expanded the borders of the empire to include Manchuria, Mongolia, East Turkestan (now known as Xinjiang), and Tibet. The Qing Empire used a variety of sophisticated ideologies and practices to rule its far-flung domains and to mediate its relations with its neighbors. The court generally required peoples of the East Asian coastal region, including Korea, Liuqiu (Ryūkyū), and Annam (Indochina), to adhere to a traditional Sinocentric tribute system, in which the empire's tributaries declared their acceptance of Qing suzerainty in return for implied security guarantees and some degree of commercial access. It pacified and governed other areas and borders through military colonization, utilization of local elites, adept use of Buddhist symbolism, and deft diplomacy. Inner Asian peoples such as the Mongols and the Zunghars presented significant challenges to Qing rule, but were ultimately co-opted or conquered.

The chief land-based competitor to Qing dominance in Asia was the empire of Tsarist Russia. Russia's eastward expansion increased the length of its empire's border with the Qing Empire and led to a number of conflicts and consequent diplomatic agreements. In the eighteenth century, a thriving Russian–Qing trade far surpassed the trade between the Qing Empire and various Western powers in the southern port city of Guangzhou (Canton).

In the nineteenth century Qing dominance in East Asia was challenged by the arrival in earnest of such Western maritime powers as the British, French, and Americans. Western powers had long sought greater access to the restricted Chinese market but were generally rebuffed by the powerful Qing court. Moreover, while European and North American demand for Chinese goods such as tea, porcelain, and silk was large and ever growing, the Western powers could provide little that appealed to the Chinese market. Thus the pre–nineteenth-century trade generally involved the exchange of foreign silver for Chinese goods.

The Qing Empire's ability to dictate the terms of its foreign relations and trade was challenged by the West's growing military superiority and the increasing competitiveness of its manufactured goods. British merchants and adventurers initially cracked open the Chinese market by illegally importing opium, usually produced in Britain's colony India, into China. Qing attempts to restrict the opium trade and punish the smugglers resulted in the First Opium War (1840–1842), in which the Qing navy's inability seriously to contend with its British counterpart was starkly revealed. The resulting Treaty of Nanjing (1842) called for the opening of five additional treaty ports on the Chinese coast and ushered in the era of unequal treaties, during which foreigners enjoyed special privileges, including extraterritoriality, in China. The use of most-favored-nation clauses generally meant that whatever privilege one outside power was able to wrest from the Qing Empire was made available to all. This was the beginning of the treaty-port system, in which foreign access and privileges were protected and promoted at the expense of Chinese sovereignty.

Opium, along with growing amounts of Western manufactured goods, particularly cotton textiles, poured into China, causing significant economic and social dislocation, especially along the coast. In addition, Western missionaries, enjoying treaty-guaranteed privileges and military protection, fanned across China in search of converts. Through a series of conflicts—the most significant being the Second Opium War (1856–1860), toward the end of which an Anglo-French expedition marched on Beijing and looted and destroyed the Qing Summer Palace (Yuanming Yuan)—foreign powers gained increasing access and privilege in China. Yet foreign powers generally did not seek directly to annex Chinese territory, two exceptions being Hong Kong and Macao. The residual strength of the Qing Empire remained significant enough to deter any would-be formal colonizer. In addition, there was no need to colonize China. For one, the commercial, diplomatic, and proselytizing access guaranteed by the treaty-port system generally protected and promoted the primary interests of foreigners in China. For another, dominating the Qing Empire as a semicolony was far cheaper and less entangling than direct territorial control.

The Rise of Japan. Tokugawa Japan (1603–1867) generally sought to restrict relations with the outside world, allowing only a handful of Dutch merchants on the island of Dejima in Nagasaki Harbor and a larger number of Chinese merchants to trade in Japan. The United States directly challenged this policy of seclusion, sending Commodore Matthew Perry and a squadron of gunboats to Edo (Tokyo) Bay in 1853 to negotiate a treaty with the Tokugawa government. The resulting treaty was followed by similar agreements with other Western powers and caused a great deal of soul searching and debate within Japan. Ultimately the Tokugawa government was overthrown, and a new group of oligarchs (*genrō*) established a regime in the name of the Meiji Emperor.

Meiji Japan (1868–1912) embarked on a course of rapid modernization and imperial expansion. After solidifying control over the northern island of Hokkaido, Meiji Japan then moved to challenge Qing Chinese claims of suzerainty over the Liuqiu Islands, successfully incorporating them in 1879. The Meiji Empire also used gunboat diplomacy to force its neighbor Chosŏn Korea (1392–1910) to open its doors to Japanese merchants and diplomats in 1876. Japan subsequently established a system of exclusive privileges for Japanese in Korea and enjoyed the benefits of duty-free trade there. Claiming the prerogatives of traditional suzerainty in Korea, the Qing Empire mediated Chosŏn Korea's first treaties with the United States, Britain, and Germany and aggressively asserted the Qing Empire's own unequal privileges in and access to Korea in a way reminiscent of the treaty-port system in China itself.

Confronted by growing Russian power to its north, restive and often rebellious populations in its western domains, devastating internal rebellions, and the serious challenge posed by Western and Japanese maritime empires along its coast, the beleaguered Qing Empire decided to devote its resources to suppressing rebellions in East Turkestan. This effort ultimately resulted in the incorporation of the region into the empire as Xinjiang

Province. However, this decision drew resources away from naval modernization, coastal defense, and other programs needed to counter the Western and Japanese threats. As a result, the Qing Empire could not defend its suzerainty in Korea and dramatically lost in the First Sino-Japanese War (1894–1895). Japan claimed the island of Taiwan as a spoil of war, but its attempt also to annex the Liaodong Peninsula on the Chinese mainland was thwarted by the triple intervention of Russia, France, and Germany. Western imperial powers strengthened their domination and began to carve up spheres of influence in China, especially after the suppression of the antiforeign Boxer Rebellion (1900). Still, the Qing Empire, limping on, successfully strengthened its hold on Xinjiang and resisted British attempts to assert control over Tibet.

While most foreign powers were content with the privileges and access afforded by the system of unequal treaties in China (as well as in Korea and Japan) and did not seek directly to annex territory, the worldwide shift to high imperialism at the end of the nineteenth century echoed in East Asia. Tsarist Russia sought to tighten its grip on Manchuria. The United States annexed the Philippines as a result of the 1898 Spanish-American War. But by far the most aggressive and far-reaching territorial grabs were Japan's expansions onto the Asian mainland. After defeating Russia in the 1903–1904 Russo-Japanese War, Japan annexed the southern half of Sakhalin Island (which it named Karafuto) and declared Korea to be a Japanese Protectorate in 1905. In 1910 it followed up by formally annexing Korea.

The fall of the Qing Empire in the 1911–1912 Chinese Republican Revolution had surprisingly little impact on the system of Western-dominated semicolonialism in China. Despite political weakness and fragmentation, the Chinese Republic was able to maintain its claims to most of the territory conquered by the Qing Empire (with the exceptions of Mongolia and Taiwan), though it could not exercise jurisdiction over foreign concessions in its own treaty-port cities. Japan remained the main imperialist power seeking greater territory. As a result of the Treaty of Versailles, which parceled up the world after World War I, Japan inherited German colonial possessions in Asia. It sought ever greater domination in Manchuria, ultimately creating the puppet state of Manchukuo in 1931. And in a series of conflicts throughout the 1930s but beginning in earnest in 1937, it ultimately engaged China in a battle for control of China proper. Japanese armies devastated northern and central China, routing the armies of Chiang Kai-shek (Jiang Jieshi) and the Nationalists (Guomindang),

and earning international opprobrium for its use of aircraft against civilian targets and for its large-scale massacre of civilians in and around the city of Nanjing. Japanese advances were stalled, however, by the sheer size of China's territory and population and by supply and resource constraints. Western-led attempts to contain Japanese expansionism and deny Japan access to oil, rubber, and other critical resources led to Japan's fateful decision to attack the United States at Pearl Harbor in 1941 and to seek control of Southeast Asia in the name of liberating Asian peoples from Western colonial rule. The resulting four years of war devastated much of East Asia and left the Japanese Empire in rubble.

The Aftermath of World War II and the Cold War. The defeat and collapse of the Japanese Empire signaled the beginning of the end of both formal colonial rule and older forms of semicolonial rule in East Asia. Japan was forced to cede all claims to its territorial acquisitions with the exception of Hokkaido, Okinawa, and a handful of disputed islets. Though Japanese motives for expansion in the first half of the twentieth century seldom matched the high-minded rhetoric of the East Asia Co-prosperity Sphere, one consequence of Japanese imperial expansion was the destruction of Western colonial regimes in Asia. After the collapse of the Japanese Empire at the end of World War II, the British, French, Dutch, and Americans all sought to reclaim their colonies in East and Southeast Asia, but nearly all of the Western colonial possessions would become independent nation-states in the decades after 1945. After an intense civil war, the Communists triumphed in China and proceeded to dismantle the treaty-port system and unequal treaties. Soon only Hong Kong and Macao remained as the last vestiges of the old system.

Yet some older conflicts and themes continued in the period following World War II. After a brief period of socialist fraternity, China and the Soviet Union parted ways in the late 1950s, and this led to competition between the two great Eurasian land empires and decades of tension and occasional armed clashes. China also sought to defend its security and assert its power in a conflict with the United States on the Korean peninsula during 1950–1953—a conflict that left hundreds of thousands of soldiers and even larger numbers of civilians dead and heightened the sense of Sino-American competition for decades.

As part of its Cold War strategy (arguably an extension of the nineteenth-century Anglo-Russian rivalry with the United States standing in for Britain), the United States maintained bases and troops in Japan, South Korea, and the Philippines, and continued to support the Nationalist regime on Taiwan. In the Second Indochina War (Vietnam War), the United States also enlisted assistance from its East Asian allies, economic assistance in the case of Japan, military assistance in the case of South Korea. All of this was done in the name of mutual security interests, but critics decried the U.S. presence in Asia as neocolonialism. Others ruefully noted the significance and power of Western ideas and culture in much of anticommunist East Asia. However, Japan rapidly reindustrialized, and this feat was followed by the industrialization of South Korea, Taiwan, Hong Kong, and Singapore, the so-called Four Tigers. As the United States and Europe came to import significant quantities of East Asian manufactured goods, West–East commercial relations were transformed. Many in East Asia spoke with increasing confidence of the importance of Asian values to economic development and of the coming Pacific Century. Then the stagnation of the Japanese economy and the significant shocks of the Asian Financial Crisis (1997–1998) eroded the easy confidence with which many viewed the future prosperity and success of Japan and the Four Tigers, but these countries remain important and increasingly independent economic and political actors in the region.

After three decades of ill-fated and often spectacularly destructive experiments in socialist revolution, the People's Republic of China also began increasingly to participate in regional and global markets with astounding success, particularly in the 1990s and 2000s. As part of its general policy of a peaceful rise to regional and even global prominence, the People's Republic has emphasized its benign intentions toward its neighbors. However, the regime continues to maintain a strong grip on its colonial possessions in Xinjiang and Tibet and has, from time to time, aggressively asserted claims to islets and their surrounding ocean territory in the South China Sea.

Japan continues to adhere to the restrictions of its U.S.-drafted Peace Constitution, but in view of the rise of China and what some see as a gradual reduction of the U.S. presence and power in Asia, some Japanese are calling for Japan to return to normalcy, which would entail acquiring an offensive military capability and perhaps even nuclear weapons. Many of Japan's neighbors and former colonies observe this internal debate with some anxiety about a future resurgence of Japanese imperialism. In the early twenty-first century, East Asia may yet again experience some of the same patterns of imperialism that it has seen in the past.

[*See also* Cultural Export in East Asia; Japan, *subentry* Japanese Foreign Relations; Japanese in China; Korean War; Manchuria; Opium Wars; Russo-Japanese War; Sino-Japanese Wars; Trade, International, *subentry* East Asia; Treaty Ports; "Unequal Treaties"; *and* Vietnam Wars, *subentry* Effect on East Asia.]

BIBLIOGRAPHY

Abernethy, David. *The Dynamics of Global Dominance: European Overseas Empires, 1415–1980.* New Haven, Conn.: Yale University Press, 2000.

Beasley, W. G. *Japanese Imperialism, 1894–1945.* New York: Oxford University Press, 1987.

Cohen, Warren. *East Asia at the Center.* New York: Columbia University Press, 2001.

Crossley, Pamela. *A Translucent Mirror: History and Identity in Qing Imperial Ideology.* Berkeley: University of California Press, 1999.

Duus, Peter. *The Abacus and the Sword: The Japanese Penetration of Korea, 1859–1910.* Berkeley: University of California Press, 1995.

Iriye, Akira. *China and Japan in the Global Setting.* Cambridge, Mass.: Harvard University Press, 1998.

Kim, Key-Hiuk. *The Last Phase of the East Asian World Order: Korea, Japan, and the Chinese Empire, 1860–1882.* Berkeley: University of California Press, 1980.

Lieven, Dominic. *Empire: The Russian Empire and Its Rivals.* New Haven, Conn.: Yale University Press, 2001.

Mancall, Mark. *China at the Center: 300 Years of Foreign Policy.* New York: Free Press, 1984.

Perdue, Peter. *China Marches West: The Qing Conquest of Central Eurasia.* Cambridge, Mass.: Harvard University Press, 2005.

KIRK W. LARSEN

Imperialism and the Environment

Imperialism has transformed the natural world on a global scale. Alfred Crosby's pathbreaking scholarship has aptly characterized biological conquest as ecological imperialism, a process that saw Europeans unwittingly introduce into their spheres of exploitation their diseases, plants, and animals. In the cases that Crosby cites for the sixteenth through the eighteenth centuries, these biological invasions dramatically transformed demography and ecology. In the Americas, for example, Europeans carried the microbes that caused influenza and smallpox, diseases that had evolved in Europe and Asia as a result of contacts between human populations and domesticated animals. Native populations did not possess either the Old World's domesticates or adequate immune responses, and when exposed to the previously unknown diseases they died in great numbers. In Crosby's view, the deadly cocktail of diseases decimated indigenous populations and subsequently opened the Americas to easy conquest by Europeans, as well as by their exotic plants and animals. The ecological exchanges tied to this phase of ecological imperialism moved in multiple directions, however. Whereas influenza, wheat, cattle, sheep, and pigs invaded America, Australia, and New Zealand, American maize, potatoes, and cassava found their way via global trade routes to Africa, Europe, and Asia, where they became an important part of agricultural ecosystems.

During the nineteenth and twentieth centuries, biological exchanges continued. However, as imperialism evolved along with Western science, technology, capitalism, and industry, the imperialist project developed both an economic and a moralistic trajectory that required nothing less than the systematic transformation of tropical environments and peoples.

New Imperialism and Science. The impetus for the effort to control tropical environments arose in part from the growing momentum of industrialization and the economic rivalries that it engendered in Europe and North America. Industrial processes required tropical commodities such as timber, rubber, cotton, vegetable oils, metal ores, and animal hides. At the same time, the increasingly wealthy populations of industrializing nations demanded luxury goods found in the tropics, goods such as sugar, tea, coffee, ivory, diamonds, silver, and gold. Increased industrial productivity required wealthy nations to seek out markets for their surplus manufactured goods. As a result, nineteenth-century industrializing nations attempted increasingly to control the production and distribution of tropical commodities, as well as market access in their growing spheres of influence. By the late nineteenth century, European nations justified their claims over the world's resources with an arrogance drawn from both their faith in bureaucratic government and also the ability of science and technology to tame tropical environments. Imperialism thus became a vehicle for extending an ideological and an ecological regime.

Government-sponsored and private organizations underwrote the expansion of imperial political, economic, and ecological influence. Agents from British, German, Dutch, French, Belgian, and U.S. firms staked claims to the natural resources of places as far flung as the Indian subcontinent, Australia, New Zealand, West Africa, Cuba, Central America, the Philippines, and Hawai'i. Their operations were unabashedly extractive and violent. In one of the worst cases of overzealous exploitation, Belgium's King Leopold II carved out his own personal fiefdom in the Congo River basin, where his agents and

their private army, the Force Publique, developed a brutally efficient system of ivory and rubber extraction in the Congo forests. Under threat of torture and mutilation, African villagers were forced to meet collection quotas for liquid latex, which they tapped from forest vines. This heinous system emptied much of the Congo forest of rubber and at the same time undermined local agricultural and social organization. Estimates have put the number of African deaths in the millions. Leopold's aggressive venture also precipitated a scramble among European nations for access to Africa's remaining natural wealth. The 1884–1885 Berlin Conference partitioned the continent into geographically bounded spheres of influence. One of the conference doctrines was that of "effective occupation," meaning that resource claims now required state oversight and investment, as well as the development of systematic scientific knowledge of the natural resources of imperial regions.

The Berlin Conference clearly linked economic power and political power to environmental control, but the process was not limited to Africa. In Latin America, American firms took advantage of weak governments eager to attract foreign capital and exploited those ecological niches suitable for development of large-scale industrial agriculture. Along the Atlantic coast of Central America, the United Fruit Company transformed species-rich lowland rain forests into massive mono-cropped banana plantations. American lumber companies laid the groundwork for plantation agriculture by cutting Philippine, Hawaiian, and Latin American forests, while the U.S. government exerted a suffocating political hegemony over the region.

Science and Technology. The evolution of ecological science during the nineteenth century dovetailed with the spread of nineteenth-century imperialism in the tropics. The explorations of naturalists like Charles Darwin, Alexander von Humboldt, and Alfred Russel Wallace led to the development of evolutionary theory and to important practical knowledge about the potential natural wealth of the tropics. These and other naturalists began a process that resulted in systematic efforts among subsequent scientists to map and to inventory tropical landscapes. In support of these efforts, imperial powers like Britain and France created specific institutions like Kew Gardens and the Jardin du Roi in order to systematize their growing knowledge of tropical plants. Satellite gardens and research stations, such as those in Ceylon (Sri Lanka), Trinidad, and Java served as collection points for the central gardens, where curators assembled collections of tropical-plant materials useful to theoretical scientific knowledge and to Europe's merchants and manufacturers. In this way, Kew's Museum of Economic Botany grew into an institution inextricably linked to imperialism.

One of the most useful of tropical-plant materials proved to be cinchona, the bark of an Andean tree from which scientists could extract an alkaloid called quinine. Quinine was truly a tool of empire; it could prevent and cure malaria, a disease that had debilitated and killed a large percentage of Europeans who entered the tropics before the mid-nineteenth century. In addition to cinchona, research scientists experimented with coffee, cacao, tea, sisal, and thousands of other plants with potential industrial or agricultural applications. Scientists disseminated their research in scientific journals specifically meant to further the aims of botanical imperialism.

By the late nineteenth and early twentieth centuries, the scope of imperial exploitation of tropical resources in many cases required the imposition of political control over indigenous land and labor. In many parts of Africa and Asia, the propagation of scientific agriculture formed part of what became in the colonial mind a moral mission to direct the transformation of indigenous production systems, and by association the land, into for-profit agriculture. The labor demands of these efforts proved extraordinarily disruptive to local communities, whose male members were often coerced to work on colonial plantations at the whim of colonial authorities, who enforced their orders with military and police power. By the early twentieth century, Africans and Asians spent much of their labor tending and harvesting coffee, cotton, sisal, and rubber on large plantations often far from their homes. Colonialism often forced transformations in small-scale agriculture as well. Where colonial authorities imposed taxes, peasant farmers began to grow marketable crops, like American maize. The changes often broke down carefully evolved cropping regimes and local ecological adaptations to climate, soils, and vegetation, creating vulnerability to drought.

In addition to forcing transformations in indigenous agriculture, colonial governments sequestered large tracts of tropical forest in order to impose a system of sustained-yield forestry. This process transformed tropical-forest ecology because it required the elimination of indigenous tree species and replanting with exotics, replacing biological diversity with sterile tree plantations. European-style forestry also restricted local farmers' access to forests, where they had traditionally farmed and grazed livestock.

Tropical environments had, as it turned out, a complex biogeography and proved difficult to manage without sophisticated knowledge of local conditions. Colonial experts, confident in their scientific superiority, neglected the most obvious source of local knowledge, that of indigenous people. Instead, colonial forestry and agricultural officials stereotyped indigenous land-use systems as inefficient at best and environmentally destructive at worst. Recent research has demonstrated the opposite to be true. In West Africa's savanna-forest transition zone, for example, farmers had historically fostered the growth of new forest vegetation in the savanna rather than diminished it, as French colonial forestry officials had argued.

The Imposition of Western Conservation Ethics. By the interwar period, European governments operating tropical colonies developed a new environmental authoritarianism based on fears of soil erosion and the international momentum toward wilderness conservation. Inspired by global drought conditions and dust-bowl scenes from the North American Midwest, colonial governments in Africa began active campaigns to control what they believed to be indigenous land-use practices that invited soil erosion and desertification. Strictly enforced rules required terracing on steep slopes, the forced removal of savanna lands from agricultural production, the introduction of new crops, and the removal of livestock from traditional grazing areas. These programs continued with a new urgency after World War II across eastern and southern Africa. Colonial officials encountered intense resistance from local communities, and the disaffection often fueled anticolonial protests.

The conservation impetus spread to wildlife as well. In many parts of Africa and South Asia, colonial governments set aside large areas initially as big-game hunting reserves for European and American elites and later as national parks for the strict preservation of wildlife. Many of these areas remain sequestered as nature reserves and thus represent a living legacy of imperial control. Indigenous people, whose ecological practices helped to fashion the preserved landscapes, have been reduced to tourist attractions living in "traditional villages" on park boundaries.

[*See also* Environment; Health and Disease; *and* Plantations.]

BIBLIOGRAPHY

Arnold, David, and Ramachandra Guha, eds. *Nature, Culture, Imperialism: Essays on the Environmental History of South Asia.* New Delhi, India: Oxford University Press, 1995. A collection of essays that treat India's colonial history of forest management, agricultural change, water management, and pollution.

Crosby, Alfred W. *Ecological Imperialism: The Biological Expansion of Europe, 900–1900.* Cambridge, U.K.: Cambridge University Press, 1986. One of the seminal works in the field of environmental history, this book follows Crosby's critically acclaimed *Columbian Exchange: Biological and Cultural Consequences of 1492* (Westport, Conn.: Greenwood, 1972).

Drayton, Richard. *Nature's Government: Science, Imperial Britain, and the "Improvement" of the World.* New Haven, Conn.: Yale University Press, 2000. A fine study in the scholarly tradition of the history of science; focuses mainly on the history of Kew Gardens and its role in British imperial expansion.

Fairhead, James, and Melissa Leach. *Misreading the African Landscape: Society and Ecology in a Forest-Savanna Mosaic.* Cambridge, U.K.: Cambridge University Press, 1996. A pathbreaking study in African environmental history and anthropology, this book focuses on the history of African land use in Guinea's savanna-forest transition zone and demonstrates the flawed nature of French colonial foresters' understandings of African land use and landscape history.

Headrick, Daniel R. *The Tools of Empire: Technology and European Imperialism in the Nineteenth Century.* New York: Oxford University Press, 1981. Still a valuable resource for students of imperial history and the history of technology.

Tucker, Richard P. *Insatiable Appetite: The United States and the Ecological Degradation of the Tropical World.* Berkeley: University of California Press, 2000. Brings the United States onto the imperial stage; focuses on U.S. exploitation of the natural resources of Latin America, the Philippines, and Hawai'i.

CHRISTOPHER A. CONTE

EMS TELEGRAM. The Ems telegram is the name given to an edited dispatch that Otto von Bismarck, minister-president of the North German Confederation—a federation of states dominated by Prussia—sent to his ambassadors on the night of 13 July 1870. It is called the Ems telegram because King William I of Prussia had a first draft of it sent to Bismarck from Ems, a spa in southeastern Germany.

The telegram grew out of a demand on the part of the French government and especially its foreign minister, the Duke de Gramont, that the Prussians withdraw, as a candidate for the vacant throne of Spain, Prince Leopold of Hohenzollern-Sigmaringen, the junior (and Catholic) line of William's family. William I, who had disliked the idea of Leopold ascending the Spanish throne all along, agreed at once to drop him. But William's decision was not good enough for the French; their aim was a humiliation of Prussia. Gramont therefore sent a second note demanding that Leopold never run for the throne again; additionally, the French demanded that William guarantee that the candidacy would never be renewed. This William refused, and he wired Bismarck. He concluded by recounting what

had happened in what were firm but moderate words: "I told the French ambassador that I could not give such a guarantee. The matter is closed. I have nothing more to say."

Just at the time when the second French demand came through, Bismarck, on vacation, returned to Berlin. He seized a pencil. He cut out all conciliatory words in William's telegram. Instead of the king's saying, "I have nothing more to say," Bismarck altered the king's reply to read, "I have nothing to say to you." The implication of these terse words was clear: Prussia had broken off relations with France.

Later on, Bismarck claimed to have provoked war with France by the Ems telegram. This explanation is remote from the truth. What finally drove the French over the brink were reports—untrue and exaggerated in order to satisfy the appetites of militants like Gramont—that the Prussians were mobilizing and must not be allowed a head start. On 15 July 1870 the French government asked its legislature for war credits; on 19 July the French declaration of war was presented in Berlin.

[*See also* Franco-Prussian War.]

BIBLIOGRAPHY
Howard, Robert. *The Origins of the War of 1870.* Cambridge, Mass.: Harvard University Press, 1924. An old but still classic work.

Steefel, Lawrence D. *Bismarck, the Hohenzollern Candidacy, and the Origins of the Franco-German War of 1870.* Cambridge, Mass.: Harvard University Press, 1962. A comprehensive though rather dry book.

Wetzel, David. *A Duel of Giants: Bismarck, Napoleon III, and the Origins of the Franco-Prussian War.* Madison: University of Wisconsin Press, 2001. A detailed account that downplays the significance of the telegram.

DAVID WETZEL

ENCILHAMENTO. The Encilhamento was an important episode of macroeconomic history related to the enactment and consequences of a massive and financially disruptive monetary policy put in place at the outset of Brazil's First Republic (1889–1930). During the brief presidential term of Marshal Manuel Deodoro da Fonseca (1889–1891), in an attempt to stimulate industrialization, Treasury Minister Rui Barbosa granted banks broad rights to issue money in the form of banknotes. The rapid formation of banks and corporations led to frantic stock market activity based on both real and speculative trading, which provoked widespread bankruptcies, pervasive financial frauds, and the crash of financial markets. The term used to describe this period came from an association between this moment of unrestrained market expansion and financial volatility and the frenzied moment in horseracing when horses are saddled up and ready to break out of the starting gate—*encilhamento*.

In an economy heavily reliant on agricultural commodity exports, the transition from slave to free labor created a significant new demand for money. The Brazilian government reasserted its political authority by imposing balanced budgets and fixed currency values, which was also a response to the demands of the international financial markets of the 1890s. The funding loan of 1898 started a major devaluation of the currency, the milreis, and led creditors to consolidate and reschedule the treasury's foreign debt. Those conditions imposed a metal standard in Brazil and transferred the effective control of Brazilian international trade revenues to overseas creditors. Banks suffered heavily in the shock of the Encilhamento. In 1900 the largest banks in Brazil failed, and the number of publicly owned banks fell abruptly.

Financial stagnation continued until 1906, when a broad package of reforms slowly restructured the banking system and initiated a unified national money market that has operated since. Currency now had a single centralized source of issue, the newly chartered Banco do Brasil, directly managed by the Treasury Ministry. During the remainder of the First Republic, domestic banking increased its share of the banking system and became increasingly stable. Between 1906 and 1930, inflation-adjusted bank deposits multiplied, and the economy and the money supply increased. The form of money shifted from currency toward bank deposits. Beyond its role in monetary policy, the Banco do Brazil served as the federal proxy for the state and acquired a dominant position in the national distribution of services within the banking system. This dominance never diminished and provided institutional stability to the system. The development of the banking system created the framework for a large and centralizing role in the economy eventually assumed by the state. This reform also set the pattern of institutionalization for the financial system, which resulted in an intimately intertwined political and financial system.

A fairly extensive historiography explains the Encilhamento, its shock, and its aftermath. Many works since the 1980s explore how the period of recovery generated real economic growth, spurred capital formation, and laid the foundations of Brazil's economic system. Researchers in political economy assert that the basis for the modern Brazilian financial system was established with the banking reform that followed the Encilhamento. Organized by an actively interventionist state, this efficient banking system became an important agent of growth that connected different regional areas of production, linked the private and public sector, and played a vital role in the consolidation of a national economy. In an important wrinkle, economic historians link the Encilhamento to a web of events ignited by both international financial conditions and economic crisis. This new approach has deepened the connections between domestic and international finance and has led to a revision of Brazil's macroeconomic history, reorienting and globalizing the world's understanding of the Encilhamento and its shock.

[*See also* Banking *and* Brazil.]

BIBLIOGRAPHY
Fritisch, Winston. *External Constraints on Economic Policy in Brazil, 1889–1930.* Basingstoke, U.K.: Macmillan, 1988.
Mitchener, Kris James, and Marc Weidenmier. "The Baring Crisis and the Great Latin American Meltdown of the 1890s." September 2006. http://www.econ.berkeley.edu/~webfac/eichengreen/e211_fa06/Mitchener.pdf.
Peláez, Carlos Manoel, and Wilson Suzigan. *História monetária do Brasil: Análise da política, comportamento e instituições monetárias.* Brasília, Brazil: Editora Universidade de Brasília, 1976.
Topik, Steven. *The Political Economy of the Brazilian State, 1889–1930.* Latin American Monograph no. 70. Austin: University of Texas Press, 1987.
Triner, Gail D. *Banking and Economic Development: Brazil 1889–1930.* New York: Palgrave, 2001.
Triner, Gail D., and Kirsten Wandschneider. "The Baring Crisis and the Brazilian Encilhamento, 1889–1891: An Early Example of Contagion among Emerging Capital Markets." *Financial History Review* 12, no. 2 (2005): 199–225.

CRISTINA MEHRTENS

ENCYCLOPÉDIE. The eighteenth century saw the birth of the encyclopedia in its modern form. But of the fifty or so published in that era, one towers above all the rest—the *Encyclopédie, ou Dictionnaire raisonné des sciences, des arts, et des métiers* (Encyclopedia, or Rational Dictionary of the Sciences, Arts, and Trades), published in seventeen volumes, with eleven volumes of plates, between 1751 and 1772. It began life in 1747 as a translation of a more modest English predecessor. But its Parisian editors, the mathematician Jean le Rond d'Alembert and the intellectual jack-of-all-trades Dènis Diderot, transformed their work into something very different, an unstoppable vehicle for the promotion of the secular, rationalist, and libertarian ideas of the Enlightenment.

Most of the luminaries of the French Enlightenment—including Montesquieu, Voltaire, Rousseau, and Buffon—contributed to the *Encyclopédie*; its 72,000 articles, which exceeded all predecessors in scope, came equipped with a scathingly witty system of cross-references and vivid illustrations; Alembert's "Preliminary Discourse," Diderot's entry "Encyclopedia," and a hundred other articles were themselves manifestos of Enlightenment principles.

The story of the *Encyclopédie*, as both daring intellectual project and risky commercial enterprise, is a tale of epic struggle and eventual triumph. On two occasions, in 1752 and 1759, conservative foes in church or state succeeded in temporarily banning its publication; a weary Alembert withdrew from the fight in 1757. But the tireless Diderot, making the *Encyclopédie* the capstone of his life's work, saw the project through to completion. By its end, some 25,000 copies of the gargantuan work were in circulation, half of them outside France, and it had inspired imitators across the European and Atlantic world.

As its editors had predicted, the *Encyclopédie* was soon rendered obsolete in regard to its primary purpose: to serve as an authoritative compendium of the most up-to-date knowledge in all fields. As supreme emblem and expression of the movement that inspired its creators, however, the *Encyclopédie* has remained a permanent fixture in modern intellectual life.

[*See also* Enlightenment.]

BIBLIOGRAPHY

Darnton, Robert. *The Business of Enlightenment: A Publishing History of the "Encyclopédie," 1775–1800.* Cambridge, Mass.: Belknap Press, 1979. The definitive study of the *Encyclopédie* as a commercial enterprise.

Donato, Clorinda, and Robert M. Maniquis, eds. *The "Encyclopédie" and the Age of Revolution.* Boston: G. K. Hall, 1992. Essays on the historical impact of the *Encyclopédie*.

Kafker, Frank A., and Serena L. Kafker. *The Encyclopedists as Individuals: A Biographical Dictionary of the Authors of the "Encyclopédie."* Studies on Voltaire and the Eighteenth Century 257. Oxford: Voltaire Foundation, 1988. Useful guide to the *Encyclopédie*'s one hundred and sixty authors.

Lough, John. *The "Encyclopédie."* London: Longman, 1971. A classic introduction in English.

Proust, Jacques. *Diderot et l'Encyclopédie.* 3d ed. Paris: Albin Michel, 1995. The major study in French of the *Encyclopédie*'s guiding figure.

JOHNSON KENT WRIGHT

ENERGY. Until the beginning of the early modern era (the period immediately following the Middle Ages and variously dated as 1493–1800, 1550–1850, or simply the sixteenth to eighteenth centuries), there was only one dominant pattern of energy conversions that determined the options and the capacities of sedentary human societies around the world: animate energies (human muscles and working animals) provided all but a small fraction of kinetic (mechanical) energy, and phytomass (wood, charcoal made from it, and assorted crop residues, mostly cereal straws) supplied the needed heat (thermal energy). Most traditional societies used sails to harness wind for ships, and windmills were relatively common in some parts of Europe and the Middle East. Similarly, the kinetic power of flowing water was converted by waterwheels only in some regions of the Old World. And in addition to woody biomass, some societies in arid regions relied on dried animal dung as a source of heat.

Though there was always some food gathering and hunting, including fishing, the bulk of the food supply came from the cultivation of a limited variety of staple crops. Tasks necessary to produce such crops were energized either by human labor or by draft animals (absent in the New World). Animals were used to perform some heavy field tasks (plowing, harrowing) and were deployed in transport (in the Americas as well). This pattern persisted for millennia largely unchanged or only marginally improved owing to better animal harnesses or better feeding. In terms of energy use, even the most advanced early modern societies of the seventeenth century were closer to the Old Kingdom of ancient Egypt or to ancient Greece—which thrived more than four thousand years ago and about two thousand years ago, respectively—than to our experience.

Early Energy Transition. The transition from societies dominated by animate labor and biomass fuels to a global civilization energized by fossil fuels and electricity has been a gradual and spatially uneven process. Its beginnings go back to sixteenth-century England, where the diminishing availability of wood led to the gradual development of excellent coal deposits. Coal was used first as both an industrial and a household source of direct heat. The earliest (Newcomen-type) external-combustion engines generated steam and converted it into mechanical power with such low efficiencies that their deployment was limited to coal mines. James Watt's famous introduction of a separate condenser and other improvements (patented in 1769) raised the efficiency by an order of magnitude and opened the way for mass deployment of a new prime mover, whose unprecedented power could be used for a multitude of industrial tasks. Watt's average engine had a capacity three to five times higher than typical contemporary waterwheels and windmills and provided power equivalent to about twenty-five horses.

Watt abhorred working with high-pressure steam, and hence the high-pressure engines suitable for mobile uses took off only after his patent expired. Commercialization of steam-driven trains and steam-propelled ships began during the 1830s. Both of these changes had truly revolutionary consequences. Steam-driven trains cut the cost of passenger and freight transport on land and increased the fastest speed by a factor of ten in just three generations— from horse-drawn carriages averaging 6 miles (10 kilometers) per hour to express trains running at more than 60 miles (100 kilometers) per hour by 1900. Steam-propelled ships reduced the length of transatlantic crossings from more than two weeks (sailing ships of the 1830s) to less than six days (ocean liners of the 1890s).

Yet steam engines were less prevalent in the early phases of Western industrialization than is generally believed. Both Atlantic Europe and the United States continued to rely for many generations on four different kinds of prime movers (in addition to human muscles). Draft animals were common in both field work and city transport well into the twentieth century. Increasingly larger and more efficient waterwheels and, since the 1830s, water turbines and windmills energized many early industrial enterprises. More advanced steam engines provided stationary power, railway traction, and ship propulsion. Finally, wood continued to be an important fuel. U.S. coal combustion surpassed total wood use only during the 1880s, whereas in Russia and Japan wood remained the dominant fuel until after 1900.

Coal-based industrialization powered by external combustion would have remained a limited affair. During the 1880s, however, two innovative technical revolutions ushered in two more flexible, more efficient, and more reliable means of energy conversion: large-scale generation of electricity and internal-combustion engines.

Thermal generation of electricity (driven by coal-fired steam engines) and water-powered generation (driven by Francis and Pelton turbines) began during the early 1880s with small units and limited direct-current transmission, dominated by numerous fundamental inventions of Thomas A. Edison. The next three decades saw rapid evolution of all the relevant techniques. Charles Parsons's steam turbine, patented in 1884, brought a new, much more efficient, and also more powerful prime mover. From the late 1880s George Westinghouse and Sebastian Ferranti, most notably, promoted less wasteful transmission by alternating current. Such transmission was made possible by efficient transformers, patented by William Stanley in 1885. Also important in the use of electricity

were a multitude of electric converters, including more efficient metallic-filament lights and, above all, electric motors, first patented by Nikola Tesla in 1888. The flexibility of electric motors made them by far the most important of all electric machines.

The first internal-combustion engines were small, gas-powered, stationary devices designed for use in workshops and factories. Those manufactured in large series were in common use by the 1870s. Mobile application came only with smaller, high-compression, gasoline-fueled engines, first designed during the mid-1880s by the duo Gottlieb Daimler and Wilhelm Maybach and, independently, by Karl Benz. Subsequent rapid improvements led first to carriages with engines, then to recognizable prototypes of modern automobiles, and during the 1890s to Rudolf Diesel's more efficient internal-combustion engine, which dispensed with sparking.

During the first decade of the twentieth century came the first flights of machines heavier than air. The Wright brothers powered their first brief trials in 1904 with their own four-cylinder engine with aluminum body and a steel crankshaft. Also appearing at this time were the first affordable, mass-produced automobiles. Henry Ford began serial production of his Model T in 1909. Commercial extraction of crude oil—initially just to produce kerosene for illumination and lubricants—began in Pennsylvania in 1859. Rapid diffusion of internal-combustion engines stimulated a worldwide search for new sources of crude oil. By 1910 the major producing areas included Texas, California, Russia, Romania, and Iran.

Only two key components of the complex energy system that dominated the twentieth century were not present before World War I: gas turbines and nuclear fission. The first gas-turbine converter was a superior internal-combustion engine in which fuel induction, compression, ignition, combustion, and exhaust proceed concurrently and continuously in different parts of the machine rather than intermittently in sequenced stages, as in Otto cycle engines. The first practical gas turbines were designed independently during the 1930s by Frank Whittle in England and Hans von Ohain in Germany, and they were first applied in jet engines during the last months of World War II. Postwar perfection of jet engines soon led not only to high-performance supersonic fighters but also to a new era of commercial jet flights. Commercial jet flights began during the 1950s and reached new levels of affordability with the introduction of the Boeing 747 in 1969.

Development of the nuclear generation of electricity was a direct spin-off of the dramatic quest to build the first nuclear bombs. The first plant was put on line during the late 1950s, and the main waves of expansion of nuclear generation extended into the 1970s.

Energy Transitions since the 1960s. The second half of the twentieth century was also a time of major energy transitions. Coal lost its dominance as hydrocarbons (crude oil and natural gas) became the most important fossil fuels and as all the industrial economies began indirectly using a larger share of fossil fuels via thermally generated electricity. Coal contributed more than half of the world's primary energy consumption until 1964, and although its absolute extraction continued to increase, its share of total global energy supply declined to 25 percent by the century's end, when it had only two principal uses: generation of electricity and feedstock for the production of metallurgical coke. The main exception to this trend was China, where coal remained a common household fuel.

Before World War II, hydrocarbons claimed large market shares only in the United States. But then came discoveries of large oil fields in Alberta, Canada, during the 1940s and 1950s; in Venezuela, Nigeria, Indonesia, and Russia—first in the Volga region, then in Western Siberia; in the North Sea, first discovered in the 1960s; and above all in the Middle East, where giant oil fields were discovered between the 1930s and the 1950s in Saudi Arabia, Kuwait, Iraq, and Iran. These discoveries led to inexpensive crude oil and the emergence of a truly global trade in petroleum and its refined products, with Europe, Japan, and (since the early 1970s) the United States being the largest importers. Once major long-distance pipelines began to deliver large volumes of natural gas—commonly associated with crude oil but also found in pure gas reservoirs—this form of energy became a leading industrial and household fuel, as well as a principal chemical feedstock. By 1950 crude oil and natural gas claimed about 35 percent of the world's primary energy supply, and by 2000 their combined share was just over 60 percent.

Major crude-oil exporters—not including Russia, nor Britain and Norway, which control the North Sea—created the Organization of Petroleum Exporting Countries, which took advantage of rising demand and engineered two rounds of steep price increases during the 1970s and early 1980s. These price increases eventually moderated the growth of global crude-oil demand, but they did not stop the worldwide increase in the ownership of passenger cars. The United States and Canada had a decades-long head start, but by the 1990s a number of European countries and Japan had the same portion of car ownership—about two people per vehicle—as did North America.

Electricity has many inherent advantages—flexibility (it can be used for lighting, propulsion, countless manufacturing tasks, heating, and chemical processing), ease of use, cleanliness at the point of consumption, and minute controllability—and these have made it the fastest-growing form of energy in the modern world. As a result, ever higher shares of fossil fuels have been converted to electricity: in 1900 about only 1 percent of the world's coal was converted to electricity, by 1950 the share for all fossil fuels reached 10 percent, and by 2000 it surpassed 30 percent. In contrast, in 2000 nearly 20 percent of the world's electricity came from hydrostations and about 15 percent from nuclear fission.

The Global System of Energy Supply. After more than a century of technical innovations and enormous investments in infrastructure for extraction, transportation, generation, transmission, and conversion, the modern world is energized by a truly global and remarkably intricate system of energy supply. This system is dominated by fossil fuels, which provide about 90 percent of all commercial primary energy; the rest comes from primary (hydro and nuclear) electricity and from biomass. Since the 1970s, new techniques for efficient, large-scale conversions of renewable energy flows have become more efficient and less expensive—the most promising being wind turbines and photovoltaic cells—but they still supply only a minuscule share of the world's primary energy, less than 1 percent. Because of the complexity, cost, and inertia of energy infrastructures and the inherently gradual nature of energy transitions, this situation is not going change swiftly.

In absolute terms, global energy use in the year 2005 amounted to nearly 450 exajoules (10^{18} joules), equivalent to about 10.5 billion metric tons of crude oil, or close to 70 gigajoules per year per capita. But access to this enormous flux is extremely skewed, with the United States and Canada averaging nearly 400 gigajoules per capita per year and the richest European Union countries and Japan about 170 gigajoules, while China's mean is only near 40 gigajoules, India's is barely above 10 gigajoules, and the modal value for the world's nearly two hundred countries is less than 15 gigajoules. Moreover, large parts of humanity do not directly consume any modern forms of energy. Rural areas of Asia, Africa, and Latin America still depend heavily on biomass fuels and on animate forms of energy. China's rapid post-1980 modernization reduced the share of wood and crop residues to only

15 percent of its nationwide primary energy consumption, but rates are in excess of 60 percent or even 80 percent in most countries of sub-Saharan Africa. Even more important, at the beginning of the twenty-first century more than 1 billion people were still living in households without any electricity.

Because energy consumption is strongly correlated with the degree of economic development and with both the physical and mental quality of life, few needs are as urgent as a notable reduction of this indefensibly huge gap in consumption. Yet even rich energy endowment (as in Saudi Arabia and Nigeria) and relatively high energy consumption (as in Russia) are not sufficient to produce open, tolerant, and prosperous societies.

Fortunately, attaining such benefits does not require North American levels of energy use. Relationships between energy use and all the important quality-of-life variables show clear inflections between 40 and 70 gigajoules per capita per year, followed by rapidly diminishing returns thereafter and virtually no gains above 110 gigajoules per capita per year. The United States consumes more than twice as much energy per capita as Japan or France but does not have lower mortalities, higher life expectancies, or happier lives, yet it does have higher crime rates and lower levels of educational achievement. The idea of voluntary restrictions on per capita energy use in the richest countries may seem preposterous today, but it may be a critical ingredient of an effective strategy needed to cope with global climate change.

Contrary to common claims, many uncertainties inherent in the extremely complex process of climate change do not allow us to make any reliable forecasts, but as rational risk minimizers, we should not discount the possibility that accumulating greenhouse gases—produced largely by combustion of fossil fuels—can result in accelerated global warming. Moderating its degree and coping with its consequences may be the greatest challenge of the twenty-first century, a price to pay for generations of affluence bought by rising consumption of fossil energy.

[See also Energy Crisis; Global Warming; Industrialization; Nuclear Energy, subentry Overview; Oil Embargo; Organization of Petroleum Exporting Countries; Petroleum; Steam Engine; and Sustainable Development.]

BIBLIOGRAPHY
British Petroleum. "BP Statistical Review of World Energy 2005." http://www.bp.com/worldenergy.
German Advisory Council on Global Change. World in Transition: Towards Sustainable Energy Systems. Translated by Christopher Hay. London: Earthscan, 2004.
Goldemberg, José, ed. World Energy Assessment: Energy and the Challenge of Sustainability. New York: United Nations Development Programme, 2000.
Hoffmann, Peter. Tomorrow's Energy: Hydrogen, Fuel Cells, and the Prospects for a Cleaner Planet. Cambridge, Mass.: MIT Press, 2001.
Houghton, J. T., et al., eds. Climate Change 2001: The Scientific Basis. New York: Cambridge University Press, 2001.
National Commission on Energy Policy. Ending the Energy Stalemate: A Bipartisan Strategy to Meet America's Energy Challenges. Washington, D.C.: National Commission on Energy Policy, 2004. http://www.nrel.gov/pv/thin_film/docs/energy_policy_report_2004_for_doe.pdf.
Smil, Vaclav. Energies: An Illustrated Guide to the Biosphere and Civilization. Cambridge, Mass.: MIT Press, 1999.
Smil, Vaclav. Energy at the Crossroads: Global Perspectives and Uncertainties. Cambridge, Mass.: MIT Press, 2003.
Smil, Vaclav. Energy in World History. Boulder, Colo.: Westview Press, 1994.
U.S. Energy Information Administration. International Energy Outlook 2005. Washington, D.C.: Energy Information Administration, 2005. http://www.eia.doe.gov/oiaf/ieo.
World Energy Council. Survey of Energy Resources 2004. London: World Energy Council, 2004. http://www. worldenergy.org/wec-geis/publications/default/launches/ser04/ser04.asp.

VACLAV SMIL

ENERGY CRISIS. The term "energy crisis" has lost its generic meaning and now applies specifically to two periods of rapidly increasing prices for crude oil—and consequently for other forms of energy as well. The first period took place in 1973 and 1974, the second one between 1979 and 1981, and prices remained high until 1986, when their gradual decline became a precipitous fall. Although there was never any physical shortage of crude oil on the world market, the combination of sudden price rises, temporary supply shortfalls of some refined products in some countries (particularly of gasoline in the United States), uncertainties created by these unprecedented events, and economic repercussions for global economic growth justifies singling out this period as an important watershed in modern history.

The first round of crude-oil price rises shocked not only because of its magnitude but perhaps even more because it took place after a century of steadily declining prices. When valued in constant U.S. dollars (in which global crude-oil trade is denominated), an average barrel of traded crude oil was selling in 1970 for less than a quarter of its price in 1870. At just $1.80 per barrel, it was a remarkable bargain (at any given time, different qualities command slightly different prices). The abundance and affordability of the fuel after World War II was among the key drivers of worldwide economic expansion, which proceeded at nearly 5 percent a year between 1950 and

Gas Lines. Long lines at an American gas station during the summer of 1979. Photograph by Warren Leffler. PRINTS AND PHOTOGRAPHS DIVISION, LIBRARY OF CONGRESS

1970. During this period, U.S. oil demand nearly tripled. During the 1960s both Western Europe and Japan converted from coal- to oil-based economies, and the incipient modernization of many low-income Asian and Latin American countries was based largely on imported oil—China and India being two important exceptions.

This rising demand offered a long-awaited opportunity for the Organization of Petroleum Exporting Countries (OPEC), which was set up in Baghdad in 1960 by Saudi Arabia, Iraq, Kuwait, Iran, and Venezuela. Later admissions during the 1960s (Qatar in 1961, Libya and Indonesia in 1962, Abu Dhabi in 1967, Algeria in 1969) and the early 1970s (Nigeria in 1971, Ecuador in 1973, Gabon in 1975) raised the total number of member countries to thirteen. As conditions began to change from a buyer's market to a seller's market, OPEC began to increase oil's posted price—the fictitious level it used for calculating taxes and royalties—as well as the tax rate paid by foreign oil companies. In 1971, Libya was the first producer to do so, and in the same year it also began to nationalize the assets of multinational oil companies. Iraq followed this example in 1972. By 1976 the process of nationalization was complete when the Saudis took over the Arabian American Oil Company and created the world's largest national oil company—in 2005 it produced about ten times as much oil as Exxon, the world's largest private operator.

Another important decision leading to the first energy crisis was made in Washington in April 1973 when the U.S. government ended limits on the import of crude oil east of the Rocky Mountains (set by President Dwight D. Eisenhower in 1959 as a fixed percentage of domestic production). The 1973 decision rapidly increased the share of foreign oil in U.S. consumption.

The Arab-Israeli War. Meanwhile, OPEC increased its posted price to $2.59 per barrel at the beginning of 1973 and then to $3.01 by 1 October. Five days later, on Yom Kippur, the Egyptian army crossed the Suez Canal, broke the Bar Lev line, and began to advance into Sinai. Israeli Defense Forces reversed the thrust, encircled Egypt's Third Army, and soon moved deep into Egyptian territory west of the canal. On 16 October 1973, OPEC raised the posted price of crude oil to $5.12 per barrel, and the next day the organization's Arab members agreed to embargo oil exports to the United States and the Netherlands (Rotterdam was Europe's largest oil terminal with the largest oil refinery) until Israel withdrew from occupied Arab territories. On 23 December 1973, OPEC announced a posted price of $11.65 per barrel starting on 1 January 1975, a 4.5-fold increase in a year. The oil embargo did not work—multinational oil companies merely rerouted their tankers—and it was soon formally abandoned, but high prices stayed, almost unchanged in

1975 and 1976, then rising slightly in 1977 and marginally in 1978 to $12.93 per barrel.

The effect of high prices was both swift and global. Their initial rise and the uncertainties created by the embargo led to car queues winding around blocks in many American cities, to fuel-rationing schemes, and to widespread fears of freezing homes and of the United States at the mercy of oil-rich Arab states. These fears eased in a matter of months as the real consequences became apparent: there were no shortages of oil, but industries, services, and households, accustomed for decades to low (and in real terms, falling) prices of oil, had to cope with nearly quintupled outlays. The world's largest economy was initially more sheltered than were the European countries and Japan. In 1974 the United States imported only about 22 percent of its oil consumption, and the prices of domestic oil remained partially controlled until 28 January 1981 when President Ronald Reagan removed the last price and allocation rules. Even so, the U.S. gross domestic product, which grew by nearly 6 percent in 1973, dropped by 0.5 percent in 1974 as overall primary energy use fell by more than 2 percent in 1974 and by nearly 3 percent in 1975.

Japan (importing 99.7 percent of its oil in 1974) and most European countries (importing in excess of 90 percent) were much more vulnerable, but at the same time they were relatively more efficient users of all forms of energy, and because they were instantly exposed to higher oil prices, they adjusted faster to these new economic realities with a combination of reduced energy use and higher reliance on other fuels and on nuclear-generated electricity. Japan's gross domestic product fell by 0.5 percent in 1974, but it was up by 4 percent in 1975 even as its overall energy use fell by nearly 5 percent, a remarkable case of decoupling energy use and economic growth. OPEC was the big winner: its revenues tripled between 1973 and 1978, though so did its expenditures. Moreover, high rates of inflation meant that between 1974 and 1978 the average oil price actually declined in real terms.

The Collapse of the Iranian Monarchy. The second oil shock was precipitated by the collapse of the Iranian monarchy. Demonstrations against the rule of Shah Mohammed Reza Pahlavi began in January 1978. By September the country was under military rule, and by the end of the year its oil production fell to a twenty-seven-year low. When the shah left Tehran for exile on 16 January 1979, OPEC's oil price averaged $13.62 per barrel. In December 1979, after the return of Ayatollah Ruhollah Khomeini to Iran and after the takeover of the U.S. embassy, the price had nearly doubled to

$25.56 per barrel. By the end of 1980 it had climbed to $32.95 per barrel, and by March of 1981 the average price reached $34.89 per barrel, with the best-quality crude oil selling for as much as $50 per barrel on the spot market. Not surprisingly, given the propensity for catastrophic forecasts, many experts saw prices of around $100 per barrel in a matter of years.

Barely recovered economies began faltering once more. In 1982 the U.S. gross domestic product fell by 2 percent. Yet record-high oil prices had the greatest negative impact on those modernizing countries of Asia, Africa, and Latin America whose industrial sectors, transportation, and urban cooking (using kerosene) were highly dependent on crude-oil imports. For example, in Brazil the cost of crude-oil imports as a share of exports rose from 12 percent in 1972 to 48 percent in 1982, and for India the rise was from 12 percent to 56 percent. But by 1982 it was clear to many observers that OPEC had overplayed its hand and pushed its average market price too high. The first round of oil price increases did not produce sufficient adjustments in demand (by 1978 both global demand and consumption in the world's largest economies rose to new highs), but the second round was high enough to do so. A combination of technical innovations (particularly in the energy-intensive metallurgical and chemical industries), simple household energy savings (urged so memorably by President Jimmy Carter in a televised exhortation), and depressed fuel demand because of an economic slowdown lowered U.S. oil use in 1983 to 21 percent below its peak level in 1978. During the same period, Japan's consumption fell by 16 percent and global demand fell by 10 percent.

Meanwhile, non-OPEC producers of oil (excluding the Soviet Union), taking advantage of high prices, began to increase their share of global oil production. In 1978 they produced 35 percent of the world's oil, and in just five years their share rose to 45 percent. Despite the falling worldwide demand and despite its falling share of production (53 percent in 1973, 31 percent a decade later), OPEC tried to hold prices at high levels, lowering the market price only to $33.63 during 1982. But by early 1983 the organization had to legitimize widespread price cutting by many of its members and so lowered the market price to $28.74 per barrel. The final denouement came in September 1985 when the Saudis—who by that time were earning much less than they were spending on their newly acquired habits of grandiose construction projects and massive subsidies—decided to regain their lost market share by doubling their output in the face of weak global demand.

By January 1986 the price fell to $20 per barrel, and in early April it was briefly below $10 per barrel, before settling around $15 per barrel. The second global energy crisis was over.

Lessons. Certainly, the most important lesson of the energy crises of the 1970s and 1980s is the obvious power that oil consumers have in setting prevailing prices. Undoubtedly, crude oil is a very convenient fuel. Its high energy density, inexpensive transport, convenient storage, and suitability for numerous final uses make it the most sought-after among fossil fuels. At the same time, uneven distribution of crude-oil resources enables an oligopolistic trading bloc of a small number of producing countries to exert a major influence on the world price. But they cannot uphold an arbitrarily high price, because the demand for oil can be considerably reduced both by technical advances and by switching to other energy sources. Except for in airplanes, other types of fuel can readily substitute for oil—fuel coal, natural gas, or renewables such as hydro, wind, or solar for generation of electricity, or natural gas and geothermal flows for space heating—and all of oil's existing converters, despite being considerably more efficient than they were during the 1970s, can still be made much less wasteful.

Cars are the best example of possible gains. The two oil price rises were behind the doubling of the average efficiency of U.S. automobiles, from 13 miles per gallon in 1973 to 27.5 miles per gallon by 1985, and this trend was a major contributor to weakened global demand for oil. Unfortunately, this commitment to efficiency was discontinued almost as soon as prices fell, and the subsequent introduction of sport utility vehicles, or SUVs (classified as light trucks and hence not subject to the performance requirement of an average 27.5 miles per gallon), resulted in a reversal of the trend. By 2005 average performance of all passenger-carrying vehicles (cars, vans, pickups, and SUVs) was only about 22 miles per gallon. For comparison, a mere continuation of the 1973–1985 rate of efficiency gains would have raised average performance to just over 50 miles per gallon in 2005, and an aggressive introduction of hybrid vehicles (averaging in excess of 60 miles per gallon) could further improve overall performance and reduce the overall demand for crude oil.

The other important lesson is that virtually none of the consequences of the two rounds of oil price rises that were expected during the late 1970s and the early 1980s actually materialized. Nobody died in dark and cold houses in embargoed countries; the wealth of the Western world did not end up in Middle Eastern (or OPEC) coffers—by 1982, OPEC countries were running deficits, and by 1983 the world's largest oil importers had smaller relative trade deficits with OPEC than they had before 1973; oil prices did not hit $100 per barrel before 1990; and global economic growth was not irreparably damaged. Rising prices finally forced both industries and households to do away with some of the worst energy conversion inefficiencies that were creating unnecessary environmental burdens (air and water pollution, carbon emissions), stimulated many technical advances in the oil and gas industry (ranging from three-dimensional geophysical exploration to horizontal well drilling, to offshore oil and gas extraction), and encouraged use of alternative energy sources.

[*See also* Energy; Industrialization; Nuclear Energy; Oil Embargo; Organization of Petroleum Exporting Countries; *and* Petroleum.]

BIBLIOGRAPHY

British Petroleum Co. Policy Review Unit. *Oil Crisis—Again?* London: BP, 1979.

Hawdon, David. *The Energy Crisis Ten Years After.* London: Croom Helm, 1984.

Lieber, Robert J. *Oil and the Middle East War: Europe in the Energy Crisis.* Cambridge, Mass.: Center for International Affairs, Harvard University, 1976.

Smil, Vaclav. *Energy Food Environment.* Oxford: Oxford University Press, 1987.

Stork, Joe. *Middle East Oil and the Energy Crisis.* New York: Monthly Review Press, 1975.

VACLAV SMIL

ENGINEERING, CIVIL. The planning, design, and construction of public works—canals, bridges, dams, buildings, walls, and so on—is not strictly a modern accomplishment, as is evidenced by the seven wonders of the ancient world, the roads and aqueducts of the Romans, or the 3,930-mile Great Wall (third century B.C.E. and later) and the 1,100-mile Grand Canal (sixth–seventh centuries) in China. Joseph Needham explained that Chinese builders, like those of other civilizations, depended upon empirical knowledge, not calculation using geometry, mechanics, or dynamics. European cathedrals were built in the same way, while Renaissance artists such as Michelangelo and Leonardo da Vinci conceived bridges, dams, fortresses, and weapons as well as river-improvement systems and chapels and churches for their patrons. As Needham commented, "Astonishing were the successes of a cumulative empirical tradition" (p. 378).

Two changes in Europe prompted the emergence of a group of experts known as civil engineers beginning in the seventeenth century. First, the needs of large permanent armies serving growing nation-states such as France encouraged specialists to work exclusively on military problems. These experts, labeled military engineers, included the Italian-born Agostino Ramelli (1531–1600), who served the Medici family and then Henry III of France; Ramelli published a book in 1588 that contained almost two hundred plates of bridges, excavators, pumps, mills, cranes, and screw jacks for military use. The most famous seventeenth-century military engineer, Sébastien Le Prestre de Vauban (1633–1707), upgraded fortresses in more than three hundred cities and towns for France's Louis XIV. The term "civil engineering" distinguished practitioners not engaged in military work, with further differentiation of specialties (mining, mechanical, electrical, and so on) emerging during the nineteenth century.

The second European change concerned how these experts approached a problem. Though not abandoning empirical knowledge, at this time Europeans began to calculate stresses and forces in structures, the volume of earth in excavations, and the flow of water in hydraulic projects. Such mathematical and eventually scientific approaches required a new kind of training. Once again, powerful nation-states, specifically the French monarchy, provided pivotal support for this development when Louis XVI established the École Nationale des Ponts et Chaussées (National School of Bridges and Roads) in 1747 as the first national engineering school. Adopting Galileo Galilei's mechanical approach to nature, the school attempted to place engineering designs on a systematic and mathematical basis. Graduates joined the state's Corps des Ponts et Chaussées, whose engineering leaders such as Pierre Trésaguet (1716–1796) oversaw construction of the best network of roads in the world and the design of ever more impressive and beautiful stone arch bridges.

An alternative style of practical, apprentice-style preparation for engineering emerged in England during the eighteenth century. British engineers, moreover, typically provided consulting services for private businesses that developed roads and turnpikes, canals, and later railroads. Thomas Telford (1757–1834), George Stephenson (1781–1848), and Isambard Kingdom Brunel (1806–1859) were lionized by Samuel Smiles in *Lives of the Engineers* (1862, 1874) for their contribution to the Industrial Revolution. Others developed municipal sanitary and water supply projects, as well as river and harbor improvements and public works.

Americans combined the French and English approaches to engineering. The first engineering school in the United States, the U.S. Military Academy at West Point, explicitly copied French textbooks and exercises. But most nineteenth-century American engineers learned through experience while constructing the Erie Canal (opened 1825), bridges, or early railroads. During apprenticeships that lasted from five to seven years, they progressed from physical labor to surveying teams and eventually to the design and planning of engineering structures. Many young engineers took classes at local colleges to learn trigonometry for surveying, but not until the last third of the nineteenth century did universities become a favored route for engineering education. By 1900, mathematics and scientific knowledge of the strength of materials or physics were more essential. Yet well into the twentieth century, engineering education in most U.S. universities devoted substantial attention to hands-on experience, including drawing and surveying. Only after 1950 did engineering science come to dominate American universities, moving them closer to the eighteenth-century approaches of the École Nationale des Ponts et Chaussées. Today every university in the world follows this approach.

Changes in educational strategies, however, have not altered the way that civil engineering shapes key features of life. Modern urban and industrial society cannot exist without the transportation, utilities, and public works infrastructures that civil engineers construct and maintain. And just as in the past, they continue to excite wonder. The American Society of Civil Engineers compiled a modern "seven wonders" that includes the Channel Tunnel, Toronto's CN Tower, the Empire State Building, the Golden Gate Bridge, Brazil's Itaipu Dam, the Netherlands North Sea Protection Works, and the Panama Canal. All demonstrate the growing scale of engineering works as engineers "tamed" nature and met broad social and economic needs—often with unexpected consequences for the environment and society alike.

Civil engineering has clearly been connected to the expansion of state power over other peoples as well as over nature. Western imperialism during the nineteenth century rested upon the adoption of engineering tools and structures designed and constructed by British, American, and other European engineers. The British in India devoted much attention to constructing a railroad and telegraph network that served the empire, which communicated with London by means of undersea telegraph cables by the 1870s. The Dutch in Indonesia attempted to introduce modern river improvements and water supply systems. Cecil Rhodes's plan for a railroad from Cairo to Cape Town at the end of the nineteenth century also reflected imperial dreams.

Industrialization efforts even more explicitly relied upon civil engineering, with Japan, Russia, and other late-comers relying heavily on Western engineers to transfer technology and knowledge. After World War II, modernization programs for the less-developed world then emerging from colonialism gave similar priority to civil engineering. Road systems, clean water and irrigation projects, and the construction of hydroelectric dams typified such efforts. All too often the outcomes were mixed. The Aswan High Dam on the Nile, for example, became the site of a skirmish in the Cold War when the Soviet Union completed the dam after the United States removed its engineers in 1956 to express displeasure with Gamal Abdel Nasser. As with many other projects, Aswan ignored environmental consequences, disrupting the Nile's annual floods that replenished the soils of the river's delta.

Thus the legacy of civil engineering in the world is dualistic. Every nation depends upon ever larger public works in transportation, water supply, waste treatment, and flood control to drive economic and social improvements. The challenge has been to do so while avoiding the unanticipated consequences that inevitably follow attempts to reshape nature. Witness New Orleans in the aftermath of the 2005 Hurricane Katrina.

[*See also* Military, *subentry* Military Technology; Science and Technology; Transportation; *and* Water and Water Management.]

BIBLIOGRAPHY

Kirby, Richard Shelton. *Engineering in History.* New York: McGraw-Hill, 1956. Though dated in some respects and Eurocentric in tone, this volume provides a good survey of the topic.

Needham, Joseph. *Science and Civilization in China.* Vol. 4, part 3: *Physics and Physical Technology: Civil Engineering and Nautics.* Cambridge, U.K.: Cambridge University Press, 1971. Part of the author's magisterial multivolume study on China, this volume is based, as always, on impeccable research and presented with superb illustrations.

Picon, Antoine. *L'invention de l'ingénieur moderne: L'École des Ponts et Chaussées, 1747–1851.* Paris: Presses de l'École Nationale des Ponts et Chaussées, 1992. The definitive history of the first engineering school.

Ramelli, Agostino. *The Various and Ingenious Machines of Agostino Ramelli (1588).* Translated by Martha Teach Gnudi and edited by Eugene S. Ferguson. Baltimore: Johns Hopkins University Press, 1976.

Rolt, L. T. C. *Victorian Engineering.* London: Allen Lane, 1970. The best discussion of British engineers during the eighteenth and nineteenth centuries.

Stapleton, Darwin H., and Roger L. Shumaker. *The History of Civil Engineering since 1600: An Annotated Bibliography.* New York: Garland, 1986. An essential finding aid for this topic.

BRUCE E. SEELY

ENGLAND. The England of 1750 was a land of fewer than 6 million people living in 50,000 square miles. Since the fifteenth century England had been united with the adjoining Principality of Wales; since 1707 England had also been bound politically to the adjoining kingdom of Scotland as the kingdom of Great Britain. The king of England was also acknowledged as king of Ireland. In addition, he laid claim to colonies (vast in territory but small in population) in North America and in the Caribbean, trading posts along the coast of West Africa, and (via the English East India Company) parts of South Asia.

Government. Unlike most other rulers of his day, King George II (1683–1760; r. 1727–1760) was a constitutional monarch. Although he named his ministers, including the prime minister, they stayed in office only if they could also satisfy Parliament (the elected House of Commons and the hereditary House of Lords), which met for several months each year. In most boroughs and counties, the electorate was small, and well-to-do landed gentlemen predominated. Even those Englishmen who lacked the right to vote could, however, claim the rights of petition, assembly, jury trial, and freedom from arbitrary arrest. Full political privileges were granted only to members of the established Anglican church.

Parliaments were most concerned with matters of war and peace and with regulating international trade and levying taxes. Local government was left largely in the hands of country gentlemen owning large estates, who served as unpaid justices of the peace. With funds from local property taxes, they also supervised the operation of the Poor Law—aid to orphans, paupers, the very old, and those too ill to work.

Society. Mid-century England was a largely rural, inegalitarian, and patriarchal land in which a small number of aristocrats and squires presided over far larger numbers of farmers, shopkeepers, artisans, and domestic servants, a yet larger number of farm laborers, and a significant number of paupers. At least three-quarters of adults were married, and the nuclear family of mother, father, and minor children was the norm. The death rate was high, however, with thirty-five as the median age; only one parent in two could expect to survive long enough to see a child grow to adulthood. The social status of women depended largely on that of their husbands, and the wives of farmers, shopkeepers, and laborers were very much part of the labor force. Upper-class wives often led comfortable lives, however, amidst elegant houses and gardens, and upper-class widows served as householders, estate owners, and even business proprietors.

G. M. Trevelyan has described eighteenth-century England as a land of "aristocracy, tempered by rioting" by members of the lower classes (*History of England*, p. 533). Well-designed furniture and Enlightenment philosophy went hand-in-hand with callousness and cruelty. Because the standing army was small and the village constable unimposing, in order to restore peace country squires were compelled to rely on their powers of persuasion as much as on the rigorous criminal law. Numerous crimes were subject to capital punishment, but a more frequent penalty was "transportation" to colonies such as Virginia.

Mid-eighteenth-century England was not solely rural; London and its immediate environs—about six hundred thousand inhabitants—served not only as the kingdom's political and legal capital but also as the site of the Bank of England and of a fledgling stock market and insurance business. Its port was large enough to find space for hundreds of sailing ships manned by the fifty thousand merchant seamen employed both in the coastal trade and in international commerce with five continents.

Wars and Politics, 1756–1783. England in 1750 was in the midst of what has been called the "Second Hundred Years' War" with France (1689–1815). In 1750 the two kingdoms were temporarily at peace, but by 1756 fighting had broken out in North America, in India, and on the Continent, where England was allied with Prussia. Early setbacks were followed by victories: the defeat of the French fleet in the Atlantic; the triumph of the English East India Company over its French counterpart in Bengal; the defeat of the French in North America. The Treaty of Paris (1763) awarded most French claims in North America and India to England, whose overseas empire reached its eighteenth-century height.

In 1760 the elderly George II was succeeded by his twenty-two-year-old grandson, George III (1738–1820; r. 1760–1820). The new English-born monarch had a deep sense of moral duty and sought to play a direct role in governing his kingdom, and the result was a series of short-lived ministries until in 1770 George III found in Lord North a prime minister pleasing both to him and to a majority in Parliament.

In the meantime politicians out of office had spurred a campaign of criticism against the manner in which George III's ministers used royal patronage powers. In 1764 a sharply critical newspaper publisher, John Wilkes, was convicted of seditious libel, imprisoned, and barred from the parliamentary seat to which he was repeatedly elected. An organization of his followers, the Society of Supporters of the Bill of Rights, provided a model for subsequent radical reform movements. Their program included freedom of the press, a redistribution of parliamentary seats, an expansion of the right to vote, and more frequent elections.

The fears expressed by Wilkes's supporters confirmed the more radical American colonial leaders in their suspicions of the government in London. Long accustomed to a high degree of self-government and freed, after 1763, from the French danger, they resented successive English attempts to make them pay a greater share of the expense of defending the empire and to enforce more strictly imperial trade regulations. The result was almost seven years of armed conflict, the American Declaration of Independence (1776), and, after the French and the Spaniards had joined the American cause, the willingness of a new English ministry to recognize the independence of the United States (1783). Diplomatic isolation, a resentment of higher taxation, and an atmosphere of domestic dissension in both England and Ireland had forced Lord North out of office a year earlier.

Population Growth, Urbanization, and Industrialization. Whereas during the first half of the eighteenth century the population of England and Wales increased scarcely at all, the numbers went up by one-half, to 8.7 million, between 1751–1801. Between 1801, the year of the first official census, and 1851 the population was to double. The reasons may include a decline of deaths from infectious diseases such as smallpox and a marginally improved diet that included the large-scale consumption of potatoes. There is also evidence of earlier marriages and larger families. A quickening of economic change became noticeable by the 1780s, when James Watt perfected the steam engine as a new source of power. New inventions galvanized the spinning and weaving of imported cotton. Between 1760 and 1830 the production of cotton textiles multiplied twelve times, making the product the country's leading export. During those same years the amount of coal mined increased fourfold, and other inventions comparably raised the production of iron. This so-called "industrial revolution" transformed Great Britain into "the workshop of the world."

During these same decades, the landscape was dotted with factory towns. Their advantages included more regular hours and wages higher than those received by farm laborers. Machines powered by steam rather than by muscle power could also more readily be operated by women and children. Their disadvantages included the devaluation of handicraft skills, a novel emphasis on discipline and punctuality, and an often greater gulf between employer and employee. It took a generation for such civic amenities as water and sewage systems to catch up with population growth. London remained Britain's largest city as a center of commerce, shipping, and government as well as of industry. Its population, estimated at 950,000 in 1801, was to grow to 2.5 million a half century later, making it the most populous city in the world. By then England had become the first large country to have more urban than rural inhabitants.

The Great War with France (1793–1815). In the immediate aftermath of the American Revolution, English politicians began to reexamine old institutions, and Prime Minister William Pitt the Younger (1783–1801, 1804–1806) established the first consolidated annual budget and restored faith in the government's ability to pay interest on the much-increased national debt. Other potential political reforms were briefly encouraged and then halted by events in France. The revolutionary French, who preached political equality and abolished old institutions such as monarchy, became embroiled in a succession of wars with their major continental neighbors. Those countries were in intermittent alliance with England (which in 1801, with the Act of Union with Ireland, formally became the United Kingdom).

During the later 1790s a successful general, Napoleon Bonaparte, took over the French revolutionary government, and in 1804 he proclaimed himself emperor. Even as Napoleon conquered the greater part of Europe with his armies, he was never able to defeat the English navy. The Battle of Trafalgar (1805) led to the death of the great admiral Horatio Nelson but foiled Napoleon's plan to invade England by sea. At the cost of rapid price inflation and lagging wages, England's government successfully focused its financial resources on the war, a conflict that encouraged farm production and the manufacture of armaments. Only the Duke of Wellington's land campaign in Spain (begun in 1810) and Napoleon's fateful decision to invade Russia (1812) caused French fortunes to wane. Wellington's victory at Waterloo (1815) and the Vienna peace treaty (1815) meant for England the onset of a century marked by naval supremacy and by numerous minor conflicts but no further world war.

Reaction and Reform (1815–1851). Rapid demobilization, economic depression, and bad harvests led to both intermittent rioting and temporary curbs on freedom of the press and of assembly, but during the 1820s moderate Tories lowered tariffs, reformed the criminal law, and eased barriers to trade union organization. Changes in the law permitted both non-Anglican Protestants and Roman Catholics to hold public office. The Whig government of the 1830s enacted a Reform Act (1832) that began the process of redistributing parliamentary seats in favor of growing industrial cities and of setting up a standard property test that gave the vote to all middle-class men and some artisans. The measure encouraged political party organization, both locally and nationally, and weakened the influence of the monarch and the House of Lords. In 1833 Parliament abolished slavery within the British Empire. Other measures created elected town councils and placed the registration of births, deaths, and marriages in state rather than church hands. The largest mass movement in English history, the Chartists (1837–1849), did not succeed at that time in securing the vote for all men.

Under the inspiration of the Anti-Corn Law League and of famine in Ireland, however, Prime Minister Robert Peel (1841–1846) moved England toward a policy of international free trade even as he divided his own Tory (Conservative) Party. During the same era, Parliament began the process of using government inspectors to regulate the poor laws, factories, mines, urban sanitation, and the steam-powered railroads that by mid-century had transformed the transportation system for both goods and people.

In 1837 the eighteen-year-old Victoria had succeeded the second of two aging uncles as monarch. She and her husband, Prince Albert, came to symbolize many of the Victorian virtues: a close-knit family life, a sense of public duty, and moral respectability. Victorian attitudes were molded also by a revival of evangelical religion and by utilitarian beliefs in efficiency and good business practices.

The Middle and Late Victorian Years (1851–1901). In contrast to the late 1830s and the 1840s and despite the Crimean War of 1854–1856, which pitted England and France against Russia, the years 1851–1873 proved to be a period of increasing prosperity and decreasing crime, with England the world's foremost industrial and trading nation. Politics came to be dominated by the rivalry of Benjamin Disraeli (Conservative) and William Ewart Gladstone (Liberal) as the Reform Acts of 1867 and 1884 extended the right to vote to most adult men and as daily newspapers became both cheaper and more popular. The secret ballot was enacted. Gladstone's first ministry set up a merit-based civil service system and a national system of tax-supported (and ultimately compulsory and free) elementary schools. Disraeli took special pride in Britain's empire, which was consolidating in India and growing in Africa and East Asia even as settlement colonies such as Canada and Australia were gaining domestic self-government. The most explosive domestic issue was

Opening of the Great Exhibition. Queen Victoria and Prince Albert inaugurate the Great Exhibition of the Works of Industry of All Nations, London, 1 May 1851. Engraving by George Cruikshank. Prints and Photographs Division, Library of Congress

Ireland. Gladstone's bills to appease Irish nationalism with Home Rule, which divided his Liberal Party, were defeated in 1886 and again in 1893.

The population of England doubled between 1851 and 1911 despite a continued stream of emigrants to the colonies and to the United States. During the final three decades of the century, much of England's agriculture was afflicted by depression even as German and American manufacturers (but not yet shipbuilders or bankers) were overtaking England in rate of economic growth. At the same time, the notion of "separate spheres," that men dominated the public world and women the domestic, was beginning to be undermined by changes in the law that made it possible for a minority of women to enter universities, vote in local elections, and keep control of their property while married.

The Edwardian Era and World War I (1901–1919). A new Education Act (1902) began a national system of secondary education, and a Liberal ministry laid the foundations of the welfare state. It instituted old-age pensions, contributory medical insurance for most workers, and even unemployment insurance, and it mandated minimum and maximum hours for coal miners. Higher rates of income tax and even higher death duties helped pay for such changes as well as for armaments. A naval race with Germany helped bring about an English diplomatic alignment with France and Russia. It was the German invasion of neutral Belgium that precipitated England's entry into World War I (1914–1918).

For England the war meant a vast program of army mobilization and (by 1916) of national conscription. It also meant the loss of hundreds of merchant ships to German submarines, the threat of starvation, the onset of food rationing, a vast expansion of labor union membership, and the increased involvement of middle-class women in the workforce. In the course of four years, tax rates rose fivefold and the nation's debt fourteenfold. In politics it meant the replacement of the prewar Liberal ministry by a predominantly Conservative coalition ministry headed by the Liberal prime minister David Lloyd George (1916–1922). At the cost of more than seven hundred thousand lives and a yet larger number of wounded, the war also led to military victory and a major role at the Paris Peace Conference and in the new League of Nations (1919). The British Empire then reached its all-time height, but during the next two decades the settlement colonies (such as Canada and Australia) became increasingly independent, India and the others increasingly stirred by nationalist agitation, and most of Ireland (as of 1922) practically independent.

The Interwar Years (1919–1939). The Reform Acts of 1918 and 1928 granted all adults over twenty-one the right to vote, and laws that had barred women from professions such as the law and from jury service were abolished. Divorce laws were eased and—as contraception became socially acceptable—families with more than two children became rare, but most middle-class women remained homemakers. Whereas England's population had more than tripled during the nineteenth century, during the entire twentieth century it grew by less than 60 percent, and during the final decades of the century, but for immigration, it would not have grown at all.

In the meantime an initially minor party, the Labour Party, committed to a socialist program of replacing private with state-owned industry, took the place of the Liberal Party as one of England's two major political parties and briefly held office (1924; 1929–1931). Even the Conservative ministries that were in power during most of the interwar era believed in a greater degree of state intervention in the economy: they ended the gold standard and, after seventy-five years, restored protective tariffs. Such measures helped only in part to cope with the international Great Depression that during the early 1930s brought high rates of unemployment to miners, shipbuilders, and textile workers. Automobile, construction, and electricity workers fared better during an era in which cars, refrigerators, and telephones became more common in English homes. Members of all social groups attended the cinema and listened to radio, broadcasts of the latter monopolized (until the 1960s) by the fee-supported BBC (British Broadcasting Corporation).

World War II and After (1939–1955). Shadowed by memories of the horrors of World War I, most political leaders preferred to appease rather than to confront an expansionist Germany led by Adolf Hitler. After the German invasion of Poland in September 1939, however, the nation declared war and, under the leadership of Winston Churchill (from May 1940 on), continued to resist Hitler even after the fall of France. England's wartime mobilization became more comprehensive than that of any other power. A German invasion plan was foiled by the intrepid Royal Air Force, but central London and parts of other cities were destroyed.

Late in 1941, after the German invasion of the Soviet Union and the Japanese attack on Pearl Harbor, Churchill forged with Joseph Stalin and Franklin D. Roosevelt the "Grand Alliance" that four years later emerged triumphant over Germany, Italy, and Japan. British forces played a central role in the Atlantic naval war, the North African land war, the decipherment of German military codes, and the invasion of France.

English Factory. The Burroughs, Wellcome & Co. factory at Dartford, Kent, 1890s. Photograph published by the Detroit Publishing Company, 1905. PRINTS AND PHOTOGRAPHS DIVISION, LIBRARY OF CONGRESS

Members of the Labour Party had played an important role in Churchill's coalition war cabinet, and in the 1945 election Labour for the first time received a decisive parliamentary majority. During the next six years, the Labour ministry advanced its socialist goals by nationalizing the coal, gas and electricity, railroad, trucking, and steel industries and by establishing a comprehensive national insurance system, a national health service, and a program of public housing.

During those same years, the nation cooperated with the United States in the Cold War, the four-decade long struggle to deter a Soviet advance into Central and Western Europe and parts of Asia and Africa. It also developed England's own nuclear bomb. By granting independence to India (1947), the Labour ministry also began the process of dismantling the British Empire, a process that during the later 1950s and early 1960s was to be largely completed under Conservative ministry auspices. Most one-time colonies remained members of the Commonwealth, an organization that fostered consultation, mutual assistance, and athletic competition in sports such as cricket. Queen Elizabeth II (crowned with pomp in 1953), served as formal head of the Commonwealth.

Prosperity and Permissiveness (1951–1979). By the later 1950s and early 1960s, the scars of war and of wartime scarcity and rationing had disappeared and been replaced by a sense of affluence and cultural revival. Conservative ministries kept in place most of the changes instituted by the postwar Labour government, but during the 1960s an increasingly secular England experienced a widespread mood of rebellion against the conventions of the past—in dress, in music, in popular entertainment such as television, and in social behavior. "Swinging London" also experienced a rising crime rate and a spreading drug culture. A Labour ministry (1964–1970) sought to make secondary education more equitable and to expand higher education. It also legalized abortion, ended curbs on homosexual behavior, lowered the voting age to eighteen, and mandated equal pay for equal work for women.

During the period of "stagflation" that followed the quadrupling of international oil prices in 1973, England was beset by disruptive labor disputes and a rate of inflation of 25 percent per year that fostered its reputation as economically "the sick man of Europe." A "time of troubles" began in Northern Ireland, most of whose inhabitants—in defiance of the Irish Republican Army (IRA)—still preferred to remain part of the United Kingdom. In the short run, the country's admission to the (then nine-member) European Union helped little, and a strike-filled

"winter of discontent" (1978–1979) led to a parliamentary vote of "no confidence" in the Labour ministry. A subsequent new general election brought the Conservative party into power for the next eighteen years (1979–1997).

Contemporary England (since 1979). Margaret Thatcher's long and controversial prime ministership (1979–1990) became associated with profound reversals in British economic life. A change in financial policy eventually reduced the rate of inflation from more than 20 percent to less than 4 percent a year. Many of the powerful trade unions (such as the miners) were tamed, and strikes became rare. Indeed, the once mighty coal mining and shipbuilding industries all but disappeared as the service sector of society grew and the giant factory declined. Major nationalized industries such as oil, airlines, gas and electricity, the telephone system, and eventually the railroads were privatized and returned to stockholder control in the interest of greater efficiency. The Thatcher ministry successfully encouraged 1.5 million of public housing renters to buy their own homes. It did not seek to abolish the popular national health service, but—at a time that new discoveries and a life expectancy of seventy-seven or higher raised medical costs—it did seek to make it more efficient. It also did its best to cope with the hundreds of thousands of immigrants coming primarily from the Caribbean, India, and Pakistan, who (making up 9 percent of the population and including 3 million Muslims) gave to the England of 2005 a far more diverse appearance than it had had as recently as 1945.

Margaret Thatcher's reputation as "the iron lady" was enhanced by her naval success in recapturing the Falkland Islands from Argentine invaders (1982). Her continuing political success was dependent also on deep divisions within the opposition Labour and revived Liberal (now Liberal Democrat) Parties. As a result, she became not only the first woman prime minister but also the first prime minister to lead a party to three successive general election triumphs (1979, 1983, 1987). Under her successor the party won one more general election (1992), but by then the Conservative Party was deeply divided over how strong the country's attachment should be to the expanding European Union. By then, too, the Soviet Union had imploded and the Cold War had ended.

By 1997 the Labour Party had chosen a charismatic new leader who persuaded his followers to forsake their traditional allegiance to nationalization and high taxation. Tony Blair led his more centrist party to a decisive parliamentary victory that year, and he was to do so again in 2001 and in 2005. By then he had altered the constitution by removing the hereditary peers from the House of Lords and by providing Scotland and Wales with their own elected assemblies, even though both areas continued to be represented in the House of Commons at Westminster. He had also succeeded in all but ending terrorism in Northern Ireland. In the aftermath of the radical Islamic terrorist attack on the United States in 2001, he cooperated with the American government in the invasion of Iraq in 2003 and the increasingly controversial war there.

Tony Blair presided over a decade of economic growth with relatively low inflation and low unemployment. His land was happily adapting to the Internet age. Despite the effective end of empire (with the hand-over of Hong Kong to China in 1997) and significant societal changes since 1945, the England of the early twenty-first century remained one of the world's most stable and prosperous lands.

[*See also* Industrial Revolution; Parliament, British; United Kingdom; *and* Victorianism.]

BIBLIOGRAPHY

Arnstein, Walter L. *Britain Yesterday and Today, 1830 to the Present*. 8th ed. Boston: Houghton Mifflin, 2001.

Daunton, M. J. *Progress and Poverty: An Economic and Social History of Britain, 1700–1850*. Oxford: Oxford University Press, 1995.

Harris, José. *Private Lives, Public Spirit: Britain, 1870–1914*. London and New York: Penguin Books, 1994.

Hilton, Boyd. *A Mad, Bad, and Dangerous People?: England, 1783–1846*. Oxford and New York: Oxford University Press, 2006.

Hoppen, K. Theodore. *The Mid-Victorian Generation, 1846–1886*. Oxford and New York: Oxford University Press, 1998.

Langford, Paul. *A Polite and Commercial People: England, 1727–1783*. Oxford and New York: Oxford University Press, 1992.

Marwick, Arthur. *British Society since 1945*. 4th ed. London and New York: Penguin Books, 2003.

Morgan, Kenneth O. *The People's Peace: British History, 1945–1990*. Oxford and New York: Oxford University Press, 1992.

Searle, G. R. *A New England? Peace and War, 1886–1918*. Oxford and New York: Oxford University Press, 2005.

Stevenson, John. *British Society, 1914–1945*. London and New York: Penguin Books, 1984.

Trevelyan, George Macaulay. *History of England*. London: Longman, 1926.

Willcox, William B., and Arnstein, Walter L. *The Age of Aristocracy, 1688–1830*. 8th ed. Boston: Heath, 2001.

WALTER L. ARNSTEIN

ENGLISH LANGUAGE.

The history of the English language covers a vast terrain, within which three issues have an undoubted importance in the modern era: (1) the widespread prescriptive concern with "proper" or "standard" English, (2) the emergence of multiple Englishes around the world, and (3) the function of English as a "world" language. Taken together, these three topics highlight how different the position and role of English are in the modern world from what they were through much of its earlier history—and they highlight how controversial a subject the English language has become.

The Concern with "Proper" English. Until the early modern era, there was very little concern with English usage: it was the mother tongue of the populace in England, certainly, but it was not viewed as a language of culture. Social and cultural prestige was tied up with Latin as the language of learning, with Hebrew and Greek as the languages of the Bible, and, into the seventeenth and eighteenth centuries, with Italian and French as the modern languages of culture. But by the late eighteenth century English had emerged as one of the recognized languages of culture in the European world—though, as yet, far behind French in its actual dissemination on the Continent.

With this elevation in status, and the concomitant domestic shift away from a bilingual cultural system (centered on the classical curriculum of the grammar schools and universities) to a vernacular dominated cultural system, there arose a new obsessive concern with "proper" English, both in speech and in writing. "Scotticisms" had to be eliminated from the speech and writing of Scottish English-speakers, just as "rustic" or "provincial" dialect had to be excised, if one wanted one's speech to sound educated and urbane in this modern context. Idioms and accents associated with the lower classes, especially the new urban accents associated with the towns of an industrializing age, were deprecated and distinguished from the usage particular to "polite" English. Where, previously, knowledge of Latin or allusions to classical authors in one's speech or writing served to distinguish the discourse of "gentleman" from that the common people, now, the use of a distinctive "elegant" and "refined" English served this purpose. This placed a fundamentally new kind of social pressure on the use of English in everyday life—one that has remained central to the politics of English into our own time.

The shift from a bilingual to a vernacular-dominated cultural system did not eliminate the verbal borderlines of caste, class, and education; it simply relocated them in relation to the use of different kinds of English—received pronunciation ("RP") versus Cockney, Standard American English versus Black Vernacular English, native-speakers' English versus foreigners' English. And, as these examples suggest, by locating these social borderlines in relation to the use of the everyday vernacular, this cultural shift also gave a new salience to issues of nationality and ethnicity in relation to language.

The Emergence of Multiple Englishes. The domestic complications of English language use in the British Isles have been supplemented, throughout the modern era, by the emergence of several distinct national varieties of English in the peripheries of the British Empire. American English, Australian English, South African English are among the products of this internationalization of English in the modern world. Where, in earlier eras, English was the language of a particular regional culture in the European world, it was now a pluricentric language, growing from roots in many parts of the world. Through much of the colonial experience of each of these regions, their local English was judged—both locally and in the imperial metropole—as deficient to the extent that it deviated from British norms. American English, in the early nineteenth century, was the first to assert its cultural independence from British suzerainty, although the cultural cachet of certain British accents can still be heard, on occasion, in both elite and mass culture in the contemporary United States. Eventually, the Englishes of the various settler colonies came to assert their own legitimacy and dignity as "native" varieties of English, although this process was not fully emergent in places like Australia until the 1960s and 70s.

The central battlefront of linguistic politics in the contemporary world is between the native-speaker Englishes of Britain and settler-colonial countries, on the one hand, and the various "second-language" Englishes of other parts of the former British Empire, especially in South Asia and in Africa. Whether Nigerian English or Indian English, for instance, are fully legitimate varieties of English or whether they (and their speakers) are in need of constant inspection and tutelage from native-speakers of English remains a charged issue, both in practice and in theory.

English as a "World" Language. The third major innovation in the modern history of English is its emergence as the major "interlanguage" of the world, that is, as the language of choice for communication between persons belonging to different language communities, even where neither of the partners in the exchange speaks English as a mother tongue. English is used as a language of international exchange not only when businesses in other parts of the world interact with U.S. or British businesses, but also when, for example, Italian and German businesses wish to speak with each other. The British Empire first established a network of areas of English proficiency around the world and then U.S. economic and mass cultural hegemony enhanced the global salience of English even further. This, combined with the domestic size and wealth of the English-speaking regions of the world, has made English the preeminent language of commerce, of science, of communications media (from BBC radio and Hollywood movies to Anglo-American popular music and the Internet). Many of the international transactions of academic scholarship, of diplomacy, of sports serve to further disseminate English as an international auxiliary language, a language familiar (at varying levels of comprehension and proficiency) to hundreds of millions of people around the globe. The emergence of English as *the* international language of the modern world has often led to a kind of triumphalist sentiment on the part of native-speakers of English, but the future of English is likely to be more complicated and more unpredictable than its present-day supremacy might suggest.

[*See also* American Literature; British Literature; Cultural Imperialism; *and* Globalization.]

BIBLIOGRAPHY

Crystal, David. *The Cambridge Encyclopedia of the English Language.* 2nd ed. Cambridge, U.K.; New York: Cambridge University Press, 2003. A rich, profusely illustrated mine of information about all aspects of the English language and its linguistic study. (Other writings by this author are also valuable resources.)

McCrum, Robert, William Cran, and Robert MacNeil. *The Story of English.* 3d ed. New York: Penguin Books, 2003. Companion to the popular BBC series on the English language. Covers the full history of the language but with major emphasis on the modern era and on international varieties of the language.

Mugglestone, Lynda. *Talking Proper: The Rise of Accent as Social Symbol.* Oxford, 2003. Provides a rich account of the emergence of notions of "proper" or "standard" English and the development of this prescriptive outlook up to the present in the British context.

Pennycook, Alastair. *The Cultural Politics of English as an International Language.* London; New York: Longman, 1994. A rich survey of issues involved in the spread of English, especially with regard to English language teaching in contexts, such as Malaysia and Singapore, outside the sphere of native-speaker Englishes.

ALOK YADAV

ENLIGHTENMENT. The Enlightenment was a pan-European cultural movement that acquired a shape and self-consciousness during the eighteenth century. Its broad goal, as defined by the German philosopher Immanuel Kant (1724–1804), was the emancipation of humanity from self-imposed submission to obsolete orthodoxies and arbitrary rule. In the view of the Enlightenment's partisans, liberation from error and liberation from oppression were part of the same desperate struggle of humanity to escape from the burdens of the past.

Origins of the Enlightenment. The roots of the Enlightenment lay in three intersecting developments. One was the epistemological revolution of the seventeenth century, during which a wave of skepticism regarding ancient truths inspired fresh efforts to rebuild knowledge on firmer foundations. Although the rationalist philosophy of René Descartes (1596–1650) shaped the epistemological goals of the Enlightenment, the philosophy of John Locke (1632–1704) had a greater influence on the movement, in part because of its affinity with the empirically grounded Scientific Revolution. The Scientific Revolution provided the Enlightenment with a model and a method for challenging other orthodoxies that stood in the way of "progress." Known as philosophes (the French word for "philosophers"), the Enlightenment's advocates proposed to extend the critical review of received ideas to all domains; no intellectual, religious, political, or social belief was, in principle, too sacred to escape rigorous reevaluation. It is no accident that the single most influential work of the Enlightenment was the *Encyclopédie*, a multi-authored, comprehensive critique of human knowledge edited by Denis Diderot and Jean le Rond d'Alembert.

The Enlightenment also resulted from the demands placed on states to modernize and streamline their methods of administration and revenue appropriation. During the eighteenth century, recurrent warfare and competitive empire-building drove up the costs of government beyond what taxpayers could or would pay, thereby forcing states to borrow so much money that they teetered on the brink of bankruptcy. In such circumstances, princes had little choice but to reexamine and reform their methods of governing. The philosophes performed critical services for governments across Europe as diplomats, financial consultants, scientific advisers, and jurists, and they provided a steady stream of new ideas to make states run more efficiently and expand the wealth of nations from which states derived their revenues. By the end of the eighteenth century, some of the less well-connected philosophes pushed their critiques so far that they began to question the very legitimacy of the ancien régime (Old Regime).

The third origin of the Enlightenment lay in the transformation of the market for high culture engendered by the growth of literacy and disposable income. Like the Renaissance humanists, who had also sought to speak truth to power, the philosophes were beholden to the princes they advised for protection, material support, and an audience for their work. Still heavily dependent on state patronage, there were few philosophes who could afford to refuse the pensions and sinecures offered them in government administration and royal academies; still fewer were willing to go to prison for expressing their often controversial beliefs. At the same time, the edge of their work was sharpened by their opportunity to communicate with a "public" that had been previously dominated by high churchmen and aristocrats, but was now much expanded to include large segments of the burgeoning middle class. This larger public not only purchased the works of the philosophes, but also provided them with an audience receptive to heterodox ideas. The expansion of the book trade (including a booming underground commerce in prohibited works), the development of a more robust periodical press, and the proliferation of new loci of intellectual and social exchange, such as coffee houses and salons (informal social gatherings usually hosted by a woman of high social and/or intellectual standing), provided venues for the expression of a more universalistic "public opinion" than existed in previous ages. The Enlightenment sought to instruct and co-opt this inchoate public opinion—which was not always inclined to "enlightened" points of view. Voltaire (François-Marie Arouet; 1694–1778) once said of his role, "I am the secretary of the public."

Vocabulary of the Enlightenment. The content of the Enlightenment has been frequently misconstrued by its enemies and its friends, who attributed to the Enlightenment notions the philosophes would have disowned. Another source of distortion has been the effort to extract from the writings of the philosophes a single coherent philosophy or program. Given the wide variation of their views, it is perhaps best to describe their thought in terms of meanings they assigned to four recurrent terms in their discourse.

Reason. Often caricatured as unbending "rationalists" in an "age of reason," the philosophes were, on the contrary, mitigated skeptics who mercilessly criticized efforts to build overarching "rationalistic" systems on weak empirical foundations. To the philosophes, "reason" properly applied entailed the analysis of complex notions into their constituent elements and their recomposition into general ideas. Since human knowledge derives from a limited set of sense experience synthesized by the mind, the philosophes contended, our notions of the world are either relatively trivial or uncertain. As regards human psychology, the philosophes believed that reason ought to keep emotions under good control, but they acknowledged the role played by emotions as an inextinguishable force essential for human creativity. Whether women were as capable of exercising reason as men remained a matter of debate.

Enlightenment. Frontispiece to the volume of plates of the *Ency-clopédie*, 1772. Engraving by Benoît-Louis Prevost after a drawing by Claude-Nicolas Chochin II. Rare Books and Special Collections Division, Library of Congress

Nature. To the philosophes, "nature" stood for the kind of mathematical regularity detected in the universe by scientists such as Isaac Newton (1642–1727). As a principle of society, nature would ideally inform all laws and institutions; the perception that in the past it had often failed to do so provided the Enlightenment with one of its critical edges. By the later eighteenth century, the philosophes were moving gradually from a neo-Stoical emphasis on natural law to the more radical focus on natural rights. This position did not lead most philosophes to the view that humanity was asocial by nature or had ever lived in an asocial state. Even the Swiss-born philosophe Jean-Jacques Rousseau (1712–1778), a great admirer of the "noble savage" and a dissenter from many of his colleagues' views, contended that humanity would be most completely fulfilled in a properly constituted political society, and he never advocated a return to the forests.

Progress. Often mistaken for naive optimists, the philosophes recognized that history had been a slaughter bench; as any reader of Voltaire's celebrated novelette *Candide* understands, they entertained many gloomy thoughts about their own world and its prospects. At the same time, most philosophes did perceive a fitful historical trend toward improvement of the human condition brought about by expansion of the economy and the advance of the sciences, arts, and other features of "civilization," a term coined in the eighteenth century. Future "progress," they believed, would result from the continued cultivation of humanity's creative capacities, but whether moral improvement would follow in the train of technical advances and increasing wealth remained a controversial and unresolved question.

Liberty. Like their progenitor John Locke, the philosophes held that "liberty" was a natural part of the human condition and that all legitimate infringements on that liberty required consent in some form. In their view, liberty was not only a natural right of individuals, but also a social necessity, since it provided far more incentive than coercion for individuals to harness their creative energies. This view did not entail belief in democracy, the razing of social differences, or popular revolution, all of which most philosophes considered utopian and dangerous, at least in the context of their own times. Within their preindustrial horizons, they expected most peasants to remain peasants, and they could not readily imagine women in social roles other than that of wives and mothers.

The Program. The reforms proposed by the Enlightenment were endless, but they may be said to cluster around three major areas of concern: the state, religion, and the economy.

Like others in their age, the philosophes questioned the efficiency and fairness of the absolute monarchies established in the previous century, and they relentlessly criticized what they perceived as obsolete systems of justice, finance, and social policy. Although most philosophes embraced monarchy as the form of government best suited for modern national states, they fretted over its tendency to degenerate into "despotism," that is, a state run without due regard for reason and law. To the more conservative philosophes, the best way to thwart despotism was to hedge monarchy with a thicket of traditional law that would contain its arbitrary tendencies and protect the liberty of its subjects. Others known as "enlightened absolutists" contended that contemporary monarchies had not been too strong, but misguided. Under this view, the purpose of the state was to provide the greatest possible utility to its citizens at the least possible cost, a goal achievable only if public opinion provided rulers with constant infusions of enlightenment. Liberalization of the state was important to ensure that the state received good advice from the best and the brightest: hence, the need for public education and a free press. At the margins of the debate between these two schools, a few philosophes entertained notions of democracy, but their voices only began to gain credibility at the end of the Enlightenment.

Because of its central place in the life of the Old Regime, the church was inevitably the subject, if not the target, of many philosophe works. In France, hostility to the established Church was especially intense, in part because dissident Catholics known as Jansenists had already launched attacks on its despotic tendencies. The philosophes campaigned strenuously for greater religious freedom, which, according to Voltaire, allowed each sect to check the despotic tendencies of the others. Although they did question and sometimes mocked belief in traditional Christian doctrine, hostility to the Catholic Church did not necessarily entail hostility to religion, which most philosophes considered a necessary institution for the inculcation of morality. Outside France, hostility to the Church was less severe, and in these countries enlightened theologians cultivated forms of religious spirituality, such as Pietism, that looked for divine guidance more to the individual soul's "inner light" than to established ecclesiastical authority. Here was another manifestation of the Enlightenment's belief in freedom.

To expand economic production by unleashing individual enterprise, the philosophes proposed the scaling back of state controls on production, prices, and wages. Although they could not foresee the industrial revolution soon to emerge in Europe, they did glimpse the possibility of a brighter, more comfortable existence through improvements in technology and the more efficient use of labor. "Sweet commerce," they contended, not only promoted civilization by raising the standard of living, but also by reducing the likelihood of war.

Impact and Legacy. Because the Enlightenment was so well integrated into many different intellectual and social contexts, any estimate of its contemporary influence is necessarily approximate, but the available evidence supports two broad generalizations. First, the Enlightenment remained primarily an affair of literate elites, who shared the philosophes' interest in the sciences and their

disdain of popular "prejudices." There were broad segments of the elite who frowned on, indeed abhorred the impieties and caustic criticisms of the philosophes, yet the fact that so many apologists of orthodoxy responded to them in a flood of antiphilosophe literature testifies to the depth of the Enlightenment's impact. Second, western and central Europe were far more profoundly touched by the Enlightenment than eastern Europe, where the middle-class public was much smaller and intellectuals remained more dependent on the state and the church. In Russia under Catherine II (Catherine the Great; 1729–1796; r. 1762–1796), the Enlightenment served to reinforce the state's repressive apparatus more than it did to lighten the burden of the serfs.

After 1789, the Enlightenment became inextricably associated with the outbreak of revolution. It is probable that the philosophes had inadvertently weakened the Old Regime by corroding traditional authority in the name of "liberty" and raising expectations of reform; but even Rousseau articulated no theory of revolution and stressed the unsuitability of democracy in large modern commercialized nations like France. The discontinuities between the Enlightenment and the age of Revolution notwithstanding, some counterrevolutionaries leapt to the conclusion that the French Revolution had been the "fault" of Rousseau and Voltaire, and on this matter the revolutionaries were in rough agreement, for they publicly celebrated these philosophes as prophets of their own cause. Throughout the nineteenth and twentieth centuries, the Enlightenment remained a battleground between those who defended it because of its secular and liberal tendencies, and those who denounced it, either because it had destroyed a cherished old order or because its program had been insufficiently radical. One school of thought portrayed the Enlightenment as a precursor of fascism because of its flirtation with technocracy, while postcolonialists associated it with Western imperialism. All these interpretations contain some measure of truth, but they also distort it by focusing on selected aspects of the Enlightenment without proper regard to context. The philosophes would undoubtedly not have welcomed these multiple misreadings of their message, but as experts on humanity's foibles, they would not have been altogether surprised to learn that their lessons had sometimes and to some extent been misconstrued.

[See also *Encyclopédie* and Scottish Enlightenment.]

BIBLIOGRAPHY
Cassirer, Ernst. *The Philosophy of the Enlightenment*. Translated by Fritz. C. A. Koelin and James P. Pettegrove. Princeton, N.J.: Princeton University Press, 1951. English translation of *Die*

Philosophie der Aufklärung, first published in 1932. The most successful attempt to elicit a coherent Enlightenment "philosophy."

Chartier, Roger. *The Cultural Origins of the French Revolution.* Translated by Lydia G. Cochrane. Durham, N.C.: Duke University Press, 1991. English translation of *Les origines culturelles de la Révolution française*, first published in 1990. Notable essay on the Enlightenment and other movements in France considered in relation to their impact on cultural "practices" rather than intellectual content.

Darnton, Robert. *The Forbidden Best-Sellers of Pre-Revolutionary France.* New York: Norton, 1995. Broad examination of the literary underground and its connections to the Enlightenment.

Gay, Peter. *The Enlightenment: An Interpretation.* 2 vols. New York: Knopf, 1966. The standard old view, emphasizing the Enlightenment's secular message and secularizing effect.

Hampson, Norman. *A Cultural History of the Enlightenment.* New York: Pantheon, 1968. Old and in some respects outdated, but a still valuable short survey.

Melton, James Van Horn. *The Rise of the Public in Enlightenment Europe.* Cambridge, U.K.: Cambridge University Press, 2001. Superb comparative study of the nature and function of the "public" in England, France, and Germany.

Outram, Dorinda. *The Enlightenment.* New York: Cambridge University Press, 1995. Perceptive essays on various aspects of the Enlightenment, including its implications for gender.

Porter, Roy, and Mikuláš Teich, eds. *The Enlightenment in National Context.* Cambridge, U.K.: Cambridge University Press, 1981. Essays of varying quality stressing the national differences within the Enlightenment movement.

THOMAS E. KAISER

ENTEBBE HIJACKING. A week-long drama in Uganda in 1976, the Entebbe hijacking was the intersection of three twentieth-century historical factors: international terrorism resulting from the establishment of Israel in 1948 and wars over land in the Middle East; Cold War competition through American and Soviet agent countries for global influence; and the reception of this competition by dictators left at the end of colonial rule in Africa.

On Sunday, 27 June 1976, two German members of the Baader-Meinhof urban guerrilla organization and two Arab members of the Popular Front for the Liberation of Palestine (PLO) hijacked Air France flight 139 from Tel Aviv to Paris after it left Athens. The hijacked flight stopped to fuel at Benghazi in Libya, then landed at Entebbe in Uganda, where additional Palestinians and Ugandan soldiers kept the 268 hostages in the old terminal building.

The flight's stops in Libya and Uganda were not happenstance; they were a result of the diplomatic history of Uganda and Israel. Israeli defense minister Simon Peres and foreign minister Golda Meir helped establish the Ugandan army and air force following Ugandan

independence in 1963. A decade of cooperation ended when President Idi Amin turned to Arab allies after Israel refused Amin's request for military assistance against Tanzania. In 1972, Amin and Libya's Muammar al-Qaddafi issued a joint statement supporting the Arab struggle against Israel, and the Israeli ambassador and Israeli residents left Uganda. Palestinian guards appeared among President Amin's security detail. The Soviet Union then invested many millions in Ugandan military forces, supplying the MiG fighter aircraft that Israel later destroyed in their raid on Entebbe.

Amin cooperated with the hijackers. Uganda Radio transmitted the hijackers' demands for the release of fifty-three convicted terrorists held in various countries, most in Israel. The hijackers separated the Israeli hostages and released the others. The Israeli government—including Simon Peres, Prime Minister Yitzhak Rabin, and opposition leader Menachem Begin—secretly planned a rescue raid. On 4 July, Israeli forces landed at Entebbe, captured the terminal buildings, and took the hostages back to Israel. During the raid, Israeli forces killed 35 Ugandan soldiers, one Israeli hostage, and 19 terrorists. Ugandan troops killed one Israeli soldier. The four Israeli planes refueled at Nairobi in Kenya and returned to Israel. The elderly hostage Dora Bloch remained, unbeknown to Israelis, in a Ugandan hospital during and after the raid. She was murdered in Uganda, and her family only recovered her remains in 1979 after Amin's ouster.

Uganda failed to gain a United Nations condemnation of Israel for violating its sovereignty. In the U.N. Security Council debates the week after the raid, Uganda claimed no involvement in the incident, and denied that Dora Bloch remained in Uganda after the rescue. An Organization of African Unity motion to censure Israel also failed. The raid on Entebbe has become important in Israel's military history, and its key figures retained importance in Israeli politics. Lieutenant Colonel Jonathan Netanyahu commanded the Israeli assault unit at Entebbe and was the only Israeli soldier to die in the raid. In the 1990s his brother Benjamin became the prime minister of Israel.

[*See also* Israel *and* Terrorism.]

BIBLIOGRAPHY

Goldberg, Michel. *Namesake.* New Haven, Conn.: Yale University Press, 1982.

Netanyahu, Iddo. *Entebbe, a Defining Moment in the War on Terrorism: The Jonathan Netanyahu Story.* Green Forest, Ark.: Balfour Books, 2003.

Stevenson, William. *Ninety Minutes at Entebbe.* New York: Bantam Books, 1976.

KATHRYN BARRETT-GAINES

ENVIRONMENT [*This entry includes eight subentries:*

See also Deserts and Desertification; Global Warming; Green Parties; Imperialism and Environment; Natural Resources; Sustainable Development; Water and Water Management; *and* Wildlife.]

Overview

For convenience, we can divide modern environmental history into three phases, roughly corresponding to the eighteenth, nineteenth, and twentieth centuries.

The Eighteenth Century. In 1700, world population was perhaps a little over 600 million; a hundred years later, it probably exceeded 900 million. The global "population explosion" of modern times had begun.

Except in the New World—where migrants arrived and the diseases European intruders had introduced two hundred years earlier receded—we have no satisfactory explanation, but the increase in numbers took two forms: dispersal on underexploited frontiers and concentration in growing cities or denser agricultural settlements.

Improved food supply played an important part. The worldwide "ecological exchange" of plants and animals increased farmers' options and extended the amount and yield of cultivable land. More people around the world got more food more regularly and survived longer to work and reproduce. Urbanization, on the other hand, made some diets worse: it interposed middlemen between city dwellers and farmers, raised the cost of food, and separated consumers from fresh local produce. In China and India, increased food production does not seem to have kept pace with population growth. Still, concentrated markets and improved shipping canals, and coastal trade made the distribution of bulk foods easier, notably in China, Japan, and Europe.

Even more significant was a new disease regime—as the lethal diseases formerly called plagues receded from some of their eco-niches. This is not likely to have been the result of improved hygiene. Even in the most technically

ambitious and sophisticated societies, until well into the nineteenth century, bigger cities meant that more people were exposed to water contaminated by human sewage and to the lice that spread typhus. Some improvements in health were clearly the result of medical science or care; but most medicine remained useless and ignorant, and nothing that was new in medicine affected the plague. Quarantine was more and more widely understood and practiced—but some diseases eluded it.

It is therefore hard to resist the impression that the global profile of disease changed without humans doing much to affect it. In part, this was a further consequence of ecological exchange. Fewer populations suffered from lack of natural immunization, as formerly localized diseases became familiar over a vast range of the world. Still, while so-called plague retreated, some deadly organisms continued to migrate. Yellow fever crossed the Atlantic from Africa and spread beyond the tropics, hitting cities as far north as Philadelphia repeatedly in the eighteenth century. The European cocktail of diseases that despoiled the Americas of Native peoples in the sixteenth and seventeenth centuries wrought havoc in newer discoveries. Toward the end of the eighteenth century, Hawai'i suffered much as the Americas had done. Tahiti's population decline started in 1769 and went from forty thousand to nine thousand by 1830. When European colonization began in Australia in 1788, smallpox ravaged the Aboriginal population.

Microbial behavior may hold the key to understanding changes in the disease regime. Some microorganisms that bear disease—especially viruses—evolve fast because they are individually short-lived. Those that kill off their hosts are not adaptively successful. They need to find new eco-niches to ensure their own survival, or they are self-condemned to disappear. For reasons we do not know—but which must be connected with their own evolutionary advantage—hostile microorganisms sometimes switch their attention away from one set of victims and find another. The improved health of parts of the eighteenth-century world may have owed less to human cleverness than to the changing habits and nature of microbes.

Increased agricultural output may have boosted immune systems. It transformed humans' relationship with the rest of nature. In Europe as far east as Poland, and in Spanish America, landowners and agricultural improvement societies promoted elements of what was virtually a common program: reducing labor costs, replacing inefficient farming with grazing, improving soils by draining and fertilizing, enhancing livestock by scientific stockbreeding, diversifying crops to maximize use of the earth, conserving exploitable forests, and fencing off underexploited land for the use of the most efficient farmers. These changes had parallels in parts of East and Southeast Asia, especially in Korea, Japan, and the Philippines.

The effects of ecological exchange complemented efforts to coax more food from the soil. From European gardens of acclimatization, plants could be redistributed around the world. Spectacular transmissions included coffee to the East Indies and the New World, the expansion of sugar production—already well established in the Americas—in the Indian Ocean, and the extension of ecological exchange to previously untransformed parts of the Pacific, including Australia and New Zealand.

Food is a form of energy. Increasing interest in new forms of energy was a pronounced feature of the period, especially in western Europe, where scientific and philosophical fashion favored investigation of mechanical ways of enhancing or replacing muscle power. It would be exaggerated, however, to speak—as historians used to do—of an eighteenth-century "industrial revolution." In most industries, development was piecemeal, and methods remained traditional. Huge gains in productivity resulted from traditional methods applied with more manpower and more capital investment to meet rising demand. Lipids (especially blubber and other animal and vegetable fats), along with muscle power, traditional fuels (wood, peat, and coal), and relatively limited exploitation of wind power and waterpower were still the only means humans had to supplement the power of the Earth and the Sun and devise ways to deliver energy. That changed in the nineteenth century.

The Nineteenth Century. In the nineteenth century traditional energy sources were no longer sufficient in an unprecedentedly populous world. By the end of the century, there were about 1.6 billion humans. A revolution in the sources of energy kept human society working: new ways to exploit the planet's resources and new ventures to release energy and redirect it to new uses.

Food production soared, partly because more land was devoted to it and partly because of new, more efficient methods of production. Fertilizers—including guano and mineral phosphates—increased productivity. Scientific agronomy multiplied crops and livestock. Industrialization revolutionized preserving, processing, and supply.

Environmental Pollution at London. *Source of the Southwark Water Works*, etching by George Cruikshank (1792–1878). John Edwards, owner of the Southwark Water Works, sits on a dome in the middle of the dark and murky Thames River, holding a trident with drowned animals on the prongs as sludge from sewers pours in from both sides. Courtesy of the National Library of Medicine, Bethesda, Maryland

Food itself became an industrial product. The greatest extension of the frontier of food production happened in the Americas. The incorporation of natural grassland to raise cattle and grow grain was the most conspicuous large-scale adaptation of the environment for human purposes ever recorded. In what people called "the Great American Desert" at the start of the century, almost nothing grew naturally that human stomachs could digest. Except in a few patches, the soil was too tough to plow without industrial technology. Yet thanks to steel blades that turned the sod, and railways that took the grain to markets, the same plains became the world's granary, with some of the most productive farming the world has ever seen.

Although global food production soared, its effects were uneven, and the ravages of famine were worse in the nineteenth century than at any other period in recorded history. But the increase had a genuinely unprecedented impact. Because so much of it was the result of new kinds of science and technology, it was achieved with a relatively small input of additional labor. Part of the vast increase of population that the food boom fed was free to engage in other kinds of economic activity. Trade, industry, agriculture, and urbanization were linked in a mutually sustaining cycle of expansion.

What we now call "fossil fuels" fueled industrialization. Peat and coal were extracted from the ground on an unprecedented scale. (Oil followed in the second half of the century and, eventually, in the twentieth century, natural gas). Fossil fuels are a form of concentrated energy. So the first effect of the release of coal from the ground was to liberate land for farming that had formerly been used to produce wood for fuel, helping along the massive growth of food production. The second was to provide energy for new forms of power, especially steam, which operated new, world-girdling forms of transport and socially transmutative factories.

But a paradox remains to be explained. In an age of increasing population, more muscle power was becoming available worldwide. So why bother to mechanize? In part, the explanation lies in the geography of industrialization. On the whole, it happened earliest and fastest in regions where labor was relatively expensive. Secondly, and perhaps more significantly, industrialization was a function of demand. Population increase accounted in part for increasing demand, but so did the multiplication of sources of wealth—the new resources unlocked from the soil, the enormous expansion of financial institutions, the growth in the money supply.

Industrialization created important regional environmental changes. Dumping of chemical wastes, plus waste pollution from growing cities, fouled the quality of many rivers in industrial areas. Smoke emissions reduced air quality around factory cities. Demand for raw materials—for example, rubber—encouraged shifts in agriculture in places like Brazil and West Africa, leading to reduction of forests and soil erosion.

The Twentieth Century. The figures of the twentieth century, when the numbers of people in the world came to exceed 6 billion, seem astonishing by the standards of earlier periods. People took up more space and depleted more resources than ever before. One result was pell-mell urbanization. For ten thousand years, most people had lived in agricultural settlements. Now centers of industrial manufacturing and services took over. Towns and cities became the normal environments for people to live in. By the end of the century, half the world lived in settlements with populations of twenty thousand or more. Cities grew even in countries where agriculture remained the economically dominant way of life. By the century's end, however, there were signs that urbanization was easing. São Paulo in Brazil and Mexico City—overgrown giants with populations approaching 20 million each by some counts—began to shrink.

As the human domain expanded, humans crowded out some life forms and blasted others into oblivion, hunting them to extinction, exterminating them with pest controls, or depriving them of their habitats or foods. At the start of the twenty-first century, the world faced the loss of more species than at any time since the end of the last Ice Age. By swapping plants and animals around the world—releasing "invading" species into unfamiliar habitats—humans condemned some of the native animals of affected zones to death by predation. Fish consumption worldwide grew fortyfold in the twentieth century, and according to the historian John McNeill, the world consumed 3 billion tons of fish, exceeding the whole catch landed during the entire previous history of the world. Some varieties were fished to near extinction. Half the deforestation of history happened in the twentieth century. In the last forty years of the century, the Amazonian forests of Brazil shrank by 10 percent. In Southeast Asia, those of Thailand, Malaysia, and Borneo in Indonesia disappeared on a similar scale. By the end of the century, Africa had lost half its tropical forests, Latin America nearly one-third. The traditional human inhabitants of these environments—foragers and seasonal farmers—survived, but their habitats shrank, and their situation grew ever more precarious. So did those of the other creatures who shared their homes.

In the long run, demand for resources hugely outstripped population growth. Between 1900 and 1950, global output rose, at 2003 prices, from $2 trillion to $5 trillion. Between 1950 and 2000, the total soared to $39 trillion. In other words, while the population of the world less than quadrupled, output rose more than nineteenfold.

Just as steam power transformed the nineteenth-century world, so electricity and the internal combustion engine transformed the twentieth century. The battery and the local generator, which was usually oil-fueled, meant that electric power could be harnessed way beyond the industrial world. The internal combustion engine came puffing and rumbling into the world in the 1890s and rapidly became the world's favorite form of locomotion. Oil gradually replaced coal as the world's major source of energy, except in China. By the end of the twentieth century, oil supplied 40 percent of the world's energy, with coal and natural gas accounting in equal measure for most of the rest. Reliance on fossil fuels carried two major disadvantages.

First, they are a limited resource. Secondly, they release carbon gases into the atmosphere when they burn. In the twentieth century, the amount of carbon dioxide in the air rose from 280 to 350 parts per million. Most of this increase was the result of the recirculation of carbon formerly locked in forests or buried underground. Global warming accelerated in consequence. The problem got worse because output of carbon-charged gases from refrigerators, air conditioners, and aerosol sprays rose, by some estimates, about 150-fold between 1950 and 1990, when international controls began to take effect.

Meanwhile, overexploitation wasted earth and water. Marginal land all over the world became ever less productive as the result of a vicious cycle of cause and effect. Farmers had to force more food from less land, while spreading deserts edged into fields. Soil that ought to be fallow had to be sown. So soil exhaustion got worse, and food supplies became more precarious. Much of the world was trapped in this cycle, especially in parts of Africa and Asia.

Traditional responses to the problem of trying to get more output from less soil are irrigation and fertilization. In the second half of the twentieth century, the amount of land under irrigation increased from under 247 million acres to almost 644 million acres. By the century's end, 40 percent of the world's food was grown on irrigated land. Demand drained much of the world's water table; giant dams, built for irrigation or hydro-electrical projects, caused salination and evaporation.

In 1909 Fritz Haber had extracted nitrogen from air for commercial fertilizers. No other single invention did more to feed the growing population of the world in the second half of the century. In 1940, the world used some 4 million tons of artificial fertilizer. By 1990, it was using about 150 million tons. Agrochemical manufacturers found ways to double-dose the soil with chemicals to stimulate crops and kill weeds.

The practice had a startling effect on the eco-systems it touched. Many kinds of insects lost weedy habitats. Creatures that fed off the insects lost their food supply. In the 1960s, an ecological movement sprang up and mobilized millions of people, especially in Europe and America, to defend the environment against pollution and overexploitation.

As fears of global food shortages became acute early in the second half of the twentieth century, agronomists had to develop fast-growing, high-yielding, disease-resistant varieties of nutritious staples for a range of different environments. In the 1950s, research concentrated on some of the traditionally most successful and most adaptable grains, especially wheat, rice, and maize. The big breakthrough came with the adaptation of dwarf varieties of wheat from Japan and of rice from Taiwan and Indonesia. By 1980, the world's average wheat yield per acre was double that of 1950. The new crops covered three-quarters of the world's grain-growing areas by the early 1990s.

The green revolution—as people called it—saved millions of lives. Even with the huge increase in global food output, failures of distribution contributed to many famines in the third quarter of the century. Without the green revolution, the death toll would surely have been much higher. Nevertheless, agronomists' success came at a price. The new varieties were heavily dependent on chemical fertilizers and pesticides.

So, as the green revolution spread, the world was—in effect—doused with poisons and pollutants. By 1985, according to the World Health Organization, pesticides had caused a million deaths, mostly among agricultural workers. Meanwhile, the new wonder crops crowded out traditional, local staples. So farmers in poor regions of the world produced ever-increasing quantities of cheap grains for survival and had little or nothing to sell to the rich consumers of the world. Global poverty was becoming institutionalized.

Booming cities cut off rural migrants from the food they formerly ate: painstakingly grown plant foods, freshly harvested and locally prepared. A massive switch to mass-produced food occurred in just about every major urbanizing environment in the world. Paradoxically, while prosperity grew and food became abundant, diets deteriorated.

At the same time, the science of dietetics failed. In the last forty years of the twentieth century, Western governments promoted massive health campaigns in favor of high-carbohydrate diets. Cheap foods, laden with carbohydrates, especially in the form of sugar, glutted the market. In combination with the problems of distribution that urbanization created, the result was a pandemic of obesity. It started in the West, especially in the United States. At the mid-point of the twentieth century, 5 percent of Americans were classified as clinically obese, and by 2001 the figure had risen to 26 percent. Well over one-third of those under the age of nineteen qualified as obese according to the standard definition. By the end of the century, the same trend was detectable in much of the rest of the globe, even in countries where obesity was virtually unknown—including China, India, and even Japan, which, starting from a low statistical base, registered the world's steepest increase in clinical obesity in the 1990s.

Beyond Human Agency. Humans are not the only makers of eco-history. Climate and disease are sources of change that humans certainly affect, but which are beyond human control. Take climate first. From the waning of the last great Ice Age some twenty thousand years ago, the world has been experiencing a protracted warming phase, except from about the fourteenth century C.E. to about the eighteenth, when, with some fluctuations, temperatures declined slightly but significantly over much of the world. Around the mid-nineteenth century, however, warming seems to have intensified. Despite a wavering in the third quarter of the twentieth century, when falling temperatures excited prophecies of a new Ice Age, global temperatures by the turn of the millennium recovered or exceeded levels last reached some eight hundred years ago. Human agency aggravates and accelerates the process, but has limited power over it. From the 1980s onward international meetings attempted to set environmental standards, particularly for emissions, but without great effect to date.

Disease is also an intractable element in the environment. Despite stunning medical achievements, humans still do not command—or even adequately understand—the microbial world in which much disease originates. Twentieth-century doctors defeated some of the most terrible killing and maiming diseases: polio, smallpox, and a whole range of illnesses formerly responsible for heartbreaking levels of infant mortality. But scientific self-congratulation over these successes masked worrying, persistent problems. Medical advances were unfairly distributed. Life expectancy in much of sub-Saharan Africa, at the end of the twentieth century, remained stuck at an average in the forties. Sub-Saharan infant mortality rates were three or four times worse than those of most of East and Southeast Asia, and immeasurably worse than those of western Europe.

And although medicine eliminated old diseases, new ones—or new forms of old ones—arose. Effects of pollution, drug abuse, sex habits, and affluence—which condemned the unwary to overindulgence and inertia—were major killers. Far more lethal was the rapid evolution of viruses. Some killers, such as Ebola, Lassar fever, and the immunity-destroying virus known as HIV, leaped from the eco-niches in which they had formerly been contained and began to attack humans. New forms of influenza appeared regularly, though none exceeded the virulence of the pandemic of 1918–1919, which claimed an estimated 30 million lives worldwide. A new strain of tuberculosis, which emerged in the late twentieth century, resisted every known drug and killed half the people infected. Bubonic plague returned to India. New strains of cholera and malaria emerged. Malaria cases in India rose a hundredfold to 10 million between 1965 and 1977. In sub-Saharan Africa at the start of the twenty-first century, malaria killed one million children a year. Yellow fever—which had almost been eradicated by the mid-twentieth century—killed 200,000 people a year in Africa in the 1990s. Measles, a disease that immunization was expected to eradicate, was still killing a million people a year at the end of the century.

Other new diseases arose in man-made eco-niches: Legionnaires' disease, which breeds in air-conditioning systems, was the prime example. Intensive farming created breeding conditions for salmonella in chickens and accumulated toxins in the food chain. Human-variant CJD, or "mad cow disease," was a brain-killing disease, apparently caused by intensive cattle-farming methods—recycling dead sheep and cattle as fodder—and was transmitted to at least some of its victims in tainted food. Twentieth-century interventions in the environment opened eco-niches for disease in overfertilized soil, stripped of much insect life in polluted waterways and in the disturbed depths of the sea, where bacteria multiply in searing hot vents that humans have only lately begun to penetrate. In an increasingly interconnected world, human carriers took diseases way beyond accustomed environments. Toward the end of the century, West Nile virus from Africa fever turned up in New York City. A few years later, variant forms of influenza from China caused widespread deaths, especially in Canada.

Broadly speaking, infectious diseases ceased to be major killers, though old ones constantly threatened to reemerge and new ones to develop. Chronic diseases, meanwhile, arose to replace infections as the major menace. Cancer and heart diseases grew spectacularly, especially in rich countries, without anyone knowing why. By the 1980s in the United States, one death in every four was blamed on cancer. In Britain, one death in three was ascribed to heart disease, which caused 10 million deaths a year worldwide by the end of the century. Some forms of cancer were "lifestyle diseases." Cervical cancer, for instance, was thought to be connected to sexual promiscuity or adolescent sexual intercourse, while smoking, according to most authorities, caused lung, throat, and mouth cancers and contributed to heart disease and strokes. Obesity and its related disorders owed their prevalence, in part, to bad eating habits. In the second half of the twentieth century, evidence began to accumulate that some medical treatments were actually contributing to the disease environment. Doctors prescribed drugs so widely that people were becoming dependent on them, while many viruses and strains of bacteria were developing immunity to them.

The record of humans' maladjusted relationship with the environment is unencouraging. The rate of depletion and pollution of the planet's resources should slow as population stabilizes. But we do not yet know how to cope with climate change if the planet continues to heat up. On the other hand, a new Ice Age may occur, and we do not know how to prepare for it. And the frequency of "health scares" in the late twentieth and early twenty-first centuries has betrayed a further anxiety: that microbial evolution could overtake medical progress.

[*See also* Deserts and Desertification; Global Warming; Green Parties; Imperialism and Environment; Natural Resources; Sustainable Development; Water and Water Management; *and* Wildlife.]

BIBLIOGRAPHY
Benedict, Carol. *Bubonic Plague in Nineteenth-Century China.* Stanford, Calif.: Stanford University Press, 1996.
Blaxter, Kenneth, and Noel Robertson. *From Dearth to Plenty: The Modern Revolution in Food Production.* Cambridge, U.K., and New York: Cambridge University Press, 1995.
Bramwell, Anna. *Ecology in the Twentieth Century: A History.* New Haven, Conn.: Yale University Press, 1989.
Cronon, Walter. *Nature's Metropolis: Chicago and the Great West.* New York: W.W. Norton, 1991.
Cronon, Walter, George Miles, and Jay Gitlin, eds. *Under an Open Sky.* New York: W.W. Norton, 1992.
Crosby, Alfred W. *Ecological Imperialism: The Biological Expansion of Europe, 900–1900.* 2nd ed. Cambridge, U.K., and New York: Cambridge University Press, 2004.
Davis, Mike. *Late Victorian Holocausts: El Niño Famines and the Making of the Third World.* London and New York: Verso, 2001.
Goodman, David, and Michael Watts. *Globalising Food: Agrarian Questions and Global Restructuring.* London and New York: Routledge, 1997.
Goody, Jack. *Cooking, Cuisine and Class: A Study in Comparative Sociology.* Cambridge, U.K., and New York: Cambridge University Press, 1982.
Grove, Richard H. *Green Imperialism: Colonial Expansion, Tropical Island Edens and the Origins of Environmentalism, 1600–1860.* Cambridge, U.K., and New York: Cambridge University Press, 1995.
Leakey, Richard, and Roger Lewin. *The Sixth Extinction.* New York: Doubleday, 1996.
McNeill, J. R. *Something New Under the Sun: An Environmental History of the Twentieth-Century World.* New York: Norton, 2001.
Paul, Rodman W. *The Far West and the Great Plains in Transition, 1859–1900.* Norman: University of Oklahoma Press, 1998.
Richards, John F. *The Unending Frontier: An Environmental History of the Early Modern World.* Berkeley: University of California Press, 2003.
Stearns, Peter N. *Fat History: Bodies and Beauty in the Modern World.* New York: New York University Press, 1997. Reprint, 2002.
Worster, Donald. *Nature's Economy: A History of Ecological Ideas.* Cambridge, U.K., and New York: Cambridge University Press, 1985.

FELIPE FERNÁNDEZ-ARMESTO

Africa

Africa's environment provides the dominant of image of the continent for many people outside of it. Africa conjures up pictures of wildlife in majestic parklands, deep green rain forests—or environmentally induced human suffering caused by famine or flood. Since 1750, dramatic changes have come to Africa's environments and the societies that inhabit them. Over the last three centuries African population grew, production of agricultural commodities and of minerals expanded dramatically, natural disasters struck and caused human suffering, fears abounded about the loss of natural beauty and diversity, and great efforts were made to preserve and conserve environments.

From the mid-nineteenth century until the mid-twentieth century, European states dominated most of Africa, first economically and then as colonies. European perceptions of African environments shaped the development of efforts to both exploit resources and protect environments. At the heart of this process lay a contradiction. European perceptions generally held that African environments had remained little altered until the very recent past, when

African societies began to overexploit them in response to increasing demand for African commodities. African views of their environments differed dramatically. These spaces had been home to settled agricultural civilizations for several thousand years, and the landscapes of the nineteenth century were not recently degraded, but were shaped by human agency over several thousand years just as agricultural and pastoral landscapes worldwide had been. Yet the colonial discourse of degradation and the necessity of control outlasted the colonial era. It remains fundamental, although challenged, in conservation efforts throughout Africa.

Environments. Africa's environments are predominantly tropical. Truly temperate climates exist only along the Mediterranean and at the Cape of Good Hope, although highland regions throughout eastern and southern Africa can have very cold weather. Africa's climates run roughly in bands across the continent with variations for altitude and other topological features. The Sahara is the largest desert in the world and merges with the Sahel in the south. Each year the movement from north to south of the Intertropical Convergence Zone (ICZ), formed by the rise of warmed water from around the equator that moves north and south tracking the sun each year, determines the amount of rainfall that West Africa receives. In West Africa, environmental zones stretch north from the Atlantic shore, with rain forest giving way to forest-savanna mosaic followed by open savanna, then the semiarid Sahel, and finally the Sahara.

Likewise, the movement of the ICZ determines the strength of the rains in East and southern Africa. Extremely wet climates create conditions for rain forests along the West African coast and into the central basin of the Congo (formerly called Zaire) River. The Rift Valley, which stretches from the Ethiopian highlands south to southern Africa, marks an effective boundary in watersheds between the Congo, the Nile, and the Zambezi. To the east, altitude determines the amount of rainfall, with large mountain blocks starting in the north with the Ethiopian Highlands and including the Eastern Arc mountains, the volcanic mountains of the crater highland, the Southern Highlands of Tanzania, and the Drakensberg in South Africa creating rainfall shadows and arid conditions behind them. The highlands of the Great Lakes region (the fabled Mountains of the Moon) create one of the most benign climates in the world, with regular rainfall and mild temperatures in what is now Rwanda, Burundi, eastern Congo, western Uganda, and northwestern Tanzania.

South of the rain forests, the extremely cold Benguela Current flowing north from Antarctica along the west coast of southern Africa keeps rainfall low from the Cape of Good Hope north through what is now Namibia and southern Angola and east toward the Drakensberg Mountains. Moving east and north, rainfall increases under the influence of the Indian Ocean monsoon, and once past the mountains, the east coast of southern Africa has a tropical climate. The Cape of Good Hope proves an exception. Sticking south slightly, the meeting of the Benguela Current with warm water from the Indian Ocean creates a storm-prone but Mediterranean-type environment.

Though geomorphic and climatological conditions have been relatively stable for the last five thousands years, in the very long run both have varied considerably. Solar radiation causes most of the variation in earth's climate, with cycles determined by orbital changes and wobbles occurring every 100,000, 41,000, and 23,000 years. This variation has led to cycles of glacial ages, which are cool and dry, and warmer, more humid interglacial ages. This variation has had tremendous impact of the flora and fauna of Africa over the course of several million years, as well as on the development of humanity and human societies in Africa. During glacial ages, the most recent of which occurred about 30,000 years ago, the climate dried, and the Sahara and the Kalahari deserts expanded. Arid regions stretched from the much larger Sahara and Sahel all the way to the southern plains to meet up with the arid regions of southern Africa. Rain forests retreated to refuges along the west and east coasts of Africa, and forests retreated up mountaintops. Lakes such as Malawi and Victoria Nyanza dried and broke up. The present warmer, wetter interglacial phase, called the Holocene, began about 14,000 years ago, and heat and moisture peaked about 9,000 years ago. Then the Sahara shrank as the ICZ moved farther north every year, forest zones expanded, and rivers ran regularly through the Sahel to feed the Niger. The Great Lakes expanded dramatically. A slightly drier, cooler period began about 8,000 years ago and peaked about 5,000 years ago. Though there have been significant variations in climate since then—for instance, a very cold, dry period around the beginning of the current era, and the so-called Little Ice Age of about 1500 to 1800 C.E.—the general climate had remained stable until the current bout of global warming began about 1850.

Animal and Plant Life. These variations, which have occurred repeatedly over the last several million years, have left a remarkable diversity of animal and plant life in Africa.

As climate varied, species expanded and modified to survive in the new fields, while others retreated and even became extinct. Hence certain "islands" on the continent, refuges surrounded by very different climates, contain large numbers of endemic species, while broadly similar environments that stretch in long bands across the continent share species.

Humanity emerged out of this variation, with modern humans present in Africa by 100,000 years ago and leaving Africa no later than 50,000 years ago. As they spread across the continent they took advantage of the diversity they found in potential food sources and suffered from the variations in climate they experienced. They developed food production systems based on the domestication of indigenous plants and animals and the incorporation where appropriate of crops of outside origins. By the time of direct seaborne European contact with African societies all parts of the continent had food-producing, urbanized, politically complex, and trading communities. African communities exploited African environments, and for the most part they did so extensively. In the grasslands and open woodlands that dominate much of Africa, farmers and herders relied on long fallow systems where land "rested" for up to twenty years after being cultivated for a few, and cattle grazed extensively across large ranges. In some areas, particularly the well-watered highlands from Ethiopia south through Mozambique and west to the eastern Congo, conditions allowed farmers to maintain permanent stands of bananas linked to grain fields and herds held on lower slopes. In the forests of West and Central Africa, bananas and plantains complemented yams and oil palms as domesticated crops. In these areas, though, loss of fertility meant that farmers abandoned land and the forest regenerated regularly. The difference between the permanent cultivation of highland regions and the more mobile regime in forest regions lay in the availability of manure from livestock that could not be kept in the rain forest because of disease. Trypanosomaisis spread through tsetse flies infected both livestock and humans. From the sixteenth century on, African farmers began to introduce New World food crops into their mix of crops. Maize and cassava spread gradually in West Africa and complemented the existing African and Asian crops that had provided the staples up to that point.

The Slave Trade. The late eighteenth and early nineteenth centuries marked both the high tide of the Atlantic slave trade and its demise. As Philip Curtin has famously argued, the Atlantic slave trade itself was in part a response to environmental differences among the tropical Americas, Africa, and Europe. European conquest brought Old World diseases to the New World, which devastated New World populations. In the tropical parts of the New World, malaria became endemic after conquest. Europeans faced higher mortality rates in the tropics as a result. West African populations proved better able to survive in the tropical New World than either Native Americans or Europeans. As a result, European and American traders bought and captured at least 13 million Africans for transport to the New World between about 1500 and about 1850. The environmental impact of the slave trade has been the subject of some debate. Many have thought that it led to depopulation in parts of western Africa. Others have suggested that rates of forced emigration could easily be replaced by reproduction within Africa.

About the transformations that took placed as the trade in slaves to the New World began to decline there can be no debate. Large parts of Africa began to export agricultural or other commodities. The nineteenth century saw the dramatic expansion of the production of agricultural commodities in West Africa, including palm oil, ground nuts, and even rubber. In East Africa ivory became a major export, along with spices and sugar. The intrusion of Europeans and the spread of modern firearms (replacing less advanced ones) meant that hunting increased dramatically in its efficiency. The result over the nineteenth century was a period throughout much of Africa of disruption and political realignment that concentrated human populations. Disease also spread more rapidly as communication quickened with the growing volume of commerce. Smallpox epidemics and cholera both made major impacts on the population of East Africa.

The European Struggle to Conquer Africa. In South Africa, the nineteenth century saw the expansion of European settlement and the displacement of much of the African population from the land itself. Most important, the discovery of diamonds (1860s) and gold (1880s) created conditions for a land scramble among European countries and a struggle to conquer Africa. The Scramble for Africa eventually resulted in the introduction of the cattle disease rinderpest into Africa for the first time, and in the devastation of African herds and of wildlife in the 1890s. In much of Africa, population declined during the last few decades of the nineteenth century and into the early twentieth century. European conquerors worried that they might not have any people to rule and contemplated expanded settlement in Africa by Europeans. Although Europeans survived better in the tropics by the beginning of the twentieth century than they had at any time before because of advances in medicine, particularly the use of quinine to treat malaria, only in isolated areas outside of South Africa, often in temperate highlands such as in Kenya, did European settlement become pronounced.

As colonial rule commenced at the end of the nineteenth century, European-led governments sought to create rational ways of controlling and exploiting their new colonies. With soldiers and administrators came scientists and technical workers. The earliest forms of European exploitation of African resources often took the form of resource mining under the protection of new-founded colonial governments. In eastern and southern Africa, white hunters continued to slaughter elephants for ivory. In the rain forests of central and western Africa, concessionary companies used forced labor to harvest wild rubber in a manner that often resulted in the destruction of the plants. In southern Africa, white settlers created large estates worked by African labor to feed the growing population of the mining areas of South Africa. Wildlife populations declined dramatically throughout Africa in the late nineteenth and early twentieth centuries because of both hunting and disease. In southern Africa extensive hunting by whites cleared land of wildlife, which reduced the threat of trypanosomiasis and opened it for settlement. In eastern Africa, conversely, the spread of the tsetse fly into areas from which humans and livestock departed after the rinderpest epidemic gave wildlife a chance to recover in the early twentieth century.

Even where Africans remained in nominal control of their own lands, new pressures for commodity production brought dramatic changes to African agriculture and landscapes. In West Africa, a variety of crops became subject to export production by African landholders that caused them to clear forest regions. Palm oil, cocoa, and coffee production expanded dramatically during the early twentieth century. Africans both cleared forest land for agriculture and shifted land formerly used to produce food to the new cash crops. In many parts of Africa, European colonial states made intensive efforts to introduce or enforce cotton production as a means of supplying a commodity thought to be of vital strategic importance. Portugal, France, Britain, and Germany all created massive schemes to force African farmers to grow cotton. Although in a few areas cotton proved a moderately successful small-holder crop, in many areas only force made Africans grow cotton, and in German East Africa, forced labor on cotton fields helped spark the Maji Maji rebellion of 1905.

World War I and Its Aftermath. In many ways World War I proved a critical turning point in the colonial exploitation of African resources. Africa became the scene of fighting in East Africa, while Allied forces quickly occupied German colonies in West and southern Africa. However, the demand for resources from colonial governments to support the war and the lack of ability to feed resources back into Africa created enormous strains. Drought in West Africa caused a major famine throughout the Sahel and Sudanic regions after 1917. In East Africa, a German guerrilla campaign that lasted until November 1918 helped create tremendous suffering. The influenza pandemic of 1918 also struck across the continent just as the war was ending.

In the aftermath of the war, British, French, Belgian, and Portuguese colonial states developed a more intervention-oriented approach to resource management. Self-governing South Africa (which also controlled the former German colony of Southwest Africa) promoted a policy of consolidation of settler control of agricultural land and development of mining and industry. It also took the lead in developing the idea of conservation of the African continent. It created the first national park in what became known as Kruger National Park in 1898 in the aftermath of the rinderpest epidemic. The Germans in East Africa followed suit, declaring the first game reserves in the Serengeti ecosystem around the turn of the century. Such wildlife preservation efforts remained relatively small and focused on protecting game for hunting by whites in eastern and southern Africa. Throughout Africa, colonial regimes also put early efforts into conserving valuable resources, especially timber. Forest reserves with varying degrees of restriction of access by local people spread across the continent as governments sought to protect revenue-earning timber from African use and to protect landscapes considered vital for the protection of hills and mountains from erosion and for the protection of watersheds.

Such efforts exploded after the end of World War I. Several interrelated factors created a climate where "development," "betterment," or *mise en valeur* became the goal of colonial agency. Such efforts usually sought to increase agricultural productivity while conserving both soil and landscape. Although the Depression of the 1930s reduced the funds available for such efforts, the crisis if anything increased the urgency with which colonial regimes sought to combat what they identified as degradation caused by "primitive" and unscientific exploitation by Africans.

Such paternalistic attitudes also pervaded views of the necessity for increased efforts at wildlife conservation. Conservation and hunting groups in Europe became alarmed at the decline in game numbers throughout the continent as both sport and subsistence hunting continued. By the 1920s an international movement had developed to promote the creation of game preserves and American-style national parks. Some of the land claimed for these early parks had been long used by African farmers, herders, and hunters. In some cases—for example, the territory that came to be known as the Serengeti ecosystem in northern Tanzania and southern Kenya—Africans had temporarily abandoned the lands in the aftermath of the rinderpest epidemic of the early 1890s. The depopulation, loss of cattle, and loss of wildlife because of the disease allowed bush to grow much more thickly than it had before, which encouraged the spread of tsetse and trypanosomiasis. Hence only in the 1920s, as population recovered in all three groups, did the need to "preserve" the "wilderness" become apparent. Much the same situation existed in Kruger National Park in South Africa. Africans expelled from parks and reserves, or merely prevented from hunting or using seasonal grazing, did not take loss of access to such resources lightly. Conflict over conservation efforts became widespread and has continued into the post-independence era.

Population Growth. The critical change in human interaction with the environment by the middle of the twentieth century became the increasing population of sub-Saharan Africa. African population growth had been suppressed in the eighteenth century by the slave trade and in the nineteenth by the disasters of the last decades of that century. Gradually after 1920, the African population began to recover and at some point, perhaps just after World War II, perhaps a little later, exceeded its historic highs. Population has continued to expand into the beginning of the twenty-first century. The reasons that the African population could expand are several, but it is difficult to say that any one of them caused the growth. Crisis mortality declined after World War I as epidemics became less common and improved transportation allowed for greater mobility of food and people during food shortages. Agricultural production and productivity increased across the continent as new techniques and crops spread. Gradually after World War II a variety of public health efforts reached many parts of Africa, bringing seemingly simple solutions to some of the age-old problems of African populations. Almost all demographic measures, including female fertility, show increases across Africa after World War II, with population growth only beginning to slow down in some areas at the end of the century.

The rapid increase in population of course led to the now familiar discussion of a population explosion threatening

to destroy the earth's ability to support life. In Africa commentators over the course of the late-colonial and post-colonial periods argued that African environments were becoming increasingly degraded because of the expansion of population. They noted what they thought was the rapid loss of forest cover in almost all parts of the continent and argued that the loss of fallow in Africa's long-fallow agricultural systems meant that agricultural productivity would decline. They predicted widespread famine and social crisis as a result. As valid as such statements may seem at first glance, it is important to note that in most of Africa productive systems have kept up with population growth. Much of the population growth has occurred in the form of urbanization, and food production has expanded generally to meet that growth. In many cases famine has been caused more by political strife or state weakness than by natural disaster. In such cases minor variations in conditions can lead to widespread hunger if political strife prevents normal responses by people affected and emergency aid from outside.

During his independence address in 1961, the then prime minister of Tanganyika (now mainland Tanzania) Julius Nyerere remarked about a serious food shortage in the country, "we [Africans] are fighting nature not man now." It has not quite worked out that way. African societies still struggle to find a sustainable way to survive in their environments. International demand for some commodities such as petroleum and precious metals and stones continues to lead to resource mining with little in the way of support for development. Nevertheless, many African nations have made substantial commitments to both conservation and sustainability. In some places, such as Kenya, Tanzania, South Africa, and Botswana, national parks have become a part of national identity in much the same way that they have in places like Canada, Australia, and the United States. Yet this slightly optimistic view of the future of Africa and its environments carries many caveats. While African environments have proven resilient, continued social disorder threatens that ability to recover. At the other extreme, the continuing industrial exploitation of resources such as petroleum and other minerals could cause great damage to many of Africa's environments. The effects of global warming will be unpredictable. Warming is likely to bring greater moisture to some parts of Africa—the melting snows of Kilimanjaro, which are predicted to disappear in the next few decades, serving as a symbol of the cost. But the effects on the ocean currents that actually govern much of the earth's climate are unknown and could cause dramatic change in weather patterns, which would require massive human adjustment. In short, the picture in Africa may not be as bleak as it is often painted, but the future is extremely uncertain.

[*See also* Famine, *subentry* Africa; Global Warming; *and* Natural Disasters, *subentry* Africa.]

BIBLIOGRAPHY

Anderson, David, and Richard H. Grove, eds. *Conservation in Africa: Peoples, Policies, and Practice.* Cambridge, U.K.: Cambridge University Press, 1987.

Beinart, William, and Peter Coates. *Environment and History: The Taming of Nature in the USA and South Africa.* New York: Routledge, 1995.

Curtin, Philip D. "Epidemiology and the Slave Trade." *Political Science Quarterly* 83, no. 2 (1968): 190–216.

Davis, Mike. *Late Victorian Holocausts: El Niño Famines and the Making of the Third World.* New York: Verso, 2001.

Fairhead, James, and Melissa Leach. *Reframing Deforestation: Global Analyses and Local Realities: Studies in West Africa.* London: Routledge, 1998.

Jacobs, Nancy J. *Environment, Power, and Injustice: A South African History.* Cambridge, U.K.: Cambridge University Press, 2003.

Kingdon, Jonathan. *Island Africa: The Evolution of Africa's Rare Animals and Plants.* Princeton, N.J.: Princeton University Press, 1989.

Leach, Melissa, and Robin Mearns, eds. *The Lie of the Land: Challenging Received Wisdom on the African Environment.* Portsmouth, N.H.: Heinemann, 1996.

Maddox, Gregory H. *Sub-Saharan African: An Environmental History.* Santa Barbara, Calif.: ABC/Clio, 2006.

McCann, James C. "Climate and Causation in African History." *International Journal of African Historical Studies* 32, no.2–3 (1999): 261–279.

McCann, James C. *Green Land, Brown Land, Black Land: An Environmental History of Africa, 1800–1990.* Portsmouth, N.H.: Heinemann, 1999.

McCann, James C. *Maize and Grace: Africa's Encounter with a New World Crop, 1500–2000.* Cambridge, Mass.: Harvard University Press, 2004.

Reader, John. *Africa: A Biography of the Continent.* London: Penguin, 1998.

GREGORY H. MADDOX

East Asia

In East Asia, large populations from early times and, more recently, a need to industrialize rapidly to counter Western imperialism have adversely affected the environment, leading to some of the worst conditions in the world.

Preindustrial East Asia. Without human impact, most of East Asia, except for what are now the far northwest and southwest portions of China, would be forested. There would be tigers throughout the Korean peninsula and China proper, elephants in most of China proper, and wolves in most of Japan. But the peoples of East Asia, particularly China, have a long and well-documented history of transforming the environment even before the eighteenth century. For more than three millennia the Han (ethnic Chinese) expanded to fill most of China proper, in the process clearing trees, killing large animals, building water-control systems, and carrying out intensive agriculture wherever the land could be made to allow it. Elephants were confined to the south by about a thousand years ago and to only the southwest about five hundred years ago. In Japan, so many trees were cut to build palaces and temples during the Heian period (794–1185) that, by late in the period, large wooden sculptures could rarely be made from single trees.

Despite the influence of Confucianism, Buddhism, Daoism, *fengshui* (Chinese geomancy), and Japan's animistic Shinto religion, and despite strong traditions of admiration of nature in poetry and painting, there was never a single view of nature. Nor did behavior always follow philosophy. Buddhist temples, for example, typically preserved large trees on their grounds, but they could be built only by cutting down many such trees. Calligraphy and paintings created a huge demand for black ink, made from the soot of the pine trees they often celebrated.

China, because of its population, was the first country in East Asia in which environmental crises became chronic and severe. Its agriculture required a large input of labor but was highly productive. By the late eighteenth century the population began to exceed the available food supply for the first time. The population may have tripled or quadrupled between 1650 and 1850, reaching more than 400 million (see Table 1). Yet over these two centuries the amount of cultivated land only doubled, and there were no great changes in agricultural technology. The resulting distress was one cause of the rebellions that were endemic from the late eighteenth century into the twentieth century, as well as of the increased deforestation and

TABLE 1. *Population (millions)*

	CHINA	JAPAN	KOREA
1700	160	29	6.2
1750	225	29	7.0
1800	330	28	7.5
1850	435	32	9.0
1900	475	45	12.0
1950	590	84	30.0
2005	1,300	127	71.6
			(South: 48.6)
			(North: 22.9)

SOURCES: Colin McEvedy and Richard Jones, *Atlas of World Population History* (New York: Facts on File, 1978), pp. 167, 177, and 181; *World Factbook* (Washington, D.C.: Central Intelligence Agency, 2005).

TABLE 2. *Population density and arable land per person*

	CHINA	JAPAN	SOUTH KOREA	NORTH KOREA
Population density (persons/hectare)	1.39	3.37	4.88	1.90
Arable land (hectares/person)	0.12	0.04	0.04	0.12

SOURCES: United Nations Economic and Social Commission for Asia and the Pacific, *Asia-Pacific in Figures 2004* (http://www.unescap.org/stat/data/apif/index.asp); *World Factbook* (Washington, D.C.: Central Intelligence Agency, 2005).

erosion caused by desperate people moving into agriculturally more marginal areas.

Japan's population did not begin to exceed the numbers that could be fed by traditional agriculture until the twentieth century, by which time food could be imported from colonies and elsewhere, and domestic productivity could be increased with agricultural chemicals and later through small-scale mechanization. Effective systems of forest management and a stable population in the eighteenth and early nineteenth centuries prevented the sort of large-scale deforestation and erosion seen in China (see Table 2).

Industrializing East Asia. Japan was the first non-Western nation to industrialize, and therefore to experience the new environmental problems brought by modern economic and technological development. Pollution from the Ashio copper mine north of Tokyo, the best-known example, resulted in the first major environmental protest movement. With newly discovered lodes and modern technology, the mine produced two-fifths of Japan's copper output by 1891, but it also destroyed much of the surrounding forest, causing serious floods that destroyed the biological habitats of the Tone and Watarase rivers with acidic runoff. Tanaka Shōzō, the area's charismatic parliamentary representative, led residents in protesting the loss of their livelihood from farming and fishing in a struggle that continued for several decades. Before World War II, Japan also developed a large offshore fishing and whaling industry, which ranged around the world and had a significant effect on fish and whale populations. The war gave marine life a temporary reprieve but augmented deforestation, erosion, and industrial pollution.

Postwar economic development made Japan the third largest economy in the world by 1968. This industrial production and a population roughly half that of the United States were condensed into the coastal zones of a nation about the size of California. The tragic effects of the resulting air and water pollution on human beings were visible sooner than in most other parts of the world. This dark side of high growth was symbolized by the mercury poisoning around Minamata in southern Japan, an incident at the center of the postwar environmental movement. The Chisso Corporation chemical factory discharged organic mercury into the sea from 1932 to 1968, and in 1956, Minamata disease was first recognized in people who had consumed fish and shellfish that had absorbed and concentrated the mercury. The mercury, which destroyed brain and nerve cells, eventually affected tens of thousands of people and killed hundreds. By the late 1960s, Minamata disease was one of the big four cases of pollution, along with a similar disease in Niigata, smog-induced asthma in Itsukaichi, and cadmium poisoning (*itai-itai* or "ouch-ouch" disease) in Toyama. Victims of these diseases attracted nationwide support in the late 1960s and sued the polluters, all winning their cases between 1971 and 1973. The government was forced to create an environmental agency and to pass strict pollution control laws that significantly reduced air and water pollution.

Korea, especially in the north, began its industrialization as a Japanese colony from 1910 to 1945, but the peninsula was devastated by the Korean War from 1950 to 1953. North Korea, despite its greater industrial plant and natural resources, was overshadowed by South Korea's rapid industrial development, which began in the 1960s. By the 1980s growth had brought the south prosperity, a middle class, and severe pollution problems such as the cadmium pollution in Onsan, which caused symptoms similar to *itai-itai* disease in Japan. A vibrant antipollution movement developed alongside the democracy movement. By the time the Doosan conglomerate contaminated Daegu's drinking water with phenol in 1991, this movement was strong enough to force a public corporate apology and the resignation of the minister and vice minister of the Environment Administration.

China's industrialization before the mid-twentieth century was slowed by imperialism, rebellions, and wars, but the stresses on its land and forests continued. During the Maoist period from 1949 to 1976, massive projects and mass campaigns severely impacted the environment, as did continued population growth. Thousands of dams were built, including a huge dam on the Huang (Yellow) River that was completed in 1962 but quickly silted up and became virtually useless. Many other dams collapsed. Deforestation greatly accelerated when trees were cut to fuel the small, ineffective "backyard" furnaces built around the nation to make steel during the Great Leap

Forward at the end of the 1950s. Dogmatic attempts to transplant the farming practices used in model communes into areas for which they were not appropriate caused erosion and desertification. Wetlands were filled in to create more farmland. Persecution of intellectuals and fear of criticizing Mao stifled opposition. Millions of city dwellers were sent down to the countryside during the 1966–1976 Cultural Revolution, and they put further stress on the land.

The economy grew rapidly in post-Mao China. The population passed 1 billion, but its increase was finally limited. Incomes tripled in the 1980s, though income gaps widened. China's greatly increased production and consumption affected its environment more than ever before. Private ownership of automobiles was allowed, and the air quality in many major cities became among the worst in the world (see Table 3). Long-standing plans for a huge dam in the Three Gorges area of the Chang (Yangtze) River were finally implemented, despite international and domestic opposition. Yet this opposition was a sign of change: domestic environmental groups appeared, and the government began to show an awareness of the need to stem environmental destruction.

The East Asian Environment in the Twenty-first Century. Japanese citizens' groups in the 1990s and beyond were active in opposing dams and supporting recycling and safer foods. Local governments competed with each other to reduce waste and promote recycling, boasting of the number of categories into which residents sorted

TABLE 3. *Average annual air-pollution levels in Beijing, Seoul, and Tokyo*

	SO$_2$, μg/m^3	NO$_2$, μg/m^3	SPM, g/m^3	PM$_{10}$, μg/m^3
Beijing, 1990–1995	96	NA	378	NA
Seoul, 1990–1998	64	66	103	66 (1995–1998)
Tokyo, 1990–1995	21	66	NA	48
Guideline	50 (WHO)	40 (WHO)	60–90 (WHO)	50 (EPA)

NOTES: SPM = suspended particulate matter; PM$_{10}$ = particles less than ten microns in diameter; WHO = World Health Organization; EPA = U.S. Environmental Protection Agency.
SOURCE: Gary Haq, et al., *Benchmarking Urban Air Quality Management and Practice in Major and Mega Cities of Asia, Stage I* (Seoul: Korea Environment Institute, 2002; http://www.test.earthscape.org/r1/ES16122/APMA_Benchmarking_report.pdf), p. 101.

their trash. In Taiwan and South Korea, environmental groups took advantage of the expanded freedoms accompanying the shift from dictatorship to democracy to promote environmental concerns. There is talk of preserving the environment of Korea's Demilitarized Zone between north and south, a strip of land four kilometers wide that has been virtually untouched since the Korean War and that shelters a great diversity of wildlife.

China's huge economy, population, and land area put it at the center of concerns about the global environment. Farmland continues to be lost to desert, and China's growing appetite for oil has meant increased imports and air pollution. Yet there are hopeful signs as well. The government has cooperated with domestic and foreign nongovernment organizations to protect giant pandas and their habitat. The Nu River dam project in Yunnan Province was suspended to allow an environmental assessment after intense pressure from Chinese and international environmental groups. Yet it remains unclear whether the government can succeed in its double balancing act: allowing room for domestic environmental activism without allowing democracy, and furthering economic growth while limiting damage to the environment.

[*See also* Chang River; Mekong River; Natural Resources, *subentry* East Asia; *and* Water and Water Management, *subentry* East Asia.]

BIBLIOGRAPHY
Elvin, Mark. *The Retreat of the Elephants: An Environmental History of China.* New Haven, Conn.: Yale University Press, 2004.
George, Timothy S. *Minamata: Pollution and the Struggle for Democracy in Postwar Japan.* Cambridge, Mass.: Harvard University Asia Center, 2001.
Ku Do-Wan. "The Korean Environmental Movement: Green Politics through Social Movement." *Korea Journal* 44, no. 3 (2004): 185–219.
Shapiro, Judith. *Mao's War against Nature: Politics and the Environment in Revolutionary China.* Cambridge, U.K.: Cambridge University Press, 2001.
Totman, Conrad. *Pre-industrial Korea and Japan in Environmental Perspective.* Leiden, The Netherlands: Brill, 2004.
Ui, Jun, ed. *Industrial Pollution in Japan.* Tokyo: United Nations University Press, 1992.

TIMOTHY S. GEORGE

Latin America

By 1750 the population descended from the original inhabitants of South America was beginning to recover from the disastrous impact of diseases introduced by the European conquerors, but their place in rural areas had already been taken by large numbers of cattle and sheep. Cultivated fields were often replaced by extensive grazing lands. Where whole communities had died of disease or resettled, the vegetation grew over the village sites and the formerly cultivated fields. Many areas of hillside terraces were cultivated less extensively or were abandoned. So the area of natural vegetation cover increased in some areas.

New towns and cities established by the Spanish and Portuguese expanded. The fuel for domestic and industrial use came from charcoal or from trees and bushes, so some reduction in scrub and forested areas in places within reach of cities occurred. The forests of the wet lowlands in both Central and South America were little changed.

In the latter part of the nineteenth century the pace of environmental change quickened. New technology—machines to power ships and to propel coaches on railroads—helped the production and transportation of food and raw materials for the cities and factories of the late Industrial Revolution in the Northern Hemisphere. A wave of immigration from southern Europe and beyond grew in the last quarter of the century and continued until the 1930s. The new arrivals, particularly in the Southern Cone of South America—southern Brazil, Uruguay, and Argentina—followed the spreading rail tracks into new territory, where the vegetation of grasslands and scattered areas of forest were soon replaced by sown pastures and cultivated fields. In parts of the lowlands of Central America, forests were replaced by banana plantations owned by U.S. corporations.

Even greater changes occurred after World War II as the world economy recovered and the rich world—principally the United States and the European Community, together with Japan—sought cheap clothing and in particular cheap food year-round. Latin American cities grew rapidly, and a predominantly rural continent became one where by 1980 the majority of the population lived in towns and cities. During this period, too, increasing numbers of people sought land to farm in the lowland forest margins, and in the last decades of the twentieth century, capital-rich individuals and corporations cleared forested areas to farm both livestock and soybeans for export to the global North.

Major Regions of Change. In Mexico and Central America the most profound environmental changes took place in the coastal lowlands. Although there have been important changes in the crops grown in the highlands, these have not resulted in major environmental changes other than increasing chemical residues, as from the application of industrial agrochemicals to control disease, weeds, and pests.

In Mexico during the 1930s, improved irrigation allowed farmland to replace the desert in many valleys along the Pacific coast. Toward the end of the nineteenth century new land for coffee cultivation had been cleared in forested areas along the eastern edges of the highlands in Veracruz and on the Pacific-facing slopes of Chiapas.

In Central America the nature of farming in the highland areas changed as commercial farming developed, but the most striking environmental changes took place on either side of the spine of mountains that traverse the area from Mexico to western Panama. From the end of the nineteenth century, U.S. fruit companies began to grow bananas for export to the north. This involved the development of a transport and communications infrastructure to facilitate efficient production. Large areas of forest were cleared in parts of the Caribbean coast in every Central American country from the 1880s onward, but by the 1920s disease forced the clearing and development of further banana plantations in the more humid areas on the Pacific coast.

In South America the main environmental changes were also related to the increasing population and expanding areas of agriculture oriented to export crops. The area of most notable change is from central Brazil in the state of São Paulo, where extensive coffee plantations replaced subtropical forest from around 1850, and further south into Uruguay and Argentina, where the rolling grassland and occasional woodlands were soon converted to pasture for cattle and sheep and were plowed for cereals south to the dry territory of Patagonia and west to the foothills of the Andes. Native populations were eliminated or forced to retreat.

Change to the tropical forest of the Amazon basin occurred in association with the rubber boom in the mid-nineteenth century and then again a century later as logging increased. As the twentieth century ended, vast areas on the drier margins of the forest were cleared to raise cattle and grow soybeans. This took place mostly in the Brazilian Amazon but, particularly in the second half of the twentieth century, also in each of the Andean nations whose eastern lowlands included part of the Amazon—Ecuador, Peru, and Bolivia. In Ecuador there was also clearance of large areas of forest in its humid central western lowlands in the twentieth century in association with a boom in cacao production until the 1940s, followed by another boom in banana production in the 1960s and 1970s. In the extreme southwest of Colombia much forest has been cleared since the late 1990s as coca production for cocaine extended to the Pacific lowlands.

Changing City and Mountain Environments.
Mexico City and São Paulo are two of the largest cities in the world (19 and 18 million inhabitants, respectively, in 2005), and like Buenos Aires (13 million) and Rio de Janeiro (12 million), each covers hundreds of square miles. It should not be surprising therefore that the growth of large and sprawling cities represents one of the most striking environmental changes of the later twentieth century in Latin America. Atmospheric pollution, alongside the physical contamination of the extensive neighborhoods inhabited by the poorest households, presents challenges to everyday living. Cities such as Mexico City and Lima, located in areas where there are often periods with little wind, regularly experience intense air pollution as a result of the large numbers of vehicles and factories generating high levels of contamination. The tendency of people to migrate to urban centers irrespective of the center's size means that all cities have severe environmental problems. These are associated with road building and with informal housing on steep slopes subject to landslides during heavy rains or beside watercourses that flood periodically; also, small- and large-scale industrial development uses scarce water and creates waste as well as air pollution. However much deforestation is discussed by environmentalists and some politicians as a major environmental issue, the degradation of the urban environment is of far more immediate importance to the majority of people living in Latin America.

Mountainous areas in Latin America contain much of the population of Mexico, Peru, and Bolivia, and many of the mines that created great wealth from the colonial period to the present were located in the mountains. The mines changed landscapes by their areas of debris, by polluting streams and rivers, and also by their need for fuel, which was supplied by cutting available trees. For thousands of years farmers, hunters, and graziers have changed mountain environments, and forests remain only on the steep slopes facing the coasts or in the Amazon basin. New forest environments were created in some areas in the second half of the twentieth century, often using fast-growing species of conifers.

Strangely to many people visiting highland Latin America for the first time, eucalyptus trees adorn Andean landscapes. They were introduced during the late nineteenth century and have long supplied much of the wood used for poles, house beams, and even planks. Although native species are planted by some farmers and are promoted by foresters, they grow slowly and represent only a small proportion of the area that has been reforested. Soil erosion, gullying, and the creation of badlands and areas of moving sand dunes all occur in many places in the mountains of Latin America. This is often a result of poor resource management and the lack of access by poor people to more suitable farmland, but the nature of rainfall and the cycles of climatic change also contribute to what is a normal process of landscape evolution. In some parts of the Andes what appears to be striking contemporary erosion actually occurred tens of thousands of years ago, and the eroded hillsides have never been able to recover.

Lowland and Marine Environments. From the earliest periods of human occupation of Latin America, lowland areas have been the site of settlement and consequently of environmental change. Major civilizations developed in Mexico and Peru in lowland and coastal areas, and water management enabled people to grow crops and live in the deserts of western South America. Since 1750 the most important environmental changes in the lowlands have been the advance of commercial farming on large estates both in many parts of the lowlands of Mexico and Central America and in coastal northeastern Brazil, as well as in the drier forest and grasslands of southern Brazil, Uruguay, Paraguay, and Argentina.

Forested areas in the humid tropics—mainly in the Amazon basin—have experienced much change since the 1970s as a result of logging and forest clearance by both poor and well-off farmers and corporations. Large farms grow crops such as soybeans and produce cattle for export to the growing cities of their own country and the global North. Although the most rapid forest loss between 1990 and 2000 in Latin America occurred in El Salvador, Guatemala, and Panama, more than 60 percent of the forest area lost was in Brazil. It is probably more important to humankind that many species of plants, birds, and animals have been wiped out through deforestation, and the long-term impact on global climate is also considerable.

Marine environments have also been subject to much change from increasingly efficient fishing, sometimes by fishing boats from Europe, Japan, and North America, which has reduced fish stocks. Mangroves have been destroyed in many coastal areas, particularly in Ecuador and Central America, to make way for urban development but also for the industrial production of shrimp for global markets.

[*See also* Agriculture, *subentry* Latin America; Bananas; Coffee; Empire and Imperialism, *subentry* Imperialism and the Environment; Forests and Deforestation; Land, *subentry* Land Reform in Latin America; *and* Urbanism and Urbanization, *subentry* Latin America.]

BIBLIOGRAPHY

Furley, Peter. "Environmental Issues and the Impact of Development." In *Latin American Development: Geographical Perspectives*, edited by David Preston, pp. 70–115. Harlow, U.K.: Longman, 1996. A useful and well-explained review of major environmental issues.

Smith, Nigel J. H., et al. *Amazonia: Resiliency and Dynamism of the Land and Its People.* Tokyo and New York: United Nations University Press, 1995. A valuable series of thoughtful essays on issues relating to the largest rain-forest area in the Americas.

United Nations Environment Programme (UNEP). *Latin American and the Caribbean, Environmental Outlook 2003.* Mexico: United Nations Environment Programme, 2003. http://www.unep.org/geo/pdfs/GEO_lac2003English.pdf. An excellent digest of information.

DAVID PRESTON

Environment and Pollution in Southeast Asia

Southeast Asia's history of environmental change and pollution in the modern era is intimately connected to the region's experiences of violently contested political change in the transition from colonial to postcolonial societies. These environmental changes are complex, as the region encompasses an extremely heterogeneous variety of ecosystems, ranging from the islands around Papua New Guinea to the Himalayan foothills. Located along the world's most trafficked sea routes between India and China, the region's environment, since the early decades of the spice trade in the fifteenth century, has been closely tied to the globalizing effects of various commodity markets. From the spice trade of the sixteenth century to the rubber plantations in the early twentieth century and the garment factories of the twenty-first century, Southeast Asia's environments and societies have been intimately connected with the ebb and flow of global commodities. It is only by placing the Southeast Asian environment in the context of the transition from colonial economies to postcolonial globalizing economies and examining the impact of this transition on the diversity of the region's ecosystems—forests, agriculture, coasts, river dams, marine environment, and atmosphere—that changes in environmental conditions and pollution levels in the modern era can be assessed.

The Forests. For most of Southeast Asia's history, until the early nineteenth century, much of the interior regions were covered in dense, impenetrable forests. The human population of Southeast Asia was a fraction of that of the early twenty-first century, with most people living along alluvial rivers or the coastline of the larger islands. For centuries, forests had been inhabited by groups who typically spoke different languages than those of the Southeast Asians living in the more recognized kingdoms: Vietnam, Burma, Siam, and various Malay-speaking Muslim sultanates. Especially in the Philippines and the Malay Peninsula, these people were descendants of the earliest human inhabitants of the region, Melanesians, and they continued to practice swidden (slash-and-burn) agriculture and hunting in lieu of the more intensive sedentary forms of agriculture—transplanted rice, sugar cane, taro—found on the coasts and river deltas. With colonial expansion and the growing demand for wood such as teak and other forest products, this isolation ended abruptly in the mid-nineteenth century, and from that time to the 1997 fires in Kalimantan, forests have been one of the major fronts for environmental destruction and its associated bitterly contested social upheaval. Early in the twenty-first century, large multinational companies continued to cooperate with national governments in rapidly, and often illegally, removing large trees to satisfy the growing demand for building materials in the booming cities of China. Besides causing widespread extinction of many endangered species, such actions were leading to increased levels of siltation in rivers, depletion of soils, deadly mudslides, and impoverishment of many thousands of people, such as the Dyaks on Kalimantan, who for centuries have lived in these forested areas.

Rain forests, such as those in the Boloven Plateau between Vietnam and Laos, were subject to rapid and uncontrolled deforestation under French colonial rule. Then, during the Cold War, they became an important part of the Ho Chi Minh Trail, which North Vietnamese troops, with Soviet and Chinese equipment, traveled through to fight South Vietnamese and U.S. forces. From 1962 the U.S. military began using chemical defoliants commonly known as Agent Orange to eliminate the forest cover. An estimated one-third of Vietnam's total forest cover was lost during the years of U.S. military intervention in Indochina from 1954 to 1975.

Agriculture. Perhaps one of the single most important influences on Southeast Asian environments in the modern era has been the introduction of plantation or industrial agriculture, beginning in the nineteenth century and continuing to the early twenty-first century. Southeast Asia, with its previously forested interiors, became the world's single largest producer of rubber in the early twentieth century, with tire companies such as Michelin basing most of their operations there. The demand for rubber and other products, such as gutta-percha, a resin used to insulate submarine cables, resulted in conversion of several hundred thousand acres of forest into orderly rows of rubber trees. In nonforested areas, other crops—such as tobacco, rice, cotton, sisal, and sugar—soon replaced staple crops and the communities that depended upon them. Before 1945 conversion of lands into plantations did not typically lead to higher levels of industrial pollution. However, the consolidation of these lands into the hands of a relatively powerful, wealthy minority typically resulted in thousands of Southeast Asian farmers fleeing tenant obligations and clearing new land in the forested frontiers in a effort to continue their traditional way of life, or often merely to survive.

The Coast. Southeast Asia's coastlines have for most of the region's history been vibrant centers of human society and commerce in the region. Beginning with Srivijaya in the seventh century, as attested by Chinese accounts, Southeast Asian coastlines have been the primary contact zones for people and products traveling inland from overseas and coastward from the forested interiors. The merchant fleets of the Dutch East Indies Corporation (as well as smaller, faster vessels from China, the Persian Gulf, Malay sultanates, and Java) tied together such port cities as Hoi An (Vietnam), Batavia (Jakarta), Melaka, Bangkok, Rangoon, Surakarta, and Singapore in a web of commerce. This network helped produce a self-regulating, coherent regional identity in Southeast Asia similar to that of the Mediterranean world. The effect of this centuries-old commerce reaching into the modern era has been to produce Southeast Asia's densest cities— Bangkok, Kuala Lumpur, Manila, Singapore, Ho Chi Minh City (formerly Saigon)—all within 30 miles (about 48 kilometers) of the sea, typically along the banks of coastal rivers. Since 1954, rapid industrialization around these urban cores has resulted in widespread contamination of freshwater supplies, as well as frequent spills of wastes and chemicals into coastal estuaries. Quite often in Southeast Asia, the largest cities continue to operate using water and sewage infrastructure designed a century ago for a population less than one-tenth its size. Thus, one of the biggest concerns in these emerging coastal megacities, as well as in rapidly multiplying suburbs and outlying towns, is the danger that high levels of organic and inorganic contamination pose to public health. In the early 2000s, outbreaks in the region of severe acute respiratory syndrome (SARS) and bird flu caused high economic losses and discouraged tourists from visiting the area.

River Dams. Closely related both to the surging growth in population and the politics of development in the Cold War has been the construction of hydropower dams and irrigation infrastructure along Southeast Asia's largest rivers. The Mekong River, first surveyed in 1952 for a series of eight mainstream dams, has since then repeatedly been a site of protest and debate over the effects of dams in the region. Typically, river dams are located in mountainous areas of Southeast Asia, and the filling of their reservoirs often displaces the same ethnic minority groups that have traditionally lived in forest areas. While such dams displace thousands and accelerate the loss of biodiverse forested ecosystems, especially in such sites as the Nam Theun Valley in Laos, they are generally viewed by urban constituencies as vital to the continuing growth and survival of the affected cities. The reservoirs frequently provide drinking water to the cities, and the hydroelectric plants supply power to local users as well as to a growing Chinese market. While work has yet to commence on mainstream dams on the Lower Mekong River, work is partially complete on a proposed twelve-dam cascade on the Upper Mekong (or Lancang) River in Yunnan, China.

Marine Environment. Perhaps one of the least understood environments in Southeast Asia is the marine environment, including coastal estuaries and coral reefs. Alfred Russel Wallace, the less-well-known cofounder of the theory of evolution, remarked in his visits to the Malay Archipelago (Sulawesi, Bali, Lombok) of the teeming, colorful diversity one encountered just below the surface of the crystalline blue water. These tropical marine Edens, which continue to lure thousands of tourists as well as scientists, have been rapidly disappearing as a result of increased releases of phosphate fertilizers, warmer sea temperatures, overfishing with cyanide or dynamite, and chemical spills. Reefs in these environments are comparable to tropical rain forests for their fragility, their species diversity, and the genetic potential they present for the development of medicines and other substances.

Atmosphere. Finally, the atmosphere in Southeast Asia has become a subject of environmental concern because of increasing levels of pollution resulting from burning forests and urban smog. The "Asian Brown Cloud," observed by the U.N. Environment Programme since 1995, is a two-mile-thick layer of haze that covers much of Southeast Asia during the winter monsoon from December to April. It results from burning forests and unregulated vehicle exhaust and industrial emissions. The Indonesian forest fires of 1997, caused in part by a prolonged dry season and higher than average temperatures, resulted in near-zero visibility in nearby Kuala

Lumpur, and the plume of smoke from this burn spread west to India and north to Hong Kong and Taiwan. This newest form of pollution has begun to draw serious attention toward control of emissions and burning of biomass.

The Future. Historically, Southeast Asia has been one of the ecologically most biodiverse regions on earth. Out of this extreme diversity came highly valued natural commodities, which shaped the intricate patchwork of human societies living in these various ecosystems. The region's political fragility in the face of twentieth-century superpower geopolitical struggles and global climate change have led to considerable destruction of its ecosystems. As a result, at the beginning of the twenty-first century it is one of the front lines of continuing struggles over increasingly scarce, fast-disappearing resources.

[*See also* Economy, *subentry* Southeast Asia.]

BIBLIOGRAPHY

Cooke, Nola, and Li Tana. *Water Frontier: Commerce and the Chinese in the Lower Mekong Region, 1750–1880*. Singapore: Singapore University Press, 2004.

Reid, Anthony. *Southeast Asia in the Age of Commerce, 1450–1680: Expansion and Crisis*. New Haven, Conn.: Yale University Press, 1995.

Rigg, Johnathan. *Southeast Asia: The Human Landscape of Modernization and Development*. New York: Routledge, 1997.

DAVID BIGGS

Environmentalism

Environmentalism, broadly defined, is a modern ideological and political philosophy dedicated to protecting the earth's environment from degradation and destruction by human action. Many strands of environmentalism are active in different parts of the world in the early twenty-first century, and the broad tendency draws on a variety of intellectual roots. Environmentalist thought and organizations can be roughly but usefully divided into two general groupings. Ecocentric environmentalism emphasizes the need to treat the natural world as if it had rights in the same way that humans do. Ecocentric movements often argue for the restoration of natural purity and for, in the long run, a reconfiguration of human society that lives within natural limits. Anthropocentric movements emphasize the earth as instrumental to the support of human society. Such views are environmentalist in that they emphasize the need to protect and restore the environment; however, they argue from a moral position that such stewardship is necessary to support a sustainable

and just human society. Both ecocentric and anthropocentric views have generally superseded and built upon older concepts of preservation versus conservation of the environment. Conservation sought to manage the environment for sustainable use, while preservation sought to protect at least parts of the environment from any human-induced change. The twenty-first-century debate among environmentalists is between those who see growth and development as inevitable and positive and those who see it as destructive and unsustainable.

Conservation and Preservation. Environmentalism as a philosophy has its direct origins in the late eighteenth and early nineteenth centuries. While premodern and non-European thought often emphasized an identification of nature with the divine and recognized the need to conserve resources for the future, the systematic development of knowledge about the environment and how it has changed through human agency came with the European Scientific Revolution. In the eighteenth century efforts at conservation of scarce resources such as timber in Europe led to the first forest reserves and the development of forestry as a profession. Some authors have argued that imperialism, which brought other parts of the world under European rule, played a critical role in forcing some Europeans to recognize that unbridled exploitation could lead to environmental degradation. The case of Mauritius is often cited as an early example of where exploitation caused the extinction of several animals—including the famous dodo—before colonial rulers began to support conservation.

A second major spur to the development of environmental thought and activism was the expansion of the United States as a continental power in the second half of the nineteenth century. Preservation made its first impact in American thinking. The rapid despoliation of much of the trans-Mississippi west after the Civil War, with American bison almost wiped out and Native Americans confined to reservations, led writers like John Muir (1838–1914) and later Aldo Leopold (1887–1948) to champion "wilderness" protection. Such areas would be free of any sustained human use. In the late nineteenth century the creation of areas preserved in a "pristine" state meant the removal of Native Americans and settlers. In general, preservationists and conservationists both regarded this alienation as the price that a civilized society must pay for preserving the environment. By the turn of the century the idea of establishing national parks as places preserved for natural beauty or scientific value became accepted. It was a middle-class consensus with little concern for the poorer people who still made their living off the land.

Conservation found its champion in Gifford Pinchot (1865–1946). Pinchot became the first American trained in forestry and under President Theodore Roosevelt became head of the U.S. Forestry Service, which managed the vast amounts of forest under the control of the federal government. Conservation also took the form of government assistance to farmers in protecting soil fertility and providing support for irrigation. The decade-long drought in the 1930s that produced the Dust Bowl in the middle of the United States both showed the limits of human ability to manipulate the environment and also strengthened the hands of those who called for greater regulation of the environment.

In Europe and its colonies a similar consensus developed after the turn of the century. Governments engaged in efforts to promote conservation of resources and sustainable development. They also began to develop both at home and in their empires areas preserved as wilderness. In many cases preservationist action came after a decline in wildlife, which led groups such as the British-based Society for the Protection of Wild Fauna of the Empire to promote wildlife reserves. As in the United States, such areas often had human populations that had to be removed in order to realize the ideal of wilderness. Wilderness became the preserve of the wealthy and eventually the middle class to the exclusion of indigenous people. In both the United States and Europe, science and scientists were expected to provide solutions to the problems of conservation.

Postwar Fears and a Growing Environmentalist Movement. While the issue of conservation and preservation remained important, in the era after World War II a new emphasis on several issues that many people saw as threatening global survival helped create modern environmentalism. These issues grew out of the enormity of modern industrial capitalism and its ability to consume resources and create commodities. In many parts of the industrial world, pollution became apparent and even sometimes a threat to life. The burning of hydrocarbon fuels, both those based on coal and those based on petroleum, created air pollution. Industrial pollution released sometimes-toxic fumes into the air and wastes into the water. Pesticides and fertilizers from agriculture also fouled water and air.

Rapid population growth, particularly in the former empires or Third World, also stimulated concern about an impending Malthusian crisis in which population growth would outstrip the world's ability to produce food. By the 1970s, oil shortages joined food shortages as causes of fears about insufficient resources. In the developing world, environmentalist movements often developed as movements to restore indigenous rights over resources that had been alienated by the state.

Finally, the development of both nuclear weapons and nuclear energy in the years after World War II stimulated fears of global catastrophe. The threat of nuclear war, which reached the point of "mutual assured destruction" between the Soviet Union and the United States in the 1960s, led many to oppose any use of nuclear power. A series of accidents at nuclear plants across the globe also led to resistance to the spread of nuclear power plants.

A growing environmentalist movement developed. A number of important works began to inspire people to environmental activism by the 1960s, while quality-of-life issues such as pollution made environmental protection a popular issue with the public in developed countries. Rachel Carson's *Silent Spring* (1962), which documented the devastating effect that pesticides, especially DDT, had on wildlife in the United States, helped create political support for a variety of environmental-protection measures. Groups such as the Sierra Club and the Wilderness Society support efforts to regulate pollution and expand the lands protected from development. Across the globe, groups like the World Wildlife Fund (renamed the Worldwide Fund for Nature) and Greenpeace took the lead. Throughout the developed world, legislation was passed and enforced that sought to protect the environment, often with the grudging support of industry itself.

By the 1980s, however, a period of slow economic growth in the industrialized West and the collapse of Communism in Eastern Europe led to a backlash against what were seen as policies that limited economic growth. Though parts of the environmentalist agenda had become mainstream, other parts came under attack. Business-oriented political leaders often portrayed environmentalism as the enemy of economic growth. In Europe the fall of Communism and the decline of socialist orthodoxy left an opening for the development of genuinely environmentalist politics. Most notably in Germany, the Green Party developed as an avowedly environmentalist political movement dedicated to restructuring society in order to consume less and become more sustainable. Its influence stretched across Europe.

Global Warming. The emergence of global warming as a major concern both stimulated and polarized the environmental debate. The phenomenon of global warming had been recognized as early as the 1960s. Scientists could not find a consensus on its magnitude or cause, however, until the 1980s. Then, as warming increased, they recognized that the emission of greenhouse gases from burning hydrocarbons was one of the major causes of global warming. By the 1990s global warming had become the central debate in environmentalism. In 1996, under U.N. sponsorship, most of the nations of the world signed the Kyoto Protocol designed to limit and eventually reduce the emission of greenhouse gases. The protocol used a sliding scale that called on industrialized nations to limit their emissions first, while assisting developing nations in their efforts. In the United States in particular, opposition to the protocol grew, and the administration of George W. Bush withdrew U.S. participation from the program. Most of the remaining signatories continued to follow the protocol (except most notably Australia), but the failure of the United States, the largest producer of greenhouse gases, to participate undermined the effort.

The fate of the environment will remain arguably the most important issue facing human society in the years to come. The effects of human-induced climate change and the shortage of critical natural resources will make their effects felt on societies across the globe. However, environmentalist hopes of promoting lower consumption and emphasizing sustainability in resource use remain unpopular with publics in parts of the developed world, as well as in the developing world. The effects of global warming will become more obvious over the next decades, and these effects may lead to renewed support for environmental action across the globe. The issues of poverty and power remain embedded in environmental concerns, and it is no sure thing that protecting the environment will weigh most heavily in debates over those concerns.

[*See also* Climate and Climate Change; Ecotourism; Empire and Imperialism, *subentry* Imperialism and the Environment; Green Parties; *and* Sustainable Development.]

BIBLIOGRAPHY

Carson, Rachel. *Silent Spring.* Boston: Houghton Mifflin, 1962.

Grove, Richard H. *Green Imperialism: Colonial Expansion, Tropical Island Edens, and the Origins of Environmentalism, 1600–1860.* Cambridge, U.K.: Cambridge University Press, 1995.

MacKenzie, John M. *The Empire of Nature: Hunting, Conservation, and British Imperialism.* Manchester, U.K.: Manchester University Press, 1988.

Muir, John. *The Mountains of California.* New York: The Century Company, 1894. Reprint. New York: Modern Library, 2001.

Muir, John. *Our National Parks.* Boston: Houghton, Mifflin, 1901. Reprint. San Francisco: Sierra Club Books, 1991.

Pepper, David. *Modern Environmentalism: An Introduction.* New York: Routledge, 1996.

Rothman, Hal K. *Saving the Planet: The American Response to the Environment in the Twentieth Century.* Chicago: Ivan R. Dee, 2000.

Worster, Donald. *Nature's Economy: A History of Ecological Ideas.* 2d ed. Cambridge, U.K.: Cambridge University Press, 1994.

GREGORY H. MADDOX

Environmentalism and Environmental Movements in Southeast Asia

While environmentalism and environmental movements are traditionally associated with American and European contexts, they are also historically tied to earlier scientific and colonial experiences in Southeast Asia. As the historian Richard Grove has pointed out in his study of British-controlled teak forests in India, many European and American ideas about conservation and protection of wilderness derived from early experiences in colonial Asia, Africa, and the Americas. Colonial forestry departments, politically able to remove forest dwellers for the sake of protecting wood as a valuable trade commodity, engaged in practices that would be untenable in their home countries. Because of its intense tropical biodiversity, Southeast Asia was also important to scientific research such as Alfred Russel Wallace's studies in the 1850s on evolution and to archaeological research in the early twenty-first century on early hominids on the Indonesian island of Flores. Thus, as a colonial laboratory, Southeast Asia was instrumental to the development of such fields as evolutionary biology, anthropology, and forestry—fields that became important in efforts to protect the world's biodiversity and counter the effects of climate change. Since the 1960s more conventional forms of environmental movements, following examples initiated in the West, have spread to Southeast Asia. More recently, largely because of problems in the colonial foundation on which such movements were formed, local nongovernmental organizations (NGOs) as well as larger international conservation organizations have begun to pay closer attention to environmental movements expressed through indigenous rather than imported frameworks.

Some key steps in the development of environmentalism as a social and political movement began with the experiences of primarily European observers in various colonial contexts. Beginning in the 1880s colonial governments in Southeast Asia, as well as the independent Siamese kingdom, began rapidly to expand an industrial infrastructure of railroads, roads, telegraph lines, canals, and electric streetcars outward from old capital cities into previously distant hinterlands. With this expansion came significant political and economic changes expressed through booming cities, rising rates of land tenancy, and local uprisings. In addition to the global depression that hit the region in 1930–1931, widespread agricultural catastrophes were brought on by the depletion of soils, siltation of waterways, and widespread, uncontrolled burning of forests. In response to these problems, a wide array of anthropologists, human geographers, and agricultural engineers visited particularly impoverished regions; these experiences, parallel to those of American farmers during the Dust Bowl in the Great Plains, led to some of the first revisions in European thought toward traditional modes of farming, such as the centuries-old techniques used in farming rice. Observation of traditional agricultural landscapes in the Red River delta quickly led René Dumont to criticize colonial policies and argue for a rapid return of lands to small farmers. Dumont's experiences in Southeast Asia helped him develop a career of scholarship that in 1974 catapulted him into the French political scene as the first Green Party candidate for president. Other researchers, notably the anthropologist Georges Condominas, followed similar paths, watching in disbelief as communities with unique traditions were torn apart by colonial or war-related decimation of forest environments. During the Cold War, experiences in Vietnam, from which footage of defoliated forests and napalmed villages reached the living rooms of millions, helped fuel widespread American political demonstrations in 1969 and 1970, ending with the single largest political protest in history, Earth Day 1970.

Starting in the 1960s conservation organizations first affiliated with U.S. and Western aid agencies began efforts modeled after American and European programs to establish national parks in Southeast Asia. This was followed in the 1970s with the establishment of international NGO offices such as the World Wildlife Federation (WWF), the World Conservation Union, and the United Nations Environment Program in various capital cities of the region. Southeast Asian governments in turn expanded forestry departments and established departments of environmental protection following Western models. However, research such as the political ecologist Nancy Peluso's studies of Indonesian forestry practices in central Java show that in many cases Southeast Asia's postcolonial governments largely continued colonial practices and institutions. International agencies, notably the WWF, had also by the 1980s drawn increasing criticism from local farmers, activists, and media for their failure to help people living on the margins of national parks while attempting to protect those parks, often through support of greater police enforcement and the use of fences.

Locally initiated environmental movements, such as indigenous people's movements and coalitions against further encroachment on traditionally held forests and agricultural lands, rapidly multiplied beginning in the 1990s. Adopting political tactics used by such groups as the Chipko tree-hugging movement in India, local groups began to demand a greater role in the management of forests and protection of some areas from urbanization or deforestation. One of the central objects drawing protest throughout the region has been hydropower dams. Projects such as Nam Theun 2 in Laos and San Roque in the Philippines have mobilized complex, technologically savvy networks of local residents, indigenous peoples, NGOs, and foreign allies in efforts to stop the projects or mediate their terms. Such movements indicate an increasing globalization not only of the companies and financing pushing for more dams but also of environmental protest movements. However, some communities have given up these models of Ghandi-influenced nonviolent protest or armed conflict in favor of more homegrown models of resistance and environmental management. Perhaps one of the most interesting forms of such environmentalism is occurring in the forested regions of northern Thailand, where Buddhist monks assist local villagers in ordaining trees through popular rituals. Such recognition of trees and forests in popular spiritual life has been more effective than political routes in successful conservation.

In the early twenty-first century, along with most of the world's tropical regions, Southeast Asia is at a critical juncture in which human and climate-induced environmental change is threatening the integrity of many ecosystems and the prospects for a large percentage of its people to escape poverty. Solving these environmental crises will require engagement with problems of globalization in the present and the legacies of colonialism and Cold War development projects in the past.

[See also Economy, subentry Southeast Asia; Empire and Imperialism, subentry Imperialism and the Environment; and Natural Resources.]

BIBLIOGRAPHY

Condominas, Georges. *We Have Eaten the Forest: The Story of a Montagnard Village in the Central Highlands of Vietnam.* New York: Hill and Wang, 1977.

Grove, Richard H., Vinita Damodaran, and Satpal Sangwan, eds. *Nature and the Orient: The Environmental History of South and Southeast Asia.* Oxford and New York: Oxford University Press, 1998.

Peluso, Nancy Lee. *Rich Forests, Poor People: Resource Control and Resistance in Java.* Berkeley: University of California Press, 1992.

DAVID A. BIGGS

Environmental Disasters

Environmental disasters fall into two broad categories: natural disasters and human-induced catastrophes. The former refer to abnormal and extreme climatic, geological, and other natural phenomena whose occurrence causes substantial environmental damage, often with deleterious effects on humanity. The latter refers to incidents caused by human activity and, often, negligence. This article provides examples of both types of disasters, as well as a third common type of environmental disaster where the devastating impacts of natural events are exacerbated by human activities.

Natural Disasters. Earthquakes and volcanoes are two examples of the first type of environmental disasters. When an earthquake estimated to have been between 8 and 9 on the Richter scale struck Lisbon, Portugal, in 1755, the townspeople had no advance warning and two aftershocks destroyed thousands of the city's buildings, and killed upward of 100,000 people in Lisbon and beyond. The earthquake caused a subsequent tsunami that devastated other coastal areas of Portugal. This first major environmental disaster of the modern era was a catalyst for the development of seismology, as systematic studies were begun into the timing, location, and strength of earthquakes. These efforts, however, failed to help the approximate ten thousand victims of an October 1891 Japanese earthquake estimated to have been 8.4 on the Richter scale. The event killed roughly seven thousand people and devastated an area of 4,200 square miles (6,758 square kilometers).

Despite advances, the twentieth century illustrated that earthquakes remain among the most deadly and expensive of environmental disasters. The destructive power of earthquakes in the twentieth century was evident in the 1906 San Francisco earthquake. It destroyed the city and claimed approximately two thousand lives. While the loss of life was not as severe as with other earthquakes, at 8.2 on the Richter scale it was at the time the largest quake ever to hit the United States and led to the subsequent development of stringent building codes. However, the new codes could not prevent $10 billion in damages in a 1989 earthquake in San Francisco that resulted in sixty-seven deaths. The damage and loss of life in 1989 pales in comparison to the earthquake in Kashmir in October 2005. The 7.6 magnitude earthquake caused an estimated seventy-five thousand deaths, with thousands of other injured, and about 3.3 million left homeless.

A similar sense of predictive progress but lingering destruction has occurred regarding volcanoes. When Mount Tambora in Indonesia erupted in 1815 about twelve thousand people were killed instantly with an additional eighty thousand dying over the subsequent months from starvation due to the fallout of ash which fell as far as 800 miles (1,287 kilometers) from the eruptions. This particular disaster had a global impact, as the ash it sent into the atmosphere reduced the amount of sunlight reaching the earth, which led to global cooling. Nearly a century later in 1902 in Martinique the Mount Pelée volcano exploded and wiped out the city of Saint Pierre and killed all but one of its estimated thirty thousand citizens. The destruction did not prevent others from resettling the area, but when another eruption occurred in 1929 there was sufficient advance notice to evacuate the population and as a result no lives were lost.

Similarly, in 1980 when Mount Saint Helens in Washington state spewed ash and debris 12 miles (19 kilometers) high, thirty-six were killed but many other likely victims were evacuated. The relatively low death count was largely a reflection of logistic abilities and the financial wherewithal to orchestrate an evacuation. By comparison, five years later twenty thousand Columbians in the town of Armero lost their lives due to an erupting volcano.

Human-Induced Disasters. Human-induced environmental disasters have been a persistent part of the story of the modern world. In general, industrialization has brought great prosperity and improved living standards for the peoples of the developed world, with developing countries striving to match the quality of life and prosperity enjoyed by the industrialized world. However, there have been severe environmental costs. Three of the most dramatic examples in the modern era of environmental disasters being caused by human activity occurred in 1952, 1984, and 1986.

The United Kingdom has a long history of dealing with air and other pollution; in fact, the painter Claude Monet is said to have captured the extent of air pollution in London in his impressionist paintings from 1899 to 1901. London's air pollution once again became a focus of attention in December 1952 when an influx of warm Atlantic air trapped colder smog-filled air at the surface. Caused by the burning of wood and coal, the weekend-long disaster led to about four thousand direct deaths with an estimated eight thousand additional subsequent deaths. The disaster led to the development and implementation of clean-air legislation that virtually banned the burning of coal in London.

In 1984 the Union Carbide plant in Bhopal, India, released forty-two tons of the toxic gas methyl isocynate into the environment, killing about 2,500 instantly and injuring an additional 200,000. Many died in their sleep, while others died attempting to run from the spreading poisonous cloud. The lingering effects of the disaster have caused the deaths of more than 16,000 individuals in the years since. The corporation never faced criminal charges, but in 1989 Union Carbide reached a compensation settlement with the Indian government for $470 million. Victim's families received $3,300 if they had a member who died, and $800 if they suffered a permanent disability. Union Carbide has abandoned Bhopal, but the legacy of the 1984 disaster continues to haunt the people there.

Two years later in 1986 another environmental disaster created a legacy that will persist long into the future. On 26 April 1986 a Soviet nuclear reactor in Chernobyl, Ukraine, experienced a reactor meltdown and released substantial amounts of nuclear material into the atmosphere that killed thirty-two people. Some thirty thousand nearby residents were evacuated, and local crops and cattle were ruined. It took another two days for the Soviet government to acknowledge the disaster officially. In the intervening period, the poisoned air had spread as far as Ireland and Scandinavia. The full long-term impact of increased radiation levels on individuals in the immediate area and across Europe will never be fully understood. The incident highlighted the international interconnectedness of environmental disasters and showed how local events can have broader catastrophic consequences.

Beyond isolated incidents, recurrent activities, such as oil spills, have also attracted substantial public attention because of their devastating consequences for marine and other life. In the 1960s and 1970s, such disasters helped to pique public interest in a then-nascent environmental movement. The tanker *Torrey Canyon* went aground in the English Channel in 1967 and spilled more than 118,000 tons of oil. The incident killed more than thirty thousand seabirds and damaged long stretches of the Welsh coast. Remediation efforts to clean up the spill made matters worse as toxic emulsifiers further damaged marine organisms that had struggled but survived the disaster. In subsequent oil spills less-toxic substances were used in remediation efforts.

The largest oil spill in history occurred in 1989 when the *Exxon Valdez* spilled 11 million gallons of crude oil off of Alaska, killing thousands of seabirds and causing damage worth millions of dollars. The salmon fishery was hit hard,

as it was closed for the 1990 season, and Exxon was forced to pay $302 million in damages. The company spent an additional $105 million on clean-up activities. Salmon were not the only wildlife affected; over 1,000 sea otters were killed, and an estimated 375,000 to 435,000 seabirds died as a result of the accident.

Human-Exacerbated Natural Disasters. The third type of environmental disasters involves human activities that serve to exacerbate naturally occurring phenomenon and turning them into environmental disasters. Famines and hurricanes provide examples. The best-known early-modern-era famine occurred in Ireland from around 1845 to 1849. This disaster was, in part, the result of over-dependence of Irish farmers on a single crop, potatoes, which were devastated by blight. Over the course of the decade from 1841 to 1851 the Irish population dropped by 20 percent—from about 8,200,000 to 6,514,000—owing to death and emigration. Beyond the impact of the famine on its individual victims and the Irish diaspora, the story of the famine of the 1840s has become an integral part of Irish history, politics, and folklore.

While the Irish numbers are striking, they pale in comparison to the estimated 5 to 10 million victims of the Soviet famine from 1932 to 1934. That disaster was, in part, the result of the seizures of farms, drought, and social upheaval.

More recently, the Ethiopian famine of 1984–1985 captured the world's attention and led to an unprecedented charitable response. The famine was caused by a combination of drought, overpopulation, and a civil war. It was evident to Western governments in August 1984 that thousands were dying of starvation and that upward of 6 million people were at risk. However, it was not until television pictures began to broadcast the plight of the famine victims that governments stepped up relief efforts. Assistance did not end with politicians and aid workers, as the international music community, led by Boomtown Rats singer Bob Geldof, organized the one-day concert *Live Aid* that raised millions of dollars. Subsequent events such as the formation of the supergroup Band Aid and their single "Do They Know It's Christmas?" raised millions more. While the aid money helped to some degree to alleviate the crisis, famine returned to Ethiopia again in the late 1990s and in 2003.

Although droughts have been an integral part of the equation for famines, human activities have served to transform natural phenomena into full-fledged environmental and humanitarian disasters. That same pattern has been evident with hurricanes as well.

Hurricanes in the modern era have become increasingly destructive and costly due, in part, to increased populations living in hurricane areas, greater property values of areas affected, and an apparent trend toward stronger windstorms. When Typhoon Vera struck the Japanese island of Honshu in 1958, it killed approximately five thousand people, with more than thirty-two thousand additional people missing and a further 1.5 million left homeless. The toll also included 510,000 acres of destroyed farmland and a total damages bill of more than $2 billion. In 1969 Hurricane Camile devastated the Mississippi coast. Three years later Hurricane Agnes caused $1.7 billion in damages. In 1988 the strongest ever-recorded hurricane, Gilbert, killed hundreds of Caribbean residents and Mexicans. More recently in 1998, Hurricane Mitch devastated Central America with 180 mph winds. The death toll reached an estimated eleven thousand people. That year's hurricane season caused more deaths than at any time in the previous two hundred years. Furthermore, the period 1995–1998 saw thirty hurricanes develop, the most ever over a four-year time span.

Public attention was focused on increasingly devastating hurricanes in August 2005 when Hurricane Katrina destroyed New Orleans in Louisiana. With damages estimated at $100 million, a death toll of about thirteen hundred (an estimated twenty-one hundred others were missing), and the destruction of 330,000 homes leaving about 770,000 citizens homeless, Katrina was the costliest environmental disaster in American history. Beyond statistics, Katrina was important in exposing the consequences of insufficient planning and poor governance in responding to the crisis. Decisions taken in previous years had reduced the size of protective wetlands off the coast by more than 3,100 square miles (4,988 square kilometers). Those wetlands had served as an initial line of defense against hurricanes. Moreover, the levees that protected the sub–sea-level city were not sufficient to withstand the over 120 mph winds and subsequent storm surge from the ocean.

Since the beginning of the modern era, circa 1750, humanity has greatly improved its prediction and response capabilities to respond to environmental disasters. Over the same period, increasing global wealth and industrial activity has, arguably, tended to exacerbate natural and other phenomena that lead to environmental disasters. Substantial scientific evidence argues that future environmental disasters, such as hurricanes and droughts, are likely to become more frequent and intense due to human-enhanced global warming. Whether scientists' fears materialize or not, environmental disasters of the three kinds discussed in this article will continue to remain part of the human condition into the future.

[*See also* Famine; Natural Disasters; *and* Potato Famine, Irish and Scottish.]

BIBLIOGRAPHY

Archibald, Andrew, and Trefor Munn-Venn. *Tough Times in the Big Easy: Lessons from a Catastrophe.* Ottawa: Conference Board of Canada, March 2007.

Cawthorne, Nigel. *100 Catastrophic Disasters.* London: Arcturus Publishing Limited, 2006.

Freedman, Bill. "Environmental Damages." Chap. 5, *Environmental Science.* Toronto: Pearson Education Canada Inc., 2004.

Hirschberg, S., G. Spiekerman, and R. Dones. *Comprehensive Assessment of Energy Systems: Severe Accidents in the Energy Sector.* Villigen: Paul Scherrer Institut, November 1998.

International Strategy for Disaster Reduction. *Building Disaster Resilient Communities.* Geneva: United Nations, June 2007.

Mungall, Constance, and Digby J. McLaren, eds. *Planet under Stress: The Challenge of Global Change.* Toronto and New York: Oxford University Press, 1990.

Swiss Reinsurance Company. *Natural Catastrophes and Reinsurance.* Zurich: Author, 2003.

Woodham-Smith, Cecil. *The Great Hunger, Ireland 1845–1849.* London: New English Library, 1965.

JASON L. CHURCHILL

EPIDEMICS. Epidemic diseases have a marked effect on society, defined by dramatic mortality (death) and morbidity (sickness) rates. In modern public-health terms, epidemics are distinguished by disease rates that far exceed disease expectancy for a given population. An epidemic can be contrasted with "endemic" diseases, diseases present in a population continuously. Epidemics are anomalies to everyday illness, distinguishable in their sudden onset, swift consequences, and gradual disappearance.

There is no numerical definition or ratio for diseases classified as epidemics. The scale of an epidemic disease is determined in relation to "normal" disease rates, although the line between epidemic disease and endemic disease is not always clear. For example, the respiratory infection tuberculosis (TB) was widespread in Europe and the Americas throughout the nineteenth century and into the twentieth century. TB was endemic in some parts of the Western world, yet TB's epidemic effect in the West was most dramatic among the urban poor during the first half of the nineteenth century.

Epidemics are most often associated with infections, or diseases that are communicable. In Western scientific models, disease rates are directly linked to the transmission of bacteria, viruses, or other infectious agents.

Communication of disease occurs through direct human contact (for example, sexually transmitted diseases), through indirect human contact (for example, airborne illnesses), and through indirect transfer through a nonhuman agent (for example, the role of animals or insects in disease transmission). Thus the root causes of epidemic diseases, including the place of origin and mode of transmission, were central to prevention and eradication efforts in the nineteenth and twentieth centuries.

Strictly biological models that trace the contagion and location of widespread disease do not often consider the social environment that produces an epidemic. Sociopolitical and economic conditions define the terrain of disease transmission and the relative effect of disease on society. Malnutrition and poor sanitation are primary causes for disease susceptibility. Often social and political conflicts are the precursors to diseases that reach epidemic scale. In the modern world, wealth disparities and resource barriers determine the incidence and effect of an epidemic upon a population.

Temporal and spatial descriptions are often included in scientific and nonscientific definitions of epidemic disease. Large-scale diseases have emerged in varied form for different time periods. Historical accounts of everything from cholera to the plague use disease to describe a time of dearth, including times of agricultural failures or high prices. By the early twentieth century the duration and effect of different epidemic diseases upon Western society had changed with the proliferation of allopathic medicine, most notably through vaccination campaigns and the discovery of penicillin. As the Western world set out to prove the end of disease and the triumph of modern sanitation and medicine, epidemics appeared mostly to affect only the underdeveloped Third World.

Epidemics also are associated with spatial or geographic regions. For example, early modern medical interventions around epidemics in both the West and the non-West "sanitized" urban spaces associated with the poor in order to combat disease. Geographic associations of disease were significant in the development of Western medicine itself. The strategic use of Western medicine by European colonizers directly related to the advancement of colonialism in the Americas, Africa, and Asia. For example, the association of cholera with India led to British imperial policies that sought to control the "natural home" of the disease. Other diseases affiliated with Asia and parts of Africa, including malaria, yellow fever, and sleeping sickness, became a separate branch of study for diseases of the tropics, or "tropical medicine."

From the eighteenth century on, geographic expansion associated with colonialism directly impacted the character of epidemic disease, including which diseases spread, where they spread, and, significantly, who was most affected by disease. The international movements of peoples expanded the regional effects of an epidemic, often leading to a pandemic—an epidemic that affects a larger geographic region. The geographic bounds of disease transformed through the course of the twentieth century, seen most notably in the movement and expansion of human immunodeficiency virus (HIV), often described as a global epidemic, or the AIDS (acquired immunodeficiency syndrome) pandemic. Greater governmental and international oversight, including the role of the World Health Organization, may affect the potentials of epidemics, as in early-twenty-first-century efforts to curtail the potential of avian flu.

Several disease outbreaks have significantly affected the modern world, including outbreaks of cholera, tuberculosis, and the so-called Spanish flu. Most literature on disease discusses epidemics in relation to the Western world or colonial expansion. Only in the early twenty-first century has scholarship begun to address not only the incidence but also the effects of epidemics upon people in the non-Western world. Further, alternative perceptions and treatments of epidemics in the non-Western world are still largely unexplored. Thus any account of major epidemics in the modern world remains incomplete.

Cholera. Cholera's dramatic symptoms and high mortality rates distinguished it as one of the most visible and feared epidemic diseases of the nineteenth and early twentieth centuries, although historians argue that its actual statistical effect was slight in comparison to that of its contemporaries—most notably, tuberculosis. Although cholera's impact on mortality and morbidity in the nineteenth century may have been less than contemporaneous diseases like tuberculosis, cholera is a pivotal epidemic disease because of its impact on politics, popular knowledge, and Western medicine. Contracted through the ingestion of water or food contaminated by bacteria, cholera is now attributed to sewage-contaminated rivers and water supplies. Cholera comes as an attack of profuse vomiting and often uncontrollable excretion. The dehydration and stress on the body causes tissues to collapse and often leads to swift heart and kidney failure.

The first outbreak, from 1817 to 1823, originated in India and spread through Southeast and East Asia. Cholera cases during this period totaled more than 6 million, with at least 3 million deaths directly attributed to the disease. The second pandemic broke out again in India in 1826, spread from China across Europe to North Africa, and eventually reached the eastern seaboard of North America. In the nineteenth century three more waves of cholera dramatically spread, eventually reaching North, Central, and South America, North and sub-Saharan Africa, Europe, China, and Southeast Asia.

At a time of growing industrialization and migration in both North America and Europe, cholera incited much debate in the West around its incidence and prevention and created conflict between "contagion" and "miasma" theories. Contagion theories declared that cholera directly spread from one individual to another, while miasma theories maintained that environmental factors led to infection. When cholera emerged in Russia during the 1820s, the tsar ordered the quarantine of all infected with the disease, but to no avail, and many thousands died despite attempts to isolate the epidemic.

The failure of quarantine techniques in Russia and the inability of scientists to produce the contagion itself elevated belief in miasmic causes for disease. Western popular and scientific understanding looked for an "Asian" causation for cholera. Great sanitarians, taking the lead from colonial perceptions of disease in India, distinguished cholera as a social disease related to poverty and hygiene. Those in support of miasmic causations sought sanitary and poverty reform through legislation that addressed water supply, sewage, and overcrowded living conditions.

By the second half of the nineteenth century the gospel of sanitation was coupled with germ theory, which again sought contagions as the source of cholera. Areas of Germany successfully adopted strong quarantine and isolation procedures against cholera under the advice of Robert Koch (1843–1910). By the sixth wave of the cholera epidemic in the 1890s, Europe saw little infection, while cholera continued to ravage sub-Saharan Africa and South and Southeast Asia. Sanitation and germ theories came together in the West to say that the disease could be controlled and potentially defeated.

Tuberculosis. Tuberculosis (TB), or consumption, is now generally considered the greatest epidemic killer of the nineteenth century in the West. Pulmonary tuberculosis, the primary tubercular infection of the nineteenth and twentieth centuries, is attributed to infection by the organism *Mycobacterium tuberculosis*, which passes from person to person. An extraordinarily high incidence of pulmonary TB emerged in the early decades of industrial urbanization as a result of crowded living conditions and poor nutrition. By the end of the nineteenth century in most of the Western world, TB rates were on the decline

as a result of individual resistance and social and environmental changes. Deliberate preventive actions, like those of sanitation and both residential and labor regulations, contributed greatly to the decline of TB in Europe and North America. With the introduction of antibiotic treatments in the 1920s and 1930s, TB retreated even further, becoming rare in the West.

In contrast, TB was and continues to be endemic in Africa and Asia. Western domination led to social and economic changes that directly affected the spread of disease in colonial states, including increased urban migration and population, repressive policies of spatial segregation, and widespread resource deprivation. Colonial rule disrupted existing social structures and undermined local knowledge and healing systems. For example, tuberculosis had declined among Europeans in South Africa by 1914. In contrast, industrialization and stringent state policies increased poverty and population density for black South Africans, leading to serious epidemics of tuberculosis accompanied by episodes of typhus throughout the first half of the twentieth century. At the beginning of the twenty-first century, TB has coupled with HIV and independently formed antibiotic-resistant strains, reemerging as a global pandemic that disproportionately affects people of the non-Western world.

Malaria and Yellow Fever. So-called tropical diseases, including malaria and yellow fever, became maladies of central concern for colonial medicine, as well as for colonial rule. Malaria, now understood to be spread by indirect transfer of protozoa through mosquitoes, causes varied symptoms including fever, and without treatment it causes high rates of mortality. Yellow fever also causes fever and extremely high mortality rates. Europeans were highly susceptible to these diseases, endemic in areas in South and Central America, South and Southeast Asia, and sub-Saharan Africa. In the 1820s and 1830s, colonial troops from France and Britain experienced mortality rates that ranged from 10 percent in India to 50 percent in Sierra Leone from tropical diseases. Colonial prejudices are acutely felt in both popular and scientific writings that consider these tropical diseases and cholera as inherent features of the "backward" and "unsanitary" people of the colonies. Though Western science and colonial policy had largely controlled the infection of malaria and yellow fever through selective prevention efforts like drainage reform and European use of treatments like quinine, the diseases of the tropics continued to afflict colonial populations.

The Spanish Flu. The most devastating epidemic of the modern world struck in 1918 as World War I raged, a

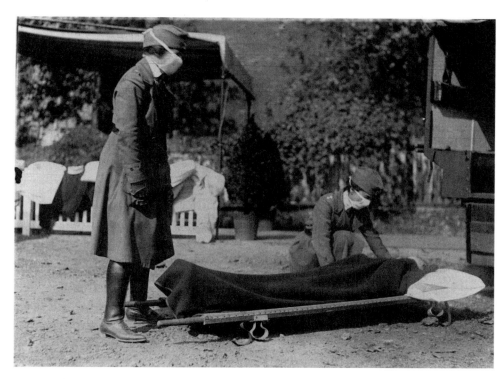

Epidemic Drill. Demonstration at the Red Cross Emergency Ambulance Station in Washington, D.C., during the influenza pandemic of 1918. PRINTS AND PHOTOGRAPHS DIVISION, LIBRARY OF CONGRESS

disease popularly known as Spanish influenza. Infection by the influenza virus caused immediate fever and swift death. During its first outbreak in April, "the fever" affected both foreign troops and civilian populations in France, with a simultaneous outbreak occurring in parts of China and Japan. The second wave of influenza was more lethal, moving from China in July to western Asia and France by August. The Spanish flu covered the globe, killing an estimated 22 million people in two months and infecting many more. It has been estimated that of the 22 million influenza deaths, 12 million people died in India alone. In certain parts of the Pacific islands, mortality rates exceeded 20 percent. In the United States, infection rates were estimated at almost 30 percent. With the discovery of the virus in 1933, inoculation against the virus became widespread.

HIV and AIDS. By the end of the twentieth century, Western biomedicine had identified and isolated the causes of most of the world's epidemics and had pushed for vaccination, sanitation, and treatment efforts across the globe. In 1980 this effort was confronted with the emergence of an entirely new virus, HIV, which held the potential of pandemic results and no curable treatment. HIV weakens the immune system; thus its symptoms

and mortality are dependent on the invasion of various infections into the body.

Many modes of transmission of HIV were initially assumed and feared, although by the early twenty-first century medical researchers had conclusively agreed that HIV passes from one person to another through the exchange of bodily fluids. HIV reached global epidemic proportions, with up to 11 million people infected in its first decade, over half of which were in sub-Saharan Africa. By the end of the twentieth century, AIDS disproportionately affected disadvantaged peoples (upward of 25 million) in the non-Western world. As the pandemic continues to spread in the twenty-first century, HIV symbolizes global systems of inequality that perpetuate disease and offers complex challenges to modern ideas of the epidemic.

[*See also* AIDS and HIV; Cholera; Germ Theory; Health and Disease; Influenza; Malaria; Medicine and Public Health; Smallpox; Tuberculosis; *and* Yellow Fever.]

BIBLIOGRAPHY
Arnold, David, ed. *Imperial Medicine and Indigenous Societies.* Manchester, U.K.: Manchester University Press, 1988. A group of groundbreaking articles looking at the interplay between colonial medicine and people under colonial rule.

Hays, J. N. *The Burdens of Disease: Epidemics and Human Response in Western History.* New Brunswick, N.J.: Rutgers University Press, 1998. A history of changing ideas of disease in the West. Has a comprehensive bibliography of general works on the history of disease and medicine.

Hudson, Robert P. *Disease and Its Control: The Shaping of Modern Thought.* Westport, Conn.: Greenwood Press, 1983.

MacLeod, Roy, and Milton Lewis, eds. *Disease, Medicine, and Empire: Perspectives on Western Medicine and the Experience of European Expansion.* London: Routledge, 1988.

Marks, Geoffrey, and William K. Beatty. *Epidemics.* New York: Charles Scribner's Sons, 1976. A good empirical overview of most major epidemics of the nineteenth and early twentieth centuries.

Porter, Roy, ed. *The Cambridge Illustrated History of Medicine.* Rev. ed. Cambridge, U.K.: Cambridge University Press, 2006.

Ranger, Terence, and Paul Slack, eds. *Epidemics and Ideas: Essays on the Historical Perception of Pestilence.* Cambridge, U.K.: Cambridge University Press, 1992. A thoughtful group of essays that consider epidemics in relation to social and political change in both the West and the non-West.

Rosenberg, Charles E. *Explaining Epidemics, and Other Studies in the History of Medicine.* Cambridge, U.K.: Cambridge University Press, 1992.

DURBA MITRA

EQUATORIAL GUINEA. Equatorial Guinea consists of two of the Guinea Islands: Bioko (formerly Fernando Póo), the largest and closest to the African continent, and Annobón (formerly Pagalu), the smallest and farthest out to sea, as well as a small block of mainland territory between Cameroon and Gabon, Mbini (formerly Río Muni). The capital, Malabo (formerly Santa Isabel), is located on Bioko. The indigenous inhabitants of Bioko, the Bubi, are of Western Bantu origin. The Fang dominate the mainland and make up 80 percent of the modern population of Equatorial Guinea.

Spanish colonialism incorporated the islands and mainland into one colonial state. In 1777, the Spanish-Portuguese Treaty of San Ildefonso, which stabilized the frontier of southern Brazil, provided for the Portuguese cession to Spain of Annobón and Fernando Póo and exclusive Spanish trading privileges on the coast between the Niger Delta and Cape Lopez. Spain had hoped by this transaction to gain a national source of slaves for its American colonies; however, Spanish involvement in the Atlantic slave trade was not particularly successful until after 1800 when a Cuban-based trade circuit developed that was suppressed by the British after 1840.

Systematic development of Fernando Póo began in 1827 when the British made it an annex to their anti–slave trading base at Freetown. Re-captives and other mainland Africans began to produce and market palm oil and later took up cocoa planting. Between 1827 and 1841, the British almost purchased the island from Spain; however, in 1843, Juan José Lerena reconfirmed Spanish possession of Fernando Póo and named its capital, calling it Santa Isabel in honor of the Spanish queen.

The first official Spanish governor, Carlos Chacón, took office in 1858. Although the explorer Manuel Iradier negotiated a number of protectorate treaties on the mainland, most of the ensuing Spanish claims were rejected at the Berlin West Africa Conference (1884–1885), thus accounting for the smallness of Río Muni.

Spain renewed its efforts to develop Fernando Póo after losing the 1898 Spanish-American War. It began taking steps, after 1926, to dominate the interior of Río Muni. The colony as a whole profited from Spanish neutrality in World Wars I and II. Coffee production, already successful on Fernando Póo, began in Río Muni in 1926.

The Francisco Franco regime that came to power after 1936 stimulated a major spurt of investment in Spanish Guinea. By 1960, plantations and cooperatives devoted to cocoa and coffee, particularly on Fernando Póo, were setting records for productivity and per capita income in Africa, underpinning education and a literacy rate in Spanish of 80 percent. Río Muni, however, remained less developed than Fernando Póo.

After 1963, with eventual decolonization in mind, the Franco regime began to push Equatorial Guinea toward democratic social and political institutions. Unfortunately, the disparities in the levels of development of Fernando Póo and Río Muni were reflected in the political arena following the 1964 and 1966 grants of autonomy. The leadership of the moderate nationalist Bonifacio Ondo Edu, who wished to retain certain political and economic links with Spain, was challenged by Francisco Macías Nguema, a radical anti-Spanish Fang clan leader. He led the country to independence on 12 October 1968.

Macías Nguema quickly emerged as one of the most bizarre and brutal dictators in Africa as he moved to wreck the inherited economy that benefited Spanish and Fernando Póo/Bubi interests. Macías Nguema's nephew and close collaborator, Teodoro Obiang Nguema Mbasogo, had him deposed and executed on 29 September 1979, replacing him as president.

After 1996, Equatorial Guinea became a major exporter of high-quality crude oil and liquefied natural gas. Although the first strikes were made by American companies, other oil-consuming countries, particularly China, have become involved in exploiting Equatorial Guinean oil and gas. Given the worldwide competition for hydrocarbons, the major consumers have tacitly agreed to avoid provoking instability by challenging Obiang's dictatorial and corrupt leadership and his sequestering of oil and gas revenues for the benefit of himself and his entourage.

[*See also* Africa, *subentry* Central Africa.]

BIBLIOGRAPHY

Fegley, Randall. *Equatorial Guinea: An African Tragedy.* New York: Lang, 1989.

Roberts, Adam. *The Wonga Coup: Guns, Thugs, and a Ruthless Determination to Create Mayhem in an Oil-rich Corner of Africa.* New York: Public Affairs, 2006.

Sundiata, Ibrahim K. *From Slavery to Neoslavery: The Bight of Biafra and Fernando Po in the Era of Abolition, 1827–1930.* Madison: University of Wisconsin Press, 1996.

LELAND CONLEY BARROWS

ERIE CANAL. One of the greatest developments of the nineteenth century in the United States was the Erie Canal, which links Lake Erie with the Hudson River, a rise of 173 meters (568 feet). Initially suggested in 1699 by the French engineer Sébastien Le Prestre de Vauban, serious efforts began in 1798 with the creation of the Niagara Canal Company. Approval by New York's state legislature was enacted in 1808, and construction began in 1817 with completion in 1825. It was 363 miles (584 kilometers) long, 40 feet (12 meters) wide, and 4 feet (1.2 meters) deep with 18 aqueducts, 83 locks, a towpath 10 feet (3 meters) wide, and the capacity to carry boats with 10 tons of freight and an expected annual tonnage of 1.5 million tons. Its considerable success resulted in several later enlargements and the construction of feeder canals. In 1918 the Erie Canal was replaced by the larger New York State Barge Canal, which followed much the same route and incorporated many existing canal sections while abandoning others. This was renamed the New York State Canal System in 2006. The Erie Canal Corridor now covers 524 miles (843 kilometers). Following the creation of the U.S. railway network in the late 1800s and the road system of the twentieth century, canals became defunct as carriers of freight and people. Since the 1990s efforts have focused on transforming the canal system into a tourism venue.

The Erie Canal made an immense impact on the settlement patterns of the United States, its people, and its economy. In its vicinity, the canal brought prosperity to the state of New York, especially to the small towns of Schenectady, Buffalo, Syracuse, Rome, Utica, and Rochester, where populations were boosted by immigrant workers attracted initially by plentiful work related to freight and passenger shipping and construction. Within twenty years these towns had become cities as trade increased and industries, such as food processing and textiles, capitalized on the ease of transport and the availability of water power from rivers. Nationally, the canal linked midwestern agriculture with the markets of the East Coast and so stimulated agricultural development, notably grain and meat production. It thus contributed to the opening up of the West and to the growth of East Coast cities, especially New York, which became the major Atlantic port. Its success also stimulated canal construction and hence development elsewhere, for example the Illinois and Michigan Canal of Chicago. On the international stage, the waterway linked the continental interior with the Atlantic Ocean to Europe, where there was a growing market for grain, especially wheat. It also facilitated trade between the United States and Canada. These developments further encouraged agricultural expansion and innovation, and the establishment of industry as well as immigration.

The Erie Canal is a landmark development in United States history. Constructed at a time of considerable international and national socioeconomic and political change it helped to unite the eastern, central, and western regions of the country and so create a national identity from a disparate array of states at the time of a rapidly shifting frontier.

[*See also* New York City; United States, *subentry* Nation Building and Westward Expansion; *and* Water and Water Management, *subentry* Water Management and Dams in the United States.]

BIBLIOGRAPHY

Bernstein, Peter L. *Wedding of the Waters: The Erie Canal and the Making of a Great Nation.* New York: W. W. Norton, 2005.

Larkin, F. Daniel, Julie C. Daniels, and Jean West. *Erie Canal: New York's Gift to the Nation, A Document-Based Teacher.* Peterborough, N.H.: Cobblestone; Albany, N.Y.: New York State Archives Partnership Trust, 2001.

A. M. MANNION

ERITREA. The modern state of Eritrea was created in the mid- to late-nineteenth century as a result of Italian colonialism. The different areas of Eritrea have had different influences throughout history and only since 1889 have they been united in one country. It is, however, the relationship with Ethiopia that has dominated modern history for Eritrea.

Eritrea consists of four distinct geographical areas: the central highlands; the western lowlands, the Danakil depression, and the northern highlands. The central highlands have always had close political relations, hostile as well as friendly, with the Ethiopian highlands. There are close ethnic and cultural ties between the regions, whose inhabitants share religion and language and have close social ties. The western lowlands, on the other hand, have always been oriented much more toward Sudan. Many ethnic groups live on both sides of the border, and they share religion and many other similarities. The Danakil depression is very sparsely populated, mainly with Afar people, who are closely related to the Afar in neighboring Djibouti.

Italian colonial ambitions began around the time the Suez Canal was opened and the Red Sea's importance to Europe increased. Initially the Italians settled on the coast, and only later did they venture into the steep and almost inaccessible highlands. The Italians were checked by the Ethiopian Empire, not least in the famous battle of Adwa, where the Italians took a heavy beating from the Ethiopians in 1896. This led to the treaty of Ucchiali in 1889, which effectively created the colony of Eritrea.

The capital of Eritrea was modernized during the 1930s to prepare for the Italian invasion of Ethiopia in 1935. When the Italians were forced out of Ethiopia in 1941, during World War II, the British handed over administration of Ethiopia to the Ethiopian emperor Hailie Selassie, but the British themselves took over administration of Eritrea, though officially Eritrea was still an Italian colony.

The British military administration of an Italian colony was an untenable situation, and in 1952 a United Nations (UN) resolution established a federation between Eritrea and Ethiopia. The federation was abolished in 1962, a year after smaller groups of Eritrean liberation fighters had initiated what became a thirty-year liberation war. Throughout the war, the Eritrean liberation fighters held the northern highlands around the town of Nakfa. The war ended in 1991 with Eritrean independence. This was confirmed in a referendum in 1993, and Eritrea became an independent state.

Ethiopia was the first country to recognize Eritrean independence, and relations were good for some years. They turned sour, however, and in 1998 a border war broke out between the two countries. A peace agreement was signed in late 2000, but border issues were still unresolved, and relations remained tense.

[See also Africa, subentry East Africa; and Ethiopia.]

BIBLIOGRAPHY

Negash, Tekeste. *Italian Colonialism in Eritrea, 1882–1941: Policies, Praxis, and Impact.* Uppsala, Sweden: Uppsala University, 1987.
Trevaskis, G. K. N. *Eritrea: A Colony in Transition, 1941–1952.* London: Oxford University Press, 1960.

MICHAEL MAHRT

ESPERANTO. Esperanto is a planned language intended for international use, created by Ludwik Lejzer Zamenhof (1859–1917) and published in Warsaw in 1887. With Latin's decline in the sixteenth century as the language of scholarship in the West and the rise in literacy in national languages, interest in creating a universal language grew in the seventeenth and eighteenth centuries, attracting the French philosopher René Descartes, the German logician Gottfried Leibniz, the English scientist Isaac Newton, and others. Such projects were based on the idea of creating a "philosophical" language, logical in structure and capable of fully reflecting the order of things. In the nineteenth century, stimulated by the emergence of an educated urban middle class interested in travel and in knowledge of the larger world, advances in transportation, the emergence of telegraph and telephone, and growing interest in international standards, language projects based on simplified combinations of existing languages were proposed for use in addition to local or national languages. A few, such as Volapük (1880), the work of the German Johann Martin Schleyer (1831–1912), attracted a following, but only Zamenhof's Esperanto established itself as a speech community and has endured.

As a Jew, Zamenhof was also inspired by a desire to overcome the virulent anti-Semitism of his time and region. His language is in part a modernization of Latin, but it bears many of the earmarks of structuralism and is often characterized as essentially non-European in conception. Zamenhof, a medical doctor who practiced as an ophthalmologist, understood perhaps better than the linguists of his day that a language is the expression of a community. He set about creating such a community by establishing local Esperanto clubs (Nürnberg, Germany, was first, in 1888), promoting correspondence in Esperanto, launching a magazine (*La Esperantisto*, 1889), and translating literary works (he himself translated Shakespeare's *Hamlet*, the entire Old Testament, and other works, and his followers also produced numerous translations and original works in Esperanto). He explained that any formal changes in the language must come from this community, meaning that the language belonged to the community, not its creator.

Despite bans by the Russian censor, the language spread beyond central and eastern Europe to France, Britain, the United States, and East Asia. In France it attracted progressive business people and academics. The first World Congress of Esperanto was held in Boulogne-sur-Mer (1905), and membership organizations and structures emerged. Reform proposals divided the movement in the following years, most Esperantists maintaining a conservative approach but some, led by French academics, favoring Ido, a reformed Esperanto. The reformists remained fractious, Ido never took hold, and some went on to projects of their own devising. In Asia Esperanto was embraced by Chinese anarchists, by the movement for Latinizing the Chinese writing system, and by leftist causes in Japan. Following World War I Esperanto expanded into all parts of the world, attracted the attention of the League of Nations, gathered a large middle-class following, and became identified with progressive causes like socialism, the labor movement, worker education, and pacifism. But its followers were later persecuted by Stalin in the Soviet Union, and vast numbers of Jewish Esperantists, including virtually the entire extended Zamenhof family, perished under the Nazis at Treblinka and Auschwitz. After World War II the Esperanto movement was rebuilt under the guidance of the politically neutral Universal Esperanto Association (founded 1908), which won the support of UNESCO for "the aims and ideals" of Esperanto and established formal links with the United Nations.

In the early twenty-first century there were Esperantists in at least 120 countries (including active organizations in China, Iran, and several African countries), a large translated and original literature, radio programs, and an extensive periodical literature. World congresses were held annually with some two thousand participants. Internet use of the language was expanding rapidly, while conventional organizations receded in importance as less formal structures appeared. There was also an active youth movement. There were a few hundred native speakers, generally born to international couples who met through Esperanto. Fluent and active speakers numbered in the tens of thousands, but calculations based on course participation and textbooks sold put the numbers in the hundreds of thousands.

BIBLIOGRAPHY
Boulton, Marjorie. *Zamenhof, Creator of Esperanto.* London: Routledge and Kegan Paul, 1960. The standard biography of Zamenhof.
Eco, Umberto. *The Search for the Perfect Language.* Translated by James Fentress. Oxford and Cambridge, Mass.: Blackwell, 1995. An intellectual history of the idea of linguistic perfection, including discussion of language projects.
Janton, Pierre. *Esperanto: Language, Literature, and Community.* Translated by Humphrey Tonkin, Jane Edwards, and Karen Johnson-Weiner. Albany: State University of New York Press, 1993. A comprehensive overview of the linguistics of Esperanto, the demography of the Esperanto community, and literature in Esperanto.
Richardson, David. *Esperanto: Learning and Using the International Language.* Eastsound, Wash.: Orcas, 1988. Introductory essays on Esperanto and language problems, with a course on Esperanto and a reader in the language.
Tonkin, Humphrey, ed. *Esperanto, Interlinguistics, and Planned Language.* Lanham, Md.: University Press of America, 1997. Scholarly essays on Esperanto and its linguistic and social context.

HUMPHREY TONKIN

ESPIONAGE AND INTELLIGENCE AGENCIES.

The gathering of information concerning both friend and foe has been a key component of national security since ancient times. References to the use of intelligence techniques can be found in the military writings of Sun-tzu (fourth century B.C.E.) and in Kauilya's *Arthaśāstra* (also fourth century B.C.E.). Intelligence played an important role in Julius Caesar's defeat of the Gauls between 59 and 51 B.C.E., and both strategic and tactical intelligence was exploited by the Roman Empire. After a relative decline in intelligence gathering in the Western world during the Middle Ages, when Arabs gained undisputed prominence in the field of cryptography and steganography (although, in the Hundred Years' War, between 1337 and 1453, both France and England had wide networks of agents and spies in the occupied territories), intelligence revived during the fifteenth century. Diplomatic missions were used to gather intelligence during the Italian Renaissance, as testified to by government reports of Venetian ambassadors. England, too, has a long tradition of strategic intelligence, dating back to Thomas Cromwell (c. 1485–1540), King Henry VIII's chief minister, and—in a more modern sense—to Sir Francis Walsingham (c. 1532–1590), Elizabeth I's principal secretary of state, who operated an extensive network of agents at home and abroad. Until the late eighteenth and early nineteenth centuries, intelligence agents were mostly nonprofessional figures, such as diplomats, merchants, or travelers. However, a professional class of cryptographers and cryptanalysts, expert in deciphering letters, producing false handwritings, and breaking and repairing seals without detection, was well established by the sixteenth century, as attested to by the life and work of Thomas Phelippes, a leading figure of the first English cipher school.

The Birth of Modern Intelligence. During the eighteenth century, Frederick the Great (r. 1740–1786), king of Prussia, made skillful use of intelligence in his wars against Austria (War of the Austrian Succession, 1740–1748), and later against a coalition among Austria, Russia, and France (Seven Years' War, 1756–1763); as did General George Washington during the American Revolution (1775–1783). Comparatively, during the French Revolutionary and Napoleonic Wars (1792–1815), intelligence played a minor role, although the almost continual state of conflict during this period fostered the development and formalization of intelligence establishments throughout Europe. In Great Britain, political control over intelligence was strengthened in 1797, when Parliament voted for the first time the annual disposition of a secret service fund, aimed at financing British propaganda on the Continent, paying informants and diplomatic bribes, and carrying out secret operations. After a decline following the end of the Napoleonic Wars, around 1850 technological progress in the fields of transport and communication and enhanced competition among the great powers led to a revival of intelligence. In 1871, after the unexpected outbreak of the Franco-Prussian War (1870–1871), an intelligence branch was established within the framework of the reorganized British Army's Topographical and Statistical Department, to monitor the Russian advance in Central Asia and to support colonial expansion. In 1882 the U.S. Office of Naval Intelligence was established, followed by the Army's Military Intelligence Division in 1885. Finally, in 1886 the British Naval Intelligence Department was created, while in Italy and France preexisting structures—generally attached to the foreign ministries and/or military establishments—were adapted to meet the increasing need of overseas expansion and national security. Japan, too, developed military and naval intelligence structures between the 1870s and the 1890s.

At this stage, human intelligence (HUMINT)—intelligence collected by human beings—predominated, although signal intelligence (SIGINT), generally obtained by tapping into the enemy's telegraph wires, had been successfully exploited, for example during the American Civil War (1861–1865). Around 1900, the Russian intelligence service (Okhrana) developed an effective SIGINT division, which cooperated with its HUMINT section for code breaking. In 1909 the establishment of the Secret Service Bureau, upon the recommendation of the Committee for Imperial Defence, marked the first time that Britain had a formally established and permanent intelligence service. The bureau's dual tasks were to counter foreign espionage in the United Kingdom (Home Section) and collect secret intelligence abroad on Britain's potential enemies (Foreign Section). The Home Section was eventually transformed into the Security Service (MI5), while the Foreign Section became the Secret Intelligence Service (SIS, sometimes known as MI6).

The development at the beginning of the twentieth century of new communication systems such as wireless telegraphy and radiotelegraphy, the worldwide extension of the cable telegraph network, and the progress in telephonic communication gradually fostered the role of SIGINT. However, during World War I HUMINT was most important, with neutral Holland and Switzerland as main theaters of the spy game. During the conflict, over three thousand British agents operated in Belgium alone. During the 1920s, Soviet intelligence, organized as the Ob'edinennoe Gosudarstvennoe Politicheskoe Upravlenie (OGPU), or Joint State Political Directorate, made significant inroads in HUMINT. Among other things, it penetrated the British security establishment through the so-called Cambridge Five (the double agents Harold "Kim" Philby, Donald Maclean, Guy Burgess, Anthony Blunt); other effective or supposed Soviet agents were John Cairncross, James Klugman, Leo Long, Michael Straight, Dennis Proctor, and Alister Watson. Soviet intelligence also penetrated the U.S. embassy in Moscow, probably through the U.S. military attaché Colonel Philip R. Faymonville; the United States government; and the top-secret Manhattan Project through the Julius and Ethel Rosenberg spy ring, Donald Maclean, and the scientists Klaus Fuchs and Theodore Hall.

World War II and the Cold War. In the field of SIGINT, between World War I and World War II the United States broke enemy codes, deciphering both the German and the Japanese encryption systems. Almost in the same period, cryptanalysts of the Polish Cipher Bureau (Biuro Szyfrów), in Warsaw, penetrated the German Enigma encryption device and built a decoder (the cryptologic bomb, or *bomba kryptologiczna*), which was the model for the British "Bombe," a machine used after 1940 to gather the so-called Ultra intelligence on U-boats in the Atlantic. Although no service was able to predict the German invasion of the Rhineland (1936) and Austria (1938), after the outbreak of World War II Ultra intelligence—together with its U.S. counterpart, Magic—provided the Allies with important strategic and operative advantages. However, these advantages were not always fully exploited, and devastating intelligence failures took place, including the sinking of Convoy PQ-17 (June/July 1942), owing to the misinterpretation of information on the whereabouts of a German naval group led by the battleship *Tirpitz*. The Japanese raid on the U.S. Navy station at Pearl Harbor (7 December 1941) revealed the absence of coordination between intelligence officers—who were largely aware of the impending threat, and even of the date of the attack—and field commanders, who failed to take effective measures to thwart it.

During World War II, the process of institutionalization that had begun in the early 1900s and advanced during World War I fueled interservice rivalries. In 1940 Britain created the Special Operations Executive (SOE), which was disbanded soon after the war, while in 1942 the United States created the Office for Strategic Services (OSS), which overlapped with preexisting entities. Alongside traditional propaganda, covert operations, code breaking, and cipher, the technological dimension gained increasing importance. The development of aerophotography and aerial reconnaissance led to refinements in

imagery intelligence (IMINT), the development of which dates back to World War I. The 1950s saw the introduction by the United States of U-2 aircraft for aerial surveillance (the first flight of a U-2 over the Soviet Union occurred on 4 July 1956); reconnaissance satellites were first installed in the 1960s. In the same period, developments in electronics widened the field of application of SIGINT, gradually evolving into the three main branches of communication intelligence (COMINT), electronic intelligence (ELINT), and foreign instrumentation signals intelligence (FISINT) and their respective subcategories.

After the end of World War II and the beginning of the Cold War, both the United States and the Soviet Union greatly enhanced their positions in the SIGINT field and technological intelligence, establishing ad hoc structures to deal with specific intelligence needs. The U.S. National Security Agency (NSA) was established on 4 November 1952, to oversee the collection and analysis of foreign communications and to coordinate, direct, and perform highly specialized activities aimed at producing foreign signals

Director of Central Intelligence. U.S. President John F. Kennedy with the newly appointed Director of Central Intelligence John McCone, Washington, D.C., November 1961. Photograph by John Rous. AP IMAGES

intelligence information. The USSR entrusted its SIGINT activities to the Komitet Gosudarstvennoy Bezopasnosti (KGB), or Committee for State Security, and the Glavnoe Razvedyvatel'noe Upravlenie (GRU), or Chief Intelligence Directorate of the General Staff. American reliance on SIGINT further increased after the Vietnam War, especially between 1977 and 1981, when Admiral Stansfield Turner was director of the Central Intelligence Agency (CIA). The CIA had been established in 1947—together with the National Security Council (NSC), under the provisions of the National Security Act—to coordinate the nation's intelligence activities and correlate, evaluate, and disseminate intelligence affecting national security. It had inherited the experience of the OSS (disbanded in October 1945), the Federal Bureau of Investigation (FBI), whose Special Intelligence Service was entrusted with intelligence activity in Latin America during World War II, the National Intelligence Authority (NIA), and the Central Intelligence Group (CIG), the latter founded in January 1946, partly to replace the OSS. Turner's reliance on SIGINT and nonhuman intelligence sources led to dramatic curtailments in the number of operatives, and in a general decline of American HUMINT, sometimes blamed for international setbacks suffered by the United States in the late 1970s.

Aftermath of the Cold War. U.S. overreliance on SIGINT was partially corrected by Turner's successor, William Casey, who was CIA director from 1981 to 1987. During this period, a wave of international tensions led to a general reorganization of intelligence establishments in both the Western countries and the Communist bloc. Organizations were generally streamlined, although compartmentalization increased to limit enemy penetration. SIGINT retained its relevance, due to the importance of electronic communications, and HUMINT revived, as attested to by the host of HUMINT operatives exposed in the 1980s and 1990s both within the Western and the Soviet establishments. Moreover, in the period leading up to the collapse of the Soviet Union, the HUMINT efforts of the superpowers increased in Europe and other critical areas, such as Latin America, Afghanistan, and the Middle East, with the aim of both gathering information and carrying out covert operations.

In the 1990s, instability following the Soviet Union's demise further enhanced the role of intelligence. In this period, the abatement of the threat of U.S.–Soviet nuclear confrontation and of the ideological confrontation between East and West led to the emergence of a new and multifaceted concept of security, which charged the intelligence establishment with new tasks in the fields of counterterrorism, counterproliferation, drug trafficking, and international financial crime. New challenges arose from an ever-changing strategic environment. The widespread access to information made possible by developing communication technologies, for example, posed difficulties for SIGINT systems, dramatically increasing the amount of data to be collected and analyzed and the number of subjects to be monitored, while traditional military and security apparatuses, such as the so-called Echelon eavesdropping system, created in the 1960s to monitor the military and diplomatic communications of the Soviet Union and its allies, were criticized for being outdated and irrelevant in the new security climate. The terrorist attacks of 11 September 2001 only reinforced this criticism. The inability of the U.S. intelligence establishment to predict or prevent the attacks has been seen as proof of the limits of a system designed to cope with a well-known threat (the Soviet Union) in a relatively stable environment (that of the Cold War). Defenders of the intelligence establishment have blamed the perceived parochialism of the intelligence community in the period leading up to September 11 on a failure of political leadership to reassess intelligence structures after the Cold War.

The American security debate reflected on the entire intelligence community, as demonstrated by the adoption of the Intelligence Reform and Terrorism Prevention Act of 2004 (IRTPA), which drastically reorganized the U.S. intelligence apparatus and created the director of national intelligence (DNI), a cabinet-level position. IRTPA is aimed at promoting greater integration and cooperation among the different components of the intelligence community, a better circulation of information, and a reduction of interservice rivalries. Above all, it seeks to promote greater integration between SIGINT and HUMINT, the relevance of which was once again on the rise in the early twenty-first century given the particular nature of terrorist threats.

[*See also* Central Intelligence Agency; MI5; *and* National Security Agency.]

BIBLIOGRAPHY

Aldrich, Richard J. *The Hidden Hand: Britain, America, and Cold War Secret Intelligence.* London: John Murray, 2001. A good general history of Western intelligence during the Cold War.

Andrew, Christopher. *For the President's Eyes Only: Secret Intelligence and the American Presidency from Washington to Bush.* New York: HarperCollins, 1995.

Andrew, Christopher, and Oleg Gordievsky. *KGB: The Inside Story of Its Foreign Operations from Lenin to Gorbachev.* New York: HarperCollins, 1990. A brief history of the Soviet intelligence establishment under its different labels.

Berkowitz, Peter, ed. *The Future of American Intelligence.* Stanford, Calif.: Hoover Institution Press, Stanford University, 2005. Contains a series of articles on a broad range of topics and on the problems that come with major reorganizations of intelligence structures.

Carlisle, Rodney P., ed. *Encyclopedia of Intelligence and Counterintelligence.* 2 vols. Armonk, N.Y.: Sharpe Reference, 2006. A standard reference book, including brief accounts of notable espionage cases.

Dupuy, Trevor N., et al., eds. *International Military and Defense Encyclopedia.* 6 vols. Washington, D.C.: Brassey's, 1993. Entries in volume 3, from "Intelligence Analysis, Military" to "Intelligence, Tactical," cover the various components of intelligence.

Fischer, Benjamin B., ed. *At Cold War's End: U.S. Intelligence on the Soviet Union and Eastern Europe, 1989–1991.* Washington, D.C.: Central Intelligence Agency, Center for the Study of Intelligence, 1999. Contains a compendium of U.S. national intelligence estimates and assessments referring to the last years of the Soviet Union.

Handel, Michael I. *War, Strategy, and Intelligence.* London and Totowa, N.J.: F. Cass, 1989. A wide collection of noteworthy historical material.

Handel, Michael I., ed. *Intelligence and Military Operations.* London and Portland, Ore.: F. Cass, 1990.

Keegan, John. *Intelligence in War: Knowledge of the Enemy from Napoleon to al-Qaeda.* New York: Alfred A. Knopf, 2003. A collection of case studies from the Napoleonic Wars to the war on terror; contains useful information on the breaking of Enigma and on U.S. military intelligence during World War II.

Robertson, K. G., ed. *British and American Approaches to Intelligence.* New York: St. Martin's, 1987.

GIANLUCA PASTORI

ESTONIA. In the mid-eighteenth century the territory that became the Republic of Estonia after World War I was a western borderland of the Russian Empire, gained from Sweden by the Treaty of Nystad in 1721. Since the thirteenth century the dominant elites in the region had been Baltic Germans—nobles in the countryside and merchants in the cities. Lutheran since the Reformation, the region's religious life was also controlled by a Baltic German clergy. Ethnic Estonians, more than 90 percent of the population, were peasant serfs or formed a small urban underclass. By the second half of the nineteenth century, following serf emancipation between 1816 and 1819 and the subsequent onset of modernization, an Estonian national movement developed, focusing initially on cultural aims in view of the repressive political system of tsarist Russia. During the Russian revolution of 1905 the goal of political autonomy was raised for the first time.

An independent Estonia emerged between 1918 and 1920 when both the Russian and German empires collapsed and the Estonians showed themselves capable of demanding and implementing self-determination. A liberal democratic political system functioned for some fifteen years, but a lack of experience in participatory politics and the impact of the Great Depression led to an authoritarian regime from 1934 to 1940 under Konstantin Päts, one of the founders of Estonian independence. Socioeconomic development advanced significantly in the interwar era, strongly aided by a successful land reform that redistributed the lands of the former Baltic German estates. Particularly important was the consolidation of a modern Estonian culture in this period, including an educational system conducted in the Estonian language from elementary school through university.

The eclipse of independence came in June 1940 when Joseph Stalin forcibly annexed Estonia, cashing in on the territorial division of Eastern Europe that he and Adolf Hitler had agreed to. World War II brought occupations by both Germany and the Soviet Union and extensive loss of life. Under postwar Stalinism the human losses continued, especially through deportations, and Estonia faced the wrenching experience of the collectivization of agriculture and the destruction of traditional rural life. De-Stalinization after Stalin's death in 1953 laid the basis for important changes, including some economic decentralization, a higher standard of living, and cultural renewal, especially in the 1960s. Nevertheless, the externally imposed Soviet system never achieved legitimacy among the ethnic Estonian population, and when the opportunity arose to claim self-determination once again in the late 1980s, the Estonians took full advantage.

Along with Lithuania and Latvia (the other two Baltic states), Estonia played a major role in challenging Soviet rule under Mikhail Gorbachev; and following the failed coup by hardliners in Moscow in August 1991, the country was able to restore its independence, remarkably without violence. In the transition from Communism among former Soviet republics, Estonia served as a pacesetter by becoming the first to adopt a democratic constitution and its own currency in June 1992. Estonia sought to balance its often tense relations with the Russian Federation by integrating more closely with the West, a goal that reached fruition with membership in NATO and the European Union in 2004.

[*See also* Russia, the Russian Empire, and the Soviet Union.]

BIBLIOGRAPHY

Raun, Toivo U. *Estonia and the Estonians.* 2d ed. Stanford, Calif.: Hoover Institution Press, 2001. Comprehensive survey of Estonian history.

Taagepera, Rein. *Estonia: Return to Independence.* Boulder, Colo.: Westview Press, 1993. Focuses on the late Soviet period and the restoration of Estonian independence.

TOIVO U. RAUN

ETHICAL POLICY. "Ethical Policy" (*Ethische politiek*) was the stance of Dutch colonial policy in Indonesia after 1900. By the 1890s it appeared that colonial Indonesia was not reaping benefits from the abolition of the cultivation system in 1870. Famines in 1900 and 1902 seemed to prove that the core island of Java was sliding into poverty. The subsequent change in colonial policy had several origins. In the Netherlands the lawyer Conrad Theodor van Deventer was critical of Dutch colonial policy. In an 1899 article in *De Gids* he argued that the Netherlands had drained wealth from Java under the cultivation system and had incurred a debt of honor of 200 million guilders. He advocated a colonial policy to improve the welfare of Indonesians. In 1901 the journalist Pieter Brooshooft, the editor of *De Locomotief* in Semarang, argued that colonial Indonesia required an "Ethical Policy," which included altruistic measures by the Dutch government to further prosperity in Java.

The leader of the Dutch Anti-Revolutionaire Partij (the Calvinist Christian Democrats), Abraham Kuyper, had long advocated an end to economic exploitation of Indonesia. In 1901 he became prime minister of a coalition government that changed Dutch colonial policy. In her annual speech to the Dutch parliament, Queen Wilhelmina mentioned that it was the "moral duty" of the Netherlands to combat the causes of perpetual poverty and improve the welfare of people in colonial Indonesia.

The new policy stance became known as the Ethical Policy. A clear definition of the goals and means of the policy has never been provided. Consequently, the term meant different things to different people. Fervent supporters saw it as the Dutch "white man's burden," a selfless experiment to transform and modernize Indonesian society. As he put it in a 1908 article in *De Gids*, van Deventer foresaw the emergence of a Western-educated elite, leading a country "indebted to the Netherlands for its prosperity and higher level of civilization" and working to cement a lasting bond between the two countries. Brooshooft stressed decentralization of colonial administration and measures to spur the welfare of Indonesians. A popular slogan summarized the Ethical Policy as "irrigation, migration, and education."

Initial expectations were that financial assistance from the Netherlands would bring the expected changes. In 1904 the Dutch parliament agreed to provide loan guarantees to the colonial government, and it granted 40 million guilders for development projects. Although sizable, the grant was small compared to the sums required to foster development in Indonesia. Most policy initiatives were funded with revenues generated in Indonesia, which restricted their development potential. Still, the colonial government pursued a range of initiatives, which involved the creation of new public services. Some international observers of Dutch colonial policy praised the benevolence of the Dutch colonial regime and considered the Ethical Policy to have been without precedent in the colonial world.

Improvements of irrigation works in Java were prominent. Already in the 1890s, but particularly after 1905, weirs and primary and secondary irrigation channels were improved with modern construction methods. Schedules for water distribution and management were established in river systems. Schemes for the operation and maintenance of irrigation structures were put in place. The aims included raising rice yields, increasing double-cropping of rice fields, and reducing crop failure. Despite some failings, such as the grandiose Solo valley works in 1905, irrigation improvements sustained the growth of rice production in densely populated Java.

Migration to sparsely populated parts of Indonesia was considered a way to relieve population pressure in Java. Government-sponsored migration schemes started in 1905 with a project in Lampung (South Sumatra). Later projects were initiated in Kalimantan and Sulawesi. But between 1905 and 1930 only 37,800 people migrated under these projects, while the population in Java increased by 9 million.

Education improvement involved the establishment of village schools after 1906. School enrollments of Indonesian children increased quickly, even though the quality of their education remained inferior to that of European children and children of the indigenous elite. Still, bright Indonesian children increasingly qualified for education at European primary and secondary schools and at tertiary institutions. This nurtured the rise of a small but well-educated indigenous elite who eventually expressed growing anticolonial feelings. By the end of the 1930s the adult literacy rate was just under 19 percent.

Other services were established. For example, an agricultural extension service propagated improved crops, superior farming methods, and the use of fertilizers. The Public Health Service spread information about common diseases and basic personal hygiene. A small-scale credit service reduced dependence for credit on usurers and crop forestallers in an effort to combat indebtedness and usury, establishing a system of village and district banks. Another service supported the formation of cooperatives.

Decentralization of government and greater political participation of Indonesians in political processes were other aspects of the Ethical Policy, achieved through municipal and regency councils and, in 1918, a surrogate national parliament (the Volksraad), all with participation of Indonesians. In the late 1920s three provinces with a degree of administrative autonomy were established in Java.

In the 1920s the phrase "Ethical Policy" became associated with budding Indonesian nationalism that assumed radical tendencies, and the term fell into disuse. Despite the grandiose visions that some entertained and the good intentions and genuine candor of colonial administrators, the impact of the Ethical Policy on Indonesian prosperity was modest at best. A major reason was that budget limitations made it difficult to expect a large impact. However, the welfare services were all reestablished after Indonesia's independence in 1949 and formed the basis for later efforts to improve prosperity through such measures as education, health care, agricultural extension, and popular credit.

[*See also* Cultivation System; Empire and Imperialism, *subentry* The Dutch Colonial Empire; *and* Indonesia.]

BIBLIOGRAPHY

Cribb, Robert. "Development Policy in the Early Twentieth Century." In *Development and Social Welfare: Indonesia's Experiences under the New Order*, edited by Jan-Paul Dirkse, Frans Hüsken, and Mario Rutton, pp. 225–245. Leiden, The Netherlands: KITLV Press, 1993.

Dick, Howard, Vincent J. H. Houben, J. Thomas Lindblad, and Thee Kian Wie. *The Emergence of a National Economy: An Economic History of Indonesia, 1800–2000.* Honolulu: University of Hawai'i Press, 2002. See especially pp. 117–121 and 146–148.

Locher-Scholten, Elsbeth. *Ethiek in fragmenten: Vijf studies over koloniaal denken en doen van Nederlanders in de Indonesische Archipel 1877–1942.* Utrecht, Netherlands: HES, 1981.

Miert, Hans van. *Bevlogenheid en Onvermogen: Mr. J. H. Abendanon (1852–1925) en de Ethische Richting in het Nederlandse Kolonialisme.* Leiden, The Netherlands: KITLV Press, 1991.

Van der Eng, Pierre. *Agricultural Growth in Indonesia: Productivity Change and Policy Impact since 1880.* New York: St. Martin's Press, 1993. See especially chapter 3.

PIERRE VAN DER ENG

ETHIOPIA. Ethiopia entered the modern world in political decline, in a period of decentralization known as the Era of the Princes. Regionally based noblemen competed for autonomy vis-à-vis one another and for control of the vestigial national institutions. This period persisted until 1855 and the appearance of Téwodros II (1818–1868; r. 1855–1868), who, with his successors Yohännes IV (c. 1831–1889; r. 1871–1889) and Menilek II (1844–1913; r. 1889–1913), struggled to recreate monarchical institutions and to rebuff imperial threats, first

from Egypt, then from the Italians. Victory over the Italians at Adwa in 1898 ensured the country's political independence, but under conditions of dominance by Britain, France, and Italy, whose colonial territories now surrounded it.

From 1900 onward, Ethiopia struggled against European imperialism and to incorporate modernity. The years—punctuated by Italian occupation from 1935 to 1941—were dominated by Ras (Duke) Täfari Mäkonnen (1892–1975), first as heir apparent (from 1917) and then, from 1930, as Emperor Haile Selassie I. His title, *negusä nägäst* (king of kings), dated to the early centuries of the Christian Era. Haile Selassie's rule was an unresolved tussle between modernization and autocracy. The emperor's overthrow in 1974 ushered in the contemporary period, shaped by revolutionary elites. Two subperiods were marked by the proclamation in 1987 of the People's Republic of Ethiopia (overthrown in 1991) and in 1995 of the Federal Republic of Ethiopia, whose constituent units were ethnically defined.

The historical succession of states in Ethiopia was based on a plateau the controlling center of which was usually located around 2,000 meters above sea level. Its social basis was a plow-cultivating peasantry. Starting more than three millennia ago, Ethiopian farmers adapted the Middle East staples of wheat, barley, and pulses and crops of African origins, some of their own domestication. Ethiopia's farming communities have struggled to sustain innovation and environmental adaptation and to ward off the demands of ruling warriors and priests. In the fourth century Ethiopia's rulers adopted Alexandrian Christianity, and by the end of the millennium Christianity was deeply embedded in highland farming communities. The political ideology, which Ethiopia's modern monarchs struggled to revive, had emerged in 1270 with a new dynasty, claiming descent from the biblical Solomon and Sheba and the political legacy of the classical empire of Aksum. Though Solomonic rule rested on plow agriculture, Orthodox Christianity, and Semitic languages, its subjects and neighbors included Muslims and adherents of ancestral religions, pastoralists, and speakers of Kushitic languages. In the late nineteenth century, Ethiopia expanded to embrace this diversity. While a majority of its population remained Orthodox Christians and spoke Semitic languages, the country now included many Muslims. Expansion was achieved primarily by conquest, followed by social subjugation and then by the alienation of agricultural land in favor of immigrants from the kingdom's heartland. The country's connection to the global economy rested on the export of skins and hides and coffee. Through the creation of a modern system of education from the 1940s onward, Haile Selassie attempted to assimilate the country's diverse peoples to Orthodox culture and the Amharic language. This policy, which never had resources adequate to its goal, reinforced cultural resentments created by conquest and land alienation. The bitterness of subjugation expressed itself in uprisings at the time of the Italian invasion of 1935 and 1936. However, when the monarchy was finally overthrown, it was by forces from the center, not the periphery.

In 1974 urban discontent spurred by inflation caused by drought and rising international oil prices led to the overthrow of the monarchy and domination by political elites, who used Marxist-Leninist language to frame competing discontents, some of them originating in the class structures of the now defunct empire, others in the country's ethnic diversity. Power at the center was challenged most notably by Eritreans, Tegreans, Somali, and Oromo. In the 1950s Ethiopia had sought unsuccessfully to absorb Eritrea, created as an Italian colony in 1890. Eritrean armed resistance was assisted by the struggle for regional autonomy within Ethiopia in neighboring Tegray province. Irredentism in the Somali Republic (independent in 1960) increased the discontent of Ethiopia's Somali subjects and led to wars in 1964 and 1977. Together the Eritrean and Tegray movements overthrew Ethiopia's first revolutionary government in 1991 and established Eritrea's independence in 1993. Somalia, defeated in 1978 and torn by internal strife, imploded. Ethiopia, as of 1995 an ethnic federation, faced the continual decline of its agricultural sector and the failure of its Tegrayan rulers adequately to capture the allegiance of the country's two-largest ethnic groups, the Amhara and the Oromo—the latter much influenced by secessionist goals constituting perhaps the country's gravest continuing political challenge.

[*See also* Africa, *subentry* East Africa; *and* Eritrea.]

BIBLIOGRAPHY

Tareke, Gebru. *Ethiopia, Power, and Protest: Peasant Revolts in the Twentieth Century*. Cambridge, U.K.: Cambridge University Press, 1991. One of the few studies based on Ethiopian government archives, it provides important insights into social relations and social conflict in Ethiopia from the 1940s through the 1960s.

Tiruneh, Andargachew. *The Ethiopian Revolution 1974–1987: A Transformation from an Aristocratic to a Totalitarian Autocracy*. Cambridge, U.K.: Cambridge University Press, 1993. The last of a succession of books analyzing the Ethiopian revolution, it ably summarizes the earlier literature and provides its own insights, which rest on a careful reading of legal documents.

Zewde, Bahru. *A History of Modern Ethiopia 1855–1991*. 2nd ed. Oxford: James Currey, 2001. The most authoritative survey of its subject, it rests on a wide reading of both the primary and secondary sources (not least of which are theses and dissertations by students at Addis Ababa University) and makes excellent use of contemporary photographs.

DONALD CRUMMEY

ETHNIC CLEANSING AND DEPORTATION.

Ethnic cleansing is the practice of deliberate and systematic displacement or removal of an identifiable group from a given geographic area. Ethnic cleansing is usually used to describe state or quasi-state policies of targeting oppositional populations, most often civilian, during war or civil conflict. There is no general agreement on the definition of the term "ethnicity," and the word is generally used to signify a collection of characteristics that human populations share, usually cultural or behavioral, and that can be used to classify groups. The concept is often understood as a moniker of differentiation within larger taxonomies or a subclassification of larger meta groupings. Ethnicity is typically conceptualized in opposition to broader and commonly understood interhuman distinctions such as race, gender, and perhaps sexual orientation. The primary distinguishing elements of ethnicity are religion, language, territorial location, and, most significantly, culture. In many ways the term "ethnicity" was a replacement for problematic and definitionally inconsistent terms such as race, class, or nationality.

Although the use of ethnicity as a category or differentiation is necessary for ethnic cleansing, other terms were used in the past. Ethnicity implies an intergroup differentiation as opposed to physiognomic concepts such as race. In other words, ethnicities could be understood to be subgroupings of races. Despite the clear evidence provided by social scientists about the social construction of both race and ethnicity, the terms are still a part of popular discourse. In many ways ethnicity was used to describe the cultural or linguistic differences between members of broad racial categories. This complicates the use of the term "ethnic cleansing," but also this paradox is the very reason the term was brought into use. Thus the plantation policies of Queen Elizabeth I of England would have been phrased as Scottish and English "races" displacing the Irish "race" in the eighteenth and nineteenth centuries; however, they are usually discussed in late twentieth- and early twenty-first century terms as ethnic or political conflicts. The differences between Irish and English were largely cultural and religious and not necessarily racial in the nineteenth-century biological sense of the word.

Furthermore, this then makes instances of displacement, deportation, and organized population transfers not ethnic cleansing in the strict sense of the term. The removal of Native Americans to reservations and western areas in the early nineteenth century involved threat and terror, as well as organized execution, but involved a racial rather than ethnic classification. The ancient Assyrian policy of moving whole populations away from their traditional homelands after conquest would be a form of ethnic cleansing for those Semitic tribes the Assyrians conquered. The Sumerian, Babylonian, Chaldean, Amorite, and other tribes differed from the Assyrians only in some custom and speech characteristics; otherwise they were indistinguishable from the armies that deported them to far-flung ends of the Assyrian Empire.

Significant instances of racial or national deportations and group cleansings include the Haitian post-revolution expulsion from and forbidding of return to Haiti for Creole or European whites. The expulsion of South Asians from Uganda in the late 1970s and the early-twenty-first-century expulsion of Bantu Africans from the Darfur region of Sudan are also instances of racial deportations. Australian policies of expulsion and deportation of Aboriginal tribes to remote locations in the Australian outback is also a case of racial deportation.

Systematic Ethnic Cleansing. Ethnic cleansing has developed from the banishment and exile of groups in the Greek and Roman worlds to enormous and spectacularly violent mass expulsions in the nineteenth and twentieth centuries. The sowing of salt into the sand of Carthage by Roman armies and the expulsion and enslavement of the Carthaginian population was an act of ethnic cleansing, but the scale would increase dramatically over the course of the next sixteen centuries. Massive deportation and terror-induced flight occurred after the *Reconquista* in Spain in the fifteenth century as hundreds of thousands of Muslim and Jewish Iberians were expelled from Spain and forbidden to return. This was simply one example of many of state-sponsored expulsion of Jews from the Roman period until the end of World War II.

The eighteenth-century expulsion of the Acadian population of the Canadian Maritimes by the British government was an act of ethnic cleansing as nearly all Acadians were ejected whether they claimed loyalty to the British Crown or not. In the twentieth century there would be massive population transfers and governmental policies of establishing ethnically "pure" areas. The Armenian and Pontian Greek

populations of the Ottoman Empire were largely forcibly removed from their homelands. Many policies of the Ottoman government during World War I have been characterized as genocidal. There were massive population exchanges between the Ottoman Empire, Greece, Bulgaria, and Serbia after the Balkan Wars (1912–1913). There were nearly 2 million people who were exchanged between Turkey and Greece in 1922–1923.

World War II saw enormous acts of ethnic cleansing and deportations, most infamous of which is the Nazi genocide. The Soviet Union forcibly deported millions of its citizens in internal displacements. Millions of Jews, Gypsies, and Slavs were ethnically cleansed from entire regions of eastern Europe, and evidence of their very existence was removed by the German occupation governments. Similar population policies were enforced in the Independent State of Croatia, Macedonia, and Slovenia. After the war the second largest act of ethnic cleansing occurred when as many as 14 million ethnic Germans were expelled from eastern Europe. This scale would only be surpassed by the massive population exchanges between India and Pakistan in 1947.

Other acts of ethnic cleansing include the expulsion from Kosovo, Macedonia, and southern Serbia of hundreds of thousands of Serbs during the Ottoman-Austrian wars of the late seventeenth century. Expulsion of Circassians and other Caucasian tribes to the Ottoman lands by the Russian Imperial armies occurred throughout the nineteenth century. Outside of Europe the apartheid policy of the South African government in the second half of the twentieth century involved wholesale population deportations, although some of this was not ethnic but racial cleansing. After the formation of the state of Israel hundreds of thousands of Jews were driven from Arab states, and the Nakba or Palestinian displacements created a several-hundred-thousand-person refugee population throughout the Middle East. In 1994 ethnic cleansing was practiced by Tutsi and Hutu armies in the states of Rwanda, Burundi, and Congo in Central Africa.

Temporary or Partial Ethnic Cleansing. The goal of ethnic cleansing can be temporary degradation of an enemy population's ability to support or sustain combat actions. This usually takes the form of moving a population out of a war zone so that the forces of the ethnic cleansing have secure rear areas and limit the ability of enemy forces to enlist or ally with local sympathizers or rebel populations. This form of ethnic cleansing is usually small in scale in that it is necessarily temporary, although return of the populations removed might be quite a long time in the future. The removal of ethnic Chechen, Volga

German, and Crimean Tatar groups from the southern Soviet Union to Central Asia during World War II or the removal of Hmong and Montagnard tribal groups from their villages to relocation areas in government-defended regions during the Vietnam War are examples of temporary ethnic cleansing.

Limited or partial ethnic cleansing is the policy of expulsion of an identifiable group from a given area when the organization conducting the expulsion does not have the sufficient means to conclude the ethnic cleansing. Often this type of ethnic cleansing will be targeted to a demographic within the group to be ethnically cleansed. Usually the intelligentsia, political, and religious leaders and military-age men are singled out for expulsion. This is usually accomplished by threat, terror, intimidation, sexual and physical humiliation, theft, deportation, arson, and murder. Limited ethnic cleansing is designed to weaken and demoralize an enemy population so that the organization applying the expulsion pressures can exercise current and future hegemony. The people left are powerless to resist domination and thus are more easily cowed into a submissive position, often as restricted or second-class citizens. Limited ethnic cleansing was conducted in Chechnya, Darfur, the Independent State of Croatia during World War II, Macedonia after the Balkan Wars, and the Palestinian Territories.

Genocide and the "Pure" State. The third and most severe form of ethnic cleansing is when a group or entity attempts to create an ethnically "pure" state. The attempt to completely remove a population through deportation or to cause refugees to flee a given area through organized terror is how most contemporary ethnic cleansing is understood. Hence the term is most often applied when there is evidence of a systematic attempt to remove a population using the techniques described above and taking steps to bar or make difficult a return to the ethnic status quo ante. The destruction of religious or cultural artifacts or monikers of identification designed to both remove the traces of the deported culture and to reorient the local social fabric to foster homogeneity combined with the actual expulsion are genocide. Thus the elements of systematic use of terror, state or organized terror and deportation, total or wholesale attempts to remove an entire group based on their shared ethnic characteristics, and the deliberate attempt to restrict return are defining features of twenty-first-century ethnic cleansing. Populations expelled from their homelands and who settle elsewhere but who retain links with kindred expelled groups are collectively known as diasporas.

Genocide and Ethnic Cleansing. The forced deportation of civilian populations during wartime is covered

Ethnic Cleasing in Croatia. A unit of Ustashe militia point their rifles at a group of bodies lying at their feet, 1940. UNITED STATES HOLOCAUST MEMORIAL MUSEUM

under international law and the treaty obligations of the participants in the various Geneva Conventions and their protocols. Article 49 of the Geneva Convention of 1949 specifically forbids the forcible transfers and deportations of protected persons from an occupied territory to another territory. Other provisions govern internal or civil conflict, and the *jus cogens* or international customary law has a controlling authority in cases of ethnic cleansing brought before national or international courts. The 1977 protocols added to the 1949 Geneva Convention specifically address crimes of internal conflicts within states.

A great deal of controversy and debate has been generated around the use of the terms "ethnic cleansing" and "genocide." Many aspects of ethnic cleansing fit criteria for characteristics of genocide. There are arguments that the popular use of the term "ethnic cleansing," which entered common usage in the early 1990s specifically in relation to the Yugoslav wars of succession, was a deliberate attempt to find an alternate term to the word "genocide." In simplistic terms most historical acts of ethnic cleansing have been genocidal, that is, attempting to destroy in whole or in part an identifiable group, but some have not. Thus limited ethnic cleansing has elements of genocide, but the attempts to create an ethnically "pure" area have been clear cases of genocide. While temporary, ethnic cleansing has often not been genocidal. For these reasons genocide and ethnic cleansing are not synonyms despite their close association and shared characteristics.

If genocide is defined and established, then certain legal obligations are actuated by both state and nonstate actors. Thus the violence in the Balkans was labeled ethnic cleansing rather than genocide to limit liability by the various European super entities and the United Nations. The term was originally a local Balkan term, *etnčiko čišćenje.* This term was used in the context of population transfers and deportations in the Balkans during World War II and was most often used in reportage from the war in Bosnia from 1992 to 1996. Media covering the civil strife in the former Yugoslavia began using the term because it best described both the physical actions on the ground and addressed the complex and intricate classifications of populations of the area who appeared to outside observers as being physically indistinguishable from each other. It should be noted that many academics try to avoid the use of the term because of the negative connotation associated with the "cleansing" of people. The construction implies an unhygienic or biologically metaphoric aspect to human beings that implies both purity and impurity. However, the term is still often used in media and popular discourse.

[*See also* Diasporas; Ethnic Conflict; Genocide; *and* Refugees and Displaced Peoples, *subentry* Overview.]

BIBLIOGRAPHY

Bell-Fialkoff, Andrew. *Ethnic Cleansing.* New York: St. Martin's Press, 1996.
Carmichael, C. *Ethnic Cleansing in the Balkans.* London: Routledge, 2002.
Mann, Michael. *The Dark Side of Democracy: Explaining Ethnic Cleansing.* New York: Cambridge University Press, 2005.
McCarthy, Justin. *Death and Exile: The Ethnic Cleansing of Ottoman Muslims, 1821–1922.* Princeton, N.J: Darwin Press, 1995.
Kaufman, Stuart. *Modern Hatreds: The Symbolic Politics of Ethnic War.* Ithaca, N.Y.: Cornell University Press, 2001.
Lieberman, Benjamin. *Terrible Fate: Ethnic Cleansing in the Making of Modern Europe.* Chicago: Ivan R. Dee, 2006.
Naimark, Norman. *Fires of Hatred: Ethnic Cleansing in Twentieth-Century Europe.* Cambridge, Mass.: Harvard University Press, 2001.
Pohl, Otto J. *Ethnic Cleansing in the U.S.S.R, 1937–1949.* Westport, Conn.: Greenwood Press, 1999.

M I C H A E L J . H A L L I D A Y

ETHNIC CONFLICT [*This entry includes two subentries, an overview and a discussion of ethnic conflict in Southeast Asia. See also* Ethnic Cleansing and Deportation; Genocide; *and* Refugees and Displaced Peoples.]

Overview

Ethnic conflict is the competition, hostility, enmity, or direct warfare between two or more groups of human populations. There is no general agreement on the definition of ethnicity, and the term is generally used to signify a collection of characteristics that human populations share, usually cultural or behavioral, which can be used to classify groups. The concept is often understood as a moniker of differentiation within larger taxonomies or a subclassification of larger meta groupings. Ethnicity is typically conceptualized in opposition to broader and commonly understood interhuman distinctions such as race, gender, and perhaps sexual orientation. The primary distinguishing elements of ethnicity are religion, language, territorial location, and most significantly, culture.

Ethnic conflict occurs when populations or portions of populations are mobilized to interact with oppositional ethnic groups in a hostile manner in order to secure political, social, cultural, or religious hegemony or primacy. The emnity between ethnic groups is usually mutual, though it not necessarily need be so. Ethnic conflict may be a dichotomal relationship or multivalent. In multivalent ethnic conflicts ethnic groups or factions may join in coalition with other groups against a prominent ethnic group. Although ethnicity and ethnic groupings may be seemingly unchanging, the fluid nature of the elements of ethnicity and human identities often makes ethnic labels difficult to assign, variable over time, and situational.

Primordialist, Constructivist, and Instrumentalist Schools. Ethnic conflict is a historically recent concept. Although notions of exclusivity of membership to a group based on language and culture existed in the ancient and premodern world, the idea of contemporary ethnicity has generally been associated with the rise of the modern nation-state. Some contemporary human populations are tribal in nature, and there are many complicated customs regarding exogamy and group differentiation. The notion of tribe and the kinship networks associated with tribalism were probably how most human populations conceptualized a binary opposition of self and other. These arguments about long-standing ethnicities based on tradition and historical memory are broadly known as the primordialist school. This view of ethnicity frequently examines themes of ethnogenesis, folk tradition, and genealogies.

However, throughout the twentieth century social scientists gave a great deal of weight to theories of social construction of ethnicity. This theory indicated that social structures and institutions gave shape to the elements of ethnicity and developed this framework of classification in response to and in relationship with the eighteenth- and nineteenth-century phenomenon of the Industrial Revolution, the European Enlightenment, and the growth of capitalism. These theories are generally known as the constructivist school. In this analysis of ethnicity, groups are made or formed by social institutions and amalgamated by a constructed history, culture, or shared experiences.

Some social scientists have examined ethnic conflict as a modified form of constructivism know as instrumentalism, which is where very conscious political choices are made to forge constituencies out of already formed or to-be-formed ethnic groups. This analysis was actively put forward to challenge the argument that ethnicity is an organic phenomenon. Instrumentalists charted the historical changes in European thinking of jus sanguinis, or "law of blood," and jus soli, or "law of state." The civic national identity of the United States, for example, proved a problem for theorists of primordialism, Marxist theorists of class consciousness, and even in the notion of social construction, as Daniel Moynihan and Nathan Glazer have argued relating to the resilience of ethnic politics in America. In the last

Ethnic Conflict. Ethnic Albanian refugees carry elderly relatives from the village of Istinic, in the Serbian province of Kosovo, September 1998. Photograph by Marco Di Lauro. AP IMAGES

few decades most works draw from all three theoretical compositions.

Because resources and populations are involved, all ethnic conflicts are political. In other words, ethnic conflict is not simply a natural or predetermined response of defined groups in conflict. Most ethnic conflict has a specific relationship to political representation, economic development, and cultural or religious rights in geographically defined nation-states. Most ethnic conflict is a question of majority-minority tension vis-à-vis political power. Ethnic conflict is complicated when multiple ethnicities are involved or when ethnic conflicts spill over internationally recognized interstate borders.

Phases of Ethnic Conflict. Ethnic conflict in the modern sense has developed through at least five distinct phases. The period from the beginning of the French Revolution through the revolutions of 1848 could be described as the foundational period of the development of nationalism. The romanticist movements in the arts and literature, and the establishment of codified folk traditions, as well as the beginnings of language standardization, coincide with this time frame. Significant examples of ethnic conflict in this era were the attempts of the Hungarian revolutionaries of 1848 to form their own state, separate from the Habsburg monarchy, and the revolts of Serbian and Greek populations against the Ottoman Empire.

In the second half of the nineteenth century various European peoples agitated against the supranational empires of the time for their own ethnically and geographically defined states. Outside of Europe people in African and Asian areas were engaged in internal ethnically driven conflicts with neighboring peoples and reacted to the increasing European and Western imperialism of the age. European colonial powers utilized and reified ethnic divisions within non-Western areas to facilitate hegemony over these lands. At the same time European thinkers were formulating other than ethnically defined criteria for identity, such as class and biology. The twin competing philosophies that interacted with ethnicity for how states and peoples would define themselves were Marxist socialism and social Darwinism. This era would culminate with World War I, which was largely driven by imperial and nationalistic rivalries.

The period from 1918 until World War II was a crucial period in understanding the role of ethnicity and state. After World War I the map of Europe was redrawn to accommodate "small peoples," and the right of self-determination of ethnically defined populations entered into the lexicon of international law. Colonies outside of Europe would internalize these restructuring changes and the new international emphasis on ethnicity and state versus province and empire. For non-European peoples the ethnic conflict would take the form of decolonialization movements and later post-colonization ethnic conflicts for indigenous control of resources.

The post–World War II international system was fundamentally changed by the enshrinement in the UN documents of the freedom of groups based on cultural affinity or ethnicity to have representation and protections from dominant groups in political power. The dynamics of the Cold War and the massive decolonialization movements further shaped the ethnic conflict of the mid-twentieth century. During this period most ethnic conflicts would be filtered through the Soviet and American superpower paradigms. Ethnic conflicts began to be both mobilized and fought with ideological underpinnings, and ethnic groups used the Cold War alliances to fund and arm their own struggles, either as proxies of communist or capitalist states or as regional actors.

By the end of the Cold War the binds that tied many former areas together in regional or federated nation-states began to unwind due to the disengagement of Cold War sponsors. This period saw ethnic conflict in former socialist areas like the former Yugoslavia, Transnistria, Georgia, Azerbaijan, Armenia, Chechnya, Ethiopia, Somalia, Eritrea, and Afghanistan. Numerous other conflicts occurred in former colonial territories in Africa and Asia. Often fueled by ethnic diasporas in other countries, the ethnic conflicts were nearly always territorial disputes, usually armed groups focused on secession from a larger state or ethnic groups advocating irredentism to establish a territorial link with them and their kindred groups across international borders. The battle for an ethnic homeland was and is the primary long-term goal of most armed groups involved in ethnic conflict.

When ethnic conflict is unconstrained by multinational controls or domestic pluralism that mediates ethnic mobilization, severe ethnic conflict may develop. In some cases ethnic nationalism is so acute that attempts are made to permanently diminish or destroy other ethnic groups' abilities to continue the conflict or exist at all. One mechanism that has been resorted to in addressing long-standing ethnic conflict is ethnic cleansing. The forcible removal or expulsion of opposing ethnic groups from a given territory, based on the characteristics of an ethnic group that differentiates them as outsiders, is ethnic cleansing. An attempt to exterminate such a group is genocide, and both methods were common facets of ethnic conflict from the late 1980s until the present time.

Addressing Ethnic Conflict. International attempts to address ethnic conflict include the founding of the United Nations, international war crimes tribunals, and truth and reconciliation commissions. Political scientists have explained possible solutions for ethnic conflict as assimilation, indigenization, or acculturation of one or more ethnic groups to blur the lines of differentiation. Other methods include accommodating minority ethnicities, as in the case of the Quebeçois in Canada, border alterations, third-party arbitration, cantonization, and consociationalization or ethnic quotas for participation in government. Regional autonomy is also a method of ethnic conflict reduction. Other methods of ethnic conflict resolutions include ethnic cleansing and genocide, ethnic suicide, partition and secession, and forced population transfers outside of large-scale ethnic violence, as was conducted between Greece and Turkey in the early 1920s.

[*See also* Ethnic Cleansing and Deportation; Genocide; *and* Refugees and Displaced Peoples.]

BIBLIOGRAPHY

Coakley, John. "The Resolution of Ethnic Conflict: Towards a Typography." *International Political Science Review* 13 (1992), no. 4: 343–358.

Cornell, Stephen, and Douglas Hartmann. *Ethnicity and Race: Making Identities in a Changing World.* Thousand Oaks, Calif.: Pine Forge Press. 2007.

Horowitz, Donald. *Ethnic Groups in Conflict.* Berkeley, Calif.: University of California Press, 1985.

McGarry, John, and Brendan O'Leary, eds. *The Politics of Ethnic Conflict Regulations: Case Studies of Protracted Ethnic Conflicts.* London: Routledge, 1993.

Moynihan, Daniel, and Nathan Glazer. *Beyond the Melting Pot.* Cambridge, Mass.: M.I.T. Press, 1970.

Roshwald, Aviel. *The Endurance of Nationalism: Ancient Roots and Modern Dilemmas.* Cambridge, U.K.: Cambridge University Press, 2006.

Smith, Anthony. *Nationalism: Theory, Ideology, History.* Cambridge, U.K.: Cambridge University Press, 2001.

Toft, Monica Duffy. *The Geography of Ethnic Violence: Identity, Interests, and the Indivisibility of Territory.* Princeton, N.J.: Princeton University Press, 2003.

MICHAEL J. HALLIDAY

Southeast Asia

Ethnic conflict in Southeast Asia today has its causes in the creation of artificial geographical boundaries and the privileging of certain ethnic groups during the colonial era.

The eleven nation-states that make up Southeast Asia (Brunei, Burma, Cambodia, Laos, Indonesia, Malaysia, the Philippines, Singapore, East Timor, Thailand, and Vietnam) have each experienced ethnic conflict since colonial times. This is because colonial powers disregarded local ideas of sovereignty and imposed arbitrary geographical boundaries that did not take into consideration local power- and resource-sharing arrangements, thus forcing peoples of diverse ethnicities into a constructed "nation" in which the majority ethnic group was privileged. This is also the case in Thailand, which, although never colonized, assimilated Western concepts of sovereignty and government. Although many ethnic minority groups were co-opted into nationalist movements and fought against European hegemony, once independence had been secured they were once again marginalized by the state apparatus, usually dominated by the majority ethnic group. This has led to constant conflict between ethnic minorities and the state (vertical conflict) or between minority groups themselves (horizontal conflict) throughout the modern era. As more and more groups agitate for self-determination and an autonomous existence, the Western ideal of sovereignty is undermined and global stability threatened.

Indonesia and Burma. Indonesia and Burma (Myanmar) have the greatest ethnic diversity in the region and, in direct correlation, the highest incidence of ethnic conflict. In Burma, the ethnic majority is Bamar (Burman), comprising some 66.9 percent of the total population in 2003. Other significant ethnic groups include the Shan (10.5 percent), Karen or Kayin (6.2 percent), and Rakhine (4.2 percent). Mon and Chin make up around 2 percent, and over 5 percent is made up of other ethnic minority groups, including Indians, descendants of British intracolony migration policies. Ethnic conflict among the Burman, Shan, Mon, and Rakhine can be traced back as far as the eleventh century when each established autonomous kingdoms and were subjugated by one of the others time and time again. The British encountered these peoples in the eighteenth century at a time when Burman hegemony was paramount and other ethnic groups were governing themselves but acknowledged the suzerainty of the Burman king, to whom they paid a nominal tribute. Certain ethnic minority groups, particularly the Karen, fought alongside the British against the Burmans in the three Anglo-Burmese wars (1823–1826, 1852–1853, and 1885–1886). When the British subjugated the Burman kingdom in 1885, they inherited the arrangement between the state and the ethnic minorities at the periphery. They retained the nonintegrated government model by separating the former Burman kingdom, now called "Burma," from the outlying areas populated by non-Burman ethnicities, which they called "Scheduled Areas," for purposes of administration.

The many ethnicities within Burma and the Scheduled Areas never received any opportunity to conceive of themselves as inhabitants of one nation, save for the Burmans, who were incorporated into the British civil service within Burma. Further adding to the ethnic confusion, the British encouraged non-Anglo citizens from their other dominions to migrate to Burma. The Burmans resented these immigrants because they were primarily Indians, who were privileged within the colonial framework. As Burman nationalism grew, the British sought support from ethnic minority groups who opposed Burman superiority and preferred British to Burman hegemony. Yet it was the Burman nationalists who fought against the Japanese in World War II and successfully routed British attempts to reinstate colonialism in the years immediately thereafter. Thus the freedom of all peoples within the geographic area of "Burma" had been gained by the Burmans. Independence had been delivered by the Burmans, and they believed themselves entitled to rule as a result. Although certain ethnic minorities, such as the Shan and Karen, had been promised autonomous states by the British, these were not fulfilled by the government of independent Burma, realized in 1948, nor by any subsequent government. Insurrection followed hot on the heels of "Burmese" independence and has continued into the twenty-first century.

Like Burma's, Indonesia's ethnic composition is diverse. The 2000 census states that the majority ethnic group is Javanese (40.6 percent), followed by Sundanese (15 percent), Madurese (3.3 percent), Minangkabau (2.7 percent), Betawi (2.4 percent), Bugis (2.4 percent), Banten (2 percent), and Banjar (1.7 percent). Nearly 30 percent of the population, however, is made up of ethnic groups that are themselves below 1 percent. Indonesia has been subject to both vertical and horizontal forms of conflict. Following independence in 1945 (although the Dutch did not recognize this until 1949) the Indonesian government declared a policy of "unity in diversity" in which all ethnicities and religions encompassed by the geographical boundaries of Indonesia were welcomed and equality reigned. But this was far from the truth. Historical hatreds between certain peoples, in some cases present for hundreds of years, endured. The Indonesian government attempted to employ a strategy of divide and conquer by implementing a scheme in which families from one area would be funded to start afresh on the other side of the nation—thus, it was hoped, diluting ethnic identity and replacing it with a common identity based on nationalism. It was also anticipated that intranational immigration would discourage local power frameworks in favor of the state mechanism. This was not to be.

Conflict in Kalimantan has taken place between the Dayaks and Madurese (1997 and 2001) and between native Malays and Madurese (1999) wherein one ethnic group has perceived the other as usurping resources or prominence traditionally theirs. Some horizontal conflicts in Indonesia have had a religious basis—for example, in Ambon, Maluku, where Christian Ambonese clashed with Muslim migrants from Sulawesi (Bugis and Makassarese), and in Poso, Central Sulawesi, between Pamona (Protestants) and Bugis (Muslims)—yet many ethnic groups define themselves on a variety of characteristics excluding religious persuasion. This is most evident in the vertical ethnic conflict in Indonesia wherein certain ethnic groups seek self-determination and autonomy from the state. In 2007, the Acehnese and Papuan minorities fell into this category. Semiautonomous when part of the Dutch East Indies, the leaders of these and many other small polities were co-opted into nationalist movements led by the Javanese—who, like the Burmans, received the most benefit from educational policies implemented by the colonial power—and fought against the Japanese during World War II. Later, many joined the struggle for independence, believing that their peoples would receive equal representation in a future federation or outright independence. Continued oppression by and privileging of other ethnic groups (mainly Javanese), however, and co-opting of local resources in state interests has ensured persistent conflict. Only East Timor (now Timor-Leste) has been successful in waging war against the Indonesian state in terms of vertical conflict.

Vietnam. A little-known ethnic conflict in Southeast Asia, the persecution of the Montagnards (non-Kinh peoples of the Central Highlands in Vietnam, including Jarai, Bahnar, Ede or Rhadé, Mnong, Koho, and Stieng), is nonetheless an illustration of the impact that globalization is having on ethnic minorities. The Kinh constituted 86 percent of the total Vietnamese population (approximately 66 million people) in 1999. Relations between the highland peoples of the Central Highlands and the state in Vietnam—under successive regimes—have been problematic for centuries. The Kinh historically referred to the highlanders as *Moï*, loosely translated as "savage" but with underlying connotations of servility due to the tradition of enslaving the peoples of the Central Highlands. They remained largely autonomous until the imposition of colonial rule in the second half of the nineteenth century. After relying on a military presence to maintain a limited control of the area, the French began mooting the idea of an autonomous Montagnard state in 1935.

It was first recognized as a separate area for administrative purposes in 1939, but the Japanese presence from 1941 prevented the realization of this objective until 1950, when the Pays Montagnard du Sud-Indochinois (PMSI) came into being, defended by a special division of multiethnic Montagnard soldiers. This fostered a sense of common identity among the highlanders and provided a base for future combined action. The creation of the PMSI was the fulfilment of a promise made to the peoples of the Central Highlands in 1946, when the French enlisted the assistance of the Montagnards against the Vietminh. After 1954, however, the PMSI was reintegrated into the Vietnamese nation-state despite Montagnard resistance, the newly appointed prime minister Ngo Dinh Diem perceiving ethnic diversity as an impediment to national integration. Ongoing Montagnard resentment toward forcible attempts at assimilation led to the creation of several resistance movements, most notably the Front Unifié de Lutte des Races Opprimées (United Front for the Struggle of the Oppressed Races, or FULRO) in the early 1960s, which received support from dissidents within Cambodia and, in 1965, from the Cambodian government itself. This group fought against both North and South Vietnam between 1958 and 1975. An estimated two hundred thousand Montagnards died during the Vietnam War.

Since reunification in 1975, the Vietnamese state apparatus has looked on the highland groups with suspicion because of their past divided loyalties. Suspected leaders of antistate movements (extant before and after reunification) have been imprisoned or executed or have "disappeared." Practitioners of "nonsanctioned religions" (including a form of Christianity subscribed to by many Montagnards) were arrested and their congregations suppressed. Adoption of a policy of highland "development" has resulted in large numbers of Kinh settlers migrating to the Central Highlands, usurping access to Montagnard ancestral lands and limiting available resources. The state has also confiscated land belonging to Montagnards in order to fulfil quotas for coffee and rubber production. These state plantations have been primarily staffed by ethnic Kinh. In February 2001, Montagnards initiated a series of protests against the state. Reasons for the protests have included general persecution on religious and political grounds, a secret state agenda of the eradication of Montagnard culture manifested in a refusal of the state to allow education in indigenous languages, confiscation of Montagnard ancestral lands, the massive influx of Kinh to the Central Highlands since 1975, and the privileging of Kinh over Montagnards that this has engendered. The state responded by a massive saturation of the Central Highlands with military and civilian police, mobilization of tanks and helicopter gunships to the area, and the arrest and detention of perceived ringleaders. Practitioners of religions not officially sanctioned by the state (such as Tin Lanh Dega, the form of evangelical Protestantism popular among Montagnards) were also arrested. Over a thousand Montagnards subsequently fled across the border to the Cambodian provinces of Mondulkiri and Ratanakiri in April and May 2001.

In each of the cases explored above, conflict with an ethnic dimension—be it vertical or horizontal—has originated from a majority ethnic group privileged during the colonial era imposing a "national" identity (often favoring the culture of the dominant group itself) on other ethnicities within the boundaries of the postcolonial nation to the detriment of those in the minority.

[*See also* Ethnic Cleansing and Deportation.]

BIBLIOGRAPHY

De Silva, K. M., Pensri Duke, Ellen S. Goldberg, and Nathan Katz, eds. *Ethnic Conflict in Buddhist Societies: Sri Lanka, Thailand, and Burma.* Boulder, Colo.: Westview, 1988.

Engelbert, Thomas, and Jana Raendchen, eds. *Colloquium and Round-Table Discussion on Ethnic Minorities and Politics in Southeast Asia.* Sudostasien Working Paper No. 23. Berlin: Humbolt University, 2003.

Ganguly, Rajat, and Ian Macduff, eds. *Ethnic Conflict and Secessionism in South and Southeast Asia: Causes, Dynamics, Solutions.* New Delhi, India; Thousand Oaks, Calif.; and London: Sage, 2003.

Snitwongse, Kusuma, and W. Scott Thompson, eds. *Ethnic Conflicts in Southeast Asia.* Singapore: Institute of Southeast Asian Studies, 2005.

Tarling, Nicholas. *Nations and States in Southeast Asia.* New York: Cambridge University Press, 1998.

Wijeyewardene, Gehan, ed. *Ethnic Groups across National Boundaries in Mainland Southeast Asia.* Singapore: Institute of Southeast Asian Studies, 1990.

TRUDY JACOBSEN

ETIQUETTE AND MANNERS. Interest in the history of manners is fairly new and has grown together with interest in the history of emotions, mentalities, and everyday life, all of which only became serious topics of research in the Western world from the 1960s onward. Until the 1960s, manners were discussed mainly in the context of the "problems" of behavior among the lower classes and of children having to learn such things as table manners, as well as of social climbers and nouveaux riches who were usually seen as being too loud and too conspicuous. Since then the topic has gained ascendancy, and manners have become the object of an increasing number of studies. They are increasingly taken to be an important part of any culture: within the relationships in which they grow up, all people are more or less attuned to the dominant manners of their society. In all societies a regime of manners mirrors and reinforces the distribution of power, status, or respect.

Norbert Elias's *The Civilising Process*. When it appeared in German in 1939, Norbert Elias's *The Civilising Process* was the first systematic study of the history of manners and emotion management. Pivotal to this work was an analysis of the extensive European literature on manners from the fifteenth to the nineteenth centuries. Elias focused particularly on manners regarding basic human functions such as eating, drinking, sleeping, defecating, and blowing one's nose, as well as on those regulating sexual and aggressive impulses. Because such manners are universal—in the sense that humans cannot avoid these activities or their regulation, no matter what society or age they live in—they are highly suitable for historical and international comparison.

Take the example of sharing a bed with a stranger. A manners book from 1729 warns that "it is not proper to lie so near him that you disturb or even touch him; and it is still less decent to put your legs between those of the other." In a few decades, to share a bed with strangers became embarrassing. The 1774 edition of the same book noted only that to be forced to share a bed "seldom happens," and if it does, "you should maintain a strict and vigilant modesty" (quoted in Elias, p. 137). As with other bodily functions, sleeping gradually became more intimate and private. From the mid-eighteenth century onward, the code of the courtly upper classes was beginning to resemble the more general usage of later centuries.

In general, what was first allowed later became restricted or forbidden. Heightened sensitivity with regard to several activities, especially those related to the "animalic" or "first nature" of human beings, coincided with increasing segregation of these activities from the rest of social life: they became private. Again and again, what was once seen as good manners later became perceived as rude or, at the other extreme, so ingrained in behavior as to be taken completely for granted. Social superiors made subordinates feel inferior if they did not meet their standard of manners. In this shaming process, fear of social superiors and, more generally, the fear of transgression of social prohibitions took on the character of an inner fear, shame.

Gradually the social commands controlling such actions as sleeping, nakedness, and excretion came to operate with regard to everyone and were imprinted as such in children.

Thus all references to social control, including shame, became embedded as assumptions and as such receded from consciousness. Adults came to experience social prohibitions as "natural," emanating from their own inner selves rather than from the outer realm of "good manners." As these social constraints took on the form of more or less total and automatically functioning self-restraints, this standard behavior became "second nature." Accordingly, manners books no longer dealt with these matters or did so far less extensively. Social constraints pressed toward stronger and more automatic self-supervision, the subordination of short-term impulses to the commandment of a habitual longer-term perspective, and the cultivation of a more stable, constant, and differentiated self-regulation. This is, as Elias calls it, a "civilizing process."

According to his civilizing theory, the main driving force of the directional process is the pressure of social competition and of an increasing division of functions, integrating increasing numbers of people into expanding and increasingly dense networks of interdependence. Elias emphasizes the importance of processes of European state formation, in which the use of physical violence and its instruments were progressively centralized and monopolized, together with taxation. Thus the inhabitants of states were increasingly constrained to settle conflicts in nonviolent ways, pressuring each other to tame their impulses toward aggressiveness and cruelty. Displays of superiority, particularly violent ones, were successfully branded as degrading.

With the rise of bourgeois groups who were no longer dependent on privileges derived from the crown, royal or "private" state monopolies were gradually transformed into societal or "public" ones. The transition was most dramatic in the American and the French Revolution in the late eighteenth century. The transition from the eighteenth-century "courtesy genre" of manners books to the nineteenth-century "etiquette genre" reflects this change. The new genre presented a blend of aristocratic and bourgeois manners. Etiquette books were directed at sociability in the centers of power and their "good society," that is, the circles of social acquaintance among people of families who belong to the centers of power. Their manners serve as a model. To be introduced, accepted, and entertained in good society was an important and sometimes even a necessary condition for success in business and politics. In the nineteenth century, upper- and middle-class women came more or less to run and organize the social sphere of good society.

The Fifteenth to Late Nineteenth Century. The period from the fifteenth until the late nineteenth century shows a long-term process of formalization in which the regimes of manners and emotions expanded and became increasingly strict and detailed, while a particular type of self-regulation in relation to a particular conscience formation developed, spread, and became dominant. The long-term trend of formalization reached its peak in the Victorian era, from the mid-nineteenth century to its last decade; the metaphor of "the stiff upper lip" indicated ritualistic manners and a kind of ritualistic self-control, heavily based on an authoritative conscience functioning more or less automatically as a second nature. This process allows one to perceive the history of manners in Europe and the United States as a long-term process toward the formalization of manners and the disciplining of people.

However, while the trend toward restricting the expression of feelings of superiority and inferiority continued in the same direction, in other respects the trajectory of change in codes of behavior and feeling was unique to the twentieth century. It points to a process of informalization: manners becoming increasingly relaxed, subtle, and varied. The lessening of power inequalities and a growing expectation to proceed through mutual consent have been conducive to greater informality in manners. As rising groups came to be increasingly represented in the centers of power and their good societies, behavioral extremes, expressing large differences in power and respect, came

to provoke moral indignation and were banned, while for the rest the codes of social conduct have become more lenient, more differentiated and varied. Rising mutually expected self-restraints allowed for an increase of socially accepted alternatives, as all kinds of formal rules and emotional controls were subjected to a "controlled decontrolling." Emotions that according to these formal rules previously had been repressed and denied, especially those concerning sex, violence, and death, being "dangerous emotions" that could lead to humiliation or worse, were again "discovered" as part of a collective emotional makeup; there was an "emancipation of emotions."

Thus the overall emancipation and integration of "lower" social groups in Western societies has been a necessary condition for the emancipation and integration of "lower" impulses and emotions in the personality structure. Both emancipations demanded a more strongly ego-dominated process of self-regulation, because drives, impulses, and emotions, even those that could provoke physical and sexual violence, tended to become more easily accessible, while their control became less strongly based upon an authoritative conscience, functioning more or less automatically as a "second nature."

The Twentieth Century and After. The turn of the twentieth century, the Roaring Twenties, and the permissive decades of the 1960s and 1970s were periods in which

Eighteenth-Century Manners. "The Englishman in Paris," anonymous print (London: C. Sheppard, 1777 or 1778). British Cartoon Prints Collection/Prints and Photographs Division, Library of Congress

whole groups collectively became involved in emancipation processes, both in Europe and in the United States. They were also periods with strong spurts in the informalization of manners. A frequent misunderstanding is to perceive informalization as just the undoing of formalization. It usually treats "informalization" as a synonym of "permissiveness" and "the permissive society," expressions that only refer to the loosening of social codes. However, to be able to "let go" without losing control or run wild demands a higher level of self-control. Therefore, in contrast to growing permissiveness, the "controlled decontrolling" or "letting go" that is involved in informalization processes raises stronger demands on self-regulation (or emotion management), thus demanding a higher level of self-restraint. The two processes should be disentangled, the tightening of restraints from the loosening of the social codes.

Increasingly subtle, informal ways of obliging and being obliged have demanded greater flexibility and sensitivity to shades and nuances in manners of dealing with others and oneself. As manners turned from a set of general rules into guidelines differentiated according to the demands of the situation and relationship, they demanded and allowed for the shift from a second nature self-regulating conscience that to a great extent functions automatically, to a "third nature" personality with a more reflexive and flexible self-regulation. For such individuals it becomes increasingly natural to attune oneself to the pulls and pushes of both first and second nature, as well as to the dangers and chances, short term and long term, of any particular situation or relationship. As national, continental, and global integration processes exert pressure toward increasingly differentiated regimes of manners, they also exert pressure toward increasingly reflexive and flexible regimes of self-regulation.

In the course of these centuries, the widening of the circles of readers of manners books reflected a widening of the circles of those who were directing themselves in terms of the dominant code, which, therefore, increasingly became the national code. These integration processes were carried by the successive ascent of larger and larger groups. As their status and power relative to other groups increased and they came to be represented in the centers of power and their good society, their members increasingly came to adopt the same code of manners and feeling, and they came to experience others as belonging to their own group or nation. Most changes in manners are related in some way or another to the representation of new groups in the centers of power and in good society. Apparently, codes of manners function to include some groups and to exclude others, but they also function to allow newcomers in. No group of established people has ever been able to keep its ranks entirely closed. The opening of the ranks of the established, the particular mix of ways in which these openings were to some extent forced and to some other extent offered, and the demands that newcomers had to meet—demands of social position, wealth, lifestyle, manners—have been different processes in each country. The specific processes of social integration in each country, particularly the ways in which the ranks of the falling strata of social superiors have been opened up by the rising strata—emancipation—and to the rising strata—accommodation—appear to have been decisive for the ways in which their distinctive codes of manners and self-regulation have influenced the type of mixture that finally resulted as the national habitus.

Some changes in manners, however, are symptomatic of changing power balances between states. As France became the dominant power in Europe, French courtly manners increasingly took over the modeling function previously fulfilled by the manners of the Italian courts. In the nineteenth century, with the rising power of England, the manners of English good society came to serve as a major example in many other countries. Around the turn of the twentieth century, according to many German and Dutch etiquette books, English manners had become the main model all over Europe.

After World War II, when the United States became a superpower, American manners served more easily as a model. Before that war, the United States had already been rising in this regard, in particular because of the relatively early development of a youth culture in that country and of an appealing entertainment industry closely connected with it, summarized and symbolized in the name "Hollywood."

The influences of European or American manners hardly form the only story of manners in modern world history. Many societies retain distinctive manners even amid globalization. Korean department store clerks routinely bow to passing customers; many Africans insist on a level of precedence for the elderly that goes well beyond Western standards. East Asian gift-giving traditions remain a strong part of social encounters, and affect international manners when people from these societies are involved. Many groups participating in global business or academic or diplomatic exchanges in the modern world learn at least two sets of manners, one appropriate for international contacts, and often reflecting considerable Western influence, the other for one's own family and community.

Other factors influence manners in recent world history as well. Revolutionary leaders deliberately attacked traditional manners in places like China, because manners encouraged undue deference. Manners in many revolutionary societies became less formal, certainly less obviously hierarchical. The spread of global consumerism also has implications for manners, for example in reducing the formality of clothing and encouraging greater informality in relationships between young people and adults.

[*See also* Adolescence; Civilizing Mission; Clothing; Emotions; *and* Family and Kinship.]

BIBLIOGRAPHY
Elias, Norbert. *The Civilising Process: Sociogenetic and Psychogenetic Investigations* (1939). Translated by Edmund Jephcott. Cambridge, Mass.: Blackwell, 2000.
Wouters, Cas. "Etiquette Books and Emotion Management in the Twentieth Century: American Habitus in International Comparison." In *An Emotional History of the United States*, edited by Peter N. Stearns and Jan Lewis, pp. 283–304. New York: New York University Press, 1998.
Wouters, Cas. *Informalization: Manners and Emotions Since 1890*. London: Sage, 2007.
Wouters, Cas. *Sex and Manners: Female Emancipation in the West since 1890*. London: Sage, 2004.

CAS WOUTERS

EUGENICS. The eugenics movement dates back to Victorian Britain and was at the center of the era's debates over evolution and heredity. The movement's avowed goal was to speed up the process of natural selection through selective breeding, as well as through the proposed sterilization of supposedly genetically defective individuals. The term "eugenics" itself, coined in 1883 by Francis Galton, an English aristocrat and cousin of Charles Darwin, derives from the Greek and means "well born." Eugenics has often been indicted as a legitimating factor in genocides such as the Holocaust, yet its legacies succeeded in crossing the ideological and political barriers of the twentieth century.

The Nineteenth Century. Victorians thought of eugenics as a respectable scientific discipline whose methods and findings could be helpful in the fields of anthropology, sociology, psychology, and the social sciences. The publication of Charles Darwin's *On the Origin of Species* (1859) put the concept of human evolution at the forefront of cultural, social, and scientific debates. The formulation of eugenic ideas was located at the conjunction of scientific findings on human evolution with their social application to the human condition. Proponents of social Darwinism such as the British philosopher Herbert Spencer theorized that class structure was the product of natural selection.

Consequently, class stratification in industrial societies mirrored underlying and innate differences between classes.

Observing the apparent human mastery over nature and displaying the faith in progress typical of the Industrial Revolution, Francis Galton believed that humans should take charge of their own evolution. He advocated a containment of social aid and medicine, which could lead to the spreading of weak individuals, and advocated for breeding by the "better elements" of the population. In *Hereditary Genius* (1869), where he compiled a eugenic catalog of eminent Victorian families, Galton concluded that families of status were more likely to produce able descendents than families belonging to lower classes and that the biological inheritance of leadership qualities had determined the social status of Britain's ruling classes. In Galton's view, the role of the environment in shaping the character and abilities of an individual was limited when compared to the influence of heredity. Anticipating some of the darker developments of eugenics in the twentieth century, Galton connected the discipline with theories of racial inferiority. He suggested, for example, that the decline of American Indians was linked to their inherently defective moral character.

Twentieth-Century Developments. Eugenics became institutionalized by the beginning of the twentieth century with the foundation of the Eugenics Education Society of London and the creation of a professorship in eugenics at the University of London, initially held by the social theorist Karl Pearson. Pearson's work is a typical example of the application of eugenics to the issue of efficient social management. In his *Grammar of Science* (1892) he argued that eugenic management of society could prevent genetic deterioration and ensure the existence of intelligent rulers. From these premises, two forms of eugenics emerged: "positive" and "negative." Positive eugenics proposed legislation to encourage the marriage of the hereditarily fit, while negative eugenics favored segregation and sterilization of the supposedly feebleminded or inferior races. Starting in the last decades of the nineteenth century and continuing well into the twentieth, eugenics influenced immigration and social policies on both sides of the Atlantic.

A similar process of institutionalization took place in the United States. In 1910 the Harvard embryologist Charles Davenport established the Laboratory for Experimental Evolution at Cold Spring Harbor, New York, in an attempt to fuse early genetics with the eugenics movement. Eugenics played with racial and ethnic anxieties: Davenport raised the money to fund his laboratory by exploiting the fears of wealthy American families about unrestricted immigration and consequent racial degeneration, while eugenicists administering IQ tests, such as Henry Goddard, claimed that more than 80 percent of the immigrant population was mentally defective. Supposedly scientific studies that proved the biological inferiority of southern and eastern European populations became common reading in America at the beginning of the twentieth century. The Eugenics Record Office demanded a survey to determine the national origins of "hereditary defectives" in American prisons, mental institutions, and other charities. Such a survey was finally carried out by Harry Laughlin, who appeared before Congress in 1924 to support a eugenically crafted immigration restriction bill. His testimony resulted in the Immigration Restriction Act of the same year, which was designed to limit the arrival of dysgenic aliens such as Italians and eastern European Jews, reducing their immigration quota from 45 percent to 15 percent of the total. The 1924 act ended the greatest era of immigration in American history and remained effective until 1965, when the quota system was repealed by the Immigration and Nationality Act.

Throughout the twentieth century, eugenics displayed a remarkable if chilling ability to cross ideological and national boundaries. In an 1896 tract entitled "The Difficulties of Individualism," the British Fabian Socialists Beatrice and Sidney Webb decried the high fertility of the "improvident," which produced "degenerate hordes . . . unfit for social life."

At the opposite end of the political divide, German National Socialist (Nazi) leaders showed a keen interest in eugenics and its potential to create a pure, Aryan race. German scientists began to search for viable means of establishing "pure" Aryan bloodlines. In the process of breeding Germans to an Aryan perfection, "lower races" such as Jews, Gypsies (Roma), the mentally handicapped, and homosexuals were to be erased. Laws forbidding the marriage of Jews and Aryans were passed in Germany in the mid-1930s, while compulsory programs of mass sterilization began to target the mentally retarded. The ideological foundations of eugenics have also been blamed for the ethnic cleansing that occurred in the Balkans in the 1990s.

Though the most extreme state-directed eugenics program in history was carried out in Nazi Germany, programs of compulsory sterilization were carried out in the United States, where sixty thousand people were sterilized by 1970, and in countries like Sweden, Japan, Switzerland, Austria, Belgium, and Canada. Many of

these programs were not abolished until the 1970s, and in some cases even later. Scientific support for eugenics started to wane in the second half of the twentieth century, when patterns of inheritance were more correctly understood and the assumption that natural selection operates to improve the species was exposed as a blatant lie. At the same time, an increasing emphasis on individual rights made the state's authoritarian interventions in human lives less acceptable.

[*See also* Body, The; Darwinism; Ethnic Cleansing and Deportation; Evolution; Genetics; *and* Social Darwinism.]

BIBLIOGRAPHY

Degler, Carl N. *In Search of Human Nature: The Decline and Revival of Darwinism in American Social Thought.* Oxford and New York: Oxford University Press, 1991.

Depew, David J., and Bruce H. Weber. *Darwinism Evolving: System Dynamics and the Genealogy of Natural Selection.* Cambridge, Mass.: MIT Press, 1995.

Kevles, Daniel J. *In the Name of Eugenics: Genetics and the Uses of Human Heredity.* Cambridge, Mass.: Harvard University Press, 1995.

Kühl, Stephan. *The Nazi Connection: Eugenics, American Racism, and German National Socialism.* New York: Oxford University Press, 1994.

Larson, Edward J. *Sex, Race, and Science: Eugenics in the Deep South.* Baltimore: John Hopkins University Press, 1995.

LUCA PRONO

EUNUCHS. There have been eunuchs throughout recorded history, although proportionately fewer of them have come from western Europe or North America than other parts of the world. There are basically two types of eunuchs. For most eunuchs, usually only the testicles are removed (a process now labeled as castration), but in many areas there is also total castration, which involves the removal of both the testicles and the penis. The second type has a much higher mortality rate than the first. In imperial China, where eunuchs in the royal court remained important until the twentieth century, total castration was usually performed on prepubescent or adolescent youths; the individual might be castrated either under family pressure or decide entirely on his own to become a eunuch. In India, among the *hijras,* an Indian male cult, asceticism and renunciation of sexual desire are proven by total castration in an operation called *nirvan,* a term for the state of mind where the individual is liberated from the finite human consciousness and approaches the dawn of higher consciousness. Within modern Christianity, the Russia sect of Skoptsi regarded procreation as the greatest of evils and therefore practiced castration. They were declared to be a harmful sect by

Tsar Nicholas I (r. 1825–1855). Many of them fled to Romania, but in Russia as late as 1920 their numbers were estimated at 100,000 believers, and in spite of Soviet persecution they continued to survive. Many if not most eventually adopted the idea of spiritual castration, that is, total abstinence, rather than physical castration.

In some parts of the Arab world where eunuchs still exist, the term *khasi* describes a eunuch who has his testicles removed, while a *madjub* has both his testicles and penis removed. In Europe, until almost the beginning of the twentieth century, boys in Catholic countries were often castrated to preserve their soprano voices. The Christian church banned castration officially in the fourth century, but there was no ban on using the services of eunuchs, who were known in the Catholic world as "castrati." One researcher claimed that records on such surgical operations from the eighteenth century indicated that more than two thousand boys were castrated in the Papal States. It was not until 1878 when Pope Leo prohibited the use of castrati in church choirs that the practice declined. Castrati in opera were replaced in the twentieth century by women playing the roles that formerly relied on castrato voices, but some castrati were still active in the early twentieth century and were recorded.

In China and the Middle East, eunuchs historically were preferred for many positions in royal courts because they presumably could not disturb the ruler's wives and concubines. Correspondingly, some families made one or more sons into eunuchs to take advantage of political opportunity. In the nineteenth century eunuchs sometimes parlayed their power in the palace to larger government roles, assuming key functions as bureaucrats and participating in bureacratic in-fighting.

In western Europe and the United States the largest number of castrations in the twentieth century were probably performed for eugenic reasons—that is, to prevent epileptics or those perceived as feebleminded, insane, or socially undesirable from reproducing. Victims of forced castration also often included poor immigrants, the poverty stricken, and habitual criminals. Such eugenic practices were ultimately discredited because of the extremes practiced by the Nazis. Most American laws involving eugenics were repealed following the end of World War II, although elective vasectomies and tubal ligations are often still done as a form of birth control. Today, a growing numbers of individuals undergo castration or ovariectomies in order to change their sex. Castration or the making of eunuchs has sometimes been advocated as punishment for sex criminals, particularly for those involved in intergenerational sex. One of the limitations of such punishment, however, is that removal of the testicles does not necessarily eliminate sexual arousal, since a male could continue to receive testosterone through his adrenal glands, which is one reason many professionals are unwilling to urge castration as a "cure" for sexual criminals.

BIBLIOGRAPHY
Bullough, Vern L. "Eunuchs in History and Society." In *Eunuchs in Antiquity and Beyond*, edited by Shaun Toughter. Swansea, Wales, U.K.: Classical Press, 2002.

VERN L. BULLOUGH

EUPHRATES RIVER. *See* Tigris and Euphrates Rivers.

EUREKA STOCKADE. The Eureka Stockade, an 1854 uprising of gold miners on the Ballarat goldfields against a heavy-handed government, was easily crushed, but its symbolism has guaranteed its place in Australian history.

The discovery of gold in Australia in 1851, soon after the Californian rush of 1849, led to a rush of diggers, particularly to the new colony of Victoria, whose administration was rapidly overstretched. To raise revenue to police the goldfields and to maintain control over Crown land, the lieutenant governor, C. J. La Trobe, instituted a licensing system. The license caused resentment among the miners, both because it taxed miners whether or not they were successful and because it was administered ineptly. In 1854, Sir Charles Hotham replaced La Trobe, and the miners hoped for some relief, but Hotham tightened the licensing system.

The miners' immediate grievances were with the licensing system and with corrupt policing of the goldfields, but their rhetoric took up broader issues, informed by British Chartism, the 1848 European revolutions, and American republicanism. The spark to action was provided by the murder of a digger, James Scobie, who had sought an after-hours drink at the Eureka Hotel. James Bentley, the hotel's owner, was among those arrested but was, despite strong evidence, exonerated by a court dominated by his friends. After a protest meeting the hotel was burned down by some of the crowd, and three diggers were arrested as scapegoats. In response on 11 November, a large meeting formed the Ballarat Reform League, which called for manhood suffrage and other Chartist demands, land reform, and an end to licensing; the league argued that "taxation without representation is tyranny." A deputation met with Hotham on 27 November to "demand" the release of those arrested; Hotham objected to the word "demand" but held out hope of future concessions following a commission of inquiry into the goldfields. He had also sent for more troops, and when the deputation reported back on 29 November, licenses were burned and stones thrown at troops. There were further arrests, but under a hastily sewn flag representing the Southern Cross—designed by a Canadian, Captain Ross—about five hundred men took an oath to "fight to defend our rights and liberties," with Peter Lalor, an Irishman, as leader.

The rebels built a rough stockade on the Eureka claim, although they came and went—some organizing food, many returning to their claims to sleep, others just drifting away. On Sunday, 3 December, at 4 in the morning, with about 120 diggers at the stockade, government forces attacked, and after fifteen minutes' skirmishing and unnecessary atrocities, some twenty miners and four troopers were dead. From more than a hundred prisoners, thirteen were chosen to be tried for treason. Lalor himself escaped and remained in hiding. From the first trial it was clear that the juries would refuse to convict, despite the government's best efforts. Hotham appointed a Gold Fields' Commission a week after the battle, and the following year it recommended the replacement of the license with a cheaper Miner's Right (which carried the right to vote), an export duty on gold, and the opening of Crown land to smallholdings. With self-government in 1856 the Australian colonies—Victoria in particular—embraced democracy. The contribution of the events at Ballarat to the process has been disputed; many of the changes were under way even before 1854.

The meaning of Eureka was immediately contested. One participant, the flamboyant Raffaelo Carboni, who had been a member of Young Italy, saw it as a romantic resistance to arbitrary government; Karl Marx read it as potentially revolutionary. Commissioner Robert Rede, responsible for order on the goldfields, believed opposition to the license was "a mere cloak to cover a democratic revolution," while Hotham did his best to paint it as the work of foreigners. Some emphasized the role of the Irish among the more defiant diggers, while others marked Eureka as the birthplace of Australian democracy or national independence. Later historians drew attention to the fact that the diggers were small-scale individual capitalists.

The Eureka heritage has been claimed variously by the Catholic Church, the Australian Labor Party, Communists, small business, the Builders Labourers Federation, and the National Front. More recently the multiculturalism of the rebels has been stressed. A memorial was raised in the 1880s commemorating the dead on both sides, although debate continued as to exactly where the stockade had been built. In 2004 the Australian prime minister John Howard refused to participate in any commemoration of the rebellion's sesquicentenary.

[See also Australia and Gold and Gold Mining.]

BIBLIOGRAPHY

Carboni, Raffaello. *The Eureka Stockade: The Consequences of Some Pirates Wanting on Quarter-deck a Rebellion.* Adelaide: Public Library of South Australia, 1962. Originally published in 1855.

Molony, John. *Eureka.* New York: Viking, 1984.

Serle, Geoffrey. *The Golden Age: A History of the Colony of Victoria, 1851–1861.* Melbourne, Australia: Melbourne University Press, 1963.

RICHARD WHITE

EUROPEAN COAL AND STEEL COMMUNITY.

In the late 1940s France attempted to exploit Germany's defeat and accelerate its own economic development. The United States, by contrast, championed Germany's rapid recovery for broader economic and strategic reasons, especially with the onset of the Cold War. The Americans convinced a reluctant France to acquiesce in the establishment of the Federal Republic of Germany in April 1949. Next, they pressured France to relax the occupying powers' controls on the production of German coal and steel.

Jean Monnet, a senior French official, responded with a proposal for a common market for coal and steel under the direction of a supranational High Authority. Monnet convinced Robert Schuman, the French foreign minister and an advocate of Franco-German reconciliation, to promote the plan. Schuman did so publicly at a famous press conference in Paris in May 1950.

France, Germany, Italy, Belgium, the Netherlands, and Luxembourg established the European Coal and Steel Community (ECSC) in July 1952. Apart from the High Authority, it included a Council of Ministers, an Assembly, and a Court of Justice. Economically, the ECSC never amounted to much—cheap imported oil soon undercut coal and demand for steel during the postwar boom assuaged national concerns about market share. Instead, the legacy of the ECSC was primarily political: it epitomized the postwar settlement between France and Germany and set a precedent for European integration. Unlike the communities that followed, however, the ECSC from its inception was intended to exist for a fixed period (fifty years). It ceased to exist after July 2002.

[*See also* European Integration *and* Trading Blocs and Common Markets.]

BIBLIOGRAPHY

Gillingham, John. *Coal, Steel, and the Rebirth of Europe, 1945–1955.* Cambridge, U.K.: Cambridge University Press, 1991. The definitive history of the origins and establishment of the ECSC.

Poidevin, Raymond, and Dirk Spierenburg. *The History of the High Authority of the European Coal and Steel Community: Supranationality in Operation.* London: Weidenfeld and Nicolson, 1994. A comprehensive account of the ECSC in action, written by a French historian, Poidevin, and a member of the original High Authority, Spierenburg.

DESMOND DINAN

EUROPEAN COMMON MARKET. *See* European Integration.

EUROPEAN INTEGRATION. European integration is the process whereby countries transfer responsibility for policy making in certain areas from the national to supranational level of governance and engage in policy making at that level. The process of European integration has resulted in the establishment of the European Union (EU), which as of 2007 had twenty-seven member states and embraced almost every aspect of public policy to some extent or other. Widening and deepening—the acquisition of new members and additional policy responsibilities—are two of the most intriguing aspects of the process. Despite the continuous challenge of enlargement, a wider EU has not necessarily meant a weaker EU. That may be changing, with the EU struggling since 2004 to cope with the accession of ten new member states, plus an additional two added in 2007—most of them poor former Communist countries in Central and Eastern Europe—and facing the prospect of eventual Turkish membership.

The EU has also been struggling since the early 1990s with growing public dissatisfaction with its institutional arrangements and policy output. Such dissatisfaction came to the fore in 2005 when strong electoral majorities in France and the Netherlands, two of the EU's founding member states, rejected the Constitutional Treaty that national governments had recently concluded after more than two years of negotiations. The decision to shelve the Constitutional Treaty represented a major political setback for the EU.

Origins. The idea of European unity is as old as Europe itself. European integration is a variation of that ancient theme, but is rooted in the historical circumstances of the mid-twentieth century. At the end of World War II, the most pressing question was what to do with defeated Germany. Britain, France, the Soviet Union, and the United States were the four occupying powers. The onset of the Cold War answered the German question to a certain extent. The country was partitioned, with the Soviet zone becoming a separate state under the control of a Communist government firmly tied to Moscow.

Anticipating that development and appreciating Germany's importance for the recovery of Europe as a whole, the United States wanted the three Western powers to unite their zones into a new state, which should then be allowed to develop economically, without hindrance from its erstwhile enemies. Britain was agreeable, but not France, which had suffered so much at Germany's hands in the previous seventy-five years and wanted to take advantage of Germany's weakness in order to accelerate its own industrial modernization.

Reluctantly, France acquiesced in the establishment of the Federal Republic of Germany in April 1949 but continued to insist on controlling Germany's coal and steel output. Under American pressure, Jean Monnet, a senior French official responsible for economic planning, proposed in May 1950 that responsibility for the production and distribution of French and German coal and steel be vested in a new supranational organization, the European Coal and Steel Community (ECSC). Robert Schuman, French foreign minister and an advocate of Franco-German rapprochement, steered the plan through a divided cabinet. Konrad Adenauer, chancellor of the Federal Republic, enthusiastically supported the plan, which offered Germany the prospect of international rehabilitation and economic recovery in collaboration rather than in conflict with France. Following intense intergovernmental bargaining about institutional and operational arrangements, the ECSC came into being in July 1952. It included a High Authority with limited supranational power, a Council of Ministers through which national governments could shape policy, an Assembly to symbolize democratic accountability, and a Court of Justice to adjudicate disputes.

The ECSC was an unglamorous organization. It was a far cry from what advocates of European integration, many of them ardent federalists, had hoped would emerge in the ferment of the early postwar period. They had put their hopes in the Congress of Europe, a gathering in 1948 of non-Communist politicians from most Western European countries. Largely owing to differences between the British delegates, who generally eschewed supranationalism, and their Continental counterparts, the ensuing Council of Europe had little integrative potential. By contrast, the ECSC was limited to only six member states—France, Germany, Italy, Belgium, the Netherlands, and Luxembourg—and to the coal and steel sectors, but it enshrined the principle of supranationalism. Moreover, it epitomized the postwar settlement between France and Germany.

By the end of the 1950s there were two additional supranational organizations in Europe with the same membership as the ECSC: the European Economic Community (EEC) and the European Atomic Energy Community (Euratom). Yet there was no automatic spillover from coal and steel to other sectors, resulting in the emergence of the two communities. Instead, the EEC originated in a Dutch proposal for a customs union as a means of stimulating trade among participating states. Some French leaders subscribed to the idea, but had great difficulty convincing their more protectionist colleagues to go along with it. By contrast, the French generally supported a call by Monnet for an organization to promote atomic energy research and development, along the lines of the ECSC. By linking the proposals for a customs union and an atomic energy community, and broadening the customs union to include a common agricultural policy (CAP) and concessions to former colonies, French negotiators managed to secure sufficient domestic support to ratify the Treaties of Rome, which established the EEC and Euratom, in March 1957.

Widening. Britain had stood aloof from these developments. No sooner was the EEC up and running, however, than Britain applied to join. Economic necessity—the necessity of unrestricted access to the European market—rather than support for supranationalism was the basis for Britain's decision. Denmark, Ireland, and Norway followed suit. Britain's application ended in ignominy in January 1963 when French President Charles de Gaulle invoked his famous veto. Strategically, de Gaulle resented Britain's special relationship with the United States, against which he sought to assert Western Europe's independence. Economically, he disliked Britain's preference for global trade liberalization and suspected that Britain would prevent completion of the CAP, a cherished French objective. De Gaulle vetoed Britain's second application in November 1967, essentially for the same reasons.

Only when de Gaulle resigned in 1969 did British accession seem imminent. Georges Pompidou, the new French president, was a Gaullist who understood that France could not keep Britain out of the EEC indefinitely. However, not until the CAP was finally put in place with the budget agreement of April 1970 did he allow the resumption of Britain's accession negotiations. Pompidou saw British membership as strategically advantageous to France at a time when Germany was becoming more assertive politically under Chancellor Willi Brandt. Britain finally joined in January 1973, as did Denmark and Ireland (a slim

European Integration. Jean Monnet and Robert Schuman. © EUROPEAN COMMUNITY

majority of Norwegians had rejected membership in a referendum the previous year).

Britain became (and has since remained) an awkward member of the EEC. With its small agricultural sector and long-standing policy of importing cheap food, Britain never liked the CAP. Despite being a relatively poor member state, Britain contributed a disproportionate amount to the EEC budget and got little in return, not least because most of the EEC's expenditure was for agricultural subsidies. Harold Wilson, who came to power soon after Britain joined the EEC, followed up on a preelection pledge and renegotiated Britain's membership terms. He won some concessions on the budget, on the basis of which a large majority of Britains voted in an unprecedented national referendum in June 1975 to keep Britain in the Community. But that was not the end of the British budgetary question. No sooner did Margaret Thatcher become prime minister in May 1979 than she returned to the charge, demanding "Britain's money back." Five years of wrangling followed before Thatcher accepted a generous rebate on Britain's contribution as part of the wider budget reform of June 1984.

By that time Greece had joined the EEC and Portugal and Spain were completing their accession negotiations. All three countries had emerged from right-wing, authoritarian rule in the mid-1970s and had immediately sought EEC membership as a means of consolidating their fledgling democracies and strengthening their weak economies. When Portugal and Spain joined in January 1986, it looked as if the EEC had expanded as much as it possibly could. The Iron Curtain cut off Central and Eastern Europe, and the Western European neutrals would not apply because of their strategic orientation. Turkey was the only country still aspiring to EEC membership, but its uncertain democracy meant that it could not seriously hope to join for many years to come.

The enlargement scenario changed dramatically at the end of the Cold War. With neutrality no longer a barrier to membership, Austria, Finland, and Sweden entered the newly launched EU in January 1995, following relatively straightforward negotiations. No sooner had the Cold War ended than the newly independent countries of Central and Eastern Europe announced their intention of "rejoining Europe." Like the Mediterranean countries before them, the Central and Eastern European countries wanted to consolidate their democracies and develop their economies. What better way of doing so than joining the EU and availing of its generous farm subsidies and regional assistance grants?

It was precisely the prospect of funding the Central and Eastern European countries on such a lavish scale that concerned the existing member states. By the end of the 1990s enlargement fatigue had set in. But having advocated a united Europe for decades, the member states had little choice in the matter. Making a virtue of necessity, the EU enlarged yet again in May 2004, this time acquiring eight Central and Eastern European countries, plus Cyprus and Malta, and Bulgaria and Romania joined in 2007. The EU put off the day of financial reckoning by offering the new member states lower agricultural subsidies than those already available to existing members and by limiting the size of financial transfers under cohesion policy. The reckoning arrived in 2005 and 2006, when the EU had to agree on a new multiannual budget for 2007 to 2013 and each new member state had to fight for equality with the other members.

Regardless of Central and Eastern European enlargement, there was no enthusiasm in the EU for Turkish accession. Nevertheless, Turkey had come a long way since the late 1980s and now met the so-called Copenhagen criteria (covering basic political and economic preconditions) for prospective EU membership. Given Turkey's strategic importance, the EU could not reject the country's candidacy out of hand. Indeed, pushed by Britain, the EU officially opened accession negotiations with Turkey in October 2005. These were expected to last at least a decade. Moreover, the ensuing agreement would be put to a referendum in a number of member states known to oppose Turkish membership. The obvious but unstated subtext was not only that Turkey was too poor and too populous, but also that, as a Muslim country, it was not really "European."

Even if it were not a case apart, Turkey's candidacy became troublesome at a time when the EU was having difficulty integrating so many new members. Managing an EU of twenty-seven countries was hard enough; managing an ever-larger EU seemed out of the question, especially following the failure of the Constitutional Treaty. Like Turkey (but unlike it in almost every other respect), Croatia is also a candidate for EU membership. Other Balkan countries are eager to join, as are Ukraine and Moldova. Although it is hard to say where exactly the boundaries of the EU should be, it is certainly the case that a majority of European citizens believe the EU has expanded far enough already.

Deepening. Notwithstanding the repeated challenges of enlargement, on balance the EU deepened rather than weakened as it widened its membership. The EEC that

Britain, Denmark, and Ireland joined in 1973 consisted largely of a customs union plus a common agricultural policy. As part of the budget agreement of 1970, the EEC acquired its "own resources"—customs duties and a small percentage of value added tax that went directly into the Community's coffers. That completed the first phase of the construction of the EEC, as outlined in the Treaty of Rome. The treaty did not specify what the next phase would be, apart from calling generally for the eradication of nontariff barriers to trade, which would involve a laborious process of legislative harmonization among member states.

Eager to reinvigorate European integration in anticipation of expansion, EEC leaders agreed in 1970 that deepening should accompany both completion and enlargement. That was the genesis of the Werner Plan for economic and monetary union (proposed by Luxembourg's Pierre Werner), which called for a common monetary policy by 1980 at the latest. But the oil crisis and ensuing stagflation blew European integration off course in the 1970s. Far from tackling nontariff barriers, member states responded to intense domestic pressure by introducing new protectionist measures. Economic and monetary union (EMU) became a pipe dream, although member states managed in 1979 to launch the European Monetary System, an arrangement that reduced radical swings in exchange rates among participating currencies and helped promote price stability.

Greece joined the EEC in January 1981, during this period of stasis. By the time Portugal and Spain had completed their accession negotiations, the EEC was emerging from a decade of stagflation and economic disintegration. Partly in response to that experience, and partly in anticipation of further enlargement, EEC leaders agreed in the mid-1980s to reinvigorate European integration by launching the single-market program, an ambitious plan to facilitate the free movement of goods, services, capital, and people by the end of 1992. In effect, the program reanimated the original Treaty of Rome. As if to reiterate their "marriage" vows, member states signed the Single European Act (SEA) in February 1986. An amendment to the original treaty, the SEA committed the member states to completing the single market by the stipulated target date through the use of qualified majority voting—a powerful instrument of supranational decision making—for regulatory harmonization.

Every national leader, ranging from the neoliberal Thatcher to the socialist François Mitterrand, could agree on the single-market program. Thatcher parted company with the others when it came to cohesion policy, the idea that poor (peripheral) parts of the EEC should receive generous transfers from the budget to help close the gap between them and the rich (central) parts, a gap that might otherwise widen following implementation of the single-market program. The issue was pressing because of the imminent accession of Portugal and Spain, two poor countries. Thatcher dismissed cohesion policy as little more than bribes paid to the prospective new member states to win their votes for the single-market program, which they might otherwise try to block in the Council of Ministers. In her view, market integration would suffice to stimulate economic growth in the poorer countries.

Led by Commission President Jacques Delors, the vast majority of member states endorsed cohesion policy, which they enshrined in the SEA. In 1988, a year after implementation of the SEA, member states agreed to overhaul the EEC's budget and double the amount of money spent on structural funds, the instruments of cohesion policy. The structural funds were again doubled in 1992, when the poorer member states, again with Delors's support, successfully linked cohesion policy to the implementation of the Maastricht Treaty's provisions for EMU.

Apart from EMU, implementation of the Maastricht Treaty (also known as the Treaty on European Union) greatly strengthened European integration. Under the terms of the treaty, the EEC was subsumed into the EU, which also included intergovernmental cooperation on foreign and security policy and on justice and home affairs (immigration and asylum policy in addition to police and judicial cooperation). The intergovernmental aspects of the new treaty were a direct response to recent geopolitical developments, notably German unification and the collapse of Soviet control in Central and Eastern Europe. The Maastricht Treaty also included institutional reforms intended both to improve decision making and to close the so-called democratic deficit (the gap between the governed and the governing at the EU level). In particular, new decision-making procedures strengthened the legislative role of the directly elected European Parliament.

The Maastricht Treaty represented the high point of European integration. The Danish electorate's rejection of it in a June 1992 referendum signaled growing public concern about the institutions and policies of the EU. The path to the final stage of EMU—implementation of a common monetary policy and the adoption of a single currency in 1999 (euro notes and coins were introduced in 2002)—fueled public unease. The EU seemed increasingly intrusive without being sufficiently effective in tackling troublesome issues ranging from the Balkan wars of the 1990s to high unemployment and low economic growth.

Giving more power to the European Parliament had failed to close the democratic deficit, as the declining voter turnout in direct elections clearly showed.

The EU tried to respond to the related challenges of public unease and imminent expansion into Central and Eastern Europe with a series of treaty changes, beginning with the Treaty of Amsterdam in 1997 and culminating in the Constitutional Treaty of 2004. Neither the Treaty of Amsterdam nor the follow-up Treaty of Nice in 2001 included far-reaching institutional reforms—hence the decision to hold a Convention on the Future of Europe (2002–2003) to overhaul the founding treaties to meet the twin challenges of enlargement and public disquiet. The Constitutional Treaty was far from ideal, but probably the best that could have been expected given the political constraints on drafting such a document for a supranational entity with so many disparate states. As the results of the French and Dutch referenda showed, however, by 2005 public dissatisfaction with the EU was too deep to keep the Constitutional Treaty afloat.

Assessment. Rejection of the Constitutional Treaty does not mean the end of European integration. Despite their dissatisfaction with the EU, most European citizens appreciate the benefits of a frontier-free Europe. The message is clear: Europeans want their leaders to concentrate on first principles—economic growth, employment, and social welfare. The EU has the means to tackle these issues. Indeed, national leaders agreed at a summit in Lisbon in March 2000 on a strategy for economic modernization and reform (the so-called Lisbon Strategy). Nevertheless, many of them are unwilling or unable, due to domestic political constraints, to take the necessary steps. Only when they do so, however, and reinvigorate economic integration, can the EU hope to overcome its current malaise.

[*See also* European Coal and Steel Community; European Union; *and* Trading Blocs and Common Markets.]

BIBLIOGRAPHY

Dinan, Desmond. *Europe Recast: A History of European Union.* Boulder, Colo.: Lynne Reinner, 2004. A good overview of the history of European integration.

Dinan, Desmond, ed. *Origin and Evolution of the European Union.* Oxford, U.K.: Oxford University Press, 2006. Contains chapters, written by experts, on particular aspects of European integration and on the historiography of the EU.

Gilbert, Mark. *Surpassing Realism: The Politics of European Integration Since 1945.* Lanham, Md.: Rowman & Littlefield, 2003. A thorough synopsis of the European integration process.

Gillingham, John. *European Integration, 1950–2003: Superstate or New Market Economy?* Cambridge, U.K.: Cambridge University Press, 2003. A comprehensive and controversial history of European integration.

Milward, Alan S. *The European Rescue of the Nation-State.* 2d ed. London: Routledge, 2000. Milward, the best-known historian of European integration, argues that by pooling sovereignty, the founding members of the EU strengthened rather than weakened national control over increasingly complex socioeconomic issues.

Wallace, Helen, William Wallace, and Mark Pollack, eds. *Policy-Making in the European Union.* 5th ed. Oxford, U.K.: Oxford University Press, 2005. This is the gold standard of EU textbooks.

DESMOND DINAN

EUROPEAN UNION. The European Union (EU) came into existence in November 1993 following implementation of the Treaty on European Union, better known as the Maastricht Treaty. The EU is built on three pillars. The first comprises the European Economic Community (EEC) and the European Atomic Energy Community (Euratom). Originally, it also included the European Coal and Steel Community (ECSC), but that organization ceased to exist in July 2002 under the terms of its founding treaty, which limited its life span to fifty years. The second pillar is security and defense policy cooperation, and the third is cooperation on justice and home affairs (immigration and asylum policy in addition to police and judicial cooperation). The key difference between the pillars is that the EU's member states (twenty-seven as of 2007) have agreed to share sovereignty in the socioeconomic policy areas covered by the first pillar—ranging from agricultural policy, to trade policy, to monetary policy—but cooperate on an intergovernmental basis in the politically more sensitive areas covered by the second and third pillars. Among other important changes, the failed Constitutional Treaty of 2004 would have abolished the pillar system and given the EU legal standing (as it is, only the EEC and Euratom have legal standing or personality).

The EU emerged as a result of the acceleration of economic integration in the late 1980s. In response to the economic setbacks of the previous decade, the leaders of the then EEC agreed on a target date of 1992 to complete the single-market program, which aimed to establish a borderless area for the free movement of goods, services, capital, and people. Implementation of the single-market program coincided with discussions already under way between French and German politicians for a common monetary policy to replace the European Monetary System, a regime in place since 1979 to limit exchange rate fluctuations among participating currencies. A common monetary policy was the centerpiece of economic and monetary union (EMU), a long-standing objective of European integration. In order to achieve EMU, however, member states would have to negotiate a new treaty or a revision of the existing EEC treaty. Buoyed by the success of the single-market program, they agreed to begin the requisite intergovernmental conference in December 1990.

By that time the Berlin Wall had come down and German unification seemed imminent. That development strengthened the German government's commitment to EMU—giving up the deutsche mark would send a powerful signal that a united Germany remained firmly committed to European unification—and also added a strategic dimension to the discussions then taking place about the future of the EEC. As a result, EEC leaders decided to hold a second, parallel intergovernmental conference on political union, meaning institutional reform, and cooperation on foreign policy, justice, and home affairs. Both sets of negotiations ended at a summit in Maastricht in December 1991—hence the popular name for the Treaty on European Union.

Danish voters' rejection of the Maastricht Treaty in a referendum in June 1992 delayed the launch of the EU and cast a pall over the entire initiative. For three decades European integration had proceeded on the basis of a permissive consensus. Since the acceleration of integration in the late 1980s, however, Europeans had begun to question the accountability and representativeness of the EEC's institutions. European leaders had anticipated such concerns by strengthening the legislative role of the European Parliament, the only directly elected institution at the European level of governance. Yet the declining voter turnout in successive direct elections showed that European leaders would have to do more in order to close what soon became known as the "democratic deficit" (the gap between the governed and the governing at the EU level).

An opt-out from participation in EMU, granted to Denmark in December 1992, facilitated the success of a second referendum and implementation of the Maastricht Treaty in November 1993. EU leaders have struggled since then to address the democratic deficit in a series of intergovernmental conferences. The first two of these resulted

in the Treaty of Amsterdam in 1997 and the Treaty of Nice in 2001, both of which reformed the treaties that established the EEC and EU. Because those reforms hardly made a dent in public dissatisfaction with the EU's institutional arrangements, however, EU leaders decided in December 2001 to convene a Convention on the Future of Europe, consisting of representatives of national and European institutions, to draft a new treaty for the EU. The so-called Constitutional Convention met over a period of eighteen months (2002–2003) and produced a draft document that national leaders haggled over in the requisite intergovernmental conference (2003–2004).

The ensuing Constitutional Treaty included a number of institutional reforms but did not radically overhaul the EU's organizational architecture. Nor would it have appeased critics of the democratic deficit. Arguably, an entity such as the EU cannot meet the standards of democratic legitimacy commonly applied to national political systems. Partly because of the chronic criticism of the EU's democratic credentials and partly because of specific policy and political concerns, voters in France and the Netherlands, two of the EEC's founding states, rejected the Constitutional Treaty in referenda in the spring of 2005. Reeling from that double rejection, EU leaders decided in June 2005 to put the Constitutional Treaty on hold for the indefinite future.

The fate of the Constitutional Treaty suggests that the EU is in serious difficulties. Indeed, the EU is unpopular and seemingly incapable of tackling unemployment and promoting economic growth among its member states. Political leaders in some of those member states, notably France and Germany, are unwilling to take the necessary steps to reinvigorate their economies, steps that the EU itself has long endorsed. At the same time, the EU faces an unprecedented challenge of enlargement. Enlargement itself is not new—the EEC enlarged from six to twelve members, and the EU from twelve to twenty-seven members by 2007. However, those rounds of enlargement brought ten poor, formerly Communist Central and Eastern European states into the EU, thereby taxing its administrative capacity and expenditure policies (particularly agriculture and cohesion policy). The prospect of further enlargement in Eastern Europe and the Balkans, and especially of Turkish accession, fills the existing member states with foreboding. The attractiveness of the EU to prospective members highlights one of the greatest strengths of European integration, while at the same time exacerbating the EU's organizational weakness and political problems.

[See also European Integration; and Trading Blocs and Common Markets.]

BIBLIOGRAPHY

Bomberg, Elizabeth E., and Alexander Stubb. *The European Union: How Does It Work?* 2d ed. Oxford: Oxford University Press, 2007. Provides a good introduction to the institutions and key policies of the EU.

Dinan, Desmond. *Ever Closer Union: An Introduction to European Integration.* 3d ed. Boulder, Colo.: Lynne Rienner, 2005. Explores the history, institutions, and policies of the EU.

Hix, Simon. *The Political System of the European Union.* 2d ed. New York: Palgrave Macmillan, 2005. Presents the EU as a political system comparable to those of familiar nation-states.

Wallace, Helen, William Wallace, and Mark Pollack. *Policy-Making in the European Union.* 5th ed. Oxford: Oxford University Press, 2005. The oldest and most authoritative textbook on EU policies and policy-making.

DESMOND DINAN

EVANGELICALISM. Evangelicalism is a term with several descriptive usages: first, it summarizes a large theological subset of Protestantism; second, it titles a social movement inaugurated in the Reformation and continuing to the present day; and third, it describes a mode of religious expression whereby missionary activity is the primary objective. The word has its origins in the Greek work *evangelion*, meaning "the good news" or the "gospel." From this root, we get the verb "to evangelize," and the nouns "evangel," "evangelist," and "evangelical" (the latter also may be applied as an adjective). Throughout Christian history, believers have been distinguished by their efforts to spread the good news, or to evangelize. However, subsequent to the Reformation, the word acquired a meaning limited to Protestant expressions of Christianity. Included under this canopy is an assortment of traditions, including Dutch Reformed churches, Anabaptists, Pentecostals, Southern Baptists, Churches of Christ, some Episcopalians, and the majority of African American Protestant sects. Holiness churches, Missouri Synod Lutherans, traditionalist Methodists, and many branches of the Presbyterian family also may be described as evangelical. As George Marsden has noted, the only test to determine whether a Christian is an evangelical is whether they possess a strong Christian identity which supersedes denominational location. However, such a vague identifier is an unsatisfactory classificatory marker; in what follows, specificity will be brought to the term through a profile of its theological content, historical background, and missionary tactics.

Evangelicalism as Theology. Although many Christian theologians might be described as evangelical, evangelicalism does not possess a systematic theological genealogy. The British historian David Bebbington has suggested that evangelical theology rotates around four emblems: the cross, the Bible, the mission, and the conversion experience. Like all condensed rubrics of evangelical belief, such a quartet obscures the array of evangelical expressions. Nevertheless, taken individually, these symbols do offer access to the style which signifies evangelicalism.

First, evangelicals have been described as *crucicentric*, since their theological expressions consistently emphasize Jesus Christ's death on the cross. Most Christians, Protestant and otherwise, would place Christ's sacrifice at the center of their theology; for evangelicals, however, the stress is on the suffering of their savior, on the specific torture of the cross. Focus on the cross means that evangelicals study Jesus' path to death (the Passion) over and above his teachings in life. The source for all knowledge of Jesus and God is the Bible and, in particular, the New Testament, which forms the center of evangelical devotional life.

Evangelicals have a unique relationship to the Bible, believing that individuals can interpret the text without the guidance of universal creeds; this is not an unbounded interpretive relationship, though, since evangelicals believe that the Bible offers coherent and final authority on God's revelation. This second scriptural signifier of evangelical belief is also a way of demarcating subsets within evangelicalism: whereas all evangelicals would claim the infallible authority of the Bible, some evangelicals believe that the Bible was written with inerrant textual precision. These evangelicals are known as fundamentalists, and comprise a minority within global evangelicalism (Marsden).

Commitment to the Bible is not a sedate venture for evangelicals. Rather, evangelicals are activists on behalf of their faith; the pursuit of missions and evangelism might be said to be the primary practice of evangelical believers. The Christian life requires righteousness not only in thought and prayer, but also in deed; sharing the message of the evangel through missionary labor is what it means to be an evangelical. The signifying event in any missionary relationship is the conversion experience, which is the result of sustained study, conversation, and prayer. Evangelicals believe that lives need to be changed, and that a singular experience of personal conversion (which some refer to as being "born again") is a necessary first step to living a life sanctified by Jesus Christ. Related to this emphasis is the evangelical quest for Christ's forgiveness: each believer must account to Christ for his or her particular sins in order to pursue a godly life here

and eternal life hereafter. The evangelical stress on a conversion experience may be sourced in the theological writings of Jacob Arminius (1560–1609), who argued that an individual had the ability to choose or refuse salvation.

Despite the prominence of human ability in evangelical theology, it would be inaccurate to suggest that evangelicalism is mere self-expression. Most evangelicals would describe their world as crowded by the supernatural and suffused with the active and gracious presence of a triune God. God is the ultimate arbiter and source of evangelical salvation: God directs lives, motivates history, heals loyal followers, and empowers the many toward righteousness. Indeed, it is this "power of the Holy Spirit" which leads many evangelicals to distinguish themselves from "churchmen" who they believe rely more on grace through sacraments than on grace personally experienced. Such talk of the sanctifying Holy Spirit infuses evangelical rhetoric and is used by believers to measure themselves against other Christian adherents.

This sketch of evangelical theology suggests that many features might mark a Christian believer as evangelical: an investment in the Bible's inerrancy, a pronounced conversion experience, a vivid sense of Jesus Christ's sacrificial death, or the prominence of the supernatural in daily life. Since it is difficult to pick just one signifier of evangelicalism, scholars have struggled to assess the number of evangelicals in the United States. Merely asking surveyed subjects if they are "born again" is unsatisfying, since many Christians do not use this phrase to describe their faith process, even if they do read the Bible as inerrant and perceive the Holy Spirit to be active in their lived experience. For example, if a disabled Lutheran man said he had been healed by an itinerant evangelist following a profound conversion experience, could he be called an evangelical? It seems that when compared to other Christian classifications, the answer should be yes. Considering the list of markers over the entirety of the American Christian population, most scholars estimate the number of evangelicals at somewhere between 30 and 35 percent of the population, or about 100 million Americans. With the rapid expansion of evangelicalism, the global tally is significantly higher, although as yet not tabulated.

Evangelicalism as a Historical Movement. Perhaps as a result of its diffuse content, evangelical theology has been described as a reactive stance toward a variety of intellectual movements: as a retraction from seventeenth-century Calvinism, as a counterbalance to eighteenth-century Enlightenment deism, and as a moral compromise to emergent nineteenth-century industrial democracies.

The rapid success of evangelicalism in the British colonies and subsequently in the United States has led many historians to equate evangelicalism with revolutionary fervor or to describe it as a democratic Protestantism (Hatch). Since it is likely the most widespread and demographically successful religious movement in the modern period, it is tempting to draw such generalized conclusions from its dissemination. Yet the diffuse nature of evangelical theology and the anti-authoritarianism of its many proponents prohibit obvious institutional correlates between evangelicalism and capitalism. Any analysis of evangelicalism that seeks to connect it to broader forces must first acknowledge that "evangelicalism" as a historical agent has never existed within the confines of a single bureaucracy, charismatic figurehead, or common creed. Rather, it has been applied—by historians and adherents, by pastors and critics—in an inconsistent and often contradictory manner.

Standard histories of the Christian West focus on the original German usage of "evangelical." The first formal application of the term was by German Lutherans, who called their church the Evangelische Kirche. However, since the seventeenth century, "evangelical" has corresponded to the denominational offshoots of an Anglo-American revival pattern. (A revival is group experience of reawakened piety.) Within Protestantism, the most pronounced revivals occurred around multiple itinerant figures during the eighteenth-century, including the founder of Methodism, John Wesley (1703–1791), and the charismatic English evangelist George Whitefield (1714–1770). When coupled with the spread of Arminianism, revivals led by these men (along with scores of minor traveling preachers) were the major engine behind America's conversion to Christianity. By the third decade of the nineteenth century, evangelicalism was the majority form of religious expression in the United States. Revivalism continued as the central mode of evangelical dissemination, and was perfected by evangelists like Charles G. Finney (1792–1875), who codified rules and procedures by which mass numbers could undergo the conversion process. The social consequences of this popularization were enormous, as thousands of Americans committed to a worldview which prescribed the moral perfectibility of this world. Due in part to evangelical epistemology, the United States quickly cultivated a "Benevolent Empire" of moral reform crusades, welfare associations, and missionary efforts that defined its emergent position on the world stage.

At the close of the nineteenth century, evangelicals controlled the majority of American denominations. However, the expanding immigrant population and new social scientific research threatened the evangelical stronghold. Higher biblical criticism questioned the consistency of the Bible as a written document, and the growth of urban centers offered new challenges to traditional forms of Protestant piety. Still, major evangelists, like former professional baseball player Billy Sunday (1862–1935), toured urban centers with their tabernacle tent spectacles, commanding souls to confession and enjoining believers to commit to "old time religion." Following World War I, a series of denominational schisms related to scriptural interpretation diluted the mainline might of evangelical America. The plurality of religious bodies in America meant that evangelicals no longer defined the public sphere; as a result, subsequent to the World War II many institutions developed to sustain a unified Christian perspective within the cacophonous theological options of modernity. Educational organizations, like Moody Bible Institute and Wheaton College, centralized intellectual life among evangelicals, and voluntary organizations, such as the National Association of Evangelicals and Youth for Christ, offered bureaucratic tabernacle tents for trans-denominational Christian conversation.

During the closing decades of the twentieth century, evangelical identity increasingly became an elective affinity for those needing to distinguish themselves from the mass of unbelief perceived within the broader non-Christian world. Until the 1970s, evangelicals were involved in the public sphere through bridge agencies, such as the benevolent societies of the early nineteenth century. The emergence of presidential candidate Jimmy Carter, a self-described "born again" Christian, brought evangelical identity to the forefront of political discourse. The progressive disappointments of the 1960s, taken together with the cultural decadence of the counterculture, were funneled into a critique of secular government. Organizations like the Moral Majority, the Concerned Women for American, and the Christian Coalition emerged as a powerful, if minority, voice for conservative evangelical political action. This "Religious Right" has been credited with the election of Republican presidential candidates and attempts to teach creationism or intelligent design in the public schools of Kansas and other states. Future scholarship will weigh the publicized power of this faction against the electoral reality of its base.

Evangelicalism as a Global Mission. Despite recent forays into legislative lobbying, personal piety and mass revivals remain the most obvious expressions of evangelical piety. Chief among the hoped for results of such conversion efforts is the continuation of the Christian mission. For two thousand years, Christians have been

International Evangelicalism. The American pastor Paul Northrup (*center*) with worshippers in the Evangelical Church of Canaan in Miller, near Santa Clara, Cuba, November 2003. Photograph by Jose Goitia. AP IMAGES

motivated to spread the gospel, following Jesus' so-called great commission (Matthew 28:19, and parallels). Although missionaries from Great Britain, Australia, and the European continent have labored in foreign fields, representatives from the United States have made the most substantial international progress. Alongside the Protestant revivals of the antebellum era emerged the first national foreign missions societies. The United Foreign Missionary Society, the American Board of Commissioners for Foreign Missions, the Baptist Board of Foreign Missions, the Missionary Society of Connecticut—all of these organizations were founded and well-funded within the first twenty years of the nineteenth century. Following the divisive tumult of the Civil War, missionary societies regrouped and redoubled their efforts, supporting missions throughout East and Southeast Asia, the South Pacific, Africa, and South America. The 1886 founding of the Student Volunteer Movement, an organization focused on the recruitment of college-age volunteers, provided the organizational center for missionary activity. With the massive influx of young missionaries, missions became the central effort of American Christianity. The number of American foreign missionaries, which stood at 934 in 1890, reached nearly 5,000 a decade later and over 9,000 in 1915. This late-nineteenth-century missionary activity reflected the increased wealth of Protestant congregations,

the general optimism of a prosperous nation, and a geopolitical obsession with imperial power. Missions provided the "moral equivalent" of imperialism, an on-the-ground translation of colonial power in religious terms (Hutchison).

The result of this empire-building was the development of many international nongovernment agencies that provide continuing spiritual guidance and critical social services to the local population. A paradigmatic operation is the Word of Life, a group with headquarters in Uppsala, Sweden. Combining a gospel of financial success and physical well-being, Word of Life was founded in 1983 by Ulf Ekman (b. 1950), who studied at a Bible training center in Oklahoma. Although seemingly out of place in socialist Sweden, Word of Life now boasts the largest church in Europe and the largest Bible school on the Continent. With an evangelical theology and Swedish operators, Word of Life epitomizes the way evangelicalism has become a prime American export, translating a conservative economic agenda into a theological affirmation of individual nation-states, and the therapy of Arminian self-reliance to diverse landscapes (Vasquez). Organizations like Word of Life suggest that the success of evangelicalism abroad has more to do with its brilliant combination of capitalist epistemology and individual habit. Within the countless options of contemporary life, evangelicalism continues to offer a commonplace pragmatism infused with spiritual fervor.

[*See also* Great Awakening; Great Awakening, Second; Methodism; Missions, Christian; Protestantism; *and* Religious Revivals.]

BIBLIOGRAPHY

Bebbington, David W. *The Dominance of Evangelicalism: The Age of Spurgeon and Moody.* Downers Grove, Ill.: InterVarsity Press, 2005.

Blum, Edward J. *Reforging the White Republic: Race, Religion, and American Nationalism, 1865–1898.* Baton Rouge: Louisiana State University Press, 2005.

Griffith, R. Marie. *God's Daughters: Evangelical Women and the Power of Submission.* Berkeley: University of California Press, 1997. An exceptional ethnography of Women's Aglow Fellowship, an international, interdenominational group of evangelical women who meet outside the formal church structure for prayer and testimonial. Offers a subtler analysis of gender politics within evangelical discourse.

Hatch, Nathan O. *The Democratization of American Christianity.* New Haven, Conn.: Yale University Press, 1989. Provides lengthy evidentiary support for the thesis that Americans learned to be democratic through the widespread dissemination of evangelical Christianity. Critics of his work suggest that evangelicalism was as much a force for social conservatism as it was for populist activism.

Hunter, James Davison. *Evangelicalism: The Coming Generation.* Chicago: University of Chicago Press, 1987. Through a survey of students and faculty at sixteen evangelical colleges and seminaries, Hunter provides a definitive sociological profile of evangelical theology.

Hutchison, William. *Errand to the World: American Protestant Thought and Foreign Missions.* Chicago: University of Chicago Press, 1987.

McLoughlin, William G., ed. *The American Evangelicals, 1800–1900: An Anthology.* New York: Harper & Row, 1968. A representative selection of sermons by prominent American preachers.

Marsden, George M. *Understanding Fundamentalism and Evangelicalism.* Grand Rapids, Mich.: Eerdmans, 1991. A compilation of essays by the author of *Fundamentalism and American Culture: The Shaping of Twentieth-Century Evangelicalism, 1870–1925* (New York: Oxford University Press, 1980; 2nd ed., 2006), the authoritative statement on the fundamentalist subset of American evangelicalism.

Vasquez, Manuel A., "Tracking Global Evangelical Christianity." In the *Journal of the American Academy of Religion* 71, no. 1 (March 2003): 157–173. An excellent review of current scholarship addressing global evangelicalism, including a detailed assessment of Simon Coleman's *The Globalisation of Charismatic Christianity: Spreading the Gospel of Prosperity* (Cambridge, U.K.: Cambridge University Press, 2000), an ethnographic survey of the Word of Life.

KATHRYN LOFTON

EVEREST, MOUNT. At approximately 29,035 feet (8,850 meters), Mount Everest is the highest mountain on earth. The discovery, documentation, and climbing of this Himalayan peak have captured the world's imagination and constitute an integral part of South Asian history. The southern face of Mount Everest is situated in the Kingdom of Nepal, while its northern ridges lie in the Tibetan Autonomous Region of the People's Republic of China. Although it straddles the Sino-Nepalese border, for official purposes the mountain is located in Nepal at 27°59′ N and 86°56′ E.

The mountain goes by many names, including Sagarmāthā in Nepali and Sanskrit and Chomolungma in Tibetan. The mountain was identified as the highest in the world in 1852, thanks to trigonometric calculations by the Indian mathematician Radhanath Sikdar (1813–1870). Previously referred to as Peak XV by English speakers, the mountain was named Everest in 1865 in honor of Sir George Everest, the British surveyor-general of India from 1830 to 1843 and director of the final stages of the Great Trigonometric Survey of India. Some Indians believe that Mount Everest should be named after Sikdar.

Some controversy exists about the mountain's exact elevation. Variations in light refraction, gravity deviation, and the snow level of the summit all contribute to varying readings of Mount Everest's height. In 1999 a U.S. team took precise GPS (Global Positioning System) measurements, which confirmed the height at 8,850 meters plus or minus 2 meters.

Since the 1920s, mountaineers have attempted to climb Everest, usually by way of the South Col via the Khumbu icefall from Nepal, or across the northern ridge from the Tibetan side. The climbing window is short because of summer monsoon rains and winter snows, so most summit attempts are made during April and May. A 1953 British expedition led by John Hunt (1910–1998) included Edmund Hillary (1919–2008) from New Zealand and Tenzing Norgay (1914–1986), a Sherpa from the Nepal-Tibet border who had connections to Darjeeling in India. They took the southern route through Nepal, and at 11:30 A.M. on Friday, 29 May 1953—coincidentally the day of Queen Elizabeth II's coronation—Hillary and Norgay became the first climbers known to have reached the summit.

Twenty-nine years earlier, on 8 June 1924, George Mallory (1886–1924) and Andrew Irvine (1902–1924), both from the United Kingdom, had perished in an Everest summit attempt. Recent research expeditions have reignited the debate about whether Mallory reached the summit before his death. A year earlier, on a speaking tour in the United States, to the question, "Why climb Everest?" Mallory famously replied, "Because it is there." A 1996 attempt on the summit ended in disaster with the deaths of eight climbers in a storm, sparking a debate about the merits of commercial expeditions. In 1997 the journalist Jon Krakauer (b. 1954), himself in the climbing party, published *Into Thin Air*, a controversial best seller that chronicles the tragedy.

Despite the high cost of climbing permits, Everest remains a popular destination for mountaineers. Modern expeditions are careful to minimize environmental impact, often collecting trash and spent oxygen cylinders left by earlier climbers, or searching for the frozen dead bodies of colleagues. The Sherpa community, whose homeland lies along the southern slopes of the mountain, continue to practice seasonal trade and traditional agriculture alongside mountain tourism and guiding.

[*See also* Mountain Climbing *and* Tourism.]

BIBLIOGRAPHY
Firstbrook, Peter L. *Lost on Everest: The Search for Mallory and Irvine*. Chicago: Contemporary Books, 1999.
Krakauer, Jon. *Into Thin Air: A Personal Account of the Mount Everest Disaster*. New York: Villard, 1997.

MARK TURIN

EVOLUTION. The theory of evolution, most commonly associated with the English naturalist Charles Darwin (1809–1882), did not spring forth from his mind like Athena from the mind of Zeus. Rather, Darwin developed his theory in light of his predecessors and attempted to provide a compelling scientific account of the "mystery of mysteries," the origin of new and diverse species. It is important to point out that Darwin did not use the word "evolution" to describe his theory. In the first edition of *On the Origin of Species* (1859) the word "evolution" does not appear. Darwin, however, did use the verbal form "evolved" as the last word of the text in the famous line, "from so simple a beginning, endless forms most beautiful and most wonderful have been and are being evolved." Darwin referred to his own theory as the theory of descent with modification and preferred this characterization because he thought it helped to distinguish his theory of species change from preceding ideas.

The Meaning of the Word. The word "evolution" comes from the Latin verb *evolvere*, defined as "to unfold or disclose." This definition carries with it an implication of teleology, or a predictable process or a directional sequence of events with a particular outcome. By the mid-nineteenth century the word had both vernacular and biological uses that were consistent with this definition. The citations in the *Oxford English Dictionary* demonstrate the common usage as far back as the seventeenth century. It was then that a biological meaning was also attached to the word. An anonymous English reviewer of

Jan Swammerdam's *Historia insectorum generalis* wrote that when Swammerdam (1637–1680) was discussing the insect metamorphosis "nothing else [is] to be understood but a gradual and natural Evolution and Growth of the parts."

This association of the word "evolution" with embryology and development led Darwin to avoid its use as a descriptor for his theory. Darwin was at pains to distinguish his theory of descent with modification from the teleology of the developmental process and to demonstrate in the *Origin* that the process of divergence and speciation occurred, not according to some predetermined plan or in a particular direction toward a certain outcome, but rather in response to constantly shifting and changing environmental conditions.

The History of an Idea. Western conceptions of the nature of species originated with the ancient Greeks, but the immutability of species was generally assumed until the seventeenth century. Modern theories of species change resurfaced as a result of the rise of the mechanical philosophy and the scientific revolution of the Enlightenment. Indeed, in the third edition of *Sylva Sylvarum; or, A Naturell History in Ten Centuries*, published posthumously in 1631, Francis Bacon (1561–1626) wrote "the Transmutation of Species is, in the vulgar Philosophy, pronounced Impossible . . . seeing there appear some Manifest Instances of it, the Opinion of Impossibility is to bee rejected; and the Means thereof to bee found out" (p. 132).

The materialist philosophers of the Enlightenment sought explanations for the existence of life that did not invoke supernatural intervention. Life was the result of the interaction of natural causes, including spontaneous generation, and therefore was not guaranteed the stability of divine guidance. The possibility of species change then seemed plausible. Most natural philosophers, however, remained more interested in the origin of life—the possibility and process of spontaneous generation—than in the process of species change.

It is also important to recognize that most Enlightenment natural history was concerned with the desire to classify rather than to explain. This is perhaps most evident in the work of the Swedish naturalist Carolus Linnaeus (Carl Linné, 1707–1778). In his *System of Nature* (1735) Linnaeus sought to understand the pattern of creation. Building on the idea of the great chain of being—an ordered hierarchy of nature from the simple to the complex culminating in humankind—Linnaeus created the basis for modern taxonomy. He realized, however, that the world is not simply based on a formal pattern of relationships but that it also had to work in practice. Linnaeus thus created taxonomic groupings based on visible relationships between species.

This system was not hierarchical in the sense of higher and lower forms; it was more similar to the relations of countries on a map. For example, a lion was not higher or lower than a hyena, they were simply different kinds of carnivores. Linnaeus initially believed that species were immutable; he did, however, come to accept that new species might appear in the course of time. Linnaeus suggested that this might result from the mechanism of hybridization from original kinds.

Contemporaneously, the great French anatomist and founder of the Jardin du Roi, Georges-Louis Leclerc de Buffon (1707–1788)—also initially opposed to the idea of species change—became a convert to, and an important influence on, later theories of transmutation. Buffon's account of the origin of new species depended, however, on degeneration rather than hybridization. In his 1766 article "On the Degeneration of Animals," Buffon suggested that the original species of animals had, through the influence of the environment, degenerated into the diversity of species currently existing.

The ideas of Buffon and Linnaeus were important precursors to the later transmutationist theories of Erasmus Darwin (1731–1802; Charles's grandfather) and Jean-Baptiste de Monet de Lamarck (1744–1829). These theories indicated an increasing awareness of and interest in the cause of species diversity. Erasmus Darwin described a theory of species transformation in *Zoonomia* in 1794–1796. Here he presented the idea of an original "living filament" that had become transmuted over time into the higher forms of life.

According to the theory, the process of transmutation was brought about by a self-improving force imparted to all organisms by God. Transmutation was also shaped by external environmental influences that elicited the development and inheritance of new organs, traits, and behaviors. In this respect, Erasmus Darwin's theory was not much different from Lamarck's, particularly with respect to the inheritance of acquired characteristics, the idea most commonly associated with Lamarck: that traits that are developed in the course of the parent's lifetime will be passed on to the offspring. Both Erasmus Darwin's and Lamarck's theories are committed to a directional process from lower to higher or from simple to more complex, a commitment that was challenged by the theory that would be published in 1859 by Erasmus's grandson Charles.

Darwin's Theory: Descent with Modification. The publication of Charles Darwin's best-known work, *On the Origin of Species by Means of Natural Selection, or The Preservation of Favoured Races in the Struggle for Life* (1859), marked the beginning of a long scientific and social debate about the process of species change. Though the scientific success of Darwin's theory was not instantaneous, it has become the cornerstone of modern biology. Nevertheless, there has been a continuing challenge to the validity of Darwinian theory from various social, political, and religious groups that persists into the present, especially in the United States.

The scientific status of Darwin's theory of descent with modification has generally been a story of increasing influence and success. Historians of science, however, have come to recognize that the initial response to Darwin's theory was not universal acceptance. There have been many disputes regarding the rate of evolution (whether it was steady or episodic) and the mode of evolution (whether change was effected largely by selection or by other mechanisms, including the inheritance of acquired characteristics).

Indeed, for many, the establishment of Darwin's theory as the organizing principle of biology did not occur for another half a century after the *Origin* was published. In the late nineteenth and early twentieth centuries, the work of the German biologists Ernst Haeckel (1834–1919) and August Weismann (1834–1914) played an important role in the status of Darwin's theory. Haeckel was the most successful popularizer of the theory, and he used his considerable artistic talent to provide some of the most iconic images of the process of evolution. Weismann's theory of the germplasm undermined scientific support for Lamarck's mechanism of inheritance of acquired characteristics and established natural selection as the most important factor in evolution.

In the years immediately after World War I, there was a great deal of concern about the negative effects of nationalism; the increasing power of big business; the rise of labor movements and their associated political radicalism; communism; and immigration. In various religious communities in the United States these concerns were often combined with a fear of increasing secularization of American culture and a rejection of higher criticism—the examination of the Bible as a historical document rather than as the word of God. Darwin's work was enmeshed in these fears because of a widespread belief that Darwinian natural selection motivated the brutality of war, criticism of the Bible, social unrest, and political radicalism. The portrait of nature as a field of open competition that many saw

Evolution Trial. The defense attorney Clarence Darrow at the Scopes evolution trial, Dayton, Tennessee, July 1925. John Scopes is at the defense table behind Darrow, leaning forward with his hand on his sleeve. PRINTS AND PHOTOGRAPHS DIVISION, LIBRARY OF CONGRESS

depicted in Darwin's work led to a number of attempts to appropriate or excoriate evolutionary theory. In the early twenty-first century, elements of this debate were revived by some conservatives in the United States.

Contemporary Evolution. The combination of the Darwinian theory of descent with modification and natural selection with the theory of heredity by Gregor Mendel (1822–1884) brought about the modern evolutionary synthesis in the early and mid-twentieth century. The genetics of Theodosius Dobzhansky (1900–1975), the taxonomy and systematics of Ernst Mayr (1904–2005), the paleontology of George Gaylord Simpson (1902–1984), and the development of mathematical population genetics by J. B. S. Haldane (1892–1964), Ronald A. Fisher (1890–1962), and Sewall Wright (1889–1988) coalesced around Darwin's ideas laid out in 1859 and became the standards of modern biology. Through genetics, the mechanisms of evolution could be more fully explained.

In another area, discoveries in the late twentieth and early twenty-first centuries added data about the diversity of extinct species and the rich and unexpectedly long history of hominid apes and early human species. The disparate fields of the life sciences now had a central organizing idea. Indeed, Dobzhansky could write in 1973 that "Nothing in biology makes sense except in the light of evolution."

[*See also* Creationism; Darwinism; *and* Social Darwinism.]

BIBLIOGRAPHY

Bowler, Peter J. *Evolution: The History of an Idea.* 3d ed. Berkeley: University of California Press, 2003. A comprehensive treatment of the idea of evolution in the West.

Dobzhansky, T. D. "Nothing in Biology Makes Sense Except in the Light of Evolution." *American Biology Teacher* 35 (March 1973): 125–129.

Hodge, Jonathon, and Gregory Radick, eds. *The Cambridge Companion to Darwin.* Cambridge, U.K.: Cambridge University Press, 2003. An excellent collection of historical and philosophical analyses of Darwin's life and work.

Mayr, Ernst, and William B. Provine, eds. *The Evolutionary Synthesis: Perspectives on the Unification of Biology.* Cambridge, Mass.: Harvard University Press, 1980. The best collection of essays on the modern synthesis; authors include some of the main participants of the synthesis.

Richards, Robert J. *The Meaning of Evolution: The Morphological Construction and Ideological Reconstruction of Darwin's Theory.* Chicago: University of Chicago Press, 1992. A compelling but controversial argument for the influence of German Romanticism on Darwin's development of the theory of evolution.

Ridley, Mark, ed. *Evolution.* 3d ed. Oxford: Blackwell, 2004. An exceptionally useful collection of primary papers by the most important scientists and scholars on evolution, beginning with Darwin. The papers represent a broad range of areas, including biodiversity, human evolution, adaptation, and natural selection.

Ruse, Michael. *The Darwinian Revolution: Science Red in Tooth and Claw.* 2d ed. Chicago: University of Chicago Press, 1999. This work represents the standard in the history of science and carefully describes Darwin's work in the Victorian scientific and social context.

MARK E. BORRELLO

EXERCISE. *See* Health and Disease; Physical Fitness.

EXPLORATION [*This entry includes two subentries, an overview and a discussion of exploration in Africa.*]

Overview

By most historians' accounts, the so-called European age of exploration, discovery, or reconnaissance began with the travels of the Venetian merchant and traveler Marco Polo through the Middle East, South Asia, and China (1271–1295) or the Iberian-sponsored expeditions to the Americas, Africa, and Asia in the fifteenth century. Much of this early modern European exploration was directed by a desire to find and secure first an overland and then a maritime route to the East Indies. Famously, this quest drove the four Spanish-funded expeditions of the Italian explorer Christopher Columbus to the Caribbean and South America between 1492 and 1504, as well as Ferdinand Magellan's circumnavigation of the globe (1519–1522) via the southern tip of the Americas. Meanwhile, Portuguese expeditions headed eastward, encouraged by Bartolomeu Dias's voyage beyond the Cape of Good Hope in 1488 and Vasco da Gama's first successful voyage to southwestern India in 1497–1498.

As English, French, Dutch, Russian, and other explorers followed suit over the next two centuries, exploration and geography soon became closely tied with nation-building and imperial rivalry. For example, Richard Hakluyt and his acolyte Samuel Purchas, in his *Hakluytus Posthumus, or, Purchas His Pilgrimes* (4 vols., London, 1625), compiled histories of "English" discovery (even if explorers themselves were not English) that defined geographical discovery, trade, and colonization as national and providentially inspired projects. Competition with Spanish America in particular drove efforts such as the three expeditions in the Atlantic of Martin Frobisher from 1576 to 1578 or those of Humphrey Gilbert and Walter Raleigh in 1578, Francis Drake's circumnavigation between 1577 and 1580, or the late-seventeenth-century explorations of the Mississippi River and French Louisiana of Jacques Marquette, Louis Jolliet, and René Robert Cavelier, Sieur de La Salle. Explorers and their patrons also sought new and better routes to Asia, putting particular hope in the fabled Arctic "northwest" and "northeast" passages.

Nonetheless, not all exploration was funded or driven by national states. For example, much early geographical information about China came from Catholic priests and missionaries, particularly Jesuits. Others explored in the service of companies, like Abel Janszoon Tasman's charting of coastal Australia and New Zealand for the Dutch East India Company. Still others, such as William Dampier, who succeeded in three circumnavigations, gathered geographical information in various roles, as naturalists, traders, naval officers, and pirates.

Enlightenment and Exploration. On these foundations, and stimulated by the intellectual and political trends of the Enlightenment, eighteenth-century Europeans led a concerted effort to explore the globe. The so-called Linnean classificatory system pioneered by the Swedish botanist Carolus Linnaeus (Carl Linné) fed a seemingly insatiable curiosity about the natural world and provided a conceptual framework to collect, catalog, and taxonomize the lands, seas, flora, and fauna of the world. Geographers also became deeply interested in what some termed "moral" geography. The study, classification, and hierarchizing of the people, languages, and cultures encountered by European explorers nurtured new social and racial theories as well as a "stadial" or "conjectural" philosophy of history, which saw in these various peoples and societies what the Irish orator, politician, and author Edmund Burke famously referred to as "the Great Map of Mankind": evidence of human civilization at its various stages of development, most often culminating in Enlightenment Europe.

This growing knowledge about the rest of the world reinforced a sense of Europe's advanced place among world civilizations. At the same time, the popularity of exploration journals and accounts provided a novel language for situating social and political critique. These often came in the form of thinly veiled utopian and dystopian travel narratives. Christened by Thomas More's *Utopia* (1516), the genre perhaps reached its apotheosis with Montesquieu's *Persian Letters* (1721). Other examples include Jonathan Swift's *Gulliver's Travels* (1726), Daniel Defoe's *Robinson Crusoe* (1719–1720), and myriad less famous accounts of fictional places, peoples, and explorers—including space

Exploration of the South Pole. Captain Roald Amundsen and crew capture seals during their expedition to the South Pole, 1910–1911. PRINTS AND PHOTOGRAPHS DIVISION, LIBRARY OF CONGRESS

John Harrison's "H4" clock, developed in the 1750s, made it possible for the first time to keep accurate longitude at sea. Captain James Cook's expeditions to the Pacific did a great deal in particular to establish the reputation of a new kind of travel, which merged political and military objectives with scientific goals. Yet, while accompanied by new scientific instruments (like the H4), artists, and naturalists, Cook's voyages also attracted a more visceral interest in the South Seas, particularly Tahiti, which came to be depicted as an erotic and exotic paradise. European fascination with the Pacific was embodied in the figure of Omai, the Tahitian brought back to London by Joseph Banks on Cook's first voyage.

Cook's expeditions and those of his French rival Louis-Antoine de Bougainville did a great deal to popularize exploration generally toward the end of the eighteenth century. In 1788, a London dining club, led in part by Banks, created the African Association, the first concerted European effort to explore the African interior. Continuing expeditions to the Pacific, including those of George Vancouver and other former members of Cook's crews, kept alive the search for a northwest passage. Alexander von Humboldt's travels (1799–1804) in South America, his vast collections, and thirty volumes of writings also helped mark the birth of the era of "scientific" exploration and geography. In the newly formed United States, his and others' efforts contributed to an emerging fervor for geographical and natural knowledge, most vibrantly expressed in the cross-continental expedition of Meriwether Lewis and William Clark from 1803 to 1806. Meanwhile, in South Asia, as the English East India Company expanded its territorial and political power, it also supported and directed geographical discovery, culminating in the Great Trigonometric Survey of India, begun in 1802 under the direction of William Lambton.

Exploration and Empire in the Nineteenth Century. As exploration gained in popularity and attention through the first half of the nineteenth century, its support became much more widespread. Global wars of the eighteenth century, particularly the Seven Years' War (1757–1763) and the French Revolutionary and Napoleonic Wars (1792–1815), as well as the expansion of empire, particularly in British India and the American West, gave Western states more incentive and interest in patronizing exploration. As the Industrial Revolution began to take hold, commercial and industrial interests also found use in exploration. Church and missionary societies saw in exploration the opportunity both to spread the gospel as well as, particularly in Africa, to stem the

and time travelers—often meant to reflect and lampoon problems at home.

Exploration was also tied to Enlightenment culture in the form of a growing fervor for observation, collection, and display of curiosities and the exotic. Expeditions around the world fed new institutions, like the British Museum and the Royal Botanical Gardens at Kew, as well as those of private individuals, such as those of the eighteenth- century's leading patron of exploration and a former explorer, Sir Joseph Banks. Meanwhile, geographers like Guillaume de L'Isle and J. B. B. D'Anville in France and James Rennell in Britain ushered in a technical and aesthetic revolution in cartography, replacing older, ornate maps with more austere and "scientific" style, which spoke to the Enlightenment's emphasis on precision, empiricism, and progress. No less rhetorical than their predecessors, these maps were vibrant expressions of the paucity of European knowledge, making clear the need for further exploration while also directing it.

New technologies and techniques in the late eighteenth century also fed into this exploratory fervor. For example,

tide of the slave trade. Exploration also continued to grow in European popular culture, increasingly available in travelogues, news accounts, and juvenile literature by and about explorers.

This broad range of interests found their expression in a new kind of institution: the geographical society. The Société de Géographie de Paris was founded in 1821, followed by one in Germany in 1828, Italy in 1867, the Netherlands in 1873, and Spain in 1876. None of these societies, however, was as actively engaged in patronizing exploration as Britain's Royal Geographical Society (RGS), created in 1830. These societies represented the union among the commercial, imperial, scientific, religious, and cultural impulses gathering behind the quest for geographical knowledge of the globe. They established standards for "correct" and "accurate" geographical knowledge, channeled resources toward exploration, and created venues for the codification, distribution, communication, and cataloging of its findings. At the same time, institutions like the RGS as well as provincial and colonial geographical societies and other bodies, like the Royal Asiatic Society, continued in an older tradition of exploration patronized by learned societies and clubs.

By the nineteenth century, exploration was also indelibly linked with the expansion of European empire. Technological and scientific innovations, such as the isolation of the malarial prophylaxis quinine in 1820 or the advent of photography after the 1830s, only aided in the expansion of exploration abroad and the proliferation of its popularity in Europe. These transformations were perhaps felt most dramatically in the exploration of Africa. After the 1830 discovery by the brothers Richard and John Lander of the outlet of the Niger River, a good deal of attention turned to finding the elusive source of the Nile. This quest defined some of the most famous expeditions of the period, including those of Richard Burton and John Hanning Speke, David Livingstone, and Henry Morton Stanley. Burton also traveled in Asia and Arabia, famously passing as a Muslim and visiting the holy city of Mecca. Others joined in European penetration of the Levant, perhaps most notably Charles Montagu Doughty, whose *Travels in Arabia Deserta* (1921) bears an introduction by T. E. Lawrence (Lawrence of Arabia). Though the British and the French took an early lead in these nationally sponsored expeditions, by the end of the nineteenth century, as their colonial empires expanded, so too did German, Portuguese, Belgian, and Italian exploration, particularly in southern and eastern Africa.

Though it has long been recounted as a series of achievements and adventures of great men, women, like Gertrude

Bell in the Levant and the American journalist Elizabeth Bisland in East Asia, played a profound role in this period of exploration. A French scholar of Buddhism, Alexandra David-Néel undertook five separate expeditions into Tibet, publishing *My Journey to Lhasa* in 1927. Amelia Edwards's travels in East Africa led, among other things, to her posthumous endowment of the University College London chair of Egyptology. Isabella Bird traveled perhaps most widely, exploring in the American West, India, Persia, Korea, Japan, China, and north Africa. Meanwhile, the voyages of Mary Kingsley through West Africa, including her climb of Mount Cameroon, captivated the British reading public, particularly through her *Travels in West Africa* (1897), one of the most popular books on African exploration in the century.

Onward, Downward, and Upward. While Europeans continued to explore within their newfound Asian and African empires, the line between exploration, imperial administration, commerce, tourism, and travel increasingly blurred. At the same time, late-nineteenth- and early-twentieth-century explorers increasingly turned their attention back to one of the earliest geographical problems—the search for the Northwest and Northeast Passage—and the remaining mysteries of the poles. Russian and Scandinavian explorers continued to explore Siberia and the West Coast of North America. In 1878, the Finnish mineralogist Adolf Erik Nordenskiöld with a largely Swedish expedition navigated the eastward Arctic route to the Pacific in its entirety. Meanwhile, British expeditions by John Ross and William Edward Parry in the opening decades of the century mapped much of the western Arctic coastline, reinvigorating the centuries-old quest for the Northwest Passage. The disappearance in 1845 of Sir John Franklin and his crew—and the controversy over rumors that the party turned to cannibalism—led to forty American and British expeditions to the Arctic to find him, including that of John Rae, who won £10,000 in 1854 for authoritatively discovering Franklin's fate. Still, it was a Norwegian explorer, Roald Amundsen, who first successfully navigated the Northwest Passage, leaving Oslo in 1903 and arriving in Alaska in 1906, and an American naval officer, Robert Peary, who first reached the North Pole. In 1912, Amundsen also became the first European to reach the South Pole, beating the Briton Robert Falcon Scott by one month.

Though much of the earth's land and sea was now mapped, the second half of the twentieth century gave rise to a new set of geographical problems that still fueled national and personal rivalries. After decades of attempts by various expeditions from around the world, in 1953, the New Zealander Sir Edmund Hillary and the Nepalese Tenzing Norgay became the first to reach the highest peak on earth, Mount Everest, in the Himalayas. In the 1960s and 1970s, Jacques Cousteau popularized deep-sea and oceanographic expeditions. Perhaps most importantly, the successful launch in 1957 of the Soviet satellite *Sputnik I* initiated a "space race" driven by competition between the two global superpowers, the United States and the Soviet Union. Also like their eighteenth- and nineteenth-century predecessors, such exploration was followed by a growth in travel, leading many, including Hillary, to warn of impending ecological disaster as sites like Everest became popular tourist destinations. In 2001, the first private tourist was sent to space, and in 2006, the Iranian-American Anousheh Ansari became the fourth individual and the first female "space tourist." In 2004, the entrepreneur Sir Richard Branson announced plans for Virgin Galactic, a company promising to run regular commercial space flights.

BIBLIOGRAPHY

Ballantyne, Tony, ed., *Science, Empire and the European Exploration of the Pacific.* Aldershot, Hants, U.K., and Burlington, Vt.: Ashgate, 2004.

Birkett, Dea. *Spinsters Abroad: Victorian Lady Explorers.* Oxford and New York: Basil Blackwell, 1989.

Blunt, Alison. *Travel, Gender, and Imperialism: Mary Kingsley and West Africa.* New York: Guilford Press, 1994.

Claeys, Gregory, ed. *Utopias of the British Enlightenment.* Cambridge, U.K., and New York: Cambridge University Press, 1994.

Drayton, Richard. *Nature's Government: Science, Imperial Britain, and the "Improvement" of the World.* New Haven, Conn.: Yale University Press, 2000.

Driver, Felix. *Geography Militant: Cultures of Exploration and Empire.* Oxford: Blackwell, 2001.

Edney, Matthew H. *Mapping an Empire: The Geographical Construction of British India, 1765–1843.* Chicago: University of Chicago Press, 1997.

Fulford, Tim, and Peter J. Kitson, eds. *Travels, Explorations and Empires, 1770–1835.* 8 vols. London and Brookfield, Vt.: Pickering & Chatto, 2003–2004.

Hanbury-Tenison, Robin, ed. *The Oxford Book of Exploration.* Oxford and New York: Oxford University Press, 2005.

Kitson, Peter J., ed. *Nineteenth-Century Travels, Explorations, and Empires: Writings from the Era of Imperial Consolidation, 1835–1910.* 8 vols. London and Brookfield, Vt.: Pickering and Chatto, 2003–2004.

Livingstone, David N. *The Geographical Tradition: Episodes in the History of a Contested Enterprise.* Oxford and Cambridge, Mass.: Blackwell, 1992.

Mackay, David. *In the Wake of Cook: Exploration, Science, and Empire, 1780–1801.* New York: St. Martin's, 1985.

Marshall, P. J., and Glyndwr Williams. *The Great Map of Mankind: Perceptions of New Worlds in the Age of Enlightenment.* Cambridge, Mass.: Harvard University Press, 1982.

Sachs, Aaron. *The Humboldt Current: Nineteenth-Century Exploration and the Roots of American Environmentalism.* New York: Viking, 2006.

Stafford, Robert. *Scientist of Empire: Sir Roderick Murchison, Scientific Exploration, and Victorian Imperialism.* Cambridge, U.K., and New York: Cambridge University Press, 1989.

PHILIP J. STERN

Africa

Until the late eighteenth century, the interior of Africa remained largely a mystery to Europeans. Notwithstanding several noteworthy early modern expeditions by the fifteenth-century Portuguese and scattered seventeenth-century English, French, and Dutch efforts, European knowledge remained largely confined to the coasts. Ancient Greeks and Romans, particularly Herodotus, Ptolemy, and Pliny the Elder, were still considered the best authorities on African geography, preferred to the often more accurate medieval Arab geographers and travelers, such as Leo Africanus, Abu Abdallah Muhammad al-Idrisi, Ahmad al-Biruni, Ibn Battuta, and Abu al-Fida. Early modern cartographers filled in the blanks in European knowledge with a curious combination of scholarship, conjecture, fantasy, and myth, a habit lampooned by the eighteenth-century English author Jonathan Swift in his *On Poetry: A Rhapsody* (1733): "Geographers in *Afric*-maps / With Savage-Pictures fill their Gaps; / And o'er unhabitable Downs / Place Elephants for want of Towns."

A number of factors were responsible for precluding systematic or sustained European contact with the African interior. Strong political and economic powers, such as Muslim caravan traders in the north and the West African states of Ashanti and Dahomey, could prove resistant to European incursions. Diseases like malaria, yellow fever, and dysentery led to such extraordinary mortality rates that the Guinea Coast of West Africa earned the reputation of being the "white man's grave." Though Europeans fantasized about accessing the North African gold trade, contemporaries were also not convinced that exploration would yield commercial, economic, political, or imperial advantage. With the notable exception of the transatlantic slave trade, much of the early modern exploration of the African littoral was primarily undertaken in the service of maintaining a maritime route to the East Indies. For their part, slavers, well supplied by an internal African slave trade, tended to regard with great suspicion any ambitions to open the interior.

Exploration in the Enlightenment. Despite these impediments, in the late eighteenth century a number of political, intellectual, and social forces in Europe encouraged a more sustained interest in the exploration of Africa. James Bruce's explorations in East Africa from 1768 to 1773 and his successful navigation of the Blue Nile had, in the words of the eighteenth-century English author and satirist Horace Walpole, brought Africa "into fashion." S. M. X. Golberry's travels in West Africa from 1785 to 1787 had a similar effect in France.

More broadly, the Enlightenment's stress on empirical knowledge and the coincident passion for collecting, cataloging, and displaying the flora, fauna, curiosities, and exotica from around the globe rendered a more systematic geography of Africa one of the great desiderata among European intellectuals and the elite. Evangelical Protestants came to see exploration as one way of undermining the African slave trade, while merchants in the early phases of the Industrial Revolution also began to speculate about the commercial possibilities of Africa.

Finally, especially following Napoleon's invasion of Egypt in 1798, European states began to take a greater interest, as European conflicts were brought directly to Africa. At the same time, these wars increasingly brought Africa to Europe, in the pages of the newspapers, in conversations of the coffeehouses and clubs, and in the collections of the museums and learned societies.

The body that did the most to direct and foster this interest was a London gentleman's dining club, which in 1788 and under the stewardship of Sir Joseph Banks created the Association for Promoting the Discovery of the Inland Parts of Africa, or the African Association, the first successful organized European effort to explore sub-Saharan Africa. The African Association's first goal was to send the first modern European to the Niger River. The first few expeditions ended in failure. However, in 1796, its fourth explorer, Mungo Park, reached the Niger from West Africa and confirmed its direction, as Park wrote, "flowing slowly *to the eastward.*" Park's *Travels in the Interior Districts of Africa* (1799) ran through several editions, and Park became an instant celebrity.

The African Association's next explorer, Friedrich Hornemann, set out from North Africa in 1797 for Tombouctou (Timbuktu), traveling as a Muslim. Though he died in the interior, the African Association published his materials in 1802, further popularizing its mission.

The Nineteenth Century. Despite this exploratory fervor, by the early nineteenth century, Europeans did not know much more than they did decades or even centuries earlier. In 1805, Mungo Park set out on a grander government-funded expedition, but the entire crew perished en route or on the Niger. Following Park, a number of explorers raced their way toward the western African interior. In 1826 the Scottish explorer Alexander Laing was the first to reach Tombouctou, followed in 1828 by the Frenchman René Caillié.

The fractious expedition of Hugh Clapperton, Walter Oudney, and Dixon Denham in 1821–1825 and another by Clapperton and Richard Lander gave support to an argument about the Niger's course that contradicted the theories of some of the greatest authorities in Europe, including the African Association geographer James Rennell (who thought the Niger flowed eastward into the interior) and the second lord of the British Admiralty, Sir John Barrow (who thought the Niger met the Congo River). In 1830, Lander and his brother John confirmed their hypothesis, following the Niger to its terminus in the oil rivers of the Bight of Benin on the coast of present-day Nigeria.

In 1832, Macgregor Laird and his short-lived African Inland Commercial Company organized the first merchant expedition to the Niger. Though the ship reached the Benue, the Niger's main tributary, most of the crew, including Richard Lander, died. Laird tried again in 1854, now with support from the British Admiralty. This expedition returned with no casualties, demonstrating the effectiveness for explorers of steamship travel and of the malarial prophylaxis quinine, isolated from the chicona bark by Joseph Pelletier and Joseph Caventou in 1820 and after the 1850s used widely by Europeans and Americans in the tropics.

New technologies, like photography, also began to broaden the scope and reach of explorers, as did new institutions like the Royal Geographical Society (RGS), created in 1830. After absorbing the African Association in 1831, the RGS took the lead in the patronage and direction of African exploration, accompanied by provincial geographical societies and similar bodies across Europe: Paris (1821), Berlin (1828), Italy (1867), and Madrid (1877).

By the middle of the nineteenth century, African exploration had come to be an almost ecumenical concern of government, commercialists, industrialists, financiers, missionaries, and humanitarians alike. This was most evident in the career of the nineteenth century's most famous missionary, Dr. David Livingstone. His four expeditions between the 1840s and 1870s in southern and eastern Africa had religious, commercial, political, and scientific aims and were sponsored alternatively by the London Missionary Society, the RGS, the British government, and the

RGS again. It was this final expedition in 1866 to find the source of the Nile that the *New York Herald* reporter and explorer Henry Morton Stanley notoriously set out to find, best remembered by Stanley's ironic question upon their meeting at Ujiji on Lake Tanganyika: "Dr. Livingstone, I presume?"

As with the course of the Niger before it, finding the source of the Nile became the guiding passion of mid-nineteenth-century African explorers. Perhaps the most notorious among them were Richard Burton and John Hanning Speke, who in 1858 became the first Europeans to reach Lake Tanganyika. Speke and a small party also "discovered" Lake Nyanza, christening it Lake Victoria and declaring it the source of the Nile. Burton disagreed, and the controversy ruined their partnership, friendship, and perhaps even Speke himself: the day before the two were to debate the issue at the RGS in September 1864, Speke died from a self-inflicted gunshot wound, which some contemporaries and historians assumed to be suicide.

Despite the popularity of the Nile, explorers, traders, surveyors, missionaries, natural historians, and hunters explored farther in southern and western Africa. Scientific, commercial, and religious interests, including a growing desire to supplant the African slave trade with so-called legitimate trade in European products and goods, combined, as in the 1850 expedition of James Richardson, Heinrich Barth, and Adolf Overweg toward Tombouctou and Lake Chad. Moreover, despite the historical attention given to the men and the search for the Nile, a number of women explorers captivated contemporaries, particularly Mary Kingsley with her 1897 best seller *Travels in West Africa.*

Empire and Exploration. By the last decades of the nineteenth century, to Livingstone's motto for African exploration—"Christianity, commerce, and civilization"—one must also add "colonization." During the so-called scramble for Africa following the Berlin West Africa Conference of 1884–1885, geographical knowledge and maps of Africa became crucial tools for defining borders, erecting transport networks, exploiting resources, governing colonial states, and policing colonial subjects.

German, Portuguese, and British explorers and surveyors extended European maps farther into southern and eastern Africa. Henry Stanley explored farther in Central Africa on behalf of the ruthless Belgian king Leopold II. French surveyors mapped vast territories of the western Sahara. Explorers also made possible Italian imperial ambitions in Eritrea and Somaliland and later in Libya and Abyssinia. Explorers and geographers became strategically and politically crucial in the extension of Fascist Italy and Germany's colonial ambitions in Africa, as well as on both sides during and between the two world wars. Of course, European geographers and cartographers also played a crucial role in defining the decolonization of Africa.

[*See also* Colonialism; Empire and Imperialism; *and* Niger.]

BIBLIOGRAPHY

Baker, J. N. L. *A History of Geographical Discovery and Exploration.* London: George G. Harrap, 1931.

Bell, Morag, Robin Butlin, and Michael Heffernan, eds. *Geography and Imperialism 1820–1940.* Manchester, U.K., and New York: Manchester University Press, 1995.

Boahen, A. Adu. *Britain, the Sahara, and the Western Sudan, 1788–1861.* Oxford: Clarendon Press, 1964.

Curtin, Philip D. *The Image of Africa: British Ideas and Action, 1780–1850.* 2 vols. Madison: University of Wisconsin Press, 1964.

David Livingstone and the Victorian Encounter with Africa. London: National Portrait Gallery, 1996.

Godlewska, Anne, and Neil Smith, eds. *Geography and Empire.* Oxford and Cambridge, Mass.: Blackwell, 1994.

Hallett, Robin. *The Penetration of Africa: European Enterprise and Exploration Principally in Northern and Western Africa Up to 1830.* London: Routledge and Kegan Paul, 1965.

Kennedy, Dane. *The Highly Civilized Man: Richard Burton and the Victorian World.* Cambridge, Mass.: Harvard University Press, 2005.

McEwan, Cheryl. *Gender, Geography, and Empire: Victorian Women Travellers in West Africa.* Aldershot, U.K., and Burlington, Vt.: Ashgate, 2000.

Stone, Jeffrey C. *A Short History of the Cartography of Africa.* Lewiston, N.Y.: Edwin Mellen Press, 1995.

PHILIP J. STERN

F

FABIANISM. Fabianism is a gradualist nonrevolutionary theory of socialism. The term "Fabianism" refers to the political theory associated with the Fabian Society, a socialist group formed in the United Kingdom in 1884 and still operating in the twenty-first century. The founders of the society chose the title "Fabian" to indicate an affinity with the Roman general Fabius Maximus Cunctator (the delayer), who was said to have won his campaigns by avoiding pitched battles in favor of patient attrition.

The Fabian Society. The Fabian Society was one of several socialist groups founded in the United Kingdom in the late nineteenth century. Though many of these groups were Marxist, the Fellowship of the New Life was more concerned with personal behavior and utopian communities than with social revolution. The fellowship split when some of its members decided that they wanted to pay more attention to social reform. These members formed the Fabian Society on 4 January 1884. They included Hubert Bland, Frank Podmore, and Edward Pease. Over the next five years the society attracted an extraordinary array of talent. New members included Annie Besant, who at the time was a leading light within the National Secular Society but who soon joined the Theosophical Society; George Bernard Shaw, who was about to make the transition from struggling novelist to world-famous playwright; Sydney Olivier from the Colonial Office; Graham Wallas, who became one of the leading political scientists of his generation; and perhaps most important, Sidney Webb, an energetic thinker and writer who did much to define the society's particular brand of socialism, writing copiously (often in collaboration with his wife, Beatrice) on political economy, sociology, public administration, labor history, and contemporary politics. It was this group of people who in 1889 published *Fabian Essays*, a book that remains the leading historical expression of Fabianism.

Although the Fabian Society was formed in Britain, its ideas soon spread across the British Empire, the Commonwealth, and elsewhere. Fabianism had a notable influence, for example, on progressive nationalists in India such as Jawaharlal Nehru. The Fabian Society defined its role more as providing ideas than campaigning; it was a precursor of what we now call think tanks. Nonetheless, although the society—unlike a more campaigning organization—never showed much inclination to form branches in the United Kingdom, there are even today prominent Fabian groups in countries such as Australia and New Zealand.

Fabian Socialism. The Fabian Society was committed to democratic means rather than revolutionary ones. Its members believed that universal suffrage and representative government made violence unnecessary. They looked to a program of systematic progressive legislation by impartial elites rather than the pursuit of class war. Typically the Fabians regarded the superiority of socialism as a rational truth that could be shown scientifically. Hence they sometimes advocated a strategy of permeation. This strategy began with the careful and patient collecting and sifting of facts, which then provided the basis for specific policy recommendations of a socialist hue. These policy recommendations were then presented to key decision makers—politicians, civil servants, trade unionists, and the like—who, it was thought, would gradually implement them. Several Fabians thereby suggested that the gradual triumph of socialism was inevitable since socialism alone could resolve the complex problems of modern societies. They thus argued that socialism would come about gradually through democratic processes and social evolution.

Fabians typically equated socialism with the extension of state activity to promote social justice. Like most socialists, they envisaged an egalitarian society free of exploitation and poverty. Typically they argued that such a society could be achieved by means of progressive taxation to generate income that the state then could use to provide collective goods and social welfare. Many Fabians also advocated state or municipal ownership of the leading economic resources of the nation. Some of them even favored extensive public ownership of the means of production. In their view, public ownership would help to overcome economic power and privilege, as well as promote efficiency by removing the waste and duplication associated with economic competition.

Although Fabianism is often taken to be a peculiarly Anglophone movement, it has had a much wider influence. In particular, the Fabians did much to inspire Eduard Bernstein's revisionist rethinking of Marxism. It is thus arguable that Fabianism was the fountainhead of much of twentieth-century social democracy.

Legacies. The impact of the Fabians on British social democracy remains hotly debated. On the one hand its leading figures were, at least intermittently, hostile to the formation of a separate Labour Party. The impetus for the Labour Party lay more in the links forged between trade unionists and a later socialist group, called the Independent Labour Party. On the other hand, leading Fabians soon played a prominent role within the Labour Party, while many of the most active members of the Independent Labour Party either were also members of the Fabian Society or were heavily influenced by Fabian ideas. The Fabians sent a delegate to the meeting in 1900 of trade unionists and socialists that founded the Labour Representation Committee—which soon became the Labour Party. The society became and still remains affiliated to the party as a socialist society. Sidney Webb drafted the party's constitution of 1918, which included its first explicit commitment to socialism. Webb and Olivier both served as cabinet members in Labour governments between the wars.

Many of the Labour Party's leading thinkers and politicians have been Fabians. Between the two wars these included G. D. H. Cole, Harold Laski, and R. H. Tawney, as well as Prime Minister James Ramsay MacDonald. After World War II they included Anthony Crosland and Richard Crossman, as well as Prime Minister Harold Wilson. In the early twenty-first century the society has around six thousand individual members, including Tony Blair and Gordon Brown. Nonetheless, it is rightly best remembered for the pioneering role that its early members played in forging a democratic strand of socialism based on state provision of common goods and social welfare.

[*See also* Socialism, *subentry* Europe.]

BIBLIOGRAPHY

MacKenzie, Norman Ian, and Jeanne MacKenzie. *The First Fabians*. London: Weidenfeld and Nicholson, 1977.

Pease, Edward. *The History of the Fabian Society.* 1916. Reprint. New York: Barnes and Noble, 1963.

Pugh, Patricia. *Educate, Agitate, Organize: 100 Years of Fabian Socialism*. London and New York: Methuen, 1984.

Shaw, George Bernard, ed. *Fabian Essays in Socialism*. London: Fabian Society, 1889.

MARK BEVIR

FACTORY GIRLS. Beginning in Britain in the eighteenth century and spreading rapidly to other parts of the world, the Industrial Revolution replaced human skill and effort with the work of machines. A new and almost unlimited supply of productive energy transformed agriculture, transportation, and communication. But it was the transformation of manufacturing—specifically textile manufacturing—that laid the economic and cultural foundations for "factory girls."

Mechanization. The introduction of machinery radically changed the older processes by which cotton was made into cloth. Traditionally, raw cotton was "put out": delivered by a textile merchant to a household, where a family would clean and spin the cotton into yarn or thread. When that task was completed, the merchant would return to exchange the spun cotton for more raw cotton, and the process was repeated. Other households had similar manufacturing relationships with textile merchants, weaving the spun cotton into cloth.

This "cottage industry" worked well until households were unable to keep pace with the demand for spun cotton and woven cloth. To meet orders, cotton processing and cloth production were rapidly innovated: cleaning and preparation of the cotton fibers would be done by a carding machine; weaving would be done by a water frame or, as factories became electrified, a power loom. To increase efficiency, these elements of production were also brought together under one roof, marking—by the early 1800s in the United States—the birth of the factory, a combination of technological and organizational innovation.

It is no secret, however, that the rise of factories destroyed cottage industry and, by extension, severely threatened the economic survival of entire families. Desperate to recapture their livelihoods, many family members took jobs in the burgeoning textile factories, tending the machines that now performed the spinning and weaving that these workers had once done by hand at home. Their particular skills, however, were not important to the functioning of the factories; rather, it was their dependability as monitors that mattered: men would periodically calibrate the machines, and women would serve as "operatives," standing next to the rapidly moving parts to supervise the processes and replacing bobbins and spindles or knotting broken threads when necessary.

Factory Girls. Shoe workers, Lynn, Massachusetts, 1895. FRANCES BENJAMIN JOHNSTON COLLECTION/ PRINTS AND PHOTOGRAPHS DIVISION, LIBRARY OF CONGRESS

Mechanization, in short, removed the need for strength or special skills from textile production, making it "something a woman could handle." Women were widely employed in textile factories in early industrial Britain, France, and, later, Japan. The opportunity to employ women workers was most extensively developed in the United States through the Waltham-Lowell system of textile mills, established in Massachusetts in 1814. Young single women from the farming communities around New England, who had experience in producing yarn and cloth at home, were recruited to work as operatives. Many women were drawn to Lowell and Waltham by the chance to escape the routine of farm life and to earn money that might be used to improve their own or their families' circumstances.

Although the rural families, as victims of industrialization, were in need of the added income, they nevertheless expressed concern about sending their teenage daughters to a one- to four-year commitment in the mills. Anticipating these fears, the Boston Associates, who established the Waltham-Lowell system, designed a regimented boarding environment to both protect and enrich their "factory girls." Waltham-Lowell system recruitment techniques drew more than forty thousand women to the mills by 1830. They made up the majority of all workers in the cotton textile industry and nearly half of the workforce in the woolen textile manufacturing industry.

The enormity of this labor pool ensured the competitive superiority of American mills over those of Britain and, consequently, generated huge profits for mill owners. Being a member of such a large labor force also provided each of the factory girls with a confidence of voice, which by the 1880s was raised in loud protest against the mills' working conditions. For sixteen hours a day the girls operated fast-moving machinery that could—and frequently did—scalp or impale them. Pay for this dangerous work was, per contract, "as the company may see fit to pay" and, in the strictly controlled environment, "subject to the fines imposed by the company" for the slightest rules infraction. It seems, therefore, that the Lowell-Waltham system, initially viewed as a means of survival for rural families and an enriching opportunity for their daughters, turned out to be a perilous system of indenture. Factory girls reacted to these conditions by striking; through the 1920s these women became an important part of the unionist labor movement, helping to fight for laws governing hours and wages.

World War II. When next the term "factory girls" was applied to working women it took on a more romantic, less radical connotation. During World War II, in response to severe labor shortages, 6 million women—most married, over thirty-five, and not previously employed— took jobs as welders, electricians, and assembly-line workers in large defense factories. Rosie the Riveter, memorialized by Norman Rockwell in the *Saturday Evening Post*, slim and beautiful in her overalls and with her work tools, became the symbol for the entire group of women who helped to fill wartime production quotas. To American society, Rosie signified that these women could do a man's job—temporarily—without losing her feminine charm. While embracing the ideal of Rosie, many of these factory girls also balked against its temporariness, hoping to continue their jobs beyond 1945. But in the postwar peacetime economy most factory girls were stripped of their title and pushed back into lower-paying, "feminized" clerical work.

Contemporary "factory girls" are the young, unmarried women who assemble products manufactured in many of the newly industrialized, export-oriented countries. Also included in this cohort are the female—legal and illegal—immigrant laborers who fill the sweatshops in the garment districts of many American cities. All of these workers are truly girls, children really, who must work to help their families survive and are snatched up for their inexpensive labor. With few enforced legal protections, they toil for long hours under threatening emotional and physical conditions.

The exploitation of these young women and the gender biases they face link them to the earliest factory girls created by the effects of the Industrial Revolution in Britain and the United States and to the sisters of Rosie the Riveter. But their existence in the twenty-first century also places them within the parameters of a global economy, making their identity as factory girls more multinational in scope. Regardless of era, however, the nimble and reliable fingers of these women, whether spinning cotton, welding aircraft, or assembling computer parts, create through their cheap labor the wealth on which national and international industrial power has been built.

[*See also* Child Labor; Globalization; Industrialization; *and* Industrial Revolution.]

BIBLIOGRAPHY

Clark, Gracia, ed. *Gender at Work in Economic Life.* Walnut Creek, Calif.: Altamira Press, in cooperation with the Society for Economic Anthropology, 2003. Collection of articles that examine the ways in which women deal with the everyday challenges of making a living.

Foner, Philip S., ed. *The Factory Girls: A Collection of Writings on Life and Struggles in the New England Factories of the 1840s.* Urbana: University of Illinois Press, 1977.

Fuentes, Annette, and Barbara Ehrenreich. *Women in the Global Factory.* Boston: South End Press, 1983. Detailed international analysis of how the multinational corporations are affecting the lives of female workers.

Louie, Miriam Ching Yoon. *Sweatshop Warriors: Immigrant Women Workers Take on the Global Factory.* Cambridge, Mass.: South End Press, 2001. Examines the practices and policies that propel women into dangerous and low-paying jobs.

CYNTHIA GWYNNE YAUDES

FALANGE. Falange assumed official political life in 1933. José Antonio Primo de Rivera, a member of a prominent Madrid family and a lawyer by profession, was the mastermind behind this new organization. His father, General Miguel Primo de Rivera y Orbaneja, had been appointed in 1923 by King Alfonso XIII, head of the government, to lead what is known as the first modern dictatorship in Spanish history. He stayed in power until 1930, and the municipal elections held the following year led to the declaration of the Second Republic on 14 April 1931 and sent the king into exile. Clearly modeled after Italian fascism, Falange was part of the right-wing movement that mushroomed in the Spanish political scene during the Second Republic. José Antonio edited the right-wing journal *El Fascio*, signaling his profound admiration for the Italian movement. In 1934 Falange merged with another minor fascist group, Juntas de Ofensiva Nacional-Sindicalista or JONS. This group was created by a university graduate, Ramiro Ledesma Ramos, in an effort to emulate the Italian Fasci Italiani di Combattimento. The merger of these two groups became Falange Española de las JONS. Falange had developed an official program, the so-called Twenty-Six Points. Its belief in authority, hierarchy, and order linked Falange with other European fascist groups. It differed, however, from the rest of them by wedding Catholicism to the Falangist ideology. Along with the male organization, a women's section of Falange was created in 1934 under the leadership of Pilar Primo de Rivera, sister of José Antonio. Pilar became the guardian of Falangist principles, especially after José Antonio was executed in an Alicante prison in 1936. His influence continued posthumously as the larger-than-life icon "el ausente" (the absent one).

During the republican radical period Falange was declared illegal and its members were arrested, but the outbreak of the civil war (1936–1939) opened the door to political preeminence for the organization. The Falangists supported the uprising of the army led by General Francisco Franco in a coup d'état against the democratic government of the Popular Front, newly elected in February 1936. After three years of horrific fratricidal conflict Francisco Franco proclaimed the Nationalists victorious and himself head of state (a position he would hold until his death in 1975). Falange provided the ideological mantle for Franco's military dictatorship during the 1940s. By unification decree in April 1937 Franco proclaimed Falange (now called Falange Española Tradicionalista y de las JONS, or FET de las JONS) the official state party. The new party would champion the Falangist "Twenty-Six Points" but also included ideas from other rightist and monarchist groups. This measure led to a split within Falange between those who believed in José Antonio's revolutionary message and those who enlisted in the new leadership of Franco. Meanwhile, the women's section of Falange was officially entrusted, by the decree of December 1939 (establishing the mandatory social service), with the task of indoctrinating Spanish women in the practice of becoming good Catholic wives and fertile mothers for the regime. The Axis defeat in World War II meant isolation and economic autarky for Spain, which had been supported on the Nationalist side by Hitler and Mussolini during the Spanish civil war and had declared itself neutral during the world conflict. The Cold War changed the international political scene and ensured the domestic ostracism of Falange within Spain. The U.S. economic and military Pact of Madrid in 1953 propped up Francoism until 1975 and eased the transition from autarky to consumerism. The women's section remained crucial to keeping alive the Falangist values until 1977. Two Falangist organizations remained active in the early twenty-first century, the Falange Auténtica and the FET de las JONS.

[*See also* Fascism and Protofascism, *subentry* Europe; *and* Spain.]

BIBLIOGRAPHY

Ellwood, Sheelagh M. *Prietasias filas: Historia de Falange Española, 1933–1983*. Barcelona: Editorial Crítica, 1984.

Payne, Stanley G. *History of Fascism, 1914–1945*. Madison: University of Wisconsin Press, 1995.

Richmond, Kathleen. *Women and Spanish Fascism: The Women's Section of the Falange, 1934–1959*. London and New York: Routledge, 2003.

AURORA G. MORCILLO

FALKLANDS ISLANDS WAR. The Falklands Islands War between Britain and Argentina occurred between April and June 1982. It arose from historical roots and immediate causes, respective government policies, and timing misjudgments. Both sides had limited objectives: for Buenos Aires the seizure of islands it believed were part of her patrimony, and for London the reestablishment of sovereignty over British territory. Although a war of intense tactical combat, this was limited to the islands and the waters and air around them. It involved the most significant naval and air engagements between forces at sea since World War II and the first major amphibious operation since Inchon, Korea, in 1950.

The Falklands consist of over one hundred islands in the main grouping, as well as South Georgia and the South Sandwich Islands hundreds of miles east-southeast of them. They lie in the South Atlantic 300 miles (483 kilometers) east of the Straits of Magellan, 1,200 miles (1,930 kilometers) from Buenos Aires, 8,000 miles (12,872 kilometers) from Britain, and 3,000 miles (4,827 kilometers) from the nearest British base (Ascension Island). There are two main islands, East and West Falkland, with the main settlement and capital at Port Stanley on the eastern side of the former. The islands have a windswept, cool, and damp climate, with rolling terrain covered with peat and major rocky peaks. Both main islands lack physical infrastructure.

The roots of the conflict lie in the colonial era of South America. Argentina asserted her claims inherited from Spain, while the British rested theirs on discovery and the eighteen hundred Britons living there. Diplomatic negotiations referencing the islands occurred over decades. Two complicating factors affected them: Argentine emotional feeling that they were part of that country's *patrie*, and London's rejection of any settlement contrary to the islanders' desires.

After a military coup in Buenos Aires, the new junta under General Leopoldo Galtieri in August 1981 commenced planning the seizure of the islands. London, meanwhile, misjudged Argentine intentions, believing no military action would occur; the British government also commenced a major fleet reduction, which included the South Atlantic ice patrol ship HMS *Endurance*. An emotional incident then occurred on South Georgia on 19 March 1982, when Argentine workers dismantling abandoned whaling stations flew their national flag over the site. *Endurance* was ordered to resolve this but not in a provocative manner. Then, on 28 March, an Argentine invasion force sailed for the Falklands.

The British had maintained a Royal Marine presence on the islands for many years. That spring it totaled seventy-nine marines and sailors, double normal strength as a relief was occurring. However, officers who had commanded it candidly admitted nothing could prevent an Argentine capture of the islands—a correct assessment as on 2 April, after initial resistance, Governor Rex Hunt surrendered. The captured troops on the islands (South Georgia capitulated on 3 April) were quickly repatriated to Britain.

The government of Margaret Thatcher decided not to accept what Buenos Aires believed would be a fait accompli. An expeditionary force was quickly assembled and dispatched to the South Atlantic. It consisted of three elements: a naval task force of two aircraft carriers and over thirty destroyers and frigates; a maritime amphibious and support shipping force of over sixty vessels; and a landing force of 3 Commando Brigade (that is, three Royal Marine commandos, and two para battalions), later augmented by 5 Brigade (two Guards battalions and one of Gurkas). No on-the-scene joint task force commander commanded in the South Atlantic; rather, Admiral Sir John Fieldhouse commanded from his headquarters in Northwood, England. Meanwhile, a 200-mile (322-kilometer) maritime exclusion zone around the islands was proclaimed on 7 April.

Combat operations soon commenced. On 25 April, Royal Marines recaptured South Georgia, with the Argentine submarine *Santa Fe* lost. On 1 May, Royal Air Force Vulcan bombers, flying from Ascension Island, then struck the airfield at Port Stanley; although only one bomb hit the runway, this resulted in no Argentine fighters being based there—an important factor in ensuing air operations. Then, on 2 May, the submarine HMS *Conqueror* sank the Argentine cruiser *Belgrano*; after this, the rest of the Argentine surface navy remained in port, including the aircraft carrier *Veinticinco de Mayo*. The Argentines countered on 4 May, sinking HMS *Sheffield*. One other Argentine submarine sailed and launched three torpedo attacks on British ships, but torpedo malfunctions ensured failure. On 14 and 15 May, British special operations forces attacked the Argentine air base on Pebble Island off West Falkland, neutralizing a potential threat to the ground force's landing area.

By mid-May the islands appeared to be well defended, with over eight thousand Argentines at Port Stanley, mostly army conscripts augmented by a marine battalion; one thousand at Goose Greene; and other scattered detachments. Defenses were augmented by antiaircraft missiles. Argentine air operations, primarily air force but augmented with naval aviation, flew from Argentina against the incoming fleet in support of the ground defenders, while logistics aircraft continued to use the airfield at Port Stanley.

The British ignored basic amphibious doctrine as Argentine air operations challenged their command of the air and sea in the objective area. Regardless, on 21 May, British forces landed on the northwestern end of East Falkland at San Carlos, a classic case of landing where defenders least expected. That day, HMS *Ardent* was lost, and on 23 May, HMS *Antelope*. On 28 May, elements of the landing force captured Goose Greene, southwestern East Falkland. Meanwhile, on 25 May, HMS *Coventry* was sunk but, more importantly, the container ship *Atlantic Conveyer* was lost—with almost all of the helicopters of the landing force. This meant that the movement of most of the ground force toward Port Stanley would be made overland on foot—which was accomplished due to the training of 3 Commando Brigade. Meantime, the Royal Fleet Auxiliary *Sir Galahad* was lost via an air strike on 8 June, with the loss of fifty sailors, and HMS *Glamorgan* was hit on 12 June. Gradually, the British encircled Port Stanley from the ground and, with the capital and its defenders isolated from the mainland, Argentine forces surrendered on 14 June 1982. They were quickly repatriated back to Argentina.

The war cost Britain 255 killed, 6 ships sunk and 10 others badly damaged, and 34 aircraft lost. Argentine losses were over 700 killed; over 1,100 wounded or sick; the destruction of the cruiser *Belgrano*, the submarine *Santa Fe*, and over 100 aircraft; and a collapsed government. Over a quarter of a century later, the status of the Falkland Islands and their inhabitants is still unresolved. As a 7 January 2007 headline in the *Washington Post* proclaimed, "Falkland Islands an Unsettled Issue 25 Years after the War: Contending Claims by Argentina, Britain Burden Relations as Anniversary Nears."

[*See also* Argentina.]

BIBLIOGRAPHY

Badsey, Stephen, Rob Havers, and Mark Grove, eds. *The Falklands Conflict Twenty Years On: Lessons for the Future*. London and New York: Frank Case, 2005. Proceedings from the conference held at the Royal Military Academy Sandhurst on the twentieth anniversary of the war.

Freedman, Sir Lawrence. *The Official History of the Falklands Campaign*. Vol. 1: *The Origins of the Falklands War*. Vol. 2: *War and Diplomacy*. London and New York: Routledge, 2005. As the titles imply, the British official history of the South Atlantic Conflict.

Hastings, Max, and Simon Jenkins. *The Battle for the Falklands*. New York: W. W. Norton, 1983. One of the first histories of the war published after the conflict, and often used as a text in professional military education schools.

Middlebrook, Martin. *The Fight for the "Malvinas": The Argentine Forces in the Falklands War*. London and New York: Viking, 1989. An Argentine perspective of the war, albeit by a British author.

Middlebrook, Martin. *Operation Corporate: The Falklands War, 1982*. London: Viking, 1985. Considered by many British military personnel to be the best overall history of the war.

DONALD F. BITTNER

FALLUJA, IRAQ. Falluja (al-Fallujah), a small Iraqi town of approximately 300,000 inhabitants located some 37 miles (60 kilometers) west of Baghdad, came into the limelight of the world media in 2004 when it was twice the target of major U.S. military operations. Though the town's population largely had benefited during the regime of Saddam Hussein through employment in the military, police, or intelligence, certain anti-Saddam sentiments were clearly noticeable after the fall of the regime. This is mainly attributable to the conservatively religious (Sunni Muslim) and tribal makeup of the town.

This religious traditionalism immediately came into conflict with the American occupational forces after the town's conquest on 23 April 2003. Before the arrival of American troops, Falluja had been notable for its relative success in maintaining law and order and avoiding much of the widespread looting witnessed elsewhere in Iraq. This was primarily because of the establishment of a Civil Management Council by local leaders and religious figures, which relied on patrimonial ties and family networks to maintain order.

Tensions grew with the arrival of American troops, chiefly because of poor communication and the U.S. failure to understand local sensibilities, norms, and traditions. On 28 April (Saddam's birthday), a small demonstration of about two or three hundred people shouted anti-American and anti-Saddam slogans outside the U.S. headquarters in the town. Though Iraqis claim that the demonstrators were unarmed, the U.S. military maintains that armed gunmen hid among the crowd and fired on the troops. American soldiers returned fire and, according to Iraqi eyewitnesses, fired automatic weapons indiscriminately for approximately ten minutes. The incident, which according to the Falluja hospital director left seventeen dead and seventy-five wounded, was followed by another similar incident on 30 April in which three were killed and sixteen wounded, according to the same source.

Continuous attacks and counterattacks took place in the following months, and on 4 June 2003 the U.S. military sent an additional fifteen hundred troops to Falluja. On 6 April the following year, the Americans launched Operation Vigilant Resolve. This major all-out assault on the town saw one-third of its population flee and resulted in some eight hundred reported deaths, mostly civilian, including over three hundred women and children, according to Iraq Body Count, an independent group that monitors the news media. On the American side, eighty U.S. soldiers were killed. Though it failed completely to quell the fighting, the United States announced a unilateral cease-fire in May 2004.

During autumn 2004, the situation again escalated, and on 8 November, ten thousand American troops, together with four Iraqi army brigades, launched another major attack on the town with the aim of completely sealing it off and eliminating all resistance fighters in it. However, many of them had left the town in advance, together with the approximately two hundred thousand inhabitants who fled their homes prior to the attack. By 15 November, the main part of the operation was over. In the midst of the thirty to fifty thousand civilians who were believed to have remained in the town, a fierce battle raged for a week, destroying much of the city and killing and maiming numerous people. The U.S. military claimed to have killed more than twelve hundred insurgents while losing thirty-eight American and six Iraqi soldiers.

The scope of the destruction and the scores of killed and injured innocent inhabitants, coupled with American admissions a year later that troops had employed white phosphorous as "an incendiary weapon" (*Guardian*, 16 November 2005) during the battle, severely damaged the image of the American-led occupation of Iraq among its supporters and further deteriorated, along with other scandals such as Abu Ghraib, its already dwindling image in the Middle East and the wider Muslim world.

BIBLIOGRAPHY

Bouckaert, Peter, and Fred Abrahams. "Violent Response: The U.S. Army in al-Falluja." *Human Rights Watch* 15, no. 7 (June 2003): 1–19.

Wilson, Jamie. "US Admits Using White Phosphorous in Falluja." *Guardian* (London), 16 November 2005.

JOHAN FRANZÉN

FALLUJA, PALESTINE. Battles in the Negev during the 1948 Arab-Israeli War, particularly around the area of the "Falluja pocket," defined the latter half of twentieth-century Egyptian history. Gamal Abdel Nasser, a major serving in Falluja, observed that events between October 1948 and February 1949 encouraged him to question "old guard" leaders and initiate (along with several colleagues) events that led to the 1952 Free Officers movement in Egypt.

The October 1948 Israeli offensive, "Yoav," sought to divide Egyptian units in the Negev. Although Egyptian forces initially held the high ground, Israelis secured hilltop locations by 17 October and forced the retreat of several Egyptian units to the Gaza Strip by 21 October. Four isolated groups of Egyptian forces remained, including four thousand men in the Falluja pocket (roughly twenty-five miles northwest of Beersheba).

Despite calls for aid, Arab reinforcements never came. Beleaguered Egyptian forces held Falluja until the armistice of 24 February 1949. In the meantime, the Egyptian brigadier Said Taha Bey, being committed to preserving Egyptian honor despite the hopelessness of the position, refused to meet with Israeli commanders. Israeli forces entrenched at Falluja were unable to aid units elsewhere, and as a result Egyptians defeated Israelis along the coast in late December. Despite this brief morale boost, the lack of unity among Arab armies and aid from the Egyptian hierarchy clearly signaled weakening state structures. In February the pocket's four thousand soldiers, arms in hand, marched back to Egypt. Despite military honors granted by their Israeli opponents, the Egyptians felt alienated from their own government.

[*See also* Arab-Israeli Conflict *and* Egypt.]

BIBLIOGRAPHY

Abu Izzeddin, Nejla M. *Nasser of the Arabs: An Arab Assessment.* London: The Third World Centre for Research and Publishing Ltd., 1981.

Herzog, Chaim. *The Arab-Israeli Wars: War and Peace in the Middle East from the War of Independence to Lebanon.* London: Arms and Armour Press, 1985.

JOHAN FRANZÉN

FAMILY AND KINSHIP [*This entry includes eight subentries, an overview and discussions of family in Europe; China; Japan; Korea; Mongolia; the Middle East and North Africa; and Central Asia. See also* Marriage and Divorce.]

Overview

All societies past and present have had social microstructures called families. Adults provide the infant with a safe environment until he or she becomes independent or is turned over to some other group for care. The variations on this global theme are legion. The "nuclear family"—husband, wife, children—which has played so important a role in the social history of Western societies should therefore be considered one of numerous types of "family." As far as the historical record goes, and according to the research of social and cultural anthropologists on relatively recent and contemporary societies, some kind of "family" has always been in charge of the human infant.

History of the Family. Historians in Western societies began a systematic study of the history of the family as a social structure only relatively recently. Before the 1960s, historians had referred to "families" in their various narratives, but more often than not these references were impressionistic and based on a handful of case studies. There was strong belief that in any given society or period there was a "family type," or perhaps a small number of "types," and that when this type or types were described, the matter was exhausted. Variation and diversity over time and place was hardly ever dealt with, even within single societies. Moreover, there was a strong belief also in development over time, in which all families everywhere across the globe were seen to be changing structurally from relative complexity to relative simplicity, depending on how close societal evolution had come to "modernity." The systematic, source-based, comparative research started in the 1960s showed quickly that these models, premises, and assumptions were misleading, and that the history of the family was far more complicated and required much more research than it had been accorded (Goode). A true global history of family structures has yet to be written in the early twenty-first century.

The Kinship Group. As historians began to look at the family more systematically, they discovered also that a conceptual distinction had to be made between "family" and "kinship." Such distinctions had already been drawn in the research of social and cultural anthropologists, but the insight had not penetrated the work of historians. The distinction was needed for several important reasons. Available historical records frequently provided empirical evidence that the family group lived together in a single household, but records that would present evidence about persons involved in a larger kinship group—however defined—were few and far between. It was plain from other sources, however, that kinship groupings, where they existed, had much larger populations than family households. Terms for kin-based groups, such as "clan" and "lineage," suggested not only that many family households could be tied together by supra-household loyalties but also that individual families belonging to such groups could be stratified within the larger group in ways that were not obvious. Thus for example, wide-ranging clan ties provided a means of military recruitment in moments of crisis; lineages sought over time to keep landed property from being dispersed to nonmembers; and wealth and prestige were deployed differentially among family units belonging to the same larger kin grouping. Simply put, there was another step to be taken in microstructural family research, namely, an investigation of the larger kinship groups in which families were embedded. This was a much more difficult assignment because the work of anthropologists had already suggested that variation and diversity among kinship groups, when viewed from a global perspective, was also substantial. It was simply not sufficient to study historical changes in the structure of the family group; it was also necessary to understand historical changes in the nature of these larger kin-based groupings.

Two Centuries of Change. The nineteenth and twentieth centuries brought momentous changes to all countries of the world, their cultures and their populations. Until the late 1980s, these changes were frequently described in terms of modernization theory. This complex set of ideas held that all societies were following a trajectory of change that eventually would bring them to a condition of modernity, characterized by industrial economies, technologically advanced communications systems, dense urban and suburban areas, and social stratification that included a large and vibrant middle class. Western Europe and much of North America were said to have become the first "modern" societies; other societies throughout the world would eventually "catch up" to the West at different speeds, having at some point entered a phase of "take-off" toward modernization.

The familial dimension of this theory held that in the modernization process population dynamics and family structures would become very different than they had been in the past. The high fertility/high mortality regimes of the past would be replaced by low mortality/low fertility regimes as societies went through a demographic transition. Because of the rapid growth of migration—both emigration and immigration—families would tend toward simplicity, the nuclear family form being the most suitable for modern societies. The relatives that in the past stayed in or moved into the family household—unmarried siblings of the head, married offspring, elderly retired parents—would live elsewhere for various reasons, in part because the "modern" nuclear family placed a high premium on privacy. Larger kinship networks would break up because incessant movement of peoples in search of greater opportunities would leave few related persons in any particular locality, as people came and went. Modernity, in other words, would transform family and kinship much as it transformed everything else.

Modernization theory in all of its variants is no longer as attractive as it once was both with respect to its explanatory and its predictive value. Research on the history of the nineteenth and twentieth centuries has shown familial change of all kinds much less likely to be explained by a set of logically linked propositions called a theory. As a consequence, researchers on the history of the family are less willing to place their empirical findings in any theoretical framework that describes predictable trajectories. Looking at all of the world's societies, few researchers would now predict a "Western" model in all of their futures. Moreover, no consensus has emerged about why Western societies took

the paths they did, which means that their stories cannot be summarized in a single model applied to all non-Western societies. Researchers are more likely to explore social change—including familial change—during the nineteenth and twentieth centuries based on a premise that all societies have moved into the modern world—defined chronologically—at the same time so that none can be labeled "advanced" or "backward." Each society has its own history at all social levels, and there is no reason to believe that all societies progress through identical steps toward some final phase of "modernity." While there may be short-term processes in various societies that resemble one another and therefore can be studied comparatively, these processes are not markers or indicators that a particular society has reached some particular phase of development.

Seen from this current vantage point, the history of family and kinship during the nineteenth and twentieth centuries throughout the world has become much less unitary. Even in European societies the passage of time did not always mean the growing predominance of family nuclearity, and kinship networks often demonstrated themselves to be far more flexible and adaptable and capable of survival than had been thought. Consequently, it is impossible to describe the history of family and kinship, from the global point of view, by reference to any global chronology or to inevitable "turning points." It is possible, however, to organize such changes by reference to general categories and to suggest the kinds of consequences such changes brought into being. Several factors have challenged kinship ties though amid great variety of settings and cultural preferences.

Population Behaviors and Movements. Researchers in the history of the family and kinship have learned that the structures of families, family households, and kinship groups are deeply affected by the numbers of people included in such social groupings. If all offspring die in infancy, a particular family group will never become complex; if many of an adult siblings group migrate and stay away, there will be few joint families in the community; long-term decline of general and marital fertility will diminish the number of persons capable of forming complex families. Such interactions are complicated, and the influences may not always flow in the same direction from place to place. During the past two centuries significant changes in demographic patterns have left their mark on family and kinship structures. Demography is not the sole variable, however, since economic constraints and cultural values also come into play. But the facts of there being not enough people to populate a certain kind of family and kinship structure, or too many, influence the dynamics of family formation and the developmental cycle. Both facts have also influenced kinship groups by depleting them of membership, or swelling them to the point of internal strife and division.

How these demography-family-kinship interactions have played out across the globe in particular societies during the past two centuries is a story still in need of a coherent narrative substantiated by much comparative analysis. We know that in the European continent a drawn-out fall of fertility and mortality rates—referred to as the "demographic transition"—over the past two centuries has led, generally speaking, to the near-disappearance of complex families and households, as social norms, even though such complexity can revive in the short term as a response to economically stressful situations. The efficacy of kinship networks has also been diminished by the same forces, combined with cultural changes refocusing loyalty and obligation away from kin and into the nuclear family. Kinship nomenclature on the European continent still reflects the importance of close kin beyond fathers, mothers, and siblings, but the intensity of obligation between kinfolk has been severely diminished.

Fertility and mortality declines became characteristic of many non-European populations as well during the twentieth century, in part because of the diffusion of new technologies of birth control (for example, in India and Africa) and in part through government policies limiting the number of children (for example, China). The actions of central governments to address the causes of infant and child mortality have reduced overall mortality levels. The general impression is that the "European model"—the demographic transition having readily documentable consequences in the domains of family and kinship behavior—cannot explain such relationships in these societies readily. There is ultimately no good reason why cultural preferences, values, and behaviors, should react in the same way everywhere to demographic change. Cultural dictates may have been felt more intensely in some places than in others, and in such societies it is possible for culture to have sought to shape demographic change as long as possible. The effects of permanent out-migration, combined with lessening fertility, however, have made demography trump culture and many of the world's societies, reducing severely the numbers of persons who can be included in microstructures other than the nuclear family.

Economic Change. During the past two centuries, all of the world's societies have undergone substantial economic changes, the main one being reductions in the population working in agriculture. The economies of a

American Family. The Faro Caudill family eating dinner in their dugout, Pie Town, New Mexico, October 1940. Photograph by Lee Russell. Farm Security Administration–Office of War Information/Prints and Photographs Division, Library of Congress

number of such societies have become irreversibly indus-trial, a larger number of them have become mixed, and a smaller number remain primarily agricultural. The growth of large- and small-scale industry has also triggered popu-lation movements from rural to urban areas, though at different rates in various places. With respect to basic eco-nomic systems, a large proportion of the world's societies have free market economies, an equally larger propor-tion mixed—free-market and governmentally managed—economies, while a much smaller number at the end of the twentieth century retained government-controlled econom-ies. Since the mid-twentieth century there has been a major expansion of regional economic organizations as well as at-tempts, such as the World Trade Organization, to diminish destructive economic competition on a worldwide basis. Within many regions there has developed a clear trend toward the free flow of labor across national boundaries, and the relatively free flow of capital became particularly marked during the last decades of the twentieth century.

The collective impact of these changes on family, house-hold, and kinship structures has not been assessed systematically. Without doubt, greater mobility of the labor force has become a cause of increased migration. Without doubt also, the increased per capita wealth in many of the world's societies is an indicator of what in times past was designated as the "growth of the middle class," whose members have everywhere shown a clear preference for nuclear family structures and for major investments in the futures of the (fewer) children that middle-class families do have. Relatively greater wealth, especially in Western societies, has led to various kinds of welfare-state measures, ensuring that certain caretaker functions (of the elderly, of parentless children, of the indigent, and so on) have been moved out of the family domain into the public sector. These factors translated into changes in family values, wherein the family feels a strong obligation toward members who could not yet work or who could no longer work. Greater job opportunities have also empowered those family members who contribute to family incomes, enhancing their role in family decision-making and family strategizing. Such changes have started at different times in different societies and have proceeded at different tempos, and there is no ineluctable link between, for example, the degree of industrialization and urbanization and the extensiveness of the so-called socioeconomic safety net. In many societies, an increased gross domestic product (GDP) has meant more rigid social stratification, with the benefits of economic change coming only to relatively small proportion of the population.

Expansion of the Modern State. The diverse histor-ies of the 190 member states of the United Nations General Assembly reveal that most are of recent vintage and therefore could not have exerted much influence on fam-ilies and kinship groups during the last two hundred years. Even the largest, oldest, and most influential states were limited in their ability to override local and regional customs and traditions. Before such state machinery existed, however, powerful local and regional lords could wield such influence through tax policies imposed on indi-vidual households, through the institutions of serfdom that imposed labor service obligations, through mandating ages at marriage, through the imposition of fines on those who were not married, and by compelling households to serve as caregivers of the old, indigent, and orphaned. Such measures, however, were patchy because methods of enforcement were often ineffectual. With respect to kinship networks, local rulers, themselves members of lineage groups, did battle with other lineage groups for control. Generally speaking, however, it is doubtful that these measures and efforts were ever strong enough for state policy at this level to become the prime determinant of social microstructures.

The modern state with its extensive bureaucratic apparatus and national codes of law became much more successful in implementing measures to change and mod-ify custom and tradition. Such efforts, however, became more determined in Western societies in the second half of the nineteenth century and in much of the rest of the world in the twentieth. Only more recently has it been possible to speak of governments having family-focused policies of wide application. Some countries introduced "pro-natalist" policies by granting subsidies to young parents for each child. Others, fearing overpopulation, fined families for hav-ing more than a set number of children. The tax codes of many countries frequently incorporated special deductions for family units. Moreover, with the growing belief that the state had clear responsibilities in the family realm came measures that provided support for fractured family units, for the elderly who had no living caretakers, and for parent-less children. Increasingly, the efficacy of social legislation was determined by how it did or did not aid the family unit.

The state could also influence the power of kinship relations in at least two ways. First, government appoint-ments based on kinship or friendship shifted to ones made on the basis of talent (civil service). Also, through progressive income tax and inheritance taxes govern-ments sought to diminish the accumulation of vast fortunes that would enrich all members of a particular kinship group. The success of such legislation has been hard to measure, but efforts made during the twentieth century to diminish the familial dimension in state appointments and wealth accumulation was viewed as being "progressive."

In the creation of social "safety nets" of various kinds the modern state in the late twentieth century was accused of enacting anti-familial policies through measures that subsidized single-parent households and single-person households. It is said that such measures go beyond mere assistance and permit, if not encourage, the creation of familial units that do not resemble the traditional father-mother-offspring family model, that promote divorce, and that encourage out-of-wedlock childbirth. It is not at all clear whether such familial configurations are a result of state policy or changing social mores and customs.

Technological Change. The diffusion of technological changes throughout the world in the past two centuries affected family and kinship both directly and indirectly. The development of increasingly effective means of birth control, especially after the middle of the twentieth century, meant the decoupling of sexual intercourse from conception, marriage, and child-bearing. If couples so chose, they could regulate fertility more efficiently and effectively than in the past. Similarly, sexual relations were no longer contingent on marriage. As a result, in Western societies at least, the ideal number of children per couple tended to decrease, settling at about two. In the last decades of the twentieth century, however, the number of children per couple in many Western societies fell below the replacement rate, and governments began to worry about the future of the indigenous labor pool. The direct effects of technological advances in contraception tended toward the same result: the reduction in the number of children. The onset of these trends in different societies was chronologically diverse, and in some they had not yet made an appearance even at the turn of the twenty-first century.

Indirect effects of technological change on family and kinship showed up generally in the ease with which family members could decide to live and work apart from each other, for economic and other reasons. Improvements in urban and suburban transportation systems meant that the workplace and the home could be far apart, resulting in long absences from family members during the waking hours of each day. Frequent relocations of entire families for work reasons meant that kinship ties beyond the nuclear family were stretched, an effect modified somewhat by improvements in communications. Modern communications systems also meant a vast expansion in available information, and the introduction of "virtual role models" into the everyday life of children, with behaviors and values substantially different than those of parents. The seemingly miraculous aspects of technological innovation called into question religious belief systems and their behavioral codes, so that entirely secular values could spread very easily and cause substantial generational friction.

By the end of the twentieth century, the increased pace of technological change and its diffusion throughout almost all human societies separated communities into those who embraced such changes enthusiastically, those who sought to integrate changes into existing belief and behavioral systems, and those who rejected such changes outright, often citing their negative effects on family life as the main reason for rejection. Technological changes appeared to be promoting individual self-sufficiency and self-absorption, reducing if not eliminating the need for any kind of family grouping at all. The huge increase of single-person households came to be seen as the harbinger of a society in which even the nuclear family, let alone more extensive kin-based family groupings, appeared at best anachronistic and at worst unnecessary for human self-fulfillment and happiness.

Gender and Authority in the Family. In Western societies during the last quarter of the twentieth century significant changes were showing up within the family group, as the roles of adult members were redefined. Men and women, in their roles as husbands and wives, began to think of marriage more as a partnership and less as a patriarchal institution (Mitterauer and Sieder). Such redefinitions were helped along by the trends that altered the perceptions of each new generation. Legal reform as well as custom equalized inheritance shares for both sexes. In higher education the proportion of women in institutions of higher learning reached parity with that of men. The opening of professions and of labor markets, heretofore closed to women, reduced the importance of the husband as the sole "breadwinner" and forced the reconsideration of household roles and duties, as women earned an increasingly larger share of family income. Legal systems were also becoming less tolerant of the physical abuse of wives by husbands and of children by parents. The relaxation of requirements for divorce expanded the number of exits from unsatisfactory partnerships, creating the need for elaborate legal arrangements for support of underage children. As a consequence of such changes, familial roles increasingly became subjects of constant negotiation. Even in Western societies, however, these changes tended to be class-specific, appearing first in the upper- and middle-income families whose relative affluence minimized collective concerns for family survival. And women often retained a disproportionate role in maintaining kinship contacts. From a global perspective, by the beginning of the twenty-first century, such alterations had changed gender roles and authority distribution in only a small portion of the world, and it remained to be seen whether and how quickly other societies would follow suit.

Conclusion. Various factors in modern world history unquestionably challenged traditional kinship relations, beyond the nuclear family. Urbanization and long-distance migration and lower birth rates were crucial developments. Many stories from many places—like Chinua Achebe's *No Longer at Ease*, set in 1920s urban Nigeria—told of people lured by jobs and consumerism to the neglect of the extended visits and hospitality essential to traditional kinship. But kinship ties maintained importance in many settings. Arab reliance on kinship ties, and knowledge of relationships, continued strong. Indian immigrants to places like the United States or Canada could use modern transportation and communication to retain vigorous contacts with kin back home. The same applied to Latino migrant workers in the United States, or the rural migrants in China who worked in urban factories but returned annually, on the Chinese New Year, to regroup with kin. New pressures were undeniable, but patterns remained both varied and complex.

[*See also* Marriage and Divorce, *subentry* Overview.]

BIBLIOGRAPHY

Bailey, Joanne. *Unquiet Lives: Marriage and Marriage Breakdown in England, 1660–1800.* Cambridge, U.K., and New York: Cambridge University Press, 2003.

Bulatao, Rodolfo A., and John B. Casterline, eds. *Global Fertility Transition.* New York: Population Council, 2001.

Engelen, Theo, and Arthur P. Wolf, eds. *Marriage and the Family in Eurasia: Perspectives on the Hajnal Hypothesis.* Amsterdam: Askant, 2005.

Federici, Nora, Karen Oppenheim Mason, and Solvi Sogner, eds. *Women's Position and Demographic Change.* Oxford: Clarendon Press, 1993.

Goldscheider, Calvin, ed. *Fertility Transitions, Family Structure, and Population Policy.* Boulder, Colo.: Westview Press, 1992.

Goode, William J. *World Revolution and Family Patterns.* New York: Free Press, 1963.

Hajnal, John. "European Marriage Patterns in Historical Perspective." In *Population in History*, edited by D. V. Glass and D. E. C. Eversley, pp. 101–143. London: E. Arnold, 1965.

Ingoldsby, Bron B., and Suzanna D. Smith, eds. *Families in Global and Multicultural Perspective.* 2d ed. Thousand Oaks, Calif.: Sage, 2006.

Kertzer, David I., and Marzio Barbagli, eds. *The History of the European Family.* 3 vols. New Haven, Conn.: Yale University Press, 2001–2003.

Laslett, Peter, and Richard Wall, eds. *Household and Family in Past Time: Comparative Studies in the Size and Structure of The Domestic Group Over the Last Three Centuries.* Cambridge, U.K.: Cambridge University Press, 1972.

Lee, James Z., and Wang Feng. *One Quarter of Humanity: Malthusian Mythology and Chinese Realities, 1700–2000.* Cambridge, Mass.: Harvard University Press, 1999.

Maynes, Mary Jo, et al., eds. *Gender, Kinship, Power: A Comparative and Interdisciplinary History.* New York: Routledge, 1996.

Mitterauer, Michael, and Reinhard Sieder. *The European Family: Patriarchy to Partnership from the Middle Ages to the Present.* Oxford: Blackwell, 1982.

Plakans, Andrejs. *Kinship in the Past: An Anthropology of European Family Life, 1500–1900.* Oxford: Blackwell, 1984.

Sabean, David Warren. *Kinship in Neckarshausen, 1700–1870.* Cambridge, U.K., and New York: Cambridge University Press, 1998.

Segalen, Martine. *Fifteen Generations of Bretons: Kinship and Society in Lower Britanny, 1720–1980.* Translated by J. A. Underwood. Cambridge, U.K., and New York: Cambridge University Press, 1991.

Simon, Rita J., and Howard Altstein, eds. *Global Perspectives on Social Issues: Marriage and Divorce.* Lanham, Md.: Lexington Books, 2003.

Wall, Richard, Jean Robin, and Peter Laslett, eds. *Family Forms in Historic Europe.* Cambridge, U.K., and New York: Cambridge University Press, 1983.

ANDREJS PLAKANS

Europe

Four decades of research on the related subjects of family and kinship on the European continent has changed our knowledge substantially. In historical accounts written before the mid-1960s, changes from the eighteenth to the twentieth centuries were depicted as movement from complex and large family structures to increasingly simpler ones, and from tightly knit and well-populated kinship networks to kinless, atomized individuals. These changes, it was said, were brought about by various kinds of "modernization": industrial growth, expansion of urban populations, mass migrations of various kinds, changing demographic patterns. All of these together pushed to center stage the nuclear family—father, mother, children—and gradually diminished the social significance of kin, both close and distant. Scholars now know that this narrative is a caricature of what actually happened, and revisionistic scholarship has yielded a much more nuanced picture.

The History of the Family. To counter the complex-to-simple paradigm, the researchers in the Cambridge Group for the History of Population (Laslett and Wall; Wall, Robin, and Laslett) proposed another, which they called the "null hypothesis": families and households in the premodern European past should be assumed to have been simple; it was complexity that had to be demonstrated to have existed. Research showed that at the end of the eighteenth century European family structures spanned the whole spectrum of predominantly simple (for example, England) to predominantly complex (for example, Russia). Whatever had gone before, by the end of the eighteenth century the European continent was already characterized by diversity in family structures. This meant that the various dynamics of modernization, when they began to change European societies in the nineteenth century, would have been changing differently from the beginning. Clearly, the complex-to-simple paradigm would not work in the European northwest region, where families and households had demonstrated prevailing simplicity for a very long time already. The complex-to-simple paradigm could possibly work in the European east, where at the starting point familial complexity was far greater than in the west. The starting points for other European regions were much more ambiguous than those of the English and Russian polarities.

The large-scale socioeconomic changes of the nineteenth century affected familial structures everywhere on the European continent, but their impact was delivered by different instruments. In the western parts of the continent, as well as in some regions of central Europe, the main engine of change was the growth of factory-based industrial production. The labor needs of factories were magnets for rural persons seeking a better life, and the resulting rural-to-urban migration swelled existing urban centers and created new ones. Both families and individuals migrated, producing a variegated structural picture in the new industrial towns. The transition for some people was quite sharp; for others, who came from rural districts where some form of small-scale industrial enterprise (termed "protoindustrialization") had already taken hold, the transition was less traumatic. But in the European regions where the nuclear family household had already been predominant, the changes associated with industrialization did not dramatically alter the prevailing structure. Perhaps the proportion of single-individual households increased, as well as the proportion of family households without children, but the dominant characteristics stayed the same.

In the European east, the principal instrument of change was serf emancipation and agrarian reform during most of the nineteenth century, followed by growth of factory industry in the last decades. The starting point in these regions was different: here complex family households,

while not universal, were certainly a very prominent aspect of everyday family life. Serf emancipation by monarchical decree transformed millions of enserfed peasants into persons with full-fledged civic identity. In most places, however, severe restrictions on migration were relaxed only slowly, keeping most people in the communities where they were born. Agrarian reform sought to transform the landless into smallholders, with variable success. Eventually, in the European east there began massive rural-to-urban migration as well, which affected rural family structures as it had in western Europe. In the east, however, the whole process was much more condensed, and perhaps, much more traumatic to the families concerned. By the end of the century, in both parts of Europe, the nuclear family had emerged as the principal familial form in all national censuses.

During the twentieth century changes in basic family structures in all parts of the European continent continued to trend in the same direction, namely, toward the dominance of the nuclear family unit: husband, wife, children. This structure, as mentioned, was no stranger to earlier European society, having been the preferred form of the domestic group in large areas of the European continent in the centuries before the twentieth. But now, and especially after the mid-twentieth century, millions of Europeans in adapting to the socioeconomic circumstances came to prefer this form of coresidence. Increasingly, neolocality typified post-marital residence: a new marriage meant the creation of a new household. Increasingly also, welfare state institutions offered to aging parents an alternative to living with their children. Increasing total employment and a regular paycheck provided to many young couples an economic base to establish and sustain an independent household. The search for employment opportunities through migration also became much more possible. In a word, many of the reasons why in earlier times households contained more than one married couple fell by the wayside, as married siblings, married children, married parents, and married aunts and uncles no longer expected to coreside under the same roof and dispersed They might indeed be still living in the same neighborhood or the same locality, but not together.

There were exceptions to these trends, of course. Anthropologists dealing with the southern Balkan regions immediately after World War II could still analyze the kin-based patrilineally defined multiple-family household (the *zadruga*, in Serbian), which was in fact a property-owning corporation. The hard times caused by the ups and downs of the business cycle periodically required families to reconstruct multiple family structures as a measure of economic survival. Twice in the twentieth century two major world wars created wartime and postwar conditions when survival of the family unit was at stake and nonnuclear forms provided greater sustenance.

Paralleling the growing importance of the nuclear family were trends in family development that often led to the dissolution of family ties and indeed reflected the choice by individuals to live out their lives outside the family structure. Changes in legal systems made family dissolution easier through separation and divorce. Increasingly, artificial means of birth control separated conception from sexual intercourse, permitting couples to remain childless if they so chose. Employment at high levels and the institutions of the welfare state gave support to single-parent families as well as single-person households, since social opprobrium no longer attached to these structures. Even within the nuclear family choices were being made that diminished the family as supplier of the future labor force: overall, marital fertility fell below replacement levels (one child or less) in many European societies.

Changing Kinship Networks. In the domain of kinship ties beyond the family household, the twentieth century also brought changes but perhaps different ones than researchers had expected. With factory industry and urban sites becoming population magnets and with the elimination of legal barriers to migration one could have predicted that the strong kinship ties created by life in small communities over long periods of time would eventually erode completely, as people left for work elsewhere, married out, and dispersed over distances too long for ties to be sustained with any degree of force. This effect of the various aspects of modernization did make itself felt, of course, but research has also pointed out how in generation after generation even in an urban-industrial society kin ties beyond the nuclear family continued to be maintained, reinforced, and put to use when needed. The trend in kinship relations was not so much toward the atomized individual with no ties at all, but toward the instrumental use of kin ties even if kin lived far apart. The genealogical positions to which social significance was accorded diminished in number, but kin positions at two steps from an individual continued to be valued (grandparents, uncles, aunts, cousins, brothers- and sisters-in-law, grandchildren). Their economic significance diminished with the growth of welfare-state "safety nets" but they continued to have both a symbolic and an emotional significance.

A more significant change in the European family since the 1950s has come not in structure but in relational content. The nuclear family unit, now the predominant structural form, was always available to Europeans and indeed was widespread historically in some societies. The internal relational change, beginning after World War II and still continuing, reconfigured the relationship between husband and wife, and parents and children, introducing a trajectory of what some have called "from patriarchy to partnership" (Mitterauer and Sieder). The redefinition of familial roles has not been smooth and has proceeded much farther in some European societies than in others. This redefinition, and the opting out of increasingly larger portions of contemporary European populations from marriage and family (but not necessarily from active kinship ties), will continue to affect the history of the European family well into the twenty-first century.

[*See also* Marriage and Divorce, *subentry* Europe.]

BIBLIOGRAPHY
Gullestad, Marianne, and Martine Segalen, eds. *Family and Kinship in Europe.* London and Washington, D.C.: Pinter, 1997.
Hajnal, John. "European Marriage Patterns in Historical Perspective." In *Population in History*, edited by David Glass and D. E. C. Eversley, pp. 101-143. London: E. Arnold, 1965.
Kertzer, David I., and Marzio Barbagli, eds. *The History of the European Family.* 3 vols. New Haven, Conn.: Yale University Press, 2001–2003.
Laslett, Peter, and Richard Wall, eds. *Household and Family in Past Time: Comparative Studies in the Size and Structure of the Domestic Group over the Last Three Centuries.* Cambridge, U.K.: Cambridge University Press, 1972.
Mitterauer, Michael, and Reinhard Sieder. *The European Family: Patriarchy to Partnership from the Middle Ages to the Present.* Translated by Karla Oosterveen and Manfred Hörzinger. Oxford: Blackwell, 1982.
Sabean, David Warren. *Kinship in Neckarshausen, 1700–1870.* Cambridge, U.K., and New York: Cambridge University Press, 1998.
Wall, Richard, Jean Robin, and Peter Laslett, eds. *Family Forms in Historic Europe.* Cambridge, U.K., and New York: Cambridge University Press, 1983.

Andrejs Plakans

China

Family ideals in the late imperial period (1750–1911) were shaped by the Confucian ideology that had shaped elite and, to some extent, popular culture beginning as early as the second century B.C.E. Most people aspired to an extended family of "five generations under one roof," though only the wealthy reproduced early enough and lived long enough to achieve it. Mencius's concept of the five key bonds—emperor and minister, father and son, husband and wife, elder brother and younger brother, and friend and friend—was central to traditional perceptions of the family and its place in the world. Four of the five relationships were hierarchical and reciprocal: the inferior owed respect and obedience to the superior, and the superior guided and cared for the inferior. Three of the five involved the family. Confucians believed that a harmonious empire rested on a well-ordered family. Women supervised the inner world of the home, while men ran the outer world. The inner and outer worlds were closely connected, and both genders contributed to an orderly world. This differs from the Western conception of mutually exclusive public and private spheres.

Until the 1920s, parents arranged children's marriages. Marriages were decided in accord with family interests. Husband and wife rarely saw one another until the groom lifted his wife's heavy red silk veil at the conclusion of the marriage ceremony. The new wife usually left her home and village to live with her husband and his family. Ties of affection and mutual aid persisted between a woman and her natal family after her marriage, and the isolation of marriage was sometimes alleviated by the custom of marrying maternal first cousins, which made a woman's aunt her mother-in-law.

Separated from family, married to a stranger, and without status until they produced a male heir, women poured their energies into their children. Mothers secured family authority and economic stability through their sons. For this reason, the relationship between a mother-in-law and a daughter-in-law could become tense if the wife competed for the loyalty and love of her husband. Although not included in the five bonds, the relationship between a woman and her children and between a mother-in-law and her daughters-in-law were crucial to a family's happiness and prosperity.

Children's lives were relatively carefree until the age of five, when boys and girls were segregated and began their educations. Boys studied the Confucian classics, began to farm, or learned a trade. Daughters of the elite were often educated along with their brothers and cousins. Most girls were secluded, underwent the ordeal of foot binding, and learned sewing and embroidery. Because well-bound feet bespoke a family's discipline and a sequestered daughter attested to the family's virtue, these qualities improved a girl's chances of making a good marriage. Women were to remain chaste, even after the death of their husbands, and the commemoration of chaste widows flourished during the Ming (1368–1644) and Qing (1644–1911) dynasties.

The Republican Era (1912–1949). Traditional family ideals came under attack during the New Culture Movement (1915–1923), a period when Chinese students and intellectuals questioned every aspect of traditional culture. New Culture radicals insisted on the right to marry for love. They argued that love made people happy, that happy individuals were productive, and that increased productivity would make China strong. They wanted to replace the traditional extended family with the conjugal family. According to this ideal, husband and wife married for love, supported themselves, and lived on their own.

In the mid- to late 1920s, the ideal of the conjugal family was adopted by progressive urban circles. By the early 1930s and 1940s, petty urbanites, reform-minded entrepreneurs, and the elite of China's modernizing cities had accepted it. In 1931 the Nationalist government promulgated marriage laws that guaranteed the right to choose one's spouse and gave men and women equal rights to divorce. Families in rural China continued to follow tradition. The exceptions were the Communist-run soviets, where the Chinese Communist Party promoted gender equality and freedom of marriage and divorce insofar as these policies did not alienate its peasant constituency. During World War II, millions of families suffered death and dislocation, but what that meant for family structure and gender roles is still unknown.

The People's Republic of China (Since 1949). In 1950, less than a year after it took power, the Communist government promulgated the New Marriage Law. Although the Chinese Communist Party claimed to be the only champion of family reform in China, in fact its code closely resembled the Nationalist code of 1931 and reflected the ideals of the New Culture Movement. The real Communist contribution to marriage and family reform was its success in carrying reforms into the countryside.

The three most momentous policies for family structure and dynamics since 1949 have been rural land and labor reforms, the one-child policy, and post-Mao economic reforms. Land redistribution, which began in 1950, gave land to every adult. Collectivization in the late 1950s pulled women further into the agricultural and community labor force. The effect of these policies were mixed. Often the patriarch controlled all family members' land or work points, and so family structure and gender roles remained intact. But, some studies suggest, young women, both married and single, experienced a rise in status and autonomy because of their participation in productive work. Mothers-in-law, however, lost status, as they often took over household and child-rearing chores for daughters-in-law who worked outside the home.

The one-child policy, enacted in the late 1970s and still in effect in the early twenty-first century, has stemmed population growth and created opportunities for women by reducing childbearing, but it has also created problems. Women bear the burden of contraception, suffer forced abortions and sterilization, and suffer the blame for bearing a girl. Rural parents need a son to support them in old age because few have pensions. In the countryside sons often live with their parents after marriage, and men still earn more than women do. Consequently, parents still prefer boys. In an effort to produce a son, a family may apply for permission to have another child. Often families have unauthorized children and pay the penalties. Some hide the birth of a first born girl. Some use ultrasound to detect female fetuses, which they usually abort. And some abandon or kill female (and disabled) infants. In some rural areas, the ratio of females to males is only 80 to 100. The shortage of wives has led in some instances to the kidnapping and selling of girls and women.

Many urban families, however, now prefer girls. They believe girls are less likely to get into trouble and more likely to care for their parents after marriage. Chinese worry about the consequences of individuals raised as spoiled only children; the absence of cousins, aunts, and uncles; and the burden on couples who must care for four aging parents.

The post-Mao market economy has reshaped and challenged the family in a number of ways. Even under Mao Zedong's state-controlled economy, women workers earned less than men did and were treated as a surplus labor supply that could be sent home when no longer needed. In new markets dominated by private enterprises operating largely without government oversight, gender discrimination is worsening. Employers often argue that men need work more than women do because men have families to support. The state implicitly endorses a family economy: The mandatory retirement age for women is fifty-five, ten years earlier than that for men. This reflects in part the expectation that older women will have a grandchild to care for. In fact, many retired women take on child care and household chores for their married children, even though married children usually have their own homes. These duties may continue into old age. In contrast, men generally enjoy a retirement of leisure.

In the cities, prostitution and the keeping of mistresses have reemerged. In the twenty some years of the post-Mao period (1976–2007), the divorce rate rose from nearly zero to about 20 percent. Cities provide some freedom for dating and intergender socializing, though high school students and even many college students eschew romance as an illegitimate distraction.

Because there is too little work in the countryside and earnings there remain low, about 300 million young unmarried men, unmarried women, and, to a lesser degree, married men have moved to the cities, leaving adult married women in the countryside to raise crops, rear children, and keep house. Even in this new environment, families still funnel resources to boys. It is not uncommon for a daughter to work in order to pay for her brother's education. Girls are more likely to be kept home from school to help with farm work. As a result, female literacy continues to lag.

In the countryside, where intergender socializing is still suspect, young people depend on parents to help find a mate. This may be changing among those who have migrated to the cities. Distance and economic independence have led some to make their own decisions about marriage and work. Some young women save their money with the hope of setting up their own businesses when they return home. How this will affect family and gender dynamics remains to be seen. Despite the changes of the twentieth century, the family remains central to the lives and identities of most Chinese.

[*See also* Gender, *subentry* Gender Relations in East Asia; Marriage and Divorce, *subentry* East Asia; *and* Women, *subentry* East Asia.]

BIBLIOGRAPHY

Barlow, Susan, and Jeffrey Wasserstrom, eds. *Chinese Femininities, Chinese Masculinities*. Berkeley: University of California Press, 2002. This collection covers traditional China, the Republican period, and the People's Republic of China. Includes essays by such leaders in the field as Susan Mann and Gail Hershatter.

Diamant, Neil. *Revolutionizing the Family: Politics, Love, and Divorce in Urban and Rural China, 1949–1968*. Berkeley: University of California Press, 2000. The author uses previously unexploited sources to argue that divorce was not as rare as once thought.

Glosser, Susan. *Chinese Visions of Family and State, 1915–1953*. Berkeley: University of California Press, 2003. Glosser traces the development of the conjugal-family ideal in China and demonstrates how intellectuals, entrepreneurs, the Nationalists, and the Communists all used the ideal to articulate their visions of a stronger China. She suggests that the authoritarianism of the People's Republic is rooted in the New Culture Movement, a movement that had been understood as one of unadulterated iconoclasm and liberalism.

Honig, Emily. *Sisters and Strangers: Women in the Shanghai Cotton Mills, 1919–1949*. Stanford, Calif.: Stanford University Press, 1986. This book provides a close look at the lives of working women. Honig demonstrates how the lives of these working-class women reveal much about the nature of Communist organization and the rise of the Communist state.

Johnson, Kay Ann. *Women, the Family, and Peasant Revolution in China*. Chicago: University of Chicago Press, 1983. Johnson's book provides a wide-ranging discussion of the place of women and family in the Communist revolution. It presents the issues concerning women and the family that absorbed many of China's prominent thinkers and politicians in the twentieth century and also demonstrates the limits of the Communist Party's dedication to family and marriage reform and to women's rights.

Judd, Ellen. *Gender and Power in Rural North China*. Stanford, Calif.: Stanford University Press, 1994. This study of rural women in the People's Republic is by one of the foremost authorities on gender and women in contemporary rural China.

SUSAN GLOSSER

Japan

In Tokugawa Japan (1603–1867), the family generally followed a stem-family system of inheritance and household formation. The family, called an *ie*, was often also part of a larger lineage organization called a *dōzoku* (clan).

A stem-family system is characterized by single inheritance, with one child remaining home with his or her spouse to inherit the household, and the other children leaving the family home to join other families through adoption or marriage, establishing new households, or remaining home unmarried to contribute labor to the household. Thus a society with a stem-family system will have both three-generation stem households and one- to two-generation nuclear-family households. A stem-family household consists of two or more coresiding married couples of different generations. It is called a stem family because the majority of the members belong to the stem line of grandparents, parents, children, and grandchildren, with few members of collateral or cadet lines— married uncles, aunts, siblings, nieces, nephews, and cousins—related to the head of the household. These collateral family members appear in stem-family households, but usually when unmarried and for short periods of time.

Inheritance in a stem family usually refers to headship succession. In the European form of the stem family, headship succession usually took place at the marriage of the heir and in many places, like Finland and Austria, was combined with a retirement contract detailing the rights of the retiring couple for support by the new head couple. The Japanese *ie* was similar to the European stem family but had some important differences. In Europe, although there is some room for debate, headship succession meant also the transfer of ownership and control of the land, with variations on how the movable assets would be divided by the heirs. In Japan, headship succession was defined as the transfer of the responsibility to manage the assets (including the labor necessary to maintain those assets), represent the family in community politics and in legal contracts, provide economic support for members of the family, perform ancestral rites, and ensure that the family would continue to the next generation.

Ownership seems to have been vested in at least the *ie* as a whole and often in the extended lineal descent group. Moreover, the headship was transferred upon the retirement or death of the former head or head couple, not upon the marriage of the heir. Finally, demographic research has shown that nearly everyone married, so Japanese households rarely included adult siblings of the head or married heir. Japanese *ie*, like European nuclear-family households, also included many nonkin domestic servants or employees.

Throughout most of Japan there was a general preference for passing the family headship to the eldest son. However, the lack of ability or will to take on the responsibility of managing the land or business, labor, assets, and public roles could cause the headship to pass to a younger or adopted son. These alternatives were also important when a couple had no sons. The preferred alternatives and whether they were taken only when sons were not available or for other reasons varied by region and status. Warrior-class families were legally restricted to passing the headship to the eldest son or adopting from within the patriline if there were no sons. In farming households, daughters were used to recruit sons-in-law to adopt when no sons were available to inherit, so succession could pass through the female line.

In central Japan, where there were many opportunities for income from commerce and industry, the headship might go to a younger son if the eldest son found better opportunities elsewhere. Family businesses sometimes bypassed a son and adopted a particularly skilled manager-employee, tying him to the lineage through marriage to a daughter or a niece. Since the headship was held by a couple, the widow of a family head could retain the headship and control and even recruit another skilled head as her husband or adopted son.

A *dōzoku* is a lineage organization comprising stem, branch, and subbranch households. If a family owned a lot of land, ran a particularly profitable business, or had possibilities for expansion through land reclamation, it would split assets and subsidize a family member to establish a branch. Branch families were formed by younger sons, daughters with their spouses, and nonkin servants or employees in a large family business.

Branch families in a *dōzoku* were under the oversight of the larger organization, often managed by a council consisting of the heads of each branch, the head couple of the stem branch, and the retired couple of the stem branch. Each *dōzoku* had its own way of controlling assets and branches. In some cases the branches were independent parts of the organization, providing labor and capital as necessary and following policies set by the stem family or the council. In others, all assets and profits were pooled, and ownership was shared.

Changes under Meiji. The *ie* system underwent major changes in the late nineteenth century under the Meiji regime (1868–1912), particularly under the Meiji Civil Code (in effect from 1898 to 1946). After the Meiji Restoration of 1868, the new regime began the task of establishing or remaking political and legal institutions to fit Western models in an effort to gain the respect of and equal treatment by Western imperialist nations. The new civil code was part of that process.

One important legal change was that headship succession was redefined to be the inheritance of assets with complete patriarchal control. At the same time, the choice of who could inherit was also redefined. Under the new civil code, the eldest son must inherit unless the family disowned him, and the inheritance was no longer partible. Hence younger sons could not inherit assets, and adoption was limited to cases where no sons were available. Moreover, the responsibility for the head to support members of the *ie* now had the qualification that he could refuse to support them if they did not obey him—a circumstance that further strengthened the patriarchal power of the head.

The Meiji Civil Code also proffered a new image of the state as a large household or lineage organization. The emperor was a patriarchal head, and individual heads of households were little emperors. Sons, even adult sons, were subordinated to males of elder generations, women were subordinated to men, and all subjects of the emperor were given well-defined roles, with women in charge of producing and educating the next generation of subjects. This code represented an attempt to reshape tradition to match Confucian and Victorian ideals of family and gender roles.

Changes after World War II. After World War II the Allied occupation authorities under General Douglas MacArthur took control of Japan with a mandate to ensure that Japan would never again be a threat to world peace. They believed that Japan's patriarchal family system in general and its large family business concerns in particular were major factors behind the war, so the occupation authorities revised the constitution and the civil code to remedy these problems. At the same time, MacArthur's staff included many liberals, who used this chance to experiment with reforms that they thought would be beneficial back home.

One of the more drastic changes to family law was that inheritance was made partible, and all legitimate descendents were equally entitled to an inheritance. Other changes removed legal support for the patriarchal authority of the head of a household and strengthened women's right to equal pay for equal work. The ownership ties of large family-business concerns were broken by abolishing holding companies, and a large inheritance tax was imposed so that no family would retain economic power and control for generations. Finally, Japanese families stopped employing large numbers of domestic servants.

Occupation authorities changed the legal framework of Japanese family practice, but this could not change people's thinking and habits regarding succession and coresidence. More important in this regard were the changes in Japan's economic structure that took place during the rapid economic growth of the 1960s. Most families came to see themselves as middle class, and labor was restructured around the "salaryman," who could work long hours because he had a housewife who ran the household. Women took time out from participation in the labor force for marriage and childbirth and reentered as part-time labor for lower pay when children entered school. Medium to large firms also instituted a system of regular transfers, which changed patterns of coresidence. The new system forced women to choose between career and marriage, and some women began choosing careers—a tendency that has increased.

At the beginning of the twenty-first century, Japanese families still include some stem-family households and also many nuclear ones. There is a tendency toward matrilocal stem households in order to take advantage of grandmothers willing to care for children. At the same time, the aging of society, together with lower fertility rates, has burdened women with increased duties to care for the elderly.

[*See also* Gender, *subentry* Gender Relations in East Asia; Marriage and Divorce, *subentry* East Asia; Salaryman; *and* Women, *subentry* East Asia.]

BIBLIOGRAPHY

Hanley, Susan B., and Arthur P. Wolf, eds. *Family and Population in East Asian History.* Stanford, Calif.: Stanford University Press, 1985.

Nagata, Mary Louise. *Labor Contracts and Labor Relations in Early Modern Central Japan.* London: RoutledgeCurzon,

2005. This study explores the Japanese *ie* and lineage organization as business in early modern Japan.

Nakane, Chie. *Kinship and Economic Organization in Rural Japan*. London: Athlone Press, 1967. A classic study on the Japanese *ie*.

Nishikawa Yūko. "The Modern Japanese Family System: Unique or Universal?" In *Multicultural Japan: Palaeolithic to Postmodern*, edited by Donald Denoon, Mark Hudson, Gavan McCormack, and Tessa Morris-Suzuki, pp. 224–232. Cambridge, U.K.: Cambridge University Press, 2001. This paper argues against the uniqueness of the Japanese family.

Ochiai Emiko. *The Japanese Family System in Transition: A Sociological Analysis of Family Change in Postwar Japan*. Tokyo: LTCB International Library Foundation, 1996.

Ueno Chizuko. "Modern Patriarchy and the Formation of the Japanese Nation-State." In *Multicultural Japan: Palaeolithic to Post-modern*, edited by Donald Denoon, Mark Hudson, Gavan McCormack, and Tessa Morris-Suzuki, pp. 213–223. Cambridge, U.K.: Cambridge University Press, 2001. This paper argues that the patriarchal *ie* was a construction of the Meiji state.

MARY LOUISE NAGATA

Korea

The family and kinship system in Korea at the beginning of the twenty-first century reflects four lines of influence: the Confucian tradition established during the Chosŏn (or Yi) dynasty (1392–1910), Japanese colonial rule (1910–1945), the establishment of the Republic of Korea in 1948, and the rapid economic and social changes since the 1970s.

The Traditional Family System. The Korean family system during the Chosŏn dynasty was based on Confucian ideals emphasizing proper roles and relationships based on gender, generation, age, and social class. The basic purpose and function of the family was the preservation of the family line and prosperity of the family. The family headship was passed from father to eldest legitimate son. Inheritance of wealth was limited to the sons, and the eldest son was entitled to a much larger share of the father's wealth than other sons. Among the East Asian countries that share the Confucian tradition, Korea was different from such countries as China and Japan in its strict adherence to the rule of primogeniture and its limitations on who could be adopted as a son in the absence of a biological son. In traditional Korea, only a paternally related male of the appropriate generation was eligible for adoption. Other males, including sons-in-law, were not eligible for legal adoption as an heir to the family headship.

Relatives having a common ancestor within five generations were considered close kin, with social obligations to help one another. A clan consisted of paternally related men, their wives, and unmarried children. Under this family system, filial duties toward living and deceased ancestors were regarded as the most important principle of social behavior. To continue patrilineal descent, the most important obligation of a person was to marry and produce a son. Marriage was mandatory, and early marriage was common. A woman could attain high status within the family by bearing and rearing a son.

Men and women assumed strictly separate roles, and interactions between men and women were restricted and reserved. Segregation of husband and wife was so extensive that spouses' respective domains in the home were regarded as completely separate: the external space for the husband and the inner space for the wife. The literati class and wealthy commoners practiced these family ideals, but it is likely that poor commoners and lower-class people lacked the means to practice them.

The Influence of Japanese Colonial Rule (1910–1945). The Japanese colonial government introduced into Korea a modern legal system fashioned after the civil code of Meiji Japan. The Korean civil code institutionalized a family system based on Confucian traditions, such as designating a family head and identifying clans in the family registration system. Held up as ideals were strict separation of the roles of women and men and the education of women to become "wise mothers and good wives."

One notable difference between the Korean and Japanese family systems concerned family names. Koreans, men and women, kept the same family name throughout life. Women did not change their family name upon marriage, and since adoption was done within the patrilineal clan, the adopted son did not have to change his family name. In 1930 the Japanese colonial government revised the civil code to allow adoption of a male with a different family name, including a son-in-law. This was perhaps intended to provide a legal basis for Japanese men to enter into Korean families and inherit their wealth. In 1939 the Japanese colonial government drastically changed the civil code, imposing the Japanese system of last names: the wife adopted the husband's family name upon marriage, and all members of a family shared the same family name. The civil code also required all family names to be Japanese names.

The Republic of Korea and the Modernization of Korean Society. The end of World War II in 1945 brought the liberation of Korea from Japan and, in 1948, the establishment of the Republic of Korea in the south and the Democratic People's Republic of Korea in the north. Little information is available about the North Korean family and kin system. The discussion below is limited to the situation in South Korea.

The interim Korean government repealed the 1939 revision of the civil code regarding family names, and the constitution of the Republic of Korea guarantees equal rights for men and women. But for family headship, adoption, inheritance, and the extent of kin, the civil code continued to reflect the traditional patriarchal family system, which gave men a higher status than that given women. The legal basis for equal rights for women continued to improve through a series of revisions, one of which is the revision of 2005, which abolished the system of family heads.

With rising levels of education for women, rapid economic growth, urbanization, and greater geographic mobility since the 1970s, family relationships and the composition of the family began to change substantially. Typical family size decreased from four or five children to two children. Women and men began to marry at an increasingly later age, and the proportion of people who never married increased. It became less common for grown children to reside with their parents. Most women work outside home before marriage, and a substantial proportion continue to work after marriage.

However, the persistence of traditional norms in South Korea has resulted in patterns different from those experienced in the West. The strong patrilineal and patriarchal family traditions, for example, have kept out-of-wedlock childbearing at very low levels. The civil code, reflecting the patrilineal family system, requires registration of the birth of a child in his or her father's family registry. The father of a child born out of wedlock may not register the child's birth, or the child may be registered in some other family registry, such as the mother's, as someone else's child. A child growing up with an unidentified father experiences serious social stigma.

The divorce rate in South Korea was low until the 1990s. Although women, including married women, are participating in paid employment at increasingly higher levels, men hardly take on domestic roles. The continuing importance of having a son, even while fertility levels and the typical family size drastically fell, produced unusually more reported boy babies than girl babies in the late 1990s, before the preference for sons began to weaken. Young married couples have closer ties with husbands' parents than with wives' parents in terms of coresidence, visitations, and economic obligations. And the importance of preserving the family line and making the family prosperous, together with the importance of being a good mother for women, has resulted in great investment in children's educations.

[*See also* Gender, *subentry* Gender Relations in East Asia; Marriage and Divorce, *subentry* East Asia; *and* Women, *subentry* East Asia.]

BIBLIOGRAPHY

Choi, Jai-Seuk. "Comparative Study on the Traditional Families in Korea, Japan, and China." In *Families in East and West: Socialization Process and Kinship Ties*, edited by Reuben Hill and René König, pp. 202–210. The Hague: Mouton, 1970. An excellent description of the traditional Korean family system from comparative and historical perspectives.

Kim, Doo Hun. "Historical Review of Korean Family System." *Korea Journal* 3, no. 10 (1963): 4–9 and 332. An excellent description of the Korean family system from a historical perspective.

Mason, Karen Oppenheim, Noriko O. Tsuya, and Minja Kim Choe, eds. *The Changing Family in Comparative Perspective: Asia and the United States.* Honolulu, Hawai'i: East-West Center, 1998. A collection of essays describing aspects of contemporary family life in South Korea and other Asian countries and the United States from a comparative perspective.

Mattielli, Sandra, ed. *Virtues in Conflict: Tradition and the Korean Woman Today.* Seoul, South Korea: Samhwa, 1977. A collection of essays on traditions and contemporary conditions affecting women's lives in Korea. Includes an excellent chapter by Martina Deuchler on Confucian influence on the traditional Korean family system.

MINJA KIM CHOE

Mongolia

Despite anthropological cliché about nomadic peoples forming strong patrilineal kin groups, most of the Mongolian people since the eighteenth century have lived in nuclear or stem families, with shallow genealogies and bilateral kin ties. In some areas of the Gobi, matrilineal clans were dominant. Only the Buriat Mongols in southern Siberia maintain strong patrilineages and extensive genealogies in the twenty-first century. With most Mongols living in small and flexible kin units, the transition to the urban nuclear-family model promoted in Communist Mongolia was not too traumatic.

Mongolian nomadic herders traditionally nomadize in small camps (*khot ail*) of about two to eight yurts (Mongolian *ger*), each yurt housing a married couple with unmarried children, or sometimes an older adult. Many household and pastoral tasks are assigned by gender, but others are performed by adults or children without regard to gender. Camps are formed freely according to paternal or maternal kinship, friendship, or marriage.

Before the 1921 revolution, up to 15 percent of the men lived as celibate Buddhist monks, leaving significant numbers of never-married women. The Mongol nobility, whose titles had to be confirmed by the supreme authorities in Beijing, secured their successions by formal marrying of their sons to, preferably, a young virgin bride. Among commoners, however, little stigma was attached to nonmarital sex and illegitimacy, and formal marriage, confirmed by traditional bridewealth payments, was in decline. Despite this decline in marriage, however, both formal Buddhist teachings and traditional proverbs emphasized an authoritarian patrilineal family structure, criticized youthful romance, enjoined daughters-in-law to obey their mothers-in-law, and exhorted all to repay the kindness shown them by their elders and betters with grateful service. Literacy rates were sharply divided by gender.

After Mongolia's 1921 revolution, supported by Soviet Russia, and the proclamation of a people's republic in 1924, the new regime legislated gender equality and voluntary marriage, while the Youth League encouraged rebellion against patriarchal mores. After the monasteries were destroyed in 1937–1940, marriage became essentially universal. After World War II, urbanization strengthened the tendency toward nuclear families and brought women into the paid workforce, and the literacy gap disappeared. Civil marriage registration was created in 1951. Infant mortality rates declined, sparking a baby boom that peaked in 1963 when the fertility rate reached eight children per family. Despite a ban on contraceptives and abortion, however, the fertility rate later declined to 4.5 by 1990. Social values under Communism emphasized equal participation of both men and women in paid labor, the stable nuclear family, and a natural affinity of women with family and housework.

With the economic collapse of the Soviet bloc, Mongolia's fertility rate declined sharply and the new democratic government in 1990 promptly legalized abortion and contraception. Age at first marriage and the divorce rate also climbed rapidly. Social values have been buffeted by a revival of Mongolia's ancient traditions, an influx of feminist ideas, and signs of anomie among the male population. Even so, the popular ideal has remained the nuclear family with the husband as the predominant breadwinner.

[*See also* Mongolia.]

BIBLIOGRAPHY

Randall, Sara. "Issues in the Demography of Mongolian Nomadic Pastoralism." *Nomadic Peoples* 33 (1993): 209–227.

Vreeland, Herbert Harold, III. *Mongol Community and Kinship Structure*. 2d ed. New Haven, Conn.: Human Relations Area Files, 1957.

CHRISTOPHER P. ATWOOD

The Middle East and North Africa

"Family" can be defined as a group of individuals bound together through ties of kinship, whether biologically determined or socially constructed. As the basic social unit, family often serves as the site where social, cultural, political, and economic change and phenomena come to bear, and where moral crises of societies in flux and experiencing accompanying shifts in values are manifested through changing patterns of gender roles and social relationships among family members. Since the 1980s interest in family as a category for historical, social, and cultural analysis has grown among scholars of the Middle East and North Africa, initially stemming from scholarship that addressed women and gender from different disciplinary perspectives.

Kinship patterns among inhabitants of the Middle East exhibited certain similarities in rural and urban settings. Kin groups are, generally speaking, patrilineal, and members of a specific kin group might share a specific patronymic, whether or not they actually share blood ties. At some level the authenticity of blood relations is irrelevant; affinity to a larger kin group is, like the notion of family, socially and politically constructed—not necessarily biologically determined. For instance, the social group in Palestine known as the *hamula* is an affiliation of families who claim descent from a common ancestor and share economic and political interests. Tribal societies exhibit similar forms of kinship patterns, in the sense that tribes are loose confederations of families who claim descent from a common ancestor and that membership in the tribe often translates into specific privileges and expectations. Though patrilineal descent is primary in determining one's inclusion in a kin group, maternal affiliations are also important and play a significant role in kinship patterns that involve cousin marriages. Because of the prevailing legal systems that are based on Sharia and customary practices, patriarchal and patrilineal families continue to be the norm across the Middle East.

Before the Nineteenth Century. It seems that the predominant structure of the family in urban centers during the early modern era (sixteenth through eighteenth centuries) was the nuclear family—that is, a household consisting of one husband, one wife, and their children. Despite its perception as quintessentially "modern," the nuclear family (or the simple family household) demonstrates remarkable historical resilience as the most common type of family unit in the urban Middle Eastern world. The nuclear family unit also seems to have been equally prevalent among rural households in some parts of the Ottoman Empire.

In urban settings before the nineteenth century, families were patriarchal and patrilineal, but not necessarily patrilocal. In seventeenth-century Anatolian and Syrian towns, for instance, a newlywed couple would set up residence in a home that was separate from the paternal home, though it was not uncommon for "stem families" to live in close proximity to the father's home or for relatives to reside close to one another. The seventeenth-century Palestinian mufti Khayr al-Din al-Ramli encouraged husbands to provide each wife with her own residence that would be separate from the patriarchal home. Polygamy was sanctioned by Islamic law and was limited to four wives, but it does not seem to have been commonly practiced by most men, possibly because of the financial burden it imposed on the husband. When practiced, polygamy rarely exceeded two wives. This prerogative of Muslim men also seems to have been unwelcome to urban women, at least in the Arab Middle East. Many women in Syria and elsewhere often included prenuptial agreements in their marriage contracts that granted them divorce (*taq*) should their husbands take a second wife.

Marriage was socially expected and encouraged. In the Muslim Middle East, marriage between a man and woman was, at its most basic level, a contract between two parties. Yet the marriage contract carried both social and religious significance. After the bride expresses her consent to marriage—if she is not a minor, in which case her male guardian contracts the marriage on her behalf—the groom presents the bride with a bride-price (*mahr* or *sadaq*), usually paid in two installments: the *muqaddam*, or advance, and the *mu'akhkhar*, which is debt owed to the wife and paid to her only if she is widowed or divorced. Once the marriage contract is executed, conjugal relations between the man and wife become permissible in the eyes of God and the community. Whereas the husband is permitted to engage in sexual relations with up to four wives and female slaves, the wife is permitted sexual relations only with her husband.

As with marriage, laws that governed divorce, child custody, and inheritance arguably favored men over women. Like other contracts, marriage can be terminated, although the right of divorce (*talaq*) without grounds is granted exclusively to the husband. In extreme cases, such as abandonment or mental deficiency, a wife may petition the Islamic court for a divorce, which a judge may grant her on behalf of the husband. If such extreme circumstances do not exist, yet a wife desires to end her marriage, she may petition for an annulment, or *khul'*, in which case she forfeits her rights to her *mu'akhkhar* and to her material

or financial support (*nafaqa*) during the waiting period after divorce (*'idda*), and she may sometimes even pay her husband to "redeem" herself.

According to Judith Tucker (1997), Islamic law, in particular Hanafi law, had rather clear delineations of the roles of mothers and fathers. In cases of divorce or orphaned children, women as mothers—and by extension the maternal family, especially the maternal grandmother if alive—were perceived as being more suitable custodians or caretakers of infants or young children because of their natural disposition toward affection, which children needed for healthy development. When boys reach the age of seven, and girls the age of nine, the father—and again, by extension the paternal family—is deemed the more suitable custodian of the children, because nurturing children after this age requires certain skills that men were deemed to be better at than women.

Devolution of property as delineated in Islamic inheritance law is likewise gendered in favor of male heirs, particularly sons over daughters. The principle behind this is arguably the notion of maintaining as much as possible a family's assets within the control of male family members. However, as Beshara Doumani (1998) has shown, in the first half of the nineteenth century, Syrian families often maneuvered within and around legal principles of inheritance through the establishment of family *waqfs* (endowments) in order to formulate inheritance strategies that in some cases might be more favorable for female descendants.

The Nineteenth Century: State, Modernity, and Nationalism. The nineteenth century witnessed changes in configuration of the family that resulted from global economic transformations and further integration of the Middle East into the world capitalist system; locally, these transformations meant shifts in agricultural production, trade networks, industry, labor, and relationships of production. There was also a change in the articulation of what family meant and an elaboration of its role in society. Ottoman reformers and Middle Eastern thinkers used the concept of the "family" rhetorically by invoking it as the backbone of the new nation and the new modern society that came with it; often they referred to the nation metaphorically as a family.

For the nineteenth century the changes in the organization and structure of the rural and urban family can be traced. Specific economic and political changes that affected the agricultural sector of the Middle East also affected the structure and organization of rural family life. Prior to the reforms and policies of Muhammad ʿAli

Pasha (r. 1805–1849) in Egypt, gender divisions of labor in rural families were predicated on their respective needs for survival and prosperity. The historian Judith Tucker (1985) argues that subsequent to the policies of Muhammad ʿAli, which led to increased state involvement and intervention in the agricultural sector, new divisions of labor and relationships of production ushered in a shift in the configuration of rural family life. Kenneth Cuno has shown that in nineteenth-century rural Egypt, wealthy landowning families tended to live together in extended joint households rather than splinter off into nuclear units.

With the spread of nationalism and the growth of nationalist sentiments, ideologies, and identities—Arab, Turkish, and Iranian—in the late nineteenth century and early twentieth century, a concurrent shift in the articulation of "family" took place. Statements by writers and thinkers were made about what the character of Turkish, Arab, or Iranian family should be. These statements incorporated both an awareness of the centrality of family to the success of the idea of the nation and also the recognition that the family, along with the school perhaps, is the primary site where notions of nationalism and citizenship and the values associated with them were most effectively inculcated, reinforced, and reproduced.

Thinkers and writers, both men (Qasim Amin, Ziya Gökalp) and women (Bahithat al-Badiya, Zaynab Fawwaz), perceived the education of women as essential to ensure the proper raising of children as future citizens of the modern state, and also as the cornerstone of a successful companionate marriage. A vigorous women's press appeared in Egypt, and to a lesser extent in Syria, which promoted the cult of domesticity by instructing women on how to be good wives and mothers in terms that were not unlike middle-class Victorian sensibilities. This attitude toward marriage was reciprocated elsewhere, but through different means: Akram Fouad Khater notes that Lebanese immigrants to the Americas returned to their hometowns with similar bourgeois attitudes toward family, marriage, and gender roles. Despite increased rural-urban migration, the simple family unit, or nuclear family, continued to be the most widespread household structure in the early twentieth century. According to Alan Duben and Cem Behar, only 16 percent of Muslim households in Istanbul were extended, and these constituted 20 percent of the city's population in 1907; in 82 percent of those extended-family households, the extended-family member was a grandparent.

Twentieth and Twenty-First Centuries. In the twentieth century the establishment of nation-states in the Middle East introduced the concepts of citizenship and national affiliation. Citizenship and nationality competed with kin-based group affiliations, in the sense that the newly independent nations are predicated on the assumption that citizens of the state will deem their family or tribal affiliations secondary to national ones. Yet because of the political nature of Middle Eastern state formation and governance, family, kin groups, and tribal affiliations continue to play an important and practical role in the daily functioning of these societies.

Patrilineal kinship continues to play a major role in conferring citizenship: legal codes in many Middle Eastern countries have established patrilineal ties as the paramount factor in determining the citizenship rights of individuals, superseding the role of birth or residence in the country as the requirement for citizenship. Additionally, most Middle Eastern countries allow for citizenship to pass from the husband to the wife if she is a foreign national, but not vice versa. This underscores both the unequal status of male and female citizens and also the primacy of paternal lineage over maternal descent. One exception is Morocco, which in 2007 passed legislation to rectify sexist nationality laws. Sometimes, as in the case of Jordan, the decision to deny citizenship to children of Jordanian mothers and non-Jordanian fathers, as well as to non-Jordanian husbands—the majority of whom are stateless Palestinians—is fueled by demographic and political concerns rather than purely patriarchal concepts of nationality.

The state's intervention in matters of marriage and divorce terminated, in some countries like Turkey and Tunisia, the Muslim male prerogative to practice polygamy, although most Middle Eastern countries permit the practice. Divorce laws continue to favor husbands over wives, although the bureaucratization of the divorce has made it more tedious for men than in the past. Recent modifications to family legal codes in Egypt and Morocco, for instance, have done much to mitigate the situation of women in unhappy marriages by granting wives greater rights to initiate divorce proceedings.

[See also Law, *subentry* The Middle East, North Africa, and Central Asia; Tribes and Tribalism, *subentry* The Arabian Peninsula; *and* Women, *subentry* The Middle East and North Africa.]

BIBLIOGRAPHY

Ali, Kamran Asdar. *Planning the Family in Egypt: New Bodies, New Selves.* Austin: University of Texas Press, 2002.

Cuno, Kenneth M. "Joint Family Households and Rural Notables in 19th-Century Egypt." *International Journal of Middle East Studies* 27, no. 4 (1995): 485–502.

Doumani, Beshara. "Endowing Family: Waqf, Property Devolution, and Gender in Greater Syria, 1800 to 1860." *Comparative Studies in Society and History* 40 (1998): 3–41.

Doumani, Beshara, ed. *Family History in the Middle East: Household, Property, and Gender.* Albany: State University of New York Press, 2003.

Duben, Alan, and Cem Behar. *Istanbul Households: Marriage, Family, and Fertility, 1880–1940.* Cambridge, U.K.: Cambridge University Press, 1991.

Eickelman, Dale F. *The Middle East and Central Asia: An Anthropological Approach.* 4th ed. Upper Saddle River, N.J.: Prentice Hall, 2002. Good overview of kinship patterns and group formations in the Muslim Middle East and Central Asia.

Gerber, Haim. "Anthropology and Family History: The Ottoman and Turkish Families." *Journal of Family History* 14, no. 4 (1989): 409–421.

Khater, Akram Fouad. *Inventing Home: Emigration, Gender, and the Middle Class in Lebanon, 1870–1920.* Berkeley: University of California Press, 2001.

Meriwether, Margaret L. *The Kin Who Count: Family and Society in Ottoman Aleppo, 1770–1840.* Austin: University of Texas Press, 1999.

Mir-Hosseini, Ziba. *Marriage on Trial, a Study of Islamic Family Law: Iran and Morocco Compared.* London: I. B. Tauris, 1993.

Tucker, Judith E. "The Fullness of Affection: Mothering in the Islamic Law of Ottoman Syria and Palestine." In *Women in the Ottoman Empire: Middle Eastern Women in the Early Modern Era,* edited by Madeline C. Zilfi, pp. 232–252. Leiden, Netherlands: Brill, 1997.

Tucker, Judith E. *In the House of the Law: Gender and Islamic Law in Ottoman Syria and Palestine.* Berkeley: University of California Press, 1998.

Tucker, Judith E. *Women in Nineteenth-Century Egypt.* Cambridge, U.K.: Cambridge University Press, 1985.

DIANA ABOUALI

Central Asia

Kinship formed the main basis on which Central Asian societies were constructed. Historically, the living members of a clan considered themselves to be under the effective protection of its dead members, and thus the principal sacred duty of the living members was to produce offspring in order to ensure the clan's future. Traditionally, large families are closely associated with honor, respect, and self-esteem. When relatives or friends greet one another after a long separation, they do not ask "How are you?" but rather "How many children do you have?" From the pre-Islamic (or pre-Buddhist in Mongolia) custom of worshiping dead members of a clan developed a remarkable tradition of showing respect to the elderly, who had accumulated wisdom and experience, enabling them after their deaths to solicit heavenly masters for their clan's prosperity.

Younger family members have traditionally looked after their parents. When the eldest son marries, he and his wife live with his parents until the second son marries. Then the second son and his wife live with their parents, and this pattern continues until the youngest son marries. Then his family takes care of the parents until they die. Clans consist of complete families of two or three generations. They are headed by the oldest male member, whose position makes him an omnipotent decision maker. Historically, closely related large families (clans) constituted self-organized communities or neighborhoods, the *makhallyas,* headed by the elected councils of eldermen or *aksakals.* Islamization in the eighth century encouraged communities to assert their Muslim identities through elaborate myths of origin. Their legendary founders (shamans or *ongons*) turned into Muslim holy men (*Baba Tukles,* or "friends of God") who had an intimate relationship with God and could intercede with him on behalf of ordinary kin Muslims. After their deaths, their mausoleums (*mazars*) became shrines, places of pilgrimage, and foci of communal identity. Legends ascribe to these bringers of Islam Arab origins (or relationship to Genghis Khan among nomads), but they were also fully indigenized as ancestors. Celebrations in their honor, annual holidays, and life-cycle events, showing respect for elders, gender distinctions, the position of women, and traditional norms of etiquette, were essential to communal existence. The dual process of localizing Islam and Islamizing local traditions led to sacralization of local customs and indigenization of Islam.

Marriages were seen as a contract between two families rather than two individuals. Matchmakers helped in arrangements. Under Islamic law (sharia) the marriageable age was nine for women and twelve for men; however, in real life there was no standard of marrying age. The amount of *qalin* (bride-price given to the father of the bride) could be negotiated if there were differences in family wealth. Sometimes the groom who could not pay *qalin* abducted the bride instead. *Mahr* was the gift from the groom to the bride, two-thirds of which was given at the time of marriage and one-third in the case of divorce. The bride's family gave gifts of clothes to the groom and his male family members; the bride also received gifts of jewelry and clothing from her family. Men could marry up to four women, but women could marry only one man. According to sharia, wives could be divorced without alimony, child custody, or cause. A husband could legally divorce his wife by repeating the word "leave" (*talog*) three times.

Among sedentary Uzbeks and Tajiks women's seclusion in the *ichkari* (women's quarter of home), as well as the wearing of a heavy cotton robe (*paranji*) covering the entire body and a veil of woven horsehair (*chachvon*), were basic facts of social order, connected with the concepts of honor, shame, respect, and hierarchy. In the nomadic communities of Turkmen, Kazakhs, Kyrgyzs, and Buddhist Mongols, where families traditionally lived in yurts or *kibitki*, women enjoyed more freedom and worked outside the home.

The Soviets (1917–1991) considerably equalized men's and women's rights in marriage. However, if a woman inherited land, it ultimately fell into the hands of male relatives. Collectivization undermined productive functions of clans. Forcible unveiling and the end of seclusion (*hujum*) involved women in work beyond the household and removed children from the clan environment. These and other changes diminished the role of traditional norms of family and social order. All the same, in the process of the collapse of Soviet regimes in the 1980s and 1990s many old ways underwent vigorous rejuvenation. Polygyny, hidden under the Soviets, has become open again. All boys are being circumcised. A civil wedding ceremony goes along with the Muslim one. Specific parts of family dwellings, such as women's quarters, have reappeared. Weddings, births, and funerals are marked by the lavish feasts. The wedding party is the biggest event for Central Asian families. Women from the entire neighborhood arrive at the home of the bride's parents to chop hundreds of pounds of carrots that will go into a huge pilaf. Several sheep are slaughtered. The host serves two or three meals in one day. Actors and entertainers are hired, and there will be music and dancing.

Such feasts are possible today because of another important aspect of traditional customs: the rules of mutual guarantees. Networks of mutual obligations based on kinship or common places of origin guarantee security in the face of the impersonal machinery of the modern state. They are held together by the exchange of favors, gifts, and mutual assistance. This system allows common people to survive by relying on their more successful relatives when, for example, they have become unemployed. In turn ordinary kinsmen or fellow countrymen show obedience and vote to promote their patrons to the most lucrative positions. Since the late Soviet period such forms of networks have come to enmesh practically all Central Asian states. Some experts argue that this system of kinship (real or fictive) produces corruption, uncompetitive economies, and poor policies. Throughout the region, politically powerful clans have retained control over the national wealth, validating themselves as bearers of the will of nations.

[*See also* Central Asia; Marriage and Divorce; *and* Paternalism.]

BIBLIOGRAPHY

Collins, Kathleen. "The Logic of Clan Politics: Evidence from Central Asian Trajectories." *World Politics* 56 (2003–2004): 224–261.

Kamp, Marianne. *The New Woman in Uzbekistan: Islam, Modernity, and Unveiling*. Seattle: University of Washington Press, 2006.

Khalid, Adeeb. *Islam after Communism: Religion and Politics in Central Asia*. Berkeley and Los Angeles: University of California Press, 2007. One of the best efforts to demonstrate the evolution of family traditions and forms of kinship during and after the Soviet period.

Khalid, Adeeb. *The Politics of Muslim Cultural Form: Jadidism in Central Asia*. Berkeley: University of California Press, 1998.

Northorp, Douglas. *Veiled Empire: Gender and Power in Stalinist Central Asia*. Ithaca, N.Y.: Cornell University Press, 2004. By far the fullest treatment of this material, showing that Islamic norms of family life became synonymous with tradition and were subordinated to powerful ethno-national identities that crystallized during the Stalin period.

ANATOLY V. ISAENKO

FAMILY PLANNING. *See* Abortion; Birth Control; Infanticide.

FAMINE [*This entry includes four subentries, an overview and discussions of famine in Africa, East Asia, and India.*]

Overview

The term "famine" has several dimensions. First, it denotes a distinctive event of economic and social crisis caused by an exceptional degree of food deprivation. Because it is not a periodic event, a famine is usually defined by a particular time and location. Famines also reveal long-term structural issues that underlie food access and food scarcity, including political strife, environmental disasters, and the relations of power that control resource distribution.

Historically, mass hunger has been vivid in collective social memories because of its devastating symptoms and dramatic effects on society. As collective disasters that affect high numbers of people, famines extend beyond immediate mass hunger in the form of infection and chronic disease, low birthrates, and political and social upheaval. Historical accounts reveal that mass hunger was often recurrent, provoking widespread fear of food deprivation and its effects for years to come. Fear of food deprivation is especially acute in oral and written histories of peasants and hard laborers, populations that most deeply experience the persistent devastation of subsistence crises.

In demographic terms, mass hunger is marked by its profound impact on mortality rates. Famine has often been described purely in statistical terms—that is, the number of people who died directly as a result of food deprivation. But mortality statistics based on starvation alone cannot account for the large-scale, long-term impact of hunger and the persistent syndromes that precede and follow famine. Included among these long-term effects of mass hunger is the relationship between famine and epidemic disease. In most famines, deaths related to disease surpass deaths directly attributed to starvation. The appearance of disease in times of dearth reveals the profound effect of social upheavals caused by famine. During the industrialization of both the Western and non-Western worlds, crowded living and working conditions in urban spaces coupled with famine conditions to create high rates of infection and death among the working classes.

Causes of Famine. The root causes and varied social and political meanings of famine continue to provoke new debates in scholarship. Theories addressing the roots of famine have considered several issues as central in the making of famine conditions, including climate change, population growth and distribution, and food entitlement and availability. Among these theories, natural causes like climatic disaster (for example, floods, droughts, and cyclones) have dominated explanations of famine causation. In natural descriptions of famine causation, food shortage is directly attributed to dramatic effects of climatic disruptions on food production. For example, monsoon rains were either short or absent before every major famine in nineteenth-century India, often causing shortfalls in the harvest of staple foods.

Historians now contest the seemingly direct relationship between these natural disasters and the traumatic famines that followed. Instead, by considering policies and social upheavals caused in large part by the rule of the British Raj, many scholars claim that climate was only one part of a complex set of both natural and social conditions that produced famine in India. In the contemporary world, climate alone is also unable to explain the uneven appearance of famine after natural disasters in some areas of the modern world, especially Asia and sub-Saharan Africa, and the virtual absence of famine in response to similar climatic conditions in Europe and North America.

Second among popular hypotheses of famine causation are those theories that link famine to ideas of overpopulation. In 1803, Thomas Malthus (1766–1834) wrote and extended his *Essay on the Principle of Population* in response to English Poor Laws that, in his view, stimulated population growth among the lower classes without expanding food production. For Malthus, famine existed as a law of nature that reduced an excessive population that strained inflexible resources of a given society. Malthus did not consider the potential consequences of uneven resource distribution on lower classes of society, nor did he consider an agricultural sector that responded to increased demands for food. His narrow subsistence parameters continuously failed in nineteenth-century Europe, which saw expansive growths in population and a generally higher standard of living for both the upper and lower classes.

Malthus's theories reappeared in the middle of the twentieth century with the recurrence of famine in Africa and Asia and the simultaneous absence of dramatic famines in the Western world. In these theories, Third World peoples had become too populous, while agricultural practices were limited by the effects of overproduction. Famine was the logical consequence of overpopulation. The so-called laws of nature were tied to racist perceptions and policies that represented the non-Western world as a place that was unable to civilize its people enough to control its population. But theories of population growth that see overpopulation as a singular cause for famine overlook significant cultural and political factors that prevent food output and distribution in colonial and postcolonial states. The concept of overpopulation in the so-called Third World disguises increasing disparities in resource access and distribution between people of the Western and non-Western worlds.

Finally, a significant intervention in contemporary discussions of famine is the Nobel Prize–winning economist Amartya Sen's hypothesis linking "food entitlement" to famine causation. In *Poverty and Famines*, published in 1981, Sen critically examines the way in which food is distributed in a given population. He links famine causation not to volumes of food available but to the access that different parts of a population have to food resources. To explain uneven resource distribution, Sen puts forth a theory of "exchange entitlements." Sen considers an entitlement as legally sanctioned rights that give control over food or goods and labor that can be exchanged for food resources. Entitlements are uneven in a population, and thus power to control food resources and distribution is concentrated in certain social groups. Sen analyzes the Bengal famine of 1943–1944, pointing out that famine was not caused by shortages in the rice supply itself but instead was accelerated by the inability of the poor to exchange goods or labor for rising prices of rice. Sen's theory points out the discriminatory impact of mass hunger and the diminishing power of certain peoples to gain access to food in the face of famine.

Though the idea of entitlements has transformed discussions of both contemporary and historical famines, scholars have pointed out that Sen's theory is unable fully to account for famines caused by long-term social and economic decline that make certain societies and social groups particularly vulnerable. Climatic and population variation may combine with uneven access to food resources to create famine conditions.

Notable Famines in the Modern World. From the 1750s on, famines disproportionately appeared and affected areas of the non-Western world. With industrialization and the unequal distribution of resources as a result of colonial expansion, Europe began to see fewer famines. In contrast, Asia has been most often associated with recurring and devastating famines. Among these areas, China and India are considered to have the highest rates of famine mortality in the world. But in the late twentieth century, famine rates in Asia slowed, making the recurrent appearance of famine in sub-Saharan Africa more visible.

In the modern world, Europe experienced famines at a comparatively low rate in relation to the non-Western world. Significant among European famines is the great Irish potato famine of 1845–1849, which led to the immediate deaths of more than a million people, mass emigration of Irish people out of Ireland, and population decline for the following century. During World War II, famine affected at least 3 million people throughout Europe as a result of war tactics and resource blockades used by German and Allied troops.

Droughts in northern China in the late nineteenth century are directly linked to consecutive famines that led to the deaths of an estimated 13 million people. The largest famine of the twentieth century, and some argue of all time, is the Great Leap Forward famine that occurred in China in 1958–1961 as a result of the attempted industrialization policies of Mao Zedong. The large-scale transformation from a largely agricultural-based economy to modern production techniques undermined food production. Although famine was eventually recognized by Mao's regime as a widespread problem, little was done to counteract the disaster. Deaths from the Great Leap Forward famine are estimated at upward of 30 million.

Famines in British India from the late eighteenth century to independence were marked both by climatic events like uneven rainfall and by British administrative policies that increased prices of food and exported a large percentage of staple crops. The Bengal famine of 1770 is estimated to have taken more than 10 million lives, leading to significant social shifts that in turn led to the permanent settlement of Bengal by the British. Throughout the nineteenth century, famines interacted with epidemic diseases like cholera, creating devastating effects on populations throughout India, including famines in Orissa, Tamil Nadu, and recurrent mass hunger in Bengal. Famines of the nineteenth century in India are estimated to have killed between 30 and 40 million people. During World War II, Bengal experienced a massive famine leading to the death of more than 4 million people. The most devastating famine to hit postcolonial South Asia occurred in Bangladesh in 1974, leading to potentially a million deaths in a period of six months.

The colonial encounter in Africa directly impacted the appearance and recurrence of widespread famines in the nineteenth and twentieth centuries. In 1888 the breakout of the cattle disease rinderpest in the Sahel region was accompanied by the appearance of epidemic disease and shortages in agricultural production. These conditions were exacerbated by the increasing presence of European colonial rule, leading to a devastating famine whose statistical effects remain unknown.

Colonial policy led to increasing frequency of famines by the twentieth century in many parts of sub-Saharan Africa, including Nigeria, Rwanda, and Malawi. Famine appeared in great force in the 1970s as a product of declining pastoral and agricultural economies that suffered under the colonial rule and the increasing dependence of peoples throughout sub-Saharan Africa on single staple foods. In Ethiopia, famine affected millions of people, beginning in 1972 and reappearing from 1982 until 1985. Colonial rule and postcolonial civil conflicts have resulted in heavy depopulation, with the roots of this depopulation almost certainly tied to famine and epidemic disease. Since 1998, Sudan has felt the effects of persistent conflict and recurrent drought, with famine conditions persisting into the twenty-first century. The demographic effect of mortality related to famines in different regions of Africa remains unknown.

[See also Agriculture; China, *subentry* Historical Overview; Empire and Imperialism, *subentry* Imperialism and the Environment; Epidemics; Food; Global Warming; *and* India.]

BIBLIOGRAPHY

Alamagir, Mohiuddin. *Famine in South Asia: Political Economy of Mass Starvation.* Cambridge, Mass.: Oelgeschlager, Gunn & Hain, 1980.

Arnold, David. *Famine: Social Crisis and Historical Change.* Oxford: Blackwell, 1988. A theoretical piece that considers ideas of famine causation and the historical implications of mass hunger; useful especially for its discussion on famines and peasant populations.

Davis, Mike. *Late Victorian Holocausts: El Niño Famines and the Making of the Third World.* New York: Verso, 2001.

Newman, Lucile F., ed. *Hunger in History: Food Shortage, Poverty, and Deprivation.* Cambridge, Mass.: Blackwell, 1990.

Sen, Amartya. *Poverty and Famines: An Essay on Entitlement and Deprivation.* Oxford: Clarendon Press, 1982. Sen's classic essay considers the causes and implications of famines in the modern world.

Vaughan, Megan. *The Story of an African Famine: Gender and Famine in Twentieth-Century Malawi.* Cambridge, U.K.: Cambridge University Press, 1987. A groundbreaking study that looks at the relationship between gender hierarchies and the effects of famine.

DURBA MITRA

Africa

Sustained hunger has long been a challenge for many Africans, just as in much of the world. However, it is important to separate catastrophic famines from seasonal periods of dearth that many African societies dependent on agriculture have long expected over the course of an average year. Famines are often set off by climatic and environmental disturbances such as droughts or floods, but they also entail a number of social crises that interfere with food production, distribution, and the ability of communities to prepare for adversity and to obtain food. The economist Amartya Sen has argued that famines are in fact a crisis of exchange entitlements that provide people with the ability to obtain food; thus famines can take place even in areas where sustenance is still available. Although some African famines, especially those before the late nineteenth century, may have involved a complete absence of food throughout an entire region, some communities have managed to retain access to food while others perish. Although it is impossible to give a generic set of explanations of famines, it is clear that warfare and conflicts over scarce resources combined with environmental disturbances together have brought on famines in Africa.

Nineteenth Century. In the nineteenth century, several regions of Africa battled famines. Much of the Sudan and the Horn of Africa endured a range of famines, culminating in the catastrophes of 1835–1837 and 1888–1892. These shortages coincided with the climatic atmospheric shifts known as the El Niño–Southern Oscillation (ENSO) that radically alter rainfall patterns in much of the world and are associated with periods of drought in much of Africa, India, and China. However, it would be a mistake to argue that environmental factors were the only ones at

work. The rise of the Madhist state in the Sudan against Egyptian rule and the neighboring kingdom of Ethiopia led to warfare and chronic instability that sent much of the Sudan into famine. Droughts combined with slave raiding to supply ivory hunters and meet the burgeoning demand for slaves in Zanzibari coastal and French Mascarene plantations caused a crisis of hunger in southern Malawi in 1862 and 1863. A lack of rain in southern Africa devastated Zulu, Xhosa, and other chiefdoms between 1876 and 1879, but the resulting crisis of food production also owed much to the sudden growth of labor demands from the booming gold and diamond mines, as well as to British and Boer efforts to break the autonomy of African leaders. In grasslands in what is now the Central African Republic, famines came as much from the depredation of slave raiders from the Sudan and Chad as they did from periods of low rainfall.

One of the worst periods of famine in much of Africa coincided, not surprisingly, with the onslaught of imperialist expansion that began in the 1880s. The rinderpest epidemic that killed great numbers of cattle between 1895 and 1905 hit at the same time that colonial armies attacked African communities in much of eastern and southern Africa. This destruction of livestock, vital for the livelihood of many communities and their ability to obtain food, made it difficult for many to eat. The long battles between the French military against the West African military leader Samori Touré (1830–1900) led to a collapse of farming because of raiding and instability brought on by both sides. Portuguese forces in Angola often struck African opponents during times of dearth, and African soldiers in the employ of the Portuguese coerced farmers to surrender food. Efforts of Shona leaders to retain independence from English settlers in the 1890s brought on conflict that made obtaining and conserving food difficult, and draconian policies of German forces against Namibians led to much death by starvation. The use of forced labor in many colonies drew male labor away from villages—labor needed to prepare fields—and regulations restricting hunting and forest use often undermined the ability of communities to acquire food.

Africans resisting colonial occupation could coerce farmers to surrender crops and livestock in the battles against European rulers. Eastern African leaders of the anti-German Maji Maji revolt in 1905–1906 often raided villagers in the interior of East Africa for food in the same ways that German military columns did. The changing political landscape also undid previous forms of paternalist policies that some African states had employed to conserve and supply food in times of hardship. For example, leaders in the Sokoto caliphate in northern Nigeria and Cameroon moved away from their earlier commitment to store and give out grain during times of drought after the British defeated them at the turn of the century.

World War I. One of the forgotten consequences of World War I was the range of famines that struck Africa between 1914 and 1918. Warfare in African colonies, such as battles between French and German forces in Cameroon and Gabon in 1914–1915 and conflicts among English, Portuguese, and German forces in eastern Africa, created a series of conditions perfect for creating famines: the destruction and forced migration of communities, increased demands for rubber and other natural resources that were satisfied through forced labor, obligatory service by men as soldiers and porters, the spread of epidemics by passing armies, and shortages of guns and powder that limited the ability of Africans to protect their fields from wild animals. Food prices rose dramatically from Nigeria and Gabon to Kenya by the end of the war.

From the 1920s onward, famines became increasingly an issue of the declining ability of some Africans to acquire food rather than the utter disappearance of food from an entire region. With the rise of a cash economy and the determination of colonial governments to reserve fertile land for European concessions, African farmers in Kenya, Zimbabwe, and South Africa became more vulnerable to famine in times of hardship. The rise of cash crops and a wage economy could weaken the ability of some to obtain food, especially rural women and elderly and disabled people who had less ability to find work for wages. Some migrant workers also could suffer from dependence on employers who were trying to cut costs at the expense of their diets, as occurred among timber camp workers in Gabon during the 1920s. However, communities developed innovative ways to increase their food production practices to avoid hunger, as northern Angolan farmers did by migrating to new areas or as Ethiopian farmers did by using wages to hire workers. These innovations did not necessarily aid everyone within a group, though; poor and landless people without access to sufficient resources often became more vulnerable to famine as a result. For example, the 1949 famine that blighted parts of southern Malawi hit those who were deemed unworthy of government assistance and those groups (especially women) that lacked access to wage labor outside of agriculturally based professions. Few outright famines took place in the 1930s and 1940s, with the exception of the dearth that may have killed three hundred thousand people in Rwanda in 1943–1944. This disaster came largely thanks to Belgian efforts to requisition cattle and intensify forced labor during World War II.

Colonial regimes developed varied responses to famines, but they often shared a disdain for African initiatives and a preference for harsh means of enforcing policies. French authorities in West Africa promoted mandatory labor in state-run camps as part of the Office du Niger project, while British authorities limited aid during famines out of fear of raising state expenditures and making Africans dependent on state largesse. South African authorities used narrow scientific models of nutrition to place the blame of famine and malnutrition on African diets rather than taking into account overcrowded African reserves that lacked adequate fertile land and the consequences of male migrant labor in the mines. Colonial officials, whether during the Gabon famines in the 1920s or in Rhodesia between the wars, regularly blamed the supposedly primitive farming techniques of Africans for causing famines rather than taking into account social and economic changes brought by colonialism.

The 1970s and After. The optimism of the late colonial period and the early 1960s regarding the end of famine in Africa proved sadly ill-founded in much of the continent. Much of the West African interior, from Mali to Chad, fell victim to a major famine caused in part by a major drought in 1973–1974. Ethiopia became most notorious example of famine in Africa in the postcolonial period. Camel herders and poor tenant farmers in northern Ethiopia encountered a brutal famine in 1973–1974 caused by both drought and the widespread confiscation of land by ruling elites, which the regime of king Hailie Selassie (1892–1974; r. 1930–1936 and 1941–1974) ignored, just as it had ignored previous famines in the two preceding decades. Students and military officers used the famine as justification for overthrowing the imperial regime in 1974. Land reform under the Marxist Dergue regime in 1975 promised an end to famines, but within a decade famine struck much of Ethiopia. Scorched-earth policies by the dictatorship of Mengistu Haile Mariam (b. 1937) against antigovernment movements in Eritrea and Tigray provinces in 1983–1984 included curtailing food supplies to enemies of the regime and the resettlement of thousands of farmers. High prices and drought also contributed to the catastrophe, as did Mengistu's greater concern for celebrating his tenth anniversary of attaining power than for dealing with famine. Widespread media attention of the famine led to a burst of international fund-raising efforts, such as the musician Bob Geldof's BandAid campaign of 1985, but much of the funding fell under the control of the Ethiopian government, which refused to allow food to reach rebel territory. War, high food prices, drought, and

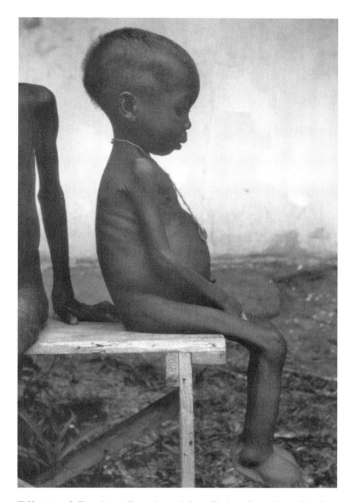

Effects of Famine. Starving girl suffering from kwashiorkor during the Nigerian-Biafran War, late 1960s. PUBLIC HEALTH IMAGE LIBRARY, UNITED STATES CENTERS FOR DISEASE CONTROL AND PREVENTION

the manipulation of humanitarian aid all worked to form a famine.

Civil wars brought on famines in Africa, from the failed efforts of the Biafra government to break away from Nigeria in the late 1960s onward. Divided Sudan became a repeated site of famines in the 1980s and 1990s. Pressure from the International Monetary Fund (IMF) and the U.S. Treasury toward Sudan, an American ally against Soviet-bloc member Ethiopia in the early 1980s, led to greater freedom for private grain traders, a decline of local state patronage, and the diminution of government welfare. When drought struck the province of Darfur in 1984–1985, the government of General Jaafar Nimeiri (b. 1930) tried to ignore the famine, which only grew worse as a result. After Nimeiri's fall in a 1985 coup, famine became

a major problem in southern Sudan, where government forces closed food relief to rebel factions fighting against them. Battles between rebel forces also cut many Sudanese off from food. The central government in Khartoum in 1990 used its control over food supplies to ensure loyalty and to punish its opponents after another crippling drought struck, as did different rebel factions later in the 1990s. The indiscriminate attacks against civilians and rebel groups in Darfur by armed nomadic groups backed by government patronage helped to unleash another famine after 2002.

In similar fashion the collapse of dictatorships after the loss of foreign aid with the end of the Cold War helped prepare the way for famines. Marginalized groups in southern Somalia, often the descendants of slaves, were victimized by clan leaders struggling for power after the fall of Mohammed Siad Barre (1919–1995) in 1989. However, Somalis with connections to prominent clans were able to obtain food, while living only a short distance from those starving. U.N. and other from nongovernmental organizations became a battleground for different clan leaders vying for power through control over food. Famines remain a pressing concern in many African countries, in large part because of the lack of political will among African governments to ensure a willingness to work to end famine and encourage food production as part of a genuine and democratic social contract.

[*See also* Agriculture, *subentry* Africa; Animal Husbandry; Environment, *subentry* Africa; Food; *and* Poverty, *subentry* Africa.]

BIBLIOGRAPHY

Davis, Mike. *Late Victorian Holocausts: El Niño Famines and the Making of the Third World.* New York: Verso, 2001.

De Waal, Alexander. *Famine Crimes: Politics and the Disaster Relief Industry in Africa.* Bloomington: Indiana University Press, 1997.

Iliffe, John. *The African Poor: A History.* Cambridge, U.K.: Cambridge University Press, 1987.

Mandala, Elias. *The End of Chidyerano: A History of Food and Everyday Life in Malawi, 1860–2004.* Portsmouth, U.K.: Heinemann, 2005.

Vaughan, Megan. *The Story of an African Famine: Gender and Famine in Twentieth-Century Malawi.* Cambridge, U.K.: Cambridge University Press, 1987.

Von Braun, Joachim, Tesfaye Teklu, and Patrick Webb. *Famine in Africa: Causes, Responses, and Prevention.* Baltimore: Johns Hopkins University Press, 1999.

Watts, Michael. *Silent Violence: Food, Famine, and Peasantry in Northern Nigeria.* Berkeley: University of California Press, 1983.

Wylie, Diana. *Starving on a Full Stomach: Hunger and the Triumph of Cultural Racism in Modern South Africa.* Charlottesville: University of Virginia Press, 2001.

JEREMY RICH

East Asia

Famine has occupied a central place in China in the modern era, spanning three political regimes, and was present in Tokugawa Japan as well. Though the nineteenth century was a period that witnessed the highest incidence of famines, the most severe catastrophe occurred in twentieth-century China under the Maoist regime—the Great Leap famine of 1958–1961—when as many as 30 million people are estimated to have died in excess of the normal mortality rate. Table 1 summarizes the major famines that occurred in different parts of East Asia in the eighteenth through twentieth centuries.

Underlying Causes. The underlying cause or causes of famines has been the subject of an intense debate. The conventional view sees famines as largely the result of a sudden decline in food availability, which in turn is caused primarily by natural disasters such as droughts and floods. For instance, the Temmei famine of 1782–1787 in Tokugawa Japan occurred after a decadelong drought, disastrous floods, and the eruption of various volcanoes. The great North China famine of 1877–1878 was similarly triggered by a prolonged drought in the area. Recently it has been suggested that this particular famine—and others in this period—was probably the result of El Niño Southern Oscillation (ENSO), a great periodic fluctuation in ocean temperature and air pressure in the equatorial Pacific with a significant impact on normal rainfall patterns over much of the globe.

The effect of the vicissitudes of the climate is not random, however; "endowment" has likely played an important role in determining how well an area can cope with an exogenous shock. Specifically, areas that receive the least amount of rainfall tend also to experience the greatest variability. In turn, inadequate water and its unreliability permit only a single-crop culture, which provides no buffer in times of weather adversity. It is thus not surprising that the greatest famine in China in the nineteenth century occurred in the north, because rainfall in the north is concentrated in mostly July and August (North Korea shares similar climatic characteristics).

Though natural calamities are typically what trigger famines, the severity of famines is determined by factors that go beyond nature. Two factors appear especially germane in this regard. The first has to do with high or basically unaffordable food prices, whereas the second factor is a government's ability—and willingness—to provide relief. In contrast to conventional wisdom, which sees high food prices in famine times as basically the consequence of

food shortages (or FAD, food availability deficit), the Nobel Laureate economist Amartya Sen contends that unaffordable food prices are in fact the result of the speculative, hoarding behavior of merchants in imperfectly integrated markets that fail to attract food supplies from outside, even when prices in the affected locales have remained high, owing to problems of transportation and other bottlenecks.

But famine severity is also determined by the effectiveness of state response or, specifically, government relief action. Famines tend to be more severe when the government fails to intervene effectively either in delivering the needed food to the famine victims or in stabilizing food prices, or both. But the reasons for this government failure vary from one instance to another. In Tokugawa Japan, the highly secluded administrative structure of the *bakufu* (shogunate) provided little incentives for individual daimyo (warlords) to dispatch food from their fiefs to help their neighbors in need. But even in the more encouraging instance of a unified Qing China, in which the regime did have the benign intentions of providing famine relief, primarily through disbursements from local granaries, declining fiscal and organizational capability over time—during the nineteenth century in particular—eventually forced the regime to rely increasingly on the local gentry for relief provisions. Such provisions failed, however, to compare with state provisions, especially in instances where famines involved vast geographical areas and lasted for long periods of time.

The importance of government action or response in famine situations has eventually led to the development of a theory that purports to provide a tighter link between politics and famine. Contrasting India's success since independence in averting famines with China's Great Leap catastrophe, Sen develops the grand hypothesis that famines are unlikely to occur under democracies. His thesis is premised on the reasoning that electoral pressure or accountability would prevent a democratically elected government from concealing a famine the way the Communist regime in China did in its heady days of utopian communism. Moreover, an independent and free press, which is unlikely to exist under an authoritarian regime, will vigilantly disseminate information about any impending food crisis so that any precariously famished condition would be quickly dealt with by a concerned government.

The fact that two of the largest famines in the twentieth century occurred under an authoritarian regime—the Soviet Union in the 1930s and China in the late 1950s (and more recently North Korea)—provides prima facie

TABLE 1. *Famine in East Asia, 1700–2000*

COUNTRY	INCIDENCE	EXCESS DEATH (MILLION)	POPULATION	AS A % OF TOTAL POPULATION	NATURE OF DISASTER
Japan	1782–1787 (Temmei famine)	0.2–0.9	26,010,600 (est. 1780)	0.77–3.46	drought, flood, cold wind, and the eruption of various volcanoes
	1832/33–1836/39 (Tempo famine)	"worse than the Temmei famine in 1782"	27,063,907 (est. 1834)	—	flood and cold weather
North Korea	1997–1999	0.2–3.5	25,904,124 (est. 1996)	0.77–13.51	"unprecedented floods" in 1995–1996
China	1877–1878	9.5–13	308,803,939	3.08–4.21	drought across north China plains
	1892–1894	1	335,134,795	0.30	drought
	1920–1921	0.5	456,200,000	0.11	drought
	1928–1929	3	446,649,832	0.67	drought
	1938	1	479,084,651	0.21	levee breach of the Yellow River
	1958–1961	16.5–30	659,940,000	2.50–4.55	drought and floods in different parts of the country

vindications of the powerfully provocative claim of the existence of an underlying relationship between regime type and famine incidence. There are some qualifications to such a grand theory, however.

The first qualification is that the complex nature of famine occurrence renders a single theory of famines untenable; more often than not major famines have had multiple causes. In the case of China's Great Leap famine, for instance, recent research has shown that excess death in this major catastrophe was the outcome of a number of factors. Weather and the misallocation of resources from agriculture to nonagricultural pursuits (most notably irrigation and steel campaigns in the countryside) had adversely impacted food availability, a factor that unambiguously affected excess deaths. The excessive procurement of grain—which reflects as much a systematically biased policy against the rural populace as "misinformation"—was also a culprit. Not the least, casualties were notably more severe in provinces where their leaders had engaged the rural people excessively in the extremely undercapitalized—and thus energy-consuming—tasks of steel production and irrigation works. In contrast, the institution of communal mess-hall dining did not have a significant impact, perhaps because unrestricted consumption may not have been universally practiced or was short-lived.

The recent North Korean famine represents another case in point. Unlike the Soviet and Chinese famines, it did not occur at the time of agricultural collectivization but forty years after it—a time when food self-sufficiency had long been achieved. Also, the economy was already predominantly urban and industrial and had a well-functioning public distribution system when the deadly famine occurred. This unexpected, curious famine in North Korea, it

has been argued, was not the result of either an ill-intended dictator or foolish planning mistakes (the authoritarian nature of its regime notwithstanding), but instead was the result of a combination of natural calamities (unprecedented floods) and an abrupt withdrawal of trade subsidies from, especially, the Soviet Union, which inadvertently afflicted an agriculture heavily dependent on imported oil for inputs (for chemical fertilizers, for instance).

The other qualification pertains to the consequence of major catastrophes. Specifically, can governments—regardless of regime type—learn from past mistakes, to the extent that they would put an end to such fatal blunders by, for instance, designing a tacit "political contract" of sorts? The answer appears to be yes. Postindependence governments of India seem to have learned from the colonial blunders that precipitated the Great Bengal famine of 1943. Likewise, and despite the continuing absence of a democracy, the Chinese adopted the safeguarding practice of rationing a fixed quantity of food grains to rural people based on minimum caloric requirements, regardless of actual work contributions in a team-based production organization (c. 1962–1979). Moreover, even after the Chinese eventually decollectivized their agriculture in order to provide greater material incentives to the peasantry, around the early 1980s, members of the village community became adequately protected by an institutional arrangement that guaranteed villagers an equal entitlement to land use and income rights.

The extent to which famines have had repercussions for social and regime stability also varies between countries and regimes. Though peasant uprisings had occurred in both China and Japan, evidence suggests that famines in Qing China likely had a more discernable impact on the

Famine Control. Distribution of rice during a famine in Jiangsu Province, China, 1946. Photograph by Arthur Rothstein. PRINTS AND PHOTOGRAPHS DIVISION, LIBRARY OF CONGRESS

society and polity than in Tokugawa Japan. In nineteenth-century China in particular, the local gentry were forced to compete with a segment of the society—the "Triads," an organized crime network—that sought to wreak havoc on the Chinese society and whose rise could be linked intimately to the perennial precarious subsistence of the peasantry. Though famines were clearly not responsible for the fall of the Qing dynasty, they did reinforce the regime's declining governability. On the other hand, despite the extreme severity of the Great Leap famine, the Communist regime, with its legitimacy bolstered by a series of important economic reforms, survived into the twenty-first century.

[*See also* Great Leap Forward; *and* Natural Disasters, *subentry* Asia.]

BIBLIOGRAPHY
Davis, Mike. *Late Victorian Holocausts: El Niño Famines and the Making of the Third World.* London: Verso, 2001.
Kuhn, Philip. *Rebellion and Its Enemies in Late Imperial China: Militarization and Social Structure, 1796–1864.* Cambridge, Mass.: Harvard University Press, 1980.
Kung, James Kai-sing, and Justin Yifu Lin. "The Causes of China's Great Leap Famine, 1959–1961." *Economic Development and Cultural Change* 52, no. 1 (2003): 51–73.
Mallory, Walter H. *China: Land of Famine.* New York: American Geographical Society, 1926.
Seavoy, Ronald E. *Famine in Peasant Societies.* New York: Greenwood Press, 1986.
Sen, Amartya, and Jean Drèze, eds. *The Political Economy of Hunger.* 3 vols. Oxford: Clarendon Press, 1990–1991.
Will, Pierre-Étienne. *Bureaucracy and Famine in Eighteenth-Century China.* Translated by Elborg Forster. Stanford, Calif.: Stanford University Press, 1990.
Woo-Cummings, Meredith. "The Political Ecology of Famine: The North Korean Catastrophe and Its Lessons." Asian Development Bank Institute Research Papers No. 31. Tokyo, Japan: Asian Development Bank, 2002.
Yang, Dali. *Calamity and Reform in China: State, Rural Society, and Institutional Change since the Great Leap Famine.* Stanford, Calif.: Stanford University Press, 1996.

JAMES KAI-SING KUNG

India

Occasional acute famines occurred in India well before colonial rule, but also in eastern India in 1769–1770 and 1791, in North India in the 1830s, and more generally in the 1860s and then repeatedly every year or so until the early twentieth century. After the 1880 and 1901 Famine Commissions, acute suffering was eventually reduced, probably aided by measures to improve property rights, agriculture, and communications, by agricultural loans, and by other famine relief, even though work camps contributed to the spread of disease. But wartime disruption and policy failure led to the Bengal famine of 1943. Famine conditions also continued occasionally after independence.

Climate—the El Niño effect has been blamed—played a part in the late nineteenth-century famines, through both flooding and drought. Much of this is now known because of pioneering weather records collected in India. The famines were identified by other measurements, too, notably of prices, "excess" death rates, and the taking up of work at "distress" wages. Famines were hotly debated among colonial officials and by nationalists, all blaming or exonerating some aspect or other of state policy: revenue demands, the export of food, commercialization, allegedly falling productivity, the breakdown of village community, the rising population, and so on.

In the modern era at least, the cause of the famines was lack of work more than lack of food. Epidemic and endemic disease played a major part in the very high death rates. For colonial rulers and their successors, believing as they did in technology, progress, and the state, it was convenient to blame exceptional local shortages of food or work and the effects of profiteering or panic. Some townspeople, beggars, and the landless would be early victims, but many cultivators—those with a little land but few reserves—were also severely affected. Some sectors of the population had become relatively more vulnerable than before; and thus most significant, whatever the changing frequency of "famine" crises, was the inadequacy of the "normal" food supply, and hence fundamental questions about morbidity and the distribution of wealth.

[*See also* Empire and Imperialism, *subentry* The British Colonial Empire; *and* Natural Disasters, *subentry* Asia.]

BIBLIOGRAPHY
Bhatia, B. M. *Famines in India: A Study in Some Aspects of the Economic History of India, 1860–1945.* New York: Asia Publishing House, 1963.
McAlpin, Michelle Burge. *Subject to Famine: Food Crises and Economic Change in Western India, 1860–1920.* Princeton, N.J.: Princeton University Press, 1983.
Sharma, Sanjay. *Famine, Philanthropy, and the Colonial State: North India in the Early Nineteenth Century.* New Delhi, India, and New York: Oxford University Press, 2001.
Stone, Ian. *Canal Irrigation in British India: Perspectives on Technological Change in a Peasant Economy.* Cambridge, U.K., and New York: Cambridge University Press, 1984.

PETER ROBB

FARABUNDO MARTÍ FRONT. The Frente Farabundo Martí para la Liberación Nacional (FMLN; Farabundo Martí National Liberation Front) was formed in 1980 by the five main revolutionary armies seeking the armed overthrow of the military-dominated regimes that had ruled in El Salvador for most of the twentieth century. The extremely violent twelve-year civil war (1980–1992) brought profound changes to the country's political and economic landscape. The insurgent movement failed militarily. Yet after signing a peace agreement in 1992, the FMLN became El Salvador's second major political force, governing many of the nation's major cities and holding a plurality of the seats in the legislature.

The roots of the FMLN can be traced to centuries-old grievances over structural inequality and political exclusion, particularly in an agrarian economy dominated by large coffee, cotton, and cattle estates. Social discontent was contained only by brutal military repression. Frustrated by massive electoral fraud in the 1970s that kept reformist movements from power, several leftist factions broke with the Christian Democrats and the Communist Party to organize guerrilla armies. Guided by revolutionary socialism and Christian liberation theology, guerrilla leaders amassed support behind a growing popular movement.

Although many of the rebel leaders were middle class and educated, the FMLN was largely a peasant army. The insurgent movement named itself in honor of Farabundo Martí, the Communist leader of a failed peasant revolt in 1932. Boom-bust cycles of agrarian modernization in El Salvador concentrated great wealth among a small class of wealthy families and marginalized most of the rural labor force. When one hundred thousand migrants to Honduras were turned back prior to the brief 1969 war between the two countries, the pressure of rural landlessness and growing urban squalor led many to explore more radical options.

As an umbrella organization, the FMLN represented a pragmatic unity among the diverse ideological currents that divided the political Left over revolutionary strategy, leadership, and external alliances. Lack of unity prior to 1980 prevented the FMLN from responding to the assassination of the beloved Catholic archbishop Oscar Romero, perhaps the only moment when popular insurrection may have been possible. Following the blueprint of military success by the Nicaraguan FSLN (Sandinistas) in toppling the dictator Anastasio Somoza Debayle in July 1979, the FMLN called a major offensive in January 1981 but failed to ignite popular insurrection. Ill-equipped, FMLN forces survived two years of severe violence before accumulating enough capacity nearly to defeat the Salvadoran military by late 1983.

Only the full weight of U.S. counterinsurgency backing, and the election of the Christian Democrat José Napoleon Duarte as president in 1984, staved off the collapse of the Salvadoran military. Following the murder-suicide of the two top FMLN commanders, the insurgents shifted strategy to a more prolonged war of guerrilla tactics that many misread as disintegration. At its peak militarily with no more than twelve thousand armed combatants supported by a complex scaffolding of civilian collaborators, the FMLN methodically deepened control within a third of national territory. There the FMLN erected parallel governance structures guided by a mix of collectivist agrarian production and democratic centralism.

As international events turned less favorable to the insurgency, the FMLN carried out the most audacious offensive of the war in November 1989, failing again to spark insurrection but effectively convincing the United States and the Salvadoran elites that the war could not be won militarily. Despite profound internal crises and tremendous tactical disadvantages, the FMLN demonstrated remarkable resilience and became the most effective insurgent army in Latin America during the 1980s.

After eighty-five thousand deaths—mostly civilians at the hands of the government security forces—the FMLN settled for a peace agreement that brought fundamental reforms to El Salvador's political system. The FMLN ceded control of the economy to the ruling right-wing Alianza Republicana Nacionalista (ARENA; Nationalist Republican Alliance) in exchange for legal recognition as a political party, institutional reforms to the military and police, and economic reinsertion for former combatants. Land inequality, a key factor in the war, was only modestly redressed, with the redistribution of about a quarter of all farmland.

Impressive postwar electoral gains, increasingly dependent on urban support, secured the FMLN's place as the principal opposition party in El Salvador but at the same time caused recurrent internal divisions over political strategy. Though surviving three major splits and achieving significant leverage in the legislature by 1997, the FMLN failed to win the presidency in three tries, which severely limited its ability to advance alternative economic policies, especially for its rural base. Postwar reconstruction favored ARENA, which controlled the presidency since 1989. FMLN power at the legislative and municipal level strengthened democracy in El Salvador and increased the voice of the poor, but it left many of the structural issues at the root of the civil war unresolved.

[*See also* El Salvador; *and* Guerrillas and Guerrilla Movements, *subentry* Latin America.]

BIBLIOGRAPHY

Durham, William H. *Scarcity and Survival in Central America: The Ecological Origins of the Soccer War.* Stanford, Calif.: Stanford University Press, 1979.

Karl, Terry Lynn. "El Salvador's Negotiated Revolution." *Foreign Affairs* 71, no. 2 (Spring 1992): 147–164.

Paige, Jeffrey M. *Coffee and Power: Revolution and the Rise of Democracy in Central America.* Cambridge, Mass.: Harvard University Press, 1997.

Williams, Robert G. *Export Agriculture and the Crisis in Central America.* Chapel Hill: University of North Carolina Press, 1986.

Wood, Elisabeth Jean. *Insurgent Collective Action and Civil War in El Salvador.* Cambridge, U.K.: Cambridge University Press, 2003.

VINCENT MCELHINNY

FARMS AND FARMERS IN THE UNITED STATES. Farmers created hybrid American farms after 1750, drawing on agrarian traditions of farmers living in compact villages, working common lands. Huron, Iroquois, Pueblos, and other Indians farmed communal, clan-controlled, or village-managed lands into the nineteenth century, but even non-Indians did not farm alone. American farmers shared tasks in gendered, family economies and managed land with family and nonfamily workers. They borrowed money, tools, and help, and depended on commercial, transportation, education, and social networks. Through 1900, the number of farms, farmers, and acres farmed steadily increased, even as farmers declined as a percent of total population. After 1900, farmers sacrificed agrarian lifestyles to business-oriented agriculture. By 2000, farmers were a tiny minority numbering less than 1 percent of a total population, but their mythic identity still swayed public policy.

Early Landholding. Land management varied with farmer ethnicity. French colonists established farms closely spaced in long lots extending back from narrow river frontages on the banks of the Saint Lawrence, the Illinois, the Mississippi, and smaller waterways draining into the Great Lakes and the Gulf of Mexico. Their closely spaced farmhouses formed extended rural neighborhoods connecting each family closely with immediate upstream and downstream neighbors, with river traffic, and with the long fields and open country behind each farmhouse.

Colonial English farm settlements ranged from New England covenant towns like Dedham to the dispersed plantations of southern tidewater areas. By the 1750s, farmers of German origin moved into interior Pennsylvania, New

Jersey, and New York. Scots-Irish and Scots-Highlander farmers more often settled the Appalachian backcountry from Pennsylvania through the Carolinas and traded in localized, barter economies connecting individual farmsteads along clan lines for subsistence and limited commercial production. Covenanted New England farmers lived in ordered towns, with individual farms radiating out from a village core. Tidewater planters lived on plantations scattered along Chesapeake Bay and other navigable waterways, directly shipping cash crops of tobacco, wheat, rice, and indigo to intermediate wholesalers. Though remote from neighbors, they were attuned to commercial markets and most likely to invest in slave labor.

Farmers in Spanish settlements north of Mexico were more oriented around local communities. Franciscan missionaries in California managed church estates with Indian and mestizo workers, producing food and textiles for military and civilian markets and mission subsistence. Elsewhere, the crown awarded encomiendas to prominent subjects, who leased or granted land to immigrant families, mestizo workers, Indian converts, and refugee slaves from other colonies. Farmers on encomiendas marketed commodities to military presidios and colonial outposts like Saint Augustine and San Antonio de Bexar, through the Mexican era. Pueblo communities, however, were more reliable producers of agricultural surpluses. Zuni and Pima farmers worked village lands, producing commercial quantities of maize, wheat, cotton, sheep, and other livestock in a gendered system of labor where women tended and processed crops while men managed herds, prepared fields, and constructed or tended irrigation systems.

Colonial Farms and Farm Labor. Specialization in cash crops required shared, hired, or bound labor. Most British-origin farmers minimized labor costs with unfenced fields, free-ranging their hogs and cattle, but German immigrants in Pennsylvania, New Jersey, and New York favored ordered farms with squared fields, substantial outbuildings, larger acreages, and controlled livestock. Successful farmers purchased slaves or servants for threshing, loading, and hauling grain to overland markets via Conestoga wagons that German craftsmen developed in Pennsylvania. They also preferred German-speaking indentured servants, whose labor, along with African slaves, established Philadelphia as the leading port for wheat exports after 1750.

Farmers in English and French colonies commonly divided work into gendered spheres. Women managed household production of poultry, butter, cheese, and produce. Men focused on barn- and fieldwork with livestock and cash crops. Women and men shared barnyard work, and German women commonly assisted with fieldwork, although fewer men assisted with household production. In the nineteenth century, men assumed dairying, poultry, and vegetable operations on farms specializing in those commodities. Gendered spheres for bound labor often aried from these norms.

Farmers in the Yeoman Republic. Individual, yeoman farmers symbolized republican virtue in the new republic, unless they joined together. In the ratification debates (1787–1789), essayists assumed agrarian identities like "Federal Farmer" or "A Farmer," and addressed "freeholders" and "yeomen." When western farmers protested a federal tax on whiskey during George Washington's presidency, however, Washington's secretary of the treasury, Alexander Hamilton, attacked their agrarianism with military force in western Pennsylvania. Still, voters, in 1800, overwhelmingly preferred Thomas Jefferson's hopeful vision of a republic of public-spirited, educated yeomen, owning and farming their own land.

Jefferson's Democratic Republicans virtually monopolized federal power through 1840, but large plantations, bound labor, public debt, and rampant land speculation belied their agrarian rhetoric. Federal land sales, under the Land Ordinance of 1785, generated federal revenue but sparked rampant speculation, especially after minor reforms in 1820 loosened restrictions. Investors purchased large blocks of cheap public land and resold it at inflated prices and in smaller parcels to actual farmers, on credit. Speculative land prices collapsed in the 1837 financial panic and ensuing depression, however, bankrupting indebted farmers. The farm crisis fueled urban anxieties about collapsing public virtue, encouraging business-led moral reforms. Rural populations increased from 8.9 million in 1820 to 19.6 million in 1850, but urban populations grew faster, from 0.7 million in 1820 to 3.5 million in 1850.

Farming in the Capitalist Transformation. Capitalist investors restructured market networks in ways that linked farmers more closely with urban centers and encouraged cash-crop specialization. Farmers reorganized fields and processes to efficiently exploit new machinery that replaced semiskilled labor with animal-powered technology, including steel plows (1837), mechanical reapers (1833), and cotton presses (1837). Household production of butter, cheese, poultry, and produce declined as a source of farm revenue, relative to field crops, and women's roles narrowed to other household activities, mimicking middle-class standards.

Specialization in cotton with slave labor emerged after 1790, paralleling other capitalist transformations. Most southern farmers owned no slaves at all, but plantation agriculture skewed markets, available technologies, transportation systems, and labor trends. Upwardly mobile farmers aspired to slave ownership, and landless owners leased slaves to planters. Small-scale farmers sold produce to and worked for planters. Female slaves gardened to supplement plantation rations, and planters encouraged male slaves to hunt. These gendered roles mimicked freehold spheres of authority, but whatever slaves produced merely maintained their subsistence while increasing their owners' wealth.

Wartime Markets and Industrialized Farming. Civil War and Reconstruction centralized marketing, purchasing, credit, and transportation. The war shattered prewar networks and depleted labor resources. Military procurement favored large producers and new market networks centered in Chicago, while labor shortfalls encouraged farm mechanization. Marauding armies disrupted southern farms, while homestead legislation and railroad land grants linked new, western farmers into the Chicago system. Market-oriented, commercial farmers and early adaptors of new technology flourished during the war, but after 1865, military procurement ended, demobilized soldiers and freed slaves took up abandoned farmland, and crop surpluses soared. From 1867 through 1900, these forces trapped mechanized farmers in a cost-price squeeze: deflationary monetary policies increased the cost of repaying debts, while depressed commodity prices undercut farm revenues.

Agrarian discontent fueled the Greenback Party, the Farmers Alliance, and the People's Party (Populists) into the early twentieth century, especially in the West and South. After 1860, southern farmers lost prewar plantation markets and lacked access to the Chicago system. Soaring debt burdens and limited transportation, marketing, or social capital options (family, friends, or voluntary organizations) similarly constrained Western farmers. In their 1892 Omaha Platform, Populists proposed an agrarian commonwealth, but farmers were less important than agricultural output to urban voters, who rejected the platform. Farm production increased every decade after 1860, and the total number of farms increased each year through 1920, but other economic sectors grew faster and employed more people.

Abandoning Agrarianism. Farmers mostly aligned with business interests after 1900, except between the world wars, when global surpluses and transportation bottlenecks collapsed commodity prices. Agrarianism briefly reemerged, including the Non-Partisan League, the Farmers

Tenant Farmers. A farmer and his children work on a cotton farm, Anniston, Alabama, 1936. Photograph by Dorothea Lange. PRINTS AND PHOTOGRAPHS DIVISION, LIBRARY OF CONGRESS

Educational and Cooperative Union, the Farmer-Labor Party, and the Farm Holiday Association, but most farmers followed business-oriented leaders rather than producer-class movements. Farm-ownership organizations, notably the American Farm Bureau Federation, lobbied Congress for legislation protecting farm owners, not farm labor or consumers. The Agricultural Adjustment Act of 1933 finally split farm owners from agricultural workers, tenant farmers, and sharecroppers. The resulting price-support legislation through the late twentieth century favored farmers with larger farms, more capital assets, and corporate organization.

By mid-century, automobiles, radio, and television linked farmers with urban life, and farm population dropped from 25 percent of the total population in 1935 to less than 1 percent by 2000. As better-connected farm children chose urban professions over farming, the average age of farmers increased, and the average farm family shrank. Electrical appliances and motors helped farm women manage routine chores, while supermarkets displaced household production. Educated farm women more commonly took off-farm jobs. Gasoline, electric, and diesel motors, meanwhile, powered machinery that reduced the time and muscles needed for field work, feeding livestock, or transporting commodities. This energy revolution helped older people farm longer while expanding operations and consolidating farmland, blocking out the next generation.

Professional Farmers and Idealizing Farming.
After 1970, farmers were more commonly college-trained managers of land-owning businesses that purchased water, soil amendments, and seed; hired farmworkers to assemble those components; and deployed resources in extended operations spread across several miles and thousands of acres. Patriarchal norms prevailed, but the proportion of farms owned by women increased from 11 percent to 21 percent between 1946 and 1988. Farm owners more commonly hired unrelated workers of different ethnic or racial backgrounds. Farm labor unions, notably the United Farm Workers (1966), approached farmers as antagonists, not fellow producers. A new breed of urban professionals meanwhile, established numerous, smaller, part-time farms on the periphery of urban areas, producing specialty crops for local or upscale markets.

The proliferation of exurban, part-time farmers illustrates the continuing, mythic allure of farming for twentieth-century urbanites. The country music star Willie Nelson's annual "Farm Aid" concerts highlighted "the farm crisis" through the 1990s, and a country of urban and suburban voters regularly reelected politicians who approved federal subsidies to farmers whose capital assets far exceeded the average wealth of most voters. The yeoman ideal survived mostly in myth, while the business of agriculture proceeded on farms operated by an ever more exclusive club of management professionals.

[*See also* Agriculture.]

BIBLIOGRAPHY
Clanton, Gene. *Populism: The Humane Preference in America, 1890–1900.* Boston: Twayne, 1991. Explores the last gasp of Jeffersonian agrarianism.

Fite, Gilbert. *American Farmers: The New Minority.* Bloomington: Indiana University Press, 1981. Explores agrarian decline after 1900.

Friedberger, Mark. "The Rural-Urban Fringe in the Late Twentieth Century." *Agricultural History* 74, no. 2 (Spring 2000): 502–514. Considers the part-time, exurban farming movement.

Genovese, Eugene D. *Roll, Jordan, Roll: The World the Slaves Made.* New York: Random House, 1972. Explores slave-planter relations.

Lemon, James T. *The Best Poor Man's Country: A Geographical Study of Early Southeastern Pennsylvania.* Baltimore: Johns Hopkins University Press, 1972. Explores early farm systems and ethnic differences.

Merchant, Carolyn. *Ecological Revolutions: Nature, Gender, and Science in New England.* Chapel Hill: University of North Carolina Press, 1989. Considers gendered roles and farm-family economies.

Ransom, Roger L., and Richard Sutch. *One Kind of Freedom: The Economic Consequences of Emancipation.* Cambridge, U.K.: Cambridge University Press, 1977. Details postwar adjustments.

Schlebecker, John T. *Whereby We Thrive: A History of American Farming, 1607–1972.* Ames: Iowa State University Press, 1975. Synthesizes earlier standards and includes numerous illustrations.

Shover, John L. *First Majority, Last Minority: The Transforming of Rural Life in America.* DeKalb: Northern Illinois University Press, 1976. Explores the expansion and contraction of farming as a defining feature of American life.

Weber, David J. *The Spanish Frontier in North America.* New Haven, Conn.: Yale University Press, 1992. Places missions and encomiendas in a continental framework.

MAX G. GEIER

FASCISM AND PROTOFASCISM [*This entry includes three subentries, an overview and discussions of fascism in Europe and in Japan.*]

Overview

Fascist movements arose in Europe in the aftermath of World War I, most prominently in Italy and Germany. Later, fascist or protofascist movements emerged in other parts of the world. The term "fascist," first popularized in Italy, stemmed from the Latin word *fasces*, the term for a bundle of rods strapped together around an axe. In ancient Rome, this object served as a symbol of state authority and was carried before a high official in public processions. It was an appropriate symbol for modern fascists, who preached violence and exalted the state.

War, Hierarchy, and the Divine Leader. The bloody and desperate nature of World War I intensified nationalism and ethnic hatreds throughout Europe. These turbulent currents fed the stream that flowed into the fascist phenomenon. Preying upon desperate men who had learned how to kill, fascism recruited thousands of veterans unhappy with their devastated or impoverished homelands. Fascism showed them the faces of the culprits and scapegoats— government officials, international communism, the Jews, and many other groups. From the Baltic to Italy, war veterans unhappy with the depression and chaos of their homelands answered the demagogic appeals of leaders who, like them, had fought in World War I. They formed a generational cohort, for whom the heroic war and its tawdry aftermath were formative influences. Fascist movements also attracted some middle-class adherents opposed to democracy, socialism, pacifism, and the treaty arrangements that had ended that war. Some fascist parties were racist, others less so, but they shared certain dominant important characteristics. They were hierarchical and military in structure, and vehemently antidemocratic. Fascists preached obedience to one charismatic leader, the führer in Germany or the duce in Italy, for example. Later, there would be quasi fascists bearing similar titles: a caudillo in Spain, a *conducator* in Romania, a *poglovnik* in Croatia. In Hungary, Romania, and Croatia, fascist movements had substantial (but minority) strength. In Croatia and Hungary, the Ustacha and the Arrow Cross, respectively, came to power during World War II as German protégés. In Romania the strong Iron Guard movement fell victim to Germany's alliance with the military dictatorship of Marshal Ion Antonescu (1882–1946).

Fascists everywhere created their own heroic myths and images, and exploited them to dazzle and intimidate their countrymen and countrywomen. In Italy the so-called March on Rome was heralded as the greatest event in modern history. In Germany, the annual salute to the Nazis killed in Munich in November 1923 became a kind of religious cult. To some, fascism was a substitute religion, imposed upon willing followers during an age of skepticism.

The Male Cohort, Women, and Labor. Fascist movements embodied an extreme kind of nationalist militarism, some of which can be traced back to the nineteenth century. Intellectual forebears or protofascists were men like Charles Maurras (1868–1952) and Gabriele D'Annunzio (1863–1938), who had attacked democracy, international

law, peace, and socialism as decadent forces to be rooted out by force. Aggressive and strutting, fascists declared that strength was a supreme virtue, and pity a vice. The worst words in the fascist lexicon were terms like "effeminate," "humanitarian," and "pacifist." Men tested in war were alone fit to lead the nation. Fascists worshiped violence. Where did this leave women?

Fascism represented an attempt to preserve or restore male gender hegemony. Women thus played a subordinate or negligible role in fascist movements, except as objects of propaganda. Fascist parties stressed masculinity, warfare, and heroism, and they often worked to place women in the kitchen rather than in the workplace. Fascism was a kind of home for restless males touched by World War I. Its leaders violently opposed most of the gains made by women in modern times. Hitler and Mussolini rewarded women and families who bore and raised many children, and subsidized rents and childrearing as a form of day care for future soldiers. Vehemently antifeminist, fascists rarely appeared in public in civilian dress. Their uniforms, which women had not worn in combat, sent a powerful and often appealing message to men threatened by democracy, women's rights, the growth of divorce, and other alleged abominations of the 1920s. Yet fascism was not devoid of appeal to some women. They, too, worried about high crime rates, lower birth rates, and the lack of housing, and fascists promised new, more efficient societies based on social justice.

The fascists argued that the state would provide for its people. Trade unions would be smashed, and their members enrolled in party-sanctioned organizations. Strikes would be illegal and productivity would soar. These fascist promises won over many industrialists, members of the middle class, and others beguiled by rhetoric and promises. The fascists, however, differed from the conservative elites in important respects. They were more brutal and less scrupulous. And fascists, unlike the old elites, prided themselves on their common, sometimes plebeian origins. Their movements offered upward social mobility to persons of humble background, unlike the institutions governed by the conservative elites of Europe. As a result, fascists and Nazis attracted substantial, if minority, working-class support.

Terror, the Old Elites, and the Seizure of Power. More important was the role of terror in the rise and consolidation of fascist rule. Fascism brought the violence of World War I home, where over the next twenty-five years fascists engaged in political intimidation, murder, and sometimes revolution. Postwar fascists often formed paramilitary units like the Sturmabteilungen in Germany and the fasci di combattimento in Italy. They wore military-type uniforms. Reflecting middle-class and conservative fears of international Communism after the 1917 Bolshevik Revolution, these fascists vowed to crush the militant Left.

Communist and Marxist interpretations early on labeled fascism a bourgeois and capitalist invention, that used terror in order to prevent the rising proletariat from establishing its own socialist dictatorship. Stalin famously called fascism the openly terrorist dictatorship of the bourgeoisie. He neglected to add that Communist attacks on the Social Democrats in Germany helped to make possible Hitler's accession to power. Other views stress nationalism and postwar crises as the seedbeds of fascism. Still other commentators have linked fascism to the plebiscitary democracy of the French Revolution, with its mass armies and public terror.

It is true that fascists sometimes despised their upper-class betters, and spouted anticapitalist rhetoric. At crucial moments, however, successful fascist parties made deals with conservatives in order to come to power. Such agreements were reached in Italy in October 1922, and in Germany in January 1933. For their part, fascists accepted private property and capitalism, but only if they served fascist purposes. Fascists recognized no constitutional legal rights, nor the right to own property. The state, which controlled the courts, could legally abolish such antiquated concepts if need be. Under fascism, all private and individual considerations and groups were subordinate to the will of the leader and the needs of his state.

The Fascist State and Totalitarianism. Fascists preached conquest and expansion, and once in power, engaged in acts of aggression. Fascists were xenophobic, and at home, they often looked to a politicized, romanticized history for their models—to the Roman Empire in the case of Italy, or to the movement eastward of German settlers in the Middle Ages in the case of the Nazis. They repudiated the postwar peace treaties as oppressive and vowed to change or eradicate them.

The first successful fascist movement was that led by Benito Mussolini (1883–1945) in Italy. It came to power in 1922, and established a dictatorship in 1925. Like other fascists, Mussolini claimed that the fascist device called the corporative state abolished class warfare and created a new kind of state-directed society. Adolf Hitler (1889–1945) came to power in 1933. Hitler's National Socialism displayed all of the above characteristics, including a German version of state-directed corporative bodies, but its powerful racism and anti-Semitism made it the most murderous of all fascist movements. Fascists claimed to be totalitarian, that is, they aimed to control the bodies, minds, and souls of their citizens. The term was first used in Italy, but it applied better to the Nazi regime.

One has to use the word "souls" with caution, however. Fascist regimes claimed to be carrying out the will of God. They could not be atheist, because Marxism, their great enemy, denounced religion as a delusion. But the fascists treated humans as chattel to be used, not as creatures made in God's image. In Italy, children were taught to worship the state and the duce. In Germany, they worshipped the *Volk* and the Aryan race and the führer. Men and women were biological material, to be molded and bred and sometimes exterminated. Fascism denied the soul except in its rhetoric. But the fascist era encompassed phenomena of the left, too.

The Soviet state glorified the supreme leader Joseph Stalin (1879–1953), was totalitarian, permitted but one party, ruled by terror, and inundated the nation with propaganda. It was not accidental that Nazis and Communists sometimes moved from one party to the other. They also borrowed each other's march music, and divided eastern Europe in a treaty signed in 1939. True, fascist Europe followed Hitler into Russia in 1941, but that decision could not obliterate the similarities between his regime and that of Joseph Stalin. Later, Stalin's anti-Jewish purges and policies further underlined the similarities between his regime and that of his erstwhile ally. So did his mindless imposition of crazed theories upon Soviet science. Often, these doctrines were Marxist mirror images of Hitler's biological determinism. Fascism ultimately rests on force, so free inquiry is an enemy to be crushed at all times. The same was true of the Soviet Union under Stalin.

Fascism and the Democratic World. Countries with strong democratic traditions, such as England and the United States, were more resistant to the fascist assault. In Britain, the British Union of Fascists under Sir Oswald Mosley (1896–1980) had its moment in the sun, but it was a brief one. In the United States, the Silver Shirts garnered some publicity and sold some uniforms, but ultimately they got nowhere.

In the democratic West, fascist regimes were viewed in various ways at different times. Many people preferred them to communism, even when Hitler threatened the peace of Europe. Some conservatives admired the fascists for crushing communism, but then feared a fascist attack upon their own nations. Other Western leaders hoped to appease the fascists and prevent the outbreak of another, bloodier war. War, many fascists believed, was inevitable. There was no liberal world order, merely submission and domination. The fascist powers called themselves "have not" nations, and demanded a new world order in which they gained access to raw materials and dominated the seas.

Italy and Germany, the two leading fascist states, dispatched forces to Spain, where they fought on the side of General Francisco Franco (1892–1975) during the civil war. They supported one another when Italy attacked Ethiopia, and Germany remilitarized the Rhineland. In 1937 the two powers signed the Anti-Comintern Pact, which committed the signatories to a common struggle against Communist subversion. By this time, German and Italian propagandists began to talk about a new "Axis," around which the world turned. In September 1940, Germany, Italy, and Japan (later joined by several other fascist or quasi-fascist states) signed the Tripartite Pact. This treaty represented a three-way division of the British Empire, whose demise the Nazis repeatedly announced.

Regimes Influenced by Fascism. Other regimes borrowed some elements of fascism, such as exaltation of the state and hierarchy, but lacked most of its other attributes. The Japanese leadership was militarist and xenophobic to an extreme, but its power rested upon the military elites and the emperor, not upon a mass party controlled by a charismatic popular leader. In Spain, Franco used, then largely discarded, the fascist movement once led by José Antonio (1903–1936). Franco's power rested upon the army, and the Catholic Church, and the landlords, not on his absent charisma, or mass rallies and organizations. Vichy France or the French state under Marshal Henri-Philippe Pétain (1856–1951) ultimately included fascist parties in its regime, but it lacked a mass fascist movement and failed to coordinate society along fascist lines. In Argentina, Juan Domingo Perón (1895–1974) appealed to the "shirtless ones" with inflationary concessions, orated from a balcony, and told his people to look to Hitler's victorious Germany as a model. Yet like Pétain and Franco, he wisely refrained from entering the war on the side of the fascist states. Ultimately, he proved to be an old-style dictator rather than a modern fascist. His power rested on the army and his own personality, along with that his wife Eva (1919–1952). When she died, his popular appeal ebbed, and within a few years he was easily overthrown.

Fascism was born of the violence that engulfed Europe after 1914. Fascist movements provoked World War II, which then destroyed them. Smaller fascist-style movements exist today (2005) throughout Europe, but they are pale and diverse imitations of their defunct forebears. They lack strong leaders and mass support, two prerequisites for fascism, and in no case are they capable of overthrowing a state.

[*See also* Communism; Japanism; Nativism, *subentry* Japan; World War I; *and* World War II.]

BIBLIOGRAPHY
Broszat, Martin. *The Hitler State: The Foundation and Development of the Internal Structure of the Third Reich.* Translated by John W. Hiden. London: Longman, 1981. A thorough exploration of the nature of Nazi totalitarian rule.
Cassels, Alan. *Fascist Italy.* London: Routledge & Kegan Paul, 1969. A good introduction to the subject.
Gregor, A. James. *The Ideology of Fascism: The Rationale of Totalitarianism.* New York: The Free Press, 1969. Traces the evolution of fascist ideology.
Griffen, Roger, ed. *Fascism.* New York: Oxford University Press, 1995. A useful compendium of original sources.
Kershaw, Ian, and Moshe Lewin, eds. *Stalinism and Nazism: Dictatorships in Comparison.* Cambridge, U.K.: Cambridge University Press, 1997. Provocative comparative histories of totalitarian and fascist movements.
Laqueur, Walter, and George L. Mosse, eds. *International Fascism, 1920– 1945.* New York: Harper & Row, 1966. Good introductory essays covering most of Europe.
Rogger, Hans, and Eugen Weber, ed. *The European Right: A Historical Profile.* Berkeley: University of California Press, 1965. Important for understanding the interaction between conservatives and the radical right.

ROBERT EDWIN HERZSTEIN

Europe

Fascism is a form of political practice distinctive to the twentieth century that arouses popular enthusiasm by sophisticated propaganda techniques for an antiliberal, antisocialist, violently exclusionary, expansionist nationalist agenda. Fascism arose in response to European democracies' alleged failure to deal with the unprecedented stresses of World War I and the spread of Bolshevism after 1917. It promised to mobilize mass opinion across all classes in defense of the nation, against the socialist threat, and against liberals considered too soft to meet these challenges.

Italy. The term "fascism" was coined in 1919 by Benito Mussolini (1883–1945), an Italian war veteran and ex-socialist leader. The Italian Socialist Party had expelled Mussolini in 1914 for urging Italian entry into World War I. After the war, he wanted to gather veterans in a new mass movement that would be simultaneously nationalist, antisocialist, and radical. He derived the movement's name from the Italian socialists' term for a militant brotherhood, a *fascio*.

At the beginning it was not clear whether fascism was right or left. Mussolini's first program, in 1919, cultivated this ambiguity by combining nationalist expansionism with radical economic, social, and constitutional aims— confiscation of war profits and clerical lands, worker participation in management, women's suffrage, and abolition of the senate and monarchy. Mussolini seemed at first to be trying to create a rival socialism for war veterans.

Right-Wing Dictatorships in Europe, 1919–1939

Similar movements appeared throughout Europe, especially in countries defeated in World War I or threatened by socialist revolution. But these movements reached power only where they moderated their initial radicalism and found conservative allies. Italian fascists became a force in the agricultural Po Valley by helping landowners fight socialist farmworker organizations. In 1921–1922 fascist squads conducted punitive raids on socialist offices and newspapers and occupied socialist-led towns in northeastern Italy, supported by the army and by conservative local authorities. When fascist squads sought to occupy Rome in October 1922, King Victor Emmanuel III (r. 1900–1946), doubting that the army would repel them, tried to domesticate Mussolini by naming him prime minister in coalition with conservatives. After 1925, Mussolini established a personal dictatorship, accepted by conservatives who believed him efficient, orderly, and willing to discipline labor.

Germany. Defeated Germany was also ripe for antisocialist nationalism. Adolf Hitler (1889–1945), a failed art student in Vienna who became a decorated German war veteran, gave his small but noisy National Socialist German Workers' Party (Nazi Party for short) prominence in the

1920s by his passionate oratory for German revival and against Germany's alleged enemies: Jews, Marxists (the same to him), internationalists, and weak-kneed bourgeois liberals. Although Hitler differed from Mussolini in his biological racism, he was inspired by Mussolini's example.

Hitler profited from the weakness of the Weimar Republic (1919–1933), blamed for accepting the harsh Treaty of Versailles (1919) and for Germany's postwar troubles. When those troubles worsened with economic depression in 1929, Germany's democratic and centrist parties shriveled, while Nazism mushroomed. The Communist Party also grew. President Paul von Hindenburg (1847–1934) and his conservative advisors installed Hitler as chancellor of Germany in January 1933 because the Nazis seemed the best barrier to the Left. When a Communist drifter burned the Reichstag (parliament building) in February, Hitler exploited fears of insurrection to establish his personal dictatorship by summer 1933.

General Characteristics. Fascists excelled at propaganda and stagecraft, such as torch-lit parades and dramatic arrivals by fast car or plane. Although they declared their doctrines inviolable, fascists had contempt for the intellect and relied more on visceral appeals to patriotism, toughness, unity, and hatred for demonized enemies such as Jews and leftists. Early socioeconomic radicalism and paganism were quietly ignored when fascists formed alliances with conservatives and religious leaders for power.

In power, fascist dictatorships suppressed individual liberties, imprisoned opponents, forbade strikes, authorized unlimited police power in the name of national unity and revival, and committed military aggression. Mussolini conquered Ethiopia in 1935–1936, and Hitler rearmed Germany, in violation of the Versailles Treaty, and encroached on neighboring lands. His invasion of Poland on 1 September 1939 opened World War II, during which Nazi racism culminated in the mass murder of Jews and others.

Defeat in 1945, combined with the revelation of fascist genocide, discredited fascism. Only a few die-hard fascists persisted in postwar Germany and Italy. Spain and Portugal remained dictatorships until 1975, but they ruled through traditional conservatives rather than through fascist parties, and though they had ruthlessly crushed their enemies, they had preferred stability to war.

After the 1970s, when Western European democracies encountered difficulties—inflation, unemployment, unassimilated immigrants—extreme right-wing movements arose that resembled fascism in some respects, though they avoided overt use of fascist symbols and slogans. Like the classic interwar fascisms, they were nationalist, anti-socialist, and sometimes violent against outsiders and immigrants. On the other hand, they did not advocate

Fascist Leaders. Adolf Hitler and Benito Mussolini, Munich, Germany, c. June 1940. Eva Braun Collection/United States Department of Defense

expansionist war, managed economies, or political dictatorship. Above all, circumstances were less catastrophic than in interwar Europe, and the existing elites were less tempted to call upon fascists as the best barrier against left-wing revolution.

After 1989. As Communism declined after 1989, protofascism became the main vehicle for protest voting in Europe. Skinheads assaulted foreigners in many European countries, but their Nazi regalia aroused revulsion. More influential were parties that played down their fascist associations and attracted embittered jobless and anti-immigrant voters. The British National Party and the French Front National exploited anger over alleged national decline and immigrants' supposed criminal behavior and refusal to assimilate. The British National Party won 53 local council seats in 2006. The Front National received nearly 20 percent of the French vote in 2002, while the Allianza Nazionale (declaring itself "post-fascist") entered two Italian governments after 1994. The Freedom Party entered the Austrian government in 2000 despite ties to former Nazis, and 15 percent of Flemish-speaking Belgians supported the xenophobic separatist Flemish League.

In newly liberated Eastern Europe, hopes for acceptance into the European Union limited protofascist appeal. Post-Communist Russia, where the sudden adoption of democracy and the market led to misery and resentment over national decline, appeared to offer ideal conditions for protofascism, but an ex-Communist elite retained firm control. For the moment, no protofascist movement seems likely to reach power alone in Europe unless economies crash or states suffer catastrophic national humiliation.

[*See also* Action Française; Falange; March on Rome; Nazism; *and* Neo-Nazism.]

BIBLIOGRAPHY

Bosworth, Richard J. B. *Mussolini.* London: Oxford University Press, 2002. The best biography in English of the creator of Italian fascism.

Ignazi, Piero. *Extreme Right Parties in Western Europe.* Oxford: Oxford University Press, 2003. Best analysis of the conditions under which far-right parties have arisen in western Europe since the 1970s.

Kershaw, Ian. *Hitler.* 2 vols. New York: W. W. Norton, 1998–2000. Superb study of Hitler and his rapport with the German public.

Paxton, Robert O. *The Anatomy of Fascism.* New York: Knopf, 2004. Discusses how fascism began, and under what circumstances it grew, attained power, and exercised power.

Payne, Stanley G. *A History of Fascism, 1914–1945.* Madison: University of Wisconsin Press, 1995. The most complete survey of fascist movements and regimes worldwide.

Robert O. Paxton

Japan

Whether Japan became fascist between 1931 and 1945 remains a contentious issue. Applying the concept of fascism to Japan seems natural because the Axis Pact of September 1940 created an alliance among Japan, Nazi Germany, and fascist Italy during World War II. Indeed, during the 1930s trends in Japan toward militarization, domestic oppression, and an aggressive foreign policy resembled those in Germany under Adolf Hitler and in Italy under Benito Mussolini.

By contrast, the previous decade in Japan had witnessed significant steps toward more democratic government under the Meiji Constitution of 1889, steps that, though emphasizing the supreme rule of the emperor, established a bicameral legislature (the Diet), including an elected lower house that had the authority to create a budget and enact laws. In the 1920s the Diet implemented universal suffrage for men, party cabinets evolved, and the military's share of the national budget fell sharply. Japan also embarked on a policy of cooperative diplomacy with the Western powers based on agreements at the Washington Naval Conference of 1921–1922 on naval limitations and respect for the territorial integrity of China.

In 1931, however, Japan seized Manchuria in northeastern China (the Manchurian Incident). Within a few years junior military officers had assassinated a prime minister, cabinets led by political parties ended, military expenditures soared, the suppression of left-wing and liberal dissent tightened, and Japanese diplomats asserted that Japan should lead an East Asian bloc.

According to the influential analysis of the political scientist Masao Maruyama, Japan became a fascist state in the 1930s by dint of its militarism, extreme nationalism, and totalitarianism. Maruyama recognized, though, that the Japanese experience differed from that of Germany and Italy because a mass fascist party did not triumph in Japan. Instead, he argued, Japanese fascism followed a unique progression through three stages.

The first, preparatory stage in the 1920s featured the rise of numerous civilian right-wing groups. In the second stage between 1931 and 1936, young military officers became active in promoting nationalistic and authoritarian policies. In February 1936 young army officers in Tokyo led fifteen hundred troops to mutiny against the government to have martial law declared and the country placed under direct imperial rule. The failure of this rebellion, representing Japan's version of a fascist movement from below, ushered in the third stage: fascism from above. As the government bureaucracy and the military mobilized for war against China in 1937 and the Anglo-American powers in 1941, state controls gradually intensified.

For a long time most Western historians of Japan eschewed the concept of fascism. Some scholars have bemoaned the lack of consensus on defining the concept of fascism, whether in or outside of Europe. To others, the institutional differences among Italian fascism, German Nazism, and the Japanese state were too large. Aside from lacking a mass fascist party, Japan did not produce a charismatic dictator comparable to Hitler or Mussolini. Moreover, Japan did not experience an abrupt transfer of power similar to Mussolini's March on Rome in 1922 or Hitler's election as chancellor in 1933 and the subsequent passage of an Enabling Act that granted him dictatorial powers. In Japan the structure of the government remained intact, and elections for the Diet continued.

More recently, the topic of fascism in Japan has attracted more attention. Some studies have suggested that even if the Japanese state was not fascist, fascist influences were significant. Reformist intellectuals dedicated to ending the inequities of capitalism in Japan and the exploitation by Western imperialism in Asia took great interest in the strategy of Germany and Italy to use the state as a force for reform; in the specific policies of creating a single mass organization for the nation, imposing central economic controls based on cartel organizations, and molding labor unions into a single national front; and in the goal of creating a regional new order. Gregory J. Kasza has argued that these policies also influenced some powerful Japanese officials, the "reform bureaucrats." Like Maruyama, some historians, such as E. Bruce Reynolds, argue that the similarities in the authoritarian and aggressive policies of Japan, Germany, and Italy as they sought a "third way" between Communism on the one hand and liberal democracy and capitalism on the other outweigh the three nations' institutional differences.

Fascist ideas and policies had a large impact on Japan from 1931 to 1945, but categorizing the Japanese state as fascist confronts the challenges of precisely defining fascism as a concept and of taking into account clear differences in institutional developments in Japan, Germany, and Italy during this period.

[*See also* Military, *subentry* Military Organization in Japan; *and* Nationalism, *subentry* East Asia.]

BIBLIOGRAPHY

Kasza, Gregory J. "Fascism from Above: Japan's *Kakushin* Right in Comparative Perspective." In *Fascism outside Europe: The European Impulse against Domestic Conditions in the Diffusion of Global Fascism*, edited by Stein Ugelvik Larsen, pp. 183–232. Boulder, Colo.: Social Science Monographs, 2001. Rejecting the argument that the Japanese state was fascist, Kasza emphasizes the influence of European fascism on Japanese "reform bureaucrats" and the policies that they implemented.

Maruyama, Masao. *Thought and Behavior in Modern Japanese Politics*. Edited by Ivan Morris. London: Oxford University Press, 1963. The second essay, "The Ideology and Dynamics of Japanese Fascism," pp. 25–83, based on a lecture given by Maruyama in 1947, presents his interpretation of Japanese fascism.

Reynolds, E. Bruce, ed. *Japan in the Fascist Era*. New York: Palgrave Macmillan, 2004. This book makes the most comprehensive case in English-language studies for applying the concept of fascism to Japan. See especially the concluding essay by Reynolds, "Particular Characteristics: The Japanese Political System in the Fascist Era," pp. 155–197.

W. MILES FLETCHER III

FASHION. Fashion since the eighteenth century is documented by garments that have survived, by contemporary literature, paintings, and drawings, and later by fashion illustrations and media representations. The increases in media representation of fashion parallel how fashion, once the privilege of the few, became available to the many. France was the main source of innovation in Western women's fashion up until the 1950s. Much of what we consider to be aspects of the modern fashion industry originated there.

The Rococo Period and the Influence of France and England. The rococo period (1725–1775), an age of graceful elegance, pastel colors, and flowers, coincided with the reign of Louis XV of France. The French aristocracy and a new middle class created a society where clothing, furniture, and the arts became more widely important. Women were influential in determining taste, and Parisian society became the center for women's fashions. Fashion magazines disseminated French styles. Women wore structured gowns divided down the front, revealing a long petticoat and a triangular panel called a stomacher that covered the middle and chest area. Underneath a corset and pannier, a large structure of hoops, formed the shape around which outer garments were assembled. The stomacher was often embellished with embroidery, jewels, ribbons, and fabric flowers. Variations over time created the *robe à la franaise*, *robe à la polonaise*, and the *robe à l'anglaise*. Embroidered silks and heavily patterned brocades were used. "Anglomania" occurred toward the end of the rococo, stimulating plainer, more practical English styles and an interest in outdoor activity, resulting in the walking dress, pelisse, and redingote (adapted from the English riding coat), worn with bonnets or hats. Men's fashion comprised a decorative knee-length embroidered coat (a habit), short knee-length fitted trousers (breeches), and silk stockings. A long waistcoat, frilly cuffs, and neck pieces completed the look. Finally English tailoring, strongly influential, resulted in the more practical frock coat and trousers. Imported Indian and Chinese goods were also popular and became copied. The *indienne*, a printed gown made of Indian chintz, was so popular it led to the expansion of the textile industry.

The Empire Style. The French Revolution (1789) coincided with changes in clothing styles, partly as a political reaction to fashions associated with the aristocracy but also as a reflection of the cultural movement of Romanticism. Women started wearing tubular, lightweight long gowns, gathered under the bust, with a lower neckline. The one-piece chemise dress made from cotton muslin became very popular, and heavy undergarments disappeared. The style of the chemise owed much to interest in the world of the ancient Egyptians, Greeks, and Romans. It marks the Directoire (1795–1799) and Empire styles (1800–1830) in France and the Regency and Georgian periods in Britain. The chemise skirt gradually grew fuller while the waistline dropped and sleeves puffed up. Woven shawls were introduced and were to become a typical item of women's outdoor clothing until the early twentieth century. The chemise dress in its last stage took on a Gothic form in keeping with the more brooding qualities of Romanticism. Men wore pantaloons or trousers. Male fashion was epitomized by the dandies in England, particularly the elegant, sharp, sober style of Beau Brummel.

The Development of Fashion as an Industry. The 1850s saw the crinoline introduced, a hooped structure that shaped the petticoat (now underwear) and large dresses. Typically women wore a close-fitting bodice and skirt. As the century progressed, round skirts became flattened at the front and more pronounced in the rear through the introduction of the bustle, an undergarment. There were different gowns for different parts of the day.

The nineteenth century is important in terms of the establishment of the fashion industry. The American inventor Elias Howe patented the first mechanical sewing machine in 1846, which allowed one person to do the work

Fashion. "Monstrosities of 1818," drawing by George Cruikshank (London: G. Humphrey, 1818). BRITISH CARTOON PRINTS COLLECTION/PRINTS AND PHOTOGRAPHS DIVISION, LIBRARY OF CONGRESS

of five. During the American Civil War (1861–1865) the demand for men's uniforms resulted in ready-made clothes rather than clothes made in the home or made to order by tailors. Women's clothing would follow suit. The industrialization of fashion and textiles meant fashion became available to a wider social spectrum. Science introduced new materials and processes, such as aniline dyes, rayon, and dry cleaning. In Paris in 1858 the English designer Charles Frederick Worth established the House of Worth. Considered "the father of couture," he created many of the features of the haute couture system. Worth produced high-quality one-off pieces but also seasonal collections, shown on live models, from which women could order garments.

The Twentieth Century. In the late nineteenth and early twentieth centuries, the period called the Belle Epoque, the heavy garments of the earlier nineteenth century gave way to an *s*-shaped silhouette in keeping with the aesthetics of art nouveau. The status of women changed and new work and leisure opportunities arose for them; they also became fashion designers. With a growing middle class and mass-produced clothing, fashions changed more rapidly. People's wardrobes become more complex, incorporating garments for leisure activities, work, and

special occasions. In 1908 Paul Poiret did away with corsetry and returned to dress forms reminiscent of the early eighteenth century. Designers controversially offered trousers for women. Coco Chanel fused male and female elements of dress to produce definitive and comfortable outfits for women, including the women's suit and the little black dress. The most influential fashion designer of the century, she was also the first designer to have a perfume named after her. In the 1920s dresses were flattened at the chest, and hemlines rose as far as knee height during the period of the flappers. In the 1930s dresses provided angle and volume around the shoulders, drew in at the waist, and had generously cut skirts. Austerity during World War II led to "utility" style, a tailored look using the minimum of fabric. In 1947 Christian Dior introduced his influential "New Look," and in the following decade women's wear accentuated the female waist, with styles ranging from haughty sophistication to primness to concealed sexuality.

In the second half of the twentieth century fashion was strengthened by its relationships with popular music, the media, advertising, celebrity culture, and retailing. Practical and functional clothing entered the vocabulary of fashion. Military, sports, and work clothing dominated casual and leisure wear. Iconic styles of dress evolved in relation to popular music. In the 1950s rock and roll raised the status of youth culture and created a globally successful look that could be cheaply copied. Thereafter youth and popular culture became an essential part of fashion trends. In the 1970s haute couture's influence waned, and facing financial difficulties, it turned to branding more accessible goods such as perfumes. Inexpensive fashion items, such as denim jeans and white T-shirts, competed with high fashion for influence. Fashion could arise from either couturiers or from popular cultural movements, a phenomenon described by Ted Polhemus as the "trickle down bubble up" effect. A series of American and British youth subcultures created iconic looks between the 1950s and 1990s, including hippy, punk, hip-hop, and grunge. Vintage and ethnic styles of clothing contributed to a culture of eclectic dressing. Sportswear became strongly associated with black youth music and street culture and influenced mass fashion.

New Technologies and the Globalization of Fashion. Computer technology, transport, and communications affected the supply chain, the linkage of raw materials, fiber and fabric production, garment construction, and retailing. The fashion industry sped up, became more global in character, and was increasingly dominated by

Fashion Model. Victoria Station, London, 1951. Photograph by Toni Frissell. Toni Frissell Collection/Prints and Photographs Division, Library of Congress

new business and retail practices. Companies looked for the cheapest places to manufacture, while concerns arose about exploitation of fashion workers in developing nations. Asia became the main source of garment production. New synthetic materials became available, notably nylon, polyester, and lycra, revolutionizing the price and characteristics of clothes. Consumers preferred more casual and easy-wearing garments that were also easy to look after. By 2000 high-tech clothing fabrics could protect the wearer against sunlight or suppress bacterial and fungal growth. The use of nanotechnology, bioengineering, genetics, and flexible manufacturing suggested new types of clothing in the future.

Western clothing spread through the world, either as a result of colonization or through the desire of states or rulers to modernize their nations. Clothing could symbolically represent new attitudes and cultural change. Tsar Peter the Great, in modernizing Russia in the early eighteenth century, forced his nobility to wear Western styles. Similarly, at the end of the nineteenth century Thailand and Japan introduced Western clothing. Conversely, in the twentieth century some Asian, Middle Eastern, and African countries deliberately rejected Western fashion for ideological reasons; typically Western clothing was seen as immodest, morally corrupting, or a remnant of colonial oppression. Another reason to reject Western dress was the desire to sustain or affirm cultural heritage. However, even if elements of Western dress styles are not universally accepted, the economic and political template of the Western fashion industry has reached global proportions. In turn, global influences have blurred the boundaries of a distinctive, separate Western fashion. Globalized fashion is pluralist and diverse, with prices and styles to suit most consumers everywhere.

[*See also* Clothing; Luxury; *and* Textiles.]

BIBLIOGRAPHY

Breward, Christopher. *The Culture of Fashion: A New History of Fashionable Dress.* Studies in Design and Material Culture. Manchester, U.K., and New York: Manchester University Press, 1995. This illustrated historical survey of fashion investigates its cultural and social meanings. It provides a guide to the changes in style and taste and challenges existing fashion histories, showing that clothes have always played a pivotal role in defining a sense of identity and society. Broad in scope, it also covers some of the more controversial aspects of fashion, particularly those relating to sexuality and the body.

De La Haye, Amy, and Cathie Dingwall. *Surfers, Soulies, Skinheads, and Skaters: Subcultural Style from the Forties to the Nineties.* London: Victoria and Albert Museum, 1996. This book attempts to codify British subcultural dress by dividing it into fifty categories spanning fifty years since World War II. It provides strong evidence of the energy and creativity that causes youth fashion to "bubble up" and compete with the fashion establishment.

Fukai, Akiko, Tamami Suoh, Miki Iwagama, Reiko Koga, and Rie Nii. *Fashion: A History from the 18th to the 20th Century.* Cologne, Germany: Tascher, 2006. A luscious photographic history incorporating annotated, detailed, and informative photographs of garments from the Kyoto Costume Institute. An authoritative written summary is given of each century.

Gale, Colin, and Jasbir Kaur. *Fashion and Textiles: An Overview.* Oxford and New York: Berg, 2004. An academic and comprehensive overview of the fashion and textile industry at the end of the twentieth century. Themes and issues relating to materials, cultural roles, fashion consumption, business and industry, and high-tech fashion are all discussed. It incorporates an extensive, wide-ranging bibliography.

Polehemus, Ted. *Streetstyle: From Sidewalk to Catwalk.* New York and London: Thames and Hudson, 1994.

Steele, Valerie, ed. *Encyclopedia of Clothing and Fashion.* Farmington Hills, Mich.: Charles Scribner's Sons, 2005. Provides both the historical and global perspectives. A useful and comprehensive reference to the sometimes bewildering complexity of fashion.

Watson, Linda. *Twentieth-Century Fashion.* Buffalo, N.Y.: Firefly Books, 2003. The world of twentieth-century haute couture and high fashion is charted first decade by decade and then designer by designer. Changes in fashion are contextualized by social and political history as well as by the biographies of individual designers. Published in association with *Vogue*, iconic pictures are perfectly matched with a strong and lucid text.

COLIN GALE

FASHODA INCIDENT. The Fashoda incident might well have brought France and Britain to war in 1898, but instead it led to diplomatic reconciliation and an agreement that later led to an alliance and cobelligerence in World War I. The incident involved the seizure of Fashoda, a fortified oasis in modern-day Sudan, by a French force in 1898. The British saw Fashoda as critical to the defense of their interests in Egypt and sent a force to take it back. The resulting standoff led to a major diplomatic impasse. Public opinion in both countries became increasingly belligerent, with calls for war coming in both nations from politicians, newspaper editors, and crowds.

French diplomats sought to defuse the situation because they knew that France's major rival was Germany, not Great Britain. They brokered an agreement that gave Fashoda back to Britain in exchange for British recognition of a French sphere of influence in Morocco. The agreement allowed both sides to emerge with their honor intact and opened up a diplomatic channel that soon led both sides to recognize their shared interests. In 1904 the two states signed an Entente Cordiale that allowed each side to eliminate the other as a threat. Thereafter the two navies could operate as potential allies rather than as enemies, and their armies could begin to work more closely together. The Fashoda incident also revealed the marginality of local African officials, none of whom was consulted in the course of the negotiation. The Sudan thus became British, and Morocco became French.

[*See also* Colonialism; Morocco; *and* Sudan.]

BIBLIOGRAPHY

Neiberg, Michael. *Warfare and Society in Europe, 1898 to the Present.* London: Routledge, 2003. Treats Fashoda as the start of a new era in European military and political affairs.

Wilkinson, Samuel, Jr. *The Politics of Grand Strategy: Britain and France Prepare for War, 1904–1914.* Cambridge, Mass.: Harvard University Press, 1969. Reprint. London and Atlantic Highlands, N.J.: Ashfield Press, 1990. A good source for the analysis of Fashoda's impact on Franco-British relations.

MICHAEL NEIBERG

FAST FOODS. Fast foods like hamburgers, French fries, pizza, and tacos are available not just in restaurants and street stands but in frozen-food sections of the grocery store. Packaged for easy and quick preparation, the category of "fast foods" also includes items like microwaveable popcorn and dinners and even the minimeals available from vending machines and convenience stores, like chips, pastries, fruit, and "sports" drinks. Indeed, it is difficult to find a store that does not sell "fast" versions of meals in one form or another—almost as difficult as it is to find a busy intersection lacking a fast-food chain restaurant.

The history of "fast food" could be traced back well into prehistory. From the earliest days of hunting and foraging, humans have needed food "on the go." On long journeys away from reliable sources of food, travelers had to carry forms of nourishment that were easily prepared, not bulky, and nutritious if not also satisfying. Drying was a common strategy for meat, and salting added to the preservative effect. "Pocket soup," the equivalent of the modern bouillon cube, kept for years. And many Americans still know of the dried cornmeal pancake, the johnnycake, through nursery rhyme if not from experience. The need for traveling foods has been with us always.

The Industrial Revolution brought a major transformation in diet and new ideas about what constituted a meal. Feeding the necessarily large urban labor populations could only be accomplished by a corresponding transformation of farming practices. Eventually whole nations became almost farmless and dependent upon imports for food. This dependence helped spur improvements in canning and food preservation while it shifted attitudes about "fresh" foods, decreased tolerance for seasonal availability, and introduced palates to a more global grocery market.

The first fast-food restaurant in the United States, White Castle, opened in the 1940s. (Popular English fish and chips constituted a variant on fast foods, with outlets spreading from the 1920s onward.) These first American restaurants typically featured hamburgers, hot dogs, french fries, and soft drinks. Within a decade Richard (Dick) McDonald and his brother had introduced the concept of franchise restaurants, and the "Golden Arches" as well as Burger King, Kentucky Fried Chicken, and others were popping up all over the country. The rapid expansion of this industry could be explained in large part by social and economic forces present in the United States in the middle of last century. Increasingly, households consisted of a single working parent, or two parents who both worked. With all the household adults working, there was less time for shopping, preparation, serving, and cleanup of meals at home. These families increasingly turned to restaurants for meals, whether eaten there, taken out, or delivered, and the so-called fast-food restaurants were the most convenient and inexpensive alternatives for those without the time or incentive to cook for themselves.

The typical American diet has therefore changed dramatically since the mid-twentieth century. Since 1977 soda has outranked coffee, beer, milk, fruit juice, and bottled water as the drink of choice, and as Bonnie Liebman has noted, "this doesn't include the eight gallons [per person per year] of uncarbonated soda that masquerades as 'fruit' drinks" (p. 8); Americans eat slightly less ice cream than they did in the 1970s, but their cheese intake continues to skyrocket and has now surpassed beef as their largest single source of saturated fat; they eat less beef than they did in the 1970s, approximately 111 pounds of red meat per person per year; and they eat more fruits and vegetables. One food epitomizes this process of globalized food production: the chicken nugget, which some manufacturers create by using polyphosphates and gums to bind together meat that has been mechanically recovered. Despite certain improvements in diet, such as less red meat and more fruits and vegetables, overall these dietary changes have contributed to epidemic proportions of obesity and diabetes in the United States. These and other related health problems are an increasing concern for the very young, who are the target of a multimillion-dollar annual advertising industry for "fast" and "junk" foods.

Since the 1980s fast-food chains have responded to consumer complaints about the nutritional quality of their foods. Of particular concern has been the high calorie, sodium, fat, and cholesterol content. Chains made efforts to reduce the saturated fat in their cooking oils, offer grilled alternatives, and include new menu items such as salads, baked potatoes, and soups, but these efforts have also helped fast-food giants and global food corporations work their way into schools and educational materials. Eager to reach this captive audience, these companies offer financial incentives to schools in return for multi-year contracts that guarantee them exclusive selling and advertising rights on campus. Advertisements aimed at young children and other strategies for "branding" help develop loyal brand consumers from an early age. Public health advocates have called for greater regulation and oversight of this type of marketing campaign aimed at children. Such strategies will be important if, as Elaine McIntosh predicts, a greater demand for fast foods is ahead: "Demographic trends, such as the aging of the population, the increase in single-family households, the rising proportions of women working outside the home, the booming ethnic population, and the shift in income distribution, will bring changes in food patterns, creating new food markets" (McIntosh, p. 222).

Despite its dangers, some argue that fast food has become the American cuisine, our culturally shared set of foods. Sidney Mintz suggests that fast foods have become so common to the American diet that they are producing an overall homogenization of American food habits. He explains that many American food favorites, such as hot dogs, hamburgers, ice cream, and pizza, are actually the national cuisines brought by immigrants from other nations. Mintz suggests a "national cuisine" must be drawn from regional specialties like "maize dishes, lobsters and terrapins, the steaks and pork roasts, the Boston baked beans, soft shell crabs" (Mintz, p. 114). But since these are not easily packaged, preserved, or shipped, they are unlikely to make it to our fast, global, and industrial food market.

The spread of fast foods from the United States to other countries has been a major feature of consumer globalization since the 1970s. McDonald's and other outlets have gained wide popularity in Europe, East Asia, Russia, and elsewhere, partly because they seem to represent international fashion. Adaptations to local diets—for example, vegetarian burgers in India, teriyaki burgers in Japan—accompany the extension. Local firms have imitated the pattern, adding to fast food's impact; by the late 1980s, 20 percent of all French restaurant meals were taken in fast-food outlets, domestic or foreign. Attacks on fast-food centers have gained notoriety as well, as means of protecting regional identities, but fast food continues to spread.

[*See also* Food *and* Health and Disease.]

BIBLIOGRAPHY

Coakley, Anne. "Food or 'Virtual' Food? The Construction of Children's Food in a Global Economy." *International Journal of Consumer Studies* 27, no. 4 (2003): 335–340.

Goody, Jack. "Industrial Food: Towards the Development of a World Cuisine." In *Food and Culture: A Reader*, edited by Carole Counihan and Penny Van Esterik, pp. 338–356. New York: Routledge, 1997.

Liebman, Bonnie. "The Changing American Diet: A Report Card." *Nutrition Action Healthletter* 29, no. 10 (December 2002): 8–9.

McIntosh, Elaine N. *American Food Habits in Historical Perspective.* Westport, Conn.: Praeger, 1995.

Mintz, Sidney W. *Tasting Food, Tasting Freedom: Excursions into Eating, Culture, and the Past.* Boston: Beacon Press, 1996.

Simon, Michelle. "Junk Food's Health Crusade: How Ronald McDonald Became a Health Ambassador, and Other Stories." *Multinational Monitor* 26, nos. 3–4 (2005): 31–35.

Tannahill, Reay. *Food in History.* New ed. London: Review, 2002.

Watson, James L. *Golden Arches East: McDonald's in East Asia.* 2d ed. Stanford, Calif.: Stanford University Press, 2006.

CAROLYN SMITH-MORRIS

FATAH, AL-. *See* Palestine.

FEDERAL BUREAU OF INVESTIGATION. The Federal Bureau of Investigation (FBI) is the main investigative arm of the U.S. Department of Justice with headquarters in Washington, D.C. Founded at the beginning of the twentieth century, the bureau has evolved from a small group of special agents into a large agency with a complex structure and various tasks. These include the protection of the United States from terrorist attacks and foreign intelligence operations, the prevention of cyber-based and high-technology crimes, the eradication of public corruption and white-collar crimes, the protection of civil rights, and the research of the appropriate technology to carry out all these duties efficiently. The bureau has eleven divisions that employ about twelve thousand special agents and twenty-eight thousand support employees. The FBI director is nominated by the president and confirmed by the U.S. Senate. The director reports to the U.S. attorney general. The FBI was routinely challenged throughout the twentieth century for its involvement in covert murder operations and for what its critics consider its frequent breaches of privacy and civil liberties. After the events of 11 September 2001, the bureau

suffered a major setback because of its failure to prevent the terrorist attacks. The Patriot Act, which grants the FBI more power to enforce its tasks, has stimulated debates on the FBI's infringement of people's privacy through the issuance of National Security Letters, a form of administrative subpoena forcing a particular entity or organization to turn over various records and data pertaining to individuals.

The first nucleus of the FBI was formed in July 1908 by Attorney General Charles J. Bonaparte, who appointed a small group of special agents, mostly trained accountants, to serve as the investigative force of the Department of Justice. It was Bonaparte's successor, George Wickersham, who gave the group of agents the name of Bureau of Investigation in 1909. In this initial phase the bureau was mainly concerned with the investigation of financial transactions. During the 1910s, the bureau's jurisdiction and organization expanded, especially due to the passage of the Espionage, Selective Service, and Sabotage Acts, which allowed the investigation of enemy aliens during World War I. However, the bureau experienced its most significant transformation and expansion under the leadership of J. Edgar Hoover, who was its director from 1924 to 1972. A graduate of George Washington University Law School, Hoover established more rigorous guidelines to employ well-qualified and competent agents as well as more regular inspections and performance appraisals. As a part of this new emphasis on effective training for agents, the FBI National Academy was created in 1935. During the Depression, the sharp increase in crime made the bureau the major law enforcement agency, and its agents were allowed to carry guns and arrest suspects. Hoover was also skillful in exploiting the press to report the bureau's operations against famous criminals such as Al Capone, John Dillinger, Bonnie Parker and Clyde Barrow, and against the revived Ku Klux Klan. In spite of the bureau's spectacular arrests of many major crime figures in the 1930s, Hoover soon found a privileged target in the political and labor agitators who appeared on the American scene during the Depression. To combat the spread of radicalism in America, President Franklin Delano Roosevelt gave the FBI the authority to deal with all subversive activities endangering American democracy in 1939. The Smith Act, passed a year later, further increased the powers of the bureau, criminalizing the campaigns for the revolutionary overthrow of capitalism advocated by radical left-wing groups.

America's entry into World War II shifted the main focus of the FBI from criminality to espionage and subversion. To this end, the bureau started to gather information on people and organizations that were considered a threat to national security. In particular, during the war, Americans of Italian, German, and Japanese descent were investigated. The FBI was also active in actions of counterintelligence, exposing foreign spy rings, and monitoring the flow of information from double agents back to the Axis powers. These activities of intelligence continued and intensified with the end of World War II and the advent of the Cold War. The FBI was affected by the nationwide hysteria about the Red Scare, and the data it collected through its investigations were instrumental in the hearings of Senator Joseph McCarthy's House Un-American Activities Committee (HUAC). In the late 1950s, the bureau expanded its targets to include not only Communists and the Communist Party but also socialist organizations, black nationalist groups, New Left activists, and civil rights organizations. Through the Counterintelligence Program (COINTELPRO), first established in 1956, the FBI employed illegal methods to undermine the leadership of all those organizations that Hoover considered a threat to national security. This abuse of power, characterized by illegal surveillance technique, systematic leaking of derogative information, and planned assassinations, continued into the 1960s. During this decade, the complacency of the 1950s was replaced by the activism and the demand for social justice of the movements against the Vietnam War and for civil rights, women's emancipation, and homosexual liberation. The COINTELPRO was only dismantled in 1971, a year before Hoover's death.

Under Hoover, the FBI grew into a strong and powerful law enforcement agency. Yet, Hoover's legacy was not unproblematic. As hundreds of documents indicating the illegal activities of the FBI became known, Congress, the media, and the American public questioned whether the FBI methods of collecting data for domestic security breached the constitutional rights of American citizens. These debates, together with the periodic rise and fall of the bureau's reputation, have characterized the history of the FBI in the last decades of the twentieth century, when the end of the Cold War and the appearance of Islamic terrorism have posed new challenges to the FBI. After the fall of the Soviet Union in 1991, containing Communism was no longer a priority and many of the bureau's agents were reallocated to fight violent crimes on American soil. The bureau scored important successes with the arrest of the Unabomber Theodore Kaczynski and of the drug-trafficker Juan Garcia Abrego. Yet, the events of 11 September 2001 pointed to the necessity of restructuring the FBI to meet the new challenges posed by international terrorism. This was confirmed by the bipartisan 9/11 Commission that, in 2004, issued a report pointing to several important communication mistakes within the FBI.

[*See also* COINTELPRO *and* Police.]

BIBLIOGRAPHY

Blackstock, Nelson. *COINTELPRO: The FBI's Secret War on Political Freedom.* New York: Pathfinder Press, 1988.

"Federal Bureau of Investigation." http://www.fbi.gov

Gentry, Curt *J. Edgar Hoover: The Man and the Secrets.* New York: Plume, 1991.

Potter, Claire Bond. *War on Crime: Bandits, G-Men, and the Politics of Mass Culture.* New Brunswick, N.J.: Rutgers University Press, 1998.

Theoharis, Athan G., et al., eds. *The FBI: A Comprehensive Reference Guide.* Phoenix, Ariz.: Oryx Press, 1999.

LUCA PRONO

FEDERATED MALAY STATES. *See* Malaysia.

FEDERATED SHAN STATES. *See* Malaysia.

FEMININITY. Research in history or other social sciences that focuses explicitly on "femininity" is rare. This is in sharp contrast to the historical study of "masculinity," which is a booming field. As of 2006, for example, there were at least thirty books on the history of British masculinity alone, not counting those that focus on masculinity in literature and a growing interdisciplinary field of scholarly endeavor termed "masculinity studies." Many books and articles refer to "masculinities" in the plural, highlighting this variety. "Femininity" seems to have a much narrower range of possible meanings and variations than does "masculinity," and the plural—"femininities"—has not become the solution. Many historians have studied what it means to be female, but they generally define their subject with phrases such as "women's roles," "the gender order," and "norms and ideals for women" rather than "femininity."

The study of both femininity and masculinity has its roots in the feminist movement. During the 1970s advocates of women's rights in the present looked at what they had been taught about the past and realized that it described only the male experience, though often portrayed as universal. This realization, combined with increasing numbers of women going into the field of history, led to the development of women's history. Historians familiar with studying women then began to discuss ways in which systems of sexual differentiation affected both women and men and, by the early 1980s, to use the word "gender" to describe these systems. They differentiated primarily between "sex," by which they meant physical, morphological, and anatomical differences (what are often called "biological differences"), and "gender," by which they meant a culturally constructed, historically changing, and often unstable system of differences. The boundaries between sex and gender were fuzzy and frequently contested, but scholars who explored masculinity or femininity in their research were clearly looking at gender.

Differing Standards. If the term is used in a broader way, "femininity" has varied nearly as much as has "masculinity." Some of this variety has been among social groups within a single area. In New Spain (present-day Mexico) in the eighteenth century, for example, high-status Spanish-born white women (*peninsulares*) and Mexican-born white women (*creoles*) were advised to be rarely seen in public, maintain their sexual honor at all costs, and marry a husband who was higher than they in social status and whose bloodline could be certified as "pure"—that is, who had no ancestors who were Native American, Jewish, African, or Muslim. The number of suitable husbands was often much smaller than that of women seeking them, so large numbers of elite women went into convents. This provided them with an alternative to marriage that was socially acceptable, for piety and devotion to the Catholic Church were an important part of femininity in New Spain and throughout Latin America. For mixed-race women (*castas*) religious devotion was also a quality viewed as positive, as was caring for children and fidelity to a long-term partner. This fidelity was not necessarily sanctioned by formal marriage, however; though the Catholic Church officially condemned women who had sex outside of marriage as "fornicators," community norms were based on the quality of the woman's relationships rather than their legal form. Enslaved African or mixed-race women were sometimes described as "exotic temptresses," as European men created an ideal that centered on sexual allure and availability; from the perspective of most white or mixed-race masters, this sexual availability was combined with the ability to work hard. For indigenous women, hard work, childbearing, and clan loyalty were important norms, with devotion to particular aspects of Christianity, such as veneration of the Virgin Mary, often part of the mixture as well. Because they could only rarely read and write, poor mixed-race, enslaved or indigenous women left few records about the ideals they set for themselves, though court records and later oral interviews, letters, and other sources indicate that motherhood and support

for one's family were ideals that arose from inside as well as outside.

In just this one time and place, then, definitions and norms of femininity varied by social class, race, and ethnicity. Any one group might also experience conflicting standards, as can be seen in the variant church and community ideals for women of mixed race. In addition, theoretical norms and actual behavior could be quite different from one another. Despite all the emphasis on sexual honor for white women, about one-third of the children born to white women in central Mexico in the early eighteenth century were out of wedlock. The church quietly legitimated many of these children, and the women rarely suffered any serious decrease in social standing. Close examination of any culture would reveal standards of femininity different from those in New Spain, but with a similar pattern of variations and contradictions.

Colonialism, Nationalism, and War. In New Spain, norms of femininity that often had their origins elsewhere were modified by interactions between cultures. This was true in every colonial context. In colonial South Asia, European (especially British) norms shaped the behavior of European women and also shaped the attitudes of European men toward Hindu and Muslim society, which had very different standards of femininity. Conversely, South Asian nationalists used idealized female figures—the devoted mother, sometimes conceptualized as Mother India, and the loving and sacrificing wife—as symbols of their opposition to the British. Actual Hindu and Muslim women sometimes altered their own notions of acceptable female behavior as they engaged in public political protests, established women's periodicals, and set up organizations to work for improvements in women's rights and education.

Nationalist movements throughout the world in the nineteenth and twentieth centuries frequently led to changes in ideals for women or conflicts between standards of acceptable female behavior. In China traditional Confucian norms held that daughters should be submissive to their fathers, wives to their husbands, and widows to their sons. In the early twentieth century nationalist and communist groups with male and female members created new ideals; foot binding was ended, women's opportunities for education were expanded, and the New Woman who wore unisex clothing, worked in a factory, and understood the political sayings of Chairman Mao Zedong became the ideal of Chinese femininity. In Nigeria in the 1920s Igbo women demonstrated against chiefs who cooperated with the British, using a long-established ritual in which they sang jeering songs and mooned the officials in order to dishonor them. British soldiers were so offended and startled by these actions, which did not fit with their ideas of proper female conduct, that they shot the women, killing nearly twenty of them. This massacre enhanced anti-imperialist sentiments, which eventually led to Nigerian independence. In many other areas as well, including Ireland, Iran, Poland, and Argentina, women and men used nationalist or revolutionary ideologies to create new symbolic and real roles for women, often centered on their position as actual or potential mothers.

Wars of all kinds created new types of femininity. The most famous of these is Rosie the Riveter, a figure created as part of a propaganda campaign in the United States during World War II to encourage women to take jobs in defense factories. The thousands of real women who worked as welders, machinists, and assembly-line workers came to see Rosie, a muscular woman in overalls, as a symbol of their labor and their contribution to the war effort. World War I also led to changes in women's roles, as women took over jobs such as postal clerk and streetcar conductor that had previously been held by men, with uniforms adapted to make them look less masculine. In some wars, including the last Cuban war for independence from Spain in the 1890s and the long Vietnamese war against the Japanese, French, and United States, women served as combatants and were praised by their co-combatants as idealized "woman warriors."

Increasingly during the twentieth century, some standards of femininity were being set by consumer culture—ideals of physical beauty, for example, increasingly emphasized slenderness and youthfulness, first in the West and then to an extent more globally. Consumer-based femininity was not itself changeless: in the 1950s it tended to emphasize domestic functions for the ideal woman but later shifted to include educational and work roles. Reactions to this source of feminine standards also varied, with some individuals and societies accepting new cosmetic standards, for example, but others resisting in the name of religious or other traditions.

Similarities and Continuities. Though norms of femininity change over time and differ widely, a few characteristics have been shared by many societies in the modern world, particularly for women in the dominant racial or ethnic group, what we might term "hegemonic femininity." Women have been viewed as being more closely tied to children and the household than men; war or revolution might thrust them into new jobs and positions, but when these are over domestic ideals of femininity reemerge. Chastity before marriage, sexual fidelity during marriage, and physical beauty have usually been viewed as more important for women than men. Women have been and continue to be seen as the most important bearers of "tradition," whereas men represent "modernity." This can be seen visually in the fact that women often wear "traditional" dress, either regularly or for special occasions, whereas men dress in Western suits. (In many cases, "traditional" clothing is actually a product of modern nationalist movements and was not worn before the nineteenth century.) Women as well as men have been active agents in creating such standards, but the limited role they envision for women may explain why, in contrast to masculinity, femininity often seems too narrow and unchanging a topic for historical enquiry.

[See also Christianity; Colonialism; Consumption and Consumerism; Empire and Imperialism; Feminism; Gender; Hegemony; Hinduism; History; Indian Nationalism; Irish Nationalism; Islam; Machismo; Marianismo; Masculinity; Nationalism; Postcolonialism; and Women.]

BIBLIOGRAPHY

Blom, Ida, Karen Hagemann, and Catherine Hall, eds. *Gendered Nations: Nationalisms and Gender Order in the Long Nineteenth Century.* Oxford and New York: Berg, 2000. Includes essays discussing many countries.

Gal, Susan, and Gail Kligman, eds. *Reproducing Gender: Politics, Publics, and Everyday Life after Socialism.* Princeton, N.J.: Princeton University Press, 2000. Examines new gender relations and gender identities in eastern Europe.

Landes, Joan B. *Women and the Public Sphere in the Age of the French Revolution.* Ithaca, N.Y.: Cornell University Press, 1988. Analyzes the impact of the French Revolution on ideals for women and women's actions.

Meade, Teresa A., and Merry E. Wiesner-Hanks, eds. *A Companion to Gender History.* Malden, Mass., and Oxford: Blackwell, 2004. Includes articles that discuss changing norms and roles for women from many areas from prehistory to the present.

O'Brien, Patty. *The Pacific Muse: Exotic Femininity and the Colonial Pacific.* Seattle: University of Washington Press, 2006. Uses both written and visual evidence to examine the colonial stereotype of the exotic Pacific Island woman from the eighteenth century to the beginning of the twenty-first.

Pettus, Ashley. *Between Sacrifice and Desire: National Identity and the Governing of Femininity in Vietnam.* New York: Routledge, 2003. Explores the role of women in the politics of national identity in Vietnam from the 1950s through the 1990s.

Sarkar, Tanika. *Hindu Wife, Hindu Nation: Community, Religion, and Cultural Nationalism.* Bloomington: Indiana University Press, 2001. Analyzes the function of different images of women in Hindu nationalist ideology and contemporary postcolonial theory.

Stern, Steve J. *The Secret History of Gender: Women, Men, and Power in Late Colonial Mexico.* Chapel Hill: University of North Carolina Press, 1995. Examines the ideals set out for many different types of women, including widows, peasants, and workers.

MERRY WIESNER-HANKS

FEMINISM [*This entry includes six subentries, an overview and discussions of feminism in Britain, Europe, East Asia, South Asia, and Southeast Asia. See also Women.*]

Overview

Feminism is a set of beliefs focused on the improvement of women's status in society, politics, the economy, and culture in order to gain for them the approximate value placed on men. Actual feminist activism dates from the modern period and is often connected to the spread of ideas drawn from the English, American, and French revolutions of the seventeenth and eighteenth centuries. Since then activists have pooled feminist efforts to work for equal opportunity in the workforce, equal rights under the law, and equal duties and privileges as citizens of modern nations. Since the mid-twentieth century feminists from all regions of the world have drastically expanded the meaning of feminism to include freedom from violence, hunger, filth, and disease, and from women's mandated ignorance through lack of schooling. Racism, human rights, and sexuality and sexual identity have also been important issues in feminism. Thus the demands of feminism have varied from place to place, while overall the issues covered by feminism have expanded. Feminists have also seen the need to forge alliances with other reform and human rights groups.

Women in the United States, Europe, and the antipodes were among the first to benefit from feminist activism when they received access to education—including higher education—from the mid-nineteenth century on, the right to vote in the first half of the twentieth century, and legal reform in the late nineteenth and early twentieth centuries. After mid-century, feminists and other reformers in these countries remained active, thereby achieving greater access to good jobs, contraception, abortion rights, health care, and in some cases political influence.

Women in non-Western regions such as Africa had traditionally held powerful local positions, and in parts of Asia and the Pacific world they also served as heads of state. These positions were usually the result not of feminist activism but of the familial power that the women inherited if they were capable. Nonetheless, the leadership of women such as Indira Gandhi of India or Corazón Aquino of the Philippines proved inspirational to women in countries such as the United States or Germany, where male privilege was especially strong and where women had failed to achieve such stature.

Feminism and Nationalist Movements. Women in Turkey, Egypt, South Africa, India, and Vietnam provide examples of activists on behalf of women, activists whose feminism intersected with movements for national independence from colonial rule. Late in the nineteenth century Egyptian and Indian women, for instance, had formed feminist organizations, founded magazines, and engaged in public activities such as philanthropic work. Activists promoted improvement in the condition of women and greater calls for improved education and involvement in serious matters such as politics. Like feminists elsewhere, they promoted dress reform, which—reversing the European trend, which sought out more comfortable garments from Asia—often meant adopting Western clothing. As the twentieth century opened, many feminists combined their activism on behalf of women with nationalist causes. They were active in the Iranian revolution of 1905–1911 and in the Turkish revolution of 1908. In the 1920s Huda Sharawi in Egypt made unveiling into a national cause. She and other colleagues in the feminist movement joined nationalists active on behalf of independence from the British.

Women's activism in South Africa was directed almost from the start at the developing apartheid system, though that system was not institutionalized until after World War II. Early in the twentieth century the government in South Africa instituted laws requiring special work and identity passes for nonwhites. Women protested these laws, demonstrating against them and holding boycotts. A leader of the anti-pass movement, Charlotte Maxeke, a teacher, helped women organize to resist being made domestic laborers and to resist other forms of deterioration in their condition. Women across Africa were losing both their agricultural rights and their high political status under colonialism because Western officials redistributed land and high positions in colonial governments to whites and to local men.

In 1929, Ibibio and Igbo women in West Africa conducted what became known as the Women's War against British colonial policies that would impose new taxes on them. Their conduct of the war included practices known as "sitting on a man," in which they demonstrated according to their customs, painting their bodies and performing warlike rituals. Although British officials tried to get the women to admit that their men were behind their protests, the women steadfastly maintained their independence.

As World War II increased exploitation, urbanization, and poverty in Africa, women's activism increased and took on new dimensions. Activists aligned their protests

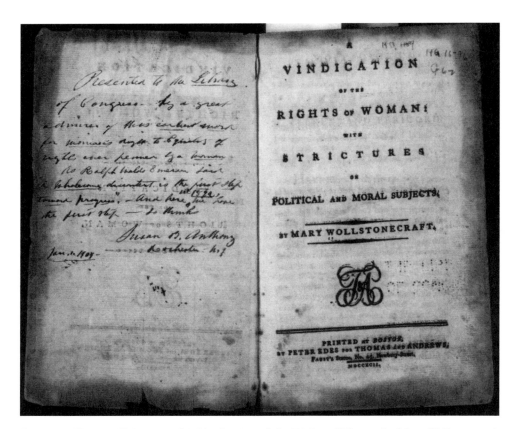

Feminist Classic. Title page of *A Vindication of the Rights of Woman* by Mary Wollstonecraft (Boston, 1792). On the blank page is a dedication by Susan B. Anthony: "Presented to the Library of Congress by a great admirer of this earliest work for woman's right to equality . . . ever penned by a woman." Rare Books and Special Collections Division, Library of Congress

with nationalist movements. Market women worked to protect their economic interests from the incursions of both the colonial government and their own men. In Lagos some ten thousand poor market women formed the Lagos Market Women's Association to oppose price controls and wartime taxation. Though women's activism proved crucial to nationalist movements, after African independence male nationalist leaders accused women of being too backward and not really fit for power. One exception was South Africa, where the new constitution of 1996 declared as one of its fundamental principles "non-racialism and non-sexism." Even though men dominated the government, women's participation was strong because of their previous activism in the antiapartheid cause.

Latin American Feminism. Nation-building developed public educational institutions across Latin America, and constitutions codified the unequal position of women in many Latin American states, leading women to organize to reform their position, increase opportunities for jobs, change laws, and obtain the vote. Their efforts for suffrage helped

obtain the vote in all of Latin America between 1929 and 1961. Middle-class feminists were also concerned with the condition of poor children in Latin America, while indigenous and poor women grew active to improve wages and job opportunities and to gain protection from exploitation by multinational corporations. Their activism became especially powerful after World War II and remained so into the twenty-first century. Although women's efforts achieved representation of some six to eight percent in representative assemblies, male dominance in politics remained strong. Nonetheless, in 1990, Violeta Chamorro was elected president of Nicaragua, while in 2006, Michelle Bachelet of Chile became South America's first woman president.

In Latin America, women organized in neighborhoods, and although many of these organizations were not avowedly feminist, they specifically addressed the cause of women and their families. A particularly effective example appeared in the city slums of Brazil, where women lacked basic public facilities such as water, garbage collection, and other sanitary services. Their organization of these services—sometimes with government help—while providing adult courses to teach literacy and other skills, also promoted women's leadership. Other organization of women locally included ad hoc protests against military regimes that attacked dissident children and murdered families. Women's demonstrations in the 1970s and 1980s, such as the Mothers of the Plaza de Mayo in Argentina, became for many models of effective feminist activism. These women's protests were undertaken in dangerous conditions, yet the participants themselves remained steadfast and eventually drew worldwide attention.

International Feminism. International feminism arose out of contacts among women in the nineteenth century. Women in Europe corresponded with one another, many of them beginning with the abolitionist movement. Because that movement was transoceanic, women in North America also had contact with European activists, especially those who came to lecture in the United States. "Our movement is cosmopolitan," the U.S. activist Ernestine Rose announced in 1860. "It claims the rights of woman wherever woman exists" (Anderson, p. 180). Later in the nineteenth century, ties among European, North and South American, North African, and Asian activists developed, and these connections were solidified with the formal creation of the International Woman Suffrage Alliance in 1904 after several international women's suffrage conventions. In 1915 activists from the alliance met at the Hague to try to persuade combatant nations in World War I to end the slaughter.

In the 1920s and 1930s women from South and North America met in the Inter-American Commission on Women, a group that arose from more informal meetings of the American states. The IACW aimed to promote women's rights in all spheres, including work, politics, and the family. Another international venture was the International League of Iberian and Hispanic American Women, founded in 1921. This group worked for women's rights, such as the right to divorce, but it also unified women against U.S. domination in the region.

Among notable international meetings during the Cold War, women met in conjunction with the development of the United Nations. Many were eager to get women's issues firmly on the United Nations agenda, but Cold War issues kept preventing consensus at these meetings. Nonetheless the United Nations eventually became a leader in monitoring women's issues: it was crucial in sponsoring international conferences such as those in Nairobi (1985) and Beijing (1995); in 1997 it established U.N. Women-watch to provide Internet services and information to women around the world.

In 1995 women held the most publicized feminist congress yet in Beijing, China. The meeting was marred when the Chinese government refused to accept the credentials of many would-be delegates, but it had many successes. These included the extraordinary camaraderie that marked the meeting and the lessons about feminism learned by women from wealthy countries. The most tangible result of the Beijing Conference was a weighty document, the result of debate and compromise, stating feminist positions globally on issues such as the well-being of women and girls, violence committed toward women, and women's access to education, food, employment, and shelter. Delegates from a number of countries appended their disagreements with certain provisions—most notably on women's right to control fertility—to the end of the Beijing Platform. The conference had much less success in getting governments to pursue policies called for in the document.

Cultural Feminism. While feminism has developed pro-women political programs and reforms over the past three centuries, women have also expressed feminist sentiments in a variety of cultural media, including novels, poetry, art, and films, and with increasing globalization these have come to attract audiences worldwide. A sampling shows the first influences in the poet Sappho of ancient Greece writing lyrical poems about loving women; the authors Murasaki Shikibu and Sei Shōnagon described sex roles in the Japanese court in the tenth and eleventh centuries, providing models for writing down to the present.

In 1905 the Muslim author Begum Rokeya Sakhawat Hossain published "Sultana's Dream," one of the most interesting utopian, feminist tales ever written. It is set in the imaginary country Ladyland, where the men are in seclusion and the women rule a well-ordered and highly advanced state. A visitor asks how this can be, considering that men's brains are bigger than women's: "Yes, but what of that? An elephant also has got a bigger and heavier brain than a man has," the guide replies (Hossain, p. 12). In Ladyland the women have harnessed solar power and collected water from the atmosphere to provide clean energy and abundant resources for farming and industry. There is no crime because the troublemaking men are in seclusion.

Similarly exuberant in their celebration of women are the paintings of Indian women artists and works like *Dinner Party* (1974–1979) by the U.S. artist Judy Chicago, which exhibits plates in honor of pathbreaking women, aligning them in a large triangular table. In the twenty-first century the Iranian author Azar Nafisi produced *Reading Lolita in Tehran* (2003), a work showing a persecuted university teacher taking up the uncensored reading of literary classics with students in her home. The group is not all feminist, but rather is a complex array of women battling over literary, religious, and political ideas. This book was widely translated and read.

Another cluster of feminist literature and occasionally visual arts reflected the grim side of gender inequality. At the end of the eighteenth century the feminist theorist Mary Wollstonecraft expressed her views in the novel *Maria, or the Wrongs of Woman* (1798). That novel's heroine is betrayed not only by a loutish husband but by the legal system that strips her of her property in his favor. Many feminist novels about the oppression of women followed in the West, and their influence was widespread: by the end of the nineteenth century such novels were seen in the hands of Egyptian and other women as they traveled or read at home. The Egyptian author Huda Sharawi (1879–1947) wrote vivid memoirs of her girlhood and her turn to feminist activism. Readers saw her experiencing unequal conditions of marriage, though some criticized her for ignoring the plight of downtrodden women of the most impoverished classes.

However, novelists remained most influential. Bessie Head, for example, presented vivid if pessimistic portraits of women in southern Africa in the second half of the twentieth century. *Maru* (1971) describes the power of men and the racial prejudice Africans felt toward one another. Similarly, Maxine Hong Kingston and Hualing Nieh provided accounts of the mental stress of transnationalism in the global age. Though Kingston's *Woman Warrior: Memoirs of a Girlhood among Ghosts* (1976) testifies to various degrees of overcoming the heritage of Chinese womanhood, Nieh's *Mulberry and Peach* (1981) depicts a heroine who becomes mentally ill as she moves from China to Taiwan to the United States.

Feminist Activism in the Twenty-first Century. Though activism continues in the form of international congresses, grassroots organizing, participation in public debates and policy making, and the production of films, books, and other cultural goods with some feminist slant, opposition is powerful. In some countries the entire weight of government is thrown against women's equality; other places have seen attempts to discredit feminism by calling it names such as infidel, lesbian, man-hating, and other terms that shame and menace women who want equality. This opposition may be inspired by the fact that feminism

has become a cause embraced by tens of millions of women around the world. Moreover, feminism has influenced employers, nongovernment organizations, and politicians to see that women have economic and political potential that can help serve economies and nations. By the first decade of the twenty-first century every major continent except North America has seen women serve as distinguished heads of nations.

[*See also* Gender *and* Women.]

BIBLIOGRAPHY

Anderson, Bonnie S. *Joyous Greetings: The First International Women's Movement, 1830–1860.* New York: Oxford University Press, 2000.

Badran, Margot. *Feminists, Islam, and Nation: Gender and the Making of Modern Egypt.* Princeton, N.J.: Princeton University Press, 1995.

Baron, Beth. *The Women's Awakening in Egypt: Culture, Society, and the Press.* New Haven, Conn.: Yale University Press, 1994.

Berger, Iris, and E. Frances White. *Women in Sub-Saharan Africa.* Bloomington: Indiana University Press, 1999.

Fleischmann, Ellen L. *The Nation and Its "New" Women: Feminism, Nationalism, Colonialism, and the Palestinian Women's Movement, 1920–1948.* Berkeley: University of California Press, 2002.

Hossain, Rokeya Sakhawat. *Sultana's Dream: A Feminist Utopia and Selections from "The Secluded Ones."* Edited and translated by Roushan Jahan. New York: Feminist Press, 1988.

Johnson-Odim, Cheryl, and Nina Emma Mba. *For Women and the Nation: Funmilayo Ransome-Kuti of Nigeria.* Urbana: University of Illinois Press, 1997.

Kaplan, Temma. *Taking Back the Streets: Women, Youth, and Direct Democracy.* Berkeley: University of California Press, 2004.

Lavrin, Asunción. *Women, Feminism, and Social Change: Argentina, Chile, and Uruguay, 1890–1940.* Lincoln: University of Nebraska Press, 1995.

Miller, Francesca. *Latin American Women and the Search for Social Justice.* Hanover, N.H.: University Press of New England, 1992.

Rupp, Leila. *Worlds of Women: The Making of an International Women's Movement.* Princeton, N.J.: Princeton University Press, 1997.

Smith, Bonnie G., ed. *Global Feminisms since 1945.* London and New York: Routledge, 2000.

BONNIE G. SMITH

Britain

Modern British feminism is dated from the late eighteenth century when both men's and women's rights were debated within the context of the scientific and rationalist ideas of the Enlightenment and the American and French revolutions. Mary Wollstonecraft's *A Vindication of the Rights of Woman* (1792), which critiqued women's inferior education and subordination within marriage and argued for women's greater inclusion in civic life, is one of the period's key feminist texts. Though the term "feminist" was not used in Britain until 1895, it has been used to describe a range of activities through which women have sought to fight against oppression and secure political, economic, and civil rights.

Eighteenth and Nineteenth Centuries. Eighteenth-century feminism did not lead to change in Britain's politically stable environment, but women were increasingly active in public life and reform efforts in the early nineteenth century. This activity was spurred by religious revivalism sweeping through Europe and America, the "feminization" of religion, and beliefs in women's moral superiority and fitness for reforming society. Religion has played a significant role in British feminist history, often providing women with the moral authority to speak out against injustice and offering a framework through which to critique society. Key events during these years included the growth of a utopian feminist philosophy, which promoted communities based on sex equality, and women's participation in such reform efforts as Chartism and the international antislavery movement, which fostered women's political activism and furthered critiques of women's subordination.

Debates on the "woman question" became a part of mainstream discourse after 1850. A formal women's movement was founded, and feminist campaigns focused on such issues as women's sexual exploitation through prostitution, unequal marriage laws, and women's access to higher education and the professions; a demographic "surplus" of women led to interest in middle-class women's employment rights. The movement had many successes during these years, including the passing of the Married Women's Property Acts (1870 and 1882), which gave married women a right to their earnings and property, the founding of a women's college at Cambridge University (1873), and the British Medical Association's decision to admit women doctors (1892). Feminists have traditionally garnered some active support from men, and such influential texts as John Stuart Mill's *The Subjection of Women*, which espoused liberal feminism and argued for women's enfranchisement, was published in 1869.

Throughout the nineteenth century, political citizenship for men had been increasingly expanded through the Reform Acts of 1832, 1867, and 1884, yet women were specifically excluded (some gained voting rights in local elections in 1869). Women's suffrage became an important cross-class, feminist concern, and organizations such as the National Union of Women's Suffrage Societies (1897) and the Women's Social and Political Union (1903)—headed by Millicent Garrett Fawcett (1847–1929) and Emmeline

Pankhurst (1858–1928), respectively—were created. After a lengthy campaign, which was divided between militant and constitutional suffragists in the years before World War I, enfranchisement was granted to women over the age of thirty in 1918 (Representation of the People Act).

Early Twentieth Century. After 1918, feminists continued campaigns for women's equal franchise (granted in 1928) and began new campaigns to focus on other inequalities (for example, married women's nationality). Interwar feminism was divided between "egalitarian" feminists, who focused on "pure" equality issues such as employment rights, and difference, or "new," feminists, who were interested in women's needs as wives and mothers (for example, housing and birth control). The leading new feminist Eleanor Rathbone (1872–1946) headed a successful campaign for the 1945 Family Allowances Act, which gave mothers financial support for their children and was one of many feminist-driven welfare reforms. Feminism has been a significant part of Britain's intellectual and cultural landscape, and the interwar years witnessed the publication of Virginia Woolf's *A Room of One's Own* (1929), which argued for the importance of private space for women's self-development, and *Three Guineas* (1939), which linked militarism and patriarchy.

Ideological differences between new feminists and egalitarian feminists were less pronounced during the 1940s and 1950s. Feminists were heavily influenced by a pervasive domestic ideology and focused on women's rights in both the home and the workplace. Few feminists challenged the sexual division of labor before the 1960s, and Alva Myrdal and Viola Klein's influential text *Women's Two Roles: Home and Work* (1956) argued that women's lives should be divided into periods devoted to motherhood or employment.

Feminism was reinvigorated in the 1960s by the Women's Liberation Movement (WLM), and by women who had been involved in the Campaign for Nuclear Disarmament and anti–Vietnam War demonstrations. Feminists in the 1960s campaigned for sexual and personal liberation, and the first national WLM conference (1970) called for such things as twenty-four-hour nurseries and legal abortion. Reproductive rights campaigns were instrumental in the provision of free contraception through Britain's health service, and the 1967 Abortion Act made abortion legal under certain conditions.

Feminism since the 1970s. Ideological differences among feminists led to the WLM's demise in the late 1970s. However, feminist campaigning has continued through women's involvement in party politics, trade unions, and other organizations, and gender equality and women's rights have remained important political issues. This can be seen through later legislation such as the 1985 Sexual Offences Act, as well as the attention given to such issues as domestic violence and rape. Feminism has also affected the Church of England, which now allows women to become priests and is removing obstacles to the bishopric.

International work has been an important facet of British feminism. Feminists have worked in such transnational organizations as the International Alliance of Women (1904) and have worked with both the League of Nations and the United Nations. Though such work has had many positive effects, feminists active during the age of empire often positioned themselves as protectors of, and spoke for, colonized women; this "imperial feminism" has shifted in the postcolonial era, but historians are still determining the nature of interwar and post–World War II international feminism. Feminist activism also grew within colonized countries in the British Empire, challenging both British imperialism and Western feminism.

The legacy of women's political citizenship has been uneven, and women's position at the end of the twentieth century made it clear that achieving, and defining, equality is difficult. British suffragists believed that the vote would provide women with a voice in the running of the nation, but women have not achieved equal governmental representation, and women's equality remains an important goal.

[*See also* Gender, *subentry* Gender Ideals in Britain; Gender and Empire; Women; *and* Women's Suffrage.]

BIBLIOGRAPHY
Caine, Barbara. *English Feminism 1780–1980.* Oxford: Oxford University Press, 1997.
Law, Cheryl. *Suffrage and Power: The Women's Movement, 1918–1928.* London: I. B. Tauris, 2000.
Liddington, Jill. *The Road to Greenham Common: Feminism and Anti-Militarism in Britain since 1820.* Syracuse, N.Y.: Syracuse University Press, 1991.
Rupp, Leila. *Worlds of Women: The Making of an International Women's Movement.* Princeton, N.J.: Princeton University Press, 1997.
Wilson, Elizabeth. *Only Halfway to Paradise: Women in Postwar Britain, 1945–1968.* London: Tavistock, 1980.

JESSICA THURLOW

Europe

European feminism in the modern period has roots in a long tradition of women's writings and activism and in increasing contact with women in the rest of the world. Eighteenth-century reformers drew on the insights of Sappho (fl. c. 610–c. 580 B.C.E.), Christine de Pizan (1364–c. 1430), Mary Astell (1666–1731), and many others to fortify their sense that for centuries women had spoken out bravely to combat inequities in their treatment. At the same time, travelers like Lady Mary Wortley Montagu (1689–1762) gained the impression from visiting places like the Ottoman Empire that women had more rights and power outside of Europe. Organizing groups for the discussion of serious philosophical and literary matters, the "bluestockings" in London and women leaders of salons across Europe are also seen as precursors of modern feminism because they acted to establish women's cultural influence. In the eighteenth century, women's activism in hard times also contributed to a burgeoning feminism; many issues of women's rights received publicity in the Enlightenment and during the French Revolution (from 1789), when women's groups and individuals demanded a variety of reforms changing their unequal position, including their right to serve in the military. Finally, in Protestant countries active evangelicals created a tradition of women's preaching before crowds and vocally concerning themselves with public issues.

Reformers and activists on women's behalf, such as Germaine de Staël (1766–1817) and Mary Wollstonecraft (1759–1797), became role models for feminists in the nineteenth century, when a mass feminist movement gradually emerged. In the first half of the century working- class women were active in England promoting women's rights to political and economic opportunity. "The most direct cause of women's misfortune is poverty. . . . From that comes the subjection of women," one Belgian activist wrote in the 1840s. In Paris, utopian socialists lauded women's special qualities, such as compassion and love, that could help soften the rough edges of an increasingly commercial society. Both the demands for equal rights and the promotion of women as particularly compassionate fed into the creation of a mass feminist ideology. Though fractured by seemingly competing beliefs in women's equality and their special differences, the many women's groups of the nineteenth century consistently worked for an array of issues, including economic and political ones. Equal rights for prostitutes subject to illegal searches, economic opportunity for working women, access to quality higher education, and relief for destitute, criminal, and ill women were all causes that feminists undertook. Many of these reformers were middle class because they enjoyed the household help, political connections, and leisure that facilitated their activism.

Quest for Suffrage. By the end of the nineteenth century, feminists determined to focus on achieving suffrage as their main goal; getting the vote, they believed, would then facilitate other reform. England's Women's Social and Political Union (WSPU), founded in 1903 by Emmeline Pankhurst (1858–1928) and her daughters Christabel and Sylvia, was only the most visible—even notorious—of the suffrage groups. Using the destruction of property, public demonstrations, and civil disobedience to gain their ends, members of the WSPU went to jail and undertook hunger strikes. "We don't want to be lawbreakers," Emmeline Pankhurst wrote. "We want to be lawmakers." This group, like other suffrage groups in Europe, received some support from working women, who agreed that the vote would help improve their economic situation.

The suffrage movement met opposition from organized Socialist feminists, however, who saw suffragists as privileged women unconcerned for righting economic wrongs. Socialists worked within the many socialist, social democratic, and labor parties that organized for workers' rights generally without specifically focusing on the woman question. Before World War I, feminists had gained divorce, child custody, educational, and property reform in many countries, but they had not achieved the vote.

It is often said that women were rewarded for their war work with the vote, which suddenly materialized between roughly 1915 and 1925. This saying discounts the long history of feminist activism, the careful building of alliances, and the deployment of rational arguments. Feminists did not quit their activism with the accomplishment of the vote, however. In the new countries of eastern Europe such as Czechoslovakia, women turned their activism toward building a nation in which women's interests were fully recognized and programs on their behalf were implemented. In Soviet Russia women headed for Muslim and peasant communities to help women become modern in their thinking and behavior, teaching them to read, keep hygienic households, and dress in a secular, urban way. Still other women directed their energies to a variety of other causes, such as social welfare, so firmly did some believe in the power of suffrage.

After the War. The Depression, World War II, the Holocaust, and the powerful antifeminist ideas of fascists across Europe took their toll on feminism if not on women's contributions to society, the economy, and politics—including the resistance to fascism itself. Yet in the immediate aftermath of the war, Simone de Beauvoir (1908–1986) wrote one of the most globally influential books analyzing the condition of women, *The Second Sex* (1949), while

European Feminist. Simone de Beauvoir, author of *The Second Sex*, 1965. AP IMAGES

other European women agitated for equal pay for civil servants, the right to birth control, and better access to goods and services. It was only late in the 1960s, however, that individual causes merged their efforts to form a recognizable feminist movement—often called "Second Wave feminism." Feminist groups took shape in small and large European cities, many of them emerging out of antiwar protests and student activism in universities. "There is no revolution without the liberation of women," Italian feminists challenged their male colleagues.

From the late 1960s and throughout the next decade European feminists demonstrated for the rights to divorce, to obtain legal abortions, and to benefit from equal economic opportunity. More strikingly, feminists tackled cultural issues such as the representation of women as primarily sexual objects in advertising and their depiction as either foolish or castrating on television programming. Feminists along with gay activists tackled the relentless discrimination meted out to those of unconventional sexual orientation. Feminists also allied with and even played leadership roles in the burgeoning environmental movement of the late 1970s that led to the formation of green parties in many countries.

The growing number of major women politicians, the narrowing of the gap between men's and women's wages, changes in divorce and reproductive legislation, and improved educational and employment opportunities even in such stubbornly resistant countries as Germany and the Netherlands demonstrate the efficacy of the Second Wave feminist movement. Feminists have also contributed to the alleviation of discrimination against gays, lesbians, and bisexuals and have allied themselves to promote multiculturalism across Europe as the population becomes more racially, ethnically, and religiously diverse. These more recent initiatives growing out of the 1970s activism are sometimes called Third Wave feminism.

[*See also* Gender; Women, *subentry* Europe; *and* Women's Suffrage, *subentry* Europe.]

BIBLIOGRAPHY

Akkerman, Tjitske, and Siep Stuurman, eds. *Perspectives on Feminist Political Thought in European History: From the Middle Ages to the Present*. London: Routledge, 1998. Excellent treatment of the intellectual roots of feminism.

Allen, Ann Taylor. *Feminism and Motherhood in Western Europe, 1890–1970: The Maternal Dilemma*. New York: Palgrave Macmillan, 2005. Studies an issue of major concern to feminists.

Banaszak, Lee Ann, Karen Beckwith, and Dieter Rucht, eds. *Women's Movements Facing the Reconfigured State*. Cambridge, U.K.: Cambridge University Press, 2003. Studies of contemporary issues.

Bull, Anna, Hanna Diamond, Rosalind Marsh, eds. *Feminisms and Women's Movements in Contemporary Europe*. New York: St. Martin's Press, 2000. Anthology covering feminism more recently.

Griffin, Gabriele, and Rosi Braidotti, eds. *Thinking Differently: A Reader in European Women's Studies*. London: Zed Books, 2002. An excellent example of Third Wave analysis and concerns.

Kent, Susan Kingsley. *Sex and Suffrage in Britain, 1860–1914*. Princeton, N.J.: Princeton University Press, 1987. The classic study of the prewar movement.

Offen, Karen. *European Feminisms, 1700–1950: A Political History*. Stanford, Calif.: Stanford University Press, 2000. A vast and comprehensive survey that includes both large and small countries.

Paletschek, Sylvia, and Bianka Pietrow-Ennker, eds. *Women's Emancipation Movements in the Nineteenth Century: A European Perspective*. Stanford, Calif.: Stanford University Press, 2004. In-depth studies of a wide variety of movements and issues.

Reagin, Nancy. *A German Women's Movement: Class and Gender in Hanover, 1880–1933*. Chapel Hill: University of North Carolina Press, 1995. A careful, insightful study of feminism at the grass roots.

Renne, Tanya, ed. *Ana's Land: Sisterhood in Eastern Europe*. Boulder, Colo.: Westview Press, 1997. A regional study of feminism in a newly independent region.

Scott, Joan Wallach. *Only Paradoxes to Offer: French Feminists and the Rights of Man*. Cambridge, Mass.: Harvard University Press, 1996. A provocative and widely influential interpretation of French feminism, with general implications for studying other feminist movements.

BONNIE G. SMITH

East Asia

Feminist thought and activism in East Asia have a history dating from the late nineteenth century. The societies of China, Japan, and Korea were feudalistic monarchies, with strict hierarchies justified according to Confucian principles. According to Confucianism, all social relationships are regulated according to hierarchical relationships of ruler-subject, parent-child, elder sibling–younger sibling, husband-wife, and friend-friend, conducted according to the principles of loyalty to the monarch, filial piety to parents, and chastity on the part of women. Women were expected to demonstrate obedience to the father in the natal family, to the husband in marriage, and to the eldest son in widowhood. By the nineteenth century, the economies of these countries were being transformed by the beginnings of capitalist relations, with which ideas of freedom, rights, and individualism were more congenial.

In Japan, discussion of ideas of freedom and popular rights became prevalent from the 1880s. As part of this more general development of liberal thought and notions of human rights, women and liberal male thinkers argued for women's rights. Socialist thinkers also debated the woman question in Japan from the first decades of the twentieth century, and women were active in socialist and labor movements. Nevertheless, the Meiji Constitution of 1890 positioned men and women as subjects of the emperor, with the franchise limited to adult, property-owning males (about 1 percent of the population). In 1925 suffrage was extended to all adult Japanese males and colonial male subjects resident in the metropolis, but not to women.

The pioneering feminist literary journal *Seitō* (Bluestocking) appeared from 1911 to 1916. Until 1922, article 5 of the Public Peace Police Law prohibited women from attending, holding, and speaking at political meetings and belonging to political organizations. Women were prevented from voting and standing for public office. After the modification of article 5 in 1922, it became possible for women to form political organizations. The League for the Attainment of Women's Suffrage, led by

Ichikawa Fusae (1893–1981), was formed in 1924. Bills for women's suffrage were passed in the Lower House in 1930 and 1931 but failed to pass in the House of Peers. Autonomous women's organizations were gradually co-opted under the total national mobilization for World War II.

In Korea and China, the discussion of feminism was linked with nationalist and anticolonial movements. Korea was a Japanese colony from 1910 to 1945. China was subject to unequal treaties with the European powers, the United States, and Japan from the nineteenth century. Students from both Korea and China also traveled to Japan, where they came into contact with feminist and liberal ideas from Japan, Europe, and the United States.

In China, from the Qing period (1644–1911) there was discussion of women's situation and women's education. From the late nineteenth century, discussion of women's emancipation was closely connected with movements for national autonomy, with the situation of women often used as a metaphor for the Chinese nation's suffering under foreign domination. The practice of footbinding was criticized by both Chinese intellectuals and non-Chinese observers. One of the leading figures of the early discussion of feminism in China was Qiu Jin (1875–1907). She traveled to Japan to study and was notorious for her cross-dressing and her support of revolutionary movements. She was executed for treason, but is remembered now as a heroine. Women were dissatisfied at the failure to grant them political rights after the revolution of 1911, which deposed the last of the Manchu emperors. Discussion of women's rights flourished as part of the May Fourth Movement of 1919. Both Nationalists and Communists included women's emancipation in their platforms for reform in the 1920s and 1930s, although women's rights were not achieved until the Communist Revolution of 1949.

In Korea too, discussion of women's rights was closely connected with nationalist movements. As in Japan and China, in Korea, Christian missionaries were among the first to create schools for women, and the Christian practice of treating men and women as equal before God was influential. Women were leading participants in the student protests against Japanese colonial domination on 1 March 1919. In the early twentieth century, journals devoted to the new woman in Korea provided a forum for the discussion of women's issues. The artist and writer Na Hye-Sok (1896–1948) is remembered as an exemplar of the new woman. Women were also active in socialist movements from the colonial period.

Japan's defeat in August 1945 is celebrated as the date of Korea's liberation. However, in the years after 1945, Korea split into North and South, the peninsula experienced the Korean War from 1950 to 1953, and at the end of the war the Demilitarized Zone was created at the border and still exists as the last remnant of the Cold War in East Asia. In South Korea, women achieved suffrage in 1948, and the Constitution guarantees gender equality. Women have been active participants in the movement for democracy and have been vital to the labor movement, as they formed a large component of the factory workforce. In 1988 with the Constitution of the Sixth Republic, a democratic system was finally achieved in South Korea.

In China, the Communist Revolution of 1949 heralded a new age for women's rights, with equal rights being affirmed in the Constitutions of 1952 and 1982. Discussion of feminism was marginalized for several decades, however, as communism was seen to hold the answers to questions of women's emancipation. In postrevolutionary China, women and men have generally been treated equally in legal terms, but in practice women have often suffered from the double burden of domestic labor and labor outside the home.

In Japan, the electoral law was amended in December 1945 to allow women to vote. In 1947 a new constitution was drafted affirming the sovereignty and equal rights of the people, and this affirmation was supported by a more egalitarian Civil Code. In postwar Japan, women were initially active in groups as mothers. In the 1970s women who had become disillusioned with the sexism of the new left formed women's liberation groups to explore issues of sexuality, reproductive control, and identity. International Women's Year in 1975 and the subsequent United Nations Decade for Women provided a focus for reformist groups.

The United Nations Decade for Women (1975–1985) and the follow-up meetings in Beijing in 1995 and in New York in 2000 provided a forum for feminist demands throughout East Asia. Japan ratified the Convention on the Elimination of All Forms of Discrimination against Women and passed the Equal Employment Opportunity Act in 1985. Issues of gender equity are now handled by the Office of Gender Equality in the Japanese Cabinet Office, in line with the Beijing Plan of Action, which enjoins states to establish national machinery for gender policy. In South Korea, gender issues are handled by the Korean Women's Development Institute. In China, the All-China Federation of Women, a mass national women's organization with regional branches, is concerned with women's interests.

At the beginning of the twenty-first century, feminists in East Asia are concerned with issues related to the globalization of labor markets, working conditions in the tourist industry and multinational corporations, neoliberal policies and the cutback of welfare policies, military sexual violence, and the legacies of World War II. The issue of forced prostitution by the Japanese military during World War II has led to coalitions that bring together women from throughout Asia. These coalitions culminated in the Women's International War Crimes Tribunal on Japan's Military Sexual Slavery in Tokyo in December 2000. Post-structuralist, postmodern, and postcolonial thought have also had an influence on feminist thought in East Asia during this period, with major works being translated from European languages and local theorists adapting these theories to the local country's own situation.

[*See also* Footbinding; Gender, *subentry* Gender Relations in East Asia; Paternalism, *subentry* East Asia; *and* Women, *subentry* East Asia.]

BIBLIOGRAPHY

Barlow, Tani E. *The Question of Women in Chinese Feminism.* Durham, N.C.: Duke University Press, 2004.
Jayawardena, Kumari. *Feminism and Nationalism in the Third World.* Rev. ed. London: Zed Books, 1986.
Mackie, Vera. *Feminism in Modern Japan: Citizenship, Embodiment, and Sexuality.* Cambridge, U.K.: Cambridge University Press, 2003.

VERA MACKIE

South Asia

Under the influence of British colonialism South Asian history has been conceptualized as ancient, medieval, and modern (the emergence of the latter conventionally dated to the revolt of 1857, also known as the Indian War, or Sepoy Mutiny). However, it would be misleading to see these periods as more than rough correspondences to Hindu, Muslim, and colonial rule. Thus, while such historical figures as the scholar Gargi from the (ancient) Vedic period, or queens such as Razia Sultana from the medieval era, or the Rani of Jhansi, who led a regiment of her soldiers against the British army in 1857, have been incorporated into popular discourses about powerful women throughout South Asian history, they have emerged as elements of modern discourses of nationalism and cannot

be taken as early examples of "feminism" in any straightforward way. "Feminism" as a set of ideas and movements is a product of modernity, however variously dated.

In South Asia, the first strands of feminist thought and agitation for women's rights emerged in the context of anticolonial nationalism. Even in Afghanistan, which was never subject to British colonial rule, the late nineteenth and early twentieth centuries saw a progressive monarchy institute reforms designed to foster women's education and to limit the cost of weddings and the tribal bride-price system. In the South Asian subcontinent, then, Muslim modernists and Hindu social reformers alike addressed issues of women's status, rights, and duties through a variety of media.

In British-ruled India, the debates about practices concerning Hindu women, such as sati (or widow immolation), female infanticide, child marriage, and widow remarriage, rarely involved women themselves until the late nineteenth century. By then, women's magazines in Tamil, Marathi, Hindi, Urdu, Bengali, and numerous other South Asian languages began to address women's own concerns about their condition. The Marathi writer Tarabai Shinde wrote a scathing critique of the treatment of women in her "A Comparison between Women and Men" (1882). Increasing literacy of the middle and elite classes meant that educated women also began writing in English. The Bengali-Muslim social reformer Rokeya Hossain published in the Madras (now called Chennai) *Indian Ladies Magazine* a 1906 short story "Sultana's Dream," which imagined a gracious, nonviolent, and Utopian world where men, not women, were secluded at home and forced to observe purdah. Her satire predated by several years Charlotte Perkins Gilman's better-known effort, *Herland* (1915).

The late-nineteenth-century emergence of Indian nationalism built upon women's involvement in caste reform politics of the Brahmo Samāj and Jyotirao Phule's non-Brahmin movement. It would expand to include women's mass-based participation in the Gandhian non-cooperation and civil disobedience campaigns of the 1920s and 1930s, in Communist organizations in the late 1930s, in the Indian National Army (under the "Rani of Jhansi" regiment led by Captain Lakshmi Seghal) in the early 1940s, and in peasant struggles against landlords in the Telengana movement of the late 1940s–1950s. Women from prominent families who had been active in the anticolonial struggle, such as Vijayalakshmi Pandit and Fatima Jinnah, found places in the governments of India and Pakistan. After independence, women were allowed entry into Pakistan's navy, while sex equality was enumerated in Article 14 of the Indian Constitution. The legacy of women's participation in the anticolonial movements of South Asia was to have a far-reaching impact upon women's movements in the postcolonial period.

If we see feminism as an "awareness by women that as women they are systematically in a disadvantaged position; some form of rejection of enforced behaviors and thought; and attempts to interpret their own experiences and then to improve their positions or lives as women" (Badran and Cooke, p. xiv), then we are probably on stronger ground for interpreting South Asian women's writing and participation in the social reform debates that concerned their status throughout the nineteenth and twentieth centuries. This is because the term "feminist" itself was sometimes explicitly rejected by such Indian nationalist leaders as Sarojini Naidu and the Begum Shah Nawaz. Cristobel Pankhurst's 1908 claim that since the British had created the very idea of sex equality, it was wrong for women in the colonies to expect political equality before British women seemed to illustrate for many an uncomfortable relationship between feminism and imperialism.

Today, while many South Asian activists concerned with women's issues are comfortable with calling themselves feminists, it is not uncommon for them to reject "Western" feminist agendas seen to prioritize sexuality, identity issues, and reproductive rights, when there is still concern over the lingering economic impact of colonialism and the introduction of neoliberal policies into the region that affect the basic economic and class survival of South Asian women. At this writing, a variety of women's movements is flourishing across South Asia, from autonomous women's organizations in India that grew out of a dissatisfaction with left-based parties' treatment of women's issues, to religious and party-based organizations, to a number of nongovernment organizations focused on women's issues in Pakistan, Bangladesh, Nepal, and Sri Lanka. From the rights of sex workers to anti-dowry, anti-rape, and sexual harassment legislation campaigns, women's organizations in South Asia have organized national conferences and have found international representation at Cairo and Beijing. In addition, many of the social movements concerned with water, environmental degradation, big dam development, HIV/AIDS education, and trade-union, anti-caste, and anti-communal politics across South Asia, while not focused on women's issues, are either women-centered or women-led. The movement in Okara to reclaim farmland from the Pakistani army is led by women, the National Association for People's Movements (NAPM) has been led by Media Parker for many years, and growing criticism of microcredit is emerging from local organizations in Bangladesh and Sri Lanka.

[*See also* Gender, *subentry* Gender Relations in Southeast Asia.]

BIBLIOGRAPHY

Badran, Margot, and Miriam Cooke, eds. *Opening the Gates: A Century of Arab Feminist Writing*. Bloomington: University of Indiana Press, 1990.
Kumar, Radha. *A History of Doing: An Illustrated Account of Movements for Women's Rights and Feminism in India, 1800–1900*. London and New York: Verso, 1993.
Mumtaz, Khawar, and Farida Shaheed, eds. *Women of Pakistan: Two Steps Forward, One Step Back?* London and Atlantic Highlands, N.J.: Zed Books, 1987.

KAMALA VISWESWARAN

Southeast Asia

Although scholars of "movements" in Southeast Asia have tended to emphasize formal male activism over women's collective actions, it is well documented that individuals, groups, and activities that express an awareness of and resistance to women's political, socioeconomic, and religio-cultural oppression appeared in Southeast Asia in the late nineteenth and early twentieth centuries. One of the pioneering figures of women's movements in Southeast Asia is Raden Adjeng Kartini (1879–1904), an Indonesian aristocrat who formed her feminist position through a combination of Javanese education, religious instruction, and formal Western education. Her countless letters to a pen-friend in the Netherlands, written between 1899 and 1903, became famous for their dual critique of colonial rule and of what Kartini perceived to be the key to the oppression of her female contemporaries: women's lack of access to education and the institution of polygamy. Similarly, many women's organizations that formed in the early decades of the twentieth century, such as the first formal women's associations in Burma and in Indonesia— the Wunthanu Konmaryi Athin (founded 1919) and the Federation of Indonesian Women's Associations (founded 1929) respectively—called for female education and an end to child marriage and polygamy.

Scholars note that these women's movements were invariably involved in anticolonial struggles, if not established under an explicitly nationalist rubric; they suggest that women's movements in Southeast Asia have been devoted primarily to anticolonialism and less concerned with questions of women's rights. This view, however, greatly underestimates the divergent concerns and strategies of the women's movements in the region; they have pursued both regime change and social change, and they have sought to destabilize colonial powers as well as the subordination of women. Even at the peak of anticolonialism, when national liberation constituted a principal objective of women's movements, such varied issues as labor conditions, education, universal franchise, class, and gender formed central concerns. In the Philippines, the explicitly feminist organization the Ilonga Feminist Association made women's suffrage its goal in 1906, and in 1909 the women's journal *Feminista* was founded with the goal of defending women's rights. Popular journals in Thailand and Vietnam such as *Women's Writing* and *Ladies' News* demanded marital equality and female education.

Supporters of women's movements, furthermore, were mobilized by ideologies other than nationalism. Colonial rule introduced not only racialist and Eurocentric colonial policies but also the ideas of progressive feminist groups that influenced the thoughts of women such as Kartini. The Patriotic Burmese Women's Association strove in cadence with such transnational feminist associations as The International Alliance of Women for Suffrage and Equal Citizenship in its struggle for women's right to run in parliamentary elections. They protested in alliance with Theravadin Buddhist monks against the colonial administration's intervention in the religious affairs of the country. Socialism and communism likewise served as the ideological basis for women's movements. By the end of World War II, a quarter of all Vietnamese women were members of the Vietnam Women's Union (founded 1930), a women's branch of the Vietnamese Communist Party.

The period immediately following national independence is widely understood as having ushered in a period of defeat for women's movements when male leaders of nationalist movements and nascent independent states sought to reinforce or intensify, rather than contest, restrictions on women's activities. The New Order state in Indonesia, established in 1965 under General Suharto, replaced the leftist Indonesian Women's Movement (founded 1950) with the Family Guidance Welfare Movement (also known as Pembinaan Keseiahteraan Keluarge, or PKK; founded 1970), which implemented mandatory female contraception at the village level. Islamic revivalist discourses have tended to reinforce patriarchal nationalist policies that attempt to control female reproductive roles and sexual rights. Supporters of women's movements, however, have continued to challenge patriarchal authority and state apparatuses. Various nongovernmental organizations (NGOs) in the region have raised awareness about reproductive rights, domestic violence, trafficking in women, "comfort women" issues, sexual harassment, and HIV/AIDS. Women's movements have coalesced around and against the sexual and economic exploitation of women especially in countries such as Thailand and the Philippines, where the states depend heavily on the sex industry for the expansion of the national economy. They have utilized the United Nations (UN) declaration of 1975–1985 as the International Women's Decade and the platform of the 1995 Beijing conference—Women's Rights as Human Rights—to legitimize their efforts at women's empowerment. They continue to draw on international mechanisms such as the UN Convention on the Elimination of All Forms of Discrimination Against Women and the International Labor Organization to advocate better working conditions for women, who constitute a large part of the industrial workforce.

[*See also* Gender, *subentry* Gender Relations in Southeast Asia.]

BIBLIOGRAPHY

Blackburn, Susan, ed. *Love, Sex, and Power: Women in Southeast Asia.* Clayton, Victoria, Australia: Monash Asia Institute, 2001.

Ong, Aiwha, and Michael G. Peletz, eds. *Bewitching Women, Pious Men: Gender and Body Politics in Southeast Asia.* Berkeley: University of California Press, 1995.

Wieringa, Saskia. *Sexual Politics in Indonesia.* Houndmills, U.K., and New York: Palgrave Macmillan, 2002.

CHIE IKEYA

FENIANISM. Emerging during the 1850s in the wake of the potato famine (1845–1849), the 1847 death of the nationalist leader Daniel O'Connell, known as the Liberator, and the 1848 failure of a rebellion by a revolutionary group called Young Ireland, the Fenian Society (from *fianna*, or ancient Gaelic warriors) was dedicated to the forcible overthrow of British rule in Ireland. The Fenians attracted many thousands of young men, mainly artisans and tradesmen, repudiated constitutional methods, and drew support from Irish at home and abroad over the next decade. After unsuccessful transatlantic risings in the mid-1860s, Fenianism metamorphosed into other Irish nationalist movements.

Early organizers included James Stephens of Kilkenny and John O'Mahony of County Limerick, both expatriate Young Irelanders. In 1858, Stephens founded the pledge-bound secret Irish Republican Brotherhood in Dublin, which merged with the Phoenix Society of Cork, and in 1859 O'Mahony transformed the Emmet Monument Association into the Fenian Brotherhood in New York. Both branches, called Fenians, espoused revolutionary goals. While O'Mahony organized a Fenian regiment in the American Civil War, Jeremiah O'Donovan Rossa organized local nationalist clubs in Ireland, and Stephens founded the *Irish People* in 1863 to promote the cause. In 1865, Stephens estimated that there were two hundred thousand Fenians in Ireland, many well-armed, and an additional fifteen thousand Irishmen in the British army. John O'Leary, as an editor of the *Irish People*, was the movement's leading intellectual and an important link to Ireland's literary renaissance. Although opposition from the Roman Catholic Church, the arrest of Stephens and his fellow conspirator John Devoy, suppression of the *Irish People*, and suspension of the Habeas Corpus Act in Ireland were setbacks, momentum shifted to North America, where large stores of arms and money were being accumulated by Fenians.

Upon the discharge of large numbers of Civil War veterans of Irish descent who were eager to strike a blow against England, a Fenian convention in Cincinnati decided on an invasion of Canada to challenge British imperial authority. (In a sense, Ireland occupied a status similar to Canada's, and for the North American Irish, Canada was easier to get at.) In April 1866 a force of several hundred gathered at Eastport, Maine, but its attempt to seize the island of Campobello in New Brunswick was frustrated by the arrival of six British warships and an American vessel with an artillery company under Major General George Meade that dispersed the Fenians. In June, Colonel John O'Neill led a force of fifteen hundred men across the Niagara River to capture Fort Erie, but it was forced to retreat to Buffalo, whereupon O'Neill and about seven hundred Fenians were arrested by American authorities. The United States also intercepted a smaller force at Saint Albans, Vermont, and British authorities captured a ship, *Erin's Hope*, that was attempting to land Fenian militants from America in Ireland.

In 1867, Fenianism reached its climax with risings on Shrove Tuesday, the day before the beginning of Lent, in Dublin, Cork, Tipperary, Limerick, Clare, Queen's (Laoighis), and Louth counties. But a March blizzard and a well-prepared constabulary ensured its failure. Of 169 Fenians tried, 52 were convicted and 110 pleaded guilty. Two of them were sentenced to death and two received lengthy sentences.

Of far greater consequence was a series of Fenian incidents in England. During an attempt to rescue three Irish American colleagues from a police van in February in Manchester, William P. Allen, Michael Larkin, or Michael O'Brien (William Gould) shot and killed a constable.

The execution of all three Fenians made them appear victims of British hate. Eliciting much public sympathy in Ireland, even from the clergy, they became known as the Manchester martyrs. Later in 1867 an abortive attempt to rescue a comrade from Clerkenwell Prison in London resulted in twelve deaths and many injuries from a Fenian dynamite explosion.

In succeeding years Fenianism declined. Stephens, O'Leary, and O'Donovan Rossa were either imprisoned or banished, and O'Mahony died in 1877. American Fenians, beset by personality and policy disputes, were condemned by President Ulysses S. Grant for attacking Canada and for trying to conduct an Irish government in exile. Many members joined the Clan na Gael (founded in 1867) under John Devoy, whose primary mission was to provide financial support for the Irish Republican Brotherhood in Ireland. Although governed by an impressive-sounding Revolutionary Directory in 1877, with representatives from three continents, Fenianism was a spent force.

Nevertheless Fenianism ultimately had profound consequences on the British government. Americans used the Fenian threat on British negotiators to secure a favorable settlement of the *Alabama* claims dispute in 1870, in which the United States sought damages from Great Britain because Britain, despite its declared neutrality during the Civil War, had allowed Confederate privateers, especially *Alabama*, to sail from England. More constructively, Archbishop Henry Manning and Cardinal Paul Cullen urged disestablishment of the Irish Protestant Church on Prime Minister William Gladstone as an antidote to Fenianism. Following the incidents in Manchester and London, Gladstone took up the cause, which received legislative sanction in 1869. Fenianism also influenced Gladstone to pilot passage of the Land Act of 1870, which intruded upon the sacred ground of landlord-tenant relations, providing tenants some protection against arbitrary evictions. Gladstone's nonsectarian universities bill, however, foundered for want of support from the Catholic hierarchy.

Even more significant was the Fenian impact on Irish politics. With an avowed purpose of neutralizing the revolutionary energies of the Left, the Home Rule League, founded by Isaac Butt in 1873, succeeded in attracting Fenians to key positions in its governing body. Another Fenian offshoot was Michael Davitt's Irish Land League, founded in 1879, which sought land nationalization. Within a year it had two hundred thousand members in a thousand branches. Most important, the outrage generated by the Manchester martyrs convinced Charles

Stewart Parnell to take up the Irish nationalist cause. After inheriting the home rule movement from Butt in 1879 and combining it with Davitt's Land League, Parnell launched, with Devoy in America, the "New Departure." It called for a parliamentary solution to nationalist ambitions, while not disallowing the possibility of a revolutionary settlement. A final legacy was provided by the revolutionary Tom Clarke, who, though too young to participate in the 1867 risings, identified himself as a Fenian, signed the Proclamation of Independence during the rebellion known as the Easter Rising of 1916, and became a martyr in its aftermath.

In its two decades of existence, Fenianism, by its emphasis on force, had a strong transatlantic appeal to young Irishmen seeking self-realization through their nation's liberation from England. But its exclusively nationalist ideology lacked a social component, and eventually the actions of "bold Fenian men," however inspirational, gave way to the more practical programs of middle-class politicians.

[See also Easter Rising; Home Rule; Ireland; Irish Nationalism; Irish Republican Army; and Potato Famine, Irish and Scottish.]

BIBLIOGRAPHY

Comerford, R. V. *The Fenians in Context: Irish Politics and Society, 1848–82.* Dublin: Wolfhound Press; Atlantic Highland, N.J.: Humanities Press, 1985. A scholarly study with an exclusive focus on the development of the Fenians within the broader context of Irish society.
Foster, R. F. *Modern Ireland, 1600–1972.* New York: Penguin, 1989. A general history by the foremost Irish historian of the late twentieth century.
Harmon, Maurice, ed. *Fenians and Fenianism: Centenary Essays.* Dublin: Scepter Books, 1968. A series of essays by leading American, British, Canadian, and Irish scholars relating to the Fenian impact on various individuals, institutions, and movements in the nineteenth century.
McCaffrey, Lawrence J. *Ireland, from Colony to Nation State.* Englewood Cliffs, N.J.: Prentice-Hall, 1979. A short general history by the foremost Irish American historian of the late twentieth century.
O'Broin, León. *Fenian Fever: An Anglo-American Dilemma.* New York: New York University Press, 1971. An account of the growth of Fenianism on both sides of the Atlantic, with an emphasis on military affairs.
Strauss, Eric. *Irish Nationalism and British Democracy.* London: Methuen, 1951. An early account that places Fenianism within the larger contexts of the Irish nationalist tradition and the British political system.

JOHN D. FAIR

FILIBUSTERING. Although in the early twenty-first century the English-language term "filibustering" usually refers to lengthy speechmaking in political bodies, it had a different meaning when it came into common usage around 1850. During the 1850s and for years afterward, "filibustering" most often alluded to peacetime private military expeditions against foreign territory in violation of international law and domestic legislation such as the U.S. Neutrality Act of 1818 and Great Britain's Foreign Enlistment Act of 1819. However, the term was elastic. It was used to describe various types of international and domestic belligerence including quasi-public aggressions such as the military campaigns in India of the British East India Company, James Brooke's conquests in Borneo, John Brown's raid to incite a slave rebellion at Harpers Ferry, Virginia, and, occasionally, attempts to obstruct legislation.

Filibustering was an international phenomenon, despite its being associated most often with the United States both in the nineteenth century and by later historians. The term originated in a Dutch word, *vrijbuiter,* for freebooter, and it had French and Spanish derivatives (*flibustier* and *filibustero*). Further, the act of filibustering erupted on several continents in the nineteenth century, with some of the expeditions antedating the coining of the term in English. Because the invasion of Moldavia by the Russian general Alexander Ypsilantis in 1821, the plots in the 1840s and 1850s of the former Ecuadorian president Juan José Flores to invade Ecuador from foreign bases, and some of Giuseppe Garibaldi's 1860s campaigns to unify Italy lacked governmental authorization, they were therefore filibusters. In 1885, Japanese authorities suppressed a filibuster plot against Korea. Dr. Lander Jameson's filibuster to the Boer republic of the Transvaal from Britain's Cape Colony in December 1895 seriously disrupted Boer-British relations in southern Africa and contributed to the tensions leading to the Boer War.

From the beginning of its national history, the United States provided a venue for filibustering. Most U.S. filibusters from the 1790s to the 1820s occurred against either British Canada or Spanish provinces in East and West Florida, Louisiana, and Texas. American filibuster companies in 1836 helped to secure Texas's independence from Mexico, and in the late 1830s thousands of U.S. filibusters joined refugee Canadian revolutionaries known as "Patriots" in unsuccessful filibusters to liberate Lower and Upper Canada from British rule.

In the 1850s, U.S. filibustering expeditions occurred every year, and many other plots failed for lack of resources or because of interference from the U.S. government; U.S. port officials took filibuster recruits into custody, brought filibuster leaders to trial, and seized filibuster troop transports. Many of the 1850s invaders believed in the U.S. expansionist philosophy of Manifest Destiny and hoped to extend their nation's domain, capitalist mores, and democratic political institutions, but other ideologies influenced filibusters, especially beliefs that Protestant Anglo-Americans were racially and religiously superior to the Catholic inhabitants of Latin America. Some filibusters hoped to strengthen the U.S. South's slave labor by either acquiring new territory for plantation labor or, in the case of Cuba, preempting rumored Anglo-Spanish plans to abolish slavery there.

The most prominent filibusters were Narciso López (1797–1851), who had fled to the United States in 1848 after being involved in unsuccessful revolutionary activity in Cuba against Spanish rule, and William Walker (1824–1860), a U.S. citizen. In 1850 and 1851, López embarked for Cuba from U.S. ports with hundreds of men, but he suffered defeat on Cuban soil. López was captured and executed by Spanish authorities during the 1851 attack. Walker conducted an unsuccessful filibuster to Mexico in 1853–1854, and he invaded Central America on several occasions—initially in 1855 when he was under contract to bring reinforcements to a warring faction in a Nicaraguan civil war, subsequently on his own initiative. Walker, whose goal seems to have been the eventual conquest of all Central America, achieved temporary success in 1856. Even though he lacked control of much of Nicaragua's countryside, Walker claimed its presidency on the basis of a fraudulent election. Following his inauguration on 12 July, Walker legalized slavery and altered land laws in a futile attempt to entice sufficient immigrants from the United States to stabilize his regime. At the time, Walker faced armed resistance from Nicaraguan insurgents and other Central American forces, as well as opposition from Great Britain and from the U.S. businessman Cornelius Vanderbilt (whose interests in Nicaraguan transit projects had been damaged by Walker's policies). In 1857, Walker acceded to an agreement negotiated by a U.S. naval officer that called for the filibusters' evacuation to the United States. Walker was executed by Honduran authorities on 12 September 1860, during the last of his several attempts to repossess Nicaragua.

Throughout the nineteenth century, U.S. filibusters suffered high mortality rates from battle wounds, disease, deprivation, and execution following their capture. Nonetheless, during the 1850s filibusters became icons of U.S. popular culture. Not only did filibustering attract extensive press coverage and become grist for congressional and state legislative debate and political party platforms, but novels, poetry, magazine pieces, plays, music, illustrations, and collegiate debating societies all addressed and frequently celebrated filibustering. However, foreign governments and commentators frequently condemned filibustering as piracy and accused U.S. leaders of being complicit in the expeditions, charges that were endorsed by many later historians. Reports of impending U.S. filibusters, even against targets that never were attacked, such as Ireland, many South American states, and the Hawaiian kingdom, induced several states to improve their military preparedness and consider joining defensive alliances such as a proposed Treaty of Union in 1856 among Peru, Ecuador, and Chile. Several Central American governments even deliberated forfeiting part of their sovereignty to European powers in return for assurances of protection against filibustering attacks. Diplomatic disputes from filibustering caused U.S. war crises with Great Britain and Spain over issues including search and seizure in international waters. Filibustering interfered with U.S. enterprise and travel abroad, caused destruction in invaded countries, and left an anti-American legacy in Latin America. Had Walker never attacked Nicaragua, it is possible that the eventual canal across Central America would have been located there instead of in Panama.

U.S. filibustering entered a new phase in the late 1860s and early 1870s with Fenian invasions of Canada. Late nineteenth- and early twentieth-century U.S. filibusters occurred mostly against Mexico, Honduras, and, especially before the Spanish-American War in 1898, Cuba again. As late as the Cold War, long after the original meaning of the word "filibuster" had faded from the American vernacular, U.S. authorities broke up several filibustering plots aimed at islands in the Gulf-Caribbean region.

[*See also* Empire and Imperialism.]

BIBLIOGRAPHY

Brown, Charles H. *Agents of Manifest Destiny: The Lives and Times of the Filibusters.* Chapel Hill: University of North Carolina Press, 1980. The most reliable chronologically organized study of U.S. filibustering in the 1850s.

May, Robert E. *Manifest Destiny's Underworld: Filibustering in Antebellum America.* Chapel Hill: University of North Carolina Press, 2002. An analytical account of filibustering that takes a comparative, international approach to the movement. Although it covers the entire history of filibustering, its focus is on U.S. filibustering in the 1850s.

Stout, Joseph A., Jr. *Schemers and Dreamers: Filibustering in Mexico, 1848–1921.* Fort Worth: Texas Christian University Press, 2002. Especially valuable for its consultation of Spanish-language Mexican sources and its treatment of late nineteenth- and early twentieth-century expeditions. Stout errs, however, in accepting too uncritically foreign accusations that the U.S. government consistently conspired in the expeditions.

Thomson, Janice E. *Mercenaries, Pirates, and Sovereigns: State-Building and Extraterritorial Violence in Early Modern Europe.* Princeton, N.J.: Princeton University Press, 1994. Essential for the international legal ramifications of filibustering, especially in comparison to other categories of nonstate violence.

ROBERT E. MAY

FILM [*This entry includes seven subentries, an overview and discussions of film in China, Japan, South Asia, Latin America, the Middle East, and the United States.*]

Overview

During the course of the twentieth century, film emerged as a central medium of expression and communication, one whose audience has increased dramatically with the advent of videos, DVDs, and cable and satellite television channels. Many aspects of contemporary life are influenced by films and by the fashions, the beliefs, and the ideas they disseminate. Not all films from every part of the world, however, enjoy equal chances of distribution. Although films made in developing countries are benefiting from a broader circulation in the new millennium, and Bollywood, the Hindi-language film industry in India, has become an important center of production, global markets are still monopolized mostly by American films.

Cinema was invented in the three decades preceding World War I. Different contributions, rather than a single invention, allowed films to be shown on the big screen. In the 1890s, Thomas Edison and his assistant W. K. L. Dickinson invented the Kinetograph camera and the Kinetoscope viewing box, which allowed them to make and to show moving photographs. The Kinetoscope was, however, a peephole device. It was the brothers Auguste and Louis-Jean Lumière who invented a projection system that contributed to making cinema the international commercial enterprise that it is in the twenty-first century. The Lumière Cinématographe used 35 mm film and shot films at sixteen frames per second. The brothers made their first film, *Workers Leaving the Factory*, in March 1895, and later in the same month they showed it at a public meeting of the Société d' Encouragement à l'Industrie Nationale in Paris.

The next decade witnessed the transformation of cinema from small businesses in amusement arcades to a global industry. In the United States the steady influx of southern and eastern European immigrants provided a large audience for cinematic entertainment whose predominant character was visual, not linguistic. However, the beginnings of the American movie industry were marred by struggles for patent rights among Edison, whose ambition was to control the American market, and the main firms of the period such as American Mutoscope (later American Mutoscope and Biograph) and Vitagraph. Italian and, above all, French companies, including the Lumière Cinématographe, Pathé, and Gaumont, took a leading position throughout international markets until the outbreak of World War I. The Frenchman Georges Méliès, still celebrated today for his fantasy films, emerged as the most important and innovative director of the period. In the United States, Edwin S. Porter drew upon Méliès's techniques to create the first American story film, *Life of an American Fireman* (1903).

The Early Days in Hollywood. Following the expansion of cinema audiences, the United States soon turned into the largest market in the world, and small movie theaters—called "nickelodeons" because admission was a nickel—spread throughout the country. The Warner brothers, Carl Laemmle, Louis B. Mayer, Adolph Zukor, William Fox, and Marcus Loew, the creators of the Hollywood studio system, all started their careers as nickelodeon owners. Stylistically, films changed rapidly, and the different national industries mutually influenced each other. Movies became longer, their narratives were enhanced by editing techniques and explanatory intertitles, and the camera started to adopt a greater variety of movements.

World War I had a negative impact on European cinema. It drastically reduced French and Italian productions, and the newly founded Hollywood gained a dominant position in global markets. As cinema grew as an art form, editing became more sophisticated, camera movements became more complex, and acting became more varied, crystallizing the filmic conventions that are still used today. D. W. Griffith, with *Birth of a Nation* (1915) and *Intolerance* (1916), was the most significant director of the era, establishing many of the principles of Hollywood filmmaking.

Classical Hollywood narratives were soon challenged by the European avant-garde movements that emerged in the late 1910s and produced films until the early 1930s: French impressionism, German expressionism, and Soviet montage. The need to differentiate their films from mainstream American productions led these European movements to use unconventional techniques that often went against the linear chains of cause and effect that constituted the norm in Hollywood. Films such as *Napoléon* (1927) by Abel Gance, *The Cabinet of Dr. Caligari* (1920) by Robert Wiene, and *Battleship Potemkin* (1925) by Sergei Eisenstein all share a reaction against realism in the direction of an extreme distortion of reality and filmic linearity.

Hollywood firms responded by refining the classical narrative style and by engineering a process of vertical integration that combined production, distribution, and exhibition. From 1920 to 1925, for example, Adolph Zukor, the head of Famous Players–Lasky and its distribution company, Paramount, started to buy movie theaters to ensure wider circulation of his films. The merger between Loew's, Inc. and Metro produced MGM, which followed the same strategy of vertical integration, becoming the second largest company in Hollywood. Paramount and MGM, together with First National, are usually grouped under the name of the "Big Three" because these firms controlled most of the American film industry. The "Little Five"—Universal, Fox, the Producers Distributing Corporation, the Film Booking Office (later RKO), and Warner Brothers—owned fewer theaters or no theaters at all. Finally, United Artists, formed by Mary Pickford, Charlie Chaplin, Douglas Fairbanks, and D. W. Griffith in 1919, was a distribution company for independent films without any theaters or any studios for the production of films.

Expansion in the 1920s and 1930s. Hollywood acquired its monopolistic character with the expansion of major American companies in the 1920s and 1930s. Independent theaters were forced to follow the practice of block booking, which compelled exhibitors to rent films with low box-office appeal if they also wanted the more

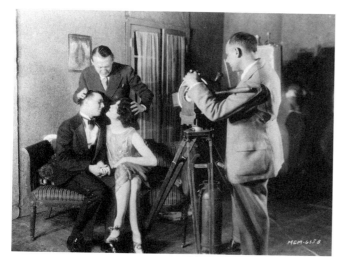

Film Directing. Edmund Goulding, MGM director, making a film with the motion picture class at Columbia University, New York, 1927. PRINTS AND PHOTOGRAPHS DIVISION, LIBRARY OF CONGRESS

successful ones from the same company. According to the American film scholar Thomas Guback, market concentration and anticompetitive behavior are the major features of the American film industry. Block booking is now illegal in the United States, but it is often imposed on foreign exhibitors, creating the American supremacy over the world's markets.

The introduction of sound coincided with the years of the Great Depression and the rise of communist and fascist totalitarianisms in Europe and Asia. It was Warner Brothers that first added music and sound to some of its films between 1926 and 1927. The innovation was soon adopted throughout the world and led to the consolidation and expansion of national industries in Britain, Japan, and India, where sound enabled the full integration of songs and choreographies within the filmic narrative that would become a trademark of Indian film industry.

During the 1930s, the impact of the Depression created many financial difficulties for the big Hollywood companies. However, the production of films continued with the rise of new genres such as the gangster film, film noir, the screwball comedy, and the musical. As the contents of some films became increasingly controversial, the Motion Picture Producers and Distributors Association (MPPDA) established the Production Code (or Hays Code) in an effort to avoid censorship from the outside. The code outlined the moral standards for the depiction of crime, sex, and violence. In Europe, the dictatorial regimes in the Soviet Union, Italy, and Germany took control of cinema, although with different strategies and degrees of censorship. In France, the current of so-called poetic realism focused on the marginal lives of working-class characters, evoking an atmosphere of nostalgia.

The second world conflict had, like the first, a major impact on film industries. European and Asian countries had to be rebuilt from the ruins of the war, and the United States seized the opportunity to assist them financially in exchange for political and military loyalty in the increasingly divided world of the Cold War. Audiences flocked to the cinemas in the first postwar years as never before. Yet by the end of the 1950s moviegoing was declining steadily both in Europe and the United States. The golden age of Hollywood studios had ended, although the American industry created new devices such as the introduction of color and the widescreen format to make movies more appealing.

With the global recovery of the 1950s, governments provided incentives for national cinemas that came to be considered important representatives of national culture.

Movie Poster. Danish poster for Jean Cocteau's *La belle et la bête* (Beauty and the Beast), starring Josette Day and Jean Marais. Nornotryk A/S, 1946. LESTER GLASSNER COLLECTION OF MOVIE POSTERS/ PRINTS AND PHOTOGRAPHS DIVISION, LIBRARY OF CONGRESS

The postwar years saw the emergence of Italian neorealism, an influential movement that eschewed the decorative rhetoric of Fascism in favor of a realistic depiction of everyday events and struggles for survival. In the 1950s Italy became an international center of production with the reconstruction of the Cinecittà studio in Rome; for the number of American films shot there, including *Ben Hur* (1959), it was called "Hollywood on the River Tiber." Developing countries such as India, Mexico, Argentina, and Brazil also consolidated their own industries, and their films acquired more visibility thanks to the festival circuits.

The 1950s and Beyond. By the end of the 1950s a new concept of the filmmaker as auteur encouraged directors to see films as the products of their own personal expression. Throughout the world, "new waves" and "young cinemas," such as the French New Wave and the British Free Cinema, contributed to revolutionizing filmic discourse, challenging past conventions in terms of both techniques and themes. These new waves soon reached the other side of the Atlantic, and a so-called New Hollywood emerged. A generation of young American directors confronted the conservatism of the old studios with films that became part and parcel of the counterculture of the 1960s.

In the face of the conflicts engendered by Cold War politics, cinema became deeply political in the 1960s and 1970s. In Third World countries that had experienced revolutions, such as Cuba and other Latin American countries, documentaries and realistic fictions became the predominant mode. However, this politicization of cinema was soon replaced by more commercial productions as many revolutions failed or became repressive dictatorships in turn.

Between the 1970s and the late 1980s, television and the growth of the home-video market led to a dramatic decline in cinema patronage. The hegemony of the United States after the fall of Soviet Communism is paralleled by the predominance of Hollywood in global markets. Hollywood films have become a new center of attraction for moviegoers also thanks to their pioneering special effects and digital technology innovations. Yet both European art films and the constant development of cinematic traditions in Third World countries continue to constitute powerful alternatives to classical cinema.

[See also Mass Media and Performing Arts.]

BIBLIOGRAPHY

Allen, Robert C., and Douglas Gomery. *Film History: Theory and Practice.* New York: McGraw-Hill, 1985.

Guback, Thomas. *The International Film Industry: Western Europe and America since 1945.* Bloomington: Indiana University Press, 1969.

Hayward, Susan. *Cinema Studies: The Key Concepts.* London: Routledge, 2000.

Miller, Toby. *Global Hollywood.* London: BFI Publishing, 2001.

Nowell-Smith, Geoffrey, ed. *The Oxford History of World Cinema.* Oxford and New York: Oxford University Press, 1999.

Thompson, Kristin, and David Bordwell. *Film History: An Introduction.* New York: McGraw-Hill, 1994.

Trumpbour, John. *Selling Hollywood to the World: U. S. and European Struggles for Mastery of the Global Film Industry, 1920–1950.* New York: Cambridge University Press, 2002.

LUCA PRONO

China

China was among the few countries first exposed to film culture. In August 1896, less than nine months after he invented cinematography, Auguste Lumière sent his assistant to show fourteen film clips in Shanghai. In the spring of 1905, Ren Qingtai, the owner of a photo shop in Beijing, made the first Chinese film, *Dingjun Shan* (Dingjun Mountain), which consisted of several episodes from a Beijing opera. In 1913, Zhang Shichuan and Zheng Zhengqiu codirected the first Chinese feature film, entitled *Nanfu nanqi* (Husband and Wife in Hard Times), in Shanghai.

China. In spite of domestic turmoil, China's film industry grew rapidly in the 1920s. In Shanghai alone there were 141 registered film studios. Sensation and sensuousness were characteristic of this period. Representative of the age was *Huo shao Honglian Si* (Burning the Red Lotus Temple, 1928, directed by Zhang Shichuan), which was such a success that it was followed by seventeen sequels.

From the early 1930s Chinese films began to criticize social injustice. Among the most influential was *Shennü* (Fairy, 1934, directed by Wu Yonggang), a story about the misery of an innocent woman named Ruan Sao (Ruan Lingyu) forced into prostitution. The first Chinese sound film was *Taoli jie* (Calamity of Students, 1934, directed by Ying Yunwei), whose theme song became the national anthem of the People's Republic of China in 1949. In 1937, Yuan Muzhi wrote and directed his influential *Malu tianshi* (Street Angel), a sentimental story about four poor talented artists.

During the Second Sino-Japanese War (1937–1945), many patriotic films were produced. Films like *Babai zhuangshi* (Eight Hundred Heroic Warriors, 1938, directed by Ying Yunwei) eulogized real patriots during the war. Others, like *Mulan cong jun* (Mulan Joins the Army, 1939, directed by Bu Wancang), used legendary characters to promote patriotism.

Soon after the war against Japan, civil war broke out (1945–1949). During this period, the sufferings and resentments of the Chinese people were expressed in film. *Yi jiang chunshui xiang dong liu* (The Spring River Flows East), cowritten and codirected by Cai Chusheng and Zheng Junli in 1947, portrays in two parts a family tragedy against the background of the Second Sino-Japanese War and its aftermath. In the meantime, a few films began to study problems and frustration in ordinary people's daily life. *Xiaocheng zhi chun* (Spring in a Small City, 1949, directed by Fei Mu), for instance, is a story about three intellectuals torn between friendship and love.

After the Communists took over mainland China in 1949 and enforced stern censorship, most films descended to the level of propaganda, but some films were artistically worthy. The most productive period was in the late 1950s and early 1960s, when the filmmakers still shared the innocent enthusiasm for Communism. *Wuduo jinhua* (Five Golden Flowers, 1960, directed by Wang Jiayi), a musical comedy, portrays romantic youth whose love seems to transcend the political boundary. Despite its dutiful ideological preach, *Wutai jiemei* (Stage Sisters, 1965, directed by Xie Jin) truthfully depicts the pathos in the suffering and friendship of two actresses.

The Cultural Revolution (1966–1976) nearly destroyed the Chinese film industry, and radicals persecuted film artists. Many of the artists did not survive the brutal decade. In 1984, however, Chen Kaige's *Huang tudi* (Yellow Earth) heralded a new era of Chinese cinema. In 1987, Wu Tianming's *Lao jing* (Old Well) won three awards at the Tokyo Film Festival. A year later at the Berlin Film Festival, Zhang Yimou won the Gold Bear award for his directorial debut of *Hong gaoliang* (Red Sorghum). In the next decade, Chinese films won hundreds of awards at international festivals.

When they began to make films, the young directors depended heavily on literature. Almost all their internationally acclaimed films of that period, such as *Da hong denglong haohao gua* (Raise the Red Lantern, 1990, directed by Zhang Yimou) and *Banwang bie ji* (Farewell My Concubine, 1993, directed by Chen Kaige), were adaptations of either novels or stories. Zhang Yimou and his comrades, who were mostly graduates from the Beijing Film Academy, are referred to as Fifth Generation directors. Unlike their predecessors, Fifth Generation directors had little sentiment or idealism for Chinese culture. For the first time, they introduced the culture to mass audiences in the West. Though their reinterpretations of Chinese history have been appreciated in the West, they have been criticized in China for selling Orientalism to the West.

Sixth Generation or New Generation directors (from 1989) are mostly apolitical. They seek to capture on film personal emotions and frustrations during a time of industrialization and modernization.

Taiwan. During the Japanese colonial period (1895–1945), all Taiwanese films had Japanese-language sound tracks, and all studios were run by the Japanese. After the Nationalists took over the island in 1948, Taiwan began to make films with Chinese-language sound tracks. Under Nationalist censorship, films made in the 1950s were mostly propagandistic. In the 1960s and 1970s, films about romantic love, martial-art legends, and Confucian paragons of virtue were promoted by the regime as Healthy Realism. Hou Hsiao-hsien, in *Tongnian wangshi* (A Time to Live and a Time to Die, 1985) and *Lianlian fengchen* (Dust in the Wind, 1986), truthfully and painfully presents Taiwan in the process of modernization. Compared with Hou, Edward Yang's films are more Western. His most successful films are *Kongbu fenzi* (The Terrorizer, 1986) and *Gulingjie shaonian sharen shijian* (A Bright Summer Day, 1991).

Hong Kong. In 1913, financed by Asia Film in Shanghai, Li Minwei directed *Zhuangzi shi qi* (Zhuangzi Tests His Wife), but for the next two decades fewer than thirty films were made. The establishment of Shaw Brothers in 1934 ushered in a new era. More than four hundred films were produced between then and 1941. During the Japanese occupation (1941–1945), no films were made in Hong Kong. After the Japanese surrender, many talented filmmakers moved from the mainland to Hong Kong. Among them was Zhu Shilin, whose *Qinggong mishi* (Secret History of the Qing Palace, 1948) was a milestone in Hong Kong film history not only for its artistic merits but also because Mao Zedong criticized it.

In the 1950s Hong Kong produced more than two hundred films annually. In 1967, King Hu directed *Dragon Gate Inn*, which glorified martial arts in China. The establishment of Golden Harvest in 1970 seriously challenged the Shaw Brothers monopoly. Three years later, Golden Harvest succeeded in coproducing with Warner Bros. *Enter the Dragon*, with Bruce Lee as the male lead. In the late 1980s John Woo embellished Hong Kong action films with traditional values in *A Better Tomorrow I* (1986), *A Better Tomorrow II* (1987), and *The Killer* (1989). In 1994 the New Wave wunderkind Wong Ka-wai attracted international attention with his *Chungking Express*.

After Fifth Generation films began to sell on the Western market in the 1980s, some Chinese directors were recruited by Hollywood to make films for a global audience. Among them, Ang Lee from Taiwan and John Woo are the most influential.

[*See also* Chinese Literature.]

BIBLIOGRAPHY

Berry, Chris, ed. *Chinese Films in Focus: 25 New Takes*. London: British Film Institute, 2006.

Berry, Chris, ed. *Perspectives on Chinese Cinema*. London: British Film Institute, 1991.

Berry, Chris, and Feii Lu, eds. *Island on the Edge: Taiwan New Cinema and After*. Hong Kong: Hong Kong University Press, 2005.

Bordwell, David. *Planet Hong Kong: Popular Cinema and the Art of Entertainment*. Cambridge, Mass.: Harvard University Press, 2000.

Browne, Nick, et al., eds. *New Chinese Cinemas: Forms, Identities, Politics*. Cambridge, U.K.: Cambridge University Press, 1994.

Cheng Jihua. *Zhongguo dianying fazhan shi* (The History of the Development of Chinese Cinema). Beijing: Zhongguo Dianying Chubanshe, 1963.

Stokes, Lisa Odham, and Michael Hoover. *City on Fire: Hong Kong Cinema*. London: Verso, 1999.

Teo, Stephen. *Hong Kong Cinema: The Extra Dimensions*. London: British Film Institute, 1997.

Widmer, Ellen, and David Der-wei Wang, eds. *From May Fourth to June Fourth: Fiction and Film in Twentieth-Century China*. Cambridge, Mass.: Harvard University Press, 1993.

Zhu, Ying. *Chinese Cinema during the Era of Reform: The Ingenuity of the System*. Westport, Conn.: Praeger, 2003.

TAN YE

Japan

Japanese film has been one of the most influential of non-Western cinemas, in part because of its perceived differences from Hollywood film. After motion picture apparatuses arrived in Japan in 1896, they were shaped by existing Japanese cultural practices, ranging from such pre-cinematic entertainments as the magic lantern to theatrical arts like Kabuki. Stage actors and directors, such as the early star Onoe Matsunosuke and the director Makino Shōzō, dominated after the first studio was built in 1908, and even *onnagata*, the male actors who traditionally played female roles, were prevalent until the early 1920s. The most notable custom was of the *benshi*, a lecturer or narrator who explained silent films, sometimes even voicing character dialogue and embellishing the story. The popularity of *benshi* was one reason the silent era lasted into the late 1930s in Japan, some ten years later than in America.

Cinema, however, was also deeply tied with the development of modernity in Japan. Authorities often frowned on its new cultural influences, censoring its depictions of crime, sexuality, and politics, and regulating moviegoing by minors until after World War II. Influenced by new realist theater (*shingeki*), intellectuals in what was called the Pure Film Movement attempted to reform the still theatrical Japanese cinema in the late 1910s by elevating its status, eliminating *onnagata*, and introducing the more cinematic editing of Hollywood. The framework for Japanese cinema was largely solidified in the 1920s, especially the primary genre division between *jidaigeki* (period films featuring samurai swordplay) and *gendaigeki* (stories set in the modern era).

From the mid-1920s and for decades thereafter, Japan boasted one of the few industries in the world that could best Hollywood both in the domestic market and in the number of films made annually. The late 1920s and 1930s was the first golden age of Japanese cinema, witnessing the rise of major stars such as Bandō Tsumasaburō and Kataoka Chiezō and the development of a virtuosic cinematic stylistics that, though influenced by foreign examples—especially from France, Germany, the United States, and the Soviet Union—could stand apart from Hollywood norms. This period included the work of the director Ozu Yasujirō (*I Was Born ...* , 1932; *Tokyo Story*, 1953), who broke many of the rules of classical continuity editing; the disorienting camera movements of Itō Daisuke (*Chūji's Travels*, 1927); the monumental long takes of Mizoguchi Kenji (*Osaka Elegy*, 1936; *Ugetsu*, 1953); and the avant-garde experiments of Kinugasa Teinosuke (*A Page of Madness*, 1926).

The coming of sound and the consolidation of an industrialized studio system in the 1930s put limits on such flourishes, as did progressively strict censorship. Leftist film movements such as Prokino were stamped out, and the 1939 Film Law gave the government considerable authority over film companies, power that was used both to promote war propaganda and to restructure and modernize the industry. Ironically, postwar occupation censorship was formally similar to that of wartime Japan, with an ideology of democratic humanism replacing the previous one of devotion to the emperor. With little soul-searching over involvement in the war, older directors merely changed hats, and new filmmakers such as Kurosawa Akira (*The Seven Samurai*, 1954) and Kinoshita Keisuke (*Twenty-four Eyes*, 1954) came to champion the new humanism.

It was the victory of Kurosawa's *Rashomon*, starring Mifune Toshirō, at the Venice Film Festival in 1951 that launched Japan's international film reputation and heralded the second golden age of Japanese cinema, the 1950s, when the movies enjoyed unparalleled commercial popularity at home and considerable critical success abroad. Each of the studios offered a particular brand of cinema: Shōchiku sold melodramas about the urban middle class; Tōhō produced businessman comedies and science fiction films like *Godzilla* (1954); Daiei focused on *hahamono*, about mothers suffering for their children, and art cinema for foreign audiences; Tōei reigned with slick samurai films and chivalrous gangster (*yakuza*) movies; Nikkatsu concentrated on youth romance and the action films of megastars like Ishihara Yūjirō; and Shintōhō offered both erotically grotesque movies and nationalistic war films.

After peaking in 1959, however, attendance suffered a precipitous decline as a result of the rise of television and changing demographics. By the 1970s the studio system had fallen apart, and independent companies, ranging from those created by stars to small-scale pink film (soft porn) producers, constituted the bulk of production. From the late 1950s, young directors such as Masumura Yasuzō began rebelling against the stylistic and social conservatism of their elders, with filmmakers like Ōshima Nagisa and Imamura Shōhei eventually leaving their studios to gain artistic and political independence. The 1960s saw a flourishing of experiment, from the flamboyant B-movies of Suzuki Seijun to the political documentaries of Ogawa Shinsuke and Tsuchimoto Noriaki.

As increasing cultural insularity hampered this new wave, the industry as a whole only suffered further decline in the 1970s as American films—some, like *Star Wars*, openly indebted to Japanese cinema—finally gained dominance at the box office, despite the efforts of new players like Kadokawa Pictures to create media-savvy blockbusters. New directors like Morita Yoshimitsu and Itami Jūzō provided spark with clever satires, but the attendance and reputation of Japanese films among domestic audiences continued to wane, with only animé providing consistent success.

Conditions finally began to turn around in the 1990s with the arrival of a new generation of filmmakers such as Kitano Takeshi (*Hana-Bi*, 1997), Miike Takashi (*Dead or Alive*, 1999), Kurosawa Kiyoshi (*Cure*, 1997), Aoyama Shinji (*Eureka*, 2000), and Kawase Naomi (*Suzaku*, 1997). Genre cinema, such as horror (for example, Nakata Hideo's *Ringu*, 1998), boomed, and the film industry was awakened from its lethargy by threats of foreign capital, government admonishments, and an influx of television money. Given the youth audience's continued adoration of things foreign, it also helped that major filmmakers such as Hou Hsiao-Hsien, Jim Jarmusch, and Quentin Tarantino produced homages to their favorite Japanese filmmakers (Ozu, Suzuki, and Fukasaku Kinji, respectively) and that American producers created remakes of Japanese hits (for example, *Shall We Dance?*, 2004) or ventured to Japan to produce their own films (*The Last Samurai*, 2003). Finally besting foreign films at the box office in 2006, Japanese cinema continued to be productive at home and influential worldwide in the early years of the twenty-first century.

[*See also* Animé.]

BIBLIOGRAPHY

Anderson, Joseph, and Donald Richie. *The Japanese Film: Art and Industry.* Princeton, N.J.: Princeton University Press, 1982. Still the most extensive history of Japanese cinema in English, if a bit dated.

Bordwell, David. *Ozu and the Poetics of Cinema.* Princeton, N.J.: Princeton University Press, 1988. A thorough account of one of Japan's most influential directors; provides a counterpoint to Burch.

Burch, Noel. *To the Distant Observer: Form and Meaning in the Japanese Cinema.* Berkeley: University of California Press, 1979. Burch's thesis about the uniqueness of prewar Japanese film is provocative and significant, if not always convincing.

Desser, David. *Eros plus Massacre.* Bloomington: Indiana University Press, 1988. A broad historical account of the Japanese New Wave from about 1960 to the early 1970s.

AARON GEROW

South Asia

The films made in South Asia—India (which produces more films than any other country in the world), Pakistan, Bangladesh, Sri Lanka, Nepal, Bhutan, and the Maldives—share certain elements, arising from both colonial and Western postcolonial influences, yet are marked by local inflections. The variety is vast; the films represent a wide range of styles, linguistic regions, and genres. Most—particularly the films made in India and Pakistan—use technology from the West to produce a hybrid product that is often described as escapist, vulgar, artificial, imitative, and mediocre. Like commercial films elsewhere in the world, however, whatever genre or genres a given film falls into (for example, historical, musical, adventure, family drama, martial arts), each South Asian film expresses its nation's modern identity. In most cases privately funded and distributed, the products of the South Asian film industry have a broad-based appeal, which in turn makes them useful as instruments to promulgate a national script.

Much of Indian cinema is immediately recognizable for its multigenre form, a distinctive style that combines a Western-style star system with elements of music, comedy, and melodrama that reflect Indian mores. Resisting the trend of salaciousness, Indian films retain the chaste love scenes that Indian cinemagoers prefer and that other conservative regional and neighboring Muslim states expect, thus securing two markets. The complex production process is a heterogeneous mode of manufacture—an assembly of several textual components, such as fight scenes, song and dance, dialogue, and comedy sequences. These units—each of which is essentially a discrete production by a separate professional team—are designed to be knitted together by a story line. They are assembled by the director, who is accountable to a distributor-financier.

Commercial filmmaking and social perspective expressed in a masala ("mix," as of spices) of genres predates modern South Asia. Beginning with the 1896 screening of the first film at Watson Hotel in Bombay (Mumbai), cinema in the region was a capitalist enterprise with potential for insurgency. The silent era, whose mythological features referenced a preindependence call to nationalism, also offered an egalitarian perspective. These themes were evident in the first talkie, *Alam Ara* (1931), which had a dozen romantic songs woven into its story, thus exhibiting the now familiar composite form of South Asian filmmaking.

This basic form has endured, but as economic conditions have improved, the rural poor, once the biggest market for South Asian cinema, are no longer its primary consumers. Exponential changes in theme, location, and format are already in evidence. The productions of Bollywood—the Bombay film industry's challenge to Hollywood's past hegemony—have long been popular in the Middle East, Pakistan, Bangladesh, Africa, and Russia; with prosperity, filmmakers are increasingly responding to a burgeoning diasporic population. For the contemporary expatriate, particularly in New York City, South Asian films—whether produced in Mumbai, Lahore, Peshawar, or Dhaka, in Hindi, Pashtu, Urdu, or Bengali—are readily available and are thus a location of memory and an evocation of home.

[*See also* Mass Media.]

BIBLIOGRAPHY

Nowell-Smith, Geoffrey, ed. *The Oxford History of World Cinema.* Oxford: Oxford University Press, 1996.

Parasher, Prajna Paramita. *Retrospective Hallucination: Echo in Bollywood Modernities.* New Delhi, India: UBS Publishers' Distributors, 2002.

PRAJNA PARAMITA PARASHER

Latin America

In 1896, shortly after audiences across Europe and New York marveled at the first moving pictures, the Lumière Brothers' portable Cinématographe was projecting its wonders all over Latin America. Before the end of the century, young pioneers were readily capturing images of the continent and showing them as an exotic extravaganza. However, while the California-based manufacturers were already churning out thousands of one- and two-reelers

and Italian studios were creating epic features, filmmaking in Latin America was a craft yet to be developed. Between 1908 and 1919 local productions—mainly documentaries and newsreels—began to have a place beside the imports from Europe and the United States. But after World War I the U.S. film industry controlled most film markets and supplied more than 90 percent of the films to the Latin American screens. Lacking technical facilities, directorial know-how, and financial support, local filmmakers could not compete with the general expansion of a consolidated industry and the growing popularity of Hollywood stars.

The moderate output of fictional stories shot in Latin America during the silent period tended to reproduce imported genres, yet with original and local flavor. A hybrid language was emerging in films such as the Mexican *El automóvil gris* (The Gray Automobile; Enrique Rosas, 1919), a serialized story in documentary form, and the Brazilian *Limite* (Boundary; Mario Peixoto, 1929), an avant-garde experience. The contrast between the suburban and rural worlds was depicted in the works of the Argentinean José Ferreyra and the Brazilian Humberto Mauro, and in literary adaptations such as the hit *Nobleza gaucha* (Cowboy Nobility; Eduardo Martínez de la Pera, Ernesto Gunche, and Humberto Cairo, 1915).

The coming of sound opened up an unimaginable opportunity to develop national film industries. With the new technology, an innovative market came to the surface: the Spanish-language talkies.

Sound and the Golden Age. The introduction of synchronized sound in the Latin American film industries gave local producers a certain advantage over Hollywood. Language and culture was on their side, as was the chance to take hold of at least part of the growing domestic markets. Throughout the 1930s, local studios emerged in Argentina, Mexico, and Brazil, many of which rose as keen Hollywood competitors. The rest of the Latin American nations had sporadic film productions but were avid consumers of the novel Latin American genres.

Songs, comedies, and melodramas merged in the new musicals: Argentinean *tangueras*, Mexican *comedias rancheras*, and Brazilian *chanchadas*. By 1933 *Tango* (Luis Moglia Barth) and *Los tres berretines* (The Three Amateurs; Enrique Susini) inaugurated industrial films in Argentina. That was also the role of the hit *Allá en el Rancho Grande* (Out on the Rancho Grande; Fernando de Fuentes, 1936), which opened up the international film trade for Mexico. A Latin American star system was on the way, and by the 1940s it was established with Mexican performers such as Dolores del Río, Pedro Armendáriz,

Mexican Film. María Félix and Pedro Armendáriz in a scene from *Enamorada*, a Mexican film directed by Emilio Fernández and released in 1946 by Panamerican Films, S.A. AGRASÁNCHEZ FILM ARCHIVES

María Félix, Pedro Infante, and Cantinflas; Argentineans such as Carlos Gardel and Libertad Lamarque; the Brazilian star Carmen Miranda; and the Cuban Ninón Sevilla, among many others. Some of them also crossed over to Hollywood but, except for Miranda (whose fruity hat image became an oversimplified icon of "Latin Americanness") and Gardel (whose untimely death made him a cult figure), none equaled their success south of the Rio Grande.

In 1939 Hollywood released 761 films and still dominated between 75 and 90 percent of Latin American screens. Argentina and Mexico, the most prolific local producers, made fifty-one and thirty-five features, respectively. But the effects of World War II would alter such a ratio. Since Mexico aligned with the Allies, and Argentina, conversely, kept a suspiciously neutral stance, Hollywood drastically curtailed the delivery of film stock to Argentina, allowing the Mexican film industry to expand. The impact can be traced in Table 1.

The golden age of Latin American cinema lasted from the mid-1930s to the mid-1950s. National identity and local customs were pitted against the so-called Hollywood

TABLE 1. *Feature Film Production during World War II*

YEAR	MEXICO	ARGENTINA	BRAZIL	CUBA	CHILE
1940	27	49	13	4	4
1941	46	47	4	1	0
1942	49	57	4	1	5
1943	67	34	8	3	3
1944	78	24	9	0	4
1945	79	22	8	0	6

invasion. In a continent struggling between provincialism and industrialization, between tradition and change, emerging national cinemas helped audiences—many of which were illiterate—to understand the ways of the modern world. It was also the time in which Latin American films began to be internationally recognized. The work of the director Emilio Fernández and the cinematographer Gabriel Figueroa, for instance, captured in films like *María Candelaria* (1943), portrayed indigenous themes that both cultivated nationalistic sentiments and pleased international audiences. While the golden age declined, a new seed of a combative cinema was germinating—a cinema of social and political interests that would challenge everything that came before.

Revolutionary Cinema. During the 1950s Italian neorealism had a paramount influence over many young Latin American filmmakers, such as the Argentinean Fernando Birri. A political conscience or the need to document injustices and inequalities dominated the Latin American intelligentsia. Film was established as an ideological weapon of liberation not only from oppressive governments but also from capitalism itself. Therefore Hollywood's commercial cinema, or what was otherwise termed cultural imperialism, came under attack.

A decade later, filmmakers throughout Latin America were responding to the new call. To have cinema serve the transformation of underdeveloped societies required crafting alternative and often marginal modes of production, distribution, and reception. After the triumph of the Cuban Revolution, Julio García Espinosa proposed the making of an "imperfect cinema." Cuba soon became the heart of the novel cinematic culture by creating a vibrant state industry radically different from the Hollywood industrial paradigm. In Brazil Glauber Rocha and the Cinema Novo (New Cinema) movement envisioned an "aesthetics of hunger." In Bolivia the Ukamau Group and Jorge Sanjinés produced a "revolutionary cinema," making the disenfranchised indigenous population its main focus. And in Argentina Fernando Solanas and Octavio Getino conceived a "Third Cinema"—a term that later served to gather all such movements under the same banner. With Salvador Allende's presidency, Chilean cinema became the voice of the Popular Unity coalition that led him to power. Film activists from Venezuela, Colombia, Uruguay, and Mexico also vigorously participated in the groundbreaking movements that were traversing the continent.

Many of the filmmakers who initially rallied around the militant culture and the cinematic experimentation of the New Cinema progressively replaced avant-garde aesthetics with rather more conventional narratives in order to lure larger audiences. The previously underestimated commercialism was pursued later on, and states were compelled to create new policies and establish transnational alliances that would favor a new Latin American film market.

Transnational Film Industries. In 1984 state representatives from Spain, Portugal, and ten Latin American countries met in Madrid and determined that the Ibero-American market was a considerable one to cater to, given approximately 1.2 billion annual spectators. In a market with two principal languages and numerous cultural commonalities, investments in film production and distribution seemed viable and profitable. Moreover, it would be advantageous culturally to place more products against the Hollywood machine.

Several marketing agreements have been signed since that meeting. However, the instability of state support in the different nations has made it quite difficult to maintain a single regime of production and exchange. New monetary regulations during the 1980s and the impact of the end of the Cold War during the 1990s tripled in a decade the budget of an average feature. Additionally, many of the institutions that supported film production were dismantled. In 1990, for instance, Brazil's Embrafilme was closed down by the Fernando Collor administration as part of a master plan to privatize state-owned enterprises. And the Mexican president Salinas de Gortari, in accordance with International Monetary Fund free-market policies, reduced state participation in the film industry.

By the mid-1990s a confluence of national film laws and transnational alliances with Europe and the United States contributed, nonetheless, to a "new wave" or "renaissance"

TABLE 2. *Box Office for Internationally Successful Latin American Films*

FILM	PRODUCTION	U.S.A.	SPAIN	UK	WORLDWIDE
Central Station	Brazil, 1998	$5,595,428		£210,552	Aprox. $21m
Amores Perros	Mexico, 2000	$5,383,834	1,298,049	£361,485	$20,908,467
Nine Queens	Argentina, 2000	$1,221,261	2,254,571	£262,726	$12,413,888
Y tu mamá también	Mexico, 2001	$13,622,333	1,190,241	£980,438	$33,616,692
The Son of the Bride	Argentina, 2001	$624,153	7,229,043		
The Crime of Father Amaro	Mexico, 2002	$5,709,616	1,401,432		$26,996,738
City of God	Brazil, 2002	$7,563,397	910,518	£2,371,159	$27,387,381
Carandiru	Brazil, 2003	$213,954			$10,781,635
Maria, Full of Grace	U.S./Colombia, 2004	$6,517,198			$12,450,821
The Motorcycle Diaries	Brazil et al., 2004	$16,756,372		£2,255,536	$57,641,466

SOURCES: www.imdb.com; *Variety International Guide* (London: Faber and Faber, 2002 and 2003); www.boxofficemojo.com; Andrew Paxman, "Crossover Dreams," *Variety* 374, 10 May 1999.

of Latin American cinema that has continued into the twenty-first century. In 2003 fifty-three features were released in Argentina—the highest output in fifty years—and Brazil premiered forty films, more than doubling the amount of the year before. Conversely, Mexico, the only country to have achieved a production of over a hundred features per year in the past, reached its lowest figure since the silent period in 1997, producing only seven films. And although by 2002 the figure had doubled, President Vicente Fox's state policies continually deferred cinematic ventures.

Large U.S. production companies have entered the region through alliances with local film industries. Spain has participated in dozens of Ibero-American coproductions and maintains official agreements with many Latin American nations. Such enterprises evidently entail the cultivation of an international audience for Latin American films, as the profits of some of the most successful features illustrate (see Table 2).

The strategic alliances with U.S.- and Spanish-based media conglomerates are representative of the new synergic dynamics that chiefly put in motion the current output of commercial cinema in and about Latin America. With local film industries still weak and in many cases dependent on state subsidies, Latin American film production in the early twenty-first century was certainly more prolific than it had been a decade earlier. However, beyond national incentives, transnational cooperation through globalized channels has definitely changed the geography of what we used to call Third Cinema.

BIBLIOGRAPHY

Chanan, Michael. "The Changing Geography of Third Cinema." *Screen* 38, no. 4 (1997): 372–388. Special Latin American issue. The article presents part of the theoretical debate over Third Cinema in the Anglo world. The issue itself provides several articles on different aspects of Latin American cinema.

Getino, Octavio. *Cine y televisión en América Latina: Producción y mercados.* Santiago, Chile: LOM Ediciones, 1998. A thorough study of the Latin American film and television industries during the 1980s and 1990s.

King, John. *Magical Reels: A History of Cinema in Latin America.* New ed. London: Verso, 1990. A comprehensive overview of the different national cinemas of Latin America.

King, John, Ana M. López, and Manuel Alvarado, eds. *Mediating Two Worlds: Cinematic Encounters in the Americas.* London: BFI, 1993. A collection of essays that offers new insights about past Latin American cinemas and highlights current debates in the field.

Shaw, Lisa, and Stephanie Dennison, eds. *Latin American Cinema: Essays on Modernity, Gender, and National Identity.* Jefferson, N.C.: McFarland and Company, 2005. Explores modern and historical topics from a contemporary perspective.

Usabel, Gaizka S. de. *The High Noon of American Films in Latin America.* Ann Arbor, Mich.: UMI Research Press, 1982. A well-researched history of the film industry in Latin America in relation to Hollywood's interests in it, from the silent period to the 1950s.

LUISELA ALVARAY

The Middle East, North Africa, and Central Asia

Encompassing a great swath of geography, history, and culture, the Middle East, North Africa, and Central Asia are home to three dominant languages: Arabic, Turkish, and Persian. Some countries with a cinematic tradition, most notably Lebanon, Syria, and Israel, are not discussed in this article. However, the three largest countries in terms of film audience and output, Egypt, Turkey, and Iran, are especially emphasized, in terms of state involvement, audience, and artistic developments. Also under consideration is the emergence of "auteur cinema," from North Africa to Central Asia, as the alternative presented to the global commercial dominance of Hollywood, which also exercised great influence in the region from the 1920s onward.

The Middle East: Egypt, Turkey, and Iran. In Egypt, the pioneering silent filmmaking period in the late 1920s and early 1930s was not the work of amateurs. Most of these pioneers had an illustrious background in theater, including Aziza Amir (producer of and lead actress in the first full-length feature, *Layla*, 1927). With the introduction of sound, and awash in profiteering capital produced by World War II, the postwar Egyptian film industry became firmly planted. The most successful producers of this period, such as Togo Mizrahi and Anwar Wagdi, relied heavily on a domestic star system, often freely blending musical, melodramatic, comic relief, and dance genres to produce extravagant spectacles. Beginning in the early 1960s the Egyptian film industry was nationalized. The period of state ownership, while commonly praised as producing many of the golden age classics of Egyptian cinema (including Henri Barakat's *The Sin*, 1965; Salah Abu Seif's *Cairo 30*, 1966; Hussein Kamal's *The Postman*, 1968; and Youssef Chahine's *The Land*, 1970), is also widely criticized for its inefficiency and eventual bankruptcy. The slump did not continue for long however. Along with the advent of color, the industry rebounded in the 1970s with the explosive growth of the videocassette market. New stars such as Adil Imam popularized a wave of farcical urban comedies for the young male market now supplanting the middle-class family audience of a decade earlier. In a divergent direction, "auteur cinema" also emerged during this period with the steady rise in the international reputation of Youssef Chahine, who often coproduced his films in other Arab countries in order to escape bureaucratic and censorial control over his work at home. By the 1990s other directors had made a name for themselves as constructors of unique cinematic visions, such as Sherif Arafa's political thematic (*Terrorism and Kebab*, 1992) and Daoud Abdel Sayed's social commentaries (*Kit Kat*, 1991).

Turkish film production, which began in earnest with the shortages of foreign films during World War II, soared in the 1960s as Hollywood withheld its movies in retaliation for quotas and taxes imposed by the state to promote local industry. Production rose from around one hundred films in 1961 to a peak of nearly three hundred by 1972. Production levels strained to meet the local demands of nearly three thousand theaters and 15 million viewers. Unlike Egyptian films, which netted half of their proceeds from foreign returns, and thus slumped in the 1960s as regional demand receded, domestic exhibition in Turkey met the needs of the local industry. Like Egypt, producers were capital poor and financed films through advances from distributors; this led to a similar star system as well as melodramatic, action, and comedic genres. Migration was the source of a new audience as well as a source for new movies, such as Şerif Gören's *Yol* (1981). The new urban migrants swelling the cities and theater audiences preferred a new generation of directors, such as Metin Erksan (*Dry Summer*, 1963), and Yilmaz Güney (*Friend*, 1974) over the pioneering generation of Muhsin Ertuğrul; as well as new stars such as Cüneyt Arkin and Türkan Şoray. The 1970s saw a slump with the rise of the video market, and the liberalizing policies of the 1980s caused a flooding of the domestic market by American films. In the early 2000s Turkish theaters numbered in the hundreds, with production at around fourteen films per year. New "auteur cinema" emerged, as well as cinema by Turks in Germany. Some notable examples are Ertem Eğilmez (*Arabesk*, 1988; *Propaganda*, 1999), and Yeşim Ustaoğlu (*Journey to the Sun*, 1999).

Local cinematic production in Iran did not begin in earnest until 1948, when Mitra Film Company and Pars Film Studio started operation. Starting from the 1950s documentary cinema has been used as elsewhere in the region as an instrument of nation-building and defining national identity. In the 1970s Iran, like Turkey and Egypt, faced increasing competition from American movies, overtaxation, and widespread bankruptcy; as a result, theaters declined and audiences departed. Like these two other countries the new audience was dominated by the recent rural migrants and urban poor. This audience preferred the formulaic melodramas and comedies and especially the tough-guy film genre (*Luti* in Iran, *Kabadai* in Turkey, *Futuwa* in Egypt) as popularized by Masud Kimiai's *Gheisar* (1969) and played by such actors as Mohamad Ali Fardin, and Nasser Malekmotei. With the revolution in 1979, much of the earlier cinema was purged and banned. As in Morocco, emerging in the postrevolutionary period in Iran were two distinct cinemas, a populist commercial private-sector cinema, accounting for the majority of production, and a smaller art cinema, implicitly critiquing social conditions, with partial state funding and support, limited in output, but garnering much of the international acclaim. The Farabi Cinema Foundation (established 1983) has moved to restrict imports, lowered taxes, and facilitated bank loans to help the local industry even as it has moved to open the door to privatization. Production soared from a low of fifteen films in 1982 to a high of sixty-four in 1998, at a time when Turkish and Egyptian output plummeted in comparison. In 1990, 230 Iranian films were exhibited in 78 international film festivals, and earned 11 prizes. Although this cinema was at times criticized as being elitist, xenophilic, unpatriotic, and un-Islamic, what captured the attention of audiences is its sense of humanism, with depictions of self-sacrifice, selfless altruism, empathy, and optimism, along with a distinct visual style that is minimalist in dialogue and filled with uninterrupted long-shots. Some directors of note in the new wave "auteur cinema" are Dariush Mehrjui (*The Tenants*, 1985); Abbas Kiarostami (*Life and Nothing More*, 1992); and Rakhshan Bani Etemad (*Nargess*, 1991).

North Africa: Algeria, Tunisia, Morocco. While independent Algeria had more theaters than any other Arab country, most of these were clustered in segregated urban centers, catering largely to the non-Arabic-speaking French colonist audience. Algerian cinema was born of the eight-year war of liberation, seeking to define Algerian identity in the struggle against "the other." It was state-owned and -directed from its inception until the early 1990s. The armed struggle for liberation was the first main theme explored, as best exemplified by Mohammad Lakhdar-Hamina's *Chronicle of the Years of Embers* (1975). This was followed in 1977 by the box office success of *Omar Gatlato* by Merzak Allouache. *The Citadel* (1986) by Mohammad Shuikh and *Louss, warda al-rimal* (1989) by Rachid Benhadj are more recent examples. The downturn in the exhibition sector and the audience abandonment of the theater in favor of video during the 1970s, as well as the outbreak of civil war in 1991, dealt a blow to the already weakened industry.

Tunisian cinema, as opposed to state-inspired Algerian cinema, emerged partially subsidized by the state as well as by foreign contributions, as an intimate and individualistic "auteur cinema." The foundations of this cinema reach back to strong amateur roots before independence. Tunisia has promoted the Kelibia Amateur Film Festival (1964) and the Carthage Film Festival, for every two years since 1966. Even though local production is limited to no more than three films per year, limited by the small market and domestic venues, Tunisian cinema has carved out a niche within the international film festival circuit, gathering acclaim for *Senjane* (1974) and *Aziza* (1980) by Abdellatif Ben Ammar, *The Sultan of the City* (1992) by Moncef Dhouib, and *A Summer in La Goulette* (1996) by Férid Boughedir.

Two cinemas have emerged in Morroco. In the 1970s two filmmakers came to prominence, Abdallah Mesbahi (*Silence, No Entry*, 1973; *Where Are You Hiding the Sun*, 1979) and Souheil Ben-Barka (*A Thousand and One Hands*, 1972; *Amok*, 1982; *Lombre du pharaon* [Pharaoh's Shadow], 1995). The former represented popular commercial cinema, often modeled after Egyptian films, and the latter a more intellectual style, which has been fostered for domestic audiences as well as for acclaim in international circles. State support became active in the late 1980s and 1990s, administering a fund to support local production. In the early twenty-first century, internationally acclaimed films include Daoud Aoulad-Syad's *The Wind Horse* (2002), Faouzi Bensaïdi's *A Thousand Months* (2003), and Narjiss Nejjar's *Cry No More* (2003).

Central Asia. Film production in the Soviet Union was nationalized by Vladimir Ilich Lenin's decree of 1919, and administered by the state film company (GOSKINO), until perestroika abandoned this system in 1986 and allowed the release of hundreds of hitherto banned films. Central Asian production during the Soviet era was dominated by didactic documentaries, in spoken Russian, reproducing Marxian "Orientalism" by starkly dichotomizing between Communist progress and the "backward" Muslim population. By the 1990s, with the collapse of the Soviet Union and the emergence of newly independent states, film production in Central Asia abandoned the "epic" genre in favor of developing a sociological and psychological

approach toward their characters. The new talents emerging in Kazakhstan included Rashid Nugmanov (*Yahha*, 1986; *The Needle*, 1988) and Darezhan Omirbayev (*Shilde* [The Summer Heat], 1988). In Kyrgyzstan, Tolomush Okeyev and Bolotbek Shamshiyev pioneered production with their documentaries, and more recently Aktan Abdykalykov coproduced with France *The Adopted Son* (1998). In Tajikistan, Anvar Turayev dealt with Stalinist repression on collective farms in *Bol lyubvi* (The Pain of Love), 1990.

[*See also* Art, *subentry* The Middle East, North Africa, and Central Asia; *and* Mass Media, *subentry* Radio and Television in the Middle East and North Africa.]

BIBLIOGRAPHY

Hafez, Sabry. "Shifting Identities in Maghribi Cinema: The Algerian Paradigm." *Alif: Journal of Comparative Poetics* 15 (1995): 39–80.

Leaman, Oliver, ed. *Companion Encyclopedia of Middle Eastern and North African Film.* New York: Routledge, 2001.

Naficy, Hamid. "Iranian Cinema under the Islamic Republic." *American Anthropologist*, n.s., 97, no. 3 (1995): 548–558.

Nichols, Bill. "Discovering Form, Inferring Meaning: New Cinemas and the Film Festival Circuit." *Film Quarterly* 47, no. 3 (1994): 16–30.

Pruner, Ludmila Zebrina. "The New Wave in Kazakh Cinema." *Slavic Review* 51, no. 4 (1992): 791–801.

Sadoul, Georges. *The Cinema in the Arab Countries: Anthology Prepared for UNESCO.* Beirut, Lebanon: Interarab Centre of Cinema & Television, 1966.

Shafik, Viola. *Arab Cinema: History and Cultural Identity.* Cairo, Egypt: American University in Cairo Press, 1998.

MAGDY EL-SHAMMAA

The United States

In 1893, Thomas Edison's lab introduced the Kinetoscope, a box with a peephole that allowed a single patron to observe a moving image. The Kinetoscope became a popular novelty in the United States for a short time, but inventors quickly turned their focus toward perfecting a device that could project a moving picture before a full audience. In 1895 the Lumière brothers (Auguste Marie Louis Nicholas Lumière and Louis Jean Lumière) in France introduced such a device, dubbed the Cinématographe, and in the United States, Edison popularized a projector he called the Vitascope. This competition between Edison and the Lumière brothers also extended to filmmaking. Edison built a studio in New York City in 1900, where he brought vaudeville performers and animal acts to be filmed. Meanwhile, the Cinématographe, smaller and lighter than the Vitascope, allowed the Lumière brothers greater mobility, and they produced films of men and women in their daily lives, public ceremonies, and travelogues.

Within a few years, entrepreneurs began to open theaters devoted exclusively to exhibiting moving pictures. These early theaters, collectively known as "nickelodeons," expanded rapidly around the United States. Nickelodeon managers designed programs for broad appeal and would string together melodramas, slapsticks, sporting events, and travel films, each about fifteen to twenty minutes long. The assortment of films and cheap admission attracted large audiences, and theaters multiplied throughout the country at an astonishing rate. By 1910 there were, by some counts, ten thousand nickelodeons in the United States, and within a decade the number doubled.

Though nickelodeon theaters were available in nearly every town in the United States, the theatergoing experience was not the same for all Americans. Theaters differed by town, state, and region. Throughout the Jim Crow era, Southern movie theaters legally separated white and black patrons. In larger theaters, blacks entered from a side entrance and were required to sit in the balconies, separate from white audiences below. In neighborhoods that were heavily segregated, black and white moviegoers patronized separate theaters altogether. Segregated movie theaters continued until the 1960s when the civil rights movement forced theaters to integrate.

Improving the Product. The move away from nickelodeon theaters began in the early 1910s when theater owners began exploring means to expand their business by attracting the patrons of legitimate theater. To achieve this end, theater managers exhibited lengthier films that were comparable to theatrical productions and they also upgraded their venues.

D. W. Griffith's *The Birth of a Nation* (1915) was one of the first full-length American films and also one of the most controversial. The film, which portrayed the Ku Klux Klan as Southern heroes after the Civil War, was vigorously protested by the National Association for the Advancement of Colored People. Nevertheless, *The Birth of a Nation* was a major success. In New York City one theater charged two dollars for admission, and the film ran for nearly a year. The exhibition of full-length features proved that there was a considerable middle-class audience for moving pictures.

Another means of attracting upscale audiences was to cultivate the theatergoing experience. Theater owners began building expansive picture palaces in which the theater was as prominent as any film production in it. These theaters outdid one another with lobbies with flowing fountains, crystal chandeliers, marble columns, statues, and tapestries throughout. The auditorium of the Fifth Avenue Theater in Seattle, built in 1926, duplicated the throne room of the Imperial Palace in Beijing's Forbidden City at twice the original scale. Not to be outdone, Kansas City's Midland Theater purchased the Oriental Room from the Vanderbilts' Manhattan townhouse and had it reassembled in their women's lounge. Although the most swanky picture palaces were reserved for large urban areas, even small-town theaters were expanded and adorned. The era of picture palaces provided the trappings of wealth for largely middle-class patrons.

During this period, movies also switched from silent films to "talkies." Before sound films, movie theaters typically provided live musical accompaniment. This ranged from a simple player piano in small theaters to orchestras of fifty or more in larger venues. Then, in 1927, Warner Brothers released *The Jazz Singer*, which was the first feature film to include prerecorded musical numbers as well as spoken dialogue. Audience enthusiasm for the new technology, as well as the cost savings of dropping in-house musicians, convinced many theater owners to invest in new sound equipment. The switch to sound films was abrupt. Just three years after *The Jazz Singer* was released, prerecorded sound became standard for all feature films.

The Studio System. During the 1930s and 1940s a handful of film studios dominated the film industry. The five largest were Paramount, Loews (which owned Metro-Goldwyn-Mayer, or MGM), Warner Brothers, Twentieth Century–Fox, and Radio-Keith-Orpheum (RKO), and three prominent but smaller studios were Columbia, Universal, and United Artists. These studios had a major impact on the industry both in the United States and abroad. They accounted for 90 percent of American film production and 60 percent of film production around the world.

The studios achieved dominance by controlling three areas of the film business: production, distribution, and exhibition. Studios owned the equipment and the accommodations to produce films, and they maintained exclusive contracts with the creative personnel. MGM's stable of stars, for example, included Katharine Hepburn, Clark Gable, and James Stewart. Studios also controlled the distribution process. They oversaw a system in which films opened first at the prestigious picture palaces, where the majority of profits were made, before being shipped to smaller markets. Last, studios had a strong hand in film exhibition because they owned many of the first-run theaters in large markets. By overseeing the production, distribution, and exhibition of films, a few studios were able to define the film industry during this era.

Intervention and Competition. Yet the singular place of movies in the leisure and entertainment industry was not to last. Ticket sales crested just after World War II, and shortly thereafter the industry witnessed a precipitous drop that did not stabilize until the mid-1970s. Several factors help explain the sharp decline during this period.

First, the studios lost a federal antitrust suit in 1948 and were forced to modify their business practices. Studios dropped some of their onerous distribution processes and were divested of their theater holdings. Loews, for example, retained ownership of the theaters and spun MGM into a separate corporation. Second, the middle class fled cities for new suburban neighborhoods, leaving behind the prominent and expensive picture palaces. Studios were ill-prepared for the shift from urban to suburban markets. Last, the introduction of television in the 1950s gave baby boomers another reason to stay home and eschew the movies. In response to shifting demographics and new competition, the film industry explored new ways to distinguish its product.

New Hollywood. Starting in the 1950s the film industry began producing and marketing films for more narrow segments of its audience. Hollywood tapped into the teen market with the success of *The Blackboard Jungle* and *Rebel without a Cause*, both released in 1955. Hollywood immediately recognized the value of aiming films specifically for this audience, and teenagers have remained a prominent focus of the film industry ever since. Another example of Hollywood's gearing products toward a segment of the public was so-called blaxploitation cinema, produced and marketed for urban African Americans. This genre began in earnest in 1971 with the release of *Sweet Sweetback's Baadasssss Song* and *Shaft*, both action films with African American lead characters fighting against a corrupt, predominantly white, system. Though segmenting its audience helped keep some of the studios afloat, the industry as a whole was suffering a financial crisis that lasted until the mid-1970s when a handful of films reoriented the industry toward the production of blockbusters.

In 1975, Universal released Steven Spielberg's *Jaws*. The studio was optimistic about the film's potential revenue; it was based on a best-selling novel, and the studio stoked anticipation with a heavy promotional campaign. Still, *Jaws* succeeded far beyond expectations, earning $129.5 million, becoming one of the highest-grossing films of the decade. More significantly, *Jaws* became a cultural phenomenon, spurring a national shark craze that lasted all summer. *Jaws* revealed that through marketing and promotion, studios could manufacture an "event film" that resulted in blockbuster revenue.

Two years later, George Lucas released the science-fiction film *Star Wars*, a film that further extended the notion of a cinematic phenomenon. Not only did the film go on to become one of the most lucrative in history, but it also taught studios the power of merchandizing. Hollywood had always capitalized on movie stars' popularity, but not to the extent that *Star Wars* did: it became a movie franchise. As a result of the film's popularity, Lucas licensed toys, clothes, food, novels, trading cards, comic books, posters, and more. The success of films such as *Jaws* and *Star Wars* shifted the focus in the film industry. Hollywood studios began both to produce fewer films each year and to focus more on producing a few blockbusters that could offset less successful films. Studios also began to develop film franchises on which they could capitalize with merchandise and sequels.

Since the 1980s, new technologies have made movies even more accessible. VCRs, DVD players, cable and satellite television, and the Internet have given consumers far more options for selecting and viewing films. Yet the contemporary film scene continues to reflect the lessons it gleaned in the 1970s, marketing some films toward segments of its audience, while simultaneously developing massive event films. In this way, cinema has come full circle. A medium that began the twentieth century as a cultural phenomenon has discovered how to manufacture cultural phenomena every year.

[*See also* Disney; Leisure; Los Angeles; Mass Media; *and* Westerns.]

BIBLIOGRAPHY
Balio, Tino, ed. *The American Film Industry*. Rev. ed. Madison: University of Wisconsin Press, 1985.
Fuller, Kathryn H. *At the Picture Show: Small-Town Audiences and the Creation of Movie Fan Culture*. Washington, D.C.: Smithsonian Institution Press, 1996.
Gomery, Douglas. *Shared Pleasures: A History of Movie Presentation in the United States*. Madison: University of Wisconsin Press, 1992.
Harpole, Charles, ed. *History of the American Cinema*. 11 vols. New York: Charles Scribner's Sons, 1990–2003.
Maltby, Richard. *Hollywood Cinema*. 2d ed. Malden, Mass.: Blackwell, 2003.

SHANNY LUFT

FINANCE, INTERNATIONAL. *See* Banking, International.

FINLAND. Despite the prevalence of a non–Indo-European language, Finland had been bound to Sweden politically and culturally since the fourteenth century. Sweden's disastrous war of 1741–1743 with Russia damaged Finland and engendered Finnish nationalism. In the late eighteenth century, Finland experienced explosive population growth as peasant farmers claimed virgin lands. The Swedish king Gustav III's regime of enlightened absolutism granted lands to Finnish peasants. The early Romantic movement inspired a new interest in Finnish folk culture among the small elite. These political, cultural, and demographic developments stirred a separatist sentiment. The American Revolution inspired Georg Magnus Sprengtporten, who had served with the French in that conflict, but he left the separatist movement leaderless when he accepted a Russian military commission in 1786. Separatism revived among the minuscule community of the Finnish nobility when the Swedish king launched an attack on Russia in 1788. Gustav still commanded the loyalty of the Finnish peasantry, however, and a quick armistice ended the threat.

Under Russian Rule. In the Napoleonic Wars, Gustav IV Adolf clung to a British alliance and refused to enter the Continental System established by Napoleon. Napoleon's allies Denmark and Russia declared war on Sweden in 1808. Russia overran Finland and annexed it at the Peace of Frederikshamn (1809). Tsar Alexander I, as Grand Duke of Finland, appointed Sprengtporten governor-general. The Finnish estates met at Borgå in 1809 and persuaded Alexander that all the members of the Committee for Finnish Affairs should be Finns. The governor-general appointed by the grand duke would run a council that oversaw extant Finnish courts and departments.

Finland was a favored province for most of the nineteenth century. Alexander ordered large-scale public works projects. Nicholas I (r. 1825–1855) founded a new university in Helsinki after fire devastated the old university of Åbo in 1827. Most important, Russia favored Finnish culture and language over Swedish. The first political newspaper in Finnish was founded in 1823. Elias Lönnrot made five journeys through Finland, Lapland, and northwestern Russia collecting fragments of the Finnish epic poem *Kalavala*. He published a first edition in 1835, then published its present form of twenty-three thousand lines in 1849. Russia imposed a tariff on Swedish goods in 1817 and substituted the Russian currency system in 1840. The Saimaa Canal opened in 1856 and linked Saint Petersburg with the forests of eastern Finland. By the 1860s Finland's population had reached 1.6 million.

Alexander II (r. 1855–1881) brought more reforms in appreciation of Finland's quiescence when Poland exploded in violence in 1863. The tsar allowed the Diet to meet every five years. Finland gained its own currency and bank in 1865–1866. Finland had a small self-defense force, and the Russian military draft exempted Finns. By 1890, Finnish was the preferred language in schools.

Russian leniency receded in the reign of Nicholas II (r. 1894–1918). The tsar feared Finnish nationalism and distrusted Sweden, which favored Germany. In 1898 he appointed Nikolay Bobrikov governor. The February Manifesto of 1899 reserved power in matters affecting Russian interest for the grand duke and gave legislative authority to the Russian Imperial Council. The conscription law of 1901 dissolved the Finnish army, making Finns eligible for Russian conscription. Five hundred thousand Finns signed a petition of protest against the manifesto. When fewer than half of the draftees reported in 1902, Russia substituted a tax for military service. Bobrikov introduced compulsory Russian-language instruction in girls' schools. Matters grew worse when the tsar granted Bobrikov dictatorial powers and deported his principal opponents. On 16 June 1904, Eugen Schauman shot and killed Bobrikov and then committed suicide.

The Bobrikov years spawned several political movements that became parties. The Old Finns, mostly clergy and rich farmers, supported cooperation with the authorities. The Young Finns, led by Pehr Evind Svinhufvud, believed that constitutional rule was paramount. Swedish speakers from the lower classes backed him, as did the Social Democratic Party, founded in 1899. In nonindustrialized Finland—only 15 percent of Finns lived in cities in 1910—the Social Democrats linked city workers and rural peasants.

In 1905 a strike in Helsinki led by the Social Democrats mirrored the Russian general strike of that year. The Social Democrats rode the Russian revolution of 1905 to become the largest party in Finland. The tsar's ministry presented the Diet with a new constitution that created the most democratic parliament in Europe and gave Finnish men and women aged twenty-four and above the vote. However, the ministers were not dependent on the Diet, and the grand duke still had veto power. Svinhufvud presided over a fragmented chamber that passed virtually no constructive legislation before World War I.

Finland. The harbor of Helsingfors (Helsinki), 1890s. PRINTS AND PHOTOGRAPHS DIVISION, LIBRARY OF CONGRESS

War and Independence. Most Finns hoped for a German victory in World War I. Anger grew toward Russian war profiteers, who seemed to be exploiting Finland's raw materials. The government called advance elections for a Diet that was supposed to convene when the war concluded. Few Finns turned out to vote except the committed supporters of the Social Democrats, who gained unexpected power with the Russian revolutions of March and November 1917. Svinhufvud served as prime minister and named Gustaf Mannerheim, a Finn who had volunteered for the Russian army in 1887 and risen to the rank of lieutenant general, to command a new Finnish army.

The pro-German stance of Svinhufvud and Mannerheim caused a revolt in 1918 by Finnish Communists backed by the remaining Russian troops. The Communists seized control of the southern half of the country, while the government fled north. Mannerheim built a force from farmers of the Bothnian coast threatened by the landless proletariat, supporting the effort with credit from Helsinki banks and aid from Sweden. In bloody fashion Mannerheim moved south, then onto the Karelian Isthmus, where he ousted the Russians by April 1918. The rump Diet made Svinhufvud regent. There were eight thousand executions, and more than twelve thousand of the seventy thousand prisoners died. The defeat of Germany finished Svinhufvud's proposal of a monarchy. Mannerheim succeeded as regent, but the elections returned an Eduskunta—the unicameral parliament that superseded the Diet in the 1919 constitution—dominated by the Left and moderate republicans. The constitution established a strong presidency, and the assembly chose Kaarlo Juho Ståhlberg over Mannerheim as president. The land reform of 1922 broke up the large estates and distributed land to peasants. Industrialization, though late to reach Finland, began to accelerate.

The Great Depression brought a swing to the right. Svinhufvud won the presidency and appointed Mannerheim as head of the Defense Council in 1931. Former White Guards and disaffected youth formed a fascistic Lapua movement, named after an Ostrobothnian town. Its violence shocked even its sympathizers, who supported government action to suppress the movement in 1932. By the late 1930s Finland had recovered from the Depression and finally integrated the Social Democrats into the government.

Finland feared the Soviet Union and maintained a large military between the wars. But when the Soviet Union began to demand concessions in October 1939, the government believed that Moscow was too weak to launch an attack. The Soviets began to bomb Helsinki on 30 November 1939 after a stage-managed border incident.

The Soviet Union set up a puppet government and brought back six thousand Finnish Communists from exile. Significantly, the Communists inside Finland failed to support Stalin, and the parties came together to oppose the Soviets. On the long northern frontier with few roads or railroads, Finnish soldiers on skis held back larger Soviet forces. On the Karelian Isthmus, the Mannerheim line held until 14 February. Finland hoped in vain for foreign intervention. Only volunteer troops from Norway and Sweden aided its cause. The so-called Winter War killed or wounded almost one-third of the Finnish troops. The Treaty of Moscow moved the southeastern border to the 1721 lines, sacrificing Vyborg and the land north of Lake Lagoda. The islands in the Gulf of Finland were lost, and the Soviet Union "leased" the Hanko Peninsula. Finland relocated 12 percent of its total population in a short time.

The Soviets continued to interfere in Finnish politics and encourage Communism. Mannerheim secretly committed Finnish troops to the Nazi side. In June 1941 they occupied Karelia, but Mannerheim would not allow troops to continue into the Soviet Union proper or to besiege Leningrad with the German army. He halted a Finnish advance to cut the railroad line to Murmansk out of fear of Allied reaction. Britain severed relations with Finland in August 1941 and declared war at the end of the year.

By early 1943, Finland was looking to leave the war. Mannerheim became president in August 1944 and signed an armistice with the Soviets in September that restored the 1940 borders and agreed to pay reparations, disarm and expel any German soldiers in Finnish lands, and lease a naval base at Porkkala. In March 1945, Finland declared war on Germany. The government tried and imprisoned some wartime leaders.

The war had devastated Finland, but Swedish and American loans staved off economic collapse. Finland paid its reparations mainly in metal goods, which had the effect of expanding its industrial sector. The Communists had some electoral success at first, but the Socialists fought them bitterly in trade unions and blocked the Communists from taking over their party. A pact of 1948 pledged Finland to a defensive alliance but did not require military occupation by the Soviets. Finland stuck to strict neutrality, leaning to the Soviet side. It refused to condemn Soviet actions in 1956 in Hungary, and the Soviet Union returned the Porkkala base. Finland traded freely with the West and began rapid industrialization, though timber remained the mainstay of its exports. The northern countries established a free labor market in 1954, and this benefited Finland.

The Soviet-mandated policies of strict neutrality and a small military allowed Finland to dedicate its resources to economic development and productive spending on transport, health, and education. Finland became a world leader in electronics, with Nokia cell phones being a particular success. The World Economic Forum hailed Finland as the most competitive nation in the world. After the Eastern European revolutions of 1989 and the collapse of the Soviet Union in 1991 loosened Finland's ties to Russia, it became the strongest advocate of the European Union in northern Europe. It joined the EU in 1995 and was a charter member of the euro currency in 2002.

[*See also* Russia, the Russian Empire, and the Soviet Union; *and* Sweden.]

BIBLIOGRAPHY
Alapuro, Risto. *State and Revolution in Finland*. Berkeley: University of California Press, 1988.
Engman, Max, and David Kirby, eds. *Finland: People, Nation, State*. London: Hurst, 1989.
Jussila, Osmo, Seppo Hentila, and Jukka Nevakivi. *From Grand Duchy to a Modern State: A Political History of Finland since 1809*. Translated by David and Eva-Kaisa Arter. London and Carbondale, Ill.: Hurst, 1999.
Myllentaus, Timo. *The Gatecrashing Apprentice: Industrialising Finland as an Adopter of New Technology*. Helsinki, Finland: University of Helsinki Press, 1990.
Paasivirta, Juhani. *Finland and Europe: The Early Years of Independence, 1917–1939*. Edited and translated by Peter Herring. Helsinki, Finland: SHS, 1988.
Polvinen, Tuomo. *Imperial Borderland: Bobrikov and the Attempted Russification of Finland, 1898–1904*. Translated by Steven Huxley. Durham, N.C.: Duke University Press, 1995. Finnish original published in 1984.
Singleton, Fred. *A Short History of Finland*. 2d ed. Cambridge, U. K.: Cambridge University Press, 1998.
Upton, Anthony F. *The Finnish Revolution, 1917–1918*. Minneapolis: University of Minnesota Press, 1980.
Vehwiläinen, Olli. *Finland in the Second World War: Between Germany and Russia*. Translated by Gerard McAlester. New York: Palgrave, 2002.

C. EDMUND CLINGAN

FIREARMS. *See* Arms, Armaments, and the Armaments Industry.

FIRESTONE RUBBER CORPORATION. Founded in 1900 in Akron, Ohio, by Harvey Firestone, Firestone grew through association with the Ford Motor Company in 1905 and profits from both world wars. In the 1920s England began to regulate the international rubber market, prompting Firestone to secure its own rubber plantations in Liberia. Recruiters paid village chiefs for annual quotas of rubber tappers. Charges of forced labor in the 1920s led to the resignation of both Liberia's president and its vice president. As one of two sources of natural rubber on the Atlantic, Liberia's strategic importance inspired the U.S. government to help Firestone construct an airfield there in 1940 and secure a million acres for plantations, from which it shipped raw sap to its Akron factory. Firestone continued to rely on Liberian forced laborers, who were exempt from Liberian labor laws.

The rubber industry limited domestic agriculture in Liberia, making it reliant on imports. Firestone monopolized commercial crop exports, road construction, and banking and currency through its Bank of Monrovia. Firestone also had plantations in Singapore and synthetic-rubber factories in the United States, Canada, England, Switzerland, Spain, South Africa, New Zealand, India, Argentina, Brazil, and Venezuela. In 1936, Firestone, General Motors, and Standard Oil created National City Lines, which converted streetcar systems to gasoline-powered bus lines in forty-five U.S. cities by 1949. Firestone was a Fortune 500 company in the 1950s, but it was hurt by a shrinking tire market, product defects, scandals, and the loss of GM's business. In 1981 the Akron plant closed, and in 1988 Bridgestone acquired Firestone.

[*See also* Liberia *and* Rubber.]

BIBLIOGRAPHY

Lief, Alfred. *The Firestone Story: A History of the Firestone Tire and Rubber Company.* New York: Whittlesey House, 1951.

KATHRYN BARRETT-GAINES

FIRST INTERNATIONAL. *See* International, First.

FIRST NATIONS. Until the beginning of the nineteenth century, the First Nations in Canada were in large part able to coexist with the Europeans who settled among them, and even profit by their unique role in the fur trade. However, a series of changes during the nineteenth century had dramatic impacts on the First Nations, as they were confronted by economic deprivations, the loss of most of their lands, and a government-led systematic effort to assimilate them through the suppression of their culture. For the most part these efforts at assimilation failed, and by the late twentieth century the First Nations were reasserting themselves, arguing for self-government and pressing land claims, though with only occasional successes.

Coexistence. The early relationship of the First Nations to the European colonizers revolved around commerce, and in particular the fur trade. Unlike the British thirteen colonies, New France was a commercial colony, and did not have any interest in widespread European settlement. Though New France would be formally transferred to the British in 1763 after the Seven Years' War, a similar situation would exist in western Canada in the early nineteenth century with the Hudson's Bay Company. Since both New France and the Hudson's Bay Company sought trade instead of settlement, the First Nations could engage in profitable trading with the Europeans while retaining control over a majority of their land. Indeed, the First Nations were crucial to the success of the fur trade, and were valued commercial partners. They were able to benefit from these commercial interactions by trading plentiful furs for goods that they could acquire only from the Europeans. The fur trade constituted not only an economic interaction, but also a social one. As Sylvia Van Kirk has shown, widespread intermarriage between European traders and First Nations women was a critical component of the fur trade society. Such marriages were an important part of cementing trade relations with particular tribes, placing First Nations women in the important role of cultural liaisons. As well, these women embraced European goods and technology that made their lives easier and saw such marriages as a route to a richer material life. The experiences of these women demonstrate the extent to which the First Nations were not simply passive receivers of European goods and culture, but were active agents who influenced how the experience of European contact would shape their lives.

Another important aspect of the First Nations–European relationship in the eighteenth century was war. During the many conflicts between the British and the French, and later the British and the Americans, the First Nations were valuable military allies, providing needed manpower and vital assistance. Prior to and during the War of 1812, for example, the First Nations allies of the British were central to the defense of Upper Canada (now Ontario), as demonstrated by the Shawnee leader Tecumseh. Though these wars did result in serious dislocation of certain tribes and significant casualties, as long as they were viewed as useful allies by the Europeans, the latter had an important reason to ensure the survival of the former.

Assimilation. From the early nineteenth century the position of the First Nations changed dramatically. The normalization of Anglo-American relations after the end of the War of 1812 eliminated the need of the British for First Nations allies. In addition, the fur trade declined in the face of large-scale migration that created a significant demand for agricultural land. This process, which was in full swing in central Canada from the 1820s, spread to western Canada in the 1860s and 1870s, with the discovery of gold in British Columbia in the late 1850s signaling a rapid decline of the fur trade in that region. Once the focus of the British and later Canadian governments shifted to settlement, the First Nations went from being valued allies and trading partners to being seen as merely in the way of European settlement. The British and Canadians negotiated a series of treaties in which the First Nations surrendered their lands to the government in exchange for smaller parcels of lands they could live on (reserves) and promises of monetary assistance. While the promises were routinely ignored, these treaties, including the Numbered Treaties of 1871–1921, which covered western and northern Canada, facilitated the widespread settlement of the country. Disease and poverty also continued to reduce the First Nations population, which included the extinction of an entire tribe, the Beothuk of Newfoundland (though unlike other cases such as the Tasmans of Australia, their extinction was not the result of deliberate genocide). These developments did provoke hostile reactions, and the Métis, a mixed-race people descended from European fur traders and First Nations women, rebelled against the Canadian government in 1869–1870 and again in 1885, though on both occasions the rebellions were suppressed.

In addition to acquiring the lands of the First Nations, the British and later Canadian governments adopted a policy of assimilation from the mid-nineteenth century onward. The aim was to transform the First Nations into Canadians through the degradation of their culture and way of life. The means by which this was to be achieved has been referred to as the "policy of the Bible and the plough" (Miller, 2001). Christian missionaries played an important role in suppressing traditional religious and cultural activities of the First Nations, who were also strongly encouraged to settle in place and become farmers, a process that facilitated the acquisition of most of their land. These efforts reached an apex in the residential school system of the late nineteenth and twentieth centuries. Run by Christian churches, these schools removed First Nations youth from their family and community, forbade the use of their own languages, and attempted to assimilate them into Canadian culture, an effort that was at least partially successful. These schools were also the scene of widespread physical, emotional, and sexual abuse, and the residential school system has been accused by some First Nations groups of practicing what amounted to cultural genocide. The last residential school closed in the 1990s, and subsequently the Canadian government formally apologized for the abuses that took place and offered a compensation package to its victims.

Confrontation. From the middle of the twentieth century, the First Nations of Canada have increasingly become politically active in defending their interests and asserting their rights. An important turning point was a 1969 White Paper by the Canadian government, which argued that the problems facing the First Nations were due to their special status under the Indian Act, as opposed to being the result of poverty, broken government promises, and racism. This White Paper generated a strong negative outcry from the First Nations, who argued in favor of their special status within Canada, and it was subsequently dropped. At the same time, the First Nations were organizing politically, including the formation of the National Indian Brotherhood in 1968 (renamed the Assembly of First Nations in 1982), which represented all First Nations other than Inuit and Métis. These new political organizations looked outward for international links with other indigenous groups, and argued that together they constituted a Fourth World of oppressed and colonized peoples.

An important focus for First Nations' groups in recent decades has been advancing land claims, either on the basis of a formal claim to lands unlawfully seized from them, or on the basis of unfulfilled promises undertaken by the Canadian government as part of earlier treaties. Some progress has been made in resolving land claims, including the James Bay and Northern Quebec Agreement of 1975 and the creation of the territory of Nunavut in 1999. In many other cases, though, agreement has not been reached, and progress toward resolution has been slow and on some occasions fraught with conflict. The most famous confrontation over land claims occurred when the town of Oka in Quebec attempted in 1990 to expand a golf course onto lands that the Kanesatake Mohawk claimed were an ancient graveyard. An attempt by police to arrest protesters resulted in gunfire and the death of a police officer, and the Canadian army was then mobilized to confront the protesters. The ensuing two-month standoff saw other First Nations groups blockading bridges across the Saint Lawrence River in support, and though the protesters eventually ended their occupation of the golf course, the expansion was canceled. Other conflicts between First Nations and police over land claims have occurred at Ipperwash in 1995 and Caledonia in 2006.

Another focus of First Nations groups has been the push for self-government, and since the 1970s, they have made some gains in winning self-government, such as securing some control over education. In large part, though, the goal of self-government has not been achieved. When the Meech Lake Accord, a package of constitutional reforms, was negotiated between the federal government and the provinces in 1987, it contained provisions for declaring the province of Quebec a distinct society, but no acknowledgment was given of the right of the First Nations to self-government. The First Nations strongly opposed the agreement, and a First Nations member of the legislature of the province of Manitoba, Elijah Harper, was able to help scuttle the agreement by not allowing it to pass by unanimous consent. A subsequent package of constitutional reforms, the Charlottetown Accord, did recognize that the First Nations had an inherent right to self-government, but this agreement was defeated in a referendum and never adopted.

Despite the moderate gains achieved by the First Nations in the latter part of the twentieth century, significant problems remained. Poverty was endemic on many reserves, and racism had not been entirely overcome. Indeed, the push for self-government had been complicated by the recognition that without outside financial assistance the First Nations would be largely incapable of dealing with the issues that confronted them. Significant progress remained to be achieved to overcome the legacy of the policies directed at the First Nations by the British and Canadian governments.

[*See also* Aborigines, Australian; Canada; Native Americans; *and* Native Peoples.]

BIBLIOGRAPHY

Coates, Ken, ed. *Aboriginal Land Claims in Canada: A Regional Perspective.* Mississauga, Ont., Canada: Copp Clark Pitman, 1992. Contains articles on the status of land claims in each region of Canada and reproduces a number of important historical documents.

Fisher, Robin. *Contact and Conflict: Indian-European Relations in British Columbia, 1774–1890.* Vancouver: University of British Columbia Press, 1977.

Miller, J. R. *Skyscrapers Hide the Heavens: A History of Indian-White Relations in Canada.* 3d ed. Toronto: University of Toronto Press, 2001. One of the best works on the history of the First Nations in Canada.

Miller, J. R., ed. *Sweet Promises: A Reader on Indian-White Relations in Canada.* Toronto: University of Toronto Press, 1991. Includes a series of articles that cover a wide range of topics and historiographical themes.

Ray, Arthur J. *Indians in the Fur Trade: Their Role as Trappers, Hunters, and Middlemen in the Lands Southwest of Hudson Bay, 1660–1870.* Toronto: University of Toronto Press, 1974.

Van Kirk, Sylvia. *"Many Tender Ties": Women in Fur-Trade Society in Western Canada, 1670–1870.* Winnipeg, Man., Canada: Watson & Dwyer, 1980. An important work that brings questions of gender into the discussion of the fur trade and its impact on the First Nations.

WESLEY FERRIS

FIRST WORLD WAR. *See* World War I.

FISHING INDUSTRY [*This entry includes two subentries, an overview and a discussion of the fishing industry in East Asia. See also* Cod Fishing *and* Whaling.]

Overview

By 1750 commercial fishing was a global industry with a long history. Commercial fishing boats sailed the seas and oceans of the world and often exhibited adaptations and features particular to the cultures that created them and the conditions under which they fished. Since 1750 much of the history of commercial fishing has been a story of globalization and mechanization. However, modern-day commercial fishing remains a diverse enterprise and can encompass activities as small as a single man in a small nonmotorized boat with simple lines or traps, as large as enormous fleets of mechanized steel ships employing hundreds, or as terrestrial as aquaculture, or fish farming.

One of the first technological innovations to drastically change the face of commercial fishing after 1750 was the development of practical steam engines for boats, developed in the 1790s and early 1800s. This innovation not only led to the gradual substitution of steam power for sails but also to the adoption of steam-powered winches, which allowed for a significant increase in the size and weight of fishing gear. Simple fishing lines with few hooks were replaced by longlines, capable of bearing hundreds or thousands of hooks. A similar process occurred with fishing traps or pots. The size of fishing nets also increased dramatically, especially after the process of net making became mechanized and early twentieth-century developments in synthetic fibers allowed for the creation of longer-lasting nets that would not rot when exposed to the elements. Steam power would, in turn, be gradually replaced by internal combustion engines in the twentieth century, enabling further increases in the size and weight of fishing gear, even for smaller vessels.

Developments in industrialization and mechanization also allowed for other innovations in the commercial fishing industry. In the late 1940s the British introduced the factory trawler, a very large fishing vessel designed to both harvest and process fish yields while at sea. Technological innovations on shore, such as canning in the early nineteenth century and refrigeration and freezing in the later nineteenth century, not only allowed commercial fishing ships to remain at sea for a longer period of time but also

Fishing Industry. Cod and halibut catch. Photograph by W. B. Miller, before 1927. Frank and Frances Carpenter Collection/Prints and Photographs Division, Library of Congress

opened up new markets for seafood, thereby encouraging more fishing. By the second half of the twentieth century many commercial fishing fleets had also adopted further technologies such as sonar, initially developed for military use during World War II.

Not all commercial fishing vessels have undergone such dramatic technological transformations, however. While these types of high-tech enterprises are common in Europe, North America, China, Japan, Russia, and other powerful nations that compete in a global fishing economy, commercial fishing in poorer countries and regions has developed in other ways. Operating at a local rather than a global level, these commercial fishing vessels typically employ a combination of traditional and modern fishing practices and technologies. While their yields are significantly smaller than those of larger commercial fisheries, these industries often constitute a very important source of food to the regions that they service.

Given the ever-increasing demands for seafood and the expanding abilities of commercial fisheries to meet these demands, it is perhaps not surprising that many

of the ocean's fish stocks became subject to overfishing. Beginning in the 1970s dramatic declines in popular food fishes such as the northeast Atlantic herring, northern Atlantic cod, West African sardines, Peruvian anchovies, South Atlantic pilchard, and Irish Sea sole began resulting in the economic collapses of the commercial fishing industries associated with these catches. In 2006 the journal *Science* reported that, globally, one-third of fish populations were operating at population levels of less than 10 percent of their maximum levels, a level that biologists refer to as population collapse. Marine biologists have also reported that, in addition to the impact overfishing has had on the fishing industry, the species-specific population declines have left gaps in the food chains of marine ecosystems, leading to dramatic population changes not just within popular food fish but throughout a wide spectrum of marine life.

Attempts to reverse or slow this trend have been difficult, owing largely to the international nature of the world's oceans and the profits to be made from commercial fishing. Many nations have attempted to offer solutions, however. In 1972 Iceland set an important precedent by becoming the first nation to claim a border of fifty miles (extended to two hundred miles in 1975) around its shores. Within this border, other nations' commercial fishing fleets were disallowed and Icelandic fleets were to operate under rules designed to limit overfishing. By 1983 enough nations had followed Iceland's example that the United Nations established the Law of the Sea, an agreement under which all countries gained exclusive rights to the waters extending two hundred miles from their shores.

Such restrictions, though designed to protect marine environments and the economic security of commercial fisheries, have not gone unchallenged. Regulations like the Law of the Sea have instigated particular concern from large commercial fisheries, as these limitations greatly restrict the yield potentials of large, expensive fleets designed to take in substantial yields and travel long distances. As a result of these new restrictions, many of these fisheries have been forced to replace these costly vessels with smaller, less efficient ships. As evidenced by international incidents like the "Cod Wars," a series of conflicts over fishing rights between Great Britain and Iceland that resurfaced periodically between 1958 and 1976, diplomatic conflicts between nations have also arisen over attempts to control or limit commercial fishing.

One proposed solution to the combined problems of overfishing and high market demand for seafood is aquaculture, often popularly known as fish farming. A practice that has ancient and global roots, many varieties of aquaculture experienced a worldwide decline in popularity in the nineteenth century, as the technological improvements adopted by commercial fisheries made aquaculture a less efficient and less cost-effective method of obtaining fish and other aquatic products. However, as maritime commercial fisheries began confronting population collapses and environmental restriction laws, aquaculture once again became an attractive option. While critics of aquaculture have voiced concerns regarding the ethical treatment of fish raised through aquaculture and the potential for environmental pollution posed by this practice, aquaculture is now more popular worldwide than ever, especially in China, for species such as shrimp and salmon.

[See also Cod Fishing and Whaling.]

BIBLIOGRAPHY

Clover, Charles. *The End of the Line: How Overfishing Is Changing the World and What We Eat.* New York: New Press, 2006.

Food and Agriculture Organization of the United Nations. *The State of World Fisheries and Aquaculture, 2006.* Rome: Food and Agriculture Organization of the United Nations, 2007.

Goodrich, Frank B. *Man upon the Sea; or, A History of Maritime Adventure, Exploration, and Discovery, from the Earliest Ages to the Present Time.* Whitefish, Mont.: Kessinger, 2007.

Hannesson, Rögnvaldur. *The Privatization of the Oceans.* Cambridge, Mass.: MIT Press, 2004.

SKYLAR M. HARRIS

East Asia

This section covers the history of fisheries in East Asia since 1750.

China. Mainland China is famous for aquaculture, with a history of 2,500 years and about 4,940,000 acres (20 million hectares) of freshwater bodies producing more than 20 million tons a year, mainly Chinese carp cultured in ponds, lakes, and reservoirs in the Huang, Chang, and Zhu river basins. Pond culture as well as inland fisheries have been a sideline occupation of small-scale farmers as an integral part of the farming system using fish, pigs, birds, rice, and vegetables.

Fishing grounds in the Yellow Sea (Huang Hai) and East China Sea were dominated by the Japanese and pirates before World War II. After independence, there were three distinct periods: the first period (1949–1958), from independence to the pre–Jinmin Kosha era, saw less than 2.7 million tons of production; the second period (1958–1977), the Jinmin Kosha era, saw production of 2.7 to 5 million tons; and the third period, after 1978, saw rapid development of fisheries as a result of economic liberation policies. Seaweed culture extended for more than 808 miles (1,300 kilometers) from the port city of Dalian to Fujian Province, and fisheries production increased from 5 million tons to 45 million tons and made China the number one fishing nation in the world. Since 1986, China has exported a large amount of fish and cultured kelp, eel, and shrimp to Japan. A new fisheries law enacted in 2000 put in place a major policy change from expansion to zero growth.

Japan. Before 1750 aquaculture in Japan was limited to oysters, carp, and goldfish. After the Meiji restoration of 1868, Western technologies were imported to develop salmon and trout culture; eel, snapping turtle, pearl, and shrimp culture were also developed. Japan exported aquaculture technologies to China and Korea during the colonial period. Since the 1960s, both marine ranching for resource enhancement and aquaculture have been encouraged.

Fish marketing became popular in the late eighteenth century along with the development of marine transportation. Traditional marketing has dealt with dried, smoked, salted, fermented, and seasoned boiled seafood, as well as fertilizer. Ornamental fish, fish paste, canned fish, frozen, fresh, and live fish and shrimp, fish oil, fishmeal, fertilizer, and drugs became part of modern fish marketing.

The code of conduct of the Tokugawa Shogunate in 1615 included the first fisheries law; its principles have been succeeded by the Fisheries Law of 1948. After the Meiji restoration in 1868, the government took an industrial fisheries promotion policy and imported Western technologies like whaling and trawling. In 1906 the first powered fishing boat, *Fuji Maru*, was built. Skipjack pole-and-line fishing became popular in the late 1920s in southern waters before World War II.

After the war, tuna and skipjack fisheries recovered quickly. After the U.S. occupation ended in 1952, government policy focused on expansion from coastal to offshore and from offshore to distant-water fisheries. Long-line fishing methods for distant-water tuna were also transferred to Taiwan and Korea. As a result, Japan, Taiwan, and Korea dominated distant-water tuna fisheries in the world. This policy of expansion was successful until the oil crisis of 1973. Since then, oil price hikes, increases of fish imports resulting from free trade movement and yen appreciation, development of the third United Nations Convention on the Law of the Sea (UNCLOS III), rising wages, and lifestyle changes have resulted in Japan's fisheries' becoming less competitive. Fisheries production decreased from more than 12 million tons in the 1980s to less than 6 million tons in 2002.

Korea. In the late eighteenth century in Korea, many species of fish were dried, salted, smoked, and fermented for the market. In 1876, Korea opened its ports to foreign vessels, resulting in the development of several fishing methods, including stow net, hand trawl, and triangular set net. Beginning in 1910, Japan colonized Korea, which it used as a food supply base, and dominated Korean fisheries, which increased production from 70,000 tons in 1911 to 2 million tons in 1937. A dual structure— with industrial fisheries of Japanese fishers and subsistence fisheries of Korean fishers—resulted in the stagnation of fisheries after World War II.

In 1948 the newly established Korean government took over fisheries development policy, but the Korean War broke out in 1950. The Lee Line (Lee Seung-man Line Declaration) was established to protect fisheries resources from Japan in 1952. After the cease-fire agreement in 1953, the government subsidized fisheries with foreign assistance. A marine port authority was established in 1955 and promoted fisheries. Based on the First Five-Year Economic Development Plan of 1962, fisheries were modernized. The Lee Line was lifted at the establishment of the Korea-Japan Fisheries Agreement in 1965, and the government promoted far-sea fisheries using reparations from Japan, fisheries cooperation funds, and other international assistance.

In 1966 a fishery agency was established, and fisheries production increased from 935,000 tons in 1970 to 3,659,000 tons in 1986. However, production has been stagnant since 1987 because of the phaseout of North Pacific fisheries. In 1996 the Ministry of Maritime Affairs and Fisheries was established to integrate marine-related functions scattered among thirteen agencies.

Issues. Fisheries issues include resource depletion, overinvestment, overfishing, illegal fishing, environmental degradation of coastal waters, and withered seashore. Issues on aquaculture include water pollution, red tide, disease, drug and chemical use, and food safety and traceability. Further, Japan, Korea, and Taiwan face issues of low fish prices, high costs, conflict with other marine interests, depopulation in fishing villages, effectiveness of public investment, the role of fisheries in society, responsible fisheries, and sustainable fisheries.

[See also Food, *subentry* East Asia; *and* Whaling.]

BIBLIOGRAPHY

Kuroda, Takeya. "Aquaculture in China." In *Fisheries in the World* (in Japanese), edited by Tadashi Yamamoto and Shigeaki Shindo, vol. 2, no. 1, pp. 83–96. Tokyo: Japan International Fisheries Research Society, Overseas Fisheries Cooperation Foundation, 1999.

Matsuda, Yoshiaki. "History of Fish Marketing and Trade with Particular Reference to Japan." Proceedings of the IIFET 2000, July 10–15, 2000, Corvallis, Oregon. http://oregonstate.edu/Dept/IIFET/html/publications.html.

Matsuda, Yoshiaki. "The Japanese 'Type 1 Common Fishery Right': Evolution and Current Management Problems." *Resource Management and Optimization* 8, nos. 3–4 (1991): 211–226.

Shindo, Shigeaki. "China's Strategy on Fisheries in the 21st Century" (in Japanese). 2005. http://www.jifrs.org/.

Shindo, Shigeaki. "Fisheries in China." In *Fisheries in the World* (in Japanese), edited by Tadashi Yamamoto and Shigeaki Shindo, vol. 2, no. 1, pp. 49–82. Tokyo: Japan International Fisheries Research Society, Overseas Fisheries Cooperation Foundation, 1999.

Shindo, Shigeaki. "Fisheries in China and Its Management." In *Fisheries Management in the World* (in Japanese), edited by Tadashi Yamamoto and Shigeaki Shindo, pp. 561–589. Tokyo: Japan International Fisheries Research Society, Overseas Fisheries Cooperation Foundation, 1994.

Tokimura, Muneharu, Hideo Ohtaki, and Daiei Kim. "Fisheries in Korea." Overseas Fisheries Cooperation Foundation *Kaigyokyou* (Resource), no. 157, pp. 1–97. Tokyo, 1998.

YOSHIAKI MATSUDA

FIVE-YEAR PLANS, CHINESE. At the heart of the Chinese planned economy during the Maoist era was the concept of the five-year plan: the planned production, distribution, and pricing of commodities without relying on market mechanisms. Planning allowed China to suppress mass consumption and channel resources into rapid industrialization as well as other social priorities, such as education and health care, by regulating the availability and prices of agricultural and consumer products. China at first used yearly plans until the end of the Korean War in 1953 and the establishment of agreements with Moscow on aid. It began implementing its first five-year plan that year and, although less important, continues to formulate them in the early twenty-first century.

The first Five-Year Plan, directed by the ambitious but cautious economic planner Chen Yun (1905–1995), lasted from 1953 to 1957. This first plan was based on the Soviet model of economic growth, which diverted the agricultural surplus to finance the development of heavy industry and capital-intensive projects. The Soviet Union helped China establish some 150 such projects across the country and dispatched over 10,000 advisers. The Chinese sent almost 28,000 students to the Soviet Union for training, including the future leaders Jiang Zemin and Li Peng. From the first plan on, the statistics associated with the plans were dubious and highly politicized because the legitimacy of the Chinese Communist Party and socialism were at stake. According to the State Statistical Bureau, the first plan's already unrealistic targets were "overfulfilled," with industrial output growing by nearly 100 percent and agricultural output by about 25 percent. Despite such problems, the first plan was successful in raising output and did increase life expectancy, expand primary-education enrollment, and improve real wages.

The second Five-Year Plan began in 1958 with modest increases in production targets, but came under attack from Mao Zedong, who had already concluded that the Soviet model was inappropriate for China. As a result, the plan was significantly altered, particularly during the Great Leap Forward (1958–1960). In the aftermath of the disastrous Great Leap Forward and the ensuing famines, China implemented yearly plans, completing the second plan as late as 1965. These plans were also a reflection of the times, particularly the decision to expend precious resources building "third line" factories deep in the Chinese hinterland, where, Chinese leaders hoped, they would be safe from attack by Chiang Kai-shek's (Jiang Jieshi's) Nationalist forces on Taiwan and the United States.

The third (1963–1967), fourth (1971–1975), and fifth (1976–1980) Five-Year Plans were similarly undermined by disruptive mass campaigns and their aftermaths during the Cultural Revolution (1966–1976). With the death of Mao and the end of the Cultural Revolution in 1976, China recommitted itself to more stable planning. But planning became less important after 1978 with the reemergence of Deng Xiaoping, the introduction of market reforms, and the lifting of price controls, that is, moves away from a centrally planned economy. Nevertheless, China continues to issue five-year plans.

[*See also* Planning, Economic.]

BIBLIOGRAPHY

Howe, Christopher, and Kenneth R. Walker. *The Foundations of the Chinese Planned Economy: A Documentary Survey, 1953–1965.* London: Macmillan, 1989.

Riskin, Carl. *China's Political Economy: The Quest for Development since 1949.* New York: Oxford University Press, 1991.

KARL GERTH

FIVE-YEAR PLANS, SOVIET. The fundamental aim of the ruling Communist Party in the Soviet Union was to establish an alternative to the capitalist free-market economy, which they as Marxists considered the root of exploitation, deep cyclical changes, and "anarchy." These theoretical origins of Soviet economic planning from nineteenth-century German socialism were combined with the practical experience from the regulated economies in World War I. In the 1920s, the Soviet leadership founded Gosplan, the state committee for planning, as a central organization that was to coordinate over time and space all the economic activities in the country (investment, production, distribution, finance, consumption, and so on). Gosplan elaborated annual as well as five-year and fifteen-year plans. Gosplan's detailed directives were adopted as laws. Industrial ministeries and firms were required to fulfill the plan targets set by Gosplan and its regional and local representatives.

The first Five-Year Plan for 1928–1932 met great difficulites; the plan targets were arbitrarily changed, and overinvestment took place so that bottlenecks and deficits occurred. The forced collectivization of agriculture led to diminishing harvests in 1931 and 1932, and a catastrophic famine in 1933. The final result was that few of the original targets were achieved. The Soviet leaders set out a more sensible, second Five-Year Plan (1933–1937) that was to assimilate the investment and accomplish reasonable growth rates. The third Five-Year Plan (1938–1942) formulated a balanced development path but soon had to take into account urgent defence considerations.

The most secret sections of Soviet five-year plans were the industrial mobilization plans, whereby the whole economy (industry, transport, distribution, and labor market) was prepared to switch from peacetime targets to the changing requirements of the armed forces in case of war. The third Five-Year Plan was interrupted by the German invasion in 1941. Immediately, the Soviet economy was geared over to wartime plans. Many conversions from civilian to military production had been prepared in advance; others were improvised because of the unexpected initial advances of the German army.

The rapid industrialization of the USSR in the 1930s was, at the time, seen as evidence of the robustness of economic planning. This alternative was a challenge to the established wisdom of economic thinking. That a planned economy was even theoretically possible had been disputed in orthodox economics. Against the experience of the Great Depression of the 1930s, and in order to avoid future major crises in the capitalist economies in the West, influential economists (Jan Tinbergen and others) advocated a modified form of economic planning in capitalist economies still dominated by private ownership. Public organs gave indications to private companies on investment targets and tried to influence economic activities indirectly by taxes, subsidies, and prognoses. Such forms of indicative planning were introduced in Western Europe (Holland, France, and Scandinavia) in the 1940s and 1950s. Since the 1940s, advocates against all forms of planned economies argued that not only would planning prove to be inefficient but that political freedom would finally be linked with free entrepreneurship and a reduction of state influence on the economy.

The most significant impact of Soviet planning after World War II was in several newly independent, former colonial states, for example, India, Tanzania, and Ghana. The Soviet Union's impressive transformation within the time span of one generation, its mobilization of mass resources, and its purposely guided industrial development were attractive when the patterns of colonial dependence were to be broken up.

The first postwar Soviet Five-Year plans accomplished, in breakneck speed, a recovery from the wartime destruction of the occupied and war zones. Up to the early 1960s, the rapid growth in Soviet industry continued. The apparent successes, for example, the launching of the *Sputnik* satellite in 1957, gave credence to the efficiency of the Soviet planned economy. Even observers in the West

considered it possible that the Soviet economy might outgrow the U.S. economy within a couple of decades. This was not to be: the relatively transparent Soviet economy of the 1930s was still possible to survey and direct from a central planning organ. Conversely, the mature Soviet industrial economy of the 1960s, with millions of calculations to be made for each long-term plan, hindered rational decision-making, particularly since there was no sound price basis for such calculations. Reformers called for decentralization and for parts of the economy to be guided instead by market forces. These Soviet reform efforts were hindered by opposition of the conservative forces within the Communist Party and ministries. The attempts to adapt the Soviet planning system to the requirements of a mature industrial system failed in the 1970s and early 1980s, calling for rethinking. The ever less flexible Soviet planning system entered a crisis, which eventually called for Mikhail Gorbachev's perestroika in the late 1980s. At that time, the static inefficiency, lack of information and flexibility in the Soviet planning system, and, perhaps most important, the neglect shown to consumer demand forced the new leadership to consider the disbanding of the planning systems.

[*See also* Planning, Economic.]

BIBLIOGRAPHY

Davies, R. W. *Soviet Economic Development from Lenin to Khrushchev.* Cambridge, U.K., and New York: Cambridge University Press, 1998.

Filene, Peter G. *Americans and the Soviet Experiment, 1917–1933,* Cambridge, Mass.: Harvard University Press, 1967.

Gregory, Paul R. *The Political Economy of Stalinism: Evidence from the Soviet Secret Archives.* Cambridge, U.K., and New York: Cambridge University Press, 2004.

Hayek, Friedrich A. *The Road to Serfdom.* Chicago: The University of Chicago Press, 1944.

Nove, Alec. *An Economic History of the USSR.* 3d ed. London and New York: Penguin, 1992.

Nove, Alec. *The Economics of Feasible Socialism.* London, Boston, and Sydney: George Allen & Unwin, 1983.

Samuelson, Lennart. *Plans for Stalin's War-Machine: Tukhachevskii and Military-Economic Planning, 1925–1941.* London: Macmillan and New York: St. Martins, 1999.

Zaleski, Eugène. *Stalinist Planning for Economic Growth, 1933–1952.* Translated by Marie-Christine MacAndrew and John H. Moore. London and Basingstoke: Macmillan, 1980.

Lennart Samuelson

FOLK MUSIC. Folk music is most centrally the music of village and small-town cultures, transmitted through oral tradition, practiced outside institutions such as church and school, in repertories widely known throughout their societies, and ordinarily performed by nonprofessional musicians. A folk song or instrumental piece has no standard form but is manifested in large numbers of variants.

This general characterization applies mostly to Western culture before the twentieth century, but the concept of folk music also plays a major role in non-Western societies, in the music of specialist musicians, popular and mass-mediated music of the twentieth and twenty-first centuries, the field of formal music education, in rural and so-called low churches, and the representation of ethnicity and nationality in urban institutions such as festivals and parades. It is customary (though perhaps simplistic) to contrast folk music with "classical" or "art" music (of learned professionals and technically informed audiences, often under the patronage of courts or governments).

Although "folk music" accounted for the preponderance of music in Europe and elsewhere outside courts and cities before about 1800, the concept and term were not developed until the early nineteenth century, with the contemporary emphasis on nationalism and ethnicity. Indeed, each culture had and continues to have its distinct taxonomy of musics—which may not include terms such as "folk music." Thus, in Serbian and Croatian cultures, the primary musical distinction was between "women's songs" (lyrical folk songs) and men's songs (epics aurally transmitted but sung by recognized and usually paid professionals). In Persian culture, a classical, professionalized tradition with national provenance called "traditional music" contrasts with "regional" or "local" folk music genres, each the province of a trained professional. Once the concept of folk music was introduced in Europe in the late eighteenth century it developed national versions. The English term "folk music" suggests the music of particular activities or social contexts, while the German *Volkslied* refers more typically to a social class. In Slavic languages, the concept is usually tied to the idea of nation (*narod*).

Analysis of Tunes and Texts. Considering the paucity of written sources, comparative analysis of folk tunes and verbal texts leads to an understanding of broad historical currents. The many variants of some tunes and some text types (e.g., ballad stories) were distributed internationally and thus suggest a shared history. Crossing borders, a tune takes on unrelated sets of words, and a story may be sung to unrelated groups of tunes. Folk songs play a major role in international migrations.

Among the first prominent scholars to describe folk song were Thomas Percy (1729–1811), whose *Reliques of Ancient English Poetry* (1765) was the first collection of British narrative ballads, and Johann Gottfried von Herder (1744–1803), whose two-volume *Volkslieder* (1778) was the first international folk collection. Each included only song lyrics. The earliest collections of melodies, which represented attempts to popularize folk music in typically scornful urban society, included arrangements of Scottish and Irish songs by Ludwig van Beethoven (1770–1827) and Franz Joseph Haydn (1732–1809) that were commissioned by the Scottish publisher George Thomson (1757–1851). Folk-music collecting played a role in the negotiation of ethnic and national relationships; thus, after the Napoleonic era, the Austrian imperial government, to appease nationalist ambition and raise the self-esteem of the Czech population, instituted major song-collecting projects.

In mid-nineteenth-century Europe, folk music increasingly played a role in the consciousness of urban and educated classes in a revival that contributed to burgeoning nationalist movements. Significant events were the urban discovery of the Finnish national epic, *Kalevala* (Elias Lönnrot, 1802–1884), and of South Slavic epics chronicling the struggles between Christians and Muslims in the Balkans (Vuk Stefanović Karadžić, 1787–1864). The history of folk music in late-nineteenth-century Europe is dominated by the publication of national and regional song collections, often arranged for choirs or with piano accompaniments, and introduced into schools, student associations, and the living rooms of middle-class music lovers (for example, works by Johannes Brahms, 1833–1897; Antonin Leopold Dvořák, 1841–1904; and later, in the United States, Aaron Copland, 1900–1990). While folk music became more widely known in this period, the importance of oral transmission and the development of regional and even personal variants was greatly reduced as a few standardized versions came to dominate.

Emigration. In the various emigration movements and diasporas between 1750 and 1920, folk music played a role in fostering ethnic identity and maintaining memory of the motherland. In European American culture of the early twentieth century, folk songs and song variants sometimes no longer known in Europe were discovered in the American backwoods (as in the Appalachians by the British collector Cecil James Sharp, c. 1914–1918). Changing functions of folk songs, for example from accompanying agricultural labor to the concert stages of ethnic festivals in large cities, helped to maintain cultural cohesion while also smoothing the transition of eastern and southern European immigrants to North America. The development of a vast and varied body of folk music in African American communities (especially the blues, which combined remnants of African culture, the social contexts of slavery, and elements of Western folk musics) came to the attention of European American society significantly through the collections of John Avery Lomax (1867–1848) and Alan Lomax (1915–2002). The late nineteenth and early twentieth centuries saw folk-music materials adopted and adapted by composers of concert music and the incorporation of African American folk music in jazz.

Political Movements. Between about 1930 and 2000, folk music increased as a factor in political movements. In Nazi Germany, folk singing was a major activity of the Hitlerjugend (Hitler Youth). In the Soviet Union after World War II, orchestras and music conservatories devoted to folk music flourished, with the goal of developing a class of urban, professional folk musicians like those of classical music. In Great Britain, a folk music revival movement of traditional ballads and dance tunes flourished in the period 1950–2000, its most famous protagonists being the singers Jeanie Robertson, Ewan McColl, and Albert Lancaster "A. L." Lloyd. In Ireland, after 1960, folk music–derived popular music accompanied the Troubles.

In the United States, folk songs became the music of antiwar, pro-labor, and environmentalist movements in a musical context that combined tunes (traditional or newly composed) and accompaniments derived from older rural practices with the instrumentation of rock music and mass mediation. During the Depression, this movement was led by Woody Guthrie. After 1960 it was led by Pete Seeger, Bob Dylan, and Joan Baez, as well as by vocal ensembles such as Peter, Paul, and Mary, and the Kingston Trio. Folk music also led to the development of popular music genres, most significantly country-and-western music. And after about 1970, throughout the world, the use of traditional songs and dances (usually by professional performers) to entertain and educate tourists became a principal way of keeping folk music alive as an emblem of ethnic and national identity.

[*See also* Music.]

BIBLIOGRAPHY

Bohlman, Philip V. *The Study of Folk Music in the Modern World.* Bloomington: Indiana University Press, 1988.

Cantwell, Robert. *When We Were Good: The Folk Revival.* Cambridge, Mass.: Harvard University Press, 1996.

Ling, Jan. *A History of European Folk Music.* Translated by Linda and Robert Schenk. Rochester, N.Y.: University of Rochester Press, 1997.

Porter, James, and Timothy Rice, founding eds. *The Garland Encyclopedia of World Music.* Advisory editors Bruno Nettl and Ruth M. Stone. New York: Routledge, 1998–2002.

Ramnarine, Tina K. *Ilmatar's Inspirations: Nationalism, Globalization, and the Changing Soundscapes of Finnish Folk Music.* Chicago: University of Chicago Press, 2003.

BRUNO NETTL

FOOD [*This entry includes four subentries, an overview and discussions of food in East Asia, Latin America, and the United States. See also* Anorexia Nervosa; Famine; Fast Foods; *and* Food Safety.]

Overview

Around the world, eating has been shaped by two factors since the mid-1700s—rapid technological change brought on by the scientific and industrial revolutions, and accelerating cultural exchanges between regions. As Europe industrialized, and in turn colonized great swaths of Africa and Asia, people exchanged seeds, agricultural technologies, and eating traditions. Europe in the 1800s slowly turned outward for its food supply, as peasants moved from country villages to teeming cities, and urban workers through the 1900s slowly became accustomed to eating more processed foods. By the third millennium, industrialized nations employed only small percentages of their populations on farms, for higher crop yields meant fewer people needed to work the land. The areas of the world that remained agrarian saw different changes. Many served the interests of the industrial world by converting lands from multiple-crop subsistence farming to single-crop export agriculture. In the European colonies, Europeans and non-Europeans exchanged food traditions. Slowly, industrial and agrarian nations saw their food traditions evolve due to industrialization and mass migration, even as many governments asserted national pride and superiority through food.

A snapshot of the food landscapes in Paris, Mexico City, and New Delhi in 1750, and again in 2000, would capture both continuity and change in each city. The 2000 portrait would feature McDonald's restaurants in all three, along with other food symbols of American culture. But one would easily find in each city many of the old staple foods of 1750. In Mexico, the tortilla is still a critical component of Mexican cuisine. In France, wheat bread in one form or another serves the same purpose. And in New Delhi, the interface of Muslim and Hindu traditions that predated European rule still rings true in the vegetarian samosa—a stuffed, fried triangle of dough that originated in the Middle East. Although people in each city have been eating some of the same foods over centuries, their meals are likely created much differently today. Industrialization has meant the samosa is fried over a gas flame and the dough fashioned from factory-milled, bleached wheat flour. That same flour might be used in the Mexican tortilla or the French baguette. The samosa's filling likely includes vegetables synthesized by geneticists to make them more resistant to disease and pests. Those vegetables, though grown in India, were probably shipped in a refrigerated rail car or truck—an impossibility in 1750.

Scientific Agriculture. Machine-processed flour and genetically modified vegetables owe their origins to the increasing fusion of science and agriculture during the eighteenth century, when scientists began intensive work on plant propagation, livestock breeding, and farm machinery. In 1701, the British inventor Jethro Tull developed the seed drill. Mechanical gears were added to it in 1782, enabling farmers to inject seeds directly into the soil rather than spreading them randomly by hand. The drill evenly spaced crops and conserved seeds, decreasing costs and increasing yields. At the same time, English farmers experimented with a four-crop rotation method, whereby farmers divided land into four tracts to conserve soil nutrients. They might plant wheat and barley for humans and animals, clover to replenish the soil, and turnips for animal feed and weed control. Before the mid-1700s, sheep had been used mostly for wool, but another British inventor, Robert Bakewell, created a breed that fattened quicker. Mutton prices fell substantially due to Bakewell's livestock management techniques, making it a popular meat in England, Australia, and New Zealand. Scientific management of agriculture by Tull and Bakewell anticipated changes wrought by industrialization in the next century.

Industrialization at the Table. As European agriculture became more efficient, peasants left farms for factories. Food production and distribution slowly shifted to accommodate burgeoning urban populations. At first, parts of the farm were transferred to the city. Dairy cows toiled in crowded urban pens to slake the thirst of mill workers in Manchester and Berlin. City butchers slaughtered hogs and steers, and vegetables and fruits grew on small garden plots or were shipped short distances to city workers.

These workers were typically ill-nourished. They often suffered from vitamin C and D deficiencies, and tuberculosis was common, brought on by living in close quarters and having weakened immune systems resulting from poor diet. Most meals consisted of bread and not much else. In good times, porridge, cheese, or a bit of bacon provided variety. Tea spiked with sugar added carbohydrates and was a mild stimulant.

The potato would, over time, provide cheap vitamins and calories for many European workers, although European populations took many years to become comfortable eating the versatile tuber. Prussian royalty, for example, had to order its minions to plant it. But the potato slowly replaced bread as a staple for many Europeans, allowing them a hot meal and extra cash for meat, coffee, or alcohol. The Irish dependence on the potato proved costly in 1845, when a fungus destroyed the island's crop, causing over one million people to emigrate.

As city populations boomed, food had to be shipped longer distances. To compensate, scientists devised better food-preservation methods. Bottling, canning, and refrigeration techniques were all invented to keep fruits, meats, and vegetables safe in transit and storage. In 1795, the French confectioner Nicholas Appert invented a way to kill bacteria before sealing a bottle, previewing Louis Pasteur's sterilization methods several decades later. A method for mechanically producing tin cans was also developed in 1849, and was immediately put into use by gold-seeking miners in California's mountains. Just a few years later, Gail Borden devised a process for canning milk, enabling the Union Army to use it during the American Civil War. Canning also allowed those in northern cold-weather climates to sample exotic fruits during winter. As a result, fruit and vegetable consumption increased in industrializing nations.

Refrigeration transformed agriculture and eating habits worldwide. Before its advent, meats had to be preserved by salt or smoke. As a result, salt cod was a critical item in the Atlantic trade. When negotiating the treaty to end the American Revolution in 1782, American emissary John Adams worked diligently to secure American access to North Atlantic fishing grounds. Pork was favored, too, for it preserved better than beef. By the mid-1800s, refrigerated rail cars were being perfected, causing the California fruit and vegetable industries to boom by the 1880s, and enabling beef shipments from the Americas to reach cities worldwide. Instead of transporting the whole steer for slaughter at market, cattle could be butchered in Chicago or Buenos Aires and shipped as steaks, chops, and sausages. Beef quickly replaced pork as the meat of choice in the United States. Looking to increase their profits, meatpackers devised innovative ways to make use of all parts of the cow by turning leg bones into cutlery, entrails into sausage casings, fat into oleomargarine, and hoofs and feet into glue, oil, and fertilizer. As William

Cronon (1991) has shown, these "by-products" (see Table 1) composed a key profit margin for Philip Armour's American operation. Armour covered only about three-quarters of his costs by selling a butchered steer in New York. But the largesse of his operation meant he could hire chemists to turn waste products into money, items small butchers had to trash.

Food and Nationalism. As industrialization took hold in Europe and the United States, new nation-states were forming in Europe and the Americas. Latin American countries threw off their Spanish and Portuguese controllers, and Europeans built nations where they did not exist before. New governments used food to encourage nationalism and to foster unity. The concept of gastronomy emerged from the French Revolution in 1789, codifying eating rituals for the middle classes. They learned these rituals in a new institution, the restaurant. Previously, taverns, inns, and street vendors had been the chief sources for food away from home. The restaurant was an alternative for workers and merchants who could not return home for a midday meal or had no home kitchen facilities. Even the working classes participated in the new culture by eating in cafés, where they learned gastronomic rituals.

Following independence, Latin American nations struggled to assert new national identities that made sense of their mestizo reality. During the nineteenth century, elites in Mexico, Chile, and Peru rejected local foods, serving French cuisine at parties. This changed around the time of World War I, as governments sought divorce from the cultural legacy of colonialism. Mexican officials began to celebrate the tamale and enchilada and, later, Brazilians trumpeted the consumption of *feijoada*, a rice and bean dish of African and Native American heritage.

No matter what Latin Americans were eating, their economies shifted in the 1800s to export foods abroad. Argentina, for example, exported grains and beef to Europe with the aid and direction of British capital. Investors dredged ports, built canals and railroads, and encouraged immigrants from Italy and other parts of southern Europe to farm the pampas and man the slaughterhouses. As a result, Argentinean cuisine took on distinctive Italian qualities.

The Imperial Grocery Store. European governments grabbed territories in Africa and Asia as they asserted control over trade with the new nations of Latin America, and this nineteenth-century imperialism brought new exchanges. The British taste for Indian chutneys, curries, and tea proves the Indian palate's effect on the colonial rulers. Now a generic term for all Indian foods in Britain, "curry" gained a following there in the 1800s, and when entrepreneurial South Asians migrated in large numbers to Britain from the 1950s forward, Indian food became big business in Britain.

The term "curry" is indicative of its European timbre. The Tamil term, *kari*, means black pepper, but it was taken by the Portuguese, and then the British, to mean any spiced sauce. In India, the sauce had garnished rice, but in Europe it became a stew accompanied by a bit of rice or bread. Rather than grind spices fresh in the Indian fashion, the British manufactured curry powder, a mixture of ready-made spices. By the 1980s, large manufacturers, often run by immigrant South Asians, churned out frozen and canned curries for distribution in British supermarkets. And by the 1990s, an English opinion poll declared curry the nation's favorite food. A song, "Vindaloo" (a version of curry that ironically is a term of Portuguese origin), topped the music charts as an anthem for the 1998 English World Cup team with the refrain, "We're off to Waterloo, Me and me mum and me dad and me gran and a bucket of Vindaloo." In India, no British dish evoked nationalistic songs. The Indian diet did take on some British qualities, notably a proliferation of sweets and candies powered by refined sugar, and Indians enjoy tea as much as the British do. However, no British dish matters in Delhi as curry does in London.

If Indians changed British food culture, the reverse relationship generally occurred with the colonizers and colonized in Africa. Although some aspects of North African food culture can be seen in Europe, such as a taste for couscous, for the most part changes occurred in the colonies. Europeans held the vast majority of African

TABLE 1. *Armour's Estimates of Dressed Beef By-product Costs and Profits*

Steer, 1,260 lbs @ $3.25 per cwt* (becomes 710 lbs dressed beef)	$40.95
Cost of killing, processing, salt, icing, etc.	$1.75
Freight on 710 pounds @ $0.45 per cwt	$3.20
New York selling charges @ $0.35 per cwt	$2.48
Costs of purchase, processing, and transport	−$48.38
Sale in NYC of 710 lbs dressed beef @ 5 3/8¢ per lb.	$38.17
(Net loss on dressed beef in NYC)	−10.21
Sale of hide, 70 lbs @ $.09 per lb	$6.30
Sale of by-products	$4.50
Yield from all by-product sales	$10.80
Net profit from all transactions	$0.59

*hundred-weight
SOURCE: William Cronon. *Nature's Metropolis: Chicago and the Great West.* New York: W. W. Norton, 1991, p. 251.

territory by the early twentieth century, for the continent offered profitable opportunities for resource extraction, including new oils and fruits for European consumption. Palm and peanut oils brought from Sierra Leone and Senegal were marketed as alternatives to olive oil, and became important cash crops for European investors. Coffee and cacao plantations on the Gold and Ivory Coasts sent more money into European coffers. These single cash-crop systems changed agricultural and hunting practices in the region. Before European domination, Igbo farmers in Nigeria, for example, employed a multi-crop system of yams, taro, groundnuts, and chili peppers. Although some communities had already long engaged in trade before the European powers took hold, in many places the plantation system took males away from the villages, leaving women to replace their work at home. Furthermore, as Africans increasingly bought food with cash, they relinquished communal food sharing traditions. European colonial administrators in many regions encouraged Africans to change their diets, mostly because they did not fit European mores. African colonial administrators also took the eating habits of the Europeans to be superior, especially if they had been educated in Europe. Thus in places like the Ivory Coast, baguettes and French cheeses found their place on store shelves.

The West Indies and Brazil meanwhile were loci for the immensely profitable and transformative sugar trade, another consequence of colonial ventures. Millions of slaves were taken from Africa to farm sugar cane in the Caribbean. Later, as slavery was abolished and Caribbean republics won independence, European and American capital continued to invest in sugar production in the region. A rarity in 1600s Europe, sugar became a luxury in the 1700s, and a necessity by the mid-1800s. It provided cheap calories for the industrial masses, who spiked their tea with the crystals. Those crystals also fed slaves and laborers in the Caribbean, who grew it on what Sidney Mintz (1985) has called "agro-industrial" plantations from the 1600s forward.

Battling Famine. In the 1700s and 1800s, famine and corresponding food riots were common. Surging populations coupled with the new capitalism in Europe created uneasiness, as governments often tried to control agricultural prices. In France, for example, the 1774 liberalization of the grain trade provoked an insurrection called the Flour War. In 1798, economist Thomas Malthus said in his *Essay on the Principles of Human Population* that human reproduction typically outruns agricultural yields, so only disease, famine, or warfare can control

population growth. He was proven wrong by the twentieth century, but the early 1800s were lean times for most industrial workers and peasants. Friedrich Engels, who coauthored the *Communist Manifesto* with Karl Marx, toured northern England's working cities in the 1840s and wrote about how children and workers in those towns sorely needed a better diet. This tour proved fodder for his socialist beliefs.

Slowly, industrialization improved agricultural production. In the twentieth century, scientists made great advances in plant propagation and breeding, animal husbandry, pest control, and irrigation techniques. Corn is one food that has been intensively manipulated to create new genetic varieties. The first commercial hybrids were widely available by the 1930s, but by 2007, around 95 percent of corn was a hybrid. Current varieties enable farmers to grow 20 percent more corn on 25 percent fewer acres than they could before the 1930s.

Even as industrial technologies advanced food production, distribution remained problematic. Getting rice to drought-ridden regions was often a more difficult prospect than actually growing it. Political circumstances, especially war, forced famine upon millions in the nineteenth and twentieth centuries. As World War I ushered in modern warfare, it also emptied the stomachs of multitudes. Around seven hundred thousand Germans died of malnutrition during the war. In World War II, the German army deliberately starved millions of Soviet civilians. In Leningrad alone, between 1 million and 1.3 million civilians died during the war from starvation or malnutrition-related diseases.

War exacerbated or even caused food supply problems, but after World War II certain developing nations attempted to "solve" peacetime famines by turning to technology for a "green revolution." Mexico, the Philippines, and other developing nations used biotechnology, pest control, and advanced irrigation techniques to raise crop yields. From 1960 to 1990, famine in Mexico decreased 20 percent as caloric consumption per capita increased 25 percent.

Nutrition and the science of eating have vastly improved in the last century. The definition of "healthy" eating changed regularly, but as the twentieth century marched on, many governments launched nutrition campaigns to show the need for certain vitamins, minerals, and proteins. At the same time, in the richest countries, those of all classes saw rising rates of obesity as a result of increased access to inexpensive, calorie-packed fast food. Japanese eating trends reflect how industrializing

Food in the Soviet Union. Five scenes of workers in Soviet food processing plants, 1950. PRINTS AND PHOTOGRAPHS DIVISION, LIBRARY OF CONGRESS

societies typically shift from carbohydrate to protein and fat consumption as income rises. In *Food in Global History* (Grew, 1999), Adam Drewnowski showed that in 1910, daily per-capita food intake in Japan was 430 grams of carbohydrate (rice and beans), 13 grams of fat, and only 3 grams of animal protein. By 1989, daily carbohydrate consumption had declined to 190 grams and fat intake and animal protein consumption had risen to 59 grams and 42 grams per capita. Even the burgeoning middle classes of China and India were suffering from obesity-related diseases by the end of the twentieth century.

Hunger remained for billions, however. The Food and Agriculture Organization of the United Nations reported that in developing nations between 2000 and 2002, over 814 million people, or 17 percent of their populations, were undernourished. In sub-Saharan Africa, the total was 33 percent. In 1981, Nobel prize-winning economist Amartya Sen argued in his book *Poverty and Famines: An Essay on Entitlement and Deprivation* that in most regions after the green revolution, famine was caused not by inadequate food supplies, but instead by poor food distribution systems, high prices, and low wages. Those problems could be ameliorated with better technologies or government intervention, but political problems, not agricultural technologies, were often at issue.

Fast Food and Fusion Cuisine. In the twenty-first century, industrial technologies and global cultural exchanges have combined in the form of fast food—cheap, quick food for the masses. Over one-quarter of all food spending in the United States is on fast food, and McDonald's, the most recognizable brand of fast food, rakes in $100 billion in sales per year. The chain has been the target of critics for its supposed transmittance of American cultural values worldwide. McDonald's foods and the company's business innovations have become a part of Chinese, European, and Latin American culture. But McDonald's is not the only company responsible for making those places more American. Conversely, with mass global migration Chinese and Mexican restaurants and the cultures from which they derive have a foothold in the United States too. Many American restaurants now use McDonald's assembly-line food preparation methods and the ethnic influences of Chinese and Mexican cuisine to produce burrito-style "Asian wraps." The continued exchange of cultures and technology advances will likely create further hybrids like those wraps, shaping the continuing evolution of eating habits worldwide.

[*See also* Anorexia Nervosa; Famine; Fast Foods; Food Safety; Green Revolution; *and* Obesity.]

BIBLIOGRAPHY

Achaya, K. T. *A Historical Dictionary of Indian Food.* New Delhi and New York: Oxford University Press, 1998.

Atkins, Peter, and Ian Bowler. *Food in Society: Economy, Culture, Geography.* London and New York: Arnold, 2001.

Basu, Shrabani. *Curry in the Crown: The Story of Britain's Favourite Dish.* New Delhi: HarperCollins Publishers India, 1999.

Cronon, William. *Nature's Metropolis: Chicago and the Great West.* New York: Norton, 1991. A magnificent urban history with a stunning analysis of the meatpacking business in its formative years.

Davidson, Alan. *The Oxford Companion to Food.* Oxford and New York: Oxford University Press, 1999. 2nd ed., 2006. The exhaustive and definitive reference source on food and food history.

Grew, Raymond. *Food in Global History.* Boulder, Colo: Westview Press, 1999.

Katz, Solomon H., ed. *Encyclopedia of Food and Culture.* 4 vols. New York: Charles Scribner's Sons, 2003.

Kiple, Kenneth F., and Kriemhild Coneè Ornelas. *The Cambridge World History of Food.* 2 vols. Cambridge, U.K., and New York: Cambridge University Press, 2000.

Mintz, Sidney W. *Sweetness and Power: The Place of Sugar in Modern History.* New York: Viking, 1985. Reprint. New York: Penguin, 1986.

Pilcher, Jeffrey M. *Food in World History.* New York: Routledge, 2006. This excellent brief survey covers a wide range of important topics.

Sonnenfeld, Albert. *Food: A Culinary History from the Antiquity to the Present.* Translated by Clarissa Botsford, et al. New York: Columbia University Press, 1999. Original 1996 edition by Jean-Louis Flandarin and Massimo Montanari.

Super, John C., and Thomas C. Wright, eds. *Food, Politics, and Society in Latin America.* Lincoln: University of Nebraska Press, 1985.

Tannahill, Reay. *Food in History.* New and updated. London: Review, 2002.

Watson, James L., ed. *Golden Arches East: McDonald's in East Asia.* Stanford, Calif.: Stanford University Press, 1997. 2nd ed., 2006.

LARESH JAYASANKER

East Asia

Food constitutes a vital component of East Asian cultures and identities. It plays a critical role in the celebration of festivals and in the everyday interaction of Chinese, Koreans, and Japanese, functioning as an important means of communication. Deriving from its central role in East Asian societies, cuisine has become a significant marker of East Asian cultures in the global world as well. A category of food defined as "Chinese," epitomized by a variety of ingredients stir-fried in a wok (Chinese-style frying pan), serves as a banner of Chinese culture worldwide. For Japan and Korea the same function is performed by specific elements from their cuisines, such as sushi (vinegared rice with raw fish topping/filling) and *kimchi* (pickled napa cabbage).

Culinary culture is an effective tool for identifying historical dynamics of East Asia. The three-tiered "rice/soup/side dishes" meal pattern and the use of chopsticks, along with tea drinking and the consumption of processed soyfoods—soy sauce, soybean curd, and a variety of soybean pastes—are vivid indicators of the common roots, stemming from the civilization of ancient China, which contemporary China, Korea, and Japan share.

The effects of the penetration of East Asia by Western imperialism constitute another source of parallels within East Asian foodways. From the late nineteenth century onward, fashion for dining Western-style began to spread among local elites, inspired by the increasing presence of Westerners in treaty ports. They were able to maintain their distinctive lifestyle owing to regular shipments of canned food and other provisions from Europe and the United States, supplemented by a growing infrastructure of restaurants, bakeries, and dairies that developed around Western settlements throughout East Asia. Japan, as the forerunner of modernization and reform in East Asia, proved most successful in accommodating Western food into its consumption patterns. When the Japanese Empire embarked on its own mission of colonizing East Asia, Japanese armed forces and entrepreneurs facilitated the spread of Western-style food and drink, and methods of their production, across the region. Along with the expansion of a Japanese sphere of influence, beer breweries, canneries, and Western-style restaurants and eateries emerged in Formosa, Korea, and Manchuria. Consequently, Japanese versions of Western food, such as curry on rice and deep-fried breaded pork cutlets, can now be found in former Japanese colonies. The mass migration of people within the East Asia Co-Prosperity Sphere, and their repatriation after 1945, also brought about the popularization of Chinese food in Japan and Korea and Korean cuisine in Japan.

During the second half of the nineteenth century, the process of culinary exchange between East Asia and the rest of the world began to intensify in the opposite direction as well. Along with the encroachment of Western imperialism, the idea of using Asians to substitute black labor in the New World became increasingly pronounced. As Chinese, and later Japanese and Koreans, migrated in great numbers across the Pacific in search for a better life, they set into motion a worldwide diffusion of East Asian cuisines. Because restaurants and other establishments necessary for the maintenance of native foodways play an

Food Processing. Workers separate egg yolks from whites, Shanghai, China, c. 1890–1923. Frank and Frances Carpenter Collection/Prints and Photographs Division, Library of Congress

important role within each expatriate community, China-towns and Korean and Japanese enclaves within them grew steadily in North America around the areas with a high concentration of East Asian residents. From the mid-twentieth century onward, they became tourist attractions and their restaurants were increasingly frequented by the Caucasian population. The American military personnel stationed in Japan and in the Republic of Korea during the decade following the Pacific War (1941–1945) constituted the hub of the newly emerging clientele of Japanese and Korean restaurants in the United States. New health considerations appearing in the 1970s, which rejected hearty, red-meat American fare in favor of a healthy cuisine of rice, fish, and vegetables, propelled the popularization of Chinese, Korean, and Japanese cuisines in the United States. The rise of Japan as a global economic power further inspired the sushi boom that swept the world in the following two decades.

The emergence of the United States as the dominant global force in economic, political, and cultural terms during the late twentieth century had two major consequences for East Asian food. On the one hand, coupled with the migration of Chinese to Europe from the former European colonies, the American hegemony induced the worldwide diffusion of East Asian cuisines that had by then become popular in the United States. Although Chinese food proved to have been most successful in terms of global penetration, Japanese cuisine has acquired equally high worldwide recognition. The spread of Korean cuisine remained limited to residential areas of Korean communities. On the other hand, the expansion of global capitalism resulted in a rapid spread of the products of the American food industry, such as breakfast cereals, soft drinks, and ketchup, and of American fast-food chains like McDonald's and KFC throughout East Asia. It remains to be seen how these new forms of consumption will be embraced and accommodated, and what effects these developments will have on food and eating in East Asia.

[*See also* Consumption and Consumerism, *subentry* East Asia.]

BIBLIOGRAPHY

Cwiertka, Katarzyna J. "Circuits of Japanese Cuisine in Europe." *Food and Foodways* 13 (2005): 1–32.

Cwiertka, Katarzyna J. *Modern Japanese Cuisine: Food, Power and National Identity*. London: Reaktion, 2006.

Cwiertka, Katarzyna J., and Boudewijn C. A. Walraven, eds. *Asian Food: The Global and the Local*. Honolulu: University of Hawai'i Press, 2001.

Roberts, J. A. G. *China to Chinatown: Chinese Food in the West*. London: Reaktion, 2002.

KATARZYNA J. CWIERTKA

Latin America

In Latin America, "fusion cuisine" has been not a trendy fad but rather an ongoing historical process for more than five hundred years. Native American, Iberian, and African foods were already thoroughly blended in the sixteenth century. Beginning around 1850, industrialization and proletarian migrations introduced new European, Asian, and Middle Eastern influences. The twentieth-century arrival of processed foods from the United States brought further dietary changes.

Highly nutritious American crops supported great civilizations in pre-Hispanic times and transformed agriculture around the world in the early modern period. Maize, the staple of Maya cultures and the Aztec Empire, proved to be more productive than wheat and became a mainstay of peasant diets throughout the Mediterranean and in large parts of Africa. The potato, domesticated in the Andes Mountains, eventually spread through northern Europe, from Ireland to Russia, while sweet potatoes supplemented peasant diets in China. Another prolific root, cassava, spread from the Caribbean and Brazil to horticultural societies of tropical Africa and Asia. Because these crops could be grown on previously marginal land, or in different seasons than existing cultigens, they dramatically increased overall productivity and spurred worldwide population growth.

Yet the Columbian Exchange of foods met with considerable resistance in Latin America. Taste played a part, as Native Americans compared European bread with dried maize stalks, and Spanish conquistadores complained about unfamiliar rations of corn tortillas and cassava flatbreads. Climate also influenced the course of dietary development. Wheat grew poorly in the tropics, and settlers eventually grew accustomed to local staples such as Brazilian *farinha* pastries. Because the Americas had few domesticated animals, European livestock offered a significant source of animal protein to Native Americans, although they often had to make do with organ meats. Thus, *anticuchos* (grilled beef hearts) are a favorite street food among indigenous Andeans. African domesticates that were imported as slave rations, including yams, okra, cowpeas, and various greens, became characteristic of the cuisines of the Caribbean and Brazil, where sugar plantations dominated the landscape. Within the racial hierarchy of colonial Latin America, European products denoted high social status, while the lower classes ate Native American and African foods.

Nineteenth-century industrialization heightened demand for agricultural exports from the Americas. Brazil's Atlantic rainforest was decimated to plant coffee, while bananas became a staple throughout the Caribbean and Central America. Plantations operated as isolated enclaves, often run by North American managers, who relied on poorly paid local and migrant labor. Indigenous peoples were driven from fertile lands such as the Argentine pampas to raise cattle and wheat for European markets. Yet Latin Americans also participated actively in the industrialization process; for example, Mexican inventors mechanized tortilla production, sparing women from arduous manual labor grinding corn.

Fin de siècle elites lavished export revenues on French delicacies, while new immigrants contributed to popular cuisines. Exclusive restaurants from Mexico City to Buenos Aires served elaborate French concoctions, accompanied by champagne, and the middle classes purchased cookbooks to reproduce these recipes at home. Nevertheless, these dishes were adapted to local tastes and often had little resemblance to Parisian fare. Meanwhile, proletarian immigrants brought their own specialties. Italians and Germans introduced macaroni and sauerkraut, respectively, to South America, along with their skills in making wine and brewing beer. The descendants of Chinese indentured servants, imported to work in the sugar plantations of Peru and Cuba after the abolition of the slave trade, made fried rice popular in these countries. Finally, Lebanese migrants introduced gyros to Mexico, where they became known as *tacos arabes* and *tacos al pastor*.

Populist movements emerging around World War I rejected the Europhile elites and sought a return to Creole national cuisines. Mexicans invented tales about the colonial origins of *mole poblano*, a mixture of indigenous chili peppers and Old World spices that represented the nation's racial mixture. Likewise in Brazil, the elaborate *feijoada* consisting of black beans, rice, collard greens, and beef jerky became a national dish. Nor were these meals entirely symbolic; progressive governments enacted welfare programs to ensure that the entire nation shared in the bounty. Juan Domingo Perón's populist regime

(1946–1955) in Argentina subsidized the beef industry to avoid unrest among the urban workers craving *asados* (grilled meats). Beginning in 1968, the Peruvian revolutionary government diverted fish meal exports from Europe to feed impoverished highland Indians. Yet economic crises and government instability invariably undermined these efforts at redistribution. Although Fidel Castro was dedicated to overcoming the health inequalities in Cuba, a U.S. trade embargo and the fall of Communism in Eastern Europe caused endemic food shortages.

The contemporary globalization of food has reinforced inequalities. Supermarket chains and fast food restaurants have opened in wealthy neighborhoods and tourist zones. Governments throughout the region have also encouraged the development of exclusive restaurants showcasing native specialties: grill houses in Argentina and Uruguay, seafood restaurants in Chile and Peru, and the so-called *nueva cocina mexicana* serving upscale tacos prepared with French flourishes. Among the poor, industrial processed food and drinks were introduced in the export enclaves of fruit and mining firms, which shipped them as a convenience to expatriate managers on the return passage of otherwise empty cargo hulls. Local workers purchased cans of soda and boxes of crackers at company stores, thereby passing a taste for exotic luxuries along to their neighbors back home.

Public health authorities identified a growing trend of replacing complex carbohydrates and vegetable proteins with sugar and fats. Mexican studies have found that well-to-do peasants and working-class urban residents derive an average of 20 percent of their calories from processed foods including soft drinks, beer, chips, and candy. The rural poor, unable to afford such snacks except on special occasions, dump heaping spoons of sugar into weak coffee. As a result, increasing numbers of people have encountered an epidemiological trap, falling victim to the dietary diseases of the rich world without escaping the nutritional deficiencies of the poor world. Heart disease, diabetes, arteriosclerosis, and various forms of cancer have likewise grown more common, even with the continuing prevalence of serious malnutrition in the region.

BIBLIOGRAPHY

Bauer, Arnold J. *Goods, Power, History: Latin America's Material Culture.* Cambridge, U.K.: Cambridge University Press, 2001.

Ochoa, Enrique C. *Feeding Mexico: The Political Uses of Food since 1910.* Wilmington, Del.: Scholarly Resources, 2000.

Pilcher, Jeffrey M. *¡Que vivan los tamales! Food and the Making of Mexican Identity.* Albuquerque: University of New Mexico Press, 1998.

Striffler, Steve, and Mark Moberg, ed. *Banana Wars: Power, Production, and History in the Americas.* Durham, NC: Duke University Press, 2003.

Weismantel, Mary J. *Food, Gender, and Poverty in the Ecuadorian Andes.* Philadelphia: University of Pennsylvania Press, 1988.

JEFFREY M. PILCHER

The United States

From the beginning of European colonization, North America was a fabled land filled with abundance. It attracted numerous culturally, linguistically, religiously, and racially diverse groups. While each of these contributed to early American life, English culture put down the deepest roots, and British food—modified by New World foods and conditions—predominated in America.

For the first two hundred years, most Americans lived on farms, which were culinarily self-sufficient. Those who lived in small towns acquired their food in public markets and occasionally maintained their own gardens. The few Americans who lived in cities, such as Philadelphia, Boston, New York, San Francisco, and New Orleans, had fairly sophisticated foods available, both from the hinterlands as well as imported foods from abroad.

Industrialization of American Food. The transition from local foodways to a national system began with the construction of the Erie Canal, which connected the Great Lakes with the Hudson River. Mills using new technology developed by Oliver Evans were constructed along the route of the canal and in the Midwest: wheat could conveniently be milled into flour and sold inexpensively to consumers hundreds of miles away. Additional transportation revolutions, such as the construction of railroads and highways, created a single national food market.

The industrialization of American food began in earnest after the Civil War (1861–1865). During the war, the federal government had let contracts to manufacture canned goods to feed its military forces spread out over thousands of miles. After the war, the cost of canning and bottling declined as manufacturers gained experience with mass-production techniques. Competition drove down prices and created the need for massive advertising for manufacturers to sell their products. New products required new distribution systems. Farmers' markets and small grocery stores gave way to large national chains by the beginning of the twentieth century. Massive supermarkets offered a great variety of inexpensive foods to many Americans.

Wartime Food Shortages. An FDA poster urges Americans to keep their home gardens growing to support the war effort, 1918. Poster by William McKee. Prints and Photographs Division, Library of Congress

Convenience and Fast Foods. Convenience foods had been around for generations, but it wasn't until the post–World War II era that they became a crucial component in American meals. Technology contributed to this shift: for instance, widespread sales of refrigerators and freezers and the invention of the microwave oven made the use of frozen foods an everyday habit in homes and restaurants. Swanson's TV dinner typified this shift; millions of complete frozen meals were sold after its introduction in 1953.

Fast food, an invention of the early twentieth century, was partly a natural progression of this tendency toward culinary convenience and partly a response to the rise of the automobile. Although fast food had been around for decades, the McDonald brothers and Ray Kroc carried the concept to its ultimate conclusion. Their efficient operation permitted them to speed up service and lower prices. The surprise effect was how quickly fast food would take over a large proportion of the American diet. Today, fast food is one of the mainstays of the American culinary experience, with an estimated 25 percent of Americans visiting a fast-food establishment every day.

Ethnic and International Food. Early immigrants to America came mainly from the United Kingdom and Ireland, with a smattering from other western and northern European countries. In the 1880s this immigration pattern changed as people from southern and eastern Europe flooded into the United States. The pace of immigration exploded between 1900 and 1910, when 9 million people arrived in American cities. Most immigrants tried to keep their culinary traditions alive, but it wasn't until after World War II that mainstream America began to adopt a sometimes bastardized version of ethnic foods, such as pizza, hard-shelled tacos, and bagels.

Beginning in the late 1930s, food writers, such as M. F. K. Fisher, stirred up interest in culinary matters, but it was the publication of *Gourmet* magazine in 1941 that launched a culinary revolution. Other culinary magazines appeared in *Gourmet*'s wake, creating even greater interest in fine food. In 1957 the *New York Times* hired its first food columnist, Mississippi-born Craig Claiborne. Other papers followed the *Times*' lead, and a cadre of authoritative newspaper food editors helped attune millions of Americans to the finer points of food and cooking. Despite these developments, for most Americans, foreign food—especially French food—was costly and needlessly complex. Julia Child and her television

Food Recommendation. U.S. Farm Security Administration consumer education photograph that recommends letting cooked foods cool to room temperature before placing them in the refrigerator, February 1942. FARM SECURITY ADMINISTRATION–OFFICE OF WAR INFORMATION COLLECTION/PRINTS AND PHOTOGRAPHS DIVISION, LIBRARY OF CONGRESS

program, *The French Chef*, helped demystify French food for Americans. Gradually, other foreign and ethnic cuisines became part of "American" food.

The American Food Scene Today. Beginning in the late 1960s, the American food scene changed radically yet again. Great strides were made in American agriculture during the twentieth century, but with progress came protest. As farming and food processing became more centralized, mechanized, and chemically enhanced, some Americans voiced concerns about the quality, safety, and palatability of the food supply. The food counterculture, which emerged around 1970, included a broad cross-section of individuals and groups opposed to corporate agriculture, corporate manufacturing of food, and perceived government protection and subsidy of corporate food producers. From the counterculture came communes, urban gardens, and food co-ops, and the reemergence of greenmarkets and organic farming.

One notable individual to emerge from the countercultural revolution was Alice Waters, who in 1971 founded Chez Panisse in Berkeley, California. Waters, along with a number of other chefs, helped launch "California cuisine," which has encouraged Americans to eat the freshest and best seasonal ingredients. The next trends to hit included southwestern cooking (Tex-Mex and Cal-Mex), Cajun cuisine, and fusion foods in the 1990s.

At the dawn of the twenty-first century, the American foodscape remained vibrant and contrasting. The Food Network, established in 1993, and television programs on other networks regularly launched celebrity chefs who quickly became the country's most influential arbiters of food and cooking. In their homes, restaurants, and supermarkets, Americans faced a multiplication of food choices: high-quality restaurants with diverse menus served well-to-do Americans, and for the working-class Americans, fast-food chains continued to expand in diversity and in number. Supermarkets continued to thrive, bringing tens of thousands of food products to millions of Americans, while farmers' markets returned and artisanal bakers and cheese makers developed loyal followings. American food corporations were at the forefront of genetic engineering research and applications, while organic and fresh foods became increasingly available to most Americans.

BIBLIOGRAPHY

Cummings, Richard Osborn. *The American and His Food: A History.* Chicago: University of Chicago Press, 1940.

Hooker, Richard J. *Food and Drink in America: A History.* Indianapolis, Ind.: Bobbs-Merrill, 1981.

Levenstein, Harvey A. *Paradox of Plenty: A Social History of Eating in Modern America.* New York: Oxford University Press, 1993.

Levenstein, Harvey A. *Revolution at the Table: The Transformation of the American Diet.* New York: Oxford University Press, 1988.

Shapiro, Laura. *Perfection Salad: Women and Cooking at the Turn of the Century.* New York: Farrar, Straus, and Giroux, 1986.

ANDREW F. SMITH

FOOD SAFETY. Making sure that foodstuffs are safe for consumption is an age-old concern. Food safety in premodern societies rested largely with the consumers, who themselves gathered or grew the food they prepared. Since the advent in the eighteenth century of the Industrial Revolution, however, food safety has increasingly come under the purview of governments, scientists, and researchers.

The transition from an agricultural to an industrialized economy revolutionized European society. Food safety serves as an important case in point. As urban populations swelled from the influx of agrarian laborers looking for jobs, so, too, did the need for readily available foodstuffs. Urbanization made food-safety issues more acute because the newly emergent working class had to rely almost wholly on markets for food. The commercialization and segmentation of the food industry meant an increased potential for spoilage and contamination during production, shipping, and storage as the distance between the consumer and producer grew. Commercialization also allowed for the deliberate adulteration of food to reach appalling levels as merchants cut corners to increase profits. For example, bakers used chalk and bone ash in breads to lessen costs and heighten appearance; brewers increased supply by watering down beer and adding picrotoxin, a poisonous stimulant; floor sweepings were added to pepper to increase volume; and copper was used to improve the color of pickles.

Such practices were so widespread that it became clear that consumers should be made aware of the health risks and that food adulteration should be criminalized. The German-born chemist Friedrich Christian Accum (1769–1838) was one of the earliest and loudest in this regard. While living in London, Accum published *A Treatise on Adulterations of Food and Culinary Poisons: Exhibiting the Fraudulent Sophistications of Bread, Beer, Wine, Spirituous Liquors, Tea, Coffee, Cream, Confectionery, Vinegar, Mustard, Pepper, Cheese, Olive Oil, Pickles, and Other Articles Employed in Domestic Economy, and Methods of Detecting Them* in 1820, which sought to expose the nature and extent of food adulteration in Britain as well as indict those associated with it.

Although it made him hugely unpopular, his early work and that of a host of others laid the basis for greater government involvement in consumer protection and ultimately resulted in national protective legislation like the 1875 U.K. Sale of Food and Drugs Act.

Advances in science and technology both helped and hindered food safety. One of the most important advances was made by Nicolas François Appert (1750–1841), a Parisian confectioner. At the behest of Napoleon Bonaparte, Appert competed for a prize of twelve thousand francs for developing a method of food preservation that would adequately supply Napoleon's troops while on campaign. After years of research, Appert submitted his invention in 1809 and won the prize. It consisted of hermetically sealing cooked food in glass containers and boiling them, a process now commonly known as canning. A year later he published his findings as *L'art de conserver, pendant plusieurs années, toutes les substances animales et vegetables* (The Art of Preserving All Kinds of Animal and Vegetable Substances for Several Years). Though Appert did not understand why his method actually worked—Louis Pasteur's advances in germ theory were still a half century away—his fundamental approach remains the same today. Other advances, like those in refrigeration and microbiology, certainly made it possible to deliver safe foods to more people and over greater distances, but science was used for disingenuous purposes as well. Progress made in organic chemistry allowed for the manipulation of unwanted tastes, odors, and colors of putrid victuals.

As industrialization spread throughout much of Europe and North America in the nineteenth century, food safety problems proliferated as well. The meat and dairy industries illustrate this point. Adulterations and hygienic problems in the milk trade were partly to blame for Germany's high infant-mortality rate. In the United States the horrifically unsanitary conditions of meatpacking plants, like that of the Union Stockyard and Transit Company in Chicago, Illinois, were publicized by the muckraking journalist Upton Sinclair in 1906. His exposé, *The Jungle*, which chronicled rodent-infested storage facilities and heaps of rotten meat, led to an investigation by Theodore Roosevelt's administration. Coupled with the efforts of the consumer health and safety advocate Dr. Harvey Wiley (1844–1930) and his famous "poison squad," these actions resulted in the 1906 Pure Food and Drug Act, the first federal legislation of its kind in America.

Yet spoilage and adulteration are only part of the food-safety equation. Foodborne hazards stem from a variety of sources. Environmental dangers like lead and mercury contaminate foodstuffs through soil and water. While on the farm, during processing, or during preparation in homes or restaurants, foodborne diseases like botulism, staphylococcal food poisoning, or *Salmonella* remain potential threats. In the United States in the early twenty-first century there were more than three hundred thousand hospitalizations and five thousand deaths from foodborne illnesses reported each year. Eating too much or not enough of the right foods also poses severe health risks. Better food-labeling regulations and improved handling practices have done much to educate consumers about their role in food safety.

Keeping the food supply safe is not an easy task, and failures are costly in both health and monetary terms. Despite the fact that contaminated beef had been documented by the British government a decade earlier, it was not until 1996, when BSE or "mad cow" cases surfaced at nearly one thousand per week, that the government spoke out. The effects were manifold. The transmissibility of the disease to humans, coupled with a potentially long incubation period, brought public scrutiny not only on the government but also on the beef industry, abattoirs, and supermarkets. In the end the gamble with public health proved economically disastrous as the European Union, whose food industry and agricultural sector account for some 800 billion euros in annual production and more than 10 million jobs, immediately announced a worldwide ban on U.K. beef and cattle imports.

Food Safety. Lester P. W. Wehle, a live-poultry inspector for the city of New York, inspects the crop of a chicken. Photograph by Al Ravenna, 1951. NEW YORK WORLD-TELEGRAM AND THE SUN NEWSPAPER PHOTOGRAPH COLLECTION/PRINTS AND PHOTOGRAPHS DIVISION, LIBRARY OF CONGRESS

It seems clear that no matter how technologically advanced or far-reaching food safety systems become, risks will remain. The outbreak of avian influenza (bird flu) in Asia in late 2003, which infected and killed hundreds of people and spread to Africa, the Near East, and Europe, serves as an important reminder. Globalization added problems by the early twenty-first century, with massive food exports from places like China where government standards and inspections remain inconsistent at best. And although international food-safety institutions like the World Health Organization, the Food and Agriculture Organization, and the European Food Safety Authority differ markedly in their approaches to food safety regulation, it is clear that research and consumer education and vigilance, as well as governmental oversight, can greatly reduced the threat.

[*See also* Bird Flu; Food; Health and Disease; Mad Cow Disease; Medicine and Public Health; *and* World Health Organization.]

BIBLIOGRAPHY

Burnett, John, and Derek J. Oddy, eds. *The Origins and Development of Food Policies in Europe.* London: Leicester University Press, 1994.

Connor, Elizabeth. *Internet Guide to Food Safety and Security.* New York: Haworth Information Press, 2005.

Heijden, Kees A. van der, et al., eds. *International Food Safety Handbook: Science, International Regulation, and Control.* New York: Marcel Dekker, 1999.

MARK B. COLE

FOOTBALL. Football had its origins in British schoolboy games. In 1823 students at Rugby School began playing a game that would take the name of its parent institution. Soccer, too, had its origins in 1820s England. Around the same time a group of students at Princeton University in Princeton, New Jersey, (the school was then named the College of New Jersey) began playing a similar game known as "ballown." The goal of ballown was simply for one team to advance a ball past the opposing team, with players using fists and feet to fight their way through the opposition. At Harvard University, in Cambridge, Massachusetts, the freshman and sophomore classes competed in a game similar to Princeton's ballown on the first Monday of each school year. The roughness of the contest earned the event the moniker "Bloody Monday." Despite the violence, however, the game spread throughout Boston by the early 1860s.

After the American Civil War, in 1867, the football was patented. That year, Princeton established a set of rudimentary rules for the game. Rutgers College in New Brunswick, New Jersey, established its own set of rules, and the relatively short distance between the two New Jersey institutions led them to organize an intercollegiate game on 6 November 1869 at Rutgers. Because the game took place in New Brunswick, the contestants followed the Rutgers rules. The teams used a soccer-style round ball and played on a field 120 yards long and 75 yards wide. There were twenty-five players on each team, and no officials regulated the contest. Rutgers scored six goals to Princeton's four. At a banquet following the game, Princeton challenged Rutgers to a rematch on its field, and thus with its rules, the following week. In the second contest, Princeton won eight goals to none.

In 1873 representatives from Princeton and Rutgers joined representatives from Columbia and Yale Universities at a meeting in New York to formulate a set of uniform rules for football. There the universities formed the Intercollegiate Football Association (IFA) to act as a governing body for the new sport. The IFA mandated that fifteen players per team would take the field. Two years later, in 1875, they replaced the round soccer-style ball with an oblong, leather-covered rugby-style ball.

But it was Walter Camp, the Yale football coach and a dissenter against the fifteen-player rule, who ushered in the final stage in football's evolution from rugby-style play. Camp headed the IFA's rules committee and used his position to change the number of players from fifteen to eleven. He reduced the size of the field to 110 yards. In 1882, Camp and his rules committee ended the continuous motion of the game, finally severing its ties with its sporting antecedents. The committee mandated three attempts to advance the ball five yards. Success would lead to another set of attempts, called "downs." In 1906 the distance was lengthened to ten yards, and in 1912 a fourth down was added.

In the late nineteenth century and early twentieth, increasing concern over the brutality of the game led some colleges to ban it. Many players had suffered serious injury. Eighteen players had died. In 1905, President Theodore Roosevelt publicly called for reform. Harvard, Princeton, and Yale—the three schools singled out by Roosevelt—met and agreed upon the need for a new governing body for the sport. A second meeting, also in 1905, was attended by more than sixty participating universities. The schools established the Inter-Collegiate Athletic Association (ICAA), the most prominent feature of which was a seven-member rules committee that was dedicated to making the game safer. In 1911, the ICAA

Football Game. The Harvard-Dartmouth football game, 14 November 1903. Prints and Photographs Division, Library of Congress

changed its name to the National Collegiate Athletic Association, the NCAA.

In 1906 the ICAA rules committee legalized the forward pass. Without it, team strategies centered on formations such as the "flying wedge," in which a ball carrier was surrounded by a wedge of teammates. The most effective method for a defender to break through the wedge was to throw himself onto the legs of onrushing foes, particularly dangerous without the use of helmets. The ICAA rules committee prohibited rough mass plays such as the flying wedge, shortened the game from seventy to sixty minutes, and established the neutral zone, separating the teams by the length of the ball before every play.

Scoring evolved as well. In the Princeton-Rutgers matches, as well as in other early games, each time a team advanced the ball across the goal in any fashion, that team earned one point. In 1883, however, the first uniform scoring system emphasized kicking. Field goals earned five points, while touchdowns and conversions earned four. In 1897 the value of a touchdown was raised to five points, with a successful conversion adding another point. The points offered for a field goal fell to four in 1904 and to three in 1909. The touchdown received its modern six-point value in 1912.

These changes were administered by the IFA, the ICAA, and the NCAA—collegiate organizations—and football remained predominantly a college game through the first half of the twentieth century. College football's true cultural importance came when state identity became tied to the success of the state university team, and this change came largely in places that lacked economic success—the South, in particular. The watershed for college football's move from the northeast to the South was the 1926 Rose Bowl between the University of Alabama and the University of Washington. Alabama won, and returning by train the team witnessed thousands of southerners waiting for them along their route, bringing flowers and applauding. The following year the University of Georgia traveled to Yale and defeated the northeastern power. But this identity formation happened not only in the South. In the decade before the 1926 Rose Bowl, a small Catholic university in northwestern Indiana, Notre Dame, rose to dominate much of college football in the twentieth century, forming a bond with Catholics nationwide.

But the game also became a professional endeavor. Though attempts at leagues were made as early as 1895, it was in 1920 that the American Professional Football Association (APFA) was formed. In 1922 the APFA became the National Football League (NFL). As the century progressed, the NFL became more and more successful. Though it was less popular than baseball and its college counterpart, professional football became profitable enough to spawn attempts at rival leagues. The most viable of these organizations was the American Football League (AFL), formed by Lamar Hunt in 1959 and beginning play the following season. The AFL began paying higher salaries than the NFL and thus stole players from its rival. The watershed AFL signing came after the 1964 season when the New York Jets signed the Alabama quarterback Joe Namath to the richest contract in professional football history.

With the AFL's popularity rising, the two leagues agreed to a merger in 1966, instituting a common draft and a championship game between the winners of each league.

The first of these world championship games occurred on 15 January 1967, when the Green Bay Packers defeated the Kansas City Chiefs. By the third year of the merger, the contest had become known as the Super Bowl. The merger was complete in 1970, and the combined National Football League has grown in popularity ever since, becoming the highest revenue-generating sports league in the United States.

[*See also* Soccer *and* Sports.]

BIBLIOGRAPHY
Bernstein, Mark F. *Football: The Ivy League Origins of an American Obsession.* Philadelphia: University of Pennsylvania Press, 2001.
Patton, Phil. *Razzle Dazzle: The Curious Marriage of Television and Professional Football.* Garden City, N.Y.: Dial, 1984.
Peterson, Robert W. *Pigskin: The Early Years of Pro Football.* New York: Oxford University Press, 1997.
Watterson, John Sayle. *College Football: History, Spectacle, and Controversy.* Baltimore: Johns Hopkins University Press, 2000.

THOMAS AIELLO

FOOTBINDING. Footbinding began in China in the tenth century, when six- to ten-year-old girls had their feet tightly bound to yield idealized three-inch "lily feet." Only women bound their feet, and they did so because women with small feet had better marriage prospects and a life of less toil than those with unbound feet. In 1636 and 1664 the Manchu Qing rulers banned footbinding without success, after which the practice became an ethnic marker and a symbol of civility for the Han Chinese majority (except for the Hakka), since Manchu and other minority women left their natural feet alone.

In the mid-nineteenth century, Western missionaries and Chinese reformers viewed footbinding as a victimization of women. They founded antifootbinding associations to persuade mothers to stop binding their daughters' feet and to unbind their own feet. Missionaries and anthropologists focused on removing the pain that derived from mutilated feet, and reformers condemned footbinding as a backward patriarchal tradition and a barrier to China's modernization. In 1912 the constitution of the Republic of China abolished footbinding, but some girls in remote villages (as in Yunnan Province) still had their feet bound in the 1920s and 1930s. Recent scholarship explores many perspectives—including women's agency, sexuality, and attire and fashion—in an attempt to explain the resistance, voiced by not a few women, to the antifootbinding movements in the mid-nineteenth and early twentieth centuries.

[*See also* Gender, *subentry* Gender Relations in East Asia; Paternalism, *subentry* East Asia; *and* Women, *subentry* East Asia.]

BIBLIOGRAPHY
Ebrey, Patricia. "Gender and Sinology: Shifting Western Interpretations of Footbinding, 1300–1890." *Late Imperial China* 20, no. 2 (1999): 1–34.
Ko, Dorothy. *Cinderella's Sisters: A Revisionist History of Footbinding.* Berkeley: University of California Press, 2005.

JENNIFER W. JAY

FORCED LABOR. As European colonizing powers began to assert hegemony in much of sub-Saharan Africa during the early twentieth century, forced labor became a common and cheap form of African labor organization. Across the continent, gangs of bonded laborers toiled on public infrastructure projects, building roads, bridges, and dams, as well as working for private interests in mines and on plantations. The colonial state institutionalized forced labor through its laws. The ideological justification for forced labor alluded to trusteeship, a vague notion that African development was contingent upon a sacred trust between European colonizers and African subjects, to be maintained until some point in the future when Africans could better manage their own affairs. The myth of the lazy African male, unresponsive to economic incentives and lethargic owing to the labor of his womenfolk, fueled the justification of forced labor as an aspect of progressive rule. Although all colonial powers used forced labor, the frequency and intensity of the practice varied across region and time period.

East Africa. In British East Africa, although coercion was pervasive in all the colonies, the European settler element determined the extent of forced labor in Kenya. European settlers lacked adequate capital to mechanize agricultural production intensively but offered only low wages as incentives for Africans. Many Africans still had access to land and went into the labor market only if they were poor or for specific reasons that determined the extent of their engagement. As a result, between 1909 and 1939, settlers filled the op-ed pages of local newspapers with cries of a labor crisis, provoking the state to enter the market and force Africans to labor through laws and penal sanctions. Forced labor developed, in part, as a means of inducing Africans to work either for Europeans or for the state.

The Native Authority Ordinance of 1912 and its subsequent amendments served as the cornerstone of forced labor legislation. This ordinance gave colonial chiefs and headmen the power to coerce able-bodied men for so-called communal projects for up to twenty-four days a year. Local headmen were usually given instructions from the district commissioner concerning the need for labor on a certain project for a set number of days. They would then go to their villages with armed retainers and extract the required number of workers. The process of extraction was usually abrupt and would disrupt the everyday routine of people. The work was supposed to involve projects such as watercourses, light dams, bridges, and footpaths that were deemed part of the traditional obligations of an ethnic group, but laborers frequently would be put to work on heavy transport roads that in reality benefited the state and the European settlers more than the African communities. Communal labor was unpaid, making it the most detested form of coerced labor.

An amendment to the Native Authority Ordinance in 1920 gave chiefs and headmen the power to force labor for up to sixty days per year for work on state infrastructure projects. Although the laborers for these projects received wages, the wages were usually below market rate so as not to compete with settlers for African labor. As with communal labor, Africans could gain exemptions if they had labored for Europeans for three months.

In addition to state forced labor, the forced recruitment of African labor by administrative officials for private European employers was also prevalent. Although illegal by 1913, it was widely practiced in Kenya until the mid-1920s.

Peasants working on forced labor details were subject to abuses. Although the law governing communal labor called for able-bodied men, young women and children were frequently found doing road work. The young girls who worked on communal labor details were prey to sexual exploitation by their guards. In some cases workers were given inadequate provisions or housing. For example, in 1925 a number of coerced laborers working on the Uasin-Gishu extension of the Uganda railway in Kenya died owing to underprovisioning and poor living conditions.

By the early 1930s, however, domestic scandals and public criticism pressured the administration in Kenya to stop relying upon paid forced labor, with the exception of emergencies and porterage. In 1930 the International Labour Organization (ILO) passed a Forced Labour Convention, which Britain signed. It severely sanctioned forced labor for private purposes and called for the end of forced labor in the foreseeable future, as well as requiring signatory powers to submit reports on their progress toward this goal. Despite these measures, however, state use of communal forced labor continued until independence.

West Africa. Like the British in East Africa, the French conscripted West African labor for both state projects and private interests. The French nominally placed the responsibility for collecting the conscripts on the Africans themselves. According to a 1912 decree governing corvée labor, each local community, through the chiefs and elders, was responsible for turning out a certain number of able-bodied men for a set period each year for construction work. The labor was unpaid but the administration was supposed to provide rations. The length of the conscription period varied by colony but normally fell between eight and twelve days per year. The corvée was not supposed to be exacted during harvest, and after 1925 the laborers were not supposed to work farther than three miles (five kilometers) from home. Elderly people and Africans who worked for the military and other facets of the administration were normally exempt.

Labor abuses were rife under the corvée system. Villagers frequently had to work long distances from home and were often overworked. Rations were usually inadequate or not forthcoming, forcing Africans to supplement their food with donations from family members. Armed guards were necessary to limit desertions, which were common.

European settlers in French West Africa also required paid forced labor for their plantations. In areas like Ivory Coast they came to depend upon forced labor recruited by the chiefs and local headmen. The recruitment pressure was so intense at times that laborers fled to neighboring territories to escape conscription. In some areas of French West Africa the government used concessionary companies to procure natural resources like salt, groundnuts, and lumber, and these companies also came to depend heavily upon forced labor.

After the French signed the ILO Forced Labour Convention in 1937, they began to reduce forced labor for private concerns and community projects. But despite some reforms, the decline in forced labor would not begin in earnest until after the Brazzaville Conference in 1944, when the French attempted to readjust their colonial policies in Africa, leading to a call for the end of forced labor within five years. African agitation induced the French to act faster, however, and legislation ending forced labor passed in 1946.

Southern Africa. In Southern Rhodesia the problem of acquiring African labor was acute early on because of the prominence of private mining and agricultural interests and company rule. The British South Africa Company under Cecil Rhodes ruled by charter in Southern Rhodesia from 1889 until 1923. Although the concession that led to the charter only gave mineral rights, the charter gave the company legislative, administrative, and judicial powers, plus a mandate to improve the land.

Although the anticipated gold potential of Southern Rhodesia was never realized, rampant mine speculation in the early twentieth century stimulated European immigration. Rhodesia quickly became the most populous settler colony after South Africa. As in Kenya, many of the settlers were undercapitalized, and they also faced the competition for African labor from the mines in Transvaal in South Africa. As a result, to meet the demands for labor, the state began to conscript Africans.

The Rhodesia Native Labour Bureau (RNLB) was created in 1903 to oversee the supply of labor to mines and later to farms. The RNLB rationalized the labor supply by using forced labor or *chibaro*, as the Africans called it, which meant "slave." The labor was paid but at rates that did not compete against the market standard. Africans were normally forced to adhere to a contract for up to twelve months. In many cases the administration procured *chibaro* labor simply by rounding up African males and carting them off to the mines. This *chibaro* labor also came to be used extensively on the European agricultural estates.

Chibaro labor was very unpleasant and the mine work was very dangerous, with a high death rate for Africans. Africans resisted through desertion, or they simply sought higher wage labor in the Transvaal mines. But by the 1920s many of the labor procurement problems for the mines, and thus the use of coercion, had begun to decline. The RNLB was disbanded in 1933 because of the legacy of conscription abuses.

Central Africa. By far the most egregious use of forced labor occurred in the Belgian Congo. State use of forced labor and recruitment for private concerns led to a number of abuses and eventually to an international campaign against forced labor in the early twentieth century.

To accomplish their aim of extracting natural resources like rubber, lumber, and tin from the Congo, the Belgian administration and the various concessionary companies needed cheap African labor, and the state entered the labor market early on to meet the need through coercion. Under an 1891 law African chiefs and headmen were responsible for supplying tribute, usually in the form of laborers for porterage and building. This law was later used to acquire labor for the extraction of rubber on government-controlled land. The labor was paid but arduous. By 1922 government forced labor was used primarily for the construction of

roads and bridges. Africans were liable for up to sixty days a year.

Forced labor recruitment for rubber resulted in a litany of abuses. In many cases Africans were simply rounded up and taken to work sites. Communities that did not meet their rubber tax were attacked and villagers were killed or mutilated, with some having their hands and feet chopped off. The appalling abuses sparked an international campaign against the Belgian regime. By 1908, when the Belgian parliament took over administration of the Congo, the state began to mitigate some of the more heinous aspects of forced labor by substituting heavier taxation. In 1912 the Belgian administration abrogated the hated rubber tax, which had made Africans responsible for a certain amount of labor on rubber plantations. By the 1930s, with the exception of wartime and emergency, the government had stopped directly recruiting African labor for private concerns. The passage of the ILO Forced Labour Convention further limited the use of coercion in other areas like cotton growing.

In Africa the impoverished state needed cheap African labor to develop the infrastructure of the burgeoning colonies. In areas with European settlement the demands for cheap African labor increased the pressure for conscription. Extra-economic forms of coercion that dominated in the early period of colonial rule, however, eventually gave way to market forces in determining African entry into the labor market. The passage of international conventions against forced labor further ameliorated the practice. Still, despite this gradual transformation, in some regions aspects of coercion remained throughout the colonial period.

Since independence, forced labor has continued to exist in some parts of Africa but is more associated with extreme situations of slavery, coerced child labor, and warfare. Because of pervasive poverty, child labor is prevalent and entrenched in Africa. However, in some of the worst cases of child labor, children are forced to work as indentured labor or sex workers. For example, in Ghana children are sometimes sold as indentured laborers in the fishing industry. In the case of slavery, forms of servitude associated with particular ethnic groups still exist in some areas of Africa. For example, in the Central African Republic forest-dwelling Khoi-San–speaking ethnic groups are sometimes forced to supply forest products and women to Bantu-speaking ethnic groups. In Sudan, because of the long-running civil war, ethnic groups in the southern portion of the country, like the Dinka, have become victims of enslavement. In the Darfur region of Western Sudan women and children have been abducted and enslaved by

Arab militias. In Northern Uganda, owing to the warfare between the Lords Resistance Army and the Movement government of Uganda, women and children have been abducted and forced to become soldiers or wives of commanders in the Lords Resistance Army.

[*See also* Africa; Belgian Congo; Colonialism, *subentry* Africa; *and* Slavery, *subentry* Africa.]

BIBLIOGRAPHY

Babacar, Fall. *Le travail forcé en Afrique-Occidental française (1900–1946)*. Paris: Karthala, 1993.

Cooper, Frederick. "Conditions Analogous to Slavery: Imperialism and Free Labor Ideology in Africa." In *Beyond Slavery: Explorations of Race, Labor, and Citizenship in Postemancipation Societies*, by Frederick Cooper, Rebecca Scott, and Thomas Holt, pp. 107–151. Chapel Hill: University of North Carolina Press, 2000.

ILO. *A Global Alliance against Forced Labor*. Washington D.C., 2005.

Northrup, David. *Beyond the Bend in the River: African Labor in Eastern Zaire, 1865–1940*. Athens, Ohio: Ohio University Center for International Studies, 1988.

Nzula, A. T., I. I. Potekhin, and A. Z. Zusmanovich, *Forced Labour in Colonial Africa*. Edited by Robin Cohen. Translated by Hugh Jenkins. London: Zed, 1979.

Phillips, Anne. *The Enigma of Colonialism: British Policy in West Africa*. London: J. Currey; Bloomington: Indiana University Press, 1989.

Zegeye, Abebe, and Shubi Ishemo, eds. *Forced Labour and Migration: Patterns of Movement within Africa*. London and New York: Zell, 1989.

OPOLOT OKIA

FORDISM. In 1914 the Ford Motor Company announced that it was paying wages of five dollars a day at its plant in Highland Park, Michigan, and reducing its working hours from nine to eight hours. Ford's innovation was based on a marketing philosophy of cheap costs and high sales volume and on new production methods including greater division of labor, standardized components, assembly lines, and continuous conveyor belts. Paying five dollars a day guaranteed a reliable workforce and avoided costly job turnover. Shortening the workday enabled Ford to engage in round-the-clock production with three eight-hour shifts. As Alfred D. Chandler and others have shown, all of these practices can be found in the prewar period, but Ford carried them to new heights.

Dubbed "Fordism" by contemporaries, Ford's practices attracted much analysis. Contemporaries including the Russian Communist leader Vladimir Ilich Lenin believed that Ford had applied the scientific management theories of Frederick Winslow Taylor (1856–1915) to auto production. Both Taylor and Ford employed mechanization, increased division of labor, and deskilling, but Taylor criticized Ford for his failure to educate workers and win their support, as well as for his reliance on hierarchical control and his distrust of teamwork.

American labor emphasized the realities of Fordist practice. Ford's eight-hour day allowed the worker only one fifteen-minute lunch break. Workers were not permitted to talk to one another and were subject to arbitrary firing and periodic speedup. Also, Ford workers and their families were subject to surveillance by Ford's Service Department. Labor organizers, even labor sympathizers, were brutally beaten by thugs connected to the Service Department. Finally, in the early 1930s, Ford backtracked, cutting its minimum wage to four dollars. Ford's retreat was not simply a result of the Depression. His theory that the public bought the cheapest car ("any color so long as it's black") was disproved by General Motors' variety of automobile makes and models.

Although the golden age of Fordism was brief, it attained new life in Marxist theory. Lenin advocated the introduction of Fordism to a war-wrecked Soviet Union. European socialists briefly expressed interest in Fordist technologies that might give workers more leisure and better pay. From prison Antonio Gramsci pondered whether Fordism foretold a new age of capitalist expansion, but he also saw it as part of a puritanical American culture. Gramsci's idea of Fordism as bound up with an entire social order was later adopted by the regulation school of neo-Marxism. It identified Fordism as a post–World War II social structure, a regime of capitalist accumulation characterized by stability and economic growth and underpinned by specific laws, institutions, traditions, and political hegemonies.

Fordism has been used as a shorthand term for the introduction of a variety of technologies, for several sets of industrial relations policies at various times, and for various hegemonic social orders. Each of these elements is complex, and there is no evidence that they vary together. Fordism originated in a claim that assembly-line workers would be paid high wages and work fewer hours. Though the claim proved fleeting, it set off debates about the future of work in modern capitalist society that still echo, but efforts to expand its definition have generally lacked both clarity and empirical support.

[*See also* Assembly Line; Automobile, *subentry* The Automobile Industry; Capitalism; Ford Motor Company; Labor and the Labor Movement; *and* Scientific Management.]

BIBLIOGRAPHY

Chandler, Alfred D., Jr. *Scale and Scope: The Dynamics of Industrial Capitalism.* Cambridge, Mass.: Belknap Press of Harvard University Press, 1990. The great historian of industrial organization.

Gramsci, Antonio. "Americanism and Fordism." In *Selections from the Prison Notebooks of Antonio Gramsci,* edited and translated by Quintin Hoare and Geoffrey Howell Smith, pp. 278–318. New York: International Publishers, 1971. Gramsci's classic musings on Fordism.

Lipietz, Alain. *Mirages and Miracles: The Crises of Global Fordism.* Translated by David Macey. London: Verso, 1987. A view of Fordism from a regulationist perspective.

Meyer, Stephen. *The Five Dollar Day: Labor, Management, and Social Control in the Ford Motor Company, 1908–1921.* Albany: State University of New York Press, 1981. An important study.

Raushenbush, Carl. "Fordism: Ford and the Workers." *League for Industrial Democracy* 5 (1937): 8–38. A view of Fordism by a pro-labor U.S. economist.

MICHAEL HANAGAN

FORD MOTOR COMPANY. The founder of the Ford Motor company, Henry Ford, was born into a well-to-do farmer's family in 1863 in Wayne County, near Dearborne, Michigan. He attended school only four years. As an engineer at Edison Illuminating Company he constructed the self-powered Quadricycle. In 1899 he started the Detroit Automobile Company, which went bankrupt after two years. In 1903 he and eleven associates founded the Ford Motor Company (FMC), which started producing the Model T in 1908. With more than 15 million sold, the "Tin Lizzy" was the first mass-produced car. Manufacturing cars was Ford's first vision; organizing that process on a mass scale was his second. The conveyor belt was used in the slaughterhouses in Chicago, and in 1913 Ford succeeded in transferring that technology to car production, thus developing the assembly-line system. While rationalization from below (work) became associated with Frederick Taylor, rationalization from above (organization) became related to Ford (Fordism). Ford's third vision was to make his mass-produced car affordable, and consequently he lowered the price every year. When shareholders opposed this policy as well as the massive investment in the giant complex in Dearborne, Ford bought the shares back. In 1918 every second car in the United States was a Model T. His son Edsel became president of the company in 1919, but little was decided against Henry's will. Believing that his workers should be capable of buying their own product, Ford raised wages and lowered working hours to eight per day. He thus paved the way for a fuller consumer society. While fighting labor unions, he simultaneously put most of his fortune into the Ford Foundation for the benefit of all in 1936. Typically for a family firm, differences occurred between father and son about changes. Edsel wanted a new model. After sales of the Model T stagnated, the Model A was introduced in 1927, and by 1931, 4 million of them had been sold.

The successful company used all means of internal and external expansion. Backward investment into India rubber plantations failed, but all other efforts succeeded. In 1925 FMC bought Lincoln Motor Company to cover the high-price end of the market, and with the introduction of the Mercury brand the medium-price segment was successfully targeted. Already in 1911 FMC produced the "Tin Lizzy" in the United Kingdom, taking 30 percent of the market in 1913. Investment into other countries followed in the interwar period, including a large investment into Germany in 1925. FMC also diversified into trucks and tractors (Fordson). During World War II, Ford Germany produced for the Germans while the bulk of FMC sustained the Allied forces; political fate divided the firm. In the United States, FMC suffered such great losses that President Roosevelt considered a state credit to maintain the necessary war production.

From 1945 to 1960 Henry Ford II provided strong leadership, and FMC flourished again. He introduced the

Tin Lizzies. Model Ts come off the Ford assembly line, Detroit, Michigan, c. 1917. PRINTS AND PHOTOGRAPHS DIVISION, LIBRARY OF CONGRESS

Thunderbird as a sporty brand and took the company public again in 1956. Earlier than other companies FMC understood the dynamics of market integration, and in 1967 it merged its European companies into Ford of Europe; North American Automotive Operations was created in 1971, more than two decades before the North American Free Trade Agreement (NAFTA) was born. Starting in the 1980s FMC made hectic acquisitions and sales of divisions and other car manufacturers, reflecting mounting globalization pressure. In 1985 FMC acquired New Holland (agricultural machines) but sold the whole division six years later. FMC took over (entirely or at least 50 percent) the companies Aston Martin in 1987, Jaguar in 1989, Mazda in 1992, Volvo in 1999, and Land Rover in 2000. Thus FMC diversified mainly into the upper-end segment of the market, which was closed for the Ford brand name. During the same period large parts of production were outsourced. The car-rental company Hertz, acquired in 1994, was sold in 2005. The Focus model became the world's best-selling car in 2000, in spite of FMC's economic difficulties. The company had great success in environmental protection, being the first car producer worldwide to receive the ISO 14001 norm (an environmental management standard for companies) for all its plants. At the turn of the twenty-first century FMC, then the world's second-largest car producer, employing 350,000, was again led by a family member, William Clay Ford. His announced vision was to make FMC again number one in the world.

[*See also* Assembly Line *and* Automobile.]

BIBLIOGRAPHY
Benham, Russ. *The Ford Century: Ford Motor Company and the Innovations That Shaped the World.* New York: Artisan, 2002.
Ford, Henry, and Samuel Crowther. *My Life and Work.* Garden City, N.J.: Garden City Publications, 1922.
Sinclair, Upton. *The Flivver King: A Story of Ford-America.* Detroit: United Automobile Workers of America, 1937.

HARM G. SCHRÖTER

FOREIGN AID. Foreign aid comprises systems by which grants, loans, goods, personnel, knowledge, policy formulas, and norms are directed abroad for geostrategic, developmental, and humanitarian purposes. Managed mainly from wealthy and powerful countries, foreign aid is supposed to benefit poor countries. Prominent since the middle of the twentieth century, today's foreign aid is a distinctly modern phenomenon.

Forerunners. Episodes of geopolitics suggest some precedents. Britain provided subsidies to Prussia in the eighteenth century and to an Italian nationalist movement led by Giuseppe Garibaldi (1807–1882) in the nineteenth century. In what has been termed the first humanitarian war, the United States sent supplies and personnel to the Philippines and Cuba after its 1898 triumph over Spain. Episodic assistance later gave way to routine systems. Colonial rule in Asia and Africa prefigured today's foreign aid. Europeans defined the problems, then provided solutions through such things as public institutions and infrastructure, mission schools and health services, research and associational life. A rationale of British colonialism was the so-called dual mandate: one purpose was to govern and subordinate colonized peoples on the basis of trusteeship, while the other was to marshal those peoples' economic assets on terms favoring colonial interests. Much of today's foreign aid shows traces of the dual mandate.

Emergence of the Aid Regime. Following World War II, foreign aid became a regime—that is, a complex hierarchy of institutions whose practices converge around a set of rules. The aid regime's inception may be dated from President Harry Truman's 1949 inaugural address, which first gave currency to terms like "underdevelopment" that continue to shape discussion of aid. Though coincidental with public welfare systems in industrialized countries, foreign aid was designed not for statutory redistribution from rich to poor but for the discretionary exercise of power. In the Cold War decades, the United States deployed foreign aid as a multiple-use device to promote its interests. Western Europe benefited from early aid initiatives by the United States, epitomized in the high-cost, high-impact Marshall Plan from 1948 to 1952. Effective U.S. aid programs followed in postwar South Korea and Taiwan.

Europe's aid systems developed in the 1960s, most reflecting continuity of relations with former colonies. Scandinavian aid reflected domestic social-democratic values. From weaker economic and cultural positions, the Soviet Union and other eastern bloc countries managed aid programs—usually admixtures of military and engineering products—on their peripheries and in lands where affiliated Communist parties held state power or were struggling to attain it. After 1973 a number of petroleum-exporting states, led by Saudi Arabia, formed a temporarily significant donor bloc, directing petrodollars to poorer oil-producing Islamic countries. After 1990, countries of Eastern Europe and the former Soviet Union became aid targets instead of providers.

Purposes. Aid serves a multitude of purposes, reflecting the range and complexity of the problems that it claims to address and the diversity of constituencies that it has acquired over time. Fundamentally, foreign aid is an instrument of statecraft. Only rarely does it stem from altruism and solidarity. Geopolitical, mercantile, and military interests determine who gets what aid when and how. Domestic agendas emanating from such sectors as agribusiness, pharmaceuticals, and consulting services can loom large. Other nonprofit institutional actors such as municipalities, universities, and charities have a stake in aid. Political constituencies, such as diasporas focused on homelands, can influence who gets aid and on what terms. Public support for aid varies greatly from country to country, but it is everywhere strong in cases of humanitarian catastrophe. The success of child sponsorship as a fund-raising approach testifies to foreign aid's power to respond to deep psychological needs of donors.

Combating poverty began to figure regularly at the top of official aid agendas only at the end of the 1990s—fifty years after the aid regime's inception. But powerful forces at work in politics, trade, finance, culture, and ideology—both in rich countries and in poor—continue to tower over foreign aid, and to frustrate if not nullify its new antipoverty aims, thereby exposing serious problems of policy incoherence.

Channels. Aid interactions follow channels that may be clustered in three categories:

1. Private aid operates via charities, foundations, large firms, and groups expressing solidarity. The smallest category of aid providers in financial turnover, this is the most diverse in motivations, ideas, and forms of engagement.

2. Official development assistance (ODA) works through statutory agencies for purposes of socioeconomic development and relief of suffering. This category accounts for the largest quantity of funds and most of the doctrine and knowledge associated with the official aid regime. Aid statistics normally refer to this category, which in the case of Eastern Europe and for the former Soviet Union is called "official assistance."

3. Government-to-government subsidies reflect geostrategic aims. This assistance may not be counted as ODA because its chief purposes are not developmental or humanitarian. But government-to-government subsidies are of particular importance for big powers wishing to arm or otherwise support allies and client states for purposes not officially recognized as developmental.

About two-thirds of net ODA operates bilaterally—that is, through agencies, such as USAID and Britain's Department for International Development, that answer to national governments. About one-third of net ODA operates multilaterally—that is, through institutions, such as regional development banks and U.N. agencies, that account formally to collectivities of national governments. Informally, however, the United States has a decisive voice in determining the scope and purposes of work, staffing, and headquartering of most multilateral institutions, especially those at the strategic heights of the aid system, namely the International Monetary Fund and the World Bank. Set against the highly limited formal powers of recipient countries, the preponderance and nontransparency of key multilateral agencies reflect the challenges posed to democratic process within the aid system.

Donor institutions channel their resources, implement their projects, and carry out research through long and complex chains of intermediaries, including for-profit and nonprofit bodies and various public and private actors at receiving ends.

Historically, donors have preferred the project format, which allows for external supervision. In the 1980s, large official donors began making loans and grants directly to governments on condition that they adopt certain policies determined by the donors. Thus a large amount of aid became a payment for policy change. After two decades of failure, donors began to replace this intrusive and coercive style of conditionality with agreements to encourage national ownership of, and responsibility for, development initiatives based on agreed plans that have particular emphasis on poverty alleviation. However, donors have not abandoned their insistence that recipients pursue macroeconomic and trade policies preferred by the donors.

Recipients. Contrary to popular understanding, most aid is not directed toward the poor. Lower-middle-income countries such as Indonesia and Egypt account for the bulk of aid flows; the lowest-income countries have historically accounted for less than a third of net ODA, and hardly any other (non-ODA) flows. Sectors of direct relevance to poor people, such as basic education, basic health, water, and sanitation, account for only small fractions of total aid flows, despite some shifts toward antipoverty purposes since 1999. Direct beneficiaries in targeted countries are found chiefly in the salaried and entrepreneurial strata and the political classes. Recipients at various levels have learned to use aid systems to regulate their relations with powerful outsiders.

Most aid funds are spent in, or flow back to, donor countries themselves, where they are absorbed by firms, organizations, and individuals providing goods and services. Together with counterparts lower along aid chains, they make up what is called the aid industry. These actors constitute aid's most active lobby. However, with the advent of greater recipient control—such as direct support to government budgets and implementation by host nationals—some aid chains may get shorter, and benefits accruing at their upper ends may diminish.

Outcomes. Foreign aid has made significant contributions to political and economic recovery, particularly in its early decades. In Western Europe, South Korea, and Taiwan, aid was geared to national economic planning and industrial protection, as well as to major public investments in health, education, and social protection. Aid has promoted successful state building, as in Botswana. When combined with vigorous diplomacy, aid has helped bring about delicate political transitions. In South Africa, for example, aid for the movement against apartheid helped speed the advent of democracy. Aid has helped curb some tropical diseases and promote women's reproductive rights. Humanitarian relief aid has sometimes been of great symbolic and political importance, but it usually accounts for only a small fraction of the total material response to emergencies; national public agencies and local people normally carry most of the burden, even if that is never recorded.

However, in many cases, aid's impact has been disappointing and even destructive. Where aid funds and coercive conditionalities have been most intense, economic growth and equitable consumption have frequently been frustrated rather than advanced. Western official aid met its political goal of containing Communism, but at a huge cost. It has often weakened reciprocity between people and rulers, whose attention and accountability are fixed on donors rather than on citizens. Particularly in sub-Saharan Africa, the aid regime has done nothing to halt—and according to some observers has helped bring on—the breakdown of reciprocity between political leaders and citizens, the hollowing out of sovereignty and self-determination, the flight of capital and trained people, and the acquisition of crippling foreign debts.

Aid commands a great deal of attention in the West. Yet the massive stream of studies and statistics and public commentary may be out of proportion to its relative importance amid far larger forces of global trade and financial circuits, the military, and geopolitics. Nevertheless, foreign aid's many constituencies, powerful institutions, and manifold uses as an instrument in world politics would seem to guarantee it a long life well into the twenty-first century.

[See also "Debt Crisis" and Development, Economic.]

BIBLIOGRAPHY

Anderson, Mary. *Do No Harm: How Aid Can Support Peace—or War*. Boulder, Colo.: Lynne Rienner Publishers, 1999. A seminal treatment of the humanitarian branch of aid.

Easterly, William. *The White Man's Burden: Why the West's Efforts to Aid the Rest Have Done So Much Ill and So Little Good*. New York: Penguin Press, 2006. A wide-ranging overview by a former World Bank economist who is now a dissenter from the mainstream.

Reality of Aid. *An Independent Review of Poverty Reduction and International Development Assistance*. Manila. A reliable and accessible annual publication about donor practice, with statistics. See http://www.realityofaid.org.

Sogge, David. *Give and Take: What's the Matter with Foreign Aid?* London and New York: Zed Books, 2002. A historical and political analysis.

Stiglitz, Joseph. *Globalization and Its Discontents*. New York: W. W. Norton, 2002. A critical analysis of economic doctrines promoted by the aid regime, written by an insider and a Nobel laureate in economics.

Uvin, Peter. *Aiding Violence: The Development Enterprise in Rwanda*. West Hartford, Conn.: Kumarian Press, 1998. An incisive case study of aid's political impact in Africa.

Wedel, Janine. *Collision and Collusion: The Strange Case of Western Aid to Eastern Europe 1989–1998*. New York: St. Martin's Press, 1998. An anthropologist's insights into aid's effects on transitions from state socialism.

DAVID SOGGE

FOREIGN INVESTMENT [*This entry includes two subentries, on East Asia and on the United States.*]

East Asia

Because governments restricted foreign investments from the nineteenth century to the early twenty-first, there were few periods during which unrestrained foreign investment was possible in East Asia. The governments feared that they would lose national independence if they let wealthy foreign institutions or individuals control key parts of their economy. As a result, foreign investment usually was possible only under certain circumstances: a weak central government authority, a foreign minority stake in the form of joint ventures, and during more advanced stages of economic development during the last decades of the twentieth century.

Early Avenues for Foreign Investment. From about the mid-nineteenth century, major East Asian countries acceded to demands for the establishment of diplomatic relations and the permission to engage in international trade by concluding treaties with foreign powers—China in the Treaty of Nanjing (1842), Japan in the Treaty of Kanagawa (1854), and Korea in the Treaty of Kanghwa (1876). These and later so-called unequal treaties also permitted foreigners to reside in designated treaty ports such as Shanghai, Yokohama, and Pusan, to own property in those places, and sometimes to engage in limited local manufacturing activity. In order to circumvent prohibitions against foreign capital investments or land ownership, some foreign entrepreneurs sought the cooperation of local businessmen, but large-scale foreign industrial investment in East Asia became possible only when Japan defeated China in 1895 and concluded the Treaty of Shimonoseki, which approved industrial activity in Chinese treaty ports where Japanese established in subsequent decades a substantial number of firms, especially in the textile industry.

Railways became another important avenue for foreign investment in East Asia. Although the earliest railroad in China opened before the first Japanese railroad was opened in 1872, Japan succeeded in constructing a network ten times larger by the time it nationalized its railways in 1906. Not only was China comparatively slow in its railway expansion; parts of its rail system were constructed and controlled by foreign powers, which then used the railways as a means for regional domination. The Russian state obtained the right to build and operate a railway through Manchuria to link its Siberian railway with Vladivostok, its port in the Far East. After its takeover of the Kwantung Peninsula, Russia also laid a line through southern Manchuria, connecting Port Arthur (Lüshun) to the city of Harbin. The Japanese inherited these privileges after defeating Russia in 1905. In subsequent decades Japan's South Manchurian Railway company turned into a major industrial conglomerate that dominated the modern economy in its sphere of influence.

Japanese imperial expansion changed investment flows in the East Asian region. After Japan annexed Taiwan (1895) and Korea (1910), Japanese state and business agencies poured funds into local infrastructure such as transportation and industry, especially in the 1930s. Japanese administrators and managers promoted economic development from agriculture to state-of-the-art chemical companies. With the Manchurian Incident of 1931 and the declaration of the state of Manchukuo (Manzhouguo), a vast new territory was opened for Japanese capital investment in such fields as mining and heavy industries. With the increase of Japan's economic strength and heightened military concerns, countries in Asia erected higher barriers to foreign investment—such as Japan's effectively closing down the Japanese operations of American car companies. During its war with China from 1937 and the United States from 1941, the Japanese military requisitioned plants in conquered overseas territories, and investments usually served to shore up production to satisfy immediate military demand. In 1945, Japanese managerial and technical staff left overseas plants, which were sometimes taken over by former local managers or investors, especially in Korea, whereas China nationalized captured Japanese industries.

Postwar Decades. During the first postwar decades the state acted as a gatekeeper for the national economy in many East Asian countries by scrutinizing the flow of funds. Japan was the first country in Asia to experience unprecedented economic growth rates of around 10 percent, which it did from the mid-1950s until the oil shock in 1973, turning it into the world's second largest capitalist economy. This new strength encouraged Japanese companies to invest abroad as they established an industrial presence overseas, where labor was often cheaper or they could be closer to their consumer markets. From the late 1970s until the early twenty-first century, Japanese have always invested more abroad than foreigners have invested in Japan. Nevertheless, the largest outflow of funds was after the yen appreciation and during the stock market bubble when $160 billion left Japan in 1985–1990—with $51 billion alone in the peak year of 1990.

The 1990s saw a major shift in the direction of foreign direct investment in East Asia as China became a worldwide target. Many were seeking to reap the rewards from China's huge market potential after China, similar to what Japan had done earlier, sustained an average annual growth rate of 9.5 percent in 1978–2001. Funds to China came from all over the world but especially from overseas Chinese, the United States, and Japan. The drastic increase in inflow to China can be seen in the investment explosion from $0.6 billion in 1983 to an annual intake of $54 billion twenty years later, when in

TABLE 1. *Foreign Direct Investment in East Asia, 2004 (in billions of U.S. dollars).*

	FOREIGN DIRECT INVESTMENT STOCK		FOREIGN DIRECT INVESTMENT FLOW	
	INWARD	OUTWARD	INFLOW	OUTFLOW
World	8,895	9,732	648	730
China	246	39	60	2
Hong Kong	457	406	34	40
Japan	97	371	31	8
Korea, Republic of	55	39	8	5
Taiwan	39	91	2	7

SOURCE: UNCTAD, *World Investment Report 2005*, pp. 303, 306, 308, and 311.

2003 China surpassed the United States as the world's top recipient of foreign direct investment. Some observers claim that China's government is more welcoming to foreign multinationals than are those of other East Asian countries such as Japan, South Korea, and Taiwan. China encouraged especially export-oriented and technologically advanced foreign direct investment. As a result, foreign investment played a proportionally larger role in China's high-growth development than it had done in Japan's. In 2001, foreign-invested enterprises in China produced 29 percent of industrial output and half of China's exports. Although most foreign direct investment is now in services, manufacturing is still a key investment area in China.

[*See also* Corporation, The; Corporatist State, *subentry* East Asia; Industrial Policy in Japan and East Asia; Merchants: Western Merchants in East Asia; Neomercantilism in East Asia; Railroads, *subentry* East Asia; Trade, International, *subentry* East Asia; "Unequal Treaties"; *and* World Economy.]

BIBLIOGRAPHY

Duus, Peter, Ramon H. Myers, Mark R. Peattie, eds. *The Japanese Informal Empire in China, 1895–1937*. Princeton, N.J.: Princeton University Press, 1989. Several chapters are about Japanese investment and industry in China and Manchuria during the first part of the twentieth century.

Ito, Takatoshi, and Anne O. Krueger, eds. *The Role of Foreign Direct Investment in East Asian Economic Development*. Chicago: University of Chicago Press, 2000. Conference volume on foreign direct investment in fostering economic growth in various East Asian economies.

United Nations Conference on Trade and Development. *World Investment Report 2005: Transnational Corporations and the Internationalization of R&D*. New York: United Nations, 2005. http://www.unctad.org/en/docs/wir2005_d&s_en.pdf. Annual report on worldwide investment trends by a key U.N. agency, which also maintains a Web site with statistical information at http://www.unctad.org/fdistatistics.

Wade, Robert. *Governing the Market: Economic Theory and the Role of Government in East Asian Industrialization*. Princeton, N.J.: Princeton University Press, 1990. Analysis of the state's role in fostering trade and economic development in postwar East Asia, especially in Taiwan.

HARALD FUESS

The United States

From the start the emerging United States was within the reach of European direct investments, to set up fresh industry (shipyards, textile, metallurgy, tobacco) and commerce (ship owning, wholesale trading, and so on). These scattered investments came mostly from Great Britain—despite the American Revolution, when British assets were confiscated, later to be compensated for—and from the Netherlands (leading until the 1790s) and France. The financing for the American Revolution came from France, Spain, and the Netherlands; foreign debt reached 22 percent of the total federal debt.

Even when the first Industrial Revolution and the commodities trade encouraged self-financing among U.S. companies, the competitive edge of British industry, the U.S. technological gap, and the need for huge basic transportation equipment to move into the Western frontier all explain the thirst for European capital during the nineteenth century. British merchant banks had affiliates in the United States (J. P. Morgan from Morgan Grenfell) and correspondents among local investment banks (Goldman Sachs, Kühn Loeb, Dillon Read) in New York. They established bridges with the City of London to issue bonds and launch underwriting operations in London, where securities were brokered on the Continent to banks' customers, which favored foreign portfolio investments (FPIs). The U.S. railways bonds met great success when regional (from the 1850s) and then transcontinental or transregional lines—53,000 miles (85,000 kilometers) in 1870, and 250,000 miles (402,000 kilometers) in 1913—absorbed large amounts of European capital.

The growth of the U.S. balance of revenues (thanks to the export of raw materials), the creation of an internal financial market, and the upsurge of U.S. banks contributed to fostering local cash flows. FPIs were helpful in expanding railway networks and building steel plants; indeed, a quarter of U.S. Steel equity was held abroad in 1914. The first foreign direct investment (FDI) poured to the United States because a few companies capitalized on their technical skills—for instance, Lever and Nestlé in foodstuffs; Telefunken, Marconi, and Philips in electronics; Courtaulds in textiles. Globally, in 1914, FDI and FPI reached $7 billion, and U.S. investments abroad reached $3.5 billion.

World War I led to a thorough reversal of the U.S. financial position, from debtor to creditor. Numerous fighting countries had to sell their U.S. assets to gain cash for their imports (food stuff, raw materials, armaments); Germany was further deprived of its foreign assets by the peace treaties. Between the two world wars, FDI in the United States took shape in parallel with mere FPI; they were achieved by a few multinational companies—French Air Liquide, British-Dutch Unilever and Royal Dutch Shell, German pharmaceuticals or chemicals, these latter also concluding patent-sharing agreements—which dispatched overseas their technical skills because they wished to circumvent customs barriers and to take advantage of booming U.S. markets. FPI kept momentum, with less railroad and land-resource investment and more industrial and utility investment. These assets had to be sold out to finance World War II purchases in the United States or were confiscated by the winners, and Germany lost affiliates (for instance, two Schering firms, the U.S. and the German ones) or patents (Bayer aspirin). But foreign investment had dwindled against the U.S. ability to self-finance the second Industrial Revolution and even to export it—for instance, the plants that Ford and General Motors built abroad.

Such a favorable situation was confirmed after World War II because the United States was rich in dollars, and European countries suffered from the "dollar gap." Conversely, from the 1960s, U.S. protectionism, purchase power, standard of life, and growth lured foreign competing transnationals: they established connections with U.S. regional markets and took part in industries from building equipment (cement, raw materials) to daily life (pharmaceutics, publishing and television like the Australian Rupert Murdoch and his News Corporation). Foreign firms controlled 3 to 4 percent of the U.S. economy and 7 to 10 percent of the manufacturing sector at the end of the 1980s. In 1986 the United Kingdom and the Netherlands topped Japan, Canada, West Germany, and Switzerland as the main FDI providers.

The surge of Japan as an economic world power enticed its firms to impose their competitive edge: car plants were built in the United States by Toyota, Honda, and Nissan to transplant "toyotism" (superiority in productivity and quality) and also to draw the upper classes with premium brands; electronic consuming goods and medias were another target, mixing devices and image or music, alongside the so-called Sony business model. Cash availabilities delivered by the 1960s–1970s boom favored the constitution of huge portfolios of assets through FPI, borne by subsidiaries of banks or through real estate with the purchase of large blocks—stirring anger when movie companies and Rockefeller Center in New York City were

bought. Such an invasion was stopped when the Japanese markets crashed in the 1990s, and only industrial firms pursued their investments afterward.

They were more and more joined by European transnationals, which constituted 70 percent of direct investment in the United States in 2004—the United Kingdom leading with 16 percent of the total stock of FDI in the United States, ahead of Japan (12 percent) and the rest of Asia (14 percent). Firms increased their industrial basis in the United States (Michelin, Bosch, BASF, Philips, mining, and so on), even if some unions failed because of clashes of corporate culture (Chrysler and Daimler). Transatlantic mergers caused by difficulties of some U.S. companies set up worldwide groups in telecommunication equipment (Lucent-Alcatel), energy (Westinghouse and Hitachi), or medias (publishing and music). The United States became the largest host country for inward FDI as transnationals' strategy conceived it as their second-rank "domestic market." The concept of "foreign investment" was thus blurred because foreign companies became more U.S.-like or binational, such as BP-Amoco since 1998. Foreign companies in the United States employed 5.3 million U.S. citizens in 2006—4.7 percent of private industry employment—and contributed to 20 percent of exports. Such inflows of capital contribute to wages, U.S. manufacturing, research and technology, tax revenues, jobs, and productivity.

But short-term foreign investments in the United States kept the key role they won from the mid-1980s: world reserves in dollars ("oil dollars," "Asian dollars," and so on) were recycled to subscribe U.S. state bonds and face the huge budget deficits that were caused by recessions (1978–1982, 1993–1995, 2001–2002) or the Iraq War (2003–). But the deficit of the payments balance started earlier, as early as 1978–1982 when the U.S. surplus, which had prevailed from 1960, gave way to deficit, thus opening doors to stronger private FPI in the form of, for example, assets management funds. By the early twenty-first century, given trade deficits, the American economy depended more and more heavily on the European, Middle Eastern, and Asian investments, the latter now including China.

[*See also* Corporation, The; Multinational Corporations; Trade, International; United States; *and* World Economy.]

Table 1. *Investment in the United States*

Percentage against U.S. GNP	FDI and FPI	FDI
1914	19.5	4.7
1918	3.9	1.3
1939	10.0	3.2
1945	3.7	1.3

BIBLIOGRAPHY

Adler, Dorothy R. *British Investment in American Railways, 1834–1898.* Edited by Muriel E. Hidy. Charlottesville: University Press of Virginia for the Eleutherian Mills–Hagley Foundation, 1970.

Arpan, Jeffrey S., Edward B. Flowers, and David A. Ricks. "Foreign Direct Investment in the United States: The State of Knowledge in Research." *Journal of International Business Studies* 12, no. 1 (Spring–Summer 1981): 137–154.

Graham, Edward M., and Paul R. Krugman. *Foreign Direct Investment in the United States.* 3d ed. Washington, D.C.: Institute for International Economics, 1995.

Jenks, Leland Hamilton. *The Migration of British Capital to 1875.* New York: Alfred A. Knopf, 1927.

Jones, Geoffrey, and Lina Gálvez-Muñoz, eds. *Foreign Multinationals in the United States: Management and Performance.* London and New York: Routledge, 2002.

Li, Jiatao, and Stephen Guisinger. "How Well Do Foreign Firms Compete in the United States?" *Business Horizons,* November–December 1991.

Veenendaal, Augustus J., Jr. *Slow Train to Paradise: How Dutch Investment Helped Build American Railroads.* Stanford, Calif.: Stanford University Press, 1996.

Wilkins, Mira. *The History of Foreign Investment in the United States to 1914.* Cambridge, Mass.: Harvard University Press, 1989.

Wilkins, Mira. *The History of Foreign Investment in the United States, 1914–1945.* Cambridge, Mass.: Harvard University Press, 2004.

HUBERT BONIN

FOREIGN WORKERS. *See* Guest Workers; Migrant Workers.

FORESTS AND DEFORESTATION. Since humans have been on earth they have been cutting, using, and eliminating trees. Trees provide fuel for domestic heating and cooking, smelting metals, and making ceramics, and are the raw material for constructing dwellings and implements. Once eliminated, new land is created for cultivation and grazing.

Expansion, Consumption, and Deforestation. During the middle of the eighteenth century a new phase of global destruction began with the expansion of Europe overseas. After 1492 Europe had burst through the confines of the continent, and with over two hundred years of experimentation behind it was now in the process of creating a global economy through trade and colonization. The capitalist society that emerged commoditized nearly all it found in the wider world, creating wealth out of nature, whether it was land, trees, animals, plants, or people. The raw materials and food from the newfound territories entered into trade, most of which were destined for the western European core where increasing population, greater urbanization, and rising affluence led to rising consumption among all classes. At first it was only the very rich who could afford the new crops like sugar,

tea, coffee, cocoa, cotton, maize, and rice, but as prosperity filtered downward so did the consumption of these goods, which moved from being luxuries to necessities. Huge fleets of ships (mainly English and Dutch) carried goods in unprecedented bulk, while the tropical forests were cleared to grow more of them.

One measure of the impact of the European expansion was the percentage that it and its direct offspring settlements were of total world population. The proportion rose from 22 percent of the world's population of 769 million in 1750, to 30 percent of 957 million in 1850, to 35 percent of 1.65 billion in 1900.

Stepping-Stones to the New World. Although mere pinpricks in the ocean, the islands of the Azores, Canaries, Madeira, and ultimately the Caribbean were strategic stepping-stones and experimental venues for colonization of new crops, especially sugar. Barbados was the classic example. Between 1647 and 1665 four-fifths of the original semitropical vegetation had been replaced by sugarcane, but the introduction of slaves in 1650 undermined the livelihood of the poorer English freeholders who migrated to New England. Similar stories can be told for other islands. In addition, the Dutch and then Portuguese established an extensive sugar economy based on slavery in the northeastern province of Brazil (Bahia). Mexico and Central America were the source of cocoa and precious metals, while on the eastern seaboard of North America cotton and tobacco flourished in the southern states, and general pioneer settlement elsewhere. In all locations there was direct settlement by Europeans either as freeholders or as plantation owners with slaves, both resulting in new crops and the alteration of large sections of the original forest biomes. In contrast, in Asia, Europeans rarely settled permanently but created trading posts to collect the produce (spices, china, textiles) of the sophisticated and industrious peasant societies of, for example, southern India, China, Indonesia, and Southeast Asia generally.

The United States. All of these early island experiments resulted in insignificant deforestation compared to the settler colonization of the forests of the United States. Here the virtues of agriculture, freehold tenure, dispersed settlement, "improvement," and personal and political freedom were extolled, leading to the rapid and successful expansion of settlement in a landscape already depopulated by disease in earlier centuries.

The technology of clearing was simple; all that had changed over thirty-five hundred years was the substitution of metal for stone axes, which increased productivity over tenfold. The main ingredient of clearing was still a combination sweat, skill, and strength, aided by fire. The pioneer was regarded as the heroic subduer of a sullen and untamed wilderness. The biggest trees were regarded as indicators of soil fertility, and consequently they were felled quickly to make way for farms. "Such are the means," marvelled the French traveller the Marquis de Chastellux in 1789, "by which North-America, which one hundred years ago was nothing but a vast forest, is peopled with three million of inhabitants. . . . Four years ago, one might have travelled ten miles in the woods I traversed, without seeing a single habitation" (Chastellux, vol. 1, p. 47).

The clearing continued unabated, and by 1850 about 113.7 million acres (46 million hectares) of former forest was in farms. During the latter half of the nineteenth century increased immigration from Europe and the general expansion of the economy resulted in a further 300 million acres (121.4 million hectares) being cleared (Williams, *Americans and Their Forests*). Clearing was widespread, universal, and an integral part of rural life. It was one of the biggest deforestation episodes ever.

The archetypal image (and reality) of the pioneer hacking out a life for himself and family in the forest was not confined to the United States. In Canada, New Zealand, South Africa, Australia, and Russia similar pioneer clearing occurred with similar results for the forests. In Australia, for example, perhaps 98,800,000 acres (40 million hectares) of the southeastern forests and sparse woodland were cleared or severely modified by the early twentieth century.

By the mid-nineteenth century railroads, steamships, the telegraph, medicine, and technological and military superiority, all of what Daniel Headrick calls "the tools of empire," facilitated settlement and clearing, and bound the peripheral areas closer to the core, which now had a rival center in the northeastern United States. When the mechanization of the lumber industry with steam sawmills, high-speed multiple-bladed saws, planing machinery, and railroads got under way after about 1870, the coniferous forests of the United States, Canada, Russia, and Scandinavia experienced a new onslaught of logging.

Europe. One should not forget that Europe itself was also being colonized internally during these centuries. In the mixed forest zone of central European Russia over 25,900 square miles (67,000 square kilometers) were cleared between around 1690 and 1900 (French), and everywhere, clearing was nibbling away at the edges of the forests. The insatiable demand for new land to grow crops was matched by a rising demand for the products of the forest themselves. The problem of fuel-wood for the iron industry in timber-deficient England was solved by making coke from coal and then using it to create pig iron, and increasingly coal took over as an energy source. Less easy to find a substitute for was timber for ships. The quest for strategic naval stores (masts, pitch, tar, turpentine) and ships' timbers made major inroads into the forests of the Baltic littoral from the fourteenth century onward and from the southern states of the United States after about 1700. Alternative construction timbers like teak and mahogany were discovered in the tropical hardwood forests after about 1800.

The Tropical World. In the subtropical and tropical forests, European systems of exploitation led to the harvesting of indigenous tree crops (for example, rubber, hardwoods), but also to the replacement of the original forest by crops grown for maximum returns in relation to the labor and capital inputs, often in a "plantation" system with either slave or indentured labor. Classic examples of this were the highly profitable crops of sugar in the West Indies; coffee ("green gold") and sugar in the subtropical coastal forests of Brazil, cotton and tobacco in the southern United States, tea and coffee in Sri Lanka and India, and later rubber in Malaysia and Indonesia. All flourished at the expense of the forest. In eastern Brazil, perhaps over half of the original 301,200 square miles (780,000 square kilometers) of the vast subtropical forest that ran down the eastern portions of the country had disappeared by 1950 through agricultural exploitation and mining (Dean).

A variation of this agricultural clearing occurred in southern Asia where peasant proprietors were drawn into the global commercial market. Outstanding was the deliberate expansion by British administrators of rice cultivation in lower Burma, which resulted in the destruction of about 34,740 square miles (90,000 square kilometers) of rain forest between 1850 and 1950. Throughout the Indian subcontinent the early network of railways meant an expansion of all types of crops, often for cash, that led to massive forest clearing in all parts of the country.

Attitudes to Clearing. The perception of the forest as a repugnant "obstacle" that needed to be cleared in order to "improve" the land began to have its critics in the West. The Romantic movement of the late eighteenth century began to see beauty in nature and trees, and many were planted for the sake of ornamentation and scenery. There was also an increasing concern during the nineteenth century that timber supplies were running out, and that excessive clearing was decreasing rainfall, increasing erosion, and generally causing the land to disintegrate. Forest conservation became a major movement from about 1850

Deforestation in Brazil. Deforestation near the city of Santarém in the Brazilian state of Pará, December 2004. Photograph by Victor R. Caivano. AP IMAGES

onward in Europe and its possessions, and in the United States. In Germany, the idea of trying to achieve a sustained yield (not cutting more than grew) and standardizing tree type and growth dominated forest management, and this method of forest management spread worldwide.

Non-European Impacts. Traditional societies also exploited their forests vigorously, and the commercialization of the resource was not a European invention. In precolonial southwest India, the forest was not regarded as a community resource; larger landowners dominated forest use over smaller-scale farmers and shifting cultivators. Scarce commodities such as sandalwood, ebony, cinnamon, and pepper were under state or royal control. In Hunan province in south central China, a highly centralized administration encouraged land clearance in order to enhance local state revenues so as to increase the tax base and support a bigger bureaucracy and militia. Later migrations into the forested hill country of south China were also encouraged by the state. Simply, forests everywhere were being exploited and were diminishing in size in response to increasing population numbers and increasing complexity of society. In the subtropical world it was just slower than the changes unleashed by the Europeans with their new aims, technologies, and intercontinental trade links, but no less severe. In all, as much as 83,400 square miles (216,000

square kilometers) of forest and 23,900 square miles (62,000 square kilometers) of interrupted or open forest were destroyed in South and Southeast Asia for cropland between 1860 and 1950 alone (Williams, "Forests").

Since 1990. The pace of deforestation increased markedly during the twentieth century as all the advances in mechanized handling and transporting in bulk of logs were perfected.

1900–1949. In the western, developed world new uses for wood fiber (pulp, paper, packaging, plywood, and chipboard), and relatively little substitution of other materials increased wood use, while traditional uses for energy production and construction, especially houses, increased. The indispensable and crucial nature of timber in many countries gave it a strategic value similar to that of petroleum in the twenty-first century. For example, the United States was gripped with the panic of a "timber famine" from around 1905 to 1915 when lumbering reached the last forest frontier in the Pacific Northwest. The shortage, however, was more apparent than real. New growth in old lumber areas was replenishing depleted stocks, and imports made up the shortfall. Also it was not realized that in North America and Europe farm abandonment in "marginal" areas was leading to greater forest acreage. In the eastern United States it had begun in the "difficult" and hard-to-work farmlands of New England as farmers migrated to the cities or to better land in the West, and it continued with the abandonment of cotton and tobacco growing in the South (Williams, *Deforesting the Earth*).

In the tropical world, the hitherto unrecognized massive expansion of population by more than half a billion on a base of 1.1 billion resulted in extensive clearing for subsistence. Commercial plantations for food crops, and lumbering for hardwoods, also increased in line with rising affluence in the West. Approximately 907,340 square miles (2,350,000 square kilometers) of tropical forest was lost between circa 1900 and 1949, the bulk of it to subsistence farming.

After 1950. The most publicized deforestation—the deforestation everyone thinks of when the word is mentioned—occurred after World War II. In the temperate coniferous softwood forests growth has about kept pace with the demands of industrial societies for supplies of timber and pulp. Forest inventories have continually outstripped estimates as regrowth on previously logged areas and abandoned farms (a net 67.4 million acres [27.25 million hectares] of farmland reverting to forest in the eastern United States between 1910 and 1979 alone), and reforestation programs have made significant additions to forest areas. The main concern in the early twenty-first century is that large areas are being withdrawn from production because of wildlife and biodiversity concerns (for example, the spotted owl controversy in the Pacific Northwest). Some environmentally conscious societies, like the United States and Japan, are preserving their forests and making good shortfalls with imports, often from the tropical world.

The focus of deforestation has moved firmly to the tropical world. Here better health and nutrition have resulted in a population explosion of an additional 3.5 billion people, an addition more than double the total world population of 1950. The demands of sheer survival for these landless people have resulted in cultivation penetrating deeper into the forests and farther up steep forested slopes. Most are "squatters" and have no stake in the land, and therefore have little commitment to sustainable management. In addition, the simple acquisition of a chainsaw and a truck removes logging from the hands of a few large firms to a multitude of individuals. Undoubtedly unsustainable and rapacious logging for hard cash has been encouraged by ineffective or even corrupt governments as a substitute for tackling more difficult problems of land reform, inequality, and poverty. Trees, especially tropical ones, take a minimum of one hundred years to grow, and require a long-term management strategy, not the realization of a quick profit to pay debts or line pockets. Since 1950 about 2,120,000 square miles (5.5 million square kilometers) of tropical forests have disappeared in Southeast Asia, Africa, and Central and Latin America. About 50 percent of early twenty-first-century clearing comes out of Amazonia, where official settlement schemes, speculation, pioneer clearing, and large-scale pasture development continues unabated,

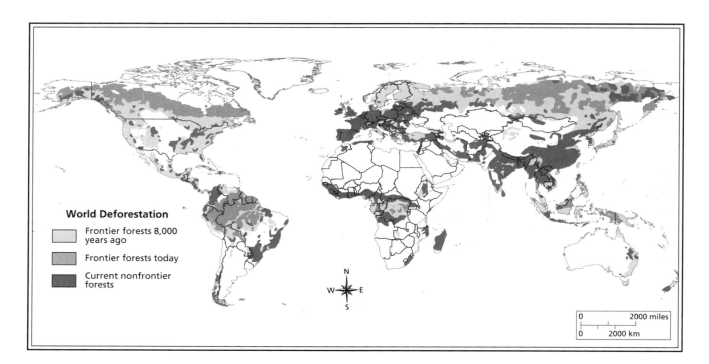

World Deforestation

- Frontier forests 8,000 years ago
- Frontier forests today
- Current nonfrontier forests

all against a background of incredible lawlessness. In addition, the tropical hardwood forests are being logged-out for constructional timber at a great rate, while wood is cut for domestic fuel in prodigious quantities in Africa, parts of India, and Latin America. Globally, fuel-wood cutting now roughly equals timber extraction—about 2.4 billion cubic yards (1.8 billion cubic meters) compared to 2.5 billion cubic yards (1.9 billion cubic meters). It is forecast to rise rapidly in line with world population increase.

The Future. The history of global deforestation is long and complex and is now reaching critical proportions. The rate of clearing (variously estimated at between 28.4 million and 37 million acres (11.5 and 15 million hectares) a year, depending on the assumptions and data used) raises concerns worldwide. Since the mid-1980s, the primary concern has been for biodiversity (over 50 percent of all known species inhabit tropical forests) and habitat loss, and the cultural extinction of indigenous peoples, climate change, and even sea level change. One thing is certain, with a continuing increase in world population (another 2 to 3 billion by 2020), many will want to exploit the resources even more vigorously, and deforestation will not end. Others will want to restrict forest use and preserve it. The tensions between exploitation and preservation will be intense and affect a wide range of political, economic, social, and, particularly, ethical issues.

[See also Amazon River and Basin; and Climate and Climate Change.]

BIBLIOGRAPHY

Albion, Robert Greenhalgh. *Forests and Sea-Power: The Timber Problem of the Royal Navy, 1652–1862*. Cambridge, Mass.: Harvard University Press, 1926. Reprint. Annapolis, Md.: Naval Institute Press, 2000.

Chastellux, Françoise Jean. *Travels in North America in the Years 1780, 1781, and 1782*. vol.1. London: G. G. L. and J. Robinson, 1787. Reprint. New York: A. M. Kelley, 1970.

Darby, H. Clifford. "The Clearing of the Woodland in Europe." In *Man's Role in Changing the Face of the Earth*, edited by William L. Thomas, pp.183–216. Chicago: University of Chicago Press, 1956.

Dean, Warren. *With Broadax and Firebrand: The Destruction of the Brazilian Atlantic Forest*. Berkeley and Los Angeles: University of California Press, 1995.

French, R. A. "Russians and Their Forest." In *Studies in Russian Historical Geography*, edited by James H. Bater and R. A. French, vol. 1, pp. 27–38. London and New York: Academic Press, 1983.

Headrick, Daniel R. *The Tools of Empire: Technology and European Imperialism in the Nineteenth Century*. New York: Oxford University Press, 1981.

Laurence, William F. "Razing Amazonia." *New Scientist*, 15 October, 2005, 34–39.

Lowood, Henry E. "The Calculating Forester: Quantification, Cameral Science, and the Emergence of Scientific Forestry Management in Germany." In *The Quantifying Spirit in the Eighteenth Century*, edited by Tore Fränsmyr, J. H. Heilbron, and Robin C. Ryder, pp. 315–342. Berkeley and Los Angeles: University of California Press, 1990.

Perdue, Peter C. *Exhausting the Earth: State and Peasant in Hunan, 1500–1850*, Cambridge, Mass.: Council on East Asian Studies, Harvard University, 1987.

Richards, John F., and Michelle McAlpin. "Cotton Cultivating and Land Clearing in the Bombay Deccan and Karnatak, 1818–1920." In *Global Deforestation and the Nineteenth-Century World Economy*, edited by Richard P. Tucker and J. F. Richards, pp. 68–94. Durham, N.C.: Duke University Press, 1983.

Thomas, Keith. *Man and the Natural World: Changing Attitudes in England, 1500–1800*. London: Allen Lane, 1983. Also published as *Man and the Natural World: A History of the Modern Sensibility*. New York: Pantheon Books, 1983.

Williams, Michael. *Americans and their Forests: A Historical Geography*. Cambridge, U.K., and New York: Cambridge University Press, 1989.

Williams, Michael. *Deforesting the Earth: From Prehistory to Global Crisis*. Chicago: University of Chicago Press, 2003. An abridged version was published in 2006.

Williams, Michael. "Forests." In *The Earth as Transformed by Human Action: Global and Regional Changes in the Biosphere over the Past 300 Years*, edited by Billie Lee Turner II, et al., pp. 179–201. Cambridge, U.K.: Cambridge University Press, 1990.

MICHAEL WILLIAMS

FORMOSA. *See* Taiwan.

FRANCE. Modern France traces its history back to the establishment of a kingdom out of a former province of the Roman Empire in 486 C.E. The rich farmland at its core provided resources that usually enabled its rulers to play a major role in European affairs.

France before 1750. The medieval period saw the establishment of a hierarchical society dominated by two privileged groups, the Catholic clergy and the landowning nobility. Beneath "those who prayed and those who fought" were the bulk of the population, peasant farmers and urban residents. The early modern period bequeathed the country a powerful absolute monarchy unhampered by consultative institutions, such as the Estates General of the Realm, which ceased to meet after 1615. French kings created an administrative machine whose efficiency in maintaining social order and extracting revenue from the population made it the envy of other rulers. This process of early modern state-building culminated under Louis XIV (r. 1643–1715). Through his system of intendants or appointed officials, he was able to impose his authority throughout the provinces and accustom his subjects to a high level of state intervention in their lives. Louis XIV's attempts to expand his domain led other European rulers to regard France as an aggressive state whose ambitions needed to be kept in check.

The Beginnings of Modernity, 1750–1789. During the reign of Louis XV (r. 1715–1774), France began to experience cultural secularization and economic growth. The end of the early modern "little ice age" and incremental improvements in agriculture and hygiene launched a period of sustained population growth: from about 20 million in 1715, the number of the king's subjects grew to about 28 million by 1789, four-fifths of them peasants. Fueled especially by a boom in colonial trade, urban communities prospered even more, and both the communities' bourgeois elites and their working classes became more educated and less respectful of traditional authorities.

The educated part of the population increasingly turned away from the religiously defined culture of the past and embraced the ideas of the secular-minded philosophes Charles-Louis de Secondat, Baron de Montesquieu, Voltaire, and Jean-Jacques Rousseau, who questioned the authority of priests and kings and exalted human reason and individualism. The impact of their writings often combined with that of a dissident Catholic tradition known as Jansenism, whose adherents challenged the church hierarchy and the royal government that backed it. In salons, coffeehouses, and the Masonic lodges that spread rapidly after the middle of the century, the new phenomenon of public opinion took shape. The judges of the kingdom's appeals courts or *parlements* appealed to this public and undermined the basis of absolutism by proclaiming that the French "nation" had a right to participate in its own government. Royal ministers also eroded traditions by attacking entrenched privileges in their efforts to make the government run more efficiently and increase its revenue.

The French Revolution and the Napoleonic Era, 1789–1815. As the end of the eighteenth century neared, France was changing in many ways, but few anticipated the monumental crisis that engulfed the country in 1789. Louis XVI, who came to the throne in 1774, was well intentioned but did not give his ministers enough support to resolve the chronic imbalance between the monarchy's steadily mounting expenses and its inadequate stream of revenue. By 1786 the government was on the brink of bankruptcy. After attempts to achieve a consensus on reforms with leading representatives of the country's privileged elites failed in 1787 and 1788, Louis XVI was forced to revive the Estates General, last convened in 1614. The elections to the Estates took place at a moment of economic crisis that had sent bread prices soaring and caused widespread unrest. In addition, the decision to follow the electoral procedures used in 1614 raised a major new problem. Under those procedures the Catholic clergy and the nobility elected their own deputies, while the remaining 97 percent of the population was lumped together as the Third Estate. If the three groups met separately, as they had in earlier centuries, the two privileged estates would outweigh the Third Estate, whose leaders were not willing to accept this secondary role.

When the deputies finally gathered at Versailles, bringing with them *cahiers* or lists of grievances drawn up in assemblies held in every French village and town, they immediately deadlocked on the issue of whether to meet together or separately. On 17 June 1789 the Third Estate took a revolutionary step by defying the privileged orders and the king and unilaterally declaring itself to be a National Assembly, representing the will of the whole French people. The popular uprising of 14 July 1789 showed that the deputies had broad support—when the ordinary people of Paris, fearing that the National Assembly was going to be dispersed by force, reacted by storming the Bastille, a fortress-prison that symbolized royal authority.

Together with a wave of peasant insurrections against noble privileges, this popular movement assured the Revolution's triumph. The National Assembly moved quickly to eliminate France's centuries-old social hierarchy and to convert the absolute monarchy into a constitutional system. Decrees voted in a tumultuous night session on 4 August 1789 abolished the privileges of the nobility, clergy, provinces, and towns. The Declaration of the Rights of Man and of the Citizen, passed on 26 August 1789, laid down new principles of liberty and equality and outlined a system of representative government. To make sure that citizens' loyalties were focused on the nation, the deputies abolished France's historic provinces, dividing the country into units of equal size called departments (*départements*) that still exist today.

The broad support that the Revolution enjoyed in its early stages soon fractured as ever wider sectors of the population took advantage of their new opportunities to voice their demands. Measures such as the Civil Constitution of the Clergy, an attempt to restructure the Catholic Church along democratic lines, encountered considerable opposition. Supporters of the Revolution demanded harsh measures to overcome resistance, while peasants and the urban poor clamored for radical measures that would benefit them. Fearing other European powers' hostility to the Revolution, the deputies declared war on Austria in April 1792, starting a conflict that lasted until Napoleon's final defeat in 1815. A series of military defeats provoked the Paris insurrection of 10 August 1792 that resulted in the overthrow of the monarchy and the constitutional system created by the National Assembly. It also resulted in the election of a National Convention pledged to create a democratic republic.

The period from September 1792, when the Convention assembled, to 27 July 1794, when the deputies unexpectedly overthrew Maximilien-François-Marie-Isidore de Robespierre, the leader of the radical Jacobin movement that dominated it, saw both a radical experiment in social and political democracy and the installation of a dictatorship whose memory inspired fears that affected French life until the twentieth century. The National Assembly of 1789 had defined equality in legalistic terms; the Jacobins promised citizens such social rights as education, welfare support, and medical care. Although women were denied political rights, they were granted equal status within the family, and illegitimate children were given the same rights as others. The National Assembly had already broadened citizenship to include France's Jewish minority and to free people of all races in the colonies; the Convention abolished slavery altogether.

While enacting these radical measures, the Convention also had to cope with war and civil unrest. Its response to these threats was the Reign of Terror. Louis XVI was tried and executed in January 1793, the first of a long series of political trials of figures accused of opposing the Revolution. Civil and political rights promised in 1789 were suspended, economic controls were imposed, and the entire population was mobilized to support the war effort. The Convention turned authority over to its Committee of Public Safety, dominated by Robespierre, which created a centralized government far more powerful than the prerevolutionary monarchy. By the summer of 1794 this revolutionary dictatorship had crushed domestic opposition and turned the tide in the war, but its arbitrary methods alienated much of the population. Robespierre had already had a number of political rivals executed; when he threatened a further purge of the Convention, the deputies turned against him, ordering his arrest and execution instead.

This coup of 9 Thermidor Year II—according to the new revolutionary calendar adopted during the Terror—ended the radical phase of the Revolution. From 1795 to 1799, France was governed by the Directory, a conservative republican regime that undid many of the radical reforms enacted under the Convention. The Directory's aggressive military policy led to the imposition of French-style republican regimes in the Netherlands, Switzerland,

and parts of Germany and Italy. The continuing war made successful generals a strong influence in French politics and ultimately allowed the most charismatic of them, Napoleon Bonaparte, to overthrow the regime in a coup d'état on 18 Brumaire Year VIII (9 November 1799). At first Napoleon claimed to be defending the accomplishments of the Revolution, but it soon became clear that the new system was a barely disguised dictatorship.

Napoleon created an efficient system of prefects, appointed officials stationed in the departments to carry out government orders, which still remains a feature of French life. In 1802 a Concordat with the Catholic Church restored that institution's important role in national life. The Code Napoléon or Napoleonic Code of 1804 emphasized the legal equality of male French citizens and the rights of individual property owners, but it repealed revolutionary legislation that had given women greater rights within the family. Napoleon's conservatism was also reflected in an 1802 law restoring slavery in the French colonies. Although Napoleon abolished the political freedoms that the revolutionaries had fought for, most of the population accepted his regime in exchange for the social order, economic prosperity, and military success it provided.

Napoleon was convinced that he needed military triumphs to maintain his prestige and to demonstrate to other governments that they had to accept French predominance. A succession of wars allowed him to extend the territories of the empire he proclaimed in 1804 until they stretched from the Baltic to Rome. Other parts of Europe were converted into kingdoms ruled by members of Napoleon's family. In these occupied areas the French restructured institutions along revolutionary lines. Rather than welcoming these reforms, local populations often asserted their own sense of national identity. An anti-French guerrilla war in Spain after 1808, supported by the British, whose naval power kept them safe from conquest, marked the beginning of the collapse of Napoleon's overextended empire. When Napoleon invaded Russia in 1812 to demonstrate the dangers of resisting his demands, he lost most of his army. Other European governments joined in a coalition against him, invading France and forcing Napoleon to abdicate in April 1814. Blunders by the Restoration government that replaced Napoleon allowed him to return to power in March 1815, but his so-called hundred days of renewed rule were cut short by his defeat at the battle of Waterloo on 18 June 1815—a defeat that marked the definitive end of the Revolutionary and Napoleonic era.

Restoration, Liberalism, and the Second Empire, 1815–1871. Between 1814 and 1871, four regimes—the

French Commemoration. Celebration on the Champs-Élyseés in Paris on Bastille Day, 14 July 1801. Etching, 1801. Tissandier Collection/Prints and Photographs Division, Library of Congress

Restoration monarchy (1814/15–1830), the liberal July Monarchy (1830–1848), the Second Republic (1848–1851), and the Second Empire (1851–1870)—tried and failed to find a balance between the principles of liberty and equality set forth in 1789 and the demand for order. Revolutions in 1830, 1848, and 1870–1871 gave France a reputation for political instability that set it apart from the rest of Europe. Paradoxically, however, these visible signs of political division masked a remarkably cohesive postrevolutionary social order based on respect for property and male authority. Nineteenth-century France thus managed to be both a hotbed of protest and a stronghold of conservatism.

Anxious to put an end to the series of wars caused by the Revolution and Napoleon, the other European powers backed a restoration of the Bourbon monarchy in 1814, with the brother of the executed Louis XVI ruling under the title of Louis XVIII. Returning to France after twenty-five years in exile, Louis XVIII realized that it was not possible to undo all the changes that had taken place since 1789. Balking at the revolutionary word "constitution," Louis XVIII issued a "charter" that provided for a bicameral legislature, regular elections, and guarantees of civil rights. Nevertheless, the regime could not quell fears that these concessions would be whittled away, especially when the cautious Louis XVIII was succeeded by his more

reactionary brother Charles X in 1824. When Charles X's ministers responded to an electoral setback in July 1830 by attempting to change parts of the charter and to control the press, they provoked a violent response. After three days of rioting in Paris, Charles X fled the capital.

Liberal leaders, anxious to keep the revolution from getting out of hand, quickly installed Louis-Philippe, head of the Orléans branch of the royal family, as a constitutional monarch, beginning the July Monarchy. The charter was revised to enlarge the small minority of wealthy men who were allowed to vote. Once in power the leaders of the new regime resisted further political reforms, but their policies fostered economic and social change. This period saw the beginning of widespread industrialization in France, symbolized by the building of the first railroads after 1835. The growth of the economy created a new class of bourgeois or middle-class entrepreneurs, who generally accepted the regime's limited version of the ideals of 1789. Economic changes disrupted the lives of much of the country's urban population, however. Living conditions in cities deteriorated as their populations swelled, and observers lamented the spread of crime, disease, and prostitution, phenomena highlighted in the novels of Honoré de Balzac and Eugène Sue. New radical movements, including France's first socialist groups, denounced the regime's inability to deal with these problems.

The regime's inept response to a severe economic crisis in the mid-1840s made it vulnerable to challenges, and in February 1848 an uprising in Paris led to the proclamation of the Second Republic. The right to vote, limited to about 2 percent of the population under the July Monarchy, was extended to all adult males. In April 1848 voters chose an assembly composed mostly of conservatives, however. The deputies soon provoked a clash with the radicalized urban workers in Paris who staged an uprising in June 1848 that was brutally crushed. To ensure the protection of law and order, the assembly enacted a constitution providing for a powerful elected president. They had not anticipated the opportunity that this system would provide for a little-known figure with a famous name: Louis-Napoleon Bonaparte. Promising to restore stability and the glory France had enjoyed under his uncle, he was swept into office in December 1848.

In December 1851, Louis-Napoleon staged a coup d'état against the assembly; a year later he proclaimed his regime the Second Empire and took the title of Napoleon III. The emperor assured other European powers that he had no intention of emulating his uncle's career of conquest, but he embarked on a series of foreign initiatives—the Crimean War against Russia and support for the unification of Italy—to assert France's central role in Europe. At home he used government power vigorously to promote economic development. With Napoleon III's support, the Paris prefect Baron Georges-Eugène Haussmann modernized the city, improving sanitation and creating the broad boulevards that still define its urban landscape.

Although he had come to power in a coup and initially used authoritarian methods to silence opposition, Napoleon III gradually permitted greater political freedom. Elections with universal manhood suffrage continued to be held, and the powers of the legislature, at first negligible, were steadily expanded. Strikes were made legal for the first time in 1864, and the formation of labor unions was made legal in 1868. In May 1870 the emperor asked voters to approve a new constitution that converted the regime into a genuine constitutional monarchy, and it won an overwhelming majority.

The Third Republic, 1871–1914. Just four months after the May 1870 plebiscite, the Second Empire collapsed altogether, plunging the country into a crisis more profound than the revolutions of 1830 or 1848. Out of this crisis, however, came a grudging consensus on a political system that proved more stable than any other France had known since 1789: the Third Republic, which lasted from 1875 to 1940.

The Second Empire fell victim to a catastrophic misjudgment in foreign affairs. Distracted by mounting opposition and unsuccessful foreign initiatives in the 1860s, Napoleon III had failed to react to the shift in the European power balance caused by the Prussian chancellor Otto von Bismarck's effort to turn the separate German states into a single country. In July 1870, Bismarck manipulated a diplomatic incident into an excuse to provoke France into war. The Prussian army won a crushing victory at the northern border city of Sedan on 2 September 1870; that defeat led to the overthrow of the imperial regime two days later.

The provisional government proclaimed in Paris on 4 September 1870 tried to continue the fight, but the Germans laid siege to Paris, reducing its population to the verge of starvation. When the French government finally sued for peace in January 1871, Parisians felt that their sacrifices had been for naught. Hasty elections held to create a government to negotiate a treaty with Germany returned a conservative legislature completely out of sympathy with the capital. The peace settlement deeply wounded patriotic feelings by requiring France to give up the territories of Alsace and Lorraine. In March 1871 the Paris population revolted against the provisional government. Supported by the city's working classes, socialist and revolutionary leaders proclaimed the Paris Commune and promised to end capitalist exploitation and create a new egalitarian society.

The provisional government, determined to show that it could maintain social order, reacted violently: some twenty-five thousand people, mostly supporters of the Commune, were killed in the bloody week that ended the uprising in May 1871. Conservative forces thought that the situation was now ripe for the creation of a restored monarchy based on traditional religious and social values. The intransigence of the Bourbon heir, hailed as "Henri V" by his supporters, who insisted on a complete repudiation of the heritage of 1789, made this impossible, and by 1875 discouraged monarchists were ready to compromise with moderate republicans. France again became a republic, as in 1792 and 1848, but with a constitution that provided multiple safeguards against any kind of social or political radicalism.

After a brief power struggle in 1877, moderate republicans wrested control from the conservatives and used the power of the government to create a strong base for the regime. Their most effective tool was the national public school system. Elementary education was made free and compulsory in 1881, and public schools for girls were created despite strong Catholic opposition. The defeat of 1871 led some to question France's future, but the artistic innovations of the Impressionist school, led by Édouard Manet and Claude Monet, kept Paris at the center of European culture. The Third Republic's leaders embarked on a program of colonial expansion in Africa and Southeast Asia to show that the country was still a major force in world affairs. By 1900 the French Empire was more than twenty times the size of European France, although only the nearby territory of Algeria, across the Mediterranean from southern France, attracted a significant number of settlers.

Opposition to the Third Republic came from Catholic conservatives, who condemned policies such as the rationalistic school curriculum, and from urban workers, who turned to socialist and anarchist movements to protest harsh factory conditions and poverty. Periodic crises also threatened the regime. The most serious erupted in the late 1890s over the fate of a Jewish captain in the army, Alfred Dreyfus, convicted of treason after a court-martial in 1895. As evidence of his innocence accumulated, army leaders and conservatives fought a losing battle to prevent review of his case, resorting to virulent anti-Semitic propaganda and attacks on republican values, while Dreyfus's defenders demanded that the Republic live up to its ideals of justice for all citizens. Dreyfus was eventually exonerated of any crime, but the divisions highlighted by the affair showed that there was still no consensus in favor of republican democracy. In 1905 in the wake of the Dreyfus affair the republican government abrogated the Napoleonic Concordat with the Catholic Church, making France officially a secular society.

The first decades of the Third Republic were a period of slow economic growth. Like other countries, France erected high tariff walls meant to protect domestic producers, but this was not enough to guard its peasants from falling prices and crop diseases. The more modern sectors of the economy generally prospered in the late 1890s and in the first decade of the twentieth century, remembered in France as *la belle époque*. The period saw a gradual development of national welfare institutions, starting with measures to aid poor children and to regulate women's working conditions. These measures were often linked to concern about France's low birthrate: France was the first country where artificial contraception became widespread.

A defensive alliance with Russia, signed in 1894, reassured the country's leaders that they would not have to fight Germany alone in any future war. An entente or unwritten understanding with Britain was reached in 1904. In June

Dreyfus Affair. Espionage trial of Captain Alfred Dreyfus at Rennes, France, 1899. Photograph by Valerian Gribayédoff. *New York World-Telegram* and the *Sun* Newspaper Photograph Collection/Prints and Photographs Division, Library of Congress

1914, France was drawn into a conflict sparked by the attack on Serbia by Germany's ally Austria-Hungary, a country protected by Russia. The German army immediately began to execute a prepared plan for a rapid invasion of France so that German forces could then be turned against the Russians. As a result, the Third Republic found itself facing a brutal test.

France in the Age of the World Wars, 1914–1945. Marching through neutral Belgium, German troops crossed France's northern frontier to within sixty miles of Paris. Despite heavy casualties, French commanders and troops did not panic, and in early September, with critical help from the small British army, they stopped the German advance at the battle of the Marne. The two sides entrenched themselves across northern France and settled into a prolonged stalemate, marked by bloody battles of attrition such as the struggle for Verdun (February–November 1916), which became a byword for the horrors of the new mechanized warfare.

Behind the lines the French government struggled to coordinate the economic production needed to meet military and civilian demands. The strain on the country was immense. By 1917 some war-weary soldiers mutinied, and antiwar sentiment was growing in the labor movement and among women. American entry into the war in April 1917 inspired hope of eventual victory, and the leadership of a determined prime minister, Georges Clemenceau, enabled the country to outlast the Germans. In November 1918 the Allied armies, under the command of the French general Ferdinand Foch, compelled Germany to ask for an armistice.

France lost 1.3 million men killed and even more wounded during the four years of fighting, and its northern regions suffered heavy damage. At the 1919 Paris Peace Conference, France sought assurance that Germany would be weakened enough to prevent it from launching another attack. The resulting treaty appeared to favor France, which regained Alsace-Lorraine and was promised the largest share of German reparations. Although German armaments were strictly limited, that country still had a larger population and industrial base, and France's wartime allies were either sidelined by revolution, in the case of Russia, or unwilling to give binding security guarantees. France thus emerged from the conflict poorer and less confident about its future.

Postwar politics took a sharp turn to the right, marked among other things by passage of a rigid ban on abortion and on most contraceptives, justified as a way of encouraging population growth. The socialist movement, which had been growing steadily before the war, split between moderates committed to working within the republican system and a new Communist party modeled after the Bolsheviks who had taken power in Russia after the 1917 Russian Revolution. The war had unleashed rapid inflation, which hurt the interests of middle-class families. In the colonies, opposition to French rule and demands for independence began to develop. The worldwide economic depression after 1929 and Adolf Hitler's rise to power in Germany in 1933 posed new threats to the Third Republic. Democracy was threatened when a massive right-wing street demonstration in front of the parliament building in February 1934 brought down a weak centrist government. The shock of this event generated a movement by antifascist groups—the Socialist, Communist, and Radical parties and the country's trade unions—known as the Popular Front. Parliamentary elections in May 1936 gave this coalition a clear majority and set off a massive wave of strikes by workers demanding immediate improvements in their lives. For the first time a Socialist, Leon Blum, became prime minister.

The Popular Front government initiated some important social reforms, of which the most notable was a law granting all workers a two-week paid summer vacation, but the effects of the Depression, the hostility of France's business classes, and the growing threat from Hitler limited its options. The increasingly poisonous atmosphere of French domestic politics and strong pacifist sentiments inspired by memories of World War I made it difficult to secure broad support for a rapid rearmament program or for serious resistance to the German threat. France did declare war when Germany attacked Poland in September 1939, but Franco-British plans provided only for a defensive strategy that left the military initiative to their foe.

The Germans launched their fast-moving blitzkrieg invasion in May 1940, and French resistance quickly crumbled. On 17 June 1940 the French cabinet voted to seek an armistice; only one junior cabinet member, General Charles de Gaulle, refused to accept the decision and flew to London, where he broadcast an appeal the next day urging a continued fight. Philippe Pétain, an aged hero of World War I, became the head of the French government, which was relocated to the small town of Vichy. The Germans occupied all of northern and western France, including Paris. Pétain and the conservative groups who supported him saw France's defeat as an opportunity to replace the democratic Third Republic with a more authoritarian and traditionalist regime. France's homegrown heritage of anti-Semitism was expressed in Vichy's *statut des Juifs*, a law enacted in October 1940 that barred Jews from many jobs and required them to register with the police; later in the war these records made it easy for the Germans to identify Jews and to deport them to death camps. The terms of the armistice agreement also allowed the Germans to exploit French resources to support their war effort: French factories and farms had to turn their products over to the occupiers at bargain prices, while French citizens suffered shortages of food, fuel, and consumer goods.

As the brutality of German policy became more obvious to the French population, opposition to the occupiers and to Pétain's collaborationist Vichy government spread. In November 1942 when American and British troops landed in the French colonies in North Africa, the Germans put the entire country under military occupation. From London, De Gaulle succeeded in imposing his leadership on the growing number of resistance movements. He established a territorial base for his Free French movement in some of the French colonies, raising their populations' hopes that the end of the war would bring them the freedom they were helping the metropole to recover.

French troops played only a minor role in the cross-channel D-day landings on 6 June 1944. It quickly became clear, however, that De Gaulle had too much support from the French population to be ignored. Once Paris was liberated in August 1944, he established a provisional government in the capital. The Vichy regime and the occupation had discredited conservatism, and the liberation government leaned heavily to the left. Large enterprises whose owners had collaborated with the Germans were nationalized, social measures favoring workers and the lower classes were enacted, and former collaborationists and Vichy leaders were put on trial and, in some cases, executed. Idealistic hopes for a purer and more democratic society were widespread, articulated by intellectuals like Albert Camus and Jean-Paul Sartre, and sympathy for Communism, the ideology of Hitler's main wartime enemy, was strong.

The Fourth Republic and De Gaulle, 1945–1969. The high hopes raised by the liberation soon faded as the population faced the realities of a crippled economy and the growing division between the United States and its allies and the Soviet bloc. The French Communists emerged as the largest party in postwar elections—the first in which women were able to vote, thanks to a decision of De Gaulle's provisional government—but fear of possible Communist domination led voters to reject a radical constitutional plan in 1945. A second constitution, resembling that of the Third Republic, was approved in 1946, establishing the Fourth Republic. By this time the wartime hero De Gaulle had withdrawn from politics to protest the return to prewar patterns of political behavior.

Despite the sour mood of postliberation politics, the period of the Fourth Republic saw important developments that foreshadowed a more stable and prosperous era. Partly thanks to aid from the American Marshall Plan, the French economy recovered more rapidly than expected. Hoping to end the national rivalries that had led to the two world wars, French leaders supported proposals for European economic integration that culminated with the creation in 1956 of the six-member European Common Market, the nucleus of what eventually became the much larger European Union.

Liberation of France. Allied tanks and half tracks on the Champs-Élyseés after the liberation of Paris, 25 August 1944. Photograph by Jack Downey. FARM SECURITY ADMINISTRATION—OFFICE OF WAR INFORMATION COLLECTION/PRINTS AND PHOTOGRAPHS DIVISION, LIBRARY OF CONGRESS

France's military security was assured by its participation in the U.S.-led North Atlantic Treaty Organization (NATO) alliance after 1949. A marked rise in France's long-stagnant birthrate, which had begun in the early 1940s, showed that ordinary citizens anticipated a better future for their children. By the early 1950s modern consumer goods, such as household appliances and automobiles, were becoming available to a wider range of the population. New media—radio and, by the second half of the 1950s, television—changed cultural patterns, and the percentage of young people completing secondary school and going on to university studies rose rapidly.

At the time, these developments were overshadowed by political quarrels resulting from France's struggle to maintain its colonies. Promises to convert the empire into a democratic French Union after the war were undermined by the brutality with which France put down protests in Algeria in 1945 and in Madagascar in 1947. In France's Southeast Asian colony of Indochina, a Communist-inspired nationalist movement led by Ho Chi Minh had taken power after the Japanese surrender in 1945. When the French tried to reassert control over the area, they became embroiled in a bitter and costly guerrilla conflict. Their defeat at Dien Bien Phu in 1954 forced France to withdraw from Indochina, leaving behind a divided Vietnam and a simmering conflict that led to an unsuccessful American intervention against the Communist regime.

The end of the French struggle in Vietnam coincided with the start of a large-scale rebellion in France's most important North African territory, Algeria. First occupied in 1830, Algeria was classified as an integral part of France, not a colony, and had a substantial European population. The leaders of the French army, battered by the defeat of 1940 and their failure to hold Indochina, were determined to defend Algeria at any cost, but revelations of the torture tactics being used against the insurgents weakened support for the war in metropolitan France. By May 1958 it had become clear that the institutions of the Fourth Republic were too weak to cope with the Algerian crisis; its leaders turned to the former Resistance leader, De Gaulle. Long dissatisfied with the institutions of the Fourth Republic, De Gaulle agreed to head a new government provided that he was given the opportunity to draft a new constitution.

Although the Algerian crisis had brought him to power, De Gaulle soon decided that the struggle there was draining the country's resources. Despite strong opposition, by 1962 he negotiated a settlement that conceded Algerian independence. In the meantime his new Fifth Republic had begun to transform metropolitan France. The new constitution provided for a powerful president, a post that De Gaulle himself naturally occupied. Although he maintained France's cooperation with its European neighbors in the Common Market, De Gaulle vigorously asserted the country's autonomy in world affairs. The successful testing of an atomic bomb in 1960 allowed France to dispense with the American nuclear umbrella, and after a series of disputes with the United States, France officially withdrew from NATO in 1966. De Gaulle accelerated plans begun in the Fourth Republic to offer France's colonies more autonomy. By 1960 all the former French colonies in sub-Saharan Africa were independent, although most of them retained important economic, cultural, and military links with France.

De Gaulle saw economic modernization as critical for France to maintain its standing in the world. His government promoted rationalization in the industrial sector and the replacement of traditional peasant farms with larger, more viable units. As the French population became accustomed to prosperity and a higher level of education, however, dissatisfaction with the Fifth Republic's authoritarian structures increased and finally boiled over in a spectacular wave of student and worker strikes that paralyzed the country for most of the month of May 1968. The seventy-eight-year-old De Gaulle and his prime minister, Georges Pompidou, succeeded in ending the strikes by a combination of concessions and appeals to groups that were tired of disorder, but the country was clearly ready for a change of leadership. De Gaulle resigned in 1969, clearing the way for Pompidou to succeed him; De Gaulle's death in 1970 marked the end of an era.

France after De Gaulle. Charles de Gaulle's successors as president, Georges Pompidou (1969–1974) and Valéry Giscard d'Estaing (1974–1981), proved that the Gaullist Fifth Republic could function without its founder. The two men, both conservatives, tempered De Gaulle's prickly nationalism, allowing the process of European unification begun in the 1950s to move ahead. Giscard's presidency saw some important changes in women's rights when the 1920 ban on contraception and abortion was finally repealed. The major problem confronting France during the 1970s, however, was economic. The sudden rise in oil prices set off by the 1973 Arab oil embargo ended the "thirty glorious years" of economic prosperity that France had enjoyed since the liberation. Manufacturing industries declined, and unemployment, almost unknown in the country during the 1950s and 1960s, began a steady rise.

In 1981, dissatisfaction with economic conditions helped ensure the election of the Fifth Republic's first left-wing government, headed by the Socialist François Mitterrand. Mitterrand's program called for nationalizations of major industries and increased rights for workers. In 1983, however, when these measures failed to stem the economic crisis, Mitterrand abandoned many of his earlier initiatives and emphasized acceleration of the process of European unity. The period of his two presidential terms saw the breakup of the traditional French Left, as the Communist Party lost most of its support and the Socialists became a centrist party no longer identified with the working class. The political landscape was also altered by the rise of a right-wing movement, the National Front, which exploited resentment of the growing number of immigrants from France's former colonies. Although high unemployment persisted throughout his fourteen years in office, Mitterrand remained popular, despite revelations that he had once been a supporter of the Vichy regime. Parliamentary elections in 1993, however, brought a sharp swing to the right, and in 1995 the conservative Jacques Chirac became Mitterrand's successor. Lacking Mitterrand's political skills, Chirac led his party to electoral disaster in 1997, allowing a Socialist, Lionel Jospin, to become prime minister.

The French economy performed well during Jospin's term of office, and he was generally expected to run strongly in the 2002 presidential elections. Instead, Jean-Marie Le Pen of the right-wing National Front succeeded in forcing a run-off between himself and the incumbent, Chirac. Chirac won overwhelmingly, but the elections revealed the strength of right-wing, anti-immigrant sentiment and concerns that France was surrendering too much of its independence to the European Union, which led to French voters' rejection of a proposed European constitution in 2005. The Chirac government led international opposition to American intervention in Iraq in 2003, but the American president George W. Bush's decision to proceed on his own underlined France's diminished weight in world affairs. In late 2005 a wave of violent riots in poor neighborhoods inhabited mostly by North African immigrants and their families demonstrated the challenge of assimilating this growing part of France's population. The country also faces increasing difficulty financing the generous but costly welfare system developed after World War II.

Like much of Europe, France at the beginning of the twenty-first century found itself wondering how much of its traditional identity could be maintained in a world dominated by a globalized economy and an unprecedented influx of non-European immigrants. France's life has become so intertwined with that of its partners in the European Union that a retreat to a more autonomous condition is unlikely, but the continuation of this process threatens fundamental aspects of French life, such as the status of the French language. Despite these challenges, France remains among the world's most prosperous countries, and the weakening of frontiers dividing it from the rest of Europe and the world has brought opportunities as well as costs.

[*See also* Alsace-Lorraine; Caribbean, *subentry* The French Caribbean; Civil Constitution of the Clergy; Civilizing Mission, *subentry* French Empire; Declaration of the Rights of Man; Decolonization, *subentry* The French Empire; Dreyfus Affair; 1830, Revolutions of; 1848, Revolutions of; Empire and Imperialism, *subentry* The French Colonial Empire; European Integration; European Union; Franco-Prussian War; French and Indian War; French Guiana; French Interventions in Mexico; French Language and Literature; French Revolution; French Union; Gaullism; Jacobins; Middle East, *subentry* Britain and France and the Middle East; Napoleonic Wars; Paris; Paris Commune; Pieds Noirs; Reign of Terror; Resistance Movements, *subentry* Europe; Rhine Basin; Vichy Regime; World War I; *and* World War II.]

BIBLIOGRAPHY

Bergeron, Louis. *France under Napoleon*. Princeton, N.J.: Princeton University Press, 1981.

Bloch, Marc. *Strange Defeat*. New York: W. W. Norton and Company, 1968. First published in 1942.

Bredin, Jean-Denis. *The Affair: The Case of Alfred Dreyfus*. New York: Braziller, 1986.

Burrin, Philip. *France under the Germans*. New York: New Press, 1996.

Conklin, Alice. *A Mission to Civilize: The Republican Idea of Empire in France and West Africa, 1895–1930*. Stanford, Calif.: Stanford University Press, 1997.

Doyle, William. *Origins of the French Revolution*. 3d ed. New York: Oxford University Press, 1999.

Gaspard, Françoise. *A Small City in France*. Cambridge, Mass.: Harvard University Press, 1995.

Gaulle, Charles de. *The Complete War Memoirs*. New York: Simon and Schuster, 1955–1960.

Jackson, Julian. *The Popular Front in France*. Cambridge, U.K.: Cambridge University Press, 1988.

Jones, Colin. *The Great Nation: France from Louis XV to Napoleon*. New York and London: Penguin, 2002.

Kuisel, Richard. *Seducing the French*. Berkeley: University of California Press, 1993.

Marx, Karl. *The 18th Brumaire of Louis Napoleon* (1852). New York: International Publishers, 1963. First published in 1852.

Miller, Michael. *The Bon Marché: Bourgeois Culture and the Department Store*. Princeton, N.J.: Princeton University Press, 1981.

Moses, Claire. *French Feminism in the Nineteenth Century*. Albany: State University of New York Press, 1984.

Moulin, Annie. *Peasantry and Society in France since 1789.* New York: Cambridge University Press, 1991.

Noiriel, Gerard. *The French Melting Pot.* Minneapolis: University of Minnesota Press, 1996.

Nora, Pierre, ed. *Les lieux de mémoire.* 7 vols. Paris: Gallimard, 1984–1992. English translations are *Realms of Memory* (3 vols.; New York: Columbia University Press, 2001–2003) and *Rethinking France* (planned 4 vols.; Chicago: University of Chicago Press, 2004–   ).

Peabody, Sue, and Tyler Stovall, eds. *The Color of Liberty: Histories of Race in France.* Durham, N.C.: Duke University Press, 2003.

Price, Roger. *The French Second Empire.* Cambridge, U.K.: Cambridge University Press, 2001.

Roberts, Mary Louise. *Civilization without Sexes.* Chicago: University of Chicago Press, 1994.

Smith, Bonnie. *Ladies of the Leisure Class.* Princeton, N.J.: Princeton University Press, 1981.

Smith, Leonard, Stéphane Audoin-Rouzeau, and Annette Becker. *France and the Great War.* Cambridge, U.K.: Cambridge University Press, 2003.

Tilly, Charles. *The Contentious French.* Cambridge, Mass.: Harvard University Press, 1986.

Tocqueville, Alexis de. *The Old Regime and the Revolution* (1856). Translated by Alan Kahan. Chicago: University of Chicago Press, 1998.

Weber, Eugen. *Peasants into Frenchmen.* Stanford, Calif.: Stanford University Press, 1976.

JEREMY D. POPKIN

FRANCO-PRUSSIAN WAR.

The Franco-Prussian War, which broke out in July 1870, was initially as lopsided as the Austro-Prussian War that preceded it by four years. The French army was in a very bad state. Napoleon III, the French emperor, who had some training as an artillery officer, was aware of this and had made its reform his overriding priority. But he ran into opposition at home. By contrast, the German army, firmly under Prussian control, was a model of efficiency and organization, and it decisively defeated the French at Sedan on 2 September 1870. The Second Empire broke up in chaos and horror; a republican government was proclaimed, and efforts were launched to liberate French soil from German troops by raising new armies. These efforts proved equally unsuccessful. Paris was choked off from the rest of the country and was battered into surrender by the Germans.

The Prussian success seemed complete. But Otto von Bismarck, the Prussian minister-president, felt depressed, not elated, by these series of events. He ruminated over what lay ahead and found himself faced by three intractable problems. The first was the Prussian military officers, who were determined to drag out the war and make decisions on their own. The second problem was closely related to the first: how to end the war without provoking the intervention of the other powers. Finally, Bismarck had to persuade the four independent states of south Germany, with Bavaria at their head, to accept a constitution that would make King William I of Prussia emperor of a united Germany.

Bismarck overcame the first problem by appealing directly to the king and by securing from him a vigorous and unequivocal directive of his own responsibility for the determination of policy. More serious still was the second problem, created by the announcement of the Russian government on 30 October 1870 that it would no longer abide by the Black Sea clauses of the treaty of Paris of 1856. This raised the specter of an Anglo-Russian war, for the British insisted that no power was free unilaterally to infringe the clauses of a treaty that had been adopted by international agreement. A conference at London arranged by Bismarck defused this crisis.

Meanwhile, Bismarck overcame south German opposition to a new German empire by agreeing to grant Bavaria substantial autonomy in the new German empire, which was created on 18 January 1871 in the Hall of Mirrors of the Palace of Versailles. The new empire included the provinces of Alsace and Lorraine, the annexation of which encumbered Franco-German relations—already badly strained by wartime horrors—with bitter memories and resentments that were not overcome until the 1950s.

[*See also* Ems Telegram.]

BIBLIOGRAPHY

Schroeder, Paul W. "The Lost Intermediaries: The Impact of 1870 on the European System." In his *Systems, Stability, and Statecraft: Essays on the International History of Modern Europe,* edited by David Wetzel, Robert Jervis, and Jack Levy, pp. 77–95. New York: Palgrave Macmillan, 2004. A brilliant and penetrating exposition.

Wawro, Geoffrey. *The Franco-Prussian War: The German Conquest of France in 1870–1871.* New York and Cambridge, U.K.: Cambridge University Press, 2003. A splendid achievement, finely written and firmly based on a thorough examination of the sources.

Wetzel, David. *A Duel of Giants: Bismarck, Napoleon III, and the Origins of the Franco-Prussian War.* Madison: University of Wisconsin Press, 2001. An analysis of the background of the war.

DAVID WETZEL

FREEMASONRY.

Freemasonry is one of the world's oldest and largest fraternal organizations. Members assemble in lodges to enact rituals that convey lessons of self-improvement and fraternal obligation; they also participate in convivial gatherings, charitable activities, and public rituals like foundation-stone–laying ceremonies.

Origins. Historians debate the relationship between "speculative" Freemasonry—the term used to describe the organization of men who adopted masonry for spiritual, intellectual, and fraternal purposes—and its "operative" antecedent—the actual practice of building with stones or bricks. Masonry's regulations, or "Ancient Charges," do date from the medieval period, but Freemasonry in its modern form was clearly a product of the late seventeenth and early eighteenth centuries. Scottish masons' guilds began admitting nonmasons, first noblemen and gentlemen and later professionals and other tradesmen, in the mid-seventeenth century when their memberships began to decline. English lodges followed suit. The guilds attracted such "accepted Masons"—including many members of the Royal Society—because of the widespread belief that the masons, familiar with architecture, geometry, and mathematics, were keepers of both practical and sacred knowledge. Over time, accepted Masons began outnumbering operative masons.

In 1717 four lodges of London Freemasons gathered to form the first Grand Lodge of Ancient, Free, and Accepted Masons. The Grand Lodge enjoyed close ties to the Whig establishment and solidified its authority. In 1723 the Reverend James Anderson composed his foundational *Constitutions of the Free-Masons*, which offered a history that connected the brotherhood to the civilizations of antiquity, outlined grand lodge regulations, and reproduced the "Ancient Charges." British Freemasonry experienced rapid growth in the 1730s and 1740s, and independent grand lodges emerged in Ireland in 1725 and in Scotland in 1736.

Teachings, Organization, Practices. Masonry teaches its members to build themselves into better men by pursuing "brotherly love, relief, and truth." It promotes belief in a universal human family, whose members are equal in the eyes of God. According to one Masonic orator, Freemasonry "teacheth Men of every Nation, of every different Faith, and of every Rank in Life . . . to embrace one another like Brethren, and give the Soul to Harmony and Love" (Alexander Spark, *An Oration Delivered at the Dedication of Free-Mason's Hall*, Quebec, 1787). To this end, the institution keeps membership requirements to a minimum. Any adult man who believes in the existence of a supreme being, described as the Great Architect of the Universe (GAOTU), is theoretically eligible for membership. To preserve a tolerant atmosphere, Masonic regulations, codified by Anderson in the wake of the religious wars of the seventeenth century, forbid the discussion of politics and religion in lodge meetings. Such rules enable Freemasons to claim that theirs is a uniquely tolerant and inclusive brotherhood.

Relief is an equally important Masonic principle. Shared ideology and ritual practices create a deep sense of fraternal obligation. The "Ancient Charges" instruct Freemasons to assist one another "before any other poor People in the same Circumstances," yet also to extend their charity to the

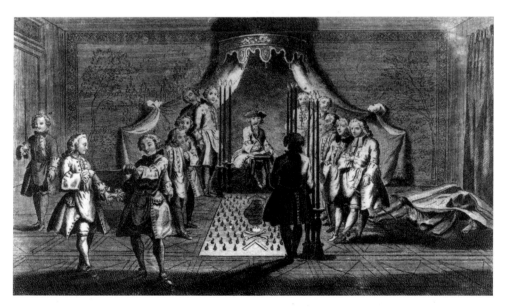

Masonic Ritual. Reception of masters into a Freemasonic lodge, eighteenth century. Bibliothèque Nationale de France

wider community. Finally, Freemasonry teaches its members to pursue truth. The brotherhood does not insist on one truth but rather urges each member to walk his own path to enlightenment and to act, as Anderson put it, "as becomes a moral and wise Man."

A Freemason learns the principles of Masonry in meetings of his lodge, the basic unit of Masonic organization. Lodges meet at least once a month. Their size has varied greatly, from a dozen to over a thousand members. Local lodges operate under the authority of a grand lodge, whose jurisdictions correspond in some cases to states and provinces and in other cases to nations. Grand lodges recognize, maintain fraternal correspondence with, and receive visiting members of other grand lodges that they deem "regular." No single international organization has ever governed Freemasonry globally.

In their lodge meetings Freemasons perform complex rituals based on the traditions of operative masons and the story of Solomon's Temple. Brethren learn a new ritual as they pass each level, or degree, in Freemasonry. Craft Masonry consists of three degrees: Entered Apprentice, Fellow Craft, and Master Mason. The allegorical rituals convey Masonic principles to initiates and members. Combined with an elaborate system of secret handgrips, passwords, and symbols, they also serve as a lingua franca for Freemasons to identify and communicate with one another. Finally, they create fraternal bonds among the brethren.

History and Diffusion. By the mid-eighteenth century Masonic lodges had emerged throughout the British Isles and the European continent. Continental lodges provoked suspicion because of their connection with English constitutionalism. Margaret Jacob has argued that participating in Masonry—with its constitutions, elections, egalitarianism, and lessons in civic virtue—was a primary way that men learned about self-governance and "lived the Enlightenment." The French police raided lodges, and the Catholic Church issued its first encyclical against the fraternity in the 1730s. Yet such challenges did not deter interested men, including Catholics, from joining Freemasonry, which proved to be one of the most popular clubs for upper- and middle-class European men in this quintessential age of associations.

Meanwhile, advancing European empires were spreading Freemasonry throughout the world. It took root most successfully in the British Empire, especially as a result of ambulatory lodges in army regiments. The first overseas lodges appeared in Gibraltar and Bengal at the end of the 1720s. Thereafter Freemasonry spread to the North American and Caribbean colonies. Two grand lodges that emerged in 1752, the Irish Grand Lodge and a rival English grand lodge, the Ancients, were particularly instrumental in planting Freemasonry abroad. The result was the creation of a vast network of lodges that connected British men across the globe. To a lesser extent Freemasonry was also increasingly evident—albeit in variant forms—in the colonies of France, Spain, Portugal, and the Netherlands.

As it spread throughout the world, Freemasonry attracted a wide range of men. British Freemasonry, for example, included Protestants, Catholics, and Jews. In 1776 a Muslim prince joined an English lodge in India, and the Mohawk leader Joseph Brant underwent initiation in London. The following decade the English Grand Lodge issued a warrant for Prince Hall and other Freemasons of African descent to establish a lodge in Boston. British Freemasonry in that age of revolution also included men of strikingly diverse political opinions who both supported and challenged the Whig oligarchy running Hanoverian Britain and its empire. Eighteenth-century Masonry was thus a relatively fluid and inclusive institution that did, at times, live up to its ideology of cosmopolitan brotherhood.

But tensions within both the ideology and the practice of Masonic cosmopolitanism were also evident at this point. Though some Catholic, Jewish, Muslim, and African men found their way into lodges, the membership was primarily white and Protestant. In the 1790s Prince Hall, having received a cold reception from his white "brothers," took it upon himself to issue warrants for new African American lodges. Thereafter, what was called Prince Hall Freemasonry followed a historical trajectory separate from that of mainstream American Masonry. Meanwhile, in India, lodges occasionally welcomed Muslims, but they closed their doors to Hindus and Parsis. Finally, British Freemasonry actively resisted the trend, evident in some Continental lodges during the eighteenth century, to include women.

The nineteenth century witnessed several important turning points in the history of Freemasonry. In 1813 the schism in English Freemasonry was healed. The new United Grand Lodge of England made a conscious effort to distance Freemasonry from its radical past by insisting on a Mason's profession of loyalty to the state and celebrating royal involvement in the brotherhood. The institution continued to flourish abroad, appealing especially to the expanding middle classes of the settlement colonies. In the United States, however, the brotherhood experienced a precipitous decline in the 1820s when a disgruntled Mason, William Morgan, threatened to expose Masonic practices and then disappeared. The incident sparked a backlash, which culminated in the formation of the Anti-Masonic Party that contested the 1832 national election. Freemasonry began recovering in the 1840s but flourished again only after the Civil War, when interest in fraternalism exploded. Millions of American men were attracted to the elaborate ceremonies, recreational opportunities, male companionship, and mutual assistance of Freemasonry and its concordant bodies, the York Rite and the Scottish Rite. They also participated in various appendant organizations, such as the Shriners, while their wives took part in auxiliary groups like the Order of the Eastern Star or Job's Daughters.

Back in Europe, Freemasonry continued to attract members but also experienced significant change in the late nineteenth century. The most important development was a schism resulting from various decisions of the Grand Orient de France. In 1877 the Grand Orient declared atheists eligible for admission. The British and North American grand lodges immediately cut off relations with the Grand Orient and other grand lodges that followed its lead. Members of "English-speaking Masonry" took pains to distinguish themselves from "Latin Masonry" by insisting that belief in a supreme being and steering clear of politics were nonnegotiable "landmarks" of Freemasonry. The Grand Orient's 1893 decision to recognize Co-Masonry, characterized by lodges that admitted women as well as men, deepened the divide. Attempts to form international Masonic bodies at the turn of the century foundered on the shoals of this schism. Nevertheless, English-speaking Freemasonry continued to prosper, especially in its capacity as a bulwark of imperialism in the years before and after World War I.

Freemasonry did not fare well in the totalitarian regimes of the twentieth century. The order was banned in Italy under Benito Mussolini and in Spain under Francisco Franco. Freemasons were among the many targets of Nazi repression. Communist regimes also declared Freemasonry illegal. Meanwhile, the end of World War II marked another moment of expansion for English-speaking Freemasonry, particularly in the United States. By 1959 more than 4 million Masons belonged to U.S. lodges. But beginning in the 1960s young men began losing interest in the fraternal culture that had so attracted their fathers and grandfathers, and Freemasonry declined.

By 2006 there were between 4 and 5 million Freemasons worldwide. The Grand Lodge of England recognizes thirty-one independent grand lodges in Europe, twelve in Africa, six in Asia and the Middle East, six in Australia and New Zealand, sixteen in South America, five in the Caribbean, five in Central America, and seventy-seven (including Prince Hall Grand Lodges) in the United States. It does not recognize dozens of grand orients in France and elsewhere. Most governments tolerate Freemasonry, but it continues to be greeted with intense suspicion by some regimes and by Christian and Muslim fundamentalists. Mainstream Freemasonry faces declining membership in most countries, though Co-Masonry appears to be growing. In both cases the Internet is playing a role in connecting Masons around the world to an unprecedented degree.

[*See also* Secret Societies, Chinese.]

BIBLIOGRAPHY

Bullock, Steven C. *Revolutionary Brotherhood: Freemasonry and the Transformation of the American Social Order, 1730–1840.* Chapel Hill: University of North Carolina Press, 1996. Key study of the brotherhood in its colonial and early national American contexts; focuses on the themes of public versus private, equality, inclusion versus inclusion, and fraternity.

Burke, Janet, and Margaret Jacob. "French Freemasonry, Women, and Feminist Scholarship." *Journal of Modern History* 68 (1996): 515–549. Documents women Freemasons in eighteenth-century Europe and traces the roots of modern feminism to lodges in which women participated.

Clawson, Mary Ann. *Constructing Brotherhood: Class, Gender, and Fraternalism.* Princeton, N.J.: Princeton University Press, 1989. Analyzes the relationship among fraternalism, masculinity, and class in American lodges, particularly during the nineteenth century.

Hamill, John. *The Craft: A History of English Freemasonry.* Leighton Buzzard, U.K.: Crucible, 1986. An accessible introduction to British Freemasonry by an official historian of the brotherhood.

Harland-Jacobs, Jessica L. *Builders of Empire: Freemasons and British Imperialism.* Chapel Hill: University of North Carolina Press, 2007. Traces Freemasonry's global diffusion and role in upholding British imperialism; examines the history of Masonry's inclusive ideology and practice in colonial settings.

Jacob, Margaret C. *Living the Enlightenment: Freemasonry and Politics in Eighteenth-Century Europe.* New York: Oxford University Press, 1991. A pathbreaking academic study of Freemasonry in the European context; argues that Masonic lodges functioned as "schools of government" for eighteenth-century men.

Jacob, Margaret C. *The Origins of Freemasonry: Facts and Fictions.* Philadelphia: University of Pennsylvania Press, 2006. Includes essays on Freemasonry and daily life, citizenship, market relations, and women.

Melton, James Van Horn. *The Rise of the Public in Enlightenment Europe.* Cambridge, U.K., and New York: Cambridge University Press, 2001. Offers excellent background on the enlightenment milieu and includes one chapter on Freemasonry.

Stevenson, David. *The Origins of Freemasonry: Scotland's Century, 1590–1710.* Cambridge, U.K., and New York: Cambridge University Press, 1988. Argues for Scotland, rather than England, as the primary site for the transition from operative to speculative Freemasonry.

JESSICA L. HARLAND-JACOBS

FREE OFFICERS. A secret Egyptian army organization led by Colonel Gamal Abdel Nasser, the Free Officers conspired to overthrow King Farouk I in July 1952. Because it was a secret cabal that would later seize control of Egypt, historical accounts vary concerning its founders and the date of its origin, but it is known that a group of officers including Nasser was meeting regularly by 1945–1946 and that it was probably founded in 1949, after the Palestine war. The group's internal structure was pyramidal, with each officer responsible for developing cells within his own military unit. Many had ties with other political groups, including the pro-Communist Hadeto, the Muslim Brothers, and the palace.

In 1949 they formulated a five-part plan to build an organization, issue propaganda, gather intelligence about the regime, contact other subversive groups, and seize power by 1954. The burning of Cairo in January 1952 led the Free Officers to move their timetable for seizing power up to August of that year; Farouk's frenzied efforts to stay on his throne and his opposition to General Muhammad Najib's election to lead the Officers' Club also speeded up their plans. The exact timing of their coup d'état was set when they learned that Farouk was planning to name General Husayn Sirri ʿAmir (whom they had just tried in vain to assassinate) as his new war minister. The coup was executed during the night of 22–23 July with the seizure of the army headquarters in Cairo. Once the Free Officers group controlled the government, it reorganized itself as the Revolutionary Command Council. It remains unique in Egypt's history as a cabal that actually took power.

[*See also* Egypt.]

BIBLIOGRAPHY

Botman, Selma. "Egyptian Communists and the Free Officers 1950–1954." *Middle Eastern Studies* 22 (1986): 350–366.

Gordon, Joel. *Nasser's Blessed Movement: Egypt's Free Officers and the July Revolution.* New York and London: Oxford University Press, 1992. Analytical account of the Egyptian revolution.

Lacouture, Jean. *Nasser: A Biography.* Translated by Daniel Hofstadter. New York: Knopf, 1973. Best early account of Nasser's rise to power.

Vatikiotis, P. J. *Nasser and His Generation.* New York: St. Martin's Press, 1978. Describes and analyzes the political and social context for Nasser and his fellow conspirators.

Arthur Goldschmidt

FREE TRADE. Free trade is the voluntary exchange of goods and services across international borders, unhindered by government tariffs, quotas, or other restrictions. Free trade is an essential component of globalization, which includes not only trade but also the international flow of capital and people and the resulting integration of national economies with each other. Since publication of *The Wealth of Nations* by Adam Smith in 1776, the debate about free trade has been one of the major battlegrounds in the broader debate about markets and economic freedom.

The expansion of international trade has become an important feature of the modern world. In the aftermath of World War II the industrial countries systematically reduced barriers to trade among one another unilaterally and through the General Agreement on Tariffs and Trade. A growing number of less developed countries also began to open their markets unilaterally, beginning in East Asia with South Korea, Taiwan, Hong Kong, and Singapore, and eventually including China, India, Mexico, Chile, and others. As a result, global trade flows have expanded rapidly since 1950, reaching unprecedented levels as a share of global output. As trade has grown in importance, it has also become more politically controversial, with its supporters crediting it for expanded global wealth and falling poverty and critics blaming it for economic dislocation, environmental damage, and growing inequalities.

Historical and Theoretical Background. Free trade was rare before the nineteenth century, when mercantilism dominated official thinking on trade. Mercantilism emphasized the accumulation of gold and other currency as the chief measure of a nation's wealth, and thus it emphasized the need to earn as much as possible from exports while spending as little as possible for imports. Governments pursued those goals through high trade barriers against imports and by expanding naval power to secure new markets for exports.

As a direct challenge to the predominant thinking of his time, the Scottish moral philosopher Adam Smith (1723–1790) published his famous work, *An Inquiry into the Nature and Causes of the Wealth of Nations.* Smith argued, through systematic logic and telling examples, that a nation's wealth does not consist in the government's stockpile of gold but rather in the ability of its people to produce goods and services that others value. Workers raise their productivity through the division of labor, with households, regions, and nations specializing in what they do best. Trade, according to Smith, creates more wealth by expanding the size of the market, thus allowing a finer division of labor among and within nations. As Smith observed,

> It is the maxim of every prudent master of a family, never to attempt to make at home what it will cost him more to make than to buy. . . . What is prudence in the conduct of every private family, can scarce be folly in that of a great kingdom. If a foreign country can supply us with a commodity cheaper than we

ourselves can make it, better buy it of them with some part of the produce of our own industry, employed in a way in which we have some advantage.

The intellectual argument for free trade was refined in 1817 when the British stockbroker David Ricardo (1772–1823) first explained the theory of comparative advantage. According to Ricardo, even if a nation's workers can produce everything more efficiently than workers in other nations, they can still trade profitably. What matters is what those workers produce most efficiently compared to whatever else they could produce. If workers in a rich country are twice as efficient at producing shoes as workers in a poor country but five times more efficient at producing computer chips, it will still be to the advantage of both nations for the rich country to specialize in computer chips and import shoes from the poor country, and vice versa. By specializing in their comparative advantages, each country can shift its productive resources, such as capital, labor, and land, to those industries where gains in productivity and output are greatest. The final result of trade and specialization is greater output of both goods and greater consumption in both countries than if their economies were closed.

Embracing Free Trade. The ideas of Smith and Ricardo, along with the end of the Napoleonic Wars in 1815, fueled the movement in Great Britain to repeal trade barriers and embrace free trade. The reformers Richard Cobden (1804–1865) and John Bright (1811–1889) led a successful effort through the Anti–Corn Law League that resulted in the repeal in 1846 of Britain's high tariffs on agricultural imports. They argued that high tariffs on food amounted to an unjust subsidy for landowners and a bread tax on workers. Cobden later joined Parliament and became an international advocate of free trade as an instrument of peace among nations. He also negotiated a trade treaty between Britain and France in 1860 that enshrined the "most favored nation" principle—that the treaty's lower tariff rates would be applied to all nations without discrimination and not just to parties of the treaty. The chancellor of the Exchequer and future prime minister William Gladstone (1809–1898) codified Britain's commitment to free trade in his 1860 budget, a policy that did not change until the 1930s.

Despite the growing intellectual arguments in its favor, free trade was not universally practiced even during the height of the first wave of globalization in the nineteenth and early twentieth centuries. Germany and the United States, in particular, used trade barriers to protect certain industries. But global trade barriers on average remained low compared to what they had been during the mercantilist era, while rapid industrialization, falling transportation costs, trade treaties, and relative political stability fueled a dramatic rise in global trade and capital flows up until World War I. Specifically, railroads dramatically cut the cost of moving grain from the American interior to seaports, and steamships reduced the cost of transatlantic shipping by 95 percent between 1815 and 1900. The carrying capacity of the global merchant shipping fleet rose dramatically during this period, from 6 million tons in 1820 to 171 million tons by 1913.

Two Global Calamities. Two global calamities brought the first era of free trade and globalization to an abrupt end. First, the catastrophic war in Europe from 1914 to 1918 disrupted trade and ushered in new economic controls that largely remained after the war. Efforts to restore the more economically liberal prewar system in the 1920s were only partially successful. Then, second, the Great Depression of the 1930s created a vicious cycle of rising trade barriers, falling trade volume, and deepening economic misery. U.S. President Herbert Hoover and a Republican Congress worsened the crisis by enacting the Smoot-Hawley tariff bill in 1930, which raised tariffs dramatically on a broad swath of imports to the United States. The tariff bill did not cause the Great Depression, but most economists agree that it did prolong and deepen the global economic crisis by cutting off access to the U.S. market and inviting trade retaliation from other nations. The economic isolationism of the 1930s has also been blamed for fanning international grievances that led to the outbreak of World War II.

The United States began to turn away from its protectionist past under the leadership of President Franklin D. Roosevelt's secretary of state, Cordell Hull (1871–1955). Like Cobden a century before, Hull believed free trade to be an instrument of peace as well as of economic progress. In 1934 a Democratic Congress passed the Reciprocal Trade Agreements Act, which allowed Hull to negotiate a series of bilateral agreements with major U.S. trading partners. The result was a dramatic fall in U.S. tariff barriers. In 1947, out of the ashes of depression and global war, the United States joined twenty-two other advanced countries to lower trade barriers through the multilateral General Agreement on Tariffs and Trade (GATT). The GATT became the forum for another seven rounds of negotiations involving a growing number of rich and developing countries, culminating in the creation of the World Trade Organization (WTO) in 1995. Multilateral trade agreements have encouraged lower trade barriers, while establishing a set of rules to arbitrate trade disputes. Many countries also continued to pursue unilateral trade liberalization.

Globalization and Technology. The reduction in global trade barriers after World War II stimulated a dramatic rise in global trade flows and cemented peaceful ties among Western Europe, the United States, and Japan. Through engagement in the global economy, the "Four Tigers" of East Asia—South Korea, Taiwan, Singapore, and Hong Kong—transformed themselves from poor to rich countries. Beginning in the 1970s, mainland China, India, Chile, Mexico, and certain other developing nations lowered their previously high trade barriers, opened themselves to foreign investment, and dramatically increased their trade with the rest of the world. The collapse of global Communism in 1989 and growing disillusionment with central planning and protectionism as tools of development further reduced barriers to trade worldwide.

Between 1950 and 2000 the volume of global trade increased eighteenfold, three times faster than global output. As a percentage of global output, trade grew from 6 percent between the world wars to 20 percent by 2000, and trade has continued to grow faster than output since then. Traded goods include both traditional commodities such as agricultural products, raw materials, and oil and also, increasingly, manufactured goods. Many developing countries have become part of sophisticated global supply chains, where components are made in several different countries and brought together for final assembly and export under the management of multinational companies. Global trade flows increasingly involve more advanced products such as automobiles, computers, semiconductors, and telecommunications equipment. Although rich Western countries still dominate the list of top traders, South Korea, Hong Kong, Singapore, Taiwan, Malaysia, Mexico, and China have also joined the list.

Technology has also helped to drive the global growth of trade. Falling communications costs have facilitated the division of the supply chain by allowing multinational companies to coordinate production across the globe. The Internet has expanded the trade in services, including outsourcing of computer programming and other information services to countries such as India. Developed countries increasingly trade financial, insurance, and other services. The development of container shipping beginning in the 1950s allows more efficient handling of manufactured products in ports. Global air freight networks have expanded dramatically.

Despite more than two centuries of economic thought and empirical evidence in support of free trade, it remains controversial in the early twenty-first century. Industries seeking relief from import competition have been joined by certain environmental groups, Third World advocates, and market critics who believe that free trade brings more harm than benefits. They argue that free trade benefits rich nations at the expense of poor nations and spurs a "race to the bottom" as multinational companies seek locations where labor and regulatory costs are lowest. Supporters of free trade counter that the wealth that trade creates allows people in less developed countries to raise their overall standard of living, as well as environmental and labor standards. And free trade is far from universally practiced. Many poor countries, especially in sub-Saharan Africa, the Middle East, and South Asia, maintain relatively high tariffs on imports. Most rich countries, including the United States, Japan, and members of the European Union, continue to restrict imports of textiles, shoes, clothing, and certain agricultural products.

Advocates and critics of free trade tend to agree that the growth of trade has exerted a profound influence on the modern world. Although the critics are correct that not all individuals or nations have reaped the benefits from expanding trade, evidence is growing that trade has played a positive role in the general progress of humankind in the past two centuries. According to the World Bank, the share of the world's population living in absolute poverty, defined as one U.S. dollar per day or less, has been cut in half since 1980, with the most dramatic progress seen in China and other countries that have opened themselves up the most rapidly to the global economy. Other indicators of human well-being, such as life expectancy, infant mortality, nutrition levels, and child labor rates, have been improving along with the rise of global trade.

Free and expanding trade has also arguably contributed to the spread of democracy and human rights. Trade and development have helped to enlarge the middle class, cultivated economic independence, and spread tools of communication in a number of formerly autocratic countries. Since the 1970s the share of the world's population living under democratic forms of government where human rights are generally protected has been rising. In countries such as South Korea, Taiwan, Chile, and Mexico, economic and trade reform have been followed by political reform. A more connected and democratic world has also become a more peaceful world. Though violent strife continues in certain countries and regions, the number of wars between and within nations and the resulting casualties have been trending downward for more than half a century. Advocates of free trade since the time of Adam

Smith would argue that expanding trade and global economic integration have played a role in creating a more peaceful and prosperous world.

[*See also* Capitalism; General Agreement on Tariffs and Trade; Globalization; Laissez-faire; Liberalism; Mercantilism; *and* Trade, International.]

BIBLIOGRAPHY
Bastiat, Frédéric. *Economic Sophisms*. Translated and edited by Arthur Goddard. Princeton, N.J.: Van Nostrand, 1964.
Bastiat, Frédéric. *Selected Essays on Political Economy*. Translated and edited by Seymour Cain. Princeton, N.J.: Van Nostrand, 1964.
Bhagwati, Jagdish. *Free Trade Today*. Princeton, N.J.: Princeton University Press, 2002.
Bhagwati, Jagdish. *Protectionism*. Cambridge, Mass.: MIT Press, 1988.
Friedman, Thomas L. *The World Is Flat: A Brief History of the Twentieth Century*. Expanded ed. New York: Farrar, Straus & Giroux, 2005.
Irwin, Douglas. *Against the Tide: An Intellectual History of Free Trade*. Princeton, N.J.: Princeton University Press, 1996.
Irwin, Douglas A. *Free Trade under Fire*. 2d ed. Princeton, N.J.: Princeton University Press, 2005.
Smith, Adam. *An Inquiry into the Nature and Causes of the Wealth of Nations* (1776). Edited by Edwin Cannan. New York: Modern Library, 1994.
Wolf, Martin. *Why Globalization Works*. London and New Haven, Conn.: Yale University Press, 2004.

DANIEL GRISWOLD

FRENCH AND INDIAN WAR. The French and Indian War (1754–1762) was the North American counterpart to the Seven Years' War. Unlike previous European wars of the eighteenth century, events in North America served as the catalyst for a wider world war involving European nations over national borders, colonial interests, and trade routes.

The seeds of the conflict lay embedded in the expansion in the Ohio Valley by the competing colonial powers of France and Great Britain. The Ohio Valley was the key to the fertile grounds of the American Midwest, as well as the headwaters of the Ohio River, which flowed to the Mississippi River. France desired to extend its control into the Ohio Valley to take advantage of trading and trapping opportunities, as well as a hedge against the expanding British colonies on the North American East Coast. Britain and her colonies saw the valley as the opportunity for expansion and to stop the influence of French Catholics into the backcountry.

From 1749 to 1753, the colonial government in New France (Canada) sent raiding parties to disrupt British control in the Ohio Valley. Parties consisting of French regulars, militia, and Native American allies attacked tribes supporting Britain and built forts to control major trade routes. In 1753, Governor Robert Dinwiddie of Virginia ordered Major George Washington to the region to order the French to leave. Major Washington's mission failed, and Governor Dinwiddie responded with a military force to take Fort Duquesne (Pittsburgh, Pennsylvania). After building Fort Necessity, Major Washington's force skirmished with the local French troops, and killed their commander. By summer of 1754, French reinforcements forced Washington and his Virginia militia to their fortification, and Washington was forced to surrender to the French on 3 July 1754.

Upon receipt of the news of the fighting in the Ohio Valley, Britain dispatched two regiments and General Sir Edward Braddock to take Fort Duquesne. General Braddock was killed and his forces were routed at the Battle of the Monongahela on 9 July 1755. French forces moved southward from Quebec to control Lake George, and were defeated by Sir William Johnson and his Anglo-American Forces on 8 September 1755. Both sides started construction of forts to control their respective ends of Lake George to control the approaches to Montreal and Albany, New York.

As the French forces secured additional strategic points in 1756, their Native American allies raided along the western Pennsylvania and Virginia borders. These raiding parties struck farms and small towns along the Great Wagon Road down to North Carolina. Britain formalized the conflict by declaring war on France on 18 May 1756. After this declaration, the European portion of the conflict began with Prussia's invasion of Saxony. On 15 August 1756, French General Louis-Joseph, Marquis de Montcalm, took Fort Oswego and secured Lake Ontario. Upon the completion of Fort Carillon (Ticonderoga) in upper New York, the French forces worked toward clearing out British control in northern New York. The French and Native American army under General Montcalm moved south and laid siege to Fort William Henry at Lake George. The fort surrendered to the French on 9 August 1757, but the victory was marred by the attack on British survivors by the French Native allies. Despite these successes, the lack of supplies forced the French army to stop their offensive toward Albany.

In June 1757, William Pitt the Elder became secretary of state, and he brought a new direction to the British war effort. He focused the nation's war resources toward attacking French colonial holdings, instead of transferring regiments to fight on the European continent. British reinforcements were sent to North America, India, and

French and Indian War. Defeat of British Gen. Edward Braddock, Virginia, 1755. Engraving by John Andrew, 1855. PRINTS AND PHOTOGRAPHS DIVISION, LIBRARY OF CONGRESS

the West Indies to cut off the French receipt of raw goods from those locations. General James Abercrombie was directed to lead an Anglo-American force of sixteen thousand from Albany northward to Montreal, New France (Canada), in summer of 1758. General Montcalm successfully defended Fort Carillon (Ticonderoga) against the British assaults, and Abercrombie was forced to turn back. The French fortress at Louisburg was taken at the mouth of the Saint Lawrence River by an Anglo-American army and opened up the invasion route into New France.

In 1759, William Pitt financed an additional twenty thousand colonial troops to assist British forces to invade New France. General Jeffrey Amherst (Abercrombie's successor) directed another British and colonial army northward from Albany and swung around the French defenses to take French fortifications at Lake Erie and Ontario. This maneuver forced the French to abandon Fort Carillon, and by August 1759 the French forces had retreated to their defenses along the Saint Lawrence River. On 13 September 1759, General James Wolfe defeated Montcalm's French forces at the Battle of the Plains of Abraham, and the victorious British army captured Quebec. Montreal was captured in September 1760. The military aspects of the French and Indian War were basically over except for Native American raiding parties operating throughout the Appalachian Mountains, which forced the English colonies to build blockhouses along their western frontier.

The French and Indian War (as well as its European counterpart, the Seven Years' War) ended with the signing of the Treaty of Paris on 10 February 1763. The Treaty of Paris dealt mainly with Great Britain and France and the determination of ownership of land in the New World. New France (Canada) became a British colony, as well as the Spanish colony in Florida. France received the island of Guadeloupe, the port of New Orleans, and the Louisiana Territory stretching into western North America. Incidentally, the European portion of the war was settled by the Treaty of Hubertusburg, which returned the national boundaries back to their prewar status.

Great Britain had become the dominant European power in North America, as well as in other locations, such as India through the British East India Company. Despite controlling commerce from new markets overseas, Britain now needed to pay for the military conflict that enabled it to control a continent, which in turn, would bring the nation into conflict with its colonies in North America.

[*See also* Plains of Abraham *and* Seven Years' War.]

BIBLIOGRAPHY

Anderson, Fred. *A People's Army: Massachusetts Soldiers and Society in the Seven Years War*. Chapel Hill, N.C.: University of North Carolina Press (Institute of Early American History and Culture), 1984. An excellent study into the raising of troops on the colonial level.

Cave, Alfred A. *The French and Indian War*. Westport, Conn.: Greenwood Press, 2004. A good overview of the conflict in North America.

Jennings, Francis *Empire of Fortune: Crowns, Colonies, and Tribes in the Seven Years' War in America*. New York: Norton, 1988. A great overview of the competing imperial forces in North America, and their interaction with the Native American tribes.

Schwartz, Seymour I. *The French and Indian War, 1754-1763: The Imperial Struggle for North America*. New York: Simon & Schuster, 1994. A great survey of the conflict, and its role in the international politics at the time.

Ward, Matthew C. *Breaking the Backcountry: The Seven Years' War in Virginia and Pennsylvania, 1754–1765*. Pittsburgh: University of Pittsburgh Press, 2003. An outstanding work directed toward a description of problems of protecting the colonial backcountry.

WILLIAM H. BROWN

FRENCH COLONIAL EMPIRE. *See* Empire and Imperialism, *subentry* The French Colonial Empire.

FRENCH GUIANA. In 1750 the corner of South America known as French Guiana (*La Guyane française*) was a minor and struggling outpost of the first French Empire. Although a plantation colony, it received little in the way of slaves or investment. A location inconvenient to French sailing routes, inadequate labor supply, and poor soil preparation all contributed to a self-reinforcing pattern of economic stagnation. Beyond a thin coastal strip, most of the land remained relatively unaffected by the French presence and was peopled by indigenous Amerindian groups.

The ensuing century witnessed social upheaval and a series of remarkable but unsuccessful efforts to populate the colony. The resettlement of French Canadians failed disastrously, while slaves were freed and reenslaved at different points in the French Revolution. Meanwhile, Maroons (descendants of escaped slaves) from the neighboring Dutch colony moved into border regions of the interior.

Following a new round of revolution and the final abolition of slavery in 1848, the French selected French Guiana as the site of their primary penal colony. For different periods between 1852 and 1946, convicts inhabited a series of miserable settlements on the mainland and three small coastal islands. Known in English as Devil's Island—the infamous site of Alfred Dreyfus's exile—this experiment produced lurid fantasy and economic dependency rather than a tropical version of Australia. The discovery of gold in the interior, on the other hand, prompted the arrival of miners from the greater Caribbean region, including a number of intrepid women. However, the bulk of the inhabitants remained on the coast. Largely the descendents of former slaves subsisting on small-scale agriculture, this population defined a local creole language and culture. Efforts to promote industries around products like rum, rosewood, and balata gum ultimately fizzled, and the world Depression of the 1930s did little to aid the colony's economic prospects.

Along with several other remaining colonies, French Guiana was integrated into France following World War II as an overseas département or department. This new status brought with it the seeds of dramatic social change. Formerly the poorest entity in the region, French Guiana's direct attachment to a European welfare state gradually transformed it into an oasis of relative wealth. Beyond modern infrastructure like roads and electricity, this transformation resulted in significant demographic changes. In 1964 the French moved their space program to a base near the town of Kourou. By default, the space center became a center of economic gravity for the department, while also supporting European consortium projects. One of these, the highly successful Ariane rocket, captured about half the market for commercial satellite launches in the 1980s and 1990s.

An influx of migrants from Haiti and Brazil in particular altered the region's social composition. Although still the largest single group, Guyanais Creoles no longer made up a majority of inhabitants, and French displaced Creole as the lingua franca. Alongside larger blocks of Creoles, Haitians, and Brazilians, the diverse population included smaller numbers of Europeans, Amerindians, Maroons, Chinese, and Hmong. Nonetheless, at the close of the twentieth century the density of settlement remained one of the lowest of the planet, particularly in the interior. Persistent unemployment and social tensions fueled sporadic calls for greater autonomy from France. The advent of the European Union, however, added another level of political complication and possibility. On the environmental front, French Guiana continued to have one of the world's residual stretches of primary-growth rain forest. Because of its unique political and economic context, logging had never become commercially viable on any significant scale. French Guiana thus stands in contrast with neighboring Brazil and Suriname and represents an anomaly within the larger pattern of accelerating deforestation worldwide. Increased illicit gold mining in the last years of the century, however, suggested that this relative state of exception might not endure indefinitely.

[*See also* France; *and* Prisons and Punishment, *subentry* Prison Colonies and Islands.]

BIBLIOGRAPHY
Price, Richard, and Sally Price. *Equatoria*. New York: Routledge, 1992. An account of a museum collecting trip into the interior of the country.
Redfield, Peter. *Space in the Tropics: From Convicts to Rockets in French Guiana*. Berkeley: University of California Press, 2000. A comparative study of the penal colony and space program in French Guiana.

PETER REDFIELD

FRENCH INTERVENTIONS IN MEXICO. French policy toward Mexico until 1867 showcased both the weaknesses with which the young nations of Spanish America entered the international arena after independence and the diverse forms of European imperialism in the nineteenth century. In March of 1838 France, a haphazard colonizer after 1815, inefficiently blockaded the main port of a nation whose independence it had not formally recognized but with whom it had been negotiating since 1827. The hostilities were unleashed by the Mexican government's inability to respond to a French ultimatum demanding the satisfaction of claims made by French citizens residing in Mexico, whose lives and fortunes had been affected by the country's endemic political instability. The "Pastry War," as the episode was derisively called by the Mexican press because of the extravagant demands of a French pâtissier, was resolved only through the intervention of the British minister and the display of Her Majesty's gunboats in Veracruz harbor. The Mexican government, distracted by the crisis of Texan independence, agreed to pay all indemnities.

In 1862 the allegations of aggrieved French citizens living abroad were called upon to justify French aggression, but were made to fit a grander scheme. With the United States completely absorbed in fighting its civil war, Napoleon III, emperor of the French, saw in his "Mexican adventure" an exceptional opportunity for regaining a foothold in the New World. In July of 1861, after a destructive and militarily inconclusive civil war left the national treasury in shambles, the Mexican president Benito Juárez called for a moratorium on foreign debts. Even though the amount owed French nationals was the most modest, the emperor of the French took it upon himself to lead a military intervention by Mexico's main creditors. Nevertheless, the emperor's "Great Design" went beyond teaching the upstart republic to respect its international commitments. With the support of the recently defeated Mexican Conservative Party, the expeditionary forces, after taking Mexico City in 1863, enabled the establishment of a "moderate monarchy" under the Habsburg archduke Maximilian, the younger brother of the emperor of Austria.

The French army, although only occasionally defeated in battle, failed to check republican resistance, and its relationship with Maximilian's government was strained, specially after the Austrian successfully resisted a project for direct French occupation and control of the prosperous mining region of Sonora. With the end of the Civil War, a triumphant Union government in the United States affirmed its opposition to European encroachments on the American continent and exerted strong diplomatic pressure for the removal of French forces. With the added pressure of a menacing Prussia, which had just defeated Austria and Denmark and seemed unstoppable in its ambition to unite the German peoples, by mid-1866 Napoleon had decided to cut his losses and bring the troops home. Maximilian and his generals were executed in June of 1867, the former as a filibuster, or foreign insurrectionist, the other two as traitors. Napoleon's failure was later seen as a prelude to his regime's disastrous fall in 1870.

In sending thirty thousand troops to Mexico and in placing an Austrian prince on a Mexican throne, Napoleon III claimed to be protecting the "Latin race" and preserving French access to an important market. But if those who supported the endeavor sang the glories of a civilizing mission and the praises of Mexico as a privileged crossroads between East and West, its silver production was the true underlying attraction. As Shirley J. Black has shown, bimetallist France had struggled under its growing shortage of silver since the 1847 gold rushes in Australia and California. This experiment in low-cost, informal colonial domination may have failed politically and diplomatically, but it did, nevertheless, increase France's silver reserves by over £350,000 a year, over forty times previous yearly amounts, enabling it to ease, a few years later, the economic crisis that accompanied defeat.

In Mexico the two crises highlighted the young nation's inability to hold its ground in a game in which it was by far overmatched, but Mexican resistance to France's ambitions contributed to consolidating nationalist feeling and imagination. The struggle and ultimate victory against a monarchical regime, sponsored by the world's "first soldiers," was canonized as a "Second War of Independence" and fed into a strain of nationalism that glorified the down-to-earth qualities and heroism of the common Mexican. After the liberal victory of 1867, this popular, localist, republican version of patriotism became official, the stuff of public celebration, monuments, and textbooks.

The story of the brave little republic that put European imperialism in its place, with the complexities of Mexican collaboration written out, was enshrined into a practically unshakeable patriotic myth.

[*See also* Latin America, *subentry* Foreign Military Intervention; Mexico; *and* Reforma, La.]

BIBLIOGRAPHY

Black, Shirley J. *Napoleon III and Mexican Silver*. Silverton, Colo.: Ferrell Publications, 2000. A valuable monograph that studies previously ignored financial and monetary aspects of the Mexican expedition.

Dabbs, Jack Autrey. *The French Army in Mexico, 1861–1867: A Study in Military Government*. The Hague: Mouton, 1963. The most thorough analysis of the policies of the army, based on the archive of its commander, Achille Bazaine, it perhaps falls a little short when taking into account the priorities and actions of Maximilian's government.

Lecaillon, Jean-François. *Napoleon III et le Méxique: Les illusions d'un grand dessein*. Paris: L'Harmattan, 1994. A balanced and sympathetic examination of Napoleon III's overt reasons and motives, measured against the background of Second Empire politics.

Meyer, Jean A. *Yo, el francés: La intervención en primera persona: Biografías y crónicas*. Mexico City: TusQuets Editores, 2002. A group portrait of the French officer corps. Remarkable in its success in weaving thorough historical and sociological analysis of the expeditionary leadership with the narrative of individual reminiscences.

ERIKA PANI

FRENCH LANGUAGE AND LITERATURE. The French language has its origins in the Latin carried out into the provinces of the Roman Empire over several centuries. A tenth-century Latin historical chronicle offers the earliest extant text recorded in a language that was no longer Latin, yet not fully French: the words of an oath of allegiance pronounced at Strasbourg in 842 C.E. by Charles the German in the *romana lingua*, or Romance language, of his brother Louis's army. Over the next two centuries, Old French appeared in religious and didactic texts and in the *chansons de geste*, verse romances of heroic exploits including the *Song of Roland*, said to have been performed for Norman soldiers before the Battle of Hastings in 1066. By the thirteenth century, French had largely supplanted Latin in literary writing, though as the language was gradually developed and standardized, it remained in competition with Latin as the vehicle for intellectual expression until well into the eighteenth century. While French continues to evolve, adapting to new realities over both time and space, the formal literary language has essentially changed little since the time of the founding of the French Academy in the seventeenth century,

although the barriers between literary and colloquial language are blurred, if not subverted or ignored, by many modern writers.

French literature has conventionally been organized into "centuries": the medieval period (the eleventh through the thirteenth centuries), Middle French (fourteenth and fifteenth), the Renaissance or early modern period (sixteenth), classicism (seventeenth), the Enlightenment (eighteenth), Romanticism, realism, and naturalism (nineteenth), and the modern period (twentieth to the present). More recently, French literature has broadened its scope to encompass literatures of French expression written outside of France, including the Francophone literatures of North Africa, sub-Saharan Africa, the Caribbean, French Polynesia, and Quebec.

Internationally, the French language gained greatest influence in the eighteenth and nineteenth centuries when it was the most common language of international diplomacy and was widely used by upper classes throughout Europe, including Russia, and parts of the Middle East. This role ceded to English in the twentieth century, and defenders of the French language were increasingly on the defensive against adoption of English words even in France. However, the importance of French for literature and global access in many former French colonies warns against exaggerating the language's decline.

French literature underwent a series of major changes beginning in the eighteenth century. After the French Revolution (1789), writers began to break away from the tradition of giving voice to the eternal and epic struggles facing humankind, and in the manner of Jean-Jacques Rousseau (1712–1778) turned their attention to the individual, in accord with the nineteenth-century French Romantic movement that sought to free the individual, and the forms of literature itself, from the tenets of classicism that were seen as impediments to artistic expression. Victor Hugo, in his famous 1834 reply to those who criticized his choice of language, boasts of having "mis un bonnet rouge au vieux dictionnaire" (put the red cap of the revolution on the old dictionary; *Les contemplations*, VII: *Réponse à un acte d'accusation*).

The Romantic revolution gave rise to a series of literary movements that frequently developed in reaction to what had gone before. Writers of the realist movement such as Stendhal (Marie-Henri Beyle; *Le rouge et le noir*, 1830) and Honoré de Balzac (*La comédie humaine*, ninety-five novels and stories published from 1830 to 1850) sought to depict society without embellishment. Marked by the massive scientific advances of their age, naturalist writers applied the scientific method to their craft, writing as if their works were scientific experiments based on minutely documented observations of events: Émile Zola's cycle of novels, *Les Rougon-Macquart* (1871–1893), was subtitled "the natural history of a family." Nineteenth-century poetry was marked most significantly by the Symbolists, among whom we may cite Charles Baudelaire, who in his collection of poems *Les fleurs du mal* (1857; English trans., *The Flowers of Evil*) depicted themes of corruption, misery, and suffering by means of poetic "correspondences" between natural phenomena and eternal truths, and Stéphane Mallarmé, whose poem "Un coup de dés jamais n'abolira le hasard" (A Throw of the Dice Never Will Abolish Chance, 1897) was set in type to resemble a musical score.

The twentieth century elicits another reference to a dictionary. David Coward observes that a new abridged dictionary called the *Petit Larousse*, in its first edition in 1905, sold 200,000 copies, a reflection of the dramatic spread of literacy that had occurred over the previous century and would continue throughout the next. Literature, no longer the province of an educated elite, became a part of modern life in all its aspects and uncertainties. Marcel Proust ushered in the modern era with *À la recherche du temps perdu* (1913–1927), which sought "remembrance of time past" through memory and artistic creation. Proust represents a break with the naturalistic, mechanistic past, observing in *Du côté de chez Swann* (1913; English trans., *Swann's Way*, 1918) that "notre personnalité sociale est une création de la pensée des autres" (our social personality is a creation of the thought of others). Reality is subjective, a creation of others, and subjective realities will dominate the century. In poetry, Guillaume Apollinaire followed Mallarmé in doing away with conventional forms of punctuation and arrangement of words on the page (*Calligrammes*, 1918), paving the way for the surrealist movement that sought a complete break from traditional forms of expression and perception. Following World War II, Jean-Paul Sartre (*L'être et le néant*, 1943; English trans., *Being and Nothingness*, 1956) questioned the meaning of human existence within the existentialist dilemma of finding one's "being" in the middle of "nothingness," a dilemma mirrored in the movement of "le théâtre de l'absurde," through which Samuel Beckett and Eugène Ionesco sought to illustrate the absurdity of mankind's existence.

In more recent times, French literature has been both the province and the product of new ways of thinking about texts and their creation, leading to experimental approaches to writing such as the *nouveau roman* (Michel Butor, Marguerite Duras, Alain Robbe-Grillet, Nathalie Sarraute), which sought to engage the reader as an active participant in the process of writing. According to structuralist principles founded on the work of the Swiss linguist Ferdinand de Saussure (1857–1913), all linguistic signs were arbitrary—and so all language, all literature, all interpretation. The text became, as David Coward puts it, no longer the creation of a particular author but a phenomenon that could no longer be accounted for, since there were no universal concepts, like Beauty or Order, by which it could be measured.

Freed from the bonds of the "universal concepts" that had defined what literature had to be and who was granted the privilege of being a writer, contemporary French literature has left aside the theoretical questions of textual genesis and of literary form, and in the latter half of the twentieth century gave expression to new voices and turned its attention to issues confronting multiple social, economic, linguistic, and geographic realities. These include women's writing; for example, the *écriture féminine* movement that developed from the works of Hélène Cixous and rejected male language, viewpoint, and perspective; *Beur* literature produced by second-generation North African writers born in France (Azouz Begag, Nina Bouraoui); and outside of France, Francophone literatures, originally conceived as extensions of metropolitan France, now flourishing in their own right.

[*See also* Empire and Imperialism, *subentry* The French Colonial Empire; France; *and* World Literature.]

BIBLIOGRAPHY

Battye, Adrian, Marie-Anne Hintze, and Paul Rowlett. *The French Language Today: A Linguistic Introduction.* 2d ed. London: Routledge, 2000. Presents, in a friendly, accessible, and nontechnical way, the historical development, sound system, and word and sentence structures of French, with special attention to stylistic, social, and regional variation.

Birkett, Jennifer, and James Kearns. *A Guide to French Literature: From Early Modern to Postmodern.* New York: St. Martin's, 1997. A chronological history of French literature in its relationship to social and political history, new directions in contemporary thought, and contemporary critical theory.

Coward, David. *A History of French Literature: From "Chanson de Geste" to Cinema.* Oxford: Blackwell, 2002. Discusses the various French literatures over the centuries in their historical and social contexts. Includes an especially lucid discussion on the development of critical theory in the twentieth century.

Hollier, Denis, ed. *A New History of French Literature.* Cambridge, Mass.: Harvard University Press, 1989. Essays by 165 scholars viewing literary works through the lens of a particular date in literary, cultural, social, or political history.

JEFFREY T. CHAMBERLAIN

FRENCH REVOLUTION. Although liberty and legal equality—ideas associated with the Enlightenment—had caused considerable political turbulence in the eighteenth century, most notably during the American Revolution, the French Revolution catapulted these ideas into public consciousness in an unprecedented way. Because France had a social and political system more like that of other counties and was also the West's most populous country, its turn toward these new ideas had far greater immediate impact than any of the other eighteenth-century experiments. Furthermore, as the Revolution wore on, the wars that followed led to the direct export of these ideas.

The impact of the Revolution proved to be international, but its source was also local. Although historians continue to debate the causes of the Revolution, most would agree that the French had lost significant confidence in their monarchy by the late 1780s. Despite French success in the American Revolution, much of the eighteenth century had been a dreary succession of martial defeats, embarrassment at royal cupidity and debauchery, social and political problems, and sudden and faulty diplomatic shifts in the face of a desire for change and royal accountability. Still, this ramshackle monarchy might have creaked into the nineteenth century had it not been for the enormous debt that piled up after the American Revolution. Unable to borrow at any reasonable rate because of the doubts of creditors, in 1788 the monarchy called the Estates-General, a roughly representative body, to pass taxes that would lead to solvency.

Having opened up the door to what might have emerged as some kind of constitutional monarchy, the monarchy faced a society that wanted much greater change. Armed with powerful doctrines of sovereignty, the middle classes endeavored to steer the Revolution in their direction. Popular classes followed, but they developed their own agenda as well. By the end of the summer of 1789, the king was at the mercy of the revolutionaries, who had claimed sovereignty, had replaced Old Regime privileges with civic equality and citizenship, and had passed a bill of rights and were writing a new constitution.

Although many scholars believe that the first two years of the Revolution were relatively moderate in intent and in reality, others have seen them as part of the movement toward the bloodshed that increasingly characterized the Revolution. By 1792 the situation had changed so dramatically that France was an increasingly polarized nation, with the supporters and opponents of the Revolution

French Revolution. The heads of the Marquis de Launay and Jacques de Flesselles carried on pikes, 14 July 1789, following the taking of the Bastille. Mezzotint and engraving, 1789. FRENCH POLITICAL CARTOON COLLECTION/PRINTS AND PHOTOGRAPHS DIVISION, LIBRARY OF CONGRESS

increasingly at odds. In part, the decision to nationalize the Catholic Church and to demand that its priests and other officials swear allegiance to the Revolution had nearly split the church and France.

But what pushed the country further into opposing divisions was the war between France and her European neighbors. Even if the neighbors did not actually want war, their kings made enough threats to validate the bellicose intentions of leading revolutionaries who believed war against the monarchies to be valid and politically popular. The war also encouraged the destabilization of France, because though the revolutionaries gained victories, defeats were common enough to increase the rift. This division—exacerbated by the trial and execution of the king in January 1793—grew within the revolutionary elite as well as between those supporting the Revolution and those against it.

Eventually in June 1793, the Jacobins, radical defenders of the Revolution who were associated with the urban populace, held power alone and faced a counterrevolution in the west, the opposition of moderates in several major cities, and war on the frontiers. To combat their foes, the Jacobins entrusted power to a few men in the Committee of Public Safety. Using revolutionary justice known as the Terror, the leadership, most famously Maximilien-François-Marie-Isidore de Robespierre, rallied supporters and suppressed challengers. Domestically and internationally, the radicals prevailed. Ironically this success made the Committee of Public Safety superfluous, and its most prominent leaders were executed on 8 Thermidor (27 July) 1794.

During the next several years an interesting dynamic developed in France. In reaction to the radicalism and the Terror, the remaining revolutionary officeholders—the Thermidoreans—sought a centrist direction, essentially embracing bourgeois notions of property rights and of property-based political rights. To avoid any repeat of the dictatorship of the Committee of Public Safety, the Thermidoreans also constructed a government—the Directory—weakened by dilution of authority. Arrayed against the ruling party were, on the one hand, nostalgic royalists desirous of a return of the Bourbon monarchy and, on the other, those wishing a resurgence of the Jacobins. The centrists stayed the course by relying on the military to deal with enemies, while simultaneously carrying on the popular policy of dominating Europe militarily.

By 1799, France was embattled in a worldwide conflict, having achieved expanded borders and a series of buffer states in Europe. Success abroad was more elusive as Haiti, the crown jewel of French possessions, remained under the control of the independent former slave Toussaint-Louverture. Overall success in foreign exploits, however, could not stabilize the government, and in 1799 leaders of the Directory unseated the regime in order to replace it with a more powerful, less democratic consular government. For military backing, they turned to the military again—in particular, to Napoleon Bonaparte.

Within a month after the coup on 18 Brumaire (9–10 November) 1799, the consular government was founded. Napoleon, however, dominated it. By 1804 he crowned himself emperor and increasingly transformed the government to enhance his power. Though with less commitment to liberty and more emphasis on his own personality, Napoleon reigned largely in the spirit of his immediate predecessors—defending property rights

French Revolution. Attack on the National Convention, Paris, 5 October 1795. Print by Pierre Berthault, 1795. Prints and Photographs Division, Library of Congress

and undertaking exploits abroad—until his regime was ended by military defeat in 1814 and again after his return in 1815.

The legacy of the French Revolution is enormous. Domestically the Revolution abandoned the nominal economic protectionist policies of the Old Regime for a greater commitment to capitalism. Despite political vacillations, the Revolution became synonymous at home and abroad with liberty and equality, social as well as legal. The Revolution modeled these economic, political, societal, and legal shifts, it spread nationalism, in part in emulation of the military dominance possible when the nation ruled instead of a king. But an even more potent nationalism emerged as a response to invading French armies. Ultimately for Europe, such national movements may have done more to reshape the continent in the succeeding centuries than the ideals of liberty. The rest of the world would have to react to this mixed legacy.

[*See also* Declaration of the Rights of Man; France; Jacobins; Nationalism; *and* Reign of Terror.]

BIBLIOGRAPHY

Censer, Jack R., and Lynn Hunt. *Liberty, Equality, Fraternity: Exploring the French Revolution.* University Park: Pennsylvania State University Press, 2001.

Godineau, Dominique. *The Women of Paris and Their French Revolution.* Translated by Katherine Streip. Berkeley and Los Angeles: University of California Press, 1998.

Klaits, Joseph, and Michael H. Haltzel, eds. *The Global Ramifications of the French Revolution.* Cambridge, U.K., and New York: Cambridge University Press, 1994.

Lyons, Martyn. *Napoleon Bonaparte and the Legacy of the French Revolution.* New York: St. Martin's Press, 1994.

Stone, Bailey. *Reinterpreting the French Revolution: A Global-Historical Perspective.* Cambridge, U.K., and New York: Cambridge University Press, 2002.

JACK R. CENSER

FRENCH UNION. The French colonial empire was a jigsaw puzzle of territories with different statutes (for example, colony or protectorate), all dependent on colonial tutelage and marked by social inequity and negligible investments in education that limited the creation of local elites. For those territories loyal to Gaullist Free France during World War II, the Brazzaville Conference of October 1944 paved the way for a project of cultural, social, and political emancipation, but these promises were vague. While the Antilles, for example, benefited from assimilation, other territories moved toward reaction, embracing nationalism and even communism (as in Indochina). In France, economic pressure was applied by

groups (for instance, the Comité de l'Empire Français, which organized the États Généraux de la Colonisation Française) to protest against the weakening of French interests overseas. The spirit of the liberation from the German occupation was torn apart by partisan struggles when the tripartite alliance of socialists, communists, and centrists—and Gaullists in the 1944–1946 period—failed. This political failure explains the compromise in governance reached in 1946 by means of the Union française (French Union), which was established through the constitution and adopted by referendum (mainly in France) in October 1946.

The notion of "empire," which implied domination, was replaced by that of "union"—the establishment of limited equal rights, but the rejection of "federalism." Decentralization prevailed throughout overseas territories; each territory could retain its own statutes: *départements d'outre-mer* (overseas departments: the Antilles, Réunion, French Guiana), *territoires d'outre-mer* (overseas territories: the majority of the former empire), direct colony (Algeria), and several to-be autonomous territories, either both under French tutelage (Togo, Cameroon since 1918), or *États associés* (associated states: Cambodia, Laos, and Vietnam). Paradoxically, the protectorates of Morocco and Tunisia were not admitted to the French Union because—by a political fiction—they maintained their independence from the French Foreign Ministry and were not considered colonies. Budgets and administrations were to be decentralized. Some institutions promoted reforms. In much the same way that Queen Victoria reigned over the British Empire, the French president presided over the Union, aided by the Haut Conseil de l'Union Française. This executive branch could rely on a legislative organ, the Assemblée de l'Union Française, an assembly of 230 representatives including 105 from overseas territories and 125 from France itself (party delegates and individuals with business links overseas—half of whom were elected by parliament). This body served as a consultative assembly, surveying legal matters overseas and submitting resolutions and proposals to the parliament and to the government.

The Union was marked by a spirit of generosity, reform, political openness, and economic and social progress, and it expressed political diversity through the participation of progressives from the opposition parties. The Union might have led to some kind of federal overseas system, with a steady evolution toward autonomy, a process that might have helped promote "moderates" among nationalists, for example, in the Maghreb or in sub-Saharan Africa and perhaps even in Indochina.

But the Union proved to be a façade: overseas elections were largely orchestrated, and politics in the protectorates (Morocco and Tunisia) became dominated by the police, army, and colonial lobbies. The dual electoral college in Algeria (Europeans and Muslims) met a deadlock because Nationalists were barred from election in the Muslim college in favour of straw men for domination by the colonial residents. The French Union proved nothing more than a kind of artificial institutional architecture, with the Haut Conseil gathering for only a short period (1951–1954) and the Assembly lacking real legitimacy in nationalism circles. The only substantive reform for the overseas territories was the *Code du travail* (labor regulation law), an achievement that was long delayed owing to resistance by overseas business interests. In short, the Union was unable to assert itself as an institution of dialogue and negotiation that could have tackled issues of overseas civil and political rights. Repression prevailed in the Maghreb (Morocco and Tunisia) by the 1950s, and then from 1954 to 1955 in Algeria; France was forced to leave Indochina following the Geneva agreement in 1954.

The Union functioned somewhat as a "club" of elites while opening some doors to dialogue: moderate nationalists participated in its institutions; political networks were formed; and enlightened businessmen were persuaded to balance calls for political autonomy with the preservation of overseas interests. The process led to negotiations with nationalists in Tunisia and Morocco, and particularly in sub-Saharan Africa, and ultimately resulted in independence agreements in Tunisia and Morocco (1957) and to the *loi-cadre Defferre* (framing law) in 1956, a legal framework that enabled the establishment of transition governments. The result was parties and elites that remained pro-France following independence in 1960, and *Françafrique* relationships that preserved French economic interests and influence in Africa.

The fate of the French Union was sealed when the Fourth Republic disappeared in September 1958; the new constitution replaced it with a temporary Communauté between 1958 and 1960, which proved less successful but ushered in the process that led to independence in most territories. "Direct rule" and democracy prevailed thereafter in the overseas territories still within France's orbit, but no other institutions were dedicated to the expression of special rights for overseas territories.

[*See also* Brazzaville Conference; Empire and Imperialism, *subentry* The French Colonial Empire; *and Loi Cadre.*]

BIBLIOGRAPHY

Borella, François. *Lévolution juridique et politique de l'Union française depuis 1946.* Paris: Librairie générale de droit et de jurisprudence, 1958.

Bouche, Denise. *Histoire de la colonisation française.* Vol. 2: *Flux et reflux (1815–1962).* Paris: Fayard, 1991.

Droz, Bernard. *Histoire des décolonisations au xxᵉ siècle.* Paris: Seuil, 2006.

Liauzu, Claude, ed. *Dictionnaire de la colonisation française.* Paris: Larousse, 2007.

Mus, Paul. *Le destin de l'Union française, de l'Indochine à l'Afrique.* Paris: Seuil, 1954.

Pervillé, Guy. *De l'empire français à la décolonisation.* Paris: Hachette, 1991.

Revue d'économie politique. *L'économie de l'Union française d'outre-mer.* Paris: Sirey, 1952, 1954.

Thobie, Jacques, Gilbert Meynier, Catherine Coquery-Vidrovitch, and Charles-Robert Ageron. *Histoire de la France coloniale.* Vol. 2: *1914–1990.* Paris: Armand Colin, 1990.

HUBERT BONIN

FREUDIANISM. The effects of Freudian psychoanalysis have been widespread, from the promulgation of the idea of an arational human being driven by desire and the subsequent break with Enlightenment notions of human perfectibility, to the securing of the bourgeois internality of the modern individual and the provision of staple interpretive strategies from disciplines as different as anthropology and literary theory. Throughout this diffusion, the basic contours of Freudianism—the internal drives, the function of the ego and superego, and the belief in infantile sexuality as mediated by the Oedipal drama—have remained the same, though its applications have varied wildly.

Although the Austrian neurologist Sigmund Freud (1856–1939) wrote *The Interpretation of Dreams* in 1899, he wanted his most important work yet to be associated with the new century, so he published it the next year. Here, Freud laid out the bare bones of his psychoanalytic structure: the theory of infantile sexuality, repression, and the unconscious. He wished to rise in fame and notoriety and understood that his work's uniqueness had yet to prove its therapeutic value, and though Richard von Krafft-Ebing and Havelock Ellis had written their pioneering works on human sexual behavior, Freud had not, at the time *The Interpretation of Dreams* was written, completely consolidated his theory. He makes comments in both directions in that work, but his leaning is clear: he believes that children have sexual feelings. Freud even wrote to his teacher, Wilhelm Fliess, that his next book might be a full account of a theory of sexuality. This theory, though, would come only in segments and was certainly not finalized until well beyond Freud's revolutionary *Three Essays on the Theory of Sexuality* in 1905.

Origins of Freudian Psychoanalysis. The psychoanalytic movement began in Vienna in 1902 at the urging of a contemporary of Freud's, Wilhelm Stekel. Stekel proposed to Freud, who was still perfecting his theory of sexuality, that he and some colleagues should gather around Freud and learn from him and possibly spread what was now becoming psychoanalysis. Stekel was a Viennese doctor who had been somewhat successfully treated by Freud for impotence and was, at least early on, a firm believer in the value of Freud's theories, though he later broke from Freud.

Sending out three initial invitations, Freud invited three other Viennese physicians: Max Kahane, Rudolf Reitler, and Alfred Adler. Early adherents also included the Viennese musicologist Max Graf, whose son became Freud's famous "little Hans" case. Graf was interested in the psychological experience of conceptualizing and actualizing music. These men and others met every Wednesday at Freud's apartment, reading papers and winding up with increasingly vehement discussions.

Early on, Freud encouraged variety in his adherents, feeling comfortable enough with his own position to both influence his Viennese interlocutors and also help them with their own individual applications, interpretations, and extension of psychoanalysis. This changed, however. The older the club got, the more some of its participants grew anxious and uncomfortable with their leader's doctrines. The anxiety increased with the growth of the organization, as key members began espousing their own interpretations, some even flagrantly disagreeing with Freud's central conceptions of sexuality. The Wednesday Psychological Society, as it came to be called, grew over the years, and in 1908, when it became the Vienna Psychoanalytic Society, the membership stood at more than twenty members.

International Spread of Freudianism. During his time as facilitator and mentor of the Wednesday Psychological Society, Freud saw its numbers and its scope increase significantly; it quickly became an international movement. And it did not take long before Freud became devoted to his new converts, hailing from Budapest, Zurich—the home of Jung's clinic, the Burghölzli—and

Sigmund Freud and His Colleagues. Seated (*left to right*): Freud, Sándor Ferenczi, and Hans Sachs. Standing (*left to right*): Otto Rank, Karl Abraham, Max Eitingon, and Ernest Jones. Photograph by Becker & Maass, Berlin, 1922 Prints and Photographs Division, Library of Congress

London. Carl Jung, head clinician at the Burghölzli, followed his associates Max Eitington and Karl Abraham to Berlin, all three becoming Freud's protégés. Eitingon and Abraham went to Berlin to practice, while Sándor Ferenczi went back to Hungary to start his own school of psychoanalysis there; Ernest Jones carried Freud's flag in London. Besides these, there was also Freud's fiery Vienna contingent. The movement grew quickly.

Jung was especially important to Freud because he was a Gentile—a tall, imposing, blue-eyed one at that. Freud thought that Jung's leadership could demonstrate that psychoanalysis was not just a Jewish movement but had instead a true international and interracial application, with the capacity to become a science. In 1908, Freud and his constituents initiated the project under a new, more ambitious scope, calling their new organization the International Psychoanalytic Association (IPA). It would be the new medium for the teaching and training, the bureaucratization and distribution of Freudian psychoanalysis.

Jung eventually broke with Freud, following his persistent feeling that Freud exaggerated the importance of infantile sexuality. Jung's break over the role of sexuality was bitter for Freud, who had installed Jung as his successor as president of the International Psychoanalytic Association. Jung did not stay in the presidency long, and he returned the IPA back to its original ownership, but by that time Freud's Viennese contingent had become unnerved by Freud's decision to support Jung so blindly. Alfred Adler and Wilhelm Stekel heatedly broke from the group, leaving the future of psychoanalysis in doubt. The major repercussion that stemmed from the disagreements with Jung, Stekel, and Adler was that the psychoanalytic press, affiliated in many ways with the International Psychoanalytic Association, was left largely in the hands of Freud's rivals. Jung, though, soon relinquished the reigns of the International Psychoanalytic Association and broke with Freud completely after Freud accused him of anti-Semitism in 1914.

Freudianism spread internationally through Freud's most prized students but was changed by them as well. Ferenczi's devotion to Freud and his skill as a teacher eventually led him to begin what was later known as the Budapest school of Freudian psychoanalysis. Though Ferenczi was sincerely beholden to Freud, his leadership of the Budapest school took psychoanalysis in a new direction, focusing much more on the curative capacity of the endeavor, a capacity that Freud was at best ambivalent about.

This turn came from Ferenczi's different attitude about patients. Where Freud saw them as merely feeding the psychoanalytic machine, Ferenczi was interested most in helping them, in curing them, and he saw the analyst's role as one of loving leadership. Ferenczi and the Budapest school focused much time on the role of the analyst and the productive capacity of love as countertransference. The Budapest school, under Ferenczi's leadership, set out to quash the harsh and uncaring tendencies in Freudian analysis and to underpin the process with a mutual trust, respect, and even love between the analyst and the patient.

The International Psychoanalytic Association's international ties and influence built steadily into the twentieth century and maintained a stronghold in certain areas, Paris included. Paris was home to many wandering analysts, including Otto Rank, the youngest member and the original paid secretary of the Vienna Psychoanalytic Association, who practiced there for ten years. The major figure in French psychoanalysis, however, was Jacques Lacan. Lacan saw himself as a Freudian and considered his project as a pursuit of Freud, but his own elaborations on and changes to Freudian ideas eventually made him a threat to the doctrinaire Freudians in the IPA. Lacan left that organization in the 1950s, though he continued his own brand of Freudian psychoanalysis well into the latter half of the twentieth century.

Paris remains today a major hot spot for psychoanalysis. Though in other places biological psychiatry has eclipsed the import of analysis, the French, through Lacan's legacy, maintain close ties with Freud's original impulse, including a widespread distaste for Carl Jung, who Lacan believed did everything but psychoanalysis.

Freudianism in the United States. In 1938, following the Nazis' harassment of Jews in Vienna, Freud and his family, including his daughter Anna Freud, escaped to London. From the 1950s Anna Freud often traveled and spoke in the United States, and she influenced Freudianism there. Although Anna Freud's legacy remains important in the United States, its luminescence has been dimmed by her lack of professional training. Freud, who was keen about soliciting his youngest daughter's company, even analyzing her and writing about it, would not allow the bright young woman to participate in higher education. Consequently, her ideas remained diffuse and her presentation of those ideas largely unsatisfactory.

Other American currents of psychoanalysis stem from Sándor Radó, Ferenczi's Hungarian student and an original member of the Hungarian Psychoanalytic Society. Radó immigrated to the United States, where he served as the head administrator and therapist of the New York Psychoanalytic Society and participated in establishing the Psychoanalytic Institute at Columbia University's medical school. Like Ferenczi, Radó was his own animal and became interested in the negative impact of the analyst's enforcing of transference upon a patient, saying that that process disallowed patients from determining their own self-discovery and belief in their own ability to self-heal and change. These views eventually made Radó an outcast in doctrinal psychoanalytic circles.

Other schools of quasi-Freudian psychoanalysis arose in Britain and United States almost immediately after Freud's famous visit to Clark University in 1909. Object relations theory dominated British psychoanalysis well into the 1950s and eventually spread to the United States as well. Object relations theory emphasized the "affects" one has for different objects (people included): attachment, frustration, and rejection. The theory held that these affects are the essential building blocks for both personality and interpersonal relations.

The second major outgrowth of psychoanalysis in the United States came from Harry Stack Sullivan. Sullivan believed that people's interpersonal interactions gave insight into their particular mental disorders, particularly where what Sullivan called selective inattention was concerned. This selective inattention functions so as to push certain elements of experience from the mind, elements that often manifest themselves later in the form of mental disorders. Sullivan's contribution was that he lifted the closed, individual realm of the internal mental workings of a patient to the realm of the observable social world. This, of course, was deemed heresy by the Freudian powers that be, even though it relied on a strictly Freudian understanding of the function of the ego.

Today, Freud's theories have been diffused throughout the humanities and social sciences as strategies for interpreting, not just human individuals, but groups, institutions, and all facets of personal and even political economy. And though not a primary factor in contemporary psychology, Freud's ideas live on in other disciplines, such as literary theory, philosophy, and anthropology, having forged a tight grip on the modern mind and having articulated a sense of humanity that, as culture demonstrates, people are unwilling to relinquish.

[See also Psychiatry and Psychology.]

BIBLIOGRAPHY

Gay, Peter. Freud: A Life for Our Time. New York: Norton, 1988. The definitive biography of Freud; pays special attention to the cultivation and development of Freud's theories and their reception among his followers.

Hale, Nathan. Freud and the Americans: The Beginnings of Psychoanalysis in the United States, 1876–1917. Oxford and New York: Oxford University Press, 1971. The best treatment of Freud's early influence on American thinkers; essential to tracing Freud's legacy in North America.

Lear, Jonathan. Freud. Oxford: Routledge, 2005. An insightful, sensitized understanding of Freud's past and his relation to numerous contemporary philosophical concerns.

Mitchell, Stephen A., and Margaret J. Black. Freud and Beyond: A History of Modern Psychoanalytic Thought. New York: Basic Books, 1995. Traces Freud's influence into the contemporary moment, including insights into Freud's influence in America.

Roazen, Paul. The Trauma of Freud: Controversies in Psychoanalysis. New Brunswick, N.J.: Transaction Books, 2002. The best treatment of the areas in the psychoanalytic tradition where breakages and rifts occur; essential to understanding the spread of Freudianism and the changes inherent therein.

Wollheim, Richard. Sigmund Freud. Cambridge, U.K., and New York: Cambridge University Press, 1971. Valuable intellectual biography of Freud.

JASON BARRETT-FOX

FRONTIER [*This entry includes four subentries, an overview and discussions of frontiers in South Asia, Latin America, and the United States. See also* Borders.]

Overview

Frontier societies in the modern period included Russia, Canada, Australia, the United States, and several Latin American countries, but there were others as well. Indeed, these frontiers should be seen as part of a larger canvas because of continuities with and differences from premodern frontiers. Scholars generally see frontiers as zones with vague definitions, whereas boundaries and borders are lines. Frontiers, especially in the United States, are often still seen through ideas developed by Frederick Jackson Turner in the late nineteenth and early twentieth centuries. Turner argued that egalitarianism in the United States was rooted in its frontier processes and peoples. Many writers have since challenged this view of the United States. Globally it is both too particularistic and generally wrong. Since 1750 there have been many different kinds of frontiers on every populated continent.

Varieties of Frontiers. Many writers distinguish two categories of frontiers: those where different societies come into contact and those where "civilizations" or states contact "wilderness." Familiar examples of the former are the frontiers between the agrarian states and the many pastoral groups who lived in Central Asia. These frontiers existed for millennia, well into the modern era. Australia until recently was thought of as a "wilderness" frontier. On closer inspection, Australia, like most wilderness regions, was populated. Even where zones were unpopulated, they had been emptied by migration, conquest, conversion, absorption, genocide, disease, or some combination of these.

Some frontiers are zones where older forms of social organization are preserved, called "regions of refuge." Typically they are populated by people who fled change. These frontiers seem to be more common in colonized areas, though such frontiers were quite common in Africa before European colonization. Finally, there are frontiers along the edges of a state as opposed to those that are internal to it. The latter can be zones that had been skipped over and were filled in later—the Great Plains in the United States is a familiar example.

Finally, some writers distinguish frontiers between approximately similar societies and those between more and less complex societies. The fractured frontier zones between states in Southeast Asia exemplify the former. The latter used to be described as areas where civilization encountered barbarians. In less pejorative terms, these are frontiers where states encounter nonstate peoples. Frontiers between nonstate peoples have rarely been discussed by historians but have more commonly been discussed by anthropologists. Familiar examples are frontiers between coastal and "outback" Aboriginal populations in Australia or between Inca and Amazonian peoples in South America. After 1750 frontiers between states and nonstate societies became more common.

Frontier Processes. Frontiers are associated with differences in physical geography, including climatic and vegetational zones—for example, the steppe and the sown or hill and valley. As technology became more robust, many states were better able to move or transcend these frontiers. Thus early in the modern era such physical differences could be crucial, but with new technologies in agriculture, transportation, military practices, and administration, their significance often declined.

Because of technological changes and migrations, frontiers have seldom remained stationary. In short, a frontier is a freeze-frame of a dynamic region. Social relations in frontier regions are much more flexible and volatile than in central areas because centers often cannot impose their rules in frontier zones. Many compromises must be negotiated locally.

Gender imbalances, common in frontier zones, often led to interbreeding and intermarriage. Intermarriage was often a way of establishing political relations, but it was also a vehicle for many other kinds of exchanges. Where intermarriage persisted, a new ethnic group developed. The Metís, produced by intermarriage of French fur traders with indigenous women in Canada, are a familiar

example. New groups also can be formed by coalescences, divisions, or reorganizations. Thus ethnogenesis, the formation of new ethnic or racial identities, is common in frontier areas.

Cultural exchanges and adaptations across frontiers are quite common. The "spread of civilization" bias in many older frontier studies overemphasizes how the less complex group "learned"—often at bayonet or gun point— from the more complex group. Though scarce in the past, studies of exchanges in the other direction are increasing. Despite the common use of force on frontiers many exchanges were voluntary. Goods, technologies, languages, ideas, and knowledge were adapted and adopted to fit local traditions. Many Creole and pidgin languages are familiar examples.

Frontiers are zones where differences blur. Even while differences were blurring, boundaries were sometimes strengthened. Fredrik Barth advanced this surprising and counterintuitive position when he argued that the "boundary" and not the "stuff" it surrounded was what was being maintained. Many ethnographic studies reveal instances where individuals, or more typically families, crossed such boundaries repeatedly. Each time they changed their ethnic identity. On frontiers it is not rare for individuals, families, or groups to hold several different, at times competing or conflicting, identities simultaneously. Thus frontiers are excellent locales for understanding how identities (personal, ethnic, or racial) are socially constructed.

The Tribal Zone Effect. The effects of changes in contact zones often ripple far beyond the frontier, especially for nonstate societies. A familiar example is the diffusion of the horse in North America far beyond zones of contact between Europeans and indigenous peoples. Diseases have spread far beyond the zone of initial contact, typically along indigenous trade pathways. War and conflict also spread quite far, as one group might raid another to acquire valuable goods like furs or captives to trade with state peoples for metal pots, guns, or animals like horses or sheep. Such conflict, which Brian Ferguson and Neil Whitehead called "war in the tribal zone," could spread far beyond the frontier.

The tribal zone effect has distorted understanding of nonstate peoples when some scholars relied too heavily on early firsthand observations to gain insights into precontact conditions. Even the very first observers might not witness conditions at all like precontact times. Rather, the very processes that brought them to the frontier as witnesses could have already caused drastic changes. One glaring example was the assumption by early settlers in the Mississippi Valley that some lost race must have built the many mounds they discovered because the Native Americans were too few to have built them. Though racism may have played a role in such assumptions, the major problem was that groups had been severely disrupted by warfare and disease, which might have killed as much as 90 percent of the original population. Thus the survivors were too few to have built the mounds, but their ancestors, archaeology shows, did build the mounds. A solution to this situation is to weigh firsthand accounts against archaeological evidence on precontact conditions. Work of this sort by many scholars is leading to the rewriting of many frontier histories.

Local and Global Interactions. Though events and processes in frontier zones are quintessentially local, they are often shaped by external or global factors. What outside group is causing the contact? Is it a mercantile state or an industrial state? Is its economy capitalist, socialist, or something else? What is the purpose of the expansion that leads to the encounter? Is the state seeking new territory for colonists? In that case, prior residents are often seen as obstacles. Is the state seeking new resources? In that case, the prior residents may be enticed or coerced into harvesting those resources—furs, minerals, forest products, and so on.

Is the state trying to make a preemptive claim to prevent a rival from getting to the resource? For instance, the Spanish province of Nuevo Mexico (New Mexico, which originally included parts of what are now Texas, New Mexico, Arizona, Utah, Colorado, and Nevada), founded in 1598, was soon discovered to lack valuable minerals and had too few natives to staff large haciendas. Despite these deficiencies it was maintained for more than two centuries, into the modern era, to serve as a buffer zone. Its primary function was to keep other Europeans from gaining access to the most productive silver mines in the Americas farther south in and around what is now the Mexican province of Durango.

The Spanish administration wanted to maintain New Mexico as a buffer zone as economically as possible. Thus there was little effort to develop the region. Though such policies could keep a region poor, they could also give residents time to adapt to the new conditions and to adopt new customs. This could also allow more time for ethnic change. Such conditions often originated before 1750 but lasted well beyond that date.

Local residents also shaped the frontier. When they had the technological and demographic resources, they could resist outsiders or attenuate their effects. When they had

goods that outsiders wanted, they might establish beneficial trade relations. Harsh treatment by outsiders could provoke resistance. Where labor was in short supply or where the outsiders faced strong enemies, frontiers tended to be hierarchical, not egalitarian. These conditions were common throughout the world after 1750.

The Puzzle of Frontiers. Frontiers present a common puzzle: Why is it that on first inspections frontiers all seem similar, but almost always on closer inspection each seems unique? Combining the factors listed here—five types of states, three reasons for expansion, four different types of native peoples, four kinds of geographical differences—yields two hundred and forty possible types of frontiers.

But frontiers do not vary randomly. In any one region only some kinds of states and some kinds of nonstate peoples are present. Thus frontiers in any one region often share similarities. Even when focusing on modern frontiers, the history of contact can be critical. In Central Asia, interactions between nomadic pastoralists and sedentary farmers go back at least two and half millennia. In South Asia, state-nonstate interactions have occurred over millennia. In Southeast Asia nearly every local group has had a long history of conflict and peace with various neighbors, so ethnic mixing is quite complex. And of course there are the overlays of Chinese, South Asian, and Arabic interactions. In Africa, interactions and frontiers long predate even the earliest slave trade. There are precontact frontiers in the Americas. Yet in all these regions premodern frontiers were rearranged, sometimes radically, by interactions with European states after 1750, and throughout Asia they were rearranged by changes in Chinese, South Asian, and Southeast Asian states.

Finally, while there are general patterns and trends, each frontier has a history shaped by the details of the interactions of local, regional, and global forces and actors. Frontiers are complex places with complex histories. They must be studied from a variety of perspectives simultaneously: from the various states that helped create and transform them, from the local people who resisted and reshaped the efforts of external states, and especially from the volatile ethnic and racial groups who lived in the frontier zone. Often a student of frontiers must master several different histories to examine their interactions. The work is difficult, but it can yield deep insights into how humans form, transform, and destroy various groups and identities.

[*See also* Borders and Borderlands.]

BIBLIOGRAPHY

Barth, Fredrik, ed. *Ethnic Groups and Boundaries*. Boston: Little, Brown, 1969. The title essay is the classic statement of the role of boundaries in marking group differences, with seven detailed examples.

Batten, Bruce L. *To the Ends of Japan: Premodern Frontiers, Boundaries, and Interactions*. Honolulu: University of Hawai'i Press, 2003. Though on a millennium of Japanese history, the introductory chapters have excellent reviews of theories of frontiers, ethnicity, and identity.

Ferguson, R. Brian, and Neil L. Whitehead, eds. *War in the Tribal Zone: Expanding States and Indigenous Warfare*. Santa Fe, N.M.: School of American Research Press, 1992. The title essay explains the "tribal zone" concept, with nine detailed examples.

Guy, Donna J., and Thomas E. Sheridan, eds. *Contested Ground: Comparative Frontiers on the Northern and Southern Edges of the Spanish Empire*. Tucson: University of Arizona Press, 1998. Includes an excellent introductory essay and eleven detailed comparisons of frontiers of the Spanish Empire.

Hall, Thomas D. "Using Comparative Frontiers to Explore World-Systems Analysis and International Relations." *International Studies Perspectives* 2 (2001): 253–269. Analyzes frontier processes and suggests ways to teach about frontiers; includes an extended bibliography.

Kopytoff, Igor. *The African Frontier: The Reproduction of Traditional African Societies*. Bloomington: Indiana University Press, 1987. The title essay reviews analyses of frontiers and discusses how Africa is different, with nine detailed examples.

McNeill, William H. *The Global Condition: Conquerors, Catastrophes, and Community*. Princeton, N.J.: Princeton University Press, 1992. An excellent global view of frontiers.

Parker, Bradley J., and Lars Rodseth, eds. *Untaming the Frontier in Anthropology, Archaeology, and History*. Tucson: University of Arizona Press, 2005. A multidisciplinary collection of essays that investigate frontiers, with an excellent introduction and nine detailed examples.

Weber, David J. *Bárbaros: Spaniards and Their Savages in the Age of Enlightenment*. New Haven, Conn.: Yale University Press, 2005. A thorough comparisons of the treatment of non-state peoples throughout the Americas by Spanish colonizers.

THOMAS D. HALL

Frontiers and Borderlands in South Asia

The place of frontiers and borderlands in South Asian history since 1750 is linked to the colonization and decolonization of the Indian subcontinent. The policies of territorial annexation and imperial frontier-making embarked on by the British East India Company between 1757 and 1857 brought the entire subcontinent under its direct and indirect rule and culminated in the establishment of the outer limits of the British Indian Empire. A continuing theme on the subcontinent is the quest to consolidate and stabilize the two types of frontiers left behind by colonial rule: an inner political frontier and an outer strategic frontier.

The frontiers of an old-civilization area like the Indian subcontinent are as much a product of its history as its geography. The high Himalayan ranges to its north and the vast Indian Ocean to the south proved to be formidable barriers setting the subcontinent apart as a stand-alone geopolitical region within the world system. Influencing Indian thinking on frontiers over the centuries are a sense of impregnability to the outside world, myths concerning the sacred geography of the Himalayas, and custom and usage.

Frontiers and borderlands are meeting grounds of civilizations and have acted as bridges as well as barriers since ancient times. The three frontier zones of continental India—the Northwest, the North, and the Northeast—have seen an intermingling of three major Asian civilizations: the Indic, Sinitic, and Islamic. The Northwestern frontier has been renowned throughout history also as a corridor for invading into the Indus and Gangetic plains from Central Asia, Afghanistan, and Iran. The borderlands of the Northeast have played a similar role as a gateway from Southeast Asia to the Brahmaputra River Valley and Assam plains. Within the region, the Deccan ramparts have historically played the role of a frontier zone between the continental North and peninsular South. Peninsular India, which has a distinctive maritime history, formed the center of trading and culture of the Indian Ocean sphere. Consequently, it has had more interaction with Western Asia and Southeast Asia than with the empires to its north until the breaching of the Indian Ocean frontier by the European sea nomads during what has been called the "Vasco da Gama epoch" of Indian history (1498–1945).

The arrival of European maritime powers effectively changed the course of South Asian history by presenting an entirely new set of challenges to the land-based regional powers of the subcontinent. Not only were the routes and methods of invasion different, with the Europeans penetrating from the periphery to the center; pressure from the sea had a relentlessness about it that tribal incursions by land nomads did not possess. Control over sea lanes also enabled European powers, particularly the British, who gained supremacy over the French and other European rivals by 1761, to establish bases in coastal towns like Madras (now Chennai) and Calcutta (now Kolkata) and extend their reach over both continental and peninsular India.

The concept of an outer frontier versus an inner frontier is crucial in understanding the place of frontiers in Indian history. For the Mughal Empire (1526–1707) and the other regional kingdoms of that period (the Maratha,

Sikh, Mysore, and Hyderabad kingdoms), the inner frontier was the frontier that fluctuated with the waxing and waning of their power. The two major battles of the mid-eighteenth century that were fought in the transitional period between the Mughal decline and rise of British power and that transformed the political map of India were primarily wars for the control of the inner frontier. Thus, Robert Clive's victory in the 1757 battle of Plassey established the British bridgehead in Bengal, and the Afghan forces' defeat of the Marathas in the 1761 battle of Panipat stopped the northward expansion of Maratha power.

The success of British territorial domination of India over all other contenders for power (European and regional) was the result of their naval power, superior arms, greater manpower, and wealth. But the drive behind the British policy of conquest and annexation was the same as that of prior empires: to consolidate the inner frontier to the natural boundaries of the Indian subcontinent. The British annexation of the trans-Indus territory of Sind in 1843 and their subjection of the Sikh kingdom of Punjab in 1849 completed Britain's expansion of the inner frontier and made British India coterminous with the geographical India in the Northwest. Britain's search for a stable frontier in the Northeast led to the conquest of Assam and three Anglo-Burmese Wars (1824–1885), which in turn led to the annexation of Burma.

What most differentiated European territorial boundaries from traditional frontier-making was that, whereas the latter evolved through custom and usage, the former focused on the demarcation and consolidation of the outer boundary of the subcontinent so as to take the shape of a modern sovereign state, which meant introducing lines on maps that embraced or annexed peoples and territories, even those that had never formally been part of the Indian political system (Burma). It also meant creating buffer states, "which had to remain friendly" with the British Empire, such as Afghanistan and Tibet, to deter more distant external threats.

In the nineteenth and early twentieth centuries, Britain, in its imperial frontier-making, sought to expand its strategic and economic interests in India to create a balance of power in Inner Asia between British India, Tsarist Russia, and Manchu China. This geopolitical rivalry led to a Great Game, played to counter the threat from Russia's alleged search for warm-water ports in the Persian Gulf and its long-term quest for domination in Central Asia. The Great Game flared up into three Anglo-Afghan Wars, which led to the creation of the Northwest Frontier Province, bringing

the Pushtun tribal belt within the orbit of the British Empire. This was followed by the formal stabilization of the northwestern frontier at the turn of the twentieth century through a series of treaties and accords, which could be concluded because all three empires had nearly reached geographical and economic limits of diminishing returns in inner Asia. Britain followed a similar policy in the Northeast to counterbalance France in Southeast Asia, where Anglo-French rivalry had triggered the Third Anglo-Burmese War (1886). The Anglo-Russian and Anglo-French accords (both concluded in 1907) guaranteed Afghanistan and Siam (Thailand) their autonomy, but only as buffer states.

The situation was different along the northern frontier, where geography dictated the terms. The Himalayas were so high that a military invasion was not feared. The northern frontier was therefore considered dead and was treated as a static frontier. Also, Manchu China was perceived as a minor threat until the Chinese Revolution of 1911, which destabilized Tibet. It prompted the British to stabilize the eastern sector of the Indo-Tibetan border, an act that resulted in the drawing of the McMahon Line in 1914. In the process the sub-Himalayan states of Nepal, Bhutan, and Sikkim were reduced to vassal states to form an inner line of defense for British India.

The decolonization and partitioning of the subcontinent in 1947 undid the strategic unity of the outer frontier of British India. Pakistan inherited the northwestern frontier, while India retained the northern and northeastern Himalayan frontier. The partition also broke up the geographical continuity of the Indus and Gangetic plains to accommodate the demand for a Muslim homeland. The Radcliffe Award delineated a new set of inner frontiers to separate the Muslim regions of continental India, creating the anomalous situation of an Indian state flanked by the two wings of Pakistan. The partition also left a legacy in which contemporary South Asia faces unstable borders that cut across ethnic, linguistic, and religious divides.

The retreat of the colonial powers from Asia in the aftermath of World War II also brought to an end the former conditions of stability and stagnation in the frontier regions of South Asia. Old imperial structures became problematic in the new Asia. Both the Durand Line and McMahon Line were later repudiated as colonial constructs by Afghanistan and Communist China, but were also defended where perceived national interests were at stake, as in Pakistan's maintenance of the Durand Line against Pushtun national aspirations. The northern frontier became a live zone between India and China in 1962, when these countries fought a short border war over the political and legal status of the McMahon Line. The national aspirations of some of the Naga and Mizo peoples of the Northeast, divided between India and Burma (Myanmar), get short shrift from these two former colonial states, which have their own hegemonic ambitions in the region.

Since decolonization in 1947, there have been have a number of boundary conflicts in the borderlands of South Asia as China, India, Pakistan, and Afghanistan readjust their strategies for their borders, which reflect both precolonial and colonial patterns. The policy of annexation dating from the Qing and Mughal eras has continued, with China occupying Tibet in 1959 and India absorbing Sikkim in 1975. The notion of a buffer state is not quite dead in the Northwest, where Afghanistan is reemerging as a zone of conflict involving first the Soviets and later the Islamic jihadists. In the North and Northeast, the competing influences of China and India loom over Nepal, Bhutan, and Burma.

The most outstanding issue of colonial-era boundary making is the status of India's Jammu and Kashmir states, which in 2007 is yet to be resolved. Here the competing interests of India, China, and Pakistan meet and overlap. Thus it would appear that the time-honored strategy of stabilizing the outer frontier and consolidating the inner frontier still holds in modern South Asia.

[*See also* Afghanistan; Afghan-Soviet War; Anglo-Afghan Wars; Anglo-Burmese Wars; Bangladesh; Bhutan; Great Game; India; Indo-Pakistan Conflict; Nepal; Pakistan; Plassey, Battle of; *and* Tibet.]

BIBLIOGRAPHY

Lattimore, Owen. *Studies in Frontier History: Collected Papers, 1928–1958.* London: Oxford University Press, 1962.

Panikkar, K. M. *Asia and Western Dominance: A Survey of the Vasco da Gama Epoch of Asian History, 1498–1945.* New Edition. London: G. Allen and Unwin, 1959. First published in 1953.

Schwartzberg, Joseph E., ed. *A Historical Atlas of South Asia.* 2d impression, with additional material. New York: Oxford University Press, 1992.

Woodman, Dorothy. *Himalayan Frontiers: A Political Review of British, Chinese, Indian, and Russian Rivalries.* London: Barrie and Rockliff, 1969.

JAYITA RAY

Latin America

The frontier in Latin America, regions on the periphery of more developed areas, played a critical role in historical development. The Spanish first colonized certain islands in the Caribbean, primarily Hispaniola, Cuba, and Puerto Rico. Explorers and slave raiders fanned out from the first island settlements and encountered advanced hierarchical and sedentary native societies in Mexico, the Andean Highlands, and Central America, among other places. The Spanish created a system of indirect rule that drew on previous colonial experiences in southern Iberia and the Canary Islands, and they modified existing native government institutions to produce wealth. This system of indirect rule did not function well when the Spanish encountered native peoples organized in tribal or band societies that did not already have the government institutions that the Spanish could use to govern. The Portuguese, too, encountered peoples living in tribal societies on the coast of Brazil who could not be easily shaped and transformed to create a colonial system.

Types of Frontiers and Institutions. There were different types of frontiers, which evolved based on a variety of factors. These included mining frontiers, where the Spanish and the Portuguese encountered gold, silver, and diamonds that attracted adventurers in large numbers but that also developed unstable populations living in mining camps that could be short-lived depending on the types of mineral deposits found. Examples of mining frontiers included Nueva Vizcaya and Sonora in northern Mexico and Minas Gerais in Brazil.

A second type was the mission frontier, where the mission was the most important colonial institution and where the Spanish placed greater emphasis on the religious conversion and sociocultural transformation of the native peoples. There generally were no mines to attract Spaniards, and in some instances native groups resisted colonization. Examples of mission frontiers include Baja California and California in northern Mexico and Moxos, Chiquitos, and Paraguay in South America.

A third type was the strategic or geopolitical frontier, areas occupied because of their strategic importance in response to the colonization schemes of rival European powers. Florida, Texas, and California in northern Mexico were examples of this type of frontier. Finally, there were agricultural or ranching frontiers, areas where settlers developed commercial and often plantation agriculture and ranching to produce crops, hides and tallow, wool, meat, and horses and mules for local, regional, and particularly European markets. The Brazilian sugar plantation frontier in Bahia was one example, and a second was the Pampas region of Argentina, which became a major wheat-producing area in the late nineteenth century. The Pampas of the Río de la Plata also was an important ranching frontier.

The Spanish and Portuguese developed different institutions to colonize frontier areas. The most important was the mission, which attempted to convert native peoples to Catholicism and radically transform their culture, social and economic organization, and worldview. The model for the mission was the *pueblo real*, the autonomous native communities in Mexico, Peru, and other core areas. The Portuguese established similar native communities known as *aldeias*. The goal was to transform native peoples from tribal or band societies into sedentary town-dwelling vassals of the king. Members of missionary orders such as the Jesuits, Franciscans, Dominicans, and Mercedarians staffed the missions, and the missionaries generally represented the interests of both the church and the state because the government subsidized the missions.

Central to the mission program was the congregation of native groups not living in nucleated communities that both conformed to the Spanish ideal of the town as the seat of civilization and also facilitated the process of evangelization and sociocultural change. In many instances the missionary created a new community from whole cloth and brought the natives to live on the missions. The mission was primarily a colonial-era institution, and those mission groups that survived beyond independence were generally seen as colonial anachronisms and were phased out by the new national governments. There were, however, several exceptions, such as the Chiriguano missions in eastern Bolivia and missions in the Chaco, that continued to function well into the twentieth century.

The frontiers of Latin America were often contested with rival European powers or with native groups that challenged and resisted Spanish or Portuguese domination, such as the Apache and Comanche on the north Mexican frontier, the groups in the Chaco and Pampas in South America, and the Mapuche in Chile. The Spanish established military garrisons on some frontier regions to protect frontier communities. On the north Mexican frontier, for example, these garrisons known as presidios existed from Texas to Sonora, as well as in the Californias. A symbiotic relationship often evolved between the military and missions, with varying levels of trade between the missions and presidios and with presidio personnel filling roles as overseers on some missions, as in California. In some instances soldiers were also stationed on the missions to help preserve order. On the other hand, the lax morals of the soldiers, as perceived by the missionaries, were often a cause of tension. In other regions, such as the Río de la Plata, military defense was carried out on more of an ad hoc basis. The Jesuits in Paraguay organized a mission militia to defend the establishments from slave raids by *bandeirantes* from São Paulo in the 1630s and 1640s. Local government officials mobilized the mission militia on numerous occasions to serve in campaigns against the Portuguese or rebellious colonists.

The Portuguese in Brazil did not invest in frontier defense as Spain did, and generally they left military relations in the interior in the hands of local settlers. One exception was in the Río de la Plata region, an area contested by Spain and Portugal, particularly in the eighteenth century. Portugal established Colonia do Sacramento in 1680 at a site in modern Uruguay opposite Buenos Aires. The establishment of Colonia asserted Portuguese territorial claims in the region, but the outpost also served as a center for illicit trade with the Spanish. In the eighteenth century, Spain and Portugal fought a series of wars for control over the Banda Oriental (modern Uruguay) and Rio Grande do Sul. The collapse of Spanish authority in the Río de la Plata region after 1810 set off a new round of wars that lasted until the end of the 1820s.

Frontier regions tended to be sparsely populated, which was a cause of concern for Spain, particularly in areas contested by other rival European countries. Spain promoted frontier settlement and introduced Iberian forms of municipal government with autonomous town councils. The discovery of mineral wealth on the frontier attracted Spanish settlers, but in regions with no apparent source of wealth there was little incentive for settlement. The Spanish government organized and funded the establishment of frontier towns and often recruited settlers to populate the new settlements. The Spanish government also encouraged settlement near the military garrisons on the north Mexican frontier.

A perceived underpopulation of the frontier concerned the Spanish government, which feared rival European colonization on the fringes of its American territories and also feared, after 1783, the expansionism of the newly independent United States. The Louisiana Purchase in 1803 placed the United States on the border of Texas, and filibustering expeditions from Louisiana into Texas between 1810 and 1821 only fueled Spanish paranoia. In the 1820s Spain and later the newly independent Mexican government initiated land grant programs to attract settlers to the frontier. The Texas empresario system brought some ten thousand Anglo-Americans to settle between 1822 and 1830. In California several governors made more than eight hundred grants of land in the 1830s and 1840s.

Closing the Frontier. The frontier in Latin America closed in the late nineteenth and early twentieth century, and new technology accelerated the process. The construction of railroads linked frontier regions to growing international markets and made the export of minerals, hides, and meat profitable. The repeating rifle, machine guns, and the telegraph, which made rapid communications possible, made it easier for governments to defeat hostile Indian groups. In 1880, Argentine forces under the command of General Julio A. Roca crushed Indian resistance in the Pampas in a military action known as the Conquest of the Desert. The brutal defeat of the Pampas Indians brought the "desert" into "civilization" and paved the way for the development of the Pampas as a productive grain-producing and ranching region. During the War of the Pacific (1879–1883), the Chilean government diverted troops from the campaign against Peru and Bolivia to crush the Mapuche in the southern part of the country. In the last decades of the nineteenth century the Mexican and United States governments finally defeated the various Apache bands that had harassed settlers.

The late-nineteenth-century growth in the use of bicycles in places such as the United States created a demand for rubber for tires, produced using rubber from stands of wild trees found in the Amazon Basin. There was a boom in rubber that lasted until 1912, when international rubber prices collapsed because of production from Malaysian plantations, created by seeds spirited out of Brazil. World War II and the Japanese conquest of Malaysia created a second short-term boom, but Brazil never regained its near monopoly. In 1970 the Brazilian government initiated construction of the Trans-Amazon Highway, designed to promote the settlement of the Amazon basin. The highway stretches 3,001 miles (4,830 kilometers) to the Peruvian border.

The frontier created historical and stereotypical images that continue to contribute to the formation of national identity, such as the gaucho, the cowboy of the Pampas of Argentina, Uruguay, and Rio Grande do Sul. The resistance of native groups such as the Mapuche of southern Chile has become a symbol of anticolonialism. In a more pragmatic sense, economic development of frontier regions, particularly in the late nineteenth century, contributed to national development. Two examples of this are the expansion of grain production in the Pampas of Argentina, an area considered a desert because Indian resistance slowed or stopped settlement, and the north Mexican mining economy, which grew in the late nineteenth century and significantly contributed to Mexican economic expansion. The growing importance of the Mexican north reached a logical conclusion with the political dominance of the

country by caudillos, who led the successful factions during the Mexican Revolution (1910–1920).

[*See also* Empire and Imperialism, *subentries* The Portuguese Colonial Empire *and* The Spanish Colonial Empire; Missions, Christian, *subentry* Catholic Missions in Latin America; Rubber, *subentry* The Rubber Boom in Latin America; *and* Settler Societies.]

BIBLIOGRAPHY

Jackson, Robert H. *From Savages to Subjects: Missions in the History of the American Southwest.* Armonk, N.Y.: M. E. Sharpe, 2000.

Jackson, Robert H. *Missions and the Frontiers of Spanish America: A Comparative Study of the Impact of Environmental, Economic, Political, and Socio-cultural Variations on the Missions in the Rio de la Plata Region and on the Northern Frontier of New Spain.* Scottsdale, Ariz.: Pentacle, 2005.

Jackson, Robert H., ed. *New Views of Borderlands History.* Albuquerque: University of New Mexico Press, 1998.

Jackson, Robert H., and Edward Castillo. *Indians, Franciscans, and Spanish Colonization: The Impact of the Mission System on California Indians.* Albuquerque: University of New Mexico Press, 1995.

Langer, Erick. "Liberal Policy and Frontier Missions: Bolivia and Argentina Compared." *Andes: Antropología é Historia* 9 (1998): 197–213.

Langer, Erick, and Robert H. Jackson, eds. *The New Latin American Mission History.* Lincoln: University of Nebraska Press, 1995.

Scobie, James R. *Revolution on the Pampas: A Social History of Argentine Wheat, 1860–1910.* Austin: University of Texas Press, 1964.

Weinstein, Barbara. *The Amazon Rubber Boom, 1850–1920.* Stanford, Calif.: Stanford University Press, 1983.

ROBERT H. JACKSON

The United States

The American frontier was a buffer zone between territories that had been fully economically developed by white settlers and those that remained undeveloped. It was a major factor in the economic development of the modern-day continental United States from the early seventeenth century through 1890, when the U.S. Bureau of the Census declared it closed. There were several different frontiers: a fur traders' frontier, a farmers' frontier, a ranchers' frontier, and a miners' frontier.

Fee simple title (unqualified private ownership) to frontier land was acquired in a variety of ways from the original Native American owners: for money or goods in kind, by outright theft, by military conquest, and by treaty. The United States also acquired sovereignty (supreme authority) over the rapidly moving frontier in a

American Frontier. Sylvester Rawding family in front of a sod house, north of Sargent, Custer County, Nebraska, 1886. PRINTS AND PHOTOGRAPHS DIVISION, LIBRARY OF CONGRESS

variety of ways. Sometimes this was achieved by military conquest, as in the case of the Mexican-American War of 1846–1848. At other times sovereignty was purchased from neighboring countries. The United States acquired sovereignty from France over the central part of North America with the Louisiana Purchase for $15 million in 1803. Later, modern-day southern Arizona and New Mexico were acquired in the Gadsden Purchase from Mexico for $10 million in 1854. The most audacious acquisition was that of the contemporary state of Alaska from Russia for $7.2 million in 1867. American settlers also unilaterally seized sovereignty in Texas and the Hawaiian Islands through the Texas Revolution of 1835–1836 and the Hawaiian Revolution of 1893, respectively, in advance of annexation by the United States.

The first major analytical study of the history of the frontier was by Frederick Jackson Turner in his seminal paper to the American Historical Association in 1893, "The Significance of the Frontier in American History." The historian Margaret Walsh argues that the most important part of his thesis is that the abundance of cheap land and resources provided the United States with opportunities to expand quickly through the efforts of millions of settlers. Turner contended that American history is explained by the "Great West" rather than the eastern seaboard. He believed that American democracy evolved on the frontier.

He subsequently argued that the frontier also served as a social safety valve during times of economic depression, which explained why the United States escaped the revolutionary upheavals of nineteenth-century Europe. Turner also saw the frontier as a struggle between civilization and savagery. On the one side were white Protestant English, Scotch-Irish, German, and Scandinavian settlers transformed by the frontier into individualistic self-sufficient Americans. On the other side were the "savage" Native Americans.

Over time the frontier thesis became very popular with American historians. The historian Ray Allen Billington observes that many of Turner's followers made extravagant claims for the thesis that were not supported by their mentor. As Walsh argues, Turner never intended his paper to be definitive. At about the time of Turner's death in 1932 there was a backlash against the thesis. The rugged individualism of Turner's frontiersmen had little appeal during the 1930s New Deal, when the emphasis was on cooperation. During the 1930s and 1940s historians challenged many aspects of the "frontier thesis," including the safety-valve concept, frontier individualism, and Turner's emphasis on American nationalism. They argued that there was no evidence that the frontier served as a safety valve—in fact the cities acted as a safety valve for excess farmworkers—that the frontier was an area of cooperative activity, and that democracy originated in England rather than the forests of the West.

During the 1960s there was a partial revival of the Turner thesis. Ellen von Nardhoff argued that the frontier had acted as a "resources" safety valve and as a "socio-psychological" safety valve. So it had counteracted labor unrest. John D. Barnhart also highlighted the development of a unique brand of American grassroots democracy on the American frontier. However, historians have subsequently identified further weaknesses in the Turner thesis. Turner was wrong to describe western land as "free," since he overlooked the cost of exterminating or removing the original Native American inhabitants. Patricia Limerick also highlights Turner's failure to criticize the brutality and immorality associated with this process. Furthermore, Walsh argues, most pioneers purchased their land from the federal government or speculators. Even if they received land as a grant or were temporary squatters, they required further capital to develop it. On the other hand, land was relatively cheap compared with the eastern seaboard or Europe. Limerick also observes that Turner ignored important aspects of the frontier experience beyond his native Midwest, such as the survival of Native American communities, the Mexican-American community, Chinese immigration, and other interactions with the Asia-Pacific region. Indeed, contrary to Turner, the American frontier began with the Spanish colony of Saint Augustine in 1565 rather than the English colony of Jamestown in 1607.

Many historians contend that the frontier did not end in 1890. It can be argued that the values of the "frontier" have continued to resonate in American society since the 1890s. This has been reflected in mass-market novels, paintings by artists such as Frederic Remington, Wild West circus shows, the Hollywood "Western" movie genre, and "Western" television series. Throughout the twentieth century American politicians drew upon frontier values. Theodore Roosevelt, for example, claimed he would never have been president if it had not been for his experiences in the frontier community of North Dakota. Ronald Reagan successfully captured the imagination of the American electorate by evoking pioneers and frontiers. In the twenty-first century George W. Bush continued this tradition when he was filmed on his Texas ranch engaged in activities such as clearing brush and chopping wood.

Even if Turner's thesis is correct, it can be argued that a frontier still exists in Alaska and has yet to be closed. At the beginning of the 1960s President John F. Kennedy also used the concept of the frontier in support of the Apollo manned space program. Some Americans see space as the last frontier, including President George W. Bush, who authorized a manned mission to Mars.

[*See also* United States, *subentry* Nation Building and Westward Expansion; *and* Westerns.]

BIBLIOGRAPHY

Banner, Stuart. *How the Indians Lost Their Land: Law and Power on the Frontier.* Cambridge, Mass.: Harvard University Press, 2005. A comprehensive account of how frontier land was acquired from the Native American owners.

Limerick, Patricia Nelson. *Something in the Soil: Legacies and Reckonings in the New West.* New York: W. W. Norton and Company, 2001. Places the frontier thesis within the context of western American history. It suggests that the history of the American West did not end in 1890 and so considers the twentieth-century experience as well.

Turner, Frederick Jackson. *The Frontier in American History.* 1920. Reprint, New York: Dover, 1996. Includes all of Turner's major work on the history of the frontier.

Walsh, Margaret. *The American West: Visions and Revisions.* New York: Cambridge University Press, 2005. An excellent analysis of the frontier thesis and the evolution of the frontier. Also places the frontier thesis within the context of the new Western history that has emerged since the late 1980s.

RICHARD A. HAWKINS

FULBRIGHT PROGRAM. The origins of the educational exchange program were modest compared to its future success. In 1945, J. William Fulbright (1905–1995), a first-year Democratic senator from Arkansas, proposed that the government use foreign currency earned through the sale of surplus military supplies to finance international exchange opportunities. World War II had ended just a month before with the bombings of Hiroshima and Nagasaki, and the United States, global superpower, would soon undertake initiatives such as the Truman Doctrine and the Marshall Plan to offer the political stability and financial resources necessary to rebuild Europe's economy. The proposal by Fulbright, who spent three years studying in England as a Rhodes scholar in the 1920s, offered the resources to build the world's intellectual capital and promote cultural relations between the United States and other countries.

Since its inception in 1946, the Fulbright Program has funded more than 250,000 students, scholars, and professionals from the United States for study, research, and work opportunities abroad, as well as funded their foreign counterparts engaging in similar activities in the United States. By 2006, as the program marked its sixtieth anniversary, its model of educational cooperation had fostered international partnerships. The program's bilateral nature has been a distinguishing feature since its beginning. Arrangements with each participating nation came through executive agreements; local boards allowed partner countries to influence the form of cooperation. In addition, participants came from nations big and small, industrialized or not. Early agreements, for example, resulted in programs in England and Nationalist China, Greece and the Philippines.

Questions of funding followed the program throughout—the foreign currency earned from the sale of military surplus did not last long—and funding battles allowed the program's foes to attack it politically. The onset of the Cold War, the conflict in Korea, and the rise of McCarthyism led congressional representatives to ask whether appropriations should continue, or whether the government should incorporate the program directly, in line with the country's information and propaganda policies. Soviet propaganda, meanwhile, charged that the program already was a tool of American imperialism. Indeed, a State Department sympathetic to McCarthyist influence had imposed loyalty oaths on American participants going abroad, as well as on foreign participants coming to the United States. Sensitive to the impact that these attacks would have on the program's integrity, officials were successful by the early 1960s in ensuring that a clear division existed between the Fulbright Program and information agencies.

The program's impact abroad was substantial. One major accomplishment was the establishment of American studies programs around the world. In Europe, for example, virtually no universities in Europe taught U.S. history in 1945. By 1964, all Western European nations offered American studies programs. In regions that did not have a strong university tradition, such as Africa and Latin America, the program worked to develop decentralized systems of higher education and university-based research. The program, said William Fulbright's Oxford tutor, Ronald Buchanan McCallum, was "the largest and most significant movement of scholars across the earth since the fall of Constantinople in 1453."

[See also Marshall Plan; Truman Doctrine; and Universities.]

BIBLIOGRAPHY

Johnson, Walter, and Francis J. Colligan. *The Fulbright Program: A History.* Chicago: University of Chicago Press, 1965. Covers the program's first twenty years.

Woods, Randall Bennett. *Fulbright: A Biography.* Cambridge, U.K., and New York: Cambridge University Press, 1995. A biography of the program's founder that covers the program's founding and places it within a larger context.

JOSEPH ORSER

FUNDAMENTALISM [*This entry includes two subentries, an overview and a discussion of fundamentalism in the United States.*]

Overview

Any definition of fundamentalism must acknowledge the diverse range of religions to which it has been applied. A "fundamentalism" has been identified within nearly every religious tradition; however, many scholars contest such rampant application as undisciplined and universalizing. Moreover, among postcolonial critics, fundamentalism has been increasingly identified as a post-Enlightenment category of Western origin inappropriately exported to non-Western societies (Antes). Within Western scholarship, "fundamentalism" has emerged as a shorthand referent for any movement in which beleaguered believers attempt to preserve their distinctive identity as adherents through articulate opposition to an actively inscribed modernity. This opposition is consistently sourced in a reification of a particular scriptural text, or set of scriptural interpretations, advocated vociferously as the primary fortification against encroaching secular decadence. Committed practitioners participate in a vast subculture of activities meant to provide viable alternatives to existent modern institutions. These activities include retail centers, educational venues, and paramilitary organizations intended to maintain the sovereignty of the enclave. Although it has been popular to describe fundamentalism as antimodern, a growing cohort of scholars emphasizes the consistent use of popular media, new technologies, and academic platforms to propagate and refine fundamentalisms. In addition, fundamentalism has been deployed as a derogatory label for reactionary cultural nativism; again, such a perspective fails to acknowledge the racial diversity, political variety, and range of theological proposals included under the auspices of self-proclaimed fundamentalist movements.

Fundamentalism has therefore always been a contested category, both by the scholars who identify it within social movements and by its primary theological advocates. In no fundamentalist tradition can one find consensus about texts, social habit, or political positioning. Indeed, one could argue that the contestation of its very meaning defines the fundamentalist project, as religious fundamentalism has become the principal source of violent conflict since the late 1980s and early 1990s. The collapse of the Cold War and its attendant spin-offs in Asia, Africa, and Latin America refocused social action around sectarian plots for a return to a golden age. It is dangerous to reduce every contemporary conflict to religious ideology (as opposed to ethnic difference or nationalist fervor). But religion as a primary source of military and political action seems to have returned to the center stage of global politics after a century of ideological conflict derived from Marxist-Leninist, National Socialist, and anticolonialist philosophies. What all of these ideological vantages share is a commitment to the overthrow of the liberal capitalist West in favor of a radically egalitarian social order. Whereas Marxist-Leninists premised this overthrow on an economic revision of society, fundamentalisms emphasize the necessity of a wholesale revival in personal piety and moral restrictions to refine and equalize the cultural condition. Four features consistently separate fundamentalism from other ideological movements: a commitment to literal readings of sacred texts, the formation of separatist enclave communities, the description of an oppositional modern agent, and conservatism in public politics. These features are paired below with representative fundamentalisms within Christianity, Islam, Judaism, and Hinduism.

Scriptural Inerrancy. Fundamentalism requires modernism. "Modernism" here may refer to any variety of post-Enlightenment scriptural rebuttals, usually framed by fundamentalists as threatening to the eternal truth enshrined in sacred texts. As a theological designate, "fundamentalism" first emerged in the United States during the early twentieth century within a specific scholarly discussion. The spread of evolutionary theory, the emergence of biblical criticism (also referred to as the Higher criticism), and the perception of an increased moral decadence goaded conservative Protestants to preserve what they understood as the core elements of a transhistorical, ecumenical Christianity. This trend culminated in the publication of *The Fundamentals*, a series of ninety articles by sixty-four authors reinscribing "the fundamentals of the Christian faith." These articles were devoted to scholarly examinations of the scriptures, parrying intensely with the new archaeological and textual criticisms that suggested that the scriptures were the constructs of history, not God. Included in these "fundamentals," then, was the preservation of beliefs relating to the Virgin Birth, the bodily resurrection of Christ, and the literal reality of Christ's eventual Second Coming. Early fundamentalism in the United States was defined by a scholarly labor to iron out narrative inconsistencies in the text to prove the inerrant logic of the Gospels.

A belief in the inerrancy of scripture distinguishes Christian fundamentalists from other conservative Christian groups. Media observers tend to oversell the influence of inerrancy in American Christian thought; in reality, inerrancy is a belief held by a loud but numerically small group of believers. In the United States, the issue that has provoked the strongest vitriol surrounding inerrancy is evolution. Theories of evolution are seen by Christian fundamentalists as assaults on faith in the name of science. Fundamentalists perceive "science" as its own form of fundamentalism, promoting a moral code and ritual practice exclusive to other totalistic claims about reality. In order to substantively counter scientific epistemology, fundamentalist Protestants developed curriculums devoted to theories of "intelligent design" and "scientific creationism" to incorporate divine work and biblical plot lines into evolutionary schematics. This investment in the rewriting of modern scientific scholarship highlights the ways fundamentalisms are more reactive than reactionary, more modern than traditional. At home with the instruments and actions of modernity, fundamentalists utilize sacred scriptures with the syntactic skill of academic text critics, preserving and reinscribing the internal logic of a given text (for Christians, the New Testament; for Hindus, the Vedas) to combat the multiplicity of source materials offered by the vast print culture in the modern age. The scriptural asceticism of textual inerrancy might be then seen as a thoroughly modern project, endorsed by the practices of the emergent universities and academic disciplines where many early fundamentalists were employed and subsequent believers were trained. There is a limit to this correlation, however: For many contemporary fundamentalists, modern institutions of higher learning have become so poisoned by diversity and cultural excess that they are now seen as dens of iniquity. Although fundamentalism as a reading practice originated in the university, its subsequent advocates became antagonistic to this point of origin, believing that the expansive methods of scholarship trumped the particularistic truths of scripture.

Enclave Communities. Fundamentalist logic focuses on the fortification of borders. A belief in scriptural inerrancy results in the careful, ceaseless policing of theological interpretations and ritual strategies among fundamentalist believers. In order to best monitor the lived religion of fundamentalists, many cohere in local enclaves that promote a panoptic observation of daily life. The preservation of "traditional" values and "original" interpretations of scriptures cannot be done in individual isolation; it is best constructed through constant mitigation and corporate analysis. The varieties of Jewish fundamentalism offer instances of these sorts of communities. Scholars have disagreed vociferously about the application of "fundamentalism" to Jewish movements (Harris). For example, to many the practices of ultra-Orthodox groups such as the Haredim are clearly fundamentalist, with their privatized communities, archaic gender roles, and devotion to a literalist scriptural exegesis. Likewise, the religious settlers of the Gush Emunim (the Block of the Faithful) have been described as "fundamentalist." Yet these two groups have very different ideas about the role of nation in their theologies: whereas many Haredim still refuse to recognize the legitimacy of the state of Israel, the Gush Emunim are devoted to the protection of Israel as a primary religious practice.

These differences are resolved into common accord, however, when it comes to practices of social cohesion. Both the Gush Emunim and the Haredim advocate exile from the world into separatist enclaves. The Gush Emunim occupy contested land in order to retain Palestine and its territories in trust for the coming Messiah. This work is both publicly activist and privately domestic, with participants constructing squatter communities as physical symbols of their differentiation and devotional occupation. The Haredim wear frock coats, broad-brimmed hats, and the ringlets of the eighteenth-century Jewish ghettos of eastern Europe. Close-knit and autonomous, these ghettos were ruled by Jewish law, not the laws of secular nations. The process of modernization and secularization is seen by Orthodox Jewish groups as detrimental to the spiritual and cultural welfare of mankind. More specifically, the process of secularization alienates Jews from the task of restoring society to the time of King David. This is a monocular restoration. The enclave culture created by such fundamentalists rejects modern diversity, and modern protection of diversity, in favor of a return to limited choices and cultural homogeneity. Many fundamentalists are thus often interpreted as antimodern because they choose a retreat to ways of life they describe as "traditional" and that may appear to the Western observer as regressive. In fact, the very rejection of modernity and the terms of that rejection merely underline the ways in which fundamentalisms are possible only within the context of modernity. The separation into enclave communities expresses the very particularized notions of social identity that have defined modern subjectivity.

The Modern Enemy. Living in social enclaves is a geographic expression of an epistemic rejection. Fundamentalists universally define themselves against an antagonistic and encroaching enemy, usually framed in terms of its modern decadence. Features of this enemy vary from fundamentalism to fundamentalism: some fundamentalists reject new technologies, globalization, and the market economy, whereas others establish pluralism and diversity as the troublesome foe. As the twenty-first century began, the terrorist acts of 11 September 2001 brought this particular epistemology into strong relief through the antagonistic actions of Islamic fundamentalists.

The designation of "fundamentalism" within Islam is not an easy one. Since the vast majority of believing Muslims are qur'anic inerrantists, textual inerrancy is not a useful definitional prism for Islamic fundamentalism. Instead, the focus must be on the social cohesion formed through the particular goal of Islamic fundamentalists: the removal of corrupt or pro-Western governments. Rather than live under governments ordered by laws imported from the West, Muslim fundamentalists argue for governments derived from the "indigenous" Sharia code derived from the Qur'an and the sunna (custom) of the prophet Muhammad.

Within Islam, "tradition" refers to the accumulated body of interpretation and practice developed over the centuries by the 'ulema, the learned men who constitute Islam's clerical class. Throughout Islamic history there have been reformers who challenged the authority of the 'ulema; reformation is a hallmark of every global religious tradition. What differentiates contemporary contestations of the 'ulema with those of previous centuries is the deconstruction of a particularly modern consensus about the productivity of liberal societies and free market economies. What makes contemporary Islamic reformers fundamentalists, and what makes their medieval counterparts not properly "fundamentalist," is their focused antagonism towards systems and processes only present subsequent to the Industrial Revolution.

Such fundamentalisms are found in varying degrees of strength in every Muslim-majority country. The social history of these movements can be sourced to two organizations: the Muslim Brotherhood in the Arab countries and the Jama'at-e Islami in the Indian subcontinent. These organizations emerged as antagonists to British colonialism. In particular, they represented protests against the oppression of Muslim residents in British colonies, as well as rejections of modernist Muslim acquiescence to European ideas. Islamic fundamentalists describe contemporary society as being in a state of *jahiliyya*, or "ignorance." This is the modern enemy of Muslim fundamentalism: the abandoned morality and Western economy of postcolonial culture. The only way to escape this ignorance is through *hijira*, or flight, from the current world in order to reclaim the golden age of the prophet Muhammad and his immediate caliphate successors. The re-creation of this precolonial epoch drives much of the violence associated with Muslim fundamentalists as they seek to retrieve a world beset by illicit sexuality, criminality, drugs, and capitalist solipsism.

Political Conservatism. Media renditions of global fundamentalisms tend to focus exclusively on the political consequences of fundamentalist ideology. As we have seen, the principles constituting fundamentalist logic are social and theological; such principles frequently develop political consequences. It would be wrong, however, to imagine fundamentalisms as political positions dressed in religious language. Fundamentalist movements nearly always have their roots in theological disputes or religious antagonisms. While such disputes may arise in contexts of political discord, the political consequences of fundamentalisms may be best understood as a late-stage development in these histories. Nonetheless, any religious group of the modern period necessarily finds itself occupying a political position, as it must argue itself into meaning under the auspices of ostensibly secular modern nation-states. Many scholars have argued that nationalism is the enemy of fundamentalism, as nationalism is the product of modern industrialization whereas fundamentalism is a protest against such modernist hegemony. Such a summation fails to recognize both the religious symbols and ritual deployed in most secular nationalisms as well as the distinctively nationalist language of many fundamentalisms.

No family of fundamentalisms better represents this interaction between politics and religious investments than those found in India. Many scholars have been wary of describing Hindu nationalism as a fundamentalism, since Hinduism does not possess an orthodoxy premised on a single scriptural tradition (Juergensmeyer). Yet there are reasons to include Hinduism in a comparative analysis of fundamentalisms. India is constitutionally secular with a Hindu majority. That Hindu majority does not have a religiously disinterested stance toward India's nation; in fact, the idea of the sacred land of India and her people is central to the development of Hinduism. Hinduism is not just an elective religious identity, but potentially a spiritual and practical prerequisite for Indian citizenship. Although debates about the relationship between India and Hindu cosmology are longstanding, Hindu nationalism has a more recent history, rooted in anticolonial maneuvers against the British attempt to catalog India's religious communities into sects easy to "divide and rule." Writings by reformers like the swami Dayananda Sarasvati (1824–1883) advocated a reification of the Vedas as scriptures including the sum of all knowledge sourced in a particular place (India) and among a particular people (Hindus). Dayananda's ideas have been immensely influential in the formation of the Bharatiya Janata Party (BJP), which today leads India's governing coalition, and actively advocates a Hindu worship of the nation, referred to as Hindutva. "Hindutva secularizes Hinduism by sacralizing the nation, bringing the cosmic whole within the realm of human organization," writes Malise Ruthven (p. 176). The consequences of this fundamentalist nationalism have been explicitly material: Hindu fundamentalists demolished the Babri Masjid Mosque at Ayodhya in 1992, believing Babri Masjid to be the birthplace of the deity Rama. Such violence against Muslim sacred sites, coupled with a promotion of sati (the suicide of widows) reflects the global political conservatism of fundamentalisms. The BJP, like many fundamentalist movements, pursues social programs designed to reshape the family in accord with values described as "traditional," frequently placing severe restrictions on women and children as necessary to the overall resuscitation of ancient Hindu glory. Although such social programming suggests fundamentalisms worldwide seek solely to repress the progress of modernity, any theory of fundamentalism must necessarily account for its scrupulous usage of modern scholarship, technology, and notions of nation to promote these politics and practices of theological nostalgia.

[*See also* Christianity; Hinduism; *and* Islam.]

BIBLIOGRAPHY

Antes, Peter. "Fundamentalism: A Western Term with Consequences." In *Perspectives on Method and Theory in the Study of Religion*, edited by Armin Geertz and Russell T. McCutcheon. Leiden, Netherlands: Brill, 2000.

Harris, Jay M. "Fundamentalism: Objections from a Modern Jewish Historian." In *Fundamentalism and Gender*, edited by J. S. Hawley. New York: Oxford University Press, 1994.

Juergensmeyer, Mark. "The Debate over Hindutva." In *Religion* 26 (1996): 129–136.

Marsden, George M. *Fundamentalism and American Culture: The Shaping of Twentieth-Century Evangelicalism, 1870–1925*. 2d ed. New York: Oxford University Press, 2006.

Marty, Martin E., and R. Scott Appleby, eds. *Accounting for Fundamentalisms: The Dynamic Character of Movements*. Chicago: University of Chicago Press, 1994.

Ruthven, Malise. *Fundamentalism: The Search for Meaning*. New York: Oxford University Press, 2004.

KATHRYN LOFTON

The United States

"Fundamentalism" has been deployed as a generic term denoting any conservative religious theology and as a specific title of a historical movement within American Protestantism. Application of the term must take into account both definitions, because prejudicial renderings of the former may skew documentary assessment of the latter.

Among scholars of religion, the word "fundamentalism" has received detailed treatment across sectarian lines, most notably by the Fundamentalism Project, directed and edited by Martin E. Marty and R. Scott Appleby and operated out of the University of Chicago from 1988 to 1995. This research concluded that as a generic category, "fundamentalism" refers to a set of family resemblances found among a variety of observed "fundamentalists": for example, fundamentalists understand truth to be revealed and unified, envision themselves as a part of a cosmic struggle, demonize their opposition, are disproportionately led by males, and seek to overturn the accepted distribution of power. Although the particular embodiment of these resemblances varies from culture to culture and from sect to sect, they are generally applicable to the form of fundamentalism that began in late-nineteenth-century American Christianity.

Cyrus Scofield. When looking for an initiating incident in the history of fundamentalism in the United States, students of American theology usually point to the nineteenth-century popularization of the eschatology of Cyrus Scofield (1843–1921). As a premillennialist, Scofield rejected the possibility that Christ would return after the millennium; instead, Scofield and his followers endorsed a trajectory of man marked by decline and decay. Presuming scriptural inerrancy, Scofield's writings outlined the various "dispensations" of God's self-revelation to humankind. According to Scofield, man was currently in the midst of the sixth dispensation, which would be concluded by the rapture of the church and an epoch of profound human tribulation.

Scofield's theological outlook could have easily become a historical curiosity had it not been for his affiliation with the wildly successful nineteenth-century revivalist Dwight Lyman Moody (1837–1899). Scofield toured with Moody and eventually joined him at the Niagara Conferences, a series of Bible and prophecy meetings that had been convening near Niagara Falls since 1883. These meetings became critical sites of ecumenical dissemination for Scofield's particular take on mankind's prophesied destiny. Yet despite the common conflation of Scofield's theology as the definitional center of American Protestant fundamentalism, his eschatological perspective did not gain canonical admittance to *The Fundamentals* (1910–1915), the twelve-volume series of books published to codify the conservative position.

The Fundamentals. Conceived during the same year as the publication of the Scofield Reference Bible (1909), *The Fundamentals* was the brainchild of Lyman Stewart, founder of the Union Oil Company of California. Stewart designed *The Fundamentals* as a series of ninety articles by sixty-four authors reinscribing "the fundamentals of the Christian faith." Moderate in tone, the articles avoided political topics entirely, focusing on a grounded defense of the scriptures. Approximately one-third of the essays guarded the Bible against the new criticism, arguing that the Old and New Testaments were without inconsistency. Another third of the essays discussed foundational theological questions, such as the meaning of the Trinity and the role of sin. The remaining essays were a diverse smattering, addressing everything from the modern "heresies" (such as Christian Science, Roman Catholicism in the United States, and Mormonism) to missionary ambitions. Any definition of "fundamentalism" that relies on *The Fundamentals* would overwhelmingly emphasize the scholastic bent of the movement, a scrupulous scholarly effort to reconcile Christianity with new criticism.

Nowhere in *The Fundamentals* do Scofield's ideas make an appearance. Moreover, in the first explicit deployment of the descriptor "fundamentalist," Curtis Lee Laws, editor of the Baptist *Watchman-Examiner*, explicitly avoided any mention of Scofield or his dispensations; rather, in his 1920 article he argued that the fundamentalist was merely prepared to "do battle royal for the Fundamentals." This discordance between Scofield and the intellectual mainline divided conservative Christian conversation during the first two decades of the twentieth century. On the one side, the scholarly essays canonized in *The Fundamentals* advocated a strict, rigorous reading of biblical texts; on the other, sermons and pamphlets propagated by Scofield and his disciples endorsed a bleak view of the modern moment, condemned by cosmic destiny to sin and suffering. Whereas *The Fundamentals* encouraged a relentless scholasticism, Scofield goaded Christians to interpret the obvious troubles of the modern world as signs of an impending epoch of trial.

In the 1920s fundamentalism simultaneously hit the climax of its public presence and the denouement of its denominational sway. Fundamentalists committed to dispensationalism and premillennialism alienated their allies, leading to loud confrontations within the major Protestant denominations, including the Presbyterians (both North and South), the Northern and Southern Baptist conventions, and the Disciples of Christ. The majority of Protestant adherents could accept the biblical adamancy of *The Fundamentals* but found the pessimistic separatism of Scofield's theology too divisive. The more militant fundamentalists broke from their home denominations, founding either new congregations or interdenominational fundamentalist organizations. Thus rather than serving as an intellectual subset within American Protestantism as a whole, fundamentalists quickly became defined by their belligerent separatism. The 1925 Tennessee trial of John Thomas Scopes for teaching evolution offered a national advertisement for fundamentalist anti-intellectualism rather than a showcase for the scholarly prowess exhibited in *The Fundamentals*. Despite the immediate legal condemnation of Scopes, journalists like H. L. Mencken were so successful in their skewering of fundamentalist attitudes that the movement went underground.

Following these sectarian splits and creationism embarrassments, fundamentalists retrenched. Some left the movement altogether, forming a conservative wing of American evangelicalism. Others, like Robert R. "Bob" Jones Sr. and J. Frank Norris, took an increasingly sectarian stance and established educational institutions to propagate their theological outlook. After the internationally renowned evangelist Billy Graham (b. 1918) accepted the sponsorship of the ecumenical Protestant Council in 1957, the majority of Protestants focused on collaborative, rather than separatist, efforts. This was the trend until the public return of separatist fundamentalism in the late 1970s under the auspices of Jerry Falwell's Moral Majority.

This fundamentalism owed more to the negative historicism of Cyrus Scofield than it did to the scholarly labors represented in *The Fundamentals*. Rather than emphasize the theological specifics of Scofield's vision, however, this manifestation of Protestant belief focused on the dismal failures of American culture and national policy. Instead of scripture, ministers like Falwell appealed to romanticized visions of the American past, a past in which patriotism, Christian commitment, and family stability were purportedly assured. Though the "moral majority" never represented a statistical majority even within American evangelicalism, its political consequences were far-reaching. Through the subsequent decades, Falwell's dedication to Christian conservatism in American politics could be discerned in vitriolic public debates over family planning, scientific research, and public morality.

[*See also* Christianity; Creationism; Evangelicalism; Great Awakening; Great Awakening, Second; *and* Religious Revivals.]

BIBLIOGRAPHY

Gaebelein, Frank E. *The Story of the Scofield Reference Bible: 1909–1959*. New York: Oxford University Press, 1959. Although overly sympathetic to Scofield's theological outlook, this monograph remains the only sustained treatment of Scofield's work.

Carpenter, Joel A. *Revive Us Again: The Reawakening of American Fundamentalism*. New York: Oxford University Press, 1997. A historical summary of fundamentalist offshoots since the 1920s.

Harding, Susan Friend. *The Book of Jerry Falwell: Fundamentalist Language and Politics*. Princeton, N.J.: Princeton University Press, 2001. Excellent ethnography of Jerry Falwell and his followers in Lynchburg, Virginia, with an emphasis on the theological and discursive strategies of the Moral Majority.

Marsden, George M. *Fundamentalism and American Culture: The Shaping of Twentieth Century Evangelicalism, 1870–1925*. New York: Oxford University Press, 1980. Definitive description of the relationship between fundamentalism and the modern world, including vivid profiles of fundamentalist social habits, technological expertise, and charismatic figures. See also Marsden's subsequent encyclopedic analysis of the category in the *Encyclopedia of the American Religious Experience: Studies of Traditions and Movements*, edited by Charles H. Lippy and Peter W. Williams (New York: Charles Scribner's Sons, 1988).

Marty, Martin E., and R. Scott Appleby. "Conclusion: An Interim Report on a Hypothetical Family." In *Fundamentalisms Observed*, edited by Martin E. Marty and R. Scott Appleby. Chicago: University of Chicago Press, 1991. Offers a discussion of the "family resemblances" shared among global fundamentalisms.

Sandeen, Ernest R. *The Roots of Fundamentalism: British and American Millenarianism, 1800–1930*. Chicago: University of Chicago Press, 1970. Prehistory of the fundamentalist movement; includes detailed assessment of the intellectual sources for *The Fundamentals*.

KATHRYN LOFTON

G

GABON. Gabon's proximity to the Atlantic Ocean allowed coastal communities to act as middlemen with Europeans searching for slaves and natural resources. Gabonese identified themselves by clan rather than by language or by their region. Leading men within clans struggled for access to trade and for control over female dependents, and slave traders in the late eighteenth and early nineteenth centuries followed by European businesses seeking ivory and rubber made violent competition endemic to the entire region until 1914.

Although visits by European merchants led coastal people to develop Atlantic connections, the region remained independent. Between 1839 and 1846, French naval officers intimidated Mpongwe clan chiefs around the Gabon estuary to surrender their independence. American Congregationalist and French Catholic missionaries also arrived in the 1840s; they set up schools that gave coastal peoples opportunities to work as clerks and interpreters. Women had the option of becoming the mistresses of visiting European men. French authorities slowly expanded their authority from the coast as officers like Pierre Savorgnan de Brazza (1852–1905) pushed for expeditions into inland Gabon between 1873 and 1900. These forays into Gabonese communities brought fighting. French concessionary companies were given free reign to dominate much of the poor colony between 1900 and 1920, bringing about even more destruction with their rapacious policies.

Between 1914 and 1940, Gabon underwent dramatic transformations. World War I brought famines and epidemics. The timber industry boom in the 1920s led thousands of men from inland regions to work in timber camps. Many men were forced to leave their homes to work. Ethnic identities beyond the clan developed in the camps, as did new religious movements like *bwiti* that stitched mission influences with religious practices from all over Gabon. The 1920s and the Great Depression led to a dramatic rise in church membership as well. Some women fled husbands to live in the camps or the small cities of Libreville and Port-Gentil.

After 1940, Gabonese politicians developed close ties to France. The politicians Léon Mba (1902–1967) and Jean-Hilaire Aubame (1912–1989) struggled to best one another by appealing to rural and urban frustrations with colonial rule. Mba won out, but he depended on French patronage after formal independence in 1960, especially after a failed coup in 1964. His successor, Omar Bongo (1935), ran a pro-French one-party dictatorship strengthened by oil and mining profits from 1968 to 1990. Oil has brought riches, but only for a few. Democratic protest movements forced Bongo to agree to elections in 1993, but Bongo and his Parti Démocratique Gabonais (PDG; Gabonese Democratic Party) did not relinquish power. Today, corruption and authoritarian rule still dominate the country. Rapid urbanization and dramatic economic inequalities frustrate the vast majority of Gabonese, who are unable to receive patronage profits. West African migrants profit from the high cost of living but face harassment from state officials. Immigration since the oil boom of the 1970s also has promoted an illicit trade in child slaves from West Africa to work in Gabon. Though Gabon is politically stable, declining oil reserves and political paralysis augur poorly for the country's future.

[*See also* Africa, *subentry* Western Africa; Colonialism, *subentry* Africa; *and* Petroleum, *subentry* Africa.]

BIBLIOGRAPHY
Bernault, Florence. *Démocraties ambigües en Afrique centrale: Congo-Brazzaville, Gabon, 1945–1965.* Paris: Karthala, 1996.
Gray, Christopher. *Colonial Rule and Crisis in Equatorial Africa: Southern Gabon, c. 1850–1940.* Rochester, N.Y.: University of Rochester Press, 2002.

JEREMY RICH

GAELIC LANGUAGE. Gaelic, a Celtic language closely related to Irish and Manx, was spoken in most parts of Scotland in the eleventh century. It subsequently retreated

411

slowly northward as the Scots language (related to English) grew in strength in the urban centers of southeastern Scotland over succeeding centuries. By the eighteenth century, Gaelic was confined to northern and western Scotland, within the so-called Highland line. The nineteenth and twentieth centuries saw the slow retreat of Gaelic speech from most of the Highlands to the Hebrides, where it still remains a community language in some places. The number of speakers of Gaelic has declined from an estimated 290,000 (23 percent of the Scottish population) in 1769 to 210,000 (5 percent) in 1891 to 58,000 (1 percent) in 2001. The rapid rate of decline has been arrested in recent decades thanks to the efforts of campaigners, but it has not yet been reversed. Parallels can be drawn with the experience of the Welsh and Irish languages under similar pressures with differing responses. Gaelic, in common with many minority languages, suffers from the pressure and prevalence of world English.

The Gaelic Highlanders of Scotland were often portrayed (misleadingly) as being united in support of Jacobitism. Gaels, however, fought on both sides at the battle of Culloden in 1746, the final conflict in the Jacobite wars. The Jacobite defeat and its aftermath was nevertheless perceived as an opportunity to quicken the impetus toward achieving social and linguistic uniformity, a goal long held by the Scotto-British polity (from 1603). The subversive book of poetry *Ais-eiridh* (1751)—one of the first books published in modern Gaelic—written by the Jacobite Alasdair mac Mhaighstir Alasdair (c. 1695–1770; known in English as Alexander MacDonald) was supposedly burned at the mercat cross in Edinburgh; this was, perhaps, symbolic of things to come.

Increasing commercialism and the wider English world had already impinged on the Gaidhealtachd (Gaelic-speaking areas) prior to 1746. Legislation in 1747 curbed Highland chiefs' powers and accelerated the shift in emphasis from chief to landlord and from clansman to commodity or crofter (farmer), straining one of the main social pillars supporting Gaelic speech. Concomitant commercial pressures saw the movement of large numbers of people out of the Highlands, either voluntarily or by forcible "clearance." Although some security of tenure was obtained by crofters (ending compulsory clearance) in 1886, migration to Scottish cities and emigration abroad continued throughout the twentieth century. This net mass exodus from the Highlands, estimated at more than 250,000 people between 1750 and 1950, included many thousands of Gaelic speakers. Of the communities where

exiled Gaels clustered, Nova Scotia alone has had some success in maintaining Gaelic as a transgenerational community language. Unabated outward migration from the Gaidhealtachd meant that by the twenty-first century many Scottish Gaels lived in Scottish urban centers—45 percent as of 2001—rather than in the traditional Gaidhealtachd, while most migrants who move into Gaelic-speaking areas do not speak Gaelic. Learners, often more proactive vis-à-vis language issues than "natives," form a new and increasingly important element in the Gaelic world.

Agencies based in the Scottish Lowlands from 1709 were much concerned with spreading their religion, "civility," and, as a corollary, the ability to read the Bible. The agencies eventually realized that the fastest route to salvation, education, and English skills was through teaching people in their own language. These agencies supported the publication of the Bible in Gaelic in 1767 and 1801, and until 1872 they supported a network of Gaelic schools. Worship continued thereafter as the main focus for formal Gaelic usage, although this varied depending on the linguistic makeup of the individual parish. The Education Act of 1872, however, was a watershed. It replaced sporadic Gaelic instruction with compulsory and universal state schooling conducted in English. There was no significant place for Gaelic in schools thereafter, other than as a subject for study. Consequently most Gaels, while literate in English, were largely illiterate in their first language.

Parental pressure in the Gaidhealtachd after 1980 bucked the trend and forced the authorities, reluctantly, to back the establishment of some Gaelic-medium education for primary schools. The undoubted success of these schools—many now outside the Gaidhealtachd in Scotland—draws attention to the current limited provision of Gaelic-medium secondary education. The Gaelic radio service, slow-growing and still limited in terms of hours, is now available nationally. This success has not yet been matched by other branches of the media. The new Scottish Parliament (1997–   ) introduced *Achd na Gàidhlig* (the Gaelic Language Act) in 2005, as well as an advisory group, *Bòrd na Gàidhlig*, which hopes to address issues contributing to the decline of Gaelic.

[*See also* Language *and* Scotland.]

BIBLIOGRAPHY

Devine, T. M. *The Scottish Nation, 1700–2000.* London: Allen Lane, 1999.

McLeod, Wilson. "Gaelic in the New Scotland: Politics, Rhetoric, and Public Discourse." In *Journal on Ethnopolitics and*

Minority Issues in Europe, July 2001, pp.1–27. Available as an electronic resource at http://www.ecmi.de/jemie/.

Thomson, Derick S., ed. *The Companion to Gaelic Scotland.* Oxford: Blackwell Reference, 1983.

Withers, C. W. J. *Gaelic in Scotland, 1698–1981.* Edinburgh: John Donald, 1984.

AONGHAS MACCOINNICH

GALLIPOLI. The Gallipoli campaign of 1915, fought on the narrow Gallipoli peninsula at the entrance to the Dardanelles, turned out to be a disaster for the Anglo-French forces involved and a defensive success for the underestimated Ottoman army, which had only recently entered World War I. (Historians often refer to the defenders of Gallipoli as the Turkish army, or the Turks, but modern Turkey was founded only in 1923. Prior to this, the Ottoman Empire and its army contained many nationalities, although Turks formed the largest group in the Ottoman army in World War I.)

The Gallipoli conflict began with the adherence of the Ottoman Empire to the Central Powers (Germany and Austria-Hungary) in late October 1914, following political and maritime maneuvering between German and British diplomats and naval forces. In particular, the arrival of the German ships *Goeben* and *Breslau* at the Dardanelles Straits in August 1914 forced the hand of the Ottoman government. However, even before the opening of hostilities, Winston Churchill, first lord of the Admiralty, and Lord Kitchener, secretary of state for war, had considered an attack on Gallipoli, and this inclination was reinforced in early January by appeals from the Russians, who were pressured by Ottoman army attacks.

The British cabinet and Lord Kitchener came to a confused agreement to proceed with the Gallipoli attack, with Churchill believing in a "ships alone" approach and others wanting a joint army-navy attack, while Lord Fisher, the mercurial head of the Royal Navy, was generally opposed to the project. In this uncertain atmosphere, the French agreed to be involved, and an Anglo-French naval attack began in February 1915 with an attack on the forts of the Dardanelles Straits. The aim was to pass through the straits, enter the Sea of Marmora, and bombard Constantinople (Istanbul). However, destruction of the forts and shore artillery could only be achieved if Ottoman mines in the straits were first cleared. But this could not be done because the Ottoman shore artillery fired on the civilian-crewed minesweeping ships. Ultimately, it was decided to force the Dardanelles Straits, with French and British battleships moving in close to the Ottoman forts and shore batteries and destroying them. This attack took place on 18 March 1915 and failed, with three Allied battleships sunk by mines and three other battleships badly damaged.

Hence, if the Dardanelles Straits were to be opened, it would have to done by the army. An Anglo-French force was prepared, General Sir Ian Hamilton was appointed commander in chief, and the landing was planned for 25 April 1915. The main Allied landing sites were to be at Cape Helles at the south end of the Gallipoli peninsula because the Allied navy could best support this area. A further landing site near Gaba Tepe on the west side of the peninsula was selected for an Australian and New Zealand force. A French force was to land on the Asian side to protect Cape Helles from shelling. For the defenders, the overall commander of the Fifth Ottoman Army on Gallipoli was the capable German officer General Liman von Sanders.

The Allied landings succeeded at Cape Helles, but at terrible cost at a number of beaches because of strong Ottoman defenses and the inability of the British navy to accurately cover the landings. An innovation at one beach was the use of a "Trojan horse" ship, *River Clyde*, to land troops, but the ship grounded too far from land. Similar heavy casualties took place near Gaba Tepe (later known as Anzac Cove), where Australian and New Zealand troops were landed too far north, and where an outstanding Ottoman defender, Lieutenant Colonel Mustafa Kemal, led a spirited defense. On the Asian side the French landed successfully and later joined British troops at Cape Helles as planned.

After severe fighting over several days at Cape Helles and Anzac Cove, the Allies were unable to advance very far inland, but neither could the Ottomans push the Allies into the sea. A costly series of Allied attacks at Cape Helles from April to June 1915 produced limited results, and Hamilton's staff was forced to seek alternatives. A large number of reinforcements were landed, and in August 1915 a surprise Allied offensive was launched from the Anzac area, supported by landings further north at Suvla. These attacks briefly succeeded in obtaining the high ground overlooking the straits before Mustafa Kemal's troops swept them away. The Suvla operation also failed due to poor Allied leadership and strong Ottoman defense.

With the failure of the August offensive, the Gallipoli campaign became stalemated. Intense political maneuvering in London did not provide any realistic alternatives, and Allied troops were withdrawn from Gallipoli in December 1915 and January 1916.

Ultimately, the February–March 1915 Allied Gallipoli naval campaign failed because of the inability to deal with Ottoman minefields, forts, and artillery. The Allied land campaign failed partly because the campaign occurred early in the war before still-evolving technical developments allowed offensive operations to succeed. In 1915 defensive technology was simply too strong for attacks to work. Also, excellent Ottoman and German leadership and abundant tough Ottoman manpower proved too great an obstacle, while some senior British commanders lacked ability. Casualties in the campaign (killed, wounded, missing) amounted to approximately 205,000 British, 47,000 French, and 289,000 Ottomans.

Results of the campaign included the continuation of the Ottomans in the war, especially in the Middle East. The Allied failure meant that Britain and France focused even more strongly on the western front, while Australian and New Zealand forces emerged with a strong sense of nationalism. For individuals, Churchill lost his post as first sea lord, although he later returned to the cabinet as minister of munitions. Lord Kitchener showed poor ability in handling this campaign and probably would have been replaced except for his untimely death at sea in 1916. By the end of 1915 Mustafa Kemal fell out with German officers and Ottoman political rivals, but he emerged as a fine commander at Gallipoli, later commanded an Ottoman army in the Middle East, and then led the resurgence of Turkish forces after the war and founded modern Turkey, being given the title Atatürk.

[*See also* World War I.]

BIBLIOGRAPHY
James, Robert Rhodes. *Gallipoli.* New ed. London: Pimlico, 1999. Originally published in 1965, this new edition is still one of the best single-volume books on the Gallipoli campaign.

Mango, Andrew. *Atatürk: The Biography of the Founder of Modern Turkey.* Woodstock, N.Y.: Overlook Press, 2000. Contains useful chapters concerning Mustafa Kemal on Gallipoli and after.

Steel, Nigel, and Peter Hart. *Defeat at Gallipoli.* London: Macmillan, 1994. Well-researched, with useful and gripping firsthand accounts.

Travers, Tim. *Gallipoli 1915.* Stroud, U.K.: Tempus Publishing, 2004. The most balanced view of the campaign yet, including use of Turkish/Ottoman archives.

TIM TRAVERS

GAMBIA. The Republic of the Gambia, situated on the western coast of Africa, is 15 to 30 miles (24 to 48 kilometers) wide on either side of the Gambia River, and almost 200 miles (320 kilometers) long. Except for its small Atlantic coastline, the nation is entirely surrounded by the Republic of Senegal. The population is estimated at approximately 1.3 million. The capital, Banjul, known as Bathurst until 1973, is located where the Gambia River flows into the Atlantic Ocean.

The nation's peculiar shape and size are a result of territorial compromises made during the colonial period of the nineteenth century by Britain, which controlled the Gambia River, and France, which ruled the neighboring colony of Senegal. Prior to European colonial rule, the Gambia River region was dominated by a series of small Muslim Mande and Fulbe (or Fulani) kingdoms. Agriculture and fishing dominated the local economy. The first Europeans to arrive in the area were the Portuguese in the 1440s, followed by the English, French, and Dutch, all of whom traded with local kingdoms on the river, seeking agricultural products and also slaves. By the eighteenth century, the British dominated trade, which was centered on slave exports. After the abolition of the slave trade in the early nineteenth century, peanut cultivation dominated the colonial economy of the Gambia, which was the poorest and smallest colony in British West Africa.

Because of its small size and weak economy, moves toward self-rule in the Gambia lagged behind those in other West African nations, and independence was only granted in February 1965. The Gambia became a republic in 1970, and Dawda Kairaba Jawara (b. 1924), initially elected in 1962 as prime minister, became president. Jawara ruled until his ouster by a military coup in 1994. The military, headed by Yahyah Jammeh, permitted elections in 2001. Jammeh, who retired from the military to run for office, was elected president, and his political party won a slim majority in the national assembly. Opposition groups and some foreign observers accused the military government of using fraud and intimidation to influence voters. Jammeh and his party won elections in 2001 and again in 2006, amid allegations of intimidation.

The Gambian economy has consistently and overwhelmingly been based on the production and export of peanuts. During the 1970s and 1980s, the Gambian environment and economy were seriously affected by the Sahelian drought from which it has never completely recovered. Approximately 85 percent of residents make a living primarily from agriculture, with peanuts being the only significant cash crop. Farmers also grow millet and sorghum. Fisheries and tourism are also foreign exchange earners, although tourism as well as foreign aid declined precipitously after the 1994 military coup. Neither the

Jawara nor the Jammeh regimes have made serious efforts to diversify the economy.

The Jawara regime was characterized by corruption, nepotism, and mismanagement. The country relied primarily on foreign assistance for survival. The Gambia did, however, have relatively strong respect for individual liberty and human rights until the military takeover in 1994. The Jammeh regime has imposed serious restrictions on freedom of speech and assembly.

[*See also* Africa, *subentry* Western Africa.]

BIBLIOGRAPHY

Gailey, Harry A. *Historical Dictionary of the Gambia.* 2d ed. Metuchen, N.J.: Scarecrow Press, 1987.

Wright, Donald R. *The World and a Very Small Place in Africa: A History of Globalization in Niumi, the Gambia.* 2d ed. Armonk, N.Y.: Sharpe, 2004.

ANDREW F. CLARK

GAMBLING. Gambling, broadly defined as risking something of value on an uncertain outcome for a chance at winning a prize, has changed a great deal throughout the modern period. Traditionally games of chance were primarily social, pitting opponents with equal stakes and equal odds of winning against each other (e.g., today's poker). In the early modern period social games of both cards and dice took place in public spaces (taverns) and private ones (homes, particularly of the upper classes), even when illegal, with a slight class bias against dice, considered a less refined medium than cards. Beginning in the fifteenth century and intensifying in the sixteenth, Europeans developed mercantile gambling, in which a single banker (the "house") took on all comers. Unlike social games, in which every player had a mathematically equal chance of winning, mercantile games had a built-in statistical edge favoring the banker that guaranteed a profit on fairly run games. This opened the door for government-sanctioned professional gambling establishments such as casinos and lotteries.

The earliest recorded lottery took place in L'Écluse, Flanders, in 1444, and lotteries became permanent fixtures after their introduction to France in 1520 and Venice in 1522. In a period when governments were experimenting with revenue-raising measures, lotteries proved popular ways to fund internal improvements, private enterprise, and a range of philanthropic endeavors. Lotteries run by private and public institutions flourished throughout Europe and its American colonies until the middle of the nineteenth century.

The period from 1650 to 1800 saw a "gambling mania" sweep Europe, spreading from the Italian peninsula, particularly Venice and Genoa, to France, and from there to the rest of the continent. In France all social classes enthusiastically gambled. The first public gaming rooms, called *academies de jeux* (gaming academies), appeared in the late sixteenth century, but gambling reached new prominence during the reign of Louis XIV (r. 1643–1715) and grew afterward; Giacomo Casanova helped to found what eventually became France's Royal Lottery in 1758, and illegal gambling dens called *enfers* (hells) saturated much of France. In 1777 Paris licensed and taxed twelve gaming houses, signaling gambling's increasing role in public life. The Revolution didn't diminish French play—indeed, the game of roulette coalesced in Paris during the 1790s.

The English were particularly sensitive to an upswing in gambling that accompanied the moral lassitude of the Restoration (1660). Several traditionalists charged that Charles II and his retinue brought gambling back to England from France, though in fact it had long roots in English culture, with ample reference to gambling in the works of Shakespeare and Chaucer. Horseracing gradually gained popularity in the eighteenth and nineteenth centuries, eventually displacing earlier blood sports like cockfighting and bearbaiting in Britain and elsewhere.

Both France and England exported their gambling; they colonized and established commercial or military outposts in much of the world during the height of the gambling mania. French colonists, traders, and adventurers from the Caribbean to Canada gambled, and one of the first acts of British officials opening a new trading post or colony in India and East Asia (where gambling was already well entrenched) was often to establish a racecourse and supervisory jockey club. In North America, the Spanish, British, and French encountered several cultures with elaborate gambling rituals and games of their own. Many Native Americans wove new arrivals, such as playing cards, into their existing games.

Even when gambling was at its most popular in Europe, it was usually illegal. Some games, such as the card game whist, received polite sanction and were rarely criminalized, while others, particularly those embraced by the working classes, subjected their devotees to prosecution. In the nineteenth century opposition to gambling hardened because of the conflict with the new work ethic, and antigambling forces secured several triumphs, including the outright prohibition of all gambling in France (1836) and Prussia (1873) and bans on lotteries

Gamblers. Roulette players, Las Vegas, Nevada, 1940. Photograph by Arthur Rothstein. PRINTS AND PHOTOGRAPHS DIVISION, LIBRARY OF CONGRESS

(1826), gambling houses (1845), and betting houses (1853) in Britain. Throughout the world the nineteenth century saw the nadir of legal gambling. Once prevalent in health resorts such as Spa, Baden-Baden, and Bad Homburg, casino-style gambling was confined, by the end of the century, to Monaco's Monte Carlo casino. In much of the Anglophone world, betting at racetracks was the sole remaining legal outlet for gamblers.

In the twentieth century governments around the world, accepting the reality that gambling continued to thrive when outlawed, and wishing to recapture a portion of the moneys spent for themselves, embarked on an unprecedented spree of gambling legalization. France legalized casinos (1907) and a lottery (1933); Nazi Germany reopened the Baden-Baden casino in 1933, though German casinos did not fully return until the 1950s. Even the Soviet Union conducted a lottery, and after the fall of Communism lotteries continued and casinos sprang up

throughout the erstwhile Eastern bloc, particularly in Russia and the former Yugoslavia.

Though the Communist Chinese banned all gambling in 1949, casinos continued to prosper in the Portuguese enclave of Macau. Gambling and casinos expanded throughout Asia in the second half of the twentieth century, with casinos in Malaysia, North and South Korea, Nepal, and the Philippines. In the previous century Chinese expatriates had brought games such as fan-tan and *pakapoo* (keno) to communities throughout the world, and in the 1920s the Chinese game of mah-jongg became a worldwide sensation. In much of the Muslim world, gambling (prohibited by the Qur'an) was accepted in small casinos that catered chiefly to noncitizens, and many African nations, both north and south of the Sahara, followed a similar model.

The United States, like Canada and Australia, saw a state-level liberalization of restrictions against gambling that, by the end of the twentieth century, gave the appearance of national sanction. Government sanction of gambling in the United States has included pari-mutuel betting on horseracing (beginning in the 1920s), lotteries (starting with New Hampshire, 1964), and casinos (Nevada, 1931; proliferation during the 1980s and afterward). Games invented in the United States, including craps, but more spectacularly bingo, slot machines (as fruit machines in Britain and pokies in Australia), and poker, have in turn become popular throughout the world.

[*See also* Las Vegas *and* Leisure.]

BIBLIOGRAPHY

Asbury, Herbert. *Sucker's Progress: An Informal History of Gambling in America*. 1938. Reprint, New York: Thunder's Mouth Press, 2003. A decidedly nonacademic look at American gambling, filled with many illuminating anecdotes.

Munting, Roger. *An Economic and Social History of Gambling in Britain and the USA*. Manchester, U.K.: Manchester University Press; New York: St. Martin's Press, 1996. A straightforward comparative study of the evolution of gambling in the United Kingdom and United States.

Reith, Gerda. *The Age of Chance: Gambling and Western Culture*. London and New York: Routledge, 1999. Traces the evolution of the idea of chance, as distinct from metaphysical will, throughout history.

Schwartz, David G. *Roll the Bones: The History of Gambling*. New York: Gotham Books, 2006. An all-encompassing narrative of gambling from its earliest recorded appearances to the present, including all major games and genres of play.

DAVID G. SCHWARTZ

GAMES. See Recreation; Toys, Children's Games, and the Toy Industry.

GANGES RIVER. The mystical located in the most inescapable of realities, the Ganges (Ganga) could be said to center India. According to legend, its flow is so overwhelming that it could only be allowed onto the Earth by having its strength broken by first cascading through Shiva's hair. Beginning with ancient records, the civilizations of the Indo-Gangetic plain can be traced as the source of both religious and philosophical thought (Mother Ganga) and a rich ecosystem that supported the rapid growth of village communities into the complex cities of the fifth century B.C.E. The river continued to be the prime mode of transportation and commerce as centers of political power shifted, until political instability ceased with the rise of the Gupta Empire in 320 C.E. Subsequent empires, including Lodhi and Mughal, enriched the complex topography and cultures along the banks of the Ganges, building new and larger cities so that with the arrival of large numbers of Europeans, it was already a major venue for trade and communication.

The source of the Ganges is identified as an ice cave 10,300 feet above sea level in the southern Himalayas. Its headstreams, the Bhagirathi, Alaknanda, Mandakini, Dhauliganga, and Pindar, all originate in the state of Uttar Pradesh. The river flows about 1,560 miles through agricultural regions so densely settled that the original flora and fauna have all but vanished, replaced by intense agricultural and industrial development, each dependent on the water that still maintains its reputation as the holiest and, at the northern end, the purest in the world. Irrigation, both by flooding and by canal systems, competes for water with industrial, domestic, and municipal requirements. Two major dams have been erected, one at Haridwar built by the British in 1854 for irrigation purposes, and another at Farakka, near the border of Bangladesh. The hydroelectric dam at Farakka and the diversion of the waters into West Bengal were until recently a source of dispute between the two countries.

In addition to its uses in agriculture and industry, the Ganges has ritual importance for Hindus, whose cremation ghats allow relatives to bring those who have died to the holiest of rivers for interment. This practice has been the subject of controversy since incompletely burned bodies, and sometimes wholly untreated bodies, are found floating in water still used for drinking and cooking by those who live along its banks. Nor is this the only source of pollution. Although its self-purification capacity is remarkable, factory waste, farming run-off, municipal sewage, and disposal of dead animals all add to the Ganges's burden of contamination. Progress has been

TABLE 1. *Average annual flow of the Ganges in millions of cubic meters*

Haridwar	24,000
Allahabad	150,000
Patna	360,000
Farakka	450,000

made. New and improved urban sewer systems and water-treatment plants along with regulations to control effluvia coming from water-dependent industries such as tanneries have had some effect on what will be a long-term project involving multiple local interventions. The Ganges's centrality as a working water system cannot be separated from the use of its image as an emblem of female power. From Tantric art to Bollywood film, the face of the river cannot be thought of as separate from the face of India.

[*See also* India.]

BIBLIOGRAPHY
Lannoy, Richard. *The Speaking Tree: A Study of Indian Culture and Society.* London and New York: Oxford University Press, 1971.
Shukla, A. C., and A. Vandana. *Ganga: A Water Marvel.* New Delhi, India: Ashish Publishing House, 1995.

SANDY STERNER

GANG OF FOUR. The Gang of Four were leading members of the Chinese Communist Party Politburo arrested in the wake of Party Chairman Mao Zedong's death in September 1976 and charged with "counterrevolution" and attempting to usurp state power. They included Mao's widow Jiang Qing (1914–1991), senior public perception managers Zhang Chunqiao (1917–2005) and Yao Wenyuan (1931–2005), and Party Vice-Chairman Wang Hongwen (1932–1992), who as recently as 1974 had been groomed as Mao's successor. Its members having risen to power in the course of the Cultural Revolution, the gang was at the time intimately associated with the most radical aspects of that catastrophically misguided movement. The members of the Politburo who engineered their arrest made the gang into scapegoats for most of the excesses of the Cultural Revolution. In the case of Jiang Qing, these were said to have included the attempted destruction of much of China's traditional culture; in the case of Zhang and Yao, the allegedly fundamental perversion of the ideals, theory, and practices of socialism. In 1981 the four were tried by a special court in Beijing, which sentenced

Gang of Four Trial. Jiang Qing, the widow of Chinese leader Mao Zedong, stands handcuffed in the Supreme People's Court during the Gang of Four Trial, Beijing, January 1981. XINHUA/AP IMAGES

Jiang and Zhang to death with a two-year reprieve, Wang to life imprisonment, and Yao to twenty years of imprisonment. While most historians inside and outside China still justifiably characterize them as Maoist leftists, the original charges against them are now widely discredited, and the brunt of the responsibility for almost everything of political import once blamed on the gang is laid squarely at the feet of Mao Zedong.

[*See also* Cultural Revolution *and* Maoism.]

BIBLIOGRAPHY
Bonavia, David. *Verdict in Peking: The Trial of the Gang of Four.* London: Burnett, 1984.

MICHAEL SCHOENHALS

GARVEYISM. Garveyism is a political ideology and socioeconomic philosophy associated with the Universal Negro Improvement Association (UNIA) and its founder, Marcus Moziah Garvey (1887–1940). Considered to be a critical post–World War I response to the development of other movements centered upon the self-determination of people of African descent (the New Negro movement, the African Black Brotherhood, black internationalism, Pan-Africanism, the Harlem Renaissance, trade unionism, Communism, socialism), Garveyism was an international phenomenon from 1914 to 1930. The Garvey movement was attractive to working-class people of African descent who disagreed with the accommodationism of Booker T. Washington (1856–1915) and the liberal reformist strategies of W. E. B. Du Bois (1868–1963). Unlike Washington, Garvey believed that African Americans should construct a world of their own as an alternative to mainstream society, developing their own businesses, social networks, and culture. Unlike Du Bois, Garvey did not seek cooperation with other racially progressive groups or gradualist reformism.

The UNIA was established first in Garvey's native Jamaica in 1914, then moved to Harlem in 1916, growing rapidly to include approximately 2 million Garveyites by 1919. Exhorting his followers to join in a mass struggle for the redemption of Africa, Garvey became the central figure of a movement that has been characterized as black nationalist, separatist, and radical. Through *Negro World*, a weekly newspaper, Garvey denounced racism, segregation, discrimination, lynching, and political exclusion; at the same time he encouraged economic independence, a religious philosophy based upon self-determination of people of African descent, the reaffirmation of black masculinity, the liberation of Africa, and the reunification of African people throughout the world. Garvey did not believe in intermarriage between racial groups and drew criticism from all sides by meeting with the Ku Klux Klan in 1922. Inside the United States, there were organized Garveyite groups from Florida to Seattle and New York to Los Angeles and in larger cities in between.

Garvey believed that the strongest factor in generating support for Garveyism was the global movement of people of African descent. Not only did he seek the return of African Americans to Africa, he advocated for the emigration, migration, and immigration of blacks to and from the Caribbean as an effort to solidify and institutionalize. Outside of the United States, Garveyism was influential in the semi-independent nations of the Gulf South—Jamaica, Cuba, Costa Rica, Panama, Honduras—transported largely by the movement of migrant laborers outward from the Caribbean. In countries that were still controlled by colonial governments, like Haiti, Trinidad, and Bermuda, Garveyism was virulently repressed. Garveyite groups were founded in many locales in West Africa—Senegal, Dahomey (Benin), French Togo, Cameroon, Sierra Leone, Gambia, the Gold Coast (Ghana), and Nigeria. In South Africa, Garveyite groups existed in Johannesburg, Natal, and Cape Town. Seeking to begin the return of African Americans to Africa, in the mid-1920s Garvey selected Tanganyika (Tanzania) as the place for his Garveyites to settle, but he was told by the League of Nations to relocate elsewhere. After protracted negotiations with the government of Liberia, his plan to return to Africa was unsuccessful and Garveyism, as an international movement by then counting 400 million members, went into decline. This decline was exacerbated by Garvey's 1925 incarceration and subsequent deportation, causing a crisis of leadership in the black nationalist movement in the context of extreme nativism spurred by waves of immigrants entering the United States. Although African Americans engaged in the struggle for self determination were forced to seek other means to achieve their goals and develop new strategies, the legacy of Garveyism continued to linger and inspired many future generations.

[*See also* Afrocentrism.]

BIBLIOGRAPHY

Lewis, Rupert, and Maureen Warner-Lewis. *Garvey: Africa, Europe, the Americas*. Kingston, Jamaica: Institute of Social and Economic Research, University of the West Indies, 1986. A collection of essays from the International Seminar on Marcus Garvey organized by the African Studies Association of the West Indies, Mona, Jamaica, 2–6 January 1973.

Vincent, Theodore G. *Black Power and the Garvey Movement*. Berkeley, Calif.: Ramparts Press, 1971. This text explains and examines the relationship of the 1960s black power movement and the 1920s Garvey movement.

KELLIE HOGUE

Marcus Garvey. Portrait, 1924. PRINTS AND PHOTOGRAPHS DIVISION, LIBRARY OF CONGRESS

GATT. *See* General Agreement on Tariffs and Trade.

GAULLISM. Gaullism (*le gaullisme*) originated as a French political ideology derived from the ideas of Charles de Gaulle (1890–1970). Springing out of the French Resistance movement of World War II, Gaullism is predominantly concerned with the continuation of the historical and national sovereignty of France. Its basic tenets include the creation and preservation of a strongly centralized state and a refusal to enter into international obligations at the expense of national interests. Today the term "Gaullism" is not restricted to any one party, or even to France, but can refer to any political entity that seeks to create a centralized, protectionist state.

In 1958 Charles de Gaulle became president of the Fifth Republic, ending the political uncertainty of the Fourth Republic and ushering in a new era of Gaullist mass politics. De Gaulle's domestic policy included currency reform, the development of a national industrial policy, and a nuclear weapons program. His foreign policies centered on national independence and the protection of French interests. De Gaulle was suspicious of European integration and so was opposed to reliance on supranational organizations like the North Atlantic Treaty Organization (NATO) and the European Economic Community (EEC). He believed that France should not be subservient to the burgeoning superpower the United States nor to the Union of Soviet Socialist Republics, and thus he blocked the entrance of the United Kingdom, an ally of the United States, into the EEC, and he defended the right of the Vietnamese to self-determination during the Second Indochina War

(Vietnam War). De Gaulle withdrew France from and granted independence to Algeria in 1962. He drew the ire of the international community in February 1966 when he withdrew France from the integrated military command of NATO and refused to allow on French soil troops that were under foreign command.

De Gaulle's political party was the conservative Union des Démocrates pour la République (Union of Democrats for the Republic). De Gaulle relied on personal charisma to govern effectively; after his resignation in 1969, Gaullism became a more fluid ideology, encompassing both right- and left-wing doctrine. Georges Pompidou, a moderate Gaullist, served as president of France from 1969 until 1974; most notably he voted to allow the United Kingdom's entry into the EEC in 1973. No Gaullists occupied the office of the president from 1974 to 1995, though the Socialist president François Mitterrand (president 1981–1995) valued some Gaullist principles, including maintaining the nuclear deterrent and France's independence in foreign policy.

Jacques Chirac's center-right Union pour un Mouvement Populaire (Union for a Popular Movement) is the dominant neo-Gaullist party in contemporary France. Since becoming president in 1995, Chirac has practiced a more pragmatic Gaullism that favors international cooperation. Though France banned nuclear testing in 1996, Chirac stated in 2006 that the nuclear arsenal would be reconfigured to deter terrorism. Although he was once a staunch anti-Europeanist, Chirac's later policies favor national security within the broader context of European collective security. Chirac is a great champion of the euro, and in 2005 he sponsored a referendum to ratify the proposed constitution of the European Union. The referendum was defeated.

[*See also* France.]

BIBLIOGRAPHY
Knapp, Andrew. *Gaullism since de Gaulle*. Aldershot, U.K.: Dartmouth Publishing, 1994. A scholarly treatise on the many permutations of Gaullism since de Gaulle. Written before Chirac's presidency; a revised edition with an analysis of Gaullism as it exists today remains to be written.
Mahoney, Daniel J. *De Gaulle: Statesmanship, Grandeur, and Modern Democracy*. Westport, Conn.: Praeger, 1996. Comprehensive study of Charles de Gaulle as a political thinker and of his contributions to modern democracy, based on his own writings.

ANNE CARTER MULLIGAN

GAYS AND LESBIANS. See Homosexuality; Lesbianism.

GAZA STRIP. Bordering the Mediterranean, Israel, and Egypt, the Gaza Strip lies outside any current political state. Named after the historic city of Gaza—the center of an area that became isolated with the establishment of Israel in 1948—the Gaza Strip includes cities such as Rafah and Khan Yunis. More than 70 percent of its 1.4 million inhabitants are refugees or descendents of refugees from territories that became part of Israel. They live in very densely populated camps—for instance, seventy-four thousand people per square kilometer in Jabalya—that are run by the United Nations Works and Relief Agency (UNRWA).

In 1967 following the Six-Day War, Israel occupied the Gaza Strip, curtailing the population's basic civil and political rights. Municipal elections were banned, and Gazans were subject to arrests and expulsions without due process. By 1980 their meager agricultural economy had been absorbed, with about 70 percent of Gaza's labor force employed in Israel. Israel began building illegal settlements and by 1988 had confiscated nearly half of the Gaza Strip's land for the exclusive use of a few Jewish colonies.

In December 1987 a mass protest movement called the Intifada started in Gaza and swept through the occupied Palestinian territories. Groups associated with the Palestine Liberation Organization (PLO) conducted a policy of nonviolent resistance, while a new political Islamist movement, Hamas, emerged and became a leading power.

After the 1993 Oslo Accords, the Palestinian Authority (PA)—a quasi-governmental body—was established in 1994, and a Legislative Council was elected in 1996. Palestinian opposition groups marginalized by the political process organized protests against PA policies and Israeli restrictions and initiated attacks on the Israeli army as well as on settlers and civilians.

The failure of the peace process resulted in a new uprising, the al-Aqsa Intifada, in 2000. By 2002 the PA was in a near total collapse, and the Gaza Strip was in chaos. Under Israeli siege, Gaza was partitioned, and its infrastructure—including its airport and seaport—was destroyed. Militant groups responded with a bombing campaign against Israeli settlements and towns. Israel withdrew its settlers and destroyed its colonies in the Gaza Strip in 2005, leaving the status of Gaza in limbo.

[*See also* Arab-Israeli Conflict; Israel; Palestine; Palestine Liberation Organization; Palestinian Refugees; *and* West Bank and Gaza Strip.]

BIBLIOGRAPHY

Butt, Gerald. *Life at the Crossroads: A History of Gaza.* Nicosia, Cyprus: Rimal, 1995. One of the few available histories of Gaza.

Roy, Sara. *The Gaza Strip: The Political Economy of Development.* Washington, D.C.: Institute for Palestine Studies, 1995. The first and most comprehensive study of its kind on the Palestinian economic development of the Gaza Strip from 1967 to the mid-1990s.

Roy, Sara. "Praying with Their Eyes Closed: Reflections on the Disengagement from Gaza." *Journal of Palestine Studies* 136 (Summer 2005): 64–74. Analyzes the Israeli disengagement plan and reflects on its possible effects on the Strip and on the question of Palestine.

ISSAM NASSAR

GDAŃSK. The city of Gdańsk is Poland's principal seaport, an industrial center, and the capital of the Pomeranian *voivodeship* (administrative territory). Famous Gdańsk natives include Arthur Schopenhauer (1788–1860) and Günter Grass (b. 1927).

In 1793 the Polish city of Danzig (modern Gdańsk) was incorporated into the kingdom of Prussia, but Danzig was designated an independent free city by the Peace of Tilsit on 9 July 1807. Then on 2 January 1814, Prussian troops occupied the city, and Danzig was reannexed by Prussia according to the Congress of Vienna. On 10 January 1920, as a result of the Treaty of Versailles, Danzig was again declared a free city.

During the 1930s the National Socialist German Workers' (Nazi) Party achieved dominance in the Danzig assembly because of German nationalist sentiment, tension with rising numbers of Polish immigrants, and economic uncertainty. On 23 August 1939 the Danzig gauleiter Albert Förster staged a coup d'état. On 1 September 1939 the German ship *Schleswig-Holstein* opened fire on the Polish-defended Westerplatte fort from the bay of Danzig, beginning World War II.

The Red Army recaptured Danzig from Germany on 28 April 1945. Following the Potsdam Conference on 2 August 1945, Danzig was renamed Gdańsk and was returned to Poland. Through the 1950s hundreds of thousands of Germans were expelled from the city. In 1970 the West German chancellor Willi Brandt formally renounced Germany's territorial claims on Gdańsk, a renunciation that was confirmed by the Treaty of Warsaw.

In December 1970, Gdańsk was the scene of bloody antigovernment demonstrations, forcing the resignation of the Polish Communist leader Władysław Gomułka. In September 1980, striking workers at the Lenin Shipyard established *Solidarność* (Solidarity), which played a major role in ending Communist rule in the Eastern bloc. The leader of Solidarność, Lech Walesa, was awarded the Nobel Peace Prize in 1983 and became president of Poland on 9 December 1990. *Solidarność* remained a dominant political party until it lost in Sejm (lower parliament) elections in 2000.

[*See also* Poland; Solidarity; *and* World War II.]

BIBLIOGRAPHY

Davies, Norman. *Heart of Europe: A Short History of Poland.* Oxford: Clarendon Press, 1984. Moves backward chronologically from the *Solidarność* movement to illustrate the continuity of themes in the past and present.

ANNE CARTER MULLIGAN

GENDER [*This entry includes five subentries:*

Overview
Gender Ideals in Britain
Gender Relations in East Asia
Gender Relations in Latin America
Gender Relations in Southeast Asia

See also Femininity; Gender and Empire; Masculinity; Sexuality; *and* Transgender Issues.]

Overview

Gender has marked the way men and women look, determined the spaces in which they conduct their lives, and awarded the power that they wield in the family and the wider world. In the modern world men have generally earned more money than have women, enjoyed more privileges because of their sex, and held the major political offices locally, nationally, and internationally. The higher positions and greater privileges of men throughout the modern period are currently attributed to the fact that masculinity is more highly valued than femininity because of the operation of gender norms that have had remarkable resilience over time. Nonetheless, since the nineteenth century women have come to contest male privilege and the arbitrariness of the greater value given men that has resulted in women living in greater poverty, working harder, and enduring domestic and other violence simply because of their sex. The rise of feminism as a form of activism contesting gender definitions has produced some modification in the political, economic, social, and cultural power that men hold because of gender.

It is hazardous to offer a periodization of gender on a global basis, for regional patterns often predominate even today. Changes in Western attitudes toward gender in the eighteenth and nineteenth centuries, toward emphasis on women's superior beauty and morality but also their special vulnerabilities and family responsibilities, had some global impact as Western influence spread. It could lead to reduction of women's traditional public roles, as in parts of Africa and among Native Americans. It could also lead, by the later nineteenth century, to some reform efforts, including missionary-sponsored educational programs for women in places like India and China or attacks on footbinding in China. By the later twentieth century, sparked in part by feminism, international agencies began to try to assert some global standards for women's rights, another component in patterns of gender change.

Current Definitions of "Gender". The term "gender" is commonly used simply to refer to women; thus "gender gap" and "gender history" are sometimes understood as synonymous with the way that women vote or with women's history. Many academics today use the term "gender" in another way: to refer to the differences between men and women, usually understood as leading to different roles for each sex and to differentials in power and influence. "Gender" in this usage is about the cultural hierarchy that makes men more valued than women. Some historians of women have viewed gender as the primary human difference, determining, for example, who gets a good job, receives health care, and enjoys personal security. Others suggest that the determining factors in human history and in current social conditions depend on the intersection of gender with other factors such as race, ethnicity, class, sexuality, and religion. One result of seeing gender in terms of male and female (and not just women) is that men have come to be studied as gendered historical, sociological, and anthropological subjects.

Another main ingredient of current gender theory is that the differences between men and women are constructed or artificial. This understanding began with the global work of anthropologists such as Margaret Mead, whose books from the 1930s and 1940s describe societies in which men performed "feminine" tasks and women performed "masculine" ones. Mead pinpointed many variations in men's and women's roles globally, leading to the conclusion that gendered behavior was determined by customs rather than by nature. The philosopher Simone de Beauvoir provided a second buttress to a slowly emerging theory of gender when she wrote in her 1949 best seller *Le deuxième sexe* (English trans., *The Second Sex*, 1953) that "One is not born, one is made a woman." From then on, there was steady intellectual movement toward uncovering the artificial nature of all gender distinctions.

The Body and Gender. Clothing, other accoutrements, and rituals helped give the human body its gender and organize society along gender lines and values. In eighteenth-century Europe there was more gender similarity in that both men and women of the upper class dressed in peacock-like fashion, sporting brightly colored and luxurious garments. If anything, the male body was emphasized in the leg-hugging tights and the corsets that pinched in the male waist and thrust out the chest. Breeches still announced male genitals if they did not always cling to them. After the French and American revolutions, upper-class men's makeup and wigs evolved over the course of the century from being luxurious to being more Spartan.

In other parts of the world, however, there was often even less difference in men's and women's dress. In Southeast Asia, for instance, men and women wore similar pajama-like garments. Kimonos were appropriate dress both for men and women in Japan, and caftan-like garments clothed both sexes in western Asia, making clothing a less visible marker of gender and power than it soon became in Europe and North and South America, where clothing became a sharp indicator of gender hierarchy. In the nineteenth century, men in these regions adopted the dark-colored suit—a slim but unrevealing garment much like the pajama of Southeast Asia. Simultaneously clothing for women became more lavish and garish, as well as constricting. It involved complicated undergarments including massive petticoats, hoops, bustles, and dangerous corsets, which constricted women's waists even to the point of causing illness. Globalization and colonialism late in the nineteenth century began spreading these styles and this new articulation of gender hierarchy to other parts of the world.

By the late twentieth century there had been some diminution of dimorphism in dress as a marker of gender. Men and women's clothing adopted the Asian custom of being more similar than different and generally slim and utilitarian. In some instances, however, sexual dimorphism became more pronounced. In countries of the Middle East that experienced Islamic revolutions, women returned to garb that covered their hair, faces, or entire bodies. Where Islam grew strong, as in North Africa or the Muslim diaspora, women whose mothers may have worn secular dress began covering themselves more extensively. In India, many women wore saris, the dress of nationalist India, while their husbands continued the style of slim pants, belts, shirts, and leather shoes. Women moving into globalized factories often resisted any return to complex and highly differentiated dress.

Food dimorphism also marked gender around the world to heighten difference. Skeletons from prehistoric times show similar height and weight for men and women, whereas by the eighteenth century, farmers, for example, scrupulously allotted less food to women servants than to men. Studies of working-class households in late-nineteenth-century London showed that men received any meat that the family might have, children received the next largest share of food, and mothers received the smallest amount. By the twenty-first century anorexia was a global problem, indicating a belief among women that to be feminine (and marketable) they needed to be excessively thin and not eat. Women had practiced most of the dieting in the West until that time, but men in the early twenty-first century had joined the concern for buff if not entirely slim bodies.

Finally, coming-of-age and other rituals constructed gender differences. For men this could entail circumcision, tattooing, piercing, and scarification. For women, genital cutting, a variety of different, specifically feminine piercing and other bodily manipulations, and practices such as the breaking and binding of the foot created femininity. With nationalist projects to modernize states, some of the most visible or painful manipulations of the body to create gender came under attack and, in the case of footbinding, disappeared.

Migration. Nothing characterizes the modern world more than migration, and in it gender played a complex part. Increasing global movement created diasporas in virtually every region, gendered in different ways. During the height of the slave trade in the eighteenth century, African leaders often wanted to keep female slaves for work on their own lands, filling many ships bound for the Western Hemisphere with men. On the other hand, women were preferred slaves in parts of the New World for the same reason as in Africa: they were skilled agricultural workers, and they could reproduce the next generation of slaves. The global slave trade was additionally gendered by the sex work that made women especially desirable captives, even though men were often valued for the heavier work that they were seen as able to perform.

Imperialism also produced massive migration that was freighted with gendered baggage. The image of the achieving man of conquest and accomplishment became dominant in U.S. and European culture in the nineteenth century, and as male imperialists spread across Asia and Africa, they did so with this gendered paradigm. Imperialism itself was described in gendered terms by which the thrusting Western imperialist came to improve a feminized and thus pathetically backward civilization. Toward the end of the nineteenth century, governments encouraged the migration of white women to colonies in order to replicate the superior Western home and domestic manners and to end the concubinage that characterized the first stages of Western colonization. The exploitation of natural resources under imperialism contributed to further gendering of migration, as men left their dominant roles in African villages, for instance, to work in mines. Colonized men were further gendered as soldiers for the imperialist armies, leading to their migration to other continents, particularly during World Wars I and II. However, it was on the basis of this gendered experience that many claimed leadership in nationalist movements from the 1920s on.

In the late twentieth century the gendering of work continued to determine migration patterns. Immediately after World War II global migration expanded, with colonized men and a few women heading for labor-short regions, particularly in Europe. Later in the century, women headed for areas such as Italy, Greece, the Middle East, East Asia, and North America, where there was strong demand for cheap domestic labor. The global marketplace created by multinational corporations was also gendered as female, encouraging the migration of Chinese, Malaysian, South Korean, and other women from the rural areas to the city to work as low-paid factory laborers. Gendered migration also occurred in the decades after World War II because of postcolonial civil wars and genocide, with men often conducting the civil wars and women refugees leaving to escape them.

Where global labor migration occurred, the gendered expectations of old and new worlds met and often clashed. Maxine Hong Kingston's heroine in *Woman Warrior* (1976) relates the "talk stories" of her Chinese-born mother. These stories of the Chinese woman warrior Mulan and also of an aunt "No Name" who becomes pregnant and kills herself in the well resonate menacingly in the psyche of the Chinese American teenager. The heroine struggles with conflicting images of femininity among migrants. Edward Rivera's *Family Installments: Memories of Growing Up Hispanic* (1982) tells of an impoverished Puerto Rican teenager learning to relate to the image of Western masculinity as he struggles through Shakespeare's *Julius Caesar* in school. More rollicking, if similarly poignant, are the many migrants to England and their descendants in Zadie Smith's *White Teeth* (2000). These complex people from South Asia and the Caribbean interact with the English and ponder their histories, always melding the gendered expectations of their new countries with the gendered rules, aspirations, and codes of conduct that travel with them from their homelands.

Education and Gender. In some parts of the world women's illiteracy remained high by comparison with men's—and was even close to 100 percent in places—down to the twenty-first century. This disparity worked to construct male superiority and female inferiority—and thus gender. However, education and training in literary and other arts allowed women to gain an esteemed place in the cultural world. For example, in China and Japan women groomed to entertain men, including sexually, went through years of training to perfect their skills in poetry, song, and calligraphy. East Asian women of the nineteenth-century floating world, even though they might accomplish great feats as artists, kept their lower place in the gender hierarchy because their high accomplishments were offset by their lack of sexual respectability.

Although Samuel Johnson, the eighteenth-century essayist and lexicographer, claimed to his friend Boswell that "a woman's preaching is like a dog's walking on his hind legs. It is not done well; but you are surprised to find it done at all," many European women (some of his acquaintance) were accomplished beyond preaching in the realms of novel, history, and poetry writing. Famed artists like Élisabeth Vigée-Lebrun painted the royalty of Europe in the eighteenth century and made a good living doing it. By the nineteenth and twentieth centuries women around the world appeared to break gender hierarchies through their artistic talents, with Selma Lagerlöf, Grazia Deledda, and Gabriela Mistral all becoming poet laureates in literature in the first half of the twentieth century. However, women's cultural accomplishments were usually interpreted as exceptions that proved the truth of men's superiority.

The idea of male superiority embedded in the capacity to learn and think—to develop their reason—had deep roots. In Jewish culture, for instance, men alone were allowed to study the Torah, enshrining women's inferiority in the most meaningful realm of life. So it was the gradual development of public education for women, along with the slow if imperfect acceptance of the credo that "the mind has no sex," that undercut the idea of men's superiority in learning and thinking. One goal of the Russian Revolution—a goal that was, astonishingly, almost realized within two decades—was ending women's illiteracy as part of the credo of gender equality.

The path to gender equity in education has been a rough one, and there have been attempts to turn back the clock. After the Iranian Revolution of 1978, women's study abroad was made more difficult, requiring the permission of a guardian and allowing no financial aid. In the 1990s the Taliban in Afghanistan sought to put women in their proper place by refusing them education. The World Bank made loans to emerging nations in the 1980s and 1990s with the proviso that they cut back on government spending, which often entailed cutting back on seats for girls in schools. African feminists, who had received a good education as their nations became independent, noted that succeeding generations of women had received hardly any education, so strict was the World Bank in its conditions for loans. Restricting the education of girls has been one way to restore gender hierarchy in places where it weakened.

Gender and Work. In general, work was distributed along gender lines, with men in agrarian society usually plowing fields, caring for large animals, and marketing grain and animals and with women tending to clothing, food preparation, and vegetable gardens and dairying. Although young children of either sex could do household work such as gathering wood, tending ducks and geese, or fetching water, training for the gender assignment of work also began at a young age with boys accompanying their fathers as shepherds to learn occupational skills. Girls similarly learned food preparation and spinning and weaving, but either sex could be assigned the monitoring of small children.

The arrangement of work thus showed the arbitrariness of gender, and this arbitrariness lasted into the adult years, even as many regions of the world industrialized. Weaving, whether of silk, cotton, or wool, was gendered male in some regions of the world and female in others. Even within the same country, entire cities could have only male weavers, while nearby there would be only female ones. Moreover, occupations could switch their gendering over the course of time: domestic service around the world in the eighteenth century was both male and female, but by the twentieth century domestic service was usually gendered female. Service-sector jobs such as bank teller, store clerk, and secretary also metamorphosed in the late nineteenth century and thereafter to being dominated by women and seen as appropriately low-paying female work.

However, in the twenty-first century, switching occurred once again as nursing, grammar school teaching, flight attending, and other service work came to include ever more men. The global workplace of the late twentieth and twenty-first centuries affected gender conditions paradoxically, luring women to work for minimal wages and in bad conditions for the multinationals from the 1970s but improving the education, access to birth control, and confidence of women in South Korea and elsewhere. Nonetheless, the wage differential attached to gender is currently what it has been for centuries: about 50–75 cents paid women for every dollar paid men.

Gender, Nation-Building, and Politics. The rise of the nation-state in which the state and its peoples are said to have a unified set of interests has had highly gendered contours. From the late eighteenth century on, nation-states in Europe and North and South America created a gender arrangement by which men became full citizens with equal rights and privileges, including the privilege of ruling over women in private homes. By awarding men the right to their wives' property and wages and by concomitantly stripping women of their property, rights as citizens, and full protection under the law, the nation-state was thus the major guarantor of gender hierarchy. Simultaneously, an ideology developed in which this marital form of theft from women was actually described as romantic love. Heterosexual romantic love replaced the older idea of marriage as simply a procreative unit involving the familial organization of production. Thus, while the nation-state enshrined women's impoverishment, men's chivalry and devotion to the weaker sex was said to ensure women's and children's well-being.

As the nation-state form spread to once colonized regions of the world, these gendered and heterosexualized values often spread along with it, though sometimes with less theft of women's wages and property. From the late nineteenth century on, nationalist men and women in India, Egypt, and Iran—to name a few—demanded independence from European control or influence to forge new nation-states that could thrive in the modernizing world. Feminists in these countries joined forces with their nationalist brothers because these men often enshrined improvement in the condition of women as a centerpiece of nation-building. The goal, in the words of one nineteenth-century Iranian reformer, was "to bring [women] out of darkness and ignorance into the open field of the city of humanity and civility" (Najmabadi, p. 186). Modernization in the form of nation-building demanded an end to female degradation and its conversion into women's partnership as good wives and informed mothers to the nation's citizens—but always in the gendered conditions whereby the more powerful male citizen would protect them.

As work in the global marketplace became a force for the modernization of nation-states, movements arose to eliminate markers of femininity such as bound feet and headscarves. Feminists around the world found, however, that once nation-building had been achieved, women remained subordinated, and men's privileges were once again guaranteed. The new version of gendered privilege for men was taken as a particular betrayal, especially among women who participated fully in the anticolonial struggles after World War II. In Kenya, women fought alongside men in the Mau Mau movement, while in Vietnam they had fully engaged the French and U.S. forces from the 1940s through the 1970s.

Politics throughout this period were generally deemed masculine, and indeed heterosexual. John F. Kennedy, for example, had extreme difficulty interacting with the Indian prime minister Jawaharlal Nehru because he wore skirts and flowers. Where women were politically active, it was outside formal institutions, including the food riots and feminist protests of the nineteenth and early twentieth centuries.

This informal politics has continued to the present. During the Brazilian dictatorship in the 1980s, women living in the slums of São Paulo took action in their neighborhoods to improve health and other sanitary conditions by arranging for the pickup of garbage and the cleaning of streets. They organized consciousness-raising sessions and informal schools to help themselves learn to read so that they could be more informed and more effective in their activism, but this activism gendered the informal political realm as increasingly feminine. "I think we women should participate in political parties, not just the popular movements, because we can learn a lot more but most women . . . aren't interested," reported a twenty-three-year-old after moving from neighborhood to national politics (Smith, p. 89).

The military regimes in Argentina and Chile were similarly gendered male, while in protests against them women used their situation as mothers (such as the Mothers of the Plaza de Mayo in Argentina) to demand the release of their children or the return of their bodies. Those regimes also used gendered forms of torture, as did those during the civil wars in the former Yugoslavia, raping and otherwise torturing women civilians sexually. It remains to be seen whether the increasing number of women heads of state since the end of World War II has worked a permanent regendering of politics.

[*See also* Anorexia; Body, The; Clothing; Dieting; Empire and Imperialism; Femininity; Feminism; Gender and Empire; Masculinity; Sexuality; *and* Transgender Issues.]

BIBLIOGRAPHY

Bederman, Gail. *Manliness and Civilization: A Cultural History of Gender and Race in the United States, 1880–1917*. Chicago: University of Chicago Press, 1995.

Ferro, Katarina, and Margit Wolfsberger, eds. *Gender and Power in the Pacific: Women's Strategies in a World of Change*. Münster, Germany, and London: Lit, 2003.

Kaplan, Temma. *Taking Back the Streets: Women, Youth, and Direct Democracy*. Berkeley: University of California Press, 2004.

Kent, Susan Kingsley. *Gender and Power in Britain, 1640–1990*. London: Routledge, 1999.

Mann, Susan. *Precious Records: Women in China's Long Eighteenth Century*. Stanford, Calif.: Stanford University Press, 1997.

McDevitt, Patrick F. *May the Best Man Win: Sport, Masculinity, and Nationalism in Great Britain and the Empire, 1880–1935*. New York: Palgrave Macmillan, 2004.

Meade, Teresa A., and Merry E. Wiesner-Hanks. *A Companion to Gender History*. Oxford: Blackwell, 2004.

Najmabadi, Afsaneh. *Women with Mustaches and Men without Beards: Gender and Sexual Anxieties of Iranian Modernity*. Berkeley: University of California Press, 2005.

Ouzgane, Lahoucine, and Robert Morrell, eds. *African Masculinities: Men in Africa from the Late Nineteenth Century to the Present*. New York: Palgrave Macmillan, 2005.

Sinha, Mrinalini. *Specters of Mother India: The Global Restructuring of an Empire*. Durham, N.C.: Duke University Press, 2006.

Smith, Bonnie G., ed. *Global Feminisms since 1945*. London: Routledge, 2000.

BONNIE G. SMITH

Gender Ideals in Britain

Since 1986 or so scholars have begun to appreciate the power of gender analysis in studying how systems of authority were created, operated, and in many cases persist. It is important to draw a distinction between women's and gender history, as they are not necessarily the same project. Women's history is concerned with writing women's stories—the important roles that women played in past events, systems that circumscribed their participation, and their resistance to these systems. In ways that may overlap with women's history, gender history studies how ideas about sexual difference have been formulated and used to create and justify other hierarchies, of politics, society, culture, science, and economy. It takes as a fundamental point that traits apparently indicating "gender" are not self-evident and unchanging phenomena but rather *constructed* ideals—in other words, not based on biological "fact" but on cultural and social views that shift with time and place and usually work to prescribe sexual difference rather than observe it. Because "gender" comes

from thinking about sexual *difference*, to study gender is to study how the range of ideas about both femininity *and* masculinity have been forged and reworked over time. In studying how society decides on, for example, who gets to vote or who gets to own property, scholars have come to realize that ideas about gender have often overlapped with ideas about race, class, the nation, empire, and sexuality. Anxiety about the permanency of male-dominated power structures often led to concerns about the general makeup of British authority and identity, at home and abroad.

Separate Spheres. The most influential gender ideal in the 1800s was that of "separate spheres." Most incarnations of this ideology adhered to this model: the public or political sphere was deemed masculine and best suited for men to participate in; the private or domestic sphere was feminized, and women were valued as its superintendents, so-called angels of the house. Within this sphere, women were to create for their families and themselves a space of respectability, taste, comfort, and spiritual and moral uplift. By remaining in a cloistered space, their feminine "virtue"—compassion, chastity, piety, and political naïveté—was to be nurtured and protected from the violence of life in the "real" (or "masculine") world of war, labor, poverty, crime, commerce, and politics. Husbands, fathers, and sons, as "breadwinners," were expected to provide the means by which women could establish their separate sphere. Men who could not serve as the major wage earner of the family were ridiculed as "improper" men; women who found that they had to work outside the home were deemed unrespectable: sexually promiscuous and morally corrupt. These women were said to exhibit a dangerous kind of femininity, one that played on long-held, negative depictions of Eve in the Garden of Eden, whose ambition and desire resulted in humanity being expelled from paradise. Beginning in 1780 and into the 1830s, these ideals were arduously asserted, indicating how important contemporaries considered the inculcation of gender roles for the stability of the British imperial nation.

In the late eighteenth century, economic trends came together to produce the consumer, financial, and industrial revolutions. Changes in farming techniques, land management, increased urbanization, and participation in the lucrative imperial-colonial trades in slaves, tobacco, and sugar, as well as the development of modern banking systems, meant that there was a lot of wealth coming into the metropole and more to be made by investing in trade and factories. Just as emerging middling classes had more to spend, goods such as tobacco, cloth, spices, and household wares from Asia and the West Indies poured into European markets. The factory system developed rapidly; instead of producing piecework from their homes according to their own schedules, laborers were hired to work under supervision in factories, using heavy machinery. Women, having always played a fundamental role to the success of a household's economy, could now earn and spend wages *outside* the home, independent of their husbands or fathers, and unprecedented numbers entered the "public sphere." Alongside these unsettling economic changes were political ones: the establishment of a constitutional monarchy in 1688 indicated to contemporary intellectuals that Britain was following a "liberal" path, in line with other Enlightenment ideas of rational thought, industrial capitalism, and responsible government. By the 1780s, "social justice" movements advocated the end of the slave trade, and radicals such as Mary Wollstonecraft proposed female suffrage. This was also the time of unprecedented political revolutions and war, namely in the United States (1775–1783), France (1789–1815), and Haiti (1791–1804). As British imperial authority collapsed in America, a monarchy-led class structure similar to Britain's was violently discarded in France, and slaves and former slaves, upon whom a great portion of the British economy rested, successfully revolted in Haiti against French authority. For many it seemed that all traditional bastions of authority were crumbling. Those who sought to preserve the status quo in Great Britain channeled their anxieties into discussions of gender, attempting to combat upheaval by more clearly delineating how men and women ought to behave, formulating an ideology of separate spheres with a middle-class bias. Frowning upon women working outside of the home regardless of their economic situations, this ideology derogated female factory workers and highly visible monarchs like Charlotte Sophia (of England) and Marie-Antoinette (of France) alike. Victoria came to the throne in 1837, and the conundrum of her reign became the difficulty of exhibiting respectable femininity while being so clearly in the public eye. The concept of separate spheres was so pervasive that it was even taken up within the working classes: Chartists, organizers for workers' rights, pressed for legislation that would limit the number of women in factories, arguing that for working males to perform their chivalrous roles as "proper" men they needed to be the breadwinners of the household.

Gender and Empire. The separate spheres ideology, though powerful, was a fiction. Women continued to perform crucial wage-earning roles for the family outside the home and to intervene in politics, by lobbying their husbands or fathers and even directly investing in the market economy. Moreover, as is evident with the Chartists, men and women manipulated the separate sphere ideology to suit their own politics. As the public sphere was thought to be brutal in nature, a premium was placed on the "civilizing influences" of the domestic sphere to create men of rationality *and* compassion. It was this idealization of "home" and the domestic as the seat of British civilization that attempted to crystallize respectable white, middle-class womanhood as *the* symbol of all that was progressive about Britain, fostering the era of the "cult of domesticity," as some historians have termed it. Cultures across the world that did not share Britain's separate sphere ideology were ranked as less civilized. In this conception, imperialism was condoned for the sake of civilizing other cultures, and enabled mainly white, middle-class women to assert themselves in national-imperial politics. Beginning in the 1780s and eventuating in the illegalization of slavery in imperial Britain in 1833, the abolitionist movement owed much of its success to female supporters who, among other things, organized consumer boycotts of such staples as slave-produced sugar and tea. Female public intervention was justified by arguing, in extremely racist terms, that Africans were "childlike" and "barbarous," requiring Britons to parent and civilize them—areas that respectable women were idealized as having expertise in. This linkage of respectable femininity with the "civilizing mission" came to be an important way for feminists after 1850 to claim their right to participate in British politics, particularly following colonial unrest in India, Jamaica, Ireland, and southern Africa. They were able to gain support by arguing, in pro-imperial, racist terms, that if the metropole allowed nonwhite, colonized peoples to have a say in their government, how was Britain justified in denying respectable white women political rights?

By the 1850s, the cult of domesticity was a gender ideology heavily entwined with the class system and an ever-developing sense of superiority that "white" Britons attained from racial ideology. Bound up in Britain's role as a world imperial power, acts of resistance to British authority in the colonies had the potential to disrupt social hierarchies in Britain and other colonies. Exaggerated reports of mass rapes of British women during the so-called Great Mutiny in India (1857) led to widespread panic in the metropole, cultivating a pervasive sentiment that to defile respectable white femininity was to defile Britishness. This, in turn, challenged definitions of British masculinity: "unmanly" Indian soldiers were not only rebelling against supposedly superior masculine authority but exposing it as an ineffective protector of "proper" femininity. Heightening this terror was the idea that sex between British women and Indian men could result in mixed-race progeny, disrupting racial hierarchies. Fear of racial mixing or "contamination" at home and in the colonies manifested itself in the Contagious Diseases Acts (or CD Acts) of the 1860s, legislation that blamed "public women" and prostitution for Britain's social ills by contaminating manhood. Feminist groups organized as never before against these acts, exposing in the first instance the state's double standard in regards to painting female sexual desire as improper and dangerous while deeming male sexual desire natural and masculine. In the 1880s, as the economy faltered in a worldwide economic depression, more women had to find work outside the home, increasing their public visibility.

Medicine. Sexuality and the physiological differences between the sexes was a key concern of nineteenth- and early-twentieth-century medicine, a discipline that provided biological arguments for dominant gender ideals and served to naturalize the link between masculinity and authority. Sex and gender was conflated and the figure of "woman" was pathologically described as being controlled by her ovaries, at once possessing dangerous sexual urges that could compel her toward hysteria or, still at the mercy of her body, lacking all sexual desire and only living by her instincts to nurture. The male body, in contrast, was heralded as a specimen of perfection, naturally dominant, and possessing a healthy sexuality.

Twentieth Century and Beyond. Many scholars have identified the turn of the twentieth century as a "crisis of masculinity"—a moment of confusion over what constituted "proper" masculine roles and authority. From the Boer War through the World Wars, men were expected to be physically fit enough to be successful soldiers: the Boy Scout movement and physical education curricula were fostered, national nutritional and education services were implemented, and boys were encouraged to hone their masculinity through sports or by spending time in the wilderness. As men were deployed on the battlefields, women became valued members of the workforce at home, and the successes of the feminist movement as well as patriotic war-work efforts were partially recognized in 1918 when women over thirty who owned a minimum standard of property won the vote. At the end of World War II, with the end of British empire in sight and the country requiring extensive reconstruction, many

contemporaries deemed it important to reestablish gender roles as they had been before the wars, yet this was impossible: civil rights, feminist, and nationalist movements both at home and abroad continually forced the nation, particularly in the 1960s and early 1970s, to reevaluate its ideas about gender, race, sexuality, class, and Britishness. On an economic downswing in the late 1970s and 1980s, a majority of voters were compelled toward Margaret Thatcher's platform of fiscal conservatism and a "return to Victorian values." Like Victoria in the nineteenth century, Thatcher was able to espouse gender ideals that would have been familiar to many Victorians—nuclear families headed by a male breadwinner with his wife as caregiver—while living a different reality. As scholars continue to explore the many ways in which gender ideals are culturally contingent, it is instructive to see how receptive the public is to biological, often genetic, arguments about the innate differences between the sexes or innate sexual proclivities. In other words, the battles between "nature versus nurture" advocates continue and gender ideals remain central to constructions of Britishness. When *Alison Lapper Pregnant* was unveiled in Trafalgar Square in September 2005, some heralded the sculpture—of a British artist born without arms, depicted naked and pregnant—as a long-overdue celebration of the strength of womanhood in Britain. Others criticized the work for enshrining femininity-as-motherhood and masculinity-as-protector, juxtaposed as it was with martial representations of Lord Nelson and other "Great Men" in the square. Just as gendered ideals in Britain display important changes (as well as continuities), the statue itself was not a permanent display and left Trafalgar in 2007.

[*See also* CD Acts; Chartism; Civilizing Mission, *subentry* British Empire; Domesticity; Empire and Imperialism, *subentry* The British Colonial Empire; Femininity; Feminism, *subentry* Britain; Gender and Empire; Masculinity, *subentry* Overview; Sexuality; Suffrage, *subentry* Britain; *and* Victorianism.]

BIBLIOGRAPHY

Burton, Antoinette. *Burdens of History: British Feminists, Indian Women, and Imperial Culture, 1865–1915.* Chapel Hill: University of North Carolina Press, 1994. Best-known study of the linkages between British feminism and imperialism, particularly in the case of India.

Clark, Anna. *The Struggle for the Breeches: Gender and the Making of the British Working Class.* Berkeley: University of California Press, 1995. Excellent study of gender, the Chartist movement, poorhouse legislation, and workers' movements.

Davidoff, Leonore, and Catherine Hall. *Family Fortunes: Men and Women of the English Middle Class, 1780–1850*. Chicago: University of Chicago Press, 1987. Classic work on "separate sphere" ideology.

Hall, Catherine. *Civilising Subjects: Colony and Metropole in the English Imagination, 1830–1867*. Chicago: University of Chicago Press, 2002. Building from her earlier groundbreaking work on separate spheres, this argues the importance of placing gender and politics in an imperial context.

Kingsley Kent, Susan. *Gender and Power in Britain, 1640–1990*. London and New York: Routledge, 1999. An excellent overview, complete with suggestions for further reading in specific areas.

Midgley, Clare. *Women against Slavery: The British Campaigns, 1780–1870*. London and New York: Routledge, 1992. Detailed look at gender and race dynamics in women's abolitionist campaigns.

Tosh, John. *A Man's Place: Masculinity and the Middle-Class Home in Victorian England*. New Haven, Conn.: Yale University Press, 1999. The benchmark work on masculinity in Britain.

Walkowitz, Judith R. *City of Dreadful Delight: Narratives of Sexual Danger in Late-Victorian London*. Chicago: University of Chicago Press, 1992. Best-known work on prostitution, misogyny, the Contagious Diseases Act, and the Jack the Ripper murders in 1888.

DANIELLE C. KINSEY

Gender Relations in East Asia

In modern East Asian history, attitudes toward gender have been tightly bound with nationalism and shifting notions of national identity. In the nineteenth century, this could be seen in the subordinate position of women throughout the region, which led many Western critics to label the region as socially "backward." This in turn prompted many male reformers to argue that women needed to be educated to be better mothers of the nation, that is, the next generation of sons.

Notions of gender, however, were always more complicated and varied than either critics or defenders suggested. Although women largely lacked property, inheritance, and other legal rights, their opportunities and stature, as well as men's, was primarily a function of economic class and social position. Nevertheless, there did exist throughout the region a generic Confucian gender ideal in which women were treated paternally and men were encouraged to seek a rich Confucian cultural education and martial training. In practice, these attributes were commonly separated. Samurai warriors in late Tokugawa Japan (1603–1867), despite their role as urban administrators, cultivated and propagated martial ideals as normative male virtues, while Chinese officials during the Qing dynasty (1644–1911) cultivated the stooped posture and long fingernails of a scholar to set themselves apart from the rough, less cultivated military classes.

In the late nineteenth century the Japanese Westernizing reformer Fukuzawa Yukichi declared that the untamed and unrefined energy of the idealized samurai of the Tokugawa era was inappropriate for the new era of civilization. He and other reformers identified civilized gentility as an essential component of success in the new modern era. Many others criticized the dandified Westernized male ideal, arguing that it conflicted with native notions of masculinity and culture. The conflict over gender definition persisted in Japan at least through World War II. In the Meiji era (1868–1912), female gender identity was given a new, much more rigid subordinating legal definition in the new civil code. Not only were women denied property and other rights but also their role was increasingly enshrined as that of being "good wives and wise mothers." Under this strict division of gender roles, women's domestic labor was construed as contributing to national aims. In contrast to this emphasis on ordered home-front domesticity, one feature of Japanese imperial expansion into Manchuria, Korea, China, and Russia in the early twentieth century was the presence of many single Japanese women coming from poor backgrounds and working as entertainers and prostitutes. These women served the front-line troops of colonial expansion, Korean observers wrote.

The presence in East Asia of Western women working as teachers, doctors, and missionary wives resulted in the misperception that in the West, men and women had equal status, and this encouraged East Asian feminists to insist on careers for women, including military careers (as soldiers in China, as Red Cross volunteers in Japan), in addition to more internationally accepted women's roles as teachers, nurses, occasionally doctors, writers, and journalists. Meanwhile, increasing numbers of working-class women were employed in city factories, particularly in the textile industry. These arduous jobs were seen as a step up from family farming, as they gave a degree of financial independence and social mobility. For Japanese men, the shared experience of military service was a rite of passage into full citizenship, and also served as a model for the authority structures of the overwhelmingly male industrial conglomerates (*chaebl* in Korea, *zaibatsu* in Japan). By contrast, the domestic obedience demanded of girls was usually considered sufficient preparation for factory work, in which women were a vital source of the cheap labor that powered industrialization.

Though women won suffrage rights following World War II, South Korea and Japan constructed nations as patrilineal communities of men for which women were necessary but subordinate. The resulting androcentric economic development produced pronounced gender inequalities, reflected in everything from the use of gendered language to the expectation that women would give up work when they started a family, and the pressure on married men to work long hours with the support of their wives, whom they were expected to support financially. Since the Asian Financial Crisis of 1997, however, there are fewer salaried jobs for men, and recent equal-opportunity legislation in Japan has made it illegal to define women's jobs as noncareer. From the early twentieth century, feminists have contested the boundaries of their social roles in such efforts as the "housewife-feminist" and "fighting women" movements in the 1970s. Even so, women's employment rates by age still follow an M-shaped curve, with many women leaving jobs to care for children throughout their school years.

In China, despite state support for women's work rights, women were still expected to sacrifice their aspirations to support their husbands' work in the service of the public good. This was made particularly clear in the mid-1950s, when high urban unemployment led the Communist Party to encourage women to "go back home." Since the 1980s, reforming state-owned enterprises again laid off large numbers of women. Images from the 1950s through the 1970s of sturdy militia women and working women have been replaced with fashionable, sexually attractive urban consumers. Devaluation of women's economic contributions has been accompanied by a reemphasis on their roles as wives, mothers, and supporters of men's economic activity.

Throughout the region, male homosexuality had been widely recognized and acknowledged, and in Tokugawa Japan, love between adult samurai warriors and young boys was widely idealized. Following the Meiji Restoration in 1868, male homosexuality came to be officially defined as a perversion, but Christian moralizing in Japan on sexual restraint and the dangers of excessive promiscuity or masturbation were considered exaggerated. In China, anal intercourse between males had been prohibited for centuries. Nevertheless, Buddhist and Daoist monks had the reputation of frequently having liaisons with novice youths, whom they idealized in feminine terms. A more visible form of homosexual activity was relationships with the men who played female roles in traditional theater, roles that were prohibited to women. In Korea, despite references to such relations in a variety of popular-culture venues, they were much less accepted.

Although historical references to lesbianism are rare, by 1911 two lesbian couples' attempts at suicides in Japan became media sensations, and female "passionate friendships" made frequent appearances in the new women's periodical literature. Around the same time in China, literature and the Western vocabulary of (homo)sexuality was being translated, often via Japanese. The increasing availability of single-sex schools for both boys and girls doubtless contributed opportunities for same-sex relationships. Additionally, some working-class women, having been sent to work in the coastal treaty-port cities of South China, chose to reject marriage in favor of communal life in "sisterhoods" with other women. To enter such communities, women often had to pay back monies that their families would have received from future in-laws, and also undergo a ceremony in which they vowed never to marry.

The idea that sexual identity defines a person's social identity is extremely rare in East Asia. Only since the late 1980s has such a notion become visible in the form of gay bars, associations of publicly gay citizens, and gay periodical literature. In many cases, these institutions were initiated by American or European homosexuals during extended stays in East Asia and have grown from these beginnings. There is a nascent movement for gay rights, but the vast majority of those living nontraditional gender roles do so under the radar of public visibility.

[See also Feminism, subentry East Asia; Footbinding; Gender and Empire; Homosexuality; Lesbianism; Paternalism, subentry East Asia; and Women, subentry East Asia.]

BIBLIOGRAPHY

Brownell, Susan, and Jeffrey N. Wasserstrom, eds. *Chinese Femininities, Chinese Masculinities: A Reader.* Berkeley: University of California Press, 2002.

Intersections: Gender, History, and Culture in the Asian Context. http://wwwsshe.murdoch.edu.au/intersections. An online refereed journal on gender in Asia.

Kendall, Laurel, ed. *Under Construction: The Gendering of Modernity, Class, and Consumption in the Republic of Korea.* Honolulu: University of Hawai'i Press, 2002.

Kim, Elaine H., and Chungmoo Choi, eds. *Dangerous Women: Gender and Korean Nationalism.* London: Routledge, 1997.

McLelland, Mark, and Romit Dasgupta, eds. *Genders, Transgenders, and Sexualities in Japan.* London and New York: Routledge, 2005.

Molony, Barbara, and Kathleen Uno, eds. *Gendering Modern Japanese History.* Cambridge, Mass.: Harvard University Asia Center, 2005.

Roberson, James, and Nobue Suzuki, eds. *Men and Masculinities in Contemporary Japan: Dislocating the Salaryman Doxa.* London and New York: RoutledgeCurzon, 2003.

Rofel, Lisa. *Other Modernities: Gendered Yearnings in China after Socialism.* Berkeley: University of California Press, 1999.

BRIDIE ANDREWS MINEHAN

Gender Relations in Latin America

"Marianismo" and "machismo" are terms used to describe gender-based honor and shame in a value system of Mediterranean culture. This value system has unified Mediterranean culture from ancient times to the present, from Iberia through Sicily and Greece to the Islamic states of North Africa and the Middle East, and Iberian conquistadores brought this system with them to America. Sexuality and power are at the core of the value system. For men the system defines honor and specifies relations among men. Because female sexual behavior defines honor in the social group, it is strongly policed. The system places great importance on virginity, which in Catholic and Orthodox traditions relates to the Virgin Mary.

Mary represents ideal womanhood because she was sinless, sexually pure, and the perfect suffering mother. Latin American society has expected women to be like Mary, hence the term "marianismo." The Latin American patriarchal family, headed by a father who dominates his wife and children, is central to Latin American gender ideology. The patriarchal social system has rested on a firm foundation of law, culture, and religion. According to this social system, men are allegedly morally and intellectually superior to women. Men guide and control; women obey. Machismo, or manliness, defines how men should conduct themselves in the public arena and includes a sexual dimension that permits, even requires, men to pursue and conquer many women. The object of this pursuit is not love, which is seen as a weakness, but possession of the woman, especially a woman under the protection of another man.

The Enlightenment brought liberal notions about women to Latin America through the works of French philosophes and Pedro Rodríguez, Count of Campomanes, who wrote that women should contribute their labor to society. Schooling opportunities for girls increased, and in major cities, *tertulias*—cultural societies modeled on the French salon—provided women with a new mode of socializing. During the Latin American wars of independence, women transformed *tertulias* into political organizations to fund and support revolutionary armies. Independence in Latin America was a family affair that required the mobilization of all resources, financial and human. When men went off to war, women stayed behind to manage diminished estates and petition the royal government on behalf of their kinsmen.

The newly independent states extended educational opportunities to women and broadened their roles in civil society. The Buenos Aires experiment was the most ambitious because it authorized a women's benevolent society to direct and finance female education. Governments in Peru and Bolivia established *colegios de educandas* (schools for girls), which provided free secular education to girls from the late 1820s. The triumph of liberalism over conservative clerical forces in the late nineteenth century opened secondary and university education to women. Liberals hoped to replace inherited codes of honor and shame with a cult of domesticity, which recognized women as morally superior. Liberals believed that a scientific secular education would wean women from their dependency on religion and make them better mothers and wives, while also preparing them for eventual full citizenship.

Liberal regimes that supported limited representative democracy also supported rights for women, and a feminist movement began among middle-class women educated in public schools. Liberals rewrote marriage laws to give women greater legal authority over their children and common property, supported procedures for dissolving marriage, and eventually approved divorce. Liberal regimes equated national health with that of the lower-class family and addressed themselves to sanitary housing, the proper nutrition of children, maternity benefits for women, and the medical licensing of prostitutes.

Entrenched social inequality throughout the region radicalized politics in the early twentieth century and mobilized women first through labor unions and later through peasant organizations. But the achievements of radical politics were limited. Revolutionary Mexico and Peronist Argentina equated orderly family life with an orderly state based on patriarchal values. In Chile, Marxist unions constructed a male identity based on worker solidarity and discipline, but they placed women in a dependent position within the working-class family. Marxist gender codes stressed a family wage but discriminated against wage-earning women, who faced gender-specific problems such as low wages, sexual harassment, and single motherhood. Fear of the influence of the Catholic Church remained great throughout Latin America, and male politicians assumed that priests would most influence how women voted. Hence it was not until 1961 that all women were enfranchised. Despite advances in education and civil rights, traditional sex roles remained unchanged, and women's sexuality still defined family honor. The Cuban Revolution used literacy and reeducation campaigns to change thinking about women's social roles. Its rhetoric addressed responsible fatherhood, and it passed legislation that requires husbands to perform half of domestic tasks. It liberalized access to divorce, birth control, and abortion. Despite much progress, machismo remains an integral part of Cuban culture and compatible with socialism.

Relational feminism, with its emphasis on the rights of women as women and their preferred role of motherhood, has dominated in Latin America through the twentieth century to the beginning of the twenty-first. It shares roots with forms of Continental European feminism and differs from the Anglo-American feminist tradition, which is based on individual rights regardless of gender. In the 1970s a new women's movement emerged in Latin America to confront massive state violence inflicted by brutal dictatorships. Many activists ranked gender inequality below ethnic and class inequality. Women organized to defend human rights and to demand the return of "disappeared" children. In international forums Latin American feminists joined with representatives from Africa and Asia to support economic development. Because so many Latin American women live in poverty, and because of a tradition of class-based politics, Latin American feminism must address class issues more than North American or European feminism does.

Latin American feminism at the beginning of the twenty-first century is maternal, community-based, and pragmatic. It views motherhood as political and has used motherhood to build coalitions across political and class lines. Viewing economic inequality as a complex problem, it partners with international agencies that provide foreign funds to raise the standard of living. The resilience of machismo as a cultural phenomenon has brought many poor Latinas to Pentecostalism—converts are 63 percent women—because it censures abusive male behavior, which drains money from family income.

[*See also* Gender and Empire; Machismo; Marianismo; Marriage and Divorce, *subentry* Latin America; Masculinity, *subentry* Latin America; Prostitution, *subentry* Latin America; Women, *subentry* Latin America; *and* Women's Suffrage, *subentry* The Female Vote in Latin America.]

BIBLIOGRAPHY

Deutsch, Sandra McGee. "Gender and Sociopolitical Change in Twentieth-Century Latin America." *Hispanic American Historical Review* 71, no. 2 (1991): 259–306. An important essay that compares Argentina, Mexico, Chile, and Cuba.

Dore, Elizabeth, and Maxine Molyneux, eds. *Hidden Histories of Gender and the State in Latin America.* Durham, N.C.: Duke University Press, 2000. A collection of essays documenting how the state constructs gender in various nations.

González, Victoria, and Karen Kampwirth, eds. *Radical Women in Latin America, Left and Right.* University Park: Pennsylvania State University Press, 2001. A collection of essays documenting contemporary feminism in various nations.

Hahner, June E. *Emancipating the Female Sex: The Struggle for Women's Rights in Brazil, 1850–1940.* Durham, N.C.: Duke University Press, 1990. An excellent country study.

Hallum, Anne Motley. "Taking Stock and Building Bridges: Feminism, Women's Movements, and Pentecostalism in Latin America." *Latin America Research Review* 38, no. 1 (2003): 169–188. A literature review that argues that Pentecostalism fits into newer approaches of feminism and women's movements.

Klubock, Thomas Miller. *Contested Communities: Class, Gender, and Politics in Chile's El Teniente Copper Mine, 1904–1951.* Durham, N.C.: Duke University Press, 1996. An excellent study of gendered working-class culture.

Lavrin, Asunción. *Women, Feminism, and Social Change in Argentina, Chile, and Uruguay, 1890–1940.* Lincoln: University of Nebraska Press, 1995. Excellent for breath, quality scholarship, and comparison.

GERTRUDE M. YEAGER

Gender Relations in Southeast Asia

Gender roles in premodern Southeast Asia were complex, with women enjoying some degree of freedom owing to their often significant role in political and economic activity, particularly in times of crisis. Yet women were still expected to fulfill male expectations of being socially submissive preservers of tradition. In the modern period, these relations persisted, but their nature became increasingly determined by such new forces as European colonization and decolonization, the efforts of Southeast Asians to develop national cultural identities, and, since the mid-1990s, globalization. While Southeast Asian men and women have participated in these processes, it is women who have borne the burden of continuing tradition in the face of sudden changes. This burden has hindered women's access to education, employment, and political participation.

The imposition of European control and social norms on Southeast Asian cultures in the eighteenth and nineteenth centuries had far-reaching consequences. Europeans foisted their own patriarchal frameworks on Southeast Asian societies, precluding women from areas in which they had exercised relative autonomy in the past. This included women heads of household and landowners. At the same time, many colonial administrations did nothing to alter the traditional practices of the local elite in many societies, practices that privileged men over women, such as denying women equal access to education. Gender inequality grew as these local elite values, which drew on both traditional and modern-colonial gender relations, became the model for people at all levels of society.

European colonial populations found what to them was the exotic and comparatively free sexual life of Southeast Asians a pleasant contrast from the strict social mores of their home countries. However, the relationships they formed with local women were not looked upon favorably by the metropolitan government, as they yielded children who were neither European nor Southeast Asian but a hybrid that represented a threat to the formerly clear divisions between metropole (the seat of the empire) and colony. Métissage effectively undermined the perceived superiority of the white race. Southeast Asian women, although submissive, also compromised social boundaries, as their influence over European men negated the presumed superiority of the colonizing peoples over the colonized.

As nationalist movements sought to develop an identity separate from that of the colony, local traditions, going back to times before subjugation, were resurrected as an intrinsic component of the new cultural character. Most Southeast Asian precolonial literature privileged men and relegated women to the roles of wives and mothers. Gender roles in precolonial society were taken up as models for societies free of imperial presence. In this way values and traditions would be maintained. Thus in Southeast Asian revolutionary and independence movements, women were often mobilized, yet after nationalist objectives had been achieved, their status always reverted to one of inferiority.

Some postcolonial governments sought to enshrine the position of women in state ideology. New Order Indonesia, for example, wished to establish gender equality within the boundaries of women's "natural" roles as wives and mothers, through an ideology known as *ibuism* (motherism), which gave a woman total freedom to pursue the well-being of her family, group, social class, work environment, or the state itself, but without expectation of recognition, privilege, or elevated prestige. Similar ideologies have existed throughout much of Southeast Asia in the modern period, legitimized by texts drawn from precolonial times, such as the "Cbpab Srei" (Code of Conduct for Women in Cambodia). Women thus were made the guardians of cultural aspects deemed to be traditional in the new national cultural identity.

Ideologies and constructs that seek to restrict women to domestic life have constrained the ability of Southeast Asian women to acquire an education. In most Southeast Asian countries, female education after primary schooling is lamentably low: only 2 to 3 percent of women in Cambodia and Laos go on to tertiary education. Other nations have figures ranging from 9 percent in Vietnam to 38 percent in Thailand. Singapore is the exception, with a relatively high rate of female tertiary education, exceeding 70 percent. Women's literacy rates are similarly low compared to those of men. This hinders women in being selected for civil-service positions, from which they could launch political careers. Governments claim that low female education and literacy rates reflect traditional perspectives toward women and education. Poor families send boys rather than girls to school, as it is believed that they will have better chances of getting jobs and that girls are better placed assisting their mothers in domestic concerns. Moreover, the education infrastructure past primary school is so poor in most Southeast Asian countries that attending secondary school often means a long commute between home and school, which is perceived as dangerous for girls. Yet these same governments do nothing to overturn "traditional" views that result in gender disparity.

The expectations that women embrace roles as wives and mothers and the lack of consistent access to education for girls has led to a dearth of women in Southeast Asian political life. The portion of women officeholders in any Southeast Asian country at any time since independence has never been higher than 10 percent, although all Southeast Asian nations ratified the right of women to vote and stand for election in the 1930s, 1940s, and 1950s, with the exception of Brunei, which has not recognized these rights. A handful of women have been elected to the highest political position in their respective countries, but all of the women concerned—Corazón Aquino, Megawati Sukarnoputri, Gloria Macapagal-Arroyo, Aung San Suu Kyi—were connected to men who were key political figures themselves. In the construct of Southeast Asian women as repositories of tradition, these women embodied the values of their fathers and husbands, and hence it was thought that they would perpetuate these same values.

Outside the political arena, women are expected to participate in the same activities as men in agriculture and industry. Women farmers constitute a large proportion of agricultural labor, ranging from 35 percent in the Philippines to more than 60 percent in Thailand. Yet because of their association with domesticity, women are also expected to care for children, elderly family members—and their husbands, who may be expected to perform similar agricultural tasks by day but have no expectations placed upon them after the "working" day is done. Work in the domestic sphere is also viewed as unimportant in comparison with the "real work" that is remunerated in markets or subsidized by the state, and that is carried out beyond the confines of the home. As the environmental resources that women depend on—such as land close to the home in which to grow food or pasture animals—are destroyed, women must devise new ways to continue to meet their social obligations. This has led to large-scale interregional migration of unskilled female labor.

The sex industry has provided an alternative for women who may have no other means of supporting their families. Other women are coerced. Nearly 70 million women and children have been victims of sex trafficking in Southeast Asia in the last decade alone. This is largely due to the pressures of international and intraregional tourists seeking disease-free sexual partners. Once initiated into the sex industry, women have little choice but to remain, as their prospects for marriage (and a respectable life) vanish. Women's premarital sexual activity, including rape, is seen as indicating a lack of morality on the part of such women, although most Southeast Asian cultures view male patronage of sex workers, often in the company of friends and colleagues, as normal.

The need to maintain a national cultural identity in the face of rapid change has led to an association of women with tradition and of men with modernity in Southeast Asia. As a loss of traditional values would result in a loss of cultural identity, few governments, which are dominated by men, are willing to implement policies that will enforce gender equality.

[*See also* Birth Control, *subentry* Southeast Asia; Feminism, *subentry* Southeast Asia; *and* Gender and Empire.]

BIBLIOGRAPHY

Blackburn, Susan, ed. *Love, Sex, and Power: Women in Southeast Asia.* Clayton, Victoria, Australia: Monash Asia Institute, 2001.

Ireson, Carol J. *Field, Forest, and Family: Women's Work and Power in Rural Laos.* Boulder, Colo.: Westview Press, 1996.

Law, Lisa. *Sex Work in Southeast Asia: The Place of Desire in a Time of AIDS.* London: Routledge, 2000.

Manderson, Lenore, and Linda Rae Bennett, eds. *Violence against Women in Asian Societies.* London: RoutledgeCurzon, 2003.

TRUDY JACOBSEN

GENDER AND EMPIRE. Until the late twentieth century, scholars who studied the history of imperialism and colonialism did not have much to say about the relationship between gender and empire. Beginning in the 1980s,

however, historians became increasingly interested in the ways in which imperial and colonial systems of rule were legitimized and maintained through policies and ideologies based, at least in part, on gender. By "gender," these historians refer not simply to biological sex, but to socially constructed ideas about how people of different sexes are supposed to interact and behave. They argue, indeed, that policies based on ideas about "normal" gender roles and gender hierarchies—even though often implicit and unstated—were fundamental to the maintenance of social boundaries, to policies of divide and rule, and to cultural transformations as a result of the colonial encounter in both the colonies and the imperial home countries.

From the late nineteenth century until the end of World War II, all of the most powerful nation-states in the world, including some who aspired to great power, pursued policies of imperial expansion. These included the European powers of Britain, France, Russia, and—to a lesser extent—Germany, Belgium, and Portugal, as well as the United States and Japan. Between 1885 and 1914, for example, nearly all of Africa was subjected to colonial control by the various European powers, and Britain's empire alone grew to encompass one-quarter of the world's land and population. Yet although the empires of this period dominated much of the globe, they varied dramatically in terms of policy, law, and style of rule. Each empire also exhibited tremendous internal diversity, because there was a variety of types of colonial possessions: some were settler colonies, for example, while others were ruled indirectly through indigenous elites. Some colonies were founded for strategic purposes, while others were important for resource extraction. Colonies also varied widely in terms of the culture, law, and characteristics of their indigenous inhabitants. Yet despite these important differences, ideologies about gender were important to the policies and structure of every colonial system. Indeed, several broad similarities across both space and time can elucidate the ways in which gender functioned to maintain and legitimate empire.

Boundary Maintenance. One of the most common ways that gender ideologies helped maintain colonial rule was in the ways that such ideologies were used to shore up the social and physical boundaries between rulers and ruled. Colonial states—including the Dutch, British, American, German, Belgian, and French—were deeply concerned with the most private affairs of colonial subjects: they cared very much about who was having sex, who was getting married, and who was having children with whom. Colonial governments were especially anxious

Gender and Empire. A Suriname planter and a female slave. Engraving by William Blake in John G. Stedman, *Narrative of a Five Years' Expedition, against the Revolted Negroes of Surinam in Guiana, on the Wild Coast of South America, from the Year 1772 to 1777* (London, 1796).

to regulate sexual contact and marital relations between colonizers and colonized peoples. All colonial governments of this period acknowledged that sexual relationships were bound to occur between colonizing men and indigenous women. In fact, colonial officials believed in the commonly held, deeply gendered belief that men needed to have sex regularly. Accordingly, most colonial states made sexual provisions for its colonizing men through the use of indigenous prostitutes or concubines.

Yet these relationships caused anxiety for colonial governments on two counts. First, many colonial governments feared that intimate sexual contact might cause colonizing men to grow too close to indigenous cultures or, put crudely, that they might "go native." This, colonial officials believed, would undermine colonial claims to cultural superiority, and with that the entire colonial project. Second, colonial officials believed that the children who would inevitably result from colonizer-colonized sexual

relationships would hopelessly blur the line between colonizers and colonized. Were such children members and citizens of the home culture or were they colonial subjects? Did the colonial state owe them special status and rights, or were they to be treated like all other indigenous peoples?

Some colonial states never encouraged long-term, public relationships between colonizers and colonized; the British Indian government, for example, did not encourage such relationships between British men and Indian women, and it did not recognize the children of such unions as British subjects. Other colonial states, like the Dutch East Indies, initially encouraged Dutch men to take concubines but then reversed course in the early twentieth century when it became clear that such relationships—not to mention the thousands of children that resulted from them—made it difficult to maintain the racial and cultural distinctions between the Dutch and the people of the East Indies. In each case, however, ideas about appropriate sexual and/or marital relationships were marshaled to maintain the boundaries between the rulers and the ruled.

Social Control. Ideas about gender were also used by most colonial states—including France, Britain, the United States, Germany, and the Netherlands—as a means of social control. Since most colonial systems were exploitative and often oppressive, colonial states invested a great deal of energy in trying to maintain control over indigenous men who, it was believed, were more likely to rebel than indigenous women were. One way that this control was achieved was by closely monitoring the movements and actions of indigenous men whenever they were in the living and working spaces of the colonizers. A persistent theme in many colonial regimes was the idea that colonized men possessed voracious and brutal sexual appetites, and that they secretly desired to rape European women. The fear of rape, and the need to protect European women from it, hence came to justify the strict control of both colonized men and European women. Colonized men were routinely excluded from positions in which they might have even a remote chance of exercising power over European women. In addition, they often found themselves at risk of severe punishment, and even death, if they were believed to have transgressed the strict social and sexual boundaries that were supposed to separate them from European women. In times of high colonial tension, fears and accusations of rape tended to increase and sometimes prompted the use of state violence against indigenous males.

Divide and Rule. Beliefs about gender also contributed to imperial policies of divide and rule—that is, policies that emphasized differences between subgroups of colonized peoples as a way of minimizing opposition to imperial rule. In places as far-flung as India, Indonesia, Kenya, and Algeria, to mention only a few, such policies encouraged preferential treatment of certain indigenous groups, which tended to pit them against other, less-preferred groups. Moreover, colonizing powers often bestowed favor on groups who seemed to embody colonizers' own notions of ideal masculinity. In British India, for example, the colonial state sought to protect itself by incorporating those men believed to be most manly, most loyal, and most warlike into the Indian army, and to pit such men against the civilian Indian population.

After the mid-nineteenth century the Indian army was increasingly recruited from the Punjab and Nepal, because British officers came to believe that these regions produced the best fighting men in India. Moreover, British officials juxtaposed these manly "martial races" with other Indian groups—especially the Anglicized, middle-class Hindu elite that had grown critical of British rule. Indeed, British officials depicted this elite as effeminate, deceitful, soft, and hysterical in contrast to the hypermasculine martial races. These perceptions of gendered difference were not trivial or superficial. Rather, they encouraged preferential treatment for the martial races, pitted Indian groups against one another, and deeply influenced British policy in India. In this way the employment of gendered language in imperial situations helped prevent indigenous populations from recognizing common interests based on colonial subjugation.

Cultural Transformations Based on Gender. Colonial encounters between rulers and ruled had profound social, cultural, political, and economic effects all over the world. In virtually every colonial encounter the gender ideals of the colonizing powers helped to shape colonial practice, law, and culture. However, the ways in which such ideals were translated into policy depended upon the response of colonized peoples, and thus their effect was neither uniform nor predictable. Moreover, the disruptive effects of the colonial encounter on gender ideals were not a one-way street, because they influenced gender ideals in imperial home countries as well.

In some cases, as in many parts of sub-Saharan Africa, the imposition of colonial law resulted in a deterioration of colonized women's legal status because European law tended to define men as heads of households and to assign to men control of both land and property. In northern Ghana, for example, the implementation of the British judicial system brought about a deterioration in indigenous women's legal status. In particular, colonial rule sought to introduce and enforce the notion that wives were the property of their husbands—a notion that, although foreign to Ghanaian gender ideals, allowed men to claim increasing legal control of their wives. At the same time, African women were not merely passive victims of a patriarchal partnership between colonizers and indigenous males. Rather, African women in many colonial states manipulated colonial court systems for their own benefit, ventured into independent economic enterprises, and moved into new occupations—as teachers or midwives—opened up to them by the colonial encounter.

Colonial encounters also shaped gender relations and gender ideologies in imperial home countries. In Britain, imperialism informed the gender identities of both men and women and often provided the context within which claims about appropriate gender roles were made. A case in point was late-nineteenth-century ideals of British masculinity. In this period, Britain's huge imperial commitments overseas led a number of influential authors, officers, journalists, and artists to insist that British men needed to possess certain characteristics if the empire was to be maintained. Faced with ruling over so much of the world, they argued, British manhood should include physical fitness, self-sacrifice, and the spirit of adventure. In this conception of masculinity there was little room for supposedly feminine qualities such as sensitivity.

[*See also* Colonialism; Empire and Imperialism; Gender; Orientalism; *and* Women.]

BIBLIOGRAPHY

Allman, Jean, Susan Geiger, and Nakanyike Musisi, eds. *Women in African Colonial Histories*. Bloomington: Indiana University Press, 2002. An anthology that charts the effects of colonialism on women's lives in a variety of sub-Saharan countries.

Clancy-Smith, Julia, and Frances Gouda, eds. *Domesticating the Empire: Race, Gender, and Family Life in French and Dutch Colonialism*. Charlottesville: University Press of Virginia, 1998. An anthology that focuses on little-known aspects of the French and Dutch empires.

Dawson, Graham. *Soldier Heroes: British Adventure, Empire, and the Imagining of Masculinities*. London: Routledge, 1994. Explores the ways that empire affected British ideas about masculinity.

Levine, Philippa, ed. *Gender and Empire*. Oxford and New York: Oxford University Press, 2004. An anthology that explores the relationship between gender and empire from the eighteenth to the twentieth century and in a variety of colonial contexts.

Sangari, Kumkum, and Sudesh Vaid, eds. *Recasting Women: Essays in Indian Colonial History*. New Brunswick, N.J.: Rutgers University Press, 1989. An anthology that explores Indian women's lives under colonialism.

Sinha, Mrinalini. *Colonial Masculinity: The "Manly Englishman" and the "Effeminate Bengali" in the Late Nineteenth Century*. Manchester, U.K.: Manchester University Press, 1995. Takes as its subject the British practice of representing Indian middle-class men as the polar opposite of virile British masculinity.

Streets, Heather. *Martial Races: The Military, Race, and Masculinity in British Imperial Culture, 1857–1914.* Manchester, U.K.: Manchester University Press, 2004. Explores the effects of selective recruiting on the Indian and British armies as well as on British popular culture.

HEATHER STREETS

GENERAL AGREEMENT ON TARIFFS AND TRADE.

A supposedly temporary agreement that lived much longer than originally planned, the General Agreement on Tariffs and Trade (GATT) provided a structure for the liberalization of trade from 1 January 1948 through 31 December 1995, when it was replaced by the more comprehensive World Trade Organization (WTO). International trading relations collapsed with the shock of the Great Depression and the response of widespread protection by means of beggar-thy-neighbor trade policies, which continued through World War II. Many policymakers believed that an international agreement among leading trading nations was needed to focus on details of how to avoid a new collapse, ideally with the support of a permanent institution.

On the Road to the GATT: The Havana Charter and the ITO.

Though international trade agreements of some sort—formal or informal—had existed alongside trade throughout the years, the GATT was the first explicitly multilateral agreement, recognizing the mutual interest of countries cooperating to clarify trade rules. It is often referred to as one of the three Bretton Woods international institutions and agreements, alongside the International Bank for Reconstruction and Development (more generally known as the World Bank) and the International Monetary Fund (IMF), although technically the GATT did not emerge from the same set of negotiations, nor was it a formal institution in the same sense as the other two.

The negotiations for these financial institutions took place in 1944 at Bretton Woods, New Hampshire, with the participation of monetary authorities, but the need for a third institution to address international trade issues was acknowledged. Thus the newly created United Nations began negotiations on this topic in October 1946, and negotiations of an International Trade Organization (ITO) were led by the United States, which provided original drafts and the push to conclude agreements. The drafts reflected significant discussions with the United Kingdom

that had begun in Washington, D.C., in 1943, language and concepts from the U.S. Reciprocal Trade Agreements Act of 1934, and concepts underlying a series of pre-1914 nondiscriminatory agreements among European countries. Discussions and negotiations were later also held in London and Geneva. The major leap forward was in providing a multilateral umbrella so that a single set of rules would apply, although actual tariff (import tax) obligations would result from bilateral negotiations.

Originally, the GATT was merely one part of a much broader agreement and institution, the International Trade Organization (ITO), but the ITO was never to be. The United Nations Conference on Trade and Employment, held in Havana, Cuba, from November 1947 to March 1948, led to the adoption of the Havana Charter for the International Trade Organization. In the struggle to arrive at the broader Havana Charter, its Chapter of Commercial Policy (chapter 4) was converted to the GATT as a framework for the tariff-negotiation component. In the struggle over the Havana Charter the wish of the United States, the new superpower, for nondiscriminatory trade opposed the wish of the United Kingdom, the fading superpower, for state intervention to achieve the goal of full employment. The resulting charter was detailed and expansive, and many viewed it as a flawed and inconsistent document. The Havana Charter never entered into force, principally as a result of the failure of the United States to ratify it.

The GATT itself was applied in a peculiar way to ensure that it would not run afoul of U.S. law, and thus it never achieved formal international institutional status in the style of the World Bank and the IMF. Instead of members, the GATT had "contracting parties." The provisional application of the GATT allowed countries (including the United States) to implement the tariff negotiations of the Havana Charter and other provisions to the extent that they did not conflict with existing domestic law. The awkward legal status of the GATT caused confusion and uncertainty about the quasi-institution that eventually emerged, as well as the impetus for clarification of institutional issues within the Uruguay Round that established the successor World Trade Organization (WTO).

The twenty-three signers of the Protocol of Provisional Application were Australia, Belgium, Brazil, Burma (Myanmar), Canada, Ceylon (Sri Lanka), Chile, China, Cuba, the Czechoslovak Republic, France, India, Lebanon, Luxembourg, Netherlands, New Zealand, Norway, Pakistan, Southern Rhodesia (Zimbabwe), Syria, South Africa, the United Kingdom, and the United States.

These countries accounted for more than half of world trade at the time. China later withdrew in 1950. Significant additions occurred with the accession of Japan in 1955 and of Poland, the first centrally planned economy to become a contracting party, in 1967.

Developing countries did not participate in large numbers because they believed that their interests were not served by the GATT, with its focus on industrial tariffs. As a result, developing nations pushed to establish the United Nations Conference on Trade and Development (UNCTAD) to consider their concerns in 1964. In response, in 1965 the contracting parties of the GATT added three new articles addressing issues relating to the promotion of economic development to its original thirty-five. Given the GATT's role as the principal negotiating forum, and the lack of enthusiasm of the industrialized world for addressing such issues, more and more developing countries acceded to the GATT, while continuing their more vocal efforts through UNCTAD and other United Nations organizations.

The Long Life of the GATT's Rules and Processes. Key concepts underpinning the system, as well as the modalities under which later negotiating rounds took place, emerged from the negotiation of the original ITO charter and the GATT. The central concept of nondiscrimination of goods at the border, termed most-favored-nation or MFN, and of foreign suppliers within borders, termed national treatment, became key terms in trade discussions, even among those not active in the GATT system. Another key concept, reciprocity, has been interpreted in different ways at different times and by different negotiators but generally is understood to mean that both sides must give up something in exchange for a tariff reduction from its partners.

Nations agreed to set their tariffs at the rates negotiated for specific items, setting a ceiling above which they could not then increase their applied tariffs without provoking the right to compensation from its trading partners in that item. The item-by-item offer-request basis of bilateral negotiation among principal suppliers in the original negotiations led many economists to complain that this approach of negotiations promoted a continuation of mercantilist thinking. However, this approach originally appeared as a practical effort to avoid controversial decisions about how to calculate the benefits and costs of various other alternatives (such as across-the-board cuts or more complicated formulas, many of which were used later) and allow countries to focus on the items of most interest to them. This pragmatism became a hallmark of the GATT system, which veered far from the theoretical world of free trade to focus on the art of the possible, thus providing for general liberalizing principles accompanied by escape clauses, safety valves, and exceptions as needed for political approval and implementation.

The GATT provided a structure and framework within which successive rounds of multilateral trade negotiations could occur. Rounds were named either for the location of their initiation or for their key leaders. The first five rounds—Geneva in 1947, Annecy (France) in 1949, Torquay (England) in 1950–1951, Geneva in 1955–1956, and the Dillon Round in 1960–1961—continued to focus on tariffs. In the sixth round, the 1963–1967 Kennedy Round, nontariff measures—antidumping and customs valuation—became topics for negotiations for the first time. The Tokyo Round, initiated in 1973 and concluded in 1979, broadly expanded the range of nontariff measures covered, mostly through the use of voluntary codes of conduct.

Though this à la carte approach allowed forward progress despite the objections of many—generally the developing countries—it was thought to have weakened the overall trading system by limiting its ability to deal with the true barriers to trade. Given the GATT's success in lowering tariffs over the years, nontariff measures increasingly became the real trade barriers. Thus a different approach can be seen in the negotiations that followed. The Uruguay Round of negotiations began in Punta del Este, Uruguay, in 1986, and concluded in Marrakech (Marrakesh), Morocco, on 14 April 1994, with formal agreements on nontariff topics both new and treated in earlier voluntary codes and on controversial pathbreaking agreements on agriculture and clothing.

The Transition to the WTO. By 1994 the broad GATT system referred to more than two hundred treaty instruments plus numerous reports and decisions. Some were multilateral, applying to all contracting parties, while others—those negotiated and agreed by a subset of contracting parties—became known as plurilateral agreements.

During the Uruguay Round, the original GATT was modified slightly to include several understandings about specific articles, with the original known as the GATT 1947 and the broader revised version known as the GATT 1994. The GATT 1994 continues to be the base of the broader WTO Marrakesh Agreement and is at the heart of the WTO rules, procedures, and specific agreements. The WTO agreement converted almost all plurilateral agreements into multilateral binding agreements under the concept of a single undertaking and finally created a truly legitimate international organization—now called the World Trade Organization.

[*See also* Free Trade; Trade, International; Trading Blocs and Common Markets; *and* World Trade Organization.]

BIBLIOGRAPHY

Hoekman, Bernard M., and Michel M. Kostecki. *The Political Economy of the World Trading System: The WTO and Beyond.* 2d ed. Oxford: Oxford University Press, 2001. Excellent review of both the processes/mechanics and the content of the GATT negotiations, including the transition to the WTO.

Hudec, Robert E. *The GATT Legal System and World Trade Diplomacy.* 2d ed. Salem, N.H.: Butterworth Legal, 1990. The authoritative legal history of the pre-GATT negotiations and the pre–Uruguay Round GATT legal procedures, with an emphasis on dispute settlement issues.

Jackson, John H. *The World Trading System: Law and Policy of International Economic Relations.* 2nd ed. Cambridge, Mass.: MIT Press, 1997. The classic text on the GATT and now the WTO by a leading scholar on the GATT/WTO jurisprudence.

Trebilcock, Michael J., and Robert Howse. *The Regulation of International Trade.* New York: Routledge, 1995. Comprehensive discussion of international trade rules from knowledgeable Canadian economists, including significant discussion of bilateral agreements outside the GATT structure but consistent with its rules.

"WTO." http://www.wto.org. The official site of the World Trade Organization, where all of the official GATT documents can be found. An excellent source for primary official documents.

ROBIN A. KING

GENERAL CONFEDERATION OF LABOR.

The Confederación General del Trabajo (CGT), Argentina's umbrella union confederation, is among the strongest such confederations in the world. The CGT does not bargain collectively, but it holds discussions with employer associations and government officials, speaks for labor in the mass media and in international organizations, and declares general strikes. The CGT is formally nonpartisan, but most of its leaders have been followers of Juan Domingo Perón, who was Argentina's populist president from 1946 to 1955 and from 1973 until his death in 1974.

In 1930, when union leaders founded the CGT, Argentina already had Latin America's strongest labor movement. The CGT maintained a nonpartisan stance throughout the 1930s, a period of rapid industrialization. A coup in 1943 initiated three years of military government during which Perón, an army colonel serving as the secretary of labor, sponsored laws that raised wages, improved working conditions, and strengthened unions. These laws, together with his shows of symbolic solidarity with labor, contributed to

Perón's victory in free presidential elections in 1946. During his nine years as president, Perón, together with his wife Maria Eva "Evita" Duarte de Perón (who died in 1952), made the CGT an instrument of government policy, but by encouraging industrialization and unionization they set the stage for the confederation to become a powerful political actor.

After Perón was overthrown in a 1955 coup, a military government placed the CGT under trusteeship. It was returned to union leaders in 1961. Despite internal conflicts and a brief split in 1968, the CGT from 1961 to 1976 proved to be a formidable political force, launching a huge factory occupation campaign in 1964 and a successful general strike in 1975 against a conservative faction in the government of Perón's wife and successor, Isabel Martínez de Perón (María Estela Martínez Cartas).

In 1976, amid hyperinflation and political violence, Isabel Perón was overthrown. The 1976–1983 military government, during which thousands of Argentines "disappeared," closed down the CGT and repressed workers. In 1982, after its failed invasion of the Falkland Islands (Islas Malvinas), the military returned the CGT to union leaders and called elections for 1983.

The winner of the 1983 presidential election was Raúl Alfonsín of the Unión Cívica Radical, the Peronists' main rival. Under Alfonsín the CGT launched thirteen general strikes, deepening an economic crisis that facilitated the election of Carlos Menem, a Peronist, as president in 1989. Menem had run on a populist platform, but hyperinflation and the prevailing international ideological climate inspired him to enact free-market economic policies including privatization, civil service layoffs, spending cuts, and trade liberalization. Meanwhile, the Peronist-led congress passed laws that decentralized collective bargaining, made it easier to fire workers, and reduced union control over cash-rich health maintenance organizations (*obras sociales*).

Partly because of allegiance to Peronism, the CGT largely accepted Menem's reforms. Some labor leaders broke away from the CGT and set up rival confederations, however, and protest escalated from 1999 to 2001, when Menem's successor, Fernando de la Rúa of the Unión Cívica Radical, resigned amid a major financial crisis. In 2004, a year after the presidential victory of the Peronist Néstor Kirchner, many of the dissidents returned to the fold, and by 2005 the CGT was largely united behind Kirchner's increasingly nationalist economic policies.

[*See also* Argentina; Labor and the Labor Movement, *subentry* Latin America; *and* Unions, Labor.]

BIBLIOGRAPHY

McGuire, James W. *Peronism without Perón: Unions, Parties, and Democracy in Argentina.* Stanford, Calif.: Stanford University Press, 1997.

Murillo, Maria Victoria. *Labor Unions, Partisan Coalitions, and Market Reforms in Latin America.* New York: Cambridge University Press, 2001.

JAMES W. McGUIRE

GENERAL STRIKE OF 1926. On 3 May 1926 at one minute before midnight, 1.75 million British workers walked out in support of more than 1 million coal miners who were resisting a cut in wages and hours. Until the strike ended at 12:20 P.M. on 12 May, industries such as utilities, transport, and construction came to a halt. Although not all union members were called out, ordinary life was brought to a standstill in a strong display of working-class strength and solidarity. The General Strike of 1926 is remarkable for several reasons. It was the only time in British history that there occurred a substantial national strike. Contrary to governmental fears of revolution and widespread violence, the strike was largely peaceful. And, most surprising, the industrial action ended swiftly with no concessions by the government and no guarantees for the coal miners. Initially, it seemed a total defeat for the British labor movement, despite the determination and sacrifice of the rank and file. In the long run, though, the General Strike did not signal death for unions or even for the bargaining power of coal miners. There was an immediate loss of power and funds within the leadership of the Trades Union Congress (TUC), but within ten years the movement had recovered and the parliamentary Labour Party was stronger than ever.

Background. As a product of the economic and social conflicts of the interwar years, the strike now seems bound to have happened at some point. The problems within the coal industry had not been solved after the war. The volatile mix of reactionary owners who received the mines back in 1921 and the depressed price of coal in the international market ensured that poor industrial relations would continue.

In the economic uncertainty of the postwar years, the Conservative Party with Winston Churchill as Chancellor of the Exchequer determined that Britain must return to the gold standard, that the budget needed balancing, and that the national debt must be repaid. The result of these stringent policies ranged from deflation to high unemployment, and when these hardships were combined with the determination to reduce wages, it was clear that there had to be a confrontation with the labor force. This was made worse by the efforts of the TUC to establish trade union unity with a central executive authority in control.

In an effort to avert the looming crisis in the coal industry, Sir Herbert Samuel, a Liberal, was appointed chair of the Royal Commission on the Coal Industry. In 1926 the Samuel Commission recommended a plan whereby the coal industry would be modernized by joining mines in order to improve industrial relations through profit sharing and national wage agreements. As part of the overall streamlining, though, the commission noted that the plan would take years to implement and that in the short term the government should reduce wages and discontinue the coal subsidy.

The Samuel Commission recommendations may have been logical, but the conclusions pleased no one. Stanley Baldwin was a Conservative prime minister, and he did not wish mining to be nationalized. The miners were totally opposed to wage reductions and indicated their unwillingness to negotiate with their slogan: "Not a penny off the pay, not a second off the day." The TUC supported the Samuel Commission, but there was no hope because this small group of union leaders was no match for the coal miners or the government.

At the urging of right-wing cabinet members such as Secretary for India Lord Birkenhead (F. E. Smith) and Chancellor of the Exchequer Winston Churchill, Baldwin began to prepare for the conflict in early 1926. A Supply and Transport Committee was appointed to make sure that necessities would be readily available in the event of widespread stoppage. Home Secretary Sir William Joynson-Hicks was convinced that the Communists were behind the looming strike, and he determined to stockpile resources, recruit volunteers, and ready armed enforcement. These preparations were reinforced with full access to the broadcasting facilities of the British Broadcasting Corporation (BBC), ensuring that the dispersal of all information was filtered through the government.

The Strike and Its Aftermath. In contrast, Ernest Bevin of the General Council of the TUC did not receive the authority to begin organizing until May 1926 and could do little to prepare. The reluctance of the 465 local trade unions to give power to a national executive was crucial in reducing the effectiveness of the General Strike. Despite the internal struggles in the labor movement, however, the majority of workers responded and remained loyal to the strike call. Bevin did a good job of placing the strikers in key positions, and although the TUC never was able to shut down the ports or power structure of London, the General Strike was widespread and disciplined.

Baldwin's government remained clearly in control throughout the nine days. Despite the presence of armed authorities—Churchill had wanted to place machine guns on the streets of central London but was overruled—which created a dangerous situation, there were no serious incidents. In Plymouth the strikers played football in the streets with the police constables. Although society ladies and university students eagerly showed up to work as strike breakers, most had to content themselves with posing for pictures because volunteers were hardly needed.

The end of the strike was swift and unexpected only to the rank and file who were determined to continue until victory. Sir Herbert Samuel again tried to help construct a compromise. He made it very clear that he did not speak for the government, nor did he have the power to enforce any agreement; within these parameters he offered the Samuel Memorandum, which again called for the reorganization of the coal industry and a wage reduction but offered the creation of an impartial National Wages Board to maintain control of pay scales. Repeating the intractable slogan "Not a penny off the pay . . . ," the miners rejected the memorandum immediately, but Arthur Pugh, the chairman of the General Council of the TUC, was desperate for a settlement, in part because of the anti-Constitutional charges and because of the monetary costs to the unions. He seized on the Samuel Memorandum, ignored the lack of guarantees, and called for an end to the General Strike in order to continue negotiations.

It was predictable that both sides would claim success, but it was soon apparent that the Samuel Memorandum was not to be the settlement. The TUC had failed to secure any concessions before ending the strike, and employers began to demand retribution against workers in almost every community, especially in the railways. The Conservative government also determined to break the power of trade unions. In the short-term flush of success, the Commons passed the Trade Disputes and Trade Union Act in 1927. This punitive act forbade sympathetic strikes, cut the automatic financial contribution of unions to the Labour Party, and tried to reduce the influence of the TUC.

Assessment. In the time since the General Strike, historians and economists have struggled to understand the causes of this unprecedented action. A few conclusions can be drawn. There was no flurry of industrial militancy that led up to the events of 1926. Employers and unions had avoided conflicts in general during the war, and this continued in the early 1920s with a decline in industrial activity. The Communist Party of Great Britain had only very isolated local influence, and there was only one Communist member of Parliament in 1926.

The long-term consequences of the failure of the General Strike were not as grim nor as far reaching as they first seemed. Even though the labor movement temporarily lost prestige and power, the trade union movement had regained the lost members and had strengthened its influence within ten years. Even the Trade Disputes Act was rescinded in 1946. The General Council of the TUC understood the limits of the trade union movement and began to seek more effective representation through the parliamentary Labour Party. Employers were wary of the economic and political costs of an unyielding harshness when dealing with workers. And political parties were wary of exercising too much power over industrial relations because of the large voting potential of the working class and the competition of the Labour Party. The General Strike of 1926 is important in that it reflects all the issues of the interwar years: declining industries faced with rationalization, tensions created when economic policies put pressure on wages, and class conflict sparked by the growing political power of the working class.

[*See also* Labor and the Labor Movement, *subentry* Britain; *and* Unions, Labor, *subentry* Britain.]

BIBLIOGRAPHY

Laybourn, Keith. *The General Strike of 1926.* Manchester, U.K., and New York: Manchester University Press, 1993.

Mason, Anthony. "The Government and the General Strike." *International Review of Social History* 14 (1969): 1–39.

Morris, Margaret. *The British General Strike, 1926.* London: Historical Association, 1973.

Perkins, Anne. *A Very British Strike.* London: Macmillan, 2006.

Phillips, G. A. *The General Strike: The Politics of Industrial Conflict.* London: Weidenfeld and Nicolson, 1976.

CYNTHIA CURRAN

GENETICS. When men and women began breeding animals and plants, they also began to study patterns of inheritance—resemblances among parents and children and the occasional resemblance to grandparents or more distance relatives. In the eighteenth and nineteenth centuries these patterns became the objects of more formal study as hybridists began to record and quantify the transmission of traits across generations. Gregor Mendel, the nineteenth-century Moravian monk often thought of as the founder of modern genetics, was one such hybridist who was trying to create new stable varieties of both plants and animals. Unlike other hybridists at the time, Mendel proposed several numerical generalizations from his work; most notably that the offspring of parents with paired traits would produce offspring with a three-to-one distribution of the two parental traits. Although not fully appreciated at the time, these generalizations were rediscovered in 1900 by Hugo De Vries, Eric Tschermak von Seysenegg, and Karl Correns.

In the thirty-four years between Mendel's paper on hybrids and his rediscovery, August Weismann, Wilhelm Roux, and other biologists developed a deeper understanding of the material basis of heredity and proposed different theories of hereditary particles. In the hands of Mendelians, such as William Bateson and Wilhelm Johannsen, these hereditary particles became known as genes and were distinguished from the traits to which they ultimately contributed. This distinction between genotype (genes) and phenotype (traits) helped resolve early disputes over different forms of inheritance. Whereas Mendel worked with discrete traits (his peas were either yellow or green), many other biologists were interested in continuous traits, such as human height, which occurred as a continuous distribution of individual heights. Untangling genes from traits allowed early geneticists, such as Herman Nilsson-Ehle, to propose that a continuous trait such as the range of seed color in wheat could be the result of many genes for seed color.

As biologists sought to clarify and expand Mendelian principles, Theodor Boveri and Walter Sutton proposed that chromosomes in the cell nucleus behaved just as Mendelian particles should. This chromosome theory of heredity was developed and supported by the ground-breaking work of Thomas Hunt Morgan. With his students Alfred H. Sturtevant, Calvin Bridges, and Hermann J. Muller, Morgan used the small fruit fly *Drosophila* to track the process of hereditary transmission. Beginning with a mutant that changed *Drosophila* eye color from red to white, Morgan and his group established that genes were in fact located on chromosomes and behaved in a Mendelian manner. Taking advantage of *Drosophila*'s short (two-week) life cycle, they found many other mutants and were able to establish the linear order of genes on chromosomes and the recombination of genes as chromosomes exchanged segments in events called crossing over. Using the frequencies of recombination, Sturtevant was able to create the first genetic map. These early discoveries culminated in a theory of the gene that established it as

the unit of structure, function, recombination, and mutation in genetics. The work of Morgan's group also established the central place of *Drosophila* as a model research organism in genetics.

In subsequent decades, work on elaborating the theory of the gene included Barbara McClintock's research on gene action and chromosome behavior as well as Muller's very important discovery in 1926 that radiation could create mutations. At the same time, eugenicists sought to apply genetic principles to understand and control human heredity. Muller, who like many early geneticists was sympathetic to eugenics, understood the genetic danger that radiation posed and became a vocal advocate of limited exposure during the atomic testing of the Cold War. During the postwar period human genetics also developed as a branch of genetics as researchers realized that many diseases had a genetic component.

After World War II, the classical genetics of the early twentieth century was transformed into modern molecular genetics. Geneticists had long realized that genes must both make copies of themselves and make all the other molecules in an organism. As Morgan's gene concept was revised in light of new discoveries, many biologists became interested in understanding genetics from a biochemical perspective. In 1944 Oswald Avery, Colin MacLeod, and Maclyn McCarty demonstrated that genes were composed of deoxyribonucleic acid (DNA). By the time that Alfred Hershey and Martha Chase confirmed this result in 1952, Francis Crick and James Watson had begun to search for the structure of DNA. Their discovery of the double-helix structure in 1953 immediately suggested how DNA might replicate, thereby solving one of the key problems of genetics. The problem of how DNA contributed to the millions of proteins in an organism was more daunting.

A network of biologists from several countries contributed to what Crick called in 1958 the central dogma of molecular biology, which linked DNA to proteins through ribonucleic acid (RNA). A network of researchers in France and the United States working on how genes make proteins and how that gene action was regulated elucidated the important intermediate role of RNA. Marshall Nirenberg and his colleagues in the United States helped crack the DNA code by discovering that triplets of nucleotides in DNA were translated by transfer RNAs into the amino acid building blocks of proteins.

Although the turn to molecular genetics was marked by tremendous progress in the central problems within genetics, it did not replace other areas of research in the field. Instead it contributed new concepts and techniques as well as new problems. Of special significance was the rise of research related to protein and DNA sequences. Comparisons of sequences from different species fostered the creation of the fields of molecular evolution and bioinformatics. Beginning in the 1980s scientists, first in the United States and then internationally, sought to map and sequence the human genome. Thanks in part to technical innovations, such as the polymerase chain reaction, a working draft of the sequence was published in 2001. Genomes from many other species continue to be sequenced, as well as an array of human sequences as part of the Human Genome Diversity Project. The major challenge of postgenomic research lies not in accumulating more sequences but in understanding how those sequences function and how their products interact to create immensely complicated organisms.

[See also Eugenics.]

BIBLIOGRAPHY
Bowler, Peter J. *The Mendelian Revolution: The Emergence of Hereditarian Concepts in Modern Science and Society.* Baltimore: Johns Hopkins University Press, 1989. An accessible overview of the development of classical Mendelian genetics.

Kohler, Robert E. *Lords of the Fly: Drosophila Genetics and the Experimental Life.* Chicago: University of Chicago Press, 1994. A history of how Morgan and his group of researchers transformed experimental genetics with the fruit fly.

Morange, Michel. *A History of Molecular Biology.* Translated by Matthew Cobb. Cambridge, Mass.: Harvard University Press, 1998. A historical survey of the rise of molecular genetics and its impact on biology and biotechnology.

MICHAEL R. DIETRICH

GENEVA CONVENTIONS. Universally recognized as international law, the Geneva Conventions, as of 2006 ratified by 194 nations (though not for all associated protocols), regulate the treatment of individuals in conflict situations as well as certain aspects of the conduct of war.

Framework. The Geneva framework began with the organizing efforts of the Swiss businessman Jean-Henri Dunant, who had been horrified by the treatment of wounded soldiers he observed after the 1859 Battle of Solferino between France and Italy. Dunant's efforts led to the creation of the International Committee of the Red Cross (ICRC) and the first Geneva Convention, which was assembled in the course of setting up the ICRC and signed by representatives of a dozen nations in 1864, officially known as the "Convention for the Amelioration of the Condition of the Wounded in Armies in the Field." It provided that aid stations housing wounded and sick soldiers were to be immune from attack, that all the wounded should be treated equally by all sides in a conflict, and that the Red Cross would be recognized as a symbol identifying persons and property protected by the convention. The ratified treaty took effect in 1867.

The original Geneva Convention has been periodically revised and expanded by conferences in 1906, 1925, 1928–1929, 1948–1949, and 1977. The convention of 1906 broadened the original agreement to include maritime warfare. In 1925, protocols were added prohibiting the use of poison gas and are now regarded as part of the Hague Convention (1899, 1907) system that creates treaty law for weapons used in armed conflict. A third convention, negotiated in 1929, regulates the treatment of prisoners. An International Red Cross conference in August 1948 revised all three conventions and a further session in Stockholm a year later drafted a fourth convention that covers the treatment of civilians in wartime. A review of these protocols in 1977 further defined international humanitarian law applicable to armed conflicts and began to extend the Geneva framework to armed conflicts not international in character. They also prohibit the use of weapons causing long-term damage to the environment. A more recent protocol (2005), not yet widely accepted, provides for recognition of a nonreligious emblem (a red crystal) in place of the red cross, red crescent, or star of David as a distinguishing visual identification for medical and humanitarian personnel and facilities. Countries that are party to the Geneva Conventions are required to enact their own statutes as necessary to give the framework provisions status in national law. In the United States, Article VI of the U.S. Constitution makes ratified treaties such as the Geneva Conventions part of the supreme law of the land.

Difficulties in Implementation. The major difficulties in implementation of the Geneva framework have arisen in cases where some parties to a conflict have not been signatories of the conventions. In World War II, the Soviet Union on the Allied side and Japan on the Axis side were not Geneva partners, a situation that affected German prisoners in Russia, Soviet prisoners in Germany, and Allied captives in the hands of the Japanese. While most belligerents chose to follow Geneva Convention provisions that specified humane treatment for prisoners, Germany engaged in egregious violations of the conventions in requiring labor service from prisoners of war. There were also specific violations in combat, such as the Nazi massacre of American prisoners at Malmedy, Belgium, in late 1944, that constituted war crimes.

During the Vietnam War, the United States was a Geneva signatory, but the Democratic Republic of Vietnam (North Vietnam) and the Republic of Vietnam (South Vietnam) were not, though the latter's declaratory policy was to follow the U.S. lead in observance. There were nevertheless notable excesses in South Vietnamese handling of prisoners and imprisoned civilians. North Vietnamese treatment of U.S. prisoners of war was atrocious, extending to the use of torture and proscribed interrogations, and met no Geneva standards. The Vietnam experience, including warfare involving guerrilla insurgents difficult to distinguish from civilians, became one factor in the 1977 adoption of Protocol I to the Conventions, which refined the definition of "combatants" in situations where nonuniformed forces participate in conflict. The United States, Iran, and Pakistan have signed this protocol but not ratified it. Nations which never signed include Israel, Afghanistan, and Iraq. Some 166 countries have signed and ratified this addition to the Geneva framework.

Several Geneva Conventions or protocols include sections with identical language. These "common articles" define minimums for treatment but have become controversial in the context of the war on terror. The United States's handling of prisoners at a base in Guantanamo Bay, Cuba, and in a network of secret prisons operated by the Central Intelligence Agency (whose existence was admitted in 2006) violated Geneva standards. The common articles prohibit torture and outrages upon personal dignity such as humiliating or degrading treatment and they apply even to those not classified as prisoners of war. Conversely, Geneva protections include assurance that passing of sentences must be by regularly constituted courts, affording defendants all recognized judicial guarantees. Other provisions prohibit physical suffering or corporal punishment and collective penalties, or any other form of coercion. In addition, they assure that prisoners of war shall be allowed to receive books, devotional articles, examination papers, scientific equipment, and other items. The United States maintains that its captives are not prisoners of war. The Geneva Conventions provide that its standards must be applied to *all* captives at least *until* some different status is accorded to them by competent tribunal. The controversy entailed significant political and diplomatic problems for the administration of President George W. Bush, which attempted to evade application of the Geneva Conventions to its actions.

Given such controversies, the growing importance of nonstate actors in conflicts, and heightened concern over international law, along with loopholes that still exist within the Geneva framework, it is likely that the international community will move to further revise the Geneva Conventions or to add new protocols.

[*See also* Red Crescent; Red Cross; Vietnam Wars; *and* War Crimes.]

BIBLIOGRAPHY

Bothe, Michael, and Karl Joseph Partsch. *New Rules for Victims of Armed Conflicts: Commentary on the two 1977 Protocols Additional to the Geneva Conventions of 1949.* The Hague: Martinus Nijhoff, 1982.

Committee of the Red Cross, *Geneva Convention and Additional Protocols.* Widely available.

Trooboff, Peter D. ed. *Law and Responsibility in Warfare.* Chapel Hill: University of North Carolina Press, 1975.

JOHN PRADOS

GENOCIDE [*This entry includes three subentries, an overview and discussions of genocide in Africa and in Southeast Asia. See also* Ethnic Cleansing and Deportation.]

Overview

The term "genocide" emerged in a specific historical moment: that of the Nazi Holocaust. It is now used to describe atrocities committed both before and after those committed by the Nazis in the 1930s and 1940s and denotes the most extreme forms of abuses inflicted by humans on fellow humans.

Raphael Lemkin, a Polish Jew and international lawyer, sought a meaningful term to describe the atrocities perpetrated against the Armenians in the early twentieth century and those perpetrated by Adolf Hitler and the Nazi regime. In an effort to convey the scale of the violence perpetrated against various groups in Europe, Lemkin rejected the terms "mass murder," "denationalization," and "Germanization." He believed that these terms inadequately described the full-scale attempts not only to exterminate entire populations but also to erase and exploit various markers of community identity. In his definitive work *Axis Rule* (1944), Lemkin settled on a hybrid term: one that combined the Greek work *geno*, meaning "race" or "tribe," and the Latin *cide*, derived from the Latin verb *caedere*, meaning "to kill."

In the aftermath of the defeat of the Nazi regime in 1945, the victor nations indicted and prosecuted captured Nazi leaders in Nürnberg, Germany, on charges of crimes against humanity. These charges encompassed only actions taken during the war and excluded any atrocities committed before the war. Lemkin, among others, believed that the adoption and incorporation of genocide into international legal codes would allow for atrocities occurring outside the bounds of war to be adequately prosecuted.

In 1946 the General Assembly of the United Nations passed a resolution that condemned genocide as "the denial of the right of existence of entire human groups." The United Nations commissioned the drafting of a convention on genocide to address and define the parameters of genocide, as well as the responsibilities of member nations in the prevention of future acts of genocide.

On 9 December 1948 the U.N. General Assembly adopted the Convention on the Prevention and Punishment of the Crime of Genocide. Its Article 2 defines genocide as

> any of the following acts committed with intent to destroy, in whole or in part, a national, ethnical, racial or religious group, as such:
>
> A. Killing members of the group;
> B. Causing serious bodily or mental harm to members of the group;
> C. Deliberately inflicting on the group the conditions of life calculated to bring about its physical destruction in whole or in part;
> D. Imposing measures intended to prevent births within the group;
> E. Forcibly transferring children of the group to another group.

Although this definition addresses the need to account for a particular scale of atrocities and allows for genocide to occur outside the bounds of international war, the contours of the definition have in the latter part of the twentieth and the beginning of the twenty-first century caused considerable confusion as to what kind of violence constitutes genocide. For a series of atrocities to constitute genocide rather than mass murder, one must prove that a particular set of persons has demonstrated absolute intent to destroy another national, ethnical, racial, or religious group. This condition has proved difficult to meet in the international legal sphere.

The Herero of Namibia (1904–1907). Although the term "genocide" emerged in the context of those atrocities perpetrated during the Nazi regime, it has also been used to describe particular events occurring before the Holocaust. Recent scholarship on nineteenth- and twentieth-century imperialism has explored the forms and extent of violence employed by European colonial forces against indigenous peoples.

Germany extended colonial control over German Southwest Africa (now Namibia) in 1884. During the course of the next twenty years German Southwest Africa witnessed the arrival of more German settlers than any other German overseas holding. As part of colonial rule the Germans dispossessed African tribes of their land, resulting in impoverishment and political subordination. In January 1904 the Herero rose up against German rule. Although the Herero vastly outnumbered German forces, the German colonial military, under the leadership of General Lothar von Trotha, possessed decidedly superior military technology. To others, General von Trotha boasted of his desire to "annihilate the rebelling tribes with rivers of blood and rivers of gold. Only after a complete uprooting will something new emerge."

The German colonial forces thus embarked on a campaign to eradicate the Herero through various strategies, such as killing cattle, driving the Herero on forced marches into the Namibian desert, and herding surviving members into detention camps. In the span of several years, between forty and seventy thousand Herero were killed, with only fifteen to twenty thousand surviving. It is worth noting that the same colonial administrators and medical personnel involved in the Herero massacre went on to inform Nazi policy on race and eugenics.

The Armenian Genocide (1915–1918). In the last quarter of the nineteenth century the Ottoman Empire perpetrated a series of massacres against the Christian Armenian minority (1894–1896 and 1909). The Ottoman government aimed to quell the growth of Armenian political groups that had formed in response to repressive religious and social policies enacted by the sultanate. These massacres resulted in the deaths of thousands of civilians—estimates run from between one hundred to three hundred thousand—and the dislocation and impoverishment of many thousands more.

In 1915 the empire embarked on a systematic program to drive out and eradicate Armenians. The Ottoman government used the pretext of World War I to justify the deportation of Armenian Christians. In conjunction with the systematic expulsion and extermination of Armenians, the Ottomans confiscated the property and possessions of dislocated and deceased Armenians and destroyed many historical and religious sites. By 1922 approximately 1.5 million people had been killed.

The Holocaust (1935–1945). The Nazi regime, led by Adolf Hitler and a powerful propaganda machine, was informed by theories of racial purity, specifically Aryan superiority. Beginning in the 1930s the Nazis embarked on a series of measures targeting "degenerate" groups including Jews, Slavs, Poles, Roma (Gypsies), homosexuals, disabled people, and dissenting religious groups. The Nazis initially employed exclusionary methods such ghettoization, forced sterilization, employment barriers, strict marriage laws, and the wearing of symbols displaying one's status.

By the late 1930s the Nazi regime pursued a more aggressive policy of extermination, introducing concentration camps throughout Germany and Poland. An integral component of these concentration camps were gas chambers designed to dispose efficiently of the so-called degenerate groups. These gas chambers represented a technological advance from the mobile gas chambers employed by the Nazis against Jews and Roma several years earlier. By the time of their defeat by Allied forces in 1945, the Nazis had killed some 7 to 9 million people, as a result of their internment in concentration camps, gassing, or summary execution. Of this number, approximately 6 million were Jewish and 1.2 million Polish.

The Cambodian Genocide (1974–1978). The Khmer Rouge, led by Pol Pot, was strongly influenced by Maoist Communism and engaged in guerrilla warfare against the Cambodian monarchy for several years before it came to power in 1974. Pol Pot advocated a return to an agrarian state and a rejection of Western society. The Khmer Rouge liquidated cities throughout Cambodia and targeted anyone resembling a Western intellectual for immediate execution. Those who survived were forced to work in rice fields throughout Cambodia and were given starvation rations.

Pol Pot and his government were intensely suspicious of any Western, particularly CIA, interference or espionage in Cambodia. Consequently, the Khmer Rouger accused countless people of spying for the United States. Those accused of such crimes were transported to facilities like Tuol Sleng (known as S-21 and located in Phnom Penh) and tortured until a confession was obtained. Of the nearly ten thousand people known to have been held and tortured in Tuol Sleng, only five are known to have survived.

Over a four-year period thousands of Cambodians fled across the border into Thailand, and in 1978 the Vietnamese invaded the country and forced the Khmer Rouge into exile. In its wake the Khmer Rouge left approximately 1.7 million people dead—from summary execution, starvation, disease, or torture. As of the early twenty-first century no leader of the Khmer Rouge had been prosecuted for crimes of genocide.

Bosnia (1992–1995). The first attempts to prosecute individuals for the crime of genocide occurred in the aftermath of the Bosnian war of 1992–1995. The conflict that set the killing in motion originated in part after the dissolution of Yugoslavia in 1991. Slovenia seceded from the Republic of Yugoslavia, followed by Croatia. As a result Bosnia found itself in a difficult position: if it remained part of Yugoslavia, its Serb population would receive preferential treatment at the expense of Muslims and Croats, but if it declared independence, Muslims would become particularly vulnerable to attack. Bosnia chose to secede in March 1992, and subsequently hard-line Bosnian Serbs formed an independent Bosnian-Serbian state within the borders of the former Serbia.

Members of the new Bosnian-Serbian state had compiled lists of prominent non-Serbs—primarily Muslim and Croat civilians—and shortly after Bosnia's secession from Yugoslavia they began to round up and in many instances kill non-Serbs. Violence against this ethnic group soon escalated and involved the establishment of concentration camps and the systematic use of sexual violence against women, summary execution, and torture. The international community was slow to respond to the overwhelming evidence of a well-organized effort to eradicate the Bosnian Muslim population. The United States for its part hesitated to designate the atrocities as "genocide" and declined to dispatch U.S. forces to accompany a U.N. peacekeeping force to the region. A NATO force, with U.S. troop support, did ultimately enter the region. The Dayton Accords, supported by the administration of President Bill Clinton, ended hostilities in 1995. The United Nations established the International Criminal Tribunal of Yugoslavia (ICTY) after the cessation of hostilities to investigate and prosecute the crimes committed between 1992 and 1995.

Rwanda (1994). Concurrent with the genocide occurring in Bosnia, Rwanda erupted into civil war in 1994 with the invasion—one of a series—of the Rwandan Patriotic Front (RPF). After achieving independence from Belgium in 1959, the Rwandan government had been controlled by increasingly radical Hutu factions. In response to the incursions of the RPF, an organization composed of Tutsi refugees living in exile in Uganda, relations between Hutus and Tutsis progressively deteriorated throughout the early 1990s, with an increasingly hostile Hutu media referring to Tutsis as *inyenzi* or "cockroaches."

On 6 April 1994 the Rwandan president Juvénal Habyarimana's plane was shot down as he returned from Tanzania, where he had attended a meeting on the implementation of the 1993 Arusha Accords that sought to normalize relations between warring Hutus and Tutsis and establish a multiethnic ruling coalition. Hours later, blockades were set up throughout the capital city of Kigali, and the national radio station, Radio Milles Collines, began to incite extremists, broadcasting kill lists of moderate Hutu intellectuals and politicians along with prominent Tutsis. Within days the killing of Tutsis and moderate Hutus spread throughout the country, and it accelerated once the United Nations was compelled to pull out all its personnel from Rwanda because of the escalating violence.

Over the course of 100 days, between 800,000 and 1 million Tutsis and Hutus were killed by the Interahamwe (a radical Hutu Power youth militia) and other Hutus. Perpetrators used machetes, hoes, and other tools as weapons. In the aftermath of the genocide, many scholars, legal analysts, and human rights advocates noted the rapidity with which people were exterminated.

The killing ended with the taking of Kigali by RPF forces in early July. Since 1994 the International Criminal Tribunal of Rwanda (ICTR), located in Arusha, has indicted, tried, and convicted several government officials and local leaders for the crime of genocide.

Genocide is universally condemned. However, despite repeated exhortations to prevent genocide from occurring, genocidal violence continues to occur throughout the world. Violence in the Darfur region of Sudan has reached genocidal proportions. Though many nations and aid organizations are attempting to relieve the human suffering felt by the African population at the hands of the Janjaweed militia, no one has yet been able to end the violence.

[See also Armenia; Bosnia and Herzegovina, Intervention in; Cambodia; Ethnic Cleansing and Deportation; Herero Revolt; Holocaust; Human Rights; Janjaweed; Khmer Rouge; Namibia; and Rwanda.]

BIBLIOGRAPHY

Arendt, Hannah. *The Origins of Totalitarianism.* New York: Harcourt, Brace, 1951.

Gewald, Jan-Bart. *Herero Heroes: A Socio-Political History of the Herero in Namibia, 1890–1923.* Oxford: James Currey, 1999.

Gutman, Roy. *Witness to Genocide: The 1993 Pulitzer Prize–Winning Dispatches on the "Ethnic Cleansing" of Bosnia.* New York: Macmillan, 1993.

Hinton, Alexander. *Why Did They Kill? Cambodia in the Shadow of Genocide.* Berkeley: University of California Press, 2005.

Hovannisian, Richard, ed. *Remembrance and Denial: The Case of the Armenian Genocide.* Detroit, Mich.: Wayne State University Press, 1998.

Mamdani, Mahmood. *When Victims Become Killers: Colonialism, Nativism, and the Genocide in Rwanda.* Princeton, N.J.: Princeton University Press, 2001.

Power, Samantha. *"A Problem from Hell": America and the Age of Genocide.* New York: Basic Books, 2002.

Schabas, William A. *Genocide in International Law: The Crime of Crimes.* Cambridge, U.K.: Cambridge University Press, 2000.

KATHERINE G. V. FIDLER

Africa

The category of "genocide" emerged in the aftermath of World War II. Formulated as a response to the war crimes of the Nazis, the term was first coined in 1944 by the scholar Raphael Lemkin and was later codified and criminalized by the United Nations in 1948.

Under the 1948 Convention on the Prevention and Punishment of the Crime of Genocide, Article 2 defines genocide as an act in which there exists "intent to destroy, in whole or in part, a national, ethnical, racial or religious group, as such." Under international law, individuals from Yugoslavia and Rwanda have been charged with—and convicted of—the crime of genocide as defined by the U.N. Genocide Convention. In addition, several countries including Spain, France, Belgium, Finland, the United Kingdom, and the Netherlands have criminalized genocide as a particular crime in their domestic codes.

Genocide in the Colonial Period. Although genocide exists as a legal category, the term is also used to describe and understand colonial violence against African populations in the modern period. Advancing under the banner of *la mission civilisatrice*, or the civilizing mission, European colonial forces exploited and expropriated mineral resources and land throughout Africa in the eighteenth, nineteenth, and twentieth centuries. The genocidal violence of colonialism in Africa accelerated with the arrival of European settler communities throughout southern Africa and the discovery of valuable mineral and plant resources such as gold, diamonds, and rubber in the nineteenth century.

In the early nineteenth century, British forces engaged in a series of frontier wars with the Xhosa, a southern African tribe. These frontier wars were designed to remove the Xhosa from the Western Cape of contemporary South Africa. By the 1840s settlers and British military forces, with the help of sophisticated long-range weapons such as the Minie rifle and rockets, deployed a genocidal policy against the Xhosa. British commanders urged their soldiers and settlers not only to defeat but also to exterminate the Xhosa population. Although the efforts to exterminate the Xhosa completely were ultimately unsuccessful, British military forces and settlers were able to force the Xhosa into the Eastern Cape and into a position of subservience that lasted throughout the nineteenth and much of the twentieth century, until the end of apartheid in 1994.

The use of violence against the Xhosa population is an example of settler genocide in which European settlers used racist ideology to justify the attempted extermination of African populations to claim the most arable and productive land; likewise, European colonial forces used genocidal violence in the course of seizing valuable resources. A particularly apt example is what occurred in the Congo Free State in the late nineteenth and early twentieth centuries. Under the "humanitarian" directive of King Leopold II (r. 1865–1909), Belgian forces extracted massive amounts of rubber and ivory from the Congo Free State (known in the early twenty-first century as the Democratic Republic of the Congo) through slave labor. Leopold's agents authorized and oversaw such coercive measures as amputating limbs, caning, whipping, and incarcerating women and children. Natives were subjected to forced deportation to mineral-rich areas where they performed slave labor and were killed if their yield did not meet specific quotas set by their European masters. It is unclear how many Africans died while performing slave labor for King Leopold II, but most scholars have concluded that a substantial percentage, if not the majority, of the population in the region was killed during the course of Leopold's rule. Although it might be difficult to prove the intent to exterminate the African population within the parameters of the U.N. Genocide Convention, it is clear that Leopold's agents employed extraordinary violence that targeted native populations simply on the basis of race.

The first clear case of genocide perpetrated in Africa during the twentieth century occurred in German Southwest Africa (now Namibia). German colonial forces first occupied and claimed this region in 1884. In the twenty years that followed, a substantial settler population came to reside in the region and began to push out native populations. These native populations were also subjected to discriminatory practices by German settlers. In 1904 the largest tribe in the region, the Herero, rose up against the settlers. The German empire dispatched to the region a large military force of approximately fifteen thousand men under the command of General Lothar von Trotha. General von Trotha declared that the Herero were no longer under the protection of the German empire and that all Herero must leave the colony of German Southwest Africa or face immediate death. German forces proceeded to drive the Herero across the barren Kalihari Desert.

On receiving imperial orders rescinding this directive, German forces then proceeded to force the remaining Herero population into concentration and slave-labor camps. In these camps German doctors and ethnographers "studied" and experimented on the Herero. Their findings contributed to the development of eugenics as later implemented by Nazi doctors in the 1930s and 1940s. Although it is difficult to document the exact numbers of Herero killed by German military forces, the 1985 Whitaker report, issued by Benjamin Whitaker, U.N. special rapporteur on genocide, estimated that approximately sixty-five thousand Herero—80 percent of the population—were killed as a result of General von Trothar's genocidal decree. The German government eventually in 2004 admitted that it had committed genocide against the Herero, but it has subsequently refused to pay any compensation to the remainder of that indigenous population.

The Rwandan Genocide. The Rwandan genocide of 1994 is perhaps the best known and most devastating of genocides perpetrated in Africa during the modern period. Rwanda, originally a German colony, became a Belgian colony in the aftermath of World War I when Germany was forced to relinquish all its colonies under a League of Nations mandate. The Belgian colonial administration, employing a form of indirect rule, identified the minority Tutsi ethnic group as the ruling class in Rwanda. The Belgians based this choice on a series of questionable ethnographic observations in which the Tutsi appeared to hold the majority of wealth and power in Rwandan society. As a result, the Belgian colonial administration allowed the Tutsi elite to exert repressive controls over the Hutu population. However, when faced with the realities of decolonization in the mid-1950s, Belgium switched its political support from the Tutsi elite to a developing Hutu elite. Upon independence in 1962, open elections in Rwanda brought a Hutu party to power.

In the years following independence, Tutsi refugees in Uganda used the emergence of a repressive Hutu government as a rallying point around which to organize armed groups and stage attacks against Hutu targets. In addition, the postindependence Hutu government led retaliatory killings against Tutsi civilians in Rwanda throughout the 1960s. A Tutsi resistance movement based in Uganda, the Rwandan Patriotic Front (RPF), eventually invaded Rwanda in October 1990, sparking a civil war. In response, the regime of Juvénal Habyarimana sought to normalize relations between the Rwandan Hutu government and the RPF, culminating in the 1993 Arusha Accords. However, this attempt to develop a multiethnic coalition infuriated an extremist movement, Hutu Power, and contributed to the development of a genocidal anti-Tutsi ideology. On 6 April 1994, returning from a meeting in Tanzania that focused on the implementation of the earlier Arusha Accords, the plane carrying President Habyarimana was shot down. Within hours of this incident, Hutu

Rwandan Genocide. A survivor prays over the bones of the 1994 Genocide victims at a mass grave, Nyamata, Rwanda, 6 April 2004. AP IMAGES

Power youth groups known as the Interahamwe set up roadblocks, armed with kill lists of prominent Tutsis and moderate Hutus.

Within days the killing of people identified either through identity cards or by physical traits thought to characterize the Tutsi had spread throughout the country. With only a small number of U.N. peacekeeping forces in Rwanda at the time and the international community's explicit refusal to intervene in the slaughter, members of the Interahamwe and other Hutus within a 100-day period perpetrated a genocide in which between 800,000 and 1 million people were killed on the basis of their ethnicity. The only military action taken by the international community during the course of the genocide was the French-led Operation Turquoise, which was later revealed to have provided, ironically, a safe haven for the Hutu government and its allied militias. The Hutu government and these associated groups in fact repeatedly took advantage of this operation to perpetuate massacres and moved the radio station being used to incite and coordinate the genocide within the confines of the safe zone secured by the French in southeastern Rwanda.

In the absence of any concrete action to prevent the genocide, the international community, slowly and at times haphazardly, attempted to establish a means by which to address the atrocities committed in Rwanda. Initially, citing budgetary constraints, the United Nations Security Council proposed to subsume at the Hague a tribunal for Rwanda under the ongoing criminal tribunal for the former Yugoslavia by adding extra trial chambers and hiring additional staff. However, after the transitional government in Rwanda, composed primarily of Tutsi refugees from Uganda, expressed considerable opposition, an independent tribunal for Rwanda—called the International Criminal Tribunal for Rwanda or ICTR—came into existence as the mechanism for transitional justice and a means by which to hold the perpetrators of the Rwandan genocide accountable.

Although the ICTR has been beset by a number of bureaucratic and political woes, including the Rwandan government's withdrawal of support in the early twenty-first century, the tribunal has arrested, tried, and convicted a number of accused perpetrators, including Jean-Paul Akayesu, a local Rwandan mayor, on the count of genocide. Akayesu was the first person to be convicted of the crime of genocide in an international court since the drafting of the U.N. Genocide Convention. The decision against Akayesu also expanded the legal definition of genocide to include the crime of rape.

Genocide in Contemporary Sudan. In the early twenty-first century the Darfur region of western Sudan witnessed escalating violence. Human rights groups such as Human Rights Watch and Amnesty International accused the Sudanese government of supporting genocidal acts by the Arab-based Janjaweed movement against the non-Arab population in the region. The Janjaweed military has engaged in such violent acts as the destruction of villages, the forced deportation of civilians, rape, and murder. Estimates in 2004 suggested that more than fifty thousand people had been killed and more than 1 million forced from their homes into refugee camps or unofficial settlements. Although a humanitarian crisis resulting from extraordinary acts of violence still existed in mid-2007, it is difficult to determine if genocide in the legal sense of the term has occurred because such a legal conclusion depends on whether or not organizations like the Janjaweed are targeting specific groups on the basis of their race, religion, or ethnicity.

To add to the human tragedy, international aid has been slow to come to the region. Although many international leaders, including a number of U.S. government and U.N. officials, have suggested or explicitly stated that genocide continues to occur in Darfur, as of mid-2007 there had been no attempt to intervene legally or militarily, and humanitarian aid in the form of food and medicine remained intermittent at best. The crisis in Sudan continues and threatens the national security of the country, as well as that of neighboring countries, including Chad and the Central African Republic.

[*See also* Belgian Congo; Civil Wars in Africa; Colonialism, *subentry* Africa; Darfur; Herero Revolt; Janjaweed; Namibia; Rwanda; *and* United Nations, *subentry* Involvement in Africa.]

BIBLIOGRAPHY

Flint, Julie, and Alexander de Waal. *Darfur: A Short History of a Long War.* London: Zed Books, 2005.

Gewald, Jan-Bart. *Herero Heroes: A Socio-Political History of the Herero of Namibia, 1890–1923.* Oxford: James Currey, 1999.

Hochschild, Adam. *King Leopold's Ghost: A Story of Greed, Terror, and Heroism in Colonial Africa.* Boston: Houghton Mifflin, 1998.

Human Rights Watch. "Entrenching Impunity: Governmental Responsibility for the International Crimes in Darfur." December 2005. http://hrw.org/reports/2005/darfur1205/.

Human Rights Watch. "Leave None to Tell the Story: Genocide in Rwanda." March 1999. http://www.hrw.org/reports/1999/rwanda/.

Mamdani, Mahmood. *Citizen and Subject: Contemporary Africa and the Legacy of Late Colonialism.* Princeton, N.J.: Princeton University Press, 1996.

Mamdani, Mahmood. *When Victims Become Killers: Colonialism, Nativism, and the Genocide in Rwanda.* Princeton, N.J.: Princeton University Press, 2001.

Prunier, Gérard. *The Rwanda Crisis: History of a Genocide.* London: C. Hurst, 1998.

KATHERINE G.V. FIDLER

Southeast Asia

Southeast Asia has not had an incident that fits within the parameters of the 1948 United Nations Convention on the Prevention and Punishment of the Crime of Genocide. If more liberal definitions that include the persecution of social and political groups are entertained, however, then genocides have taken place in at least three Southeast Asian nation-states since the middle of the twentieth century: Indonesia (1965–1966), Cambodia (1975–1979), and East Timor (Timor-Leste; 1975–1999).

Indonesia. The persecution, torture, and execution of alleged members of the Parti Kommunis Indonesia (PKI, the Indonesian Communist Party), between October 1965 and March 1966, during which more than 500,000 people died or disappeared, resulted from the failed coup attempt of 30 September 1965. Suspected PKI members, including the Gerakan Wanita Indonesia (Gerwani), a Communist women's organization, were identified, arrested, and detained for questioning regarding the PKI's purported orchestration of the coup. Government military units carried out direct executions of those believed responsible after extracting confessions by torture. Gerwani members were sexually assaulted. Local anti-Communist groups (Muslim, Christian, and nationalist) carried out summary punishments and executions with the support of the armed forces, although many seem to have taken this opportunity to exact retribution for perceived slights, in some cases going back generations and disguised as outrage over the coup.

Cambodia. An estimated 2.52 million people died as a result of execution, torture, disease, malnutrition, and overwork in Democratic Kampuchea—the name by which Cambodia was known between 17 April 1975 and 7 January 1979—because of the policies and mismanagement of the Khmer Rouge. Cities were evacuated, people who had worked for the previous governments were killed along with their families, and large numbers of ethnic Vietnamese and Cham people were executed. Anyone who could speak a foreign language, had been educated—doctors, lawyers, engineers—or had owned a business was targeted. Individualism was outlawed, men and women alike being required to dress in black, cut their hair short, and eschew adornment. Everyone was relocated to the countryside in order to plant and harvest rice, build dams, hew new courses for waterways, and "build solidarity." Family connections were broken down, with children being placed in children's cooperatives where they, too, worked, collecting chicken waste for fertilizer and firewood. Marriages were carried out en masse and with little or no decision making from the parties involved.

The crimes of the regime are forever documented in the Tuol Sleng Genocide Museum in Phnom Penh and the "killing fields," the mass graves in which the Khmer Rouge buried their victims. The People's Republic of Kampuchea (PRK) held a genocide tribunal for the "leaders of the Pol Pot–Ieng Sary clique" in August 1979, but this has been categorized as inadequate in the eyes of the international community. The International Criminal Court was scheduled to convene the Extraordinary Chambers for the Period of Democratic Kampuchea in order to bring the surviving leaders of the regime to justice.

East Timor. Indonesia invaded East Timor on 7 December 1975 in response to the declaration of independence by the Frente Revolucionária de Timor-Leste Independente (Fretilin), the popularly supported independence movement. Its main political rival, the União Democrática Timorense (UDT), had been receiving support from the Indonesian army for some time, in return for which UDT agreed to support East Timor's integration into the Indonesian nation-state. By February 1976 more than sixty thousand East Timorese had been killed, and human rights violations committed by the Indonesian army, including rapes and other assaults, were widespread. The United Nations never recognized the annexation, and Jose Ramos-Horta of Fretilin led an East Timorese government-in-exile for the next ten years.

Another 100,000 to 200,000 people died between 1975 and 1981, and 800,000 more died between 1974, when the Indonesian armed forces are alleged to have begun their campaign of terror and intimidation, and the arrival of the advance United Nations peacekeeping mission on 20 September 1999. The governments of the United States and Australia, who are alleged to have given tacit approval for the 1975 invasion, ignored the situation until the Dili Massacre of 12 November 1991, when Indonesian soldiers opened fire on people attending the burial of a student who had himself been killed by the armed forces. Kay Rala Xanana Gusmão spoke openly about the incident, generating international condemnation of the continued occupation of East Timor.

Mounting international pressures caused the Indonesian government to agree to a referendum for East Timor, held on 30 August 1999, during which the Indonesian armed forces attempted to intimidate people into voting against independence through still more violence. Independence was declared on 20 May 2002 and the country was renamed Timor-Leste. The Commission for Reception, Truth, and Reconciliation in East Timor was devised as a mechanism for reconciling the perpetrators and victims of violence between 1974 and 1999.

Because all these incidents are not classified as genocides according to the 1948 convention, and the acknowledgement of them as such would involve investigation of current heads of state and the past indifference of the international community, their perpetrators carry on with impunity.

[See also Cambodia; East Timor; Ethnic Conflict, subentry Southeast Asia; Indonesia; and Khmer Rouge.]

BIBLIOGRAPHY

Cribb, Robert, ed. *The Indonesian Killings, 1965–1966: Studies from Java and Bali.* Clayton, Australia: Center for Southeast Asian Studies, Monash University, 1990.

Kiernan, Ben. *The Pol Pot Regime: Race, Power, and Genocide in Cambodia under the Khmer Rouge, 1975–1979.* 2nd ed. New Haven, Conn.: Yale University Press, 2002.

Saul, Ben. "Was the Conflict in East Timor 'Genocide' and Why Does It Matter?" *Melbourne Journal of International Law* 2, no. 2 (2001): 477–523.

TRUDY JACOBSEN

GEORGIA. Georgia is a small mountainous country (26,900 square miles, or 69,700 square kilometers) in the South Caucasus, the isthmus between the Black and Caspian seas, to the south of Russia, west of Azerbaijan, and north of Armenia, Iran, and Turkey. Its population is just over 5 million, with more than a million living in its capital city, Tbilisi (Tiflis). Georgians speak a number of Kartvelian languages or dialects (for example, *kartuli* [Georgian], *svan*, *megreli* [Mingrelian]) and call their country *sakartvelo*. Other large cities include Kutaisi in the western part of the country and Batumi on the Black Sea. A former Soviet republic (1921–1991), Georgia includes the Abkhaz Republic, the Adjarian Autonomous Republic, and the South Ossetian Autonomous Region. Its economy is principally agricultural, though the Soviet government developed industry, notably the Rustavi steelworks.

The Origins of the Georgian State. The earliest tribal groups that might be considered Georgian or proto-Georgian are mentioned by the Greek historian Herodotus (c. 484–430/420 B.C.E.) as living under the Persian Empire. Western Georgia was known to the Greeks as Colchis, the land to which Jason and the Argonauts went to steal the Golden Fleece. In his trek across Asia Minor to the Black Sea, the Greek historian Xenophon (c. 431–c. 352 B.C.E.) mentioned local tribes that he called "the most valiant of all the peoples they passed through." The Greeks referred later to the *Iberoi* or Iberians, and Georgia has since been referred to as Iberia. In the Georgian chronicles, the *kartlis tskhovreba*, the first kingdom in eastern Georgia was that of Parnavzi with its capital at Mskheta. Conquered by Alexander III (Alexander the Great; 356–323 B.C.E.) and later by the Romans, Georgian kings and princes managed to maintain a degree of local autonomy. The country's social structure was highly influenced by the Iranians, with the king at the apex of power, the noble *aznaurni* his principal servitors, and the mass of common people below. More than ancient Armenia, Georgia of all Caucasian states most closely resembled early European feudal society.

The great transformation of the Caucasus came in the early fourth century C.E., when Armenians and Georgians adopted Christianity as their official religion. Saint Nino, the illuminatrix of Kartli-Iberia (eastern Georgia), began preaching in 328, and King Mirian of Kartli-Iberia soon converted. At first the major Christian communities in the Caucasus were part of a single Christian community, but in the sixth century the Kartvelian church freed itself of Armenian dominance and identified with the Greek Orthodox Church of Byzantium. Still, the early sources proposed a common ancestry of Armenians and Georgians, a single forefather and descendent of Noah, Togarmah (Targamos), whose first son was Haos/Hayk, the eponymous founder of the Armenians, while the younger son, Kartlos, was the founder of the Georgians. The chronicles even claim that Georgians spoke Armenian before the (mythical) invasion of Alexander the Great and only then created *ena kartuli* (the Georgian language).

Georgians in the Middle Ages identified with their language, the particular religion embraced by the king (first paganism, then Christianity), and the developing historical tradition set down in the chronicles after the invention of the first Georgian alphabet. In the seventh century Islamic armies moved into Georgia, but the various kingdoms remained semi-independent, from the late eighth century under the Bagratid (Bagratuni) kings who would continue to rule the Georgian states until the early nineteenth century. In the Bagratid period identity was wrapped around religion, and these kings sought to unite all Orthodox Georgians under a single state authority. The Georgian Bagratids established the autocephaly of the Georgian church and then argued that that religious independence had existed since the church's foundation by the apostles Andrew and Simon the Zealot. Over time the Georgian Bagratids distanced themselves from their Armenian cousins, obscured their common ancestry, and emphasized instead Georgian uniqueness.

Eastern Georgia reached its apogee in the late eleventh and twelfth centuries under David II (III) (the Builder; r. 1089–1125) and Queen Tamar (r. 1184–1212). Their kingdom reached its greatest expansion, incorporating the whole of South Caucasia. From that period dates the national poem, "The Man in the Panther's Skin," by Shota Rustaveli. Ravaged in the thirteenth century by the Mongols, Georgia fragmented into smaller states. When Alexander I (r. 1412–1442), the last king of united Georgia, retired to a monastery, his kingdom fell to his feuding sons. Three major kingdoms contended with one another: Kartli, Kakheti (far easterly Georgia), and Imerti (western Georgia). Both the Ottoman Empire and Persia fought for influence in Georgia, and by the eighteenth century the battered Georgian states were desperate enough to call on their great northern neighbor, Russia, for assistance. In 1783 the king of Kartli-Katheti, Erekle II (r. 1762–1798), signed the Treaty of Georgievsk and placed his Georgia under the protection of Empress Catherine II (Catherine the Great; r. 1762–1796). In 1801 Tsar Paul I (r. 1796–1801) abolished the kingdom of eastern Georgia, and through the next decades Russia incorporated the remaining Georgian regions into the empire.

Georgia under Russian and Soviet Rule. For the first time in centuries almost all the Georgian lands were under a single government, tsarist Russia. After initial resistance to Russian rule, Georgian nobles and intellectuals accommodated themselves to the new order, traveled to the north, and imbibed the European education then offered in Russia. From these encounters with the modern world Georgians developed a deeper sense of their own national uniqueness and the value of their own culture. Until the 1890s strong Russophilic tendencies marked the relations of the Georgian elites, while ordinary peasants resisted the imposition of Russian-style serfdom on their villages. But the heavy hand of Russia in the Caucasus encouraged a younger generation to turn to revolutionary opposition to tsarism. In the last decade of the century young Marxists, led by Noe Zhordania, combined antagonism toward Russian officialdom with hostility toward the influential Armenian middle class to forge a massive movement that mobilized workers and peasants against the government. By 1905 western Georgia was in full rebellion against tsarism, and in the following decade the Georgian Marxists, now aligned with the Menshevik wing of the Russian Social-Democratic Workers' Party, represented the Georgian provinces in the central Russian parliament.

After the collapse of the tsarist empire in the Russian Revolution of 1917, the Georgian Mensheviks declared Georgia's independence (26 May 1918). For nearly three years the Social Democrats ruled a beleaguered but democratic republic. In February 1921 Soviet troops overthrew the Georgian government and established a Soviet republic that lasted until 1991. In 1922 Georgia became a constituent republic in the new Union of Soviet Socialist Republics as a member of the Transcaucasian Soviet Federated Socialist Republic. In 1936 it became a separate union republic. Along with other republics Georgia developed industrially and culturally during the Soviet period. Masses were educated in the Georgian language, and Georgian literature and art flourished. From a peasant country, Georgia became an urban society. But Georgia was no longer sovereign; Moscow determined the limits of national expression, and Georgians suffered from the repressions of the Joseph Stalin years (1928–1953), when thousands were exiled or executed for fabricated political crimes. Some 350,000 Georgians died defending the Soviet Union against the Nazi invasion during World War II, an enormous loss for a small country.

After Stalin's death in 1953, national consciousness grew in the republic, even as illegal economic activity and corruption increased. In 1972 Eduard Shevardnadze became the leader of the Georgian Communist Party and attempted to curb corruption and nationalism. When in 1978 the Soviet government tried to disestablish Georgian as the official language of the republic, thousands protested and Shevardnadze conceded to their demands. With the coming to power of Mikhail Gorbachev in 1985 and the general liberalization of the Soviet regime, Georgians mobilized for greater national independence. On 9 April 1989 Soviet troops brutally repressed a nationalist demonstration, killing twenty and injuring hundreds. A year later the nationalist leader Zviad Gamsakhurdia was overwhelmingly elected leader of Georgia.

A New Nation-State. Georgia declared its independence on 9 April 1991, but only after the collapse of the USSR was it officially recognized internationally as an independent state. The rule of the erratic Gamsakhurdia stimulated secession from Georgia in Abkhazia and South Ossetia, and a civil war broke out among Georgians. As the country fell into chaos and violence, Shevardnadze returned to power (1992) and managed to bring a degree of order and stability to the country. But Tbilisi's influence did not extend to the rebellious regions of Abkhazia and South Ossetia, whose defiance was supported by Boris Yeltsin's Russia. In 1995 Shevardnadze was reelected president under a new constitution, but as his initial democratic reforms foundered and corruption spread, the president became steadily more unpopular. Twice he survived assassination attempts. His electoral victory in 2000 was suspect, and the parliamentary elections of November 2003 were so evidently manipulated that protests broke out in the streets. Led by the charismatic Mikhail Saakashvili, crowds surged into the parliament and drove Shevardnadze from power in what was dubbed the "Rose Revolution."

Saakashvili was elected president in January 2004 and immediately began a campaign against corruption. He amended the constitution to increase his powers; brought the autonomous province of Adjaria under Tbilisi's control; and pressured Vladimir Putin's Russia to remove its military bases from Georgia. The United States backed Georgia's efforts, and President George W. Bush made a triumphal visit to Georgia in May 2005 to reinforce American support for democratization.

[See also Caucasus; Commonwealth of Independent States; and Russia, the Russian Empire, and the Soviet Union.]

BIBLIOGRAPHY

Allen, W. E. D. *A History of the Georgian People from the Beginning Down to the Russian Conquest in the Nineteenth Century.* London: K. Paul, Trench, Trubner, 1932.

Lang, David Marshall. *The Last Years of the Georgian Monarchy, 1658–1832.* New York: Columbia University Press, 1957.

Lang, David Marshall. *A Modern History of Soviet Georgia.* New York: Grove, 1962.

Rhinelander, Anthony L. H. *Prince Michael Vorontsov: Viceroy to the Tsar.* Montreal: McGill–Queen's University Press, 1990.

Suny, Ronald Grigor. *The Making of the Georgian Nation.* Bloomington: Indiana University Press, 1988.

Suny, Ronald Grigor, ed. *Transcaucasia, Nationalism, and Social Change: Essays in the History of Armenia, Azerbaijan, and Georgia.* Rev. ed. Ann Arbor: University of Michigan Press, 1996.

RONALD GRIGOR SUNY

GERMAN COLONIAL EMPIRE. *See* Empire and Imperialism, *subentry* The German Colonial Empire.

GERMANY. Germany in the mid-1700s possessed a mix of institutions partly familiar, partly unfamiliar to the modern eye. Serfdom remained everywhere entrenched, although not as harshly as in Russia. Many German rulers had taken steps to ameliorate its worst abuses. The guilds, though not as dominant as before, retained most of their old monopolistic privileges. Individual freedom of religion and expression, as well as other modern-day civil liberties, did not exist. The nobility possessed exclusive social and legal privileges, and absolute rulers brooked no political opposition. The various German lands were loosely organized in the unusual Holy Roman Empire, a decentralized conglomerate of 61 church-run bailiwicks, 51 imperial cities, and 350 secular territories, including militarily potent powers like Austria and Prussia.

For centuries, however, the Holy Roman Empire and its Austrian Habsburg emperors had been yielding authority to "states" like Prussia, Saxony, Bavaria, and other German entities that had become sovereign in everything but name. Even Austrian rulers came to realize that their real power base lay in the army recruits and tax revenues of Habsburg ancestral territory around Vienna, not in the complicated institutions of the Holy Roman Empire. This was a modern development, for it meant central government and rapidly expanding, increasingly well-equipped standing armies, especially in Austria and Prussia. Military expansion and frequent warfare spawned technological change—particularly in mining and metallurgy— while in the countryside the first factories had begun to sprout up away from stifling guild controls. There were even political and cultural bright spots. By guaranteeing certain "free imperial" cities and other small states protection against the expansionism of Austria and Prussia, for instance, the legal and political institutions of the Holy Roman Empire seemed to many Germans a guarantee of independence. The smaller states, inspired by the example of Saxe-Weimar and its liberal duke, Karl August, also permitted an increasing number of literary, legal, historical, and semipolitical publications, while also pouring money into a thriving world of culture. One thinks of the music of Wolfgang Amadeus Mozart (1756–1791) and the literary masterpieces of Johann Wolfgang von Goethe (1749–1832) and Friedrich von Schiller (1759–1805). Because of these peculiar freedoms, some modern historians (such as Gagliardo) see much more of worth in the Holy Roman Empire than did late-nineteenth-century nationalistic detractors like Heinrich von Treitschke, who demeaned the empire as a roadblock to German power in Europe.

Impact of the French Revolution and Napoleon (1789–1815). The French Revolution of 1789 had a profound impact on German Europe. At first the effects manifested themselves in a debate over the significant intellectual, social, and political changes that were sweeping through France. While reform-oriented progressives and radicals saw great promise in these Western developments, conservatives decried them as unthinkably devilish and threatening to the authority of the church, the nobility, and the absolute rulers of German lands. The contrast between French and German institutions exploded into conflict in 1792 when Austria and Prussia responded to a French declaration of war by invading the land of revolution.

A rapidly assembled French army defeated the German powers at Valmy and then advanced into the Rhineland. In subsequent years numerically superior French forces—organized along new lines, open to talent, and inspired by the abolition of serfdom and other radical changes—were able to win many victories over German armies consisting of serf recruits and noble officers chosen by their class, not their merit. In 1798 the Holy Roman Empire was forced to cede the entire left-bank Rhineland to France, thereby introducing far-reaching change to this region. Serfdom and guild privileges were eliminated, and scores of church-run territories and free imperial cities came under French rule. The larger German states began annexing smaller territories, too, and by 1803 only one ecclesiastical state and six city-states remained. After the

French routed the Austrians and Russians at Austerlitz in 1805, their great emperor, Napoleon Bonaparte (r. 1804–1815), abolished the Holy Roman Empire. Attempting to challenge this outcome, the Prussian king Frederick William III (r. 1797–1840) led his armies to a humiliating defeat at Jena and Auerstadt in 1806.

In the meantime, Napoleon had organized the bulk of the surviving German states outside of Austria and Prussia into the so-called Confederation of the Rhine. By 1808 thirty-nine states belonged, led by the newly established Kingdom of Westphalia under Napoleon's brother Jerome. Jerome introduced French reforms there, and soon many of the larger states like Bavaria, Württemberg, and Baden began to consider representative institutions, as well as the abolition of serfdom and guild privileges. These developments forced Austria and Prussia to decide whether to emulate French reforms or preserve the old order. Austria, under the arch-conservative emperor Francis I (r. 1804–1835), tried to preserve the old order, limiting itself to army reorganization along French lines—modern-style divisions, corps, and army groups— in order to keep pace with the "revolution in military affairs" that had propelled France to European hegemony. Prussia also adopted French army institutions but went much further with reforms, opening the officer corps to middle-class talent, granting rights of self-governance to municipalities, substituting free enterprise for guild regulations, promoting technology in rural enterprises, abolishing the legal basis of serfdom, and giving land title to the best-off former serfs—about 10 percent of peasant households. Aside from increasing state revenues, Prussian reformers like Gerhard von Scharnhorst (1755–1813), Heinrich Friedrich Karl vom und zum Stein (1757–1831), and Karl August von Hardenberg (1750–1822) strove to transform downtrodden subjects into patriotic citizens willing to fight for their homeland.

In 1812, Bonaparte's grip on Germany began to loosen with his disastrous invasion of Russia. Though patriotism may have played a role in the subsequent liberation of Germany from Napoleon, it did so within the regular units of the Prussian army and its allies, not the voluntary "free corps" that figured so prominently in late-nineteenth-century nationalistic accounts. In 1813, Prussia, Austria, and Russia finally united to defeat the great conqueror at Leipzig, after which the French-dominated Confederation of the Rhine began to unravel. The final defeat of Napoleon by British, Belgian, and Prussian armies took place at Waterloo, outside Brussels, in 1815.

Restoration, Revolution, and Unification (1815–1871). The abolition of the Holy Roman Empire, which had been popular among many politically conscious Germans, sparked intense discussion and negotiation concerning what might possibly replace it. A political compromise between the two dominant German powers, Austria and Prussia, produced an answer in 1814–1815: the German Confederation, a sort of league among the thirty-nine sovereign states that survived the Napoleonic Wars. The primary purpose of the confederation initially was to facilitate military cooperation among member states, thereby avoiding the divide-and-conquer strategy that Napoleon had used to dominate German Europe.

Although this compromise did not upset a majority of the people, there was nevertheless a vocal minority among university professors and students, veterans and former free corps fighters, and other nationalistically minded Germans who were angry that war and sacrifice had not produced federal institutions with more central power than the Holy Roman Empire. Many also expressed outrage that a national parliament like the old imperial Reichstag—or at the very least, representative assemblies in the various German capitals—had not been created, despite commensurate promises in states like Prussia. Matters came to a head after an irreverent protest rally at the Wartburg Castle in 1817. Feeling the pressure, Bavaria, Württemberg, and Baden introduced constitutions, and Prussia seemed to be on the verge of doing so. However, the assassination of the conservative poet August von Kotzebue (1761–1819) by a crazed university student in 1819 allowed reactionary forces to prevail. Frederick William III backed away from his parliamentary promises, while Austria's conservative chancellor, Klemens von Metternich (1773–1859), prodded members of the confederation into accepting the draconian Carlsbad Decrees, which brought the universities under political surveillance, introduced confederation-wide measures to root out subversives, effectively blocked the establishment of parliaments in states that had none, and put limits on the powers of representative assemblies in the southern states.

Although another round of disturbances rocked Germany in the early 1830s, leading to constitutional governments in Hanover, Brunswick, Hesse-Kassel, and Saxony, the forces of political conservatism were not seriously shaken because, as in 1819, Austria and Prussia used the confederation to inhibit parliamentarism. Though there had been some political progress in Germany since 1815, it is still useful to label this period "the era of restoration." Reactionary policies dominated the confederation, in fact, until 1848.

Somewhat more progress was registered in gradually ending serfdom before mid-century. Freedom had come to

the Rhineland by the late 1790s. In southern Germany, where emancipation had already been under discussion before 1815, reforms freed the bulk of the serfs—in Bavaria, for instance, 76 percent of them became free farmers. In northern Germany, rates ranged from 40 percent in Hanover to 60 percent in Prussia. This mix of the old and the new came at a price, however, because rising expectations among those who still suffered under serfdom, sometimes living beside those who were free farmers, caused disgruntlement and unrest throughout the confederation, especially in Austria, where no reforms were introduced. Peasants went on a rampage in western Galicia in 1846, for example, killing fifteen hundred noblemen.

A much greater degree of change occurred in the realm of industry and technology—indeed the entire period after 1815, with the exception of the depressed early 1820s, is now seen by economic historians as the time of early industrialization. The impact of tariff union on railroad construction and of the railways on coal mining and iron production was so pronounced after the mid-1830s that the term "industrial take-off" still finds favor. These developments created new sources of income at all levels of society, but they also generated new frictions. The handicraft guilds bristled, for example, at the unwelcome competition of factories, especially as states like Prussia abolished guild privileges or simply did not enforce the old laws, as in Saxony. Factory workers began to organize the first labor associations, and they occasionally rioted or struck. Even the industrialists themselves, much more numerous by the 1840s, were displeased by the lack of political representation to modify tariff, monetary, technology, and other economic policies that were considered restrictive. Thus industrialization, like reactionary politics and agrarian reform, laid the foundation for revolution.

All of this anger and resentment boiled over in March 1848 when news of the latest revolution in France spread into the lands of the German Confederation. Peasants burned noble estates and destroyed feudal records, urban mobs besieged royal palaces demanding reforms, and long-frustrated nationalists planned elections for an all-German constitutional assembly. Too shocked and frightened to react, rulers throughout the confederation, including those in Berlin and Vienna, established parliaments, appointed liberal ministers, and approved reforms like the abolition of the remnants of serfdom. Meanwhile, voters selected some eight hundred representatives that spring for a constituent assembly that gathered in Frankfurt am Main.

The high hopes of the revolutionaries turned to bitter disappointment, however, as 1848 yielded to 1849. Because the Frankfurt parliament was fragmented into nine separate party coalitions, polarized between radicals and conservatives, divided between Catholics and Protestants, and further split over whether to include Austria in the German state—the "large Germany" option—or exclude it—the "small Germany" solution—little agreement was reached on important issues. Already by summer 1848, monarchs in Prussia and Austria had come to realize that the deliberators in Frankfurt possessed no real military power—a huge failing in any revolution—and thus represented less of a threat than had first been assumed. After both Francis Joseph of Austria (r. 1848–1916) and Frederick William IV of Prussia (r. 1840–1861) refused to participate in the new Germany and swept away parliamentary governments at home, the radical faction in Frankfurt attempted to raise an army and settle matters by force. The Prussian army defeated them in June 1849, thus ending the nationalist experiment.

Historians are still divided over viewing the decade of the 1850s as "the reactionary fifties" (Blackbourn), as it has traditionally been seen, or as a time with more of a mixture of repression and progress (Brose, Brophy). The old ways had certainly not disappeared, for revolutionaries were executed, exiled, or imprisoned, 1848 constitutions were revoked (Hanover, Saxony, Württemberg, Baden, Austria) or revised (Prussia), noble and church privileges were restored, and the stifling institutions of the German Confederation were reinstalled. However, a new spirit of political realism designed to ward off another revolution reigned in German Europe. The abolition of serfdom proceeded in Prussia, for example, and was not overturned in Austria. Prussia permitted a limited form of parliamentary government, as did most of the major German states outside Austria. Prussia continued to promote economic unity through the expanding Zollverein (customs union), while also introducing a series of pro-business measures to accommodate some of the demands of bankers, mine owners, railroad promoters, and other entrepreneurs. Austrian opposition prevailed, on the other hand, when the Prussian king Fredrick William IV tried to establish a Prussian-dominated league of German states loosely connected to the people by a plutocratically elected German parliament.

The initial support for Prussia's plan by more than thirty German states reflected the lingering desire of Germans high and low for some form of national union. So did a wave of fervently nationalistic festivals and demonstrations during the late 1850s and early 1860s. Working more behind the scenes, the Nationalist Society, a lobby of prominent businessmen and professionals primarily from Protestant north-central Germany, looked for Prussia to lead the nationalist movement, if necessary by crushing Catholic Austria militarily. Similar sentiments lay behind much of the opposition of the Prussian Diet to army expansion and modernization that began in the early 1860s, for unless the new king, Frederick William IV's brother, William (king of Prussia, 1861–1888; German emperor, 1871–1888), was willing to defy Austria and unify the north, increased military expenditure could possibly translate into repression of parliament and its "small Germany" agenda.

The rejection of the king's budget requests and resulting political deadlock in Berlin—the so-called constitutional crisis—was not resolved until William's new tough-minded premier, Otto von Bismarck (1815–1898), prodded his monarch into a war with Austria and the German states that fought with it in 1866. The victory of Prussian arms so pleased the parliamentary opposition that they approved, retroactively, four years of essentially illegal expenditure, an act traditionally interpreted as a caving in to state power in Prussia. As later historians (including Hamerow and Gall) demonstrate, however, the liberal opposition had not been crushed so much as accommodated. Thus a Berlin-dominated north German state with limited parliamentary institutions came into being in 1867, followed by the accession of Bavaria, Württemberg, and Baden to a similarly constituted German empire after the all-German defeat of France in 1870. Economic concessions like the introduction of a pro-business commercial code, the establishment of a German currency and central bank, and the abolition of remaining guild privileges sweetened the political compromise for former opponents of Bismarck and his sovereign. That traditional conservatives were angered by all of these changes is perhaps the best measure of how much the liberals had actually won.

Imperial Germany (1871–1918). Like the Kingdom of Prussia, whose king was the German emperor (kaiser), the so-called Second Empire featured considerable executive authority. Kaisers William I (r. 1871–1888), Frederick (r. 1888), and William II (r. 1888–1918) controlled the military establishment, foreign policy (including declarations of war), and appointment of ministers, as well as the Imperial Diet (Reichstag) insofar as they retained veto power over parliamentary legislation. Bismarck and his successor imperial chancellors, who typically were premiers in Prussia, also possessed great influence through their domestic and foreign political expertise, regular access to the sovereign, and constitutional right to cosign

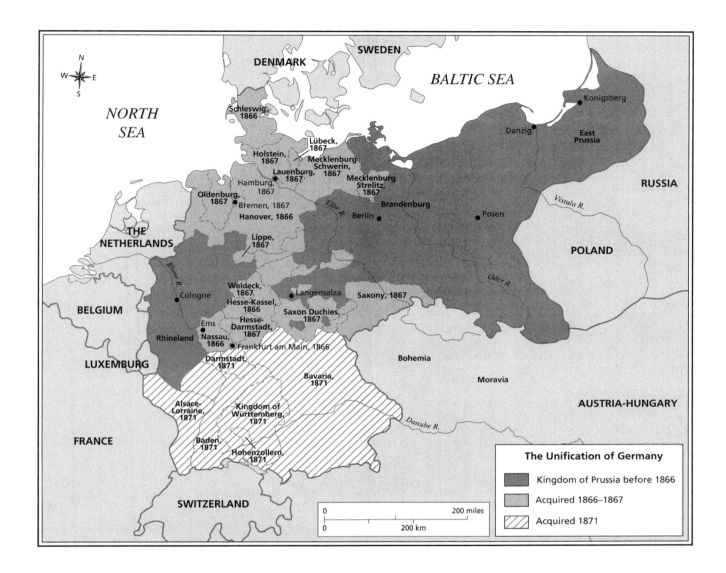

The Unification of Germany

■ Kingdom of Prussia before 1866

■ Acquired 1866–1867

▨ Acquired 1871

legislation. An upper chamber representing the federal states, the Bundesrat (Federal Council), had the right to approve all legislation, which amounted to an extension of monarchical authority because of the control that king and premier in Prussia wielded over the powerful, veto-wielding Prussian Bundesrat delegation. However, the executive could not bypass the Reichstag, for it could approve or reject all bills put before it, including the all-important military budget of the empire. Like Prussia after the constitutional crisis, the German empire was not an absolute monarchy; hence the importance of histories that underscore the critical compromises of the pre-1871 period.

Once installed, parliamentary institutions tend to gain in power (consider nineteenth-century Italy)—and this is what the liberal Reichstag parties anticipated. But this was not the case in Germany during Bismarck's tenure as chancellor (1871–1890). The Reichstag had arguably lost stature, in fact, when the "Iron Chancellor" stepped down. He accomplished this by playing various party groupings off against one another, or occasionally by calling for new elections and then heaping nationalistic abuse on parties that had voted against budget proposals. In other ways, however, the Reichstag undermined its own strength. For example, Liberal Protestants pressed for discriminatory laws against the Catholic Church, with the result that worsening religious divisions weakened opposition unity.

Class divisions were a more significant factor in the long run. The party that championed the workers' cause, the Social Democratic Party of Germany (SPD), gained so steadily at the polls as the century ended that the previously pro-parliamentary middle-class parties began to doubt the wisdom of their goals. Indeed the SPD's Marxist propaganda, transparent preference for republican democracy, and parliamentary demands for radical labor legislation like the eight-hour day and unemployment insurance—reforms that went much further than the minimal social insurance programs introduced by Bismarck in the 1880s—shed a frightening light on the prospects of greater parliamentary (that is, Social Democratic) control of the state. This antisocialist stance made the Marxist credo of inevitable class struggle more credible, thereby strengthening the SPD's appeal to workers as German industrialization and the accompanying growth of the working class accelerated. And all of this rapid economic, social, and political change in turn made William II and his ministers balk at building on Bismarck's reforms, which only enhanced Social Democratic momentum.

By the eve of World War I, Imperial Germany was badly polarized along class lines. While waiting in vain for the progressive labor laws demanded by the SPD, proletarians had grown angrier as the central government and nonsocialist Reichstag parties approved tariff (1902) and tax (1909) bills that increased the cost of living. The refusal of the government to democratize Prussian voting laws in 1910 added to the unrest, propelling the Social Democrats to a dramatic victory in the Reichstag elections of 1912: they became the largest party in parliament, with 35 percent of the popular vote. Having lost working-class votes, two parties to the right of the SPD, the Progressives and the Center Party, swung left in 1913, approving imperial tax legislation that tapped wealth for the first time. Significantly enough, these were later the same three parties that democratized Germany in 1918–1919. The government, strapped for money to fund its arms race with rivals Britain, France, and Russia, acquiesced.

That same year, 1913, Reichstag conservatives, prodded by extra-parliamentary allies like the militaristic and rabidly antisocialist Pan-German League, spoke out not only against unacceptably leftist, seemingly democratizing party agendas, but also against the government's alleged pandering to them. Personal scandals and controversies surrounding William II strengthened the longing in right-radical circles for a tougher, more authoritarian rule in Germany, a rule that could come, said some, only in wartime. Some historians see this rightist resurgence from below—one that did not emanate exclusively from the aristocracy or the executive establishment—as an early sign of the emergence of those populist antidemocratic forces that weakened German democracy in the 1920s and paved the way for the rise of Adolf Hitler (1889–1945) and the Nazis in 1933. Thus Germany's leftist and rightist alternatives to monarchy had already surfaced before 1914.

These disruptive, polarizing trends worsened after the outbreak of World War I in 1914. The SPD and their allied trade unions, joined by the Center Party, the Progressives, and the allied unions of these parties, pressed the last imperial chancellor, Theobald von Bethmann-Hollweg (1856–1921), to implement far-reaching social and political reforms. The army leaders Paul von Hindenburg (1847–1934) and Erich Ludendorff (1865–1937) resisted these demands, however, as well as the Reichstag's call in 1917 for peace negotiations. That year they convinced the increasingly marginalized William II to dismiss Bethmann, hold out for total victory over Germany's many enemies, and preserve monarchical authoritarianism, behind the façade of which the army would carry on its "silent dictatorship." Supporting this draconian agenda was the Party of the Fatherland, a political amalgam of conservatives, radical nationalists, and militarists, including the Pan German League and the fellow-traveling Army League—whose leaders went so far as to pressure Ludendorff, unsuccessfully, for a full-fledged military dictatorship. The military defeat of Germany in November 1918, accompanied by the kaiser's abdication, revolutionary violence in the streets, and the proclamation by SPD leaders of a democratic republic, seemed to indicate that the forces of the left had defeated their right-wing adversaries.

The Weimar Republic (1919–1933). Germany now tried democracy. Prospects for success appeared positive at first. Dubbing themselves "Spartacists," Communist revolutionaries who wanted, Bolshevik style, to seize power were crushed by special free corps units armed by the old imperial army and deployed by the young republic. Although this was a disturbing beginning to republican rule, the violence did not derail the constitutional process. The political forces of the right lost heavily in elections to the constituent assembly, while the reform-oriented parties of prewar days—the SPD, the Center, and the Progressives, now renamed the German Democrats—won nearly 80 percent of the vote. The new regime was legitimated and the old was discredited as delegates gathered in Weimar to write the constitution. The three victorious parties, the so-called Weimar Coalition, completed a document by August 1919 that gave men and women the vote and guaranteed social justice.

The acceptance by the government that summer of the punitive Treaty of Versailles began the process of undermining democracy because, even though there was no realistic alternative to signing, many Germans began to question the patriotism of the new leadership. Hindenburg fueled these doubts by charging that the Reichstag Left had pursued selfish political ends during the war rather than providing for the army's needs. Economic catastrophe in the form of raging inflation cut further into the electoral base of the Weimar Coalition. By 1924 the coalition had slipped below 42 percent, and it never again achieved a majority. The election of Hindenburg to the presidency in 1925 confirmed for many the wisdom of the quip that Germany had become "a republic without republicans." This is not to say, however, that the electorate favored a return to the monarchy. Thus the two rightist parties with the most avid monarchists, the German People's Party and the German National People's Party, lost nearly eight percentage points between 1924 and 1928. The inability of the Weimar Coalition as well as of the old right-wing politicians to rebuild national prestige or fully restore economic prosperity drove increasing numbers of Germans—a third of the 1928 voters—toward the radical departures espoused by the Communists and splinter parties representing small businessmen, farmers, and veterans. Among these splinter parties was Hitler's Nazi Party. German democracy survived the 1920s, but only because the antidemocratic majority was too splintered to agree on an alternative.

The onset of the Great Depression in 1929–1930, which sent unemployment levels soaring to nearly 40 percent by 1932, created a political opportunity that the Nazis seized more successfully than any other party did. Hitler's followers grasped 18.3 percent of the vote in 1930, up from a mere 2.6 percent in 1928, and then 37.4 percent in 1932. The charismatic oratory of the party's self-proclaimed Führer (leader) partly explains this success, but there were many other factors at work. The Nazis had the best local organization, catering opportunistically to the economic grievances of every occupational group and social class. Moreover, they beat the nationalistic drum louder than the others, which appealed to voters tired of Germany limping from one national catastrophe—the Great War—to another—the Great Depression. The party also toned down its rabid anti-Semitism in public in an effort to appeal to those Germans—perhaps one-half of the electorate—who favored a rescinding of Jewish civil rights but were repulsed by more violent "solutions" to the so-called Jewish Question. With the largest Reichstag

delegation behind Hitler, President Hindenburg saw no political alternative to appointing the Nazi leader chancellor in January 1933.

Nazi Germany (1933–1945). Over the next eighteen months the Nazis swept away Germany's struggling democracy and established one-party rule. Alleging that the Communists plotted revolution, Hitler obtained emergency powers from Hindenburg to deal with the threat. Civil liberties were eliminated temporarily in February, and then more permanently in March when a Reichstag majority of Nazis and older right-wing parties passed the Enabling Act. Hoping for concessions to the Catholic Church, the Center Party, controlled now by its own right wing, joined the majority. With these far-reaching powers the Nazi-controlled police and the party's paramilitary organization, the Sturmabteilung (SA; Storm Troopers), arrested Communists, socialists, and trade unionists and commandeered trade union assets. Frightened by these developments but also aiming to win favor with the Nazi regime, the other, non-Nazi parties, including the Center, abolished themselves that spring and early summer. Hitler's minions took over local governments across the country, while also bringing all of the heretofore influential state governments under central control. Social and recreational clubs were Nazified in this process of *Gleichschaltung* (coordination). Even the leadership of the powerful SA was purged so that the SA would not pursue an independent agenda. With the death of Hindenburg in the summer of 1934, accompanied by the army's oath of allegiance to Hitler, the last impediments to Nazi dictatorship were removed.

Hitler, a common soldier in World War I, now set his sights on foreign policy in pursuit of his monomaniacal desire to overturn the negative verdict of that conflict. In 1935 he made public the rearmament process, illegal under the Treaty of Versailles, that had been under way secretly since 1933. The next violation of Versailles occurred in 1936 with the military reoccupation of the Rhineland, followed in 1938 by the annexation of Austria, which had been blocked by the allies in 1919. The British and the French hoped to appease Hitler in September 1938 by forcing Czechoslovakia to cede Germany the Sudetenland, but the appeasers' hopes faded when the Nazis marched into Prague in March 1939. The German invasion of Poland in September 1939 finally triggered war with Britain and France.

The ensuing six-year conflagration underscored the recklessness of Hitler's foreign policy, for additional declarations of war on both the Soviet Union and the

Nazi Germany. Adolf Hitler receives the congratulations of the Reichstag after announcing the Anschluss between Germany and Austria, Berlin, March 1938. United States Department of Defense

United States produced an enemy coalition so powerful that even the German-dominated continent of Europe could not prevail. The tragic result was a Germany beaten and bombed into submission by May 1945. Millions of German soldiers and civilians had paid the ultimate price for Hitler's insanity.

The tragedy of World War II was deepened by the unfolding Nazi genocide against the Jews. Hitler and his henchmen moved cautiously at first, contenting themselves with purging the civil service in 1933 and banning German-Jewish marriage and removing Jewish citizenship rights in 1935. As war approached in 1938, however, Nazi policy radicalized further—witness the horrible *Kristallnacht* (Night of the Broken Glass) pogrom in November 1938. Hundreds of Jews died in this night of violence and its aftermath, a frightening sign of things to come during the war, when nearly 6 million Jews perished. The war and the Holocaust left a terrible legacy for German survivors as they attempted to rebuild their ruined state.

From Division to Reunification (1945–2007). The victorious Grand Alliance originally intended to administer Germany as one country. Within three years of VE Day, however, this joint administration had deteriorated,

a victim of the antithetical political and economic systems of the Western democracies and the Soviet Union. In 1948 the United States, Britain, and France moved toward the establishment of a separate West German state, the Federal Republic of Germany (FRG). Its founding in 1949 induced the Soviets to establish their own Communist state in East Germany, the German Democratic Republic (GDR). Germany remained divided for the next forty-one years.

Under the leadership of Konrad Adenauer (1876–1967; chancellor, 1949–1963), head of the Christian Democratic Union (CDU) and its sister party, the Christian Social Union (CSU), the FRG reestablished democratic procedures. By the late 1950s West Germany possessed a smoothly functioning three-party system: the SPD sat in opposition, while the Free Democrats sat either in opposition or in coalition with the CDU/CSU. Perhaps the only blemish on West German democracy was its slow coming to grips with the Nazi past. Well into the 1960s a majority of Germans refused either to admit the mistakes of Nazism or, if they did, to engage in the kind of discussion required to make genuine amends—and without such admissions and engagement with the tragedy of the past, the danger of once again slipping away from democracy seemed real to many outside observers of the FRG. Not until a younger generation moved into political life in the 1970s and voted in large numbers for the SPD and its charismatic leader, Willi Brandt (1913–1992; chancellor, 1969–1974), did West Germany complete the process of dealing with the evils of Nazism. Brandt's famous kneeling in 1970 at the memorial to the victims of the Jewish uprising in Warsaw, crushed by the Nazis in 1943, was a poignant symbol of this transition.

Meanwhile in the GDR Communist rule had tightened by the 1960s. Millions of East Germans had fled to the FRG by traveling to the Western-controlled sections of West Berlin, but this was no longer possible after the Communists constructed a wall around free Berlin and along the border with the FRG in 1961. Dissatisfaction with police-state abuses and poor economic performance, especially for consumers, simmered throughout the 1970s and 1980s, however, coming to a head in 1989 with protest marches in Berlin, Leipzig, and other cities. After the beleaguered regime opened the wall for travel to the FRG in November 1989, what was left of governmental legitimacy crumbled. In this position of weakness the Communists allowed free elections in March 1990 that returned a majority in favor of joining the FRG. The reunification process was completed in October when the five states of the former GDR became states of the FRG.

Reunification did not come without its difficulties. The cost of modernizing East German industry and infrastructure was much higher than the CDU/CSU head Helmut Kohl (b. 1930; chancellor, 1982–1998) anticipated, a miscalculation that led to government deficits, inflation, and unemployment, especially in the "new federal states" of the East. These problems made the transition to democratic rule there more difficult, a dilemma that continued during the government of the SPD leader Gerhard Schröder (b. 1944; chancellor, 1998–2004). It is a measure of the gradual stabilization of the reunited state, however, that Angela Merkel (b. 1954), a former citizen of the GDR, advanced to the chancellorship after the CDU/CSU electoral victory of September 2004. Another, perhaps more important, sign of Germany's successful completion of the long struggle for liberal and democratic institutions is the leading role that Germany has played in the establishment and expansion of the European Union, a beacon of democracy and peace in a Europe that had experienced little of either throughout most of the twentieth century.

[See also Austro-Prussian War; Bavaria; Berlin; Carlsbad Decrees; European Union; Franco-Prussian War; Gestapo; Hanover, Kingdom of; Holocaust; Holy Roman Empire; Kulturkampf; Munich Agreement;

East Germany. Thousands of East German citizens sit on the street in front of the Palace of the Republic on the eve of the election of the new head of state of East Germany, October 23, 1989. AP IMAGES

German Chancellor. Helmut Kohl campaigning in Büsum, Schleswig-Holstein. Photograph by Christ of Stache. AP IMAGES

Nazism; Occupation of Germany; Prussia; Reunification of Germany; Rhine, Confederation of the; Rhine Basin; Saarland; Saxony; Schleswig-Holstein; SS; World War I; World War II; *and* Württemberg, Kingdom of.]

BIBLIOGRAPHY

Allen, William Sheridan. *The Nazi Seizure of Power: The Experience of a Single German Town, 1922–1945.* Rev. ed. New York: F. Watts, 1984. Looks at the rise of the Nazis in the Hanoverian town of Northeim. Excellent vehicle for studying the Nazi coordination of society from below.

Anderson, Margaret Lavinia. *Windthorst: A Political Biography.* New York: Oxford University Press, 1981. An excellent biography of the late-nineteenth-century Catholic political leader Ludwig Windthorst. Also a good means of studying the increasingly frustrated and demoralized Reichstag at the end of Bismarck's tenure as chancellor.

Berghahn, Volker R. *Imperial Germany 1871–1914: Economy, Society, Culture, and Politics.* Providence, R.I.: Berghahn Books, 1994. A comprehensive history of prewar Germany; includes valuable and extensive statistical appendices.

Blackbourn, David. *The Long Nineteenth Century: A History of Germany, 1780–1918.* New York: Oxford University Press, 1997. The best comprehensive, short (about 500 pages), readable, and still largely current history of this period.

Böhme, Helmut. *Deutschlands Weg zur Grossmacht: Studien zum Verhältnis von Wirtschaft und Staat während der Reichsgründungszeit 1848–1881.* Cologne, Germany: Kiepenheuer & Witsch, 1966. See also Hamerow.

Brophy, James M. *Capitalism, Politics, and Railroads in Prussia, 1830–1870.* Columbus: Ohio State University Press, 1998. Illuminates the "negotiated settlements" between conservatives and liberals, especially after 1848, as opposed to the traditional emphasis on the continuity of reactionary policies.

Brose, Eric Dorn. *German History, 1789–1871: From the Holy Roman Empire to the Bismarckian Reich.* Providence, R.I.: Berghahn Books, 1997. Shorter (382 pages) and more current than the works by Sheehan and the relevant volumes of Wehler.

Brose, Eric Dorn. *The Politics of Technological Change in Prussia: Out of the Shadow of Antiquity, 1809–1848.* Princeton, N.J.: Princeton University Press, 1993. Assesses the role of the state in early industrialization, finding both positive and negative influences; also challenges the older view that state reformers had clearly modern visions and agendas. Includes extensive concluding comments on the 1850s and 1860s.

Chickering, Roger. *Imperial Germany and the Great War, 1914–1918.* Cambridge, U.K.: Cambridge University Press, 1998. A short (227 pages) but comprehensive history of Germany during World War I.

Eley, Geoff. *Reshaping the German Right: Radical Nationalism and Political Change after Bismarck.* New Haven, Conn.: Yale University Press, 1980. Argues that radical nationalism in Germany before 1914 was a populist phenomenon as opposed to manipulation from the state establishment, emphasized by Hans-Ulrich Wehler in *The German Empire, 1871–1918.*

Eyck, Erich. *A History of the Weimar Republic.* 2 vols. Translated by Harlan P. Hanson and Robert G. L. Waite. Cambridge, Mass.: Harvard University Press, 1962–1963. The English translation of *Geschichte der Weimarer Republik,* first published in 1954–1956. A classic, the traditional "top-down" approach.

Fremdling, Rainer. *Eisenbahnen und deutsches Wirtschaftswachstum, 1840–1879.* Dortmund, Germany: Gesellschaft für Westfälische Wirtschaftsgeschichte, 1975. See also Rostow.

Fritzsche, Peter. *Germans into Nazis.* Cambridge, Mass.: Harvard University Press, 1998. Sees the ultimate triumph of the Nazis not merely as a product of the lost war and the misery of the Great Depression but primarily as a product of populist forces unleashed by the war—forces that activated radical antidemocratic movements like the Nazis, who opposed not only the Weimar Coalition but also the traditional right.

Fulbrook, Mary. *Anatomy of a Dictatorship: Inside the GDR, 1949–1989.* New York: Oxford University Press, 1995. A fine study of the gradual consolidation of the GDR in the 1960s and 1970s, followed by the gradual loss of central control in the 1980s.

Gagliardo, John G. *Reich and Nation: The Holy Roman Empire as Idea and Reality, 1763–1806.* Bloomington: Indiana University Press, 1980. An important corrective to German nationalistic accounts that viewed the Holy Roman Empire as an anachronism.

Gall, Lothar. *Bismarck: The White Revolutionary.* Translated by J. A. Underwood. London: Allen and Unwin, 1986. Emphasizes Bismarck's realistic turn toward liberal nationalist demands after 1865.

Hamerow, Theodore S. *The Social Foundations of German Unification, 1858–1871.* 2 vols. Princeton, N.J.: Princeton University Press, 1969–1972. An indispensable analysis of the economic rivalry between Austria and Prussia, as well as the classic investigation in English of the political compromise between liberals and conservatives before 1871. See also Böhme.

Herf, Jeffrey. *Divided Memory: The Nazi Past in the Two Germanys.* Cambridge, Mass.: Harvard University Press, 1997. Analyzes the avoidance of dealing with the Nazi past both in the GDR, which saw the Hitler period as a bourgeois problem, and in the FRG, which throughout the 1950s and 1960s swept these issues under the rug to appease Nazi sympathizers who might otherwise have created Weimar-style difficulties for the young democracy.

Holborn, Hajo. *A History of Modern Germany, 1840–1945.* New York: Alfred A. Knopf, 1969. See also Pinson.

Hull, Isabel V. *The Entourage of Kaiser Wilhelm II, 1888–1918.* Cambridge, U.K.: Cambridge University Press, 1982. A fascinating, insightful study of Wilhelm II's problematic relationship with the army, as well as of scandals and controversies during his reign (such as the Daily Telegraph Affair and the Eulenburg trial).

Jones, Larry Eugene. *German Liberalism and the Dissolution of the Weimar Party System, 1918–1933.* Chapel Hill: University of North Carolina Press, 1988. Traces in great detail (660 pages) the collapse of German democracy through the history, first told here, of the left-of-center German Democratic Party and the right-of-center German People's Party.

Kershaw, Ian. *Hitler, 1936–1945: Nemesis.* New York: W. W. Norton, 2000. The definitive and most current biography of the Nazi leader.

Kitchen, Martin. *The Silent Dictatorship: The Politics of the German High Command under Hindenburg and Ludendorff, 1916–1918.* New York: Holmes and Meier, 1976. The classic study of military politics during the Great War, especially the army's role in the erosion of monarchical control of the state.

Knox, MacGregor. "Mass Politics and Nationalism as Military Revolution: The French Revolution and After." In *The Dynamics of Military Revolution 1300–2050,* edited by MacGregor Knox and Williamson Murray, pp. 57–73. Cambridge, U.K.: Cambridge University Press, 2001. The book contains numerous articles dealing with German military history from the early nineteenth century to World War II. The article advances the notion of "revolutions in military affairs," which involve successful organizational and operational responses by military establishments to far-reaching political change or technological change or both.

Peukert, Detlev J. K. *The Weimar Republic: The Crisis of Classical Modernity.* Translated by Richard Deveson. New York: Hill and Wang, 1992. English translation of *Die Weimarer Republik,* first published in 1987. Probes everyday life, culture, and politics in an attempt to explain the intensifying contradictions of Germany's advanced industrial society that led ultimately to breakdown and the nightmare of Nazism.

Pinson, Koppel S. *Modern Germany: Its History and Civilization.* New York: Macmillan, 1954. Holborn also emphasizes the failure and defeat of nineteenth-century German liberalism, but is somewhat more balanced.

Rostow, Walt W. *The Stages of Economic Growth: A Non-Communist Manifesto.* Cambridge, U.K.: Cambridge University Press, 1960. The theoretical underpinning for later works, like Fremdling's, emphasizing the tremendous impact of railroads on German industrialization. There is consensus today, however, that economic growth was also robust *before* 1840.

Sheehan, James J. *German History, 1770–1866.* New York: Oxford University Press, 1989. Still the best in-depth (969 pages) study in English of the period, despite having become somewhat dated.

Turner, Henry Ashby, Jr. *The Two Germanies since 1945.* New Haven, Conn.: Yale University Press, 1987. An excellent overview of political and economic developments in the FRG and GDR.

Vogel, Barbara. *Allgemeine Gewerbefreiheit: Die Reformpolitik des preussischen Staatskanzlers Hardenberg (1810–1820).* Göttingen, Germany: Vandenhoeck & Ruprecht, 1983. Argues convincingly that Hardenberg and his aides strove for rural, not urban industrialization.

Wehler, Hans-Ulrich. *Deutsche Gesellschaftsgeschichte.* 3 vols. Munich: C. H. Beck, 1987–1995. A detailed (more than three thousand pages), indispensable analysis of societal trends from 1700 to 1914, although, like Sheehan, now somewhat dated.

Wehler, Hans-Ulrich. *The German Empire, 1871–1918.* Translated by Kim Traynor. Leamington Spa, U.K.: Berg, 1985. English translation of *Das Deutsche Kaiserreich, 1871–1918,* first published in 1973.

ERIC DORN BROSE

GERM THEORY. The words "origins of germ theory" conjure up images of clusters of researchers centered around Robert Koch of Berlin (1843–1910). Beginning in 1876 with his discovery of the minute living thing ("germ") that caused anthrax (usually a cattle disease), Koch then turned his attention to the principal infectious diseases that each year, globally, killed millions of humankind. In 1882 he announced discovery of the "germ" causal agent of tuberculosis—an illness that in rapidly industrializing Europe (and later in industrializing Japan) was annually causing 7 or 8 percent of all deaths. Two years later Koch announced his discovery of the causal agent of cholera. He affirmed that cholera was carried from India to distant continents by infected humans who harbored the self-multiplying causal agent, the vibrio, in their guts. Therefore its movement outward could be blocked.

Building on laboratory techniques Koch pioneered in 1881–1882 while working on tuberculosis, during the next few years his associates discovered the specific "germ" causal agents of typhoid, diphtheria, pneumonia, tetanus, gonorrhea, cerebrospinal meningitis, and bubonic plague. Yet the mention of these powerful affirmations of that long-disputed, now precisely defined concept, "germ theory" must not let us forget that the discovery of the actual microscopic disease causal agents was not accompanied by the discovery of curative agents. This breakthrough had to await the "therapeutic revolution" of the 1940s, beginning with the wholesale use of penicillin. However, knowledge of a causal agent specific to each ailment had the potential (not everywhere taken up) to contribute to global progress in preventative medicine.

In pioneering "germ theory," Koch's best-known competitor was Louis Pasteur of France (1822–1895). Through his work on the fermentation of alcoholic beverages in the 1860s and early 1870s, Pasteur did much to disprove the rival theory of "spontaneous generation," which held that a disease causal agent need not have ancestors—it somehow created itself anew in the present. However, Pasteur never did do research into the major infectious diseases of humankind; that work was done by Koch. And as for the English, they began well and then came unstuck.

Building on Pasteur's "fermentation" theory, Joseph Lister (1827–1912) revealed in 1867 that if open wounds were covered with a carbolic acid solution during surgical operations and during recovery, they would not be made septic by "germs" floating around in the air; patients no longer need die of septicemia or gangrene. But Lister's findings were opposed by British challengers of germ theory. They were far better received in Germany. John Snow of London (1813–1858) was also belittled in his homeland after he suggested in 1849 and 1854 that cholera was caused by some sort of living, self-reproducing "germ."

At the root of British resistance to the germ theory was the low social status of medical protoscientists and the governing elite's awareness that if germ theory were recognized as true, they would have to accept the practice of quarantine and the long delay of ships and suspect crews coming from cholera-afflicted India before they could pass through the Suez Canal. This the government refused to do. Thus for reasons related to trade but unrelated to medical science, after 1868 British protoscientists were warned off germ theory research. As late as 1893 the governing class still chose to ignore "mere" scientific findings. In that year "experts" testifying to a royal commission about the safety of Thames water for human consumption failed to convince its members that the water harbored typhoid, dysentery, and other lethal "germs": so much for "germ theory." For their part, in the 1920s U.S. educators continued to bypass theoryless Britain and sent their medical students to research institutions in Germany.

Growing knowledge of germ theory dramatically transformed a variety of medical procedures, particularly in surgery and childbirth. It also underlay important hygiene movements in many parts of the world, affecting personal habits and food preparation alike. As part of broader programs in public health, efforts to reduce exposure to germs helped account for considerable reductions in mortality levels, particularly among children, in virtually every region during the twentieth century, affecting personal habits and food preparation alike. As part of the broader program in public health put in place by the World Health Organization by its Alma Ata Declaration in 1979, efforts to reduce exposure to germs helped to account for considerable reductions in mortality levels, particularly among children in those regions of the world that had access to safe water and safe waste disposal systems.

[*See also* Cholera; Drugs and Narcotics, *subentry* The Science of Drugs; *and* Health and Disease.]

BIBLIOGRAPHY

Hamlin, Christopher. "Politics and Germ Theories in Victorian Britain: The Metropolitan Water Commissions of 1867–9 and 1892–3." In *Government and Expertise: Specialists, Administrators, and Professionals, 1860–1919*, edited by Roy MacLeod, pp. 110–127. Cambridge, U.K.: Cambridge University Press, 1988. The John Burdon Sanderson lectures in the *Lancet*.

Watts, Sheldon. "The Birth of Modern Scientific Medicine: The German Lands Contrasted with the United Kingdom and British India." In *Disease and Medicine in World History*, pp. 109–125. London: Routledge, 2003.

Wootton, David. *Bad Medicine: Doctors Doing Harm Since Hippocrates*. London: Oxford University Press, 2006.

SHELDON WATTS

GESTAPO. The Gestapo (Geheime Staatspolizei, or "Secret State Police") became the centralized political detective police of the Third Reich in June 1936 after Adolf Hitler appointed Reichsführer-SS Heinrich Himmler (1900–1945) chief of the German police. When the Nazis came to power in January 1933, to destroy all opposition they had created in each federated German state such special detective police. "Political suspects" expanded beyond spies, traitors, and saboteurs to include all non-Nazi political, professional, social, and youth organizations, as well as politically active clerics and "alien races," especially Jews. The Gestapo had authority to take suspects into veritably indefinite "protective custody," without judicial review. They could commit internees to prisons or concentration camps. In 1938 the Gestapo became the executive agency for solving the "Jewish problem," originally by "encouraging" emigration. Himmler's SS (Schutzstaffel, or "Protection Corps") also had control over all concentration camps. His triangle of SS, Gestapo, and concentration camps formed the heart of the terrorist police state.

Under its ultimate head, Heinrich Müller (1900–1945), the Gestapo was part of the Sipo or Sicherheitspolizei (Security Police) of SS-General Reinhard Heydrich (1904–1942), who also commanded the SD (Sicherheitsdienst, or "Security Service") of the SS, its intelligence agency for monitoring all enemies of German society. The regular detectives, Kriminalpolizei, were the other branch of Sipo, and they acquired similar extraordinary arrest powers for eliminating all unwanted or "asocial" elements of society. Heydrich inserted SS/SD men into all levels of Sipo while simultaneously recruiting suitable detectives into SD membership. He thus pursued Himmler's long-range plan to fuse the SS and the police into a future SS detective force, thoroughly imbued with Nazi ideology and totally obedient to the Führer. Though well placed, SS penetration of Sipo never exceeded 18 percent, and although it was under SS command, the Gestapo was never part of the SS.

Beginning in 1939, Sipo and SD expanded into the conquered territories, first as part of Einsatzgruppen (special action groups) that followed the army, establishing field offices. In first Poland and then the Soviet Union they initially exterminated all potential opposition, but this soon escalated to the intended extermination of the entire Jewish population, most Senti and Roma, and millions of Slavs. In all occupied countries the Gestapo rounded up Jews and shipped them to death camps in the east. For their work the Gestapo had extensive support from regular German police, SS units, the army, and police auxiliaries from local populations. The war brought increasing numbers of women into the Gestapo in mostly clerical roles.

[See also Germany; Nazism; Police; and SS.]

BIBLIOGRAPHY

Browder, George C. Hitler's Enforcers: The Gestapo and the SS Security Service in the Nazi Revolution. New York: Oxford University Press, 1996. Covers the formative years of Sipo and SD, especially the development and nature of their personnel and work.

Gellately, Robert. The Gestapo and German Society: Enforcing Racial Policy, 1933–1945. Oxford: Clarendon Press, 1990. A pioneering analysis of the relationship of the Gestapo with the general population, and of the Gestapo's support of ferreting out "public enemies."

Johnson, Eric A. Nazi Terror: The Gestapo, Jews, and Ordinary Germans. New York: Basic Books, 1999. Case studies of regional Gestapo offices, their work, and their behavior in persecuting "enemies"; argues that the Jewish experts in particular were devoted anti-Semites.

GEORGE C. BROWDER

GHANA. Ghana's history since 1750 can be divided into four periods: independent African polities and the transatlantic slave trade (1750–1807); British expansion (1807–1902); British colonial rule (1902–1957); and independence (1957–present).

Independent African Polities and the Transatlantic Slave Trade. In 1750 the territory that is now Ghana was inhabited by many different political and cultural groups. The main integrating force in the region was the overseas trade through which gold and slaves were exchanged for European manufactures. Several European nations had established commercial locations along the Atlantic coast. The kingdom of Ashanti occupied the interior forest. Many smaller kingdoms and tribal systems occupied the grasslands of the north.

The main European commercial establishments, from Britain and Holland, occupied forts that dotted the "Gold Coast." They maintained close relations with coastal peoples, some of whom became Westernized. The traders were confined to their settlements, which they leased from the local indigenous authorities. Ashanti deliberately restricted European movements in order to maintain its control over gold and slaves. The growing trade encouraged competition between English and Dutch interests, and Ashanti expanded, incorporating most of the territory that is now Ghana and establishing direct contact with Europeans on the coast.

By this time the main features of indigenous society had crystallized. The Akan cultural group, including the Ashanti, is the largest in the country. Its traditional order reflected the importance of localized matrilineal groups and of hereditary chiefs. Settlement was based on towns composed of several wards, each occupied by a single lineage. These family groups provided their members with residential and farming land and held positions in the town's administration. Lineage membership was determined by matrilineal descent.

A town was ruled by a hereditary chief selected from a royal lineage. The chief assumed administrative and judicial authority but was bound to consult with his council, whose members represented the settlement's other lineages. He had no control over his subjects' land or crops but held subsoil rights. This entitled him to a share of any natural products, most importantly gold. He also was able to collect incomes from the sale of slaves. Town chiefs were organized into a hierarchy of divisions and states, each of which was headed by a higher-order chief. The Ashanti Union was an even larger confederation of seven states with additional conquered territories.

British Expansion and Colonial Rule. Affairs on the West African coast changed dramatically after 1807, when Britain abolished the slave trade. British activities shifted from actively trading in slaves to pursuing campaigns against slavers. Conflicts with the Dutch and Ashanti marked the century, and Britain became increasingly involved in the region to counter French and German encroachments. British merchants were joined by military regiments, administrators, and missionaries, who attempted to suppress slave trading and local slavery and to foster alternative commercial activities.

Expanding British interests led to the imposition of a protectorate over their coastal forts in 1843 and the acquisition of Dutch forts in 1872. Wars against the Ashanti between 1827 and 1901 ended with the kingdom's defeat and the imposition of British rule over Ashanti and the Northern Territories.

The key British policy in its new Gold Coast Colony attempted to construct an economy that would feed its industries by supplying raw materials and purchasing manufactured goods. This process involved direct British development of the gold mining industry. Some attempt was also made to establish British-owned plantations, but the commercialization of agriculture was predominantly undertaken by indigenous farmers. A focus on oil palm production quickly shifted to cocoa, and by 1920 the Gold Coast had become the world's largest producer. Export crop incomes and import and export duties brought wealth to the colony and funded infrastructure development.

Britain's administrative arrangements in the Gold Coast followed the policy of "indirect rule," establishing a British administration in the capital at Accra but delegating local authority to indigenous rulers. The intent of this system was to cultivate an African elite that would eventually take over from the British. Local rulers were overseen by colonial administrators, who maintained ultimate authority because of their control over finances and the police. The system generated many contradictions. Most seriously, it undermined the legitimacy of the chiefs that it attempted to elevate, since they had become accountable to the British authorities rather than to the local populace.

Colonization brought many changes to indigenous society and culture. The spread of cocoa cultivation created a commercial economy that affected farming methods, consumption patterns, and family and community organization. Cocoa farmers reinvested in new lands and migrated to pioneer regions. Land leases and sales weakened lineage tenure and generated private property and financial wealth under the personal control of individuals. Matrilineal ties were weakened as inheritance became divided according to family claims and obligations to wives and children. Movements to new cocoa-growing regions and to the cities brought people from different ethnic backgrounds together, generating arenas of cooperation, accommodation, and competition.

Economic transformations were accompanied by changes in other aspects of society. Export revenues and Christian missionary groups brought hospitals, schools, and other services. Educated Africans migrated to the cities seeking employment in commercial and government sectors. Divisions developed between urbanites and farmers and among professionals, small business owners, and wage workers.

British policy and activities on the Gold Coast quickly led to indigenous resistance. The main opposition emerged from the educated elites. Excluded from participation in indirect rule, they led a movement to mitigate colonial injustices. The Aboriginal Rights Protection Society sent numerous petitions to the British parliament protesting policies such as the creation of Crown lands and taxation without representation. These protestors were not inclined to seek support from the broader population. However, after 1945 mass discontent grew over an economic downturn and failed promises of more political freedoms. The intelligentsia took advantage of the growing dissatisfaction and brought in Kwame Nkrumah to organize a mass movement. A radical activist, Nkrumah broke ranks with his sponsors and formed a new party, which advocated and achieved independence. The nation of Ghana was inaugurated in 1957.

Independence. Nkrumah pursued an ambitious plan to modernize the Ghanaian economy. He adopted a socialist approach of state investment in industry and infrastructure. His international policy cultivated ties with communist countries to offset British and American influences, attempted to assist African independence movements, and supported continental unification. His domestic policy stripped the chiefs of all but ritual powers and established elected district councils.

The rapid implementation of grandiose projects depleted the new country's foreign reserves and development grants through mismanagement and corruption. Along with falling cocoa prices, failures of nationalist programs led to a coup in 1966. Since then, Ghana has experienced many economic vicissitudes and a succession of civilian and military regimes that resulted in an economic crisis in the 1980s. At that time Jerry Rawlings, the head of the ruling junta, negotiated a structural adjustment agreement with the World Bank to liberalize the economy. He subsequently disbanded military rule but remained in power in the new civilian government as winner of the 1992 presidential election. His party was defeated in the 2000 election by John Kufuor.

Ghana's reconstruction after 1985 showed much promise. By the mid-2000s, Democratic rule had remained in place through four election cycles; the economy had grown at an average of 5 percent per year. However many problems remained. Per capita income remained low. Industrialization had grown slowly, and the economy remained dependent on commodity exports. Improvements that did occur favored the wealthy. In spite of some attempts at decentralization, the national government retained a large share of power and was less than fully responsive to popular demands.

[*See also* Africa, *subentry* Western Africa.]

BIBLIOGRAPHY
Chazan, Naomi. *An Anatomy of Ghanaian Politics: Managing Political Recession, 1969–1982*. Boulder, Colo.: Westview, 1983. A study of the sequences of civilian and military rule in Ghana in the post-Nkrumah era.
Hill, Polly. *The Migrant Cocoa-Farmers of Southern Ghana: A Study in Rural Capitalism*. Cambridge, U.K.: Cambridge University Press, 1963. A socioeconomic study of the expansion of the Ghanaian cocoa industry and its implications for Ghanaian society.
Loxley, John. *Ghana: The Long Road to Recovery, 1983–90*. Ottawa: North-South Institute, 1991. An in-depth macroeconomic treatment of Ghana's economic crisis and the implementation of the World Bank's Structural Adjustment Program.
Rattray, R. S. *Ashanti*. Oxford: Clarendon Press, 1923. A classic anthropology of Ashanti social and political organization.
Ward, W. E. F. *A History of Ghana*. London: Allen & Unwin, 1967. First published in 1958. A detailed and comprehensive history of Ghana from its earliest settlement to the end of the Nkrumah era.

BRIAN SCHWIMMER

GIBRALTAR. Situated at the strategic juncture of the Atlantic Ocean and the Mediterranean Sea, Gibraltar (known as "the Rock") has been a British colony since 1704, when it was seized by an Anglo-Dutch force during the Wars of the Spanish Succession. Article 10 of the Treaty of Utrecht (1713) confirmed British ownership of the Rock "in perpetuity" but also stated that if Britain ever decided to divest itself of Gibraltar, Spain would have the first claim to it. Spain last attempted to retake it by force in the "great siege" (1779–1783), but ever since—especially from the 1960s—it has put pressure on Britain to transfer sovereignty back to Spain in order to restore its "territorial integrity."

That pressure was initially exercised through the United Nations, but the lack of progress in that forum, together with an overwhelming referendum vote in Gibraltar in 1967 in favor of retaining ties with Britain, followed by a new constitution, led in June 1969 to a sixteen-year blockade by Spain, when all communications between Gibraltar and the Spanish mainland were suspended. Far from starving the Gibraltarians—largely of Maltese and Genoese as well as of British origin—into submission, the isolation they suffered had the effect of creating a social cohesion that worked against Spain's ultimate objective. Gibraltarians were granted a substantial degree of self-government through their 1969 constitution, the preamble to which guaranteed that if Britain ever considered a transfer of sovereignty, it would not do so without the freely and democratically expressed wishes of the Rock's inhabitants.

With Spain set to join the European Community in 1986, requiring freedom of movement between member states, Britain and Spain established (through the 1984 Brussels Declaration) a negotiating process "aimed at overcoming all the differences between them" relating to Gibraltar, including "the issues of sovereignty." This enabled Spain to justify putting an end to the blockade, and the border gates were opened in 1985.

Negotiations on a wide range of issues took place at regular intervals until 1997, but Gibraltarian leaders could only participate in talks as members of the British delegation (and from 1988 decided to stay away), while Spain was only really interested in making progress on the transfer of sovereignty. Meanwhile, despite the loss of its major role as part of Britain's defense strategy, Gibraltar had moved to virtual economic self-sufficiency through the development of activities such as tourism, bunkering, and, above all, the exploitation of its role as an offshore financial center.

In July 2002 the British government attempted to force the issue by proposing to discuss sharing the sovereignty of the territory with Spain. While Britain and Spain struggled to reconcile their nonnegotiable issues (Britain's insistence on Gibraltarians' virtual right of veto through a referendum on any agreement, the permanence of a shared sovereignty agreement, and the exclusion of the military facilities—all opposed by Spain), Gibraltarians held a preemptive referendum in November 2002 and conclusively voted against joint sovereignty. Britain and Spain had to take notice and shelved sovereignty discussions in favor of a tripartite forum, allowing Gibraltar its own negotiating voice. In December 2006 a new Constitution of Gibraltar came into force.

[*See also* Spain.]

BIBLIOGRAPHY

Gold, Peter. *Gibraltar: British or Spanish?* London and New York: Routledge, 2005.

Harvey, Maurice. *Gibraltar.* Staplehurst, U.K.: Spellmount, 2000.

Hills, George. *Rock of Contention: A History of Gibraltar.* London: Robert Hale, 1974.

Jackson, W. G. F. *The Rock of the Gibraltarians: A History of Gibraltar.* Rutherford, N.J.: Farleigh Dickinson University Press, 1987.

PETER GOLD

GIRL SCOUTS. *See* Scoutism; Youth Movements.

GLOBALIZATION [*This entry includes three subentries:*

Overview
Resistance to Globalization
Impact on Africa

See also World Economy.]

Overview

The idea of globalization formed one of the most widely discussed—and certainly widely popularized—social science concepts of the later 1990s. The basic model was simple enough: at some recent point, the intensifying level of interactions among major societies around the world, and the interconnections among different kinds of interactions, generated a new framework for the human experience. New technologies, like satellite television and then the Internet (public access introduced in 1990), vastly accelerated the rate and speed of contacts around the globe. New organizational forms, like multinational corporations, introduced an unprecedented amount of global coordination in production and distribution as the global organizational capacity increased. The spread of international consumer styles added yet another dimension. And these developments combined: a person working in a multinational corporation, watching MTV or listening to rock music exported from Japan, or staying up to the wee hours to see a soccer match halfway around the world, experienced a multifaceted series of global influences.

Globalization theories were most commonly associated with considerable optimism: the unprecedented contacts would improve economic life and possibly even conduce to more widespread democracy and greater peace. One popular theory, highly debatable in fact, argued that two societies that both had McDonald's restaurants would not go to war with each other—McDonald's here symbolizing a commitment to material indulgence that would bridle at military confrontation. Some commentators noted a similarity between globalization theory and earlier ideas about modernization, both of which assumed that major societies would move in similar directions and that the result would be progress.

It was possible, however, to believe that globalization was occurring but to view the results pessimistically. A number of social scientists argued that globalization was increasing economic inequality, particularly among different parts of the world depending on their levels of industrialization, but to an extent within societies as well. The United States probably benefited overall from globalization economically, in terms of lower consumer prices and greater access to varied goods, but some groups were displaced by international competition, which contributed to increased poverty in many cities.

Scope of the Concept. In terms of modern world history, the key issue, beyond assessments of progress or deterioration, involved the magnitude of change and the chronology of the phenomenon. The question of dates of origin was not trivial. Though globalization theory pointed to the late twentieth century as a turning point, many historians argued that a first clear round of globalization occurred a century earlier, around new methods of communication and transportation, including the opening of new ocean-linking canals.

To be sure, post–World War I revolutions and nationalisms pushed globalization back. Communists and Nazis alike rejected prevailing global ties, viewing them as too purely Western-dominated and hoping to establish alternatives, while the United States pulled away from international politics, and, soon, the Japanese worked on a separate sphere of influence in the Pacific.

These resistances to globalization, dominant in the second quarter of the twentieth century, then gradually yielded. Defeat in war brought the Japanese and Germans back to global connections with a vengeance. Later, the Chinese decision in 1978 to open their economy to international linkages, and the Russian decision in 1985 to do the same, formed a key policy framework for globalization's resumption—arguably as significant as the new, distance-shrinking technologies. But this could be seen as a renewal of globalization, not a brand-new beginning.

Debates over origins relate to the even more important question of the scope of change. Because globalization was not initially a historical theory, many social scientists assumed great novelty without actually taking the trouble to demonstrate how different a globalized society was from its predecessor. Some historians eagerly joined the globalization bandwagon, arguing at least in principle that globalization was a profound innovation in human affairs.

One "new global historian" indeed divided the human past into three chunks: traditional (origins of the species to 1500 C.E.); protoglobal, 1500–1950, when some changes began to occur that brought world societies closer together but without, as yet, decisive results; and finally global, 1950 onward, when the human condition began to differ from prior patterns more fully than ever before in the experience of the species. These were dramatic claims, not easy to test save in specific areas like speed of communication. New global historians sought to demonstrate their premises by analyzing how, for example, cities and urban life reflected conclusive changes brought by globalization, but many of the projects remained somewhat tentative.

Globalization affects childhood, for example, by accelerating trends toward schooling and lower infant mortality—but these trends had begun to spread internationally before globalization is generally believed to have started. Globalization adds shared consumer patterns, perhaps even a global youth culture, based on musical styles, blue jeans, fast foods, and the like. But many children are too poor or too isolated in rural enclaves to participate.

And against the idea of consumer homogenization was the stark fact that children's lives around the world were in many ways becoming more differentiated. Though increasing numbers of children did not work, the pressures of globalization contributed to an outright growth in child labor in South and Southeast Asia. Though infant mortality continued to decline overall, greater poverty and new patterns of disease actually heightened mortality rates in several African countries during the 1990s. Was there any definable globalization of this key aspect of the human experience?

It was also true that some global connections were not entirely new. The global spread of disease, for example, had occurred sporadically, and often tragically, for millennia. With more rapid and frequent transportation, certain diseases could spread faster; an outbreak of Severe Acute Respiratory Syndrome (SARS) in East Asia could show up in Toronto within weeks. But the fundamental phenomenon predated globalization. Migration was another old human connection. Global transportation helped spread migrations from longer distances and, perhaps more important, facilitated individuals going back and forth between their new home and their old, developing bicultural fluency in the process. But the degree of fundamental innovation could be debated.

Clear Examples. Globalization made undeniable sense in certain areas, however, if not in all. Historians can, after all, assess the differences between late-twentieth-century multinational corporations and early-twentieth-century international corporations. The earlier international corporations—the Singer Manufacturing Company, known for its sewing machines, and the United Fruit Company are examples—had production outlets in several places, in order to reduce transportation costs, and/or they set up branches to mine or harvest raw materials or foods in different parts of the world. Certainly there were many companies that exported large quantities of goods and had marketing operations in a variety of countries.

Multinationals, in contrast, continue these activities in greater volume, but they literally treat the world as a production stage, setting up plants to manufacture certain components in one place, based on advantageous resources, cheap labor, and/or lax environmental regulations, while producing other parts halfway around the world. Rapid, high-volume transportation and the ease of communication provided by the Internet explain this escalation in global activity. By the same token, multinationals, with their huge facilities and massive capital, have unparalleled impact on government policies, as well as on the lives of ordinary workers and consumers.

The environment offers another clear example of globalization. Human beings have had an environmental impact since at least the origins of agriculture. During the nineteenth century, industrial factories and growing cities worsened air and water quality in many regions. Demand for items like rubber or cotton pushed production into new areas, often causing soil erosion or reduced fertility. Never before the late twentieth century, however, had activities in one region affected distant areas or the world as a whole. Now tall smokestacks, designed to reduce local pollution, caused acid rain in forests hundreds of miles away. A nuclear accident like Chernobyl touched many parts of eastern and central Europe. The clearance of tropical forests, to generate timber for world markets or create new space for export agriculture, affected global climates, as did carbon dioxide production from vehicles and factories. Pollution became a worldwide issue, and from the 1980s onward international conferences, though limited in impact, recognized that pollution would require a global policy response.

Cultural globalization was suggested in the later nineteenth century, with the surprisingly rapid spread of European and American sports like soccer and baseball to many parts of the world and then, by the early twentieth century, with the internationalization of films, with Hollywood the reigning world capital. New media, and active export efforts by concerns like Disney or the leading Japanese video game producers, undoubtedly pushed cultural globalization still further after 1950. When the advent of television in some of the more remote Pacific islands, in the 1980s, led to outbreaks of bulimia by local girls trying to look like Western starlets, it was clear that cultural globalization was reaching new levels.

Political globalization formed a final area of interest. Initial efforts to organize international agreements, around issues such as sending mail or the treatment of prisoners of war, went back to the later nineteenth century. There is no question, however, that the establishment of the United Nations, after World War II, and subsidiary groups like the World Health Organization (1948) pushed international discussions into additional areas, yielding among other things a variety of conventions on human rights and the rights of women and children. Some sociologists refer to a shared "global culture" around some of these issues, though again there can be debate about how much is widely accepted.

The 1960s saw an acceleration of international non-government organizations (INGOs), working in areas ranging from prevention of torture to the environment to attacks on sweatshops. Global politics obviously failed to keep pace with problems like pollution, or with the power of organizations like the multinationals, but formal organizations and broader surges of world opinion did become a factor to be reckoned with.

Late-Twentieth-Century Confluence. The notion of globalization as a segmented process within modern world history, with different aspects beginning at different times

and proceeding at different speeds, does not eliminate the idea of a special confluence late in the twentieth century, fueled by additional new factors. Even at this point, of course, globalization remained uneven in both impact and reception. By 2002, for example, only about a quarter of the world's population had any access to the Internet. This was a huge figure by any historical precedent, and it would grow rapidly, but it reinforces the point that many regions were too poor, and many rural inhabitants too isolated, for most aspects of globalization to have much impact.

Even when globalization did have measurable effects, it could as often divide as unite, as was obvious in the conditions of children in different parts of the world. Economic globalization brought new goods to many consumers. It vastly accelerated world trade, and this created new jobs in many regions, including factory jobs. Early in the twenty-first century, when prosperity was increasing in the giant nations of India and China, it could even be argued that economic globalization was benefiting more people than ever.

But there were downsides. New production sites, amid cheap labor, dislocated many workers in places like the United States, where manufacturing employment began to dip, possibly permanently. Poverty increased, even as the nation as a whole seemed to prosper. In places like India or Brazil, traditional manufacturing outlets, pressed by global competition, increased their exploitation of labor, including child labor, or went out of business. Unemployment soared in many regions, leading some families to have desperate recourse to practices like the sale of body organs for medical transplants, or the export of girls to houses of prostitution in distant regions—a sordid illustration of globalization. Financial institutions like the International Monetary Fund pressed governments in poorer regions to reduce their expenditures in favor of lower taxes and freer markets, but the result often included a diminution of state aid to the poor. Huge parts of Africa, additionally burdened by disease, suffered immensely amid globalization, but there were problems elsewhere as well.

Finally, partly because of unequal economic impacts but even more because of cultural and political resentments, globalization roused resistances. Some experts even argued that conflicts among big cultural zones—the clash of civilizations that might pit Westerners against Islam—would define the world's future, not globalization at all. Beginning in Seattle in 1999, at meetings of groups like the World Bank, protesters rallied against globalization directly, mixing environmental, labor quality, and

GLOBALIZATION: Resistance to Globalization

anticonsumerist concerns. More important—for these movements remained small—were differentiations by area. Certainly, some regions accepted globalization more fully than others did. Japan had basically made its peace with the idea of global connections in the later nineteenth century, so its success in globalization was well prepared. Many Muslims, in contrast, resented global consumerism and its frequent sexual overtones; a vigorous dispute arose in the Islamic world between those who basically cast their lot with globalization and those who vowed to resist.

Terrorists in 2001, attacking the World Trade Center as a symbol of globalization as well as of American dominance, pushed resistance to an extreme. In another instance, many African countries accepted global definitions of human rights in principle, including declarations stipulating the right of women to own property, only to find courts of law arguing that African traditions that vested ownership in fathers or husbands took precedence. Even the United States, an active advocate of globalization in many respects, largely resisted international agreements—even agreements banning landmines—because it might restrict national freedom of action. Different societies accepted globalization to different degrees, and they varied also in which aspects of globalization seemed most troubling. Globalization is an important process, but it has also raised many questions of interpretation and many issues for the future.

[*See also* Brain Drain; Global Warming; Outsourcing; World Bank; *and* World Economy.]

BIBLIOGRAPHY

Frank, Thomas. *One Market under God: Extreme Capitalism, Market Populism, and the End of Economic Democracy.* New York: Doubleday, 2000.
Guha, Ramachandra. *Environmentalism: A Global History.* New York: Longman, 2000.
LaFeber, Walter. *Michael Jordan and the New Global Capitalism.* New York: W. W. Norton and Company, 1999.
Mazlish, Bruce, and Ralph Buultjens, eds. *Conceptualizing Global History.* Boulder, Colo.: Westview Press, 1993.
Ward, Kathryn, et al. *Women Workers and Global Restructuring.* Cornell International Industrial and Labor Relations Report No. 17. Ithaca, N.Y.: ILR Press, School of Industrial and Labor Relations, Cornell University, 1990.

PETER N. STEARNS

Resistance to Globalization

First investigated by the Canadian scholar Marshall McLuhan in 1964 and then further explored during the 1970s, globalization is the process through which world populations become increasingly interconnected and interdependent both culturally and economically. Such a process is often perceived by its critics—generally coming from left-wing, green, women's, queer, and labor movements—as creating a sense of standardization throughout the globe and reinforcing economic inequalities between developed and underdeveloped countries. Advanced capitalism, enhanced by technological developments such as the Internet and electronic business transactions, is seen as stretching social, political, and economic activities across the borders of communities, nations, and continents. Global connections and circulation of goods, ideas, capital, and people have deepened the impact of distant events on everyday life. Thus globalization entails two related phenomena: the development of a global economy and the rise of a global culture.

Global Economy. Critics of globalization point out that the new global economy involves a discrepancy between a huge decentralization of production processes, often to developing countries where manpower is cheaper, and a simultaneous centralization of command and control processes in rich economies. Corporations, which are accountable only to their shareholders, are perceived to have replaced governments in economic and social control. This condition has been dubbed "corporate rule."

Yet, as the antiglobalization journalist Naomi Klein points out, "the triumph of economic globalization has inspired a wave of techno-savvy investigative activists who are as globally minded as the corporations they track" (*No Logo*, p. 327). Since the mid-1990s the number of public investigations in corporate crime has increased exponentially, so much so that the American Studies professor Andrew Ross dubbed the period between 1995 and 1996 "The Year of the Sweatshop." Corporations involved in this massive exposure of exploitative labor practices include Gap, Wal-Mart, Guess, Nike, Mattel, and Disney. Antiglobal organizations are also investigating the links between transnational corporations and totalitarian regimes in developing countries.

Although Western investments in the Third World were considered as a first step in fighting poverty until the mid-1990s, antiglobal activists are now seeking to show consumers how the alliance between corporate investment and many governments in the developing world is predicated on a mutual human rights violation. Totalitarian governments are willing to protect profitable investments by disregarding human rights violations on the part of corporations against their people, while Western corporations accept the political repression and the elimination of all opposition perpetrated in some countries in order to protect their own global marketability.

Therefore, to antiglobal activists, the equation between increased foreign investment and increased democracy in developing countries is a blatant lie. On the contrary, they point out, big business frequently relies on local police and armed forces to quench any sort of peaceful demonstration and to evict peasants from lands needed by foreign conglomerates. The Nobel Prize winner Aung San Suu Kyi, who was imprisoned for six years following the refusal of the Burmese military regime to acknowledge her overwhelming victory in the 1990 election, explicitly condemned the foreign companies operating in Burma and profiting from quasi-institutionalized forced labor: "Foreign investors should realize there could be no economic growth and opportunities in Burma until there is agreement on the country's political future" (Klein, *No Logo*, p. 331).

Still more important for the development of the human rights critique of global economy was the execution in 1995 of the Nigerian author Ken Saro-Wiwa, who had taken a leading position in the Ogoni people's campaign against the human and ecological destruction of the Niger Delta as a result of Royal Dutch/Shell's oil drilling. The Nobel Prize nominee and his Movement for the Survival of the Ogoni People (MOSOP) had blamed the Nigerian dictator General Sani Abacha for the murder and torture of thousands of Ogoni to silence their exposure of Shell's exploitation of their land. Yet they had also denounced with equal force Shell's treatment of Nigerian police forces as a private militia and its financial backing for a totalitarian regime. At his farcical trial that would end with the death penalty, Saro-Wiwa told the court that "Shell is here on trial. . . . The Company has, indeed, ducked this particular trial, but its day will surely come."

The Saro-Wiwa incident was a powerful catalyst for the emergence of antiglobalization activism, because it showed the interconnectedness among issues of social justice, environmental exploitation, and labor policy. In addition, because Saro-Wiwa was a writer, his trial was also perceived by many literary authors as a denial of the freedom of self-expression. The South African writer and 1991 Nobel Laureate Nadine Gordimer went so far as to say that "to buy Nigeria's oil under the conditions that prevail is to buy oil in exchange for blood. Other people's blood; the exaction of the death penalty on Nigerians" (Klein, *No Logo*, p. 384). Saro-Wiwa's execution showed that movements with different aims and partially different constituencies could join forces on an antiglobal agenda.

Cultural Globalization. Parallel to economic globalization is the phenomenon of cultural globalization. Its supporters claim that the rise of a global culture entails multiculturalism and a hybridization of national cultures. Yet critics of cultural globalization point out its darker side, claiming that cultural globalism destroys all local traditions and regional distinctions, creating in their place a homogenized world culture. What is passed off as world culture, its detractors claim, is really the Americanization of world culture. Local cultures are replaced by a uniform and single culture, dictated by the same powerful corporations that control the global economy.

Although there is much evidence for this cultural imperialism, the sociologist Arjun Appadurai cautions us not to underestimate the power of local cultures to react to this phenomenon ("Disjuncture," p. 295). He also stresses that there are various alternative fears to that of Americanization: "It is worth noticing that for the people of Irian Jaya, Indonesianization may be more worrisome than Americanization, as Japanization may be for Koreans, Indianization for Sri Lankans, Vietnamization for Cambodians, Russianization for the people of Soviet Armenia and the Baltic republics"; he reminds us that "one man's imagined community is another man's political prison."

Antiglobal theorists stress how corporations have hijacked culture and education through their aggressive

Protesting Globalization. Spanish students attack the front of a McDonald's restaurant following a demonstration against the U.S.-led Iraq war, Barcelona, Spain, 26 March 2003. The graffiti on the wall reads "Killer Capitalism." Photograph by Cesar Rangel. AP IMAGES

marketing practices. Hidden behind slogans that stress the rhetoric of the global village (Levi's "a world-wide style culture" or IBM's "solutions for a small planet"), cultural choices are narrowing in the face of corporate censorship, and public space is increasingly occupied by brand advertising. No-global activists have stated that the real work of corporations does not lie so much in manufacturing as in the marketing process and in the production of an image for their brands.

Global Resistance. The antiglobalization movement was thrown from the fringes to the center of political debates thanks to the November 1999 protests in Seattle against the World Trade Organization. Since then, major financial and commercial summits of the G8, the International Monetary Fund, the World Economic Forum, and the World Bank have been disrupted by mass demonstrations in the streets of Washington, D.C., Genoa, and Prague. These demonstrations raised controversial debates about police and protester violence. Such debates have become all the more polarized after the events of 11 September 2001, as critics of the antiglobal movements accuse the movements, rather simplistically, of being as fundamentalist and as anti-American as Islamic terrorists.

In the activists' view, Genoa was a particularly significant example of state violence and the need of authorities to build fortresses to protect their debates, which mirrors the international creation of a global security state where rich nations are safely fenced off against poor ones. The decision of the right-wing Italian government to bar the demonstrators from certain parts of the city gave rise to popular anger. Riots exploded throughout the city, and evidence suggests they were fomented by the police, who infiltrated armed criminals within the demonstrators' ranks. The Italian police also shot Carlo Giuliani, a twenty-three-year-old demonstrator, and then backed over his body with a jeep. Activists sleeping at a local school legally granted by the city council were beaten, and false evidence of their keeping weapons was created by the police forces.

Since January 2001, annual counter meetings have been held at the World Social Forum in Porto Alegre, Brazil, under the slogan "Another World Is Possible." Antiglobal activists have attracted sympathies of left-wing political parties such as the Brazilian Workers' Party (PT) and the Italian Party of Communist Re-foundation (PRC) and Left Democrats (DS). Alternative media and communication networks such as the Independent Media Center (www. indymedia.org) have been established to turn the Internet,

one of the tools that enables globalization, into a powerful antiglobal weapon.

Yet, perhaps, as many important activists have pointed out, the label of "antiglobal" is an ironic misnomer for people who are closely tied together across national, racial, class, and gender borders. Because the corporate world is based on power centralization, antiglobal activists react by championing fragmentation and radical power dispersal. This attitude is best represented by the word of the Zapatista spokesperson Subcomandante Marcos, whose movement is taken as an ideal blueprint for many antiglobal militants:

> Marcos is gay in San Francisco, black in South Africa, an Asian in Europe, a Chicano in San Ysidro, an anarchist in Spain, a Palestinian in Israel, a Mayan Indian in the streets of San Cristobal, a Jew in Germany, a Gypsy in Poland, a Mohawk in Quebec, a pacifist in Bosnia, a single woman on the metro at 10 P.M., a peasant without land, a gang member in the slums, an unemployed worker, an unhappy student and, of course, a Zapatista in the mountains.
>
> (Klein, *No Logo*, p. 455)

[*See also* Capitalism; Corporation, The; International Monetary Fund; Multinational Corporations; World Bank; *and* World Trade Organization.]

BIBLIOGRAPHY

Appadurai, Arjun "Disjuncture and Difference in the Global Cultural Economy." In *Global Culture: Nationalism, Globalization, and Modernity*, edited by Mike Featherstone, pp. 295–310. London and Thousand Oaks, Calif.: Sage, 1990.

Appadurai, Arjun. *Globalization*. Durham, N.C.: Duke University Press, 2001.

Appadurai, Arjun. *Modernity at Large: Cultural Dimensions of Globalization*. Minneapolis: University of Minnesota Press, 1996.

Bauman, Zygmunt. *Globalization: The Human Consequences*. New York: Columbia University Press, 1998.

Hardt, Michael, and Antonio Negri. *Empire*. Cambridge, Mass.: Harvard University Press, 2002.

Jameson, Fredric, and Masao Miyoshi. *The Cultures of Globalization*. Durham, N.C.: Duke University Press, 1998.

Klein, Naomi. *Fences and Windows: Dispatches from the Front Lines of the Globalization Debate*. London: Flamingo, 2002.

Klein, Naomi. *No Logo*. London: Flamingo, 2000.

Robinson, William I. *Promoting Polyarchy: Globalization, U. S. Intervention, and Hegemony*. New York: Cambridge University Press, 1996.

Ross, Andrew. *No Collar: The Humane Workplace and Its Hidden Costs*. New York: Basic Books: 2002.

Ross, Andrew, ed. *No Sweat: Fashion, Free Trade, and the Rights of Garment Workers*. New York: Verso, 1997.

Ross, Andrew, and Kristin Ross. *Anti-Americanism*. New York: New York University Press, 2004.

Stiglitz, Joseph E. *Globalization and Its Discontents*. New York: Norton, 2003.

LUCA PRONO

Impact on Africa

"Globalization" refers to intense economic, political, social, and cultural relations across international borders, through which barriers in the areas of culture, commerce, and communication are broken down. Under the influence of globalization, free-market economics, liberal democracy, and good governance have become universal values for states. The collapse of the Soviet bloc in the late 1980s and early 1990s led to the emergence of a global economy structured by the interests of mainly Western countries and furthered the integration of most economies into the global economy. By the early twenty-first century capitalism as an economic system dominated the globe. While globalization is characterized by broadening linkages of national economies into a worldwide market for goods and services, it also involves the international division of labor: developed countries specialize in high-skill manufacturing and services and developing countries specialize in low-skill intensive manufacturing. This asymmetry has severe impacts on African countries that primarily produce raw materials for industries in the developed countries that may sell the produced goods in developing countries.

Capitalism and Marginalization. In the early twenty-first century the African continent was largely marginalized in the global economy. Already in 1996, Africa's part of world exports had dropped to 1 percent; if South Africa and the oil-producing states were excluded, the percentage would be virtually nothing. At the end of the twentieth century, economic growth in African countries slowed to 1 percent, while official aid was less than twenty dollars per head per year. Scholars such as Nigel C. Gibson emphasize that the world system has been strongly unequal since the beginning of the Industrial Revolution in the north, which was linked to the exploitation of colored and black bodies. According to Gibson, "political power has been employed to gain advantages, exploit inequalities, and crush competition" (p. 5). Because of its centrality to the triangular trade between Africa, the Americas, and Europe, Africa ironically became marginalized. European colonialism shaped modern Africa, but Africans also contributed to the rising power of Europe.

Africa was linked to other regions such as China and India, the Middle East, and the Mediterranean through trade as early as the second century C.E. In the early sixteenth century the Portuguese contributed to the partial destruction of African mercantilism in what is now Mozambique, but some African economies continued to trade with Europe until the period of European colonization in the nineteenth century. The enormous wealth linked to the slave trade, lasting for nearly four hundred years, had strong effects on the African and American continents. Walter Rodney famously argued that "the development of America meant the underdevelopment of Africa" (Gibson, p. 6). Other authors, such as S. T. Akindele, have argued that globalization is the latest form of capitalist diffusion in Africa. The continent has been opened to capitalism by structural adjustment, privatization, the World Bank, and International Monetary Fund (IMF) policies, but the result in the twenty-first century has been the marginalization of Africa as a continent of increasing inequality.

Globalization and Labor Productivity. For most African countries the first period of independence did not realize the political goals that the anticolonial struggles had aimed at. Often, national economies functioned more or less successfully by loading the largest share of the burden on the peasantry, who produced for low prices. Cheap capital loans led to high debt burdens, while the prices of primary goods for export diminished. Since the 1980s African countries have been obliged to accept the rules of the international economic system by opening up their national economies to world-market competition. The free movement of capital searched for markets and cheap labor. Since the 1960s there has been a constant movement of redundant workers from the African countryside to the overcrowded towns. These men and women may have worked, but they have often been unemployed, part-time, or occasional workers. Export Processing Zones (EPZs), which see the assembly of products, have been created in twenty-five African countries but are only important in Tunisia, Egypt, and Mauritius. They have been successful in Mauritius, where they account for 65 percent of exports. The rest of the continent is not a source of semiskilled workers from the point of view of international capitalism. But there has been an important brain drain of African intellectual elites to Western countries since the 1960s. Another element of the continent's globalization is that women's unpaid work as subsistence farmers not only has contributed to their national economies but has also given women a degree of autonomy and independence unknown in most other continents. It can be argued that Africa's marginalization from the international economy is also a result of the gendered division of labor.

The terrorist attacks on 11 September 2001 led to renewed interest in Africa's raw materials, especially oil. The United States in particular has sought control of these goods. Globalization as a myth is only affordable to an elite minority of Africans, while most other people live in situations of unemployment, illness, and starvation. As a result of structural adjustment and the debt regime, the situation of the majority of Africa's population was worse in the early twenty-first century than it was twenty-five years before. This decline has created diminished chances for youth, conflicts over resources, and social and political movements against globalization and against Western states in particular.

Globalization and a National Leadership. Instead of finding good governance, Africans are faced with political elites who tend to think more about their privileges than about improving the situation of their populations. In fact, world markets contribute to the declining power of the nation-state and its elites. Political elites are less and less able to control their national economy. International organizations such as the IMF or the World Bank are more important than national governments. Countries like Nigeria and South Africa play dominant regional roles, but most other states are weak. The possibility of instituting socioeconomic change is rather limited in African states. Even if the argument that Africa needs ethical and charismatic leaders who are responsible for their population's needs is valid, limited political autonomy presents a real challenge to African elites. Yet the early twenty-first century crisis in Africa might be a turning point: all sorts of internal crises appear, such as civil wars, ethnic and political conflicts, and high crime rates. The youths feel like "the lost generation," and having nothing to lose, they engage in political upheavals, religious fundamentalism, or cultural chauvinism.

The Impact of Globalization on African Societies. Globalization influences indigenous cultures, the environment, labor standards, productivity, and other elements of societies. Liberal economic thinking has assumed that trade would result in economic well-being for the participating states. The General Agreement on Tariffs and Trade (GATT) played a major role after World War II in reducing tariffs for developed countries, eliminating certain barriers and subsidies, broadening GATT principles to sectors such as services and investment, and applying more rules to agricultural trade. Long-term rules were established and national policies that hindered access to the market were reduced. Formed in 1995, by 2006 the World Trade Organization included 150 countries that accept its free-trade rules. The worldwide movements of capital and labor have become easier, so that even the last unlinked regions have rural migrants who send money back from their regions of residence and spend their holidays in their regions of origin. But the evidence that globalization is beneficial to most countries is mixed. Some scholars argue that, in the globalization process, the fate of the poorer countries is to be marginalized, except for those countries that can attract subcontracting enterprises. Global companies instead are concentrated in the North, and Northern countries dominate trade. The percentage of world trade is small in the Least Developed Countries (LDCs), especially in per capita figures. In 1999 the merchandise trade among these countries accounted for 14 percent of world trade. Some four or five developed countries bought 54 percent of all exports from the least developed countries.

On the other hand, some scholars think that LDCs gain from engaging in global interactions. In fact, they gain access to larger markets, and consumers gain access to a larger variety of goods and services. Domestic industries may have the possibility to serve global markets, and domestic producers gain access to necessary inputs at lower prices. A further argument is that LDCs may improve their level of technology without the high costs of research and development. They may import capital equipment that raises their productive capacity. These effects may create future growth with higher domestic savings and/or international credits. Some also argue that globalization encourages governments to follow international economic policies; countries that insist on policies that do not favor the market will no longer receive international investments.

History suggests that the wealthiest nations of the world are trade-oriented (Western Europe, the United States, Japan, South Korea, Singapore). In contrast, the poorest regions of the world, such as some Asian countries and sub-Saharan Africa, remain more or less absent from foreign trade. Countries such as India, China, and Poland that have opened their economies could strongly improve their standard of living for parts of their populations. Yet in order to benefit from globalization, there must be a sort of Marshall Plan for the developing world. Only by pursuing the welfare of all can the international community improve the effects of globalization that the poorer countries currently resent.

[See also Africa; Brain Drain, subentry Africa; Development, Industrial, subentry Africa; and Trade, International, subentry Africa.]

BIBLIOGRAPHY

Ajayi, S. Ibi. "Globalisation and Africa." *Journal of African Economies* 12, no. 1 (2003): 120–150.

Akindele, S. T., T. O. Gidado, and O. R. Olaopo. "Globalisation, Its Implications and Consequences for Africa." *Globalization* 2, no. 1 (2002): 1–20. http://globalization.icaap.org/content/v2.1/01_akindele_etal.html.

Brunel, Sylvie. *L'Afrique dans la mondialisation*. Paris: La Documentation Française, 2005.

Gibson, Nigel C. "Africa and Globalization: Marginalization and Resistance." *Journal of Asian and African Studies* 39, nos. 1–2 (2004): 1–28.

Grégoire, Emmanuel. "La difficile insertion de l'Afrique de l'Ouest dans la mondialisation." *Les Temps Modernes* 620–621 (2002): 392–409.

Momayezi, Nasser. "Globalization: Impact on Development." In vol. 2 of *Encyclopedia of the Developing World*, edited by Thomas M. Leonard, pp. 707–712. New York: Routledge, 2006.

ULRIKE SCHUERKENS

GLOBAL WARMING. Global warming of the Earth's surface—land, atmosphere, and oceans—occurs when radiation energy from the sun exceeds the thermal radiation from the Earth, thereby producing a measurable increase of the Earth's average surface temperature. "Enhanced global warming" and "climate change" are commonly used phrases that attribute Earth's elevated temperatures to a "greenhouse effect" resulting from man-made increases in greenhouse gases such as carbon dioxide and other radiatively active gases. The atmosphere exhibits a greenhouse effect when mostly visible solar radiation is transmitted to the Earth's surface. This produces a warming effect that allows the Earth, in turn, to retransmit absorbed energy as thermal or infrared radiation. Greenhouse gases can absorb and retain this radiation, thereby warming the atmosphere and subsequently Earth's land and sea surfaces.

Evidence for global climate change is suggested by the Earth's average surface temperature increase of nearly $1°F$ ($0.6°C$) over the past century, in combination with unusually warm weather in the 1980s and 1990s. The ten hottest years since temperatures were first recorded in 1861 occurred since 1990, and the greenhouse gas thought to be the major cause is the carbon dioxide released by the combustion of fossil fuels from fixed and mobile sources.

Greenhouse Effect. The origin of the term "greenhouse effect" stems from the similarity of atmospheric capture and retention of heat by glass windows in a greenhouse as first described by the French scientist and mathematician Jean-Baptiste Fourier in 1827. The coal burning and land clearing that resulted from the first Industrial Revolution in the 1800s led Svante Arrhenius to publish the first calculations of global warming resulting from anthropogenic (human-caused) emissions of carbon dioxide in the atmosphere.

Molecules of carbon dioxide, water vapor, methane, and nitrous oxide act as a natural blanket retaining heat that is retransmitted as infrared radiation from the solar energy the Earth has absorbed. The normal impact of atmospheric heat absorption in pristine air contributes close to $91°F$ ($33°C$) to the Earth's average surface temperature, thus changing a subzero world $0°F$ ($-18°C$) to one with a livable average surface temperature of $60°F$ ($15°C$).

Controversies related to global warming abound. Most scientists, environmentalists, and government leaders agree that the Earth's mean temperature increase in the twentieth century forecasts a warming trend that may average up to ($4°C$) warmer in the twenty-first century, but skeptics argue that such projections are based upon simplified computer models that do not account for temperature effects from variables such as cloud cover and water vapor in the atmosphere.

Although scientists agree that human activities involving the combustion of fossil fuels since the early 1900s have substantially increased the concentration of carbon dioxide, not everyone agrees that temperature increases directly result from increased carbon dioxide in the atmosphere, especially since global temperatures seem to have decreased between the 1940s and the 1970s. Increasing temperatures, increases in the sea level, and the size of ice sheets may be argued to stem from plate-tectonic effects, subtle changes in the Earth's orbit, volcanic debris in the atmosphere, or even changes in the energy emitted by the Sun.

Mixed Signals. At first glance, the variable effects of global warming may appear to be sometimes incoherent or even contradictory. Global warming may result in lower temperatures in one area while producing a heat wave in another area. Whether the season is wetter or drier, the extremes prevail, with more energetic hurricanes and tornadoes, intensified El Niños, worse floods, and terrible droughts. Though glaciers and Arctic sea ice are receding around the world, snowstorms may be deeper and more frequent as a result of global warming. Gulf of Mexico water temperatures above $80°F$ ($27°C$) supercharged Hurricane Katrina in August 2005, but Los Angeles experienced a two-foot snowfall in the same year. Likewise, in 2005, Mumbai (Bombay), India, received thirty-seven inches of rain in one day, allegedly resulting in more than one thousand deaths and the dislocation of 20 million people, but the U.S. Midwest had a record drought in early summer, and a sustained heat wave killed up to twenty people in Arizona. The general rule seems to be that a warmer atmosphere produces heavier rains and more-frequent extremes in all weather events.

International Efforts to Control Global Warming. In 1988 the United Nations responded to concerns about global warming by creating the Intergovernmental Panel on Climate Change (IPCC) to provide comprehensive assessments that provide reports on climate change and potential ways to mitigate the effects of climate change. The IPCC collects and assesses global warming facts to provide scientific evidence that constitutes a base for political action. IPCC publications warn that increasing global temperatures could threaten crops, melt glaciers, spread disease and pests, increase sea levels, increase storm damage, and destroy Arctic ecosystems.

Reliable data obtained from ice cores demonstrate that the atmospheric concentration of carbon dioxide has now reached the highest level in more than 400,000 years. The respective increases of 31 percent and 149 percent for heat-absorbing carbon dioxide and methane occurred as industry developed after 1750. Although preindustrial atmospheric carbon dioxide levels of 270 parts per million reached 375 parts per million in just over one hundred years, the noted paleoclimatologist William F. Ruddiman pointed out that carbon dioxide levels have been slowly increasing since humans began clearing forests for agriculture 8,000 years ago. In addition, Ruddiman documents that methane, another infrared-absorbing gas, registered increasing concentrations as humans began to grow rice and herd livestock.

The United Nations Framework Convention on climate change ultimately gained the support of 157 countries attending a conference in Rio de Janeiro in June 1992. The signing nations agreed to a protocol that recognized the reality of global warming and required developed countries by 2000 to return emissions of greenhouse gases, and especially carbon dioxide, to 1990 levels. A second part of the convention required a long-term stabilization of greenhouse gas levels to prevent dangerous changes in the global climate.

The Kyoto Protocol. By 1997 the debate between the cost of preemptive actions needed to counter global warming and the damage to particular environments led to the Kyoto Protocol. The developing nations China, India, and Brazil remained outside the Kyoto Protocol since they contended that controls would hinder development. In 2001 the United States declared that it would not ratify the Kyoto Protocol because it would wrongly exclude developing nations and damage the U.S. economy by moving jobs to developing nations.

The 1997 Kyoto Protocol covered emissions of six greenhouse gases that can be converted into an equivalent amount of carbon dioxide. The complex protocol sought a reduction of carbon dioxide emissions to 5.2 percent below 1990 levels between 2008 and 2012. The withdrawal of the United States from the Kyoto Protocol slowed the legal adoption of the Kyoto accord since it required the ratification by enough developed nations to account for 55 percent of carbon dioxide emissions in 1990. The U.S. share of 36 percent created a major deficit that was offset four years later by inclusion of Russia's 17 percent share of 1990 emissions of carbon dioxide. As a result of Russia's ratification, the Kyoto Protocol came into effect on 16 February 2005, setting legally binding limits for greenhouse gas emissions, although there remained some concerns that the accord might provide an incentive to encourage logging as a result of carbon credits that could be earned by reforestation.

The Bonn Agreements in 2001 limited reforestation credits for carbon dioxide removal from the atmosphere to lands that did not contain forests on 31 December 1989. A weakness of the accord appeared to be the possible renegotiation of the 1989 time limit and the precedent this might set for further extension of the deadline. By 2003, countries applying for ten-year extensions of the deadline included Canada and Indonesia. Although Landsat satellite images can document deforestation and reforestation changes, much of the forest area can be subjected to a harvesting technique that removes only the biggest and most valuable trees without Landsat detection.

By pushing the Kyoto treaty over the top without the inclusion of the United States, the Russian Federation hopes to gain a windfall of payments earned under Kyoto's emission credits for closed factories and reduced agriculture. Under this trading plan, European countries and Japan would pay Russia billions of dollars to compensate for their failure to meet Kyoto reductions. A flaw in Russia's emission reduction claim remains the weakness in its emissions inventory. Reviews by a U.N. panel in 1997 revealed significant weaknesses in both data collection and methodology. Three years later, a second U.N. review team was not completely satisfied with the new data, and the Russian petroleum industry, which is now the world's largest producer, does not even provide information to the Russian Federal Service for Hydrometrology and Environmental Monitoring (Roshydromet).

Beyond Kyoto. The 157 nations ratifying the Kyoto Protocol were obligated to begin negotiations no later than 2005 for a second commitment period beyond 2008–2012 that would be stronger and include developing countries. The 6:30 A.M. conclusion of a Montreal, Canada, follow-up conference on 9 December 2005 dispelled all rumors of an early demise of the Kyoto Protocol by extending and agreeing to deeper emission cuts, while launching a dialogue with the United States. With the Annual Greenhouse Gas Index released by the Climate Monitoring and Diagnostics Laboratory in Boulder, Colorado, in September 2005 registering a 20 percent increase in greenhouse gas effects since 1990, local and regional initiatives following the Regional Greenhouse Gas Initiative in nine northeastern states of the United States began actively drafting plans to provide incentives to spur power plants to become more efficient or to switch to less polluting fuels.

On 5 February 2007, the U.N.-sponsored Intergovernmental Panel on Climate Change (IPCC) released an update for the Fourth Assessment Report of the IPCC. Measurements of global average air and ocean temperatures during eleven of the twelve years from 1995 to 2006 rank among the twelve warmest years that have been recorded since 1850, and a continued increase in global average sea level coincides with recorded temperature increases. The fourth report offers evidence that advances in climate change assessments now rely on a larger number of climate models that provide best estimates for temperature increases for six scenarios.

[*See also* Antarctica; Arctic; Climate and Climate Change; Environment; Famine; Kyoto Protocol; *and* Natural Disasters.]

BIBLIOGRAPHY

Houghton, John T. *Global Warming: The Complete Briefing.* 3d ed. Cambridge, U.K., and New York: Cambridge University Press, 2004.

Ruddiman, William F. *Plows, Plagues, and Petroleum: How Humans Took Control of Climate.* Princeton, N.J.: Princeton University Press, 2005. Ruddiman's reputation as one of the world's most accomplished paleoclimatologists allows him to advance a controversial hypothesis suggesting thousands of years of human alteration of Earth's atmosphere with a subsequent impact on climate over thousands of years.

Schulze, Ernst-Detief, et al. "Making Deforestation Pay under the Kyoto Protocol?" *Science* 299 (2003): 101–125.

R. MAX FERGUSON

GOA. The smallest of India's twenty-eight states, with an area of 1,429 square miles (3,702 square kilometers) and a population of 1,343,998 (2001 census), Goa is located on India's west coast, approximately 250 miles south of Mumbai (formerly Bombay). In 2003 *India Today* ranked it the best state in the country, with the highest literacy rate (82.30 percent). Its capital is Panaji; its main harbor is Mormugao, the principal iron ore–loading port of India. Despite intensive exploitation of iron and manganese ore, much of it exported to Japan and the United States, the Goa government has been environmentally conscious, working to preserve the natural beauty of a state famous for its beaches, rivers, and verdant hills. It is one of India's most popular tourist destinations, both for domestic travelers and for those from Europe and the United States.

A former Portuguese colony, acquired by Admiral Afonso de Albuquerque in 1510, only twelve years after Vasco da Gama's landing in Calicut, Goa was made the capital of the rather exuberantly named Estado da India under a governor-general with command over the Portuguese empire and navy from Sofala in East Africa to Macau off China. It was dubbed "Rome of the Orient" thanks to its cluster of Catholic religious edifices and its position as headquarters of the papal ecclesiastical enterprise in the East. Since 1553 Goa's Church of Bom Jesus has housed the "incorrupt body" of Saint Francis Xavier, which is periodically, mostly every twelve years and on special occasions, exhibited to pious pilgrims from the Catholic world, adding substantially to Goa's tourist traffic. Goa's prosperity made Luis de Camões, the noted Portuguese poet, call it "Goa Dourado," or Golden Goa.

The Portuguese acquired Goa in two phases: the Velhas Conquistas (Old Conquests) in the sixteenth century and the Novas Conquistas (New Conquests) in the second half of the eighteenth century. The districts that make up the Old Conquests suffered from the Inquisition, forced conversions, and demolition of temples, which explains the continued overwhelming majority of Catholics in that area. The relative religious liberalism during the second phase of Portuguese rule allowed the Hindu majority population in the New Conquests to follow their religion and preserve their temples. When the Portuguese were forced out of Goa in 1961, its population was 60.8 percent Hindu and 36.1 percent Catholic; there were hardly any Portuguese settlers in Goa despite Portugal's hold of over four and a half centuries.

Before Portuguese rule, Goa was part of the neighboring kingdoms from the time of the Mauryan empire in the third century B.C.E. It was a prosperous port under the Silaharas, the Kadambas, the Chalukyans, Vijayanagar, and Adil Shahi of Bijapur. Its language, Konkani, adopted as Goa's state language, is spoken along the west coast of India and is written in the Devanagari script.

In 1951 the Portuguese dictator Antonio de Oliveira Salazar declared Goa a province of Portugal, entitled to NATO's protection. That created a conflict with India, which regarded its independence incomplete without Goa. Portuguese rule in Goa ended in December 1961, after a brief two-day Indian military action.

[See also Empire and Imperialism, subentry The Portuguese Colonial Empire; and India.]

BIBLIOGRAPHY

Pearson, M. N. The Portuguese in India. Cambridge, U.K., and New York: Cambridge University Press, 1987.

Rao, R. P. Portuguese Rule in Goa, 1510–1961. Bombay: Asia Publishing House, 1963.

D. R. SarDesai

GOLAN HEIGHTS.

GOLAN HEIGHTS. Following the 1967 Arab-Israeli War (the Six-Day War), Syrian-Israeli relations have centered on the return of the Golan Heights to Syrian sovereignty. Syria attempted to regain its territory during the 1973 Arab-Israeli War (the Yom Kippur War) but was repelled by Israeli forces. Ending the conflict, Syria and Israel agreed to a United Nations–supervised buffer zone in the Golan between the two nations.

Since 1973 the Golan Heights front has remained quiet, yet steps toward a peaceful settlement remain elusive. In 1991, Syria and Israel attended the Madrid Conference, cosponsored by the United States and the Soviet Union, which sparked subsequent negotiations, but the two nations failed to reach a permanent peace deal. Since then leaders on both sides have made favorable statements regarding an end to the conflict, but these accolades have yet to renew significant formal negotiations.

Some of the difficulties in resolving the status of the Golan Heights include the assassination of the Israeli prime minister Yitzhak Rabin in 1995, the death of the Syrian president Hafiz al-Asad in 2000, the flare-up of the second Palestinian Intifada, and uncompromising demands on both sides. In the early twenty-first century, Syria continued to call for unconditional Israeli withdrawal from the Golan, while Israel remained concerned over Syrian state sponsorship of several terrorist groups, including the Palestinian Islamic Jihad and the Lebanese Hezbollah. On the Israeli side, concerns often centered on the potential strategic use of the Golan Heights as staging grounds for Arab artillery or rocket attacks against the Galilee region. Since 1967, Israel has established several settlements in the Golan, and in 1981 the Israeli Knesset annexed the Heights despite significant international criticism.

[See also Arab-Israeli Conflict; Israel; and Syria.]

BIBLIOGRAPHY

Ginat, Joseph, Edward J. Perkins, and Edwin G. Corr, eds. The Middle East Peace Process: Vision versus Reality. Norman: University of Oklahoma Press, 2003. Chapters 19 and 20, respectively authored by Moshe Ma'oz and Eyal Zisser, provide in-depth information relating to Israeli-Syrian negotiations and the potential for a future peace deal.

The Middle East. 10th ed. Washington, D.C.: Congressional Quarterly Press, 2005. One of the most comprehensive and systematic reference works on the modern Middle East.

Van Creveld, Martin L. The Sword and the Olive: A Critical History of the Israeli Defense Force. 2d ed. New York: Public Affairs, 2002. Provides an excellent analysis of Israeli strategic and military history relating to the Arab-Israeli conflicts.

Matthew R. Johnson

GOLD AND GOLD MINING.

GOLD AND GOLD MINING. People have used gold as money and a store of wealth for the past 2,500 years, because gold is both hard to destroy or damage, yet malleable, and found on every continent, but still rare. These characteristics became increasingly important during the seventeenth and eighteenth centuries with the development of global trade systems. Despite its abandonment as a world monetary standard during the twentieth century, gold remains valuable today. Technological advances have led to a consolidation of gold mining by large corporations, raising questions of sovereignty in poorer countries around the world. Gold is a mineral that has proven its importance throughout world history and continues to be important today, in such diverse areas as medicine, electronics, chemical processes, and jewelry.

As economies around the world became ever more connected by transoceanic trade, gold became one of the most important trading items linking Atlantic and Indian Ocean trading centers. Early European explorers in both Africa (along the aptly named "Gold Coast") and South America searched for "El Dorado," a mythical land of gold. European countries realized that controlling the world supply of gold would guarantee economic dominance.

South America was site of the most important gold mines during the eighteenth century. Spanish settlers in Ecuador around 1699 established some of the earliest gold mines, using the labor of indigenous peoples and slaves of African descent. The problems they encountered with maintaining a reliable labor supply, however, led the Spanish to abandon most mining. The harsh labor required for mining was to prove a problem for many mine owners. More successful was Minas Gerais, a mine located in Brazil's southeastern interior. The discovery of gold there in 1693 led to the first international gold rush in history. With the gold rush, massive numbers of people arrived in the interior of Brazil and opened up the interior of Brazil to European colonization. During this century, Minas Gerais possessed one of the largest slave populations in the Americas. The Portuguese government, demanding a royal fifth (*quinto*) from the profits, attempted to control and restrict the use of the land in Minas Gerais. Brazilian gold mining also spread in the eighteenth century to locations such as Mato Grasso and Goiás.

Early gold mining relied upon riverine sources of gold; prospectors would recover it on the shores of a river after a heavy rainstorm, or by panning a river's water. Digging deep mines, by contrast, required considerable technological advances, which the Portuguese tried to develop during the eighteenth century. Although shaft mining was used successfully in Spanish-American silver mines during the eighteenth century, the capital invested by the Portuguese proved insufficient to expand mining in Brazil. With this failure to develop shaft mining, Portuguese-sponsored mining began declining at the end of the eighteenth century.

The British were responsible for implementing innovations in Brazilian gold mining. Deep-shaft mining, technology learned in Cornwall by the British, relied upon waterpower to dig deep into the earth. British capitalist enterprises, led by the St. John d'el Rey Mining Company, developed the largest gold mine in South America in 1830. Based at Minas Gerais, this conglomerate also sponsored the development of power plants and a railway in the region, in order to lower transportation costs. The St. John Company controlled the land in the region and was the largest employer and taxpayer in Brazil during the nineteenth century. This British mining company turned a rural community of miners and slaves into an industrial city, and the massive investment of British capital led to

Gold Miners. Miners washing gold-bearing sand in the Ural Mountains, Russian Empire, 1910. SERGEI MIKHAILOVICH PROKUDIN-GORSKII COLLECTION/PRINTS AND PHOTOGRAPHS DIVISION, LIBRARY OF CONGRESS

another gold rush in the nineteenth century. The St. John Company, despite British rhetoric on the abolition of the slave trade and slavery, continued to employ slaves in their mines. As always in the history of gold mining, the demands of mining meant coercion and profit went hand-in-hand.

The discovery of gold in California on 24 January 1848 had a profound effect on the history of the United States. The subsequent gold rush attracted massive migrations to the western United States, with migrants traveling from the east in prairie schooners or across the Pacific Ocean. These gold miners, known as "Argonauts," came from around the world, from places as diverse as Chile, Australia, China, Mexico, the Caribbean, Europe, Peru, and Hawaii. In the space of ten years, a land that previously was home to a small population of Native Americans and people of Spanish and Mexican heritage had produced about three hundred million dollars in gold. Immigrants unseated long-time residents and pursued their economic livelihoods in a location distant from the controls of a central government. The gold rush had a permanent effect on the United States, leading to the development of a transcontinental railroad and making the United States of America a Pacific power.

Gold miners in California lived transient lives, and life on the frontier proved to be vastly different from anything they had previously experienced. Women were scarce in the west, for example, and with their absence men had to learn to live without their customary services. The exodus of men from the eastern United States also affected women and their families. Two years later, however, women began arriving in California, taking up occupations in places such as gambling halls. By 1869, with the initial flurry of excitement calmed down and the transcontinental railroad complete, gold-mining communities began to assume a more permanent status. Capitalized mining companies assumed control of mining sites, and other entrepreneurs developed other industries in California to support the migrant population.

The California gold rush presaged a number of mid- and late-nineteenth-century gold rushes around the Pacific Rim. Improvements in sea and land transportation allowed mass migrations of people during this century. For example, the discovery of gold in New South Wales led to massive migrations from China into the Australian colonies. As in California, gold-rush areas were centers of constant conflict, despite attempts by the government to license access to gold deposits. The quick boom from the mid-1850s to the mid-1870s slowed down with the decrease in easily accessible surface deposits. In the end, new technology such as steam pumping was required for the continuation of mining. A similar pattern of development occurred decades later in Western Australia, where there was a gold rush in the 1890s. A gradual consolidation of mining companies followed the shift from alluvial mining to deep-level mining. Labor issues remained confrontational in gold mining areas, with immigrant mineworkers involved in unions and politics.

As these individual gold rushes ran out, Anglo-European groups moved around the Pacific, searching for new gold opportunities. At the end of the nineteenth century, for example, gold was discovered in the Klondike River in northwest Canada. People from North America, unprepared for the hostile environment they would encounter, flocked to the Yukon with "Klondike Fever." A strong desire for individual wealth helped to create a new sense of transnational community among the gold miners.

In 1886, a gold rush in the Transvaal Republic (Witswatersrand) attracted both British mining investors and California mining engineers. Nearby Johannesburg attracted a global community of those seeking to profit from this newly discovered gold mine, which ended up being the largest gold field in the world. The mines in the Rand, however, had to be dug at deep levels, in a process that required a large investment of capital and labor. The mines were worked by unskilled African workers and imported Chinese labor.

Tensions between the government, seeking to profit from the mines, and the mine owners—as well as between the owners and their impoverished labor force—ran high throughout the nineteenth and twentieth centuries. High levels of racial violence manifested as a form of labor control. White workers struggled to maintain their high levels of pay in comparison with their black colleagues. White workers were responsible for supervising the gangs of twenty to twenty-five African workers who performed the manual labor in the mines. Despite these labor problems, the gold mines in South Africa attracted migrant laborers from around the African continent, drawn by the promise of wage labor. Between the years of 1920 and 1970, thanks to a centralized recruiting system headed by the Chamber of Mines, miners came from as far away as southern Tanzania to work in South Africa. Gold mining, in many senses, subordinated the entire subcontinent of Africa to the South African economy. This seemingly limitless supply of laborers willing to relocate and work for low wages allowed the mining companies to accumulate large fortunes.

These gold rushes, from the eighteenth to the twentieth centuries, were spurred by the development of global trading. For instance, British pressure for global free trade rested upon the gold standard, which allowed different global powers to trade in gold for other desired commodities. In general, the nineteenth century was the century of the gold standard—use of the gold standard was necessary for a country to participate in the world economy. Prior to 1821, England and other west European countries depended on a bimetallic standard. European governments used gold for large transactions and silver for smaller. The bimetallic standard, however, proved complicated when governments attempted to trade internationally. The gold standard was adopted in Britain in the early nineteenth century during a technological revolution in minting that allowed the mass production of coins with steam-powered machinery. When the price of silver plummeted in the 1870s, more countries joined the gold standard.

The gold standard was also crucial to industrial expansion in the United States. The California gold rush introduced new liquidity and stability to the United States economy. The government used gold to finance the construction of America's railroads, for example. The Coinage Act of 1873 led to the dropping of the silver standard and the complete adoption of the gold standard. Despite this law, debates about the gold standard recurred during the 1896 election between William Jennings Bryan (bimetallism) and William McKinley (gold standard). Once he became president, McKinley successfully worked for the passage of the Gold Standard Act of 1900. It was not until 1971 that the United States formally left the gold standard, making the central bank of the country responsible for backing the currency. Other countries, such as Brazil, were less committed to the gold standard.

If the nineteenth century was the era of the gold rush, the twentieth century ushered in a time of conflict over mining resources and state control, conflicts that continue today. Due to the high levels of capital necessary for profitable gold mining, mines are now predominately controlled by international conglomerates. Most new gold mines, however, are in poor, underdeveloped countries. Countries such as Ghana and Kyrgyzstan are torn between protecting their limited resources and gaining the investment and employment provided by international mining companies. These struggles are between economic profit and ownership.

Some countries, such as Fiji, allow international mining groups to use indigenous people for labor in their mines. Others refuse to sign over control of their gold deposits, sacrificing crucial employment opportunities for their people. Ghana, for example, has a long history of gold mining, and the Ghanaian government has refused to allow a large number of European mining companies to operate in the country. Some external investors dangle carrots in front of countries—Chinese companies promise to improve the infrastructure in Kyrgyzstan if Chinese firms are allowed to participate in the local gold-mining industry. The Chinese government, on the other hand, has only recently opened up its gold industries to outsiders. One of the most striking conflicts occurred in Nicaragua in 1928, when Augusto César Sandino (1895–1934) seized control of, and destroyed, two American-owned mines in Nicaragua along the Mosquito Coast. Sandino led followers fueled by anger against American hegemony in the region, a result of the large mining concessions the Nicaraguan government had made to American companies.

Such conflicts in poorer countries are endemic now that large gold reserves have been exhausted in the rest of the world. Environmental concerns are increasing as, over time, it is becoming more apparent that mining can be permanently destructive to local ecosystems. This is an even larger issue as gold-mining explorations are occurring in previously isolated ecosystems. Underwater mining, for example, popularized in the 1960s and 1970s, raises new concerns over sovereignty and the environmental impact of such mining. New technology also brings with it new worries over the high levels of capital now required for productive gold mining. Gold mining has moved from being an economic activity millions participated in, hoping to get rich quick, to the preserve of well-funded conglomerates trying to squeeze profits out of an ailing industry.

BIBLIOGRAPHY

Dumett, Raymond E. *El Dorado in West Africa: The Gold-Mining Frontier, African Labor, and Colonial Capitalism in the Gold Coast, 1875–1900.* Athens: Ohio University Press, 1998. Dumett describes the development of gold mining in West Africa, providing an interesting contrast to studies of mining in South Africa.

Flynn, Laurie. *Studded with Diamonds and Paved with Gold: Miners, Mining Companies, and Human Rights in Southern Africa.* London: Bloomsbury, 1992. Charts the connections between violence, racism, and mining in nineteenth- and twentieth-century South Africa.

Gedicks, Al. *Resource Rebels: Native Challenges to Mining and Oil Corporations.* Cambridge, Mass.: South End Press, 2001. Describes how indigenous groups successfully form a movement to oppose large mining corporations.

Higgins, Kathleen J. *"Licentious Liberty" in a Brazilian Gold-Mining Region: Slavery, Gender, and Social Control in*

Eighteenth-Century Sabará, Minas Gerais. University Park: Pennsylvania University Press, 1999. Higgins discusses the lives of slaves, freed slaves, and colonists in the interior of South America during the eighteenth century.

McCalman, Iain, Alexander Cook, and Andrew Reeves, eds. *Gold: Forgotten Histories and Lost Objects of Australia.* Cambridge, U.K.: Cambridge University Press, 2001. The editors present a series of studies on the impact of the discovery of gold and gold mining in Australia.

Redish, Angela. *Bimetallism: an Economic and Historical Analysis.* Cambridge, U.K.: Cambridge University Press, 2000. Describes why the British abandoned bimetallism for the gold standard.

Rohrbough, Malcolm J. *Days of Gold: The California Gold Rush and the American Nation.* Berkeley: University of California Press, 1997. Rohrbough uses gold-rush diaries, letters, and newspapers to produce a different picture of the gold rush and its effect on the nation.

Sargent, Thomas J., and Francois R. Velde. *The Big Problem of Small Change.* Princeton, N.J.: Princeton University Press, 2002. Provides a useful discussion of the relation of changing technology to monetary systems.

JANE HOOPER

GOLD COAST. *See* British Colonial Empire; Ghana.

GOLDEN TRIANGLE. The "Golden Triangle" refers to the area where the northernmost regions of Burma (called Myanmar by the current government), Thailand, and Laos intersect. This region has long been associated with opium production and its derivative, heroin. During the period from the 1940s to the 1970s, before the rise of opium agriculture in Afghanistan, the Golden Triangle was considered the leading source of world heroin supplies. The poppy, from which opium and heroin is derived, has long been a staple crop for the peoples inhabiting the Golden Triangle, including the Hmong and Yao of Laos and the Shan of Myanmar (Burma). Mule trains traditionally carried poppies and flower pulp to drug laboratories in the Thai-Burmese border area for processing into heroin.

Government efforts to stem opium production have repeatedly fallen afoul of political or international interests. For example, Chinese Nationalist troops retreating from mainland China toward the end of the civil war there (1927–1950) established themselves in northern Burma and have trafficked in drugs ever since. French secret services in Indochina attempted to control poppy exports from Laos as a means of financing its activities during the Franco-Vietnamese war (1945–1954). The net result was to stimulate production and to transform a traditional trade in opium into one in heroin. Golden Triangle

production of opium was estimated at about eighty tons at the end of World War II. By the 1960s, opium production had fallen, and heroin was moving by the hundreds of tons annually. The main export route seems to have been to towns in northern Thailand and then through Bangkok to the international marketplace.

Studies of the heroin problem during this period find that the drugs were routed to the French mafia (*Union Corse*) for onward shipment to Europe through Turkey and other countries. Repeated allegations of Central Intelligence Agency involvement in Laotian drug trafficking during the American war in Vietnam (1959–1975) were not proven, but Royal Laotian Government involvement in the traffic is widely acknowledged. Heroin use became problematical among U.S. troops in Indochina during the latter conflict, and significant amounts of the drugs were smuggled directly from Laos into the Republic of Vietnam (South Vietnam). United States interests in pursuing its Vietnam War and maintaining alliances with Laotian and South Vietnamese leaders precluded strong enforcement activity, as on many other occasions when official corruption or reasons of state have impeded efforts to curb the international trafficking in illicit drugs.

More recently, the drug profile of the Golden Triangle has changed. The post–Vietnam War exodus of the Hmong from Laos much reduced poppy cultivation in that country and efforts to eradicate the crop have continued under the postwar communist government. Thailand has also made great inroads against poppy agriculture, and in Myanmar estimated exports fell by two-thirds over the decade beginning in 1995. The United Nations maintains a very active illicit drug suppression program in Southeast Asia. According to its figures, Myanmar was the source for over 90 percent of the 350 tons of opium poppy produced in 2006, and is the world's second supplier after Afghanistan. The Burmese drug labs are reported to be shifting into production of methamphetamine, however, as both local and foreign users demand the new drugs.

[See also Drugs and Narcotics, *subentry* Illegal Drugs and the Drug Trade; Laos; Myanmar; Opium; *and* Thailand.]

BIBLIOGRAPHY

McCoy, Alfred W. *The Politics of Heroin: CIA Complicity in the Global Drug Trade.* New York: Lawrence Hill & Company, 1991.

United Nations, Office on Drugs and Crime. *Opium Cultivation in the Golden Triangle: Lao PDR, Myanmar, Thailand.* Geneva: United Nations, October 2006.

JOHN PRADOS

GOLF. Although the origins of golf are contested, it is accepted that the modern game originated in Scotland. The first rules and golf club were established in Leith, a seaside link close to Edinburgh, in 1744. The Royal and Ancient Golf Club of Saint Andrews, fifty-five miles (eighty-eight kilometers) northeast of Edinburgh, is regarded as the cradle of golf because in the late nineteenth century it determined the standard of golf courses and developed golf's rules. Nowadays regulations are defined in conjunction between the Royal and Ancient and the U.S. Golf Association.

In the eighteenth century the game was extensively played in Scotland but scarcely known elsewhere. Most of the historical accounts about golf in Scotland describe it as a popular game during the eighteenth and nineteenth centuries. Yet studies in the 1990s suggested that golf might not have been as democratic as it has been portrayed. In late-nineteenth-century England the game became fashionable among upper-middle- and some upper-class people. In contrast, few working-class people could afford playing the sport.

The early internationalization of the sport is associated with the expansion of British colonialism. Golf clubs were erected in India (Bangalore, 1820; Calcutta, 1829; and Bombay, 1842), Ireland (Curragh, 1856), Australia (Adelaide, 1870), Canada (Montreal, 1873), South Africa (Cape Town, 1885), and China (Hong Kong, 1889).

Although it is not clear when and where golf was first played in the United States, the Saint Andrew's in New York (1888) is considered to be the first golf club founded there. The growth of the sport in late-nineteenth-century Britain and the United States was incredibly fast. In the United States between 1888 and 1900 nearly 1,040 clubs were founded. Many scholars suggest that the Victorian values and individualism connected to golf, as well as the countryside settings and privacy of the clubs, may have been some of the cultural factors that attracted new golfers so rapidly.

The global dissemination of the sport during the twentieth century was linked to economic and political trends. In the first half of the century Britain and the United States were its biggest supporters, but after World War II, Japan embraced golf as well. These three countries have played a key role in spreading golf, either through expatriate business communities that have imported it to new places (for instance, Mexico in the 1900s) or through political involvement in some countries, which indirectly have made local elites adopt the sport (for instance, South Korea in the 1950s).

Until the early 1970s golf preserved an amateur nature. Although professional leagues existed in many countries, they were not particularly important. This trend was first changed in the United States, where the Professional Golf Association (PGA) played a substantial role in commercializing golf. Since the 1990s international tourism has encouraged a boom of the sport on a global scale. Diverse countries are constructing or plan to construct new courses to attract tourists. Nowadays many golf tournaments, such as the U.S. Open or British Open, are globally watched. Golf is played in almost every country, yet at a global scale it has retained an upper-middle- and upper-class identity.

[*See also* Sports.]

BIBLIOGRAPHY

Lowerson, John. "Golf and the Making of Myths." In *Scottish Sport in the Making of the Nation: Ninety-Minute Patriot?*, edited by Grant Jarvie and Graham Walker, pp. 75–90. Leicester, U.K., and New York: Leicester University Press, 1994. Approaches in a critical way the notion that golf was a democratic pastime in Scotland. Provides a good number of historical sources to show how the origins of golf need a new interpretation.

Moss, Richard J. *Golf and the American Country Club.* Urbana: University of Illinois Press, 2001. Does not approach the game in the same critical way that Lowerson does; however, it is a good historical account of the expansion of the sport in the United States from the late nineteenth century to the present. Chapter 7 ("An Endangered Species") develops an interesting analysis of gender and racial exclusion in country and golf clubs in the United States.

HUGO CERON-ANAYA

GOOD NEIGHBOR POLICY. President Franklin D. Roosevelt (1882–1945; president 1933–1945) is accurately credited with crystallizing the Good Neighbor Policy, but it was President Herbert Hoover (1874–1964; president 1929–1933) who originally laid down the vocabulary for the plan. On a stop in Honduras during a 1928 goodwill trip to Latin America, president-elect Hoover announced that the United States had "a desire to maintain not only the cordial relations of governments with each other, but also the relations of good neighbors." Demonstrating his willingness, Hoover promised not to repeat previous U.S. interventions into the region, and he withdrew marines from Nicaragua and Haiti. Despite revolutionary activity in South America during his term, he did not intervene, keeping his word to leave these nations to their own business.

Franklin D. Roosevelt entered the presidency determined further to improve U.S. relations with the nations
of Central and South America, and he organized his
administration to emphasize that friendship with these
nations was essential to the security of the United States.
His March 1933 inaugural address summed: "In the field
of world policy, I would dedicate this nation to the policy of
the good neighbor—the neighbor who resolutely respects
himself and, because he does so, respects the rights of
others." In December of the same year, Roosevelt sent his
secretary of state, Cordell Hull, to the Pan-American Conference in Montevideo, Uruguay, to reinforce the sentiment. While there, Hull backed a declaration favored by
most nations in the Western Hemisphere: "No state has
the right to intervene in the internal or external affairs
of another."

Exceptions were made, however, and the now-labeled
Good Neighbor Policy was tested, beginning in the next
year. In Cuba, a nation of vital economic and strategic
importance to the United States, intervention continued
to be a way of life. In 1934, at Roosevelt's direction, the
State Department used its considerable leverage to establish in Havana an "acceptable" government: one more
amenable to North American business interests. But with
Sergeant Fulgencio Batista y Zaldívar's cooperative regime
in place, the United States returned to its former level of
neighborliness. Roosevelt agreed to renounce America's
right to intervene in Cuba to preserve internal stability
or independence—previously allowed by the 1903 Platt
Amendment—in return for permission to keep a huge
naval base at Guantánamo Bay.

The ability of the United States to abide by its own policy
faced its most serious test even closer to home that same
year, 1934. The Mexican president Lázaro Cárdenas had
begun a national recovery program called "Mexico for the
Mexicans" by proposing to nationalize the agricultural and
mining properties of all foreign corporations. He promised
"fair compensation" of $10 million to all nations with cor-
porate holdings in Mexico, but American and British oil
companies, demanding $262 million in the nationalization
process, saw Cárdenas's offer as meager. The Roosevelt
administration went to great lengths finally to convince
Mexico to pay $40 million in compensation for the foreign-
owned lands it had seized and another $29 million for the
oilfields.

Even if sharply nudged toward "good neighborliness,"
Latin American states did respond to their part of the policy
by rallying to the Allies' cause during World War II. This
was the high point in the life of Roosevelt's principle,
however, as U.S. anti-Communist activities throughout
Europe and Asia renewed distrust in the Americas, leading
to the gradual, but ultimate, eclipse of the Good Neighbor
Policy.

[*See also* Monroe Doctrine; New Deal; Roosevelt Corollary; *and* United States, *subentry* American Foreign
Policy.]

BIBLIOGRAPHY
Brewer, Stewart. *Borders and Bridges: A History of U.S.–Latin
    American Relations*. Westport, Conn.: Praeger Security Inter-
    national, 2006. Examines collaboration between the United
    States and Latin America, including the Good Neighbor Policy,
    and changing social and political relationships.
Pike, Fredrick B. *FDR's Good Neighbor Policy: Sixty Years of
    Generally Gentle Chaos*. Austin: University of Texas, 1995.
    Explores the applications of the Good Neighbor Policy and
    concludes that it is not so much an anticipated aberration
    from interventionist policies as it is a natural complement to
    the New Deal.

CYNTHIA GWYNNE YAUDES

GRAMEEN BANK.   An antipoverty bank owned by
its village borrowers and headquartered in Dhaka,
Bangladesh, the Grameen Bank pioneered and institutionalized "microcredit" lending on a massive scale and widely
influenced practices in the area of international development. Microcredit involves the extension of small, uncol-
lateralized loans for self-employment, usually to individuals
living in poverty who otherwise would be denied access to
credit at reasonable rates of interest. During 2006 the
Grameen Bank (meaning "bank of the villages" in Bangla)
extended $730 million in loans to 6.9 million people, 97
percent of them women, living in 75,000 Bangladeshi
villages. Its methodology has been replicated or adapted
in more than 100 countries. By 2006 the Grameen Trust, a
sister organization, and the Grameen Foundation USA,
based in Washington, D.C, had supported microcredit
programs in 37 countries serving 3 million borrowers.
Numerous studies have demonstrated that, when well
administered, microcredit can reduce poverty, empower
women, improve nutrition, increase contraceptive use,
and help poor families with crises.

The Grameen Bank grew out of a project initiated by
the economist Muhammad Yunus when he was teaching at
Chittagong University in Bangladesh. In response to
the suffering he witnessed during Bangladesh's 1974
famine, in which hundreds of thousands starved, Yunus
began fieldwork with his graduate students in the nearby
village of Jobra, exploring avenues for development.

His encounters with "landless" villagers, particularly women, who were frequently exploited by moneylenders and traders, inspired him to launch the Grameen Bank Project in 1976, which extended its first loans totaling 856 takas (worth about $55 at the time) to 42 villagers.

Over the next seven years, the project, under Yunus's direction, and financed by government-owned banks in Bangladesh, expanded to 58,000 borrowers in the district of Tangail. However, Yunus found partnership with the formal banking system to be unworkable, and he successfully lobbied the government to incorporate an independent bank that would extend credit in rural areas only to the poor. In 1983 the Grameen Bank was established by a special act of parliament. According to its bylaws, the bank may extend loans only to individuals whose total net worth is valued at less than a half-acre of moderate-quality land. It lends money for income-generating activities, housing, and higher education, and provides savings and insurance services. By 2006, through its Housing Loan Programme, the bank had financed 642,000 homes, and through its Struggling (Beggar) Members Programme, had extended loans totaling $1.25 million to to 81,000 beggars.

Early in its history, the Grameen Bank focused on women borrowers, largely because the bank found that this approach markedly improved the socioeconomic conditions in poor families and had a more pronounced positive impact on children. From 1976 to 1994 the Grameen Bank's growth was funded through a combination of grants, concessionary loans, and loan guarantees from development sources, including the International Fund for Agricultural Development, and the governments of Canada, Germany, Sweden, and Norway. Since 1995 the bank has financed its activities exclusively through deposits and commercial borrowings, including a $150-million bond offering. By 2006 its borrowers had amassed some $650 million in savings.

Since 1990 the Grameen Bank's influence has spread internationally. Thousands of microcredit, or microfinance, organizations have been established worldwide. According to the Microcredit Summit Campaign, by early 2006 these programs were providing credit and other financial services to approximately 100 million families around the globe. The Grameen Bank has also established a series of social benefit enterprises in Bangladesh that address a range of development needs, including health, education, nutrition, energy, and communications technology. For continuing efforts to aid the disenfranchised, Muhammad Yunus and the Grameen Bank were jointly awarded the Nobel Peace Prize in 2006.

BIBLIOGRAPHY

Bornstein, David. *The Price of a Dream: The Story of the Grameen Bank and the Idea That Is Helping the Poor to Change Their Lives.* New York: Simon & Schuster, 1996. Rev. ed. New York: Oxford University Press, 2005.

Todd, Helen. *Women at the Center: Grameen Bank Borrowers after One Decade.* Boulder, Colo.: Westview Press, 1996.

Yunus, Muhammad, with Alan Jolis. *Banker to the Poor: Micro-Lending and the Battle Against World Poverty.* New York: Public Affairs, 1999.

DAVID BORNSTEIN

GRAN COLOMBIA. The original Republic of Colombia, founded 17 December 1819 at an improvised meeting at Angostura in what is now Venezuela, is called Gran (Great) Colombia to distinguish it from the Colombia of today. It encompassed all the Spanish Viceroyalty of New Granada, equivalent to the present Venezuela, Colombia, Panama, and Ecuador, most of which was still under Spanish rule. However, by his victory in the Battle of Boyacá (7 August 1819), the South American revolutionary leader Simón Bolívar, the Liberator, freed the heart of the viceroyalty, including its capital Santafé (soon renamed Bogotá). He was determined to keep northern South America united, and the Congress gave its consent.

Union already existed de facto between patriot-held areas of Bolívar's native Venezuela and those of New Granada proper (present-day Colombia), since revolutionaries in both had recognized Bolívar's leadership as he campaigned back and forth, ignoring colonial divisions. The Liberator furthermore believed that only such a large nation, with its complementary resources, would be taken seriously abroad. In reality, those resources were mostly undeveloped, and there were significant social and cultural differences between Venezuela, with its plantation agriculture and livestock-raising plains, Ecuador with its highland textile workshops and heavy Native American population, and New Granada, which shared some characteristics of both and had gold as its principal export. Even during the independence struggle, frictions developed between regions; great distances and primitive transportation and communications were other obstacles to integration. Nevertheless, Colombian forces steadily reduced the areas under Spanish rule: the last royalist holdout, Puerto Cabello, surrendered in November 1823.

Meanwhile an 1821 constituent convention established a highly centralized yet generally liberal form of government and enacted some fundamental reforms including abolition of the Inquisition, the Indian tribute or yearly head tax required of Native Americans, and a start toward abolition of slavery under the free-birth principle, whereby at least the children of slaves born henceforth would be free on reaching a certain age. It elected Bolívar constitutional president and, for regional balance, made the New Granadan Francisco de Paula Santander vice president. Since Bolívar continued leading armies in the field—even into Peru to complete the independence struggle there—Santander became acting chief executive in the nation's capital. Santander proved a capable administrator and worked closely with Congress in adopting additional reforms, which were generally moderate, but controversial when touching ecclesiastical or military prerogatives.

Gran Colombia was the first Spanish American republic to obtain United States recognition, in 1822; three years later recognition by Great Britain followed. Thanks to its international prestige it raised a $30 million foreign loan on favorable terms. But it soon proved impossible to maintain debt service, for the nation's basic economy was less impressive than its military might, and neither New Granada's mining nor Venezuela's agriculture had fully recovered from wartime damages. Gran Colombia hosted the first inter-American conference, at Panama City, in 1826. However, the meeting accomplished little, and by the time it met, the union was beginning to unravel.

In Venezuela José Antonio Páez launched a rebellion against Santander's central administration in April 1826. Apart from specific complaints, Venezuelans resented their subordination to Bogotá, hoping for greater autonomy or even separation; other protest movements arose in Ecuador in imitation of Venezuela though stopping short of outright rebellion. Both Páez and Ecuadoran dissidents reaffirmed allegiance to Bolívar. But the latter, well aware of growing discontent, had his own agenda, featuring a suspension of overhasty liberal innovations and revamping of Colombian institutions in line with the constitution he had drafted for Bolivia, the key element of which was a president serving for life. Bolívar therefore returned from Peru in late 1826, settled the Venezuelan revolt by negotiation with Páez, and in September 1827 took personal command of the central government, displacing Santander. He hoped that a constitutional convention that met in April 1828 would introduce necessary changes. When it failed to do so, Bolívar yielded to his followers' demands that he assume dictatorial powers.

As dictator Bolívar satisfied some, not all, demands for the rollback of liberal reforms. He survived an assassination attempt in September 1828, and a brief border conflict with Peru ended in victory for Colombia.

But that war was unpopular, as was a proposal of Bolívar's ministers (not Bolívar himself) to create a monarchy in Colombia on his death or retirement. Other complaints were not lacking. Even before a disheartened Bolívar resigned the presidency in April 1830, Venezuela was again in revolt, aiming at full independence. Ecuador soon seceded as well; what was left of Gran Colombia became the Republic of New Granada. Although some historians have attributed this outcome to the intrigues of foreign powers and shortsightedness of local elites, more have concluded that Gran Colombia was too ambitious a creation for its time. Three of its successor states (Colombia, Ecuador, and Venezuela) retained the yellow-blue-red color scheme of the Gran Colombia flag in their own banners, and over the years the shared history of the Gran Colombian union was often invoked in rhetorical solidarity or even in such formal arrangements as the Gran Colombian Merchant Fleet (founded in 1946 but finally liquidated in 1996).

[*See also* Colombia; Ecuador; Latin American Wars of Independence; Panama; *and* Venezuela.]

BIBLIOGRAPHY

Bushnell, David. "The Last Dictatorship: Betrayal or Consummation?" *Hispanic American Historical Review* 63, no. 1 (1983): 65–104. Similar in scope to the next item, but treating the final years of Gran Colombia as well as historiographic controversies.

Bushnell, David. *The Santander Regime in Gran Colombia.* Newark: University of Delaware Press, 1954. A study of domestic politics and administration (to 1827).

Jaramillo, Juan Diego. *Bolívar y Canning, 1822–1827: Desde el Congreso de Verona hasta el Congreso de Panamá.* Bogotá, Colombia: Banco de la República, Biblioteca Luis-Angel Arango, Talleres Gráficos, 1983. Examines the most significant dimension of Gran Colombian foreign relations.

Uribe-Uran, Victor M. *Honorable Lives: Lawyers, Family, and Politics in Colombia, 1780–1850.* Pittsburgh, Pa.: University of Pittsburgh Press, 2000. An analysis of the social bases of politics, from late colonial antecedents to New Granada after the breakup of Gran Colombia.

DAVID BUSHNELL

GRAND CANYON. One of the world's outstanding landmarks, the Grand Canyon is situated in the state of Arizona, United States. It is a steep-sided gorge, which has been created by the erosion of sedimentary rocks by the Colorado River over many millions of years. The canyon begins at Lees Ferry and ends at Grand Wash Cliffs, an area through which the Colorado River meanders a distance of 277 miles (446 kilometers). Its width and depth vary, with maximum width being approximately 15 miles (24 kilometers) and maximum depth being approximately 6,000 feet (1,829 meters). The oldest basal rock exposed is the Vishnu Schist, approximately 2,000 million years old, and the youngest is the Kaibab Limestone, approximately 230 million years old. Downcutting began five or six million years ago, and erosion continues today to reveal multicolored sediments of marine, desert, and swamp origin to produce a landscape of world renown, which today is in a U.S. National Park of 1,904 square miles (4,931 square kilometers). Other attractions include varied plant and animal life, which reflect many different ecosystems ranging from various desert types to boreal forest. There are approximately 1,500 plant, 355 bird, 89 mammalian, 47 reptile, 9 amphibian, and 17 fish species, many of which are endangered and/or endemic. Artifacts attesting to human presence date back twelve thousand years, and the canyon's many archaeological features include rock paintings of the Desert Archaic people and rock shelters of the Anasazi and Puebloan people, ancestors of the present-day Hopi Indians.

Although the canyon region was inhabited by native people prior to European arrival and visited by Spanish explorers in the sixteenth century, it was not until the mid-1800s that European Americans explored the region. In particular the Civil War veteran Major John Wesley Powell led the first party to sail through the canyon in 1869. Soon afterward mineral prospectors arrived in search of lead, zinc, and silver and established camps along the rim. Cattle- and sheep-rearing enterprises were established by the 1880s, but overgrazing ensued and ranching failed as grass was replaced by sage brush. By 1900 tourists were beginning to visit, a trend accelerated by the construction of the railroad from Williams to the canyon rim, and the first accommodation specifically for tourists was constructed in 1917. The significance of the Grand Canyon as a national environmental and cultural asset was first acknowledged in 1893, when it was given the status of Forest Reserve by the federal government. It became a National Preserve in 1906 and then a National Monument in 1908. In 1919 it was designated as a National Park, the seventeenth such park in the United States, just three years after the establishment of the National Park Service. International recognition was bestowed in 1979, when it became a World Heritage Site.

The Grand Canyon is of local, national, and international importance. Beginning well before the era of mass tourism (which began around 1960) it has brought prosperity through tourism for over 120 years. Activities include hiking, rafting, and running, as well as general sightseeing and scientific research. There are more than 5 million visitors per year to what has become an iconic symbol of the western United States.

[*See also* National Parks.]

BIBLIOGRAPHY
Anderson, Michael F. *Polishing the Jewel: An Administrative History of Grand Canyon National Park.* Grand Canyon, Ariz.: Grand Canyon Association, 2000.
Rudd, Connie. *The Grand Canyon.* Las Vegas, Nev.: KC Publications, 1990.

A. M. MANNION

GREAT AWAKENING. The Enlightenment introduced a sense of rationalism to religious practices in Europe and prerevolutionary America, stressing the free will of individuals to lead a moral life and achieve salvation. For some, this idea was comforting in its democracy—including in the church all who worked to live decent Christian lives, not just those who believed they were saved by grace. Others thought Christian rationalism was heretical in its movement away from the belief that salvation came only from grace.

It was these individuals who, fearing the Enlightenment's effect on traditional religion, pushed to reaffirm the primacy of grace to the process of salvation. Their zeal coalesced into a series of religious revivals, known as the Great Awakening. Spreading from Europe between 1720 and 1760, waves of revivalism convulsed British North America, dividing churches and threatening social and political authority. Using an animated preaching style, immigrant and native ministers canvassed the northern and southern colonies, emphasizing the importance of powerful, personal conversion to salvation. They visited established churches or founded their own, urging congregants to engage in a process of self-judgment—feeling despair as sinners damned to hell, then rejoicing in the conviction that God, through saving grace, had rescued them from this fate. "New Lights" (as these ministers were called) contrasted dramatically with "Old Lights": classically trained theologians who emphasized reasoned commitment to a godly life. Congregations broke apart along this Old Light–New Light fault; as church authority weakened, religious controversy spilled into the secular realm.

A large number of college students found New Light beliefs applicable to their experiences. At Yale University, for example, they challenged authoritative curriculum, questioned whether their teachers were saved, and, despite punishments, bequeathed the Great Awakening's intellectual legacy to higher learning: a sense of spiritual power and independence among the many.

The Great Awakening inspired this linkage between evangelicalism and secular change. A second round of revivalism secured it. Labeled the Second Great Awakening, these revivals began around 1800 and lasted through the 1830s. With the First Great Awakening, the Second shared views on the importance of piety over theology and the power of emotional, extemporaneous speech over a written sermon. But it was also wider-reaching and more secularly complex than its predecessor.

During the Second Great Awakening's lifetime, thousands of people streamed west to settle the American frontier. Eastern clergy worried that these settlers would leave religiosity behind. Consequently, they sent evangelicals across all parts of the expanding nation to preach from wagons and in tents. So numerous and well-attended were these camp meetings that they shifted the denominational base of American religion toward evangelical churches (like Baptists and Methodists), which grew rapidly in the heated atmosphere of frontier conversion.

Indeed, frontier culture seemed to warp the very shape of evangelicalism. Usually the first social organizations in frontier communities, these churches served both basic communal and religious needs. To this extent, preachers began placing greater stress on human ability and individual will. Seen by some as a return to Enlightenment ideals, this might also be viewed as pious optimism, born from the struggle to exist in the rugged west and the call to spread the message of salvation. Ultimately, the Second Great Awakening is a testament to the growing confidence in social reform, and it laid the foundation for Progressivism in the next century.

[See also Evangelicalism; Great Awakening, Second; Protestantism; and Religious Revivals.]

BIBLIOGRAPHY

Bourne, Russell. *Gods of War, Gods of Peace: How the Meeting of Native and Colonial Religions Shaped Early America.* New York: Harcourt, 2002. Examines the ways in which colonial and native religions clashed and meshed. A central analytical point is the Great Awakening.

McClymond, Michael J. *Embodying the Spirit: New Perspectives on North American Revivalism.* Baltimore, Md.: Johns Hopkins University Press, 2004. Provides a political, economic, and social analysis of America's revival traditions.

CYNTHIA GWYNNE YAUDES

GREAT AWAKENING, SECOND. The term "Second Great Awakening" refers to an evangelical Protestant religious revival in the United States in the first half of the nineteenth century, similar in some respects to the Great Awakening of the 1740s. The Second Great Awakening began in the wake of the revolutionary ethos as a democratic reaction to the Deism of the Enlightenment and the radicalism of the French Revolution and drew strength from the missionary preaching of the Presbyterian Charles Grandison Finney in Utica, New York. Rejecting the colonial-era pattern of church establishment and Calvinism's belief that God shaped our destiny, the charismatic Finney said that people were morally free agents who won salvation by their own effort. The dominance of the Congregational, Anglican, and Presbyterian churches gave way to a voluntary church membership that placed all denominations on an equal footing and spurred growth in Baptist, Methodist, and other sects. By 1831 central and western New York State was dubbed the burned-over district because of Finney's successful conversion of one hundred thousand people and the consequent increase in church membership. Finney and other dynamic preachers used colorful vernacular language to inspire hardworking people to think for themselves and ignore the criticism of social elites.

This revival, dubbed the shopkeepers millennium, had important economic consequences because American capitalism benefited from the evangelists' admonitions to avoid sin, work hard, read the Bible, and learn self-discipline. Its idealism and belief in perfectionism stimulated many reform movements, including temperance, abolitionism, sabbatarianism, public education, missionary societies, prison reform, women's rights, and philanthropy. Especially the poor, the enslaved, the downtrodden, and women found this religious message appealing. Phoebe Worrall Palmer, the Second Great Awakening's leading female preacher, established a Methodist mission in the Five Points slum of New York City, offering various programs for the poor.

Rural people in Appalachia and those migrating west to the frontier found the itinerant Baptist and Methodist preachers more appealing than the more traditional eastern clergymen. By 1800 outdoor ecumenical revivals known as camp meetings attracted large frontier crowds for a weeklong religious and social gathering. Noteworthy for the shouting, shaking, falling, rolling, and barking sinners inspired by the emotional hellfire-and-damnation sermons, camp meetings brought the young and unchurched into local churches and into newly founded sects like the Disciples of Christ and the Church of Christ. Following camp meetings, Methodist circuit riders—young unmarried ministers who traveled from one frontier congregation to another—were noted for converting (or reconverting) lapsed Christians. Baptist congregations, on the other hand, were often led by lay preachers, untrained but earnest men who farmed during the week and preached to their neighbors on Sunday. Both churches relied on music and hymns to teach theology because literacy and schools were lacking on the frontier. Joseph Smith, who founded Mormonism in 1830 in the burned-over district, created the most unusual offshoot of this movement, one that flourished in the West.

The Second Great Awakening changed public behavior because those who were converted or saved attended church, did not drink or swear, practiced charity, and encouraged their neighbors to accept religion. It also forced the established Anglican and Congregational churches to liberalize to compete for congregants with the more democratic evangelical churches. Although the movement was somewhat anti-intellectual, its strong connection to abolitionism led Ralph Waldo Emerson and many transcendentalists to join the antislavery crusade by 1844. Evangelists also founded some colleges, including Dartmouth College, Oberlin College, and Illinois Wesleyan University. After the Civil War (1861–1865) the Second Great Awakening continued to be influential, especially in the evangelical preaching of Dwight Lyman Moody and Billy Sunday.

[See also Christianity, subentry The United States; Evangelicalism; Great Awakening; Protestantism; and Religious Revivals.]

BIBLIOGRAPHY

Bilhartz, Terry D. *Urban Religion and the Second Great Awakening: Church and Society in Early National Baltimore.* Rutherford, N.J.: Fairleigh Dickinson University Press, 1986.

Hankins, Barry. *The Second Great Awakening and the Transcendentalists.* Westport, Conn.: Greenwood Press, 2004.

McLoughlin, William G. *Modern Revivalism: Charles Grandison Finney to Billy Graham.* New York: Ronald Press, 1959.

PETER C. HOLLORAN

GREAT BRITAIN. *See* England; Scotland; Wales; United Kingdom.

GREAT GAME. One of the more remarkable aspects of the British Empire was its inherent fragility. Throughout the nineteenth century, British politicians, soldiers, and diplomats feared the intervention of a foreign power that could overthrow British rule in India, whether directly or by inspiring an uprising among the Raj's subjects. After the defeat of Napoleon, Britain saw the most likely threat to India coming from the new great power in Europe, Russia. Both empires would dramatically expand their holdings in Asia throughout the course of the nineteenth century, and it did seem as though a direct clash between the two was inevitable. That conflagration never occurred, though it did help spawn a number of smaller conflicts, including two invasions of Afghanistan and the Crimean War.

From the Russian perspective, expansion into Central Asia was their own version of imperialism, a move to acquire resources and markets and to extend military power in the ever-elusive quest for a warm-water port. The khanates of Central Asia, were, like India, just far enough behind militarily that small numbers of European troops could overcome much larger armies of poorly trained and equipped Muslims. Although thousands of miles separated the respective frontiers at the beginning of the nineteenth century, Russia's rapid sweep southward alarmed Britain, just as the British move northward alarmed Russia.

As Russians swept southward, British control advanced north, butting up against what would become the natural, logical boundary of the Himalayas and Hindu Kush. In time, this expansion acquired a self-reinforcing logic, as each strategic advance required another to guarantee the security of the former. Although there were other areas of concern, it was always the northwest frontier and the Khyber Pass, the traditional avenue for invasions of India, that attracted the most attention.

Large-scale military adventures were the exception in the Great Game, which was instead largely played by small groups of explorers, surveyors, and spies, whose jobs were frequently all of these tasks in one. Early on in the Great Game, the geographic knowledge of Central Asia each power possessed was surprisingly limited. It was the job of explorers on both sides to fill in the gaps on the map. In many ways this ignorance magnified fears, since the extreme difficulty of any attempt to march an army from the Caspian Sea to the Khyber Pass or vice versa was unknown to them. The early explorers for both sides concluded that Afghanistan was the only logical route for an invasion from Central Asia into India, even if this route presented enormous logistical difficulties for an invader. In any event, any expedition Russia or Britain sent would have to cover thousands of miles, through difficult terrain and hostile populations unless the khanates of Khiva, Bokhara, and Samarkand, as well as Afghanistan and the Punjab, were first subdued.

Much to the alarm of the British, this is precisely what the Russians did to the Muslim states on the steppe of Central Asia by the 1870s. The khanates were vulnerable to invasion because of their isolation and lack of modern military resources. Also, the khanates were still bastions of slave trading, and accounts of Russians taken as slaves provoked popular resentment in much the same way that David Livingstone's accounts of African slavery inspired British intervention there.

The strategic goal of the Raj therefore became securing the line of the Hindu Kush by bringing the Punjab, Afghanistan, and other smaller mountain states into a secure orbit. While diplomacy was tried, military action became the ultimate solution. Persia, a potential back door, was also propped up as a buffer state against further Russian advances. Russian attempts to weaken Afghanistan, particularly aiding a Persian attack on Herat, led to a direct attempt by the British to place a more reliable king on the throne of Afghanistan. The result was the first Anglo-Afghan War, which ended in disaster for Britain.

Rather than flocking to the banner of Shah Shuja, Britain's choice to rule Afghanistan, the Afghans instead saw him as a puppet of a foreign invader. In the end, the British position in Kabul was untenable, leading to a disastrous retreat in mid-winter of 1840–1841, from which only one member, Dr. William Brydon, returned. The humiliating setback the British suffered in Afghanistan dramatically lowered their prestige in the khanates of Central Asia. British emissaries to Bokhara were executed, and it appeared as though the Russians had the upper hand.

In what was an indirect continuation of the geopolitics of the Great Game, the continuing decline of the Ottoman Empire consumed Britain and Russia in the middle of the nineteenth century, leading to a direct clash of the powers in the Crimean War. In the immediate aftermath of the Crimean War, the British were occupied with putting down the revolt of 1857 (the Great Mutiny) in India. In the long run the mutiny became a key part of British concerns about Russian moves. Which troops in India could the British count on? How would India react to even a relatively small Russian force that attempted an invasion? In answer, the army was rebuilt along "martial race" principles favoring Pathans and Sikhs who remained loyal in the mutiny. Politically, a school of thought known as "The Forward Policy" emerged, advocating further advances into Central Asia to preempt Russian moves there.

Russia's rapid advance in Central Asia in the 1860s and 1870s reinforced these concerns. With cotton supplies low during the U.S. Civil War, the potential of Central Asia to become a cotton supplier helped drive Russia into a more aggressive stance. The three major states of Khiva, Bokhara, and Khokand would fall under a rapid Russian onslaught. Russia was also able to bully large concessions out of China in the east, acquiring huge territories without firing a shot.

Britain did not actively intervene against the Russians, and it focused most of its efforts in mapping and intelligence gathering. These Pundits, as the surveyors were called, wandered Central Asia in disguise collecting geographical information and military intelligence, and kept a wary eye for their Russian counterparts. It was this part of the Great Game, combining adventure, espionage, and exoticism that Rudyard Kipling would memorialize in arguably his greatest novel, *Kim* (1901).

The Russians' sweep through Asia had now brought them close to the borders of the Raj, and the Pundits recognized that the geographic obstacles were no longer insuperable. The Russo-Turkish War of 1877–1878 again escalated tensions, and Russia saw an opportunity to hit back at Britain by stirring up trouble in Afghanistan. When a Russian emissary was allowed into Kabul, and a British mission denied, the viceroy, Edward Robert Bulwer-Lytton, a member of the "Forward" school, saw no option but a military response. In spite of some setbacks, Britain did establish Afghanistan as a buffer state with a relatively friendly ruler, Abdur Rahman. Lord Roberts's military victories erased the sting of a humiliating defeat at Maiwand, and reestablished British prestige in Central Asia.

Roberts, on his accession to the position of commander in chief of the Indian Army, became the most prominent member of the Forward school. Russian advances on Merv in the aftermath of the second Afghan War reinforced his mistrust of Russian intentions. The year 1885 marked a peak year for Russophobia. The flashpoint was the oasis at Pandjeh, seized by a small Russian force. England considered this Afghan territory, and the press became particularly jingoistic in pushing for a confrontation. In the end, Abdur Rahman helped press for a diplomatic solution that delineated Afghanistan's boundaries. From here, the Great Game would shift eastward into the Karakorum.

When George Curzon made his train trip through Central Asia in 1888, he became acutely aware of the change that the railways made in the strategic balance, something his Russian hosts undoubtedly wanted him to see. A decade after this trip, Curzon would be viceroy of India. His two main advisers in the Great Game would be Roberts and a frontier officer, Francis Younghusband.

Younghusband undertook one of the great adventures of the Great Game, mapping the regions between Afghanistan and the Chinese border in the Pamirs. Encountering a Russian party on his travels, Younghusband became a forceful advocate of the danger Russia posed in the Pamirs. The result was a military intervention in Chitral in 1892 to forestall a Russian advance and to secure the pass.

Russia's ambitions extended beyond Chitral, and the steady weakening of China opened new possibilities for expansion. Tibet would be the last playing field in the Great Game. Curzon authorized Younghusband to lead a military expedition into Tibet when word of a Russian party in Lhasa reached India. This expedition in 1903 was in many ways the last classic Victorian military adventure, though the result was sordid. No Russians were found, and the accounts of Maxim guns cutting down poorly armed Tibetans turned public opinion against the expedition.

Events outside Central Asia would bring an end to the Great Game. Russia's defeat in the Russo-Japanese War ended her Far Eastern ambitions, and the revolution of 1905 made Russia look toward her internal problems. In the aftermath, a series of negotiations between Russia and Britain resulted in the Anglo-Russian Convention of 1907, which set clear boundaries for each power's sphere of influence. The Great Game would briefly revive in the aftermath of World War I as the British attempted to keep Central Asia out of the hands of the Bolsheviks. In an ironic twist, the Russian invasion of Afghanistan in 1979 started another shift in Central Asia, hastening the collapse of the Soviet Empire and creating a new group of Islamic states in Central Asia, a process that some scholars refer to as the "new Great Game."

[See also Afghanistan; Anglo-Afghan Wars; British Raj; Central Asia; Empire and Imperialism, subentry The British Colonial Empire; India; and Indian War.]

BIBLIOGRAPHY

Allworth, Edward. Central Asia: 130 Years of Russian Dominance, a Historical Overview. 3d ed. Durham, N.C.: Duke University Press, 1994.
Curzon, George. Russia in Central Asia. London and New York: Longmans, Green and Co., 1889.
Hopkirk, Peter. The Great Game: The Struggle for Empire in Central Asia. New York: Kodansha International, 1994.
Kipling, Rudyard. Kim. Reprint. New York and London: Oxford University Press, 1987.
Meyer, Karl E., and Shareen Blair Brysac. Tournament of Shadows: The Great Game and the Race for Empire in Central Asia. Washington, D.C.: Counterpoint, 1999.
Rich, Norman. Great Power Diplomacy, 1814–1914. New York: McGraw-Hill, 1991.

JEREMY NEILL

GREAT LEAP FORWARD. The Great Leap Forward (1958–1960), the worst disaster of the Maoist era, was a utopian attempt to achieve the economic goals of catching up with advanced capitalist countries overnight without creating a new elite class of experts, which would be contrary to the goal of socialism. The Great Leap Forward also represented a final break with the Soviet Union and a departure from the Stalinist model of industrial development.

Mao Zedong first outlined his strategy at the Beidaihe Conference of August 1958. At the heart of the Great Leap Forward was the mass mobilization of Chinese labor and the use of revolutionary enthusiasm, rather than material incentives, to increase production. The state engineered massive water and land reclamation projects to expand the amount of land under cultivation. Other policies aimed to increase agricultural productivity by dedicating more labor to the land. At the same time, Mao decentralized industrial production by sponsoring small-scale local industry and relied on modern industrial output to produce exports to pay for imported capital goods and plant construction.

In the countryside, the attempt to intensify agricultural production involved the creation of people's communes in agriculture, which Mao dubbed "sprouts of communism." The first commune was created in the summer of 1958, and within six months virtually the entire rural population was organized into 26,000 communes having an average of 10,000 farmers and as many as 100,000. The creation of communes transferred power down from the Ministry of Agriculture but also up from smaller production units, such as brigades. Ideally, the devolution of power to the communes would spread across China the benefits of modern life, including access to health care and education. Similarly, the promotion of labor-intensive, small-scale production would help China overcome its technological and capital shortages without exacerbating the urban-rural and technological divisions that Mao saw in the Soviet Union. But commune leaders also endorsed the most radical and ultimately destructive policies, such as the construction of a million "backyard furnaces" to smelt iron, experiments in planting rice seedlings too close together, deep plowing, mass canteens, and the systemic fabrication of production figures.

These policies ultimately created record famines that claimed from 15 to 30 million lives. Although agricultural production was actually decreasing, inflated crop reports informed Beijing that record harvests had doubled output in 1958. These reports allowed Beijing to requisition a growing percentage of the harvest. By early 1959 the looming disaster was obvious, but few dared to oppose Mao openly. When Chinese Communist Party leaders met at the mountain retreat of Lushan, defense minister Peng Dehuai, who had fought beside Mao for thirty years, attempted to convince Mao to reverse course. Mao responded by labeling Peng's critique "bourgeois," dismissing him and his allies, and launching a nationwide campaign to purge "rightist" critics of the Great Leap Forward. Yet at the same time the Party backed away from such Great Leap Forward excesses as unrealistic production targets. The Great Leap Forward squelched elite political debate and exacerbated deep rifts in Party leadership over the relationship between economics and politics—rifts that reignited a few years later in the Cultural Revolution (1966–1976).

[See also Chinese Revolutions and Maoism.]

BIBLIOGRAPHY
Bachman, David. *Bureaucracy, Economy, and Leadership in China: The Institutional Origins of the Great Leap Forward.* New York: Cambridge University Press, 1991.
MacFarquhar, Roderick. *The Origins of the Cultural Revolution.* Vol. 2: *The Great Leap Forward, 1958–1960.* New York: Columbia University Press, 1983.

KARL GERTH

GREAT POWERS. There is no comprehensive definition of the term "Great Power," though different states have claimed this status on the basis of legal rights, military power, or membership of certain institutions, such as the Security Council of the United Nations. It is perhaps best to adopt the "duck" principle: if it acts like a Great Power and is treated like a Great Power, then it is a Great Power. Membership can change because of the shifting relationship between states and the ways in which different kinds of power—military, economic, financial, cultural, and so on—operate within the international system at any particular time.

The Emergence of the Five European Great Powers, 1750–1815. That said, one of the remarkable features of the international system in the two centuries from the beginning of the Seven Years' War (1756–1763) to the end of World War II was the relative stability of the Great Powers. During the conflicts of the eighteenth century, five states emerged to dominate the European states system. Britain, France, and Austria already enjoyed Great Power status, but the Prussia of Frederick II and Russia emerged to replace the exhausted powers of Spain, Sweden, and the Dutch Republic as the leading states in Europe.

Some of these powers also had a global reach, with the rivalry between France and Britain played out in Asia and North America between the late seventeenth century and the end of the Napoleonic Wars in 1815. The exertions of the Seven Years' War exhausted the five Great Powers, and their rulers became more anxious to maintain international stability and limit conflict. Yet the American War of Independence saw France and Britain dragged into another conflict. Britain lost its North American empire, and Old Regime France proved incapable of dealing with the financial pressures of Great Power rivalry, leading to a domestic political crisis and the French Revolution in 1789.

During the French revolutionary wars of the 1790s, the French republic claimed that it was fighting Old Regime despots, bringing an ideological dimension to Great Power conflict. Yet ideology was more an instrument than a driving force in foreign policy in this period. Indeed, the course of the French revolutionary wars was partly influenced by the traditional Great Power concerns of the eighteenth century—partitioning weaker states, such as Poland and Turkey. By creating a centralized administration, the Revolution enabled the French state, especially under Napoleon, to exploit its massive resources and to challenge the European states system. Napoleon nearly extinguished Prussia and Austria as Great Powers. Although the dominant power in Europe, Napoleonic France finally overstretched its resources when it tried to bring Russia into its orbit in 1812. A coalition of Britain, Russia, Austria, and Prussia finally defeated France between 1813 and 1815.

Great Power Politics in the Nineteenth Century. The ending of the Napoleonic Wars saw the preservation of the five Great Powers—a remarkable achievement given the scale of the conflict between the early 1790s and 1815. The five Great Powers drew up a general European settlement at the Congress of Vienna. By 1815, Britain and Russia had emerged as the two major global hegemons, considerably more powerful than their European rivals. Their hegemony and interest in European stability contributed to the maintenance of peace for four decades. The only revisionist power, France, was too weak to challenge the system.

The five Great Powers regulated European politics among themselves, intervening in revolutions around Europe to prevent or manage political change. The Great Powers, especially Russia, combined to defeat the nationalist aspirations of revolutionaries in 1848 and 1849. The stability of the Vienna order collapsed during the Crimean War (1854–1856), which saw France and Britain defeat Russia in a struggle for influence in Turkey, one of the key strategic areas in global politics.

After the Crimean War, Russia and Britain, both disappointed at their lackluster performance in the conflict, became more interested in internal reform. This created the opportunity for a revisionist French challenge to the European states system. Napoleon III (r. 1852–1871) supported Italian unification, completed in stages between 1859 and 1870, but France was defeated by Bismarck's Prussia, which forced the pace of German unification. At the same time that these processes of national unification, with their consequences for the Great Power system, were occurring, the American Civil War resolved the future geopolitics of the North American continent. The United States, however, concentrated on internal consolidation and expansion rather than on global competition. In East Asia, the Meiji Restoration in Japan in 1868 marked the emergence of another potential Great Power.

Nonetheless, global politics continued to be dominated by the European Great Powers, with Italy now joining the club. International relations between 1871 and 1914, often seen as dominated by the considerations of military power, did not witness any wars among the Great Powers. Even Japan's victory over Russia in 1904–1905 was not sufficient for other states to grant Japan the label. Statesmen continued to be wary of going to war, so that international relations in this period could be characterized as a form of restrained competition.

This competition took place on the peripheries of the European continent, in Africa, China, and South America. In the late nineteenth century, theorists began to identify "world powers," who, it was thought, would dominate the twentieth century. According to world power theory, it was no longer sufficient to be a Great Power, because only world powers, with their vast demographic, economic, and military resources, could be truly independent.

Although it was not even recognized as a Great Power, the United States seemed to epitomize the future world power—technologically advanced, economically powerful, and dominant in its region. Russia, Britain, and Germany were seen as the other states most likely to make the transformation to world power status. There was a growing awareness in Europe that its era of global dominance was nearing an end, though the desire for global dominance could be couched in the racist garb of fears about the "Yellow Peril."

The End of the European Great Power System. The two world wars hastened Europe's demise and brought about the most significant transformation in the Great Power system since the mid-eighteenth century. Although vastly superior in terms of economic resources and population, France, Russia, Britain, and, from 1915, Italy, could not defeat Germany and its allies in World War I. German dominance in eastern Europe seemed secure after the Russian Revolution in 1917; however, just as Russia entered a period of internal convulsion, the United States entered the war. This transformed the stalemate on the western front. It was also the first time that the United States exercised its power on the global stage, making 1917 as much of a turning point in the history of the twentieth century as 1914 had been.

World War I witnessed the collapse of only one of the Great Powers, Austria-Hungary, which was dismembered in 1918. However, the European states, including the victors, had been greatly weakened by the conflict. The loss of population, the destruction of industry, and the financial burdens of the war exhausted France, in particular. The peace settlements of 1919 did provide some hope of renewed stability in Europe, but Britain and the United States were unwilling to enforce its terms, and France was too weak to do so alone.

By the 1930s the revisionist Great Powers—Germany, Soviet Russia, Italy, and Japan—had seized the initiative in shaping the global system. Their policies ultimately led to World War II, during which European dominance of the international system ended. Adolf Hitler, for whom war was an end in itself, declared that Germany would be a world power or it would cease to exist. Italy's and Japan's brief bids to establish themselves firmly as Great Powers ended in defeat.

At the end of the war, five states became permanent members of that symbol of Great Power status, the United Nations Security Council: the United States, China, the Soviet Union, France, and Britain. The last three of these had dominated European politics in the eighteenth and nineteenth centuries. But this seeming continuity masked the reality that two powers, the United States and the Soviet Union, were truly Great Powers, or as they now were known, superpowers. Even then, the United States was far more powerful than its Cold War rival. This rivalry was played out in wars, in competition for the hearts and minds of people, and in an arms race between the late 1940s and the late 1980s.

The absence of direct military conflict between the two superpowers reflected the increasing ability of the leading states to manage their rivalries and reflected their awareness that wars were costly for the victor as well as for the defeated. The efforts to manage Great Power rivalry in this peaceful way dated back to at least the 1720s, when a series of congresses of leading European states had met. It was a slow process, with many setbacks.

The demise of the Soviet Union saw the emergence of new major, regional powers—China, India, Pakistan, and Brazil. The ebbing away of European dominance has been slow, but by the beginning of the twenty-first century there arguably was a unipolar international system, with a series of regional subsystems with their own dominant powers.

[*See also* Cold War; Empire and Imperialism; World War I; *and* World War II.]

BIBLIOGRAPHY
Blanning, T. C. W. *The Origins of the French Revolutionary Wars.* London: Longman, 1986.
Gaddis, John Lewis. *The Cold War.* London: Allen Lane, 2005.
Keylor, William. *The Twentieth Century World and Beyond: An International History.* 5th ed. Oxford: Oxford University Press, 2005.
Schroeder, Paul. *The Transformation of European Politics, 1763–1848.* Oxford: Clarendon Press, 1994.
Steiner, Zara. *The Lights That Failed: European International History, 1919–1933.* Oxford: Oxford University Press, 2005.
Taylor, A. J. P. *The Struggle for Mastery in Europe, 1848–1918.* Oxford: Oxford University Press, 1954.

WILLIAM MULLIGAN

GREAT REFORM ACT. The Great Reform Act (1832) altered arrangements for electing members to the lower house of Parliament (the House of Commons) in the United Kingdom and for determining which constituencies those members should represent. Since 1801 the number of members of Parliament (MPs) representing the four nations of the United Kingdom (England, Ireland, Scotland, and Wales) had stood at 658. The Reform Act did not change that overall number, although it gave more seats to Scotland (8, to a total of 53), Ireland (5, to 105), and Wales (5, to 29), at the expense of England, whose complement was reduced by 18 (from 489 to 471).

The key changes concerned the distribution of seats and the qualifications to vote. Fifty-six English borough constituencies with very small electorates lost both of their MPs, and thirty more lost one of their two. Twenty-two new double-member constituencies were created, mostly in the larger commercial and industrial centers such as Birmingham, Leeds, and Manchester; twenty new single-member constituencies were also created. The number of seats in the U.K. counties was increased from 186 to 253, largely because county seats before 1832 had larger

electorates and were considered less liable to "bribery" and "influence."

This act also developed the first uniform criteria to determine who could vote in Parliamentary elections. The vote was restricted to adult males who met specified qualifications. Those holding land worth at least forty shillings (two pounds) per year retained their right to vote in county constituencies. To their number were added those having copyhold land worth at least ten pounds a year and tenants occupying land worth at least fifty pounds a year. In borough constituencies adult males owning or occupying property worth at least ten pounds a year (the so-called "ten-pound householders") could now vote if they had been occupying that property for at least one year and had not received any poor relief during that period. Finally, all those entitled to vote before 1832 but not otherwise qualified retained that right during their lifetimes. For the first time also, constituencies were required to maintain an official register of those entitled to vote.

Parliamentary reform had been on the political agenda for more than half a century. Its advocates pointed to the unrepresentative nature of the unreformed system, to the grotesque anomalies between constituencies. Some had fewer than a hundred voters, others more than two thousand. They also bemoaned the lack of direct representation of many fast-growing communities whose wealth and importance had increased substantially as a result of urban growth and rapid commercial and industrial change in the early stages of the Industrial Revolution. Reformers suggested that the old system no longer represented the nation adequately and that power was sustained by corruption. Some even argued that its unrepresentative nature vitiated Parliament's legitimacy as the nation's supreme legislative body.

Until 1830 support for Parliamentary reform never had a majority in Parliament itself. Radical reformers outside Parliament grew in numbers and influence first during the ineffective struggle of 1776–1783 to retain the American colonies within the British Empire and then, particularly, in the wake of the French Revolution from 1789. Many reformers corresponded with their French counterparts and produced pamphlets and newspapers advocating not just reform of Parliament but, on the basis of natural rights and perceptions of legitimate government warranted by "citizens," an electorate of all sane adult males. In the early nineteenth century growing pressure for reform coincided with periods of economic depression and widespread unemployment, as in the years 1815–1820 and 1829–1832.

While pressure for Parliamentary reform undoubtedly increased over the period discussed, many historians now hold that the main reason why a Reform Act passed in 1832 was due to short-term factors. In particular, in the years 1827–1830 the profoundly antireformist Tory Party, which feared that reform would inevitably lead to revolution, perhaps on the French model, and which held secure Parliamentary majorities from the 1790s onward, suffered disastrous splits. The root cause was irreconcilable divisions over whether to increase political liberties for religious nonconformists and Roman Catholics. Repealing the Test and Corporations Acts (1828) and granting Roman Catholic Emancipation (1829) led directly to resignations and division. These caused the eventual resignation of the Duke of Wellington, the Tory prime minister, in November 1830. His ministry was succeeded by a coalition government headed by the Whig reformer the second Earl Grey.

Making use of the growing pressure for reform outside Parliament, although facing vigorous Parliamentary opposition, especially in the House of Lords, the new government shepherded reform through Parliament. The Reform Act reached the Statute Book with the reluctant assent of the monarch, William IV, pointedly given in absentia, on 7 June 1832.

Historians have debated how radical a measure the Great Reform Act was. The Whigs and their allies had no intention of creating a democratic franchise. Their objective was to regain the trust of all property owners and especially to win the confidence of the middle classes, people who, as the lord chancellor Henry Brougham put it, were "a class above want, having comfortable houses over their heads, and families and homes to which they are attached." The Whigs did not provide either a secret ballot or constituencies of equal size. They also reestablished the legitimacy of Parliament, although they intended (and for nearly three-quarters of a century succeeded in ensuring) that Parliament would remain numerically dominated by landowners and "the rural interest." The numbers entitled to vote increased by some 45 percent, but the new electorate still comprised comfortably fewer than 5 percent of the total population. The main direct beneficiaries were the lower middle classes, who, having limited property to protect and aware of their vulnerability to adverse circumstances, proved themselves naturally conservative in political outlook.

On the other hand, the reformed Parliament proved considerably more interventionist in social questions than those elected before 1832. The pace of legislative change quickened after 1832. The Reform Act also succeeded in increasing the sense that Parliament did represent an appropriate range of propertied interests, as the Whigs had intended. It also increased the independence of ordinary MPs over the executive. Most important, it rapidly proved not to be that "final solution" to a great constitutional question promised by the Whigs during the reform debates of 1830–1832. Further vigorous debate took place on Parliamentary reform, from the Chartist period in the late 1830s and 1840s through to the 1860s, leading first to a second, and more radical, Reform Act in 1867 and then, in stages, to a democratic electoral system in the early twentieth century. Such an outcome was no part of Whig intention; indeed it would have horrified them. It was the unintended consequence of 1832 nevertheless.

[See also Chartism; Parliament, British; and Suffrage, subentry Britain.]

BIBLIOGRAPHY
Brock, Michael. *The Great Reform Act.* London: Hutchinson, 1973.
Evans, Eric J. *The Great Reform Act of 1832.* 2d ed. London: Routledge, 1994.
Lawrence, Jon, and Miles Taylor, eds. *Party, State, and Society: Electoral Behaviour in Britain since 1820.* Aldershot, U.K.: Scholar Press, 1997.
Phillips, John A. *The Great Reform Bill in the Boroughs: English Electoral Behaviour, 1818–1841.* Oxford and New York: Oxford University Press, 1992.

ERIC J. EVANS

GREAT TREK. *See* South Africa.

GREECE. Greece as an ideal existed in the minds of western Europeans for centuries. But the Greek nation-state was created by its people out of an imperial world in the nineteenth century.

From Imperial Domain to Nation-State. Most Greek Orthodox Christians were under Ottoman rule by 1600. The Ottoman Turks organized their subjects into confessional communities (*millets*), investing the Greek Orthodox spiritual leader, the patriarch, with authority over his flock. Most Greeks were peasants whose identity derived from their faith and local community. But by the eighteenth century, the culturally Greek mercantile sector grew in size and wealth by facilitating trade with industrializing Europe. With trade came new ideas from the West, which engendered the desire for educational and political changes among the enlightened Greek diaspora. Adamantios Korais (1748–1833), this movement's most noted representative, proclaimed a new vision: the Greeks were descendants of ancient Hellas, they were a nation—a secular rather than a religious community—and they should be free of Ottoman rule.

In March 1821 a revolutionary society, the Filiki Etairia (Friendly Society) initiated a revolt, appealing to all Orthodox Christians. Despite disagreements and factional quarrels, the rebels wrote a constitution, created a provisional government, and sought aid. Initially aid came from individuals, called "philhellenes," in Europe and America. Later, in 1827, England, Russia, and France intervened to mediate a cessation of hostilities. By 1832, Greece was an independent kingdom guaranteed by the three protecting powers, indicating its dependent status.

Building a State, Making a Nation. The first foreign monarch, Otto, the son of Bavaria's king, arrived in 1833. Athens became the capital, symbolically linking the Greeks to the ancients and through them to the West. The university, founded in 1837, educated a growing state-service middle class and promoted the national vision, the *Megali Idea* (Great Idea). It envisaged the inclusion of all Ottoman territories inhabited by Greeks, impelling political leaders to expand the state's borders. Otto supported the Great Idea, but he refused to grant a constitution until compelled to do so in 1844, establishing universal male suffrage. Domestic opponents forced him out in 1862. His successor was a prince from the Danish royal house, whose family reigned until the monarchy was abolished in 1974.

Late-nineteenth-century efforts to realize the *Megali Idea* focused on lands to the north—Epiros, Macedonia, and Thrace—as well as on Crete, Cyprus, and the coastal littoral of Asia Minor. But territorial expansion without economic modernization was an illusion. Incipient industrialization occurred, but the country remained largely agrarian. Rural social issues went unresolved, leading thousands to emigrate. State bankruptcy in 1893 and an ill-considered war with the Ottoman Empire in 1897 added to the ills of the patronage-beholden political system.

Military intervention in 1909 brought a new political face, Eleuthérios Venizélos (1864–1936), Liberal Party leader, who became prime minister in 1910. His government passed reform measures affecting politics, social welfare, education, the military, and landholding. He negotiated military agreements with other Balkan states, and together they fought the Ottoman Empire in 1912. Following the Balkan wars, Greece acquired almost 70 percent more territory and 2 million new citizens, increasing its population to approximately 4.5 million people.

From World War I to Civil War. World War I engendered a deep political division between Venizélos and the king, Constantine. Venizélos supported entering the war on the side of the Entente Powers, Britain, France, and Russia. Constantine, married to the German emperor's sister, favored neutrality. By 1916 their disagreement produced two rival governments. Entente intervention in 1917 forced the king to step down, and Greece entered the war.

Following the defeat of Germany and the Ottoman Empire, Venizélos at the Paris Peace Conference sought territorial gains, especially in Asia Minor. In May 1919, Greek troops landed at Smyrna (Izmir). By 1921, however, a Turkish nationalist movement led by Mustafa Kemal Atatürk (1881–1938) challenged the Greek presence. In September 1922 the Greek armed forces were defeated, and the Greek Orthodox population was uprooted in an exchange of populations between Greece and Turkey. More than one million Asia Minor refugees settled mostly in Athens and in territory acquired in the Balkan wars. Constantine, who had returned to Greece at the end of 1920 upon the electoral defeat of Venizélos, was forced to abdicate. A revolutionary committee installed a new government, opening the way for military involvement in politics. In 1924 the monarchy was abolished, and a republic was declared. But political divisions remained, and military dictatorship ensued. Civilian government returned in 1927. In 1928, Venizélos again became prime minister.

The early 1930s saw better relations with neighbors, but the republic had foundered politically, and the world depression took an economic toll. In 1935 royalist officers restored the monarchy, and in 1936 the king agreed to the imposition of an authoritarian government by the conservative general Ioannis Metaxas (1871–1941). He emasculated the Communist Party, while traditional party leaders stayed on the sidelines. Inspiring little popular enthusiasm for his regime, Metaxas nevertheless rallied the nation to confront an attack from Fascist Italy in October 1940. Initial success turned to defeat when Adolf Hitler attacked in April 1941. Greece endured an Axis occupation until autumn 1944 that ravaged the economy and brought food shortages, famine, physical destruction, hyperinflation, and war profiteering. Almost the entire Jewish population perished.

Occupation aroused armed resistance. In autumn 1941, Communists organized the National Liberation Front (EAM). It and its military arm, the National People's Liberation Army (ELAS), welcomed opponents of the

Fascists regardless of political affiliation. Women and youth were recruited. By 1944 it was the major resistance movement, though nonleftist organizations also existed. Relations between the resistance groups deteriorated and civil war ensued as the EAM sought to eliminate its competitors. It called for new ways in government and society, hoping to dominate postwar politics. Britain and the royal Greek government in exile were opposed.

In December 1944, after the Germans departed, the two sides clashed in Athens. Fighting ended in February 1945 when the ELAS agreed to disarm in return for amnesty and a referendum on the monarchy. But the Left abstained from elections in March 1946, and a referendum in September brought the king back. Spring 1947 saw all-out civil war and the intervention of the United States. Aid from the Truman administration eventually enabled the national army to prevail. Hostilities ended in 1949, with many leftists captured. Thousands of others, including children, crossed into Communist-dominated countries. Whether they were forced out or went willingly remains contested.

Progress and Cold War Politics. Situated militarily on the Balkan front of the Cold War, postwar Greece was bound to the West through membership in NATO in 1952 and association with the European Economic Community in 1961. Postwar recovery was slow, skewed by military needs in the civil war. American aid and planning supported infrastructure projects. Devaluation of the drachma in 1953 produced monetary stability. However, little was achieved in industrialization, while agriculture needed modernizing. With little hope, thousands of rural folk migrated to the cities or emigrated. Nevertheless, emigrants' remittances, a growing merchant marine, and mass tourism fueled the economy.

Political stability returned in the early 1950s with the conservative government of Konstantinos Karamanlis (1907–1998). In 1963 disagreements between Karamanlis and the king opened the way for the center-left government of Georgios Papandreou (1888–1968). His premiership was short-lived; infighting among the Left, the Right, and the monarch led to a military coup in April 1967. Using a bogus claim of Communist danger, the junta established itself in power. The monarch fled the country, and the junta's leader, Georgios Papadopoulos (1919–1999), took over governmental power.

Foreign affairs eventually entangled the junta. Since the mid-1950s, Greece, Turkey, and Britain had been involved with the political status of Cyprus, whose population was four-fifths Greek and the one-fifth Turkish. Cyprus's independence from Britain in 1959 did not resolve issues between Greece and Turkey, and tensions on the island grew. In the summer of 1974 the junta tried to overthrow the Cypriot government of Archbishop Makarios III (1913–1977) in a bid for union of the island with Greece. The attempt failed, and Turkey reacted by occupying much of the island. These events precipitated the junta's demise. Karamanlis returned from abroad, becoming prime minister on 24 July 1974.

Populist Politics and the Way to Europe. Democratic government was reestablished and consolidated. Karamanlis steered the country through the de-juntafication process and the writing of a new constitution (1975), created the center-right New Democracy Party, and served as president from 1980 to 1985. On the left, Andreas Papandreou (1919–1996), son of Georgios, built a new party, the Panhellenic Socialist Movement (PASOK). Combining nationalist and socialist rhetoric, he came to power in 1981.

That year Greece became a member of the European Community (EC). Papandreou, premier until 1989, emphasized national sovereignty vis-à-vis the EC, NATO, and the United States. However, he kept Greece's international ties because relations with Turkey remained rocky. Domestically, PASOK initiated reforms in civil matters, while dispensing patronage. The decade ended with PASOK mired in scandals, huge government deficits, and an enlarged state sector.

A Place in the World. At the end of the Cold War, upon Yugoslavia's disintegration, new states emerged, including one calling itself the Republic of Macedonia. Greeks reacted negatively, remembering past conflicts over Greece's northern province, Macedonia. A modus vivendi on the new state's name was reached in 1995. When the Albanian Communist regime collapsed, thousands of impoverished people entered Greece seeking a better life. Officials were unprepared, and it took years to regularize the foreign population from many countries, estimated at one million people (a tenth of the population).

Once-powerful personalities left the political scene, Andreas Papandreou in 1996 and Karamanlis in 1998. With Papandreou's death, Kostas Simitis (b. 1936) became leader of PASOK. As premier, he focused on meeting the criteria for the European Monetary Union, which Greece entered in 2002. Greece declared its support for Turkey's entry into the EU and promoted business investments in the neighboring Balkan countries. In May 2004 it hosted the EU meeting that admitted ten new members, including Cyprus. Later that year Athens hosted the summer Olympics.

[*See also* Cyprus; Greeks in the Middle East, North Africa, and Central Asia; *and* Greek-Turkish War.]

BIBLIOGRAPHY

Augustinos, Gerasimos. *Consciousness and History: Nationalist Critics of Greek Society, 1897–1914.* Boulder, Colo.: East European Quarterly, 1977. Examines the cultural politics of state and nation making.

Clogg, Richard. *A Concise History of Greece.* 2d ed. Cambridge, U.K.: Cambridge University Press, 2002. Narrative account, with informative illustrations, emphasizing domestic politics and foreign affairs.

Clogg, Richard, ed. *Minorities in Greece.* London: Hurst, 2003. Essays on religious and ethnic groups.

Close, David H. *Greece since 1945: Politics, Economy, Society.* London: Longman, 2002. Balanced account noting both progress and problems of development.

Koliopoulos, John S., and Thanos M. Veremis. *Greece: The Modern Sequel from 1831 to the Present.* London: Hurst, 2002. A topical approach focusing on politics, identity, state institutions, and foreign affairs from a modernization perspective.

Mavrogordatos, George. *Stillborn Republic: Social Conditions and Party Strategies in Greece 1922–36.* Berkeley: University of California Press, 1983. Detailed coverage of electoral politics and the political dynamics of social groups.

Mazower, Mark. *Inside Hitler's Greece: The Experience of Occupation, 1941–44.* New Haven, Conn.: Yale University Press, 1993. Insightful account of the Axis occupation of Greece and its impact on the Greek people.

GERASIMOS AUGUSTINOS

GREEKS IN THE MIDDLE EAST, NORTH AFRICA, AND CENTRAL ASIA.

Spurred by seventeenth-century maritime trade, a number of Greek merchants and clerics moved to live in the Middle East. The region's geographical proximity to the Greek islands and the establishment of the Greek Orthodox patriarchates in Alexandria, Antioch, and Jerusalem helped in the growth of their community, a process later accelerated by the modernization plans of Muhammad ʿAli (r. 1805–1849), which attracted European capitalists, industrialists, military officers, artists, and civil servants. The number of Greeks in Egypt increased from 62,973 in 1907 to 76,264 in 1927, over one-third of whom lived in Alexandria, the rest being spread out in Cairo, Port Said, Suez, and some small towns in the Nile Delta. As the largest European ethnic group in Egypt (in 1927 foreigners numbered 99,793), Greeks enjoyed a versatile and rich life but continued to cling to their native tongue and to the Greek Orthodox Church.

The Greek community was a socially diverse group that ranged in occupation from wealthy bankers and tradesmen to shipbuilders, sailors, civil servants, and factory workers. They contributed greatly to the banking sector, establishing the Bank of Alexandria, the Anglo-Egyptian Bank (Sunadinos family), and the General Bank of Alexandria. In the agricultural sector, leading Greek families such as the Salvagos, Benachis, Rodochanakis, and Zervoudachis built a thriving trade empire in tobacco, and others helped develop the first systematic and scientific cultivation of Egypt's most important strategic crop, cotton. A class of wealthy Greek entrepreneurs developed, consisting of rich industrialists, tradesmen, and bankers who laid the foundation for a legacy of Egypto-Greek philanthropy. People of this class sponsored the building of schools, academies, hospitals, and institutions in both Egypt and Greece. Smaller Greek communities spread out in the Sudan, Palestine, and cities along the North African coast.

In 1855, Greece signed a Capitulatory Rights Agreement with the Ottoman Empire that granted Ottoman Greek subjects—including those in Egypt and Sudan, Palestine, and Syria—broad-ranging privileges. In 1876, Greece joined the Mixed Courts system that stipulated the trial of Western subjects for committed crimes by courts presided over by judges from the defendant's homeland as well as by an Egyptian judge. More power was allowed to the Greek community when the Ottoman Empire ceded control of the island of Cyprus to Britain in 1878 after three centuries of Ottoman rule. The Ottoman Empire had occupied Cyprus in 1571 and applied the *millet* system to its inhabitants, which allowed religious authorities to govern their own non-Muslim minorities. This system reinforced the status of the Greek Orthodox Church and the solidarity of the ethnic Greek population.

Ottoman defeat and collapse in the wake of World War I heralded a new era for the whole region and the beginning of Greek-Turkish conflict. To help divide the lands of the defeated Ottoman Empire, the warring countries signed the Treaty of Sèvres on 10 August 1920, granting parts of Anatolia (present Asia Minor) to Greece and Italy while promising the establishment of the Republic of Armenia in eastern Turkey and an autonomous area for the Kurds. In reaction, Turkish rebels led by Mustafa Kemal Atatürk rejected the terms regarding the partitioning of Anatolia and forced out the Greeks and Armenians, while the Italians failed to assert any territorial claims. Once Turkey established sovereignty over Anatolia, the Treaty of Sèvres was superseded by the Treaty of Lausanne (24 July 1923), which formally ended all hostilities and led to the creation of the modern Turkish republic. The treaty formally acknowledged the new League of Nations mandates in the Middle East, the cession of Ottoman territorial claims in the Arabian Peninsula, and British sovereignty over Cyprus (1925).

The Catastrophe. The first large-scale population exchange or agreed mutual expulsion in the twentieth century was decreed by the Treaty of Lausanne in a side agreement signed by the governments of Greece and Turkey. The 1923 population exchange between the two countries involved some 2 million people (1.5 million Greek Orthodox and 0.5 million Muslim Turks), who were forced to leave their homelands of centuries or millennia. An estimated one-third of the Greek population was expelled from millennia-old homelands, practically ending a three-thousand-year-old presence of ethnic Greek people in Asia Minor and other territories. Since signing the treaty, both sides have claimed that the other has violated its provisions. The Greek ethnic minority population in Turkey diminished from several hundred thousand in 1923 to a mere few thousand by 2007, a decline attributed to the systematic enforcement of anti-minority measures. Similarly, Turkey closed the Halki Seminary, the main school of theology of the Eastern Orthodox Church's Ecumenical Patriarchate of Constantinople, risking Greek accusations of violations of the Treaty of Lausanne's guarantees for religious freedom.

In the aftermath of the 1923 population exchange, known to Greeks simply as "the catastrophe," Greek immigrants headed toward North Africa, particularly Alexandria, Egypt, where the number of Greeks increased rapidly to 250,000 in 1940. The numbers began to decline in 1937 with the termination of foreign capitulations, and the Egyptian revolution of 1952 accelerated the process further. The Suez Crisis of 1956 reinforced the trend, although a large part of the Greek community supported Egypt. The nationalization measures taken by the Egyptian government between 1957 and 1963 further reduced the numbers of Greeks remaining in Egypt and subsequently in the Middle East; most immigrated to Australia and the United States, and a substantial number returned to Greece.

Cyprus. The island of Cyprus became a British colony in 1925. There the seeds of sectarian conflict nurtured by territorial ambitions and claims by both Turkey and Greece divided Cypriots into two factions, the Greek Cypriots who called for union with Greece (a movement known as *enosis*), and Cypriots of Turkish origin who preferred to join ranks with Turkey. After decades of factional strife, Britain granted Cyprus its independence in 1960, and a Treaty of Guarantees was signed between the Republic of Cyprus on one hand and the United Kingdom, Greece, and Turkey on the other to secure the unity of the island and guarantee its independence, territorial integrity, and security. Sectarian conflict, however, increased over implementation and interpretation of the constitution, concluding in full-fledged armed struggle supported by the Turkish and Greek governments. The armed struggle resulted in the division of the island into two main enclaves, one Greek-Cypriot and the other Turkish-Cypriot. UN peacekeepers were deployed on the island in 1964 to separate the combatants. In July 1974, the military junta in Athens sponsored a coup led by extremist Greek Cypriots against the government of President Makarios, and Turkey, citing the 1960 Treaty of Guarantees, intervened militarily to protect Turkish Cypriots, taking control of one-third of the island in the north and causing another wave of mass emigration as most Greek Cypriots fled to the south and the majority of Turkish Cypriots escaped to the north. A larger UN peacekeeping force was stationed as a buffer between the two sides, and the status quo was maintained until the Turkish Cypriots declared in 1983 an independent state under the name of the Turkish Republic of Northern Cyprus (TRNC); it was internationally recognized only by Turkey. Cyprus, the third-largest island of the Mediterranean after Sicily and Sardinia, covers a total of 5,735 square miles (9,250 sqare kilometers), of which 2,080 square miles (3,355 square kilometers) are presently under TRNC control. The population of Cyprus (Greek and Turkish zones) in 2003 was estimated by the United Nations at 802,000, of which only 18 percent lives in the Turkish area.

The first UN-sponsored negotiations to develop institutional arrangements acceptable to both Cypriot communities began in 1968; several sets of negotiations and other initiatives followed, under close monitoring by the Greek and Turkish governments. Turkish Cypriots emphasized the need for two separate zones, security guarantees, and political equality between the two communities. They favored a loose grouping of two nearly autonomous societies living side by side with limited contact. Greek Cypriots, on the other hand, demanded freedom of movement and passage, property, and settlement and the right to return to their original lodgings. They envisioned a more integrated structure that was rejected by the Turkish Cypriots, who preferred to maintain their individuality and autonomy.

On November 2002, the UN secretary-general Kofi Annan proposed a comprehensive plan to end thirty years of enmity between Greek and Turkish Cypriots.

On 16 December 2003, the European Union (EU) offered additional incentive to the two parties by extending an official invitation to the Republic of Cyprus to become a member of the EU. Cyprus entered the European Union on 1 May 2004 as a divided island, and its people continue to live separately.

[*See also* Cyprus; Greece; Greek-Turkish War (1919–1922); *and* Turkey.]

BIBLIOGRAPHY

"Annan Plan for Cyprus Settlement." http://www.tcea.org.uk/Annan-Plan-For-Cyprus-Settlement.htm. Full text of the UN plan for Cyprus.

"European Research and Information Center." http://www.emu.edu.tr/~eric/Papers1.htm. On Cyprus's admission to the European Community.

Kitroeff, Alexander. *The Greeks in Egypt, 1919–1937: Ethnicity and Class.* St. Anthony's Middle East Monographs, no. 20. London: Ithaca Press, 1989.

Mansfield, Peter. *A History of the Middle East.* 2d ed. Revised by Nicolas Pelham. London and New York: Penguin, 2003.

Masters, Bruce. *Christian and Jews in the Ottoman Arab World: The Roots of Sectarianism.* New York: Cambridge University Press, 2001.

DAHLIA ABDEL FATTAH

GREEK-TURKISH WAR. World War I ended in November 1918 with the Ottoman Empire, Germany, Austria-Hungary, and Bulgaria defeated. The victorious Allies met in Paris in 1919 to decide the fate of the defeated. Already during the war Britain, France, and Italy had indicated through secret agreements their interest in Ottoman territories. Greece, an Allied state, presented its claims at the Paris conference. These developments gave further impetus to the Turkish nationalist movement. Thus Great Power politics, Woodrow Wilson's support of national self-determination, and nationalist politics interacted.

Greece, ably represented by its prime minister, Eleuthérios Venizélos, sought territorial gains that reflected the so-called Megali Idea (Great Idea), the vision of a greater Greece. When the leaders of Britain, the United States, and France became concerned over Italian interests in Asia Minor (Anatolia), they authorized Greek occupation and administration of the Anatolian port of Smyrna (Izmir) in May 1919.

The Ottoman government of Sultan Mehmet VI (r. 1918–1922) cooperated with the Allies in hopes of a favorable peace settlement. But the Turkish nationalist movement was opposed to concessions to the Allies.

Mustafa Kemal (Atatürk), a capable Turkish army officer, arrived in eastern Anatolia in May 1919 as inspector of the Third Army. He quickly proceeded to organize and unite, militarily and politically, the Turkish resistance. A national congress at Sivas in September 1919 adopted a program for self-determination, and a Grand National Assembly at Ankara in April 1920 established a provisional government headed by Kemal.

With the Treaty of Sèvres (August 1920), the Allies disposed of the Ottoman domains. Greece gained eastern Thrace, many of the Aegean islands, and administration of the Anatolian province containing Smyrna, while the Bosphorus and Dardanelles straits were placed under international control. Relations between the sultan's government and the Turkish nationalists ruptured.

While the Turks rallied, the Greeks were weakened by domestic political disputes. Elections in November 1920 saw a royalist government replace Venizélos. At an Allied conference convened in London in February 1921 to modify the Treaty of Sèvres, the Greeks and the Turks failed to settle their differences. In March the Greeks launched an offensive against the Kemalist forces. The decisive battle occurred in August–September 1921 at the Sakarya River near Ankara: the Turks stopped the Greek advance. They also made important gains on the diplomatic front, negotiating favorable accords with the Soviets, the Italians, and the French during March–October 1921. In August 1922 a Turkish offensive forced the Greek army to retreat. On 9 September, Turkish troops entered Smyrna, and the Armenian, Greek, and European quarters of the city went up in flames. Throngs of refugees sought safety in Greece.

Peace negotiations began in November 1922. The Ankara nationalists, not the Istanbul government, represented Turkey, and the national assembly abolished the sultanate in November 1922. The Treaty of Lausanne of July 1923 confirmed Turkish sovereignty over eastern Thrace and Anatolia. The straits were demilitarized, and freedom of passage was guaranteed. Greece acquired several of the Aegean islands. There was also a compulsory exchange of populations between Turkey and Greece. The Greek Orthodox, except for the Greeks in Istanbul, left Turkey, and Muslims in Greece, excluding those in western Thrace, departed for Turkey.

For Greece the conflict meant the end of the Megali Idea and the influx of more than a million refugees. For Turkey, it was a war of independence that created the republic, solidified national identity, and resulted in a favorable peace settlement.

[See also Greece; Kemalism; Ottoman Empire; and Turkey.]

BIBLIOGRAPHY

Clark, Bruce. *Twice a Stranger: The Mass Expulsions That Forged Modern Greece and Turkey*. Cambridge, Mass.: Harvard University Press, 2006.

Mango, Andrew. *Atatürk: The Biography of the Founder of Modern Turkey*. Woodstock, N.Y.: Overlook Press, 2000. Detailed account based on published works.

Pentzopoulos, Dimitri. *The Balkan Exchange of Minorities and Its Impact upon Greece*. Paris: Mouton, 1962. Multifaceted account of the refugee settlement, concentrating on the Asia Minor Greek refugees.

Smith, Michael Llewellyn. *Ionian Vision: Greece in Asia Minor, 1919–1922*. New York: St. Martin's Press, 1973. Well-crafted narrative emphasizing the personality, politics, and diplomacy of Greece and the Great Powers.

Sonyel, Salahi Ramsdan. *Turkish Diplomacy 1918–1923: Mustafa Kemal and the Turkish National Movement*. London: Sage, 1975. Concentrates on the diplomacy of the Kemalist Turkish nationalists.

GERASIMOS AUGUSTINOS

GREEN BOOK. Six years after he led a coup d'état in Libya overthrowing the ruling monarchy, Muammar al-Qaddafi summarized the ideological tenets of his revolution in a series of three short volumes, collectively known as the Green Book. Published in 1975, the first volume, *The Solution of the Problem of Democracy: "The Authority of the People,"* develops the theoretical foundations of direct democracy, the unique political system based on congresses and committees that Qaddafi subsequently implemented throughout Libya. The second volume, *The Solution of the Economic Problem: "Socialism,"* examines the economic dimensions of Qaddafi's Third Universal Theory, his earlier effort to articulate an alternative to capitalism and communism, leading to the conclusion that socialism is the optimal economic system. The third volume, *The Social Basis of the Third Universal Theory*, explores selected social aspects of the Third Universal Theory, focusing on the family, tribe, and nation.

The first volume has proved the most enduring. The congress-committee political system in place since the mid-1970s has changed little, and Qaddafi has regularly stated that the Libyan form of direct democracy is superior to the representative democracy found in the United States and elsewhere. Nevertheless, in the late 1980s Libya began to move away from the socialist command economy, and the breadth and depth of economic reform broadened after 2003. The third volume of the Green Book has been the most controversial; Qaddafi's insular, contradictory, and even reactionary views on the tribe, women, education, minorities, the arts, sports, and other subjects are an endless source of debate.

[See also Libya.]

BIBLIOGRAPHY

Christman, Henry M., ed. *Qaddafi's Green Book: An Unauthorized Edition*. Buffalo, N.Y.: Prometheus Books, 1988.

Gathafi, Muammar Al. *The Green Book*. Tripoli, Libya: World Center for the Study and Research of the Green Book, 2005.

RONALD BRUCE ST JOHN

GREENLAND. Originally a dependency of Norway, Greenland became part of Denmark in the Middle Ages and remained so, along with Iceland and the Faeroes, when Denmark ceded Norway to Sweden in 1814. Greenland's habitable land covers about 135,000 square miles (350,000 square kilometers) and is thus eight times larger than continental Denmark; Greenland has an arctic and subarctic climate. The population of about fifty thousand people is of Inuit and European (mostly Danish) origin. The Norse population in southern Greenland in 800–1500 C.E. seems to have left no trace in the present population.

The secession of Norway from Denmark to Sweden in 1814 left the North Atlantic dependencies—Iceland, the Faeroe Islands, and Greenland—with Denmark. Colonization from Denmark began in 1721 with the purpose of converting the population to Christianity and in the hope that arctic products like blubber and hides from sea mammals could finance the colony. Various private companies tried their luck, but the king had to take over in 1774, establishing a royal company, the Royal Greenland Trade Department (Det Kongelige Grønlandske Kompagni) to run the province.

In the 1860s local councils were established as part of the administration, and in 1911 two provincial councils were formed, which were advisory to the Danish government. In the 1920s fishing became more important than the traditional seal hunting, and in the early twenty-first century fish represented Greenland's main export.

During World War II, Greenland was cut off from Denmark, but the two governors managed to keep Danish authority intact by making a defense arrangement with the United States, accepting American bases in Greenland. Financially, Greenland was self-sufficient during the war, running a trade surplus because of the high demand for cryolite for the production of aluminum.

In 1950 a major reform was launched to modernize Greenlandic society by lifting the monopoly of the Trade Department and investing in housing, harbors, health care, and modern machinery, all paid for by the Danish treasury. Encouragement was given to private enterprise, which at the time scarcely existed outside sealing and fishing. The two provincial councils became one, and in 1953 the Danish constitution was extended to cover Greenland as well, giving Greenland two representatives in the Danish parliament. Officially the colonial period was over, but planning and development was still run from Copenhagen.

The benevolent embrace nearly choked the Greenlanders, and in the early 1970s they began to request a greater say in running Greenland. Home Rule was introduced in 1979, and over the next twenty years almost all government activities were transferred to the Home Rule authorities, leaving only defense, foreign policy, and currency with Copenhagen. The Home Rule Authority receives a fixed grant—subject to price-index adjustment—from the government to cover expenses. The grant amounts to about two-thirds of the total Greenland gross domestic product, but in the early 2000s the grant was slowly diminishing in importance.

Independence has never been requested by the Home Rule Authority, but it is probably the ultimate goal for many Greenlanders. In 2004 a Danish-Greenlandic commission began to investigate ways of giving Greenland a greater say in foreign relations concerning Greenland. The proposed arrangement is called self-rule.

[*See also* Denmark.]

BIBLIOGRAPHY
Damas, David, ed. *Handbook of North American Indians*, edited by William C. Sturtevant et al. Vol. 5: *Arctic*, pp. 522–645. Washington, D.C.: Smithsonian Institution, 1984.
Greenland Home Rule. Official homepage at http://www.nanoq.gl/english.aspx.

AXEL KJÆR SØRENSEN

GREEN PARTIES. The first identifiably "Green" political parties emerged in the early 1970s in Australia and New Zealand. Soon thereafter they spread to Western Europe and North America, and by the early twenty-first century there were some eighty national parties throughout the world that embodied the principles of green politics. Though the origins and fortunes of these parties have varied tremendously according to differing political opportunity structures, there are nonetheless some general characteristics that they all, to one degree or another, share. These include a commitment to environmental protection based on a holistic ecological worldview, the pursuit of social justice, a strong opposition to warfare as a means of resolving disputes, and a devotion to a more participatory—some might say idealized—version of democracy.

Early Green Parties. In 1972 the government of Tasmania, the island state located some 125 miles (200 kilometers) south of the Australian mainland, authorized the construction of a dam that would flood Lake Pedder, a wild, mist-shrouded lake that many considered the jewel of the state's wilderness crown. Though environmentalists failed to halt the construction, their campaign nonetheless led to the establishment of the United Tasmania Group (UTG) in March 1972, an organization that many now regard as the world's first Green party.

Dr. Richard Jones, a University of Tasmania botanist who was instrumental in forming the UTG, outlined a political vision shared by many of the new generation of environmentalists of the early 1970s. Environmental activists, Jones insisted, needed to do more than merely campaign against wilderness destruction. They also needed to reach out to groups such as trade unions and to become involved in electoral politics. Jones and others saw environmentalism as part of a broader progressive agenda that also included social justice issues and the development of new forms of political organization that broke down the rigid hierarchies of the established political parties. Here, in embryonic form, were the ideas and coalitions that would later characterize Green parties throughout much of the world.

In May 1972, New Zealand's Values Party emerged as the world's first national Green party. The group was unaware of the existence of its Tasmanian counterpart and was in no way influenced by it. Rather, it was the outcome of a set of historical trends that were present throughout the world's Western industrial democracies. These included the emergence of a postmaterialist class that was less concerned with its own wealth than with the general quality of life; the recognition that the human impact on the earth, particularly in the form of nuclear weapons, toxic chemicals, and rapacious development, was threatening the quality of life for all humans as well as the very existence of many other species; a growing skepticism toward an economic system that required constant growth to sustain itself; and the various liberation movements of the 1960s, such as feminism, civil rights, and the student movement.

Though the Tasmanian and New Zealand groups can lay claim to being the first Green parties, there is little evidence to indicate that they were vital to the formation of those that followed. The historical trajectory of environmentalism throughout the world suggests that some of the most influential Green parties, such as Die Grünen in West Germany, would have emerged regardless of developments in relatively remote parts of the antipodes.

European Parties. In Europe, Green parties began to appear in the mid- to late 1970s. Whereas the impetus in Tasmania and New Zealand had primarily been the destruction of wilderness, for the Europeans it was pollution. In the United Kingdom, the Ecology Party was formed as early as 1973, though the first-past-the-post voting system hindered its electoral success.

In West Germany in the late 1970s, a diverse group of people also began to discuss the possibility of forming a Green party. Initially the idea of renegade Christian Democrats nostalgic for the preindustrial German countryside, the nascent political movement soon drew environmentalists and antinuclear activists from the political Left. For these mostly younger activists, ecology offered an all-encompassing critique of industrial capitalism, and the Green movement soon attracted a variety of political activists, thereby creating a rainbow coalition consisting of environmentalists, peace protestors, feminists, gay rights activists, socialists, communists, anarchists, and other progressive and radical groups. Numerous meetings occurred throughout the country in which these groups thrashed out their differences and attempted to jockey for power within the emerging coalition. Finally, in November 1979 an agreement was struck and a new party, Die Grünen, was born.

Unlike in Britain, the proportional representation of West Germany's electoral system was conducive to small parties, and Die Grünen soon garnered the requisite five percent of the vote that was necessary for parliamentary representation, first in the states and then, in 1983, in the Bundestag. The party's early electoral success might have been considerably greater had it not been for the split that developed between the realists or "Realos"—those who were willing to compromise in order to further the party's electoral potential—and the fundamentalists or "Fundis"—those who wished to maintain the purity of the party's original vision and abstain from joining coalitions. This was a split that became characteristic of many Green parties throughout the world. After much political bloodletting, the Realos finally triumphed over the Fundis in the early 1990s. The resulting stability enabled Die Grünen to reach the pinnacle of minor party success in 1998 when it joined the Social Democrats in a governing coalition, one that lasted for the next seven years.

In the 1990s, nationwide Green parties were formed in Australia and the United States, though the lack of proportional representation meant that neither of them had the kind of success that characterized Die Grünen, despite the fact that, in Australia at least, the Greens have garnered as much of the vote as their German counterparts have. The end of the Cold War saw a rapid escalation in the number of Green parties, particularly in the former Communist nations of Eastern Europe but also throughout much of the developing world. Though each party has tailored its program and political strategies to suit its nation's electoral system, virtually all the parties adhere to the basic principles established by the early Green parties in the Western industrial democracies. Furthermore, Green parties have made a concerted effort to involve themselves in politics at the continental and global levels, thereby establishing a degree of ideological consistency and a series of strong linkages that should ensure that they remain a stable feature of politics at various levels.

Current trends suggest that many nations, particularly the Anglo-American ones, are intensifying their commitment to the growth-at-all-costs ideology that Green parties oppose. Nevertheless, optimists among the Greens feel that the gradual evolution of the movement since the 1970s has created mature political parties that would be ready to assume the reigns of power should a change in the political opportunity structures occur.

[*See also* Environment *and* Political Parties.]

BIBLIOGRAPHY

Burchell, Jon. *The Evolution of Green Politics: Development and Change within European Green Parties.* London, and Sterling, Va.: Earthscan, 2002. Suggests that involvement in mainstream politics has significantly compromised many of the original ideals of Green politics.

Rootes, Christopher. "It's Not Easy Being Green: From Protest to Power." *Harvard International Review* 23, no. 4 (Winter 2002): 78–82. Argues that although environmental awareness may have been a necessary precondition for the formation of Green parties, their success or failure has had more to do with electoral systems and political opportunity structures than with the strength of environmentalism in any given nation.

Rüdig, Wolfgang, ed. *Green Politics.* 3 vols. Edinburgh: Edinburgh University Press, 1990–1995. Contains a variety of essays dealing with Green parties from around the world.

Talshir, Gayil. *The Political Ideology of Green Parties: From the Politics of Nature to Redefining the Nature of Politics.* New York: Palgrave Macmillan, 2002. A historical and theoretical overview of the emergence of Green parties, concentrating in particular on Germany and the United Kingdom.

Zelko, Frank, and Carolin Brinkmann, eds. *Green Parties: Reflections on the First Three Decades.* Washington D.C.: Heinrich Böll Foundation, 2006. Contains reflective and analytical essays by people who participated in the formation of Green parties in Australia, Germany, the United States, and the United Kingdom.

FRANK ZELKO

GREENPEACE. Greenpeace is an international environmental organization renowned for its use of nonviolent direct action. The organization was founded in Vancouver, Canada, in 1969. Its roots lie in the peace movement of the 1950s and the environmentalism of the 1960s, and its values and tactics were shaped by an eclectic blend of Gandhian civil disobedience, Quakerism, countercultural idealism, and New Left activism. The philosophy of the renowned Canadian media theorist Marshall McLuhan (1911–1980), with its emphasis on the importance of television and the creation of archetypal images, was particularly influential. Among Greenpeace's most prominent early members were Canadian journalists such as Bob Hunter and Ben Metcalfe, both of whom devoted considerable effort to ensuring that the group's campaigns received substantial media coverage.

Although founded in Canada, Greenpeace was largely shaped by American ideas and social movements. Americans who were leaving their homeland because of their nation's involvement in the Vietnam War (1954–1975) were a highly effective conduit for such influences. Among these, two couples—Irving and Dorothy Stowe of Rhode Island and Jim and Marie Bohlen from Pennsylvania—were particularly important. They brought with them to Vancouver their experience in the civil rights and peace movements of the 1950s and 1960s and played a vital role in establishing a broad antinuclear coalition known as the Don't Make a Wave Committee, a reference to the potential tidal wave that many felt might result from U.S. nuclear weapons testing on the Aleutian island of Amchitka.

Along with a handful of other Americans and several Canadians, they chartered a boat—which they named *Greenpeace*—and in October 1971 attempted to sail it from Vancouver to Amchitka. Poor weather prevented them from reaching the island, but along the way they stopped at several Indian villages, where they received the blessing of tribal leaders and participated in sacred native rituals. Such events were of particular significance to the countercultural members of the crew, such as Hunter, for whom Indians embodied a respect for nature that was lacking in Western culture. These encounters gave rise to the Warriors of the Rainbow mythology that became a central part of Greenpeace's identity.

Throughout the early 1970s, Greenpeace mounted several campaigns—led by a Canadian businessman named David McTaggart—protesting French nuclear testing in the South Pacific. From the mid-1970s, the organization gravitated toward a more holistic ecological philosophy—known as deep ecology—and began to conduct campaigns against whaling and the slaughter of

Greenpeace. A Greenpeace inflatable tries to hinder the shooting and eventual transfer of a minke whale by a Japanese whaling ship in the Southern Pacific Ocean, December 2005. Greenpeace photograph by Kate Davison, HO. AP IMAGES

harp seal pups in Newfoundland, Canada. The whaling campaign was particularly effective, both in bringing a little-known issue to the public's attention and in yielding the archetypal Greenpeace images of brave environmentalists in small boats taking on the giant whaling ships.

Throughout the 1970s the organization's rapid expansion caused tensions between its various branches, which culminated with the original Vancouver group mounting a lawsuit against the San Francisco office. Through deft maneuvering, David McTaggart was able to broker the dispute and in early 1980 succeeded in establishing a unified organization—Greenpeace International—with its headquarters in Amsterdam, multiple branch offices throughout the world, and himself at its head.

In 1985 in Auckland, New Zealand, French agents sunk Greenpeace's flagship vessel, *Rainbow Warrior*, killing an activist in the process. This event garnered Greenpeace a tremendous amount of sympathy and dramatically increased its membership, which was largely a "checkbook" one. Since then the organization has broadened the focus of its campaigns, which include issues such as climate change, toxic chemicals, forest preservation, and genetic engineering. In the early twenty-first century it had branches in some forty countries throughout the world.

[*See also* Environment *and* Green Movements.]

BIBLIOGRAPHY
Dale, Stephen. *McLuhan's Children: The Greenpeace Message and the Media*. Toronto: Between the Lines, 1996. A solid historical overview, as well as an examination of the evolution of Greenpeace's media strategy.
Weyler, Rex. *Greenpeace: How a Group of Ecologists, Journalists, and Visionaries Changed the World*. Vancouver, Canada: Raincoast, 2004. A detailed account of Greenpeace's first decade, written by one of the organization's early activists.

FRANK ZELKO

GREEN REVOLUTION. "Green revolution" is the term used to describe the spread of agricultural technologies that dramatically increased food production in the developing world, beginning in the mid-twentieth century, with impacts that last today. In the 1940s, to address the problem of impending famine from a growing imbalance between population and food supply, the Rockefeller Foundation provided funds for agricultural advances in developing nations and garnered a team of dedicated researchers from different parts of the world. Other national and international institutions joined this effort in the following decades. The crops developed as part of this effort were superior to locally planted crops in yield increase, yield stability, wide-scale adaptability, resistance to diseases and insects, tolerance to drought and flooding, and grain quality. Fertilizers, pesticides, and irrigation systems were also introduced in many parts of the world. The science and technology, funding sources and the policies and politics that underlay them, worldwide spread of the agricultural technologies, and remaining challenges are all important aspects to explore to understand the successes and shortcomings of the green revolution.

Science and Technology. The high yield varieties (HYVs) of staple food crops were perhaps the most important factor in the food production increase. These varieties were first developed at the International Rice Research Institute (IRRI) in the Philippines and at the Centro Internacional de Mejoramiento de Maiz y Trigo (International Maize and Wheat Improvement Center, CIMMYT) in Mexico. Three types of breeding strategies were used to develop these crops: conventional breeding (crossing parents of the same line and screening offspring for desirable traits), hybrid breeding (cross-breeding plants of different lines to produce offspring with increased vigor), and shuttle breeding (growing plants at different locations and cross-breeding between these lines to obtain offspring with widely adaptable traits under diverse growing conditions). These new HYVs of wheat, maize, and rice had improved ratios of grain to straw, shorter and sturdier stems, and better response to fertilizers. Norman Borlaug, the young plant pathologist and plant breeder who developed the shuttle breeding technique, went on to win the Nobel Peace Prize for his green revolution work.

The combination of irrigation systems, fertilizers, and pesticides with the HYV seeds was also key. When the HYVs were grown with these other inputs, they gave substantially higher yields. Local scientists, sponsored by the Food and Agriculture Organization and the Rockefeller Foundation, were given the necessary training to breed the crops themselves so that they would be able to carry out the agricultural revolutions in their own nations without continued supervision from outside. After their training, the scientists were given HYV semidwarf seeds to take back to their respective nations.

Funding, Policies, and Politics. Public sector funding and leadership were crucial to ensuring the green revolution's success. The Rockefeller Foundation is generally regarded as the "founder" of the green revolution in the 1940s, with programs committed to agriculture in the developing world. Later, the World Bank and the United

States Agency for International Development (USAID) joined in the effort. Recognizing the importance of increasing local expertise, development organizations in Western countries pooled their resources to link industrial-world scientists with developing world locations, resulting in the formation of the Consultative Group on International Agricultural Research (CGIAR). CGIAR now includes sixteen institutions worldwide, conducting research on key crops in the developing world, as well as livestock and fish, forestry, plant genetics, and food policy.

The substantial production improvement that the farmers experienced through green revolution technologies enabled them to pay off their loans quickly. Moreover, the money they earned from their surplus food production often meant that whole villages began investing in schools and roads, efforts that in the long run would further improve not only agriculture, but also other aspects of socioeconomic well-being.

Politically speaking, it has been argued that these green revolution efforts were realized in the context of a fear of famine, overpopulation, and the threatened rise of communist governments in areas considered a strategic threat to the West. Globally, it went unquestioned in the mid-twentieth century that greater food production would contribute to greater political stability in developing nations. The United States made significant commitments at the federal and philanthropic levels to promote crop breeding as part of Cold War efforts to contain the spread of communism. President Harry Truman's 1949 inaugural speech emphasized this purpose: "the United States and other like-minded nations find themselves directly opposed by a regime with contrary aims . . . that false philosophy is communism." To that end, Truman proposed four major courses of action, the fourth of which concerned alleviating hunger and disease in underdeveloped areas: "Greater [food] production is the key to prosperity and peace." In the 1940s, the Rockefeller and Ford foundations also wanted to foster the development of liberal democratic capitalism rather than see either socialism or fascism make further inroads, sharing the common goal of both humanitarian outreach and "thwarting a perceived threat of communist subversion and keeping India from going the way of China."

Worldwide Impact of the Green Revolution. The green revolution is generally considered to have been a "success" in Latin America, China and Southeast Asia, and India and South Asia. Latin America was a primary region of interest because of a combination of need and local governmental interest in improving agriculture. From 1960 to 1990, both wheat and maize production

more than doubled, so that now Mexico is a net exporter rather than importer of these crops. The green revolution also achieved significant yield increases throughout East and Southeast Asia. Before 1960, wheat yield in India and China was on par with that of Europe during the Middle Ages (600–800 kg/ha). This was adequate because the population had stayed within the bounds necessary to ensure adequate food supplies even with suboptimal agricultural practices. However, in the 1960s India and China experienced improved living conditions that prolonged life expectancy, which compounded with high fertility could have led to massive malnutrition. Instead, through green revolution technologies, rice production throughout Asia more than doubled from 1960 to 1990, and wheat production more than quadrupled.

In spite of its successes in many parts of the world, the green revolution did not create a significant impact in most areas of Africa. Overall, while average agricultural production in Asia after the green revolution increased dramatically to nearly 3 tonnes per hectare, Africa remains trapped at a production level of about 1 tonne per hectare, the average productivity of British farmers during the Roman Empire. There are several possible reasons for this lack of success. One is that the new HYV crops developed elsewhere in the world were not suited to African planting conditions, where the topsoil is thinner and weather patterns such as drought more unpredictable. Also, serious and uniquely African agricultural problems persist, such as certain insect pests, viruses, fungi, and weeds that are difficult to control. A number of the later-developed CGIAR centers, such as IITA (International Institute of Tropical Agriculture) and CIAT (Centro Internacional de Agricultura Tropical, or International Center for Tropical Agriculture) have developed improved varieties of sorghum, millet, cowpeas, cassava, potatoes, and sweet potatoes for African use. But the dramatic yield improvements scored in Asia and Latin America have not been achieved in Africa.

Infrastructural problems likely served as a barrier to green revolution success in Africa as well. Inadequate property rights blunted farmers' production opportunities and incentives, and local banks were unable or unwilling to assist in providing loans for farmers to purchase the new agricultural technologies. Moreover, the African transportation system was poorly prepared to deliver green revolution technologies to the places they were needed. Uganda and Ethiopia, for example, had as of the year 2001 fewer than 62 miles (100 kilometers) of paved roads per million people: one hundred times less than in other developing nations such as Brazil and India, and some thousand times less than in industrial nations such as the United States and France. Thus, green revolution technologies could not reach farmers reliably.

Remaining Challenges. While the green revolution had a dramatic and lasting effect for the good, it did not solve agricultural problems worldwide. Africa is a case in point. The effectiveness of the green revolution is reaching a natural limit, even in areas in which it did succeed, as human populations in the developing world continue to rise. To increase production, it is necessary to improve yields on currently existing fields beyond what green revolution technologies have been able to provide. Moreover, while the green revolution played a key role in achieving food security and reducing rural poverty, it was environmentally harmful in many settings. Some of the best-irrigated lands have become overly saline since irrigation was introduced as part of the green revolution, making planting increasingly difficult. Water tables have declined, and waterways and soils have become contaminated by pesticides and fertilizers, proving detrimental to human and animal health. Moreover, overuse of pesticides has caused pests to develop resistance to the pesticidal chemicals, rendering them ineffective.

Legacy of the Green Revolution. The green revolution has made astounding production increases in basic food crops in the developing world. It significantly increased food production in Asia and Latin America at a time when massive hunger in these areas was feared. Its success was due to a combination of circumstances: Worldwide, policymakers saw increased food production as a priority after World War II, and set the wheels in motion to facilitate that goal. At the same time, agricultural science and technology in the industrial world—hybrid seeds, pesticides, fertilizers, and irrigation systems—had advanced to the point that these technologies could be transferred to other parts of the world, and could be useful there. While it did not have a similarly vital impact in Africa, and agricultural and environmental challenges remain, the green revolution can be considered one of the most important movements in the history of world agriculture.

[See also Agriculture, *subentry* Overview.]

BIBLIOGRAPHY

Alston, Julian M., George W. Norton, and Philip G. Pardey. *Science Under Scarcity: Principles and Practice for Agricultural Research Evaluation and Priority Setting.* Ithaca, N.Y.: Cornell University Press, 1995.

Conway, Gordon, *The Doubly Green Revolution: Food for All in the 21st Century.* Ithaca, N.Y.: Comstock, 1998.

Hazell, Peter B. R., and C. Ramasamy. *The Green Revolution Reconsidered: The Impact of High-Yielding Rice Varieties in South India.* Baltimore, Md.: Johns Hopkins University Press, 1991.

Khush, Gurdev S. "Green Revolution: The Way Forward." *Nature Reviews: Genetics* 2 (2001): 815–821.

Perkins, John H. *Geopolitics and the Green Revolution: Wheat, Genes, and the Cold War.* New York: Oxford University Press, 1997.

Wu, Felicia, and William Butz. *The Future of Genetically Modified Crops: Lessons from the Green Revolution.* Santa Monica, Calif.: RAND, 2004.

FELICIA WU

GROUP OF EIGHT. The oil crisis and global recession of 1973 demonstrated the need for global governance on economic issues. The United States formed the Library Group in 1974 to discuss global economic issues, inviting senior financial officials from the United States, the United Kingdom, West Germany, and Japan to Washington. In 1975 the French president Valéry Giscard d'Estaing held a summit of the heads of government from West Germany, Italy, Japan, the United Kingdom, and the United States, marking the beginning of Group of Six (G6). In 1976 the U.S. president Gerald Ford requested that Canada be allowed to join, forming the Group of Seven (G7). Since 1977 the European Union has been represented by the president of the European Commission, completing the process of making the G7 an international organization for economic cooperation representing the largest industrial nations of the world, at that time making up 14 percent of the world population and accounting for almost two-thirds of the world's economic output.

Russia met separately with the G7 after the 1994 summit in Naples to discuss becoming a member of the group, known as Political 8 (P8) or "G7 plus 1." Russia formally joined the G7 in 1997 through the efforts of U.S. president Bill Clinton as an act of gratitude to the Russian president Boris Yeltsin for initiating economic reforms in Russia and for remaining neutral to the eastward expansion of North Atlantic Treaty Organization (NATO). The joining of Russia to form the G8 was eventually opposed by U.S. senators Joe Lieberman and John McCain in 2005 until such time that President Vladimir Putin would provide assurance of democratic reforms and political freedoms for the Russian people. Since then Russia has been excluded from G8 meetings of the finance ministers and governors of central banks.

The G8 does not have a formal administrative structure, budget, or permanent staff, as it was originally conceived as an informal forum. The presidency of the group rotates

Group of Eight Meeting. Group of Eight leaders meet in Denver, Colorado, June 1997. *Clockwise from top right*, President Bill Clinton, French President Jacques Chirac, Canadian Prime Minister Jean Chretien, Italian President Romano Prodi, European Union Commission President Jacques Santer, European Council President and Prime Minister of the Netherlands Willem Kok, British Prime Minister Tony Blair, Japanese Prime Minister Ryutaro Hashimoto, German Chancellor Helmut Kohl, and Russian President Boris Yeltsin. Photograph by Michel Lipchitz. AP IMAGES

annually, with the country holding the presidency responsible for planning and hosting ministerial-level meetings. The summit's initial concern was economic and financial issues relating to macroeconomic management, international trade, international financial institutions, and relations with developing countries, but its focus eventually expanded to include microeconomic issues ranging from employment to electronic commerce. Issues are no longer restricted to economics and finance and now include anything of mutual or global concern, such as health, law enforcement, labor, economic and social development, human rights and justice, financial crime, energy, environment, foreign affairs, terrorism, nuclear safety and security, nonproliferation of weapons, and arms control.

The finance ministers meet four times a year to review developments in their economies and to originate common approaches on international economic and financial policy issues. The central bank governors join the finance ministers at the first three meetings, with other meetings scheduled as necessary to discuss specific economic or financial issues. The finance ministers also meet shortly before the G8 summit. Any issue appearing on the agenda of one summit can be brought up again at a subsequent summit.

This enables leaders to develop and implement strategies for reforms and respond to economic and political concerns that can then be referred to the larger international community and global institutions such as the International Monetary Fund, the World Bank, and the United Nations. One example of a G8 initiative is the formation of the Global Information Society in 1994 with databases on pedophiles and terrorists. There are also separate meetings attended by finance and energy ministers from all eight member countries, with the inclusion of the People's Republic of China, Mexico, India, Brazil, and South Africa, known as "G8 plus 5." This group was formed in Scotland in 2005 to agree on a consensus to deal with the post-2012 objectives of the Intergovernmental Panel on Climate Change.

Over the years, criticisms of the G8 have centered on its failure to combat poverty among developing nations stemming from rising international debt and unfair trading policies and to combat global warming by limiting carbon dioxide emissions. The G8 has also been criticized for not dealing with the ill effects of globalization and the consequences of a strict patent policy on medicine for treating Acquired Immune Deficiency Syndrome (AIDS). Another criticism of G8 is its exclusion of the economic powerhouse of the People's Republic of China and its lack of representation from the "global south," keeping the G8 an institution of Western economic powers. Emerging nations have complained about their interests not being discussed at G8 meetings, which led to the formation of the Group of Twenty (G20) in 1999, which includes G8 members plus Argentina, Australia, Brazil, China, India, Indonesia, Italy, Mexico, Saudi Arabia, South Africa, South Korea, and Turkey.

Annual G8 summits are high-profile events subject to lobbying, street demonstrations, and even terrorist attacks, such as the antiglobalization movement protest during the twenty-seventh G8 summit in Genoa in 2001 and the synchronized terrorist bombings in London on the opening day of the 2005 summit in Scotland, which resulted in the death of innocent bystanders and the disruption of the summit agenda. As its history suggests, the G8 is an evolving institution continually revising its membership, agenda, and purpose, with a growing sense of its importance in world governance.

[*See also* Banking, International; Globalization; *and* International Relations.]

BIBLIOGRAPHY

Edwards, John, and Jack Kemp, eds. "Russia's Wrong Direction: What the United States Can and Should Do." Independent Task Force Report No. 57. New York: Council on Foreign Relations Press, 2006.

G8 Research Group. "G8 Information Centre." http://www.g7.utoronto.ca/. Sponsored by the University of Toronto.

Hajnal, Peter. *The G8 System and the G20: Evolution, Role, and Documentation.* Burlington, Vt.: Ashgate, 2007.

Wainwright, Martin. "G8 to Pool Data on Terrorism." *Guardian*, 18 June 2005.

SUBRINA MAHMOOD AND ROY NERSESIAN

GUADALUPE, VIRGIN OF. According to the traditional story of the apparitions of the Virgin of Guadalupe, she appeared in 1531, just ten years after the Spanish victory at the Aztec capital of Tenochtitlán, to Juan Diego, a poor indigenous person. She urged him, in a series of encounters, to request of the archbishop of Mexico the building of a chapel for her on the site, the hill of Tepeyac. Despite the archbishop's initial skepticism, she provided Juan Diego with convincing proof as the flowers that he had wrapped, at her direction, in his cape (a native *tilma*) were miraculously transformed into a painting of her. This miraculous image was interpreted as a sign of the Virgin's special concern for the people of Mexico. This interpretation has continued and, particularly since the seventeenth century, grown. It is associated in many reproductions with the words from Psalm 147, "*Non fecit taliter omni natione,*" that is, "It was not done thus for any other nation."

The text of the story was first recorded in Spanish by Miguel Sánchez in 1648 and in Nahuatl in 1649 by Luis Laso de la Vega, the latter account now known as the *Nican Mopohua* ("Here is recounted"). However, there are earlier artworks supporting the tradition: a 1606 painting by Baltasar de Echave Orio that nearly duplicates the well-known image, and a 1613 engraving by Samuel Stradanus that identifies Guadalupe by name and recounts a number of her miracles.

The devotion grew rather slowly through the seventeenth and early eighteenth centuries, but was given enormous impetus by her selection as patroness of Mexico City and the naming of 12 December as her feast day in 1737, when her image was invoked to abate a terrible epidemic. Other cities in New Spain (Mexico), Guatemala, and Puerto Rico accepted her as patroness over the next two decades, illustrating the reverence for her among Creoles, persons of Spanish descent or identification. Yet she was also seen as a protector of Native peoples.

A series of indigenous protests in New Spain from 1769 onward were connected with the Virgin of Guadalupe, showing the perception of her power and efficacy. As New Spain's independence movement began in 1810, she was called on by Father Miguel Hidalgo y Costilla as he rallied his Native followers by invoking her help and authority. Thereafter, she appeared on insurgent banners along with calls for "Death to bad government." Still, the Spanish and Creoles opposed to independence invoked her name as well and decried what they saw as the profane use of her image by the rebels. Even indigenous forces allied with the Spanish claimed her as protector and patroness against the forces of Hidalgo. Yet when, in 1821, Agustín Iturbide—who had come late to the insurgent cause—entered Mexico City with his triumphant forces, a sermon was delivered at Tepeyac thanking Guadalupe for the victory.

She has continued to be associated with Mexican nationalism and is a source of Mexican pride; in 1895, Guadalupe was crowned and in 1910, Pope Pius X proclaimed her the patroness of all Latin America. The honors have continued; in 1999 Pope John Paul II declared 12 December as a Liturgical Holy Day for the entire continent. In 2002, he canonized Juan Diego at her basilica during his fifth visit to the sacred site.

The reverence for Our Lady of Guadalupe continues to grow, spread by Latinos into the United States and throughout Latin America. Her basilica is the second most heavily visited Roman Catholic site in the world, surpassed only by the Vatican.

Even now, for the faithful, she is believed to appear where she is needed. In 1997, a subway worker at the Hidalgo subway station in Mexico City—named for the leader of independence mentioned above—discovered on the tiles of the floor what seemed to be an image of the Virgin of Guadalupe. Thousands began to visit the site, up to fifty visitors a minute on weekends, leaving flowers and candles and imperiling the safety of travelers. Despite the warning by the archbishop of Mexico City that the image was a result of water damage and by no means miraculous, Mexicans felt that she had appeared when needed, in answer to corruption, assassinations, poverty, abandoned children, in a space that was convenient to them all. Though the tile was removed from the station for safety reasons and placed in a small kiosk at street level, heavily protected by a thick plastic shield, the space is now venerated by believers. This continued reverence and sense of presence makes her an important unifier for the Mexican people, inside and outside of the borders of that country.

[See also Catholicism, subentry Catholicism and Folk Catholicism in Latin America.]

BIBLIOGRAPHY

Brading, David A. *Mexican Phoenix: Our Lady of Guadalupe: Image and Tradition across Five Centuries.* Cambridge, U.K., and New York: Cambridge University Press, 2001.

Peterson, Jeanette. "The Reproducibility of the Sacred: Simulacra of the Virgin of Guadalupe." In *Exploring New World Imagery*, edited by Donna Pierce. Denver, Colo.: Denver Art Museum, 2005.

Poole, Stafford. *Our Lady of Guadalupe: The Origins and Sources of a Mexican Symbol, 1531–1797.* Tucson: University of Arizona Press, 1995.

LINDA B. HALL

GUANGZHOU. Guangzhou (Canton) is the political capital of the Chinese coastal province of Guangdong. It is an important regional metropolis in the commercial network of its Pearl River Delta hinterland and of the West River basin connecting Guangdong with Guangxi Province to the west. At the outset of the modern era, Guangzhou was also an important northern port in the Southeast Asian maritime trading network, into which Europeans inserted themselves. The city has played a prominent role in transnational economic and cultural flows throughout the modern period. Because of their distinct dialect and remoteness from Beijing, the Cantonese have been portrayed as proudly independent. Yet many members of the urban elite in Guangzhou have been outsiders: northern officials or cadres, sojourning merchants, and émigré elites.

In the eighteenth century, Guangzhou and the manufacturing town of Foshan anchored a highly commercialized regional economy. Many Cantonese moved into the West River basin, distributing Guangdong salt and shipping Guangxi rice back to the Pearl River Delta, while others conducted operations in Southeast Asia. In 1757 the Qing court increased the city's economic significance by restricting trade with European merchants to Guangzhou. Europeans exchanged American silver, and later Indian opium, for Chinese tea, silk, and porcelain. In the nineteenth century, Guangzhou's salt and maritime merchants, many of whom were sojourners from outside Guangdong, invested their wealth in public works projects, such as the West River dike system, and in scholarship, often associated with Guangzhou's premier academy, the Xuehaitang (Sea of Learning Hall).

Guangzhou was the site of China's first encounter with Western imperialism. The First Opium War (1840–1842), between the Qing and British empires, was precipitated in March 1839 when the Qing official Lin Zexu (1785–1850) seized British opium at Guangzhou. During the ensuing war, British forces blockaded and partly occupied Guangzhou. Chinese remember the May 1841 Sanyuanli incident, in which a British detachment patrolling the Guangzhou suburbs was attacked and forced to withdraw, as an early victory against Western imperialism.

With the Treaty of Nanjing (1842) ending the First Opium War, Guangzhou lost its position as the sole port open to trade with Western merchants, but it instead became one of the five designated treaty ports. Many scholars believe that this had a deleterious effect on the region's economy, because trade was diverted to the Chang (Yangtze) River basin. Some suggest otherwise, pointing to flourishing silk production during the late nineteenth century and China's first silk filature, opened in 1872 on the outskirts of Guangzhou. In 1854, Guangzhou suffered a siege by Red Turban rebels, and during the Second Opium War (1856–1860) it was occupied by British and French troops.

Guangzhou is sometimes described as the cradle of the Chinese revolution because Sun Yat-sen (Sun Yixian, 1866–1925) was a native of the region, and his Nationalist Party (Guomindang or Kuomintang) made Guangzhou its base before launching the 1926 Northern Expedition to unify China. Guangzhou was also the site of a failed Communist uprising in December 1927, known as the Canton Commune. Equally significant, Guangzhou was one of the first cities in which Chinese modernist elites were able experiment with urban reform. Sun Fo (1891–1973), Sun Yat-sen's son, became the first mayor of Guangzhou's municipal government in 1921.

Beginning in the 1920s, much of the city's development shifted toward the eastern suburb of Dongshan, which was largely settled by families with ties to overseas Chinese. Female and child labor dominated a small modern industrial sector, primarily in the match and latex industries, that emerged at this time. Under the Chinese Communists, Guangzhou maintained its commercial reputation and outward-looking orientation. As one of the "later liberated areas," Guangzhou was subjected to an influx of northern Chinese Communist Party cadres, who looked askance at Guangzhou as a city tainted with bourgeois, foreign, and imperialist associations. Nevertheless, because of its remoteness from Beijing and its links to Hong Kong and overseas Chinese, Guangzhou remained a pioneering region in experimenting with market reforms.

In 1957 the semiannual Canton Export Commodities Trade Fair was initiated and became a venue for negotiating foreign contracts before the economic reforms under Deng Xiaoping (1904–1997). The Pearl River Delta was one of earliest regions to open up to foreign investment in the reform era, after 1978. Two of the four special economic zones (SEZs) designated in 1980, Shenzhen and Zhuhai, are near Guangzhou. In 1984, Guangzhou was one of fourteen coastal cities designated to attract foreign investment. Since the 1990s, consumer culture and the market economy have thrived among an emerging Cantonese middle class, particularly in the newly developed eastern suburb of Tianhe.

[*See also* China; Special Economic Zones; *and* Urbanism and Urbanization, *subentry* East Asia.]

BIBLIOGRAPHY

Ikels, Charlotte. *The Return of the God of Wealth: The Transition to a Market Economy in Urban China.* Stanford, Calif.: Stanford University Press, 1996. An anthropological survey of Guangzhou during the 1980s and early 1990s.

Miles, Steven B. *The Sea of Learning: Mobility and Identity in Nineteenth-Century Guangzhou.* Cambridge, Mass.: Harvard University Asia Center, 2006. A study of the Xuehaitang academy and the Cantonese urban elite during the nineteenth century.

Tsin, Michael. *Nation, Governance, and Modernity: Canton, 1900–1927.* Stanford, Calif.: Stanford University Press, 1999. Describes the efforts of modernist elites in Guangzhou during the 1920s.

STEVEN B. MILES

GUANO BOOM. Whereas some European countries developed processes of industrialization in the nineteenth century, Latin American countries grew export economies. In Peru this was the case with guano. The Peruvian economy, society, politics, and culture experienced extraordinary changes starting in the late 1830s as a result of guano discoveries and exploitation. The exploitation of large amounts of bird dung (guano) created an unprecedented increase in Peruvian exports, revenues for the state, and personal fortunes. Guano exports jumped from zero to close to 20 million U.S. dollars per annum during the peak boom years in the late 1860s and early 1870s; 538,767 tons of guano, for example, were exported just to Europe in 1869. The total value of all guano exports between 1841 and 1878 has been estimated at 600 million to 814 million U.S. dollars. However, the influx of this capital into the Peruvian economy created inflation. The guano capital also created a banking system, and some monies were invested in agriculture, mining, railroads, and urban developments.

The Arequipa scientist Mariano Eduardo de Rivero y Ustáriz (1798–1857) was one of the first scholars to study and advertise the qualities of Peruvian guano for increasing agricultural productivity in Europe as a natural fertilizer. Guano was abundant because of the confluence on the coast of Peru of cold ocean currents coming from the South Pole, the Humboldt current, and northern warm currents, El Niño, a confluence that generates particular ecological conditions for the reproduction and existence of very specific sea birds, *aves guaneras*, among them the *guanay* (a Quechua word). Inca and pre-Inca peoples used guano to fertilize their fields, but this practice was largely ignored during colonial times.

Since the guano deposits were on islands and coastal areas with no private ownership, the Peruvian state became the exclusive possessor of this strategic resource. Some scholars also argue that this public control of export goods in 1840s Peru follows a particular tradition of state control of business not seen in other nineteenth-century Latin American countries. The influence of foreign immigrants and foreign businesses operating from abroad was clear since the early guano contracts; the British merchant house Anthony Gibbs and Sons stands out. By the 1860s the control of the guano business shifted to Peruvian concessionaries, *compañía de consignatarios nacionales*. However, in 1868 the minister of finance, Nicolás de Piérola (1839–1913), gave control of the guano trade to the French financier Auguste Dreyfus (1827–1897).

The large amounts of capital during the guano boom had a great effect on many elements of the Peruvian economy, society, and government. The organizing of government budgets became a norm; budget surpluses occurred, as well as contracting new foreign loans. Foreign and domestic debts were also paid, favoring merchant houses and groups linked to high government officers. President Ramón Castilla (1797–1867), counting on guano fiscal resources, abolished slavery and the Indian tribute. Railroad lines were built in many parts of the country, public education increased, the university was modernized, urban areas were improved, and the Peruvian military was built up.

The laborers who worked the guano deposits were Peruvian free wage earners, prison gang workers, slaves (until the abolition of slavery), Chilean contract laborers, and, above all, Chinese coolies. During the guano boom, some one hundred thousand Chinese came to Peru to work in the guano areas as well as in agricultural plantations and haciendas. They worked in slave-like conditions and left an indelible influence on Peruvian culture, politics, and society.

[*See also* Peru.]

BIBLIOGRAPHY

Bonilla, Heraclio. *Guano y burguesía en el Perú*. 2d ed. Lima, Peru: Instituto de Estudios Peruanos, 1984.

Deustua, José R. *The Bewitchment of Silver: The Social Economy of Mining in Nineteenth-Century Peru*. Athens: Ohio University, 2000.

Hunt, Shane. *Growth and Guano in Nineteenth-Century Peru*. Princeton, N.J.: Woodrow Wilson School, Princeton University, 1973.

Méndez, Cecilia. *Los trabajadores guaneros del Perú (1840–1879)*. Lima, Peru: Seminario de Historia Rural Andina, Universidad Nacional Mayor de San Marcos, 1984.

JOSÉ R. DEUSTUA

GUANTÁNAMO. The U.S. Guantánamo Bay Naval Base (also called Gitmo) is located on the southeast corner of Cuba about 112 miles from Florida. It covers forty-five square miles surrounded by seventeen miles of fences. Since the early twentieth century Guantánamo has been a symbol of the clash between U.S. power and Cuban sovereignty. In 2002 another chapter was added to Guantánamo's controversial history when Al-Qaeda and Taliban suspects were brought there for detainment, interrogation, and trial. From 2002 to 2007 an estimated 750 individuals were imprisoned at Guantánamo, and the secrecy, lack of legal protections, and reports of torture and other abuses prompted international criticism.

In 1898, U.S. Marines landed at Guantánamo Bay during the Spanish-American War, the first of a series of U.S. military interventions. The Platt Amendment, attached as an appendix to the Cuban Constitution (1903), included provisions that the United States had the right to intervene militarily to ensure Cuban independence and was guaranteed coaling and naval stations. In 1904, the United States procured a lease of land and water from the Cuban government as a fueling station in Guantánamo Bay. A 1934 lease included a clause that termination required the consent of both the U.S. and Cuban governments or the abandonment of the base property by the United States. One of the three Cuban signatories was Fulgencio Batista y Zaldívar, who dominated Cuban politics for decades until his dictatorial rule was overthrown by Fidel Castro.

Cuban opposition to U.S. presence and interference accelerated following the 1959 Cuban Revolution, and the new government attempted repeatedly to end the Guantánamo lease. However, the United States refused, and following a series of disputes, the Cuban government cut off the water supply to the base and surrounding fields in 1964. The United States has been supplying water and food directly to Guantánamo ever since. While the U.S. Treasury sends a yearly check of over $4,000 to lease the territory, the Cuban government refuses to cash it. Hence, the stalemate continues, and Cuba maintains that the U.S. naval base at Guantánamo Bay represents illegitimate occupation of Cuban territory.

In the 1990s, the base was used as a site for "migrants," tens of thousands of Haitian and Cuban refugees fleeing their governments who were refused asylum on the U.S. mainland. There was international criticism of the detainees' poor living conditions and medical treatment, including the separate internment of Haitians with HIV/AIDS. In 2001 the George W. Bush administration determined that Guantánamo would serve as the detention center for prisoners in the war on terror. The U.S. government refers to them as "enemy combatants" rather than "prisoners," maintaining that the Third Geneva Convention on treatment of prisoners of war does not apply.

In November 2001 President Bush issued a military order on the "Detention, Treatment, and Trial of Certain Non-Citizens, in the War against Terrorism" authorizing the holding of non–U.S. citizens in custody for an indefinite time without charge. The detainees are prohibited from seeking any judicial remedy in any U.S., foreign, or international court proceedings. Trials were to be by military commission. On 11 January 2002 the first twenty prisoners allegedly connected with Al-Qaeda and the Taliban arrived at Guantánamo and were held in wire mesh cages in an area known as Camp X-Ray. While most such prisoners were captured in Afghanistan and Pakistan, over the next five years individuals from over thirty countries were brought to Guantánamo. Over three hundred prisoners were eventually released; many returned to their countries of origin and never were officially charged. There have been reports of hunger strikes and suicides, as well as revelations of torture and other mistreatment.

Legal challenges to the detention without charges and treatment of prisoners were coordinated largely through the Center for Constitutional Rights, which earlier represented Haitian detainees. In *Rasul v. Bush* (2004), the U.S. Supreme Court held that foreign nationals at Guantánamo could challenge their detention by filing habeas corpus petitions. The decision rejected the executive claim of freedom from judicial scrutiny; however, it remains unclear precisely what rights the petitioners have that might be vindicated by a habeas court petition. The struggle continues over the rights of detainees, and the passage of the Military Commission Acts (2006) includes authorizing the president to establish military commissions to try enemy combatants.

Guantánamo has come to represent a test case for the methods and effectiveness of the U.S. war on terror. Critics emphasize the assertion of executive power, disregard of traditional checks and balances, veil of secrecy, denial of due process rights, and mistreatment including torture of prisoners. As of December 2007, hundreds of prisoners remained in Guantánamo; most remained in limbo without official charges or access to counsel.

[*See also* Cuba; Prisons and Punishment, *subentry* Overview; *and* Terrorism, *subentry* Overview.]

BIBLIOGRAPHY
"The Center for Constitution Rights." http://www.ccr-ny.org.
"The Joint Task Force at Guantánamo Bay." http://www.jtfgitmo.
Margulies, Joseph. *Guantánamo and the Abuse of Presidential Power*. New York: Simon & Schuster, 2006.

JOYCE APSEL

GUATEMALA. A republic on the isthmus of Central America covering more than 42,000 square miles (110,000 square kilometers), Guatemala gained its independence from Spain in 1821. The Spanish conquistador Pedro de Alvarado conquered the Maya civilizations of the region in 1524, aided by superior technology, European diseases, and rivalries between the two dominant groups of the region, the Quiché and Cakchiquel. During nearly three hundred years of Spanish rule, ethnic tensions among Spaniards, Creoles (native-born whites), Ladino (Spanish-Indian ancestry), and Maya characterized colonial social life.

The Maya, who inhabited farming communities scattered throughout the highlands, provided temporary hard labor for a few export commodities, such as cochineal and indigo, but the absence of mineral resources limited Spanish demands on Indian labor. The Maya adopted elements of Spanish civilization, such as the Roman Catholic faith, but indigenous cultural expressions survived the conquest even as the indigenous people mixed with the Spanish immigrants. In the early twenty-first century more than two-fifths of the country's 15 million people identified themselves as indigenous, and the government officially recognized twenty-three languages.

Liberal Party Rule. Neither the colony nor the independent republic held much economic value to the Europeans and North Americans until the late nineteenth century, when Liberal reformers implemented a series of political, economic, and social reforms to develop an export economy based on coffee. The development of the coffee industry required labor and land that could be provided only by the indigenous communities. Coffee planters moved into the highlands, supported and encouraged by the national government in Guatemala City. The expansion of coffee into the highlands exacerbated existing ethnic and class tensions. Most of the coffee planters were either Creole or Ladino, and they controlled the government and the armed forces.

The Creoles and Ladinos acquired land from indigenous communities and used the state to reinstitute forced labor drafts as required to plant, maintain, harvest, and transport coffee. The loss of land suffered by the indigenous communities varied from village to village, depending in part on geography and the suitability for coffee cultivation. The new labor requirements that were imposed on both men and women led indigenous families into debt peonage or seasonal migration. Indigenous family and village life was disrupted as a result of the modernization program, with indigenous women often left to raise families and

Guatemalan Archaeological Sites. Examining a Mayan artifact, Quirigua, Guatemala, early twentieth century. FRANK AND FRANCES CARPENTER COLLECTION/PRINTS AND PHOTOGRAPHS DIVISION, LIBRARY OF CONGRESS

tend to domestic crops while men were compelled to work on the coffee fincas or road construction projects.

As coffee cultivation spread through the highland communities, the national government offered generous concessions to foreign investors to develop railroads, ports, electrical plants, and utilities. One such concession, granted to Minor Cooper Keith of Boston in 1904, allowed for the completion of the railroad line from Guatemala City to Puerto Barrios on the Caribbean coast. It also served as the foundation for the United Fruit Company (UFCO), which acquired lands on the northern coast to cultivate bananas, part of a multinational effort to develop tropical sources of supply for the expanding North American market. The United Fruit Company subsequently acquired a controlling interest in Guatemala's entire railroad network as it also became the country's largest landowner and developed bananas into the country's second-largest export commodity.

A succession of corrupt and dictatorial governments facilitated the company's growth, exposing the dictators and the company to increasingly nationalistic criticism, best expressed by the country's Nobel Prize–winning novelist, Miguel Angel Asturias. In *El Señor Presidente* (The President, 1946) and the so-called Banana Trilogy, *Viento fuerte* (The Cyclone, 1950), *El papa verde* (The Green Pope, 1954), and *Los ojos de los enterrados* (The Eyes of the Interred, 1960), Asturias exposed the corruption, brutality, and exploitation that characterized nearly seventy-three years of Liberal Party rule (1871–1944).

From Reform to Military Rule and Insurgency. In 1944 a coalition of students, workers, and junior military officers overthrew the last Liberal government and ushered in a ten-year period of reform under two democratically elected governments. Colonel Jacobo Arbenz Guzmán, one of the architects of the 1944 revolution, was elected to the presidency in 1950 with the support of labor unions and the Communist Party. Arbenz implemented an ambitious land reform in 1952, by which the government confiscated uncultivated lands from large estates and redistributed them to more than a hundred thousand rural families. The largest landowner, UFCO, lost more than three-fourths of its holdings and denounced the measure and the government as Communist. The administration of President Dwight D. Eisenhower, with close associates of UFCO in the Central Intelligence Agency (CIA) and the State Department, agreed that Arbenz posed a threat to the interests of the United States in its cold war against the Soviet Union. The CIA subsequently organized a 150-man counterrevolutionary army led by Colonel Carlos Castillo Armas, who took power after Arbenz resigned in June 1954.

A succession of military-dominated governments from 1954 to 1985 terminated the social and economic reforms initiated during the revolutionary decade and promoted capitalist development projects with United States economic assistance. Foreign investment and regional economic integration promoted agricultural diversification and a measure of industrial development. New export commodities, particularly cotton and sugar, developed on Pacific coast plantations in the 1960s, attracting increasing numbers of indigenous workers from the highland communities. Foodstuffs, cigarette, cement, and pharmaceuticals manufacturing increased substantially in the 1960s, coinciding with sharp increases in the urban working and middle classes.

With the government under the control of a firmly anti-Communist military, workers, peasants, women, students, and other reformist organizations found the political environment increasingly repressive and intolerant. In the early 1960s disgruntled military officers and former leaders of the Communist Party launched a guerrilla campaign against the government, inspired and supported by the Cuban revolutionary government. The military's campaign against the insurgents in eastern Guatemala, conducted with United States military assistance, eliminated the guerrilla bases but also strengthened the institutional autonomy of the armed forces, which grew corrupt and brutal as their power over the government expanded.

In the late 1970s the guerrilla organizations reorganized and relocated, gathering new strength among the indigenous communities in the northern highlands as they adopted a political agenda that offered land and labor reform, indigenous rights, and equality for women. Indigenous men and women joined the ranks of the guerrillas or campaigned against the military governments through organizations affiliated with them, such as the Comité de Unidad Campesina (CUC). The power of the insurgents provoked a genocidal response by the military, which launched a scorched-earth campaign in 1982 to eliminate the guerrilla organizations and the communities that allegedly sustained them. Hundreds, perhaps thousands of highland Indian villages were destroyed and their inhabitants dispersed or killed. By some estimates, more than two hundred thousand Guatemalans, the vast majority of them indigenous, perished during a war that began in the early 1960s, intensified in the late 1970s, and reached genocidal levels in the early 1980s.

The plight of Guatemala's indigenous majority was brought to the world's attention through the efforts of Rigoberta Menchú Tum, a Quiché woman who gained national and international notoriety through the publication of her autobiography. Titled *I, Rigoberta Menchú* (1983), the book was presented as the story of Menchú and all poor and indigenous Guatemalans then confronting a brutal counterinsurgency campaign under the direction of General José Efraín Ríos Montt, a born-again Christian who attempted to crush the insurgency by offering "beans or bullets" to the people. Partly as a result of the publicity generated by Menchú, human rights organizations denounced Ríos Montt and the Guatemalan military.

Transition to Democracy. International pressure, including the denial of economic and military assistance, contributed to the military's decision to initiate a transition to civilian government in the mid-1980s. By that time the

military had effectively reduced the insurgency to isolated pockets of resistance. The inauguration of the Christian Democrat Vinicio Cerezo Arévalo in 1986 marked the first time in twenty years that the military allowed a civilian to assume the presidency, but even Cerezo recognized that the armed forces still wielded supreme political power. Nevertheless, the transition to democracy also initiated a transition to a peaceful settlement of Guatemala's thirty-year civil war, one of the longest armed conflicts in Latin America.

The transition to peace and democracy suffered a setback in 1993 when the civilian president Jorge Serrano Elias attempted to institute dictatorial government through a "self-coup." Democratic forces in civil society, including Rigoberta Menchú (who received the Nobel Peace Prize in 1992), allied with constitutional factions of the military and the economic elite to restore constitutional government. Peace negotiations subsequently resumed, leading to the signing of accords in 1996.

A succession of democratically elected civilian governments have continued to promote economic diversification through neoliberal development programs that are based in large part on increased foreign trade with and investment from the United States. Reformist efforts, notably attempts to prosecute officers suspected of committing atrocities during the armed conflict, have not produced significant results. The conflict continues in other arenas, symbolized perhaps most dramatically by the denunciations of Rigoberta Menchú that followed the revelation that she may have fabricated elements of her autobiography. The armed conflict may have subsided, but the ethnic, economic, political, and social tensions that have characterized Guatemala since the Spanish conquest have not abated.

[*See also* Bananas; Coffee; Dictatorship, *subentry* Military Dictatorships in Latin America; Guerrillas and Guerrilla Movements, *subentry* Latin America; Indigenous Movements in Latin America; *and* United Fruit Company.]

BIBLIOGRAPHY
Dosal, Paul J. *Doing Business with the Dictators: A Political History of United Fruit in Guatemala, 1899–1944.* Wilmington, Del.: Scholarly Resources, 1993.
Gleijeses, Piero. *Shattered Hope: The Guatemalan Revolution and the United States, 1944–1954.* Princeton, N.J.: Princeton University Press, 1991.
Handy, Jim. *Gift of the Devil: A History of Guatemala.* Boston: South End Press, 1984.
Human Rights Office of the Archdiocese of Guatemala. *Guatemala, Never Again! The Official Report of the Human Rights Office, Archdiocese of Guatemala.* Maryknoll, N.Y.: Orbis Books, 1999.

Menchú, Rigoberta. *I, Rigoberta Menchú: An Indian Woman in Guatemala.* Edited by Elizabeth Burgos-Debray and translated by Ann Wright. New York and London: Verso, 1983.

Stoll, David. *Rigoberta Menchú and the Story of All Poor Guatemalans.* Boulder, Colo.: Westview Press, 1999.

PAUL J. DOSAL

GUERRILLAS AND GUERRILLA MOVEMENTS

[This entry includes four subentries, an overview and discussions of guerrillas in Latin America, in South Asia, and in Southeast Asia.]

Overview

Guerrillas are "irregular" warriors who take up arms outside the control of legally established armies on behalf of a political cause or to redress a social grievance. Their name comes from the Spanish word for "little war." The name gained currency in the early nineteenth century, on account of the celebrated uprising of the Spanish peasantry against the forces of Napoleonic France. Guerrillas fight in ways calculated to wear down their opponents, while avoiding pitched battles in which the superior fighting power of regular armies can be employed to greatest effect. Guerrilla tactics place a premium on elusiveness and deception. They emphasize hit-and-run raiding, traps, ambushes, terrorism, kidnapping, assassination, and so on. In tactical terms guerrilla warfare blends imperceptibly into other forms of vernacular or entrepreneurial violence—rural banditry and machine breaking, clan rivalry and vendetta, organized crime—a resemblance that is routinely seized upon by the guerrillas' opponents, who generally prefer to portray him as a criminal rather than as warrior.

Guerrilla leaders assert their military legitimacy by pointing to the political nature of their motives. In principle guerrillas can fight on the side of legally constituted authority—for instance, when partisan bands take up the cause of national defense following the surrender of the regular army. In practice, however, guerrilla warfare is virtually synonymous with revolutionary war, aiming at the overthrow of the established order or at the reconstitution of political authority amid the ashes of a failed or defeated regime. If the idea of the guerrilla as such is mainly military—the guerrilla is defined in the first instance by the way that he fights—that of a guerrilla "movement" is specifically political, and implies the use of irregular warfare for the purpose of seizing power from those who currently possess it.

Guerrilla Wars in Modern Times. Guerrilla wars have existed throughout history. They have acquired a heightened significance in modern times mainly owing to the expansion of European power and influence around the world and to the armed resistance this expansion inspires. In the heyday of imperialism such conflicts were of limited consequence, except in those rare instances in which a revolutionary movement could attract the sympathetic intervention of a major power, always an important requirement for the guerrilla's strategic success. The American Revolution (1776–1781), in which guerrilla forces fought alongside revolutionary armies organized on European lines, exemplified this pattern. The triumph of the revolution was critically dependent on the support of Britain's main geopolitical rival, France.

The Greek war of independence (1821–1832), directed against the imperial suzerainty of the Ottoman Turks, presents a similar picture. Like Britain's American colonists, the Greek guerrillas gained their victory thanks to the intervention of powerful outsiders, in this case Britain, France, and Russia, whose governments shared a common interest in reducing the sway of the Ottoman Empire in Europe.

The ability of Greeks and Americans to derive strategic leverage from the rivalries of the European states' system was not shared by the native peoples of Asia and Africa, however. Anticolonial guerrilla movements were common in the nineteenth century and produced their share of heroic figures and legendary exploits, which would fuel the nationalist mythologies of the future. But in themselves these episodes posed no threat to European hegemony, nor much of a threat even to the decrepit traditional empires of Eurasia, of which the Ottomans were an example.

The fortunes of the revolutionary guerrilla improved in the twentieth century. The world wars deprived Europeans of the material strength required to retain their place at the center of the world system and dispelled the aura of efficiency and imperviousness that had surrounded colonial regimes. These effects were amplified by the spread of communism as a global ideology. It provided guerrilla movements with a superior set of organizing tools and held out the prospect of direct assistance from the Soviet Union, which emerged after 1945 as one of the two militarily strongest nations on earth, and one at least nominally committed to the cause of world revolution.

At the same time new information technologies were transforming the practice of guerrilla warfare both tactically and strategically. Guerrilla fighters cannot risk concentrating into large formations, because doing so exposes them to discovery and engagement by the main forces of the enemy. Modern communications have compensated to some extent for this weakness, by allowing small, dispersed forces to achieve new forms of tactical coordination—to mount simultaneous attacks against widely separated targets, for instance, or to provide timely warning about enemy actions—that were impossible for the primitive rebels of the past. Advanced communications have also provided new means of connecting the guerrilla to surrounding society, on whose loyalty (or at least sufferance) he depends for his survival, and also to international opinion, whose reaction, as has been suggested, will often tip the balance between eventual victory and slow, grinding defeat. Modern revolutionary war is a drama played out before a vast audience, whose sympathy and support are the ultimate prize for which the combatants are fighting. The fact that guerrilla movements in the twentieth century have been able to address that audience on something approaching equal terms with their opponents has made an enormous difference to their chances of success.

The Chinese Revolution. The most influential guerrilla war of modern times occurred in China, following the overthrow of the Qing dynasty (1644–1912) by a fledgling national regime based on the army and the middle class. The struggle waged against it by the Chinese Communist Party became a model for similar movements around the world, not least because it culminated in 1949 in the seizure of power over the largest country on earth, a result sufficiently remarkable to speak for itself. In case it did not, the writings of the Party's supreme leader, Mao Zedong (1893–1976), provided a commentary on how it was achieved. Mao portrayed guerrilla war as dominated by political rather than tactical considerations, so that even the smallest military action had to be judged in relation to its impact on society. In the beginning, when guerrilla forces were small and vulnerable, the focus of effort must be the rural peasantry in remote parts of the country, where government forces were likely to be thin on the ground and government services poor. The guerrilla fighter must insinuate himself within this setting, by providing support and security for the population while conducting symbolic acts of violence calculated to discredit the authorities. Only after such rural bases were secured could larger operations be attempted, with a view to expanding the territory and population under revolutionary control. In time, Mao proposed, the balance of forces would gradually tip in the guerrilla's favor, to the point where conventional military operations directed against the main strength of the enemy would become possible.

Mao's ideas, even backed by the exemplary success of the Chinese Revolution, fell short of providing a recipe for success. His culminating stage, in which guerrilla forces are supposed to transform themselves into a conventional army, has proved especially elusive for his disciples. Such outcomes, when they occur, are invariably dependent upon outside assistance. The French Indochina War (1946–1954) began as a guerrilla campaign of modest dimensions and ended in a siege (Dien Bien Phu, 1954) in which a French army of fifteen thousand men was destroyed by a revolutionary force three times as large, the equipment and logistical support for which were provided by China. The final destruction of the American-backed government in South Vietnam was likewise accomplished by the regular army of the North, rather than by the guerrilla forces that it had sponsored there over the intervening twenty years.

Elsewhere, however, the conventional coup de grâce hypothesized by Mao has proved unnecessary. In Cuba (1959) and Algeria (1962) guerrilla movements seized power directly, testimony in the first case to the incompetence and corruption of the existing regime, in the second to the implausibility of France's claim of a moral right to rule a country whose inhabitants were most decidedly not French. So, too, did the Sandinistas of Nicaragua (1979) and the Taliban of Afghanistan (1989). Both were victors in hard-fought campaigns, the Sandinistas against a well-trained national army, the Taliban against the occupying forces of the Soviet Union—though in the Afghan case the leavening effects of surreptitious American aid should not be discounted.

On the whole, however, Mao was right to recognize that the fundamental problem for any guerrilla movement is how to impose a political decision upon its enemy—the object of all military violence, whatever its form. For the guerrilla, the opposite of victory is not so much outright defeat as prolonged futility. Modern history is littered with guerrilla movements that fought for years or even decades to no avail, sustained by trickles of opportunistic aid and the hope that somehow their message would finally get through. In the 1960s and 1970s such movements threatened to become endemic in Latin America, where their main effect was to force the displacement of civilian governments by military regimes, which were more willing to take whatever ruthless measures were required to enforce domestic security. Guerrilla wars have in fact become endemic in Africa, where dozens of failed and failing states provide fertile ground for insurrectionary violence on a scale more than sufficient to cripple prospects for social and economic development, but far below what would be required to seize and wield effective political power.

[*See also* Revolution; Terrorism; *and* War.]

BIBLIOGRAPHY

Beckett, Ian F. W. *Modern Insurgencies and Counter-Insurgencies: Guerrillas and Their Opponents since 1750.* London and New York: Routledge, 2001.

Bond, Brian, ed. *Victorian Military Campaigns.* New York: Praeger, 1967.

Laqueur, Walter. *Guerrilla Warfare: A Historical and Critical Study.* Boston: Little, Brown and Company, 1976.

Moran, Daniel. *Wars of National Liberation.* London: Cassell, 2001.

Snow, Donald M. *Distant Thunder: Patterns of Conflict in the Developing World.* New York: St. Martin's Press, 1993.

DANIEL MORAN

Latin America

Most Latin American guerrilla groups began as small armed bands that split from political movements when they could not, or were not willing to, pursue a democratic expression of their ideological proposals and power-sharing aspirations. Sometimes invoking Marxist-Leninist or Maoist principles but mostly inspired by the nationalistic tradition of the late nineteenth and twentieth centuries, guerrilla movements in Latin America represented, and in some countries remain, a major political inspiration. Although they rarely seized power by military means, guerrilla groups—collectively labeled "insurgency" in the U.S. military tradition and "subversion" by the French—managed in the long term to raise awareness about social injustice, or at least about the need to share power with an ampler array of political forces. Though the military tactics of surprise attacks and sudden strikes against conventional armed forces in harsh terrain derived from movements and theorists outside the region, the peculiar quality of Latin American guerrilla movements is that political violence was almost always ancillary to radical ideologies.

From Colonial Revolts to National Identities. The first recorded guerrilla warfare in Latin America was initiated by the cacique Enriquillo in 1519 against the Spanish forces in Hispaniola. For fourteen years Enriquillo and his mobile bands were able to harass the army, but after this period they were forced to submit to the colonial authorities. Later in the century Manco Inca Yupanqui and his clan in Peru struggled for three decades against the Spanish colonizers. The rebellion ended when the army seized and killed Manco Inca's son Túpac Amaru in 1572.

In Mexico a *cimarrón* (runaway) African named Yanga and other slaves initiated a rebellion and harassed their former Spanish masters for twenty-nine years before signing a peace accord in 1608.

A number of revolts in the colonial period were the outcome of violent oppression by colonial officials and governing elites over the poorest among the indigenous peoples, the African slaves, and the mestizo population. The great Andean rebellion took place in 1780 when Túpac Amaru II in Peru and Túpac Katari in Bolivia launched raids against the Spanish but were finally defeated and executed. Later revolutionary groups took the names of Tupamaros (after Túpac Amaru) and Kataristas (after Túpac Katari) in Uruguay and Bolivia, respectively.

During the Peninsular War in Portugal and Spain (1808–1814), the term "guerrilla"—"little war," from the Spanish diminutive of *guerra*—swiftly crossed the Atlantic to Latin America and inspired military tactics occasionally used by rebel and loyalist forces in the wars of independence. José Antonio Páez in Venezuela and Francisco de Paula Santander in Colombia effectively harassed the Spanish forces with hit-and-run attacks. Rural *montoneras* (peasant militias) in many parts of the region, formed by peasants of indigenous and mestizo origins, used guerrilla tactics. These forces were led by their employers, usually large landowners and caudillos like Facundo Quiroga in La Rioja, Argentina, who supported the federal central power in Buenos Aires with his mounted bands of gauchos (the cowboys of the pampas). In 1820 in Venezuela and in 1871 in Cuba, *montoneras* with expert knowledge of harsh terrain and strong support from local populations successfully assisted the Spanish colonial armies harassing the rebel forces.

Postindependence rebellions were driven less by ideology or ethnic factors than by intense social inequalities between the Creole landowning elites and mestizo agricultural workers in the countryside. The Caste War of the Yucatán (1847–1901) exploded in a region close to modern Belize when Maya indigenous groups revolted against Yucatecos of European origin who expanded their private ownership to communal lands. By 1850 most of the peninsula was under the control of the rebels, whose struggle was inspired and justified by a syncretism of European and Amerindian beliefs. Some of the rebels—known as Cruzob—formed an independent Maya community and resisted until the Mexican army occupied the area in 1901.

However, it was not until the Mexican Revolution, which started in 1910 against the authoritarian rule of

Porfirio Díaz, that guerrilla warfare in Latin America acquired its traditional social significance within the concept of class struggle in favor of the landless poor. Emiliano Zapata and his guerrillas in the area of Morelos epitomized the moral ideals of peasants and rural workers who struggled for land reform. Although Zapata was killed by forces loyal to the government, he became one of the most prominent national heroes in present-day Mexico, and groups like the Zapatistas consider themselves his ideological heirs. In 1924 in Brazil the army officer Luís Carlos Prestes led an insurrection with other young officers and conscript soldiers. Itinerant groups of rebels went to Rio Grande do Sul, then to Foz do Iguaçu, and joined the Paulista revolutionaries at Paraná province in what was later styled the Brazilian "long march" (named after the retreat of the Chinese Soviet Republic's army in 1934–1935).

Augusto César Sandino led Nicaraguan rebel forces against the U.S. army stationed in the country from 1927 to 1933. Influenced by religious, anarchist, and communist ideologies, Sandino launched a nationalistic campaign that exalted the indigenous character of Latin American peoples. His guerrilla organization suffered many defeats but eventually succeeded when the U.S. Marines withdrew from Nicaragua after the 1932 elections. Sandino proclaimed the independence of the Union of Central American Republics in the country's northern departments, but he was kidnapped and executed on 21 February 1934 by the Guardia Nacional (National Guard) commanded by Anastasio Somoza García. Two years later Somoza seized power and established a dictatorship that he passed on to his son Anastasio Somoza Debayle. The Somoza dynasty was overthrown by the Sandinista National Liberation Front in 1979.

Between Nationalism and Socialism. In the context of the Cold War a myriad of movements in the region ranged from ephemeral groups of a few men and women and limited visibility to sizable armies that effectively struck against armies and businesses and financed themselves through terrorist acts. As a part of Fidel Castro's internationalist policy, Cuban military aid and training was provided occasionally to insurgents, though it never surpassed Cuba's assistance to Angola and Ethiopia. More frequently, the United States supported government counterinsurgency units and paramilitary forces, who were also inspired by French officers with experience in the Algerian War of Independence (1954–1962).

On 2 December 1956 eighty-six members of the Cuban 26th of July Movement landed in the Oriente province of the island. Only a few eventually survived, among them Fidel Castro, his brother Raúl Castro, Camilo Cienfuegos, and Ernesto "Che" Guevara. The fighters regrouped in nearby Sierra Maestra and waged successful guerrilla warfare against the forces of the dictator Fulgencio Batista y Zaldívar until his fall two years later. The Cuban Revolution ended after Batista fled to the Dominican Republic and Castro's army rolled into Havana on 8 January 1959.

Che Guevara is probably the figure who best epitomizes the paradigm of Latin American guerrillas. Born into a middle-class Argentine family, after studying medicine Guevara gradually became involved with social movements and traveled frequently in the region. After the fall of Jacobo Arbenz Guzmán in Guatemala, Guevara met Fidel Castro and joined his movement in Mexico. After the successful campaign of the Cuban Revolution, in which he commanded the rebel forces in the decisive battle of Santa Clara, Guevara was generally regarded as second in power to Castro himself, and his national and international prestige rose with his undertaking of new responsibilities. He resumed the armed fight in 1965 and acted in the Congo and later in Bolivia, where his rebel group was ambushed and he was summarily executed by the Bolivian forces backed by the United States. Guevara was eulogized as a model revolutionary who met a heroic death at the hands of imperialist forces.

Apart from Guevara's *La guerra de guerrillas* (Guerrilla Warfare, 1961) and other writings in the context of rural combat, revolutionaries in Latin America widely read different translations of *Mini manual do guerrilheiro urbano* (Manual of the Urban Guerrilla), a guerrilla handbook published in 1969 by the Brazilian revolutionary and Marxist writer Carlos Marighella. Furthermore, an intellectual validation of guerrilla action was developed by Régis Debray, a French philosopher and specialist in mass media who taught at the University of Havana. Debray joined Guevara in Bolivia and was imprisoned there until 1970. His most influential work was first published as *Révolution dans la Révolution?* (Revolution in the Revolution?, 1967) and was well known among members of the intellectual Left, many of whom warmly embraced Guevara's "foci" theory, popularized by Debray. This theory asserts that when social inequalities in a country are unbearable, small nuclei of armed groups may start a guerrilla war that will mobilize the population against the ruling system.

From the early 1960s, inspired by these and other authors and by the example of Che Guevara, political groups resorting to guerrilla tactics mushroomed in the region. They tried to emulate the successful revolutionary struggle in Cuba by creating "two, three, many Vietnams" in Latin America (Guevara, *Message to the Tricontinental*). The same year as Castro's seizure of power, similar armed groups began operating in Panama, Nicaragua, the Dominican Republic, Haiti, and Paraguay. Further movements operated between 1962 and 1979 in Argentina, Chile, Colombia, El Salvador, Guatemala, Nicaragua, Peru, Uruguay, and Venezuela.

Among them, the National Liberation Movement (MLN; also known as the Tupamaros) in Uruguay is worth noting for its broad popularity. Conceived as an urban guerrilla organization by its founder Raúl Sendic, the Tupamaros grew into an irregular army of fifteen thousand—in a country with a population of 3.5 million—with logistic support among the population and links with politicians and military officers. Increasingly, the Tupamaros and other movements in the Southern Cone of South America resorted to terrorism to finance their struggle. Kidnapping, providing protection to wealthy individuals, bank robbery, and foreign investment of proceedings allowed these groups to generate enough revenue to support large numbers of armed troops and effective propaganda campaigns.

The Montoneros in Argentina, a group that combined nationalistic, socialist, and progressive Catholic ideologies, became known in 1970 with the kidnapping and execution of the former president Pedro Eugenio Aramburu. In 1974 the Montoneros kidnapped the brothers Juan and Jorge Born of the multinational Bunge and Born and were paid the world-record ransom of $60 million in cash. Like the Tupamaros in Uruguay, the Montoneros and other revolutionary groups were brutally but effectively suppressed by the armed forces who seized power in those countries in 1973 and 1976. In Argentina alone it is estimated that the security forces and paramilitary groups kidnapped, executed, and secretly disposed of the bodies of fifteen to twenty thousand persons in what became known as the Dirty War.

In Peru, members of the Sendero Luminoso (Shining Path), inspired by its founder, the Maoist Abimael Guzmán Reynoso, conducted one of the most violent movements in the region. Peasants, trade union leaders, and civil servants accused of collaborating with the government were frequently victims of summary executions, which allegedly included slitting throats, strangulation, stoning, and burning. This level of indiscriminate violence reduced the movement's popularity, particularly among peasants. It collapsed with the internment of Guzmán and other Senderista leaders on 12 September 1992. According to government sources, some scattered bands

remained in the Andes in the early twenty-first century, operating in collusion with drug traffickers.

The association of guerrilla movements with the drug trade has been increasing in Colombia, one of the most violent countries in the world. Since the period of La Violencia from 1948 to 1958, when intense conflict between liberals and conservatives cost the lives of at least 190,000 victims, a combination of social, political, economic, and sectarian factors ensured an enduring situation of national insecurity. The Revolutionary Armed Forces of Colombia (FARC), founded in 1964 by rural Marxist guerrillas, increasingly resorted to kidnapping and was accused by Colombian and U.S. officials of offering security services to drug crops and trade.

A movement that did not resort to narco-terrorism and indiscriminate violence, and yet successfully positioned itself as a defender of the rights of the Mexican indigenous people against imperialist practices of globalization, is the Zapatista Army of National Liberation (EZLN). Based in the poor state of Chiapas and composed of Maya women and men, the group was founded in 1983 and gained public support in 1994 among middle-class urban professionals after its opposition to the North American Free Trade Agreement (NAFTA). Its well-known spokesperson, Subcomandante Marcos, drew his rhetoric from Christian and indigenous spiritual cults, Maoist principles, environmentalist and antiglobalization activism, and even the pacifist pragmatism of Mohandas K. Gandhi, emphasizing the preponderance of ideology over military tactics.

Impact of Guerrillas in Latin America. In spite of the political importance and social significance of guerrilla

Colombian Guerrillas. Guerrillas guard a van carrying recently released captive soldiers, Cartagena Del Chaira, Colombia, June 1997. Photograph by Fernando Llano. AP IMAGES

movements in this region, only a handful achieved their goal of seizing power. Apart from Cuba, only in Nicaragua (1979), Grenada (1979), and El Salvador (1983) did revolutionaries manage to take control of their governments or at least constitute major political forces. Rebel groups in other countries were either suppressed violently by government and security forces or were too short lived, fragmentary, and unpopular to have any effect on their countries' politics.

In the debate about the merits of guerrilla warfare in promoting social change in Latin America, most observers conclude that their struggle may be labeled as a failure. However, at the turn of the twenty-first century several high-ranking government officials and leading politicians in Argentina, Bolivia, Brazil, Chile, Ecuador, Nicaragua, Uruguay, and Venezuela were former members of, or held strong connections with, revolutionary groups of the 1960s through the 1980s, indicating that guerrillas tend ultimately to pursue democratic venues for their political purposes.

[*See also* Cuban Revolution; Dirty War; Guevara, Che, as Icon; Shining Path; *and* Túpac Amaru Rebellion.]

BIBLIOGRAPHY

Castro, Daniel, ed. *Revolution and Revolutionaries: Guerrilla Movements in Latin America.* Wilmington, Del.: Scholarly Resources, 1999. A complete collection of essays by contemporary guerrilla strategists and witnesses.

Gonzalez-Perez, Margaret. "Guerrilleras in Latin America: Domestic and International Roles." *Journal of Peace Research* 43, no. 3 (2006): 313–329. Female participation in international and domestic guerrilla groups.

Gott, Richard. *Guerrilla Movements in Latin America.* London: Thomas Nelson & Sons, 1970. Classic account of regional rebel groups by the journalist who confirmed the death of Ernesto Guevara in Bolivia.

Guevara, Ernesto "Che." *Guerrilla Warfare.* Translated by J. P. Morray. New York: Vintage Books, 1961. Probably the manual most widely read by guerrillas around the world. Includes practical military tactics and recommendations to interact with the population.

Guevara, Ernesto "Che." *Message to the Tricontinental.* Nashville, Tenn.: Southern Student Organizing Committee, 1968.

Laqueur, Walter. *Guerrilla: A Historical and Critical Study.* Boston: Little, Brown, 1976. A Cold War perspective on guerrillas, including their practice considered as terrorism.

Marighella, Carlos. *The Terrorist Classic: Manual of the Urban Guerrilla.* New Translation by Gene Hanrahan. Chapel Hill, N.C.: Documentary Publications, 1985. A text widely published in Latin America, frequently clandestinely, and closely followed by rural guerrillas.

O'Neill, Bard E. *Insurgency and Terrorism: Inside Modern Revolutionary Warfare.* Washington, D.C.: Brassey's, 1990. How guerrillas need to be counterattacked, by a former U.S. Air Force officer and now expert in terrorism.

EDMUNDO MURRAY

South Asia

South Asia prior to World War II was a British colonial enterprise, with its present configuration of states emerging only with postwar independence. Though regular revolts punctuated the Raj, with guerrilla action the logical weapon of the weak, it was the second half of the twentieth century and beyond that produced the most salient instances of guerrilla action.

Allied anti-Japanese guerrilla action in Asia exposed entire populations to the specific techniques of irregular warfare. The tribal groups who had been central to the successful British resistance against the Japanese advance, from Burma into the northeast of India, were the first to pose a serious insurgent challenge to New Delhi. More than a hundred largely independent groups, all using terror and guerrilla warfare as their principal weapons, continue to convulse entire areas of the northeast. Though the 2006 death toll of 627 was down from the 715 of 2005, according to the Institute for Conflict Management (New Delhi), this was still 23 percent of the total "terrorism-related" deaths recorded for the year. Cross-border movement by guerrillas continued in 2007 to complicate relations with India's neighboring states, particularly Burma (Myanmar) and Bangladesh. India's response to these tribal insurgencies has been increasingly effective, but Manipur and Assam remain particularly affected.

Irritating as the northeast insurgencies may be, they pale in comparison to the two major upheavals that have convulsed Jammu and Kashmir (J&K), India's only Muslim majority state, and Punjab, the Sikh-dominated granary of the nation. The J&K episode exploded in 1987 as a result of electoral chicanery. Inability of local security forces to deal with challenges posed by emerging guerrilla and terror actions resulted in massive deployments of paramilitary and military forces to the small state; the intervention of Pakistan, providing arms, equipment, training, and sanctuaries; and a conflict that to date has cost more than 40,000 lives, with 1,116 dying in 2006. Terror is the tactic of choice for the several dozen insurgent groups, but guerrilla units have at times tried to amalgamate for larger actions. The most important such effort, in mid-2003, forced several brigades of 16 Corps in Jammu to conduct a major operation in the Hill Kaka area of Poonch District, resulting in considerable stockpiles being seized amid defensive positions with reinforced bunkers.

A similar dynamic marked the 1980–1993 upsurge of Sikh fundamentalism in the Punjab, with the guerrilla component overshadowed by the widespread use of terror by the followers of Sant Jarnail Singh Bhindranwale. His demise, however, came in an urban assault by security forces, Operation Blue Star in June 1984, after the militants had seized control of the Golden Temple, the holiest Sikh center. Subsequent splintering in insurgent ranks resulted in a dynamic that saw some one thousand dead per year, with a total of five thousand reached in 1991. Though terror remained the driver, it was often integral to guerrilla operations designed to dominate the population. Effective counterinsurgency ultimately led to the restoration of order and an uneasy status quo.

Emerging as the most serious challenge to New Delhi, Maoist insurgents have grown steadily. Present in fourteen Indian states (170 of 602 districts), with a demonstrated capacity to wipe out police patrols of platoon strength, the Maoists have relied overwhelmingly on guerrilla action and terror, inflicting 742 deaths in 2006, up from 717 the year before. Though Nepalese Maoist forces to the north graduated to main force action, massing for attacks, the Indian Maoists have remained as guerrillas. This no doubt reflects their healthy appreciation for the superior power of the state, as compared with feckless Nepal. Kathmandu presently finds its authority severely limited, its country in a state of chaos as it negotiates with the Maoists, and the death toll at thirteen thousand.

Both Indian and Nepali Maoists have fielded leadership figures drawn from local and even societal elites, while the manpower is overwhelmingly from the marginalized elements of particular localities. These have proved predominantly tribal, as in the northeast. This proved also to be the case in the most prominent guerrilla-led upheaval in Bangladesh, the rebellion of the Chakma tribals in the Chittagong Hill Tracts. Incensed at lowland encroachment onto their traditional homelands, the tribesmen in the early 1970s formed a political body with a military wing, Shanti Bahini (SB), and used guerrilla action to force an unsatisfactory but tenuous settlement in their favor.

In Sri Lanka, postindependence marginalization of Tamils produced, in the early 1980s, more than three dozen insurgent groups, all practicing a mix of terror and guerrilla warfare, all committed to *Eelam*, an independent Tamil homeland. Dominant was the Liberation Tigers of Tamil Eelam (LTTE). Intertwined with these developments was the emergence of a Sinhalese-dominated Maoist challenge, Janatha Vimukthi Peramuna (People's Liberation Front, or JVP), which twice (1971, 1987–1990) convulsed the state using a combination of terror and

guerrilla warfare. It was all but wiped out, but LTTE became capable of main force action, fielding thousands of combatants in massed units. Unable to deal with the potent combination of terror–guerrilla–main force warfare, Colombo was forced to negotiate an uneasy truce, which broke down in late 2006.

Separatism is also at the roots of the guerrilla action encountered by Pakistan as it seeks to assert its authority in the Pashtun tribal areas of the west and northwest. Government efforts throughout 2006 resulted in major losses as the tribal elements fell back on the same guerrilla tactics that had stymied the Soviets during their disastrous 1979–1989 intervention in Afghanistan. By 2007 Islamabad had attempted a variety of hearts-and-minds gambits, noticeably a formal agreement of nonintervention in tribal areas as long as Taliban and Al-Qaeda elements were excluded, but it became increasingly clear that the government had been tricked.

[*See also* Frontier, *subentry* Frontiers and Borderlands in South Asia; Peasants, *subentry* South Asia; South Asian Languages; *and* Terrorism, *subentry* South Asia.]

BIBLIOGRAPHY

Gill, K. P. S., and Ajai Sahni, eds. *Terror and Containment: Perspectives of India's Internal Security.* New Delhi, India: Gyan, 2001.

Maitra, Kiranshankar. *The Noxious Web: Insurgency in the North-East.* New Delhi, India: Kanishka, 2001.

Sahni, Sati. *Kashmir Underground.* New Delhi, India: Har-Anand, 1999.

Singh, Harjeet. *Doda: An Insurgency in the Wilderness.* New Delhi, India: Lancer, 1999.

Swamy, M. R. Narayan. *Tigers of Lanka: From Boys to Guerrillas.* 3d ed. New Delhi, India: Konark, 2002.

THOMAS A. MARKS

Southeast Asia

Examining guerrilla warfare, Southeast Asia is noteworthy on two accounts. First, in the modern era, it has produced a number of prominent guerrilla episodes and movements. Second, it was the scene of perhaps the most significant transitional case, Vietnam, wherein guerrilla warfare was incorporated into the larger phenomenon of insurgency in such manner as to produce a new strategic synthesis. Vietnamese "people's war" was to prove as influential as its Maoist companion.

Before World War II. Prior to World War II, guerrilla warfare surfaced in Southeast Asia early and often. Only Thailand, of the region's present ten countries, escaped colonization. Britain took what are now Burma (Myanmar), Malaysia, Singapore, and Brunei; France ruled Cambodia, Laos, and Vietnam; the Netherlands incorporated Indonesia; and the United States made the Philippines its only major colony. Diverse outside presence evoked complex response, with guerrilla war prominent in the profile of resistance.

American pacification of the Philippines, 4 February 1899–4 July 1902, was possibly the most significant case in which guerrilla war was integral to and drove the resistance. Numerous revolts (some sources list as many as thirty) during the three centuries of Spanish rule culminated in the guerrilla insurgency that was ongoing in 1898 when American forces arrived as part of the Spanish-American War. Easy conventional victory over the Spanish confronted Washington with a Filipino insurgent challenge that fielded both main and guerrilla forces. It was the latter that ultimately proved the test, particularly their use of terror. A sharp learning curve and decentralized counterinsurgency resulted in American victory but at a cost of 4,234 U.S. dead and 2,818 wounded. At least 16,000 Philippine combatants died, and as many as 200,000 civilians.

The subsequent pacification of the Moros in the south was not truly a guerrilla conflict but involved many of the same tests for the foreign power. Regular revolts punctuated the era that led up to World War II, but none of these was of such nature as to challenge the colonial regime. Invariably, though, asymmetric power relations produced a measure of guerrilla war as the insurgent tactic of choice.

Elsewhere in Southeast Asia, the process of imperial expansion often took on a similar character. From its initial takeover of Lower Burma in the mid-1820s, Britain moved steadily to the 1886 climax in Mandalay. Penetration of the Western state model with its socio-economic-political dislocation led to regular resistance, particularly in hill areas, which were ideal for guerrilla war and never completely absorbed. The Saya San Rebellion, 1930–1932, was the premier episode of rebellion and featured such a distinctly "insurgent" combination of elements, from patient construction of clandestine infrastructure, to guerrilla war, to mass upheaval, that a debate has gone on since as to the precise manner in which the upheaval should be characterized. In the event, 3,000 Burmese were killed, 9,000 captured, 350 tried and convicted, and 128 hanged; and the British were forced to deploy two entire divisions from India before order could be restored.

Dutch rule in the East Indies, or Indonesia, reestablished in 1816 after the Napoleonic Wars (1803–1815), found itself buffeted by the same process. The Dipo Negoro Revolt, 1825–1830, a jihad stimulated by grievances not unlike those the British provoked in Burma, proved the greatest test. The revolt's length alone guaranteed that guerrilla action was integral to the process.

For France, the 1862 takeover of Cochin China began a cycle of resistance, much of it guerrilla, as intense at times as that faced by the Americans in the Philippines and certainly more long-lived. Significant pacification energy was required through 1895, with a resurgence in 1909–1913. A proliferation of resistance movements, many with clandestine infrastructure, saw the communists steadily gaining in strength. They and other groups provided the leadership for the substantial uprisings in 1930–1931, beginning with the Vietnamese garrison at Yen Bay. Though violent mass action was the most prominent tactic, guerrilla war was increasingly integrated into rebel planning.

World War II and After. World War II served to draw the diverse threads of resistance together. Numerous individuals and groups gained guerrilla experience as part of the Allied effort. Deep penetration missions built on guerrilla tactics, such as Merrill's Marauders and Wingate's Chindits, moved within an extensive regional context of partisan activity directed against brutal Japanese occupation. Though movements were of varying strength, all countries of the region saw some sort of guerrilla action. This was to have severe consequences for the postwar efforts of the colonial powers to reassert their authority.

In Indochina, the Vietnam Independence League, or Viet Minh (Viet Nam Doc Lap Dong Minh), led by Ho Chi Minh, declared independence in 1945—as did the Indonesian nationalists following Sukarno—before the colonialists could return. In Malaya, the communist forces of Chin Peng, whom the British at one point called "their most trusted guerrilla," prompted the Malayan Emergency, 1948–1960. In Burma, guerrilla resistance was centered on the same tribes, especially the Kachin, whose resistance had led to virtual administrative autonomy within British Burma. Having given their loyalty to Britain, the tribes expected the same from London at the time of Burmese independence. This was not politically possible, and there followed nearly universal tribal guerrilla revolt that continues to plague Burma today. In the Philippines, a large guerrilla resistance was an integrated Filipino-American effort that was to have positive consequences for the era of independence. Ramón Magsaysay, who had been one such guerrilla, ultimately became president in what was to prove a turning point in the postwar suppression of the communist-linked People's Anti-Japanese Army or Huks (Hukbalahap, from Hukbong

Bayan Laban Sa Hapon). Even Thailand, which formally sided with Japan, produced a guerrilla resistance, the Free Thai of regent Pridi Phanomyong.

It was the turmoil of the war that set the stage for what was to follow. Most often called "revolutionary guerrilla warfare," what emerged was insurgency. Guerrilla warfare, though a key component, was but one weapon in the larger dynamic of armed political movement. A global phenomenon, it was the Southeast Asian synthesis, most particularly in Vietnam, that was of lasting import. People's war, as practiced by the Vietnamese, integrated all elements of power, violent and nonviolent, military and political, international and local. Fused in the "war of interlocking," this insurgent approach had evolved nearly simultaneously with that of Chinese people's war but took on a more finely developed form doctrinally. In particular, its ability to integrate terror, guerrilla and main force warfare, and war of position went beyond anything that Mao Zedong had envisaged.

Vietnamese victory over first the French, then the Americans and their Indochinese allies, while ultimately achieved by main forces (conventional units that could fight either in guerrilla or conventional fashion), was built on terror and guerrilla warfare. As such, it was looked to as an example by other Southeast Asian movements, as well as those much further a field, such as FMLN in El Salvador and FARC in Colombia.

Communist victory in the Vietnam War did not bring peace, and the 1978 invasion of Cambodia by the Vietnamese, and the subsequent Khmer Rouge guerrilla resistance, highlighted the extent to which guerrillas remained woven into the regional fabric. Tribal guerrilla resistance to Rangoon continues to this day. Manila is assaulted by an array of movements, from the Communist Party of the Philippines (CPP), to the Moro National Liberation Front (MNLF), to the Moro Islamic Liberation Front (MILF), to the Abu Sayyaf Group (ASG), all using various violent and nonviolent tools, but guerrilla warfare the mainstay.

Chin Peng was not to surrender to Kuala Lumpur until 1989, even as Islamist insurgents of southern Thailand produced a generational shift. Though improvised explosive devices (IEDs) were the major weapon, a growing capacity for guerrilla action clearly concerned Bangkok. Jakarta, beset by its own problems of transition, dealt with the guerrilla resistance on East Timor by granting independence but has refused to do likewise with West Papua, where guerrillas of the Free Papua Movement, or OPM (Organisasi Papua Merdeka), wax and wane.

[*See also* Decolonization *and* Terrorism.]

BIBLIOGRAPHY

Linn, Brian McAllister. *The U.S. Army and Counterinsurgency in the Philippine War, 1899–1902.* Chapel Hill: University of North Carolina Press, 1989.

Lintner, Bertil. *Burma in Revolt: Opium and Insurgency since 1948.* Bangkok: Silkworm, 1999.

Marks, Thomas A. *Maoist People's War in Post-Vietnam Asia.* Bangkok: White Lotus, 2007.

SarDesai, D. R. *Southeast Asia: Past & Present.* 4th ed. Boulder, Colo.: Westview, 1997.

THOMAS A. MARKS

GUEST WORKERS. Guest workers are migrant laborers recruited to work in a host state temporarily. Unlike immigrants, their settlement in the receiving country is neither expected nor desired. It is their temporariness that makes them appealing to employers interested in expanding their supply of flexible labor. Guest workers schemes have been employed since the late nineteenth century and may be usefully seen as a consequence of industrialization and the rise of nation-states.

The combination of steadily declining rates of mortality, improvements in the production and distribution of food, and the radical dislocation of traditional ways of life brought about by industrialization created a large pool of dispossessed laborers willing to migrate in the hope of finding work. As the pace and scope of industrialization picked up, growing numbers of immigrants from increasingly variegated sources made their way to industrial centers in Europe and North America to work in factories and mines, build railroads, plant and pick crops, and take up the other dirty, difficult, and poorly paid jobs. Receiving states typically lacked the legal and administrative means of dealing with these movements and therefore set about creating mechanisms for managing flows and their social consequences. The principle aim of early guest worker schemes was to harness international migration to meet employers' demands for labor while minimizing its impact on processes of nation-building, which relied on distinguishing between nationals and foreigners.

This double-sided impulse animated Imperial Germany's pioneering of the guest worker model. The internal migration of Germans from the rural east to industrializing west created labor shortages in Prussia's eastern provinces, which employers attempted to remedy by recruiting Polish migrant workers from the Austro-Hungarian and Russian empires. However, the arrival of these workers exacerbated nationalist fears of "Polinization," leading Otto von

Bismarck to order the deportation of some thirty thousand to forty thousand foreigners in March 1885.

Renewed demands for foreign labor compelled Bismarck's successor, Leo von Caprivi, to reconsider the ban on foreign labor recruitment. In an effort to satisfy demands for labor while simultaneously guarding against the perceived effects of migration on national integration, a system of tightly controlled temporary labor recruitment was introduced in 1890. Only unmarried laborers were permitted to enter and permission to work was granted from 1 April to 15 November exclusively. The system was enhanced through the establishment of the Prussian Farm Workers Agency in 1905 and the introduction of "compulsory domestic permit" in 1907. The permit noted foreign workers' nationalities and other personal data, along with the name of their employers.

This system of temporary labor migration facilitated massive transnational movements into Germany. On the eve of World War I, Prussia alone accounted for nearly 1 million foreign workers. Compulsory rotation helped maintain the temporary character of this migration. Of the 270,496 Poles employed in Prussia in 1913, only 3,213 remained in the country at the end of the year. While far from perfect, these regulatory mechanisms helped maintain a mass labor force that met the needs of German employers while acknowledging Prussian officials' interest in excluding "unwanted elements."

Although Germany's reliance on foreign labor decreased markedly after the war, the interwar period witnessed important changes to the guest worker system. The Labor Exchange Act of 1922 granted responsibility for recruitment and supervision of foreign laborers to the German Labor Agency and the Reich Employment Office. These bodies worked to ensure that the duration of work and residency permits was strictly limited to a maximum of twelve months. During World War II, the Nazi regime opted for more brutal means of exploiting foreign labor, relying on prisoners of war and concentration camp inmates to fuel its war economy.

The United States sought to satisfy its wartime labor needs by enacting a guest worker agreement with Mexico in July 1942. Driven by California growers' demands, the Bracero Program granted Mexican workers (*braceros*) permission to work in the United States temporarily. The program was terminated in 1947, but was reestablished during the Korean War. Although it was ended definitively in 1964, a combination of employers' demands and lax enforcement ensured that a steady flow of (now illegal) Mexican workers would continue to find employment in the United States.

Western European states also turned to foreign labor in the postwar period, with several countries, including Austria, Belgium, France, West Germany, the Netherlands, and Switzerland instituting guest worker programs. Although the precise nature of these systems differed, the desire to use foreign labor as a temporary means of enabling economic growth was broadly shared. Guest workers typically came from the less developed countries of the Mediterranean rim (including Greece, Italy, Morocco, Portugal, Spain, Tunisia, Turkey, and the former Yugoslavia), which were interested in combating domestic unemployment by reducing "excess" labor and obtaining hard currency through remittances.

The most elaborate guest worker system was developed by the Federal Republic of Germany, which centralized its recruitment operations through the Federal Institute of Labour. Announcements of job openings were sent to the Federal Employment Administration and then forwarded to branch offices in the respective sending states. Successful job candidates were directed to the German Employment Administration office and equipped with documents confirming their identity, lack of criminal record, and marital and family status. After a thorough medical examination, German officials decided on prospective migrants' suitability for work in Germany. Contracts were signed and the worker was granted a renewable twelve-month *Legitimationskarte* that served as a work permit. Upon arrival in West Germany, foreign workers registered with the local employment office and the police, who issued a temporary residence permit. Accommodations were to be provided by the employer, as per guidelines formulated by the Federal Ministry of Labour and Social Affairs. Upon expiry of their contract, foreign workers were to return home and be replaced by fresh recruits.

Guest workers were an essential ingredient in western Europe's postwar economic boom. The ready supply of foreign workers checked labor shortages and allowed employers in receiving states to increase production without having to raise wages. This kept inflation at moderate levels throughout the 1950s and 1960s, facilitating an extended period of growth. And yet by the early 1970s, western European states were questioning their reliance on foreign labor. Although most guest workers did return to their home states, many opted to stay and were being joined by their spouses and minor children. Receiving states' publics began voicing concerns regarding the transformation of their societies as a result of what was in fact significant immigration. By the mid-1970s, most western European states had suspended or radically reduced their guest worker programs. The end of the postwar boom and onset of high unemployment and slow growth in the 1980s made what were initially announced as temporary recruitment stops permanent.

While the termination of guest worker programs blocked the entry of new workers, it could not reverse the consequences of previous migratory waves. Mass repatriation was rejected for humanitarian reasons and family reunification continued largely unabated, sanctioned by court decisions drawing on liberal norms and human rights. Thus receiving states found themselves confronted with the challenge of integrating millions of de facto immigrants. This led many western European states to liberalize their citizenship laws in an effort to facilitate the incorporation of foreign workers and their children. Some states, such as Sweden and the Netherlands, experimented with official multiculturalism policies as well.

Regardless of whether pluralization was embraced, guest worker migration had a profound impact on receiving countries. Urban centers were transformed by the emergence of ethnic neighborhoods and longstanding ideas regarding the separation of church and state were called into question, as Islam emerged as one of Europe's principal religions. The emergence of ethnic minorities also changed politics in western Europe, as xenophobic parties enjoyed electoral breakthroughs by exploiting anti-immigrant sentiment.

Just as the repercussions of western European states' experiences with guest worker migration were becoming clearer, countries in the Middle East and East Asia began turning to foreign labor to staff their growing economies. By 2007, 8.2 million foreigners accounted for approximately 67 percent of Saudi Arabia's workforce, while South Korea's 2006 quota for foreign workers stood at 105,000. By the 1990s, Germany and a number of other European states were once again experimenting with modest guest worker programs to satisfy labor market needs in specific economic sectors, such as agriculture, construction, and tourism. The United States also raised the possibility of establishing a significant guest worker program with Mexico.

Several economists have argued that a revival of mass guest worker migration might assist in alleviating global poverty. They claim that extending globalization beyond trade in goods and services to include the movement of temporary migrant labor would facilitate the global redistribution of wealth without altering the fundamental character of the world's wealthy states (as would be the case in a hypothetical situation of open borders). While these arguments have yet to influence policy in any significant way, the fact that they are being voiced speaks to the durability and suppleness of the guest worker concept.

[*See also* Migrant Labor.]

BIBLIOGRAPHY

Bade, Klaus. "'Preußengänger' und 'Abwehrpolitik': Ausländerbeschäftigung, Ausländerpolitik und Ausländerkontrolle auf dem Arbeitsmarkt in Preußen vor dem Erstem Weltkrieg." *Archiv für Sozialgeschichte* 24 (1984): 91–162.

Castles, Stephen. "The Guest-Worker in Europe—An Obituary." *International Migration Review* 20, no. 4 (Winter 1986): 761–778.

Castles, Stephen. "Guest Workers in Europe: A Resurrection?" *International Migration Review* 40, no. 4 (Winter 2006): 741–766.

Park, Won-Woo. "The Unwilling Hosts: State, Society and the Control of Guest Workers in South Korea." *Asia Pacific Business Review* 8, no. 4 (June 2002): 67–94.

Pritchett, Lant. "The Future of Migration: Irresistible Forces Meet Immovable Ideas." Paper presented at the conference on The Future of Globalization: Explorations in Light of Recent Turbulence. Yale University, 10 October 2003.

Zolberg, Aristide R. "Bounded States in a Global Market: The Uses of International Labor Migrations." In *Social Theory for a Changing Society*, edited by Pierre Bourdieu and James S. Coleman. New York: Russell Sage Foundations; Boulder, Colo.: Westview Press, 1991.

TRIADAFILOS TRIADAFILOPOULOS

GUEVARA, CHE, AS ICON. The subject of admiration and the object of commodification since his assassination on 9 October 1967, Ernesto "Che" Guevara has been a fixture in the world's political and cultural imagination. He has become an icon invested with contested meanings. Cuban schoolchildren expressed their allegiance to the official socialism by claiming "We will be like Che," and Prince Harry of England wore a Che T-shirt for partying. Nepalese guerrillas displayed Che's face on their banners, and the exhibition "Che Guevara: Revolutionary and Icon," presented in New York and London, sold Che's Lipbalm. The life of a symbol, representing the integrity of a Third World social revolutionary or whatever a fashionable young rebel in the developed world wants to express, has a great deal of independence from the person it is based on.

"If we want to say how we would like our children to be educated, we should say without hesitation: we want them to be educated in the spirit of Che," Fidel Castro said after Guevara's death (Diego Garcia, p. 15). The two men had met in 1955 in Mexico. Guevara first left Argentina in 1952 for a six-month trip with his classmate Alberto Granado to discover their continent. By the summer of 1953 he graduated as a physician, traveling afterward to Central America.

If in 1952 he had discovered the starving, landless peasants, his arrival in Guatemala in late 1953 introduced him to Cuban rebels and to the experience of democratic reform under way in Guatemala. After the CIA-organized invasion of June 1954 to stop the Guatemalan reform movement, Guevara fled for Mexico. Incarcerated with the Cuban revolutionaries he joined there, he became one of the few foreigners allowed to take part in the adventurous invasion of Cuba in December 1956. According to Guevara, he learned in Guatemala that there is no social change without revolution.

Guevara became "Che" in the Cuban revolutionary war, admired as a victorious thirty-year-old *comandante* in 1959. Che rapidly became a living representation of integrity, to a certain extent a model of the *hombre nuevo* (new man) that he proclaimed would be born out of armed struggle and the day-to-day effort of building socialism. According to Castro's testimony, Guevara was looking forward to continuing the "revolutionary tasks" in different countries. Despite his positions in Cuba as the head of a failed industrialization effort and of the national bank (where he signed the bills as "Ché"), he committed himself to extending the fight for "human dignity." Criticizing the policies of the Soviet Union, he argued that Asia, Africa, and Latin America would build a new socialism, developed through small groups of clandestine fighters that, from the countryside to the cities, would gain growing support from the "wretched of the earth." He claimed that constructing many Vietnams would lead first to the overthrow of despotic regimes and finally to the end of U.S. imperialism. The new man that he envisioned, "able to feel deeply any injustice committed against any person in any part of the world," would cross borders, sacrificing life and family to continue his struggle (Anderson, p. 634).

In 1964, Guevara quietly left all his Cuban duties. His project of joining the African liberation movements took shape in 1965, when he began to build a Cuban "internationalist force" in the Belgian Congo. A failed seven-month guerrilla war showed him the differences between the local rebels and the idea of the guerrilla as a living moral example. For Guevara, the superstitious, male-centered tribal culture he found at Lake Tanganyika was the opposite of his human-centered, purifying socialism.

As rumors about Guevara's fate brought accusations of a purge by Castro, the Cuban government made public three farewell letters. In the one that Guevara left for Castro, he stated that "other lands of the world claim the presence of my modest efforts. I can do what is denied to you because of your duties in front of Cuba. . . . I will carry to new battlefronts the faith you taught me, the revolutionary spirit of my people, the feeling of fulfilling the most sacred of duties: to fight against imperialism wherever it may be" (Castro). Though the letters showed that Guevara was waging wars somewhere, his whereabouts were unknown. His fame was multiplied through rumor, and the Western intelligence services multiplied their efforts to catch him. Meanwhile, the publication of his letters made it impossible for him to reappear in Cuba. Thus the Bolivian plan was activated.

The plan was to initiate a guerrilla war in southern Bolivia, the strategic heart of South America. The southern jungles, the U.S.–backed military dictatorship, and the militant miners' unions would presumably provide a fertile ground for the spread of the revolution. Guevara's own presence would motivate ample solidarity in neighboring countries. In late 1966, Guevara entered Bolivia as Ramón Benítez. After fourteen months he could not find the support he expected, either from peasants or from the local Communist Party; his communications were intercepted, and a series of errors led to his identification. U.S. military and intelligence officers intervened to support the Bolivian army operations. By 8 October 1967, Guevara's platoon was decimated and he was captured, wounded and wearing ragged clothes. The next day he was assassinated in the village of La Higuera. The picture of his corpse, surrounded by his uniformed killers, resembled Rembrandt's *Anatomy Lesson*. His face, eyes wide open, looked like that of the *Dead Christ* by Andrea Mantegna.

With Guevara's death, his hands chopped off and his remains hidden for the next thirty years, his legend and image began to take on independent life. In 1968 his image, the most reproduced picture in the history of photography, became the main symbol of the youth rebellion, extending from Paris to Berkeley to Saigon. Che's portrait, taken by Alberto Korda in 1960, was popularized after the Italian publisher and extravagant revolutionary Giangiacomo Feltrinelli borrowed it. With the help of that image Che became a banner for landless peasants, a saint for La Higuera peasants, a model for the revolutionary Left, a hero for the Cuban pantheon and social activists, and an object of consumption, to be exhibited together with James Dean or even John Kennedy, for a depoliticized youth looking for small signs of rebelliousness.

The greatest revolutionary martyr of Latin America despite four decades of defeats for the strategy he proposed

Guevara as Icon. Sandinista supporters carry banners portraying Che Guevara during a march in Masaya, Nicaragua, June 2003. Photograph by Mario Lopez. AP IMAGES

for building socialism, Guevara incarnates the drive to overthrow the centuries-old combination of capitalism and imperialism in the Third World and is a global reference as an epic ethical radical who remained committed to his ideals to the end. As Ariel Dorfman observed, he has been erased of complexity, as is "the normal fate of any icon." Icon of consumption, icon of commitment, Guevara will stay alive for a long time. Those who try to follow in his footsteps in one way or the other, whether by fighting globalized, growing social inequalities or by buying the Che fashion statements, will preserve him from the dust.

[*See also* Cuban Revolution; *and* Guerrillas and Guerrilla Movements, *subentry* Latin America.]

BIBLIOGRAPHY

Anderson, Jon Lee. *Che Guevara: A Revolutionary Life.* New York: Grove Press, 1997.

Castro, Fidel. *Carta de despedida de Che Guevara, leida por Fidel Castro en Octubre, 1965.* Video available online: http://www.filosofia.cu/che/chet9g1.htm.

Deutschmann, David, ed. *Che Guevara Reader: Writings on Politics and Revolution.* Melbourne, Australia, and New York: Ocean Press, 2003. The most comprehensive English-language selection of articles, chapters of books, and speeches by Guevara.

Diego Garcia, Fernando, and Oscar Sola. *Che: Images of a Revolutionary.* London: Pluto Press, 2000.

Dorfman, Ariel. "Che Guevara." http://www.time.com/time/time100/heroes/profile/guevara01.html. A wonderful piece of writing on the iconic Guevara on the occasion of *Time* magazine's election of him as one of its two Latin Americans among the one hundred people who shape our world.

Löwy, Michael. *Marxism of Che Guevara: Philosophy, Economics, and Revolutionary Warfare.* Translated by Brian Pearce. New York: Monthly Review Books, 1986. A great analysis of the moral radicalism of Guevara's practice, his theoretical connections with Marxism, and his differences with the Soviet line of Communism.

Paco Ignacion, Taibo, II. *Guevara, Also Known as Che.* Translated by Martin Michael Roberts. New York: St. Martin's Press, 1997.

ALBERTO HARAMBOUR

GUIANA. *See* French Guiana; Suriname.

GUILDS. Traditionally, guilds were organizations that grouped artisans in particular crafts, like ironwork or butchery, to provide mutual protection and sociability. Some societies also developed merchant guilds, but these had mostly disappeared before 1750. Craft guilds organized in many societies that had well-developed craft production, including Japan, the Middle East, and western Europe. Guilds did not form in societies with a more modest urban tradition, like Russia, or in the new settler societies in places like the Americas, where government support, crucial for guilds to maintain regulatory functions, was simply lacking.

Role of Guilds. Guilds normally helped regulate working conditions in skilled trades, specifying how apprentices should be treated, for example, and what kind of test should be imposed on journeymen to make sure they had mastered their craft. Some guilds also helped organize travel for journeymen, helping to find work and accommodations in different cities; this gave their members wide experience early in their careers and also helped even out the distribution of the labor force.

Guilds were normally eager to make sure that not too many workers entered a craft, to protect against pressure on wages. They usually sought some rough equality among master craftsmen, preventing any master from hiring too many journeymen and rising too far above his colleagues in earnings. Guilds also tried to regulate technological innovation, again to protect skill levels and earnings. At the same time, guilds sought to protect consumers by insisting on quality work and production.

Most guilds also had a gendered quality. Though guilds might admit female members, particularly the widows of former male colleagues, and a few women's guilds developed, most guilds were masculine affairs and served to bar women from the most prestigious crafts. Guilds also served social roles, providing occasions for banquets and parades, often in uniforms distinctive to each craft. Sometimes they gained roles in urban governments. Guilds might also provide benefit funds to assist members in illness or to arrange proper funerals.

Challenges. Guilds came under attack as economies became more commercial and as populations grew. This happened first in western Europe. English guilds had been weakening before 1750, as many cities saw large numbers of people entering urban crafts, overwhelming guild regulations and protections. English guilds also progressively lost their ability to restrict technologies.

In France, guilds were directly attacked during the Revolution by the Le Chapelier law of 1791, which banned restrictions on entry to crafts and opposed worker organizations as potentially subversive. Some guilds managed to survive in secret, occasionally organizing strikes or attacking nonmembers. Artisans also soon organized partial replacements for guilds—for example, mutual aid societies that could provide death benefits. In France and elsewhere, craft trade unions, relying on the skills of members, took on certain guildlike qualities, including regulating apprenticeships.

But the disappearance of full guilds undoubtedly subjected artisans to greater competition and widened gaps between employers and workers in the crafts. Apprenticeship standards loosened, and in some cases formal apprenticeships were abolished altogether, while skill standards declined as artisans were pressed to increase their output and standardize products. Guilds and rapid industrialization did not mix well. In some crafts, like printing, the decline of guilds also signaled the entry of a certain number of women workers, though many crafts long preserved masculine dominance even after guilds were gone.

Battles over guilds were fiercer in central Europe. Laws in several German states attacked guilds during the early nineteenth century, in the name of greater competition and innovation. But artisans participating in the revolutions of 1848 asked for a restoration of guilds or their equivalents. Many German states allowed guilds, at least as social though not regulatory organizations, into the later nineteenth century and beyond. Even the Nazis, appealing to artisanal nostalgia in the 1920s, talked about restoring guilds, though again in practice the guilds really had only social functions. Debates over guilds played an important role in German politics until the defeat of the Nazis ended the era more definitively.

Without so much explicit conflict, guilds declined in China by the end of the nineteenth century, again as new levels of competition and technical innovation affected traditional crafts. Japanese guilds, the *za*, had been abolished in the seventeenth century, and more informal groups faded as industrialization took hold.

Quite generally, guilds declined or disappeared as modern commercial economies gained ground. Their legacy continued, however, in characteristic features of craft work and craft unionism, and in some cases in significant political battles in which artisans sought to maintain or regain a more traditional identity.

[*See also* Artisans; Industrialization; *and* Unions, Labor.]

BIBLIOGRAPHY

Rorabaugh, W. J. *The Craft Apprentice: From Franklin to the Machine Age in America.* New York: Oxford University Press, 1986.
Walker, Mack. *German Home Towns: Community, State, and General Estate 1648–1871.* Ithaca, N.Y.: Cornell University Press, 1998. First published 1971.

PETER N. STEARNS

GUINEA. The Republic of Guinea is a nation on the coast of West Africa. It is dominated by the mountainous Fouta Djallon (Futa Jallon) region, often called the "water tower of West Africa" because three major rivers flow from it. The country is divided into four regions: the Fouta Djallon; a coastal region marked by high rainfall and deeply indented tidal rivers that were once major bases for the Atlantic slave trade; a savanna region to the east; and a mountainous forest zone to the southeast. The Fouta was home to a strong Muslim state founded in a jihad during the eighteenth century. The French established posts on the coast in the 1860s and brought the diverse regions together into a single entity after conquest during the 1890s.

French rule was harsh. Forced labor was used to create infrastructure and produce cash crops. After World War II, a radical nationalist movement developed. By 1958, when the French president Charles de Gaulle offered colonies the choice of independence or a looser association with France, the Parti Democratique de Guinée under Sékou Touré convinced Guineans to opt for complete independence. It was the only colony to do so. The French responded by pulling French personnel out of the country and cutting trade links. Touré turned to the Russians for trade and assistance. The result was an inefficient and brutal dictatorship, which ended with the death of Touré in 1984. Lansana Conté seized power and dismantled the state-controlled economy. Since 1993, Guinea has regularly held elections, but the results and their fairness have often been questioned.

[*See also* Africa, *subentry* Western Africa.]

BIBLIOGRAPHY

Barry, Boubacar. *Senegambia and the Atlantic Slave Trade.* Translated by Ayi Kwei Armah, Cambridge, U.K., and New York: Cambridge University Press, 1998.

O'Toole, Thomas, with Janice E. Baker. *Historical Dictionary of Guinea.* 4th ed. Lanham, Md.: Scarecrow Press, 2005.

MARTIN KLEIN

GUINEA-BISSAU. Guinea-Bissau was founded in 1974. Before this, Balanta, Papel, Fulup, Biafada, Bijago, and other politically decentralized societies in western Africa had long had interactions with Atlantic merchants seeking trade goods. From 1750 through the early 1800s their major export was slaves, the bulk of whom were purchased by Portuguese traders. Some Portuguese entered into sexual relationships with African women. Their offspring, known as Luso-Africans, developed a distinct identity and a middleman role in exchange.

In the nineteenth century the Portuguese administered the coast through Luso-African representatives, the most important of whom was Honorio Barreto, who expanded Portuguese claims through treaties signed with coastal groups. These treaties were not recognized by France, which claimed some of the same territories. In response, Portugal firmed up its hold on regional groups by "pacifying" them through a series of military campaigns in the early twentieth century. During these campaigns Portugal carved out a colony, Portuguese Guinea.

Portuguese rule was particularly harsh, largely because the region's people never recognized the legitimacy of the colonial government. Luso-Africans were replaced with men sent from Portugal, who found that violence was the only means of coercing villagers to pay taxes and produce export crops, the basis of the colonial economy. The nationalist leader Amilcar Cabral tapped rural discontent in the 1960s. He led a protracted, violent revolution, the result of which was the independent country of Guinea-Bissau. In independence, Guinea-Bissau's leaders have been unable to integrate multiple decentralized groups into state apparatuses. The country has suffered political instability and economic malaise.

[*See also* Africa, *subentry* Western Africa.]

BIBLIOGRAPHY

Forrest, Joshua B. *Lineages of State Fragility: Rural Civil Society in Guinea-Bissau.* Athens: Ohio University Press, 2003.

Hawthorne, Walter. *Planting Rice and Harvesting Slaves: Transformations along the Guinea-Bissau Coast, 1400–1900.* Portsmouth, NH: Heinemann, 2003.

WALTER HAWTHORNE

GULAG. Although properly an acronym for the Soviet bureaucratic institution Glavnoe Upravlenie ispravitel'no-trudovykh LAGerei (Main Administration of Corrective Labor Camps), the term "Gulag" has come to represent the entire Soviet system of forced-labor concentration camps and internal exile that held millions of people convicted of various alleged political and nonpolitical crimes.

Though forced-labor camps existed throughout the Soviet period, they were at their largest in the Stalin era. The total population of prisons, camps, and exile reached a maximum of some 5.2 million people in the early 1950s just before Joseph Stalin's death. Throughout its history, some 24 or 25 million people passed through the various institutions of the Gulag. An unknown number, well into the millions, died there. At the same time, no less than 20 percent of the camp population was released every year from 1934 to 1953.

The largest Soviet concentration camps were scattered along the geographic extremes of the Soviet Union, though camps existed in virtually every part of the Soviet Union. Gulag inmates performed heavy and largely unskilled labor in mining, forestry, agriculture, and construction. Recent scholarship demonstrates the extreme inefficiency of Gulag labor and the tremendous expense of operating the camp system. None of this prevented the growth of the system, though, because the Gulag was a penal institution first and a productive institution second.

After Stalin's death the Gulag as the massive phenomenon containing millions of prisoners came to an end. Forced-labor camps continued to exist in the Soviet Union right up until the Gorbachev era, but they became much smaller and ever more focused on recidivists and serious criminals. Soviet dissidents made up an important but exceedingly small part of the post-Stalin camp population.

[*See also* Russia, the Russian Empire, and the Soviet Union; *and* Stalinism.]

BIBLIOGRAPHY

Khlevniuk, Oleg V. *The History of the Gulag: From Collectivization to the Great Terror*. Translated by Vadim A. Staklo, with editorial assistance and commentary by David J. Nordlander. New Haven, Conn.: Yale University Press, 2004. An English-language edition of documents from official Soviet archives on the 1930s Gulag.

Solzhenitsyn, Alexander I. *The Gulag Archipelago, 1918–1956: An Experiment in Literary Investigation*. 3 vols. Translated by Thomas P. Whitney. New York: Westview Press, 1991–1992. A combination primary source and secondary source. Still the best single study of the Gulag.

STEVEN A. BARNES

GULF WAR. *See* Desert Shield and Desert Storm.

GUOMINDANG. *See* Nationalist Party.

GYPSIES. *See* Roma.

H

HACIENDA EXPANSION. In Spanish America, the large landed estates that were owned mainly by Europeans and their descendants were called *haciendas* (in Portuguese, *fazenda*). These estates generally mixed agriculture and ranching, and included a dependent labor force of hacienda peons who rented land from the hacienda and paid in cash and labor for their plots. During the modern period, haciendas (if one includes large ranches) became the dominant form of landholding in Latin America, at the expense of peasant smallholdings, frontier lands, and Indian communities. In their heyday in the late nineteenth and early twentieth centuries, haciendas covered around two-thirds of all arable land in the region. Agrarian reforms in the mid-twentieth century largely eliminated the hacienda, though they continued to exist in many countries, such as Argentina and Colombia.

The process of hacienda expansion occurred in jumps and starts and was closely related to indigenous population fluctuation, economic incentives, and most importantly, the political power that landlords could exercise in the Latin American countryside. The first wave of hacienda expansion occurred in the late sixteenth and early seventeenth centuries, when the indigenous population suffered catastrophic decline as diseases brought over from Eurasia and Africa wiped out up to 95 percent of the Indians. Spaniards snapped up abandoned lands and created large estates to supply urban centers and silver mines with foodstuffs and other goods.

The second wave of hacienda expansion took place from the 1720s to the 1780s. As in the earlier period, a series of epidemics among the Indians weakened their grip over their land; it is in this period that in the Andes the Indian population dipped to its lowest numbers in history. Added to the impact of disease were Spanish crown policies in which the crown sold offices to the highest bidder to pay for its European wars. In return, the officers (especially Indian agents called *corregidores de indios*) were permitted to recoup their investments by selling goods to the Indians under their charge. The system lent itself to abuse, as the corregidores sold goods by force to the Indians at highly inflated prices. Many Indians were forced to go into debt and so lost their lands to ambitious landlords. This period of hacienda expansion ended by the 1780s, when a series of Indian rebellions, such as that of Túpac Amaru in Peru, forced the Spanish government to suspend the sale of offices.

The last period of hacienda expansion, in which the hacienda expanded the most, occurred after independence, in the late nineteenth and early twentieth centuries. During this period, the Latin American elites, most of European descent, implemented free trade policies that connected the region to the industrializing North Atlantic countries and provided them with raw materials. The economic boom increased land values. The elites also gained enough resources to equip modern armies and build railroads and telegraphs, which permitted the subjugation of the lower classes. Also, new ideologies imported from Europe, such as social Darwinism, predicated the superiority of Europeans and their descendants and justified the taking of lands from the natives. In the name of modernizing the country, hacienda owners absorbed independent villagers as peons into newly constituted estates. Merchants or landlords indebted villagers and then forced them to sell their land when they could not repay. This created debt peonage, in which workers were unable to pay off their debts and so had to work on the estates for life. In Mexico, the government declared that the village commons belonged to the state and gave them to surveying companies or railroads in return for their services. Frontier expansion also created large estates. The governments of Argentina, Chile, and Mexico authorized national troops to invade frontier territories, taking the land from their indigenous inhabitants and then selling it in great chunks to their cronies while the Indians were either killed, made into peons, or corralled into tiny reservations.

The expansion of the haciendas came to an end by the 1920s. In Mexico, hacienda expansion helped unleash the Mexican Revolution (1910–1940), in which the displaced rural inhabitants rose up against the usurpers. Elsewhere, revolutions engendered land reforms that returned the lands to the peasants, such as in Bolivia (1953), Peru (1969), and Chile (1972). A wave of neoliberal reforms in the late twentieth century again favored the expansion of large estates, such as in Chile (1973) and Mexico (1994), though Venezuela, Bolivia, and to a lesser extent Brazil saw new attempts at eliminating the vestiges of the hacienda.

[*See also* Land, *subentry* Land Reform in Latin America; Liberalism, *subentry* Latin America; Mexican Revolution; Peasants, *subentry* Latin America; *and* Túpac Amaru Rebellion.]

BIBLIOGRAPHY
Huber, Evelyne, and Frank Safford, eds. *Agrarian Structure and Political Power: Landlord and Peasant in the Making of Latin America.* Pittsburgh, Pa.: University of Pittsburgh Press, 1995.
Love, Joseph L., and Nils Jacobsen, eds. *Guiding the Invisible Hand: Economic Liberalism and the State in Latin American History.* New York: Praeger, 1986.

ERICK D. LANGER

HADRAMAWT.

The Hadramawt is the deep valley running parallel to the southern coast of the Arabian Peninsula, between precipitous walls rising to a high plateau that separates it from the narrow coastal plain and on the north from an arid tract merging into the sand desert of the Empty Quarter (al-Rubʾal-Khali) of Arabia.

In 1967 the ancient sultanates of Quaʾiti and Kathiri, the former British colony of Aden and the former Aden protectorate, became an independent Communist state, the People's Republic of South Yemen, later the People's Democratic Republic of Yemen. South Yemen along with Hadramawt was united with North Yemen in 1990 as the Republic of Yemen. The town of Shibam, right on the northwest perimeter of Hadrami territory, owes its importance to commercial and religious factors, since it was the main entrepôt for the incense trade, and a shrine and pilgrimage center. Frankincense, produced in the Mahra country east of Hadramawt, was transported by caravans to the west coast of Arabia for the markets of the Mediterranean and Mesopotamia. The sophisticated culture inherited from Hadramawt patterns of trade and migration was expressed in architecture with tall, mud-brick houses. The houses of Shibam, the oldest "skyscraper city" of the world, are all made out of mud bricks, and about five hundred tower houses still stand, rising five to nine storeys high. Surrounded by a fortified wall, the sixteenth-century city of Shibam is one of the oldest and best examples of urban planning based on the principle of vertical construction.

BIBLIOGRAPHY
Freitag, Ulrike, and William Gervase Clarence-Smith, eds. *Hadrami Traders, Scholars, and Statesmen in the Indian Ocean, 1750s–1960s.* Leiden, The Netherlands: Brill, 1997. A comprehensive collection of essays on the strategic role of Hadramawt.

BEATRICE NICOLINI

HAGUE PEACE CONFERENCES.

The two Hague Peace Conferences of 1899 and 1907 originated in an 1898 proposal for a disarmament conference made by the Russian tsar Nicholas II (r. 1894–1917).

Motivations. Inevitably, the tsar's motives were subjected to much cynical scrutiny by the other Great Powers, but it is likely that genuine idealism played some part, alongside more immediate concerns about Russia falling behind in the escalating arms race of this period. A particular apprehension was that Russia might not be able to compete with one of its main enemies, Austria-Hungary, at that time embarked on a major process of military modernization. However, the proposal also fitted the mood of the times in two important respects. First, what would much later come to be known as "transnational civil society"—the network of nonstate actors ranging from broad coalitions like the women's movement to single-issue activist organizations—was playing an increasingly influential role in setting the political agenda, especially in the more democratic states. Second, there was a growing awareness of the interconnectedness of what had once been seen as distinctive political, social, and economic domains and that ever-rising military expenditure might have adverse consequences such as unemployment and social unrest that might be exploited by radical political movements.

Something of this thinking was captured by the opening address of the president of the first conference, Georges de Staal: "We perceive that there is a community of material and moral interests between nations, which is constantly increasing. . . . If a nation wished to remain isolated it could not. . . . It is part of a single organism." The most important implication of this interdependence was, he felt, that "when a dispute arises between two or more nations, the others, without being directly involved, are seriously affected." This, in his view, meant that further machinery for states to submit their disputes for mediation, conciliation, or arbitration needed to be developed. The two other items on the agenda of the first conference were reform of the laws of war, which had not been changed since the Geneva conventions of 1864 and 1868, and, most important so far as the tsar and public opinion were concerned, disarmament.

Results. The conferences were the most widely attended to date, with twenty-six states attending the first, including the United States, China, Japan, Siam, and Mexico, and forty-three the second, with a much larger South American contingent. Partly because of this global representation, the conferences developed new modes of conducting their affairs that sought to move away from the Great-Power domination that characterized the main European conferences of the nineteenth century toward procedures that permitted wider participation based on the principle of equality among states. These innovations, which included dividing up business between three committees, considering disarmament, the laws of war, and arbitration respectively, were among the contributions of the conferences to later multilateral diplomacy.

Disarmament and controlling the development of military technology were always going to be the most difficult issues before the conferences. Although many delegates echoed the tsar's original sentiments, they found it harder to agree on the concrete obligations their states would have to accept if these principles were to be given substance. Not atypical in this regard were the instructions given to the American delegation by Secretary of State John Hay, who saw many of the specific proposals as impractical, and, at least in the case of prohibiting new military technology, not necessarily liable to produce the desired result, quite apart from his doubts about "the expediency of restraining the inventive genius of our people." Indeed, all subsequent disarmament and arms control negotiations have encountered the same kinds of problems: how to allow for completely new technology, how to calculate different force equivalences, and how to implement effective inspection and verification procedures. In the event, the first conference was only able to agree on three declarations: prohibiting dropping bombs from balloons, using projectiles to diffuse poisonous gases, and firing bullets that flattened on impact, such as the "dumdum" bullet favored by the British army.

The conferences were also able to agree to some further codification of the laws of war, including, in 1899, in the so-called Martens Clause: the strongest (if still somewhat vague) affirmation to date that states are bound by broad humanitarian considerations and "the dictates of the public conscience" in their conduct of war. The first conference extended the laws of war to naval warfare, while the second

conference added provisions extending them to militia and volunteer forces—an issue that was to assume increasing importance after 1945.

Arguably the greatest achievement of the first conference was the Convention for the Pacific Settlement of International Disputes. This set out various procedures by which states in dispute might seek a peaceful resolution, including accepting the "good offices" of third parties and, in the case of disputes "involving neither honor nor essential interests and arising from a difference of opinion on points of fact," commissions of inquiry. Potentially most important was the establishment of a so-called Permanent Court of Arbitration. In reality this was little more than a mechanism under which states could make use of a list of respected arbitrators, but it did attempt to institutionalize the practice of arbitration, which went back to the ancient Greeks and had been increasingly used in the nineteenth century, especially in Anglo-American relations.

The true significance of the conferences is hard to gauge. Military spending rose sharply between 1899 and 1907 and continued to do so up to World War I. Relatively little use was made of the new disputes procedures, with only eight cases submitted to arbitration before 1914, only one of which involved a potentially serious Great Power conflict (the Dogger Bank incident between Russia and Britain). Moreover, when the League of Nations was being constructed at the 1919 Paris Peace Conference, the Hague experience was generally ignored, especially by the British and Americans, who argued that the League needed to be free from association with previous ventures. Nonetheless, the conferences may be seen as marking two important points of departure in international relations whose significance did not really become apparent until after 1945. Its procedural innovations helped to usher in a new era of multilateral diplomacy in which the voices of smaller states could be more audible. Secondly, the conferences constituted the first faltering recognition by the international community that many aspects of their relations with each other needed to come under clearer and more effective legal regimes.

[*See also* Arms Limitation and Control; Geneva Conventions; Law, International; Military, *subentry* Military Technology; Red Cross; *and* War Crimes.]

BIBLIOGRAPHY

Armstrong, David. *The Rise of the International Organisation: A Short History*. London: Macmillan, 1982.

Best, Geoffrey. "Peace Conferences and the Century of Total War: The 1899 Hague Conference and What Came After." *International Affairs* 75, no. 3 (1999): 619–634.

Rosenne, Shabtai, ed. *The Hague Peace Conferences of 1899 and 1907 and International Arbitration: Reports and Documents.* The Hague: T. M. C. Asser; Norwell, Mass.: Kluwer Law International, 2001.

Scott, James Brown, ed. *The Proceedings of the Hague Conferences: The Conference of 1899.* New York: Oxford University Press, 1920. Out of print but available at many university libraries.

Scott, James Brown, ed. *Reports of the Hague Conferences of 1899 and 1907.* Oxford: Clarendon Press, 1917. Out of print but available at many university libraries.

DAVID ARMSTRONG

HAIFA. Israel's third-largest city (with a population of approximately 270,000), the area in and around modern Haifa was intermittently settled from as early as the fourteenth century B.C.E. Refounded by the regional Ottoman ruler Zahir al-ʿUmar in 1761, this mixed Muslim and Christian Arab city gained in size and prestige over the following century owing to the expansion of its shipping trade. In the years preceding World War I, rapid commercial and industrial development led Zionists and British diplomats alike to look upon Haifa as the Mediterranean port of the future. Economic modernization continued apace under British rule, exemplified by the opening of a new harbor in 1933 and completion of an Iraqi oil pipeline terminus six years later. During the 1920s and 1930s Haifa's Jewish and Arab populations both grew dramatically, with the once-small Jewish minority reaching near parity by 1939.

As elsewhere, the intersection of Jewish settlement with Arab urbanization held the potential for conflict. Yet Haifa in the era of the British Mandate could also claim a uniquely successful record of joint municipal relations, in large part because of its mayor, Hasan bey Shukri. This spirit of cooperation evaporated in the late 1930s, a product both of the Arab revolt in Palestine and efforts at "Judaization" of the city by Zionist authorities. During the final years of the Mandate, the city's port became a staging post for the attempted immigration of Jewish displaced persons as well as a target of Jewish guerrilla attacks against British industrial installations. Mass departures of the Arab population occurred in 1947 and early 1948; scholars disagree as to what, if any, role was played by Jewish authorities. Following statehood, Haifa gradually regained a substantial Arab minority. It has also remained the international center of the Bahaʾi sect. Still a hub of industrial activity, the city's shipping has declined owing to the ongoing Arab boycott and the expansion of Israel's southern port, Ashdod.

[*See also* Bahaʾi Faith *and* Israel.]

BIBLIOGRAPHY

Goren, Tamir. "'Cooperation Is the Guiding Principle': Jews and Arabs in the Haifa Municipality during the British Mandate." *Israel Studies* 11, no. 3 (2006): 108–141.

Goren, Tamir. "The Judaization of Haifa at the Time of the Arab Revolt." *Middle Eastern Studies* 40, no. 4 (2004): 135–152.

Seikaly, May. *Haifa: Transformation of an Arab Society, 1918–1939.* New ed. London: I. B. Tauris, 2002.

Yazbak, Mahmoud. *Haifa in the Late Ottoman period, 1864–1914: A Muslim Town in Transition.* Leiden, The Netherlands, and Boston: Brill, 1998.

SHIRA SCHNITZER

HAIKU. A Japanese poetic form consisting of seventeen syllables arranged in three metrical units of five, seven, and five syllables each, haiku derived from classical *haikai* (comic linked verse), the humorous form of *renga* (courtly linked verse). *Haikai* distinguished itself from courtly poetry by its emphasis on wit and its use of nonclassical language (*haigon*).

In *haikai*'s heyday in the sixteenth through eighteenth centuries, poets normally worked in groups, creating chains of verses where each link was composed extemporaneously in response to the one that preceded it. However, the *hokku* (starting verse)—the opening seventeen-syllable verse that referred to the season and circumstances of the sequence's composition—could be written separately and in advance. In the seventeenth century, poets took to writing *hokku* independently of sequences, and by the mid-nineteenth century the *hokku* became the dominant form of *haikai*.

At the end of the nineteenth century, a reform movement led by the poet Masaoka Shiki (1867–1902) established a modern form based on the *hokku*, called haiku. The haiku retained two of its predecessor's conventions—the seventeen-syllable form and inclusion of a conventional seasonal word (*kigo*)—but its thematic scope was broadened to make it better suited to expressing the experiences of the modern world. In the twentieth century, haiku became popular internationally as well as in Japan, and though each successive generation has experimented with modifications, the seventeen-syllable, season-focused form has remained relatively constant.

The most celebrated Japanese masters of haiku are Matsuo Bashō (1644–1694), Yosa Buson (1716–1783), Kobayashi Issa (1763–1827), and Masaoka Shiki (1867–1902).

[*See also* Japanese Literature *and* Poetry.]

BIBLIOGRAPHY
Blyth, R. H. *A History of Haiku* (1963). 2 vols. Tokyo: Hokuseido Press, 1998. Somewhat dated but still regarded as a classic introduction. Volume 1 traces the development of haiku from its origins in *renga* up to Issa; volume 2 concentrates on nineteenth- and early-twentieth-century haiku.

CHERYL CROWLEY

HAITI. The country known today as the Republic of Haiti occupies the western third of the island that was called Haiti, Quisqueya, or Bohio by the natives that the Europeans found there in 1492. Haiti has an area of about 10,700 square miles (27,750 square kilometers), with 8.2 million inhabitants, and is situated in the Greater Antilles chain in the Caribbean Sea. The remaining two-thirds of the island is occupied by the Dominican Republic.

Haiti was a French colony from 1625 to 1804. A slave uprising that began in 1791 concluded with an antislavery and anticolonial revolution, and the making of an independent state on 1 January 1804. Haiti took its first steps into the international arena amid hostility from the colonial powers and slavery interests of the period. France ordered an international boycott of the fledgling state, and the United States subjected it to an embargo until 1810. In the twentieth century it faced several foreign interventions, and in the early twenty-first century a United Nations peacekeeping force was there.

Early Years and Modernization Attempts. The task at hand after independence was colossal. Early efforts focused on the international recognition of the country as well as on its military defense. While the leaders were setting up schools and establishing state institutions, they were also constructing forts and citadels against a French invasion. For approximately twenty years no world power recognized Haiti as an independent state. In 1825, France agreed to recognize it in exchange for the payment of 150 million gold francs. With great difficulty Haiti paid this sum, but it represented a massive drain on its economy. England recognized Haiti in 1833, followed by the Holy See in 1860 and the United States in 1862, during the Civil War.

Subsequent to the international recognition, young intellectuals began to rethink the political, economic, and social foundations of the Haitian state. Such men as Edmond Paul, Demesvar Delorme, Louis-Joseph Janvier, and Anténor Firmin, to name just a few, proposed changes in structure and made proposals for modernization. Their ideas and proposals were opposed by others, and stifled by political realism, and failed to materialize. The advocates of a shortsighted business bourgeoisie, many being of foreign extraction or linked to their various countries of origin, were also unable to modernize the country. Many of them pulled the strings of the ruling generals and preferred to invest their capital in periodic military reviews, using political instability as a means of enrichment. At the end of the nineteenth century, Haiti was a vassal state, at the mercy of foreign powers. France, England, Germany, and the United States also disputed their international hegemony on Haitian soil.

Initially, Haiti sank deeper into French neocolonialism. Soon after independence, Haiti's power elite turned to France, seeking inspiration, education, aestheticism, and capital. The French educational system was adopted. Similarly, Haitian laws, codes, and modes of government were based on the French model. French merchants enjoyed the privileged status of "most favored nation." In 1880 the Haitian government charged a consortium of French capitalists with the establishment of the Bank of the Republic of Haiti (BNRH). Though headquartered in Paris, this bank had the privilege of issuing currency for the Haitian state and was also responsible for collecting taxes. Moreover, from 1825 to 1911 all foreign loans approved by the Haitian state were consistently floated, at usurious rates, on the French Stock Exchange.

Francophile Movement and U.S. Hegemony. In the nineteenth century the Haitian elite embarked on a Francophile movement extolling the merits of the French language and culture, promoting Haiti as France's spiritual daughter or the Black France of the Americas. In an effort to protect the country from covetousness on the part of the powers with which the Haitian elite believed it did not share the same cultural preferences, the elite proposed a strategic alliance with France, which was not accepted by France. Ultimately, the country found itself isolated, both defenseless and lacking the capital to embark on a large-scale modernization.

American capital trickled in after 1906, preceded by American merchants, who had been established in the country for several years. American political influence was already apparent in the 1890s. France progressively lost its traditional political and financial hegemony to the United States, which in 1898 had become an international power and was already carrying out military interventions in the Caribbean. The United States took possession of the BNRH in 1910–1911. In 1915 a political crisis in presidential succession provided the opportunity for the United States to occupy Haiti.

Controversies and the Search for National Identity. The American occupation lasted nineteen years. The occupants controlled the country's tax revenues, encouraged political and financial reform, and stimulated state investments. But the changes were small, and the foreign occupiers were racist. Deception and dissatisfaction reigned. Resistance to the occupation, which started from the very beginning among the peasants in the northern region of the country, received the support of members of the elite in 1919, with the launch of the Patriotic Union. The country emerged from its ashes, and a vast nationalistic and cultural political movement materialized. At a time when most Haitians were demanding that the Americans leave, they were also discovering a new cultural identity, promoting within its national culture African elements that had been long neglected or ignored. This marked the emergence of Négritude, which Dr. Jean Price-Mars codified in 1928 in his book *Ainsi parla l'oncle*.

This cultural movement led to several schools of thought and also became the political ideology of young intellectuals and professionals from the middle classes, who claimed black power on behalf of the degraded black masses who had been exploited by the traditional elite. From 1946 to 1950 the government of Dumarsais Estimé used Négritude in a more positive manner than the Duvalier regime, which in 1964 established a hereditary presidency for life and a politically authoritarian, economically regressive, and socially repressive administration.

The Duvalier dictatorship collapsed in 1986. From that moment Haiti entered into a long period of transition. Jean-Bertrand Aristide's democratic election to the presidency in 1990 was met with hope. However, a few months later he was removed following a military coup. In 1994, after a three-year international embargo that proved catastrophic for the Haitian economy, once again U.S. troops, followed by UN troops, occupied the country, reinstating Aristide. His handling of power proved to be modeled on that of the previous authoritarian regimes. Faced with a vast political protest movement, Aristide left the country. In 2004, U.S. troops returned once more, subsequently making way for the United Nations Mission to Haiti (MINUSTAH).

Haiti has experienced many convulsive moments in its two centuries of existence. Surprisingly, it achieved better

Haiti. Former President Jean-Bertrand Aristide and his wife Mildred Aristide are surrounded by children from his orphanage at his home in Tabar, Haiti, October 1996. Photograph by Daniel Morel. AP IMAGES

results in the nineteenth century than in the twentieth. In the nineteenth century, Haitians established political and educational institutions that contributed to the advancement of their country. There was an attempt at modernization from 1889 to 1896, which Anténor Firmin and the movement known as Firminism could have sustained if not opposed by foreign powers and their local allies.

In the twentieth century, Haiti experienced foreign interventions and dictatorial regimes, while the country regressed. During the first intervention, the Americans instituted the Gendarmerie d'Haiti, a military police corps that is often considered a native occupation force catering to foreign interests. From 1946 on, the corps started to play an openly political role in the country, promoting authoritarian regimes. It was involved in the various coups d'état until its demobilization during the second American occupation.

In sum, in the twentieth century Haitians lost control of their country. Furthermore, they were uncertain as to whether they should pursue their traditional Francophilia or insert themselves into the American world. The choice has always been a difficult one, just as it has also been difficult to reach an agreement on a long-term development plan.

Contemporary Haiti. The Haitian government in the early twenty-first century faced armed groups established in the slums, which challenged the authority of the state and defied UN forces. The historical social exclusion of the subaltern classes practiced by the elites in power was perhaps the greatest problem facing Haitian society.

Haiti today endures poor public health, illiteracy, and basic infrastructural problems. Exports are diminishing considerably, whereas imports are increasing. Tourism, which greatly flourished in the past, has lost its luster. Investments are lacking, and unemployment is raging— at the beginning of the twenty-first century, around 60 percent of the economically active population. Money transfers from the Haitian diaspora to their families in the country cushion a moribund economy, plagued by inflation and unstable exchange rates. The *Madan Sara*, female merchants of the informal economy, play a significant role in keeping the Haitian economy alive. These problems notwithstanding, the strength of the artistic and intellectual production in Haiti during its two centuries of history has never failed.

[*See also* Caribbean, *subentry* United States Relations with Caribbean Nations; Dominican Republic; *and* Haitian Revolution.]

BIBLIOGRAPHY

Blancpain, François. *Un siècle de relations financières entre Haïti et la France (1825–1922)*. Paris: L'Harmattan, 2001.

Denis, Watson R. "Les 100 ans de Monsieur Roosevelt et Haïti: Comment Anténor Firmin posa les fondements des études et des relations haitiano-américaines." *Revue de la Société Haïtienne d'Histoire et de Géographie* 81, no. 226 (July–September 2006): 1–41.

Denis, Watson R. "Miradas de mutua desconfianza entre dos repúblicas americanas: El expansionismo marítimo de los Estados-Unidos frente a la francofilia haitiana, 1888–1898." PhD diss., University of Puerto Rico–Rió Piedras Campus, UMI, 2004.

Gaillard, Roger. *La république exterminatrice*. Vol. 2: *L'état vassal*. Port-au-Prince, Haiti: Imprimerie le Natal, 1988.

Hector, Michel, and Jean Casimir. "Le long XIXe siècle Haïtien." *Itinéraires*, special edition, December 2004, pp. 37–56.

Manigat, Leslie. "La substitution de la prépondérance américaine à la prépondérance française au début du XXè siècle: La conjoncture de 1910–1911." *Revue d'Histoire Moderne et Contemporaine* 14 (October–December 1967): 321–355.

Nicholls, David. *From Dessalines to Duvalier: Race, Colour, and National Independence in Haiti*. Cambridge, U.K., and New York: Cambridge University Press, 1979.

Plummer, Brenda Gayle. "The Metropolitan Connexion: Foreign and Semiforeign Elites in Haiti, 1900–1915." *Latin American Research Review* 19, no. 2 (1984): 119–142.

Price-Mars, Jean. *So Spoke the Uncle* (1928). Translated by Magdaline W. Shannon. Washington, D.C.: Three Continents, Press, 1983.

Turnier, Alain. *Les Etats-Unis et le marché Haïtien*. Washington, D.C.: Imprimerie Saint-Joseph (Montréal), 1955.

WATSON R. DENIS

HAITIAN REVOLUTION. As was the case with several colonies in the Caribbean in the eighteenth century, the French colony of Saint-Domingue was driven primarily by an agricultural export economy. Saint-Domingue produced coffee, cocoa, cotton, indigo, and sugarcane. However, toward 1750, given the sustained demand for sugar on the European market, sugarcane surpassed all other crops. In Saint-Domingue the topic of the day was the "Sugar Revolution," just as the "Industrial Revolution" was the topic of the day in England. Sugarcane was one of the factors that changed not only the slave relationship but also the political and economic structures in Saint-Domingue.

From small farms (*minifundia*) in the beginning, sugarcane first transformed Saint-Domingue into a system of large farms (*latifundia*) and then into a plantation economy where agricultural crops blended with industrial production. The authorities in the metropolis had enabled French capitalists to set up workshops and factories in the colony, and thereafter some slaves worked in the new agro-industrial plants. Others even received wages and small lands in order to meet their needs. At the same time, the slave trade intensified and more slaves were landed in the colony.

The French merchant marine became very active, transporting a large number of commodities and products from Saint-Domingue to France; these were refined by French industries and later distributed on the European market. The yields were significant for the metropolis and for French merchants, who invested more and more in the colony. Saint-Domingue became a thriving economy. In 1788 its exports reached 214 million francs, or the equivalent then of about $42 million, surpassing even U.S. exports. Saint-Domingue became the jewel of the French colonial empire and supplied France with half of the wealth it derived from all of its colonies combined.

Slavery and capitalism coexisted as a hybrid system. It was difficult to reconcile the means of capitalist production with the social relations of slavery. Another complex issue for Saint-Domingue was that it was built on a hierarchical view of social relations. In 1789, Saint-Domingue consisted of 40,000 whites, 28,000 *Affranchis*—colored and black freemen—and 450,000 slaves, but skin color determined social status. This racial construct would collapse like a pack of cards.

In 1789, Saint-Domingue was plagued by a number of contradictions. The great white planters demanded political autonomy. The *Affranchis*, most of whom were landowners, clamored for civil and political equality with the whites. The slaves looked for freedom. Brought from Africa, they toiled on plantations and in production workshops and were at the mercy of the overseer's whip. On the night of 21–22 August 1791, following a political movement in the North Province under the leadership of a certain Boukman, slaves set fire to the plantations and attacked their masters. The insurrection spread to the West and South Provinces.

The fight waged by the slaves became more structured with the emergence of Toussaint-Louverture. As the commander of an army that he personally organized, he became a powerful figure in the colony. From 1794 to 1802, Toussaint-Louverture led the combat. In order to keep Saint-Domingue within its colonial empire, the French authorities came to terms with Toussaint-Louverture, promoting him to the rank of general in chief of the Saint-Domingue army and, later, governor. In such a position of power, he made freedom of blacks the focus of his international policy and made the revival of production the focus of his domestic policy.

Toussaint-Louverture forged an autonomous policy vis-à-vis France. In 1801, without the backing of French authorities, he entered the eastern side of the island, then under Spanish domination, and abolished slavery there. In the same year he promulgated a constitution for the entire island with immediate application. Nonetheless, he sent it to France for approval by Napoleon Bonaparte. In response, Napoleon deployed twenty-two thousand troops and eighty-six warships in order to subdue Toussaint-Louverture and restore slavery in the colony and in all the other French dependencies of America. The troops also had a mission to expand the French colonial empire in America, going from Saint-Domingue up to the former French possessions along the Mississippi.

The revolutionaries of Saint-Domingue were unable to withstand the assault of the French troops. Toussaint-Louverture was arrested for treason in 1802 and sent to France, where he died. When leaving Saint-Domingue, Toussaint-Louverture declared: "By overthrowing me, you have merely succeeded in cutting the trunk of

Haitian Revolution. "Revenge taken by the Black Army for the Cruelties practised on them by the French," illustration from Marcus Rainsford, *An Historical Account of the Black Empire of Hayti* (London: J. Cundee, 1805), page 337. PRINTS AND PHOTO-GRAPHS DIVISION, LIBRARY OF CONGRESS

Saint-Domingue's Tree of Liberty; but it will grow again, for the roots are deep, and many."

Prophetic words from the old leader! The resistance of the indigenous army, under the leadership of General Jean-Jacques Dessalines, changed direction: from autonomy to independence. After two years, French troops capitulated to the ragged troops of Saint-Domingue. On 1 January 1804 the independence of the colony was proclaimed under the aboriginal name of Haiti. For the first time in the history of humanity, an uprising of slaves had led to a victorious revolution. Thus Haiti became the first state to proclaim the abolition of slavery. Haiti was the first black republic of the world and was the second republic in the Western Hemisphere after the United States.

The consequences of the Haitian Revolution were considerable. It sounded the death knell for slavery throughout the world and weakened colonialism in the Americas. For example, in 1805 the Venezuelan revolutionary Francisco de Miranda received assistance from General Jean-Jacques Dessalines to liberate South America from the yoke of Spain. Similarly, in 1815 the liberator Simón Bolívar received substantial aid from the Haitian president Alexandre Pétion to fight for freedom and independence in Latin America. The Haitian Revolution remains one of the greatest revolutions of modern times and changed the perspective of human beings on slavery, colonialism, and man's exploitation of man.

[*See also* Atlantic Revolutions; Empire and Imperialism, *subentry* The French Colonial Empire; Haiti; Plantations; Slavery, *subentry* Latin America; *and* Sugar.]

BIBLIOGRAPHY

Cesaire, Aimé. *Toussaint-Louverture: La révolution française et le problème colonial.* Paris: Présence Africaine, 1962.

Corbaba-Bello, Eléazar. *La independencia de Haití y su influencia en Hispanoamérica.* Caracas, Venezuela: Instituto Panamericano de la Geografía y Historia, 1967.

Denis, Watson R. "La représentation de la Révolution Haïtienne dans le monde occidental." *Itinéraires,* special edition, December 2004, pp. 58–63.

Fick, Carolyn E. *The Making of Haiti: The Saint-Domingue Revolution from Below.* Knoxville: University of Tennessee Press, 1990.

Geggus, David P., ed. *The Impact of the Haitian Revolution in the Atlantic World.* Columbia: University of South Carolina Press, 2001.

Hector, Michel. *La Révolution Française et Haïti: Filiations, ruptures, nouvelles dimensions.* 2 vols. Port-au-Prince, Haiti: Editions Henri Deschamps, 1995.

WATSON R. DENIS

HAMAS. *See* Palestine.

HANDICAPS. "Handicaps" is a technical term that can be understood only in what has come to be known as its social context—that is, a set of various dimensions (individual, social, religious, sexual, political, historical) related to the practical concerns that give the term meaning.

Adoption of the Term "Handicap" or, More Recently, "Disability." The close of the nineteenth century revealed the destructive effects of industrialization, which included accidents and risks in general. Work accidents formed the nucleus of a debate taking place in a society that was changing from naturalistic, where mishaps were dealt with by acts of charity, to more of an insurance mentality; there was a shift in responsibility from personal fault to a societal responsibility that views ill fortune as a claim upon the social contract. The issue of on-the-job injuries lies at the heart of the friction between the old and the new ways in which people understand their behavior, their relationships, their conflicts, and their collaboration. Industrial society, realizing its own power, acknowledged the emergence of hitherto unrecognized obligations, which became known collectively in mid-twentieth-century Europe as "social security."

In some countries this new social reality, with its issues of risk and responsibility, resulted in reliance upon the state as a sort of providence, whatever institutional forms that providence might take. It also led everywhere in the West to a new standardization based on a statistical definition of "average." The theory of the average man ushered in an age where perfection was equated with normality, where the great goal of society was to become standardized. "Perfection," "duty," "good," and "well-being" came to mean being within the norms and the average.

This way of thinking transformed society's view of what was known as "infirmity." Infirmity was no longer an absolute condition but instead was defined by its distance from the norm—a distance, moreover, that could vary in terms of its burden and threat. In this theory, the negative vocabulary of "infirmity," "incapacity," "inability," and so forth, gradually yielded to a vocabulary that expressed the new social philosophy of risk, responsibility, insurance, compensation, and reparation—that is, of making up one's losses.

The calamity of World War I reinforced this vision. The countries involved in the conflict were left with at least 5 million wounded. What to do with all of these injured people? Two responses developed: disability pensions and vocational retraining. The terms "reassignment," "reeducation," "readaptation," "rehabilitation," "reinsertion," and "reintegration" marked a new social orientation vis-à-vis the infirm. Even if the negative vocabulary did not completely disappear, the degree to which the new vocabulary replaced it is remarkable. In fact, the prefix "re-" indicates a return to the person's preinjury status, hence the person's return to social normality and the common life. The former images of the infirm as poor, beggars, or at least the objects of charity were erased in favor of that of a person having a right to assistance, a person who was wounded in the service of society.

Finally, yet one more development came into play: compulsory education. As school, with its grades and levels, became progressively standardized, and as the well-known intelligence tests measured this progress, those persons who for one reason or another could not adapt to the common mentality of the standard school became more visible. Thus the concern with normalization continued to increase.

Adoption of a Handicap Vocabulary. A handicap vocabulary appeared in North America at the beginning of the twentieth century. To mention just one example: the *New York Times* during the years 1905 to 1908 devoted a number of articles to the "handicapped," the word being used in its current sense of persons disadvantaged because of some infirmity. These articles describe efforts to help these people return to work and a normal social life. In 1920, a newspaper called *Handicapped Worker* appeared in New York. All the evidence seems to point to a close connection between this terminology and the consequences of industrialization and war.

To return to the situation in Europe, the adoption of this racetrack vocabulary seems to have passed first through a literary usage of the word "handicap" to mean any kind of situation of inferiority or disadvantage suffered by one group or person in relation to another. Not until the 1950s and especially the 1960s did the handicap vocabulary blossom out and expand to apply to instances of deficiency and incapacity. This led to a sense of the need to reinsert such persons into social and professional life.

Once this necessity imposed itself on society, a second necessity arose from it: the need for actions and techniques (educational, functional, prosthetic) that could accomplish the task of normalizing such persons sufficiently to restore them to the status of average citizens. On the one hand, industrial society, with its market economy, now recognized work as the sole source of income and social recognition. On the other hand, this same society favored protection based on redistribution and contribution—that is, on insurance in a broad sense. Everyone who could do so

was expected to acquire, or to reacquire, the level of performance needed to be a fully participating citizen. Add to this the social expectations concerning appearance and physical beauty, as well as success by merit (whereby everything is obtained by examination, competition, or personal force), and a vast panorama emerges where every lack, every fault, every nonconformity must be fought, suppressed, stopped, compensated, or done away with.

Thus the racetrack terminology of "handicap" is striking; it allows infirmity to be defined as an obstacle imposed from outside but also able to be tamed. It implies that there is a course to be followed, a desire for equalization, so that even the most disparate of situations can be made comparable by applying external techniques and resources to them. The notion of handicap, to the extent that it joins together various situations that had historically been viewed as distinct (sensory deficiencies being different from motor or intellectual deficiencies), tends to define itself by the idea of maximum participation for all, of standardization to an average, of a level of performance to be reached.

The horse race, with its implications of competition, training, equal chances, and performance, is both a telling metaphor and a model that reveals much about the general perception of infirmity in the twentieth century. A handicapped race is one in which clearly unequal contestants are placed on an equal footing. And the metaphor can be carried further. Out of the entire pool of citizens, one particular subgroup is selected, just as racehorses are drawn from the general horse population. The chief purpose of this selection is to improve this subgroup, which is then grouped into different classes. Each class has its own particular forms and techniques of training and building skills—a distinct specialization. Finally, there is a test, to see whether the candidate is fit to take an equal part in the common competition. Contemporary society finds in this model a way of bridging the gap presented by infirmity. The infirm are viewed as citizens expected to perform; they are thus regarded as subjects who can, and even should, succeed. The concept of infirmity as a handicap is society's way of situating it in the framework of productive, technological, and commercial rationality, and thus admitting it into society in spite of everything.

Recent Developments and Comparisons among Different Countries. The end of this mode of thought is already coming into view. Various obstacles—sheer numbers and the severity of the infirmities that medicine, surgery, and prevention can now deal with—have all increased, while at the same time certain risks have become catastrophic. All of these factors conspire to make the standardization project impossible. In addition, the social model of disability has now come to the fore. This model gives primary importance to the social and environmental factors involved in defining handicaps, and consequently it implies a struggle against social barriers of every kind in order to make all of society totally accessible. Insistence on this point has led to new classifications that have come into being since the 1990s.

The emphasis on social and environmental factors has its origin in the activism of the persons concerned. A strong movement of speaking out and claiming rights began at the University of California, Berkeley, in the 1970s, called independent living. This movement, in turn, engendered the Disabled People's International, which sent representatives to the United Nations in the 1980s. Not only did the movement influence the recommendations of the United Nations, but also it spread to Great Britain and thence into the Council of Europe and the European Disability Forum. From that point on, emphasis was placed on nondiscrimination. The principle of nondiscrimination implies as well the idea that the persons involved should participate in all plans and decisions that concern them (the concept of empowerment) and the idea of peer emulation, because these ideas enable the handicapped to take their fate into their own hands. In this view, the need for accessibility of all public spaces for everyone ("universal design") becomes particularly urgent.

It can readily be seen that this approach to handicaps— defined by the deficiencies of the individual, predominantly medical, and having as its sole purpose compensation for the results of disease and accidents—is too narrow. A change in terminology is required. In France an attempt has been made to introduce the notion of a handicapped situation, so as to define the handicap not as an identity but as the relationship between an individual's characteristics and the environment. The English-speaking world has adopted the term "disability," which does not mean incapacity (unabled) as much as differently abled; the term carries connotations of social barriers. Since the person is simply differently abled, his or her capacities depend largely on external factors. Not all languages have the same resources, and each one must find the vocabulary that best suits its cultural setting.

What has become increasingly common is the idea of interaction among different factors, some of them being personal (both physical/functional and social/lifestyle) and others being collective and environmental (religion, climate, pollution, social interpretations of disability).

Different countries are in different situations. Some are more advanced in terms of the accessibility of public spaces (North America and Europe), others in terms of education (Italy) or professional life (Germany or France). Some have been more concerned with civil rights (voting access in Ireland, for example), others with access to sexuality (Belgium, Quebec, Switzerland). Each one has its strong and weak points. However, a consensus is emerging: internal and external factors interact to limit or promote certain physical and mental attitudes, realms of activity, and participation in social and political life for the disabled. The most important thing would seem to be to discover where these factors interact; this place may change according to time and circumstances. By all evidence, the handicap model developed in the mid-twentieth century has seen its day.

[*See also* Disability *and* Health and Disease.]

BIBLIOGRAPHY

Albrecht, Gary, Jean-François Ravaud, and Henri-Jacques Stiker. "L'émergence des disability studies, état des lieux et perspectives." *Sciences Sociales et Santé* 19, no. 4 (December 2001): 15.

De Jong, Gerben. *Handicap in a Social World*. Milton Keynes, U.K.: Hodder and Stoughton in association with Open University Press, 1979.

Fougeyrollas, Patrick, René Cloutier, Hélène Bergeron, Jacques Côté, and Ginette Saint Michel. *Processus de Production du Handicap*. Quebec: RIPPH/SCCIDIH, 1998.

Ingstad, Benedicte, and Susan Reynolds White. *Disability and Culture*. Berkeley: University of California Press, 1995.

Mauss, Marcel. "Rapports réels et pratiques de la psychologie et de la sociologie." In *Sociologie et anthropologie*, p. 293. Paris: PUF, 1950.

Oliver, Mike. *The Politics of Disablement*. London: Macmillan, 1990.

Ravaud, Jean-François, and Henri-Jacques Stiker. "Inclusion/ Exclusion: An Analysis of Historical and Cultural Meanings." In *Handbook of Disability Studies*, edited by Gary L. Albrecht, Katherine Seelman, and Michael Bury. Thousand Oaks, Calif.: Sage Publications, 2001.

Stiker, Henri-Jacques. *Corps infirmes et sociétés essais d'anthropologie historique*. 3d ed. Paris: Dunod, 2005. An English translation is available: *A History of Disability*, translated by William Sayers (Ann Arbor: University of Michigan Press, 1999).

World Health Organization. *International Classification of Functioning, Disability, and Health*. Geneva, Switzerland, 2001.

HENRI-JACQUES STIKER
Translated from the French by Johanna M. Baboukis

HANOI. Hanoi is the capital of the Socialist Republic of Vietnam and has been a political and cultural center for the Vietnamese since its founding in the early eleventh century. The city served as capital of the Vietnamese state until 1802 when the Nguyen dynasty came to power and selected the more centrally located city of Hue as its political seat. Hanoi was relegated to secondary status, serving only as an administrative center for the northern region of the country. When the French captured the city in 1873 as part of their graduated conquest of Vietnam, they restored the city's political primacy, designating it as capital of their greater Indochina colony comprising Laos, Cambodia, and the central and northern parts of the Vietnam protectorate.

The colonial regime aggressively transformed Hanoi into a city worthy of its new modern role. Although elements of the old city were retained, including the thirty-six merchant guild streets that make up the city's current historical core, the French dramatically altered the cityscape. Centuries-old temples were torn down, and lakes and canals were filled in to make way for wide tree-lined boulevards and grand administrative buildings. As a French political center, Hanoi became the site of educational and social transformations that remade Vietnamese urban society. From the Tonkin Free School, led by an early generation of scholar-patriots, to the later University of Indochina and a handful of secondary schools, art institutes, and medical facilities, the city introduced many Vietnamese to European ways of life and thought. At the same time Hanoi helped shape Vietnamese anticolonialism, for its schools produced revolutionaries and its colonial villas served to highlight the divide between rulers and ruled.

Although the Japanese occupation of Vietnam during World War II had little impact on the city, Hanoi rose to prominence again in late August 1945 when Communist-dominated Vietminh forces took the city in the aftermath of the Japanese surrender. The Vietminh made Hanoi the center of their new revolutionary government until December 1946, when returning French troops forced Ho Chi Minh's government to abandon the city. This commenced the First Indochina War (1946–1954), which dragged on until the French surrender at Dien Bien Phu in May 1954. The division of Vietnam at the Geneva Conference later that year transformed Hanoi into the capital of what emerged as North Vietnam (Democratic Republic of Vietnam, or DRV), and it soon became a city at war. From 1966 until 1972, during the Second Indochina War, Hanoi was subjected to frequent and devastating bombardment by American B-52s, a campaign that led DRV authorities to evacuate much of the city and its industrial base. Although numerous neighborhoods were destroyed in the American air campaigns, the historical city core was spared, as was much of its population.

After the war Hanoi regained its status as capital of the reunified Vietnam. Despite its political status, Hanoi's initial postwar economic recovery was slow, accelerating only in the 1990s, when it became the site of considerable foreign investment. This economic resurgence transformed Hanoi's cityscape once again, as colonial structures gave way to modern office buildings and automobiles came to clog its streets. Preservationists struggled to retain elements of the older city even as economic and political pressures, and the growing traffic nightmare, made such efforts difficult.

[*See also* Vietnam.]

BIBLIOGRAPHY
Boudarel, Georges, and Nguyên Van Ky. *Hanoi: City of the Rising Dragon.* Translated by Claire Duiker. New York: Rowman and Littlefield, 2002. English translation of *Hanoi, 1936–1996: Du drapeau rouge au billet vert*, first published in 1997. Series of essays examining life and politics in twentieth-century Hanoi.
Logan, William. *Hanoi: Biography of a City.* Sydney, Australia: University of New South Wales Press; Singapore: Select, 2000. Detailed study of the city, with strong emphasis on architecture, and a focus on the colonial and postcolonial periods.

GEORGE DUTTON

HANOVER, KINGDOM OF. George Augustus Frederick, prince regent of Great Britain and elector of Hanover (later King George IV of England), raised the former electorate of Hanover to the status of a hereditary monarchy by a declaration of 12 October 1814. As part of the restoration process in Europe after the defeat of Napoleon in 1814–1815, the territory in the northwest of today's Germany—then 14,700 square miles (38,000 square kilometers) in size and inhabited in 1814 by approximately 1.3 million people—emerged as one of five kingdoms (the others were Prussia, Saxony, Bavaria, and Württemberg) that, along with Austria, were the largest and most influential states within the German Confederation.

Because George III of Great Britain was incapacitated, the prince regent was de facto the first king of Hanover; but the history of the ruling dynasty, the house of Guelph, goes back to the Middle Ages, when Henry the Lion (c. 1130–1195) formed the beginnings of a unified Saxon territory. In 1692, Hanover was raised to the status of electorate, and the marriage of its first elector, Ernest Augustus, to Sophia Dorothea von der Pfalz created a dynastic link to the ruling British royal family. The exclusion of Catholics from the British throne led to the accession of their son George Louis as George I in 1714. Linked in personal union for 127 years, the electorate and later kingdom of Hanover both gained and suffered from its connection with the politically and economically much more powerful Britain.

After the death of William IV in 1837 the personal union broke up. Ernest Augustus, Duke of Cumberland, acceded to the Hanoverian throne, followed by his son George V in 1851. Hanover's defeat in the war against Prussia in 1866 and the formation of a Prussian-led North German League in 1866 ended the political independence of Hanover.

[*See also* Germany; Prussia; *and* United Kingdom.]

BIBLIOGRAPHY
Nipperdey, Thomas. *Germany from Napoleon to Bismarck, 1800–1866.* Translated by Daniel Nolan. Princeton, N.J.: Princeton University Press, 1996.
Simms, Brendan, and Torsten Riotte, eds. *The Hanoverian Dimension in British History, 1714–1837.* Cambridge, U.K.: Cambridge University Press, 2006.

TORSTEN RIOTTE

HARLEM RENAISSANCE. A literary movement shaped by cultural nationalism that revolutionized African American society, the Harlem Renaissance has been interpreted as an attempt to secure "civil rights by copyright," as David Levering Lewis put it. The post–World War I era was a fragmented time; African Americans had made significant social and economic gains in the war years, signified by the growth of a vibrant and increasingly successful middle class that had access and opportunity to education, literature, and travel. These gains aside, the trajectory of race relations in American society was in sharp decline. This critical historical moment had all the makings of social transformation: a growing sense of the self-determination of people of African descent through black nationalism and Pan-Africanism, the existence of revolutionary politics represented by Marcus Garvey and A. Philip Randolph, an increase in national interest in the arts and culture, a new awareness of the connection to Africa, an economic crisis caused by the fall of the stock market, continued immigration, the growth of an African American intelligentsia, the development of a literary strategy to confront mainstream notions of blackness, and the advance of new media technologies.

Caught in the middle between the conservatism of the National Association for the Advancement of Colored People and the National Urban League and the tensions of communism, socialism, and Garveyism, exacerbated by the cultural differences between West Indians and African Americans, the literary intellectuals in Harlem, New York City, during this period created their own social and economic space in which they could demonstrate to the world the greatness of African American culture and could subsequently engineer racial uplift. The group of second-generation African Americans who actively participated in the movement jointly formed a response to existing social and political trends taking place in the interwar years. The entrenched racism of the times, intensified by an increase in lynchings, the rise of black radicalism as symbolized by the popularity of Garveyism, and the nativist response represented by the Ku Klux Klan prompted African American literary intellectuals to attempt to legitimize the social position of blacks through the production of literature, music, and plays.

In the 1920s wealthy white liberal patrons championed young talented African American writers, providing them much-needed financial resources to enable them to complete a wide range of novels, plays, and music performances all drawn from and based on African American culture and folklore. These literary intellectuals continued their work during the 1930s as part of the Federal Writers' Project and other Works Progress Administration programs designed to help them stay afloat.

The Harlem Renaissance was not confined to the United States; a number of the writers were born in the Caribbean, and most of the literary intellectuals had the opportunity to visit Paris, London, Berlin, or Kingston, Jamaica. The internationalization of the movement drew global attention to the issue of race in American society.

[*See also* African Americans.]

BIBLIOGRAPHY
Cruse, Harold. *The Crisis of the Negro Intellectual.* New York: Quill, 1984. First published 1967 by Morrow. A historical-interpretation theoretical analysis of African American life, grounded primarily in culture and the arts.
Lewis, David Levering. *When Harlem Was in Vogue.* New York: Alfred A. Knopf, 1981. Widely considered the definitive interpretation of the importance of the Harlem Renaissance to African American history and life.

KELLIE J. HOGUE

HAWAI'I. The anticolonial nationalist and decolonization movements that swept Africa and Asia after World War II came late to Oceania. Much of the recent postcolonial scholarship on Hawai'i traces its roots to the 1970s Hawai'ian renaissance, which renewed the native culture, language, and *lahūi* (nation, people). Much of it also has roots in nineteenth-century Hawai'ian resistance to Euro-American campaigns aimed at the destruction of the *lahūi*. Contesting the haole (foreigner, white settler) historiography of the U.S. annexation in 1893 and statehood in 1959 as the mutually desirable outcome of a long history of cross-cultural collaboration, postcolonial scholars stress continuities among indigenous sovereignty struggles of three centuries. They challenge the still-prevalent belief that Hawai'i is and was a racial utopia whose diverse members embody an "aloha spirit" that Hawai'ians allegedly bequeathed them.

Hawai'ians had lived in the islands for a millennium before Captain James Cook (1728–1779) put them on Western maps during his third Pacific voyage of the late 1770s. Over the next half a century Hawai'ian *ali'i* (male and female chiefs), sailors, and workers made possible the U.S.-dominated sandalwood, seal-fur, and whaling industries that linked the capitalist economies of the Atlantic and the Pacific. At the same time, foreign diseases devastated the Hawai'ian people, killing 90 percent during the nineteenth century. Kamehameha I (r. 1795–1819) capitalized on internal and external upheavals in his successful quest to bring the Hawai'ian Islands under centralized rule by 1819. His successors collaborated with Congregationalist missionaries from New England to build a modern nation-state. *Ali'i* provided missionaries with converts, and missionaries schooled Hawai'ians in the tools of Western civilization—Christianity, written language, constitutional government—required to make the Kingdom of Hawai'i into a sovereign nation worthy of recognition by the leading nations and colonial rivals in the Pacific: Britain, France, the United States.

Entwined global and local factors complicated Hawaiian efforts to "purchase independence with the coin of civilization," as Sally Engle Merry puts it (p. 13). In the 1840s, the United States followed Britain and France in recognizing Hawai'i as a sovereign nation, but then it asserted that it would allow no foreign power but itself to colonize Hawai'i. The 1848 Mahele (land division) institutionalized capitalist relations of property. It dispossessed *maka'ainana* (commoners) from all but 1 percent of the land, concentrated ownership of the land in the hands of *ali'i* and the *mo'i* (monarch), and opened the land's purchase to foreigners. The Mahele paved the way for the rise of a haole-owned sugar-plantation society worked by Asian contract laborers and dismembered reciprocal relationships between *maka'ainana* and *ali'i*. Henceforth, *ali'i*, particularly the *mo'i*, struggled to serve two competing, contradictory constituents and orders: haole and U.S. imperial capitalism on the one hand and the *maka'ainana* and *lahūi* on the other.

This state of affairs came to a head during the reign of King David Kalākaua (1874–1891). Kalākaua tried to serve haole and Hawai'ians alike, but his twin efforts to advance planter interests and strengthen the *lahūi* alienated him from both. In 1887 haole forced Kalākaua to sign the so-called Bayonet Constitution, which reduced the king to a figurehead and vested governance in the hands of haole. With the support of Hawai'ians, Kalākaua's successor, Queen Lili'uokalani (r. 1891–1893), prepared to promulgate a new constitution to restore power to the monarchy. In response, a group of haole, with the unauthorized support of U.S. diplomatic and naval agents, overthrew queen and kingdom in 1893. Despite the opposition of the vast majority of Hawai'ians, the United States annexed Hawai'i in 1898 and made it a U.S. territory two years later.

For half a century the Republican haole elite acted on their belief that the purpose of the sugarcane industry was less about the production of sugar than it was about dividends. They ruled through a mixture of paternalism toward all nonwhites combined with patronage for Hawai'ians and repression of the multiracial, majority-Asian, plantation workforce. Once the martial law that the United States imposed on Hawai'i during World War II ended, self-identified locals, mostly nonwhite, organized to challenge haole hegemony and remake the political economy of Hawai'i. Organized labor rapidly made substantial economic and political gains; liberal locals made the Democrats a competitive party officially dedicated to class and racial equality and confident that U.S. statehood would aid their achievement. Few nonnatives reflected on statehood's implications for Hawai'ians. The protagonist of the novelist Milton Murayama's *Plantation Boy* (1998) did: "Statehood will be the final nail in the coffin [for Hawai'ians]. . . . But how can they turn back the clock?" But on the contrary, contemporary natives again have undertaken to revitalize the Hawai'ian people and culture and reassert their ties to the *'aina* (land) and sovereignty over the *lahūi* in a present that is rerouted but not eradicated by a long history of colonial conquest and occupation.

[*See also* American Colonial Empire; *and* United States, *subentry* American Foreign Policy.]

BIBLIOGRAPHY
Kuykendall, Ralph S. *The Hawaiian Kingdom.* 3 vols. Honolulu: University of Hawai'i Press, 1938–1967.

Merry, Sally Engle. *Colonizing Hawai'i: The Cultural Power of Law.* Princeton, N.J.: Princeton University Press, 2000.

Silva, Noenoe K. *Aloha Betrayed: Native Hawaiian Resistance to American Colonialism.* Durham, N.C.: Duke University Press, 2004.

Takaki, Ronald. *Pau Hana: Plantation Life and Labor in Hawaii, 1835–1920.* Honolulu: University of Hawai'i Press, 1983.

CHRISTINE SKWIOT

HAYMARKET RIOT. In Chicago's Haymarket Square on 4 May 1886, an anarchist-led demonstration took place to spark awareness of American workers' struggles. In spite of its peaceful protest, the crowd was attacked by local police. A bomb was thrown; in the explosion and ensuing crossfire, eight officers died and an undetermined number of demonstrators were killed. The identity of the Haymarket bomber remains unknown, but the conditions that were the catalysts for the riot, and the repercussions of the bomb that punctuated it, are traceable.

The demonstration in Haymarket Square grew out of a nationwide movement to demand an eight-hour working day. After the Civil War, workers in several states, including Illinois, successfully lobbied for eight-hour laws, but almost all of these laws contained gaping loopholes and therefore were practically unenforceable. Workers reacted to these useless statues by striking; one of the largest strikes occurred in Chicago in 1867. The strikers' actions failed, quelled in part by police violence, but they laid much of the philosophical groundwork for what happened at Haymarket less than twenty years later.

By 1886, a broad coalition of labor organizations had joined the eight-hour-day campaign, and on May Day of that year initiated a general strike across the United States to continue the battle for shorter hours. The effects of this call were particularly apparent in Chicago. More than half of the workers at the McCormick Harvesting Machine Company went on strike that day. Over the course of the three-day walkout, replacement workers and retaliatory police officers clashed with the strikers, killing two and injuring several others.

Reacting to police brutality, disgruntled workers and anarchist leaders planned a rally in Haymarket Square. They expected a crowd of twenty thousand demonstrators, but rain and unseasonable cold reduced that number to about two thousand. Against the mayor's instructions, a police official sent units to Haymarket to force the gathering to disperse. During this confrontation, the bomb was thrown.

A period of panic followed, culminating in the arrest of eight Chicago anarchists for the murder of one of the policemen at Haymarket. Despite a lack of evidence linking them directly to the bombing, seven were convicted and sentenced to death, and the eighth was sentenced to fifteen years in prison. In 1887 the defendants appealed their case to the Illinois Supreme Court, which upheld Cook County's decision, linking the anarchists' guilt to their inflammatory rhetoric.

Not all served their sentences, however. Pressured by a forty-thousand-signature clemency campaign, the Illinois governor overturned two of the seven death sentences, but he sustained the other five. Of those condemned, one committed suicide shortly before his date of execution, detonating a small bomb smuggled to him by a friend. The remaining four were hanged on 11 November 1887.

Haymarket Riot. Drawing by T. de Thulstrup from sketches and photos furnished by H. Jeaneret, *Harper's Weekly*, 15 May 1886. Prints and Photographs Division, Library of Congress

Ultimately, public opinion blamed organized labor for the Haymarket Riot, and many citizens became convinced that all union activities would likely be violent. It would take the turn of a century for American labor to regain the public sympathy and power it had lost because of the tragic events of May 1886.

[*See also* Anarchism; Chicago; *and* Labor and the Labor Movement, *subentry* Organized Labor in the United States.]

BIBLIOGRAPHY

Avrich, Paul. *The Haymarket Tragedy.* Princeton, N.J.: Princeton University Press, 1984. Classic leading original history of the riot.

Green, James. *Death in the Haymarket: A Story of Chicago, the First Labor Movement, and the Bombing that Divided Gilded Age America.* New York: Pantheon, 2006. Re-creates the story of the Haymarket Riot, including new information and placing it within the context of the race and class tensions that defined the Gilded Age.

Roediger, David, and Franklin Rosemont, eds. *Haymarket Scrapbook.* Chicago: Charles H. Kerr, 1986. An immense anthology of the Haymarket bombing and its international legacy. Reprints many of the speeches and writings of the eight accused bombers and includes an abundance of cartoons and illustrations.

Cynthia Gwynne Yaudes

HEALTH AND DISEASE

[*This entry includes five subentries, an overview and discussions of health and disease in Africa, in Latin America, in South Asia, and in Southeast Asia. See also* Body, The; Disability; Doctors without Borders; Drugs and Narcotics: The Science of Drugs; Epidemics; Germ Theory; Handicaps; Hospitals; Medicine; Mental Health and Mental Illness; Physical Fitness; Tobacco; *and* World Health Organization; *and individual articles on the following diseases and conditions*: AIDS and HIV; Anorexia Nervosa; Bird Flu; Cancer; Cholera; Heart Disease; Plague; Poliomyelitis; SARS; Smallpox; Tuberculosis; *and* Yellow Fever.]

Overview

The one hundred years following the outbreak of the French Revolution in 1789 witnessed dramatic changes in ideas about the ability of humankind to head off the worst ravages of killing disease. Inasmuch as the discipline of history is the study of change, the history of health and disease constitutes a central element in the history of humankind. After the epic events of 1789, some well-intentioned ideas led to nothing. Yet on occasion ideas about health and health-related issues—such as the existence of abject poverty and how this was related to disease epidemics—were converted into definite health policies at the national or empirewide level.

Premodern and Non-Western Health Care. Before the validation of germ theory by Robert Koch of Prussia in 1876, one of the most important ideas about disease causation invoked supernatural forces. Some devotees of the world's monotheistic religions held that their deity hurled down the arrows of disease in order to try the fortitude of each suffering victim. Others held that the deity purposefully punished wrongdoers and evil persons by afflicting them with a horrible disease. This meant that "public health policies" must necessarily take the shape of campaigns to reform public morals, and in particular the morals of the poor.

But before the early decades of the nineteenth century, the concept of "the public's health" in any of the world's polities was actually a nonstarter. "The public" as such did not exist. What existed instead were regional groupings of people whose principal sense of identity was centered on their own household, and beyond that their village. Lying perhaps many kilometers away was a market center, and beyond that the court of the regional overlord and his retainers. Superimposed over this collection of farmers and craftsmen and warriors was a network of magistrates (in imperial China they were termed "mandarins," in the Ottoman Empire "pashas") who oversaw the general administration of the province or country.

In this premodern world the social unit to which ordinary people first turned when illness struck someone in the family was the household. Then, if ordinary cures—healing broths and the like—did not have any effect, the head of the household might call in an expert—in China, a literate person who was trained in the complexities of classical Chinese medicine. Based on readings or cross-readings of the *Inner Classic of the Yellow Sovereign*, which dated back to before 165 B.C.E., this outside expert would diagnose the cause of the illness and suggest appropriate corrective measures.

Seen from the perspective of medicine that has gone well beyond the simple germ theory approach of "modern medicine," experts now recognize that what the Chinese called "the medicine of systematic correspondences" did provide the patient with the peace of mind that comes from knowing that "the experts" are doing all they can for you. Bolstered by this peace of mind, the patient's body may well have set in motion disease-combating agents such as antibodies found in its own immune system. These suppositions about the triumph of mind over body using the insights of Chinese classical medicine are complemented

Preventing Disease. Anticholera measures in Marseille, France. Wood engraving, *Harper's Weekly*, 18 November 1865. Courtesy of the National Library of Medicine, Bethesda, Maryland

by statistical findings. As of 1750, life expectancy at birth in the manufacturing provinces of coastal China exceeded that found at that time in France.

The existence of a great tradition of medicine based on ancient literary sources in China was paralleled by two great literary-based traditions of medicine in Mughal India at the beginning of the nineteenth century: Ayurvedic medicine among the Hindu elite and Unani Tibb among the Muslim elite. But among the peasant cultivators who constituted the overwhelming majority of the population of the subcontinent, the first line of defense against an ordinary illness lay in the household. Then, if traditional remedies did not work—"starve a fever," for instance—resort might be had to the village expert and communal rituals.

The indigenous population of sub-Saharan Africa in 1800 appeared to have no written great traditions of medicine. But on that vast continent, just as in pre-British India, the household was the first line of defense against illness. Beyond the expertise found among coresident family members lay the village, with its experts well versed in the special healing rituals. These were associated with the ancestors, the intermediaries with the lesser gods. Following long-established precepts of African community behavior, in time of an epidemic the kinship groups that constituted the village moved off to a safer

place. But by the year 1800 among Africans living anywhere within access of the coasts, these eminently sensible "public health" practices had been hopelessly disrupted by the Europeans' ship-borne trade in black African slaves for lifetime service on the sugar, indigo, tobacco, and cotton plantations in the New World.

Black Africa has never recovered from this hemorrhage of its population and the collapse of its social systems. In the early twenty-first century it ranked at the bottom of all public health categories (infant mortality levels, life expectancy at birth, per capita access to safe water, per capita access to health clinics, female literacy). Sub-Saharan Africa is the only major region of the world where infectious diseases (as opposed to chronic diseases, violence, and the like) are still the leading cause of death. Elsewhere in the world, the therapeutic revolution that took off in the early 1940s with the application of penicillin finally broke the hold that infectious diseases had long exercised over the human race.

Science and Public Health. Before 1492 and the disastrous voyage of Christopher Columbus, infectious diseases (with the possible exception of tuberculosis) were unknown among the millions of people living in the New World and the Pacific islands. But by 1800 the "globalization" of diseases, carried by English, Dutch, French, Spanish, Portuguese, and North American ships, was already well advanced. Yet it was white "civilized" men—Europeans who were distant cousins of those who built and manned the disease-carrying ships—who finally devised the technology and the scientific know-how required to break the hold of infectious diseases.

This effort was pursued through two mutually exclusive approaches, one German and the other English. The German approach, as it came to exist after 1840, was fully "scientific" in the way that today's scientists understand that word. Based on rigorous laboratory research and the testing and retesting of hypotheses, it laid the foundations on which modern medical science is based. The German approach culminated in the work of Robert Koch (1843–1910) and his many followers. Following Koch's first validation of "germ theory," with his discovery of the precise living organism that caused anthrax in 1876, he went on to discover the causal agent of tuberculosis in 1882. In 1883–1884 he discovered the causal agent of cholera, a major killing disease in India. In 1884 Koch's pupil Georg Gaffky (1850–1918) discovered the causal agent of typhoid. Like cholera, typhoid was also a water-borne disease, but unlike cholera it was a major killer among the urban poor in already industrialized Britain and in slowly industrializing mainland Europe. During these decades others of Koch's pupils used his newly devised laboratory methods to discover the causal agents of diphtheria, pneumonia, tetanus, gonorrhea, and cerebrospinal meningitis. Among the foreign visitors who later applied Koch's laboratory methods to their own work was Shibasaburo Kitasato of Japan (1851–1931), who codiscovered the causal agent of bubonic plague (as then found in China) in 1894.

Aristocratic British governments in London and India (from 1896 onward the subcontinent was washed over by bubonic plague) long dismissed German and other non-British discoveries in medicine. They claimed these findings were not in accord with empirical experience in the real world as known in the time of Britain's intellectual heroes, Lord Chancellor Francis Bacon (1561–1626), the Roman medical philosopher Galen (129–199 C.E.), and Hippocrates (460–377 B.C.E.), the Greek "father of medicine." Why did these "ancients" exercise such a strong hold over the British mind?

The Industrial Revolution that had rapidly converted England and lowland Scotland from a rural to an essentially urban society in the space of two decades after 1820 had been based on breakthroughs in technology (such as the steam engine). Drawing on "empirical experience" with

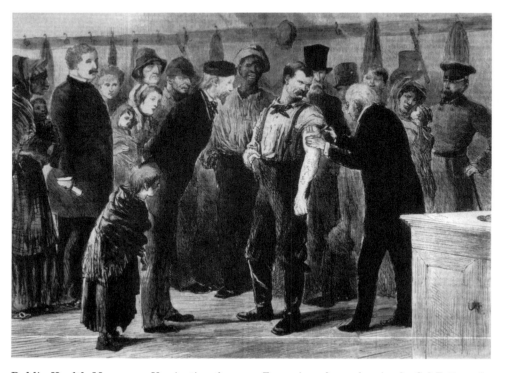

Public Health Measures. Vaccinating the poor. Engraving after a drawing by Sol Eytinge Jr. (1833–1905), *Harper's Weekly*, 16 March 1872. COURTESY OF THE NATIONAL LIBRARY OF MEDICINE, BETHESDA, MARYLAND

materials that could be readily held in one's hand and seen with the naked eye, the industrialization experience strengthened English contempt for thinking in terms of hypotheses, analogies, and abstract mathematics. Justus von Liebig (1823–1873), one of the early pioneers of German scientific medicine, famously said in his essay on Francis Bacon (published in German and English in 1863) that Englishmen's inability to think in terms of theory was a "national affliction." Yet, suffering as it did from this "national affliction," mid-nineteenth-century Britain used its technological know-how (and naval supremacy) to make itself for a time the world's richest country and to create the largest and most populous empire ever known.

After 1870 the English government finally began to apply token bits of this great national wealth to the sewerage and drinking-water needs of some of its urban populations. Beginning with Birmingham, the national government began to make long-term loans on favorable terms to urban governments for civic sanitary improvements. But for many decades after 1870, Germany and other mainland European countries were not in a financial position to follow Britain's lead.

Also differentiating early- and mid-nineteenth-century Britain from the German lands were the mindsets of their respective ruling elites. In the German lands the guiding principle was "cameralism," which held that the true wealth of a country lay in the well-being of all of its inhabitants. In a well-managed country, there need be no extreme poverty. Cameralism also held that in well-managed rival principalities, kingdoms, and duchies, governments should compete with each other in the founding and funding of universities and scientific research institutes. From the 1840s onward, one of the principal subjects under investigation in these many German research institutes was experimental physiology, the study of living organisms and their body parts. Coming out of all this in the 1870s and 1880s were Robert Koch and modern scientific medical theory. The therapeutic revolution, the creation of the drugs and practices needed to actually cure the specific diseases whose causal agents were identified by Koch and his associates, did not fully take off until the 1950s, but without Koch's validation of germ theory and his almost single-handed creation of the techniques and practices of modern laboratory-based medicine, the advent of "scientific medicine" might have been delayed indefinitely. It was the special characteristics of the German lands that made possible the creation of modern medical science.

The United Kingdom presented an alternative model of innovation in matters related to public health. The guiding philosophy of that era in Britain was laissez-faire. Based on a very partial reading of the works of Adam Smith, laissez-faire held that persons of substance should be allowed to do what they liked without interference by central government. Whether they were aristocrats with long pedigrees or shopkeepers or manufacturers who had pushed their way forward to be the dominating power in local town councils, their common attitude toward the poor was "they have only themselves to blame." If disadvantaged people (the majority of the population) were sick, it was because of their own foul habits and because they insisted on living in foul slums.

In the area of "public health" the tone was set by Edwin Chadwick (1800–1890). Born in Manchester and trained as a lawyer, Chadwick became the most active member of the General Board of Health in 1848. In his search for an easy, readily understandable answer to the question of why English cities were awash with epidemic diseases that threatened the health of "respectable people," Chadwick hit upon the old Greco-Roman idea that diseases were caused by foul smells (miasma) generated by animal and human wastes, most of which were excreted by the urban poor. To solve the problem he turned to an engineering solution: he would create a system of sewers, which in London would carry the wastes to the Thames. Chadwick was not bothered by the fact that the river was also the source of London's drinking water.

Chadwick's "sanitary ideal" was thus to create an odor-free world where the excreta of the poor would no longer threaten the health of "respectable people." Accompanying this engineering solution was his solution to the problem of poverty: the infamous Poor Law Amendment Act of 1834, which was not abolished until 1948. According to its terms, conditions in a workhouse were to be made so grim that a diseased pauper would prefer to die on the streets rather than resort to the public workhouse and its infirmary. The Poor Law medical doctors that staffed these institutions were regarded by other men in the profession as the lowest of the low (women holding degrees in medicine were not officially recognized by the British Medical Association until 1892).

On the global scale, the first concerted government-sponsored effort to block the movement of epidemic diseases into Europe from their perceived Indian or African homelands by way of the impoverished passengers who traveled in the steerage compartments of steamships was the International Sanitary Conference held in Paris in 1851. The conference was attended by medical experts from all over the Continent, many whom were already thinking in terms of some sort of germ theory. The International Sanitary Convention emerging from the conference proposed to use the techniques of "early warning": the quarantine of suspect ships and the isolation of the sick. The agreement was scheduled to remain in force for five years, by which time it was hoped that there would be further progress in medical theory about infectious diseases. Britain refused to sign the convention (all the Mediterranean powers, however, did) because it ran contrary to its guiding principles of laissez-faire and free trade.

The Paris Sanitary Conference of 1851 was the first of several such international meetings of European medical and scientific experts. Others were held in Constantinople in 1866, in Vienna in 1874, and so on. Following World War I (1914–1918) their agenda was taken up on a permanent basis by the League of Nations Health Organization. But because the United States chose not to join the league, and because Germany was not permitted to do so (it was perceived to be the nation primarily responsible for the bringing about World War I), the league's attempts at disease control came to naught.

The Therapeutic Revolution and Global Health Care. Following the end of World War II in 1945 and the collapse of British colonialism in India in 1947, attitudes of mind and developments in the realm of medical science (penicillin, sulfa drugs, the therapeutic revolution) made it seem possible that humankind's long struggle with infectious disease and other causes of premature death could at long last be brought to a triumphant close. With a few exceptions, all the infectious diseases known at the time (HIV/AIDS was not identified until 1981) could now either be cured outright or neutralized within the patient's body so that they would not infect other people.

Among the old imperial powers the therapeutic revolution was in large part responsible for a remarkable alteration in demographic structures, particularly through the reduction of child mortality. Together with greatly enhanced access to a range of food products from all over the world (the transport and distributing revolution), the therapeutic revolution led to greatly extended life expectancies. Thus in the United Kingdom life expectancy at birth for men and women in 1900 (before the therapeutic revolution) was about fifty years. By the early twenty-first century it stood at slightly more than seventy-five for men and at eighty for women. In the state of Massachusetts in 1865, life expectancy at birth for men and women was forty years. Between 1910 and 1920 the increase was more than four years. By the early twenty-first century in the United States among people of European descent, life expectancy at birth was

in the mid-seventies for men and the early eighties for women. However, among ordinary United States citizens of African descent, life expectancy at birth was not much different—upper-seventies for men and mid-seventies for women.

Building on the potential that therapeutic breakthroughs had finally created (infectious diseases need no longer be killers) after World War II, new governments put in place by revolutions as in China (in 1949), in Cuba (in 1959), and in Iran (in 1979) announced that access to appropriate medical treatment in government-financed clinics and hospitals was a basic human right. Similar conclusions were reached by long-established governments elsewhere. In post–World War II Britain and across the whole of mainland Europe and the USSR, governments announced that medical treatment should no longer be regarded as a privilege that could only be exercised by the fee-paying rich. Overseeing and assisting in the conversion of well-meaning declarations of intent into actual on-the-ground health services was the World Health Organization (WHO), founded in 1948.

One of the WHO's first decisions was to give high priority to preventive medicine in all parts of the world, especially in the impoverished non-Western regions (expectations of longevity at birth in India when the British left in 1947 were half of those found in imperial Britain itself). With the coming of independence in many nations on the African continent in 1960, new governments, in collaboration with the WHO, established local primary health care (PHC) clinics within easy access of all but the most remote communities. PHC centers were not intended to cater to the needs of the seriously ill but as installations for the prevention of disease. High priority was given to the health needs of children under five, who suffered the highest death rates of any age group, and of pregnant women. Vaccinations against preventable infectious diseases such as measles, smallpox, and polio were administered in an orderly and systematic fashion. Easily administered oral rehydration techniques, which could be applied by the mother herself, were developed to prevent an infant's death from diarrhea or dysentery; before that time, these had been major killers (they still are in Africa).

These new programs and techniques led to remarkable results. In 1977 the WHO was able to announce that free-ranging smallpox had been abolished worldwide. Going beyond this success, the mix of programs that the WHO encouraged and sponsored in "developing countries"—PHC clinics, ready access to the new range of curative drugs, and so on—did much to cut down child mortality so that these individuals would live to a reproductive age. Before large-scale interventions began in 1950, there were some 2.5 billion people in the world (there had been only 1.6 billion in 1900). Fifty years later, global population numbered more than 6 billion, with every indication that it would reach 7 billion by the mid-twenty-first century. Much of this increase took place among young people living in the formerly colonial world, in Africa, South Asia, Southeast Asia, and Latin America.

Following the WHO's success in abolishing smallpox in 1977, at Alma Ata in the USSR in 1978 the WHO proposed a program of "Health for All by the Year 2000." Twenty years later, as the millennium approached, the WHO promulgated its famous Millennium Development Goals. In addition to reducing gender inequality, illiteracy, and environmental degradation worldwide, the Millennium Development Goals set targets to reduce poverty, on the understanding that poverty greatly reduces a young individual's life chances and his or her ability to contribute positively to the economic growth of the region. The targets were also set on the not-so-new understanding that "poverty" in its widest sense causes disease.

This "truth" had been arrived at two hundred years earlier by the marquis de Condorcet and Thomas Paine, author of *The Rights of Man* (1791–1792). Both of these Enlightenment thinkers had argued that if slight adjustments were made in the way that existing national economies, tax structures, and educational systems were managed, poverty could be forever abolished. Paine's plans included state-supported medical treatment, maternity leave for mothers, and old-age pensions.

Obstacles to Progress in Public Health. In contrast to the preconditions that make it possible to envision the widening of a given population's ease of access to the new therapeutics and to state-of-the-art medical care, other preconditions stymie and even prevent change. In the years after 1980, when Ronald Reagan was elected president of the United States, the proponents of laissez-faire ideology (recrafted by members of the Chicago school of economics during the crisis of American involvement in Vietnam) claimed that the billions of dollars in wealth that multinational companies create for the benefit of their shareholders and boards of directors would eventually trickle down the social scale to benefit the whole of humanity. In the meantime, humanity must put up with the fact that a fifth of their number live in abject poverty, without access to safe water or to sanitation. They must put up with the fact that 11 million children die each year from preventable diseases and that 3 million people die

each year from HIV/AIDS. Working to ensure that the laissez-faire policies were realized on the ground in non-Western countries as well as in the West were three multinational financial organizations: the International Monetary Fund (IMF), the World Bank, and the World Trade Organization (WTO).

In the years after 1980 the IMF and the World Bank insisted that the cost of services provided by newly founded state-funded humanitarian institutions in non-Western countries should now be borne by the consumers of their services, accomplished through the imposition of so-called "cost recovery" programs: the poor paid for what had previously been free. The granting of IMF and World Bank loans to struggling non-Western countries was made dependent on compliance to these dictates.

First to fall victim to the new policies were the networks of primary health care centers. Sub-Saharan Africa was the region of the world hardest hit. As a result, in the early twenty-first century that huge collection of regions extending southward from the second cataract of the Nile to the Cape of Good Hope was the only area of the world where deaths from infectious diseases continued to outnumber deaths from chronic diseases. In the West and in Japan, the list of principal killers was topped by chronic diseases and the diseases of old age.

By the beginning of the twenty-first century the neoconservative think-tank authors of the recrafted laissez-faire policies being enforced by the World Bank, the IMF, and the World Trade Organization were confident that they represented the wave of the future. They pointed with pride to the fact that fully fledged Communism had collapsed in nearly all the countries of the world and that, with its demise, state-supported free medical treatment for all citizens had also collapsed. Coinciding with this were sharp increases in rates of mortality and sharp decreases in life expectancies. For example in Russia, in the five years following the collapse of the old Soviet Union in 1990, life expectancy at birth for men fell from 63.8 to 57.5 and from 74.4 to 71.0 for women. This dramatic decline was unprecedented in any industrialized country. A similar collapse in life expectancies was in process in China. In addition to the neoconservative think-tanks and the politicians they served, also working against the possibility that the embattled World Health Organization would be able to achieve its Millennium Goals were the policies of the great pharmaceutical companies. Running contrary to the business ethics preached by Adam Smith in his *On the Wealth of Nations* (1776) and his *Theory of Moral Sentiments* (1759), a handful of huge multinational companies have successfully swallowed up nearly all their competitors. Since the mid-1990s, working within the framework of the WTO, the top pharmaceutical companies have come to claim that they have a legitimate worldwide monopoly on the drugs they produce. Under the slogan of "intellectual property rights" and the application of judicial processes managed by the WTO itself (the TRIPS agreements), the WTO made great headway in preventing biochemists in India (the leader in the field) from the copying and reproduction of the drugs produced by the Western-based pharmaceutical companies. As one of the leading non-Western nations—and as a longtime victim of imperialists' exploitation—India felt duty-bound to sell its generic drugs to poor countries at a fraction of the cost charged by their Western counterparts. For the 1 billion people in the world who, according to the 2005 United Nations publication *In Larger Freedom*, live on less than one U.S. dollar a day, the difference between having access to an urgently required drug of Indian manufacture that is almost affordable and being limited to the U.S.-manufactured equivalent at least ten times the price is quite literally the difference between life and death.

The TRIPS agreement that gave legal protection to Western pharmaceutical companies' "intellectual property rights" was—under the strong encouragement of the United States—accepted by 125 governments in 2001. In that same year, the neoconservatives in power in Washington, D.C., began to insist that all health-related aid to non-Western countries be made dependent on the moral reformation of their population.

And in particular, Washington began to insist that adolescents and adults in Africa, Southeast Asia, and Latin America should do their bit to staunch local epidemics of HIV/AIDS by abstaining from all sexual intercourse outside of marriage. The Western moralists warned that the standard way of preventing infection during intercourse through the use of rubber prophylactics (condoms) was ineffective. This claim was not backed up by scientifically sound data. The moralists refused to accept that condoms had proven themselves wonderfully effective in Uganda, the first country in the non-Western world to have mounted an effective sex-education campaign, centered around the use of condoms. Before that education campaign took off, the incidence of HIV/AIDS was increasing incrementally. But thanks to the education campaign, in 2003 Uganda was able to announce that new incidence had stabilized and that the epidemic seemed to have been brought under control. Western moralizers have placed this and all other anti-AIDS campaigns in jeopardy.

All too often in the past, medical and scientific expertise has been relegated to the footnotes of policy statements written by politicians and economists. Those wielding effective power over the lives of millions have regarded the statements of medical doctors and medical scientists as too abstract and too theoretical to be of practical use in the real world. Speaking directly to this issue were the final conclusions of the great International Sanitary Conference on Cholera held in 1866 in Constantinople:

> The public administration of every country of the world has become convinced by reason, as well as by cruel experience, that the expenditure necessitated by preventive measures [against disease] is eminently reproductive . . . no hygienic measure is ever too costly . . . the disbursement of even the largest sums in carrying out measures of health is simply equal to laying out money at a very considerable interest. Enormous sums have been spent in bringing the means of destruction to perfection and CAN THERE be any hesitation to spend something for hygiene, which is the art of preservation, the art of sustaining life and warding off disease and death?

After a few weeks of hesitation, the British government of the day laughed these words to scorn.

At the meeting of the world's heads of state in September 2005 at the United Nations in New York, the secretary general expressed the hope that the United Nations and its agencies—the WHO—would be able to give the highest priority to the control of infectious diseases and the reduction of poverty by half by the year 2015. But in his own presentation, the head of state of the world's newest hegemonic power went out of his way to ignore the secretary general's plea. The future of global public health continued to hang in the balance.

Marked discrepancies in health conditions among and within nations constituted one of the key issues in global health by the twenty-first century. While life expectancy has increased in most countries, rates varied according to income, social status, and standards of living. In some countries in the Arab world in the early years of the twenty-first century, life expectancy deteriorated due to civil strife and the collapse of health provisioning services. In Africa and in former Soviet bloc HIV/AIDS continued to kill able-bodied young adults, wreaking havoc with traditional child-rearing practices. Another key issue was concern about the possibility of new worldwide epidemics such as Avian influenza (a rerun of the influenza epidemic of 1918 with its twenty million victims).

Partially offsetting this threat of doom was the optimism born of the success of the WHO in bringing the SARS epidemic rapidly under control in 2003. Yet a fifth of the world's population still did not have access to safe water or

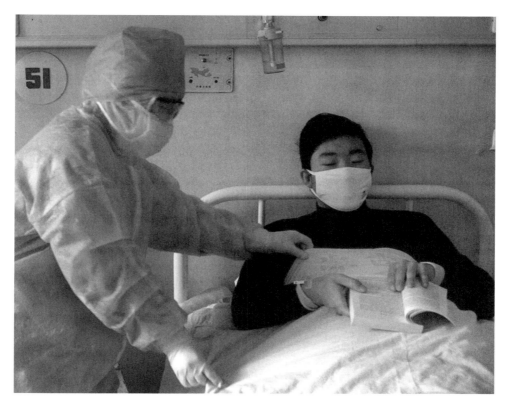

Health Care. A nurse looks after a SARS patient at Inner Mongolia Hospital in Hohhot, capital of north China's Inner Mongolia Autonomous Region, April 2003. Photograph by Li Xin, Xinhua News Agency. AP IMAGES

safe sanitation. Without those essentials it is impossible for them to enjoy "good health." The technology necessary to provide these essentials exists, but the will to make this technology universally available is obviously lacking. As had been true in 1866 when Europe's and the Middle East's medical experts presented their case at the International Cholera Conference, in the early twenty-first century, among the political leaders of the great nation states and the policymakers of several global corporations there continues to be marked unwillingness "to spend something on hygiene, which is the art of preservation" and to spend less on the production of ever-increasingly-sophisticated weapons of war.

[See also AIDS and HIV; Bird Flu; Body, The; Cancer; Cholera; Disability; Doctors without Borders; Drugs and Narcotics; Epidemics; Germ Theory; Handicaps; Heart Disease; Hospitals; Medicine; Mental Health and Mental Illness; Physical Fitness; Plague; Poliomyelitis; SARS; Smallpox; Tobacco; Tuberculosis; World Health Organization; and Yellow Fever.]

BIBLIOGRAPHY

Farmer, Paul. *Infections and Inequalities: The Modern Plagues.* Berkeley: University of California Press, 2001. An assessment of the real world in which "minority" populations in the United States and the majority of people in non-Western countries live and prematurely die. Written by a heroic figure, a practicing medical doctor with a doctorate in anthropology, who appreciates the role played by open-minded historians.

Fogel, Robert. *The Escape from Hunger and Premature Death, 1700–2100.* Cambridge, U.K., and New York: Cambridge University Press, 2004.

Jones, Gareth Stedman. *An End to Poverty?: A Historical Debate.* New York: Columbia University Press, 2004. An assessment of the role of seminal Enlightenment figures.

McKeown, Thomas. *The Modern Rise of Population.* London: Edward Arnold, 1976. His thesis buried by Simon Szreter (1988) and resurrected by Robert Fogel (2004).

McMichael, Anthony J., Martin McKee, Vladimir Shkolnikov, and Tapani, Valkonen. "Mortality Trends and Setbacks: Global Convergence or Divergence?" *The Lancet* 363 (2004): 1155–1159. A realistic assessment of where we were in the early twenty-first century.

Parry, Eldryd, Richard Godfrey, David Mabey, and Geoffrey Gill, eds. *Principles of Medicine in Africa.* 3rd ed. Cambridge, U.K., and New York: Cambridge University Press, 2004. A realistic, grim assessment of the rapidly deteriorating health situation in tropical Africa.

Pomeranz, Kenneth. *The Great Divergence: China, Europe, and the Making of the Modern World Economy.* Princeton, N.J.: Princeton University Press 2000. A major breakthrough in non-Eurocentric cultural and economic history—controversial.

Porter, Roy. *The Greatest Benefit to Mankind: A Medical History of Humanity from Antiquity to the Present.* London: HarperCollins, 1997. The now standard long work, though with a marked Anglo-American bias. Shows awareness that medical doctors share the dominant mindset of the particular society of which they are a part. Ends with an extremely useful forty-five-page bibliography.

Ruger, Jennifer Prah. "Health and Social Justice." *The Lancet* 364 (2004): 1075–1080.

Stiglitz, Joseph E. *Globalization and Its Discontents.* New York: W. W. Norton and Company, 2002. A realistic, hence controversial, assessment of the contemporary world's power elites, the 0.00005 percent of the global population whose decisions impact heavily on the remainder of humanity. Winner of the Nobel Prize for Economics, 2001.

Szreter, Simon. "The Importance of Social Intervention in Britain's Mortality Decline c. 1850–1914: A Re-interpretation of the Role of Public Health." *Social History of Medicine* 1 (1988): 1–37. A major contribution by one of the leading scholars in the field. Reassesses and buries the thesis of Thomas McKeown (1976).

Watts, Sheldon. *Disease and Medicine in World History.* New York: Routledge, 2003. A brief 160-page survey, non-Eurocentric, written in the non-West. Contains brief accounts (fifteen pages each) of medicine in China to 1840, in India before 1800, and in the Middle East before 1882 (the British conquest of Egypt); on the contrasts between medical science in the German lands in the nineteenth century and in the United Kingdom and British Empire; and on health and medicine from 1940 to the present. A thirteen-page bibliography.

Watts, Sheldon. *Epidemics and History: Disease, Power, and Imperialism.* New Haven, Conn.:, Yale University Press, 1997. Developments since 1800 assessed toward the end of each chapter and in the afterword. Contains one hundred pages of detailed annotation and bibliography.

Wootton, David. *Bad Medicine: Doctors Doing Harm Since Hippocrates.* London: Oxford University Press, 2006.

Yeo, Richard. "An Idol of the Market Place: Baconianism in Nineteenth-Century Britain." *History of Science* 23 (1985): 251–297. On the peculiarities of the "English."

SHELDON WATTS

Africa

The World Health Organization (WHO) defines health as "a state of complete physical, mental and social well-being and not merely the absence of disease or infirmity." While a state of health is never constant and even in high-income countries individuals move between well-being and disease, in most parts of Africa dire socioeconomic and political conditions make health the preserve of the privileged few.

Infant mortality rates are usually interpreted as indicators of the health status of a country. While in most developed countries today infant mortality is less than ten per thousand, in many countries in Africa the infant mortality rate is sixty-four per thousand. Between 1990 and 1999 the infant mortality rate increased in twenty of the fifty-three African countries. Africa is also the only region of the world where it is projected that the mortality rate for children under five will continue to increase. In 1960, 14 percent of deaths of children worldwide occurred in Africa. By 1980 the proportion had risen to 23 percent and by 2003, 43 percent.

In most countries in the West life expectancy at birth (the number of years lived, on the average, by a given population) improved from around forty years in the mid-nineteenth century to over seventy years in the 1970s and has remained fairly constant into the early 2000s. By contrast life expectancy in many parts of Africa is declining, largely as a result of the HIV/AIDS epidemic with life-expectancy in some countries reaching as low as thirty-four years.

Major diseases that affect and often kill people in Africa include a variety of fevers, measles, pneumonia, whooping cough, gastroenteritis, tuberculosis, malnutrition, anemia, and tetanus, most of which have been eradicated or do not kill people in the developed world. Vast numbers of people in Africa die of treatable diseases each year because they are too poor to access treatment and care. Inadequate health care in Africa, part of the overall crisis of underdevelopment across the continent, has been exacerbated by the HIV/AIDS epidemic and constitutes a global emergency.

Indigenous Medicine. Indigenous or traditional medicines have been a vital part of Africans' health-seeking practices from precolonial times to the present. Although healers and treatment options vary across the continent, many of the underlying ideas are shared across cultures. All indigenous healing systems place health and healing within broader cultural frameworks. Medicine and medical care are intertwined with cultural notions of good and evil and are an integral part of politics, kinship relations, religion, trade, farming, and sexual life.

Indigenous worldviews see the world as both a physical (material) and nonphysical (nonmaterial or spirit) reality. Traditional healers endeavor to rebalance these spheres to assist the healing process. Indigenous healers come from all walks of life and either gender. They are often responsible for offering guidance to their communities on issues of physical and psychological health as well as on community matters. Health experts might be household elders with knowledge of medical problems or they might be trained experts. The latter might be either diviners or herbalists, although their roles often overlap. Diviners are usually called to their profession by the ancestors and they heal by consulting with the ancestors. Herbalists heal based on plant medicines and other natural ingredients such as plants, barks, animal blood, and feathers. Although healers play a critical role in diagnosis and prescribing a cure, the entire community can be involved in health care delivery through taking part in healing rituals or ceremonies.

In most African indigenous health systems the idea of disease includes physical sickness, misfortune, and imbalance. Illness might be caused by ancestors who are displeased with the way the person is living or by witches or enemies who are believed to have the magical ability to bring about harm. Illness might also be linked to beliefs about pollution and the violation of taboos.

Cures deal with the individual who is sick, the unnatural or supernatural agencies seen as leading to the illness, and the community in general. Procedure for medical consultations under indigenous systems depends on the nature of the illness. In some parts of Africa chronically sick patients, people with leprosy, or those who are mentally ill stay with the healer for a period of time. Healers also conduct home visits and heal patients in their homes. Treatments have curative, protective, and preventive elements and often use physical medicines prepared from animal, mineral, or vegetable substances, or ritual methods, or a combination of these. Physical medicines may take the form of ointments or powders taken with water. Treatments also include purgative methods, such as enemas or emetics, to cleanse the system. Protective charms are often worn to guard individuals against the malicious intents of others, for self-fortification, or to ward off evil spirits. Psychological or ritual methods include charms, dancing, drumming, prayers and sacrifice to the ancestors, and reassurance or ritual to appease the ancestors or to right a social wrong. The rituals may include the slaughtering of an animal, part of which is dedicated to the ancestors, and a ceremony requesting help.

Because indigenous medicine is rooted in society, as African society changed so too did healing. As new diseases were introduced, healers had to respond and so new ways of healing developed. In the early 2000s, almost 80 percent of Africans used traditional or indigenous medicine either on its own or in combination with biomedicine. Payment was unlikely to be a barrier to treatment because it was often offered in kind or was reciprocal. Indigenous medicine was in many instances more readily available than biomedicine, and its cures and treatments fit within a broader cultural framework that people recognize and relate to.

The Effects of Colonialism. Missionary penetration into Africa and colonialism had a mixed and contradictory effect on health and health care in Africa. From the earliest contact between settlers and indigenous people the latter suffered the devastating effects of previously unknown diseases. Entire populations, such as the Khoi-San in southern Africa, were decimated by outbreaks of measles and smallpox. Yet the missionaries and the colonial officials also introduced Western biomedicine to Africa, bringing with them hospitals, dispensaries, and, especially after World War II, an array of drugs that improved health and extended life expectancy. However, these services were often concentrated in urban areas, ports, or centers of administration and commerce. They tended to serve the expatriate community as their first priority. Institutionalized biomedical services were expanded after World War II, when attempts were made to introduce reforms in order to forestall the emergence of aggressive nationalism. However, this did little to change the urban focus and the concentration of services around the needs of the colonizers rather than the colonized. For example, in the Ivory Coast in 1952 all eleven major hospitals were in the southern part of the territory where European enterprise was concentrated. That health-care facilities, medical schools, and dispensaries are often situated far away from a majority of patients and that traveling to them and accessing these services is expensive is a persistent problem in most African countries.

Colonial officials also used health as a political tool, a justification for segregation and oppression. This became known as the "sanitation syndrome." Many Europeans came to Africa with a stereotypical and grossly distorted picture of African life. In this view Africa figures as a space of sickness and death, a dark continent inhabited by savage, promiscuous individuals. These stereotypes had a major impact on colonial health care and health policy. Similarly, because states of health emerge from the basic organization of daily life as well as from social, political, and economic factors, the very nature of the colonial state had a major impact on health and disease in Africa. In early colonial West Africa, public health practices were inextricably linked to the pattern of race relations. Europeans who planned West African cities assumed that the health of colonists would be preserved if they lived at a spatial remove from their African subjects.

In 1914, when the bubonic plague struck Senegal, the French colonial medical community not only blamed Senegalese victims for the outbreak but used the outbreak to justify segregation. The colonial medical community sought to exploit the outbreak of plague to intensify their control over African property and lives in Dakar and introduced plague control measures that were both highly intrusive and coercive.

In the early years of colonial rule the colonial governments relied on forced labor. In the eastern and southern parts of the continent male workers often migrated from rural homes, leaving their families behind. In the urban areas or around their places of work they often lived in barren single-sex hostels. Here conditions were marked by poor ventilation, lack of adequate sanitation, and poor nutrition, all conditions that lead to poor health. These migrants also found themselves separated from their wives and families, who remained in the rural areas. The long-term separations disrupted kinship relations and sometimes led to the spread of sexually transmitted infections, as migrants entered into transient sexual liaisons at their place of work.

The removal of young, able-bodied men also had a detrimental effect on rural areas. Farming and other heavy labor had to be done by women and old men. This doubled the burden on women. As rural economies began to fail, the rural population became increasingly reliant on the remittances of their migrant kin. When these did not come women were often forced into transactional sexual relationships in order to survive. Often they chose as partners returned migrants who might have additional cash. These relationships formed further paths along which sexually transmitted infections could spread. In postcolonial Africa of the early twentieth century, urbanization and the movement of populations remain significant factors in the patterns of disease across the continent.

In central Africa and especially in French Africa, forced labor was different but the oppression and detrimental effect on health was similar. For example, in Ubangi-Shari (later Central African Republic), where the territory was governed by concessionary companies, Africans were brutally forced to collect rubber and other wild products. Many people fled from their homes and farms, leading to a decline in food production. During this period the population dropped, death rates rose, and fertility diminished. The declining likelihood of survival grew directly out of political and economic exploitation.

As colonial control changed so too did health problems. The 1920s saw a shift to a colonial economy based on cultivation. Local African farmers were now obliged to grow certain commercial crops, such as cotton, sorghum, and millet. These crops were highly labor intensive and drew labor away from food-crop cultivation. In combination, increased monocropping and increasingly specialized labor led to seasonal increases in malnutrition.

In addition to the detrimental consequences of the new crops, colonial control brought particular forms of social organization of economic production that had profound health consequences. In some parts of Africa, social organization of economic production entrenched racial inequality. For example, in South Africa during the colonial and apartheid eras the organization of labor in mining work meant that there was a much higher likelihood of black miners suffering disabling accidents than white miners. At the same time conditions and access to health care in the mines and for the black population in general were far inferior to those provided for whites. In many parts of Africa under colonial rule, class was the deciding factor in access to health care. For example, it was far more likely that children of bureaucrats would receive hospital care than would the children of the urban poor. Gender also played a significant role; for example, peasant women without husbands had a greater chance of raising malnourished children than those who were married and whose husbands contributed to the household resources.

By the late colonial period, colonial health systems were faced with an increasing volume of work arising from new forms of ill health that were in part a result of the colonial system itself. At the same time there was an increasing uptake of biomedical systems by Africans in the wake of World War II. By this period an increasing number of Africans were practicing Western biomedicine, making this medical system as African as indigenous systems. Among the early Africans who were trained in the West as medical doctors and who practiced in Africa were two Nigerian former slaves who had returned from England by 1859 and helped to establish Western medicine in West Africa. In East Africa, Africans were practicing Western-style medicine by the 1870s. While there were certainly exceptional individuals who trained as doctors, most Africans who practiced within the early biomedical system served as nurses or medical orderlies. In the 1920s medical schools, such as Makerere in Uganda, began to be built and this significantly increased the number of Africans who were trained in and who practiced biomedicine.

The end of the nineteenth century saw the development of tropical medicine, a form of medical practice to prevent and cure diseases thought to be specific to Africa, India, Latin America, and Southeast Asia. This meant that for much of the twentieth century colonial governments and international aid organizations focused on a limited range of parasitic diseases.

In the mid-twentieth century a series of international organizations were formed that continue to have an important effect in shaping patterns of disease on the African continent. These organizations often focused on trying to rid the developing world of the parasitic diseases that were the focus of tropical medicine. First the League of Nations and then the United Nations and the WHO were formed to address global population, disease eradication, and health issues. The gathering of statistical information and programs of international standardization were the aim of international institutions of the interwar period. By the end of the twentieth century all aspects of health, including reproductive health, were incorporated within the activities of the United Nations and the WHO.

Philanthropic organizations, mainly based in the United States, and in particular the Rockefeller Foundation's International Health Board, significantly influenced the promotion of sanitation and the spread of Western medicine across the world. Such organizations largely focused on infectious diseases such as yellow fever and malaria and did not invest in the provision of primary health care and in developing health care infrastructure.

However, global partnerships to improve health in Africa have played a critical part in eradicating specific diseases. One example can be observed in the attempt to eradicate Guinea worm disease. This parasitic disease is contracted by consuming water that is contaminated with microscopic copepods (often referred to as water fleas), which themselves have consumed Guinea worm larvae. Inside a human's abdomen, the Guinea worm larvae mature and grow, some to as long as three feet. After a year, the Guinea worm slowly emerges through an agonizingly painful blister it creates in the skin. Those infected often immerse their limbs in water, seeking relief from the burning sensation caused by the emerging worm, and thus recontaminate drinking water. The disease is limited to remote rural villages in thirteen sub-Saharan Africa countries. More than half of all cases of Guinea worm disease are reported from southern Sudan. Other countries with more than one thousand cases each year are Nigeria, Burkina Faso, Niger, Ghana, Mali, Uganda, Togo, Benin, and Ivory Coast. Smaller numbers of cases are reported from Mauritania, Ethiopia, Chad, Senegal, and Cameroon.

Many organizations, including the United Nations Children's Fund (UNICEF), the WHO, the U.S. Centers for Disease Control, the Gates Foundation, and the Carter Presidential Center, are helping the governments of countries where Guinea worm is found to eliminate the disease worldwide. Since 1986, when an estimated 3.5 million people were infected, the international campaign has eliminated much of the disease and prevented millions of cases. In 1995, the total number of infected people worldwide had dropped to about 130,000, less than 4 percent of the total in 1986. A decade later, in 1996, the WHO declared Central African Republic to be endemic for Guinea worm disease. In 2001 it was announced that transmission of the disease had been stopped from endemic villages. In 2005 it was estimated that there were about 10,600 cases worldwide.

One of the most successful disease eradication campaigns has been the fight against poliomyelitis in Africa and throughout the world. The development of polio vaccines in the 1950s and global vaccination campaigns in the 1960s and 1970s reduced the incidence of polio across the world. The Global Polio Eradication Initiative was launched in 1988 and since that time there has been a remarkable drop in the number of cases of polio each year. In 1988 there were 350,000 cases of polio worldwide, and by 2003 just 784 cases. Since 2002 the number of cases of polio has increased because of limited vaccination campaigns in India and Nigeria, but in spite of this it seems that the eradication of polio may be realized in the near future.

The attempt to eradicate malaria has been more complex. In 1957 the WHO launched a global campaign to eradicate the disease. The campaign entailed the use of DDT spray to kill mosquitoes, and while at first malaria seemed to have disappeared in some places, the disease reemerged due to a failure to involve local populations in the initiative and to provide health care infrastructure to sustain the campaign. The campaign was abandoned in the 1970s. Today approximately 300–500 million cases of malaria occur each year and over 90 percent of these infections occur in Africa. One million people die of malaria in Africa each year, the majority of whom are children under the age of five. Although there is effective treatment for malaria—artemisinin-based combination therapies—only nine of the forty-two countries in Africa in which malaria is endemic were administering these drugs. A wide-reaching campaign has been launched to provide mosquito nets to people living in areas where malaria is most prevalent. The Global Fund to Fight AIDS, TB, and Malaria was launched in 2002. The fund is financing 109 million insecticide-treated bed nets and aims to rapidly expand access to artemisinin-based antimalarial drugs, particularly in countries where drug resistance is high.

Around the middle of the 1940s advances in medical science led to a seismic shift in health care and in the health of populations across the world. Effective curative and preventive medicine became more broadly available, antibiotics were introduced, drugs were developed to treat tuberculosis, and sulphonamides, used in the treatment of puerperal fever, reduced maternal mortality by 70 percent in the West. These developments in the way in which medicine was practiced also affected the state of health of population across Africa.

Not only poliomyelitis but also some other communicable diseases such as measles and diphtheria have been virtually eradicated in most African countries through vaccination and other disease control measures. In 1974 the WHO launched its Expanded Programme on Immunization, and in 1977 it completed the eradication of smallpox. In 1978 the organization adopted a broader strategy, of assuring global primary health care. In 1979 the introduction of oral rehydration therapy together with widespread vaccination campaigns lowered infant mortality rates and increased life expectancy in most countries in Africa. In the 1980s approximately 5 million children under the age of five died each year from diarrhea. In 2000 this figure had fallen to 1.8 million, largely because of the use of oral rehydration therapy. Between 1965 and 1988 the life expectancy at birth in sub-Saharan Africa rose from forty-five to fifty-one years. Over the same period the ratio of doctors to population increased by about 50 percent and the ratio of nurses to population more than doubled.

While the immediate postindependence period saw significant improvements in health and education in many African countries, these gains have been lost in the wake of violent conflicts, environmental degradation, and increasing poverty. Misguided national health policies and the widening economic divide between the First and Third Worlds have also played a role in the health care crisis.

Conflict, Famine, and Disease. There are chronic structural problems in most African states and in the provision of health-care services across the continent, and these ongoing challenges have been compounded by humanitarian crises since the late twentieth century. The international aid organization Doctors without Borders provides medical relief to Africa (and across the world) to people threatened by war, epidemics, famine, and displacement. In 1992 Doctors without Borders physicians worked in refugee camps in Mauritania among the more than thirty thousand Tuaregs and Malian Moors interred there. The Tuaregs have been a displaced population since

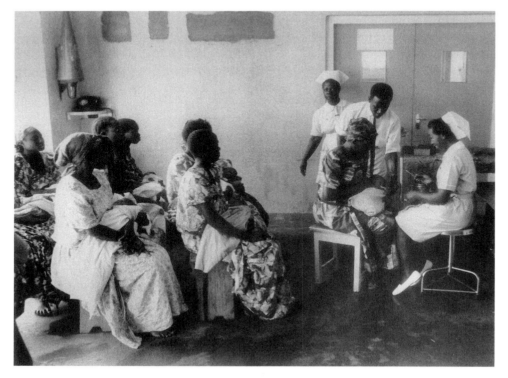

Vaccination in Africa. Mothers having their babies vaccinated against smallpox, Uganda, 1975.
Photograph by Jean Mohr. COURTESY OF THE NATIONAL LIBRARY OF MEDICINE, BETHESDA, MARYLAND

the beginning of the 1960s when countries in North Africa gained independence from France, and when the Sahara, the desert territory traditionally occupied by the Tuaregs, was divided between Algeria, Mali, and Niger. Severe droughts in the 1970s and 1980s led the Tuaregs to seek refuge in Algeria. In 1986 Algeria expelled the Tuareg refugees and in 1989 they were relocated to camps in Niger and Mali. In 1990 Tuaregs revolted in Niger and in 1992 demanded that Mali recognize their right to autonomous government of the northern regions of the country. Guerilla warfare broke out and the army responded by attacking the civilian population. Thousands of Malian Tuaregs fled to Algeria, Niger, and Mauritania. The death rate in the camps in Mauritania in 1992 was four deaths per ten thousand people per day, double what is considered the norm in emergency situations. Most of these deaths were caused by an epidemic of measles and many of those who died were children. Although a vaccination against measles exists, this example points to how social conditions—violence, famine, and oppression—combine to create the conditions for the emergence of a deadly epidemic.

In the same year a terrible drought affected most countries in southern Africa. In Mozambique, afflicted by war for twenty years, drought rapidly became famine and the United Nations estimated that approximately 3 million Mozambicans were displaced, fleeing war and the threat of starvation. In 1992 Mozambique had the highest infant mortality rate in the world (one-third of all children under the age of five died).

As of 2007, less than 40 percent of Mozambicans had access to basic health care services, largely a result of a shortage of trained health-care practitioners. As in many other African countries, medical facilities in Mozambique are insufficiently equipped and clinics and hospitals are understaffed. Health-care workers practice under extremely challenging circumstances; they receive low remuneration, they often do not have access to the equipment and drugs they require in order to treat their patients, and they face the burden of the HIV/AIDS epidemic— including high HIV prevalence rates among the health-care workers themselves. Many health-care professionals have sought work in the West, leading to a human resource crisis in many parts of Africa.

Since 2000 the increasingly totalitarian regime of Robert Mugabe, Zimbabwe's president since 1980, has resulted in political and economic crisis in Zimbabwe and has led to what UNICEF describes as "the sharpest rise in child mortality in history." Increasing levels of poverty, a forced removal campaign that left more than a million

people homeless in 2005, severe food shortages, and extremely high HIV infection rates have combined to reduce life expectancy in Zimbabwe from sixty-one years in the early 1990s to thirty-four years of age at the end of 2005. Similarly, the humanitarian crisis in Sudan has precipitated a severe health crisis. The armed conflict in Darfur has affected an estimated 3.6 million people. About one in ten Sudanese children die before the age of five, and malaria, acute respiratory infections, and diarrheal diseases kill more than 100,000 children annually. The civil war in the neighboring Democratic Republic of the Congo has claimed the lives of more than 3 million people. Although a peace accord was signed in 2003, armed conflict continues in parts of the country. There, one in five children dies before reaching age five. Sexual abuse and violence against women is widespread, and HIV prevalence rates are increasing. The life expectancy for a person living in the Democratic Republic of the Congo is forty-four years of age.

South Africa has the world's largest number of people living with HIV/AIDS. In 2003 approximately 25 percent of pregnant women tested HIV positive, and in some provinces prevalence rates were as high as 40 percent. AIDS is the leading cause of death in South Africa and causes almost half of all child deaths. Life expectancy in South Africa, one of the wealthiest countries on the continent, is now estimated to be forty-six years. The HIV epidemic is also responsible for the increase in infant mortality rates. Many women who require treatment to prevent the transmission of the virus to their babies do not have access to these drugs. The legacy of apartheid together with the failure of the post-apartheid state to address adequately the crisis of HIV/AIDS has led to the effective collapse of the health-care system in many parts of the country. In the Transkei, under apartheid a "homeland" state and now part of one of the poorest provinces in South Africa, the infant mortality rate in 1996 was more than one hundred per thousand.

Women living in the industrialized West in the early twenty-first century rarely die in childbirth, but in the developing world around half a million women per year die of pregnancy-related causes, and approximately half of these deaths occur in Africa. Maternal mortality figures for women in Africa closely resemble those for the West in the nineteenth century.

Socioeconomic conditions are also responsible for the more than half a million deaths from tuberculosis in Africa each year. While effective and inexpensive treatment for tuberculosis exists, and has done so for the last fifty years, many people living with the disease in Africa do not have access to these drugs. Prevalence rates for tuberculosis have also been rising as the numbers of people living with HIV/AIDS increases. HIV leads to people becoming more susceptible to infection with tuberculosis, and it also allows active tuberculosis to develop more quickly. Tuberculosis control efforts are severely threatened by partial or inconsistent treatment, as this leads to the emergence of forms of the disease that are resistant to multiple drugs.

An overview of health and health care in Africa brings the global and local political, social, and economic barriers to effective treatment and care into sharp relief. In his 2001 book *Infections and Inequalities*, the anthropologist and physician Paul Farmer argues that "inequalities have powerfully sculpted not only the distribution of infectious diseases but also the course of health outcomes among the afflicted" (p. 5). Farmer shows that the persistence of what he terms "the plagues of the poor" are inextricably linked to social inequalities. The relation between inequality and the health of populations is nowhere more apparent than in the case of the global HIV/AIDS epidemic, which disproportionately affects the peoples of Africa. The Joint United Nations Programme on HIV and AIDS (known as UNAIDS) estimates that of the 39.5 million people living with HIV/AIDS worldwide in 2006, 24.7 million were living in sub-Saharan Africa. In 2006, 2.9 million people died of AIDS-related diseases, and 2.1 million of these deaths occurred in sub-Saharan Africa alone.

[*See also* AIDS and HIV; Civil War; Colonialism, *subentry* Africa; Doctors without Borders; Famine, *subentry* Africa; Forced Labor; Labor and the Labor Movement, *subentry* Africa; Malaria; Medicine and Public Health, *subentry* Traditional Medicine in Africa; Missions, Christian, *subentry* Africa; Nongovernment Organizations; Racism; *and* Tuberculosis.]

BIBLIOGRAPHY

Anderson, Neil, and Shula Marks. "The State, Class, and the Allocation of Health Resources in South Africa." *Social Science and Medicine* 28, no. 5 (1989): 515–530.

Bashford, Alison. "Global Biopolitics and the History of World Health." *History of the Human Sciences* 19, no. 1 (2006): 67–88.

Cordell, Dennis, Joel Gregory, and Victor Piche. "The Demographic Reproduction of Health and Disease: Colonial Central African Republic and Contemporary Burkina Faso." In *The Social Basis of Health and Healing in Africa*, edited by Steven Feierman and John M. Janzen, pp. 39–71. Berkeley: University of California Press, 1992.

Echenberg, Myron. *Black Death, White Medicine: Bubonic Plague and the Politics of Public Health in Colonial Senegal, 1914–1945*. Portsmouth, N.H.: Heinemann, 2002.

Falola, Toyin, and Dennis Ityavyar. *The Political Economy of Health in Africa*. Athens: Ohio University Center for International Studies, 1992.

Farmer, Paul. *Infections and Inequalities: The Modern Plagues*. Berkeley: University of California Press, 1999.

Feierman, Steven, and John Janzen, eds. *The Social Basis of Health and Healing in Africa*. Berkeley: University of California Press, 1992.

Hammond-Tooke, William David. *Rituals and Medicine: Indigenous Healing in South Africa*. Johannesburg, South Africa: AD Donker, 1989.

Horwitz, Simonne. "Migrancy and HIV/AIDS: An Historical Perspective." *South African Historical Journal* 45 (2001): 103–123.

Iliffe, John. *The African AIDS Epidemic: A History*. Athens: Ohio University Press; Oxford: James Currey; Cape Town, South Africa: Double Storey, 2006.

Iliffe, John. *East African Doctors: A History of the Modern Profession*. Cambridge, U.K.: Cambridge University Press; Kampala, Uganda: Fountain, 2002.

Jean, François. *Populations in Danger: Médecins Sans Frontières*. London: John Libbey, 1992.

Labonte, Ronald, Ted Schrecker, David Sanders, and Wilma Meeus. *Fatal Indifference: The G8, Africa, and Global Health*. Cape Town, South Africa: University of Cape Town Press, 2004.

Ngubane, Harriet. "Aspects of Clinical Practice and Traditional Organization of Indigenous Healers in South Africa." *Social Science and Medicine* 15, no. 3 (1981): 361–365.

Swanson, Maynard. "The Sanitation Syndrome: Bubonic Plague and Urban Native Policy in the Cape Colony, 1900–1909." *Journal of African History* 18, no. 3 (1977): 387–410.

Vaughan, Megan. *Curing Their Ills: Colonial Power and African Illness*. Stanford, Calif.: Stanford University Press, 1991.

Worboys, Michael. "The Spread of Western Medicine." In *Western Medicine: An Illustrated History*, edited by Irvine Loudon. Oxford, U.K.: Oxford University Press, 1997.

SIMONNE HORWITZ AND KYLIE THOMAS

Latin America

The great backdrop to the modern history of health and disease in Latin America is the European expansion of the sixteenth century as a transoceanic exchange of peoples, crops, animals, and germs, with dramatic consequences at ecological, socioeconomic, and cultural levels. The Americas were not a disease-free paradise, but having been isolated from Eurasian and African pools of infection, the indigenous population had developed a very particular set of immunities that made it susceptible to many Old World pathogens. Under such circumstances, the first contact with overseas invaders was bound to be deadly for those aboriginal peoples lacking most forms of acquired or inherited protection against common European and African diseases.

The epidemics associated with these differential immunities—notably smallpox, influenza, typhus, measles, mumps, and scarlet fever—combined with other variables, played a decisive role in the demographic catastrophe of the sixteenth century that decimated indigenous populations. The African populations introduced to supplement the labor force enjoyed resistance to many Old World pathogens while remaining vulnerable to the ravages of other diseases related to their dual condition as slaves and newcomers in the Americas. The transatlantic circulation of malaria and yellow fever was a determining factor in the development of the plantation system, its demographic configuration, and the endemic condition of these diseases (in conjunction with a complex of natural selection, racial prejudice, and biomedical perceptions).

During the first two-thirds of the nineteenth century miasmatic and environmentalist approaches dominated medical perceptions of health and disease without producing major changes in sanitary infrastructure or overall mortality. Official reactions to epidemics—for example the cholera pandemics that swept the region in the 1830s and 1850s—were spasmodic and probably ineffective, while the epidemics and reactions were aggravated by the recurrent civil conflicts of the era. Answers to epidemic catastrophes were sometimes improvised, other times reflecting incipient state policies shaped by liberal nation-building reforms and international science (at that time mostly French).

The commodity export boom of the second half of the nineteenth century contributed to the spread of epidemic and endemic diseases, with an increase in international maritime traffic and immigration, combined with developing infrastructure, massive internal migration, and the concentration of ever larger numbers of people in cities and in plantation and mining export enclaves. An insalubrious reputation stuck to Latin America's great port cities in the late nineteenth and early twentieth centuries, and local elites saw this as a grave hindrance to modernization. Sanitarism and *higienismo* (hygiene reform) grew up as part of an effort to manage and control mortality and morbidity patterns dominated by diseases such as tuberculosis, yellow fever, malaria, and plague. These epidemics unveiled the poor state of collective health and the limited infrastructure of sanitation and health care, but at the same time facilitated the emergence of state initiatives in public health and accelerated the presence of the state authority, both in social policy matters and in private life.

From the end of the nineteenth century until well into the twentieth, epidemic cycles were linked to the so-called social question. Thus, with the growing acceptance of

mono-causal explanations for every illness, references to the larger context were inescapable: the precariousness of garbage disposal, sewer and drinking water systems, housing hygiene, biological or racial inheritance, daily habits, the work environment, diet and poverty, massive immigration, and the "dangerous" teeming multitudes in the cities. Often these explanations were articulated in moral terms.

At the beginning of the twentieth century, statistics became a common staple of social analysis and in some countries state agencies specifically concerned with questions of public health were created. First hygienists and later public-health physicians played a decisive role in modernizing urban facilities and the networks of public assistance, reform, and social control. At times the struggle against epidemics took on the character of quasi-military campaigns—rhetorically by defining microorganisms as enemies, and in practice by encouraging intrusive interventions in neighborhoods and houses, especially those of the poor. Perhaps for that reason, these interventions were resisted on certain occasions. At other times, the struggle also included persuasion, aiming to educate the population and disseminate so-called hygienic ways of living.

The diversity of national historical experiences is present in the epidemiological history of Latin America. Thus while tropical diseases such as malaria, yellow fever, or hookworm played a specific role in the history of certain nations such as Brazil and Costa Rica, for others like Argentina and Mexico diseases and problems somehow associated with modernization and urban and industrial growth (tuberculosis, syphilis, urban hygiene, and occupational health) came to the fore.

In any case, it is important to note that over time diseases have played different roles at the national, regional, or local levels. That which became relevant in epidemiological terms in one country might have no significance in another. In certain contexts diseases like syphilis or leprosy were classified as epidemic even though they did not massively affect the population. They were turned into national problems for social, cultural, or political reasons, legitimized by medical expertise, attracting public attention and spurring campaigns designed specifically to eradicate them. Other illnesses, which did not break out suddenly like the infectious diseases but were well established in everyday life and sometimes killed and afflicted more people than epidemic diseases, did not always manage to mobilize sufficient resources to be perceived as national problems. In different times and places, this was the case with tuberculosis and gastrointestinal diseases, or malaria and hookworm in areas where they were endemic. Because they were more widespread, more difficult to treat, more closely associated with poverty, more socially or geographically distant from centers of power, and more easily overlooked, these diseases could only be made visible to public opinion and elite consciousness with enormous effort, and therefore particular policies to combat them were often rare or nonexistent.

In the urban world, some of these diseases finally did manage to become public issues because they came to be seen as part of the "social question" or strongly associated with broader national problems. In the countryside, endemic illnesses were the ones that expanded the area of action of public-health interventions, fostering initiatives of rural sanitation that launched social policies, state expansion agendas, the centralization of power, and, more generally, nation-building processes.

Although results were uneven, during the first half of the twentieth century the prevalent epidemiological and mortality patterns based on infectious diseases that dominated Latin America began to change. Increasing efforts were made, especially after the 1940s, to deal with problems of primary care as a crucial dimension of public health and also as part of a culture of survival embodied in emergency responses, ephemeral training of lay personnel, and the creation of health posts in the poverty rings of mega-cities or in underserved rural areas. Some contemporaries were critical of these efforts, claiming that primary health care was temporary relief for ill-served social sectors or second-class medicine for the poor. Nevertheless, primary health care can be seen as a by-product of social changes and also an instrument to promote such changes.

In the reception and transfer of expertise and practices associated with the fight against malaria, yellow fever, and hookworm, as well as in the development of primary-care networks, foreign institutions played significant roles. The Rockefeller Foundation developed a series of ambitious initiatives during the first decades of the twentieth century. Its agenda aimed at organizing single-disease services and promoting technical approaches and specific cures to the detriment of more comprehensive, educational, and preventive strategies. Rockefeller missions reveal the growing influence of the United States as a new metropolitan world player with an increasing hegemonic role in the region. However, in many countries, health- and disease-related problems had already become a public issue before these missions arrived, often as a result of initiatives launched by national scientific communities. On some occasions these communities were able to develop novel and quite specific approaches to research and

intervention, sometimes even before their North American peers, and on many more occasions actively negotiated with the foundation's representatives.

In any case, the arrival of the Rockefeller missions was crucial in the orientation of sanitary reforms, particularly for rural areas and for diseases that were believed to be eradicable with little cost and in a short time. Despite varied and uneven results in different countries and with different diseases, there is no doubt that the Rockefeller Foundation projects and later NGO-promoted initiatives mobilized public opinion. This was especially true with regard to the living conditions of the rural poor. These projects also contributed enormously to centralizing sanitary efforts, reinforced the power of the central government vis-à-vis the local and regional ones, and consolidated the position of the United States as the dominant external reference in matters of public health.

As in later relations with institutions like the Pan-American Health Organization, Latin Americans played leading roles in staffing and directing these initiatives, and the relations between national and foreign medical groups were complex. In their original design, international health projects may have been conceived as purely technical endeavors in keeping with a neocolonial philanthropic or economic agenda. But when these interventions materialized they contributed, whether intentionally or not, to establishing precedents and laying the institutional foundations for future social and preventive medicine projects that local professional actors later led.

The statist public-health model of Latin America, by and large reinforced by the evolution of U.S. and international health agencies, entered into a period of crisis and reformulation following the era of neoliberal structural adjustment in the 1980s and 1990s. As some countries in the region complete the so-called demographic transition, while others suffer catastrophic indices of morbidity and infant mortality from nutritional deficiencies, infectious disease, and gastrointestinal illness, Latin America continues to show highly heterogeneous health and disease patterns.

[*See also* Body, The; Disability; Doctors without Borders; Drugs and Narcotics, *subentry* The Pharmaceutical Industry; Epidemics; Germ Theory; Handicaps; Hospitals; Medicine and Public Health, *subentry* Latin America; Mental Health and Mental Illness; Physical Fitness; Tobacco; World Health Organization. *See also individual articles on the following diseases and conditions*: AIDS and HIV; Anorexia Nervosa; Bird Flu; Cancer; Cholera;

Heart Disease; Plague; Poliomyelitis; SARS; Smallpox; Tuberculosis; *and* Yellow Fever.]

BIBLIOGRAPHY
Armus, Diego, ed., *Disease in the History of Modern Latin America: From Malaria to AIDS*. Durham, N.C.: Duke University Press, 2003.

Cueto, Marcos, *The Return of Epidemics: Health and Society in Peru During the Twentieth Century*. London and Burlington, Vt.: Ashgate Publishing, 2001.

de Castro-Santos, Luiz Antonio. "Power, Ideology and Public Health in Brazil, 1889–1930," PhD diss., Harvard University, 1987.

DIEGO ARMUS AND STEVEN PALMER

South Asia

Although the Portuguese originally introduced new forms of medicine into South Asia in the late sixteenth century, the British deserve credit for introducing their evolving therapeutic knowledge and institutions and erecting a more complex infrastructure in the nineteenth century. Despite the self-adulation of the imperial proconsuls such as Viceroy Lord George Nathaniel Curzon (viceroy 1899–1905), who claimed that the transfer of European medicine marked an unmistakable instance of benevolence, late-twentieth-century studies on the impact of medicine have exposed the disjuncture between the rhetoric and the reality. British motives and policies were often dictated by political survival, commercial profit, fiscal parsimony, and a hegemonic outlook.

Concerns over the health of British soldiers, civilians, and their families, and the Indian sepoys (or soldiers) loomed large in the minds of the officials for whom the security of their Indian empire justifiably depended on the well-being of the army. The government was committed to reducing the morbidity and mortality from malaria, smallpox, cholera, and venereal diseases. The enthusiastic but ill-executed smallpox vaccination program in the 1820s, for example, demonstrated that such undertakings must be backed by an allocation of substantial resources and the recruiting of thousands of indigenous intermediaries who would popularize the new technique among the rural population. First in a series of public health measures, the smallpox campaign accentuated that cultural sensitivity and persuasion would be more effective than bureaucratic dogmatism, arrogance, and high-handedness.

The revolt of 1857 (also known as the Sepoy Mutiny and the Great Mutiny) constituted a watershed in the government's health policies as sickness and death persisted among the British soldiers. The revolt etched in the British psyche their alleged sense of superiority, racial and social,

over myriads of Indian castes and sects that should be distanced from the military cantonments and civil settlements. The colonial government, inspired by the advocacy of Florence Nightingale in the aftermath of the Crimean War (1853–1856), enacted the Military Cantonments Act (1864) and the Contagious Diseases Act (1868) for treating and regulating the Indian brothels that the soldiers frequented. Maintaining complete social distance seemed impractical because the British were dependent on their native helpers. The rulers concluded that the Indian leaders should be taught, as part of the "civilizing mission" rhetoric, to emulate the proved sanitary measures then in vogue at home.

Between the 1860s and the 1870s several professional men and medical women publicly debated the health issues of women, Hindu and Muslim, arguing that the government had—because of male prejudice and other constraints—denied treatment to women, who would voluntarily visit the clinics and hospitals if they were run by women. In the 1880s, supported by philanthropic Europeans and Indian princes, the Dufferin Fund was established to promote the health of women and children.

Following the reforms of the 1870s and 1880s, the devolution of control over corporations and municipalities shifted the burden of sanitizing India from the imperial professionals to the wealthy and Western-educated Indians. Winning elections proved to be less difficult than raising the requisite revenue or implementing various public health measures in an unsanitary landscape where the recurrence of major famines and epidemics—such as cholera in the 1880s and the plague between 1898 and 1900—wreaked havoc. The unprecedented human toll was deplorable, especially among the poor, who were caught in a vicious cycle of poverty, malnutrition, and disease. The rulers' draconian measures to control the spread of the contagion had unleashed a public outcry against British arrogance and insensitivity.

The first half of the twentieth century saw the founding of national and regional institutions to undertake research on rabies, beriberi, and malaria. Indian nationalist leaders, chiefly Jawaharlal Nehru, envisioned that India as an independent nation should shoulder its own national health care needs. Nehru, as chairman of the Planning Commission, inaugurated in 1950 a series of measures articulated in the Five-Year Plan; the first two plans committed millions of dollars to eradicating malaria, tuberculosis, smallpox, and elephantiasis.

By 1972, India's population had exploded to nearly 600 million, exhausting the precious resources that it had earmarked for subsidized health care. As a result, poverty became widespread and infant and child mortality from preventable conditions ran high. The fourth and the fifth plans, between 1969 and 1979, allocated more than $1.2 billion for birth control and family planning, but the coercive sterilization tactics adopted by zealous bureaucrats and government agencies drew such public ire from various women's organizations and the press that the government finally capitulated by radically modifying its policies.

India has been confronted with a new scourge since 1986 when the AIDS virus was first reported. With India second only to South Africa in the number of HIV/AIDS cases—about 5.2 million in 2005—the global menace continues to invade the countryside, where vital information on prevention and treatment, as well as the adoption of safe-sex measures, is meager. Regional variations in the prevalence of the infection, the uneven commitment of national and local government agencies, and lingering conservative social attitudes militate against launching a well-orchestrated campaign.

[*See also* AIDS and HIV; British Raj; Cholera; Famine, *subentry* India; Malaria; *and* Smallpox.]

BIBLIOGRAPHY
Arnold, David. *Colonizing the Body: State Medicine and Epidemic Disease in Nineteenth-Century India.* Berkeley: University of California Press, 1993. An insightful analysis that discusses how death, disease, and medicine unleashed debates between the British and the Indian public and how the rulers systematically incorporated various indigenous elements and discourses in extending their medicine beyond the urban enclaves.
Harrison, Mark. *Public Health in British India: Anglo-Indian Preventive Medicine, 1859–1914.* Cambridge, U.K.: Cambridge University Press, 1994. A more balanced evaluation of the shifting roles of numerous actors—the European medical professionals, the British government, the colonial state, and the local Indian population—within the context of evolving public health policy debates.
Jeffery, Roger. *The Politics of Health in India.* Berkeley: University of California Press, 1988. A thorough sociological treatment, detailing India's achievements since 1947 in developing preventive health programs and creating a host of auxiliary medical personnel.

JOHN J. PAUL

Southeast Asia

In reflecting on responses to recent outbreaks of bird flu, it is particularly striking to note the persistence of an association between Western representations of the Far East, especially Southeast Asia, and the peril of widespread infection. Yet, upon closer inspection, Southeast Asia's portrait of pathological disease is complex and dynamic, in line with its remarkable sociocultural heterogeneity and longstanding participation in the globalization of goods, persons, and knowledge.

Informative sources of epidemiological data for the years 1750 to 1900 are scarce. Demographers and historians are nevertheless quite confident that at least 80 percent of the mortality in Southeast Asia during this period was due to malnutrition, parasitic infections, and probably tuberculosis. Major epidemics (smallpox, malaria, typhoid fever) still struck, often in tandem with wars, natural catastrophes, and famines. Consensus has not yet been reached on the causes of the demographic expansion that began after 1850—the region's population in 1900 is estimated at 80 million, compared with 30 million in 1800; in 2007 it exceeded 530 million. Was the growth in population a result of general improvements in living conditions and nutrition, or a rise in fertility? Or was an epidemiological transition underway, characterized by fewer acute epidemics despite the ravages of cholera and of a plague pandemic that killed up to 13 million by the end of the nineteenth century? Moreover, how did Western colonial rule, which spared only Thailand, influence health and disease in the region? That post-1945 independent states took on European-initiated public health programs, including massive vaccination campaigns, suggests the possibility that indirect, long-term benefits on the health of Southeast Asian populations stemmed from this period.

This general trend of improvements in health continued during the 1960s and 1970s but was accompanied by a diversification in pathological markers. An increasingly uneven distribution of disease can be linked to gaps in local levels of economic, technological, and urban development, but also to wide variations in national health programs, particularly regarding prevention. Events such as the chaotic construction of the state in Vietnam, or the genocides in Cambodia and Timor, have also had complex effects on the physical but also mental and social health of their populations. In the 1980s, and especially the 1990s, the impact of modernization became increasingly visible in contrasting patterns of health and disease. There have been rising rates of cardiovascular disease (the age-standardized coronary heart disease mortality in Singaporean men is 150 per 100,000, as high as that of Australians), at-risk lifestyles, mental health problems, accidents, and health conditions arising from inadequate environmental management (deforestation, the massive use of pollutants and chemicals). Yet, the gap between health indicators in Southeast Asia and those in developed countries remains wide: profound disparities persist in the distribution of health, access to primary healthcare, and sanitation along national, geographic (urban versus rural), sociodemographic (gender and ethnic), and socioeconomic lines. These disparities put obesity alongside undernutrition in Malaysia, sustain high rates of maternal mortality (650 per 100,000 live births in Laos and Timor, a rate equal to that of Haiti), and make it difficult to eradicate leprosy or manage infantile diarrhoea (accounting for 18 percent of all deaths in Myanmar in 1996). Legacies of the past and cultural and religious frames of reference may also play a role in shaping health and responses to illness. For example, the difficulties encountered in formulating effective AIDS policies in the early 1990s reflect tensions between competing views—Confucian, Buddhist, Islamic—of sexuality and "social scourges." More generally, the epidemiological weight of sexually transmitted diseases may arise from a long history of "endemic" prostitution associated with long-standing and active networks of migration within Asia, a correlation further fueled by European and Japanese domination, and then by sexual tourism, particularly to Thailand and the Philippines. As for the rising prevalence of malaria (20–40 million cases currently estimated in the region), it reveals continuity between the detrimental effects of colonial and postcolonial policies aimed at boosting agricultural productivity.

Today in Southeast Asia, healthcare is being shifted to the private sector. Populations are aging and are increasingly afflicted with chronic diseases. The region also faces the threat of reemerging infections such as dengue and tuberculosis, and the prevalence of AIDS accelerates. Finally, global warming seems set to aggravate health conditions in tropical areas. The challenges of health, disease, and well-being in Southeast Asia remain complex and changing.

[See also Health and Disease, subentry Overview.]

BIBLIOGRAPHY

Henley, David. *Fertility, Food, and Fever: Population, Economy, and Environment in North and Central Sulawesi*, 1600–1930. Leiden, The Netherlands: KITLV Press, 2005.

Owen, Norman G., ed. *Death and Disease in Southeast Asia: Explorations in Social, Medical, and Demographic History.* Singapore and New York: Oxford University Press, 1987.

Whittaker, Andrea. "Women's Health in Mainland Southeast Asia." *Women & Health* 35, no. 4 (2002): 1–119.

LAURENCE MONNAIS

HEART DISEASE. Given the growing prominence of cardiovascular disease as a major worldwide health problem in the twentieth and twenty-first centuries, it is difficult to appreciate how much less important this seemed until relatively recently. At the start of the twentieth century in Europe as well as the United States infectious disease, especially tuberculosis, was the major cause of death. Certainly this was even more true at the end of the eighteenth century, when knowledge of the types of heart disease and their treatment was even more scanty. There were, however, certain mileposts of medical progress that would serve to underpin major developments in the field over the next two hundred years or more.

One of these was the publication by Andreas Vesalius, a Belgian working at the University of Padua, Italy, of his masterpiece of anatomical illustration, *De humani corporis fabrica* in 1543. The physiological counterpart to Vesalius's anatomical work was *Exercitatio de Motu Cordis* (1628), on the circulation of the blood, by the Englishman William Harvey. Following in the steps of Harvey, Richard Lower (1631–1691) in England and his Danish contemporary Niels Stensen (1638–1686) through their dissections and experiments furthered the understanding of the workings of the heart.

Critical to the advancement in the diagnosis and treatment of any disease is the need to match the symptoms and signs found in the patient while alive and the postmortem changes found at the autopsy table (clinicopathological correlation). The father of this branch of medical science was Giovanni Battista Morgagni (1682–1771), also working in Padua, who demonstrated such correlations not only for heart disease but for other maladies through his extensive studies.

Diagnosis. Adding immeasurably to the clinical ability to diagnose abnormalities of the heart and lungs was the invention of the stethoscope by the Frenchman René T. H. Laënnec (1781–1826). His treatise, published in 1821, provided the first auditory descriptions of what might be detected as abnormal heart sounds and murmurs in the diagnosis of heart disease. Following in his wake were a succession of skillful clinicians, not only in France but also in Great Britain and Ireland, who began to predict with remarkable accuracy at the bedside what might ultimately be found postmortem in their patients, particularly those with valvular heart disease. During the eighteenth and nineteenth centuries, especially in Germany, research institutes were established in Europe to study the workings of the cardiovascular system. Later on, the discovery of X-rays and the invention of the electrocardiograph at the beginning of the twentieth century and cardiac catheterization in the 1940s added to the diagnostic capability of physicians.

In the course of such clinical work, diagnostic categories of various heart diseases were established: congenital heart disease (present at birth); hypertensive heart disease (related to elevations in blood pressure); acquired valvular heart disease (such as the aftereffects of rheumatic fever attacks); coronary heart disease (related to the building up of fatty material in the wall of the coronary arteries or sudden occlusions by blood clots); pericardial disease (involving the sac surrounding the heart); and so forth.

Treatment. Unfortunately, as late as the early twentieth century there were few medical treatments to enable physicians to relieve the suffering of their heart patients. Digitalis, a heart muscle stimulant extracted from the foxglove plant by the Englishman William Withering in 1785, relieved the fluid retention secondary to heart failure in many patients. Morphine was extracted from opium in 1803 and later used to relieve the pain and lung congestion associated with acute heart failure. Mercury had been used for hundreds of years not only to treat syphilis but also as a diuretic, but the side effects of the forms available were often so severe as to preclude their use. Not until a safe injectable form was found in Vienna in the 1920s was a truly safe and effective diuretic available to practitioners. In 1867 nitroglycerin in the form of amyl nitrite was first recommended by the Englishman Thomas Lauder Brunton to relieve the pain of coronary attacks (angina).

Perhaps the most significant recent advances in the treatment of heart disease have been surgical in nature. Before the introduction of open-heart surgery, "closed procedures" such as removal of diseased pericardium (the sac around the heart) and tying off a persistent connection after birth between the pulmonary artery and the aorta (ductus arteriosus) opened the door to the surgical approach, along with the "blue baby" operation for certain congenital heart conditions and the "finger fracture" approach (commissurotomy) to relieve narrowing of the mitral valve (mitral stenosis), the most common of postrheumatic valve disorders. Repair of most of the congenital heart defects, such as holes or defects in the walls separating the chambers of the right and left heart, required open-heart surgery with temporary complete bypass of the heart. Such surgery also made coronary bypass surgery more practicable. More recently, percutaneous catheter techniques are being employed by interventional cardiologists to open up coronary obstructions with balloon angioplasty, with or without the insertion of stents, both bare and drug-eluting. Finally, human cardiac transplantation as introduced by the South African surgeon Christiaan Barnard in 1967 and subsequently enhanced

in effectiveness by control of rejection with proper medication, became an answer for end-stage heart disease unsuitable for other types of repair. However, the large number of potential recipients and the limited number of donors have limited the usefulness of this approach for most patients with end-stage heart disease. The total artificial heart is now in development to answer the need of such patients, for whom inadequate numbers of donor hearts are available. While work continues on improving the total artificial heart, left ventricular assists devices (LVADs) of various design are being used in patients with end-stage congestive heart failure.

In addition to surgery, the introduction of cardiac pacemakers and defibrillators for lethal irregularities of the heartbeat has saved or prolonged countless lives.

Prevention. By the mid-twentieth century coronary heart disease was beginning to be recognized as the major cause of death among industrial societies and by the early twenty-first century, along with stroke, constituted the major cause of death for populations worldwide. The recognition of risk factors such as lipid factors in the blood (e.g., high cholesterol) and the roles of smoking, exercise, and obesity have added to our ability to prevent coronary heart disease as well as to treat the established disease among such patients.

With the aging of many populations, congestive heart failure as the result of long-standing cardiac disease has become a major health problem in the developed world, with over 5 million people so affected in the United States alone. Finding means to treat such patients within the bounds of our technical and financial capacity as well as new ways to prevent or delay the onset of this disease presents a major challenge.

[*See also* Health and Disease.]

BIBLIOGRAPHY

Acierno, Louis J. *The History of Cardiology.* New York: Parthenon, 1994. Probably the most comprehensive current history in English.

Bing, Richard J., ed. *Cardiology: The Evolution of the Science and the Art.* 2d ed. New Brunswick, N.J.: Rutgers University Press, 1999. A multiauthored work with Bing as editor and contributor along with others. An insightful historical view by one of the pioneers of twentieth-century cardiology.

Weisse, Allen B. *Heart to Heart: The Twentieth Century Battle against Cardiac Disease: An Oral History.* New Brunswick, N.J.: Rutgers University Press, 2002. A series of interviews with sixteen outstanding cardiologists and surgeons of this period, each preceded by an historical essay. A biographical notes section includes over two hundred entries of prominent individuals in the field in the recent and more distant past.

ALLEN B. WEISSE